Caribbean Cultural Thought

CARIBBEAN CULTURAL THOUGHT
FROM PLANTATION TO DIASPORA

Edited by
Yanique Hume and Aaron Kamugisha

IAN RANDLE PUBLISHERS
Kingston • Miami

First published in Jamaica, 2013 by
Ian Randle Publishers
11 Cunningham Avenue
Box 686
Kingston 6
www.ianrandlepublishers.com

Introduction and Editorial material
© 2013 Yanique Hume and Aaron Kamugisha

All rights reserved. While copyright in the selection and editorial material is vested in Yanique Hume and Aaron Kamugisha, copyright in individual chapters belongs to their respective authors and no part of this publication may be reproduced, stored in a retrieval system or transmitted in any form or by any means electronic, photocopying, recording or otherwise, without the prior express permission of the publisher and author.

NATIONAL LIBRARY OF JAMAICA CATALOGUING-IN-PUBLICATION DATA

Caribbean cultural thought : from plantation to diaspora / edited by
   Yanique Hume and Aaron Kamugisha

   p. : ill. ; cm.
ISBN 978-976-637-620-8 (pbk)

  1. Acculturation – Caribbean Area   2. Culture
  3. Civilization   4. Ethnicity
  I. Hume, Yanique   II. Kamugisha, Aaron

306   - dc 23

Cover Artwork: 'Faaka Tiki 1' by Marcel Pinas
Cover and book design by Ian Randle Publishers

Printed and bound in the United States of America

To the Thinkers of Our Region and the Many Voices that Give Expression to Our Existence

Table of Contents

Acknowledgements / xi

Publisher's Acknowledgements / xiii

Introduction: Caribbean Cultural Thought in Pursuit of Freedom / xix
  Yanique Hume and Aaron Kamugisha

Anti-Colonial Thought

The Equality of the Human Races: Positivist Anthropology (excerpt) / 1
  Anténor Firmin

Our America / 7
  José Martí

La Vocation d'élite (excerpt) / 13
  Jean Price-Mars

Culture and Colonisation / 28
  Aimé Césaire

The Malaise of a Civilization / 40
  Suzanne Césaire

Racism and Culture / 43
  Frantz Fanon

Hiccups / 51
  Léon Damas

I Come from the Nigger Yard / 54
  Martin Carter

Caribbean Nationalisms

Africa for the Africans / 59
  Marcus Garvey

Race and Creole Ethnicity in the Caribbean / 62
  Percy Hintzen

Caliban: Notes Toward a Discussion of Culture in Our America / 75
  Roberto Fernández Retamar

Not Just (Any)*Body* Can Be a Citizen: The Politics of Law, Sexuality and Postcoloniality in Trinidad and Tobago and The Bahamas / 91
  M. Jacqui Alexander

Song for Puerto Rico / 106
  Nicholás Guillén

The Plantation

Plantation Society: Toward a General Theory of Caribbean Society / **109**
George Beckford

Beckford and the Predicaments of Caribbean Culture / **121**
George Lamming

The Dark Complete World of a Caribbean Store:
A Note on the World System / **127**
Richard Price

Reluctant Matriarchs / **130**
Lucille Mathurin-Mair

The Origins of Reconstituted Peasantries / **135**
Sidney Mintz

Culture on the Edges: Creolization in the Plantation Context / **142**
Michel-Rolph Trouillot

Cultural Identity and Social Change

On the Social Phenomenon of "Transculturation"
and Its Importance in Cuba / **157**
Fernando Ortiz

Transatlantic African Survivals and
the Dynamism of Negro Culture / **161**
Jean Price-Mars

The Social Framework / **167**
Elsa Goveia

Caribbean Man in Space and Time / **174**
Kamau Brathwaite

Retentions and Survivals / **185**
Sidney W. Mintz and Richard Price

The "Creolisation" of Indian Women in Trinidad / **190**
Patricia Mohammed

Reputation and Respectability:
A Suggestion for Caribbean Ethnology / **202**
Peter Wilson

That Event, This Memory: Notes on the Anthropology
of African Diasporas in the New World / **215**
David Scott

Creolization and Nation-Building in the Hispanic Caribbean / **232**
Antonio Benítez-Rojo

Culture, Color and Politics / 240
Michel-Rolph Trouillot

West Indian Society 150 Years after Abolition:
A Re-Examination of Some Classic Theories / 259
Lloyd Best

Cultural Identity and the Arts –
New Horizons for Caribbean Social Sciences? / 275
Rex Nettleford

A Dialogue: Nation Language and Poetics of Creolization / 290
Kamau Brathwaite and Edouard Glissant

Caribbean Aesthetics
Of the Marvellous Realism of the Haitians / 303
Jacques Stephen Alexis

"Preface" and "Afrocubanismo" / 323
Alejo Carpentier

"What is Art?" / 333
C.L.R. James

History, Fable and Myth in the Caribbean and the Guianas / 343
Wilson Harris

The Love Axe(l): Developing a Caribbean Aesthetic / 354
Kamau Brathwaite

Articulating a Caribbean Aesthetic:
The Revolution of Self-Perception / 377
Gordon Rohlehr

The Battle for Space / 387
Rex Nettleford

Gender and Sexuality
Afterword: "Beyond Miranda's Meanings:
Un/Silencing the 'Demonic Ground' of Caliban's 'Woman'" / 397
Sylvia Wynter

"What's Identity Got to do with it?"
Rethinking Identity in Light of the *Mati* Work in Suriname / 408
Gloria Wekker

Uses of the Erotic: The Erotic as Power / 421
Audre Lorde

Theorizing Sexual Relations in the Caribbean:
Prostitution and the Problem of the "Exotic" / 425
Kamala Kempadoo

In the Night / 444
Jamaica Kincaid

Caribbean Religions and Spiritualities

Introduction to *Creole Religions of the Caribbean:
An Introduction from Vodou and Santería to Obeah and Espiritismo* / 449
Margarite Fernández Olmos and Lizabeth Paravisini-Gebert

The Spirit of the Thing:
Religious Thought and Social/Historical Memory / 467
Patrick Bellegarde-Smith

Healing the Nation:
Rastafari Exorcism of the Ideology of Racism in Jamaica / 479
Barry Chevannes

Ritual in Diaspora:
Pedagogy and Practice Among Hindus and Muslims in Trinidad / 497
Aisha Khan

Visitation: The Legacy of African-Derived Religions in Jamaica / 509
Dianne M. Stewart

Diaspora

Thinking the Diaspora: Home-Thoughts from Abroad / 557
Stuart Hall

The Diasporic Mo(ve)ment: Indentureship and Indo-Caribbean Identity / 570
Sean Lokaisingh-Meighoo

Re-Engineering Blackspace / 587
Erna Brodber

Out on Main Street / 598
Shani Mootoo

Colonisation in Reverse / 604
Louise Bennett

Inglan is a Bitch / 606
Linton Kwesi Johnson

The Star-Apple Kingdom / 607
Derek Walcott

Afterword:

Horizons of Caribbean Studies: An Afterword-Overture / 617
Aisha Khan

Acknowledgements

The creative process of writing, compiling and editing is seldom a singular exercise. We owe many of our perspectives to the legacies of the scholars who have inspired us and enriched our own thinking during the course of our academic training. We are also indebted to the scholars whose essays we have reproduced here, for their work have broadened our knowledge and enhanced our understanding of the Caribbean and its rich intellectual tradition. Christine Randle's, Managing Director at Ian Randle Publishers, immediate enthusiasm about the project has been a great inspiration. We would like to thank her and the team at Ian Randle Publishers, particularly Susan Callum and Lisa Marie Clunis, for their commitment and guidance over the last two years. To Aisha Khan, we express our heartfelt appreciation for her encouragement and contribution to the anthology. We are also indebted to a wonderful artist, Marcel Pinas, who provided the dynamic image for the cover of this volume.

At the University of the West Indies, Cave Hill Campus, we extend our gratitude to the Dean of the Faculty of Humanities of Education at the University of the West Indies, Professor Pedro Welch, for his enthusiastic support for this project from its inception. The creation of this volume in Caribbean Cultural Thought would have been impossible without generous support from the Principal's Office and the School for Graduate Study and Research at the University of the West Indies, Cave Hill Campus; and the University of the West Indies Office of Research. For these grants, I would like to especially thank Professor Sir Hilary Beckles and Professor Wayne Hunte. Thanks also to Bernadette Farquhar for her translation of Jean-Price Mars's article. Further afield, we would like to express our appreciation to Vanessa Spence, for her skill in proofreading the text, and Code Mantra, for rendering it ready for submission. We have also benefitted tremendously from the support and assistance of colleagues and friends who have helped us secure out of print documents, as well as provided their advice and comments in the selection of the articles presented in this volume. For this, we want to take this opportunity to thank Keith Nurse, Peter Hudson, and Patrick Sylvain for their suggestions and gracious input along the way.

Yanique would like to especially acknowledge Carlos Moore, for his scholarship and especially his love, friendship and counsel ...*Obrigado!* To the late Rex Nettleford, Michel-Rolph Trouillot and Barry Chevannes she owes a special debt of gratitude for their unflinching commitment to producing knowledge about the complex cultural dimensions of our existence. Special thanks go to co-editor and co-author, Aaron Kamugisha, for his valued friendship, intellectual companionship, his unique critical insights and humour, all of which were invaluable to the process of publishing this anthology.

Aaron would like to thank Percy Hintzen, Patrick Taylor and Sylvia Wynter, for their scholarship, mentorship and counsel; and so many others from his journeys in Toronto, Chicago and Berkeley, particularly Alissa Trotz, Peter Hudson and Paget Henry. Special thanks to co-editor, co-author and friend Yanique Hume, who made the long process of creating this volume intellectually exciting, and despite the inevitable tedium, fun.

Finally, we are grateful to our families who have nurtured our intellectual development and continue to provide us a space for further growth and development. Yanique would like to thank her mother Yvonne, siblings Rae, Howard, Greg, Patsy, and Steve (who is among the ancestors), her in-laws, Fern and Andrew Lewis, partner Peter Lewis and daughter Naia: words cannot fully capture the gratitude and love I have for all of you. Many thanks, Much Love and *Muito Axé*! Aaron would like to express his love and appreciation to his sister, mother and aunt, and grandmother (now among the ancestors), respectively Kemi, Stephanie, Arlette, Dorin: my love always!

Publisher's Acknowledgements

The editor and publisher would like to thank the following for permission to reproduce the material in this volume:

Anténor Firmin:
The Equality of the Human Races: Positivist Anthropology by Anténor Firmin, translated by Asselin Charles. Copyright 2000 by Taylor & Francis Group LLC – Books. Reproduced with permission of Taylor & Francis Group LLC – Books via Copyright Clearance Center.

José Martí:
'Our America,' from *José Martí Reader: Selected Writings*, by José Martí, introduction by Roberto Gonzalez Echevarria, edited by Esther Allen, translated by Esther Allen, copyright © 2002 by Esther Allen. Used by permission of Viking Penguin, a division of Penguin Group (USA) Inc.

Jean Price-Mars:
La Vocation d'élite (Port-au-Prince, Haiti: Fardin, 1976).

Aimé Césaire:
Aimé Césaire, 'Culture and Colonisation' © Revue Présence Africaine, n° 8, 9, 10, 1956.

Suzanne Césaire:
Negritude Women, edited and annotated translations by T. Denean Sharpley-Whiting and Georges Van Den Abbeele, University of Minnesota Press, Copyright 2002 by the Regents of the University of Minnesota.

Frantz Fanon:
'Racism and Culture' from *Toward the African Revolution: Political Essays* by Frantz Fanon, copyright © 1967 by Monthly Review Press. Used by permission of Grove/Atlantic, Inc. Any third party use of this material, outside of this publication, is prohibited.

Léon Damas:
The Negritude Poets, edited by Ellen Conroy Kennedy. Copyright 1989 by Ellen Conroy Kennedy. Reproduced with permission of Ellen Conroy Kennedy via Copyright Clearance Center.

Martin Carter:
'I Come From the Nigger Yard' from *Poems of Succession* by Martin Carter, published by New Beacon Books Ltd., 1977.

Marcus Garvey:
Marcus Garvey, 'Africa for the Africans' from *The Philosophy and Opinions of Marcus Garvey, or Africa for the Africans*, edited by Amy Jacques Garvey (Dover, Massachusetts: Majority Press, 1986).

Percy Hintzen:
Percy Hintzen, 'Race and Creole Ethnicity in the Caribbean' from *Questioning Creole: Creolisation Discourses in Caribbean Culture*, edited by Verene A. Shepherd and Glen L. Richards (Kingston, Jamaica: Ian Randle Publishers, 2002). Reprinted by kind permission of the author.

Roberto Fernández Retamar:
Roberto Fernández Retamar, 'Caliban: Notes Toward a Discussion of Culture in Our America' from *Massachusetts Review* Vol. 15, No. 1 & 2 (1974): 7–72 (excerpt). Reprinted by kind permission of the author.

M. Jacqui Alexander:
M. Jacqui Alexander, 'Not Just (Any) *Body* Can Be a Citizen: The Politics of Law, Sexuality and Postcoloniality in Trinidad and Tobago and The Bahamas' from *Feminist Review* 48 (Autumn 1994). Reprinted by kind permission of the author.

Nicholás Guillén:
Reprinted from *Man-making Words: Selected Poems of Nicholás Guillén*. Copyright © 1972 by Robert Márquez and David Arthur McMurray and published by University of Massachusetts Press.

George Beckford:
George Beckford, 'Plantation Society' from *Savacou* 5 (1971).

George Lamming:
George Lamming, 'Beckford and the Predicaments of Caribbean Culture' from *The Critical Tradition of Caribbean Political Economy: The Legacy of George Beckford*, edited by Kari Levitt and Michael Witter (Kingston, Jamaica: Ian Randle Publishers, 1996). Reprinted by kind permission of the author.

Richard Price:
Richard Price, 'The Dark Complete World of a Caribbean Store: A Note on the World System' from *Review* IX, 2 (Fall 1985): 215–19. Reprinted by kind permission of *Review*.

Lucille Mathurin-Mair:
Lucille Mathurin-Mair, 'Reluctant Matriarchs' from *Savacou* 13 (1977). Reprinted by kind permission of Estate Lucille Mathurin-Mair.

Sidney Mintz:
From *Caribbean Transformations* by Sidney Mintz. Copyright © 1989 Columbia University Press. Reprinted with permission of the publisher.

Michel-Rolph Trouillot:
Michel-Rolph Trouillot, 'Culture on the Edges: Creolization in the Plantation Context' from *Plantation Society in the Americas* Vol. V, 1 (Spring 1998).

Fernando Ortiz:
Fernando Ortiz, 'The Social Phenomenon of "Transculturation" and Its Importance in Cuba' from *Cuban Counterpoint: Tobacco & Sugar*, translated by Harriett de Onís (New York: Vintage Books, 1970).

Jean Price-Mars:
Jean Price-Mars, 'Transatlantic African Survivals and the Dynamism of Negro Culture' © Revue Présence Africaine, n° 8, 9, 10, 1956.

Elsa Goveia:
Elsa Goveia, 'The Social Framework' from *Savacou* 2 (1970).

Kamau Brathwaite:
Kamau Brathwaite, 'Caribbean Man in Space and Time' from *Savacou* 11/12 (1975). Reprinted by kind permission of the author.

Sidney W. Mintz and Richard Price:
The Birth of African-American Culture: An Anthropological Perspective by Sidney W. Mintz and Richard Price. Copyright © 1992 by Sidney W. Mintz and Richard Price. Reproduced with permission of Sidney W. Mintz and Richard Price via Copyright Clearance Center.

Patricia Mohammed:
Patricia Mohammed, 'The "Creolization" of Indian Women in Trinidad' from *Questioning Creole: Creolisation Discourses in Caribbean Culture*, edited by Verene A. Shepherd and Glenn L. Richards (Kingston, Jamaica: Ian Randle Publishers, 2002). Reprinted by kind permission of the author.

Peter Wilson:
'Reputation and Respectability: A Suggestion for Caribbean Ethnology,' Peter Wilson. Copyright © 1969 Peter Wilson. Reproduced with permission of Blackwell Publishing Ltd.

David Scott:
David Scott, 'That Event, This Memory: Notes on the Anthropology of African Diasporas in the New World' from *Diaspora* 1, 3 (1991). Reprinted with permission from University of Toronto Press.

Antonio Benítez-Rojo:
Antonio Benítez-Rojo, 'Creolization and Nation Building in the Hispanic Caribbean' from *A Pepper-Pot of Cultures: Aspects of Creolization in the Caribbean*, edited by Gordon Collier and Ulrich Fleischmann (Amsterdam and New York: Rodopi, 2004). Reprinted with permission from Rodopi.

Michel-Rolph Trouillot:
Haiti: State against Nation by Michel-Rolph Trouillot. Copyright 1990 by Monthly Review Press. Reproduced with permission of Monthly Review Press via Copyright Clearance Center.

Lloyd Best:
From: *Out of Slavery: Abolishment and After*, edited by Jack Hayward, Copyright (© 1985) and Frank Cass. Reproduced by permission of Taylor & Francis Books UK.

Rex Nettleford:
Rex Nettleford, 'Cultural Identity and the Arts – New Horizons for Caribbean Social Sciences?' from *Inward Stretch, Outward Reach: A Voice from the Caribbean* (New York: Caribbean Diaspora Press, 1995). Reprinted by kind permission of Caribbean Diaspora Press.

Kamau Brathwaite and Edouard Glissant:
From *Presencia Criolla en el Caribe y América Latina/Creole Presence in the Caribbean and Latin America*, edited by Ineke Phaf (Madrid: Iberoamericana, 1996). Reprinted by permission of Kamau Brathwaite.

Jacques Stephen Alexis:
Jacques Stephen Alexis, 'Of the Marvelous Realism of the Haitians' © Revue Présence Africaine, n° 8, 9, 10, 1956.

Alejo Carpentier:
Alejo Carpentier, 'Preface' and 'Afrocubanismo' from *Music in Cuba* (Minneapolis, MN: University of Minnesota Press, 2001).

C.L.R. James:
C.L.R. James, 'What is Art?' from *Beyond a Boundary* (London, Hutchinson, 1963). Reprinted with permission of the publisher.

Wilson Harris:
Wilson Harris, 'History, Fable & Myth in the Caribbean and Guianas' from *History, Fable & Myth in the Caribbean and Guianas* with an introduction by Selwyn Cudjoe. Calaloux Publications, 1995. Reprinted by permission of Calaloux Publications.

Kamau Brathwaite:
Kamau Brathwaite, 'The Love Axe (l): Developing a Caribbean Aesthetic' from *Reading Black: Essays in the Criticism of African, Caribbean and Black American Literature*, edited by Houston Baker. Africana Studies and Research Center, Cornell University. Reprinted by permission of the author.

Gordon Rohlehr:
Gordon Rohlehr, 'Articulating a Caribbean Aesthetic: The Revolution in Self-Perception' from *My Strangled City and Other Essays* (Port-of-Spain: Longman Trinidad, 1992). Reprinted by permission of the author.

Rex Nettleford:
Rex Nettleford, 'The Battle For Space' from *Inward Stretch, Outward Reach: A Voice from the Caribbean* (New York: Caribbean Diaspora Press, 1995). Reprinted by kind permission of Caribbean Diaspora Press.

Sylvia Wynter:
Sylvia Wynter, 'Afterword: Beyond Miranda's Meanings: Un/Silencing the "Demonic Ground" of Caliban's "Woman"' from *Out of the Kumbla: Caribbean Women and Literature*, edited by Carole Boyce Davies and Elaine Savory Fido (Trenton, NJ: Africa World Press, 1990). Reprinted by permission of the author.

Gloria Wekker:
From *Female Desires, Same-Sex Relations and Transgender Practices across Culture*, edited by Evelyn Blackwood and Saskia E. Wieringa. Copyright © 1999 Columbia University Press. Reprinted with permission of the publisher.

Audre Lorde:
© 1984, 2007 by Audre Lorde. Excerpted from: *Sister Outsider – Essays and Speeches by Audre Lorde*, published by The Crossing Press/Random House Inc. New York. Reprinted by permission of the Charlotte Sheedy Literary Agency.

Kamala Kempadoo:
Kamala Kempadoo, 'Theorizing Sexual Relations in the Caribbean: Prostitution and the Problem of the "Exotic"' from *Confronting Power, Theorizing Gender: Interdisciplinary Perspectives in the Caribbean*, edited by Eudine Barriteau (Kingston, Jamaica: University of the West Indies Press, 2003). Reprinted by permission of the publisher.

Jamaica Kincaid:
Jamaica Kincaid, 'In the Night' from *At the Bottom of the River* (London and New York: Vintage Books, 1997).

Margarite Fernández Olmos and Lizabeth Paravisini-Gebert:
Margarite Fernández Olmos and Lizabeth Paravisini-Gebert, 'Introduction' to *Creole Religions of the Caribbean: An Introduction from Vodou and Santería to Obeah and Espiritismo*. 2nd Edition (New York and London: New York University Press, 2011) © 2003 by New York University.

Patrick Bellegarde-Smith:
From *Fragments of Bone: Neo-African Religions in the New World*. Copyright 2005 by the Board of Trustees of the University of Illinois. Used with permission of the University of Illinois Press.

Barry Chevannes:
Barry Chevannes, 'Healing the Nation: Rastafarian Exorcism of the Ideology of Racism in Jamaica' from *Caribbean Quarterly* 36, 1&2 (1990). Reprinted by permission of the publisher.

Aisha Khan:
From *Asian Diasporas: New Formations, New Concept* by Rachel S. Parreñas and Lok C.D. Siu (Editors). Copyright © 2007 by the Board of Trustees of the Leland Stanford Jr. University. All rights reserved. Used with the permission of Stanford University Press, www.sup.org.

Dianne M. Stewart:
Three Eyes for the Journey: African Dimensions of the Jamaican Religious Experience by Stewart (2005) Chp. 'Visitation: The Legacy of African-Derived Religions in Jamaica' pp. 139–187 © Oxford University Press, Inc. by permission of Oxford University Press.

Stuart Hall:
Stuart Hall, 'Thinking the Diaspora: Home-Thoughts from Abroad' from *Small Axe* 6 (Sept 1999). Reprinted by permission of the author.

Sean Lokaisingh-Meighoo:
Nation Dance: Religion, Identity and Cultural Difference in the Caribbean, edited by Patrick Taylor, Copyright © 2001, Indiana University Press, Reprinted with permission of Indiana University Press.

Erna Brodber:
Erna Brodber, 'Re-Engineering Blackspace' from *Caribbean Quarterly*, 43, 1&2 (1997). Reprinted by permission of the author.

Shani Mootoo:
Shani Mootoo, 'Out on Main Street' from *Out on Main Street and other Stories* (Vancouver: Press Gang Publishers, 1993). Reprinted by permission of the author.

Louise Bennett:
Louise Bennett, 'Colonization in Reverse' from *Jamaica Labrish* (Jamaica: Sangster's Book Stores, 1966).

The works of Louise Bennett Coverley is copyrighted, and permission to use said material, has been obtained from the Executors of the Louise Bennett Coverley (LBC) Estate, messers: Judge Pamela Appelt, (pappelt@cogeco.ca) and Fabian Coverley B.Th (fcoverley@gmail.com).

Linton Kwesi Johnson:
Linton Kwesi Johnson, 'Inglan is a Bitch' from *Race Today* 13 (1980/81). Reprinted by permission of the author.

Derek Walcott:
Derek Walcott, 'The Star-Apple Kingdom' from *Collected Poems 1948–1984* (New York: Farrar, Straus and Giroux, 1986).

Introduction: Caribbean Cultural Thought in Pursuit of Freedom

Yanique Hume and Aaron Kamugisha

This collection of articles takes a critical appraisal of the wealth of cultural criticism on, and epistemological developments in, the study of Caribbean societies. In many ways it engages in a dialogic exercise of excavating classic texts of the past and placing them in dialogue with more contemporary interrogations and explorations of regional cultural politics and debates concerning identity, history, coloniality, diaspora, aesthetics, religion and spirituality, gender and sexuality and nationalisms. These seemingly disparate concerns are brought together under the overarching intellectual project of Caribbean Cultural Thought because we want to stress the long history of critical writing on culture and its intersection with political work in the Caribbean intellectual tradition from within the academy and beyond its confines. As an area of inquiry whose contours constantly shift, enveloping various and seemingly contradictory theoretical positions, the study of culture allows us to engage with an extensive range of themes and texts using an interdisciplinary/transdisciplinary lens. Besides this emphasis on blurring disciplinary boundaries to generate a more nuanced and complex engagement with the critical work done on cultural analysis in the region, the volume also takes as its point of departure a more inclusive and comprehensive look at the notion of a Pan-Caribbean regional totality and cultural ethos, unencumbered by the colonially induced linguistic divisions that haunt its scholarship. We hope this work will contribute towards the ongoing project of illustrating the complexity of voices from different historical, political, cultural and territorial perspectives that constitute the region.

In titling this collection *Caribbean Cultural Thought: From Plantation to Diaspora*, we seek to highlight our interest in a critical archive of writing on Caribbean culture with a distinctive, insular Caribbean inflected set of considerations and a tradition of critical engagement with North American and European traditions of writing on culture for over a century. The key words of our subtitle – plantation and diaspora – are crucial counterpoints of Caribbean cultural thought and, respectively, concepts filled with hemispheric and global resonances. However, our intention is not to signal a progression from plantation to diaspora. As we shall show, Caribbean cultural thought has been diasporic from its inception, and in its early conversations with particularly, African American thinkers, constitutes an under-recognized and profound tradition of transnational scholarship (Yelvington 2001).

Writings on the broad field of inquiry we may now call Caribbean culture have certainly existed from the inception of the colonial project in the region. However, many of the most profound studies of culture in the Caribbean have been wedded to a critique of colonial power, and the tradition of cultural thought in the Caribbean that we trace here is yoked to resistance against colonial domination. Anti-colonial thinkers knew that central to any resistance to colonialism were struggles in the domain we call 'the cultural' – and these struggles for self-determination were inseparable from imagining a future free from coloniality. *Caribbean Cultural Thought* thus commences with anti-colonial thought, as the daring of its contestation of coloniality, and the urgency of its quest for something new, resulted in the invention of groundbreaking work in the realm of folklore, critical work on race, and pioneering explorations of an African diasporic aesthetic. This field of inquiry was stimulated by the intensity of nineteenth-century 'scientific' racism and imperialism, and is best seen in the writings of José Martí and Anténor Firmin. Martí's essay 'Our America' is a justly famous and prescient response to the encircling domination of the United States of America, and arguably the classic text of late nineteenth-century Caribbean nationalism. Firmin's *The Equality of the Human Races*, largely unknown outside some Haitian intellectual circles for a century, represents the best Caribbean and African diasporic critical work on race until Frantz Fanon's post-Second World War *Black Skin, White Masks*. According to a leading Africana philosopher, 'his achievement in the text is also a magnificent example of philosophical anthropology and philosophy of human science' (Gordon 2008, 60).

It is the lifework of another Haitian polymath, Jean Price-Mars (1876–1969), that has had the most influential and enduring impact on critical traditions of writing on Caribbean culture. Inspired by the work of Firmin, and roused to action by the US invasion of Haiti in 1915, Price-Mars's *La Vocation de l'élite*, was a critical anti-colonial call to arms – but from the perspective of a national, African-based culture, the lack of which he believed facilitated American hegemony. Over his long career, Price-Mars would be inspired by the Harlem Renaissance, and in turn inspire the négritude movement, and in the process become one of the quintessential figures facilitating the thought and movement of ideas about black cultural sovereignty throughout the African diasporic world. The theories he derived from his anthropological fieldwork and social and political thought and practice – the idea of 'cultural survivals', notions of cultural relativism, and a re-semanticizing of the meaning of African diasporic cultures, rendered by colonial discourse to the barbaric – were crucial for the development of not just an indigenous anthropological tradition in the Caribbean, but the anthropology of people of African descent in the Americas (Magloire and Yelvington 2005). As Gérarde Magloire and Kevin Yelvington have shown, Melville Herskovits 'came to owe a tremendous debt to Price-Mars, both in terms of his theoretical position as well as for significant logistical support when Herskovits came to do fieldwork in Haiti' (Magloire and Yelvington 2005, 11). This rarely acknowledged (including by Herskovits himself) contribution is of considerable significance, as the argument made by Melville Herskovits about African cultural retentions in the Americas is widely acknowledged to be one of *the* decisive contributions to the anthropology of the Americas. The engagements that have followed over the last 70 years – from E. Franklin Frazier and Herskovits's contrary positions of the 1940s, Sidney Mintz and Richard Price's *The Birth of African-American Culture* thesis (often dubbed 'creolization versus creation' thesis) to latter day polemics between rival historiographical/anthropological traditions that oppose rapid creolization of newly arrived Africans to the continual, discernable role of specific African ethnic groups – remain indebted to Herskovits. However, despite his influence on the African American researchers Zora Neale Hurston and Katherine Dunham, Herskovits is perhaps best seen as a contemporary of Price-Mars (rather than *the* pioneer of the field), who worked alongside the major African diaspora figures W.E.B. Du Bois, Carter Woodson, and Fernando Ortiz in the creation of a field of criticism now called African American anthropology.

In Price-Mars we see the consolidation of two traditions – of social and political criticism animated by anti-colonial thought, and a practice of anthropological writing on culture in the Caribbean. Haiti emerges here as a talismanic site for Caribbean thought and criticism, both through the work of Price-Mars and as a result of the tremendous significance of its revolution.

Haiti was instumental to the thought of African diaspora intellectuals from Langston Hughes, Zora Neale Hurston, Katherine Dunham and in the insular Caribbean, three figures fundamental to the development of Caribbean cultural criticism: Alejo Carpentier, C.L.R. James and Sylvia Wynter. Carpentier's debt to Haiti is well known, seen best in his novel *The Kingdom of this World* (Brennan 2001). The Haitian Revolution gave James the subject for his most influential work, *The Black Jacobins: Toussaint L'Ouverture and the San Domingo Revolution*. Sylvia Wynter's elaborate description of the Jonkonnu folk dance commences with an acknowledgement of the work of Price-Mars. The power and resonance of Haiti for C.L.R. James was because 'West Indians first became aware of themselves as a people in the Haitian Revolution' (James 1963, 391). Students of Caribbean thought and criticism are aware that every historical-cultural movement and political conundrum in the wider region since – neo-colonialism, black consciousness, the debt burden and the cultural response to American imperialism – first announced itself there. If Haiti presented the Caribbean with its first nation, it also presented it, in the form of Jean Price-Mars, with a enigma that continues today – how to theorize the national-cultural question in the presence of constitutively diasporic linkages. National and regional culture in the Caribbean demands a theory, implicit or explicit, of diasporic connections – and this is central to much of the most enduring work on Caribbean culture.

If the Haitian Revolution gave the Caribbean and the world anti-colonial thought in action, and the formation of the first free black republic in the Americas, the full flowering of Caribbean anti-colonial thought would be delayed another century. In Haiti and Cuba, anti-colonial resistance to US imperialism and a burgeoning interest by a local intelligentsia in folklore, resulted in the *indigènes* movement of Haiti and *Afrocubanismo* in Cuba by the first two decades of the twentieth century. Marcus Garvey's global movement, followed by the flowering of négritude in Paris, led to both an increased juxtaposition and sharpening of the questions of colonialism and culture. In the aftermath of the Second World War, Indonesia and India's rapid decolonization, armed struggles for sovereignty from Vietnam to Algeria, and civil rights and anti-colonial struggles throughout the world gave the Caribbean intelligentsia a particularly fertile ground to consider the question of national culture. It is worth reflecting that many Caribbean intellectuals who are often more recognized for their political ideas, produced over their lifework a fascinating body of genre-defying scholarship impossible to reduce to one field of inquiry. Thus Garvey wrote poetry, C.L.R. James's first written (though not first published) book was the novel *Minty Alley*, Frantz Fanon in *Black Skin, White Masks* creates a wonderfully complex text that contains psychoanalysis, cultural analysis, philosophy and political thought. Cultural and political nationalism, predicated on a quest for self-determination away from the confines of colonialism, created powerful discourses about Caribbean identity and local and regional culture. However, Caribbean nationalisms also contained their own ideological limits, and in our consideration of them in this collection we contain recent commentaries by Percy Hintzen and Jacqui Alexander that examine the question of incorporation versus exclusion within them.

The aftermath of the Second World War coincided with the advent of another tradition of writing on culture in the Caribbean. What is now known as the 'Puerto Rico project', a joint collaboration between Columbia University and the University of Puerto Rico through which graduate students from the former visited Puerto Rico to do research, introduced the region to two scholars who would become major figures of twentieth-century anthropology – Eric Wolf and Sidney Mintz. Sidney Mintz became arguably the most influential US-based anthropologist of the Caribbean in the last half of the twentieth century, with decisive impacts on the careers of Michel-

Rolph Trouillot and Richard Price among many others. The new interest in the Caribbean as a site for social science investigation after the Second World War also stimulated the idea of a Caribbean Studies, as announced in Vera Rubin's 1957 collection *Caribbean Studies: A Symposium*. In her preface to the second edition of that collection, Rubin states the volume 'delineate(s) the principal conceptual approaches to the study of these New World societies, i.e., the plantation society as a sociohistorical determinant of contemporary subcultures; the synchronic structural-functional analysis of culture and society; the view of history as a resultant of culture diffusion and syncretism; the pluralistic theory of culture and society' (Rubin 1960). Many of the authors and discussants are figures well known in Caribbean circles as the first generation of social science researchers at the then University College of the West Indies – Lloyd Brathwaite, M.G. Smith, Raymond T. Smith. Clearly identifiable among the contributors to Caribbean Studies is another important influence – from a long tradition of African American scholarship, located then largely in historically black colleges in the United States, and given a presence in the form of contributions from E. Franklin Frazier, and Eric Williams, then Chief Minister of Trinidad and Tobago but a past professor of Howard University. This socio-anthropological literature would be paralleled in the work of Morton Klass, whose concern in his study of Indo-Caribbean communities would contribute to the increasingly familiar themes in the study of New World societies – continuity versus change, cultural persistence versus adaptation (Klass 1961).

This connection – growing out of the post-war interest in Caribbean societies and its linkages to older bodies of scholarship – is again seen in the second of Vera Rubin's collections, *Plantation Systems of the New World*. Here, one of the dominant social structures of Caribbean societies becomes a grand theory that links social dynamics in the region to earlier work on the existence of a plantation sphere in the Americas, stretching from the US South to north-eastern Brazil. The plantation is one of the most enduring social structures that have been theorized over time to examine Caribbean society, and a key site where Caribbean social thought begins, with theories of Caribbean modernity, political economy, creolization and pluralism dependent on it. The shift in the meanings associated with the term 'plantation' can be traced from its representation as a site both of unrelenting hostility but filled with meanings for a Caribbean modernity in C.L.R. James' *The Black Jacobins* through the historical anthropological concerns of *Plantation Systems of the New World* to the moment of the 1960s, where Caribbean theorists like Lloyd Best, George Beckford, Lucille Mathurin-Mair and Sylvia Wynter would identify the pervasive social structures instituted by the plantation as the root of contemporary Caribbean inequality. The creation and re-animation of concepts to describe Caribbean culture and society shows both the deep influence from the socio-anthropological work of this time and anti-colonial scholarship and activism. One of the best examples of that twinning can be found in the work of Kamau Brathwaite, whose historical scholarship, poetry, and cultural-theoretical work has always been informed by the labyrinth of ideas that have come to constitute the intellectual history of the region. The sheer intellectual creativity of this period of Caribbean scholarship, stimulated by the global movements of the 1960s, is largely responsible for the Caribbean's role as a major pioneer of many leading theories and debates about cultural and racial mixing and identity formation. Terms like 'transculturation' and 'creolization' with Pan-Caribbean provenances and articluations, are now commonplace in global Cultural Studies. Notwithstanding, the caution we should exercise in assuming the global applicability of its theoretical provocations (Khan 2001) and the elision of the Indo-Caribbean component within the African and European cultural dialectic it extols (Munasinghe 2002), the expansive discourse on interculturation developed in the region has been pivotal to understanding the process of cultural change over time and locale. The various terms coined, (e.g., *transculturación*, creolization, *antillanité*), of course, have their roots in attempts by Caribbean thinkers to theorize the nature of societies that have undergone sudden wrenching change, and to comprehend the lived realities of peoples from all over the 'old' world, yoked together in modern societies, under (post)colonial governmentality. The debates here, which continue until today, include the question of creativity or continuity of transplanted cultures in the Caribbean, pluralism vs. creolization, tradition vs. modernity, and contemporary consumer culture and globalization.

Amidst this robust discourse on the dynamic process of cultural change and identity formation, emerged a related and somewhat localized preoccupation with articulating a Caribbean aesthetic and by extention an independent, non-alienated subjectivity. Central to the (post-)colonial predicament for these scholars was the inherent space of dislocation, alienation and fragmentation from which the Caribbean subject operates within prevailing asymmetrical structures of power and persistent domination. The quest of defining a national/regional aesthetic thus drew heavily on concepts of memory, history and imagination as the scaffold for reconstructing the fractured subject and awakening an innate consciousness that would animate wider socio-political agendas and discourses. Of critical importance, therefore, was coming to terms with the particularities of the existential crisis of New World Africans and the fractured realities of the present born out of the ravages of enslavement and colonial subjugation. Although cognizant of the cultural hybridity of the region, 'Africa' as an icon of a neglected past as well as a cultural and aesthetic resource, became a master symbol for restoring and constructing a collective identity that would counter the hegemonic status quo and the valorization of Europe inherited from colonialism. The call for the revaluation of Africa, which commenced with the négritude movement, was not simply a glorification of an African past but indeed a catalyst for rehabilitating the cultural practices of the folk that remained on the peripheries of New World societies.

It is during the late 1920s and 1930s that we witness Haiti once again leading the way in this cultural process of arguing for a new aesthetic sensibility that incorporated folk culture as the new idiom for expressing Haitianness. Africa became a central theme in the movement's attempt to build a sense of cultural authenticity which would energize and unify modern Haiti. There was an emphasis, therefore, on an African emotive sensibility that stood in opposition to the rationalism of Europe. *Indigénisme*, like its Cuban counterpart *Afrocubanismo*, was influenced by the intellectual upheavals that were taking place in postwar Europe. Paris had become the centre of anti-establishment activities and artistic movements such as Surrealism and Dada and the European interest in the libratory possibilities of African cultures were making their mark on Haitian and Cuban students at home and abroad. Moreover, as Michael Dash argues, the French intellectual interest in racialized and cultural essences encouraged the Haitian artists' desire for cultural authenticity (1981). Poetry that incorporated the folk was a means through which political criticism could be made an avenue for the assertion of an authentic national consciousness and an attempt to link the artist to a larger global community. Both in Haiti and Cuba in the '20s through '30s, in response to the imposed US hegemony, artists sought to create a national artistic aesthetic that created an 'indigenous' cultural sphere through the incorporation of the folk. Although each country represents different political and cultural histories, the work of these artists are tied to a general Caribbean search for identity that is distinct from the European and American colonizer and an identity that permits one to stand in certitude against the effects of domination. In these two early literary and artistic movements, the Caribbean intelligentsia used the international vocabulary of *modernism* to carve their unique space and assert their distinct contribution to the modern world.

This 'passionate research,' as Fanon coins it, was tied to the fragmented cultures created out of the history of slavery and colonization and upon which the new modern identities of Haiti, Cuba, and the rest of the Caribbean found indigenous expression.

The Marvelous Realism as an aesthetic theory, was to emerge as a leading vernacular language for interpreting the magical reality that is life in Latin America and the Caribbean. Scholars like Carpentier relied on resucitating the wealth of folk traditions that unite the seemingly distinct cultural spheres of the region. Continuing along this trajectory, in his seminal 1956 speech 'On the Marvellous Realism of the Haitian,' which we have reproduced in this volume, Haitian novelist Jacques Stephan Alexis furthers the discussion of marvelous realism as an alternative to the model of Négritude as he cautions against the valorization of blackness and advances an argument for interpreting Haitian culture as being inherently creole. Although acknowledging the great contributions Africa has made to Haitian culture, for Alexis, the indigenous practices of the folk were not exclusively neo-African but in fact exhibited traces of Taino and European influences, which fermented to create a dynamic 'cultural syncretism'. It is within this generative mosaic of cultures from diverse origins coexisting within a wretched reality of subjugation that Alexis locates the power of the marvelous. Marvelous realism – the ability to create a new reality through marrying the real with fantasy and the imagination – was the formulation of an aesthetic sensibility that spoke to the needs of the nation but was also universal in its scope and reach.

In subsequent theorizing on Caribbean aesthetics in the immediate post-indepence period in the English-speaking Caribbean, we see further exploration of the concept of creolization and its relationship to processes of indigenization and resistance. This is most noted in Sylvia Wynter's astute reflection on the Jonkonnu, which she demonstrates represented a socio-cultural phenomenon that operated along a register of the carnivalesque and communal religiosity (Wynter 1970). Within indigenous folk expressions the once submerged and subversive self finds a voice to resist and be a counter presence, hence for Wynter, these forms are instrumental for humanizing the hostile terrain in which the once displaced are forced to inhabit. The liberatory ethos of traditional festive and sacred forms that are part and parcel of the cultural armour of the folk created a base from which Kamau Brathwaite and Rex Nettleford would explore the indigenous creative intellect of the folk. Whether through an examination of the indigenous poetics found in the creole tongues of the region, the subsequent literary formations of a canon or embodied through the dancers' body through space and time, the articulation of a national/regional aesthetic cannot be separated from the desire to make sense of a Caribbean existence. Moreover, as Wilson Harris indicates, aesthetics creates a site of historical becoming, a means by which Caribbean people define their place in the annals of history.

In the course of the past two decades the study of Caribbean culture has witnessed a mushrooming of research and publications on the particularities of the construction of gender and sexualities. While far from being a new area of study, current scholarship pushes the analysis of sexual and gendered subjectivities to address broader issues and theoretical concerns including the international sex trade, transnationalism, power and coloniality, racial subjugation, performance, as well as governance and citizenship (Alexander and Mohanty 1997; Kempadoo 2003; Barriteau 2004). When we take a stock of some of the earlier writings on the subject matter we are drawn to an extensive corpus of interdisciplinary scholarship that in a sense sets the stage for further analyses on issues as wide and diverse as Caribbean masculitinities and the performance of gendered identities. It can be argued that Caribbean Studies' entry into the discursive field of anthropology and folklore commenced with the extensive studies on Caribbean kinship structures and most notably the phenomenon of matrififocality. Studies of gender in their earliest instantiation were therefore enveloped within studies on the social formation of the West Indian family unit and mating patterns that deviated from normative Western construction of the nuclear family and social relationships. In this light, as Michel-Rolph Trouillot reminds us, 'Caribbean kinship studies have always been gender studies' (1992, 26).

Out of this body of work emerged significant analytical models for examining the cultural codes and dual value systems of Caribbean societies. However flawed or limited, one of the most enduring of these is the 'respectability and reputation' paradigm developed in Peter Wilson's 1973 study, *Crab Antics*, which outlined the dual value system that structured Caribbean social behaviour. While certainly too generic a formula to neatly fit the diverse societies and socialities of the region, what Wilson does quite well is to begin a dialogue about the socialization of Caribbean men. In many ways, the model of respectability/reputation initiates an exploration of Caribbean masculinities and in particular the role of space in ordering the social worlds of men and women. We see the longevity of this particular analysis in the work of Roger Abrahams, who later focuses on the performance of masculinities through the medium of oral culture or the 'men-of-words', followed by Richard Burton, who furthers this analysis in his reflection on the dynamic spaitialization of play and opposition in Caribbean societies.

Outside of this earlier scholarship on gender, Caribbean feminisms are often thought in the popular imagination and in some scholarly circles to be a development of the last 30 years. However, more considered reflections on Caribbean feminisms have revealed their history to be over a century old (Gregg 2005). Beyond the study of kinship structures and anthropological accounts of gender systems in the Caribbean, a self-conscious literature on women's subordination and gender asymmetries in Caribbean societies has been extant throughout the twentieth century. Activist work in the first half of this century was initially largely dominated by a liberal feminist outlook whose limits were the 'right to education, citizenship, and political participation' in the colonial state, but soon developed a growing nationalist orientation, well seen in the career of Audrey Jeffers of Trinidad and Tobago (Reddock 1990). More forthrightly, anti-colonial figures like Amy Ashwood Garvey, Amy Jacques Garvey and Una Marson would portray an internationalist conviction about the rights of colonial peoples, and the central place of gender in any quest for their liberation. At mid-century, Claudia Jones's anti-imperialism, communism, and quest for Caribbean community in the diaspora would result in an enduring legacy now rightly recuperated as part of the history of Caribbean and Africana feminisms (Boyce-Davies 2008).

Caribbean feminisms have thus always been simultaneously an intra-regional and diasporic enterprise. The selections in this volume by Audre Lorde, Gloria Wekker, Kamala Kempadoo, Jamaica Kincaid and Sylvia Wynter illustrate this, and all belie an easy association with Western feminist thought. It is often said that Caribbean feminisms are indelibly marked by race, but rather than race, it is the deep experience of coloniality which we would suggest is their dominant feature. By coloniality, we refer to a particular form of power with its genesis in the colonial relation, which now defines 'culture, labor, intersubjective relations, and knowledge production well beyond the strict limits of colonial administrations' (Maldonado-Torres 2007). It is this that lies at the heart of the colonial state. Classic and controversial texts like Sylvia Wynter's 'Beyond Miranda's Meanings' are misinterpreted when it is suggested that they privilege race over gender. Rather, it is what Wynter would later call the coloniality of being/power/truth/freedom which is her target – and has animated much of the best work of Caribbean feminisms.

It is arguable that the sphere of religion and spirituality was the area treated with the most unrelenting hostility by colonial institutions and by extension, the most misunderstood part of our contemporary cultural legacy. The engagement with religion and the spiritual landscape of the Caribbean is intimately related to the search for a tangible expression of adaptation and accomodation, which accompanies what Bastide calls, 'the interpenetration of civilizations' (1960). Indeed, religious practices were at the very centre of the creolization process. Many of the traditions existed as forms of cultural continuity, which over time became indigenized through innovative appropriations and the subsequent transformation of the iconographic, aesthetic and cosmological orientations of diverse systems of thought. From the 1920s and 1930s, North American folklorists were among the earliest scholars to explore the varied religious worlds that structured the quotidian lives and social and cultural institutions of the region's inhabitants (Beckwith 1929; Hurston 1938; Courlander 1939). These initial investigations served as catalyst for further studies that would situate religion as a critcial lens for analysing 'New World Africanisms' and the inherent fluidity of religious identities and ritual practices in the Americas (see Deren 1953, Métraux 1959, Barrett 1976, Bastide 1978, Simpson 1978). Located within the historical and social context of the (neo) colonial Caribbean, research on African derived practices revealed the embodied cultural memory of displaced Africans and the creative agency to maintain and refashion their rites and beliefs to suit their new hostile environment. Theories on syncretism would thus form the espistemological foundation for interpeting and, in a sense legitimizing, Neo-African religions and their encounter and confrontation with orthodox Christianity.

The concept of syncreticism illuminated the inventive cultural work of enslaved Africans to reformulate ancient practices, thus harnessing the power of other belief systems through strategic and systematic appropriations and revisions. As an example, chromolithographs of Catholic saints were readily appropriated by practitioners of African-derived religions for their symbolic similarities to the visual motifs associated with African deities and in some cases were interpreted as yet another manifestation of ancient spirits. With the adoption of the Christian liturgical calendar, the Afro-Creole population feasted their gods publicly cloaked in the guise of the saints. To this end, the dominant religion served at once as a mask and also as a component of the revised and expanded religious worlds of New World Africans. However, for Brathwaite, syncretism went a bit further. It not only entailed the process of cultural re-invention, adaptation and change, but also spoke to a process of what he calls, 'psychic marronage'. This entails, 'a syncretic vision of African patterns, symbols and communicative cannons (modes of walking, eating, working, inter-relating, musical, artistic, and other practices) which the subordinate maintains in everyday life even in the course of submitting to large scale socioeconomic pressures of dominance' (Brathwaite 1974). Within Brathwaite's matrix, the concept of syncretism moves beyond the limited realm of religion to that of expressing an ontology of blackness that did not wholly replicate Africa but one that was informed by an African past reconstructed anew as an alternative space, refuge and being. Brathwaite's argument thus forces us to move beyond an uncritical discourse on the functional equivalences of diverse religions cohering to form a new. Instead, his critque and development of the concept of syncretism alerts us to examine Creole religions as existing parallel to dominant systems of thought or indeed, as Chevannes argues in this volume on Rastafari, a process of selective co-optation and reconfiguration of hegemonic doctrine to construct a liberation theology and a self-conscious rejection of colonial domination. In this view, the Creole religions of the Caribbean represent a critical idiom of self-actualization; a means to express an African existence in the Caribbean.

While it is true that all religions are syncretic, as Bellegarde-Smith and Fernández Olmos and Paravisini-Gebert argue in this volume, the concept is never used to interpret world religions such as Islam, Judaism or Christianity. Unlike the bilateral contested process that is at the centre of any understanding of creolization, theories of syncretism have tended to demonstrate a unipolar dynamic wherein non-European and by extension 'inferior' cultures borrow from 'superior' Western models to construct new religious modalities. By extension, Creole religions are understood primarily as derivative forms as opposed to complexly nuanced beliefs systems with their own innate cosmological structure and orientation. The articles presented in this volume caution us to take another look at the prevailing understandings of syncretism and to explore the diversity of the Afro-Creole systems of thought as legitimate and wholistic forms that have been instrumental in giving meaning to the lives of the region's inhabitants. In so doing, they rehabilitate the subjugated indigenous and creole spiritualities and move the dialogue beyond ritual content and function to address broader ideological, political, socio-cultural and historical issues including concepts of diasporic consciousness.

The religious expressions of the Caribbean and the Americas more generally are inherently diasporic in that they were dispersed from a source and refashioned in new disparate territories. They also continue to be exported through migration. However, the literature on this dynamic cultural process has tended to exclusively focus on Afro-Creole religious formation and the subsequent migration of these traditions to urban metropolitan spaces. Aisha Khan shifts the analytical gaze to an examination of the dynamism within Indo-Trinidadian Hindu and Muslim ritual practice. To this end, she argues that religious rituals are not stable constructs but shift depending on the historical, material and ideological contexts and conditions. Likewise, diasporic consciousness forms a constitutive part of the religious identity of Indo-Trinidadians and this identity is articulated through ritual.

In a 1993 interview with Meryl F. Schwartz, the Jamaican writer Michelle Cliff said 'The Caribbean doesn't exist as an entity; it exists all over the world. It started in diaspora and it continues in diaspora' (Schwartz 1993). The Caribbean provides one of the richest sites of exploration of the meaning of the term diaspora. Its societies were constituted by migrants, forced and voluntary, from Africa, Asia and Europe, in territories haunted by the near complete genocide of their original inhabitants, and structured by relations of dominance. In the aftermath of transatlantic slavery and contemporaneous with indentureship, large internal Caribbean labour migrations would re-create the social and cultural landscape of many Caribbean countries. In the twentieth century, Caribbean migrants would create new diasporas in metropolitan cities from London to Amsterdam, Miami to Paris, an incredibly rich archive of work on the meaning of home, diaspora and community would emerge.

Diaspora is presented here not as a culmination, nor just in recognition of its constitutive role in the creation of Caribbean peoples. Rather, we wish to acknowledge a theoretical question that has been consistently raised in this introduction – the impossibility in the Caribbean of theorizing culture without an immediate gesture, and consideration, of diaspora. Whether our subject here has been religion, anti-colonial thought, nationalism, identity or aesthetics, Caribbean theorists have found the cultural unfathomable without a theory of diasporic linkages, solidarities, intimacies. Through mapping the movements and encounters of persons of African descent in metropolitan centres, Brent Hayes-Edwards (2003) reveals how transnational black cultural and intellectual formations within Europe engendered a vision of internationalism and pan-African unity. Likewise, the intellectual production around questions of the cultural has been wedded, at times implicity and explicitly to a braoder African diasporic project. Simultaneously, the highly mobile populations of the region have also engaged in lateral movements within the confines of the Caribbean archipelago and neighbouring Latin American territories, developing hybrid identities and cultural expressions in the peripheries of the global West.

Caribbean Cultural Thought: From Plantation to Diaspora

In the preceding pages, we have sketched our thoughts on the field of Caribbean Cultural Thought that we trace in this work. The intent is not to provide an intellectual history of the term 'culture' in the Caribbean, nor to produce a reader that merely reproduces some of the "best" writings on Caribbean culture over the last few generations. Rather, our interest is excavating the precise theoretical contribution that the study of the Caribbean has made to the study of culture both in and beyond the region – through its locally created terms like transculturation and creolization which now have a global reach, to its deep implication in the creation of the modern world order, and hence its constitutive relationship with the modern project in the West.

In our choice of the term 'cultural thought' in our title, we wish to advance the claim that the critical study of Caribbean culture is in many ways inseparable from a study of its intellectual traditions as well as its social, political and aesthetic dimensions. As we have outlined above, Caribbean cultural thought has emerged in a manner quite distinct from the formation of Cultural Studies in Europe and North America, and it has been significantly different enough in its historical provenances, key debates and questions, and intellectual influences to give us pause before we use the term 'Caribbean Cultural Studies'. A radical anti-colonial praxis has been central to the formation of Caribbean cultural thought, rather than the suzerainty of purely anthropological conceptions of culture in its development. Caribbean cultural theorists from the early twentieth century understood that culture cannot be seen to be shared in any simple sense among a community's members, but that societies are fundamentally divided by class, race and ethnicity. Affect, resistance, pleasure, play, power and desire are transformed by coloniality into something new. To the keywords of contemporary Cultural Studies – hegemony, discourse, articulation, governmentality – Caribbean cultural thought presents the plantation, creolization, transculturation, tidalectics and proffers searching questions to complacent theories of Western modernity, and cultural diasporas.

The choice of articles for *Caribbean Cultural Thought* has been complicated by the incredible breadth of sources that had to be considered, ranging from little known gems to classics in the Caribbean intellectual tradition. In making our selections, we have been anxious to show a fidelity to the territorial, linguistic and cultural complexity of the Caribbean, while constructing a narrative that illustrates our reading of the main trends of the cultural thought of the region. The difficulties posed by questions of the correct balance between easily available classics which demand inclusion and hard to find material which deserves a wider audience has been immense. We have sided with inaccessible material and work that has been non-country specific, conceptual and daring in its scope and has range as representative of the best work of Caribbean cultural thought.[1] The point is not to hope for the impossibility of comprehensiveness, but rather to collect a body of work indicative of major trends in theorizing Caribbean culture over the last century. The absence of sections on language and orality and the Caribbean popular may cause some surprise. Given the scope of our undertaking in this project which has exceeded our original intentions, we have decided to produce another collection provisionally titled *Caribbean Popular and Expressive Culture*, which we expect will be published by Ian Randle Publishers in 2014. It is our hope then, that *Caribbean Cultural Thought* will be read as part of the wider work on Caribbean intellectual traditions to be found in both collections, and in the allied texts *Caribbean Political Thought: From the Colonial State to Caribbean Internationalisms* and *Caribbean Political Thought: Theories of the Post-Colonial State*. *Caribbean Cultural Thought: From Plantation to Diaspora* is then, part of a wider inquiry into and survey of, unsettled questions in Caribbean thought, which we expect will guide our futures for generations still to come.

Yanique Hume and Aaron Kamugisha
Barbados, April 2013

Note
1. We regret our inability to publish Sylvia Wynter's path-breaking essays "Novel and History, Plot and Plantation," *Savacou* 5 (1971): 95-102 and "Jonkonnu in Jamaica," *Jamaica Journal* 4, 2 (June 1970): 34–48 in our reader. However, these articles are due to be published shortly in Sylvia Wynter, *We Must Learn to Sit Down Together and Talk About a Little Culture: Decolonizing Essays* (Leeds: Peepal Tress Press, 2013)

References
Alexander, M. Jacqui and Chandra Mohanty, eds. 1997. *Feminist Genealogies, Colonial Legacies, Democratic Futures*. New York: Routledge.
Barrett, Leonard E. 1976. *The Sun and the Drum: African Roots in Jamaican Folk Tradition*. London: Heinemann.
Barriteau, Eudine. 2003. *Confronting Power, Theorizing Gender: Interdisciplinary Perspectives in the Caribbean*. Kingston, JA: University of the West Indies Press.
Bastide, Roger. 1978. *The African Religions of Brazil: Toward a Sociology of the Interpretation of Civilizations*. Baltimore: Johns Hopkins University Press.
Beckwith, Martha. 1929. *Black Roadways: A Study of Jamaican Folk Life*. Chapel Hill: University of North Carolina Press.
Boyce-Davies, Carole. 2008. *Left of Marx: The Political Life of Black Communist Claudia Jones*. Durham: Duke University Press.
Brathwaite, Edward Kamau. 1974. *Contradictory Omens: Cultural Diversity and Integration in the Caribbean*. Mona, Kingston: Savacou Publications.
Brennan, Timothy. 1995. Introduction to Alejo Carpentier. *Music in Cuba*, ed. Timothy Brennan and trans. Alan West-Durán. London and Minneapolis: Minnesota University Press.
Carpentier, Alejo. 1949/1983. *El Reino de este Mundo*. *Obras Completas*. Vol. II. México: Siglo xxi.
Courlander, Harold. 1939. *Haiti Singing*. Chapel Hill: University of North Carolina Press.
Dash, Michael, J. 1981. *Literature and Ideology in Haiti, 1915–1961*. Totowa, NJ: Barnes & Noble Books.
Deren, Maya. 1953. *Divine Horsemen: The Living Gods of Haiti*. London: Thames and Hudson.
Gordon, Lewis R. 2008. *An Introduction to Africana Philosophy*. Cambridge and New York: Cambridge University Press.
Gregg, Veronica, ed. 2005. *Caribbean Women: An Anthology of Non-Fiction Writing 1890–1980*. Notre Dame, IN.: University of Notre Dame Press.
Henry, Paget. 2010. Caribbean Sociology, Africa, and the African Diaspora. In *The African Diaspora and the Disciplines*, ed. Tejumola Olaniyan and James H. Sweet. Bloomington and Indianapolis: Indiana University Press.
Hurston, Zora Neale. 1938. *Tell My Horse*. Philadelphia: J.P. Lippincott.
James, C.L.R. 1963. Appendix: From Toussaint L'Ouverture to Fidel Castro. In *The Black Jacobins: Toussaint L'Ouverture and the San Domingo Revolution*. London and New York: Vintage.
Kempadoo, Kamala. 2004. *Sexing the Caribbean: Gender, Race and Sexual Labor*. New York: Routledge.
Khan, Aisha. 2001. Journey to the Center of the Earth: The Caribbean as Master Symbol. *Cultuarl Anthropology* 16(3): 271–302.
Klass, Morton. 1961. *East Indians in Trinidad: A Study in Cultural Persistence*. New York: Columbia University Press.
Magloire, Gérarde and Kevin A Yelvington. 2005. Haiti and the Anthropological Imagination. *Gradhiva* 1:2–34.

Maldonado-Torres, Nelson. 2007. On the Coloniality of Being: Contributions to the Development of a Concept. *Cultural Studies* 21 (2,3): 240–70.
Métraux, Alfred. 1959. *Voodoo in Haiti*. New York: Pantheon Books.
Munasinghe, Viranjini. 2002. Nationalism in Hybrid Spaces: The Production of Impurity or of Purity. *American Ethnologist* 29, 3:663–92.
Reddock, Rhoda. 1990. Feminism, Nationalism and the Early Women's Movement in the English-Speaking Caribbean. In *Caribbean Women Writers: Essays From the First International Conference*, ed. Selwyn Cudjoe. Wellesley, Massachusetts: Calaloux Publications.
Rubin, Vera, ed. 1960. *Caribbean Studies: A Symposium*. 2nd ed. Seattle and London: University of Washington Press.
———. 1959. *Plantation Systems of the New World*. Papers and Discussion Summaries of the Seminar Held in San Juan, Puerto Rico. Washington, D.C.: Pan American Union.
Schwartz, Meryl F. 1993. An Interview with Michelle Cliff. *Contemporary Literature* xxxiv, 4:594–619.
Scott, David. 2004. Modernity that Predated the Modern: Sidney Mintz's Caribbean. *History Workshop Journal* 58:191–210.
Simpson, George Eaton. 1978. *Black Religions in the New World*. New York: Columbia University Press.
Wynter, Sylvia. 1970. Jonkonnu in Jamaica. *Jamaica Journal* 4, 2:34–48.
———. 2003. Unsettling the Coloniality of Being/Power/Truth/Freedom: Towards the Human, After Man, Its Overrepresentation – An Argument. *CR: The New Centennial Review* 3, 3:257–337.

Anti-Colonial Thought

The Equality of the Human Races: Positivist Anthropology (excerpt)

Anténor Firmin

Conclusion

> *Agapate allelous*
> (St. John, Chapter XIII)

> *Tous les hommes sont l'homme.*
> Man is every man.
> (Victor Hugo)

After reviewing all the possible arguments put forward in support of the doctrine of the inequality of the human races, we realize that none seems to resist the most superficial examination. We have omitted several of these arguments in our inventory of the errors and prejudices which have such a stranglehold on so many people's minds that they find it impossible even to consider more logical and accurate views. But in the course of an arduous journey, after having climbed mountains and crossed precipices, it is meet that we stop and look back on the road covered thus far. From the heights we observe with satisfaction that we have indeed explored much terrain, but we also know that there are more obscure paths to trod before we reach our destination. Still, we have such a clear view of the landscape that we are able properly to gauge the terrain on which we conduct our investigation. Such is my state of mind as I close this series of discussions of the various scientific notions which, falsely interpreted, seemed to support the thesis of the inequality of the human races.

As we recapitulate the various objections raised in order to destroy the very foundations of every method used to rank the human races, we find that we are justified in asserting that all the races are naturally equal. This equality is upset only when one particular race benefits from favorable evolutionary circumstances to achieve a level of development and acquire certain aptitudes not yet attained by the others. But lest we forget that those now on the heights had to rise from an earlier stage of inferiority, we find both in the past and today, in various places around the globe, many of their congeners living in a state obviously reminiscent of that of their ancestors.

In the beginning, all the human races on earth were equally ignorant, weak, immoral, and ugly, but they gradually evolved for the better, transferring to their descendants various faculties which successive generations would perfect. Physical and moral heredity fixes each acquisition in the family, the district, and the country. These acquisitions add up, and their cumulative effects raise to great heights creatures who started from the very ground. Each race reaches the heights by different itineraries and at different moments. Who can say, then, that one ethnic group is superior to another when we know how long it has taken the most civilized races to attain their current advanced stage and what serendipitous combination of environmental and historical factors has contributed to their development? "Art, poetry, science, morality, all these highest manifestations of humanity," says Ribot, "are akin to a late-blooming costly and delicate plant that bears fruit only thanks to the work of many generations … The ideal did not suddenly appear; it manifested itself gradually."[1]

Social evolution alone is responsible for the differences in the moral and intellectual constitution of the different segments of humanity. Perhaps it could be supposed that the physical and psychological make-up of certain races makes them superior to the others, giving them an evolutionary edge. But why make such a gratuitous supposition when such factors as climate and historical circumstances satisfactorily explain the fast evolutionary pace of these privileged races? The White nations of Europe, for example, did not all reach a similar level of development in the same historical period. We observe, to the contrary, that most of those nations formerly considered hopelessly backward now occupy a preeminent position, whereas others which enjoyed enormous power in the sixteenth and seventeenth centuries have lost all their former status.

Looking at the facts with all the impartiality required by such a serious question, we have established that the Black race, which has been labeled inferior to the rest of humanity, is to the contrary as capable of intellectual and moral progress as any other race. Must some people persist in the errors of the past despite the light which modern science shines on the truth? Must the authority of a few scientists and scholars suffice to legitimize erroneous opinions that have survived over the centuries only through legends and prejudices of which one should be ashamed in this era of freedom and progress? The answer is, a thousand times no!

High above the presumptions and prejudices of scientists and scholars stands science itself; high above the systematic errors of historians stands history itself; more powerful than all the philosophers is philosophy itself. The inventors of systems and creators of doctrines should remember this. The world does not stand still. Nations and races interact on the stage of history, exit, and return in different roles. In the larger scheme of human destiny, none of these roles is insignificant. Equally imbued with dignity, each actor takes a turn at the main role. So things will continue to be until the day when the actors on the stage can comfortably exchange roles, and support and complement one another, effortlessly and without friction, in the larger enterprise which is to carry the intellectual torch that lights the moral and spiritual world as the sun does the physical and material world.

Will the Black race some day play a prominent role in world history, picking up again the torch it had carried on the shores of the Nile to light up the way for the whole of humanity at the dawn of civilization? I think I have sufficiently proven that it lacks nothing to assume such a role. Everything suggests indeed that it will undergo a new transformation from which it will emerge to cause human genius to shine as never before. With its first steps on the road to civilization and freedom it showed such precocious aptitudes that we have every reason to believe and hope that it is destined to fulfill the highest of destinies.

Some will object that the Black race has arrived too late on the scene, that all the places are already occupied, and that nothing new and original can be added to an already old and glorious civilization. Edison in the United States, Renard and Krebs in France, and others in England, Germany, Italy, and throughout Europe have achieved such marvels that the world has become accustomed to wonderful inventions and curious discoveries. Science continues its forward march, and scientists constantly turn their attention to new fields of investigation. It seems clear that those who do not hurry will find nothing to do, for soon all problems will have been solved, all questions answered, all moral and material truths found, labeled, and classified. All we will need is a giant index, and no question will embarrass us, no natural or supernatural force will be beyond our understanding.

Fortunately, things will not reach this point, if they ever do, until the earth is peopled entirely by human beings as wise and enlightened as those superior men are supposed to be, and there are no more than twenty or so of those in a century. So until then we have a long way to go. The road to civilization lies before us, long, immense, endless. In two centuries, our great-grandchildren will find us as backward as we find the people of the seventeenth century, who themselves were so advanced in comparison with the people of the fifteenth century barely emerging from the tumult and chaos of feudalism. "In reality," says Sir John Lubbock, "we are only on the threshold of civilization. Far from slowing down, the development of knowledge and, we might add, of the power of man, seems lately to have been quickening as never before. There are many things we have not yet thought of in all our philosophy; there are many more discoveries to be made that will immortalize their authors and bring benefits to the human race which we today may not be capable of appreciating. We can say, with our illustrious countryman, Sir Isaac Newton, that we have been like children playing on the sea shore and picking up a smooth pebble here and a pretty shell there, while before us lies unexplored the great ocean of truth."[2]

Such insights are not only brilliant, they are also accurate and profound. No, it will never be too late for either an individual or a race to ascend to the world of enlightenment, to enter the domain of science. As it hurries through the necessary stages of its upward evolution, the Black race must not despair in its upward climb toward the heights of civilization now flourishing in all its European exuberance. The race indeed has no reason to despair nor to tire. It must constantly reinforce its conviction that it is equal to all the other races on the planet. To believe in equality is to make a moral commitment to spare no effort in order to translate that belief into facts and results. Once the race makes such a commitment, a new day of glory awaits. It will play a splendid role in the affairs of the world. Its main contribution to progress will be to promote justice more forcefully and, at the same time, much more tactfully, than the blasé and heartless races that have arisen in Europe or emerged on the plains of the Middle Empire and in the land of the Tartars.

The Negro race, which has been martyred, scorned, discriminated against, brutalized, and systematically exterminated, would be justified to feel righteous anger and to dream of crushing its persecutors and its former oppressors. But its generosity will prevail, for the more one has suffered, the more one is prepared to understand and exercise justice. From the depths of intellectual and moral poverty in which they had been thrown by the combined effects of various prejudices, the race has emerged endowed with a virile courage and an ineffable kindness, twin virtues which tend to foster a tempered sense of justice.

No one today doubts the courage of Blacks, for history offers enough bloody examples to convince even the greatest skeptics. Still, their courage must never turn into violence nor must it degenerate into brutality. The detractors of the Negro race have never denied it physical equality. To the contrary, in all those works which put forward the thesis of the inequality of the races with such a combination of astonishing inconsistency and rare tenacity, the authors usually suggest that the Black race is by far superior when it comes to brute force. When in asserting their claims to ethnic and social equality the children of Africa renounce more dignified methods of struggle and resort, instead, to burning and killing, they merely lend support to a false theory which inspires others malevolently and purposely to exaggerate their least faults. To achieve equality, which is a natural and imprescriptible right, given that science has proven that no human race is superior to any other in terms of abilities, the Black race must ceaselessly aspire to conquer the moral and intellectual forces which alone guarantee equality among human beings. The race must grow in intelligence and morality. Only education and justice will ensure its triumph, for these are irresistible weapons in both social and international struggles.

With an educated mind, the Ethiopian will read into the past. The wisdom of philosophy will enable him to sort out facts and to weigh past and current suggestions every time he has to pass judgment or adopt a rule of conduct. Instead of harboring hatred in his heart, he will generously spread the inexhaustible love of which he is naturally endowed, so much so that those who do not know the rich and varied qualities of his temperament will read into it a feminine trait even as they behold him at his most masculine behavior. Facing the other races, he will remember his days of humiliation under the yoke of slavery, when he was forced to pay with his sweat for the luxurious way of life of the sybaritic colonizer. But he will also go back further in history, as far actually as the protohistoric epochs. As he reviews the past, he will then remember that there had been a time when the savage Tamahou and the humble Amou, the children of Seth and Japheth, were themselves under the harsh rule of his Black ancestors. The gigantic monuments which are the glory of Egypt had been built with the labor of Whites from the East and the West. Humanity is one in time as in space; the injustices of past centuries echo those of present centuries.

There comes a stage in history, however, when long fighting antagonists feel the need to reach some sort of regenerative conciliation which would serve better their material and moral interests. While I harbor no utopian illusions and no fanatical faith, I do believe that all nations and races are now being irresistibly propelled toward this stage of equilibrium. Since the French Revolution broke down old traditions to allow man an unprecedented sense of his own greatness and dignity, people's minds everywhere have become superbly enlightened. Noble France set things in motion by inscribing the principle of equality as the underpinning of her declaration of the rights of man. The voice of France crossed mountains and oceans to be heard all around the world. It is a voice that will always be heard. Should all the legions mobilized by an obsolete, scholastic and theological mindset unite to assert that all human beings are not equal, that the races are not equal, the revolutionary voice will still resound in the hearts and minds of all like the trumpet of the Day of Judgment. The message conveyed by this voice, which underlies the evolutionary dynamics of humanity as whole, will inspire all the races in their conquest of science and civilization, late blooming but eternally beautiful flowers which burgeon on every branch and twig of the human tree.

All men are brothers. These are golden words, ceaselessly repeated ever since the day the Prophet of Nazareth lay his hand on the great and the humble, giving the same blessing to all. Anyone hiding in his heart the least doubt about the brotherhood of all human beings, which has become one of the fundamental beliefs of modern society, would be too ashamed to express his secret obsession out loud. He would be too afraid to offend the prevailing sense of morality in thus opposing the principle of solidarity by which each human being is linked to all others by bonds of solidarity. But I fear it must be said, however, that this notion of universal brotherhood has remained a mere joke for most civilized nations. The idea is still part of current thinking only because it is convenient. The problem is that logically one cannot conceive of brotherhood without equality. Such a conception would fly in the face of every notion of philosophy and modern law. Proven by science and confirmed by increasingly numerous, eloquent, and indisputable facts, the principle of the equality of the races is the true basis of human solidarity. Patent injustice can never cement a sincere alliance or a moral engagement between two parties who would feel bound for the most elevated and noble reasons conceivable in human nature.

It is to the honor of the nineteenth century to have seen the dawn of the true religion in which man will accompany his fellow man everywhere and at all times in the pursuit of the common good and the general amelioration of the species.

Once they acknowledge they are all equal, the races will be able to support and love one another. While they have generally the same abilities, each one will develop certain exquisite qualities of the heart, the mind, and the body in response to the stimuli of their respective milieus. Inevitably, then, the races will always need to complement one another if they are to live, develop, and flourish in their own environments. They can help one another in exploiting nature, for there are no inferior or superior participants in the work of universal progress, which gathers side by side workers and thinkers, both Black and White. Once those who harbor ideas of domination and supremacy over others have abandoned such pretensions, the races will move closer to one another and get to know one another. This new coexistence will foster a spirit of generosity such that even differences, appreciated without bias, will become sources of attraction. Such is the case, as we often observe, when two people of quite different races get over their initial surprise, approach each other, and speak to each other, using to communicate the exclusively human faculty of speech. The more one is struck by the physical differences of the other, the more one takes pleasure in discovering that the essence of humanity is identical and constant in all ethnic groups, that members of different races with the same level and kind of education will form the same ideas around a given object or a particular fact. True brotherhood develops out of such exchanges of feelings and ideas.

In the universal alliance of peoples and races, certainly there are, and always will be, advanced groups and backward ones. The same state of things which prevails on a small scale within each nation must naturally prevail as well on the larger scale of the community of nations. But instead of being divided into superior and inferior races, the human community will be divided into civilized nations and savage or barbarian peoples. Among the civilized nations themselves, some are first rate, others low ranking, and still many others intermediate. In other words, each national community can be studied, evaluated, and deemed endowed with a superior or inferior civilization depending on its level of sociological development compared to a certain ideal of the civilized state. There will be no question of race, for the word implies a biological and natural fatality which has no correlation with the degree of ability observable among the different human communities spread around the globe. It is no news to anyone today that there are countless Negroes who are much more civilized, intelligent, and educated than most Caucasians. There are even more striking examples among the Mongolian race. Is it not an abuse of language, therefore, to speak of superior races and inferior races? Such an abuse of language has unfortunately fathered the most harmful ideas, to which both ignorant masses and trained scientists sacrifice daily their intelligence or common sense. Thus slowly and imperceptibly arises the greatest obstacle to the development of a sense of human solidarity, the most effective stimulus of progress and prosperity for our species. We must act against this obstacle which has become an established prejudice.

My wish is that this book will enlighten minds, inspire a sense of justice in all, and compel one and all to face reality. Perhaps European scientists, who are still convinced of the superiority of their race, will stop, think, and realize that they have been the victims of an illusion. The current state of the world, the myths and legends which had shaped their thought as children, the traditions that had continuously fed their intelligence, everything necessarily led them to a doctrine, to a set of beliefs, which appearances seem to justify. But can they persevere in a proven error without renouncing the exercise of reason, the greatest endowment of humanity? Will prejudice, the belief that a more or less white complexion is a sign of superiority, remain forever in the best minds despite the facts which prove its falseness? This cannot be, for reason shall always prevail. When they see in the facts, as in a mirror, what their own intelligence had been whispering to them, they will think again. I have no doubt that they will hasten to reject all those ideas which are inconsistent with the moral and intellectual temper of our century.

Returning to the truth, they will realize that human beings everywhere are endowed with the same qualities and defects, without distinctions based on color or anatomical shape. The races are equal; they are all capable of rising to the most noble virtues, of reaching the highest intellectual development; they are equally capable of falling into a state of total degeneration. Throughout all the struggles that have afflicted, and still afflict, the existence of the entire species, one mysterious fact signals itself to our attention. It is the fact that an invisible chain links all the members of humanity in a common circle. It seems that in order to prosper and grow human beings must take an interest in one another's progress and happiness and cultivate those altruistic sentiments which are the greatest achievement of the human heart and mind.

The doctrine of the equality of the human races, which consecrates these rational ideas, thus becomes a regenerative doctrine, an eminently salutary doctrine for the harmonious development of the species. Ultimately, it evokes for us the most beautiful thought uttered by a great genius, "Every man is man," and the sweetest divine instruction, "Love one another."

Notes
1. Th. Ribot, *De l'Hérédité*, 390.
2. John Lubbock, *Prehistoric Times*, 615.

Our America

José Martí

The prideful villager thinks his hometown contains the whole world, and as long as he can stay on as mayor or humiliate the rival who stole his sweetheart or watch his nest egg accumulating in its strongbox he believes the universe to be in good order, unaware of the giants in seven-league boots who can crush him underfoot or the battling comets in the heavens that go through the air devouring the sleeping worlds. Whatever is left of that sleepy hometown in America must awaken. These are not times for going to bed in a sleeping cap, but rather, like Juan de Castellano's men, with our weapons for a pillow, weapons of the mind, which vanquish all others. Trenches of ideas are worth more than trenches of stone.

A cloud of ideas is a thing no armored prow can smash through. A vital idea set ablaze before the world at the right moment can, like the mystic banner of the last judgment, stop a fleet of battleships. Hometowns that are still strangers to one another must hurry to become acquainted, like men who are about to do battle together. Those who shake their fists at each other like jealous brothers quarreling over a piece of land or the owner of a small house who envies the man with a better one must join hands and interlace them until their two hands are as one. Those who, shielded by a criminal tradition, mutilate, with swords smeared in the same blood that flows through their own veins, the land of a conquered brother whose punishment far exceeds his crimes, must return that land to their brother if they do not wish to be known as a nation of plunders. The honorable man does not collect his debts of honor in money, at so much per slap. We can no longer be a nation of fluttering leaves, spending our lives in the air, our treetop crowned in flowers, humming or creaking, caressed by the caprices of sunlight or thrashed and felled by tempests. The trees must form ranks to block the seven-league giant! It is the hour of reckoning and of marching in unison, and we must move in lines as compact as the veins of silver that lie at the roots of the Andes.

Only runts whose growth was stunted will lack the necessary valor, for those who have no faith in their land are like men born prematurely. Having no valor themselves, they deny that other men do. Their puny arms, with bracelets and painted nails, the arms of Madrid or of Paris cannot manage the lofty tree and so they say the tree cannot be climbed. We must load up the ships with these termites who gnaw away at the core of the patria that has nurtured them: if they are Parisians or Madrileños then let them stroll to the Prado by lamplight or go to Tortoni's for an ice. These sons of carpenters who are ashamed that their father was a carpenter! These men born in America who are ashamed of the mother that raised them because she wears an Indian apron, these delinquents who disown their sick mother and leave her alone in her sickbed! Which one is truly a man, he who stays with his mother to nurse her through her illness, or he who forces her to work somewhere out of sight, and lives off her sustenance in corrupted lands, with a worm for his insignia, cursing the bosom that bore him, sporting a sign that says 'traitor' on the back of his paper dress-coat? These sons of our America, which must save herself through her Indians, and which is going from less to more, who desert her and take up arms in the armies of North America, which drowns its own Indians in blood and is going from more to less! These delicate creatures who are men but do not want to do men's work! Did Washington, who made the land for them, go and live with the English during the years when he saw the English marching against his own land? These incroyables who drag their honor across foreign soil, like the incroyables of the French Revolution, dancing, smacking their lips, and deliberately slurring their words!

And in what patria can a man take greater pride than in our long-suffering republics of America, erected among mute masses of Indians upon the bloodied arms of no more than a hundred apostles, to the sound of the book doing battle against the monk's tall candle? Never before have such advanced and consolidated nations been created from such disparate factors in less historical time. The haughty man thinks that because he wields a quick pen or a vivid phrase the earth was made to be his pedestal, and accuses his native republic of irredeemable incompetence because its virgin jungles do not continually provide him with the means of going about the world a famous plutocrat, driving Persian ponies and spilling champagne. The incapacity lies not in the emerging country, which demands forms that are appropriate to it and a grandeur that is useful, but in the leaders who try to rule unique nations, of a singular and violent composition, with laws inherited from four centuries of free practice in the United States and nineteen centuries of monarchy in France. A guacho's pony cannot be stopped in midbolt by one of Alexander Hamilton's laws. To govern well, one must attend closely to the reality of the place that is governed. In America, the good ruler does not need to know how the German or Frenchman is governed, but what elements his country is composed of and how he can marshal them so as to reach, by means and institutions born from the country itself, the desirable state in which every man knows himself and is active, and all men enjoy the abundance that Nature, for the good of all, has bestowed on the country they make fruitful by their labor and defend with their lives. The government must be born from the country. The spirit of the government must be the spirit of the country. The form of the government must be in harmony with the country's natural constitution. The government is no more than an equilibrium among the country's natural elements.

In America the natural man has triumphed over the imported book. Natural men have triumphed over an artificial intelligentsia. The native mestizo has triumphed over the alien, pure-blooded criollo. The battle is not between civilization and barbarity, but between false erudition and nature. The natural man is good, and esteems and rewards a superior intelligence as long as that intelligence does not use his submission against him or offend him by ignoring him – for that the natural man deems unforgivable, and he is prepared to use force to regain the respect of anyone who wounds his sensibilities or harms his interests. The tyrants of America have come to power by acquiescing to these scorned natural elements and have fallen as soon as they betrayed them. The republics have purged the former tyrannies of their inability to know the true elements of the country, derive the form of government from them, and govern along with them. Governor, in a new country, means Creator.

In countries composed of educated and uneducated sectors, the uneducated will govern by their habit of attacking and resolving their doubts with their fists, unless the educated learn the art of governing. The uneducated masses are lazy and timid about matters of the intellect and want to be well-governed, but if the government injures them they shake it off and govern themselves. How can our governors emerge from the universities when there is not a university in America that teaches the most basic element of the art of governing, which is the analysis of all that is unique to the peoples of America? Our youth go out into the world wearing Yankee – or French – colored glasses and aspire to rule by guesswork a country they do not know. Those unacquainted with the rudiments of politics should not be allowed to embark on a career in politics. The literary prizes must not go to the best ode, but to the best study of the political factors in the student's country. In the newspaper, lecture hall, and academies, the study of the country's real factors must be carried forward. Simply knowing those factors without blindfolds or circumlocutions is enough – for anyone who deliberately or unknowingly sets aside a part of the truth will ultimately fail because of the truth he was lacking, which expands when neglected and brings down whatever is built without it. Solving the problem after knowing its elements is easier than solving it without knowing them. The natural man, strong and indignant, comes and overthrows the authority that is accumulated from books because it is not administered in keeping with the manifest needs of the country. To know is to solve. To know the country and govern it in accordance with that knowledge is the only way of freeing it from tyranny. The European university must yield to the American university. The history of America from the Incas to the present must be taught in its smallest detail, even if the Greek Archons go untaught. Our own Greece is preferable to the Greece that is not ours; we need it more. Statesmen who arise from the nation must replace statesmen who are alien to it. Let the world be granted onto our republics, but we must be the trunk. And let the vanquished pedant hold his tongue, for there is no patria in which a man can take greater pride than in our long-suffering American republics.

Our feet upon a rosary, our heads white, and our bodies a motley of Indian and criollo we boldly entered the community of nations. Bearing the standard of the Virgin, we went out to conquer our liberty. A priest, a few lieutenants, and a woman built a republic in Mexico upon the shoulders of the Indians. A Spanish cleric, under cover of his priestly cape, taught French liberty to a handful of magnificent students who chose a Spanish general to lead Central America against Spain. Still accustomed to monarchy, and with the sun on their chest, the Venezuelans in the north and the Argentines in the south set out to construct nations. When the two heroes clashed and the continent was about to be rocked, one of them, and not the lesser one, turned back. But heroism is less glorious in peacetime than in war, and thus rarer, and it is easier for a man to die with honor than to think in an orderly way. Exalted and unanimous sentiments are more readily governed than the diverging, arrogant, alien, and ambitious ideas that emerge when the battle is over. The powers that were swept in the epic struggle, along with the feline wariness of the species and the sheer weight of reality, undermined the edifice that had raised the flags of nations sustained by wise governance in the continual practice of reason and freedom over the crude and singular regions of our mestizo America with its towns of bare legs and Parisian dress-coats. The colonial hierarchy resisted the republic's democracy, and the capital city, wearing its elegant cravat, left the countryside, in its horsehide boots, waiting at the door; the redeemers born from books did not understand that a revolution that had triumphed when the soul of the earth was unleashed by a savior's voice had to govern with the soul of the earth and not against or without it. And for all these reasons, America began enduring and still endures the weary task of reconciling the discordant and hostile elements it inherited from its perverse, despotic colonizer with the imported forms and ideas that have, in their lack of local reality, delayed the advent of a logical form of government. The continent, deformed by three centuries of a rule that denied man the right to exercise his reason, embarked – overlooking or refusing to listen to the ignorant masses that had helped it redeem itself – upon a government based on reason, the reason of all directed toward the thing that are of concern to all, and not the university-taught reason of the few imposed upon the rustic reason of others. The problem of independence was not the change in form, but the change in spirit.

Common cause had to be made with the oppressed in order to consolidate a system that was opposed to the interests and governmental habits of the oppressors. The tiger, frightened away by the flash of gunfire, creeps back in the night to find his prey. He will die with flames shooting from his eyes, his claws unsheathed, but now his step is inaudible for he comes on velvet paws. When the prey awakens, the tiger is upon him. The colony lives on in the republic, but our America is saving itself from its grave blunders – the arrogance of the capital cities, the blind triumph of the scorned campesinos, the excessive importation of foreign ideas and formulas, the wicked and impolitic disdain for the native race – through the superior virtue, confirmed by necessary bloodshed, or the republic that struggles against the colony. The tiger waits behind every tree, crouches in every corner. He will die, his claws unsheathed, flames shooting from his eyes.

But 'these countries will be saved', in the words of Argentine Rivadavia, who erred on the side of urbanity during crude times; the machete is ill-suited to a silken scabbard, nor can the spear be abandoned in a country won by the spear, for it becomes enraged and stands in the doorway of Iturbide's Congress demanding that 'the fair-skinned man be made emperor.' These countries will be saved because, with the genius of moderation that now seems, by nature's serene harmony, to prevail in the continent of light, and the influence of the critical reading that has, in Europe, replaced the fumbling ideas about phalansteries in which the previous generation was steeped, the real man is being born to America, in these real times.

What a vision we were: the chest of an athlete, the hands of a dandy, and the forehead of a child. We were a whole fancy dress ball, in English trousers, a Parisian waistcoat, a North American overcoat, and a Spanish bullfighter's hat. The Indian circled about us, mute, and went to the mountaintop to christen his children. The black, pursued from afar, alone and unknown, sang his heart's music in the night, between waves and wild beasts. The campesinos, the men of the land, the creators, rose up in blind indignation against the disdainful city, their own creation. We wore epaulets and judge's robes, in countries that came into the world wearing rope sandals and Indian headbands. The wise thing would have been to pair, with charitable hearts and the audacity of our founders, the Indian headband and the judicial robe, to undam the Indian, make place for the able black, and tailor liberty to the bodies of those who rose up and triumphed in its name. What we had was the judge, the general, the man of letters, and the cleric. Our angelic youth, as if struggling from the arms of an octopus, cast their heads into the heavens and fell back with sterile glory, crowned with clouds. The natural people, driven by instinct, blind with triumph, overwhelmed their gilded rulers. No Yankee or European book could furnish the key to the Hispanoamerican enigma. So the people tried hatred instead, and our countries amounted to less and less each year. Weary of useless hatred, of the struggle of book against sword, reason against the monk's taper, city against the tempestuous or inert natural nation, we are beginning, almost unknowingly, to try love. The nations arise and salute one another. 'What are we like?' they ask, and begin telling each other what they are like. When a problem arises in Cojimar they no longer seek the solution in Danzig. The frock-coats are still French, but the thinking begins to be American. The young men of America are rolling up their sleeves and plunging their hands into the dough, and making it rise with the leavening of their sweat. They understand that there is too much imitation, and that salvation lies in creating. Create is this generation's password. Make wine from plantains: it may be sour, but it is our wine! It is now understood that a country's form of government must adapt to its natural elements, that absolute ideas, in order not to collapse over an error of form, must be expressed in relative forms: that liberty, in order to be viable, must be sincere and full, that if the republic does not open its arms to all and include all in its progress, it dies. The tiger inside came in through the gap, and so will the tiger outside. The general holds the cavalry's speed to the pace of the infantry, for if he leaves the infantry far behind, the enemy will surround the cavalry. Politics is strategy. Nations must continually criticize themselves, for criticism is health, but with a single heart and a single mind. Lower yourselves to the unfortunate and raise them up in you arms! Let the heart's fires unfreeze all that is motionless in America, and let the country's natural blood surge and throb through its veins! Standing tall, the workmen's eyes full of joy, the new men of America are saluting each other from one country to another. Natural statesmen are emerging from the direct study of nature; they read in order to apply what they read, not copy it. Economists are studying problems at their origins. Orators are becoming more temperate. Dramatists are putting native characters onstage. Academies are discussing practical subjects. Poetry is snipping off its wild, Zorilla-esque mane and hanging up its gaudy waistcoat on the glorious tree. Prose, polished and gleaming, is replete with ideas. The rulers of Indian republics are learning Indian languages.

America is saving herself from all her dangers. Over some republics the octopus sleeps still, but by the law of equilibrium, other republics are running into the sea to recover the lost centuries with mad and sublime swiftness. Others, forgetting that Juárez traveled in a coach drawn by mules, hitch their coach to the wind and take a soap bubble for coachman – and poisonous luxury, enemy of liberty, corrupts the frivolous and opens the door to foreigners. The virile character of others is being perfected by the epic spirit of a threatened independence. And others, in rapacious wars against their neighbors, are nurturing an unruly soldier caste that may devour them. But our America may also face another danger, which comes not from within but from differing origins, methods, and interests of the continent's two fractions. The hour is near when she will be approached by an enterprising and forceful nation that will demand intimate relations with her, though it does not know her and disdains her. And virile nations self-made by the rifle and the law love other virile nations, and love only them. The hour of unbridled passion and ambition from which North America may escape by the ascendency of the purest element in its blood – or into which its vengeful and sordid masses, its tradition of conquest, and the self-interest of a cunning leader could plunge it – is not yet so close, even to the most apprehensive eye, that there is no time for it to be confronted and averted by the manifestation of a discreet and unswerving pride, for its dignity as a republic, in the eyes of the watchful nations of the Universe, places upon North America a brake that our America must not remove by puerile provocation, ostentatious arrogance, or patricidal discord. Therefore the urgent duty of our America is to show herself as she us, one in soul and intent, rapidly overcoming the crushing weight of her past and stained only by the fertile blood shed by hands that do battle against ruins and by veins that were punctured by our former masters. The disdain of the formidable neighbor who does not know her is our America's greatest danger, and it is urgent – for the day of the visit is near – that her neighbor come to know her, and quickly, so that he will not disdain her, he will remove his hands from her in respect. One must have faith in the best in man and distrust the worst. ne must give the best every opportunity, so that the worst will be laid bare and overcome. If not, the worst will prevail. Nations should have one special pillory for those who incite them to futile hatreds, and another for those who do not tell them the truth until it is too late.

There is no racial hatred, because there are no races. Sickly, lamp-lit minds string together and rewarm the library-shelf races that the honest traveler and the cordial observer seek in vain in the justice of nature, where the universal identity of man leaps forth in victorious love and turbulent appetite. The soul, equal and eternal, emanates from bodies that are diverse in form and color. Anyone who promotes and disseminates opposition or hatred among races is committing a sin against humanity. But within that jumble of peoples which lives in close proximity to our peoples, certain peculiar and dynamic characteristics are condensed – ideas and habits of expansion, acquisition, vanity, and greed – that could, in a period of internal disorder or precipitation of a people's cumulative character, cease to be latent national preoccupations and become a serious threat to the neighboring, isolated and weak lands that the strong country declares to be perishable and inferior. To think is to serve. We must not, out of a villager's antipathy, impute some lethal congenital wickedness to the continent's light-skinned nation simply because it does not speak our language or share our view of what home life should be or resemble us in its political failings, which are different from ours, or because it does not think highly of quick-tempered, swarthy men or look with charity, from its still uncertain eminence, upon those less favored by history who, in heroic stages, are climbing the road that republics travel. But neither should we seek to conceal the obvious facts of the problem, which can, for the peace of the centuries, be resolved by timely study and the urgent, wordless union of the continental soul. For the unanimous hymn is already ringing forth, and the present generation is bearing industrious America along the road sanctioned by our sublime forefathers. From the Rio Bravo to the Straits of Magellan, the Great Cemi, seated on a condor's back, has scattered the seeds of the new America across the romantic nations of the continent and the suffering islands of the sea!

The Vocation of the Elite

Jean Price-Mars
Translated by Bernadette Farquhar

Ladies and gentlemen, I tried in previous studies to identify the historical origin of the elite and it might have appeared to many of you that that was a futile undertaking. After all, rightly or wrongly, each of us holds that view that we ascribe by tacit agreement to the high and the low in our society, which is that the main events of our history, analyzed ad infinitum, are so familiar to us that if we recall them in order to make certain sociological conclusions, we run the risk of seeing interest and attention evaporate rapidly.

However, whether we like it or not, no conscientious observer can measure the extent and the complexity of the ills facing Haiti without studying its history. Furthermore, thanks to a new phenomenon, which is foreign intervention and military occupation, the question of Haiti's history is more current than ever, not only because American action has forced us to re-examine ourselves, consider our faults carefully and correct them, but also because that action infuses fervent and despairing souls with a nostalgia for the heroic past. Above all, somewhat in spite of that action and certainly in spite of ourselves, we have had the opportunity over the past two years for daily comparisons of the values through which Haitians of old and even of today meet challenges with a dignity which, to our own eyes, enhances our worth.

It therefore seemed to me neither tiresome nor useless to define the role that the elite must play in the course of the present crisis, taking into account historical information, whether we consider the *American intervention* as a part of the world war and therefore as an accident whose character will not be clearly known until that conflict itself comes to an end, or whether we consider it now from the most pessimistic of angles, that is to say as the ultimate political status of the Haitian people. In either case, since we cannot repel it, wallowing in useless regret and bitter lament is inappropriate. The time for that is past.

On the contrary, while pointing in unending protest to what is right in contrast to the brutality of the deed, we need to determine how we can adapt our society to the new regime, but we must disassociate ourselves from its aims, secret or declared, so that our discontent does not become powerlessness or a tendency towards collective suicide.

It appears, therefore, that in the struggle taking place in our country, we have a role to play which events have assigned to us whether we like it or not. Because of the foregoing considerations, no study seems more appropriate than the assessment of the real nature of the Haitian elite.

***

But first, what does that elite represent and what are its components? Those two questions were partially answered when the role of the population and of events in the formation of Haitian society was described. I sought to demonstrate, as you will recall, that the initial point of departure for the change from a colonial society to a politically and economically independent society was the elimination of the old systems and the almost automatic replacement of the landowners by the leaders of the masses in revolt. One of the points that I stressed and on which I think that I can garner the unanimous support of thinkers is that this historically established fact had unmistakable social and political implications for the future development of our nation.

It follows, therefore, that the national elite was, in the past, the slow and laborious creation of the genius of that race which brought to its country of exile the rather vague possibilities of ethnic rehabilitation. It was, in short, the result of extremely involuntary selection processes practiced from time immemorial on the sensibilities and latent knowledge of African tribes. In recent times, those processes created in this hemisphere a decisive era of evolution through cross fertilization, spawning from among the enslaved masses the leaders who freed our race from the forces of oppression and brutalization.

So, if our definition is correct, not only was yesterday's elite a product of its milieu and in perfect harmony with it, but, however imaginative we are, we cannot conceive of the possibility that our society could exist without the discipline and leadership which that elite provided. Well then, what strange and disturbing phenomenon accounts for the fact that what was the norm yesterday is now only a memory tainted with very deep regret?

How do we explain that distance which separates the elite from the masses, so much so that even the least observant can immediately recognize that our nation seems to be divided into distinct segments, like so many watertight compartments? How do we explain that we are so divided socially that our elite seem to be a foreign organism superimposed on the rest of the nation, living in an ambiguous parasitical relationship with the masses?

This discussion is dominated by two sets of information, one economic, the other psychological. Analyzing them sheds some light on this strange phenomenon and helps to dispel the obscurity that surrounds the issue.

The first set of information was adequately explained – at least I like to think so –when in previous lectures I tried to point out that the abolition of slave labour, obtained through much bloody sacrifice, only changed the condition of the masses superficially. In reality, legal slavery ceded to a hybrid form of servitude which merely entailed a change of persons and responsibilities. In spite of the subsequent exclusion and dispossession of the privileged class of large landowners, in spite of the grandiloquence of the legal documents and the good intentions of ideologues, the new indigenous society maintained, insidiously and tacitly, the old class structure. The most apparent result of this state of affairs was that, barring a few obscure changes which included the introduction of a rather crude wage system as the only tangible innovation, the lower social classes were left with the same tasks they previously had. Of course, in this wage system that continues today almost unchanged, the work contract, while not containing the principle of a day's salary for a day's work, at least entitled the labourer to payment in kind, which was a fourth and then a half of the goods produced.

But this system, by itself, scarcely denoted progress To be an indication of progress, it needed to be considered less than an end and more as a means, one of the means which marked a stage between slave labour and labour rewarded according to its real worth and the ability of the worker, one of those means used universally to raise the dignity of the individual through wealth and knowledge. Unfortunately, sharecropping, known as *de moitié* or the half and half system, was to date the only form of payment accorded to most workers by landowners. This is because management and labour not only imposed on each other a habit of routine inimical to progress and modernization of farming techniques, but also engendered other ills that our society suffers from to this day. For example, the State, as you know, took possession of most of the land by right of conquest and distributed it in large holdings or in small plots to its favourites, either as state gifts or as farms from which it collected land taxes sporadically. It therefore created a new privileged class that built on the debris of the remnants of the ruling class which survived the upheaval of the revolution. Had they been fully aware of their responsibilities, the members of this new privileged class would have become agents for change through example by making direct and intelligent use of lands on which in a not too distant past, the slave driver's whip was the only form of discipline and the only agricultural technique. Unfortunately, the privileged class had neither the energy nor the good sense and perhaps not the capital to restore the ruined plantations that they inherited through the generosity of Toussaint Louverture. Maintaining nominal control over the properties acquired, they chose residence elsewhere, in the cities, living off of the easy and more immediate profits of politics and leaving the running of their properties to the whims of ignorance and the routine of sharecroppers. Desertion of the land was therefore the first major error of the elite.

Furthermore, we must not forget that land was distributed according to the country's topography and according to its suitability for certain crops. That is to say that whereas rural holdings were divided since colonial times into mountainous zones and plains, the first more suited to such crops as coffee and the second to large crops such as sugar cane, the final division respected the old distribution to a large degree, so that even today, over 80% of the large and average-sized plantations are concentrated in the various plains, in contrast to the endless small holdings located mainly in the mountainous areas. The result was that the latter areas, broken down into a wide diversity of so-called plantations, were highly attractive to the exceedingly large number of freed dirt-poor citizens who found an opportunity to eke out a more or less comfortable existence there, not having known any alternative to that of toiling for others.

And since the question of their existence was not complicated by concerns about such luxuries as clothes and adornment, they were content to till lands that yielded well in excess of what was strictly necessary for a primitive existence, without dreams, but also without doubt or care. In this way was formed this class of mountain peasants that continued to our time. They lived in scattered enclaves in the isolation of very high areas or on slopes and in the hollows of valleys, in conditions of isolation sometimes made spectacular by a very tortured landscape. Many of them, indeed a large majority of them, once were and still are sharecroppers like those of the plains, but whereas the plain dwellers enjoyed a network of fairly developed roads, practiced industrial farming and remained in contact with the urban middle class, deriving from all of these conditions an irrefutable benefit of refinement which made them resourceful, the former, two-thirds of the country's population, were left to themselves, unaware of the tragic misery inherent in the way of life that they had accepted as their lot. The rhythmic thud of their hoes striking the earth , alternating with the click of their cutlasses, recalls the same ancestral motions that bind them to the land, making them a community different and distinct from the rest of the population through language, dress, customs and a crude, primitive mental development. In short, a mere rough sketch, like a distant, very ill-defined outline, a caricature of the elite, that other component of Haitian society.

So there you have it, ladies and gentlemen, a synopsis of the economic factors which I denounced as having a very strong influence on the separation of the Haitian social classes. To complete my very tentative explanation of that separation, I must now examine the role that psychology had in it.

One of the most unlikely results of the horror of slavery was that it instilled in those who had just thrown off the yoke of slavery through the atrocities of war, a downright revulsion for manual labour. That was in the nature of things.

If we consider that as a colony *Saint-Domingue* was nothing but a large plantation, that the various trades on that plantation were plied only by poor whites and freed slaves, who were held in contempt and ridicule by the big planters despite their freedom, if we consider that tradesmen who became rich were quick to display the same shame of their recent , we can easily understand why the freed slave harboured a certain ideal, a valuable yardstick that had nothing to do with wealth, but which, along with wealth was the unmistakable sign of social superiority. That ideal was and could only have been academic training Courage, daring and good fortune gave entry into the highest rank of the ruling class. Those features could also bring wealth and titles. Nevertheless, something mysterious and simultaneously fascinating and irritating superseded all of that. It was knowledge, to which a quiet and sometimes undeclared homage had to be paid because knowledge was efficient, distinct and rare. The prestige likely accorded to academic training was such that to the eyes of the new masters it must have appeared as a sign of nobility greater, certainly more inaccessible, than the exercise of power or even wealth itself. To support this assertion, I need only turn to the general esteem accorded by the new society not only to those of its members said to be educated, however few in number, but also to some of those with whom it had previously waged war and against whom it still boiled with rage despite its recent victory.

It was indeed for that reason that Toussaint, Dessalines, Christophe and Pétion respected priests, doctors and writers despite their French nationality, who at that time were the repositories of knowledge. Everybody knows the delightful story about Mr. Descourtilz, which he himself told without apology for the motives which prompted Dessalines to rescue him from acts of reprisal ordered against him by the General in Chief, Toussaint Louverture, in revenge for acts of atrocities committed against the nation by Rochambeau and Leclerc. The story is worth recounting here.

Descourtilz, a botanist, brought from Gonaïves to the concentration camp at Petite-Rivière along with a gang of suspects, had just been condemned to death by court-martial, but was pardoned through the intervention of Dr. Say, a French surgeon, and Madame Dessalines. Madame Dessalines even hid him under a bed in the room next to the dining room. Later, during the general conversation at a luncheon attended by the General in Chief and his officers, Dessalines exclaimed: "My goodness! That Descourtilz knows quite a few tricks! The things he knows! He can take care of the sick. He knows plants very well and no animal in the sea, air or on land is unfamiliar to him. It would be a pity if we got rid of a man like him."

Which confirms my assertion that at the birth of our nation and at a time when the might of arms was a mere mediocre tool in the restructuring of the branches of government, the prestige of knowledge held enormous sway in the new society. But it can also be easily understood that if, on the one hand, manual labour, devoid of appeal and tacitly discredited, seemed to recall abolished servitude while, on the other hand, academic training seemed to bestow a certain dignity of ennoblement, one can easily imagine that the small number of men enjoying the might of money and of knowledge presumably formed a kind of aristocracy quite distinct from the rest of the herd. That said, it must be added that at that time, the nation was still fairly close to an era in which equality of suffering and of contempt was the general rule, close to an era in which because of the threat of an external peril, shared fears led to a shared defence of rights so dearly won. That era was not sufficiently distant for this change in values to bring about a sudden distinct change in human relations. On the contrary, while a certain social solidarity more intuitive than intentional softened the antagonisms between social groups, economic and psychological factors hardened, revealing a deepening division. And there, to my mind, is where the origin of the distressing separation of the elite and the masses is to be found, such that at present, the two classes form two nations within a nation, each with its own interests and objectives.

As a result, a definition of our elite can only be understood in relation to the mental development of a minority living on the fringe of the larger society like an artificial class of Mandarins. Make no mistake about it, if there is an incontrovertible truth, it is that in all countries where the caste system does not relegate social groups to stereotyped, fixed roles, the elite are found in all spheres of occupation. In practice, they must become industrialists, businessmen and agriculturalists, not just intellectuals. By that I mean that in the complexities of modern societies and at a time when science is diversifying human tasks, the division of labour specializes skills in such a way that each occupation attains its maximum potential through the development of knowledge.

By restricting the elite to the narrow confines of just one of the roles identified above, we do present a distorted image of it and of its role in society; we repress it and prevent it from achieving its full potential. So, what had we been seeing in this country since the old days referred to earlier? We have seen a magnificent blooming of scholarship, more literary than scientific, among those at the top level of the social hierarchy, so that when we speak of the elite, it is understood that reference is being made only to our intellectuals.

Furthermore, such literary specialization was for a long time the only knowledge ideal to which we aspired. It lead to every leadership and management post and typified unmistakably the education of our political and administrative personnel. There is not a single public register, not a single book written in the first 60 or 75 years of our independence, which does not bear the hallmarks of this rather superficial bombastic literary expression in which rhetoric laden with pompous images, excessive hyperbole and metaphor, does not exceed good taste. Could this lack of moderation and lack of good taste truly have come from us? The immediate response must be that it was all the result of our education system and of the habits and tendencies of our race.

We have a reputation for being a very sensitive people, don't we? We have a very rich and quick imagination. In addition, we love finery and possessions, not to make them a measurement of what is necessary for a comfortable, happy, serene surrounding, but for the vanity of show and display.

We are strongly attracted by the external and tire quickly in the pursuit of what is hidden and profound. Slow, sustained effort is anathema to our haste to finish a task before we have even begun it.

Those are, in a very brief summary, some of our main tendencies. However, if education is an attempt to mould the individual to a particular ideal, it seems to me that every education system must first of all know the temperament of the people to whom it is addressed. That is the first consideration, I dare say the most important consideration which governs any education of a community. Now I'm sure that you are aware that such thoughts have never crossed the minds of our statesmen and spokesmen in the past and I regret to say that even today, with so much talk about reform in public education, our officials and most of our writers seem to be unaware of this basic truth.

It is certainly because of ignorance of this fundamental pedagogical law that from 1804 to the present, all of our schools have been founded on the same education principle, which is to stuff as much information as possible into the heads of our children and adolescents without caring to find out if the information can be assimilated and is assimilated by their brains, without knowing if it corresponds to their needs or the circumstances of their history and other circumstances of their society. We don't even know if, ultimately, this knowledge can develop or contribute to the development not only of their intrinsic mental qualities, but also of equally important and precious character qualities which give value to life and imbue human hearts with a sense of responsibility.

I said that the architects of our public education system adopted a universal education model throughout the school system. It is a model with a criterion guaranteed to show efficiency whenever scrutinized. In this model, the learner shows how much he has learnt by demonstrating how much he can remember. What is learnt and how it is learnt is of no importance. Consequently, the mere recitation of the subject matter as proof of knowledge led to the development of verbal memory at the expense of the other intellectual faculties. The most definite result of such a system was *verbomania*, a type of psychosis, fairly well recognized, one of those rare psychoses commonly found among our intellectuals.

Would you like to know what the main characteristics of this psychic disorder are? "It is a disorder characterized mainly by an irresistible urge to talk, to speechify; a pathological tendency, not without a certain awareness and intention, to juggle with words without really being aware of their meaning. This tendency is constitutional in origin, found among a steadily increasing number of persons of certain categories, who in their speech create situations devoid of objective reality, situations of which they have only the vaguest of notions, which are foreign to them, never personal, and which they hardly understand. Verbomania is noticeable by its excessive duration and intensity and by the unusual nature of the sufferer's verbal manifestations."[1]

It is easily observed that various degrees of this psychosis are commonly found among our intellectuals and that the condition is widespread. If you doubt me, go to social gatherings, to the Houses of Assembly and to our law courts, especially to our law courts. You will be quite astonished to discover the disturbing number of persons whose "penchant for exerting the minimum of effort is illustrated by their mental inertia, laziness of thought, their acceptance of received ideas and clichés", their obsession with the printed word learned by heart.[2] Yes indeed, those are the unmistakable characteristics of verbomania.

Shall I give you an example of verbomania, a written example, to use a contradiction in terms? The example I'm going to read is a particularly good one. It is a welcoming address directed to the President during a visit to Gonaïves. Citing it is easy, since it is recent, appearing in the *Le Matin* newspaper of the 10th of November, 1917, with the name of its author withheld.

The address begins with a quotation from Isaiah, chapter 9: "The people that walked in darkness have seen a great light." It continues:

> Mr. President,
>
> Your surprise visit to the town of Gonaïves on this the 4th day of November on the occasion of our parish festival is not of local, parish or provincial significance in the Haitian Republic, but involves and signifies, after the speeches delivered at the Town Hall with the enthusiasm of improvisation upon your arrival, where you were received and acclaimed by this benevolent population comprising all the patriots who heard you (in your relations with the country as Head of State, under the Convention), admired your wisdom with tact and skill in understanding the benefits which will arise from sentiments to be presently kindled in order to prepare our future well being, approved the effusion of your soul in the deep desire to prevent our unfortunate country from sinking into the abyss of our common ambitions imputable to us all.

That our education system is the chief offender in such a disaster as this speech is quite true and quite easy to prove if the arguments propounded earlier are accepted as well founded. But this disorder has additional causes.

We refuse to admit, don't we, that for us the French language is a borrowed language. And yet, even in the most refined circles it is only spoken along with our local patois, which, as you know, is a strange mishmash of corrupt French terms and a few English, Spanish, Carib and African words.

Creole occupies a very large place in our linguistic makeup and our mental framework. It is Creole that generated our first speech reflexes, because it was in Creole that we heard our first songs on the lips of those who nursed us, so that when we begin to learn French at school, our minds have to contend with analogies and turns of phrase which are not Creole. We internalize it all but sometimes it is only in adolescence that we are able to understand the ideas that we used to repeat parrot-fashion. It is nothing but rote memory and repetition. I need not add that for many of us, the age of penetration of the meaning of ideas often comes after real adolescence, in comparison with the real French-speaking people of France.

On the other hand, if the educators, instead of cramming our heads with a whole set of grammatical rules laced with difficulties and exceptions as is their unwise habit, had seen that as the worst possible method of teaching a modern language and had tried instead to make us speak French before teaching us its rules, perhaps we would have performed better in our studies and at an earlier stage. Unfortunately, we learn French as if it were Greek, a factor which contributes as much to this tendency towards verbalism in our young people as do the factors cited earlier.

There is, finally, one last cause of this behaviour that I must mention and it is that verbomania has found extremely fertile ground for its propagation in our ethnic traits. Whether we consider the old African tree-trunk or the European branches which have been grafted on to it, both of them ethnic traits which combined to produce the Haitian race, our predecessors have been lovers of the word to various degrees. Furthermore, throughout the long period of servitude followed by a long period of military despotism, the Haitian of every class acquired the habit of convoluted expression, captivating periphrasis and clever circumlocution, which conceal his thoughts, through fear of displeasing his masters whoever they were, fear of compromising himself by simply exposing his soul.

He has even found a word recently to describe this state of mind. The word is *calbindage* – that curious state of mind that involves juggling with words to hide one's true feelings rather than express them openly, that involves concealing the fear of action with a powerful profusion of words.

So there you have it, ladies and gentlemen -- our failed education system, our ethnic tendencies, our past history – all of which led to the development of serious deficiencies, if not real pathological disorders, among those in authority. But, one might ask in objection, is the entire elite class afflicted with this disorder? Is that class made up only of powerless talkative elements and pseudo-intellectuals?

To say that it is would be foolish and absurd. Besides, the proverb says that a tree should be judged by its fruit. Well, let's take a look at a few of the masterpieces in the Haitian library, some of the scientific work produced by Haitians, some of the artistic creations in music, sculpture and architecture that are the pride of our creativity. When we do so, we are extremely proud and justifiably boastful of the achievements of the most eminent representatives of Haitian intellectualism. And when we consider where we came from and what we have achieved in spite of a variety of obstacles along the way, we can rightfully wonder if a better coordination of our efforts, a more intelligent discipline and higher goals would not have produced better results and more quickly.

A new analysis and a revision of our values therefore become necessary, which is the purpose of this address. Because if in the course of the last two years, foreign occupation of Haiti found a fragmented and divided elite turned against itself, to the point where it is impossible to get it to take a common action in the legal domain, or to even form a moral resistance to the invader, it is because the elite class has failed in its vocation as a leading class. In short, the elite have become unworthy of their mission of providing leadership. This accusation is so serious that the brilliant results of Haitian creativity cannot be offered in excuse for the errors committed. And there, to my mind, is the root of the problem.

***

So, gentlemen, we have established first of all that the intellectual preparation of the elite is insufficient and faulty. Secondly, we have noted that in terms of general progress, that preparation has nevertheless contributed to the honour of Haitian thought through the intellectual development of a few eminent personalities. Why then were the elite incapable of foreseeing and suppressing the series of crises providing the declared pretext by which it seemed to us and to the entire world the intervention in Haiti was being justified, an intervention in which our pride as an independent nation suffered horribly? Furthermore, why since then have they appeared incapable of reorganizing themselves and tackling the enormity of the tragic results of occupation?

The first and the most decisive reason for their powerless, as I have sought to demonstrate, is primarily their development as an entity separate from the rest of the nation. A second very decisive reason for their inability to act is that while a few great men came out of that class, in each generation they were too few in number and were too far above the rest of the general population not to entertain the superior individual's petty hatred of the lowly, a kind of ransom that talent pays for the jealousy of the helpless and the unworthy.

Furthermore, these great men have never achieved the genius of action of a Toussaint Louverture, never attained the heights reached by a Pierre le Grand, so as to have the might which could make them mould the clay of greatness, so to speak, producing a new kind of Haitian.

Hence this muted conspiracy against any action taken by the ultra-elite and geared towards our intellectuals and the rest of society, a muted conspiracy which could erupt into violence of all sorts.

But we must also identify a final very pertinent source of turmoil in Haitian society, which is the marked separation between education and moral training even in the best of us. By that I mean that in Haiti, even the most educated of individuals can be almost completely devoid of a sense of morality. I mean to point out that intellectual force-feeding is decidedly quite useless in creating men of good character, even though to our astonishment and joy, it has, exceptionally, produced writers and artists from among our scholars.

Of course, this problem is neither unique to our society nor peculiar to our race. In every country, there are men who are great because of their intelligence, but for whom morality is of little importance. History can provide us with a few notable examples of such men. Here, we cite a few among thousands. There was Honoré Gabriel Mirabeau, whom Hippolyte Taine called "a miry colossal satyr"; Francis Bacon, the most progressive, most productive most original thinker of his time, but also a man of loose morals, a traitor to cherished friendship, who was also venal, misappropriating public funds despite his high office as Chancellor of the Exchequer. Marlborough was one of the most famous army captains of his time like the Turennes and Condés of military fame, but also "one of the vilest scoundrels of history", who sold state secrets, was maintained by his mistresses and betrayed James II in favour of William of Orange. And there are any number of contemporary examples that can be added to the list. You can see, then, that this problem of the coexistence of the most despicable and the most intelligent traits in a single individual is not peculiarly Haitian. What I wish to point out is that in Haiti it has alarming characteristics, occurring in a much too limited circle, which is a minority of our elite, as well as among a far too large number of the members of that class.

The immediate result of this state of affairs is a very annoying mutual mistrust. Because some speak of honour and virtue without having any, because they even practice certain acts of dishonesty on the sly and display a lack of integrity, those with whom they interact refuse to believe what they say, for fear of being made a fool of.

It therefore becomes impossible to produce anything of permanence, since the public, grown indifferent because of frequent ridicule, sees a host of personal interests, particularly narrow political interests, behind every endeavour, even one of moral benefit. To my mind, this is why the collapse brought about by political anarchy was preceded by and became part of moral anarchy, to such an extent that even the most enlightened individuals developed a messianic mentality, promising miracles.

The Messiah eventually came and many Haitians–most Haitians–prostrated themselves before the newcomer and stretched forth imploring hands, the wiliest among them believing that they could gain personally from the situation. Haitians quickly rallied around "the foreign authority" and entertained it, just as the first Caesar returning triumphant from civil wars was readily hailed. Some of our young ladies in their foolish vanity flattered themselves that they could find husbands among the soldiers while the men hoped to have their aspirations fulfilled. The bayonet was supposed to make these aspirations possible and guarantee their continuance. Unfortunately, disenchantment soon set in.

The initial enthusiasm ceded to characteristic scepticism and mistrust: Haitians realized that while the foreign intervention might claim the purest intentions of generosity, in this world always motivated by greed, it would be highly unlikely that self interest was not the primary motive behind human action. We now identify self-interest as the real motive of the foreign presence, just as very good actions were once expected of it.

We also now believe that the foreign entity is proposing an education reform which will simply reduce the entire public education system to one form of primary education. Those who know the history of the elite are highly alarmed by this threat, but in no quarter has this alarm been supported by anything other than useless talk.

Should we simply throw up our hands in despair or can we use peaceful means to oppose the implementation of such proposals? This is the question that I will now examine with your permission.

***

Four points can be identified in the analysis just made. They are:

a. that our elite are considerably lacking in moral competence and that examples of excellence produced by that class are few.

b. that neither of these deficiencies can be properly eradicated through the influence of strong stable families and are deficiencies which have as their immediate and secondary origin the poor organization and unreliable principles of public education, grafted on to racial predispositions and social environment.

c. that learning so dispensed has no educational value.

d. that like someone prone to suicide, the Haitian State seems to be consenting to the beheading of the Haitian people by abandoning the concept of free education for all. By abandoning this supreme democratic victory in our present social development, we would limit high intellectual training to the infinitesimal minority represented by the privileged class.

If these points are well founded, they place us in a very clear position. They indicate quite clearly that the threat of moral breakdown is far more serious than the loss of political autonomy. We therefore need a peaceful and lawful organization of our response to that breakdown. Sadly, I must confess that we have very few means of making that possible. In the past, the parliamentary opposition, fear of scandal and the revolt of public opinion were tools against the arbitrary policies of government. Today, alas, today, there is no counterbalance, no control against any audacious government action. We are living under an exceptional regime and that poses a major danger.

However, as far as is possible under martial law, we should try to guarantee our rights through the activities of leagues, associations, advertising houses, so as to bring the justice of our cause to public attention through petitions and press appeals and so exert moral pressure on government decisions.

We need therefore to remind government officials pointing to the American model as a justification for their policies that the only American University created by the American government and financed by the American federal treasury is Howard University. American Negroes receive free secondary and higher education in that institution. The American Government and Congress understood that if a downtrodden race up from slavery and entirely lacking in resources of any kind, is thrown into the ring to compete fully with other races of advanced civilization, it is only fair to create a forum for the moral and intellectual training of its pastors, doctors, teachers, scientists and men of letters so that its talents can be developed to the fullest extent.

In the same situation, we have the right to demand that our policy of free education, which has the same moral objectives, be respected for the same reasons.

Moreover, if one day the final political status of Haiti puts our destiny in our hands once again, we must immediately mandate a new programme of action for the authorities, one which requires the total restructuring of public education so that the moral education of the future elite is as vigorous as its intellectual education.

***

Because of the cruel events of the last two and a half years, an extremely interesting protest movement has sprung up among the young. I have been following with satisfaction the activities of all the literary and social organizations formed since the intervention. One of the most evocative of these is the *Ligue de la Jeunesse Haïtienne,* which has unfortunately ceased publication of its newspaper.

I am deeply saddened by that. Such publications contain more than promises for the future. In their members' contributions I have often found real talent and themes which will one day yield masterpieces. At least, that is my sincerest wish.

Nevertheless, I confess to you that in my personal research and my assessment of the work of the young intellectuals, I am yet to detect the real thoughts of our young elite. Do they suffer from the same lack of order as their predecessors? Does the same wind of indiscipline blow on them? Some six years ago, Pradel Pompilus, with his usual skill, described the despair, dreams, anger and suffering of his generation in a publication entitled *Les deux tendances*. I hope that a writer of the next generation will provide us with an equally skillful description of the thoughts of the present one. However, in some of the writings that I have come across, I think I have detected suggestions for the reconstruction of our country, as well as certain noble ideas which, peculiarly, seem to be scaled down imitations of foreign concepts. Unless I am mistaken, unless I am taking the thoughts of one or two writers to be representative of an entire group, it seems to me that among the ideas of concern to the youth we can detect a certain unease regarding the underlying structure of the country's laws, as well as the timid fear, even a certain trepidation, that the country might be too democratic.

I've always noticed, in regard to this last characteristic, that criticism of the ideas of egalitarianism advocated by the French Revolution, which are the bedrock of modern democracies as well as questions about religious supremacy occupy pride of place in the thinking of the young elite.[3] Assuming that they really exist, I gladly pay tribute to such concerns, which are a credit to that group. However, I am also a little concerned, because I wonder if these issues, which were of great interest in France before the revolutionary war have the same importance in Haiti today. I'm afraid not. Obviously, a religious question exists in Haiti, but I am afraid that I will not examine it here even briefly. It cannot merely be said, however, that this question means knowing how to change our people's concept of the divine.

You must have noticed, have you not, that the Haitian's conversion to Christianity is only superficial. For the overwhelming majority of the population, latent animism coexists with belief in the Christian creed. The African gods have not quite surrendered before Jesus of Nazareth. Believe me, for many of us of the elite class, who pride ourselves on being devout Christians, the juxtaposition of the two faiths and the cooperation between them is something of a double insurance against the mysteries of the hereafter.

But this situation is not recent. It flourished even centuries ago when slaves newly arrived from Africa rushed in their numbers to be baptized, although the process failed to destroy their fetishism. They simply became baptized to avoid the mockery and ragging which the *bossales* suffered at the hand of the creole slaves. If this phenomenon became the subject of research and studies today, anyone with a passion for things Haitian would be delighted by such indulgence. But in France itself, men concerned with the restoration of the monarchy associated religious revival with political designs, so much so that there was an atheistic Catholicism very much favoured by the political movement *l'Action française* and its political organ, but roundly condemned by Pious the Tenth in his famous papal letter *Pascendi dominici gregis*. Furthemore, Paul Bourget, Maurice Barrès, Jules Lemaître and others, who were in alliance with the dogmatic politicians and neo-positivists of *l'Action française*, issued a new apologetic denounced by Rome. Our young writers therefore think it fit to become obsessed with the idea of working for the restoration of the Catholic Church, when the Church is neither threatened nor under attack. Indeed, church authority has not shown any concern in this regard, not even in the pastoral letters of the Lord Bishops. I am surely left to think that once again, issues debated in France have unusual repercussions for our society, that is unable to free itself from a certain bondage.

Of course, we wouldn't mind if the youth appealed to the Church as this country's largest if not its only organized social movement, to try to effect moral unity through the cohesion of the various disparate and opposing forces in our society. It should do so in defence of our nationality as the Capuchin and Jesuit priests once did at the risk of their lives, when they devoted their moral authority to the cause of liberty for all.

We don't mind occasionally recalling the memory of *Abbé de la Haye*, of the priests at *Dondon, la Grande Rivière du Nord* and *Limbé,* who practised a shining example of charity to the point of braving the rigours of colonial justice, many of them condemned to death in the process. If, in the current crisis, the Church is to be asked to play a role, it must become national by adopting the Haitian cause and making Haitian suffering its own. If, after that, we wish to talk about neo-catholicism in terms of art or from a purely religious point of view, our sympathies should be directed towards Paul Claudel, Francis Jammes and Ernest Psichari, rather than be wasted on literary pontiffs whose philosophical influence, lacking in impartial investigations into the truth, can only have unfortunate consequences for Haitian thought.

I find no trace at all of the influence of young French catholic writers in the philosophy of our young intellectuals. I came to this conclusion after conducting surveys among Haitian intellectuals of writers and their works, particularly among our young elite.

****

To deal with the great dislike some people have of taking part in a survey, I thought I should use a bit of subterfuge by asking a few individuals the following question: "If you had to spend three consecutive months in the countryside and could only take three books with you, which would you choose?" I recognize that in that form, the question was likely to receive many insincere responses, which would of necessity contaminate the reliability and the significance of the results.

Only about thirty of the exceedingly small number of questionnaires returned were valid. This was due in some cases to laziness, in other cases to indifference, but to snobbery for the most part. It is also an unmistakable sign of stagnation and moral impotence in our society. In contrast, I received a good amount of extremely useful oral comments at the same time that the written survey was done.

Whatever the case, the responses received have an importance and significance impossible to misinterpret. While some of my respondents did not exactly identify the books that would readily become their companions during three consecutive months of solitude, they listed those that they wished they had read. All things considered, that too is an indication of their taste in books and while not enough, it says a lot.

That said, you will see the most frequently chosen writers and books identified by the thirty or so responses received.

La Fontaine's fables, the Bible, and *The History of Haiti*, were the first book choices, while Anténor Firmin, Hyppolite Taine, Melchior de Vogüé, Paul Bourget and Ferdinand Brunetière headed the list of authors. With or without a choice of books, the following names were prominent:

Max Nordeau	Rostand
Chateaubriand	Charles Wagrer
Racine	Rousseau
Alexandre Dumas (father and son)	Anatole France
Alfred de Musset	Flaubert
Hannibal Price	Pierre de Coulvain
Massillon Coicou	Alphonse de Lamartine
Émile Faguet	Janvier
The Goncourt brothers	Guizot
Walch	Gustave Le Bon
Firmin Rose	Alfred de Vigny
Jean Finot	Paul Adam
Montaigne	Oscar Wilde
Hugo	Albert Samain
Sully Prudhomme	Henry Mürger
Lemaître	Boileau
Benjamin Constant	Lenôtre
Maeterlinck	

Not bad at all, as you can see. It's even very enlightening. As I see it, if an overall view of the situation could be obtained and if the sentiments expressed were genuine, I would say to my respondents: "You have identified most of the works listed as your favourites and report that you like some of the authors which you mentioned. Congratulations. Now please demonstrate that what you have read has become "mental muscle." However, I am afraid that for some of the respondents, the preference for a given category of writer is just for show, an attempt to impress. But that should not be our objective or our concern at this time.

Our task at the moment is to contribute to a national way of thinking indicative of our feelings, our strengths and our weaknesses. We can do so by gleaning ideas generated by ideas contained in the masterpieces which are the pride of humanity's common heritage. This is the only way in which the study and assimilation of the works of the mind play an indispensable part in the enrichment of our culture.

But by the way, what is the true qualitative and quantitative worth of our intellectual achievements? That is yet another question which I have asked myself and that I have attempted to answer. As a result, I decided, for your benefit, to evaluate our intellectual strength, not only by counting the works produced here in roughly a century, but also to have a more accurate measurement of the progress we have made. It was too ambitious an undertaking and once again I failed in my objectives.

I hope that others will pursue this idea further and with greater success. Instead of a project of large scale dimensions, I limited my aspirations to the identification of new works produced for the benefit of our society in the last ten years by our secondary schools and tertiary level institutions, works which should renew and reinforce the worth of the intellectual elite, or simply maintain it at its present level. To this end, I sent the following questionnaire to heads of institutions:

1. How many graduating pupils / students has your institution turned out in the last ten years?
2. How many of your pupils / students abandoned their studies?
3. Is there a very noticeable drop-out rate in the first year as compared with the last year?
4. Have you kept track of your former students after they leave your institution?
5. Can you say how they were employed or are now employed?
6. Unless it is a breach of confidentiality, can you provide their names for further follow-up?

Yet another project which had only partial success. You can see that surveys don't do very well in our country. Indeed, of the 18 questionnaires sent to secondary level and tertiary level headmasters, headmistresses and principals, only 13 were returned, some with very vague, loose answers (a case of *calbindage* if there ever was one), others quite complete. Needless to say, the best ones came from private institutions. One point is clear, however, from the various questionnaires returned, and that is that while in the last ten years there has been a steady increase in the number of young men and women who completed their studies, that number is proportionately lower than the large number of those who dropped out. One Head even reported a drop-out rate of 90%. Various Heads stated that this large failure rate had given rise to a very worrying class of unproductive persons with claims to academic qualifications.

Consider for a moment the deficiencies of our education system which were cited earlier. Think of the consequences if our elite have had inadequate and unreliable schooling. Lastly, consider the various factors dividing our people into mistrustful, hostile groups opposing each other and you will agree with me that together, all those factors turn our social environment into an arena very ripe for the seeds of disorder and destruction. You will also agree with me that of necessity, such an environment exerts an extremely destructive force on the morale of our country, making any attempt at sustained progress impossible. You will agree in short that together, these factors continue to make us responsible for the state of affairs through which an outsider dared raise his flag on the moral ruins of our country.

So, to assist in the reconstruction of our country on a different foundation, to have the elite and the masses exist in harmony in this reconstructed arena, I launch a firm appeal to all men, to all men of good will. The task before us is immense. Whatever its future status, our bounden duty is not to abandon our country, not to let it be snatched away. If we remain with our arms folded in perpetual expectation of what will be, what will be will come about without us and against us. Our only alternative is to come together, to unite our forces through the creation of private social programmes. We have maintained an atavistic trait of mistrust one for the other and a pronounced reluctance – I almost said an inability – to unite. These are the main weaknesses used against us. Because of this impotence, we appear to be not only below other civilized peoples, but also quite below what we were when our enslaved forefathers united to oust the intruder from this land and far below our brothers in the United States.

Whenever I receive newspapers from that country, my heart is filled with joy and I applaud what our American brothers are doing, while I feel ashamed at our inferiority because we cannot imitate them. Would you like some examples? Here is what I learned from the November issue of *Crisis*, a Negro magazine published in New York:

1. "The fortieth meeting of Free Masons in Alabama collected funds for the Lodge this year totaling $118,855"
2. "At the 23rd meeting of the Lott Carey Baptist Foreign Mission in Virginia, $11,000 was collected for religious work.
3. "At a convention held in Tyler, Texas, Bishop Carter of the African Episcopal Church collected $14,000 on the spot for work in education."
4. "The Negroes of Texas have given $10,000 to the Freedman's Aid Society to assist with its school programmes."

So there you have it. In one year, our brothers in a single American state collected $24,000 tax free for religious and social work, from among only 690,049 Negroes, almost three times less the size of Haiti's population. Are we not ashamed that with a population of two and a half million we can offer nothing that even remotely resembles such initiatives and such social solidarity? Are we so selfish or so indifferent that we can't impose a certain discipline for the defence of our rights and interests? Can't we set aside a mere tenth of our resources, even a tenth of what we spend on pleasure, for educational projects on which the safeguard and the future of our children depend? Of course, we readily spend thousands on clubs for fun and games and on the cinema, but we can't support a good literary magazine, set up clinics and night schools or build good secondary schools where, in contrast to the dilapidated schools provided by a State negligent of its mission or a traitor to it, we could provide a better education for the elite of tomorrow?

Shame! Shame on you who don't have the courage to devote your energies to a worthwhile activity in cordial cooperation with other conscientious entities in order to achieve the well-being of our people and our country.

I hear it being said everyday that nothing more can be done because we have no political power. That's the resignation of slaves and the cowardice of eunuchs. On the contrary, against the State, whether local or foreign, we must pit the demands of the society united in its desire to overcome any attempts to demoralize it.

All branches of society—the Church, the school, corporate entities—must have only one doctrine and one goal, which is to save our political heritage. It can only be saved by private groups with the goal of a better provision of a better education system.

Make a methodological, rational effort and if you don't succeed, try again. It is only when you have exhausted all your initiative and good will that you can look back forlornly on the past and say with regret: "Nothing more can be done."

Until that time comes, you have an obligation to keep on trying.

Notes
1. Ossip Lourié, *Le Langage et la Verbomanie*.
2. Translator's note: The source of this quotation is not acknowledged in the text.
3. See articles by Rameau, Pressoir, Barjon and others in editions of the *Bulletin de la Ligue de la Jeunesse Haïtienne*.

Culture and Colonisation

Aimé Césaire

For the past few days we have been greatly exercised as regards the significance of this Congress.

More particularly, we have wondered what is the common denominator of an assembly that can unite men as different as Africans of native Africa, and North Americans, as men from the West Indies and from Madagascar.

To my way of thinking the answer is obvious and may be briefly stated in the words: colonial situation.

It is a fact that most native countries live under the colonial system. Even an independent country like Haiti is, in fact, in many respects a semi-colonial country. And our American brothers themselves, thanks to racial discrimination, occupy within a great modern nation an artificial position that can only be understood within the context of a colonialism that has certainly been abolished but whose after-effects still persist down to the present day.

What does this mean? It means that in spite of our desire to maintain a note of calm in the discussions of the Congress we cannot, if we are to come to grips with the situation, avoid raising the problem that has the greatest influence upon the development of native cultures, namely, the colonial situation. In other words, whether we like it or not, we cannot pose the problem of native culture without at the same time posing the problem of colonialism, for all native cultures are to-day developing under the peculiar influence of the colonial, semi-colonial or para-colonial situation.

***

But what, you may ask, is culture? It is desirable that this should be defined in order to dissipate certain misunderstandings and reply very precisely to certain anxieties that have been expressed by some of our enemies, and even by some of our friends.

The legitimacy of this Congress has, for example, been questioned. It has been said that if culture must be national, surely, to speak of negro-African culture is to speak of an abstraction.

Is it not obvious that the best way to avoid such difficulties is to choose our terms carefully?

I think it is very true that culture must be national. It is however, self-evident that national cultures, however differentiated they may be, are grouped by affinities. Moreover, these great cultural relationships, these great cultural families, have a name: they are called *civilisations*. In other words, if it is an undoubted facts that there is a French national culture, an Italian, English, Spanish, German, Russian, etc., national culture, it is no less evident that all these cultures, alongside genuine differences, show a certain number of striking similarities so that, though we can speak of national cultures peculiar to each of the countries mentioned above, we can equally well speak of a European civilisation.

In the same way we can speak of a large family of African cultures which collectively deserve the name of negro-African culture and which individually reveal the different cultures proper to each country of Africa. And we know that the hazards of history have caused the domain of this civilisation, the locus of this civilisation to exceed widely the boundaries of Africa. It is in this sense, therefore, that we may say that there are, if not centres, at least fringes of this negro-African civilisation in Brazil and in the West Indies, in Haiti and the French Antilles and even in the United States.

This is not just a theory invented for the purposes of the present argument; it is one that is, in my view, implied in a sociological and scientific approach to the problem.

The French sociologist Mauss defined civilisation as "a group of sufficiently numerous and sufficiently important phenomena spread over a sufficiently large number of territories". It may be inferred from this that civilisation tends towards universality and culture towards particularism; that culture is civilisation regarded as peculiar to one people or nation, not shared by any other, and that it indelibly bears the mark of that people or nation. To describe it from the outside, one might say that it is the whole corpus of material and spiritual values created by a society in the course of its history and by values we mean, naturally, elements as diverse as technics and political institutions, things as fundamental as language or as fleeting as fashion, the arts as well as science or religion.

If, on the other hand, one were to define it in terms of purpose, revealing its dynamism, one would say that culture is the effort of any human collectivity to endow itself with the wealth of a personality.

This is tantamount to saying that civilisation and culture define two aspects of the same thing; civilisation defining the widest outskirts of culture, its most external and most general aspects, while culture represents an internal irradiant cell that is the most unique aspect of a civilisation.

It is known that Mauss, in his efforts to find reasons for the compartmentation of the world into clearly defined "civilisation areas", found them in a profound quality that was in his view common to all the social phenomena and which he defined by the term *arbitrary element*. "All social phenomena", he declared, "are to some extent the *work of the collective will*, and when we speak of human will, we infer a *choice* between different possibilities ... It follows from this characteristic of representational collective practices that the area over which they spread, as long as humanity does not constitute a single society, is necessarily finite and relatively fixed".

Thus, all culture is specific. Specific in that it is the work a single particular will, choosing between different possibilities.

We see where this idea leads.

To take a concrete example; it is indeed true to say that there is a feudal civilisation, a capitalist civilisation, a Socialist civilisation. But it is obvious that on the compost of the same economic pattern, life, the life passion, the *élan vital* of any people gives rise to very different cultures. This does not mean that there is no determinism running from base to superstructure. It means that the relation between base and superstructure is never simple and should never be simplified. In this respect we have the dictum of Marx himself who writes (Das *Kapital,* Vol. III, p. 841 *et seq.*)

"It is always in the immediate relations between the masters of the means of production and the direct producers that we discover the intimate secret, the hidden foundation of the whole social structure. This does not mean that the same economic basis—the same, that is, as regards the main conditions—may not by reason of innumerable distinct empirical conditions, e.g. natural and racial factors, historical influences acting from without, etc., manifest itself in an infinity of variations and graduations that may only be discovered by an analysis of the empirical circumstances concerned".

No better way could be found to say that civilisation is never so special that it does not presuppose, to breathe life into it, a whole constellation of ideational resources, traditions, beliefs, ways of thought, values, a whole intellectual equipment, a whole emotional complex, a fund of wisdom that precisely we call culture.

This, I submit, is what legitimises our present meeting. All who have met here are united by a double solidarity; on the one hand, a *horizontal solidarity,* that is, a solidarity created for us by the colonial, semi-colonial or para-colonial situation imposed upon us from without; and on the other, a vertical solidarity, a *solidarity in time,* due to the fact that we started from an original unity, the unity of African civilisation, which has become diversified into a whole series of cultures all of which, in varying degrees, owe something to that civilisation.

We may accordingly consider this Congress from two points of view, both of them equally valid, namely, that this Congress is a return to the sources, a phenomenon characteristic of all communities in times of crisis, while, it is at the same time an assembly of men who must get to grips with the same harsh reality, hence of men fighting the same fight and sustained by the same hope.

For my part, I can see no incompatability between the two things. On the contrary, I believe the two aspects to be complementary and that our bearing, which may seem to indicate hesitation and embarrassment between the past and the future, is in fact only natural, seeing that it is inspired by the idea that the shortest way to the future is always one that involves a deep understanding of the past.

***

I now come to my main theme, namely, the concrete conditions underlying the problem of native cultures at the present day.

I have said that this concrete conditioning may be briefly expressed as the colonial, semi-colonial or para-colonial situation in which these cultures are developing.

The question at once arises: What influences can such conditions have upon the development of these cultures? And first of all, can a political status have cultural consequences? This is not immediately obvious. If one believes with Frobenius that culture is born of man's emotion before the cosmos and that it is no more than "παιδευμα" then there can be little or no influence of politics upon culture.

Or again, if one holds with Schubart that the essential factor is a geographical one, if one believes that "it is the spirit of the countryside that forges the soul of a people", there can be little or no influence of politics upon culture.

If, however, one believes, as common sense dictates, that civilisation is first and foremost a social phenomenon and the result of social facts and social forces, then the idea that politics can influence culture becomes crystal clear.

This influence of politics upon culture is expressly recognised by Hegel in the *Lessons from the philosophy of history* when he writes this innocent little phrase which Lenin, however, must have considered less innocent than it appears as he quoted it and underlined it twice in the *Philosophical Notebooks:*

> "The importance of nature should be neither over- nor under estimated; certainly the gentle sky of Ionia greatly contributed to the grace of the poems of Homer. Nevertheless, it cannot in isolation produce Homers. *Nor does it always produce them. No bard arises under Turkish domination".*

This can mean only one thing, namely, that a political and social system that suppresses the self-determination of a people thereby kills the creative power of that people.

Or, what amounts to the same thing, wherever colonialism has existed, whole peoples have been deprived of their culture, deprived of all culture.

It is in this sense that the historic meeting in Bandung may be said to have been not only a major political event; it was also a cultural event of the first magnitude in that it was the peaceful rising of peoples athirst not only for justice and human dignity but for what colonialism had chiefly denied them, namely, justice.

The mechanism of the death of culture and of civilisations under the colonial system is beginning to be well known. In order to flourish, a culture must have a framework, a structure. Nothing can be surer than that the elements that buttress the cultural life of a colonised people disappear or become debased as a result of the colonial system. I am referring naturally in the first place to political organisation. For it must not be forgotten that the political organisation freely evolved by a people is a significant factor in the culture of that people and, moreover, conditions that particular culture.

Furthermore, there is the question of language. Language has been called "psychology petrified". The native language, the language learnt at school, the language of ideas, once it ceases to be the official and administrative language suffers a loss of status that hinders its development and sometimes threatens its very existence.

We must fully grasp this idea. When the English destroy the state organisation of the Ashantis in the Gold Coast, they deal a blow to Ashanti culture.

When the French refuse to recognise as official languages Arabic in Algeria or Malgache in Madagascar, thus preventing them from achieving their full potentiality in the modern world, they deal a blow to Arab culture and Madagascan culture.

Limitation of the colonised civilisation, suppression or debasement of all that it rests on, how in these conditions can we feel surprised at the suppression of one of the characteristics of all live civilisations, namely the faculty of self-renewal?

It is, we know, a commonplace in Europe to disparage nationalist movements in the colonial countries by representing them as obscurantist forces priding themselves on reviving medieval ways of life and thought. This, however, is to forget that the power to *leave behind the past* is one that belongs to a live civilisation, and that a civilisation is alive when the society in which it finds expression is free. What is happening at present in Africa or in free Asia is, in my view, highly significant in this respect. I shall confine myself to remarking that it is Free Tunisia that has abolished the religious tribunals, not colonial Tunisia, and that it is Free Tunisia that has nationalised Habu properties and abolished polygamy and not the Tunisia of the colonists; that it was the India of the English that maintained the traditional status of the Indian woman, but an India freed from British tutelage that gave the Indian woman equal rights with man.

Let us not delude ourselves! Limited in its action, its dynamism hampered, the civilisation of the colonised society from the first day enters the twilight that is the precursor of the end.

Spengler, in his *Decline of the West*, quotes these lines from Goethe:

> "Thus thou must be, no man his face can change.
> So saith Apollo, thus the prophet spake
> Develop in life the form graven in thee
> That neither time, nor king, nor law can break".

The great reproach we may justly level at Europe is that she broke the upsurge of civilisations that had not yet reached full flowering, that she did not permit them to develop and achieve the full richness of the forms graven in them.

It would be superfluous to detail the process by which the death of this whole was accomplished. Suffice it to say that it was stricken at its base. At its base, and thus irretrievably.

We recall the pattern worked out by Marx in respect of the societies of India, namely, small communities that break up because the foreign admixture disrupts their economic pattern. This is only too true. And not only for India. Wherever European colonisation has occurred, the introduction of an economy based on money has led to the destruction or weakening of traditional links, the break-up of the social and economic structure of the community as well as the disintegration of the family. When a member of a colonised people makes this kind of remark, European intellectuals tend to reproach him with ingratitude and to remind him complacently of what the world owes to Europe. In France, one can still remember the impressive picture painted by M. Caillois and M. Béguin, the former in a series of articles entitled *"Reversed Illusions"*, the latter in his preface to M. Pannikar's book on Asia. Science history, sociology, ethnography, morals, technics, all are brought in. And what importance, these writers ask, can be attached to a few acts of violence, that were in any case unavoidable, as compared with such a long list of benefits? There is certainly much that is true in this picture. But neither of these gentlemen can persuade world opinion that the great revolution brought about by Europe in the history of humanity is either the introduction of a system based upon respect for human dignity, in spite of all their efforts to make us think so, or the invention of intellectual integrity; this revolution turned upon very different considerations that it would be disloyal not to face, namely, that Europe was the first to have invented and to have introduced everywhere under her sway a social and economic system founded on money and to have mercilessly destroyed everything—I repeat, everything, culture, philosophy, religions,—everything that might prevent or slow down the enrichment of a group of privileged men and peoples. I am well aware that for some time it has been claimed that the evils caused by Europe are not irreparable. It is said that by taking certain precautions, the devastating effects of colonisation could be mitigated. Unesco has been considering the problem and lately (*Unesco Courier*, February 1956), Dr. Luther Evans, the Director General, stated that "in certain conditions technical progress could be introduced into a culture in such a way as to harmonise with it". While a well known ethnographer, Dr. Margaret Mead, declared that if we bear in mind that "every culture forms a logical and coherent whole" and that "the slightest modification of any single element of a culture brings in its train changes in other respects", it should be possible by taking the necessary precautions "to introduce into certain cultures, basic education, new agricultural and industrial methods, new rules of hospital administration, etc., with a minimum of dislocation, or, at least, to make use of the inevitable dislocation for constructive ends".

All this is certainly steeped in good intentions. One must, however, resign oneself to the facts. This is not a case where there might be said to be a bad king of colonisation destroying native civilisations and attacking the "moral health of the colonised people", and another good kind of colonisation, an enlightened colonisation backed by ethnography, which could integrate the cultural elements of the coloniser within the corpus of the native civilisations harmoniously and without risk of the "moral health of the colonised peoples". One must resign oneself to the facts: the tenses of colonisation are never conjugated with the verbs of the idyllic.

We have seen that all colonisation leads in the longer or shorter run to the death of the civilisation of the conquered society. But can it be said, if the native civilisation dies, that the coloniser replaces it with another type of civilisation that is superior to the native kind, that is, by the conqueror's own civilisation?

This illusion, to parody a fashionable expression, I propose to call the Deschamps Illusion, after Governor Deschamps who, at the opening of this Congress yesterday morning, pathetically recalled that Gaul had once been colonised by the Romans, adding that the Gauls had not retained too unhappy memories of that colonisation. The Deschamps Illusion is, moreover, as old as Roman colonisation itself and might just as well be called the Rutilius Namatianus Illusion, as I find among Governor Deschamps' ancestors a man who was not Governor but Palace Chamberlain, which is not indeed without some analogy, who in the 5th century A.D. expressed in Latin verse a thought rather similar to that expressed by Monsieur Deschamps yesterday morning in French prose. Naturally such a comparison raises certain problems. One may in particular wonder if the comparison is valid for such widely differing historical situations if, for example, one can compare, on the grounds of colonisation, a pre-capitalist colonisation with a capitalist colonisation. Nor does this absolve us from wondering incidentally whether the position of Governor, or Palace Chamberlain, is one that best qualifies a man to pass impartial judgment on colonialism. However that may be, let us hear what Rutilius Namatianus has to say:

> "Fecisti patriam diversis gentibus unam;
> Profuit injustis te dominante capi
> Dumque offers victis proprii consortia juris
> Urbem fecisti quod orbis erat".

We may note in passing that no poet has ever yet been inspired by the modern colonial system; never has one hymn of gratitude resounded in the ears of modern colonialists. And that in itself is a sufficient condemnation of the colonial system... But no matter. Let us come to the heart of the illusion, namely, that just as in Gaul a Latin culture was substituted for a native culture, so there will occur throughout the world off-shoots of French, English or Spanish civilisations as a result of colonisation. But this, I repeat, is an illusion.

Moreover, the spread of this misunderstanding is not always unconscious or disinterested. In this respect we shall confine ourselves to recalling that in 1930, when a politician like Monsieur Doumer interrupted the historian Berr or the ethnographer Mauss at a meeting of philosophers and historians to define the word civilisation, it was to point out to them the political dangers of their cultural relativism and to insist that the idea that France had a mission to spread "civilisation"—by which he meant French civilisation—to her colonies must not be upset. An illusion, I say, for we must be quite convinced of the opposite, namely, that no colonising country can *give* its civilisation to any colonised country, that there is not, there has never been and there never will be scattered throughout the world, as was thought in the early days of colonisation, a "New France", a "New England, or a "New Spain". This is worth emphasising: a civilisation is a co-ordinated group of social functions. There are technical functions, intellectual functions, and functions of organisation and coordination.

To say that the coloniser substitutes his civilisation for the native civilisation could mean only one thing, namely, that the colonising nation ensures to the colonised, that is to the natives in their own country, the fullest mastery over these different functions.

What, however, does the history of colonisation teach us in this respect? That techniques in colonial countries always develop alongside the native society without the colonised ever being given the chance to master them. (The great misfortune of technical education in all colonial countries is the attempt by the colonists to bar the way to technical qualifications for native workmen; the attempt that finds its most odious and most radical expression in South Africa is, in this respect, highly significant.) That as regards intellectual functions there is no colonial country of which the main characteristic is not illiteracy and the low level of public education. That in all colonies, as regards the functions of organisation and co-ordination, the political power belongs to the colonial authorities and is directly exercised by the governor or resident-general, or is at least controlled by him.

(This, incidentally, explains the vanity and hypocrisy of all colonial policies based upon integration or assimilation—policies clearly recognised by the native peoples for the snares and booby-traps they are.)

You see the extent of the requirements. I shall sum them up by saying that, for the coloniser, exporting his civilisation to the colonial country would mean nothing less than a deliberate attempt to establish native capitalism, a native capitalist society in the image of and also as a competitor of metropolitan capitalism.

One has only to glance at the facts to realize that nowhere has metropolitan capitalism given birth to native capitalism. Moreover if a native capitalism has not arisen in any colonial country (I do not mean the capitalism of the colonists themselves that is directly connected with metropolitan capitalism), the reasons must not be sought in the laziness of the natives but in the very nature and logic of colonial capitalism.

Malinowski, who is certainly open to criticism from other angles, once had the merit of drawing attention to the phenomenon that he called the "selective gift".

"The whole conception of European culture as a cornucopia from which all blessings flow freely is fallacious. There is no need to be a specialist in anthropology to see that the "European gift" is always highly selective. We never give, and we never shall give native people living under our domination—as it would be complete madness from the point of view of political realism to do so—the four following elements of our culture:

1. —The instruments of physical power—firearms, bombers, etc. or anything that makes defence effective or aggression possible.

2. —Our instruments of political mastery. Sovereignty always remains the prerogative of the "British Crown", or the "Belgian Crown" or the French Republic. Even when we practice indirect rule such rule is always exercised under our control.

3. —We do not share the main part of our wealth and our economic advantages with the natives. The metal that comes from the African gold and copper mines never flows along African channels, apart from wages that are in any case always inadequate. Even under a system of indirect economic exploitation such as we practice in Western Africa or in Uganda when we leave a proportion of the profit to the natives, the entire control of economic organisation always remains in the hands of the western enterprise.

Nowhere is full political equality granted. Nor full social equality. Nor even full religious equality. In fact, when we consider all the points just mentioned, it is easy to see that there is no question of "giving", nor of offering "generously", but rather of "taking". We have taken from the Africans their lands and, generally speaking, it is the most fertile lands we have taken. We have bereft tribes of their sovereignty and of the right to make war. We oblige the natives to pay taxes but they do not control, or at least never entirely, the administration of these funds. Finally, the work they do is never voluntary except in name". (*Introductory essay on the anthropology of changing African cultures*, 1938).

Several years later Malinowski drew the following conclusions in *The dynamics of culture*: "It is the selective gift which, of all the elements of the colonial situation, has perhaps the greatest influence on the process of cultural exchange. What the Europeans refrain from giving is both significant and clearly determined. It is a refusal which tends to nothing less than a withdrawal from the process of cultural contact of all the economic, political and juridical benefits of the superior culture. If power, wealth, and social advantages were given to the natives the cultural change-over would be relatively easy. It is the absence of these factors, our "selective gift", that renders the cultural change so difficult and so complicated".

As we see, there is never any question of the gift being offered in its entirely, hence if there is never any question of a civilisation being offered to others, there can be no question of a transfer of civilisation. Toynbee in *The World and the West* propounds a most ingenious theory of the psychology of the impact of civilisation. He explains that when the ray of civilisation strikes a foreign body "the resistance of the foreign body refracts the cultural ray by decomposing it in the same way as the prism decomposes light rays to produce the colours of the spectrum". He holds that it is, moreover, the resistance of the foreign social body that impedes the total diffusion of one culture in another, causing a kind of purely physical selection by which only the least important and most harmful elements are retained.

The truth is very different; Malinowski is right and Toynbee wrong. The selection of cultural elements offered to the colonised is not the result of a physical law. It is the result of a political decision, the result of a policy deliberately chosen by the colonist, a policy that may be summed up as the import-export of capitalism itself, by which I mean its foundations, its virtues and its power.

***

But, it may be said, there is still another possibility, namely, the elaboration of a new civilisation, a civilisation that will owe something both to Europe and to the native civilisation. If we discard the two solutions represented, on the one hand, by the preservation of the native civilisation and, on the other, by the export overseas of the colonists' civilisation, might it not be possible to conceive of a process that would elaborate a new civilisation owing full allegiance to neither of its component parts?

This is an illusion cherished by many Europeans who imagine they are witnessing in countries of British or French colonisation the birth of an Anglo- or Franco-African or an Anglo- or Franco-Asiatic civilisation.

In support of it they rely on the notion that all civilisations live by borrowing, and infer that when two different civilisations have been brought into contact through colonisation, the native civilisation will borrow cultural elements from the colonists' civilisation and that from this marriage will spring a new civilisation, a mixed civilisation.

The error inherent in such a theory is that it reposes on the illusion that colonisation is a contact with civilisation like any other and that all borrowings are equally good.

The truth is quite otherwise and the borrowing is only valid when it is counter-balanced by an interior state of mind that *calls* for it and integrates it within the body which then assimilates it so that both become one—what was external becoming internal. Hegel's view applies here. When a society borrows, it takes possession. It acts, it does not suffer action. "In taking possession of the object, the mechanical process becomes an interior process by which the individual *takes possession* of the object in such a way as to strip it of its separate identity, transform it into a means and impart to it the substance of his own personality". (Hegel, Logic Vol. II, p. 482).

Colonisation is a different case. Here there is no borrowing arising out of need, no cultural elements being spontaneously integrated within the subject's world. And Malinowski and his school are right to insist that the process of cultural contact must be regarded mainly as a continuous process of interaction between groups having different cultures.

What does this mean if not that the colonial situation, that sets the colonist and the colonised in opposing camps, is in the last resort the determining element?

And what is the result?

The result of this lack of integration by the dialectic of need is the existence in all colonial countries of what can only be termed a cultural mosaic. By this I mean that in all colonial countries the cultural features are juxtaposed but not harmonised.

What, however, is civilisation if not a harmony and an integration? It is because culture is not just a simple juxtaposition of cultural features that there cannot be a mixed culture. I do not mean that people who are biologically of mixed blood cannot found a civilisation. I mean that the civilisation they found will be a civilisation only if it is not mixed. It is for this reason too that one of the characteristics of culture is its style, that mark peculiar to a people and a period and which is to be found in all fields in which the activity of a people is manifested at a given period. I feel that Nietzsche's remarks in this respect are worth considering; "Culture is above all a unity of artistic style in all the vital manifestations of a people. To know many things and to have learnt much are neither an essential step towards culture nor a sign of culture and could indeed go hand in hand with the opposite of culture, namely, barbarism, *which implies a lack of style or a chaotic mixture of all styles*".

No truer description could be given of the cultural situation common to all colonised countries. In every colonised country we note that the harmonious synthesis of the old native culture has been destroyed and has been replaced by a heterogeneous mixture of features taken from different cultures, jostling one another but not harmonising. This is not necessarily barbarism through lack of culture. *It is barbarism through cultural anarchy.*

You may be startled by the word barbarism. But this would be to forget that the great creative periods have always been periods of great psychological unity, periods of *communion,* and that culture does not live intensely or develop except in the presence of a system of common values. Where, on the other hand, society is in dissolution, forms splinter groups and is criss-crossed by a medley of values that are not recognised by the community as a whole, there is room only for a debased style and, in the last resort, for sterility. A further objection is that any culture, no matter how great, or rather the greater it is, is a mixture of extremely heterogeneous elements. We recall the case the case of Greek culture, consisting of Greek elements to which were added Cretan, Egyptian and Asiatic elements. We may even go further and state that in the realm of culture the composite is the rule and the uniform the harlequin's dress. This is a view of which the American anthropologist Kroeber has become the interpreter (*Anthropology*, New York, 1948):

"It is", he writes, "as though a rabbit could be grafted with the digestive organs of a sheep, the respiratory gills of a fish, the claws and teeth of a cat, a few tentacles of an octopus, a further assortment of foreign organs borrowed from other representatives of the animal kingdom, and could not only survive but reproduce itself and prosper. Organically, this is obviously an impossibility, but in the realm of culture it is a very close approximation to what actually takes place".

It is no doubt true that the rule here is heterogeneity. We must however beware; this heterogeneity is not lived as such. In a live civilisation this heterogeneity is lived internally as homogeneity. Analysis may reveal the heterogeneity, but the elements however heterogeneous are lived in the consciousness of the community as *theirs* in the same way as the most typically native elements. The civilisation does not feel the foreign body, for it is no longer foreign. Scientists may prove the foreign origin of a word or a technique nevertheless the community feels that the word or the technique is its own. A process of naturalisation, ascribable to the dialectic of *having*, has taken place. Foreign elements have become mine have passed into my being because I can dispose of them, because I can organise them within my universe, because I can bend them to my uses; because they are at my disposal, not I at theirs. It is precisely the operation of this dialectic that is denied to the colonised people. Foreign elements are dumped on its soil, but remain foreign White man's things! White man's manners! Things existing along side the native but over which the native has no power.

***

But, it may be asked, once the original unity is broken, is it not possible that the colonised people can reconstitute it and integrate is new experiences, hence its new wealth, with the framework of a new unity, a unity that will not, of course, be the old unity, but a unity nevertheless?

Agreed. But is must be realized that such a solution is impossible under the colonial system because such a mingling, such a commingling, cannot be expected from a people unless that people retains the *historic initiative,* in other terms, unless that people is free. Which is incompatible with colonialism.

Referring back to the previous statement on the dialectic of need, Japan has been able to commingle the traditional elements with those borrowed from Europe and melt them down into a new culture that nevertheless remains Japanese. Japan, however, is free and acknowledges no law but that of her own needs. It should, moreover, be added that such a commingling postulates a psychological condition, namely, historic boldness, self-confidence. This however, is precisely what the coloniser has endeavoured, right from the start, in one thousand and one ways to take away from the colonised.

And here it must be clearly understood that the famous inferiority complex that they are pleased to find in the colonised is not just matter of chance. It has been deliberately created by the coloniser.

Colonisation is a phenomenon that, among other disastrous psychological consequences, involves the following: it raises doubts regarding the concepts on which the colonised could build or rebuild their world. To quote Nietzsche: "Just as earthquakes devastate and ravage towns so that men build their dwellings on volcanic soil with misgivings, so life itself collapses, grows weaker, loses courage when then overthrow of his beliefs robs man of the basis of his security, his peace of mind, his faith in what is enduring and eternal".

This lack of courage to live, this vacillation of the will to live, is a phenomenon often remarked among colonial peoples, the best known case being that of the people of Tahiti, analysed by Victor Segalen in *"Les Immémoriaux"*.

Thus the cultural position in colonial countries is tragic. Whenever colonisation occurs, native culture begins to wither. And among the ruins there springs up, not a culture, but a kind of sub-culture, a sub-culture that, because it is condemned to remain marginal as regards the European culture and to be the province of a small group, an "élite", living in artificial conditions and deprived of life-giving contact with the masses and with popular culture, is thus prevented from blossoming into a true culture.

The result is the creation of vast stretches of cultural wastelands or, what amounts to the same thing, of cultural perversion or cultural by-products.

This is the situation which we black men of culture must have the courage to face squarely.

The question then arises: in such a situation, what ought we, what can we, do? Clearly our responsibilities are grave. What can we do? The problem is often summarised as a choice to be made. A choice between native tradition and European civilisation. Either to reject native civilisation as puerile, inadequate, outdated by history, or else, in order to preserve our native cultural heritage, to barricade ourselves against European civilisation and reject it.

In other terms, we are called upon to choose: "Choose between fidelity and backwardness, or progress and renunciation".

What is our reply?

Our reply is that things are not as simple as they seem and that the choice offered is not a valid one. Life (I say life and not abstract thought) does not recognise, does not accept these alternatives. Or rather if these alternatives are offered, life itself will transcend them.

We say that the question does not arise in native society alone that in every society there is always a state of equilibrium between old and new, that it is always precarious, that is it in a constant state of readjustment and that it has in practice to be rediscovered by every generation.

Our societies, our civilisations, our native cultures are not exempt from this law.

For our part, and as regards our particular societies, we believe that in the African culture yet to be born, or in the para-African culture yet to be born, there will be many new elements, modern elements, elements, let us face it, borrowed from Europe. But we also believe that many traditional elements will persist in these cultures. We refuse to yield to the temptation of the *tabula rasa*. I refuse to believe that the future African culture can totally and brutally reject the former African culture. To illustrate what I have just said, let me use a parable. Anthropologists have often described what one of them proposes to call cultural fatigue. The example they quote deserves to be recalled as it is profoundly symbolic. The story, which takes place in the Hawaiian Islands, is as follows: A few years after the discovery of these islands by Captain James Cook, the king died and was succeeded by a young man, Prince Kamehamela II. On being converted to European ideas the young prince decided to abolish the ancestral religion. It was agreed between the new king and the high priest that a great festival should be organised and that during the festival the taboo should be solemnly broken and the ancestral gods repudiated. On the appointed day, at a sign from the king, the high priest hurled himself upon the statues of the god, trampled them underfoot and broke them, while a great cry went up: "The taboo is broken!" Naturally, some years later the people of Hawaii welcomed the Christian missionaries with open arms. The rest of the story is well known, it has passed into history. This is the simplest and clearest example we know of a cultural subversion preparing the way for the enslavement of a people. And I ask, is this renunciation of its past and its culture by a people, is this what is expected of us?

I say distinctly, there will be no Kamehamela II among us!

I believe that the civilisation that has given negro sculpture to the world of art; that the civilisation that has given to the political and social world the original communal institutions such as village democracy, or fraternal age-groups, or family property, which is a negation of capitalism, or so many institutions bearing the imprint of the spirit of solidarity; that this civilisation that, on another plane, has given to the moral world an original philosophy based on respect for life and integration within the cosmos; I refuse to believe that this civilisation, imperfect though it may be, must be annihilated or denied as a pre-condition of the renaissance of the native peoples.

I believe that, once the external obstacles have been overcome, our particular cultures contain within them enough strength, enough vitality, enough regenerative powers to adapt themselves to the conditions of the modern world and that they will prove able to provide for all political, social, economic or cultural problems, valid and original solutions, that will be *valid because they are original.*

In the culture that is yet to be born, there will be without any doubt both old and new. Which new elements? Which old? Here alone our ignorance begins. And in truth it is not for the individual to reply. Only the community can give the answer. We may, however, affirm here and now that *it will be given* and not verbally but by facts and by action.

And this is what finally enables us to define our role as black men of culture. Our role is not to prepare *a priori* the plan of future native culture, to predict which elements will be integrated and which rejected. Our role, an infinitely more humble one, is to proclaim the coming and prepare the way for those who hold the answer—the people, our peoples, freed from their shackles, our peoples with their creative genius finally freed from all that impedes them and renders them sterile.

To-day we are in a cultural chaos. Our part is to say: "Free the demiurge that alone can organise this chaos into a new synthesis, a synthesis that will deserve the name of culture, a synthesis that will be a reconciliation and an overstepping of both old and new". We are here to ask, nay to demand: "Let the peoples speak! Let the black peoples take their place upon the great stage of history!"

The Malaise of a Civilization

Suzanne Césaire

If in our legends and tales we see the appearance of a suffering, sensitive, sometimes mocking being that is our collective ego, we look in vain for an expression of that ego in Martinique's ordinary literary products.

Why is it that in the past we have been so unconcerned about telling our ancestral worries directly?

The urgency of this cultural problem escapes only those who have decided to put on blinders so as not to be disturbed from an artificial tranquillity—at any price, be it that of stupidity or death.

As for us, we feel that our troubling times will bud here a ripened fruit, irresistibly called by the ardor of the sun to disperse its creative forces to the wind; we feel in this tranquil, sun-drenched land the fearsome, inexorable pressure of destiny that will dip the whole world in blood in order, tomorrow, to give it its new face.

Let us inquire into the life of this island that is ours.

What do we see?

First the geographical position of this parcel of land: tropical. In this case here, the Tropics.

Whence the adaptation here of an African settlement. The Negroes imported here had to struggle against the intense mortality of slavery in its beginnings, against the harshest work conditions ever, against chronic malnutrition—a reality that is still alive. And nevertheless, it cannot be denied that on Martinican soil the colored race produces strong, tough, supple men and women of a natural elegance and great beauty.

But, then, is it not surprising that this people, who over the centuries has adapted to this soil, this people of authentic Martinicans is just now producing authentic works of art? How is it that over the centuries no viable survivors of the original styles have been revealed—for example, those styles that have flowered so magnificently on African soil? Sculptures, ornate fabrics, paintings, poetry? Let the imbeciles reproach the race and its so-called instinct for laziness, theft, wickedness.

Let's talk seriously:

If this lack of Negroes is not explained by the hardships of the tropical climate to which we have adapted, and still less by I know not what inferiority, it is explained, I believe, as follows, by:

1. the horrific conditions of being brutally transplanted onto a foreign soil; we have too quickly forgotten the slave ships and the sufferings of our slave fathers. Here, forgetting equals cowardice.

2. an obligatory submission, under pain of flogging and death, to a system of "civilization," a "style" even more foreign to the new arrivals than the tropical land.

3. finally, after the liberation of people of color, through a collective error about our true nature, an error born of the following idea, anchored in the deepest recesses of popular

consciousness by centuries of suffering: "Since the superiority of the colonizers arises from a certain style of life, we can access power only by mastering the techniques of this 'style' in our turn."

Let's stop and measure the importance of this gigantic mistake.

What is the Martinican fundamentally, intimately, and inalterably? And how does he live?

In answering these questions, we will see a surprising contradiction appear between his deep being, with his desires, his impulses, his unconscious forces—and how life is lived with its necessities, its urgencies, its weight. A phenomenon of decisive importance for the future of the country.

What is the Martinican?

—A human plant.

Like a plant, abandoned to the rhythm of universal life. No effort expended to dominate nature. Mediocre at farming. Perhaps. I'm not saying he makes the plant grow; I'm saying he grows, that he lives plantlike. His indolence? That of the vegetable kingdom. Don't say: "he's lazy," say: "he vegetates," and you will be doubly right. His favorite phrase: "let it flow." Meaning that he lets himself flow with, be carried by life, docile, light, not insistent, not a rebel—amicably, amorously. Obstinate besides, as only a plant knows how to be. Independent (the independence and autonomy of a plant). Surrender to self, to the seasons, to the moon, to the day whether shorter or longer. The picking season. And always and everywhere, in the least of his representations, primacy of the plant, the plant that is trod upon but alive, dead but reborn, the free, silent, and proud plant.

Open your eyes—a child is born. To which god should he be confided? To the Tree god. Coconut or Banana, in whose roots they bury the placenta.

Open your ears. One of the popular tales of Martinican folklore: the grass that grows on the tomb is the living hair of the dead person, in protest to death. Always the same symbol: the plant. The lively feeling of a life-death community. In short, *the Ethiopian feeling for life*.[1]

So, the Martinican is typically Ethiopian. In the depths of his consciousness, he is the human plant, and by identifying with the plant, his desire is to surrender to life's rhythm.

Does this attitude suffice to explain his failure in the world?

No—the Martinican has failed because, misrecognizing his true nature, he tries to live a life that is not suited to him. A gigantic phenomenon of collective lying, of "pseudomorphosis." And the current state of civilization in the Caribbean reveals to us the consequences of this error.

Repression, suffering, sterility.

How, why this fatal mistake among this people enslaved until yesterday? By the most natural of processes, by the play of the survival instinct.

Remember that what the regime of slavery above all forbade was the *assimilation of the Negro to the white*. Some choice ordinances: that of April 30, 1764, which forbids blacks and coloreds from practicing medicine; that of May 9, 1765, which forbids them from working as notary publics; and the famous ordinance of February 9, 1779, which formally forbids blacks from wearing the same clothes as whites, demands respect for and submission to "all whites in general," etc., etc.

Let's cite too the ordinance of January 3, 1788, which obliged free men of color "to request a permit if they wished to work *anywhere but in cultivation*." It is understood henceforth that the essential goal for the colored man has become that of *assimilation*. And with a fearsome force, the disastrous conclusion forms in his head: *liberation equals assimilation*.

In the beginning, the movement was off to a good start: 1848; the masses of freed blacks, in a sudden explosion of primitive ego, incorrectly renounced all regular work, despite the danger of famine. But the Negroes, subdued by economics, no longer slaves but wage earners, submitted once more to the discipline of the hoe and the cutlass.

And this is the era that definitively establishes the repression of the ancestral desire for letting go.

That desire is replaced, especially in the colored bourgeoisie, by the foreign desire of struggle.

Whence the drama, evident to those who analyze in depth the collective ego of the Martinican people: their unconscious continues to be inhabited by the Ethiopian desire for letting go. But their consciousness, or rather their preconsciousness, accepts the Hamitic desire for struggle. The race to riches. To diplomas. Ambition. Struggle reduced to the level of the bourgeoisie. The race to monkey-like imitations. Vanity fair.

The most serious consequence is that the desire to imitate, which had formally been vaguely conscious—since it was a defense reaction against an oppressive society—now passed into the ranks of the fearsome, secret forces of the unconscious.

No "evolved" Martinican would accept that he is only imitating, so much does his current situation appear natural, spontaneous, born of his most legitimate aspirations. And, in so doing, he would be sincere. He truly does not KNOW that he is imitating. He is *unaware* of his true nature, which does not cease to exist for that matter.

Just as the *hysteric* is unaware that he is merely *imitating* an illness, but the doctor, who cares for him and delivers him from his morbid symptoms, knows it.

Likewise, analysis shows us that the effort to adapt to a foreign style that is demanded of the Martinican does not take place without creating a state of pseudocivilization that can be qualified as *abnormal, teratoid*.

The problem today is to determine if the Ethiopian attitude we discovered as the very essence of the Martinican's feeling for life can be the point of departure for a viable, hence imposing, cultural style.

It is exalting to imagine in these tropical lands, finally rendered to their internal truth, the long-lasting and fruitful accord between man and soil. Under the sign of the plant.

Here we are called upon finally to know ourselves, and here before us stand splendor and hope.

Surrealism gave us back some of our possibilities. It is up to us to find the rest. By its guiding light.

Understand me well:

> It is not a question of a return to the past, of resurrecting an African past that we have learned to appreciate and respect. On the contrary, it is a question of mobilizing every living force mingled together on this land where race is the result of the most continuous brazing; it is a question of becoming conscious of the tremendous heap of various energies we have until now locked up within ourselves. We must now put them to use in their fullness, without deviation and without falsification. Too bad for those who thought we were idle dreamers.

The most troubling reality is our own.

We shall act.

This land, our land, can only be what we want it to be.

Note

Among other things, the title plays on the French translation of Sigmund Freud's *Civilization and Its Discontents* [Malaise de la civilisation].

1. Suzanne Césaire's italics, as are all others unless otherwise noted. She is here alluding to the theories of the ethnologist Leo Frobenius. See her essay, 'Léo Frobenius et le Problème des Civilizations,' *Tropique* 1 (April 1941): 27–36.

Racism and Culture

Frantz Fanon

The unilaterally decreed normative value of certain cultures deserves our careful attention. One of the paradoxes immediately encountered is the rebound of egocentric, sociocentric definitions.

There is first affirmed the existence of human groups having no culture; then of a hierarchy of cultures; and finally, the concept of cultural relativity.

We have here the whole range from overall negation to singular and specific recognition. It is precisely this fragmented and bloody history that we must sketch on the level of cultural anthropology.

There are, we may say, certain constellations of institutions, established by particular men, in the framework of precise geographical areas, which at a given moment have undergone a direct and sudden assault of different cultural patterns. The technical, generally advanced development of the social group that has thus appeared enables it to set up an organized domination. The enterprise of deculturation turns out to be the negative of a more gigantic work of economic, and even biological, enslavement.

The doctrine of cultural hierarchy is thus but one aspect of a systematized hierarchization implacably pursued.

The modern theory of the absence of cortical integration of colonial peoples is the anatomic-physiological counterpart of this doctrine. The apparition of racism is not fundamentally determining. Racism is not the whole but the most visible, the most day-to-day and, not to mince matters, the crudest element of a given structure.

To study the relations of racism and culture is to raise the question of their reciprocal action. If culture is the combination of motor and mental behavior patterns arising from the encounter of man with nature and with his fellow-man, it can be said that racism is indeed a cultural element. There are thus cultures with racism and cultures without racism.

This precise cultural element, however, has not become encysted. Racism has not managed to harden. It has had to renew itself, to adapt itself, to change its appearance. It has had to undergo the fate of the cultural whole that informed it.

The vulgar, primitive, over-simple racism purported to find in biology–the Scriptures having proved insufficient–the material basis of the doctrine. It would be tedious to recall the efforts then undertaken: the comparative form of the skulls, the quantity and the configuration of the folds of the brain, the characteristics of the cell layers of the cortex, the dimensions of the vertebrae, the microscopic appearance of the epiderm, etc....

Intellectual and emotional primitivism appeared as a banal consequence, a recognition of existence.

Such affirmations, crude and massive, give way to a more refined argument. Here and there, however, an occasional relapse is to be noted. Thus the "emotional instability of the Negro," the "subcritical integration of the Arab," the "quasi-generic culpability of the Jew" are data that one comes upon among a few contemporary writers. The monograph by J. Carothers, for example, sponsored by the World Health Organization, invokes "scientific arguments" in support of a physiological lobotomy of the African Negro.

These old-fashioned positions tend in any case to disappear. This racism that aspires to be rational, individual, genotypically and phenotypically determined, becomes transformed into cultural racism. The object of racism is no longer the individual man but a certain form of existing. At the extreme, such terms as "message" and "cultural style" are resorted to. "Occidental values" oddly blend with the already famous appeal to the fight of the "cross against the crescent."

The morphological equation, to be sure, has not totally disappeared, but events of the past thirty years have shaken the most solidly anchored convictions, upset the checkerboard, restructured a great number of relationships.

The memory of Nazism, the common wretchedness of different men, the common enslavement of extensive social groups, the apparition of "European colonies," in other words the institution of a colonial system in the very heart of Europe, the growing awareness of workers in the colonizing and racist countries, the evolution of techniques, all this has deeply modified the problem and the manner of approaching it.

We must look for the consequences of this racism on the cultural level.

Racism, as we have seen, is only one element of a vaster whole: that of the systematized oppression of a people. How does an oppressing people behave? Here we rediscover constants.

We witness the destruction of cultural values, of ways of life. Language, dress, techniques, are devalorized. How can one account for this constant? Psychologists, who tend to explain everything by movements of the psyche, claim to discover this behavior on the level of contacts between individuals: the criticism of an original hat, of a way of speaking, of walking...

Such attempts deliberately leave out of account the special character of the colonial situation. In reality the nations that undertake a colonial war have no concern for the confrontation of cultures. War is a gigantic business and every approach must be governed by this datum. The enslavement, in the strictest sense, of the native population is the prime necessity.

For this its systems of reference have to be broken. Expropriation, spoliation, raids, objective murder, are matched by the sacking of cultural patterns, or at least condition such sacking. The social panorama is destructured; values are flaunted, crushed, emptied.

The lines of force, having crumbled, no longer give direction. In their stead a new system of values is imposed, not proposed but affirmed, by the heavy weight of cannons and sabers.

The setting up of the colonial system does not of itself bring about the death of the native culture. Historic observation reveals, on the contrary, that the aim sought is rather a continued agony than a total disappearance of the pre-existing culture. This culture, once living and open to the future, becomes closed, fixed in the colonial status, caught in the yoke of oppression. Both present and mummified, it testifies against its members. It defines them in fact without appeal. The cultural mummification leads to a mummification of individual thinking. The apathy so universally noted among colonial peoples is but the logical consequence of this operation. The reproach of inertia constantly directed at "the native" is utterly dishonest. As though it were possible for a man to evolve otherwise than within the framework of a culture that recognizes him and that he decides to assume.

Thus we witness the setting up of archaic, inert institutions, functioning under the oppressor's supervision and patterned like a caricature of formerly fertile institutions...

These bodies appear to embody respect for the tradition, the cultural specificities, the personality of the subjugated people. This pseudo-respect in fact is tantamount to the most utter contempt, to the most elaborate sadism. The characteristic of a culture is to be open, permeated by spontaneous, generous, fertile lines of force. The appointment of "reliable men" to execute certain gestures is a deception that deceives no one. Thus the Kabyle *djemaas* named by the French authority are not recognized by the natives. They are matched by another *djemaa* democratically elected. And naturally the second as a rule dictates to the first what his conduct should be.

The constantly affirmed concern with "respecting the culture of the native populations" accordingly does not signify taking into consideration the values borne by the culture, incarnated by men. Rather, this behavior betrays a determination to objectify, to confine, to imprison, to harden. Phrases such as "I know them," "that's the way they are," show this maximum objectification successfully achieved. I can think of gestures and thoughts that define these men.

Exoticism is one of the forms of this simplification. It allows no cultural confrontation. There is on the one hand a culture in which qualities of dynamism, of growth, of depth can be recognized. As against this, we find characteristics, curiosities, things, never a structure.

Thus in an initial phase the occupant establishes his domination, massively affirms his superiority. The social group, militarily and economically subjugated, is dehumanized in accordance with a polydimensional method.

Exploitation, tortures, raids, racism, collective liquidations, rational oppression take turns at different levels in order literally to make of the native an object in the hands of the occupying nation.

This object man, without means of existing, without a *raison d'être*, is broken in the very depth of his substance. The desire to live, to continue, becomes more and more indecisive, more and more phantom-like. It is at this stage that the well-known guilt complex appears. In his first novels, Wright gives a very detailed description of it.

Progressively, however, the evolution of techniques of production, the industrialization, limited though it is, of the subjugated countries, the increasingly necessary existence of collaborators, impose a new attitude upon the occupant. The complexity of the means of production, the evolution of economic relations inevitably involving the evolution of ideologies, unbalance the system. Vulgar racism in its biological form corresponds to the period of crude exploitation of man's arms and legs. The perfecting of the means of production inevitably brings about the camouflage of the techniques by which man is exploited, hence of the forms of racism.

It is therefore not as a result of the evolution of people's minds that racism loses its virulence. No inner revolution can explain this necessity for racism to seek more subtle forms, to evolve. On all sides men become free, putting an end to the lethargy to which oppression and racism had condemned them.

In the very heart of the "civilized nations" the workers finally discover that the exploitation of man, at the root of a system, assumes different faces. At this stage racism no longer dares appear without disguise. It is unsure of itself. In an ever greater number of circumstances the racist takes to cover. He who claimed to "sense," to "see through" those others, finds himself to be a target, looked at, judged. The racist's purpose has become a purpose haunted by bad conscience. He can find salvation only in a passion-driven commitment such as is found in certain psychoses. And having defined the symptomatology of such passion-charged deliria is not the least of Professor Baruk's merits.

Racism is never a super-added element discovered by chance in the course of the investigation of the cultural data of a group. The social constellation, the cultural whole, are deeply modified by the existence of racism.

It is a common saying nowadays that racism is a plague of humanity. But we must not content ourselves with such a phrase. We must tirelessly look for the repercussions of racism at all levels of sociability. The importance of the racist problem in contemporary American literature is significant. The Negro in motion pictures, the Negro and folklore, the Jew and children's stories, the Jew in the café, are inexhaustible themes.

Racism, to come back to America, haunts and vitiates American culture. And this dialectical gangrene is exacerbated by the coming to awareness and the determination of millions of Negroes and Jews to fight this racism by which they are victimized.

This passion-charged, irrational, groundless phase, when one examines it, reveals a frightful visage. The movement of groups, the liberation, in certain parts of the world, of men previously kept down, make for a more and more precarious equilibrium. Rather unexpectedly, the racist group points accusingly to a manifestation of racism among the oppressed. The "intellectual primitivism" of the period of exploitation gives way to the "medieval, in fact prehistoric fanaticism" of the period of the liberation.

For a time it looked as though racism had disappeared. This soul-soothing, unreal impression was simply the consequence of the evolution of forms of exploitation. Psychologists spoke of a prejudice having become unconscious. The truth is that the rigor of the system made the daily affirmation of a superiority superfluous. The need to appeal to various degrees of approval and support, to the native's cooperation, modified relations in a less crude, more subtle, more "cultivated" direction. It was not rare, in fact, to see a "democratic and humane" ideology at this stage. The commercial undertaking of enslavement, of cultural destruction, progressively gave way to a verbal mystification.

The interesting thing about this evolution is that racism was taken as a topic of meditation, sometimes even as a publicity technique.

Thus the blues—"the black slave lament"—was offered up for the admiration of the oppressors. This modicum of stylized oppression is the exploiter's and the racist's rightful due. Without oppression and without racism you have no blues. The end of racism would sound the knell of great Negro music …

As the all-too-famous Toynbee might say, the blues are the slave's response to the challenge of oppression.

Still today, for many men, even colored, Armstrong's music has a real meaning only in this perspective.

Racism bloats and disfigures the face of the culture that practices it. Literature, the plastic arts, songs for shopgirls, proverbs, habits, patterns, whether they set out to attack it or to vulgarize it, restore racism. This means that a social group, a country, a civilization, cannot be unconsciously racist.

We say once again that racism is not an accidental discovery. It is not a hidden, dissimulated element. No superhuman efforts are needed to bring it out.

Racism stares one in the face for it so happens that it belongs in a characteristic whole: that of the shameless exploitation of one group of men by another which has reached a higher stage of technical development. This is why military and economic oppression generally precedes, makes possible, and legitimizes racism.

The habit of considering racism as a mental quirk, as a psychological flaw, must be abandoned.

But the men who are a prey to racism, the enslaved, exploited, weakened social group—how do they behave? What are their defense mechanisms?

What attitudes do we discover here?

In an initial phase we have seen the occupying power legitimizing its domination by scientific arguments, the "inferior race" being denied on the basis of race. Because no other solution is left it, the racialized social group tries to imitate the oppressor and thereby to deracialize itself. The "inferior race" denies itself as a different race. It shares with the "superior race" the convictions, doctrines, and other attitudes concerning it.

Having witnessed the liquidation of its systems of reference, the collapse of its cultural patterns, the native can only recognize with the occupant that "God is not on his side." The oppressor, through the inclusive and frightening character of his authority, manages to impose on the native new ways of seeing, and in particular a pejorative judgment with respect to his original forms of existing.

This event, which is commonly designated as alienation, is naturally very important. It is found in the official texts under the name of assimilation.

Now this alienation is never wholly successful. Whether or not it is because the oppressor quantitatively and qualitatively limits the evolution, unforeseen, disparate phenomena manifest themselves.

The inferiorized group had admitted, since the force of reasoning was implacable, that its misfortunes resulted directly from its racial and cultural characteristics.

Guilt and inferority are the usual consequences of this dialectic. The oppressed then tries to escape these, on the one hand by proclaiming his total and unconditional adoption of the new cultural models, and on the other, by pronouncing an irreversible condemnation of his own cultural style.[1]

Yet the necessity that the oppressor encounters at a given point to dissimulate the forms of exploitation does not lead to the disappearance of this exploitation. The more elaborate, less crude economic relations require a daily coating, but the alienation at this level remains frightful.

Having judged, condemned, abandoned his cultural forms, his language, his food habits, his sexual behavior, his way of sitting down, of resting, of laughing, of enjoying himself, the oppressed *flings himself* upon the imposed culture with the desperation of a drowning man.

Developing his technical knowledge in contact with more and more perfected machines, entering into the dynamic circuit of industrial production, meeting men from remote regions in the framework of the concentration of capital, that is to say, on the job, discovering the assembly line, the team, production "time," in other words yield per hour, the oppressed is shocked to find that he continues to be the object of racism and contempt.

It is at this level that racism is treated as a question of persons. "There are a few hopeless racists, but you must admit that on the whole the population likes..."

With time all this will disappear.

This is the country where there is the least amount of race prejudice ...

At the United Nations there is a commission to fight race prejudice.

Films on race prejudice, poems on race prejudice, messages on race prejudice …

Spectacular and futile condemnations of race prejudice. In reality, a colonial country is a racist country. If in England, in Belgium, or in France, despite the democratic principles affirmed by these respective nations, there are still racists, it is these racists who, in their opposition to the country as a whole, are logically consistent.

It is not possible to enslave men without logically making them inferior through and through. And racism is only the emotional, affective, sometimes intellectual explanation of this inferiorization.

The racist in a culture with racism is therefore normal. He has achieved a perfect harmony of economic relations and ideology. The idea that one forms of man, to be sure, is never totally dependent on economic relations, in other words—and this must not be forgotten—on relations existing historically and geographically among men and groups. An ever greater number of members belonging to racist societies are taking a position. They are dedicating themselves to a world in which racism would be impossible. But everyone is not up to this kind of objectivity, this abstraction, this solemn commitment. One cannot with impunity require of a man that he be against "the prejudices of his group."

And, we repeat, every colonialist group is racist.

"Acculturized" and deculturized at one and the same time, the oppressed continues to come up against racism. He finds this sequel illogical, what he has left behind him inexplicable, without motive, incorrect. His knowledge, the appropriation of precise and complicated techniques, sometimes his intellectual superiority as compared to a great number of racists, lead him to qualify the racist world as passion-charged. He perceives that the racist atmosphere impregnates all the elements of the social life. The sense of an overwhelming injustice is correspondingly very strong. Forgetting racism as a consequence, one concentrates on racism as cause. Campaigns of deintoxication are launched. Appeal is made to the sense of humanity, to love, to respect for the supreme values …

Race prejudice in fact obeys a flawless logic. A country that lives, draws its substance from the exploitation of other peoples, makes those peoples inferior. Race prejudice applied to those peoples is normal.

Racism is therefore not a constant of the human spirit.

It is, as we have seen, a disposition fitting into a well-defined system. And anti-Jewish prejudice is no different from anti-Negro prejudice. A society has race prejudice or it has not. There are no degrees of prejudice. One cannot say that a given country is racist but that lynchings or extermination camps are not to be found there. The truth is that all that and still other things exist on the horizon. These virtualities, these latencies circulate, carried by the life-stream of psycho-affective, economic relations …

Discovering the futility of his alienation, his progressive deprivation, the inferiorized individual, after this phase of deculturation, of extraneousness, comes back to his original positions.

This culture, abandoned, sloughed off, rejected, despised, becomes for the inferiorized an object of passionate attachment. There is a very marked kind of overvaluation that is psychologically closely linked to the craving for forgiveness.

But behind this simplifying analysis there is indeed the intuition experienced by the inferiorized of having discovered a spontaneous truth. This is a psychological datum that is part of the texture of History and of Truth.

Because the inferiorized rediscovers a style that had once been devalorized, what he does is in fact to cultivate culture. Such a caricature of cultural existence would indicate, if it were necessary, that culture must be lived, and cannot be fragmented. It cannot be had piecemeal.

Yet the oppressed goes into ecstasies over each rediscovery. The wonder is permanent. Having formerly emigrated from his culture, the native today explores it with ardor. It is a continual honeymoon. Formerly inferiorized, he is now in a state of grace.

Not with impunity, however, does one undergo domination. The culture of the enslaved people is sclerosed, dying. No life any longer circulates in it. Or more precisely, the only existing life is dissimulated. The population that normally assumes here and there a few fragments of life, which continues to attach dynamic meanings to institutions, is an anonymous population. In a colonial system these are the traditionalists.

The former emigré, by the sudden ambiguity of his behavior, causes consternation. To the anonymity of the traditionalist he opposes a vehement and aggressive exhibitionism.

The state of grace and aggressiveness are the two constants found at this stage. Aggressiveness being the passion-charged mechanism making it possible to escape the sting of paradox.

Because the former emigré is in possession of precise techniques, because his level of action is in the framework of relations that are already complex, these rediscoveries assume an irrational aspect. There is an hiatus, a discrepancy between intellectual development, technical appropriation, highly differentiated modes of thinking and of logic, on the one hand, and a "simple, pure" emotional basis on the other ...

Rediscovering tradition, living it as a defense mechanism, as a symbol of purity, of salvation, the decultured individual leaves the impression that the mediation takes vengeance by substantializing itself. This falling back on archaic positions having no relation to technical development is paradoxical. The institutions thus valorized no longer correspond to the elaborate methods of action already mastered.

The culture put into capsules, which has vegetated since the foreign domination, is revalorized. It is not reconceived, grasped anew, dynamized from within. It is shouted. And this headlong, unstructured, verbal revalorization conceals paradoxical attitudes.

It is at this point that the incorrigible character of the inferiorized is brought out for mention. Arab doctors sleep on the ground, spit all over the place, etc. ...

Negro intellectuals consult a sorcerer before making a decision, etc. ...

"Collaborating" intellectuals try to justify their new attitude. The customs, traditions, beliefs, formerly denied and passed over in silence are violently valorized and affirmed.

Tradition is no longer scoffed at by the group. The group no longer runs away from itself. The sense of the past is rediscovered, the worship of ancestors resumed ...

The past, becoming henceforth a constellation of values, becomes identified with the Truth.

This rediscovery, this absolute valorization almost in defiance of reality, objectively indefensible, assumes an incomparable and subjective importance. On emerging from these passionate espousals, the native will have decided, "with full knowledge of what is involved," to fight all forms of exploitation and of alienation of man. At this same time, the occupant, on the other hand, multiplies appeals to assimilation, then to integration, to community.

The native's hand-to-hand struggle with his culture is too solemn, too abrupt an operation to tolerate the slightest slip-up. No neologism can mask the new certainty: the plunge into the chasm of the past is the condition and the source of freedom.

The logical end of this will to struggle is the total liberation of the national territory. In order to achieve this liberation, the inferiorized man brings all his resources into play, all his acquisitions, the old and the new, his own and those of the occupant.

The struggle is at once total, absolute. But then race prejudice is hardly found to appear.

At the time of imposing his domination, in order to justify slavery, the oppressor had invoked scientific argument. There is nothing of the kind here.

A people that undertakes a struggle for liberation rarely legitimizes race prejudice. Even in the course of acute periods of insurrectional armed struggle one never witnesses the recourse to biological justifications.

The struggle of the inferiorized is situated on a markedly more human level. The perspectives are radically new. The opposition is the henceforth classical one of the struggles of conquest and of liberation.

In the course of struggle the dominating nation tries to revive racist arguments but the elaboration of racism proves more and more ineffective. There is talk of fanaticism, of primitive attitudes in the face of death, but once again the now crumbling mechanism no longer responds. Those who were once unbudgeable, the constitutional cowards, the timid, the eternally inferiorized, stiffen and emerge bristling.

The occupant is bewildered.

The end of race prejudice begins with a sudden incomprehension.

The occupant's spasmed and rigid culture, now liberated, opens at last to the culture of people who have really become brothers. The two cultures can affront each other, enrich each other.

In conclusion, universality resides in this decision to recognize and accept the reciprocal relativism of different cultures, once the colonial status is irreversibly excluded.

Note
1. A little-studied phenomenon sometimes appears at this stage. Intellectuals, students, belonging to the dominant group, make 'scientific' studies of the dominated society, its art, its ethical universe. In the universities the rare colonized intellectuals find their own cultural system being revealed to them. It even happens that scholars of the colonizing countries grow enthusiastic over this or that specific feature. The concepts of purity, naïveté, innocence appear. The native intellectual's vigilance must here be doubly on the alert.

Hiccups

Léon Damas

For Vashti and Mercer Cook

I gulp down seven drinks of water
several times a day
and all in vain
instinctively
like the criminal to the crime
my childhood returns
in a rousing fit of hiccups

Talk about calamity
talk about disasters
I'll tell you

My mother wanted her son to have good manners at the table:
    keep your hands on the table
    we don't cut bread
    we break it
    we don't gobble it down
    the bread your father sweats for
    our daily bread

    eat the bones carefully and neatly
    a stomach has to have good manners too
    and a well-bred stomach never
    burps
    a fork is not a tooth-pick
    don't pick your nose
    in front of the whole world
    and sit up straight
    a well-bred nose
    doesn't sweep the plate

And then
and then
and then in the name of the Father
               and the Son
               and the Holy Ghost
at the end of every meal

And then and then
talk about calamity
talk about disasters
I'll tell you

My mother wanted her son to have the very best marks
     if you don't know your history
     you won't go to mass
     tomorrow
     in your Sunday suit

This child will disgrace our family name
This child will be our ... in the name of God
     be quiet
     have I or have I not
     told you to speak French
     the French of France
     the French that Frenchmen speak
     French French

Talk about calamity
talk about disasters
I'll tell you

My mother wanted her son to be a mama's boy:
     you didn't say good evening to our neighbor
     what–dirty shoes again
     and don't let me catch you any more
     playing in the street or on the grass or in the park
     underneath the War Memorial
     playing
     or picking a fight with what's–his–name
     what's–his–name who isn't even baptized

Talk about calamity
talk about disasters
I'll tell you

My mother wanted her son to be
            very *do*
            very *re*
            very *mi*
            very *fa*
            very *sol*
            very *la*
            very *ti*
            very *do-re-mi*
            fa-sol-la-ti-do

I see you haven't been to your vi-o-lin lesson
      a banjo
      did you say a banjo
      what do you mean
      a banjo
      you really mean
      a banjo
      no indeed young man
            you know there won't be any
            ban-or
                jo
                  or
                    gui-or
                        tar
                            in our house
They are not for *colored* people
Leave them to the *black* folks!

I Come from the Nigger Yard

Martin Carter

I come from the nigger yard of yesterday
leaping from the oppressors hate
and the scorn of myself;
from the agony of the dark hut in the shadow
and the hurt of things;
from the long days of cruelty and the long nights of pain
down to the wide streets of to-morrow, of the next day
leaping I come, who cannot see will hear.

In the nigger yard I was naked like the new born
naked like a stone or a star.
It was a cradle of blind days rocking in time
torn like the skin from the back of a slave.
It was an aching floor on which I crept
on my hands and my knees
searching the dust for the trace of a root
or the mark of a leaf or the shape of a flower.

It was me always walking with bare feet,
meeting strange faces like those in dreams or fever
when the whole world turns upside down
and no one knows which is the sky or the land
which heart is his among the torn or wounded
which face is his among the strange and terrible
walking about, groaning between the wind.

And there was always sad music somewhere in the land
like a bugle and a drum between the houses
voices of women singing far away
pauses of silence, then a flood of sound.
But these were things like ghosts or spirits of wind.
It was only a big world spinning outside
and men, born in agony, torn in torture, twisted and broken
      like a leaf,

and the uncomfortable morning, the beds of hunger stained
      and sordid
like the world, big and cruel, spinning outside.

Sitting sometimes in the twilight near the forest
where all the light is gone and every bird
I notice a tiny star neighbouring a leaf
a little drop of light a piece of glass
straining over heaven tiny bright
like a spark seed in the destiny of gloom.
O it was the heart like this tiny star near to the sorrows
straining against the whole world and the long twilight
spark of man's dream conquering the night
moving in darkness stubborn and fierce
till leaves of sunset change from green to blue
and shadows grow like giants everywhere.

So was I born again stubborn and fierce
screaming in a slum.
It was a city and coffin space for home
a river running, prisons, hospitals
men drunk and dying, judges full of scorn
priests and parsons fooling gods with words
and me, like a dog tangled in rags
spotted with sores powdered with dust
screaming with hunger, angry with life and men.

It was a child born from a mother full of her blood
weaving her features bleeding her life in clots.
It was pain lasting from hours to months and to years
weaving a pattern telling a tale leaving a mark
on the face and the brow.
Until there came the iron days cast in a foundry
Where men make hammers things that cannot break
and anvils heavy hard and cold like ice.

And so again I became one of the ten thousands
one of the uncountable miseries owning the land.
When the moon rose up only the whores could dance
the brazen jazz of music throbbed and groaned
filling the night air full of rhythmic questions.
It was the husk and the seed challenging fire
birth and the grave challenging life.

Until to-day in the middle of the tumult
when the land changes and the world's all convulsed
when different voices join to say the same
and different hearts beat out in unison
where on the aching floor of where I live
the shifting earth is twisting into shape
I take again my nigger life, my scorn
and fling it in the face of those who hate me.
It is me the nigger boy turning to manhood
linking my fingers, welding my flesh to freedom.

I come from the nigger yard of yesterday
leaping from the oppressor's hate
and the scorn of myself.
I come to the world with scars upon my soul
wounds on my body, fury in my hands.
I turn to the histories of men and the lives of the peoples.
I examine the shower of sparks the wealth of the dreams.
I am pleased with the glories and sad with the sorrows
rich with the riches, poor with the loss.
From the nigger yard of yesterday I come with my burden.
To the world of to-morrow I turn with my strength.

Caribbean Nationalisms

Africa for the Africans

Marcus Garvey

For five years the Universal Negro Improvement Association has been advocating the cause of Africa for the Africans—that is, that the Negro peoples of the world should concentrate upon the object of building up for themselves a great nation in Africa.

When we started our propaganda toward this end several of the so-called intellectual Negroes who have been bamboozling the race for over half a century said that we were crazy, that the Negro peoples of the western world were not interested in Africa and could not live in Africa. One editor and leader went so far as to say at his so-called Pan-African Congress that American Negroes could not live in Africa, because the climate was too hot. All kinds of arguments have been adduced by these Negro intellectuals against the colonization of Africa by the black race. Some said that the black man would ultimately work out his existence alongside of the white man in countries founded and established by the latter. Therefore, it was not necessary for Negroes to seek an independent nationality of their own. The old time stories of "African fever," "African bad climate," "African mosquitos," "African savages," have been repeated by these "brainless intellectuals" of ours as a scare against our people in America and the West Indies taking a kindly interest in the new program of building a racial empire of our own in our Motherland. Now that years have rolled by and the Universal Negro Improvement Association has made the circuit of the world with its propaganda, we find eminent statesmen and leaders of the white race coming out boldly advocating the cause of colonizing Africa with the Negroes of the western world. A year ago Senator MacCullum of the Mississippi Legislature introduced a resolution in the House for the purpose of petitioning the Congress of the United States of America and the President to use their good influence in securing from the Allies sufficient territory in Africa in liquidation of the war debt, which territory should be used for the establishing of an independent nation for American Negroes. About the same time Senator France of Maryland gave expression to a similar desire in the Senate of the United States. During a speech on the "Soldiers' Bonus." He said: "We owe a big debt to Africa and one which we have too long ignored. I need not enlarge upon our peculiar interest in the obligation to the people of Africa. Thousands of Americans have for years been contributing to the missionary work which has been carried out by the noble men and women who have been sent out in that field by the churches of America."

Germany to the Front

This reveals a real change on the part of prominent statesmen in their attitude on the African question. Then comes another suggestion from Germany, for which Dr. Heinrich Schnee, a former Governor of German East Africa, is author. This German statesman suggests in an interview given out in Berlin, and published in New York, that America takes over the mandatories of Great Britain and France in Africa for the colonization of American Negroes. Speaking on the matter, he says:

As regards the attempt to colonize Africa with the surplus American colored population, this would in a long way settle the vexed problem, and under the plan such as Senator France has outlined, might enable France and Great Britain to discharge their duties to the United States, and simultaneously ease the burden of German reparations which is paralyzing economic life.

With expressions as above quoted from prominent world statesmen, and from the demands made by such men as Senators France and McCullum, it is clear that the question of African nationality is not a far-fetched one, but is as reasonable and feasible as was the idea of an American nationality.

A "Program" At Last

I trust that the Negro peoples of the world are now convinced that the work of the Universal Negro Improvement Association is not a visionary one, but very practical, and that it is not so far fetched, but can be realized in a short while if the entire race will only co-operate and work toward the desired end. Now that the work of our organization has started to bear fruit we find that some of these "doubting Thomases" of three and four years ago are endeavoring to mix themselves up with the popular idea of rehabilitating Africa in the interest of the Negro. They are now advancing spurious "programs" and in a short while will endeavor to force themselves upon the public as advocates and leaders of the African idea.

It is felt that those who have followed the career of the Universal Negro Improvement Association will not allow themselves to be deceived by these Negro opportunists who have always sought to live off the ideas of other people.

The Dream of a Negro Empire

It is only a question of a few more years when Africa will be completely colonized by Negroes, as Europe is by the white race. What we want is an independent African nationality, and if America is to help the Negro peoples of the world establish such a nationality, then we welcome the assistance.

It is hoped that when the time comes for American and West Indian Negroes to settle in Africa, they will realize their responsibility and their duty. It will not be to go to Africa for the purpose of exercising an over-lordship over the natives, but it shall be the purpose of the Universal Negro Improvement Association to have established in Africa that brotherly co-operation which will make the interests of the African native and the American and West Indian Negro one and the same, that is to say, we shall enter into a common partnership to build up Africa in the interests of our race.

Oneness of Interest

Everybody knows that there is absolutely no difference between the native African and the American and West Indian Negroes, in that we are descendants from one common family stock. It is only a matter of accident that we have been divided and kept apart for over three hundred years, but it is felt that when the time has come for us to get back together, we shall do so in the spirit of brotherly love, and any Negro who expects that he will be assisted here, there or anywhere by the Universal Negro Improvement Association to exercise a haughty superiority over the fellows of his own race, makes a tremendous mistake. Such men had better remain where they are and not attempt to become in any way interested in the higher development of Africa.

The Negro has had enough of the vaunted practice of race superiority as inflicted upon him by others, therefore he is not prepared to tolerate a similar assumption on the part of his own people. In America and the West Indies, we have Negroes who believe themselves so much above their fellows as to cause them to think that any readjustment in the affairs of the race should be placed in their hands for them to exercise a kind of an autocratic and despotic control as others have done to us for centuries. Again I say, it would be advisable for such Negroes to take their hands and minds off the now popular idea of colonizing Africa in the interest of the Negro race, because their being identified with this new program will not in any way help us because of the existing feeling among Negroes everywhere not to tolerate the infliction of race or class superiority upon them, as is the desire of the self-appointed and self-created race leadership that we have been having for the last fifty years.

The Basis of an African Aristocracy

The masses of Negroes in America, the West Indies, South and Central America are in sympathetic accord with the aspirations of the native Africans. We desire to help them build up Africa as a Negro Empire, where every black man, whether he was born in Africa or in the Western world, will have the opportunity to develop on his own lines under the protection of the most favorable democratic institutions.

It will be useless, as before stated, for bombastic Negroes to leave America and the West Indies to go to Africa, thinking that they will have privileged positions to inflict upon the race that bastard aristocracy that they have tried to maintain in this Western world at the expense of the masses. Africa shall develop an aristocracy of its own, but it shall be based upon service and loyalty to race. Let all Negroes work toward that end. I feel that it is only a question of a few more years before our program will be accepted not only by the few statesmen of America who are now interested in it, but by the strong statesmen of the world, as the only solution to the great race problem. There is no other way to avoid the threatening war of the races that is bound to engulf all mankind, which has been prophesied by the world's greatest thinkers; there is no better method than by apportioning every race to its own habitat.

The time has really come for the Asiatics to govern themselves in Asia, as the Europeans are in Europe and the Western world, so also is it wise for the Africans to govern themselves at home, and thereby bring peace and satisfaction to the entire human family.

Race and Creole Ethnicity in the Caribbean

Percy Hintzen

Caribbean identity occurs within the discursive space of the "Creole". To be "Caribbean" is to be "creolised" and within this space are accommodated all who, at any one time, constitute a (semi)-permanent core of Caribbean society. Creolisation brought with it notions of organic connections across boundaries of ethnicised and racialised difference. It was the mechanism through which colonial discourses of difference, necessary for its legitimation, were accommodated. Everyone located in its discursive space, whatever her/his diasporic origin, becomes transformed in a regime of identific solidarity. At the same time, the Creole construct is integrally inserted into a discourse of exclusion as a boundary-maintaining mechanism. Maintaining a strict and rigid boundary between "Caribbean" and "non-Caribbean" (local versus foreign) has functioned strategically as a mechanism for manipulation in the maintenance of order and control.[1]

From this perspective, Caribbean ethnicity is constituted by its créolité. In their panoptic gaze, White colonisers imposed créolité to render invisible the racialised division of labour and the racial allocation of power and privilege. Historically, the discourse of racial difference has been shifted to distinctions between the Creole and non-Creole. The result has been a valorisation of White purity, located outside Creole space. This valorisation, at the root of White supremacy, became the foundation principle of colonial power, privilege, honour and prestige. Créolité went hand-in-hand with the symbolic capital of Whiteness.[2] It offered the possibility of "whitening" while demonstrating the consequences of descent into the world of savagery represented, in European discursive construction, by the colonised.

Nationalism, according to Benedict Anderson, is to be understood in terms of "the large cultural system that preceded it, out of which – as well as against which – it came into being".[3] And culture constitutes the representations and practices of ethnicity. As its precedent, créolité has imposed upon Caribbean nationalism European aspirations that have become hidden behind the veil of anti-colonialism. It has served to hide commonalties in social practice that could have formed the basis of counterdiscursive challenges to North Atlantic power. The visualisation of similarities located outside of European constructs could have come with "new possibilities for struggle and resistance, for advancing alternative cultural possibilities".[4]

Creole discourse has been the bonding agent of Caribbean society. It has functioned in the interest of the powerful, whether represented by a colonialist or nationalist elite. It is the identific glue that bonds the different, competing and otherwise mutually exclusive interests contained within Caribbean society. It paved the way for the accommodation of racialised discourses of difference upon which rested the legitimacy of colonial power and exploitation. Difference was rendered invisible in a cognitive merger created and sustained by its impositions. Competing interests and relations of exploitation and privilege became socially organised in a fluid clinal system of racial and cultural hierarchy. This was the observation of Caribbean sociologist Lloyd

Braithwaite in what has been termed a "reticulated" colour-class pattern of social stratification by anthropologist Leo Despres.[5]

To be Caribbean, then, is to occupy the hierarchical, hybridised, "Creole" space between two racial poles that serve as markers for civilisation and savagery. It is to be constituted of various degrees of cultural and racial mixing. At the apex is the White Creole as the historical product of cultural hybridisation. The Afro-Creole is located at the other end of the Creole continuum. The "creolisation" of the latter derives from transformative contact with Europe's civilising influences and from physical separation from Africa. Valorised forms of European racial and cultural purity become unattainable ideals in Creole representation and practice. Distance from the ideal European phenotype and from Europe's cultural practices determines and defines the Creole's position in the social hierarchy.

Thus, the principles of hierarchisation of Caribbean-Creole society are intimately tied to notions of European civilisation and African savagery. When applied to Europeans, creolisation implies the taint of savagery. When applied to Africans it implies a brush with civilisation. The Caribbean is the location where civilisation and savagery meet and where both become transformed. In this regard, Creole nationalism becomes a quest to be fully European.

The discourse of purity is one of the means through which disciplinary power is imposed upon Caribbean society. Under colonialism, White purity came to be represented as symbolic capital in the practices of the colonial administrators. This was contrasted with the hybridised practices of the White Creole. In the English colonies these different regimes of representation were concretised in colonial institutional practices of the nineteenth century. In the administration of governance, White Creole practices were represented in a merchant-planter-dominated financial college, which became the representative arm of the local White population. British colonial interests came to be signified and represented in the practices of a Court of Policy that served, in effect, as the legislative arm of government. Executive power was exercised through a colonial administration centred on the governor and comprising civil servants appointed by the Crown.[6] This development in political representation and practice contributed significantly to the process of White creolisation. It paralleled the development of divergent material interests between local and metropolitan capitalists. It differed across territory, irrespective of colonial jurisdiction, and presaged differences in the presence and significance of White Creoles in the development of Creole identity across the region.

The Discourse of Purity

The hybridised reality of Creole society left little room for accommodation of claims to cultural and racial purity. It is important to emphasise here that purity, like race, is socially constructed. It emerges out of discursive regimes of representation and practice. In Dominica, for example, despite a long history of racial intermixing with Blacks, cultural conversion, and the practice of Creole forms of social organisation, discourses of purity still exclude the putative descendants of the indigenous Kalinago ("Caribs") from Creole society. Purity emerged as a boundary defining and maintaining principle separating Creole society from the external world. It is a central principle in the discourse of difference that separates the "local" Creole White from the foreign "pure" European. This distinction is quite important in the assertions by the national elite of cultural claims to the new global order of North Atlantic universalism. These assertions have been made possible by nationalist rejection of White supremacy. As symbolic and cultural capital (acquired knowledge, skill and capabilities) such assertions have come to embody the new European aspirations of the nationalist elite.

To be "genuinely" White in the Caribbean is to be culturally and racially pure, untainted by absorption into the society of the former enslaved Blacks. This taint of impurity, forged out of cultural and sexual contact with the African, became the basis for exclusion of White Creoles from colonial power and privilege. Paradoxically, the organic connection to the "territory", which was at the root of such exclusion, assured the White Creole a position of privilege in nationalist construction. White inclusion in the nationalist space suggests the need for a much more nuanced view of the nationalist movement. The embrace of representations and practices of the racialised European mirrors precisely, the position of the nationalist movement toward European institutional and cultural forms. Many of the latter were adopted wholeheartedly after independence.[7] Whiteness, however tainted, retains its valorised position in Creole-nationalist construction. The rights of White Creoles to social and economic privilege and preference in the territorial space were retained, and even enhanced, with the departure of the colonial power. In many instances, White Creoles are used as international brokers in the new regimes of sovereignty. At the same time, their representation as cultural and racial hybrids and their organic claims to the territory served to protect their social and economic privilege in the crucible of anti-colonial nationalism with its anti-European and anti-White implications. Such representations rendered their "Whiteness" invisible in the face of a nationalist rejection of White supremacy. In this way, White creolisation became the mechanism for the non-problematisation of Whiteness. It legitimised a post-colonial version of racial capitalism and explains the continued domination of Whites in the private sector of the post-colonial Caribbean.

Thus, the nationalist movement was neither anti-White nor anti-European. Rather, it was a contestation of the claims of Whites and Europeans to supremacy and superiority. Its various assertions of Africanity in national expression must be understood in these terms. The meaning of such assertions continues to be subject to debate among scholars and writers in the Francophone Caribbean under conditions where nationalist ambitions have been frustrated. Rather than a shift to sovereign independent status like their Anglophone counterparts, the French Antilles have become incorporated into the administrative and jurisdictional structure of the French state as *départements*. Frustrated nationalist ambitions have fuelled the development of a Créoliste movement "agitating for the local culture and language of the French West Indies".[8] This has supplanted earlier nationalist expressions framed around notions of Négritude. Leading members of the movement have rejected Négritude's notions of Africanity that were integral to Caribbean nationalism. They consider claims to an African past to be an "illusion of Europe with that of Africa".[9] They have painstakingly pointed out the contradictions in the Négritude movement in the support provided by its leadership, headed by Aimé Césaire of Martinique, for *département* status and in Césaire's firm embrace of the party-politics of France. In all of this, what clearly emerges is the rejection of Africa and an embracing of Europe. It is an embrace that is firmly implanted in Caribbean nationalist representations and practices. Its themes are more convincingly evident in the competing versions of nationalist expression in the French Caribbean. They are not so obvious in its Anglophone versions. The necessity of challenging the authorial power of Britain rendered invisible the latter's fundamentally European character.

Creole discourse locates all with claims to purity outside of the territorial community of the Caribbean. This is the point of the Créolistes charge of African and European illusion. Indeed, they go a step further by valorising hybridity as "the vanguard of a world-wide movement".[10] In other words, créolité portends the racial and cultural hybridity of a new North Atlantic that is at the forefront of neoglobalisation. Such hybridity is essential to the notions of Creole nationalism and to the European aspirations contained within them. It substantiates the self-location of the Creole at the centre of a new globalisation of the Europeanised North Atlantic. Thus, Patrick Chamoiseau, one of the movement's leading ideologues, describes creolisation as a "great poetics of relation, which allows people to express their newfound diversity, to live it fluidly. In creolisation, there never comes a time of general synthesis, with everyone beatifically at one with one another."[11]

Thus, claims to purity, essentialised around geographic discourses of origin, cannot be accommodated in Creole discourse. This is the basis of the Créolistes' discomfort with "illusions of Africa and Europe". It is why the North must first undergo a *métissage* transformation to accommodate the European aspirations of Creole nationalism. Thus, firmly embedded in nationalist aspirations is the goal of the conversion of Europe into the pregnable, transitory and open space that is the Caribbean. This is very much what has occurred in the French Antilles. The assertion of créolité is very much a declaration of the hybridisation of European space occupied exclusively by Whites. Indeed, the term Creole, before its hybridisation, signified the representations and practices of White French Caribbeans known as *Békés*. It referred specifically to "a White person of pure race born in the Antilles".[12]

Post-emancipation indentureship imposed its own legitimating regime of exclusion. Its legitimacy rested upon the "racial" and cultural location of the new indentures outside of the European-African continuum of Creole society. But the new rationality of exclusion also applied to European and African post-slavery indentures. Portuguese indentures, imported from Madeira, were unable to make immediate claims of racial affinity with the White Creoles in Trinidad and British Guiana (now Guyana). They remained for a time outside of Creole society. For post-emancipation African indentures, the boundary maintaining distinction between African and Afro-Creole, typical of slave systems, prevailed. Once inserted into plantation society, however, Portuguese and Africans became quickly amalgamated. For the African, creolisation came with location at the lowest rung in the colour-class hierarchy.[13] The Portuguese took over from Coloureds in small-scale retailing. They followed a trajectory of incorporation into Creole society by Whites and near Whites as "trading minorities".[14] This was also the path followed by the small migrant population of Lebanese, Syrians, Jews and post-indenture Chinese who, with the Portuguese, were able to establish themselves in the retail sector, particularly in Trinidad and Jamaica.

Amalgamation has become integral to the historical reproduction of Creole identity. It calls for an abnegation of purity through sexual and cultural immersion. The Creole space "swallows everything up ... remaining permanently in motion, pushing us headlong in a movement of diversity, of change and exchange."[15] "Blending and impurity" stand as its fundamental values.[16] With the exception of the Syrians and Lebanese, whose cultural forms disappeared with their creolisation, immersion has acted, historically, to modify the African-European continuum in the Anglophone Caribbean. Rituals and practices of Creole transformation can include racial immersion through miscegenation. Cultural immersion can occur through marriage, religious conversion, association and adoption of the tastes and styles of Creole society. Cohabitation has become quite important in individual practices of creolisation. For the offspring of the ensuing unions, Creole parentage negates any claim to purity. It brings with it automatic location within the White-Black continuum. To some degree, cohabitation with White Creoles has offered the most acceptable means of immersion into Creole society for those located outside of the European-African space. As the most "desirable" of the Creoles, cohabitation with Whites serves to lessen the social opprobrium of creolisation with its implications for impurity. Thus, with the exception of the Whites who were pushed "downward" into Creole space, the thrust of creolisation has always been upward to the

European end of the racial and cultural spectrum. The quest of the nationalist movement was to penetrate the barrier of racial purity by hybridising European space.

Exclusion and Incorporation

Symbolic exclusion is the instrument of disciplinary power wielded historically against diasporic communities functionally integrated into Caribbean political economy. It rendered legitimate the systematic denial of any claims non-Creoles might make upon the resources of Creole society. This became the basis for exclusion from opportunities provided through access to these resources. While historically pervasive, the discriminatory and exploitative consequences of symbolic exclusion were not always universal. With exclusion came also the benefits of freedom from the normative strictures of Creole society. It created opportunities unavailable to those located in the colour/class hierarchy of Creole social space. The discourse of purity served historically, until well into the twentieth century, to confine Asian Indians to rural agriculture and to justify their semi-servile status. At the same time, however, Asian Indians have managed to use peasant agricultural practices as a springboard for upward mobility through business and the professions. In the process, they were able to eviscerate the social stigma of agricultural labour. Their agricultural background did not prefigure in social evaluations of their fitness for business and higher education, as it would have been for Creole subjects. As "outsiders", these standards of evaluation were rendered irrelevant.

The benefits of exclusion were evident, also, in the ability of Chinese and Portuguese (coming in as nineteenth-century indentures), Syrians, Lebanese and the small number of Jews (all arriving after World War I) to exploit economic opportunity. Their exclusion from Creole society freed them from the strictures of colour imposed by their light complexion. As such, they were able to ignore the principles of behaviour and association implicated in the colour/class hierarchy of Creole society. They established themselves in petty trade by developing highly personalised relationships with customers lower down the colour/class hierarchy. From here, they created niches in small-scale retailing, particularly in Trinidad, Jamaica and British Guiana (now Guyana). Their activities, and the pattern of associations and practices engendered by them, became the springboards for the structural and social insertion of their members into colonial Creole society. Once located in Creole space, they were able to combine symbolic capital (derived from their colour) with economic capital to move up the social hierarchy. Many came to occupy positions identical with or just below Creole Whites. What became most evident in their upward mobility was the importance of the symbolic capital of Whiteness. This pattern of amalgamation and upward mobility was not available to the over 40,000 post-emancipation Africans brought to the Caribbean between 1834 and 1867 for plantation labour.[17] Their amalgamation occurred at the lowest rung of the colour/class continuum of Creole society.

It is through racial and cultural incorporation that the transitory nature of Creole society is preserved. Incorporation allows Caribbean society to respond to the constantly changing pressures and demands from outside its borders. These must be accommodated for the very economic survival of the territories of the region. Practices of amalgamation have changed the racial and cultural character of Creole society. They have produced new forms of racial hybridity involving, particularly, Asian Indian and Chinese post-slavery additions to plantation society. Similarly, new emergent forms of cultural hybridity have become integrated into Creole practice. Thus, cultural and racial insertion has contributed to an historical reformulation of Creole identity. It has produced, over time, a modification of its racialised construction. Dark skin continues to retain the signifying power of inferiority. However, its exclusive association with African diasporic origin is no longer a firmly entrenched principle. Thus, a White-Black polarity based on colour has replaced Europe and Africa at opposite ends of the Creole continuum. This has been particularly the case as new diasporic communities with origins in Asia, the Middle East, and in the indigenous population of the region have become immersed into Caribbean reality. "Blackness", however, continues, by and large, to retain its association with Africa in an ongoing counter discourse to Creole construction. This is quite evident in the regional spread of the Rastafarian movement that originated in Jamaica[18] and in the Orisha religious movement in Trinidad.[19]

For the most part, the indigenous and diasporic communities with cultural and racial origins outside Africa and Europe remain, in representation and practice, outside Creole reality. For members of these communities, amalgamation is available through individual practices of cultural and sexual immersion. For Asian Indians, individual practices of racial miscegenation with Afro-Creoles have been significant enough to produce a distinctive Creole variant identified as "Douglas" in local lexicon. As the products of Afro-Indian unions, "Douglas" have become integral to the construction of Creole identity in Guyana and Trinidad. They have also come to symbolise the threat posed by creolisation to Asian Indian purity. The theme of "Douglarisation" emerges persistently in Asian Indian narratives of purity. It has become emblematic of the polluting consequences of sexual contact with Africans. "Douglarisation", therefore, is the process of transformation of Asian Indians into racial Creoles through miscegenation. Another route to Asian Indian creolisation is through cultural amalgamation. Asian Indians may enter the social space of Creole organisation through practices of inter-marriage, religious conversion, Creole association (including location of residence) and through the adoption of Creole style and tastes.

The representations and practices of créolité are responses to the deployment of symbolic power at the disposal of the constituents of its various segments and of those located outside its symbolic space. Each is engaged in a constant struggle to define Creole reality. Creoles activate honour and prestige as symbolic power, they activate resources of economic, social and cultural power available to them, and they activate the privilege of belonging in order to maintain créolité's existing integrity. Those excluded from créolité definition are perpetually engaged in efforts to redefine its character or to challenge its centrality in national conceptions of belonging. These struggles produce constant reformulations over time of the cognitive schemata that inform Creole identity and out of which its representations and practices are fashioned. They have also produced territorially specific manifestations of Creole constructs.

Trinidad provides an example of the complexities and idiosyncrasies of Creole construction and its implication for nationalist discursive formation. The European cultural component of Trinidadian society has been shaped quite significantly by Spanish colonialism (the former colonial power) and by the presence of a French merchant plantocracy (via Haiti after the Haitian revolution). As "local Whites", French and Spanish Creoles were historically differentiated from the administrative class of the British in colonial representation and practice. As a result, Creole identity in Trinidad became heavily infused with French and Spanish representations and with Roman Catholicism. It has also been influenced by the presence of Asian Indian, Chinese, Portuguese, Syrian and Lebanese diasporic populations and by the various racial and cultural hybridities produced in social interaction among all these groupings. In particular, hybridised rituals and symbols of Asian Indian representations and practices are gaining considerable visibility in Creole construction. This is despite the latter's historical exclusion from the creolised space of Trinidadian identific discourse. At the same time, Trinidadian créolité has amalgamated the representations and practices of "Douglas" (the products of miscegenous unions between Africans and Indians), Portuguese (by giving up their claims to Whiteness), and Chinese, Syrians and Lebanese (through cultural amalgamation and miscegenation).

At over 40 per cent of the population, the size and functional integration of East Indians in Trinidad have had profound consequences for the reproduction of Creole society. Their strategic presence has produced considerable challenges to the central role that créolité has played in nationalist construction. The fundamental contradiction between the structural integration of Asian Indians in Trinidad's political economy and their symbolic exclusion from nationalist space has produced an increasing crescendo of national conflict as well as persistent contestation of nationalist discourse. Access to Creole society has been available only to those members of the Asian Indian community prepared to reject representations and practices of purity on cultural grounds or to those who are prepared to reject patterns of racial solidarity and marriage endogamy. One avenue for rejection is through conversion to Christianity. For the smaller population of Muslim Asian Indians (which constitutes less than 25 per cent of the total Asian Indian population), religion poses less of a barrier to creolisation given their monotheism and the common foundation of beliefs that they share with Christianity. As a result, Muslims have been much more visibly included in the representation and practices of Creole nationalist expression. However, discourses of purity continue to locate the large majority of Asian Indians, as Hindus, outside the national space. Members of the Asian Indian middle classes, particularly its economic, social, and political elite, experience most profound pressures for creolisation. This derives from their high degree of functional integration into the "Creole" segments of Trinidad's political economy. To this is added their own predispositions toward creolisation as they seek to realise the benefits of nationalism that have accrued to their Creole counterparts in the post-colonial era. The pressures and predispositions have resulted in the incorporation by many Hindus of more universal western forms into their religious practices and the opening up of their religion to Creole practitioners. It has produced a form of creolisation that comes with little sacrifice to Hindu identity.[20]

Notwithstanding the pressures placed upon the Hindu middle classes and their own predispositions for Creole incorporation, there is mounting resistance to creolisation among the Hindu cultural elite. In their campaign, they activate the symbolic power of purity to petition for inclusion in the nationalist space as Asian Indians. Hindu purity is deployed as a symbolic resource by these leaders to delegitimise "polluted" Creole discourse. The leaders reject the central role that Creole representations occupy in notions of national belonging. Such rejection is organised around narratives of cultural degradation directed, particularly, at the cultural ascendance of Afro-Creole forms in nationalist discourse. There is mounting contestation of the claim made by Afro-Creoles of their own central role in nation building. Asian Indians are beginning to present themselves as the true builders of the nation. Their cultural elite has constructed an historical narrative of Asian Indians as redeemers who have, time and again, delivered the country from the abyss of Afro-Creole degradation.[21] The Asian Indian challenge to Creole nationalism is not merely a quest for nationalist inclusion. Rather, it is an attempt to retain representations and practices of cultural purity while resisting "Douglarisation". It represents a redemptive counter-discourse to Afro-Creole nationalism and presents a fundamental challenge to Trinidadian créolité. It remains a rejection of the "blending and impurity" of the form of hybridity that occupies the critical centre in the value framework of Creole's discourse.

Despite Hindu challenges, the fundamental thrust of creolisation is deeply embedded in the historical development of Trinidadian national identity. Créolité occupies the critical core of the country's national psyche. This is evident in the mythic representation of the "Spanish". As a social construction of the ideal-typical Trinidadian, it has emerged as a means of managing the complexities and conflicting pulls of disaporic identity. But "Spanish" identity is instructive in another important way – it exposes and externalises the European aspirations that exist at the root of Creole discourse and that are integral to the country's nationalist expression. It is a narrative of a simpler time in Trinidad colonial history before the introduction of plantation slavery (and hence of the complexity of the African presence). The "Spanish" construct embodies all the positive elements of the various ethnic groupings that occupy the country's territorial space (creolised or otherwise). As such, it is a trope of hybridised harmony in the face of multiple and competing representations and practices of difference.[22] But it is a harmony forged out of idealised "European" qualities, devoid of notions of ethnic, cultural and social exclusivity.

In Trinidad, the struggle for the nation occurs in the field of symbolic production and reproduction. Representations and practices of purity are raised as challenges to Creole nationalism. In Guyana, symbolic representations of nationhood that valorise Creole cultural forms are less important than practices of institutional solidarity. This is related partly, to an historical absence of White Creoles in the colour class order of Guyanese social construction. Nationalist discourse did not have to accommodate a White Creole presence through the activation of colonial notions of cultural and biogenetic hybridity. The absence of Creole discourse left a cultural vacuum in the nationalist movement that was filled by competing racial claims to the state. Such claims were activated after 1955 through deployment by competing political elites of institutional resources under exclusive racial control. This occurred in the wake of a breakdown in the multi-racial nationalist movement. It set the stage for development of an integral association between nationalist organisation and existing racialised practices of institutional inclusion and exclusion.

Between 1957 and 1964, racial claims to the state by Asian Indians were held in check by colonial overlordship and by colonial predispositions to countenance the demands of the Creole elite for control of national power and privilege. But the efforts of the British colonial office to place this elite in power through fiat collapsed after an uncertain tenure between 1964–1967. Creole elite ascendance was stymied in the face of a successful effort to place a more Africa-centred stamp on Guyanese nationalist expression. During the 1960s, the African Society for Cultural Relations with Independent Africa (ASCRIA) had become highly integrated into the structure and organisation of the Black nationalist People's National Congress (PNC) that had run the country since 1964. ASCRIA's leaders enjoyed powerful positions in the government and saw their role as ensuring the location of the Black lower class at the centre of the country's nationalist agenda. In the colour-class hierarchy of Creole society, this grouping's historical location at the bottom of the socio-cultural ladder facilitated and reinforced identific notions of its own African origin. The Black lower class comprised Afro-Guyanese rural own-account peasantry and urban proletariat, many of whom were migrants from rural villages. ASCRIA was the organisational arm of its membership. The Association's leadership mounted challenges to Creole discourse with narratives of African belonging. Under its influence, the country's foreign relations shifted to an emphasis on the development of close relations with the African continent. At its insistence, elements of the state's national policies were adopted, almost wholeheartedly, from Tanzania's version of cooperative socialism.

The emphasis on Africa conflicted with the culturally rooted aspirations and practices of the country's Creole middle classes, a significant proportion of whom were Coloured. By 1971, middle-class opposition forced the ruling party to abandon its ideology of Africa-centred nationalism.

In response, ASCRIA leaders resigned their government posts and began a scathing campaign against the ruling PNC. Added to rejection of an African-centred nationalism by the Black and Coloured middle classes was strong and organised opposition from an Asian Indian population that exceeded 50 per cent of the country's total. As a means of neutralising Asian Indian challenges to its nationalist agenda, the PNC was forced to embark upon a strategy of co-optation of the most strategic sectors of the Asian Indian political economy, particularly its businessmen, professionals and educated elite. This received added impetus from the ruling party's quest for institutional control of the public space. In turn, the Asian Indian elite came to rely upon the protection and patronage of a ruling party in control of the overdeveloped Guyanese state.

The absence of a legitimate historical cultural claim to nationhood, rendered Afro-Creole assertions of nationalism in Guyana quite problematic. Asian Indian opposition produced a need for co-optation of the Asian Indian elite. Co-optation combined with middle-class opposition to dilute Afro-Creole nationalist expression.

Through its strategy of co-optation, the ruling party exercised considerable control over the public activities of strategic sectors of the Asian Indian population. It was able, also, to neutralise the effects of Asian Indian opposition. East Indians are strategically located in all the major institutional sectors of the political economy, much more so, in most cases, than the Creole population. This is particularly true of the local private sector, where ownership and control is almost exclusively Asian Indian and is reinforced by the type of racially endogamous patterns of recruitment and hiring that typifies every sector of Guyanese political economy. There is also a significant presence of East Indians in the professional sector. They enjoy an almost exclusive racial presence in the country's agro-productive sector as cash crop producers and plantation labour.

By 1975, the international relations of Guyana's ruling party shifted to a close alliance with Eastern Europe. This occurred in the wake of state take-over of the foreign private sector and of many large local merchant and trading enterprises. In the process, the "nation" came to be constituted by the institutions of the state. The latter began to play pervasive roles in almost every aspect of public behaviour. The justifying ideology of socialism displaced cultural notions of Creole national belonging from the centre of nationalist discourse.

Socialism, a Euro-Communist orientation in foreign policy, and co-optation of the Asian Indian institutional elite all combined to produce a form of nationalist expression that was less integrally tied to créolité than was the case in Trinidad. Guyanese nationalism began to take the form of state-centered institutional cooperativism. It became identified with the institutions of governance and with the domestic institutional interests represented by and identified with the governing elite and its allies.[23] In Trinidad, competition for the national space occurs over issues of its ethno-cultural character. In Guyana, competition for the national space occurs over access to the institutional resources of power. In both cases, however, challenges to nationalist construction emerged from within the Asian Indian population. In Guyana, they were mounted by representatives of East Indian working-class interests.

Nationalist expression in Guyana has come to incorporate the symbolic capital of the governing elite and the interests it represents. In popular consciousness, these continue to be understood in racial terms despite efforts at cross-racial co-optation. The result is a racialised struggle over control of the national space that takes place in the political arena. The struggle is objectified in political competition for control of the governing institutions of the state and takes place among competing racialised political organisations – these include political parties and trade unions. In 1992, the Asian Indian political elite, organised since the 1950s in the People's Progressive Party

(PPP), regained the executive and legislative power that it lost in 1964. It proceeded to redefine the national space using the control it exercises over the executive and legislative branches of the state. In response, the campaign for control of the nation has shifted to the bureaucratic apparatus of government (including the country's police and security forces) and to the judiciary. Both remain largely under the control of a Black and Coloured bureaucratic elite.[24] These have become the locomotive centres of Afro-Guyanese challenges to an East Indian take-over of the institutionalised national space.

Asian Indians in Trinidad and Guyana have employed different strategies to challenge nationalist constructs and to redefine national identity. In Guyana, challenges have been mounted also by the Black lower classes. Each challenge represents a specific instance of the incorporation over time of multiple and competing claims to the national space. Each is a particular response to colonial and post-colonial discourses of exclusion, legitimised in the historical production and reproduction of Creole reality. Each challenge presents itself as an assault against the rituals, symbols, and institutions of Caribbean self-representation. In the final analysis, each represents a counter-discourse to the complexity of cultural and racial representations and practices constitutive of Creole identity and to the honour and prestige that underlie Creole claims to privilege and power. In Trinidad, créolité remains visible as the critical component of nationalist expression. In Guyana, it is rendered invisible by the institutional construction of national space. At the same time, it continues to be pervasive in the representations and practices of all the racialised groupings of elite. Its non-problematisation in Guyana has intensified the process of Asian Indian creolisation, producing a Creole elite distinguished from its Afro-European counterparts only by the racialised sources of its institutional power.

Creole discourse is so integral to national identity in the Caribbean that nation-state contestation seems to lead, inevitably, to the intensification of the process of creolisation for those located outside of Creole space. Efforts aimed at dislocation from the state seem to be capable of producing a more successful result. In Dominica, the Karifuna descendants of the indigenous Kalinago ("Caribs") are engaged in a struggle for autonomy against the Creole nation-state. The struggle is a manifestation of the developing organisation of indigenous peoples in Latin America and the Caribbean. It has emerged in response to colonial and post-colonial practices of exclusion and displacement organised through historical containment of the Karifuna in a Kalinago reserve. Ironically, these very practices have become bases for rejection of Creole nationalism. During colonialism, they facilitated the super exploitation of the Karifuna as they became structurally integrated into the Dominican political economy.

Karifuna contestation of nationalist authority occurs through rejection of the historical practices of marginalisation and displacement. They have engaged the legal system to make a claim for exclusive right of occupation of the very "Carib Territory" that was developed for their exploitation. In the process, the "Territory" has become transformed into the symbolic objectified centre of Karifuna identity. The demand for autonomy is accompanied, periodically, by ritual acts of purification. Such as the explusion of non "Caribs", particularly Afro-Creole males and their Karifuna female partners, from "Carib" territory.[25] What is significant here is that Karifuna claims to territory are based on notions of prior occupation. The contestation of Creole nationalist practice is organised by groups with putative claims to indigenous identity – this provides them with considerable moral legitimacy. Such legitimacy is transformed into symbolic power in the deployment of the honour and prestige that attaches to the rights of prior occupation. As such, Dominica provides an example of the strategic deployment of symbolic power in the contestation of Creole domination. This form of contestation is not confined to Dominica alone – parallel movements have emerged among "Carib" populations in St Vincent and the Grenadines.

Creole nationalism has been negotiated differently by the much larger indigenous population of Guyana. "Amerindians" occupy a much more ambiguous position in Guyanese nationalist space compared with the Karifuna in Dominica. They do not have at their disposal a single territorial location that can be converted into a symbol of identific separation from Creole society. Rather, they are scattered throughout the hinterland of the country in numerous small communities under the disciplinary authority of Creole administrators and functionaries. Their integration into Creole society and into national institutions varies with geographic location and is not uniform. This is accompanied by an uneven pattern of economic integration into the Guyanese political economy. Amerindian communities display varying degrees of cultural hybridity: most of their members have been converted to Christianity and there are varying experiences of miscegenation across the several geographic communities. "Amerindians" experience differing degrees of co-optation in the institutional arena of politics and have differing degrees of access to the institutionalised national space.

The absence of a definitive identific boundary between "Amerindian" and Creole societies has diluted demands for autonomy from nationalist representations and practices. Their indeterminate relationship to Creole practice and to nationalist expression has produced less of a predisposition to nationalist rejection than their counterparts in Dominica. This is despite participation in international and local organisations of indigenous peoples.[26]

In Barbados, Creole society has deviated little from its original colonial construction. In its historical reproduction, much of the European-African roots in its colour-class hierarchical social formation has been retained. The persistence of this ideal-typical form can be explained by a history of uninterrupted British colonial rule. There was no importation of labour for post-slavery indentureship and this minimised the possibility of counter-discourses to Creole formulation that appeared in countries like Guyana and Trinidad. A certain idiosyncrasy has emerged in the historical reproduction of Creole society. The Barbadian historical process of creolisation was fashioned much more from cultural rather than bio-genetic syncretisation. Practices of cohabitation between Europeans and Africans were significantly less than in the other territories and this is reflected in the relatively small number of persons classified as mixed. At 2.6 per cent, these "Coloureds" constitute an even smaller proportion of the population than Creole Whites who number around 3.3 per cent. Thus, the colour-class continuum is far less smooth and far more abrupt in Barbados. There is a considerably greater discernible distinction between White and Afro-Creoles in representation and practice. This distinction is only minimally mitigated by the presence of the small intermediary grouping of Coloureds. The local White Creole had considerable access to power and privilege in colonial organisation. White settlement and identification with the territory was fostered historically by colonial practices of White Creole governance. This was accompanied by a great degree of institutional exclusivity in economic, social and cultural practices. The local merchant-plantocracy, together with the colonial administrators, dominated the politics of the colony until the introduction of representative government in the mid-twentieth century. Since then, power has been shared with the Coloured and Black Creole middle classes.

Creole discourse has rendered almost impossible the accommodation of any diasporic community existing outside the European-African continuum in Barbados. The latter part of the twentieth century has seen immigration of a merchant class of South Asians that has grown to 0.5 per cent of the population. Despite an initial period of intermarriage within the local community, the social location of members of this grouping remains strictly confined to a position outside Creole nationalist space. There, they retain their cultural and racial distinctiveness as "foreign". This has contributed to the reinforcement of identific rituals of purity as Hindus and Muslims. These rituals are accompanied by strict practices of endogamy in marriage. Community organisation is tight and closed and there is an enforced social seclusion of women.[27]

The Euro-cultural aspirations of Creole nationalism are least hidden in Barbadian nationalist discourse. Anglophilia continues to be strong in Barbadian popular consciousness and is evident in the generalised pride expressed in the idea of the country as a "Little England". There has been little challenge mounted against the economic, social and symbolic power of the Creole Whites.

Conclusion

The representations and practices of Creole nationalism differ significantly across the territories of the Anglophone Caribbean. Such differences reflect the varying compositions of colonial and post-colonial societies and the different ways in which the diasporic communities have become inserted into political economy. Ultimately, they reflect, in all the manifestations of créolité, differences in the technical and social conditions of capitalist production over time and space. Conceptualisations of White purity continue to reinforce and legitimise a system of globalised dependency. Domestically, Creole nationalism continues to hide the reality of racial capitalism. Aspirations to cultural purity have prevailed in the face of hybridity and have been at the root of an endemic conflict over identity and nationalism in the region. They have also foreclosed opportunities for regional integration. Creole nationalism in the post-independence era has foreclosed possibilities for development of a social construction that can serve as an alternative to the cultural and social legacy of Europe. It has wedded the former colonies to patterns of international relations characterised by an uncritical acceptance of the North Atlantic as the center of the social, cultural, political and economic universe. This has been the tragedy of the current colonial construction of créolité in the Caribbean.

Notes

1. For an elaboration of the ideas discussed in this paper and their application to race and ethnicity in the Caribbean see Percy Hintzen, 'Race and Creole Ethnicity in the Caribbean,' in *The Blackwell Companion to Racial and Ethnic Studies*, ed. David Golberg and John Solmos (Oxford: Blackwell Publishers, 2001).
2. The use of the term 'symbolic capital' is taken from Pierre Bourdieu and pertains to the accumulation and display of symbols of honour and prestige that renders 'unrecognisable' the true exploitative nature of relationships of economic exchange. It is 'denied capital recognised as legitimate.' See Pierre Bourdieu, *The Logic of Practice* (Stanford, CA: Stanford University Press, 1990), 118, 112–21.
3. Benedict Anderson, *Imagined Communities* (London: Verso, 1983), 19.
4. Arturo Escobar, *Encountering Development* (Princeton: Princeton University Press 1995), 155.
5. See Lloyd Braithwaite, 'Social Stratification in Trinidad,' *Social and Economic Studies* 2 (1953): 5–175, and Leo A. Despres, *Cultural Pluralism and Nationalist Politics in British Guiana* (Chicago: Rand McNally, 1967)
6. Vere T. Daly, 'A Short History of the Guyanese People,' *Daily Chronicle*, 1966, 214.
7. The point here is not that white creoles should not be included in the nationalist definition. Rather, it is to point out the paradox of this embrace by a nationalist movement rooted in challenges to white supremacy.
8. L. Taylor, 'Créolité Bites: A Conversation with Patrick Chamoiseau, Raphael Confiant, and Jean Bernabé,' in *Transition* 74 (n.d.): 124.
9. See Taylor, 'Créolité Bites,' 128.
10. Ibid., 141.

11. Ibid., 136.
12. Ibid., 132.
13. Maureen Warner-Lewis, *Guinea's Other Suns: The African Dynamic in Trinidad Culture* (Dover, Massachusetts: Majority Press, 1990).
14. D.G. Nicolls, 'No Hawkers and Peddlers,' *Ethnic and Racial Studies* 34 (1981): 422–26.
15. See Taylor, 'Créolité Bites,' 142.
16. Ibid., 137.
17. J. Asiegbu, *Slavery and the Politics of Liberation, 1787–1861* (London: Longman, 1969), 189–90.
18. Barry Chevannes, *Rastafari: Roots and Ideology* (Syracuse: Syracuse University Press, 1995).
19. J. Houk, 'Afro-Trinidadian Identity and the Africanisation of the Orisha Religion,' in *Trinidad Ethnicity*, ed. K. Yelvington (Knoxville: University of Tennessee Press, 1993), 161–79.
20. See Morton Klass, *Singing with Sai Baba* (Boulder: Westview Press, 1991).
21. Kevin A. Yelvington, *Producing Power: Ethnicity, Gender and Class in a Caribbean Workplace* (Philadelphia: Temple University Press, 1995), 77
22. Isha Khan, ed., 'What is "a Spanish"?: Ambiguity and Mixed Ethnicity in Trinidad,' in *Trinidad Ethnicity*, ed. K. Yelvington (Knoxville: University of Tennessee Press, 1993), 180–207.
23. See Percy C. Hintzen, *The Costs of Regime Survival* (Cambridge and New York: Cambridge University Press, 1989), 169–71
24. Percy C. Hintzen, 'Democracy on Trial: The December 1997 Elections in Guyana and its Aftermath,' *Caribbean Studies Newsletter* 25 (1998): 13–16.
25. C. Gregoire, P. Henderson and N. Kanem, 'Karifuna: The Caribs of Dominica,' in *Ethnic Minorities in Caribbean Society*, ed. Rhoda E. Reddock (St Augustine, Trinidad: University of the West Indies, Institute of Social and Economic Research, 1996), 107–71.
26. D. Fox and G.K. Danns, *The Indigenous Condition in Guyana* (Georgetown: University of Guyana, 1993).
27. P. Hanoomansingh, 'Beyond Profit and Capital: A Study of the Sindhis and Gujaratis of Barbados,' in *Ethnic Minorities in Caribbean Society*, ed. Rhoda Reddock (Kingston: University of the West Indies, Institute of Social and Economic Research, 1996).

Caliban:
Notes Toward a Discussion of Culture in Our America

Roberto Fernández Retamar (Cuba)

A Question

A European journalist, and moreover a leftist, asked me a few days ago, "Does a Latin-American culture exist?"[1] We were discussing, naturally enough, the recent polemic regarding Cuba that ended by confronting, on the one hand, certain bourgeois European intellectuals (or aspirants to that state) with a visible colonialist nostalgia; and on the other, that body of Latin-American writers and artists who reject open or veiled forms of cultural and political colonialism. The question seemed to me to reveal one of the roots of the polemic and, hence, could also be expressed another way: "Do you exist?" For to question our culture is to question our very existence, our human reality itself, and thus to be willing to take a stand in favor of our irremediable colonial condition, since it suggests that we would be but a distorted echo of what occurs elsewhere. This elsewhere is of course the metropolis, the colonizing centers, whose "right wings" have exploited us and whose supposed "left wings" have pretended and continue to pretend to guide us with pious solicitude—in both cases with the assistance of local intermediaries of varying persuasions.

While this fate is to some extent suffered by all countries emerging from colonialism—those countries of ours that enterprising metropolitan intellectuals have ineptly and successively termed *barbarians, peoples of color, underdeveloped countries, Third World*—I think the phenomenon achieves a singular crudeness with respect to what Martí called "our *mestizo* America." Although the thesis that every man and even every culture is *mestizo* could easily be defended and although this seems especially valid in the case of colonies, it is nevertheless apparent that in both their ethnic and their cultural aspects capitalist countries long ago achieved a relative homogeneity. Almost before our eyes certain readjustments have been made. The white population of the United States (diverse, but of common European origin) exterminated the aboriginal population and thrust the black population aside, thereby affording itself homogeneity in spite of diversity and offering a coherent model that its Nazi disciples attempted to apply even to other European conglomerates—an unforgivable sin that led some members of the bourgeoisie to stigmatize in Hitler what they applauded as a healthy Sunday diversion in westerns and Tarzan films. Those movies proposed to the world—and even to those of us who are kin to the communities under attack and who rejoiced in the evocation of our own extermination—the monstrous racial criteria that have accompanied the United States from its beginnings to the genocide in Indochina. Less apparent (and in some cases perhaps less cruel) is the process by which other capitalist countries have also achieved relative racial and cultural homogeneity at the expense of *internal* diversity.

Nor can any necessary relationship be established between *mestizaje* ["racial intermingling, racial mixture"—ed. note] and the colonial world. The latter is highly complex[2] despite basic structural affinities of its parts. It has included countries with well-defined millennial cultures, some of which have suffered (or are presently suffering) direct occupation (India, Vietnam), and others of which have suffered indirect occupation (China). It also comprehends countries with rich cultures but less political homogeneity, which have been subjected to extremely diverse forms of colonialism (the Arab world). There are other peoples, finally, whose fundamental structures were savagely dislocated by the dire activity of the European despite which they continue to preserve a certain ethnic and cultural homogeneity (black Africa). (Indeed, the latter has occurred despite the colonialists' criminal and unsuccessful attempts to prohibit it.) In these countries *mestizaje* naturally exists to a greater or lesser degree, but it is always accidental and always on the fringe of the central line of development.

But within the colonial world there exists a case unique to *the entire planet:* a vast zone for which *mestizaje* is not an accident but rather the essence, the central line: ourselves, "our mestizo America." Martí, with his excellent knowledge of the language, employed this specific adjective as the distinctive sign of our culture—a culture of descendants, both ethnically and culturally speaking, of aborigines, Africans, and Europeans. In his "Letter from Jamaica" (1815), the Liberator, Simón Bolívar, had proclaimed, "We are a small human species: we possess a world encircled by vast seas, new in almost all its arts and sciences." In his message to the Congress of Angostura (1819), he added:

> Let us bear in mind that our people is neither European nor North American, but a composite of Africa and America rather than an emanation of Europe; for even Spain fails as a European people because of her African blood, her institutions, and her character. It is impossible to assign us with any exactitude to a specific human family. The greater part of the native peoples has been annihilated; the European has mingled with the American and with the African, and the African has mingled with the Indian and with the European. Born from the womb of a common mother, our fathers, different in origin and blood, are foreigners; all differ visibly in the epidermis, and this dissimilarity leaves marks of the greatest transcendence.

Even in this century, in a book as confused as the author himself but full of intuitions (*La raza cósmica,* 1925), the Mexican José Vasconcelos pointed out that in Latin America a new race was being forged, "made with the treasure of all previous ones, the final race, the cosmic race."[3]

This singular fact lies at the root of countless misunderstandings. Chinese, Vietnamese, Korean, Arab, or African cultures may leave the Euro–North American enthusiastic, indifferent or even depressed. But it would never occur to him to confuse a Chinese with a Norwegian, or a Bantu with an Italian: nor would it occur to him to ask whether they exist. Yet, on the other hand, some Latin Americans are taken at times for apprentices, for rough drafts or dull copies of Europeans, including among these latter whites who constitute what Martí called "European America." In the same way, our entire culture is taken as an apprenticeship, a rough draft or a copy of European bourgeois culture ("an emanation of Europe," as Bolívar said). This last error is more frequent than the first, since confusion of a Cuban with an Englishman, or a Guatemalan with a German, tends to be impeded by a certain ethnic tenacity. Here the *rioplatenses* appear to be less ethnically, although not culturally, differentiated. The confusion lies in the root itself, because as descendants of numerous Indian, African, and European communities, we have only a few languages with which to understand one another: those of the colonizers. While other colonials or ex-colonials in metropolitan centers speak among themselves in their own language, we Latin Americans continue to use the languages of our colonizers. These are the linguas francas capable of going beyond the frontiers that neither aboriginal nor Creole languages succeed in crossing. Right now as we are discussing, as I am discussing with those colonizers, how else can I do it except in one of their languages, which is now also *our* language, and with so many of their conceptual tools, which are now also *our* conceptual tools? This is precisely the extraordinary outcry that we read in a work by perhaps the most extraordinary writer of fiction who ever existed. In *The Tempest,* William Shakespeare's last play, the deformed Caliban—enslaved, robbed of his island, and trained to speak by Prospero—rebukes Prospero thus: "You taught me language, and my profit on't/ Is, I know how to curse. The red plague rid you/ For learning me your language!" (1.2.362–64).

Toward the History of Caliban

Caliban is Shakespeare's anagram for "cannibal," an expression that he had already used to mean "anthropophagus," in the third part of *Henry IV* and in *Othello* and that comes in turn from the word *carib*. Before the arrival of the Europeans, whom they resisted heroically, the Carib Indians were the most valiant and warlike inhabitants of the very lands that we occupy today. Their name lives on in the name Caribbean Sea (referred to genially by some as the American Mediterranean, just as if we were to call the Mediterranean the Caribbean of Europe). But the name *carib* in itself— as well as in its deformation, *cannibal*—has been perpetuated in the eyes of Europeans above all as a defamation. It is the term in this sense that Shakespeare takes up and elaborates into a complex symbol. Because of its exceptional importance to us, it will be useful to trace its history in some detail.

In the *Diario de Navegación* [Navigation logbooks] of Columbus there appear the first European accounts of the men who were to occasion the symbol in question. On Sunday, 4 November 1492, less than a month after Columbus arrived on the continent that was to be called America, the following entry was inscribed: "He learned also that far from the place there were men with one eye and others with dogs' muzzles, who ate human beings."[4] On 23 November, this entry: "[the island of Haiti], which they said was very large and that on it lived people who had only one eye and others called cannibals, of whom they seemed to be very afraid." On 11 December it is noted "...that *caniba* refers in fact to the people of El Gran Can," which explains the deformation undergone by the name *carib*—also used by Columbus. In the very letter of 15 February 1493, "dated on the caravelle off the island of Canaria" in which Columbus announces to the world his "discovery," he writes: "I have found, then, neither monsters nor news of any, save for one island [Quarives], the second upon entering the Indies, which is populated with people held by everyone on the islands to be very ferocious, and who eat human flesh."[5]

This *carib/cannibal* image contrasts with another one of the American man presented in the writings of Columbus: that of the *Arauaco* of the Greater Antilles—our *Taino* Indian primarily— whom he describes as peaceful, meek, and even timorous and cowardly. Both visions of the American aborigine will circulate vertiginously throughout Europe, each coming to know its own particular development: The Taino will be transformed into the paradisiacal inhabitant of a utopic world; by 1516 Thomas More will publish his *Utopia,* the similarities of which to the island of Cuba have been indicated, almost to the point of rapture, by Ezequiel Martínez Estrada.[6] The Carib, on the other hand, will become a *cannibal*—an anthropophagus, a bestial man situated on the margins of civilization, who must be opposed to the very death. But there is less of a contradiction than might appear at first glance between the two visions; they constitute, simply, options in the ideological arsenal of a vigorous emerging bourgeoisie. Francisco de Quevedo translated "utopia" as "there is no such place." With respect to these two visions, one might add, "There is no such man." The notion of an Edenic creature comprehends, in more contemporary terms, a working hypothesis for the bourgeois left, and, as such, offers an ideal model of the perfect society free from the constrictions of that feudal world against which the bourgeoisie is in fact struggling. Generally speaking, the utopic vision throws upon these lands projects for political reforms unrealized in the countries of origin. In this sense its line of development is far from extinguished. Indeed, it meets with certain perpetuators—apart from its radical perpetuators, who are the consequential revolutionaries—in the numerous advisers who unflaggingly propose to countries emerging from colonialism magic formulas from the metropolis to solve the grave problems colonialism has left us and which, of course, they have not yet resolved in their own countries. It goes without saying that these proponents of "There is no such place" are irritated by the insolent fact that the place *does* exist and, quite naturally, has all the virtues and defects not of a project but of genuine reality.

As for the vision of the *cannibal*, it corresponds—also in more contemporary terms—to the right wing of that same bourgeoisie. It belongs to the ideological arsenal of politicians of action, those who perform the dirty work in whose fruits the charming dreamers of Utopias will equally share. That the Caribs were as Columbus (and, after him, an unending throng of followers) depicted them is about as probable as the existence of one-eyed men, men with dog muzzles or tails, or even the Amazons mentioned by the explorer in pages where Greco-Roman mythology, the medieval bestiary, and the novel of chivalry all play their part. It is a question of the typically degraded version offered by the colonizer of the man he is colonizing. That we ourselves may have at one time believed in this version only proves to what extent we are infected with the ideology of the enemy. It is typical that we have applied the term *cannibal* not to the extinct aborigine of our isles, but above all, to the African black who appeared in those shameful Tarzan films. For it is the colonizer who brings us together, who reveals the profound similarities existing above and beyond our secondary differences. The colonizer's version explains to us that owing to the Carib's irremediable bestiality, there was no alternative to their extermination. What it does not explain is why even before the Caribs, the peaceful and kindly Arauacos were also exterminated. Simply speaking, the two groups suffered jointly one of the greatest ethnocides recorded in history. (Needless to say, this line of action is still more alive than the earlier one.) In relation to this fact, it will always be necessary to point out the case of those men who, being on the fringe both of utopianism (which has nothing to do with the actual America) and of the shameless ideology of plunder, stood in their midst opposed to the conduct of the colonialists and passionately, lucidly, and valiantly defended the flesh-and-blood aborigine. In the forefront of such men stands the magnificent figure of Father Bartolomé de las Casas, who Bolívar called "the apostle of America" and whom Martí extolled unreservedly. Unfortunately, such men were exceptions.

One of the most widely disseminated European utopian works is Montaigne's essay "De los caníbales" [On Cannibals], which appeared in 1580. There we find a presentation of those creatures who "retain alive and vigorous their genuine, their most useful and natural, virtues and properties."[7]

Giovanni Floro's English translation of the *Essays* was published in 1603. Not only was Floro a personal friend of Shakespeare, but the copy of the translation that Shakespeare owned and annotated is still extant. This piece of information would be of no further importance but for the fact that it proves beyond a shadow of doubt that the *Essays* was one of the direct sources of Shakespeare's last great work, *The Tempest* (1612). Even one of the characters of the play, Gonzalo, who incarnates the Renaissance humanist, at one point closely glossed entire lines from Floro's Montaigne, originating precisely in the essay on cannibals. This fact makes the form in which Shakespeare presents his character *Caliban/cannibal* even stranger. Because if in Montaigne—in this case, as unquestionable literary source for Shakespeare—"there is nothing barbarous and savage in that nation…, except that each man calls barbarism whatever is not his own practice,"[8] in Shakespeare, on the other hand, *Caliban/cannibal* is a savage and deformed slave who cannot be degraded enough. What has happened is simply that in depicting Caliban, Shakespeare, an implacable realist, here takes *the other option* of the emerging bourgeois world. Regarding the utopian vision, it does indeed exist in the work but is unrelated to Caliban; as was said before, it is expressed by the harmonious humanist Gonzalo. Shakespeare thus confirms that both ways of considering the American, far from being in opposition, were perfectly reconcilable. As for the concrete man, present him in the guise of an animal, rob him of his land, enslave him so as to live from his toil, and at the right moment exterminate him; this latter, of course, only if there were someone who could be depended on to perform the arduous tasks in his stead. In one revealing passage, Prospero warns his daughter that they could not do without Caliban: "We cannot miss him: he does make our fire,/ Fetch in our wood, and serves in offices/ that profit us" (1.2.311–13). The utopian vision can and must do without men of flesh and blood. After all, *there is no such place.*

There is no doubt at this point that *The Tempest* alludes to America, that its island is the mythification of one of our islands. Astrana Marín, who mentions the "clearly Indian (American) ambience of the island," recalls some of the actual voyages along this continent that inspired Shakespeare and even furnished him, with slight variations, with the names of not a few of his characters; Miranda, Fernando, Sebastian, Alonso, Gonzalo, Setebos.[9] More important than this is the knowledge that Caliban is our Carib.

We are not interested in following all the possible readings that have been made of this notable work since its appearance,[10] and shall merely point out some interpretations. The first of these comes from Ernest Renan, who published his drama *Caliban: Suite de "La Tempête"* in 1878.[11] In this work. Caliban is the incarnation of the people presented in their worst light, except that this time his conspiracy against Prospero is successful and he achieves power—which ineptitude and corruption will surely prevent him from retaining. Prospero lurks in the darkness awaiting his revenge, and Ariel disappears. This reading owes less to Shakespeare than to the Paris Commune, which had taken place only seven years before. Naturally, Renan was among the writers of the French bourgeoisie who savagely took part against the prodigious "assault of heaven."[12] Beginning with this event, his antidemocratic feeling stiffened even further. "In his *Philosophical Dialogues*," Lidsky tell us, "he believes that the solution would lie in the creation of an *élite* of intelligent beings who alone would govern and possess the secrets of science."[13] Characteristically, Renan's aristocratic and prefascist elitism and his hatred of the common people of his country are united with an even greater hatred for the inhabitants of the colonies. It is instructive to hear him express himself along these lines.

We aspire [he says] not only to equality but to domination. The country of a foreign race must again be a country of serfs, of agricultural laborers or industrial workers. It is not a question of eliminating the inequalities among men but of broadening them and making them law.[14]

And on another occasion:

> The regeneration of the inferior or bastard races by the superior races is within the providential human order. With us, the common man is nearly always a *declassé* nobleman, his heavy hand is better suited to handling the sword than the menial tool. Rather than work he chooses to fight, that is, he returns, to his first state. *Regere imperio populos*—that is our vocation. Pour forth this all-consuming activity onto countries which, like China, are crying aloud for foreign conquest. ... Nature has made a race of workers, the Chinese race, with its marvelous manual dexterity and almost no sense of honor: govern them with justice, levying from them, in return for the blessing of such a government, an ample allowance for the conquering race, and they will be satisfied; a race of tillers of the soil, the black...a race of masters and soldiers, the European race. ... *Let each do that which he is made for, and all will be well.*[15]

It is unnecessary to gloss these lines, which, as Césaire rightly says, came from the pen not of Hitler but of the French humanist Ernest Renan.

The initial destiny of the Caliban myth on our own American soil is a surprising one. Twenty years after Renan had published his *Caliban*—in other words, in 1898—the United States intervened in the Cuban war of independence against Spain and subjected Cuba to its tutelage, converting her in 1902 into her first *neocolony* (and holding her until 1959), while Puerto Rico and the Philippines became colonies of a traditional nature. The fact—which had been anticipated by Martí years before—moved the Latin American *intelligentsia*. Elsewhere I have recalled that "ninety-eight" is not only a Spanish date that gives its name to a complex group of writers and thinkers of that country, but it is also, and perhaps most importantly, a Latin American data that should serve to designate a no less complex group of writers and thinkers on this side of the Atlantic, generally known by the vague name of *modernistas*.[16] It is "ninety-eight"—the visible presence of North American imperialism in Latin America—already foretold by Martí, which informs the later work of someone like Darío or Rodó.

In a speech given by Paul Groussac in Buenos Aires on 2 May 1898, we have an early example of how Latin American writers of the time would react to this situation:

> Since the Civil War and the brutal invasion of the West [he says], the *Yankee* spirit had rid itself completely of its formless and "Calibanesque" body, and the Old World has contemplated with disquiet and terror the newest civilization that intends to supplant our own, declared to be in decay.[17]

The Franco-Argentine writer Groussac feels that "our" civilization (obviously understanding by that term the civilization of the "Old World," of which we Latin Americans would, curiously enough, be a part) is menaced by the Calibanesque Yankee. It seems highly improbable that the Algerian or Vietnamese writer of the time, trampled underfoot by French colonialism, would have been ready to subscribe to the first part of such a criterion. It is also frankly strange to see the Caliban symbol—in which Renan could with exactitude see, if only to abuse, the people—being applied to the United States. But nevertheless, despite this blurred focus—characteristic, on the other hand, of Latin America's unique situation—Groussac's reaction implies a clear rejection of the Yankee danger by Latin American writers. This is not, however, the first time that such a rejection was expressed on our continent. Apart from cases of Hispanic writers such as Bolívar and Martí, among others, Brazilian literature presents the example of Joaquín de Sousa Andrade, or Sousândrade, in whose strange poem, *O Guesa Errante,* stanza 10 is dedicated to "O inferno de Wall Street," "a *Walpurgisnacht* of corrupt stockbrokers, petty politicians, and businessmen."[18] There is besides José Verissimo, who in a 1890 treatise on national education impugned the United States with his "I admire them, but I don't esteem them."

We do not know whether the Uruguayan Jose Enrique Rodó—whose famous phrase on the United States, "I admire them, but I don't love them," coincides literally with Verissimo's observation—knew the work of that Brazilian thinker but it is certain that he was familiar with Groussac's speech, essential portions of which were reproduced in *La Razón* of Montevideo on 6 May 1898. Developing and embellishing the idea outlined in it, Rodó published in 1900, at the age of twenty-nine, one of the most famous works of Latin American literature: *Ariel*. North American civilization is implicitly presented there as Caliban (scarcely mentioned in the work), while Ariel would come to incarnate—or should incarnate—the best of what Rodó did not hesitate to call more than once "our civilization" (223, 226). In his words, just as in those of Groussac, this civilization was identified not only with "our Latin America" (239) but with ancient Romania, if not with the Old World as a whole. The identification of Caliban with the United States, proposed by Groussac and popularized by Rodó, was certainly a mistake. Attacking this error from one angle, José Vasconcelos commented that "if the Yankees were only Caliban, they would not represent any great danger."[19] But this is doubtless of little importance next to the relevant fact that the danger in question had clearly been pointed out. As Benedetti rightly observed, "Perhaps Rodó erred in naming the danger, but he did not err in his recognition of where it lay."[20]

Sometime afterward, the French writer Jean Guéhenno—who, although surely aware of the work by the colonial Rodó, knew of course Renan's work from memory—restated the latter's Caliban thesis in his own *Caliban parle* [Caliban speaks], published in Paris in 1929. This time, however, the Renan identification of Caliban *with* the people is accompanied by a positive evaluation of Caliban. One must be grateful to Guéhenno's book—and it is about the only thing for which gratitude is due—for having offered for the first time an appealing version of the character.[21] But the theme would have required the hand or the rage of a Paul Nizan to be effectively realized.[22]

Much sharper are the observations of the Argentine Aníbal Ponce, in his 1935 work *Humanismo burgués y humanismo proletario*. The book—which a student of Che's thinking conjectures must have exercised influence on the latter[23]—devotes the third chapter to "Ariel: or, The Agony of an Obstinate Illusion." In commenting on *The Tempest*, Ponce says that "those four beings embody an entire era; Prospero is the enlightened despot who loves the Renaissance; Miranda, his progeny; Caliban, the suffering masses [Ponce will then quote Renan, but not Guéhenno]; and Ariel, the genius of the air without any ties to life."[24] Ponce points up the equivocal nature of Caliban's presentation, one that reveals "an enormous injustice on the part of a master." In Ariel he sees the intellectual, tied to Prospero in "a less burdensome and crude way than Caliban, but also in his service." His analysis of the conception of the intellectual ("mixture of slave and mercenary") coined by Renaissance humanism, a concept that "taught as nothing else could an indifference to action and an acceptance of the established order" and that even today is for the intellectual in the bourgeois world "the educational ideal of the governing classes," constitutes one of the most penetrating essays written on the theme in our America.

But this examination, although made by a Latin American, still took only the European world into account. For a new reading of *The Tempest*—for a new consideration of the problem—it was necessary to await the emergence of the colonial countries, which begins around the time of the Second World War. That abrupt presence led the busy technicians of the United Nations to invent, between 1944 and 1945, the term *economically underdeveloped area* in order to dress in attractive (and profoundly confusing) verbal garb what had until then been called *colonial area*, or *backward areas*.[25]

Concurrently with this emergence there appeared in Paris in 1950 O. Mannoni's book *Psychologie de la colonisation*. Significantly, the English edition of this book (New York, 1956) was to be called *Prospero and Caliban: The Psychology of Colonization*. To approach his subject, Mannoni has created, no less, what he calls the "Prospero complex," defined as "the sum of those unconscious neurotic tendencies that delineate at the same time the "picture" of the paternalist colonial and the portrait of 'the racist whose daughter has been the object of an [imaginary] attempted rape at the hands of an inferior being.'"[26] In this book, probably for the first time, Caliban is identified with the colonial. But the odd theory that the latter suffers from a "Prospero complex" that leads him neurotically to require, even to anticipate, and naturally to accept the presence of Prospero/colonizer is roundly rejected by Frantz Fanon in the fourth chapter ("The So-Called Dependency Complex of Colonized Peoples") of his 1952 book *Black Skin, White Masks*.

Although he is (apparently) the first writer in our world to assume our identification with Caliban, the Barbadian writer George Lamming is unable to break the circle traced by Mannoni:

> Prospero [says Lamming] has given Caliban language; and with it an unstated history of consequences, an unknown history of future intentions. This gift of language meant not English, in particular, but speech and concept as a way, a method, a necessary avenue towards areas of the self which could not be reached in any other way. It is this way, entirely Prospero's enterprise, which makes Caliban aware of possibilities. Therefore, all of Caliban's future—for future is the very name of possibilities—must derive from Prospero's experiment, which is also his risk. Provided there is no extraordinary departure which explodes all of Prospero's premises, then Caliban and his future now belong to Prospero...Prospero lives in the absolute certainty that Language, which is his gift to Caliban, is the very prison in which Caliban's achievements will be realized and restricted.27

In the decade of the 1960s, the new reading of *The Tempest* ultimately established its hegemony. In *The Living World of Shakespeare* (1964), the Englishman John Wain will tell us that Caliban:

> has the pathos of the exploited peoples everywhere, poignantly expressed at the beginning of a three-hundred-year wave of European colonization; even the lowest savage wishes to be left alone rather than be "educated" and made to work for someone else, and there is an undeniable justice in his complaint: "For I am all the subjects that you have,/ Which once was mine own king." Prospero retorts with the inevitable answer of the colonist: Caliban has gained in knowledge and skill (though we recall that he already knew how to build dams to catch fish, and also to dig pig-nuts from the soil, as if this were the English countryside). Before being employed by Prospero, Caliban had no language: "... thou didst not, savage,/ Know thy own meaning, but wouldst gabble like/ A thing most brutish." However, this kindness has been rewarded with ingratitude. Caliban, allowed to live in Prospero's cell, has made an attempt to ravish Miranda. When sternly reminded of this, he impertinently says, with a kind of slavering guffaw. "Oh ho! Oh ho!—would it have been done!/ Thou didst prevent me: I had peopled else/ This isle with Calibans." Our own age [Wain concludes], which is much given to using the horrible word "miscegenation," ought to have no difficulty in understanding this passage.28

At the end of that same decade, in 1969, and in a highly significant manner, Caliban would be taken up with pride as our symbol by three Antillian writers—each of whom expresses himself in one of the three great colonial languages of the Caribbean. In that year, independently of one another, the Martinican writer Aimé Césaire published his dramatic work in French *Une tempête: Adaptation de "La Tempête" de Shakespeare pour un théâtre nègre;* the Barbadian Edward Brathwaite, his book of poems, *Islands,* in English, among which there is one dedicated to "Caliban"; and the author of these lines, an essay in Spanish, "Cuba hasta Fidel," which discusses our identification with Caliban.29 In Césaire's work the characters are the same as those of Shakespeare. Ariel, however, is a mulatto slave, and Caliban is a black slave; in addition, Eshzú, a "black god-devil," appears. Prospero's remark when Ariel returns, full of scruples, after having unleashed—following Prospero's orders but against his own conscience—the tempest with which the work begins is curious indeed: "Come now!" Prospero says to him, "Your crisis! It's always the same with intellectuals!" Brathwaite's poem called "Caliban" is dedicated, significantly, to Cuba: "In Havana that morning..." writes Brathwaite, "It was December second, nineteen fifty-six./ It was the first of August eighteen thirty-eight./ It was the twelfth of October fourteen ninety-two./ How many bangs how many revolutions?"30

Our Symbol

Our symbol then is not Ariel, as Rodó thought, but rather Caliban. This is something that we, the *mestizo* inhabitants of these same islands where Caliban lived, see with particular clarity:

Prospero invaded the islands, killed our ancestors, enslaved Caliban, and taught him his language to make himself understood. What else can Caliban do but use that same language—today he has no other—to curse him, to wish that the "red plague" would fall on him? I know no other metaphor more expressive of our cultural situation, of our reality. From Túpac Amaru, *Tiradentes,* Toussaint-Louverture, Simón Bolívar, Father Hidalgo, José Artigas, Bernardo O'Higgins, Benito Juárez, Antonio Maceo, and José Martí, to Emiliano Zapata, Augusto César Sandino, Julio Antonio Mella, Pedro Albizu Campos, Lázaro Cárdenas, Fidel Castro and Ernesto Che Guevara, from the Inca Garcilaso de la Vega, the *Aleijadinho,* the popular music of the Antilles, José Hernández, Eugenio María de Hostos, Manuel González Prada, Rubén Darío (yes, when all is said and done), Baldomero Lillo, and Horacio Quiroga, to Mexican muralism, Heitor Villa-Lobos, César Vallejo, José Carlos Mariátegui, Ezequiel Martínez Estrada, Carlos Gardel, Pablo Neruda, Alejo Carpentier, Nicolás Guillén, Aimé Césaire, José María Arguedas, Violeta Parra, and Frantz Fanon—what is our history, what is our culture, if not the history and culture of Caliban?

As regards Rodó, if it is indeed true that he erred in his symbols, as has already been said, it is no less true that he was able to point with clarity to the greatest enemy of our culture in his time—and in ours—and that is enormously important. Rodó's limitations (and this is not the moment to elucidate them) are responsible for what he saw unclearly or failed to see at all.[31] But what is worthy of note in his case is what he did indeed see and what continued to retain a certain amount of validity and even virulence.

> Despite his failings, omissions, and ingenuousness [Benedetti has also said], Rodó's vision of the Yankee phenomenon, rigorously situated in its historical context, was in its time the first launching pad for other less ingenuous, better informed and more fore-sighted formulations to come....the almost prophetic substance of Rodó's Arielism still retains today a certain amount of validity.[32]

These observations are supported by indisputable realities. We Cubans become well aware that Rodó's vision fostered later, less ingenuous, and more radical formulations when we simply consider the work of our own Julio Antonio Mella, on whose development the influence of Rodó was decisive. In "Intelectuales y tartufos" [Intellectuals and Tartuffes] (1924), a vehement work written at the age of twenty-one, Mella violently attacks the false intellectual values of the time—opposing them with such names as Unamuno, José Vasconcelos, Ingenieros, and Varona. He writes, "The intellectual is the worker of the mind. The worker! That is, the only man who in Rodó's judgment is worthy of life...he who takes up his pen against iniquity just as others take up the plow to fecundate the earth, or the sword to liberate peoples, or a dagger to execute tyrants."[33]

Mella would again quote Rodó with devotion during that year[34] and in the following year he was to help found the Ariel Polytechnic Institute in Havana.[35] It is opportune to recall that in this same year, 1925, Mella was also among the founders of Cuba's first Communist party. Without a doubt, Rodó's *Ariel* served as a "launching pad" for the meteoric revolutionary career of this first organic Marxist-Leninist in Cuba (who was also one of the first on the continent.)

As further examples of the relative validity that Rodó's anti-Yankee argument retains even in our own day, we can point to enemy attempts to disarm such an argument. A strange case is that of Emir Rodríguez Monegal, for whom *Ariel,* in addition to "material for philosophic or sociological meditation, *also* contains pages of a polemic nature on political problems *of the moment.* And it was precisely this *secondary* but undeniable condition that determined its immediate popularity and dissemination." Rodó's essential position against North American penetration would thus appear to be an afterthought, a *secondary* fact in the work. It is known, however, that Rodó conceived it immediately after American intervention in Cuba in 1898, *as a response to the deed*. Rodríguez Monegal says:

> The work thus projected was *Ariel*. In the final version *only two direct allusions* are found to the historical fact that was its primary motive force; ...both allusions enable us to appreciate how Rodó has *transcended* the initial historical circumstance to arrive fully at the essential problem: the proclaimed decadence of the Latin race.[36]

The fact that a servant of imperialism such as Rodríguez Monegal, afflicted with the same "Nordo-mania" that Rodó denounced in 1900, tries so coarsely to emasculate Rodó's work, only proves that it does indeed retain a certain virulence in its formulation—something that we would approach today from other perspectives and with other means. An analysis of *Ariel*—and this is absolutely not the occasion to make one—would lead us also to stress how, despite his background and his anti-Jacobianism, Rodó combats in it the antidemocratic spirit of Renan and Nietzsche (in whom he finds "an abominable, reactionary spirit" [224]) and exalts democracy, moral values, and emulation. But undoubtedly the rest of the work has lost the immediacy that its gallant confrontation of the United States and the defense of our values still retains.

Put into perspective, it is almost certain that these lines would not bear the name they have were it not for Rodó's book, and I prefer to consider them also as a homage to the great Uruguayan, whose centenary is being celebrated this year. That the homage contradicts him on not a few points is not strange. Medardo Vitier has already observed that "if there should be a return to Rodó, I do not believe that it would be to adopt the solution he offered concerning the interests of the life of the spirit, but rather to reconsider the problem."[37]

In proposing Caliban as our symbol, I am aware that it is not entirely ours, that it is also an alien elaboration, although in this case based on our concrete realities. But how can this alien quality be entirely avoided? The most venerated word in Cuba—*mambí*—was disparagingly imposed on us by our enemies at the time of the war for independence, and we still have not totally deciphered its meaning. It seems to have an African root, and in the mouth of the Spanish colonists implied the idea that all *independentistas* were so many black slaves—emancipated by that very war for independence—who of course constituted the bulk of the liberation army. The *independentistas*, white and black, adopted with honor something that colonialism meant as an insult. This is the dialectic of Caliban. To offend us they call us *mambí*, they call us *black;* but we reclaim as a mark of glory the honor of considering ourselves descendants of the *mambí*, descendants of the rebel, runaway, *independentista* black—*never* descendants of the slave holder. Nevertheless, Prospero, as we well know, taught his language to Caliban and, consequently, gave him a name. But is this his true name? Let us listen to this speech made in 1971:

> To be completely precise, we still do not even have a name; we still have no name; we are practically unbaptized—whether as Latin Americans. Ibero-Americans, Indo-Americans. For the imperialists, we are nothing more than despised and despicable peoples. At least that was what we were. Since Girón they have begun to change their thinking. Racial contempt—to be a Creole, to be a mestizo, to he black, to be simply, a Latin American, is for them contemptible.[38]

This naturally, is Fidel Castro on the tenth anniversary of the victory at Playa Girón.

To assume our condition as Caliban implies rethinking our history from the *other* side, from the viewpoint of the *other* protagonist. The *other* protagonist of *The Tempest* (or, as we might have said ourselves, *The Hurricane*) is not of course Ariel but, rather, Prospero.[39] There is no real Ariel-

Caliban polarity: both are slaves in the hands of Prospero, the foreign magician. But Caliban is the rude and unconquerable master of the island, while Ariel, a creature of the air, although also a child of the isle, is the intellectual—as both Ponce and Césaire have seen.

Again Martí

This conception of our culture had already been articulately expressed and defended in the last century by the first among us to understand clearly the concrete situation of what he called—using a term I have referred to several times—"our mestizo America:" José Martí[40] to whom Rodó planned to dedicate the first Cuban edition of *Ariel* and about whom he intended to write a study similar to those he devoted to Bolívar and Artigas, a study that in the end he unfortunately never realized.

Although he devoted numerous pages to the topic, the occasion on which Martí offered his ideas on this point in a most organic and concise manner was in his 1891 article "Our America." I will limit myself to certain essential quotations. But I should first like to offer some observations on the destiny of Martí's work.

During Martí's lifetime, the bulk of his work, scattered throughout a score of continental newspapers, enjoyed widespread fame. We know that Rubén Darío called Martí "Maestro" (as, for other reasons, his political followers would also call him during his lifetime) and considered him the Latin American whom he most admired. We shall soon see, on the other hand, how the harsh judgments on the United States that Martí commonly made in his articles, equally well known in his time, were the cause of acerbic criticism by the pro-Yankee Sarmiento. But the particular manner in which Martí's writings circulated—he made use of journalism, oratory, and letter but *never published a single book*—bears considerable responsibility for the relative oblivion into which the work of the Cuban hero fell after his death in 1895. This alone explains the fact that nine years after his death—and twelve from the time Martí stopped writing for the continental press, devoted as he was after 1892 to his political tasks—an author as absolutely ours and as far above suspicion as the twenty-year-old Pedro Henríquez Ureña could write in 1904, in an article on Rodó's *Ariel*, that the latter's opinions on the United States are "much more severe than those formulated by two of the greatest thinkers and most brilliant psycho-sociologists of the Antilles: Hostos and Martí."[41] Insofar as this refers to Martí, the observation is completely erroneous; and given the exemplary honesty of Henríquez Ureña, it led me, first, to suspect and later, to verify that it was due simply to the fact that during this period the great Dominican had not read, *had been unable to read*, Martí adequately. Martí was hardly *published* at the time. A text such as the fundamental "Our America" is a good example of this fate. Readers of the Mexican newspaper *El Partido Liberal* could have read it on 30 January 1891. It is possible that some other local newspaper republished it,[42] although the most recent edition of Martí's *Complete Works* does not indicate anything in this regard. But it is most likely that those who did not have the good fortune to obtain that newspaper knew nothing about the article—the most important document published in America from the end of the past century until the appearance in 1962 of the Second Declaration of Havana—for almost twenty years, at the end of which time it appeared in book form (Havana, 1910) in the irregular collection in which publication of the complete works of Martí was begun. For this reason Manuel Pedro González is correct when he asserts that during the first quarter of this century the new generations did not know Martí. "A minimal portion of his work" was again put into circulation, starting with the eight volumes published by Alberto Ghiraldo in Madrid in 1925. Thanks to the most recent appearance of several editions of his complete works—actually still incomplete—"he has been rediscovered and reevaluated."⁴³ González is thinking above all of the dazzling literary qualities of this work ("the literary glory" as he says). Could we not add something, then, regarding the works' fundamental ideological aspects? Without forgetting very important prior contributions, there are still some essential points that explain why today, after the triumph of the Cuban Revolution and because of it, Martí is being "rediscovered and reevaluated." It was no mere coincidence that in 1953 Fidel named Martí as the intellectual author of the attack on the Moncada Barracks nor that Che should use a quotation from Martí—"it is the hour of the furnace, and only light should be seen"—to open his extremely important "Message to the Tricontinental Congress" in 1967. If Benedetti could say that Rodó's time "was different from our own...his true place, his true temporal homeland was the nineteenth century," we must say, on the other hand, that Martí's true place was the future and, for the moment, this era of ours, which simply cannot be understood without a thorough knowledge of this work.

Now, if that knowledge, because of the curious circumstances alluded to, was denied or available only in a limited way to the early generations of this century, who frequently had to base their defense of subsequent radical arguments on a "first launching pad" as well-intentioned but at the same time as weak as the nineteenth-century work *Ariel,* what can we say of more recent authors to whom editions of Martí are now available but who nevertheless persist in ignoring him? I am thinking, of course, not of scholars more or less ignorant of our problems but, on the contrary, of those who maintain a consistently anticolonialist attitude. The only explanation of this situation is a painful one: we have been so thoroughly steeped in colonialism that we read with real respect only those anticolonialist authors *disseminated from the metropolis.* In this way we cast aside the greatest lesson of Martí; thus, we are barely familiar with Artigas, Recabarren, Mella, and even Mariátegui and Ponce. And I have the sad suspicion that if the extraordinary texts of Che Guevara have enjoyed the greatest dissemination ever accorded a Latin American, the fact that he is read with such avidity by our people is to a certain extent due to the prestige his name has even in the metropolitan capitals—where, to be sure, he is frequently the object of the most shameless manipulation. For consistency in our anticolonialist attitude we must in effect turn to those of our people who have incarnated and illustrated that attitude in their behavior and thinking.⁴⁴ And for this, there is no case more useful than that of Martí.

I know of no other Latin-American author who has given so immediate and so coherent an answer to another question put to me by my interlocutor, the European journalist whom I mentioned at the beginning of these lines (and whom, if he did not exist. I would have had to invent, although this would have deprived me of his friendship, which I trust will survive this monologue): "What relationship," this guileless wit asked me, "does Borges have to the Incas?" Borges is almost a reductio ad absurdum and, in any event, I shall discuss him later. But it is only right and fair to ask what relationship we, the present inhabitants of this America in whose zoological and cultural heritage Europe has played an unquestionable part, have to the primitive inhabitants of this same America—those peoples who constructed or were martyred by Europeans of various nations, about whom neither a white nor black legend can be built, only an infernal truth of blood, that, together with such deeds as the enslavement of Africans, constitutes their eternal dishonor. Martí, whose father was from Valencia and whose mother was from the Canaries, who wrote the most prodigious Spanish of his—and our—age, and who came to have the greatest knowledge of the Euro–North American culture ever possessed by a man of our America, also asked this question. He answered it as follows: "We are descended from Valencian fathers and Canary Island mothers and feel the inflamed blood of Tamanaco and Paramaconi coursing through our veins; we see the blood that fell amid the brambles of Mount Calvary as our own, along with that shed by the naked and heroic Caracas as they struggled breast to breast with the gonzalos in their iron-plated armor."[45]

I presume that the reader, if he or she is not a Venezuelan, will be unfamiliar with the names evoked by Martí. So was I. This lack of familiarity is but another proof of our subjection to the colonialist perspective of history that has been imposed on us, causing names, dates, circumstances, and truths to vanish from our consciousness. Under other circumstances—but closely related to these—did not the bourgeois version of history try to erase the heroes of the Commune of 1871, the martyrs of 1 May 1886 (significantly reclaimed by Martí)? At any rate, Tamanaco, Paramaconi, "the naked and heroic Caracas" were natives of what is today called Venezuela, of *Carib blood, the blood of Caliban,* coursing through their veins. This will not be the only time he expresses such an idea, which is central to his thinking.[46] Again making use of such heroes, he was to repeat sometime later: "We must stand with Guaicaipuro, Paramaconi [heroes of Venezuela, probably of Carib origin], and not with the flames that burned them, nor with the ropes that bound them, nor with the steel that beheaded them, nor with the dogs that devoured them."[47] Martí's rejection of the ethnocide that Europe practiced is *total*. No less total is his identification with the American peoples that offered heroic resistance to the invader, and in whom Martí saw the natural forerunners of the Latin American *independentistas*. This explains why in the notebook in which this last quotation appears, he continues writing, almost without transition, on Aztec mythology ("no less beautiful than the Greek"), on the ashes of Quetzacoatl, on "Ayachucho on the solitary plateau," on "Bolívar, like the rivers."[48]

Martí, however, dreams not of a restoration now impossible but of the future integration of our America—an America rising organically from a firm grasp of its true roots to the heights of authentic modernity. For this reason, the first quotation in which he speaks of feeling valiant Carib blood coursing through his veins continues as follows:

> It is good to open canals, to promote schools, to create steamship lines, to keep abreast of one's own time, to be on the side of the vanguard in the beautiful march of humanity. But in order not to falter because of a lack of spirit or the vanity of a false spirit, it is good also to nourish oneself through memory and admiration, through righteous study and loving compassion, on that fervent spirit of the natural surroundings in which one is born—a spirit matured and quickened by those of every race that issues from such surroundings and finds its final repose in them. Politics and literature flourish only when they are direct. The American intelligence is an indigenous plumage. Is it not evident that America itself was paralyzed by the same blow that paralyzed the Indian? And until the Indian is caused to walk, America itself will not begin to walk well. ["AAA," 337]

Martí's identification with our aboriginal culture was thus accompanied by a complete sense of the concrete tasks imposed upon him by his circumstances. Far from hampering him, that identification nurtured in him the most radical and modern criteria of his time in the colonial countries.

Naturally, Martí's approach to the Indian was also applied to the black.[49] Unfortunately, while in his day serious inquiries into American aboriginal cultures (which Martí studied passionately) had already been undertaken, only in the twentieth century would there appear similar studies of African cultures and their considerable contribution to the makeup of our mestizo America (see Frobenius, Delafosse, Suret-Canale, Ortiz, Ramos, Herskovits, Roumain, Metraux, Bastide, Franco).[50] And Martí died five years before the dawning of our century. In any event, in his treatment of Indian culture and in his concrete behavior toward the black, he left a very clear outline of a "battle plan" in this area.

'This is the way in which Martí forms his Calibanesque vision of the culture of what he called "our America." Martí is, as Fidel was later to be, aware of how difficult it is even to find a name that in designating us defines us conceptually. For this reason, after several attempts, he favored that modest descriptive formula that above and beyond race, language, and secondary circumstances embraces the communities that live, with their common problems, "from the [Rio] Bravo to Patagonia," and that are distinct from "European America." I have already said that, although it is found scattered throughout his very numerous writings, this conception of our culture is aptly summarized in the article-manifesto "Our America," and I direct the reader to it: to his insistence upon the idea that one cannot "rule new peoples with a singular and violent composition, with laws inherited from four centuries of free practice in the United States, or nineteen centuries of monarchy in France. One does not stop the blow in the chest of the plainsman's horse with one of Hamilton's decrees. One does not clear the congealed blood of the Indian race with a sentence of Sieyès"; to his deeply rooted concept that "the imported book has been conquered in America by the natural man. Natural men have conquered the artificial men of learning. *The authentic mestizo has conquered the exotic Creole*" (my emphasis); and finally to his fundamental advice:

> The European university must yield to the American university. The history of America, from the Incas to the present, must be taught letter perfect, even if that of the Argonauts of Greece is not taught. Our own Greece is preferable to that Greece that is not ours. We have greater need of it. National politicians must replace foreign and exotic politicians. Graft the world onto our republics, but the trunk must be that of our republics. And let the conquered pedant be silent: there is no homeland of which the individual can be more proud than our unhappy American republics.

Notes
1. This article appeared for the first time in *Casa de Las Américas* (Havana), 68 (September–October 1971). It is that journal, and that issue specifically, to which the author refers in the text.
2. See Yves Lacoste, *Les Pays Sous-Developpés* [The Underdeveloped Countries] (Paris: Presses Universitaires de France, 1959), 82–84.
3. José Vasconcelos, *La Raza Cósmica* [The Cosmic Race] (Madrid: Agencia Mundial de Librería, 1925). A Swedish summary of what is known on this subject can be found in Magnus Mörner's study, *La Mezcla de Razas en la Historia de América Latina* [The Mixture of Races in the History of Latin America], Jorge Piatigorsky (Buenos Aires, 1969). Here it is recognized that 'no part of the world has witnessed such a gigantic mixing of races as the one that has been taking place in Latin America and the Caribbean [Why this division?] since 1492' (15). Of course, what interests me in these is not the irrelevant biological fact of the 'races' but the historical fact of the 'cultures'; see Claude Lévi-Strauss, *Race et Histoire* [Race and History] [1952] (Paris, 1968).
4. Cited along with subsequent references to the *Diario* [Logbook], by Julio C. Salas, in *Etnografía Americana: Los Indios Caribes – Estudio Sobre el Origen del Mito de la Antropofagia* (Latin American Ethnography: The Carib Indians – A Study of the Myth of Anthropophagy] (Madrid, 1920). The book exposes 'The irrationality of [the] charge that some American tribes devoured human flesh, maintained in the past by those interested in enslaving [the] Indians and repeated by the chroniclers and historians, many of whom were supporters of slavery' (211).
5. *La Carta de Colón Anunciando el Descubrimiento del Nuevo Mundo, 15 de Febrero –14 de Marzo 1493* [Columbus's Letter Announcing the Discovery of the New World, 15 February–14 March 1493] (Madrid, 1956), 20.
6. Ezequiel Martínez Estrada, 'El Nuevo Mundo, la Isla de Utopía y la Isla de Cuba' [The New World, the Island of Utopia, and the Island of Cuba], *Casa de las Américas* 33 (November–December 1965); this issue is entitled *Homenaje a Ezequiel Martinez Estrada*.
7. *The Complete Essays of Montaigne*, trans. Donald Frame (Stanford, Calif.: Stanford University Press, 1965), 152.
8. Ibid.
9. In William Shakespeare, *Obras Completas*, trans. Luis Astrana Marín (Madrid, 1961), 107–8.
10. For example, Jan Kott notes that 'there have been learned Shakespearian scholars who tried to interpret *The Tempest* as a direct autobiography, or as an allegorical political drama' (*Shakespeare, Our Contemporary*, trans. Boleslaw Taborski. 2d ed. [London: Methuen, 1967], 240).

11. Ernest Renan, *Caliban: Suite de 'La Tempête.' Drame Philosophique* [Caliban: 'The Tempest' Suite. A Philosophical Drama] (Paris: Calmann-Lévy, 1878).
12. See V. Arthur Adamov, *La Commune de Paris (8 Mars–28 Mars 1871): Anthologie* [The Paris Commune (8 March–28 March 1871): An Anthology] (Paris: Éditions Sociale, 1959); and, especially. Paul Lidsky, *Les Écrivains contre la Commune* [Writers Against the Commune] (Paris: Francois Maspero, 1970).
13. Paul Lidsky, *Les Écrivains contre la Commune*, 82.
14. Cited by Aimé Césaire in *Discours sur le Colonialisme* [An Address on Colonialism]. 3d ed. (Paris: Présence Africaine, 1955). 13. This is a remarkable work, and I have made extensive use of its main ideas in this essay. (A part of it has been translated into Spanish in *Casa de las Américas* 36–37 [May–August 1966], an issue dedicated to *Africa en América* [Africa in Latin America]).
15. Ibid., 14–15.
16. See Roberto Fernández Retamar. 'Modernismo, Noventiocho, Subdesarrollo,' [Modernism, the Generation of 1898, Underdevelopment], paper read at the Third Congress of the International Association of Hispanists, Mexico City, August 1968; collected in *Ensayo de Otro Mundo* [Essay on a Different World], 2d ed. (Santiago: Editorial Universitaria, 1969).
17. Quoted in José Enrique Rodó, *Obras Completas* [Complete Works], ed. Emir Rodríguez Monegal (Madrid: Aguilar, 1957), 193; this volume will hereafter be cited by page number in the text.
18. See Jean Franco, *The Modern Culture of Latin America: Society and the Artist* (London: Penguin, 1967), 49.
19. José Vasconcelos, *Indología* [Indology]. 2d ed. (Barcelona: Agencia Mundial de Librería, 1927), xxiii.
20. Mario Benedetti, *Genio y Figura de José Enrique Rodó* [A Portrait of José Enriqué Rodó] (Buenos Aires: Editorial Universitaria de Buenos Aires, 1966), 95.
21. The penetrating but negative vision of Jan Kott causes him to be irritated by this fact. 'Renan saw Demos in Caliban; in his continuation of *The Tempest* he took him to Milan and made him attempt another, victorious coup against Prospero. Guéhenno wrote an apology for Caliban-People. Both these interpretations are flat and do not do justice to Shakespeare's Caliban' (*Shakespeare, Our Contemporary*, 273).
22. Guéhenno's weakness in approaching this theme with any profundity is apparent from his increasingly contradictory prefaces to successive editions of the book (2d ed., 1945; 3d ed., 1962) down to his book of essays *Caliban et Prospero* [Caliban and Prospero] (Paris: Gallimard, 1969), where according to one critic, Guéhenno is converted into 'a personage of bourgeois society and beneficiary of its culture,' who judges Prospero 'more equitably than in the days of *Caliban parle*' (Pierre Henri Simon, in *Le Monde*, 5 July, 1969).
23. See Michael Lowy, *La Pensée de Che Guevara* [Che Guevara's Thought] (Paris: Francois Maspero, 1970), 19.
24. Aníbal Pónce. *Humanismo Burgués y Humanismo Proletario* [Bourgeois Humanism and Proletarian Humanism] (Havana: Impr. Nacional de Cuba, 1962), 83.
25. J.L. Zimmerman, *Países Pobres, Países Ricos: La Brecha Que Se Ensancha* [Poor Countries, Rich Countries: The Breech that is Widening], trans. G. González Aramburo (Mexico City: Siglo XXI Editores, 1966), 7.
26. O. Mannoni, *Psychologie de la Colonisation* [The Psychology of Colonialism] (Paris: Éditions du Seuil, 1950), 71; quoted by Frantz Fanon, in *Peau Noire, Masques Blancs* [Black Skin, White Masks], 2d ed. (Paris: Éditions du Seuil, c. 1965), 106.
27. George Lamming, *The Pleasures of Exile* (London: Michael Joseph, 1960), 109. In commenting on these opinions of Lamming, the German Janheinz Jahn observes their limitations and proposes an identification of Caliban/negritude. See *Neo-African Literature*, trans. O. Coburn and U. Lehrburger (New York: Grove Press, 1968), 239–42.
28. John Wain, *The Living World of Shakespeare* (New York: St Martin's Press, 1964), 226–27.
29. See Aimé Césaire, *Une Tempête: Adaptation de 'La Tempête' de Shakespeare pour un Théâtre Nègre* [A Tempest: An Adaptation of Shakespeare's "The Tempest" for a Black Theater] (Paris: Éditions du Seuil, 1969); Edward Brathwaite, *Islands* (London: Oxford University Press, 1969): Roberto Fernández Retamar, 'Cuba hasta Fidel' [Cuba until Fidel], *Bohemia*, 19 September 1969.
30. The new reading of *The Tempest* has become a common one throughout the colonial world of today. I want only, therefore, to mention a few examples. On concluding these notes, I find a new one in the essay by James Ngugi (of Kenya). 'Africa y la Descolonización Cultural' [Africa and Cultural Decolonization], in *El Correo* (January 1971).
31. 'It is improper.' Benedetti has said, 'to confront Rodó with present-day structures, statement, and ideologies. His time was different from ours[;] ...his true place, his true temporal homeland was the nineteenth century' (*Genio y figura de José Enrique Rodó*, 128).
32. Ibid., 109. Even greater emphasis on the current validity of Rodó will be found in Arturo Ardao's book *Rodó: Su Americanismo* [Rodó: His Americanism] (Montevideo: Biblioteca de Marcha, 1970), which includes an excellent anthology of the author of *Ariel*. On the other hand, as early as 1928, José Carlos

Mariátegui, after rightly recalling that 'only a socialist Latin or Ibero-America can effectively oppose a capitalist, plutocratic, and imperialist North America,' adds, 'The myth of Rodó has not yet acted—nor has it ever acted—usefully and fruitfully upon our souls' ('Aniversario y balance' [An Anniversary and a Summing Up] [1928], in *Ideología y Política* [Ideology and Politics] (Lima: Bibliotecha, 1969), 248.
33. *Hombres de la Revolución: Julio Antonio Mella* [Men of the Revolution: Julio Antonio Mella] (Havana, 1971), 12.
34. Ibid., 15.
35. See Erasmo Dumpierre, *Mella* (Havana, c. 1965), 145; see also José Antonio Portuondo, 'Mella y los Intelectuales' [Mella and the Intellectuals] (1963), which is reproduced in *Casa de las Américas*, no. 68 (1971).
36. Emir Rodríguez Monegal, ed., *Rodó* (Madrid: Aguilar, 1957), 193–93; my emphasis.
37. Medardo Vitier, *Del Ensayo Americano* [On the Latin American Essay] (Mexico City: Fondo de Cultura Económica, 1945), 117.
38. Fidel Castro, speech, 19 April, 1971.
39. See Kott, *Shakespeare, Our Contemporary*, 269.
40. See Ezequiel Martínez Estrada, 'Por una Alta Cultura Popular y Socialism Cubuna' [Toward a Cuban Popular and Socialist High Culture] (1962), in *En Cuba y al Servicio de la Revolución Cubana* [In Cuba and at the Service of the Cuban Revolution] (Havana: Unión de Escritores y Artistas de Cuba, 1963); 'Martí en Su (Tereer) mundo' [Martí in his (Third) World], *Ensayo de Otro Mundo, Cuba Socialista* 41 (January 1965); Noël Salomon, 'José Martí et la Prise de Conscience Latinoaméricaine' [José Martí and Latin America's Coming to Consciousness], *Cuba Sí* 35–36 (4th trimester 1970–1st trimester 1971): and Leonardo Acosta, 'La Concepeión Histórica de Martí.' [Martí's Idea of History], *Casa de las Américas* 67 (July–August 1971).
41. Pedro Henríquez Ureña, *Obra Crítica* [Critical Work] (Mexico City: Fondo de Cultura Economica, 1960), 27.
42. Ivan Schulman, *Martí, Casal y el Modernismo* [Martí, Casal, and Modernism] (Havana: Universidad de la Habana, Comisión de Extensión Universitaria, 1969), 92 has discovered that it had been *previously* published on 10 January 1891, in *La Revista Ilustrada de Nueva York*.
43. Manuel Pedro González, 'Evolución de la Estimativa Martiana' [The Evolution of Martí's Critical Tools], in *Antología Crítica de José Martí* [Critical Anthology of José Martí']. comp. and ed. Manuel Pedro González (Mexico City: Editorial Cultura, 1960), xxix.
44. Nonetheless, this should not be understood to mean that I am suggesting that those authors who have not been born in the colonies should not be read. Such a stupidity is untenable. How could we propose to ignore Homer, Dante, Cervantes, Shakespeare, Whitman, to say nothing of Marx, Engels, or Lenin? How can we forget that even in our own day there are *Latin American* thinkers who have not been born here? Lastly, how can we defend intellectual Robinson Crusoism at all without falling into the greatest absurdity?
45. José Martí, 'Autores Aborígenes Americanos,' *Obras Completas* 8 (1884): 336–37; hereafter cited as 'AAA' in the text.
46. For instance, to Tamanaco he dedicated a beautiful poem: 'Tamanaco of the Plumed Crown,' *Obras completas*, 22:237.
47. José Martí, 'Fragmentos' [Fragments] [1885–95], in *Obras Completas*, 22:27.
48. Ibid., 28–29.
49. See, for example, José Martí, 'Mi Raza' [My Race], *Obras Completas*, 2:298–300, where we read: An individual has no special right because he belongs to one race or another: to speak of a human being is to speak of all rights.... If one says that in the black there is no aboriginal fault or virus that incapacitates him from leading his human life to the full, one is speaking the truth...and if this defense of nature is called racism, the name does not matter; for it is nothing if not natural decency and the voice crying from the breast of the human being for the peace and life of the country. If it be alleged that the condition of slavery does not suggest any inferiority of the enslaved race, since white Gauls with blue eyes and golden hair were sold as slaves with iron rings around their necks in the markets of Rome, that is good racism because it is pure justice and helps to remove the prejudices of the ignorant white man. But there righteous racism ends. And, further on. 'A human being is more than white, more than mulatto, more than black. Cuban is more than white, more than mulatto, more than black.' Some of these questions are treated in Juliette Oullion's paper. 'La Discriminatión Racial en los Estados Unidos Vista por José Martí,' [Racial Discrimination in the United States as seen by José Martí], *Anuario Martiano* (Havana, 1971), which I was unable to use, since it appeared after these notes were completed.
50. See *Casa de las Américas* 36–37 (May–August 1966), a special issue entitled *Africa en América* [Africa in Latin America].

Not Just (Any) *Body* Can Be a Citizen:
The Politics of Law, Sexuality and Postcoloniality in Trinidad and Tobago and The Bahamas

M. Jacqui Alexander

I am an outlaw in my country of birth: a national; but not a citizen. Born in Trinidad and Tobago on the cusp of anti-colonial nationalist movements there, I was taught that once we pledged our lives to the new nation, 'every creed and race [had] an equal place.' I was taught to believe 'Massa Day Done', that there would be an imminent end to foreign domination. Subsequent governments have not only eclipsed these promises, they have revised the very terms of citizenship to exclude me. No longer equal, I can be brought up on charges of 'serious indecency' under the Sexual Offences Act of 1986, and if convicted, serve a prison term of five years. In the Bahamas, I can be found guilty of the *crime* of lesbianism and imprisoned for twenty years. In the United States of North America where I now live, I must constantly keep in my possession the immigrant (green) card given me by the American state, marking me 'legal' resident alien; non-national; non-citizen. If I traverse any of the borders of twenty-two states even *with* green card in hand, I may be convicted of crimes variously defined as 'lewd unnatural; lascivious conduct; deviate sexual intercourse; gross indecency; buggery or crimes against nature' (Robson, 1992:58).

Why has the state marked these sexual inscriptions on my body? Why has the state focused such a repressive and regressive gaze on me and people like me? These are some of the questions I seek to understand in this paper. I wish to use this moment to look back at the state, to reverse, subvert and ultimately demystify that gaze by taking apart these racialized legislative gestures that have naturalized heterosexuality by criminalizing lesbian and other forms of non-procreative sex. It is crucial for us as feminists to understand the ways in which the state deploys power in this domain and the kinds of symbolic boundaries it draws around sexual difference, for these are the very boundaries around which its power coheres (Hall, 1994). Indeed, 'homosexual' difference is indispensable to the creation of the putative heterosexual norm. Located, then, within the very oppositional movements which the state has outlawed, I look back as part of the ongoing and complicated process of decolonization and reconstruction of the self, a project which has been seriously disrupted in most 'postcolonial' nation-states.

I want to suggest a way of thinking about state nationalism and its sexualization of particular bodies in Trinidad and Tobago and the Bahamas in order to determine whether such bodies are offered up, as it were, in an internal struggle for legitimation in which these post-colonial states are currently engulfed. What kinds of reassurances do these bodies provide, and for whom? The state's authority to rule is currently under siege; the ideological moorings of nationalism have been dislodged, partly because of major international political economic incursions that have in turn provoked an internal crisis of authority. I argue that in this context criminalization functions as a technology of control, and much like other technologies of control becomes an important site for the production and reproduction of state power (Heng and Devan, 1992).

Although policing the sexual (stigmatizing and outlawing several kinds of non-procreative sex, particularly lesbian and gay sex and prostitution) has something to do with sex, it is also more than sex. Embedded here are powerful signifiers about appropriate sexuality, about the kind of sexuality that presumably imperils the nation and about the kind of sexuality that promotes citizenship. Not just (any) *body* can be a citizen any more, for *some* bodies have been marked by the state as non-procreative, in pursuit of sex only for pleasure, a sex that is non-productive of babies and of no economic gain. Having refused the heterosexual imperative of citizenship, *these* bodies, according to the state, pose a profound threat to the very survival of the nation. Thus, I argue that as the state moves to reconfigure the nation it simultaneously resuscitates the nation as hetero*sexual*.

Yet, the focus on state power is not to imply rationality or even internal coherence. In fact, what is evident in the legislation and in other contextual gestures surrounding it are paradoxical and contradictory ways in which the state exerts its will to power. Seemingly emancipatory practices such as legal 'protections' of women's interests or provisions which constrain violent domestic patriarchy are crafted in the same frame that disciplines and punishes people with HIV infection, and women who exercise erotic autonomy. In addition, the state moves to police the sexual and reinscribe inherited and more recently constructed meanings of masculinity and femininity, while simultaneously mediating a political economy of desire in tourism that relies upon the sexualization and commodification of women's bodies. Further, the nationalist state mediates the massive entry of transnational capital within national borders, but blames sexual decadence (lesbian and gay sex and prostitution) for the dissolution of the nation. It may no longer be possible to understand the state purely within the boundaries of the nation because these global processes are rapidly transforming the ways that nations constitute and imagine themselves. This is why methodologically I foreground the economic and political processes of transnationalization to better examine the processes of sexualization undertaken in the legal text. The role of the imperial in transforming the national is therefore crucial.

These paradoxes raise some perplexing questions for feminist theorizing and for oppositional movements. Clearly feminist mobilizations have been successful in wresting certain concessions from the state and in inaugurating vigorous public discussion about sexualized violence. They have also challenged the state on its meaning and definitions of crisis. Yet feminists are also caught in the paradoxical discursive parameters set up by the state and end up helping to devise and monitor the state's mechanisms that surveille criminalized women. On what basis then, would solidarity work among different women be possible? Further, when one examines the effects of these transformations, it becomes clear that some areas of patriarchy have been challenged while others have been resolidified. Citizenship, for instance, continues to be premised within heterosexuality and principally within heteromasculinity. In the absence of visible lesbian and gay movements, can feminist political struggles radically transform these historically repressive structures? How can women inscribe their own interests within fundamentally masculinist organizations (Irigaray, 1985).

I shall begin by reading the ways in which the heterosexual is naturalized in the legal text in order to isolate its importance to the state. In the section that follows, I analyse the ways in which naturalized heterosexuality shapes the definitions of respectability, Black masculinity and nationalism. We come full circle, then, as I argue that the effects of political economic international processes provoke a legitimation crisis for the state which moves to restore its legitimacy by recouping heterosexuality through legislation. I end by suggesting that the process of decolonization, which the nationalist state had claimed as its own, has been seriously disrupted and I draw out the implications for oppositional movements and analyses.

Naturalizing Heterosexuality as Law

In 1986, the Parliament of the Republic of Trinidad and Tobago scripted and passed the Sexual Offences Act: 'An Act to Repeal and Replace the Laws of the Country relating to Sexual Crimes, to the Procuration, Abduction and Prostitution of Persons and to Kindred Offences.' This gesture of consolidation was, in the words of law commissioners, an attempt 'to bring all laws dealing with sexual offences under one heading.' It was the first time the postcolonial state confronted earlier colonial practices which policed and scripted 'native' sexuality to help consolidate the myth of imperial authority.

Many of the thirty-five provisions of the legislation, then, had prior lives, and were being reconsolidated under a different schedule of punishments. Prohibitions regarding sexual violence within the family (incest), and against women who exchanged sex for money (prostitutes) and those who aided them (brothel-keepers), or those who exploited them (pimps) had long been established in the emendations to the Offences Against the Person Acts, that one-sided pivot of British jurisprudence. In keeping with its allegiance to hegemonic masculinity, the script upheld a prior provision that defined anal intercourse between men as buggery, outlawed it, and affixed a penalty of ten years imprisonment, if convicted. It moved, in addition, to criminalize new areas of sexual activity. Established were prohibitions against employers who took sexual advantage of their minor employees at the workplace, and against men who had sex with fourteen- to sixteen-year-old girls, who would now be guilty of a statutory offence. For the first time, a category called rape within marriage was established and criminalized: 'Any "husband" who had forceful intercourse with his "wife" without her consent' could be convicted and imprisoned for fifteen years under a new offence called sexual assault; and sex between women became punishable by five years under a new offence called '"serious indecency", if committed on or towards a person sixteen years or more.'

Three years later, the parliament of the Bahamas scripted and passed its own version of the Sexual Offences Act, cited as the 'Sexual Offences and Domestic Violence Act of 1989', *its* gesture of consolidation, formulated by law commissioners 'as an attempt to provide one comprehensive piece of legislation setting out sexual offences which are indictable', seeking, in its words, 'to make better provision in respect of the rights in the occupation of the matrimonial home.' As in the case of Trinidad and Tobago, it was the first attempt to impose a veiled sexual order on the chaotic legacy of colonialism. The commission had hoped to deal not only with this chaos, but also with the disruptions and violence of conjugal relations by reasserting the primacy of the matrimonial home and the rights of '*any* person' residing therein.

Its thirty-one provisions bore close resemblance to those of Trinidad and Tobago in terms of the injunctions, prohibitions and schedule of punishments against prostitution, incest, and sexual harassment and assault in the workplace. It too, conflated buggery, bestiality and criminality: 'If any two persons are guilty of the crime of buggery – an unnatural crime, or if any person is guilty of unnatural connection with any animal, every such person is guilty of an offence and liable to imprisonment for twenty years.' This definition resembles the first civil injunction against sodomy that was legislated in 1533 in Henry VIII's parliament (Cohen: 1989). In its injunction against sex between women, it abandoned the coyness of the Trinidad legislature in favour of an explicit approach that pronounced, criminalized and penalized a sexual activity in one single gesture: 'Any female who has sexual intercourse with another female, whether with or without the consent of that female, is guilty of the offence of lesbianism and is liable to imprisonment for twenty years.' Similarly, under restrictive stipulations that were an exact replication of those in Trinidad, it moved to criminalize violent marital sex, but fell short of calling it rape. The legislation asserted: 'Any person who has sexual intercourse with his spouse without the consent of the spouse is guilty of the offence of sexual assault and liable to imprisonment for fifteen years.' The law also moved to imprison (for five years) anyone with HIV infection who had consensual sex without disclosing their HIV status.

Its new provision, relating to domestic violence, made it possible for *any* party in the marriage to apply to the Supreme Court for an injunction that would restrain the other party from molestation and from using violence in the matrimonial home. What is remarkable about this act that calls itself a domestic violence act is that nowhere is there a definition of domestic violence. Rather the majority of the provisions focus upon the disposition of private property and on the minute distinctions among 'dwelling, estate, apartment', etc. These were not the terms on which the women's movement in the Bahamas had pushed for the criminalization of domestic violence. Over a five-year period, women held public rallies, campaigned door to door and gained more than 10,000 signatures and the knowledge from women's experiences of physical and sexual violence against themselves and their daughters. It would seem then, that even in the face of violent disruptions in marriage, conjugal heterosexuality is most concerned with the patrilineal transfer of private property.

Legislative gestures fix conjugal heterosexuality in several ways. Generally, they collapse identities into sexual bodies which, in the particular case of lesbian and gay people, serves to reinforce a fiction about promiscuity: that sex is all of what we do and consequently the slippage, it is all of who we are. Yet lesbian and gay sex, the 'pervert', the 'unnatural' are all indispensable to the formulation of the 'natural', the conjugal, the heterosexual. This dialectic must be made visible, for there is no absolute set of commonly understood or accepted principles called the 'natural' which can be invoked definitionally except as they relate to what is labelled 'unnatural'. Here is a remarkably circular definition of sexual intercourse that was attached as a supplementary note to the Trinidad and Tobago Act:

> [The Clauses] do not necessarily define 'sexual intercourse' but give a characteristic of it. 'Sexual intercourse' means natural sexual intercourse in the clauses relating to rape and other offences of sexual intercourse with women, whereas the clause concerned with buggery relates to unnatural sexual intercourse.

Heterosexual sex, even while dysfunctional (as in rape in marriage, domestic violence and incest), assumes the power of natural law only in relation to sex which is defined in negation to it (what natural sexual intercourse is not) and in those instances where desire presumably becomes so corrupt that it expresses itself as bestiality. In other words, heterosexual practices carry the weight of the natural only in relational terms and ultimately, one might argue, only in its power to designate as unnatural those practices which disrupt marriage and certain dominant notions of conjugal family. Beyond that, sexual intercourse remains necessarily, remarkably unclarified.

Conjugal heterosexuality is frozen within a very specific and narrow set of class relations between 'husband' and 'wife' in 'marriage', narrow because the majority of heterosexual relationships are in fact organized outside of this domain. Even while the Bahamian legislation might appear to address violence in all 'domestic' domains, its skewed emphasis on private property immediately renders it class specific. For working-class women who do not own property and are beaten by the men with whom they live, this legislation offers no protection. And even for middle-class and upper-middle-class women who are beaten by their husbands and might own property, the problem they face is how to disentangle the web of well-connected social relationships that protect *their* middle-class and upper-middle-class husbands from being prosecuted as criminals. For most women who stand outside of the legal definitions of 'parties to a marriage', they can make no claims for relief from the state. Thus, domestic violence works as a proxy for class and facilitates the reallocation of private property in disruptive conjugal marriage.

Both pieces of legislation systematically conflate violent hetero*sexual* domination, such as rape and incest, with same-sex relations, thereby establishing a continuum of criminality among same *sex* rape, domestic violence, adultery, fornication and dishonesty. On this continuum the psyche of homosexuality becomes the psyche of criminality. By criminalizing perverted heterosexual sex, the legislation aims to expunge criminal elements from the heterosexual so that it could return to its originary and superior moral position. However, homosexuality, inherently perverse, could only be cleansed by reverting to heterosexuality. And still, not all heterosexualities are permissible: not the prostitute with an irresponsible, 'non-productive' sexuality, and not young women whom the state defines as girls requiring its protection.

Outside the boundaries of the legislation, yet informing it, state managers generated a simultaneous discourse invoking nostalgia for a Bahamas and Trinidad and Tobago when there were ostensibly no lesbians, gay men and people with AIDS. In this move, heterosexuality becomes coterminus with and gives birth to the nation. Its antithesis can unravel the nation. The state has eroticized the dissolution of the nation, producing apocalyptic (mythic) visions of dread disease and destruction (paralleled in the destruction of Sodom and Gomorrah) brought about by prostitution and the practice of lesbian and gay sex. Yet, it simultaneously enacts the dissolution of the nation through a series of political-economic gestures (adherence to the narratives and practices of modernization through allegiance to multinational capital, tourism, etc.) that it ideologically recodes as natural, even supernatural, as the salvation of the people. In this equation, tourism, foreign multi-national capital production and imperialism are as integral and as necessary to the natural order as heterosexuality. But before examining these twin processes of sexualization and internationalization more closely, one would have to understand why conjugal heterosexuality is so important for nationalist state managers and the role it plays in constituting respectable masculinity. We would have to understand the sexual inheritances of nationalism as well as the new meanings of masculinity and femininity the nationalist state has invented.

State Nationalism and Respectability, Black Masculinity Come to Power 1962, 1972

> Women, and all signs of the feminine, are by definition always already anti-national (Heng, 1992).

It would be difficult to map the minute and nuanced ways in which colonial hegemonic definitions of masculinity and femininity insinuated themselves throughout the variety of political, economic, social and cultural structures in history. We can, however, frame these definitions by examining what Kobena Mercer and Isaac Julien have called the 'hegemonic repertoire of images' which have been forged through the histories of slavery and colonization in order to identify the sexual inheritances of Black nationalism as well as its own inventions. (Mercer and Julien, 1988:132–5). I am not suggesting that ideologies simply get foisted onto people (Burawoy, 1982), for there is always an ongoing struggle to redefine power. What is crucial for my argument, however, is the intransigence of dominance and, in this instance, the continuities and discontinuities between the practices of the colonial and the 'postcolonial' around those very images.

In the repertoire of images that developed during the organization of slave-plantation economy and in the consolidation of imperial rule, the English gentleman was given primacy. In Trinidad and Tobago white militarized masculinity had to concede the right to rule to the civilian who would displace the importance of war and the more visible signs of policing and terror. Similarly in the Bahamas, the pirate, the rogue and the wrecker (white predatory masculinity) were engaged in a protracted struggle with the English gentleman for cultural and economic authority until the latter was installed as representative of the crown in 1718. It marked the triumph of respectability and honour over the boorish, the disreputable (Saunders, 1990:2).

Colonial rule simultaneously involved racializing and sexualizing the population, which also meant naturalizing whiteness. There could really be no psycho-social codices of sexuality that were not simultaneously raced. In general terms, these codices functioned as mythic meta-systems fixing polarities, contradictions and fictions while masked as truth about character. 'Laws for the governing of Negroes, Mulattoes and Indians' (Saunders, 1990:8; Goveia, 1970) made it possible for white masculinity to stand outside the law. As the invisible subject of the law, he was neither prosecuted nor persecuted within it. Since it was lawful to reinforce the ontological paradox of slave as chattel, Elizabethan statutes of rape operated to legitimize violent colonial masculinity which was never called rape, yet criminalized black masculinity for rape. This would solidify the cult of true womanhood and its correlates, the white madonna (untouchable) and the Black whore (promiscuous).

Here too, identities were collapsed into bodies. Black bodies, the economic pivot of slave-plantation economy, were sexualized. Black women's bodies evidenced an unruly sexuality, untamed and wild. Black male sexuality was to be feared as the hypersexualized stalker. These dominant constructions worked to erase indigenous (Lucayan, Carib and Arawak) sexualities. Indentured Indian femininity (in Trinidad and Tobago) was formulated as dread and desire, mysteriously wanton, inviting death and destruction, although it could also be domesticated. Indian manliness was unrestrained, violent and androgynous, the latter construction drawn from Britain's colonial experience in India. Free coloured women, who outnumbered Black women in the Bahamas, and their counterparts in Trinidad and Tobago who were believed anxious to 'acquire property and wealth by inheriting land for the natural white fathers', were also sexualized, but positioned as potential mates (Saunders, 1990:18, 19; McDaniel, 1986). Even with these differences in the construction of 'native' sexualities, however, colonized sexualities were essentially subordinated sexualities.

It would indeed require a complicated set of cognitive and ideological reversals for the British to turn the savage into the civilized, to turn those believed incapable of rule into reliable rulers. Herein lies the significance of socialization into British norms, British manners, British parliamentary modes of governance; into conjugal marriage and the 'science' of domesticity. This would operate in effect as socialization into respectability which George Mosse argues emerged in Europe at the end of the eighteenth century with the beginnings of modern nationalism. He argues that respectability emerged in alliance with sexuality and helped to shape middle-class beliefs about the body, sexual (mis)conduct, normality and abnormality, about virility and manly bearing. The control over sexuality evidenced in the triumph of the nuclear family was vital to respectability (Mosse, 1985:2–10). Whereas in Europe these processes were indigenous to the formation of the middle class, in the Caribbean it was imported through imperialism. The Black middle class would be schooled in the definitions of morality, civility and respectable citizenship in the metropolis, in the company of the British, while 'women of reduced means' and the working class would be trained at 'home'. Specialized training schools like the Dundas Civic Center in the Bahamas were established at the turn of this century to prepare cooks, general maids and hotel workers; and the Trinidad and Tobago Home Industries and Women's Self Help Organization and the Oleander

Club of the Bahamas would train Black women in housewifery, cooking, sewing and knitting (Saunders, 1990; Reddock, 1984:245).

It was the élites of the middle class who established the nationalist parties which later became part of the state apparatus. They mobilized consensus for nation building, moulded psychic expectations about citizenship and therefore consolidated their own internal power on the ideals of sovereignty, self-determination and autonomy from foreign mandates. Ostensibly this was a neutered invocation to citizenship; yet it was in the creation of the women's wing of these parties and in their organization of 'culture' that one begins to detect a gendered call to patriotic duty. Women were to fiercely defend the nation by protecting their honour, by guarding the nuclear, conjugal family, 'the fundamental institution of the society', by guarding 'culture' defined as the transmission of a fixed set of proper values to the children of the nation, and by mobilizing on the party's behalf into the far reaches of the country. She was expected to represent and uphold a respectable femininity and, in so doing, displace the figure of the white madonna. Patriotic duty for men, on the other hand, consisted in rendering public service to the country, and in adopting the mores of respectability. Thus, we can identify a certain trajectory in the establishment of nationalism which is grounded in notions of respectability, which like eighteenth-century European nationalism came to rely heavily upon sexual gestures that involved the *symbolic* triumph of the nuclear family over the extended family and other family forms.

In order to demonstrate that it had 'graduated from all schools of constitutional, economic and social philosophies' (Pindling, 1972), and that it could comport itself with 'discipline, dignity, and decorum, with the eyes of the world upon us' (Williams, 1962), Black nationalist masculinity needed to demonstrate that it was now capable of ruling, which is to say, it needed to demonstrate moral rectitude, particularly on questions of paternity. This required distancing itself from irresponsible Black working-class masculinity that spawned the 'bastard', the 'illegitimate', and that thus had to be criminalized for irresponsible fatherhood by the British. It also required distancing itself from, while simultaneously attempting to control, Black working-class femininity that ostensibly harboured a profligate sexuality: the 'Jezebel' and the whore who was not completely socialized into housewifery, but whose labour would be mobilized to help consolidate popular nationalism. Of significance is the fact that Black nationalist masculinity could aspire toward imperial masculinity and, if loyal enough, complicitous enough, could be knighted (Craton, 1986:29), although it could never be enthroned. It could never become king.

If, as Toni Morrison has suggested, rescue and indebtedness sometimes sediment as part of the psychic residue of the process of colonization, then respectability might well function as debt payment for rescue from incivility and from savagery (Morrison, 1992: vii–xxx). But a rescued masculinity is simultaneously an injured masculinity; a masculinity that does not emerge from the inherited conditions of class and race privilege. And it is injured in a space most vulnerable to colonial constructions of incivility. At one time subordinated, that masculinity now has to be earned, and then appropriately conferred. Acting through this psychic residue, Black masculinity continues the policing of sexualized bodies, drawing out the colonial fiction of locating subjectivity in the body (as a way of denying it), as if the colonial masters were still looking on, as if to convey legitimate claims to being civilized. Not having dismantled the underlying presuppositions of British law, Black nationalist men, now with some modicum of control over the state apparatus, continue to preside over and administer the same fictions.

To the extent that the sexual offences legislation polices non-procreative, 'non-productive' sex especially in relationship to women, the neutered invocation to citizenship becomes transparent. In fact we can read state practices as attempts to propagate fictions of feminine identity, to reconfigure women's desire and subjectivity and to link the terms of the nation's survival to women's sexual organs. This is what Geraldine Heng calls, in the specific case of Singapore, 'the development of a sexualised, separate species of nationalism, a nationalism generated from the productive source of the womb.' To understand it in Heng's terms, the indictment of prostitutes and lesbians inscribes 'a tacit recognition that feminine reproductive sexuality refuses, and in refusing registers a suspicion of that sexuality as non-economic, in pursuit of its own pleasure, sexuality for its own sake, unproductive of babies, unproductive of social and economic efficiency' (Heng and Devan, 1992:343–64). It registers a suspicion of an unruly sexuality, omnipotent and omniscient enough to subvert the economic imperatives of the nation's interests. From the point of view of the state, it is a sexuality that has to be disciplined and regulated in order that it might become economically productive.

State claims of a non-productive femininity are deceptive in a number of different ways. Both the People's National Movement (PNM of Trinidad and Tobago) and the Progressive Liberal Party (PLP of the Bahamas) could not have consolidated their power or secured support for popular nationalism without women's labour, women who ironically would later have to struggle for citizenship. Yet once installed, state nationalism came to stand in an authorial relationship to women's interests and women's agency. The claim also works to mask women's labour in other areas of the economy, particularly in the tourist sector where women are the majority of a proletarianized and superexploited workforce. Capital accumulations from sex tourism and prostitution have been hidden, but given what we know about tourism and postcolonialism in South East Asia, it would be most plausible to assume that for the Bahamas in particular, there would be substantial (although now unacknowledged) accumulation from prostitutes' labour (Truong, 1990:158–91). Further, women's unpaid labour compensates for the state's refusal to expand the social wage and for the disjunctures brought about by the adoption of structural adjustment programmes. It is to these questions I turn in the following section.

(Inter)national Boundaries and Strategies of Legitimation

I wish to foreground the effects of international political economic processes in provoking the legitimacy crisis nationalist states are currently confronting, and argue that the sexual is pivotal in state orchestration of a new internal struggle whose contours are different now than they were at the moment of flag independence. In an almost ideal-typical sense, the nation had come to be shaped by what it had opposed (Anderson, 1983). Public opposition to the British had provided powerful ideological fodder for independence. We had all suffered colonial injustice together, and it was out of that experience of collective suffering that a collective vision of sovereignty could be built. Since 'independence', the state has colluded in adopting strategies that have locked these nations into a world economic and political system, the effect of which is re-colonization. The internal effects of internationalization blur the boundaries of the nation; they do not constitute anything unique anymore. Further, the reproduction of private accumulation by members of the indigenous bourgeoisie has been stifled (Gibbon, 1992), local patronage networks have been disrupted and people's material and communal lives have dramatically deteriorated. Paradoxically, these same states simultaneously preside over the transfer of substantial profits to metropolitan countries. All of these effects replicate the racialized colonial pattern of poverty, private ownership and lack of access to resources. These are the very grounds on which oppositional movements have challenged the state; it is the reason that its moral claim to leadership is unravelling.

But this is not how state managers see the crisis. Both in Trinidad and Tobago and the Bahamas they sound the danger of cultural contamination from the West' which they depict simultaneously as sexual intemperance, the importation of AIDS and the importation of feminism (read lesbianism). The Bahamian state has invoked an impending population crisis, positioned Haitian communities as Immigrants', 'refugees' and repositories of crime. It has vindicated its use of military and police force to expel Haitians from the nation's borders by claiming that they are no longer legitimate citizens; they imperil the nation. There are other strategies as well, ranging from policing oppositional movements and subtle, yet coercive ideological violence where Bahamian people, for instance, believe that the ballot is not a secret ballot and fear reprisals from the state. Individual state managers develop a patronage system to build their own authority in their own political interests, not necessarily consolidating support for nationalism, but for themselves and for their political parties.

State nationalism in Trinidad and Tobago and the Bahamas has neither reformulated nor transformed the fundamental premises upon which economic and material exchange is based. Its secular adherence to a linear definition of 'development' and progress has continued to imagine an (il)logic of a movement from 'tradition' to 'modernity' in which industrialization presumably serves as the motor for economic success. The contemporary version of development now called structural adjustment, finds expression in a powerful, yet unequal alliance among foreign multinational lending agencies such as the International Monetary Fund (IMF), the World Bank, United States Agency for International development (USAID), the American state and neocolonial regimes. Their aim is to impose a set of lending arrangements that would ostensibly reduce the foreign debt through a combination of economic measures to accelerate foreign investment, boost foreign-exchange earnings through export, and reduce government deficits through cuts in spending (McAfee, 1991:67–79). In particular, the programmes have been organized to reduce local consumption by devaluing currency, increasing personal taxes and reducing wages. The economy becomes privatized through state subsidies to private vendors, lowering taxes and providing tax holidays for foreign multinational corporations, expanding investments in tourism, dismantling state-owned enterprises, and curtailing the scope of state bureaucratic power by reducing the workforce and reducing the social wage – those expenditures for a range of social services for which the state had previously assumed some responsibility.

Although the Bahamas has not formalized 'structural adjustment' programmes (SAP), the continued subordination of its economy to the political and economic imperatives of the United States of North America has resulted in an economic infrastructure that bears all the marks of a country that has actually adopted structural adjustment. The most dramatic shift is evident in the displacement of capital and labour forces from agrarian production to service which now employs more than 50 per cent of the workforce, massive increases in the size of the food import bill (people are no longer able to feed themselves), the consolidation of foreign transnational capital in the tourist industry (hotels, airlines, services and tour operators, international finance capital, real estate), and the expansion of off-shore companies.

But perhaps the most significant and dramatic effect of SAP is that it has exacerbated the triple processes of proletarianization superexploitation and feminization of the workforce which began in the mid 1960s. By proletarianization I am referring not only to the influx, or even the magnitude of industrial capital, or the making of a gendered, racialized working class, but perhaps more importantly to the access that capital has in exploiting and even expelling relatively large percentages of the workforce. What makes this impact so profound for the nation in both Trinidad and Tobago and the Bahamas is the small size of the workforce (Rothenberg and Wishner, 1978). In the Bahamas, industrial capital has access to a sizeable portion of the workforce. More than 65% of the working population is employed in service with women comprising more than 73% of all workers, performing jobs such as housekeepers, cooks, maids, cleaners and laundresses. Two-thirds of these women earn incomes of $7,000 annually. Of the total workforce, 22% have never been employed. Women's unemployment, which has always been higher than men's, is 13%, and that of men is 11.7% and steadily increasing.

In Trinidad and Tobago, the process of proletarianization which began in the 1970s has had different, yet similar effects. Private capital employs roughly the same amount of the workforce as the state, 36% and 38% respectively. Areas such as construction, the impetus for proletarianization in the 1970s, have experienced severe retrenchment. This is particularly affecting women whose rate of unemployment in that sector is now 73%, compared to the national average of 46%. (Henry and Williams, 1991:315). Like the Bahamas, there has been a significant growth in the service sector, but it has come from self-employment and within the state bureaucracy where women work as clerical workers, nurses, teachers and maids. State retrenchments under IMF restrictions have increased women's unemployment. The overall unemployment rate in Trinidad and Tobago is 19%; women's unemployment rate is 23%.

Gendered superexploitation can best be assessed by the gap between workers' real wages and the profit which capital accrues and never returns to the workforce. Overall, the rate of return from the United States' investment in the Caribbean is considerably higher (31% to 14.3%) than the returns generated from investments in other parts of the world (Barry, 1984:19). In the Bahamas, almost three-fourths of households (74%) live on an annual income of $10,000. Of these households, almost all (82%) are headed by women, at least half of whom are employed in the tourist industry. In contrast, earnings from tourism contributed 61% of the total export earnings of the Bahamian state (Rosensweig, 1988:89–100). The limitations of tourism as a national economic strategy are immediately apparent with the recognition that 81 cents of every tourist dollar spent in the Bahamas finds its way back to the United States (Barry, 1984).

In the space between foreign- and state-controlled export has arisen a substantial informal economy that operates at different levels. Some elements of it are masculinized, particularly those in the drug trade that are linked to tourism. This marks another incursion on state control because people can make quick money and improve their standard of living. Drug lords can command authority and develop a horizontal patronage system that rivals that of state managers, while simultaneously remaining outside the arm of state regulation. In fact, state managers have had to deal with an erosion of their own credibility because of their complicity in the drug trade – one of the many faces of the underside of respectability (Smith, Gomez and Willes, 1984). Not labelled an illegal activity by the state, the feminized informal economy is involved in trade and marketing, relying on kinship, long-established peer networks and communal ties. Much like farmers' co-operatives, these networks provide for people's everyday needs.

It is difficult to imagine that these massive economic disjunctures with corresponding deterioration in the quality of people's daily lives, precipitated by SAP, would not provoke a major political crisis for the state. Emerging within this crisis are serious contestations to the state's right to rule. The question is how do these movements frame their opposition to the state? Even with the importance of material struggles in people's lives, one of the more crucial elements uniting these varied constituencies is the urgency to move beyond questions of survival to, as Joan French has argued, 'creating, building community, deepening the understanding of oneself and of others, developing local, regional, and international structures for communication and participation' (McAfee, 1991:188). The focus of the challenges, therefore, is to transform the nature and definition of development from profit and exploitation to holistic, participatory models, the maps of which are still being worked out (Antrobus in McAfee, 1991:187). Not surprisingly, the most sustained, organized challenges have originated within nongovernmental organizations, a loose affiliation of groups of trade unions, churches and grass-roots organizations. Farmers' co-operatives not only challenge the state with a model of collective agricultural production, very dissimilar to the corporate profit model, but also, under difficult conditions, they are doing what the state has refused to do: feed the population. A regional feminist movement in the Caribbean as a whole and specific movements in both countries have developed some of the most sustained critiques of the devastating effects of structural adjustment as state violence. They have argued that unemployment has destroyed the identity of the male 'provider' resulting in increased violence against women for which they hold the state accountable.

State Nationalism, Globalization and Privatization

State-supported globalization of capital is crucial not only because of the internal political effects I outlined earlier, but also because these international processes help to refigure definitions of masculinity and femininity and simultaneously undermine the ideological bases upon which the state organizes, separates and draws from the 'public' and 'private' domains. International practices dovetail with state ideologies about masculinity and femininity, and in particular with ideological constructions of women's work. The most significant retrenchment with the adoption of SAP has taken place in those sectors which have been historically coded as women's work: health, clinic and hospital service, caring for the sick and elderly, social services and education. As women continue their work in the home and their work in the private or public service sector, they work, in addition, to care for the sick and elderly, and to continue the education of their children without state subsidies. The state relies upon and operates within these dominant constructions of a servile femininity, perennially willing and able to serve, a femininity that can automatically fill the gaps left by the state. Quite the opposite of a 'non-productive' femininity drawn in the legislation, these are women doing work, and ironically, state work.

International ideological registers are significant in another important regard that has to do with the presumed disjuncture between the 'public' and 'private' spheres. In one sense, one of the effects of a privatized state is that it becomes somewhat insulated from 'public' demands; what was 'public' responsibility is now shifted elsewhere, in this case on to women who compensate for retrenchment in both spheres. But there is also a paradoxical collapse of this dichotomy, for the state is now relying upon the private – private capital and private households to consolidate its own quest for economic and political power. We know that the household has been an important ideological instrument for the state. It has been indispensable in the creation of the 'public' against which it can be positioned. Because it has been an important space where a particular kind of hierarchical, patriarchal power has resided, the state must move to rehabilitate this sphere by specifically recoding women's experience of domestic violence and rape within it, and generally, by disallowing any household space for lesbians. Yet state economic practices are contributing to the demise of the 'male breadwinner' especially in working-class and working-poor households which are the ones hardest hit by SAP, and in a racialized context are actually intervening to fix racial polarities as well.

We can now return to one of the central paradoxes this paper raises, that of the nationalist state legislating against certain sexualities while relying upon women's sexualized body and a political economy of desire in private capital accumulation. Tourism is the arena in which the moves to privatize the economy through foreign investment, imperial constructions of masculinity and femininity and state constructions of sexualized woman all intersect.

The significance of tourism is that it foregrounds sexual pleasure as a commodity, based in the sexualization of land (through the old imperial trope woman-as-nation) and people. The sinister drama finds expression in commercial advertising and the production of certain fetishes that get signified as 'culture'. Bahama Mama, (there is no Bahama Papa) is a buxom, caricatured, hypersensualized figure that can be bought in the Bahamas; she can also be consumed as 'hot and spicy sausage' at any 'Nice and Easy' convenient store in the United States. Tourists upon their return home can continue to be intoxicated by the Bahamas, order Bloody Mary along with Bahama Mama, alterity as instrument of pleasure. European fantasies of colonial conquest, the exotic, the erotic, the dark, the primitive, of danger, dread and desire all converge here on virgin beaches and are traced back through the contours of imperial geography.

How does one prepare citizens for self-determination and for dependency on its antithesis, tourism, the practice of servility and serviceability, the production of maids, washers, cooks? Black women who must braid white women's hair in the market as they flirt with Blackness, for African styles can only be adopted far away from home. Difference is exotically and fleetingly adopted. These are a complicated set of psycho-sexual gestures converging in this (hetero)sexual playground; this arena which Caribbean state managers see as the economy of the future; where Black masculinity manages phantasmic constructions of Black femininity, satisfying white European desire for restless adventure, satisfying white European longing for what is 'rare and intangible' (hooks, 1992:21–39).

Mobilizing Heterosexuality: Post-Colonial States and Practices of Decolonization

My analysis suggests that the archetypal source of state legitimation is anchored in the heterosexual family, the form of family crucial in the state's view to the founding of the nation. This consolidation of domesticity in the very process of nation-building is the sphere in which a certain kind of instrumental legitimation is housed. There is an evident relationship among monogamous heterosexuality (organic representation of sexuality) nationhood and citizenship. Although presumably universal and falling on *every* body, we have seen that it is not just *every* and *any* body, for *some* bodies are not productive enough for the nation. The erosion of heterosexual conjugal monogamy is a perennial source of worry for state managers and so it is invoked and deployed particularly at moments when it is threatened with extinction. Nothing should threaten this sphere; not the single woman, the lesbian, the gay man, the prostitute, the person who is HIV infected. The state must simultaneously infiltrate this domain in order to recoup its original claim to it. It must continue to legislate its existence.

To whom do state managers believe they have access in mobilizing discourses around conservative, homophobic registers? Do they believe that a large number of citizens can be mobilized in its defence? Clearly, this mobilization serves to reassure different constituencies which historically have been important anchoring points for the state, but have currently lost political ground with feminist critiques of patriarchy. It serves to reassure men, for they are the archetypal citizen, conservative elements and religious constituencies in a context in which the religious provides important explanations for daily life, and in the case of the Bahamas, the potential tourist who presumably would not encounter diseased black bodies during his travels.

With the globalization of specific definitions of morality, the state believes itself able to conform to the international, and in its view to widely accepted and respectable definitions of morality. Even with efforts to reinvoke patriarchal modes of behaviour and patterns of thinking that are familiar and secure, these nationalist states have not been able to solve their legitimation crisis.

Part of the difficulty we face as feminists doing this kind of analysis, and ironically one of the reasons the state can at least be partially successful in mobilizing heterosexuality, is the persistence of the belief in naturalized heterosexuality, the belief that it lies outside of the sphere of political and economic influence and therefore state influence. In the absence of any visible lesbian and gay movements in the Caribbean, state managers believe they can rely upon heterosexuality even more heavily. Our analyses and mobilizations of the naturalization of heterosexuality have perhaps lagged behind analyses of naturalization in other areas, like women's work, for example. We face a challenge to traverse inherited analytic boundaries that have kept us within discrete and narrow formulations. Radical lesbian and gay movements in metropolitan countries which have demystified heterosexuality, must now take on board analyses of colonization and imperialism, for the effects of these processes loop back to the centre from which they originated. These movements in metropolitan countries need to work assiduously, however, not to reproduce practices of imperialism. If feminists have analysed the masculinization of the state, it is imperative that we also analyse the heterosexualization of the state, for these are twin processes. The urgency of a research and political agenda that continues to make the processes of heterosexualization transparent, tying them to both national and international social interests cannot, therefore, be overstated. If sexualization and internationalization have been linked in the strategies of domination, *we* must link them in our strategies for liberation, although admittedly along different registers (Moraga, 1983). It might help to reduce the impulse to conflate capitalism with democracy and the more pervasive feminist theorizing of liberal *democratic* advanced capitalist states.

More work needs to be done in disentangling the state from the nation and in figuring out differing interests. If indeed our political mobilizations are located between the spaces of state and nation, even state and party, we would need to be clearer about our allegiances and the political bases of solidarity. The analysis should help point to the political responsibility feminists inside the state apparatus have to those on the outside. At the same time, we cannot diminish the intensity of our demands to make the state more accountable.

It is both analytically, and therefore politically necessary to disentangle the processes of decolonization and nation-building. In a real sense, the work of decolonization (the dismantling of the economic, political, psychic and sexual knowledges and practices that accompanied the first five hundred years of conquest) has been disrupted, especially in light of the map I have drawn of these new sexualized strategies of recolonization and the commodification of alienated sexual desire in tourism within nation-states that are infiltrated by corporate globalization politics. The work of decolonization consists as well in the decolonization of the body. Women's bodies have been ideologically dismembered within different discourses: the juridical; profit maximization; religious; and the popular.

How do we, in our alternative movements, construct a collectively imagined future that takes account of these dismemberments, fractures, migrations, exiles and displacements that have been part of these processes of domination? How do we construct home when home is not immediately understood nor instinctively accessible? Our challenge within oppositional movements is to invent home in different spaces that cross geography. We cannot afford to let the international be one-sidedly pernicious.

Note
1. M. Jacqui Alexander is currently involved in researching questions relating to the historical construction of sexuality (particularly its legal production) in the Caribbean. An anti-racist worker, she is now at the New School for Social Research in New York City where she teaches courses grounded in feminist critiques of imperialism, colonialism and heterosexuality. An essay exploring the processes of sexualization in the Bahamas is a collection (co-edited with Chandra Talpade Mohanty entitled, *Histories, Movements, Identities: Genealogies of Third World Feminism* (New York: Routledge, 1995). Projects like the one I have undertaken could only survive in an 'intellectual neighbourhood' (the phrase is Toni Morrison's). I am especially thankful to my neighbours Chandra Talpade Mohanty, Linda Carty, Honor Ford Smith, Jinny Chalmers and Mab Segrest for their keen insights, support and friendship. I also wish to thank David Trottman, Angela Robertson and the members of the *Feminist Review* Collective.

References
Anderson, Benedict. 1983. *Imagined Communities: Reflections on the Origin and Spread of Nationalism*. London: Verso.
Barry, Tom, et al. 1984. *The Other Side of Paradise: Foreign Control in the Caribbean*. New York: Grove.
Brecher, Jeremy, et al. 1993. *Global Visions: Beyond the New World Order*. Boston: South End Press.
Burawoy, Michael. 1982. *Manufacturing Consent: Changes in the Labor Process Under Monopoly Capitalism*. Chicago: University of Chicago Press.
Cohen, Ed. 1989. Legislating the Norm: From Sodomy to Gross Indecency. *The South Atlantic Quarterly* 88(1): 181–218.
Commission of Inquiry. 1984. *Report of the Commission of Inquiry*. Bahamas: Bahamas Government Printing Department.
Craton, Michael. 1986. *A History of the Bahamas*. Canada: San Salvador.
Department Of Statistics. 1987. *A Collection of Statistics on Women in the Bahamas 1979–1985*. Bahamas: Department of Statistics.
———. 1991. *Labour Force and the Household Income Report 1989*. Bahamas: Department of Statistics.
Enloe, Cynthia. 1990. *Bananas, Beaches and Bases: Making Feminist Sense of International Politics*. Berkeley: University of California Press.
Fanon, Frantz. 1977. *The Wretched of the Earth*. New York: Grove.
Gibbon, Peter. 1992. Population and Poverty in the Changing Ideology of the World Bank. Stockholm: PROP Publication Series No. 2.
Goveia, Elsa. 1970. The West Indian Slave Laws of the 18th Century. Mona: University of the West Indies.
Hall, Stuart. 1994. Race Matters: Black Americans, US Terrain. Paper presented at Conference. Princeton University.
Henry, Ralph and Williams, Gwendolyn. 1991. Structural Adjustment and Gender in Trinidad and Tobago. In *Social and Occupational Stratification in Contemporary Trinidad and Tobago*, ed. Selwyn Ryan. Jamaica: ISER.
Hooks, Bell. 1992. *Black Looks Race and Representation*. Boston: South End Press.
Irigaray, Luce. 1985. *This Sex Which is Not One*. New York: Cornell University Press.
Laws of Trinidad and Tobago. 1986. *The Sexual Offences Act*. Port-of-Spain: Government Printing Office.
Mcafee, Kathy. 1991. *Storm Signals: Structural Adjustment and Development Alternatives in the Caribbean*. Boston: South End.
Mcdanlel, Lorna. 1986. Madame Phillip-O: Reading the Returns of an 18th Century 'Free Mulatto Woman' of Grenada. Unpublished manuscript.
Mercer, Kobena and Julien, Isaac. 1988. Race, Sexual Politics and Black Masculinity: A Dossier. In *Male Order: Unwrapping Masculinity*, ed. Rowena Chapman and Jonathan Rutherford. London: Lawrence & Wishart.
Mohanty, Chandra Talpade, et al. 1991. *Third World Women and the Politics of Feminism*. Bloomington: Indiana University.
Moraga, Cherríe. 1983. *Loving in the War Years*. Boston: South End Press.
Morrison, Toni. 1992. *Race-ing Justice, En-gendering Power: Essays on Anita Hill, Clarence Thomas, and the Construction of Social Reality*. New York: Pantheon.
Mosse, George L. 1985. *Nationalism and Sexuality: Middle-Class Morality and Sexual Norms in Modern Europe*. Madison: The University of Wisconsin Press.

Parker, Andrew, et al. 1992. *Nationalisms and Sexualities*. New York: Routledge.
Parliament of The Bahamas. 1991. *The Sexual Offences and Domestic Violence Act*. Nassau.
Pindling, L. O. Hon. 1972. Speech at the Opening Session of the Bahamas Independence Conference. London: Her Majesty's Stationery Office.
Reddock, Rhoda. 1984. Women, Labour and Struggle in 20th Century Trinidad and Tobago: 1898–1960. Amsterdam (Ph.D dissertation).
Robson, Ruthann. 1992. *Lesbian (Out)law: Survival Under the Rule of Law*. Ithaca: Firebrand.
Rosensweig, Jeffrey A. 1988. Elasticities of Substitution in Caribbean Tourism. *Journal of Development Economics* 29(2): 89–100.
Rothenberg, Jane and Wishner, Amy. 1978. Focus on Trinidad. *NACLA* (July, August): 16–29.
Saunders, Gail. 1985. *Slavery in The Bahamas*. Bahamas: The Nassau Guardian.
Truong, Thanh-Dam. 1990. *Sex, Money and Morality*. London: Zed Press.
Williams, Eric. 1960. We Are Independent. In *Forged From the Love of Liberty: Selected Speeches of Dr Eric Williams*, ed. Paul K. Sutton. Longman: Caribbean.

Song for Puerto Rico

Nicholás Guillén

Puerto Rico, member by membership
dismembered, how are you?
To the sound of guitars and coco-palms,
beneath the moon, beside the sea,
the honor is sweet to stroll arm in arm
on the arm of Uncle Sam!
In what language do you understand me?
Should I address you finally
in yes,
in *sí*,
in *bien*,
in well,
in *mal*,
in bad ... in very bad?

They who kill you swear
you're happy. Is that true?
Your pale countenance burns and
the anemia of your gaze takes on a fatal glow
as you masticate a babble
half of Spanish, half of slang;
when they stuck you in Korea with one shove
you never knew for whom you killed:
whether for yes,
for *sí*,
for *bien*,
for well,
for *mal*,
for bad ... for very bad!

Oh, how well I know your foe,
for we have the same thing here:
a partner in blood and sugar,
a member by membership dismembered.
United States *y* Puerto Rico,
that is to say, New York City *con* San Juan,
Manhattan and *Borinquen*...noose and neck;
it comes to little more than that:
not yes,
or *sí*,
or *bien*,
or well,
but *mal*,
but bad ... but very bad!

The Plantation

Plantation Society:
Toward a General Theory of Caribbean Society*

George Beckford

Every society is a product of the particular historical forces that give it shape and form. The thesis of this paper is that modern Caribbean society displays structural forms that are a direct legacy of the slave plantation system. This legacy provides the single most important clue for an understanding of contemporary Caribbean society.

The plantation was the chief instrument of European colonization and exploitation in the Caribbean, the U.S. South, the Guianas, and Northeast Brazil — an area described by Wagley as Plantation America;[1] in certain islands of the Indian and Pacific Oceans; and in Ceylon, Malaya, Indonesia and the Philippines. In all these places the structural characteristics of the plantation system have persisted and they define a particular social framework. "Plantation economy and society" is an appropriate general description of this social framework. Elsewhere, I have explored at length its economic dimension.[2] This paper briefly considers its social and political dimensions. Although the Caribbean is the main point of reference, the general conclusions apply as well to other plantation societies to which some consideration is given.

Typically, a plantation is a unit of agricultural production with a specific type of economic organization characterized by a large resident labour force of unskilled workers who are directed by a small supervisory staff. As well, the plantation is a community, its social structure and the pattern of interpersonal relations within it reflecting to a large extent the authority structure governing the pattern of economic organization. Historically, plantations came to be established in places where land was abundant relative to population. Labour was imported (to carry out production tasks) on a scale that irreversibly changed the demographic picture in most places. The terms on which such labour was incorporated into the new locations involved a high degree of coercion and control; and thereafter determined social and political relationships in very precise ways. So that wherever plantations came to engross most of the arable land in a particular country, the resulting society consisted of a series of plantation communities.

Whether or not the economic dominance of plantations has persisted to the present time, societies with this historical legacy continue to reflect the plantation influence. All types of plantations have certain features in common: they cover relatively large areas; numerous unskilled workers are involved; decision making is highly centralized; the pattern of management organization is authoritarian; and the workers are separated from the decision makers by social and cultural differences. Within the plantation community there exists a rigid pattern of social stratification based on a caste system that separates owners and managers (normally white people of European extract) from the workers (normally Africans or East Indians).

The traditional plantation is a *total* economic institution. It binds every one in its embrace to the one task of executing the will of its owner or owners. And because it is omnipotent and omnipresent in the lives of those living within its confines, it is also a total social institution.

Social relations within the plantation community are determined by the economic organization that governs production. Now imagine an economy composed of only plantation producing units. In such a case, the social structure and distribution of political power in the country as a whole would merely be a larger reproduction of that existing on the individual plantation. No country is purely an aggregation of plantations, in fact. But, as the discussion in this paper indicates, the plantation economies and sub-economies of the world reveal social and political characteristics almost identical to those found within the individual plantation community. Thus we can appropriately define plantation society as a particular class of society with distinguishing characteristics of social structure and political organization, and laws of motion governing social change. The rest of this paper develops this point.

DEMOGRAPHIC CHARACTERISTICS OF THE PLANTATION ECONOMICS

The present day composition of population in all the plantation economies of the world is a direct result of the movement of labour which the plantation system effected in the past. All the African people in the New World were brought here by the plantation. So also were all the East Indians now living in this hemisphere and in other plantation economies of the Indian and Pacific Oceans and Southeast Asia (including many of those in Ceylon). Cultural plurality is a characteristic feature of all plantation societies because the plantation brought together people of different races and cultural backgrounds to carry out the task of production. Everywhere in the plantation world today we find national population groups that consist of people and sub-groups different in race. We are not here concerned with the fact that differences in racial composition of population exist in countries where plantations are not dominant. The argument is simply that the dominance of plantations in any particular situation is *alone* a necessary and sufficient condition for the existence of a mixed population base.

Before the arrival of the plantation, the plantation areas of the New World had been peopled by the indigenous Amerindians. The plantation brought white Europeans at first, then brought black people from Africa as slaves, then brought the East Indian people as indentured labourers. The indigenous Indians never managed to survive the European conquest. And today African people, East Indians, and white people make up the populations in the New World plantation economies—roughly in the same proportion as existed on an individual plantation. Throughout the West Indies, for example, white people are a very small proportion while black people make up the bulk of the population because numerous workers were associated with individual plantations which normally have one or a few white families as owners, managers, and skilled workers. Similarly, the relative importance of Africans and East Indians in a particular country and the distribution of these two races throughout the region are linked directly with the plantation. For example, plantations in the smaller West Indian islands did not need to rely on indentured labour after Emancipation because the ex-slaves there had little choice but to continue working on the plantation as all the land had already been alienated. But in Jamaica, Trinidad and Guyana indenture was necessary and East Indians were brought in. That East Indians are a relatively small proportion of population in Jamaica in comparison with the other two reflects the fact that the resource situation was far less open in Jamaica after the abolition of slavery. The sugar industries of Trinidad and Guyana developed rather late and, for the most part, after slavery had been abolished. Consequently, the plantation need for indentured East Indian labour was greater there. These workers were brought in during the period 1836 to 1917; and today East Indians are more than 50 per cent of the population in Guyana and roughly 40 per cent in Trinidad.

Elsewhere indentured migration of East Indians also rapidly transformed the composition of populations. In Mauritius, this migration began in 1835; ten years later Indians made up a third of the island's population and by 1861 the proportion had reached two-thirds, remaining about the same up to the present time. In Fiji, indentured migration of East Indians lasted from 1879 to 1916; and today Indians outnumber the indigenous Fijians, being about one-half of the total population. To a lesser degree, the same pattern obtains for Ceylon, Malaya, and Indonesia. The Ceylon plantations drew large numbers of contract indentured workers from the south of India—mainly Tamils. Today these Indians are over 10 per cent of Ceylon's population and they are roughly 70 per cent of the labour force working on plantations. Malaya also recruited plantation labour from the same part of India beginning in the late nineteenth century. Between 1911 and 1920, these labourers were brought in at the rate of 90,000 a year. Although the indenture system was ended in 1910, the *kangany* or gang system of recruitment from India continued until the Government of India terminated it in 1938. Today the Indians are over 10 per cent of the population in Malaya; and most of them work on rubber and tea plantations.[3]

In the plantation sub-economies — that is, the U.S. South, N.E. Brazil and lowland Central America — population composition can also be linked directly with the plantation influence. The predominantly black population of the Caribbean lowlands of the Central American republics came from the Caribbean islands in the service of the plantation. And the substantial proportions of black people in the populations of the United States and Brazil are a legacy of the slave plantation. In these two countries, the proportion of black people in the plantation sub-economies is much less than would normally have been because of internal migration to other parts of the country. Today, black people are more than 10 per cent of the total population of the United States. If all these people were still concentrated in the plantation South they would represent well over half of that region's total population. In Brazil, black people are about a third of the total population which is equivalent to more than half the population of the plantation Northeast.[4] It should be pointed out, however, that these two areas differ somewhat from the other old plantation areas of the New World. In the United States South numerous "poor whites" had been involved in the plantation system (or were within its pale); while in Northeast Brazil, the indigenous Indians remained a relatively important group since they were able to minimize contact with Europeans in the vast territory available. Consequently, black people do not constitute as high a proportion of the population of these two areas as in the West Indies.

In general, then, we can conclude that the basic population characteristics of all the plantation economies of the world reflect the plantation influence very significantly. Different races that comprise the plantation work force in different countries represent significant shares of national or regional population. The presence of Africans and East Indians in the New World, and East Indians in most other plantation areas is a direct legacy of the plantation. So also is most of the European presence. In addition to these two groups, we should also expect to find a sizeable proportion classified by the censuses as "mixed". These people represent the outcome of sexual intercourse between the white plantation owners and managers and non-white women from the plantation work force. The actual percentage distribution between these three basic ethnic groups will of course vary from place to place; but these variations can be explained in terms of the relevant history of the plantation system in particular places.

The population mix that derives from the influence of the plantation system directly influences the character of society in many ways. For one thing, the different races bring with them different cultures; and cultural plurality is the result. In every plantation society in the world we find two or more racial and cultural groups living side by side but having a minimum of cultural intercourse. Black people throughout the New World plantation belt have a cultural identity distinct from that of the white plantation owner and manager groups. In Trinidad and Guyana the East Indian and African groups live together with different cultural traditions. The same is true of the "Fijians" and the Indians, the Sinhalese and the Tamils in Ceylon, the Indians and the white planter class in Mauritius, and the Malays, Chinese, Indians and white people in Malaya. However, in spite of these basic differences in cultural traditions among the groups, they manage somehow to live together. And, as will be argued subsequently, it appears that a welding influence can be attributed to the plantation system. In every instance, however, the weld is continuously under pressure because of the underlying inherent social and cultural differences.

SOCIAL ORGANIZATION AND STRUCTURE IN PLANTATION SOCIETY

The plantation influence can be traced almost directly in every important aspect of social life in the plantation societies of the world. As with plantation community, plantation society derives an ordering of social status of different groups and individuals within a country which is directly correlated with occupational status and rank in the authority structure of the plantation itself. Of course, correlation alone does not establish causality. To establish this we need to explore the historical legacy somewhat to determine what forces have moulded the pattern of social organization which we find today in these societies. The New World experience perhaps provides the clearest illustration of plantation influence on social structure. Since this area has the longest history of continuous plantation influence, the experience there should provide useful insights into the general phenomenon.

The slave plantations of the New World brought together a few white people from Europe as owners, and large numbers of black people from Africa as forced labourers. The latter came from different parts of the west coast of Africa and were generally an odd mixture of people from different tribal and cultural backgrounds who, most often, did not speak the same language; the slave groups were mixed in terms of sex but men usually outnumbered the women, as more of them were required for the arduous task of sugar and cotton plantation work. On the other hand, the white Europeans who came were chiefly plantation owners, managers and skilled labourers; and these were mostly males who viewed their association with the plantation as a temporary affair. The two groups were thrown together with one single purpose—production of the plantation crop. This meant, therefore, that the structure of authority established for this exercise would influence the entire social order on the plantation. We have already noted that the slave plantation had the character of a total economic and social institution. Raymond Smith describes such institutions in the following way:

> 'Total institutions' are organised groups with well-defined boundaries and with a marked internal hierarchical structure approaching an internal caste system. Examples would be asylum inmates and staff, prisoners and wardens, officers and men on board a ship at sea, slaves and masters ...
>
> It is characteristic of total institutions that people enter them as already socially formed human beings with a culture and a set of attitudes which need to be reformed so that the inmate can be 'handled' as a lunatic, a monk, a prisoner, a slave or whatever it might be. Mechanisms are brought into play designed to effect a clean break with the past and a destruction of the inmate's old self so that a new set of attitudes—a new 'identity'—can be imposed.[5]

The slaves were put through a process known as "seasoning" to adjust them for work on the plantation. And since then, right up to the present, the black experience in the New World has been a continuous process of acculturation and socialization to the norms of the plantation system.

The social structure of the slave plantation took shape from the social organization necessary for production. White European planters and administrators stood at the top; and were separated by a system of caste which placed the black slaves firmly at the bottom. An intermediate group of skilled white people also existed. And among the black people there emerged a group of racial and cultural half-castes resulting from the exploits of white males with black females. This group was generally more privileged than the pure blacks and frequently made up the staff of house servants whose tasks were less arduous than those of other blacks.[6] Slave plantation society as a whole was simply made up of individual plantation communities. As Smith suggested, "one may say that this was a segmentary society with the plantations constituting a simple linear series of segments having little or no organic inter-relation."[7] The society as a whole was therefore rigidly stratified by race and colour directly correlated with occupational status on the plantation; and without any kind of social mobility whatever.

On each plantation, the white owner or administrator was lord and master; and his mansion was the centre of social life for all within the community. All decisions affecting the lives of the black people emanated from there. No church, state or other social institution had direct access to the slaves. Church facilities were provided on the plantation by the master who also exercised juridicial and state functions. The political order was despotic with commands issued by the master to the slaves through an overseer. Slaves were herded together as an undifferentiated mass in compounds that had a kind of village character. Because the slaves were drawn from different cultures, they had to develop a language on the plantation in order to communicate with each other. And a common language was also necessary to facilitate the chain of command from master to slave. In the circumstances what emerged was a language which was a simplification and modification of the tongue of the masters. These are the so-called "creole" languages of the plantation societies today. This pattern of acculturation was to have a lasting effect on the lives of black people. For, as Thompson points out:

> Language is bound up with the system of social control. With its acquisition there tends to develop at the same time an acceptance of the situation. The meanings of the terms of the language develop in the general atmosphere of authority and against the background of co-operative activity involved in agricultural production. As this takes place, authority and obedience are determined more by moral and less by material factors.[8]

In the process, black people were increasingly emasculated culturally and socialized toward the culture of the planter class. However, they did succeed in retaining some of their original culture; and this was blended with the other to create what is now a clearly distinct and separate culture within plantation society today. Slave plantation society, therefore had certain distinctive features; a caste system based on race, rigidly stratified social structure based on occupational status on the plantation and divided along race and colour lines, and cultural plurality with integrative elements deriving from the common destiny to production of the crop for everyone in the plantation community. This last feature of the system is one which has largely escaped the notice of most plantation scholars. Yet it is one that is of great importance in explaining certain aspects of plantation societies today. The different groups on the slave plantation interacted with each other in one main area of activity—production of the crop; and from day to day, season by season, year in and year out, this was the chief bond between them. Because production of the crop was the only reason why these groups were brought together, it is not surprising that this dominated their lives. For the white masters who owned the slaves and governed the plantations, the pattern of tolerable social organization was one that would maximize profits on production. Rigid control of the labour supply was critical and this involved control over the movement of slaves in space and status.

Although slavery has been formally abolished for about four generations or so, the basic structure of plantation society in the New World remains today very much what it was during slavery. The reasons for this are not very hard to find. The white planter class monopolized the means of production on the land and were therefore in a position to maintain their dominant position. In addition, their ranks were reinforced with the arrival of non-agricultural enterprises owned and managed by their kith and kin in more recent times; so the means of production were further concentrated among that group. On the other hand, there was little that black people could do to improve their lot. Scarcity of land limited independent peasant production which meant continued dependence on the plantation. Barring emigration, the only significant scope for social mobility open to them was education. During slavery educational opportunities had been restricted. Slaves were only trained in skills useful to the plantation—artisan skills which could make the slave a more productive and contented servant. Illiteracy was almost universal among them because their masters believed that skills of reading and writing would not increase their productive value, and might even put ideas of insurrection in their heads! After Emancipation, educational opportunities for the ex-slaves opened up somewhat. But the assimilation of what was being offered served further to acculturate black people to the culture of the dominant white class. And this served simply to expand the ranks of the intermediate social group rather than to effect any significant change in the general social structure.

Among the ranks of black people educational opportunities opened up more for the half-castes than for the rest. What limited social mobility they could achieve as a result depended in large measure on the extent to which they could succeed in divorcing the culture of black people and in assimilating that of the whites. This set the stage for a dynamic process by which black people sought social mobility by aspiring continuously to a European way of life. Education, residence, manners of speech and dress, religious beliefs and practice, social values and attitudes, and general life style, all served to distinguish those black people who had "made it" from those who had not. The white sub-culture of plantation society was thereby reinforced by the joining of the club by some of the blacks. But even so the caste line still prevents their total acceptance by the dominant white class.[9] The sub-culture of the rest of the black people has remained basically that which they developed on the slave plantation. Consequently, plantation societies today maintain the traditional features of stratification by colour and race, as well as a certain degree of social integration. The latter derives from the fact that all black people in these societies regard the white European culture as superior and, in a dynamic sense, they all aspire to it. Those still fully immersed in the plantation subculture aspire to getting their children "out" even if they see no possibility of getting "out" themselves.

We find therefore that the plantation societies of the New World have the rather unique characteristic of exhibiting both cultural pluralism and social integration. This curious blend derives from the fact that cultural pluralism is operative in a static sense while the motivations and aspirations of people exhibit a kind of social integration. In terms of analysing the dynamics of social change the latter is the more appropriate concept. But in describing the social structure at any point in time cultural pluralism seems more relevant. Our general conclusion that the basic structure of plantation society in the New World today remains much the same as that of the slave era finds support in numerous studies by sociologists, social anthropologists and historians.[10] And of course those who live in these societies know it well.

The predominant social characteristic of all plantation areas of the world is the existence of a class-caste system based on differences in the racial origins of plantation workers on the one hand and owners on the other. And it is being argued here that for all practical purposes, this caste line still exists in New World plantation society today. It separates the superordinate white planter and commercial classes and other white people in these societies from the subordinate class of black people. All that has happened since Emancipation is that the caste line has shifted from a basically horizontal position which kept all black people more or less in the single class category of plantation labourers. Since Emancipation, increasing educational opportunities for black people and diversification of the structure of the plantation economies have made some modification to the class structure in these plantation societies. But in every instance race has been an important factor in the class divisions.

An important aspect of the post-Emancipation evolution of class structure throughout the New World plantation areas is that among the underprivileged black people, there developed within the caste group a class structure which placed those with most physical and cultural likeness to the superordinate white classes at the top, and those with the least at the bottom of an internal class hierarchy. Consequently, within this group race is supplemented by the degree of assimilation of white culture patterns in determining class positions.

POLITICAL ORGANIZATION AND DISTRIBUTION OF POWER

As in other aspects of social life already considered, the nature of political organization in plantation societies today can be linked directly with the plantation. Political organization and state power are based upon principles of authority and control (law). So is the plantation. Edgar Thompson provides a good summary of the position when he states that "in no other way except through authority and law can a group whose members represent different racial and cultural backgrounds be made to act as a unit...In fact, the plantation is best defined not in terms of territory or of agriculture but in terms of the authority of the planter."[11] We have noted already that the individual plantation is an authoritarian institution in which power is centralized in the hands of the plantation owner or manager. This power involves decision making relating not only to production within the territory but also to all aspects of the life of those in the community. Consequently, in societies which largely consist of plantation communities, we should expect to find the same characteristics of political organization on the individual plantation reflected in the larger society. The thesis we advance in this connection is that all plantation societies have in common the following features: concentration of power among a small planter class, and highly centralized political administrative structures (government).

This legacy of the plantation persists today everywhere we find plantation societies; and strong central government is characteristic of all these places. Given the distribution of economic and social power, local government can only emerge if there is adequate social organization at the local level; but it appears that everywhere plantations created loose and weak local communities. The reason for this is, basically, that strong community organization tends only to emerge in situations where smaller units of people are bound firmly together. The family is such a unit. But the plantation system is generally not based on family units; indeed, if anything, the tendency is more towards family-less people. The only unifying element within plantation community is the authority of the planter. Studies of Caribbean societies have revealed that these generally follow the pattern just described. The link with the plantation system is summarized by Wagley as follows:

> The lack of a strong and well-defined local community in the Caribbean region is the result of slavery and a plantation economy. The decimation of the Indians in the region precluded any possible aboriginal basis for local community life. The transferred population of African slaves from many tribes and nations were unable under conditions of slavery to form communities, although it is notable that escaped slaves in Jamaica and on the mainland found a basis for community organization ...While paternalism and common residence often united the slaves of a particular plantation into a neighborhood, they were unable to develop a full community life. Even after abolition the plantation system continued to exert an influence unfavorable to the development of a strong and cohesive local community ... Brazil, and to a certain extent the southern United States, share this historical heritage of the plantation and slavery and the resulting weak, divided, and amorphous community. One is tempted to generalize that wherever the plantation and slave system were present, the rural community could not become an efficient and cohesive social unit.[12]

We advance the hypothesis that the tentative conclusion reached by Wagley in the above applies not only to plantation societies with a legacy of slavery but to all plantation societies.

In spite of considerable diversification in the New World plantation economies since Emancipation, in spite of major constitutional changes in the political status of individual countries, and in spite of dramatic changes in procedures of selecting governments (involving the enfranchisement of black people who earlier had no vote), we still find that everywhere highly centralized government administration is in evidence. Part of the reason for this is that economic and social power has remained in the hands of the white planter and commercial classes which more recently have been reinforced by industrialists of the same ethnic origin. We find therefore that in those areas where full enfranchisement of black people has been delayed, legislatures still are predominantly comprised of people of the new "planter" class. Such is the case in the U.S. South and Brazil. For example, Taylor in a study of a Brazilian sugar plantation region, notes that "In 1965, every one of Pernambuco's twenty-nine usineiro families had a close relative or family member in *both* the federal congress and the Pernambuco assembly."[13]

Where full enfranchisement of black people came earlier and where these people make up the bulk of the population, as in the West Indies, a different pattern of racial composition of legislatures is observed; but the basic structure of political organization remains the same. Since the 1940's black people in the West Indies have had the right to vote in government elections. At first, the white planter class directly faced the electorate but they met with resounding defeat as the tide of the black vote overwhelmed them. The strategy then adopted was withdrawal from direct political involvement to an indirect role of providing financial backing for black political aspirants in what emerged as black political parties and trade unions. So today we find throughout the West Indies government administrations comprised of black people who essentially exercise authority and control on behalf of their financial backers—the white planter, commercial and industrial classes that remain for the most part in that background of political activity.[14] Given the terms of social mobility for black people in the system, as earlier described, the alliance between the dominant power group and the de-culturated blacks has been easy and natural. For the latter have as much contempt for the "unrefined" masses of black people as the dominant group.

The two patterns of racial composition of government administration described for the West Indies on the one hand, and Brazil and the United States on the other, are representative of the situation in all the plantation societies of the world today. Wherever there is full enfranchisement, the subordinate racial group has its representatives in government legislatures but these representatives do not rely financially on the group they represent; and have to depend on support from the superordinate economic and social group. This constrains their freedom fully to represent the interests of the subordinate group. Where full enfranchisement has not been yet achieved, the superordinate groups still directly control the legislative process. The result in either case is the same—real political and legislative power still resides with the superordinate group among whom economic and social power is concentrated. As in all societies, the distribution of real political power is identical to the pattern of distribution of economic and social power.

PLANTATION SOCIETY — A SYNTHESIS

The structural features of plantation society, outlined in the foregoing sections of this paper, indicate sufficient uniqueness that it seems necessary to treat "plantation society" as a particular type of society. Plantation society has properties which distinguish it clearly from, say, peasant society, feudal society, urban society, and other such types which social scientists have isolated for particular study. Its own special type of social and political organization sets it apart from other kinds of societies in the world today.

Plantation society is a plural society. It consists of different racial and cultural groups which are brought together only in the realm of economic activity. This single common bond provides the integrative element. The particular nature of this common economic activity determines the force and character of what social integration exists. On the plantation itself the common economic activity is production of the plantation crop. The plantation owner or manager is the immediate embodiment of the superordinate group in the wider society; and the plantation workers of the subordinate group. The economic welfare of each depends on the other. The two groups are therefore in a mutually dependent economic relationship. And since decision making resides with the owner or manager, it is the plantation "great house" that symbolizes the integrating force. In addition, because the social structure pyramids to the planter class, the social aspirations of lower status groups in the society are directed toward the social achievement of that class. One element of social integration in the society as a whole is, therefore, to be found in the area of achievement motivation.

Another element of social integration is nationalism. Plantation economy is dependent on metropolitan economy. The crop that binds different groups together in plantation society is destined for sale in metropolitan markets, Consequently, the fortunes of all groups in plantation society are bound up with relationships between plantation economy and metropolitan economy. Common attitudes concerning relationship with the rest of the world, and in particular with the relevant metropole, are to be found among all groups that make up plantation society. Although the planter class monopolize power internally, they need to marshall the support of other groups to face any outside threat to their economic interest. And since their interests in this connection coincide with that of other groups, the society usually stands together in these matters.[15]

We conclude that the elements of social integration in plantation society are to be found in three main areas: economic production, achievement motivation, and nationalism. The question that now arises is whether the degree of social integration provided by these forces is strong enough to withstand the disintegrative elements that derive from social and cultural plurality. The answer to this must be equivocal: that it depends on the nature of the pressures on or within the society as a whole at any particular point in time. Whenever pressures emanating from outside are light, internal conflict is more likely to occur. But heavy external pressure may or may not stimulate the integrative mechanism; it all depends on the nature of these pressures. For example, a prolonged period of low prices for the plantation crop is likely to heighten workers' mistrust of the plantation owners in addition to the squeeze this puts on their already low levels of living.[16] Internal social tension is likely to increase in the circumstances. All that we can say with certainty is that plantation society will necessarily exhibit a condition of underlying social tension at all times; and that internal crisis will *be* a recurrent feature in the development of this kind of society. These crises are also likely to involve racial divisions. This follows from the particular grouping of production into castes as well as from the consideration that as the society as a whole is threatened with disintegration each component finds greater security within its own racial contingent.

Furnivall arrives at similar general conclusions in his study of Indonesia, which he describes as a plural economy and society. He notes that plural economy differs from homogeneous economy because (1) whereas social demand in the latter is common to the whole society, there are two or more distinct and rival complexes of social demand in plural economy; (2) production in plural economy is grouped into castes; and (3) in plural economy, further sectionalization of demand follows when each of the constituent social demands ceases to embrace the whole scope of social life, and becomes concentrated on those aspects relating only to the separate province. The difficulty of achieving social integration is posed in the following way:

> This distribution of production among racial castes aggravates the inherent sectionalism of demand; for a community which is confined to certain economic functions finds it more difficult to apprehend the social needs of the country as a whole.[17]

Furnivall goes on to note that the basic consideration is that "In a plural society...the community tends to be organized for production rather than for social life." As contrasted to the situation in a homogeneous community, this results in abnormal conditions which create a kind of nationalism in each section that "sets one community against the other so as to emphasize the plural character of the society and aggravate its instability, thereby enhancing the need for it to be held together by some force exerted from outside."[18]

The argument is heightened by the observation that nationalism in plural society is itself a disruptive force which tends to disintegrate, rather than consolidate the social order. It is instructive to quote Furnivall at some length on this score because he highlights a fundamental problem confronting all plantation societies today.

Democratic principles imply that the preponderance of voting power shall be entrusted to the people; yet economic power remains with the other classes, and chiefly with the Europeans... we have the economic rivalry of town and country, capital and labour, industry and agriculture, aggravated by racial difference; and with economic power on the one side and voting power on the other side, the future of the country under the accepted principle of Nationalism can hardly be envisaged with composure. The principle of Nationalism provides no solution in itself, for, in a plural society, nationalism is in effect internationalism.[19]

This generalization seems applicable to all plantation societies of the world today. This is not surprising because Furnivall arrived at these conclusions from a study of Indonesia which we have identified as one of our class of plantation society. In every such society, we find the recurrent feature of serious internal conflict existing alongside rampant nationalism. The conflict situations between Indians and Africans in Guyana (and to a lesser extent Trinidad); Tamils and Sinhalese in Ceylon; Indians and Fijians in Fiji; Chinese, Malays, Indians, and Europeans in Malaya; Indians and Europeans in Mauritius; and between white people and black people throughout the New World are examples of the universality of this phenomenon among plantation societies.

Exceptions to this general phenomenon are to be found perhaps in those plantation societies where state ownership of the producing units is dominant. Cuba, for example. In such instances, the distribution of economic, social, and political power has been altered from the traditional pattern described in the present paper. Because the state now monopolizes power, sectional social demands are more likely to be integrated and internal conflict less likely to occur. Even so conflict can hardly be avoided. Much depends on the manner in which state power is manipulated. For example, if state power is used to redress the traditional distribution of power this will alienate the traditionally dominant group and thereby generate internal conflict. This has been the case in Cuba and the former dominant group there has been forced into exile but continue to fan the flames of internal conflict in various ways. It seems then that every type of plantation society fits the general pattern of internal social conflict in spite of the presence of nationalism.

We must conclude, therefore, that the strongest elements of social integration in plantation society are to be found in the areas of economic production and achievement motivation. Individuals in every group are bound by their dependence on each other for economic survival. Their source of bread is the same. And they all want the same things in life. So we find common demands for social services, such as education and health; and common aspirations for material things associated with a Great House life style, such as elaborate housing and consumer durables. This level of social integration becomes tenuous during periods of crisis; but otherwise, provides a sufficient base for holding the society together.

The basic problem goes much deeper than this. It is that the nature of social and political arrangements create several biases toward a continuous state of underdevelopment. Inherent social instability impedes investment; the rigid pattern of social stratification restricts mobility; the concentration of social, economic and political power prevents the emergence of a highly motivated population; and racial discrimination inhibits the fullest use of the society's human resources. And, as I have demonstrated elsewhere, the economic environment further reinforces this bias toward underdevelopment.

The implications are clear. The major conclusion we can derive is that Caribbean economy and society can move forward to provide a just existence for its peoples only if the plantation foundations on which the contemporary society rests are completely destroyed. How that can be achieved goes beyond the bounds of the present paper.[20]

Acknowledgement
*This paper is extracted from a chapter of my book, *Plantations and Poverty in the Third World* (Kingston and Oxford: Institute of Social and Economic Research of the UWI and Oxford University Press, 1970). A fuller treatment with comparative material is to be found in Chapter 3 of that book; in particular, the plantation influence on black people in different parts of the New World is explored in more detail there.

Notes
1. Charles Wagley, 'Plantation America – A Culture Sphere,' in *Caribbean Studies – A Symposium*, ed. Vera Rubin (Kingston: Institute of Social and Economic Research, University College of the West Indies, 1957).
2. George L. Beckford, *Plantations and Poverty in the Third World* (Kingston and Oxford: Institute of Social and Economic Research and Oxford University Press, 1970).
3. William Morgan, *Economic Survey of the Tea Plantation Industry* (Geneva: International Federation of Plantation, Agricultural and Allied Workers, 1963), 28, 46–47.
4. There are about 22 million black people in the United States as a whole whereas the figure for the plantation South is about 39 million. In Brazil, race is officially an elusive concept. The estimate of one-third is based on what the census defines as 'black' and 'pardo' which includes black people of mixed ancestry.

5. R.T. Smith, 'Social Stratification, Cultural Pluralism and Integration in West Indian Societies,' in *Caribbean Integration*, ed. S. Lewis and T.G. Mathews (Rio Piedras, Puerto Rico: Institute of Caribbean Studies, 1967), 230.
6. The structure described here is a simplification of what obtained in fact. But the abstraction is fairly representative of the situation in most cases. For a detailed exposition on the social structure of the slave plantation, see H. Orlando Patterson, *The Sociology of Slavery* (London: MacGibbon & Kee, 1967). For modifications of the general pattern described here, see, for example, W.E. Moore and R.M. Williams, 'Stratification in the Ante-Bellum South,' *American Sociological Review*, June 1942.
7. R.T. Smith, 229.
8. Edgar Thompson, 'The Plantation: The Physical Basis of Traditional Race Relations,' in *Race Relations and the Race Problem, ed.* Edgar Thompson (Durham, N.C.: Duke University Press, 1939), 211.
9. As will be argued below, we maintain that the caste line still exists in all New World plantation societies. The distinction between the caste system now operative in the West Indies and Brazil as compared with that in the United States is simply one that reflects differences in the definition of race. Whereas in the US it is 'physical race' that is critical, in the West Indies and Brazil 'social race' is the operative factor.
10. In this connection see the following: for the West Indies, R.T. Smith, op. cit. and his *British Guiana* (London: Oxford University Press, 1962); Lloyd Braithwaite, 'Social Stratification in Trinidad,' *Social and Economic Studies*, October 1953; M.G Smith, *The Plural Society in the British West Indies* (Berkeley and Los Angeles: University of California Press, 1965); and Elsa Goveia, *Slave Society in the British Leeward Islands at the end of the Eighteenth Century* (New Haven, Connecticut: Yale University Press, 1965). For the Spanish Caribbean, see Charles Wagley and Marvin Harris, 'A Typology of Latin American Sub-cultures,' *American Anthropologist*, June 1955 and Julián Steward, ed., *The People of Puerto Rico* (Urbana, Illinois: University of Illinois Press, 1957). For Brazil, see H.W. Hutchinson, *Village and Plantation Life in Northeastern Brazil* (Seattle, Washington: University of Washington Press, 1957). For the US South, see W.E. Moore and R.M. Williams, 'Stratification in the Ante-Bellum South,' *American Sociological Review*, June 1942, and Morton Rubin, *Plantation County* (Chapel Hill, North Carolina: University of North Carolina Press, 1951).
11. Edgar T. Thompson, 'The Plantation: The Physical Basis of Traditional Race Relations,' in *Race Relations and the Race Problem: A Definition and an Analysis* (Durham, NC: Duke University Press, 1939), 192–93.
12. Charles Wagley, 'Recent Studies of Caribbean Local Societies,' in *The Caribbean: Natural Resources*, ed. Curtis Wilgus (Gainesville, Florida: University School of Inter-American Studies, 1961), 189.
13. Kit Sims Taylor, The Dynamics of Underdevelopment in the Sugar Plantation Economy of Northeast Brazil (Florida, University of Florida: Unpublished thesis, 1969), 147.
14. This phenomenon and its development are described by Trevor Munroe in *The Politics of Constitutional Decolonization: Jamaica 1944–1962* (Institute of Social and Economic Research, University of the West Indies, 1971).
15. An illustration of this is to be found in the present day composition of national delegations to international commodity conferences. In most instances, the delegations from plantation economies are made up partly of people representing plantation owners and those representing plantation workers. In the West Indies, sugar manufacturers representatives and trade union officials sit together on these national delegations.
16. The question of mistrust is important. Since plantation owners have such great power and control over plantation society, workers are not going to be easily convinced that these seemingly omnipotent people have no control over the prices they receive for the plantation output.
17. J.S. Furnivall, *Netherlands India – A Study of Plural Economy* (Cambridge: Cambridge University Press, 1944), 451–52.
18. Ibid., 459.
19. Ibid., 468.
20. The reader who is interested in pursuing the question posed is referred to the last two chapters of the book from which this paper is extracted. See Beckford, *Plantations and Poverty in the Third World* (Kingston and Oxford: Institute of Social and Economic Research and Oxford University Press, 1970), Chapters 8 and 9. Analysis of the political and social economy of underdevelopment is provided in this book as well. See, in particular, Chapter 7.

Beckford and the Predicaments of Caribbean Culture

George Lamming

I don't think I ever told Beckford that sometime in 1970 I was visiting Austin, Texas, and someone wanted to introduce me to West Indian families in the region. They took me to a house where, by chance, there lived an old lady, a relative of Beckford. The name came up and she was very pleased to hear that I knew this George Beckford and asked whatever became of him. I said that he was a professor, and he had to do with agriculture and such things. She said: 'Oh I am not surprised, my first recollection of the boy was him thieving bananas.' He was five. You see, his authority in this field has a very long and curious history.

First Encounter

I first met Beckford in 1964 at St Augustine, sitting in what passed for a 'common room'. He had just arrived there and we got into a very strange conversation about a man who had thrown a cigarette butt on the floor. That night I made a note: 'Today I met a peasant who has come to teach here...this place is looking up.' By peasant I mean a certain kind of sensibility which shows the trace of its root, and which has managed, in spite of far journeys, to survive the hazards of an opposing style. He was a very plain man in conversation that evening, and he was very blunt. That was his style of courtesy and a very correct form of modesty.

I have never forgotten or overcome this early memory of GBeck at St Augustine in 1964. I think he got a little blunter with time and in ways which others might prefer to forget. But I think we judge a colleague not only by the quality of his work but by his relationship to that work, the way his thought reveals itself as an organic part of a particular personality, and the ways in which these thoughts touch the lives and work of others.

Beckford has never been a scholar in the archival sense of the word or an academic in hot pursuit of personal career. He has a certain populist instinct to put knowledge in the service of social practice. And what we call a discipline is for him an instrument which aids the process of change. That is his meaning for me.

Links

I want this evening simply to draw a few links between his continuing concerns and the predicament of others who work in the cultural sciences. And I don't only want to remind you of books. I want to remind you of what he actually said. You have to be very fond of George to be comfortable with him and I want this evening to remind you of some the things he has actually said.

I was reading recently an essay by Mintz called 'From Plantations to Peasantries' and came across a passage that is very much a Beckford text:

> It was as slaves that these Caribbean people learnt to budget their own time, to judge soil quality, to select seed, to cultivate and harvest, to prepare foods for sale and otherwise to make the proto peasant sector successful. They managed their family labour, learnt to store and conserve seed, saved their earnings, acquired new habits of consumption, raised animals for sale and for food, and all this while being subjected to the prevailing view that their capacities as individuals were too limited to enable them to survive as free persons.

This is essentially the text of Beckford, the theme that runs through everything that he writes, the insistence with which he is always drawing attention to that great reservoir of experience from down below, an experience moulded by collective struggle which established a correct equilibrium between individual worth and communal purpose.

I think it was some time around 1972 that GBeck got engaged in debate here in Jamaica about the constraints which then appeared to affect the range and variety of the National Dance Theatre Company. He was very strong on what was happening in the National Dance Theatre and how it related to something called the Jamaican landscape. I think that Rex Nettleford found this exchange very fruitful and it may even have influenced the following statement by Nettleford which appeared in his history of the company:

> The dance is not only a performing art, it is also an art of community effort that proclaims the virtue of co-operation over unrestrained individualism. It is self evident how this relates to self government, nation building, and social organization. Traditionally, government leaders have dismissed the sensitive intellectual gifts of peasant experience precisely because they have been regarded as too mundane or folkloric to guide affairs of state. And yet it is the peasant who realised that the individual dancer usually has little to offer outside of community ritual.

There was a stage in the National Dance Theatre when the peasant was not really there, and came increasingly there I think as a result of the kinds of exchanges generated by Beckford. But it is not only the government that suffers from this deficiency. I suspect that there were and still are large areas of the professional intelligentsia which have a similar difficulty.

On Authoritarian Tradition

In *Persistent Poverty*, Beckford forces us to engage seriously with the roots of an authoritarian tradition which worked as an agent of destruction against all examples of communal purpose. 'Within the plantation community', he wrote, 'interpersonal relations reflect the authority structure of the plantation. In every aspect of life, a strong authoritarian tradition can be observed. Anyone with the slightest degree of power over others exercises this power in a characteristic exploitative and authoritarian manner. Attitudes to work clearly reflect this plantation influence.'

This has engendered an ethos of dependence and patronage, It deprives people of dignity, security and self respect, and impedes the material, social and especially the spiritual advance of the majority of people. In these circumstances, we could hardly expect to find a highly motivated population displaying the kinds of characteristics that development demands.

On the basis not only of reading, but by direct observation and experience, almost all major Caribbean leaders over the past thirty years, reveal this to be the central distortion in their relation to party, to government and to the general populace. Since this legacy has been so persistent, perhaps two questions may be raised.

1. Is the political ethos of liberal democracy which has produced all these leaders adequate to initiate and carry through a radical change in the structure of our institutions?
2. Should people begin to think of forms of organizational struggle other than the conventional party politics?

Beckford is not only concerned with analysis; destruction is very much on his mind. In *Persistent Poverty* he says, 'Only by destroying this system can they be overcome'. Destroying the system involves revolutionary changes in the institutional structure, that is, in economic, social and political arrangements.

We begin therefore, by recognizing that the present dependency syndrome in our psychological makeup is a legacy of the system we are destroying, and the most intractable problem is the colonized condition of the minds of the people.

Until we de-colonize the mind there is little hope that genuine independence can be achieved. We need further to recognize that among the people of plantation society the most colonized minds are to be found within the higher ranks of the social order.

The intellectual classes cannot lead in such a struggle; they need first to de-colonize their own minds, and to develop genuinely independent scholarship in the process. And it would appear to be the de-colonized mind which produces acute ambivalence in the political leader caught in a crisis of change.

Manley and the Local Capitalist Class

This quality of Beckford – what I call this plain, blunt man (I will not bother with black this evening) – surfaced again in a seminar here in Jamaica in 1984. He is considering the responses of an element in Jamaica that is called the local capitalist class, to the changes which Manley was attempting in the 1970s.

I want you to listen to me very carefully. I have the text (Beckford 1984). Beckford is arguing that it was the character of the unequal distribution of land inherited from the plantation that was responsible for bottling up the creative energies of the peasantry, which allowed not only the land to go idle, but people to go hungry. A society where you have this amount of idle land co-existing with this scale of idle labour, where malnutrition is significant enough to distort the lives and chances of hundreds of thousands, is not a civilized society. You cannot get 'civilized' reconciled with that situation. That is what he was arguing in 1984, here in Jamaica in that seminar. And then he went on to deal with the predicament of Mr Michael Manley who had made, in my view, very honourable attempts to halt injustice, if not completely reverse it; and who had done nothing in his term of office that could be regarded as dishonourable. Mr Manley found himself the target of a class which, according to Beckford, had in fact benefited more than any other from economic policies that granted that privileged class incentives and opportunities that no previous government had given them. And yet when they got vexed, everything he did, as well as he himself, started to tremble. Beckford is saying, and I quote: 'when a movement or a party begins to confront imperialist interests, that movement or party must be prepared to mobilize the population behind this activity, or else it is lost'. And this is precisely what happened to Michael Manley in 1980 (Beckford: 1984)

By the time 1980 came, the population was tired of Manley riding two horses, trying to benefit the black masses of the population of this country, while at the same time providing incentives to the white and near white bourgeoisie, and brown petit-bourgeoisie. And as time went on, the white capitalist class and the brown leadership classes gradually abandoned Manley, while Manley himself abandoned the black workers. He was left out there on a thread when Seaga and the Americans combined to cut the thread in 1980. Very much the Beckford talking to me in 1964 about the man throwing the cigarette butt on the floor.

'A Common Cord'

There is an area in his thinking which is open to question. He opens it to question, because in *Persistent Poverty* he is saying that the dynamics of social change require a political ideology in order to mobilize action. And all he can say in this connection is that an appropriate ideology will emerge out of the dilemmas of change. He makes reference to capitalism, socialism and communism with the reservation that perhaps there are modes of thought and systems of social and economic organization which came out of very different social structures from our own: 'It might well be that political ideologies that relate to those experiences are not adequate for the social and political realities of plantation society. We cannot be entirely sure of this.'

By the time he gets to *Small Garden, Bitter Weed* (1980), there is an assertion of much greater certainty about this matter. He is now saying that only a radical transformation of the present class structures of this country can release and mobilize the intelligence. And later he made it quite clear that this ideology requires socialist content and direction. But he is thinking here also of a peculiar concept which he calls 'integral man'. He asks: how do you find the way of bringing together this dispersed and fragmented social reality into one movement of struggle? And the answer is that you have to find what he calls 'a common cord' to bind these different classes in the struggle ahead. The emphasis is placed on the necessity for sacrifice.

In the seminar on the Manley predicament, the issue raised is the nature of patriotism of a privileged class which, in the defence of its privilege, may regard the sacrifice of the nation as necessary. The issue of patriotism is central to whatever may be the possibility of striking this cord that would bring these classes together. There is this conflict of ideology at work in his thinking which is what is most refreshing about him ... he has never been doctrinal and dogmatic.

A Collective Dialogue

I want to make reference in this connection to a very rewarding essay I read by Carl Stone who is examining the failed experiments in the transformation of society in Guyana, Grenada and Jamaica. It has to do with ideology although he uses a different phrase. It says that in all three cases, efforts at transformation centered on political structures and the character of political power, without sufficient attention to spelling out and articulating the new society and the new Caribbean man that would have to be the fundamental objective of the exercise as well as the vehicle for achieving its objective and goals. Political strategies and objectives towards socialist change were often articulated but there was 'no commanding vision of the new society' to be created.

My comment on this text is that while this is a just evaluation of the limitations of political activists at the time, we should not assume that the political mind is always suitably equipped to articulate 'a commanding vision' of the new society.

The politician is overwhelmed by concrete tasks to be performed; decisions to be taken urgently, often without any pause for reflection. He is haunted by the failure to deliver. His working hours are spent in a permanent state of emergency. The shadow of parliamentary opposition, where it exists, blurs his sense of priority. He lives with intrigues, and the constant threat of betrayal within his own ranks. It is a very feverish atmosphere hardly conducive to that state of reflective self consciousness from which a commanding vision of a new society could be born.

But the political leader may arrive at such a vision if he enjoys a certain measure of collaborative support from other modes of thought and perception...that of the historian, the poet, the student of philosophy and the social sciences, the economist and the theatre director who creates the cultural history of the nation.

It is the collective dialogue between these different categories of sensibility which ultimately gives voice to a commanding vision of the new society. But it is precisely this voice which has often withdrawn its service from any form of political engagement.

There is a large category of intellectual workers who view such involvement with great misgiving. What is remarkably triumphant about GBeck is that he represents one of the very few who have always been engaged in contributing to this collective dialogue on the new society.

In *Small Garden, Bitter Weed,* Beckford focuses on what is a central cultural issue: the distinction between demand and need. The excessive demand made upon the resource base by the uncritical and almost primitive pattern of consumer tastes which the society cannot support is encouraged, for electoral advantage, by all the political parties, while in opposition.

The distinction, he says, between demand and need is crucial, because much of the existing consumer demand has been conditioned and shaped by the most dishonest advertising associated with our legacy of dependent capitalism. There is a significant gap between that demand and what is really required for the well being of our people.

I do not want to detain you with scandalous examples but in Barbados almost every building that is going up is a mall, a boutique, a supermarket, a parking lot – utterly unproductive structures invested in by the most unmentionable elements within and outside of the society. But I want to make a connection between this and people in the area of cultural work.

I have said on another occasion that fishermen and farmers are cultural workers in their own right. Social practice which has provided them with a considerable body of concrete knowledge as well as with a capacity to make discriminating judgements in their daily work make them intellectual workers. If we do not regard them as cultural workers, it is largely because of the stratification created by the social division of labour and by an educational system designed to reinforce this social stratification. All of Caribbean society has been culturally crippled by this artificial status which separates the 'educated' from the 'uneducated', although experience of our middle classes confirms the view that literacy may sometimes be a form of self enslavement.

By culture we mean that variety of ways in which men and women interpret and translate through the imagination, the meaning of their material existence in the light of their experience, whether it be through religion or philosophy or art, and the institutions which mediate our daily lives. All these – religions, philosophy, art – are influenced in one way or another by the circumstances of our material existence.

So if we aim for sovereignty, what we are aiming for is the collective power to exercise control and direction over these means of existence, and the freedom to define and re-define all those processes, material and otherwise, which make up our social reality.

One characteristic of our history has been the continuing constraints placed on the power to exercise control over the freedom of such definitions. And if there is one area in which we can identify the neglect and even the abandonment of cultural sovereignty it is in the area of food production. It may sound strange and I do not want to mention him in any positive way, but the only leader I know who took this seriously was Burnham.

The Caribbean is a fertile sea. We occupy lands which accommodate a variety of crops. It is a region which, by the gifts of nature, has the distinct potential for meeting the basic food needs of the Caribbean people within every territory. And yet, in this English-speaking region alone, we import what must now be more than one billion dollars of food a year. This is not only a matter of agriculture or economics. There is a crisis of the cultural sovereignty of a people when patterns of consumption bear no relation to basic needs and cannot be supported by the productive base of the society. It may sound very strange but a minister of agriculture in our region, whether he knows it or not is engaged in what is essentially a cultural problem: how do you decolonize the eating habits of a people who have surrendered their very palates to foreign control?

Liberal democracy does not allow you to say 'stop eating that' – and certainly not a year before an election. But it is not only the farmer who experiences this assault on his struggle for sovereignty. The native actor, the native dancer, the native writer, the musicians, all those who strive for an authentic definition of themselves and their society are in much the same position as the local farmer because they too are condemned to a hopeless struggle against the massive insult of imported television.

No governments anywhere have insulted their people like the governments of the Caribbean with the television they feed to them. Not only is it imported, there is nothing so wrong with that; not only is it bad; there is nothing so wrong with that, but it is the absolute garbage of another world, unloaded on a mesmerized and uncritical populace.

The political leadership is very innocent if it does not recognize that the mass production of culture in this form is intended to ensure and reinforce the underdevelopment of our people. Unfortunately for us, there is this enormous separation, between the head and the belly of this society; between that world that organized itself even in slave times, and how governments now see that world.

It pervades institutions like the University. The West Indian historian is not an active and informing influence in the popular consciousness of this region. The language of economic advisors conveys little or nothing to people outside their immediate circles. Novelists function without a substantial and continuing reading class even among the certificated graduates of the region's university.

The organizing agents of the communications media are vaguely aware of these creative resources; they may know their names through episodes of scandal. This failure of involvement co-exists with the widespread and vivid enthusiasm for a great volume of imported drama which advertisers make available through television.

This deprivation works both ways; it impoverishes the popular consciousness and in turn it places a very rigorous constraint on the development of the intellectual classes themselves. The reason why I would have journeyed anywhere to celebrate this anniversary is because GBeck has always stood out on a limb trying to bring the head into connection with the belly of our regional body.

The Dark Complete World of a Caribbean Store:
A Note on the World System
Richard Price

In spite of the recent advent of supermarkets, *libre services,* and *supermercados* in the cities and towns of the Caribbean, the traditional one-room-store-plus-rum-shop remains the place where rural people go to purchase their everyday needs. Buying one or two items at a time slated for immediate consumption, the various members of a household make several visits each day: the woman to buy some rice, cooking oil, or soap flakes; the children to buy candies or crackers; the man to have a drink, chat, and play some dominoes. In many Caribbean communities, such stores form the central social hub of the neighborhood. Yet what Diane Vernon (1983: 104) has called, with considerable poetic and psychological accuracy, "the dark complete world of a Caribbean store" is a complete world in another sense as well. For the products on its dusty shelves form a startling microcosm of the world-system, an astonishing testimony to the history of colonialism and the more recent organization of international commerce.

I illustrate here with a single such store, in a community I have known well for over twenty years (Price, 1964, 1966). Petite Anse is a fishing hamlet on the southwest coast of Martinique. Although relatively remote—the community does not appear on the standard rent-a-car road maps of the island—it now has electricity, piped water, and an all weather road. The main sources of income are fishing (with the surplus catch distributed to local markets), occasional construction work, and remittances from younger family members now in the metropole (who work, for example, in the P.T.T. or the Paris *métro*) and from the social security system. Since sustaining a serious injury in a fishing accident fifteen years ago, my friend Emilien and his wife Merlande have run an *épicerie-bar,* one of the half dozen such rum shop/stores in the *quartier*. Less cramped physically than most (measuring about three by four meters), the rambling, galvanized tin structure has a counter at one end for rum drinking, candy buying, and weighing and paying for groceries; there are sacks of animal feed, rice, and sugar ranged along the walls; boxes of salt cod, canned goods, and cosmetics are stacked against shelves; wire racks as well as miscellaneous wooden and glass cabinets are filled with everything from tomato paste, onions, and sardines to antimosquito coils, toothpaste, and tennis sneakers; and Hawaiian-style shirts hang from the ceiling alongside buckets and sausages. Since the coming of electricity, cold drinks and popsicles have been big sellers, and the store now has two freezers and a large refrigerator. Attached to the store is the proprietors' bedroom and kitchen, as well as an open-sided terrace with tables and chairs where patrons can drink, or sometimes eat, overlooking the sea. Trucks make deliveries to the store as part of a series of regular rounds—beer and ice cream arrive on Fridays, dried goods on Tuesdays. On a typical day, the store grosses about $120 (U.S.)—two-thirds groceries, one-third drinks and ice cream—as a result of some 185 individual sales. (In other words, the average sale comes to less than a dollar—a handful of gumballs, a loaf of bread, or a pound of dried peas.) But for present purposes, it is the provenience of this small store's inventory that interests us.[1]

During July 1983, the store stocked some 213 different items or brands. And of these, 84% were imported from outside Martinique—from 31 countries and from every continent except Australia. A glance around the store would have revealed, among numerous other items, toilet paper and garlic from Italy, onions from the Netherlands (which replaced a shipment of onions from Egypt), condensed milk and hair rollers from Switzerland, candy and matches from Belgium, bathing trunks from Thailand, cigarettes and safety pins from England, sneakers from Korea, salt and soft drinks from the Netherlands, kidney beans and cigarettes from the U.S. (the sole direct U.S. contributions in the store), sardines from Morocco, shirts from Taiwan, orange drink from Israel, underpants from Spain, beer and glue from Germany, T-shirts (proclaiming in bold letters "Martinique") from the People's Republic of China, outboard motor sparkplugs from Japan, children's shoes from Czechoslovakia, bay rum from St. Lucia (the sole manufactured product from elsewhere in the Caribbean), fish hooks from Norway, stout from Ireland, whiskey from Scotland, chewing gum from Denmark (where did they get the chicle?), flashlights from Hong Kong, raisins from Greece, and, of course, just about anything your heart might desire from metropolitan France (which contributed more than half of the store's stock), from fine champagne and Normandy butter to instant mashed potatoes, from canned paté to feminine protection. The list of products from Martinique included little more than rum (the store's single most important product), beer, soft drinks, sugar, milk, candy, margarine, honey, marmalade, and insecticide; from the sister island of Guadeloupe came only an occasional shipment of rice or sugar.

Certain patterns emerge (and they have a long history in the Caribbean). Local crops and products are systematically suppressed or undervalued in favor of "interchangeable" imports. For example, the excellent, locally grown coffee was often unavailable, and the store sold instead stale coffee that had been grown in the Ivory Coast, processed in Switzerland, imported to France, and then shipped to Martinique; cheap, locally produced charcoal was often unavailable, and the store sold expensive charcoal "briquettes" manufactured in the metropole; and traditional Martiniquan tastes for special imports nurtured during the days of slavery—for example, (Norwegian) salt cod or (Dutch) pickled herring as substitutes for local fish—remain very powerful.

Quite generally, there appears to be a rigorous separation of production from consumption, with many products undergoing a remarkably roundabout itinerary on their way to Emilien and Merlande's. Take, for example, a certain brand of orange juice, sold in the store with a label vaunting "Le soleil de Californie toute l'année." It specifies further that the contents were made from California concentrate, canned in the Netherlands, imported to Paris, and then shipped to Martinique, where (for a price) one could drink a can just outside the store in the shade of a lovely citrus tree. The store also sells numerous other tropical products whose itinerary before their reexportation in processed form from Paris to Martinique can only be guessed: cloves, vanilla, cocoa powder, and so on. Or again, there is a beauty product now much in vogue among local young women—"Realistic Professional Formula Creme Relaxer for Professional Use Only"—that is manufactured in the U.S., sent on to Dublin where it is "distributed" by Revlon Realistic, Ltd. to Paris, and only then dispatched to Martinique. And the same holds true for staples: Rice from the Caribbean nation of Suriname is shipped to the Netherlands, then trucked to France, whence it is shipped back across the Atlantic to Martinique.

Recently, Martinique was the venue for an effective critical restudy—at least in part from a world-systems perspective—of a community that had earlier been described as a relatively self-contained unit, in the standard anthropological community study fashion of the 1950's (Baber 1982, Horowitz 1959). And it was behind the counter of Emilien and Merlande's store last summer, enveloped by the pungent aroma of Norwegian salt cod and French pickled pigs' muzzle, that I read Eric Wolf's masterful historical account of the special "interconnections" wrought by European expansion and the rise of capitalism, and his gentle warnings against the continued tendency of some anthropologists to conceptualize "their village" as an isolate, to view societies as so many "sociocultural billiard balls, coursing on a global billiard table" (1982: 17). My sketchy description of one Martiniquan store—which may, nevertheless, stand for thousands of similar Caribbean emporia—is intended simply as a supportive footnote to such ideas.

Note

1. I am very grateful to Niko Price, who help run the store and, with the proprietors' permission, kept careful records of sales and inventory during the summer of 1983. Special thanks also to Emilien and Merlande Larcher for their generous hospitality over the year and to Sidney Mintz, Niko Price and Sally Price for commenting on a draft of this sketch.

References

Baber, Willie L. 1982. Social Change and the Peasant Community: Horowitz's Morne-Paysan Reinterpreted. *Ethnology* III, no. 21 (July): 227–41.
Horowitz, Michael. 1959. Morne-Paysan: Peasant Village in Martinique. Unpublished PhD diss., Columbia University.
Price, Richard. 1964. Magie et Pêche à la Martinique. *L'Homme* IV, no. 2 (mai–août): 84–113.
———. 1966. Caribbean Fishing and Fishermen: A Historical Sketch. *American Anthropologist* LXVIII, 1363–83.
Vernon, Diane. 1982. Review of Louis Doucet, *Vous avez, dit Guyane? Nieuwe West-Indische Gid* LVI, 104–5.
Wolf, Eric R. 1982. *Europe and the People Without History*. Berkeley: University of California Press.

Reluctant Matriarchs

Lucille Mathurin-Mair

The myth of the black matriarch, the mother-who-fathered countless generations of West Indians, and who in the process demoralised and feminised husband, lover, brother and son, originated historically in the concept of the slave woman as a specially privileged and authoritative person within the slave hierarchy.

She had, allegedly, unique access to white male attention: she consequently reaped the rewards of sexual collaboration.

But let us however look squarely at that white male/black female encounter. Winthrop Jordon in an analysis of the dynamics of interracial sex in the New World underlined its essentially coercive nature. "White men" he writes, "extended their dominion over their negro to the bed, where the sex act itself served as ritualistic re-enactment of the daily pattern of social dominance."[1] The relevance of this to the British Caribbean is clear.

A male witness appearing before the Parliamentary Committee of 1832 on Slavery in the West Indies stated the Jamaican situation in these terms: when asked "Do you mean that the state of slavery gives to the proprietor that extent of wealth or property which enables him to corrupt the women that are there?" he replied, "I mean particularly that it invests him with unlimited power over the body of his female slave."[2]

Legislation, or the lack of it, until nearly the end of slavery, condoned the mastery of the white man over the body of the black woman.

The Elizabethan Statute of Rape, which had been administered in Jamaica since 1731, protected only those women who were white, and/or free. It was not until 1822 that the case of an extraordinarily sadistic assault by a white planter of the parish of St. Elizabeth on a female slave child under ten years old served to stir the normally impassive creole conscience. Thomas Simpson, the accused, was tried in the Cornwall assizes, convicted and sentenced to hang. He petitioned for mercy: the Chief Justice and the Attorney General examined the legality of his trial and concluded that in fact the statute involved could not be enforced in cases "where rape is committed by a white person on a slave." Both officials deplored "this defect in the colony's criminal code" and sought a legislative remedy.[3] As a result of their representation, the Jamaican House of Assembly in 1826 extended the law of carnal abuse and rape to cover those victims who were slaves.

The image of the mighty black woman has been further projected through her supposed dominance of the Caribbean slave family in the absence of a spouse.

This stereotype of the invisible and therefore powerless father, with its corollary of the visible and therefore powerful mother, requires persistent challenging on many fronts.

It is well known, but worth recalling, that the lion's share of the rewards for the birth of a slave infant on the plantation went not to the black man who fathered it, or even to the black woman who bore it, but to the white overseer who controlled it, and who, with the slave owner, functioned in many essentials as virtual "paterfamilias."

And if the plantation did admittedly deny the black man much of his authority as father, it also usurped some of the female functions of "materfamilias." So that in the 1780's, William Ricketts, Jamaican planter of Canaan Estate in the parish of Westmoreland saw his responsibilities to his black "family" in this light, viz, ...

> ... "by having a room near my dwelling house I have raised 6 children. Feby and I have 9 more women ready to lye in here — I have now 26 from 3 years old to the breast at this place besides a swarm at my mountain, and I make it a rule to have them fed from my own table every day and in my sight which pleases their parent ..." [4]

But even the image of the plantation as surrogate parent has complex dimensions, which clearly need further exploration. For current research points increasingly to stabler black male/female relationships during slavery than are usually assumed, and this has implications of significant complementary domestic roles for men and women. Recent demographic studies of the structure of slave households in western Jamaica have unearthed relatively strong evidence of the black male presence..."the woman-and-children household type was far from dominant."...[5]

These studies also indicate that the "matriarchal" syndrome may have been of greater significance in the mulatto slave household which, in a society dominated by the ascriptive force of race and colour, should not be confused with the black household.

In assessing the status of black women in slaveholding Jamaica, an additional consideration is the well established leadership roles assumed by the black man in many areas of communal slave activity, (religious, political and economic), which questions the concept of the emasculated male acquiesing in a domestic role subordinate to the female.

It is above all in the economic field that the status of the black woman, as a member of the slave labour force, modifies any claims for her of equality, much less of superiority, to any male in the society.

It is often assumed that slavery being essentially, if not exclusively, concerned with labour productivity, resulted in a rough levelling off of the sexes, and created a work unit of neuter gender. Male slaves were costed a bit more on the market, presumably having that much more muscle power to put into the agro-industrial machine. In fact the difference in the valuation of male and female slaves reflected a difference in kind, as well as in degree, of manual output: it reflected also the difference between the skilled and the unskilled worker.

The sugar plantation of the Caribbean, which consumed the largest volume of imported African labour, is one of the earliest capital-intensive and technologically demanding undertakings of the modern era, combining both large scale agricultural cultivation with relatively sophisticated manufacturing processes. Through a conscious policy of labour deployment, such an enterprise offered slave owners and managers every opportunity for sorting out the girls from the men. And one saw a form of sexual discrimination and oppression dramatically at work, within a group which was already the object of other forms of discrimination and oppression.

A wide range of samplings of the tasks performed by men and women on Jamaican estates during the eighteenth and nineteenth centuries indicates that women, almost without exception, did field work, while men had access to artisan' skills. Even a scholar as deeply concerned as Professor Orlando Patterson is with what slavery did to the black masculine psyche cannot help commenting on the phenomenon at Green Park Estate, Trelawny, in 1823, and Rose Hall, St. James, in 1832, viz:

> "One is struck by the fact that male slaves had a much wider range of occupations to choose from than females: apart from being domestics and field-hands, the latter could only be washerwomen, cooks and nurses."[6]

Craton and Walvin's analysis of the work force on Worthy Park Estate, St. John's in Jamaica in 1789 and 1793 reveal the same trend. In 1789, 70 women out of a female slave population of 162 worked in the fields, in comparison with 29 men out of a possible 177. In 1793, 107 women out of a total of 244 were put in the field, in contrast to 92 men out of a total of 284. The authors observe, viz:

> "While the work of the female slaves was concentrated in the fields, the energy and skills of the men had to be chanelled into the great variety of functions vital to sugar production."[7]

The great variety of functions which could be performed by men included those of carpenters, wheelwrights, coopers, masons, sawyers, boilers, wainmen, boatswains, fishermen, blacksmiths: findings of other estates have shown ratios ranging from 25% to 60% of the men engaged in such skilled tasks: whereas almost 100% of the female task force have been found in individual areas to be in the unskilled area of plantation work. The semi-professional rating of the "nurse" and "midwife" proved in many instances to be a euphemism for a superannuated field worker; a male artisan was more likely than not to have acquired his techniques through apprenticeship. Domestic service, the other avenue open to the woman, with its highly debatable "privileges," in any event seldom absorbed more than 10% of female slaves, and was very largely the preserve of mulattoes.

Towards the later years of slavery, sugar estates, which dominated Jamaica's utilisation of land, labour and capital, had a marked excess of female slaves, 100 women to every 92 men.[9] As has been indicated, women were preponderant in the field gangs. By the eve of emancipation, not only were the majority of Jamaican black women labourers in the field, but the majority of Jamaica's labourers in the field were black women.

And what this did to the black female psyche has yet to be fully assessed.

"No other group of slaves, "writes Professor Elsa Goveia, "was so completely subject to the harsh necessities of slavery as an industrial system. The life of the ordinary field slave was characterised by coercion and dependence. The gangs of field slaves were worked for long hours under discipline of the whip... since the field slaves had fewer opportunities for earning a cash income than most other slaves, they relied heavily on the master for the necessities of life ... [they] were maintained by their owners on the bare margin of subsistence ... though they did the most laborious work their standard of living was generally lower than that of any other group of slaves."[10]

Occupation was in pre- and post-emancipation Jamaica, a major status-identifying factor: the emphasis on technical expertise, the dominance of the work-situation in slotting the individual into his or her social niche, was particularly crucial in a New World plantation society organised primarily towards a single economic goal. Skills opened up opportunities for profitable employment over and above what the individual estate could absorb: surplus labour could purchase material comforts, could do more: with the use of one's trained hands, it was possible to purchase freedom and to restore human status. For the woman, job-degradation closed this vital avenue to independence and respect.

One of the most remarkable movements of West Indian people in the later nineteenth and twentieth centuries has been the exodus of free black labour and, in particular, free black female labour, from estate work. In 1844, the year of Jamaica's first census, 80% of all persons at work were engaged in agriculture. A hundred years later, the proportion was 47%. The woman's participation in agriculture fell from 57% in 1921, to 28% in 1943.[11] In 1972 it was less than 20%.[12]

Escaping from the land, she headed for the towns, where 43% of Jamaica's women, (compared with 39% of its men), now live. But her mobility led her to another vocational deadend: she exchanged the oppressions of the canefields for those of the city's kitchens. 125,000 Jamaican women, or approximately 40% of the females on the labour market in 1972, were in "service" occupations.[12] Overworked and underpaid house helps, still often required to "live in," now dominate the female working population: unlike the multiple complexion of commerce which employs some 15% of working women, and favours the lighter-skinned, the colour of domestics is preponderantly black. Indices of their low status are their wage rate, averaging $8 weekly — the worst in the national economy — their unemployment rate, 34% — also the worst — and their exclusion from trade union organisation.

All of these factors reflect the society's perception of women as workers without skills, reservoirs of cheap human power, always available for exploitation: so that the sophisticated sectors of the economy carefully exclude them from access to expertise and status. Today's Caribbean's "service" industry par excellence, tourism, creates growing demands for updated skills. But the occupational hierarchy of its hotels remains stratified on sexual lines. So its female staff constitutes the largest, lowest paid and least prestigious category of worker, the chamber-maid. And in the kitchen, the male head cook, unquestionably skilled, reigns supreme.

The persistent prejudice which relegates woman and her tasks to the bottom of the vocational/technological ladder permeates new enterprises. So that the appropriately named industrial "estates" of today reproduce the structures and relationships of older plantations: and the female technician, when she is found in these enterprises (some 7% or so of her sex), rates scarcely higher than the manual untrained worker. The processes of garment factories, extensions of "women's skills," condemn her to the most exploitative conditions of the modern sector.

Any analysis of the status of Caribbean woman today has to take into account the occupational context in which the black majority functions, relative to the occupational positionings of the rest of the society. Her alleged position of influence and power in the family and community has to be judged against the ground base of the lowest status-bearing jobs which the society has always allocated to her.

The rather tired cliché of the black matriarch perhaps contains some validity in terms of the numbers of women who head their own households (approximately one-third of Jamaica's adult females in 1972) and in terms of the moral strength they can, and do, exercise within the family.

But one has to register considerable reservations about the assumption that to be a female head of a household is to have some kind of natural access to authority. A considerable number of the single female heads are among the most powerless of the society, the absence of a spouse often implying the absence of a stable family income on which the household can function decently. The economically depressed condition of such a female breadwinner makes her as sexually vulnerable as she was in the darker days of her history. Not only does she outnumber the man in the city, she is a migrant, unsupported by the traditional familial and communal resources of the countryside which she has fled. Singlehanded, she is unable to control the forces which circumscribe her life and that of her children. She turns more and more to a new paterfamilias, the state, admitting her powerlessness to deal with the one meaningful role the society leaves to her, the role she traditionally values most, that of mother. Reluctantly, she now opts out, even of that.

The single most disturbing social phenomenon of contemporary Jamaica is the physical and/or moral abandonment of children by single young mothers.[13]

It may be the newly born infant left behind in the city's hospital bed, or the difficult boy-child handed to the welfare official. Statistically the cases are still relatively few; but they have been growing significantly in the past ten years. More than any other human indicator, abandonment of a child signals near social collapse: it points to a growing sense of desperation and despair in a group historically perceived as a main effective source of human power. Economic realities, past and present, have always made that perception a flawed one. The "Matriarch" of old, nevertheless, lived with the irony, wore her title well, and the race survived.

It should not now push its luck.

Notes
1. Winthrop Jordon, *White over Black* (1968).
2. Parliamentary Papers, 1832: Minutes of Evidence taken before the Select Committee of the House of Lords on Slavery.
3. Colonial Office Papers 137/153: 1822.
4. Ricketts/Jervis Family Papers 1762-1842. Add Ms. 30001, (British Museum).
5. B.W. Higman, 'Household Structure and Fertility on Jamaica Slave Plantations' (1973).
6. Orlando Patterson, *The Sociology of Slavery* (1967).
7. Michael Craton and James Walvin, *A Jamaican Plantation, the History of Worthy Park 1670-1970* (1970).
8. Lucille Mathurin, 'A Historical Study of Jamaican Women 1655-1844,' Ph.D. Thesis, U.W.I. (1974).
9. B.W. Higman, 'The Demography of Slavery in Jamaica 1817-1834,' Ph.D. thesis, U.W.I. (1971).
10. Elsa Goveia, *Slave Society in the British Leeward Islands at the end of the eighteenth century (1965)*
11. George Roberts, *The Population of Jamaica* (1957).
12. The Jamaica Labour Force 1972; Population Census, 1970, Dept. of Statistics.
13. Erna Brodber, *Abandonment of Children in Jamaica*, (1974).

The Origins of Reconstituted Peasantries

Sidney Mintz

The history of the Caribbean region begins in 1492, and its present character shows the effects of five centuries of complicated contact. This lengthy and complex past creates genuine analytic difficulties, when one seeks to classify the peasantries of the region in any orderly fashion. An attempt is made here to describe these peasantries as expressive of forms of resistance to European enterprise, as modes of escape or of contrary adaptation. But the origins of the peasantries have been diverse: some came into being only relatively recently; others flourished—and withered—at an earlier time. We lack anything like a complete account of the present distribution of peasant peoples in the islands; and even our criteria for defining a peasantry are open to serious question.

Nonetheless, there may be some utility in seeking to describe some of the main ways in which Caribbean peasantries came into being, if only to indicate what we know of the history of these groups. By and large, Caribbean peasantries have been "interstitial" groupings, living on the margins of Western enterprise. But reflection on these "interstices" tells us something about the direction and intent of imperial strategy in the islands, and allows us to discern more clearly how the peasantries responded to such strategy. If the emphasis seems to rest unduly on conflict, on resistance, this is because only rarely and briefly have European powers or even local governments viewed the peasantry as more than an "obstacle" to development; and the reasons for this negativism, as well as the negativism itself, still persist.

It is certainly not our intent to describe the peasantries of each and every island and mainland Caribbean society as they are now constituted, nor even to examine the full list of historical processes by which such groups came into being. Rather, we shall describe a few major modes of peasantry formation, each of which enables us to perceive, from a somewhat different viewpoint, the challenge of European or state power, and the reaction of local people. Each such instance is substantially independent of the others, though commonly one mode of formation might lead eventually to the appearance of a different adaptation at a later time.

The Squatters

The first such adaptation is that which typified the early period of settlement in the Greater Antilles, in the period before Spain was seriously challenged by its North European rivals. The period begins soon after the Conquest, and continues until the rise of large-scale sugarcane plantations in Cuba and Puerto Rico and, to a much lesser extent in Spanish (that is, eastern) Hispaniola, near the start of the nineteenth century. In these large islands, held uninterruptedly by Spain until nearly the mid-nineteenth century in the case of Santo Domingo, and until 1899 in the cases of Cuba and Puerto Rico, peasantries of mixed cultural and physical origins seem to have come into being as a mode of escape from official power. The locus of settlement was invariably in the interior of the islands, and the settlers were often deserters, escaped slaves from other islands, freedmen of color, and Europeans seeking to detach themselves from government surveillance and control. Such settlers were often squatters on Crown land, engaged in what was, technically, illegal settlement. Their crop repertories and horticultural techniques are little known, but appear to have included elements originating in Amerindian (Arawak), African, and European cultural heritages. They produced most of their own needs and sold little to outsiders—most such trade, in fact, seems to have been based on smuggling through illegal ports.

Fray Iñigo Abbad y Lasierra, whose *Historia Geográfica...de Puerto Rico* was published in 1782, gives us some idea of the life and manners of this curious peasantry (Fernández Méndez 1969). He is astonished, for instance, that they preferred their hammocks (*hamacas*), an item of Amerindian origin, to regular beds; that their meat consumption was low, and that they could be satisfied with a bit of rice and land crab; that they used heavily sweetened coffee to still their hunger pangs; that they loved cockfighting and dancing; and that they were not given to long hours of hard work in the fields. But it is clear that the people Abbad is describing represent a local adaptation to nonplantation life—that they are, in fact, quite happy to be barefoot, to sleep in hammocks, and to limit their labor to their own notions of necessity.

As we have already seen, this was the group out of which the Puerto Rican sugar industry was to fashion a work force of almost 50,000 for the new plantations of the nineteenth century. In so doing, the sugar industry undercut badly the competitive position of its interior frontiersmen, and the highland areas of the island probably never fully recovered. Thus, this first category of peasants—the term is only barely applicable—consisted of people whose adaptation probably depended on the absence of a fully developed sugar industry; and the growth of the industry constituted a major element in its destruction. This is not to say, of course, that Puerto Rico's peasantry disappeared in the early nineteenth century, but rather that the balance was thereafter heavily weighted in favor of plantation enterprise.

The Early Yeomen

A second peasant category stems from the development of indentured labor systems in the islands of the Lesser Antilles, such as Barbados and Martinique, under the influence of British and French planters, in the mid-seventeenth century. Such indentured laborers received a grant of land when their term of labor ended, and it was common for them to settle down in the Lesser Antilles as a peasantry. This category approaches much more closely one part of the conventional definition of peasantries as landholders who produce much or most of their own consumption, while also producing items for sale; in most cases the former indentured servants of the Lesser Antilles produced tobacco, indigo, and other products for European markets. But the growth of the plantation system—a system which accounted in good measure for the original importation of indentured servants—was also to lead to the destruction of such peasantries. Not surprisingly, this process of destruction took on a clear racial character, since the original indentured servants were all Europeans, while those who supplanted them were African slaves. Merivale (1841: 75–76), referring to the British islands, states:

The early settlers who occupied in such numbers the soil of the Antilles, seem to have been chiefly small proprietors, who lived on the produce of their estates. When the cultivation of sugar was introduced about 1670, the free white population rapidly diminished, and continued to do so for a century afterwards. The whites in Barbadoes are said to have increased until they amounted about 1670 to 70,000; but these early calculations must be received with doubt: in 1724, there were only 18,000, there are now [1841] 16,000. Antigua contained 5,000 in the reign of Charles II, now only 2500. The history of the other Windward Islands is precisely similar. Jamaica, from its extent of surface, and fitness for a variety of productions, did not present the same diminution; yet even there the number of whites remained stationary at about 8000 from 1670 to 1720. This declining condition of the white populations, showing how unsuited these islands were to become, what their first occupiers imagined they would, the scenes of extensive colonization from Europe, chiefly proceeded from the monopoly of land, consequent on the cultivation of sugar. As mentioned in a former lecture, it was found that the small proprietor could not compete with the large one, in raising this staple product. Coffee, and still more sugar, requires a number of hands, and the simultaneous application of much labour at particular seasons. Thus this species of agriculture resembles in some respects a manufacture; and, as in manufactures, the large capitalists have great advantages....Hence all accounts of our West Indian colonies, in the first half of the last century, teem with complaints of the decay of small proprietors, and the consolidation of all classes of society into two, the wealthy planters and the slaves (Merivale 1841: 75–76).

The economic fundamentals which made the plantation more expeditious than the small farm as a medium of colonial development under mercantilism need not detain us. What matters is that the process was general in the New World area embraced by what Philip Curtin (1955: 4–7) has aptly called "The South Atlantic System." The slave plantation was, in general, an expansive agro-social enterprise, land being regarded as the expendable factor in production. Improper land utilization led swiftly to exhaustion, whereupon new land, rather than improved agriculture, became the solution. Eric Williams quotes Merivale: "It is more profitable to cultivate a fresh soil by the dear labour of slaves, than an exhausted one by the cheap labour of freemen." And Williams continues: "From Virginia and Maryland to Carolina, Georgia, Texas and the Middle West; from Barbados to Jamaica to Saint Domingue and then to Cuba; the logic was inexorable and the same. It was a relay race; the first to start passed the baton, unwillingly we may be sure, to another and then limped sadly behind" (1944: 7).

The accompaniment of this relay race was the persistent and successive extirpation or degradation of yeoman cultivators. L. C. Gray (1941) has documented part of the process in the United States South. Merivale, as cited, did much to reveal the underlying dynamics of the process for the British West Indies. Ortiz, in his *Contrapunteo Cubano* (1940), and Guerra y Sánchez in his *Sugar and Society in the Caribbean* (1964) touch on the parallel theme for Cuba. Though much work remains to be done in order to clarify how yeomen and free squatters were driven out of other parts of the Caribbean by the plantation system, everything we know makes clear that this was not a racial but an economic matter, intimately connected with the plantation system, and the support it consistently received in the metropolis, whether in London, Paris, Madrid, or elsewhere.

However, since the plantation system depended so heavily on slavery, and since slavery fell most cruelly upon African peoples, an assumed relationship has been posited between slavery and race, which conceals a significant part of Caribbean historical reality. All that we know about the social history of the Caribbean plantation system convinces us that the planters were, in one important respect, quite without prejudice: they were willing to employ any kind of labor, and under any institutional arrangements, as long as the labor force was politically defenseless enough for the work to be done cheaply and under discipline. Hence it is a serious error of interpretation to posit any necessary relationship between slavery and race, ignoring all of those instances where non-Africans were enslaved, or otherwise coerced, by the plantation system. This is by no means to say that slavery in the Caribbean region was the same as slavery in other places and at other times; throughout Afro-America, the slavery institution assumed a highly distinctive character, probably never duplicated anywhere else. But just as Caribbean slaves were sometimes Indian, so Caribbean peasants have often been African; the key to the processes by which plantations and peasantries arose or declined is fundamentally economic and political, not racial.

The Proto-Peasantry

A third category of peasantry I have referred to elsewhere as a "proto-peasantry" (Mintz 1961a), by which I meant simply that the subsequent adaptation to a peasant style of life was worked out by people while they were still enslaved. The full story of life on Caribbean plantations has by no means been written. But we may be sure of a number of general characteristics of Caribbean slave systems: the formal slave codes never represented, other than very superficially, the actual character of life in each society; each island society differed in certain important ways from every other, with regard to its treatment of the slave population; and in each and every system, the slaves were able to work out certain creative adaptations, in spite of the profoundly repressive conditions under which they were forced to live. "There is something in human history like retribution," wrote Karl Marx (1857), "and it is a rule of historical retribution that its instrument be forged not by the offended, but by the offender himself." The chronicle of Caribbean proto-peasantries seems to confirm this ringing assertion.

Repeatedly, activities which the slaves were compelled to carry out in order to benefit the planters also enabled them to demonstrate their intelligence, resourcefulness, and creativity. Repeatedly, the planters were struck by the slaves' capacities to function very differently in new contexts—when producing their own foods or going to market, for instance—from the way they functioned under the whip. The planters, of course, explained the difference in terms of the slaves' contrariety; but the slaves—and occasional foreign visitors—knew better. Often these selfsame skills turned out to be basic in establishing the freedmen's independence from the plantation after emancipation; and Part III deals with just this development.

The proto-peasantry, then, are slaves who later became peasant freedmen, either through emancipation (as in the case of Jamaica) or revolution (as in the case of Haiti), and whose particular repertoires of agricultural skills, craft techniques, crops, and all else represent important "blendings" of traditional and new materials. Commonly, among such peasantries today, one finds both African religious elements and European religious elements; African crops and European, Asian, and Amerindian crops; African food-processing techniques and food-processing techniques from many other areas; and so on. Those of a proto-peasant past form the largest Caribbean peasant category, both numerically and in terms of historical origins. But this category has remained rather poorly defined, in contradistinction to other categories of rural agrarian people in the region.

The Runaway Peasantries

A fourth category shares much with the preceding categories but also differs in important ways and deserves separate treatment. These are the "runaway peasantries," which were formed by escaping slavery rather than by submitting to it. Throughout the Caribbean region—in Mexico, Colombia, Puerto Rico, Cuba, Saint-Domingue and Jamaica, as well as in Brazil and the Guianas—the creation of maroon communities in defiance of slavery and the plantation system was a common occurrence. Such communities must be separated, for some purposes, from individual escapees—who could attach themselves to the maroon communities only when they were accepted into the maroon bands—and from instances of resistance or rebellion in situ, in which slaves attacked their masters locally. The rationale of the maroon pattern was to create a new and free kind of community outside of, and in opposition to, the slave plantocracy and, where possible, to establish diplomatic relations with the plantocracy on the basis of some kind of reciprocal treaty. The best-known instances are probably those of Jamaica and Surinam (Dutch Guiana); but maroon communities elsewhere also established treaty accords with the slave society, as in Mexico (Davidson 1966) and Cuba (Pérez de la Riva 1952), and sometimes became runaway-slave hunters themselves as part of their compact.

Since the slaveowners and the metropolitan governments carried out frequent attempts to destroy the maroon settlements, their inhabitants often lived under the threat of war, and their economic integration with the outside world was correspondingly impaired. To the extent that they were compelled to maintain complete isolation, such settlements were not, typologically speaking, "peasant communities." But the history of such groups, in general, has been one of extermination or of transformation into peasantries. Thus, to take the Haitian case, we know that substantial maroon bands survived for generations in the borderlands of Spanish Santo Domingo. We do not know whether such bands had formal contact of any kind with the Haitian revolutionary movement after it became a movement of the slaves themselves; but we are inclined to assume that the maroon bands, like the revolutionaries, became settled peasantries after the Revolution. Debbasch, in his monograph on *marronage* (1961, 1962), has indicated what evidence we have that the maroon groups of prerevolutionary Haiti maintained their previous contacts and amities after the Revolution; but it is likely that they became part of the Haitian peasantry in general in the postrevolutionary period. The relationships between proto-peasantries and maroon bands, though hardly known at all, could prove of immense significance for our understanding of slave resistance. For the moment, what we know is largely surmise.

These attempts to define certain historical trajectories in regard to peasant subcultures do not take the place of serious studies, either in the form of fieldwork or documentary research; in fact, fieldwork and research should test and refine (and, if necessary, discard) such formulations. Nor should a typological category as wide and as loose as that of "the peasantry" disguise in any way the immense cultural variety that typifies peasant societies everywhere. Certain features of the Caribbean peasant adaptation originate in the general conditions—ecological, economic, political—under which the emergence of peasant groups occurred. We are able to trace the particular effects of these conditions in single cases, as is done in some of the following chapters. Thus, for instance, in both Haiti (French Saint-Domingue) and Jamaica, the slavery regime produced two highly variant responses among the slave population: escape and struggle on the one hand, accommodation and the learning of specific skills on the other. But the general sociological conditions under which the slaves had to respond to the immense pressures put upon them do not in any way explain the contemporary differences between, for example, Haitian and Jamaican peasants, nor even, necessarily, their contemporary similarities. The heavy commitment of the Jamaican peasantry to market-oriented production of pimento (allspice: *Pimenta officinalis* Lindl.) and bananas, when contrasted with that of the Haitian peasantry's production of coffee, implicates significant differences in seasonal activity, the use of family labor, attitudes toward the land, and much else, that are dependent on the nature of the crops themselves and on the marketing arrangements imposed from outside on the peasantry. Such differences cannot be "explained" by reference to history as such, nor do they hinge on any shared characteristics of the peasantry, except in the most general sense. In other words, the delineation of a "developmental path" along which the peasantry has evolved in any particular Caribbean case is little more than a highly abstract exercise, until the necessary historical and ethnological research to confirm or disprove such postulations is carried out.

Caribbean Peasantries as a Social Science Problem

The assertion that it is useful to study Caribbean peasantries as cases of resistance to the plantation regime is likewise open to attack—though a number of young scholars (e.g., Marshall 1968) have begun to make very good use of this perspective. A core feature of the argument rests on the assumption that Caribbean populations, whether slaves, indentured laborers, or contract laborers, have consistently struggled to define themselves either within culturally distinctive *communities* or as members of family *lines*—that is, they have not *generally* responded to the plantation regimen in terms of their class identity but along other dimensions of social affiliation. A key to this assertion is the significance of land for Caribbean rural folk—a significance that far exceeds any obvious economic considerations. The slaves sought desperately to express their individuality through the acquisition of material wealth, and some of the following selections indicate the ways in which this might be done. Torn from societies that had not yet entered into the capitalist world, and thrust into settings that were profoundly capitalistic in character on the one hand, yet rooted in the need for unfree labor on the other, the slaves saw liquid capital not only as a means to secure freedom, but also as a means to attach their paternity—and hence, their identity as persons—to something even the masters would have to respect. In these terms, the creation of peasantries was simultaneously an act of westernization and an act of resistance.

Such responses were not limited to the formation of peasantries alone, however. All kinds of skills could be pressed into use to achieve the same results: craftsmanship, fishing, trade, veterinary science, hunting, and much else. In all such cases, the slaves—and at a later time, the contract laborers who succeeded them—sought to *become persons*, to define themselves, in terms of what they knew and could do. We have already seen how, on the Puerto Rican plantations, special skills were a source of prestige, wealth, and self-respect for black freedmen. This was even truer for the peasantries, and for all those who managed to escape the plantation regimen in order to define their lives outside its iron order.

This may very well be one of the most important ways in which a contrast may be drawn between the North American and the Caribbean instances. If one were asked to specify the single feature of the Caribbean past that might best account for the differences in circumstance facing the North American freedman and the freedmen of the Antilles, this—in the view of the present writer—would be the feature to explore. By what processes of disfranchisement, terror, and psychological pressure were the black freedmen of North America deprived of the means to define themselves *economically* as men? I would say that the answer to this question would explain, at least on some very general level, all of the derivative destructions of individuality, dignity, and self that white North America has sought—ultimately, in vain—to impose upon its black victims. Such an assertion remains surmise, for the most part. But the endless controversies about "culture deprivation," the supposedly nonexistent black nuclear family, and much else that now typify the North American politico-intellectual scene, cannot be resolved only by revalidating the cultural norms of black Americans; it is essential to revert at some point to lower-order explanations of a more molar kind.

All of this takes us far from the task of formulating a typology of Caribbean peasantries. But it does suggest one way in which these peasantries must be evaluated historically: namely, by assessing the means used by the Caribbean masses to resist a system designed to destroy their identity as human beings.

References

Curtin, Philip. 1955. *Two Jamaicas*. Cambridge: Harvard University Press.
Davidson, David M. 1966. Negro Slave Control and Resistance in Colonial Mexico, 1519–1650. *Hispanic American Historical Review* 46:235–53.
Debbasch, Yvan. 1961. Le Marronage: Essai sur la Désertion de l'Esclave Antillais. *L'Année Sociologique*, 1–112; (1962): 117–95.
Fernández Méndez, Eugenio. 1969. *Crónicas de Puerto Rico*. Spain: Editorial Universidad de Puerto Rico.
Gray, Lewis C. 1941. *History of Agriculture in the Southern United States to 1860*. New York: P. Smith.
Guerra y Sánchez, Ramiro. 1964. *Sugar and Society in the Caribbean*. New Haven: Yale University Press.
Marshall, Woodville K. 1968. Peasant Development in the West Indies since 1838. *Social and Economic Studies* 17:252–63.
Marx, Karl. 1857. The Indian Revolt. *New York Tribune*, September 16.
Merivale, Herman. 1841. *Lectures on Colonization and Colonies*. London: Longman, Orme, Brown, Green and Longmans.
Mintz, Sidney. 1961. The Question of Caribbean Peasantries: A Comment. *Caribbean Studies* 1:31–34.
Ortiz, Fernando. 1940. *Contrapunteo Cubano del Tabaco y el Azúcar*. Havana: Jesús Montero.
Pérez de la Riva, Francisco. 1952. *La Habitación Rural en Cuba*. La Habana: Contribución del Grupo Guamá, Antropología No. 26.
Williams, Eric. 1944. *Capitalism and Slavery*. Chapel Hill: The University of North Carolina Press.

Culture on the Edges:
Creolization in the Plantation Context*

Michel-Rolph Trouillot

Le lieu est incontournable.
—Edouard Glissant

Creolization is a miracle begging for analysis. Because it first occurred against all odds, between the jaws of brute and absolute power, no explanation seems to do justice to the very wonder that it happened at all. Understandably, the study of creole cultures and languages has always left room for the analyst's astonishment. Theories of creolization or of creole societies, assessments of what it means to be "creole" in turn, are still very much affected by the ideological and political sensibilities of the observers.[1]

It may not be possible or even meritorious to get rid of these sensibilities, but the knowledge of creolization can benefit from a more ethnographic approach that takes into account the concrete contexts within which cultures developed in the Americas. The plantation-society, the plural-society and the creole-society models—and even Bolland's "dialectical" approach[2]—all seize creolization as a totality, thus one level too removed from the concrete circumstances faced by the individuals engaged in the process. All these models invoke history; some even use it at times. Yet the historical conditions of cultural production rarely become a fundamental and necessary part of the descriptions or analyses that these models generate. Calls for a more refined look at historical particulars[3] remain unheeded. Worse, current apologists of *créolité*[4] pay even less attention to the historical record than their predecessors in cultural nationalism, perhaps because the historiography of slavery is much weaker in French than in Dutch, or especially, English.

This article, which draws primarily from the experience of Afro-Caribbean peoples, tries to give due credit to the creativity that Africans and their descendants demonstrated right from the beginning of plantation slavery. However, praise for the creativity of Afro-Caribbeans may mask the struggles that are also inherent in creolization unless we take the analysis one step closer to changing historical contexts. From a wide range of changing historical circumstances I abstract three contexts as key heuristic devices: a plantation context; an enclave context and a modernist context. I then return to the plantation context to illustrate the many ways in which such a framework may improve our knowledge of creolization.

The Afro-American Miracle

From the family plots of the Jamaican hinterland, the Afro-religions of Brazil and Cuba, or the jazz music of Louisiana to the vitality of Haitian painting and music or the historical awareness of Suriname's maroons, manifestations of Afro-American cultures appear to us as the product of a repeated miracle. For those of us who keep in mind their conditions of emergence and growth, the very existence of cultural practices associated with African slaves and their descendants in the Americas is a continuing puzzle. Afro-American cultures were born against all odds. Even if we define culture in the restricted sense of artistic and intellectual production ultimately sanctioned by power (what some anthropologists call "high culture"), the Antilles alone suffice as exemplars of the repeated wonder: in relation to their size, the Caribbean islands have given birth to an impressive array of individuals who left their intellectual mark on the international scene. But the real achievement is, of course, that of the anonymous men and women who have woven, along the centuries, in spite of slavery and other forms of domination, the cultural patterns upon which rest the highly individualized performances of the intellectuals.

Afro-Caribbean cultures came to life unexpectedly, unforeseen developments of an agenda set in Europe, by Europe and for Europe. Caribbean territories have experienced Western European influence longer than any other area outside of Europe itself. They are territories that Europe claimed to shape to fit its particular goals, territories through which Europeans moved as if they were empty lands. And indeed, they were emptied, in so far as the native population had been wiped out without even the dubious privilege of slow death on a reservation. Almost everything that we now associate with the Caribbean—from sugarcane, coffee, mangoes, donkeys and coconuts, to the people themselves, whether African or Asian in origin—was brought there as part of the European conquest.

Cultural concerns did not figure among European priorities during most of the conquest. For more than a century, the search for gold and the rivalries it provoked obliterated most other issues. Then, from the seventeenth century on, European attention slowly turned to the production of agricultural commodities in the tropical areas of the mainland and in the Antilles. Cultural considerations entered into the design of plantation America, but only as prerequisites of political and economic domination, as corollaries of the plantation system. Thus, although the Afro-Caribbean world came to life on the plantation and, in part, because of the plantation, Afro-Caribbean cultural practices emerged against the expectations and wishes of plantation owners and their European patrons. They were not meant to exist.

Because Afro-Caribbean cultures were not meant to exist, many observers came to believe that they did not exist, in spite of all evidence to the contrary. Up to the second part of this century, most observers and many speakers viewed the creole languages of the Caribbean as burlesque versions of European tongues, *"français petit nègre,"* "patois," "broken English," unworthy of serious attention from linguists and writers.

Interestingly, however, Caribbean cultural practices never became exactly what Europeans planners and owners might have expected. From the very beginnings of slavery, it was clear that the Africans and their descendants were shaping modes of behavior, patterns of thought and their expression. Caribbean languages provide good examples of this creativity. Africans brought to the Caribbean during the slave trade spoke a wide variety of African languages. Yet, in many circumstances, which we have yet to specify, they were also forced to draw from the vernacular of their respective masters. That itself is not surprising. More interesting is the fact that, once taken over by the slaves and their descendants, European languages did not remain the same. They acquired sounds, morphological and syntactic patterns unknown in Europe. More important, they were shaped to express the joys, pains and reflections of hundreds of thousands of humans. In one word, they were creolized.[5]

From Creole Linguistics to *Créolité*

For a number of reasons, these creole languages became the first products of the creolization process to attract the attention of scholars.[6] First, creole languages were obvious. The features that demarcated them from European vernaculars could not be denied.[7] On the contrary, these features had to be acknowledged if only for the purpose of communication. Even when the linguistic status of creoles was denigrated, such denigration also reinforced the acknowledgment that they were different. Second, a vibrant tradition in the observation of non-Western languages existed in Europe since at least the seventeenth century. Lastly, language was politically safe—or thought to be so. It was thought to be amenable to study without long encounters with a mass of natives. It was one of the few products of creolization least likely to engage the scholar in immediate political controversies about the people who had been creolized.

Controversies there were, however, especially on the matter of origins. Here also, wonderment played its role. Since the early nineteenth century analysts felt the need to explain the puzzle of the emergence of creole languages, to ponder the significance of their existence.[8] This obsession with origins, still central to creole linguistics,[9] gave rise to two methodological tendencies.

First, since actual slave speech was—for all practical purposes—inaccessible, creolists had to infer the past from the present. Current Caribbean speech or changing patterns in more recent non-Caribbean creoles supposedly documented what must have happened in some undetermined pan-Caribbean past. Second, since the ultimate purpose of the exercise was, more often than not, to explain or dissipate the wonder of creole emergence, creolists tended to use one exclusive all-encompassing theory after another. Either all creoles had evolved from a singular source, most probably a Portuguese pidgin (monogenesis theory); or all followed the same "West African" grammatical principles (substratum theory); or again the same genetically programmed elementary structures (bioprogram theory).

From an epistemological and methodological viewpoint, the striking similarity between these theories is their exclusiveness. Their adherents, past and present, right or wrong, tend to be virulently monocausal. In the words of Claire Lefebvre, creolists "[try] to explain everything the same way at the same time."[10] Fidelity to a unique explanation in turn tended to preclude detailed examination of changing historical contexts in spite of Sidney Mintz's crucial demonstration at the first international conference on creole languages—in Mona in 1968—that the study of linguistic change had to take into account "the sociohistorical background" of creolization.[11] Available documents were not used to their full potential. Known historical facts, periodization, empirical questions of space and time, demography and social norms, took secondary positions within pre-developed schemes. Even when creole linguistics focused on the past, even though it emphasized the process of linguistic change, it generally ignored the sociohistorical process. History was always evoked, often used, yet rarely treated in its complexities.

Since the mid 1980s, in part in response to Bickerton's bioprogram hypothesis, in part because of the influence of non-Caribbean creolists,[12] linguists are increasingly aware of the historical complexities involved in Afro-Caribbean creolization. The distance between two hallmark conferences[13] reveals a tremendous growth in historical sophistication between the late 1960s and the mid-1980s. However, such sophistication[14] has yet to inform fully the study of specific linguistic changes.

The linguistic stalemate is reinforced by the lack of exchange between linguists and non-linguists and by the weaknesses of cultural theories of creolization. First, students of sociocultural history have yet to provide as detailed answers as the more sophisticated linguists have questions. Moreover, in recent years, grand pronouncements by some cultural and literary critics have increased the gap between many linguists' empirically-oriented inquiries and sociocultural theories of creolization. For instance, the repeated announcement that the world is now in—or moving toward—a state of hybridity or creolization[15] is too sweeping to reinforce a dialogue between the cultural theorists who make such statements and historical linguists interested into knowing who actually taught what to whom and when in particular Caribbean territories.[16] On the contrary, such sweeping statements reinforce, perhaps inadvertently, the proclivity to treat creolization as a totality, thereby reinforcing the worst tendencies of the sociocultural theorists.

Indeed, both the tendency to infer the past from the present and the predilection for all-encompassing explanations, which together characterize creole linguistics, reappear in sociocultural studies of creolization with some noteworthy differences. First, the technical apparatus of creole linguistics could not be transferred to studies of creolization outside of language. Whereas linguists generally agree on micro-methodologies and definitions (e.g., what are noun phrases and how to break them down), social scientists and cultural theorists do not have this fundamental agreement on a technical apparatus. Thus, second, non-linguist students of creolization find themselves in the awkward situation of having fewer tools (at least apparently) to do yet a larger job. Sociocultural life is an object of study admittedly more fluid and harder to delimit than language, which it encompasses. Without a common technical apparatus, the theoretical claims made by students of sociocultural creolization are even less controllable than those of the linguists. Or, to put it differently, the distance between these claims and the organization of the facts into a coherent object of study is greater than in linguistics. Faced with the wonder of creolization, the need to explain a cultural emergence that seems to defy their implicit assumptions about culture, social scientists used strokes as broad as those of the linguists but on a greater range of topics. The range of topics has actually increased with time. With methodological issues further relegated to the back burner, current studies of creolization return, in a cycle, to the wonder of origins with the added value of the ideologies of the day.

The increased relevance of ideology is understandable. First, social scientists are increasingly aware that creolization still goes on. Even though analysts are not much closer to an agreement in defining creolization as an object of study than they were, say, in the 1950s, they have both the increased feeling of being witness to the ongoing wonder and the conviction that it matters how they explain it. Second indeed, the ongoing denigration of many Afro-American populations continues to incite praise for the "creoleness" that they are said to typify.[17] Third, now that globalization and hybridity have become suspiciously fashionable—some would say too fashionable[18]—the creolization process in the Afro-Americas appears, in retrospect, as an early state of grace only now accessible to the rest of humanity.[19] The cultural idealism that now so happily masks increased inequalities worldwide further fuels the ahistorical tendencies of creolization studies.[20] Indeed, if there is a difference between the *créolité* movement of the 1990s and predecessors such as Haitian *indigénisme* of the 1930s[21] and the Jamaican creole-society school of the 1950s and 60s,[22] it is the increased persistence' to further divorce the wonder of creolization from the very history that made it possible. As social theory becomes more discourse-oriented, the distance between data and claims in debates about creolization and *créolité* increases. Historical circumstances fall further into a hazy background of ideological preferences.

The Contexts of Creolization

Historical circumstances are what I would like to emphasize here: creolization cannot be understood outside of the various contexts within which it occurred.

Many features shaped such contexts. First among these was the regimentation of the populations involved, including their regimentation as labor force. The nature and degree of such regimentation necessarily skewed the daily expressions of cultural creativity. In the second half of the eighteenth century, the kind of materials needed, available, and used to "produce culture" were quite different for the member of a canefield gang in Barbados than for an enslaved coffee grower in Dominica or in Saint-Domingue. Regimentation, including labor regimentation, crystallized such differences. Differences in labor regimes in turn, proceeded from the crops involved, but also from the number of years a particular crop had been cultivated in a territory.[23] Regimentation, so construed, thus centers around labor but includes all the factors that limited daily activities of the laboring populations both before and after slavery.

Second, the frequency and nature of outside contact—in and out migrations, communications, the ease or difficulty of individual movement—also helped to define the context of creolization. Clearly, creolization must have proceeded differently in contexts marked by constant influx of enslaved Africans than in situations where such influx was negligible. Third, creolization cannot be understood without some attention to its participants as subjects of history. Edouard Glissant suggests that creolization implies some awareness of heterogeneity, the impossibility to deny mixed origins.[24] But surely, that awareness includes both an implicit sense of cultural ideals—what Mintz calls target cultures,[25] and, an implicit attentiveness to facts of power on the ground, which Glissant himself tends to neglect. Cultural ideals and power relations, including actors' understandings and interpretations of the stakes and forces available to reach their self-defined goals fundamentally shape the context of creolization.

A short example may make the point. We can assume that to practice what is now known as Haitian vodoun is to engage knowingly or not in creolization. Yet even if we assume an unchanging content to vodoun—a dubious assumption indeed—we must concede that what it meant to serve the gods changed in space and in time. Imagine first, the negotiations, trials and tactics necessary for African-born slaves just to set a ritual in colonial Saint-Domingue: how to do it away from the masters' ears; whom to include and on what grounds; which gods to evoke or invoke. Imagine, then, the relative freedom of association and the related freedom of choice in the isolated mountains of independent Haiti, away from memories of both Europe and Africa before the growth of the Catholic clergy at the end of the nineteenth century. Imagine, in turn, the fears unleashed by the US occupation of 1915–34 and renewed by the repressive campaigns of the 1930s and 1940s. Today, the change is monumental: the holders of state power in Haiti officially recognize vodoun as religion. Even before that recognition, vodoun had become truly transnational; some of its canonical rituals are routinely held in Cuba's Oriente or in Brooklyn, New York. Not all its practitioners are Haitian. Some are white North Americans. Yet the poverty of the Haitian countryside has also undermined vodoun at the base, limiting its ritual possibilities among the peasantry.[26] Throughout all this, nevertheless, vodoun has figured and continues to figure as a key manifestation of Haitian culture, an emblem of its successful creolization. There is no way to follow that thread of continuities and breaks without evaluating these changing contexts.

In short, we need a framework to approach the changing contexts of creolization. Using time, space and power relations as my main markers, I suggest three such contexts for the study of creolization: (a) a plantation context; (b) an enclave context; (c) a modernist context.

Each of these contexts emphasizes, in turn, one of the factors highlighted earlier. The regimentation of populations is the defining moment of the plantation context. The frequency and nature of outside contact help to distinguish the enclave context. The awareness of heterogeneity and power are inherent in the context of modernity. Since all three factors are always relevant, it follows that these contexts are heuristic devices. Further, in the case of the Spanish Caribbean, it may be useful to devise a pre-plantation context that would help to account for the markedly different base and outcome of the creolization process there.

At any rate, the contexts described here are not meant to duplicate real life situations, but they may help us understand such situations by focusing attention on "the specific sorts of community settings within which groups became further differentiated or intermixed."[27] They do not delineate fixed periods: often they overlapped in historical time within the same territory. What I hope they do best is to sketch with broad strokes the notably different historical dynamics of creolization as a cultural process so as to bring forward the particulars of the populations involved.

By *plantation context,* I have in mind situations defined primarily by plantation slavery both during and immediately after the centuries of legal enslavement. Most enslaved Africans and their immediate descendants throughout the Americas engaged in creolization within a plantation context until—and at times way into—the second half of the nineteenth century.

By *enclave context,* I mean situations marked by the relative autonomy and isolation of the populations under study. Early maroon societies from St. Vincent to Suriname, the Haitian peasantry from 1804 to the 1880s, highland villagers in the Windward Islands up to the first decades of this century creolized mainly within such enclaves.

The *modernist* context became dominant only with the decline of the plantation. I do not mean by this that modernity itself came late to the Caribbean or is a post-plantation phenomenon. On the contrary, the Caribbean was in many ways as modern as Europe by the first quarter of the seventeenth century, especially because of the plantation. Indeed, creolization itself is a modern phenomenon if only because it implies the awareness and even the expectation of cultural differences.[28] Further, frequency and ease of contact with the outside world marked the daily routine of many urban slaves, especially in the port cities where news of other territories circulated to an extent we have yet to appreciate.[29]

My modernist context combines elements of both modernity and modernization. It implies a different kind of technical and institutional support to creolization. It implies also a sense of global history and the awareness of progress—or backwardness, which are part of modernity, and which spread quite unevenly among Caribbean populations from early conquest until the second third of this century. The degree to which the awareness of both target cultures and facts of power become explicit and voiced, the degree to which organic intellectuals harness institutional and technical support for cultural practices help define a modernist context.[30]

These three contexts bring us closer to actual situations, yet we need to specify them further by way of a number of changing parameters. The relative proportion of populations of diverse origins, including individuals of mixed descent (see Mintz's "The Socio-Historical Background to Pidginization and Creolization"); the impact of prior moments of creolization, including the spread of institutions that solidified that creolization; and the extent of social differentiation are among such parameters. Their relevance will vary with the case under study, but the point is precisely to use these three contexts as starting points and to refine them with the relevant particulars so as to get closer to actual situations.

Thus the scheme outlined here puts on hold most theories of creolization and creole societies for trying to do too much, too fast. In that sense, I am not proposing an alternative model. Rather, I am suggesting that we have not thought enough about what went on in specific places and times to produce a framework sensitive enough to time, place, and power. I now turn to the plantation context to illustrate the complexities that we need to address.

The Plantation as Cultural Matrix

During the long centuries of the slave trade, Africa was no more static or culturally unified than Europe was at the time. We simply do not know enough of African variations and change. Ignorance and ethnocentrism may explain the general tendency to acknowledge differences among Europeans and ignore them when referring to Africans. Second, whereas European residents of particular territories usually came from similar—when not the same—milieux, enslaved Africans did not necessarily end up among tribal fellows. Further, the Middle Passage had cut the African-born slaves from their roots, without the possibility, open to many Europeans, of maintaining regular contact with their original milieu. Thus, although they kept their memories, they could not reproduce the societies whence they came.

Only since the 1980s have we begun to acknowledge the restrictions imposed by the trade and plantation slavery on African cultural transfers, but the achievement seems even more spectacular against this limiting background. As Sidney Mintz and Richard Price argue in the pathbreaking essay that launched this new awareness: given the conditions of their passage, the enslaved "were not able to transfer the human complement of their traditional institutions to the New World. Members of tribal groups of differing status, yes; but different status systems, no. Priests and priestesses, yes; but priesthoods and temples, no. Princes and princesses, yes; but courts and monarchies, no."[31]

Limitations applied as much to the collective as to individuals. Surely, no African slave came to the Caribbean carrying a drum from the motherland. But the memory of African music lingered long enough to catch up with the memory of drum making; and Afro-Caribbeans used their new environment to create drums and music that were close to those of Africa yet distinctively Caribbean. Likewise their dances may have been influenced by the minuets and waltzes they learned to play sometimes for their European masters, but their own Sunday performances were not likely to be minuets and waltzes—though some musicologists may rightfully argue that these were also influenced by minuets and waltzes. In short, Africans and their descendants had to create, so to speak, a new cultural world, with elements gathered from the many African cultures they came from and the European cultures of those who dominated them.

How was such a process of selective creation and cultural struggle—in one word, creolization—possible among the enslaved? How could Africans and Afro-Americans forge entirely new cultures out of the remnants of Old World values and patterns, both African and European? How did they come to dominate the process of cultural formation in societies such as those of the Caribbean where they were kept by daily terrorism at the bottom of the socio-political ladder?

Sidney Mintz and Richard Price suggest that the West African cultural heritage is to be found mainly in unconscious, underlying "grammatical" principles: cognitive orientations, attitudes, expectations common to the diverse communities whence most of the enslaved came. They argue that these underlying principles ordered the process of creolization by making certain choices more appealing or more significant than other possible ones.[32]

This argument needs to be refined in light of more sustained research on the institutional impact of African ethnicity on slave practices in specific territories. In other words, the underlying principles that Mintz and Price highlight had to work through tensions among Africans in order to produce meaningful practices and we need to know how and when they did so. More important, however a modus vivendi on cultural grammar was obtained among slaves, shared principles—old and new—had to survive the European exercise of power. How did they do so? When and how were they given space and time to breathe and to breed? How did they survive and reproduce themselves enough to generate new institutions?

Answers to these questions, tentative as they may be, require that we turn to the plantation. Afro-American slavery was plantation slavery. The plantation was the institution around which the system was built; it provided the model after which were shaped the actual units on which slaves labored. But to phrase it this way is already to suggest that the word "plantation" covers in fact different types of realities that we may, want to keep separate even if for heuristic purposes: the institution itself, in the restricted sense of a type of agricultural enterprise; the socio-economic and political system built upon it (in this particular case, plantation slavery); and the actual units of production modeled after this ideal type.

As a form of labor organization, the plantation is an agricultural enterprise, distinguished by its massive use of coerced or semi-coerced labor, producing agricultural commodities for markets situated outside of the economy within which the plantation itself operates. One of the better treatments of the type comes from sociologist Edgar T. Thompson.[33] Thompson suggests that, as a unit of production, the plantation is an economic institution, an agricultural unit operating with an industrial dynamic. It is also, in his view, a settlement institution, in the sense that it arranges peoples in a "new" territory; a political institution, inasmuch as it operates as a small state, with an authoritarian structure. Plantation owners claim a monopoly of violence, control over the life of the people who inhabit the plantation. The plantation is, finally, a cultural institution. It tends to generate a distinguishable way of life for owners and workers alike, but it also divides them along racial and ethnic lines. It is a race-making institution.[34]

Needless to say that few if any actual plantations ever exactly matched the prototype. Whether inferred or planned, social models are peculiar kinds of abstraction, the dual products of the typological exercise that projects them and the historical units through which they are actualized. In other words, the plantation, as such, never existed historically, not even in the Americas of slavery. Rather, thousands of plantations did, that tried to conform to the ideal type, but always within the limitations imposed by specific circumstances. This is an obvious enough assertion; but it implies that in almost every instance there were varying limits to economic efficiency, to the organization of settlement, to planters' political power, or to the cultural apartheid premised in the organization of labor. The very actualization of the institution, whether or not premised on the planter's pursuit of the ideal type, allowed the slaves much more room to maneuver than implied by the type itself.

Latitude came also from elsewhere and perhaps in more important ways. Units of production never operate alone. As units of production serving distant markets within the strict order of slavery, the plantations of the Americas felt even more the pressures of the system. Indeed, we can conceptualize an inherent tension between plantation slavery as a system and the actual units of production. This is not to suggest that the units and the system belong to the same order of things; but the fact that the system is a construct does not make it any less real than actual estates. It had its requirements, its logic; but the very fact that this logic and these requirements were not of the same kind as the daily exigencies that masters and overseers had to face within individual units of production created an inherent tension.

Reactions to *maronnage* provide us with a good entry point in this world of tensions and broken lines. In principle, throughout the Americas, slaves were forbidden to leave the plantations without authorization, and infractions to this code were punished. On the ground, however, planters' attitudes varied, according to the particulars of the case at hand: the time of the infraction, its mode of discovery, the climate of the colony, the individual slave involved, or indeed the personality of the owner or overseer. More important, beyond these variations, planters often acknowledged a difference between desertions intended to be final and temporary absences. The French even distinguished them by name, coining the former *"grand maronnage"* as opposed to the more benign forms of *"petit maronnage."* Throughout the Americas, whereas system and practice tended to overlap in cases of the first kind, planters sometimes closed their eyes on instances of *petit maronnage,* when slaves ran away to visit relatives, to take part in certain rituals, or sometimes even to make a symbolic gesture of protest.

This indulgence did not necessarily come from kindness. Its deepest roots were systemic: planters knew that the code was not always enforceable, that not all instances of unauthorized absence could be punished without encroaching on the working routine of their particular plantation. One suspects that slaves came to the same realization and took repeated risks at manipulating this systemic fissure, often to their detriment, but as often perhaps with the expected results. Communication across plantations, for instance, must have depended on such "illegal" absences as much as on the "free" time officially allotted by the planters. And as slaves repeated such manipulations, on the one hand acknowledging the system, on the other circumventing its actualization in carefully chosen instances, they solidified the *détour,* the social time and space that they controlled on the edges of the plantations.

Thus, even though *grand marronage* stands as a privileged example of Afro-American resistance under slavery, maroon societies are better seized within what I call the enclave context.[35] *Petit maronnage,* in turn, stands as a more accurate model for the kind of behavior through which most slaves established the institutional continuity of creole patterns within the plantation context. For a majority of enslaved Africans, and Afro-Americans, prior to the mid-nineteenth century, creolization did not happen away from the plantation system, but within it.[36]

I suggest that this creation was possible because slaves found a most fertile ground in the interstices of the system, in the latitude provided by the inherent contradictions between that system and specific plantations, historically situated. Afro-Caribbean cultural practices developed within the plantation system, but on the margins of the units through which the ideal type was actualized. They were born within the plantation but on the edges of particular plantations. The tensions between the logic of the system and the daily life of actual estates provided a context full of minute opportunities for initiatives among the enslaved. We need to look closely at the mechanisms by which slaves seized upon these contradictions and repeatedly turned latent opportunities to their advantage, further stretching the time and space that they controlled. But even before further empirical research on the so-called slave sector illuminates these mechanisms, we can assess the opportunities. I will give one more example of an opportunity seized upon by the slaves, one quite different from planters' attitudes to *petit maronnage,* but which ultimately makes the same point.

In many Caribbean societies, slaves were allowed by their masters to grow their own food, and at times, to sell portions of what they harvested. This was a fundamental contradiction within the plantation system. The practice of allowing slaves to cultivate their own gardens whenever they were not working on plantation crops emerged because particular planters wanted to save money, given the high cost of imported food.[37] Planters were not in the business of feeding slaves. The name of the game was profit; and it is to enhance their profits that many planters passed on to the slaves the responsibility of feeding themselves. Indeed, the extent and viability of slave provision grounds depended on a series of factors operating within the unit of production and on the impact of these factors on the planter's cost accounting. Steep and broken terrain, less fertile lands not used for the production of plantation staples, the flexibility of work regimen, all worked to reinforce the use of provision grounds within a unit. Within a given territory so did the unavailability of cash, the availability and acclimation of imported plants and animals.

Eventually however, these practices, which first emerged because they provided concrete advantages to particular owners, went against the logic of the plantation system itself. Provision grounds provided both time and space that were both within the order dictated by the plantation and yet detached from it. They provided a space quite distinct from the plantation fields congested with sugarcane, coffee, and cotton. Space where one learned to cherish root crops, plantains, bananas; space to raise and roast a pig, to run after a goat, or to barbecue a chicken; space to bury the loved ones who passed away, to worship the ancestors and to invent new gods when the old ones were forgotten.

Time used on the provision grounds was also slave-controlled time to a large extent. It was time to develop new practices of labor cooperation, reminiscent of—yet different from—African models of work. Time to talk across the fences to a passing neighbor. Time to cross the fences themselves and fish in the adjacent rivers. It was time to create culture knowingly or unknowingly. Time to mark the work tempo with old songs. Time to learn rhythm while working and to enjoy both the rhythm and the work. Time to create new songs when the old ones faded way. Time to take care of the needs of the family. Time to meet a mate. Time to teach children how to climb a tree. Time indeed to develop modes of thought and codes of behavior that were to survive plantation slavery itself.[38]

Such survival, in turn, depended on the consolidation of institutions. For instance, we know that in some colonies—Saint-Domingue, for instance—slaves sold part of their produce at urban markets. We can assume that the practice of producing and especially producing for sale involved a number of individual and economic decisions. Slaves not only had to engage in a cost-benefit analysis—as any petty producer would—but in a cost-benefit analysis that took into account their ideals (what and when to cultivate; how to profit; what to buy with the profit, for whom and why). Such a culturally-informed cost-benefit analysis, in turn, necessarily implied the distribution and consolidation of roles within the household, the distribution and consolidation of statuses across households. In short, practices of that kind—and there were many more we need to think about—influenced also the institutions that would survive slavery.

How they did so remains, of course, open to serious concrete investigation. Such investigation can only benefit from analyses that try to integrate the three contexts suggested here. As enclaves and plantations slowly gave way to populations that experienced creolization mainly in a modernist context, how did cultural content and, especially, patterns of accommodation, resistance and struggle change? For instance, how did the transformation of target cultures accommodate the perception of past practices? We can already assume that here again historical particulars played their role. Contact between different populations within and across political boundaries, influx of newcomers, impact of prior creolization, political control and social differentiation enter into the process. But my main point is that we need to rehistoricize creolization.

Creolization is a process rather than a totality. To enable us to seize it in its movement, I have suggested the use of three contexts as heuristic devices but bearing in mind that these contexts often overlapped in particular places and times. My longer exploration of the plantation context is meant as an illustration of the complexities we need to acknowledge at the very beginning. Ideally, the analysis would need to integrate the overlap of the three contexts in historically specific cases.[39] The point remains that we need to look at creolization as a process, constantly influenced not only by prior history but by the numerous factors that characterize(d) the times, the territories and the peoples to which it bears witness.

Conclusion: Plantation Coda

The provision grounds of slavery, the reluctant tolerance toward *petit marronage*, the unequal ranking and treatment of slaves constitute only conspicuous examples of tension among many to be found in the plantation context. The general lesson remains the same. Cultural practices markedly Afro-American emerged, at least in part, because of the slaves' ability to use the contradictions inherent in the fundamentals of the system and the daily workings of specific plantations. Time and space matter enormously here—that is, social time and social space seized within the system and turned against it.

This ability to stretch margins and circumvent borderlines remains the most amazing aspect of Afro-American cultural practices. It encapsulates their inherent resistance. Afro-American cultures are cultures of combat in the strongest possible sense: they were born resisting. Otherwise they would not have existed at all. For they were not meant to exist. But the resistance they encapsulate is not best seized by the epics that typify cultural nationalist treatments of creolization. The heroism of the creolization process is first and foremost the heroism of anonymous men, women and—too often forgotten—children going about the business of daily life. And for more than three centuries, such daily life was conditioned primarily by the plantation.

Afro-American cultural practices emerged on the edges of the plantations, gnawing at the logic of an imposed order and its daily manifestations of dominance. Filtering in the interstices of the system, they conquered each and every inch of cultural territory they now occupy. In that sense, the plantation was the primary cultural matrix of Afro-American populations. But it was so against the expectations of the masters. It was an imposed context, and quite a rigid one at that, an institution forced upon the slaves but one within which they managed their most formidable accomplishment, that of creating what has indeed become a New World.

Notes

* This article started as a contribution to the colloquium The Plantation System in the Americas, Louisiana State University, Baton Rouge, 27–29 April 1989. It was revised in 1996–97, mainly at the Center for Advanced Study in the Behavioral Sciences, Stanford, CA, and at Johns Hopkins. I thank Edouard Glissant, who invited me to the Baton Rouge colloquium, and all the participants who commented on the original version. Thanks also to the National Science Foundation, which supported my fellowship at the CASBS, to Marie Espelencia Baptiste, and Niloofar Haeri for sharing their views on creolization. Haeri and A. James Arnold also commented on later versions.
1. Nigel Bolland, 'Creolisation and Creole Societies,' in *Intellectuals in the Twentieth-Century Caribbean*, ed. Alistair Hennessy (Basingstoke: Macmillan Caribbean, 1992), 50–79; Annie Le Brun, *Statue Cou Coupé* (Paris: Jean-Michel Place, 1996).
2. 'Creolisation and Creole Societies.'
3. For example, Sidney W. Mintz, 'The Socio-Historical Background to Pidginization and Creolization,' in *Pidginization and Creolization of Languages*, ed. Dell Hymes (Cambridge: Cambridge University Press, 1971), 481–96; Sidney W. Mintz and Richard Price, *The Birth of an African-American Culture: An Anthropological Perspective* (Boston: Beacon Press, 1992 [1976]).
4. For example, Jean Bernabé, Patrick Chamoiseau, and Raphaël Confiant, *Éloge de la Créolité* (Paris: Gallimard and Presses Universitaires Créoles, 1989).
5. The extent of linguistic creolization varied. In some cases, creolization led to the rise of entirely new languages spoken by the entire population, like Haitian Creole, now the language of Haiti, or Lesser Antillean (also a French-based Creole, common to Martinique, Guadeloupe, and to a lesser extent Dominica and St Lucia). Sranan (Tongo) emerged in Suriname, Papiamento in Curaçao. In many of the former British territories, we witness a different phenomenon. The linguistic spectrum presents itself more like a continuum with the more Creolized forms at one end and the forms closer to the European standard at the other.

6. Of course, sociohistorical studies of the Caribbean have dealt with creolization since colonial times (Gordon Lewis, *Main Currents in Caribbean Thought* [Baltimore: Johns Hopkins University Press, 1983]), but the delineation of creolization and of its products as a specific object of scholarly research, and the subsequent labelling of creolists as specialists of the field so defined first happened in linguistics.
7. Joachim M. Magens, *Grammatica over det Creolske sprog, som bruges paa de trende danske eilande, St Croix, St Thomas og St Jans I America. Sammenskrevet og opsat en paa St Thomas indföd mand* (Kopenhagen: Trykt udi det Kongelige Wayenshusets Bogtrykkerie, af Gerhard Giese Salikath, 1770)
8. Glenn Gilbert, 'The Language Bioprogram Hypothesis; Déjà Vu?' in *Substrata versus Universals in Creole Genesis Papers from the Amsterdam Creole Workshop, April 1985*, ed. Pieter Muysken and Norval Smith (Amsterdam and Philadelphia: John Benjamins, 1986), 15–24.
9. Mervyn C. Alleyne, *Comparative Afro-American* (Ann Arbor: Karoma, 1980); Muysken and Smith, *Substrata versus Universals in Creole Genesis*.
10. Claire Lefebvre, 'Relexification in Creole Genesis Revisited: The Case of Haitian Creole,' in *Substrata versus Universals in Creole Genesis, ed.* Muysken and Smith, 282.
11. Mintz, 'The Socio-Historical Background to Pidginization and Creolization.'
12. For example, Suzanne Romaine, *Pidgin and Creole Languages* (London and New York: Longman, 1988); Gillian Sankoff, *The Social Life of Language* (Philadelphia: University of Pennsylvania Press, 1980); and Jeff Siegel, *Language Contact in a Plantation Environment: A Sociolinguistic History of Fiji* (Cambridge: Cambridge University Press, 1987).
13. Hymes, ed., *Pidginization and Creolization of Languages*, and Muysken and Smith, eds., *Substrata versus Universals in Creole Genesis*.
14. For example, Marie-Josée Cérol, 'What History Tells Us about the Development of Creole in Guadeloupe,' *New West Indian Guide* 66, nos. 1 and 2 (1992): 61–76; Gilbert, 'The Language Bioprogram Hypothesis'; Lefebvre, 'Relexification in Creole Genesis Revisited'; John R. Rickford, 'Short Note,' *Journal of Pidgin and Creole Languages* 1 (1986): 159–63; and John R. Rickford, *Dimensions of a Creole Continuum: History, Texts, and Linguistic Analysis of Guyanese Creole* (Palo Alto: Stanford University Press, 1987).
15. For example, Bernabé, Chamoiseau, and Confiant, *Éloge de la Créolité*; Ulf Hannerz, 'The World in Creolization,' *Africa* 57 (1987): 546–59; and Ulf Hannerz, 'The Global Ecumene as a Network of Networks,' in *Conceptualizing Society* (London: Routledge, 1992), 34–56.
16. For example, Rickford, 'Short Note'; Rickford, *Dimensions of a Creole Continuum*; and Cérol, 'What History Tells Us about the Development of Creole in Guadeloupe.'
17. Bernabé, Chamoiseau, and Confiant, *Éloge de la Créolité*.
18. David Harvey, 'Globalization in Question,' *Rethinking Marxism* 8, no. 4 (1995): 1–17; Brackette F. Williams, 'Review of The Black Atlantic,' *Social Identities* 1, no. 1 (1995): 175–92.
19. Paul, Gilroy, *The Black Atlantic: Modernity and Double Consciousness* (Cambridge: Harvard University Press, 1993); Hannerz, 'The Global Ecumene as a Network of Networks.'
20. Micaela di Leonardo, 'It's the Discourse, Stupid,' review of Michael Taussig, *The Magic of the State, The Nation*, 17 March, 1997.
21. Michel-Rolph Trouillot, 'Jeux de Mots, Jeux de Classe: Les Mouvances de L'indigénisme,' *Conjonction* 197 (Jan.–Mar. 1993): 29–44.
22. Bolland, 'Creolisation and Creole Societies.'
23. Ira Berlin and Philip D. Morgan, eds., *Cultivation and Culture: Labor and the Shaping of Slave Life in the Americas* (Charlottesville and London: The University Press of Virginia, 1993); B.W. Higman, *Slave Populations of the British Caribbean 1807–1834* (Baltimore and London: The Johns Hopkins University Press, 1984).
24. Edouard Glissant, *Introduction à une Poétique du Divers* (Paris: Gallimard, 1996).
25. Mintz, 'The Socio-Historical Background to Pidginization and Creolization.'
26. Gerald F. Murray, 'The Evolution of Haitian Peasant Land Tenure: A Case Study in Agrarian Adaptation to Population Growth,' PhD dissertation (Anthropology), Columbia University, 1977.
27. Mintz, 'The Socio-Historical Background to Pidginization and Creolization,' 481.
28. Edgar T. Thompson, *Plantation Societies, Race Relations, and the South: The Regimentation of Populations* (Durham: Duke University Press, 1975); Glissant, *Introduction à une Poétique du Divers*.
29. Julius Sherrard Scott, III, 'A Common Wind: Currents of Afro-American Communication in the Era of the Haitian Revolution,' PhD dissertation (History), Duke University, 1986.
30. Late twentieth-century developments in linguistic ideology and speech practice in Haiti and the geographical and social expansion of both reggae music and Rastafarianism within and beyond Jamaica

are two cases that may illustrate the point even briefly. The increased technical and institutional support to Haitian as a language – from its use in print and audiovisual media in Haiti and abroad to its official recognition as one of the two national languages – is part of a process of modernization (This modernization is now obvious, but keep in mind that Napoleon's army issued proclamations in Creole to the revolutionary slaves.) But these recent technical and institutional changes intertwine with modernity, with the recognition of indifference and the recognition of an identity that claims to be specifically Haitian. Similarly, reggae music and, by extension, Rastafarianism have benefited from the profound changes in both electronics and communication that have affected the music industry worldwide. But the opportunity that these changes offered had to be seized by artists, cultural nationalists, and local entrepreneurs quite aware of Jamaican modernity. In Jamaica as in Haiti, organic intellectuals have integrated the knowledge that the world is now their context if not always their interlocutor.

31. Mintz and Price, *The Birth of an African-American Culture*, 10.
32. Ibid., 9–10.
33. Edgar T. Thompson, *The Plantation* (Chicago: n.p., 1935); Thompson, *Plantation Societies, Race Relations, and the South*.
34. Ibid., 31–38; 115–17.
35. Richard Price, ed., *Maroon Societies: Rebel Slave Communities in the Americas* (Baltimore: Johns Hopkins University Press, 1979 [1973]).
36. Even the Haitian Revolution, which stands as the most significant act of resistance against slavery, does not actually fit the *grand maronnage* model. To start with, there is no evidence of a continuous maroon community in the northern part of Saint-Domingue, where the revolution started. Rather, in part because the local topography prevented the establishment of permanent camps where fugitives could regroup, the slaves from that region could not escape the contradictions of the system through organized forms of *grand maronnage* (Michel-Rolph Trouillot, *Ti Difé Boulé Sou Istoua Ayiti* [New York: Koléksion Lakansièl, 1977]). Indeed, our knowledge so far suggests that the original rebellion involved primarily slaves located on the plantations that were burned, even though some historians infer maroon participation. Further, there are indications that slave drivers and privileged slaves established the inter-plantation network of communication without which the widespread revolt that destroyed the northern plains and launched the revolution would have been impossible.
37. For more detailed treatment of the provision grounds in the Caribbean, see Sidney W. Mintz's article 'Was the Plantation Slave a Proletarian?' *Review* 2, no. 1 (1978): 81–98, and Michel-Rolph Trouillot, *Peasants and Capital: Dominica in the World Economy* (Baltimore and London: The Johns Hopkins University Press, 1988).
38. It is not at all surprising that when slavery ended, Caribbean slaves did the most to maintain access to their provision grounds. And almost everywhere after the end of slavery, planters unanimously condemned the former slaves' attachment to these provision grounds.
39. For instance, although a society such as eighteenth-century Saint-Domingue (between 1763 and 1789) was primarily a plantation society, one would need to examine both the impact of port cities, where creolization had a strong modernist component, and the impact of Le Maniel's enclave and of coffee frontier areas, which operated as cultural enclaves, on the creolization process. Given the location of these port cities and enclaves and the history of settlement (Yvan Debbasch, 'Le Maniel: Further Notes,' in *Maroon Societies: Rebel Slave Communities in the Americas*, ed. Richard Price [Baltimore: Johns Hopkins University Press, 1979], 143–48; Michel-Rolph Trouillot, 'Motion in the System: Coffee, Color and Slavery in Eighteenth-Century Saint-Domingue,' *Review* 5, no. 3 [1982]: 331–88), this immediately suggests that the research should eventually look at specific regions within the territory. In the 1770s, creolization around Jacmel – close to Le Maniel and close to new coffee areas – could not have worked the same way on the ground as in the northern plains.

Cultural Identity
and Social Change

On the Social Phenomenon of "Transculturation" and Its Importance in Cuba

Fernando Ortiz

With the reader's permission, especially if he happens to be interested in ethnographic and sociological questions, I am going to take the liberty of employing for the first time the term *transculturation*, fully aware of the fact that it is a neologism. And I venture to suggest that it might be adopted in sociological terminology, to a great extent at least, as a substitute for the term *acculturation*, whose use is now spreading.

Acculturation is used to describe the process of transition from one culture to another, and its manifold social repercussions. But *transculturation* is a more fitting term.

I have chosen the word *transculturation* to express the highly varied phenomena that have come about in Cuba as a result of the extremely complex transmutations of culture that have taken place here, and without a knowledge of which it is impossible to understand the evolution of the Cuban folk, either in the economic or in the institutional, legal, ethical, religious, artistic, linguistic, psychological, sexual, or other aspects of its life.

The real history of Cuba is the history of its intermeshed transculturations. First came the transculturation of the paleolithic Indian to the neolithic, and the disappearance of the latter because of his inability to adjust himself to the culture brought in by the Spaniards. Then the transculturation of an unbroken stream of white immigrants. They were Spaniards, but representatives of different cultures and themselves torn loose, to use the phrase of the time, from the Iberian Peninsula groups and transplanted to a New World, where everything was new to them, nature and people, and where they had to readjust themselves to a new syncretism of cultures. At the same time there was going on the transculturation of a steady human stream of African Negroes coming from all the coastal regions of Africa along the Atlantic, from Senegal, Guinea, the Congo, and Angola and as far away as Mozambique on the opposite shore of that continent. All of them snatched from their original social groups, their own cultures destroyed and crushed under the weight of the cultures in existence here, like sugar cane ground in the rollers of the mill. And still other immigrant cultures of the most varying origins arrived, either in sporadic waves or a continuous flow, always exerting an influence and being influenced in turn: Indians from the mainland, Jews, Portuguese, Anglo-Saxons, French, North Americans, even yellow Mongoloids from Macao, Canton, and other regions of the sometime Celestial Kingdom. And each of them torn from his native moorings, faced with the problem of disadjustment and readjustment, of deculturation and acculturation—in a word, of transculturation.

Among all peoples historical evolution has always meant a vital change from one culture to another at tempos varying from gradual to sudden. But in Cuba the cultures that have influenced the formation of its folk have been so many and so diverse in their spatial position and their structural composition that this vast blend of races and cultures overshadows in importance every other historical phenomenon. Even economic phenomena, the most basic factors of social existence, in Cuba are almost always conditioned by the different cultures. In Cuba the terms Ciboney, Taino, Spaniard, Jew, English, French, Anglo-American, Negro, Yucatec, Chinese, and Creole do not mean merely the different elements that go into the make-up of the Cuban nation, as expressed by their different indications of origin. Each of these has come to mean in addition the synthetic and historic appellation of one of the various economies and cultures that have existed in Cuba successively and even simultaneously, at times giving rise to the most terrible clashes. We have only to recall that described by Bartolomé de las Casas as the "destruction of the Indies."

The whole gamut of culture run by Europe in a span of more than four millenniums took place in Cuba in less than four centuries. In Europe the change was step by step; here it was by leaps and bounds. First there was the culture of the Ciboneys and the Guanajabibes, the paleolithic culture, our stone age. Or, to be more exact, our age of stone and wood, of unpolished stone and rough wood, and of sea shells and fish bones, which were like stones and thorns of the sea.

After this came the culture of the Taino Indians, which was neolithic. This was the age of polished stone and carved wood. With the Tainos came agriculture, a sedentary as opposed to a nomadic existence, abundance, tribal chieftains, or caciques, and priests. They entered as conquerers and imposed the first transculturation. The Ciboneys became serfs, *naborías,* or fled to the hills and jungles, to the *cibaos* and *caonaos.* Then came a hurricane of culture: Europe. There arrived together, and in mass, iron, gunpowder, the horse, the wheel, the sail, the compass, money, wages, writing, the printing-press, books, the master, the King, the Church, the banker. ... A revolutionary upheaval shook the Indian peoples of Cuba, tearing up their institutions by the roots and destroying their lives. At one bound the bridge between the drowsing stone ages and the wide-awake Renaissance was spanned. In a single day various of the intervening ages were crossed in Cuba; one might say thousands of "culture-years," if such measurement were admissible in the chronology of peoples. If the Indies of America were a New World for the Europeans, Europe was a far newer world for the people of America. They were two worlds that discovered each other and collided head-on. The impact of the two on each other was terrible. One of them perished, as though struck by lightning. It was a transculturation that failed as far as the natives were concerned, and was profound and cruel for the new arrivals. The aboriginal human basis of society was destroyed in Cuba, and it was necessary to bring in a complete new population, both masters and servants. This is one of the strange social features of Cuba, that since the sixteenth century all its classes, races, and cultures, coming in by will or by force, have all been exogenous and have all been torn from their places of origin, suffering the shock of this first uprooting and a harsh transplanting.

With the white men came the culture of Spain, and together with the Castilians, Andalusians, Portuguese, Galicians, Basques, and Catalonians. It could be called a crosscut of the Iberian culture of the white Pyrenean subrace. And in the first waves of immigration came Genoese, Florentines, Jews, Levantines, and Berbers — that is to say, representatives of the Mediterranean culture, an age-old mixture of peoples, cultures, and pigmentation, from the ruddy Normans to the sub-Sahara Negroes. Some of the white men brought with them a feudal economy, conquerors in search of loot and peoples to subjugate and make serfs of; while others, white too, were urged on by mercantile and even industrial capitalism, which was already in its early stages of development. And so various types of economy came in, confused with each other and in a state of transition, to set themselves up over other types, different and intermingled too, but primitive and impossible of adaptation to the needs of the white men at that close of the Middle Ages. The mere fact of having crossed the sea had changed their outlook; they left their native lands ragged and penniless and arrived as lords and masters; from the lowly in their own country they became converted into the mighty in that of others. And all of them, warriors, friars, merchants, peasants, came in search of adventure, cutting their links with an old society to graft themselves on another, new in climate, in people, in food, customs, and hazards. All came with their ambitions fixed on the goal of riches and power to be achieved here, and with the idea of returning to their native land to enjoy the fruits of their labors in their declining years. That is to say, the undertaking was to be bold, swift, and temporary, a parabolic curve whose beginning and end lay in a foreign land, and whose intersection through this country was only for the purpose of betterment.

There was no more important human factor in the evolution of Cuba than these continuous, radical, contrasting geographic transmigrations, economic and social, of the first settlers, this perennial transitory nature of their objectives, and their unstable life in the land where they were living, in perpetual disharmony with the society from which they drew their living. Men, economics, cultures, ambitions were all foreigners here, provisional, changing, "birds of passage" over the country, at its cost, against its wishes, and without its approval.

With the whites came the Negroes, first from Spain, at that time full of slaves from Guinea and the Congo, and then directly from all the Dark Continent. They brought with them their diverse cultures, some as primitive as that of the Ciboneys, others in a state of advanced barbarism like that of the Tainos, and others more economically and socially developed, like the Mandingas, Yolofes (Wolofs), Hausas, Dahomeyans, and Yorubas, with agriculture, slaves, money, markets, trade, and centralized governments ruling territories and populations as large as Cuba; intermediate cultures between the Taino and the Aztec, with metals, but as yet without writing.

The Negroes brought with their bodies their souls, but not their institutions nor their implements. They were of different regions, races, languages, cultures, classes, ages, sexes, thrown promiscuously into the slave ships, and socially equalized by the same system of slavery. They arrived deracinated, wounded, shattered, like the cane of the fields, and like it they were ground and crushed to extract the juice of their labor. No other human element has had to suffer such a profound and repeated change of surroundings, cultures, class, and conscience. They were transferred from their own to another more advanced culture, like that of the Indians; but the Indians suffered their fate in their native land, believing that when they died they passed over to the invisible regions of their own Cuban world. The fate of the Negroes was far more cruel; they crossed the ocean in agony, believing that even after death they would have to re-cross it to be resurrected in Africa with their lost ancestors. The Negroes were torn from another continent, as were the whites; but not of their own will or choice, and forced to leave their free and easy tribal ways to eat the bitter bread of slavery, whereas the white man, who may have set out from his native land in despair, arrived in the Indies in a frenzy of hope, converted into master and authority. The Indians and the Spaniards had the support and comfort of their families, their kin-folk, their leaders, and their places of worship in their sufferings; the Negroes found none of this. They, the most uprooted of all, were herded together like animals in a pen, always in a state of impotent rage, always filled with a longing for flight, freedom, change, and always having to adopt a defensive attitude of submission, pretense, and acculturation to a new world. Under these conditions of mutilation and social amputation, thousands and thousands of human beings were brought to Cuba year after year and century after century from continents beyond the sea. To a greater or lesser degree whites and Negroes were in the same state of dissociation in Cuba. All, those above and those below, living together in the same atmosphere of terror and oppression, the oppressed in terror of punishment, the oppressor in terror of reprisals, all beside justice, beside adjustment, beside themselves. And all in the painful process of transculturation.

After the Negroes began the influx of Jews, French, Anglo-Saxons, Chinese, and peoples from the four quarters of the globe. They were all coming to a new world, all on the way to a more or less rapid process of transculturation.

I am of the opinion that the word *transculturation* better expresses the different phases of the process of transition from one culture to another because this does not consist merely in acquiring another culture, which is what the English word *acculturation* really implies, but the process also necessarily involves the loss or uprooting of a previous culture, which could be defined as a deculturation. In addition it carries the idea of the consequent creation of new cultural phenomena, which could be called neoculturation. In the end, as the school of Malinowski's followers maintains, the result of every union of cultures is similar to that of the reproductive process between individuals: the offspring always has something of both parents but is always different from each of them.

These questions of sociological nomenclature are not to be disregarded in the interests of a better understanding of social phenomena, especially in Cuba, whose history, more than that of any other country of America, is an intense, complex, unbroken process of transculturation of human groups, all in a state of transition. The concept of transculturation is fundamental and indispensable for an understanding of the history of Cuba, and, for analogous reasons, of that of America in general. But this is not the moment to go into this theme at length, which will be considered in another work in progress dealing with the effects on Cuba of the transculturations of Indians, whites, Negroes, and Mongols.

When the proposed neologism, *transculturation,* was submitted to the unimpeachable authority of Bronislaw Malinowski, the great figure in contemporary ethnography and sociology, it met with his instant approbation. Under his eminent sponsorship, I have no qualms about putting the term into circulation.

Transatlantic African Survivals and the Dynamism of Negro Culture

Jean Price-Mars

It is evident that the foulest blot which has over besmirched the face of the habitable globe has been the Slave Trade. And when one thinks that for hundreds of years this abomination was practised by the European nations which were most proud of their standard of civilization — France, England, Holland, Spain, Portugal, etc. — the crime seems even more hateful and unforgivable. No doubt it was disguised by humanitarian and highly spiritual pretexts. It was by the intoxication of purported crusades against paganism, by the fervour of a campaign against idolatry, that an attempt was made to justify what was in truth a most pitiless economic enterprise. For if there is one fact which is obvious and long since brought to light as a shattering commonplace, it is that the prodigious impulse towards the conquest and enslavement of the Negro masses was nothing more than the passive submission of the European Powers to the pressure of economic necessities which compelled them to replace the unproductive Amero-Indian labour by more robust, more resistant and at the same time more malleable workers, so as to derive the utmost profit from the agricultural and industrial wealth to be found in exploiting the newly discovered American lands. This is the explanation of the trade which began in the first decades of the seventeenth century.

It will be remembered that the first elements in the Negro immigration were despatched to the Antilles, first to St. Kitts, and then to San Domingo.

In France Colbert regulated the trade in 1664, and after that it expanded progressively, in such a way that with the passage of years the traffic in human cattle became so intense that towards the end of the XVIII century some 30,000 to 35,000 souls were transported from Africa to America every year.

Such, at least, was the process of the Slave Trade between the French motherland and her Transatlantic colonies, among which San Domingo held the first place by reason of its extent and the wealth of its territory.

But, practically to the same extent, all the colonial establishments in Tropical America which belonged to the other European Powers — in the islands as well as on the mainland — and which obeyed the same rules of exploitation in the search for a more productive labour yield, had recourse to the same stratagems of the Slave Trade, so that the cultivation of the sugar cane, of cotton and of tobacco, undertaken by the English, the Spanish, the Portuguese and the Dutch, should lead to the greatest prosperity of their respective colonies.

Thus it followed that in the sixteenth and seventeenth centuries the slave population of the New World, composed of African Negroes had risen to more than a million in the United States by about 1800, to 1,600,000 souls in Brazil by about 1798 and 600,000 in San Domingo by about 1789. But at the moment when the Negroes in the United States were emancipated, some sixty years later, the growth of the slave population had reached a total of 4,500,000 souls. If the figures for the other islands of the Antilles and the other countries of Central and South America are added to these first figures, the number of Negro Slaves in the New World at the beginning of the XIX century seems likely to have been more than twelve million. For the rest, it has always been difficult to specify the exact numbers of this population, scattered over the different regions of America. Possibly for this reason, only the most approximate figures on this point have been put forward during the last fifty or sixty years. We can only make use of them subject to certain reservations. In the first place statistics were most frequently non-existent, and even where they existed they were generally systematically falsified from motives of prestige and even of shame, because in this way nine tenths of the primarily Caucasian communities could brazenly deny the obvious cross-breeding of many of their members. It is nevertheless clear that the Negro or negroid element spread throughout America, from the North to the South and from the East to the West. It was at its densest in North America in the Southern States of the Union on the Atlantic seaboard, in the western part of the island of Haiti and in South America in Brazil.

According to statistics published in 1900 by Sir Harry H. Johnston in his remarkable book "The Negro in the New World", the total Negro or negroid population in the New World then reached the figure of 24,591,000. Forty years later in 1940 Angel Rosenblatt in "La Problacion indigena de America desde 1492 hasta la actualidad" stated that the figure has increased to 54, 617, 416 souls.

It is unfortunate that we cannot compare the actual figures for the last sixteen years (1940-1956), since no authoritative and reliable publication is available. We may, however, assume that if the three main centres of Negro population in America give us a total of 48 millions — made up of 15 millions in the United States of America, 19 millions in Brazil and 14 millions in the Archipelago of the Antilles — it is obvious that the addition of negroid groups living in other parts of the hemisphere would bring the total of Negroes in the Americas to a figure in excess of 54 million souls.

In any event it follows from the above figures that this total of 54 million Negroes in America in this twentieth century is sufficiently suggestive to allow us to draw certain conclusions.

We shall bear in mind that his figure, which does not result from any massive immigration of Negroes from Africa or Asia, demonstrates the normal increase of population among the Negroes themselves and their cross-breeding with the other basic elements of the American populations; Whites, Amero-Indians and Asiatics. And these facts constitute the most striking evidence of the anthropobiological survival of the Negro masses led into slavery in the New World. In spite of the feeling of opprobrium attached to Negroslavery, in spite of the legal obstacles and judicial prohibitions which forbade sexual relations between Whites and Negroes, in spite of the system of racial discrimination which was the immediate consequence, in spite of the stupid negative attitude and the megalomania shown by many American communities affected by collective Bovaryism, cross-breeding is the prevailing fact, as it always has been in America, so rightly called the "melting pot". The growing number of men of every shade of colour, the innumerable varieties born of crossing the Negro with Caucasian or Mongolian types in the different regions of the New World, bear eloquent witness to the mixture of races in which the Negro imported from Africa has shared in the Western Hemisphere. It follows that his biological survival has become the decisive factor in his cultural influence in American surroundings.

That is what we shall now look at.

II

First of all, nobody would have thought, at the time when the Slave Trade was becoming established and the hard regime of servitude being set up, that the human cattle destined for slave labour and whose sole purpose was to furnish motive power for agricultural exploitation, would nevertheless proceed to an exchange of services with his master. But between the barbarian and the patrician a system of spiritual exchanges was born which survived the cruelty of slavery. This was the language which master and slave used in many colonies for the purpose of mutual understanding. We would indicate that this language, which is called *Creole,* is common, in spite of certain variations, to all the Transatlantic agglomerations colonised by the French in the XVI and XVII centuries, whether it is San Domingo, Martinique, Guadeloupe, Guiana, Louisiana, or even Réunion in the Indian Ocean. Nevertheless no similar language has become current in the communities colonised by the English or the Spanish or even the Portuguese. It is only in the Dutch colony of Curacao that a similar process, Papiamento, served as a means of communication between the Dutch colonists and their slaves. Like Creole it has survived the colonial period and remains the vernacular language in Curacao. With regard to Creole it is at the present moment the vehicle for the thought of an aggregation of more than six million people if one includes the Creole of Haiti, that of the small islands of the Antilles, part of Louisiana, French Guiana and Réunion.

It forms a real language, endowed with all the attributes of such. In origin it is linked with French from which it is derived by its historic formation.

But then a question arises in this connexion.

What is the reason for the difference in linguistic development between the English and Spanish group on the one hand and the French and Dutch on the other in creating an intermediate language suitable as a vehicle of thought between these different colonists and their slaves?

Perhaps it was easier for the Africans to assimilate the minimum command of the English and Spanish languages to enable them to grasp the thought of their English and Spanish masters than it was to go through the same psychological process with French and Dutch. Thus they had the ingenuity to include the French or Dutch vocabulary, more or less deformed, in the morphological mould of certain West African dialects, and thus invented Creole and Papiamento. At least this is the explanatory theory of the origins of Creole which prevails among the most distinguished linguists of Haiti, such as Mr. Charles Fernand Pressoir who has devoted outstanding studies to the comparison of Creole and certain African dialects, especially Dahomeyan. These linguists stress that the grammatical forms of Creole are in many respects so similar to certain dialects of West Africa that spiritual contact between Whites and Negroes for the exchange of ideas was facilitated by the speed with which the Negroes retained French vocables which they adapted to the morphology of African languages. It is useful to note further that this operation was imperative, since while the masters spoke no African dialect, the Africans on their side not only spoke no French but could not even understand each other. For it must be remembered that this was the device employed by the slave traders, to sell the Negroes in dispersed tribes so as to prevent any common understanding between them with a view to possible revolt. The twofold necessity of finding a language common to all gave birth to Creole.

In any event comparative linguistic studies of Creole and the West African dialects make it possible to refute the stupid and nonsensical explanation which uninformed teachers like Mr. Edward Larocque-Tincker still persist in giving of the origin of Creole. It is therefore surprising in an article published in the *Revue de Paris* for April 1956, to find the following propositions on the physiological difficulties which prevented the slave newly landed from Africa from speaking French: "His swollen lips" he writes "and his thick tongue made it impossible for him to pronounce in French certain words rich in vowel sounds. In his mouth *"juge"* became *"jige" "tortue", "toti", "nuit" "nouitte".* As he could not roll his r's, he decided "not to bother" and said *"neg"* for *"nègre"* and *"vend,* for *"vendre".*

As he could not either read or write, language for him was merely a matter of ear. Only the accentuated syllables of words struck him; and as soon as he could, he added the other. *"Appeler"* to him became *"pele", "capable", "capab"* and *"aujourd'hui", "jordi".*

A less superficial knowledge of linguistic studies of African dialects and a less fanatical attachment to his absurd prejudices on the biological malformation of the Negro would have helped

Mr. Larocque-Tincker to find in phonetics the true explanation of the transformation of XVI century French into Creole invented almost at the same period.

Be that as it may, Mr. Jules Faine, a distinguished Haitian linguist, puts forward another theory under which Creole derives from the old French dialects still in use in the XVI century at the time when sailors from Normandy, Britanny, Picardy and elsewhere were cruising the seas in search of adventure and trade. In this way they would have diffused an archaic tongue which was borrowed and adapted by the peoples with whom they came into contact. Whatever judgment may be passed on either of these theories, both of which deserve to be pursued by increasingly profound study of African dialects until they are either proved or disproved by incontestable demonstration, it should be pointed out that, quite apart from its African morphology, Creole contains a large number of vocables which are manifestly African and which are met with almost unchanged both in Haiti and the French colonies in America, just as they also persist in Brazil, Louisiana, Cuba, Guiana and even in some of the British colonies in the Antilles. These vocables are particularly common in relation to cooking, agriculture, religion and magic. Unfortunately no lexicographer in Haiti has so far thought of cataloguing them as Fernando Ortiz has done for Spanish in Cuba, or Renato Mendonça for Portuguese in Brazil. We will, however, cite a few by way of example:

Acassan; edible paste made of maize flour, water and salt, very popular in Haitian peasant diet.
Acra; edible paste made from flour of the cow-pea *(vigna sinensis)* seasoned with pimento.
Agogo!; an exclamation frequently uttered by Voodoo adepts during religious ceremonies.
Banza; a stringed musical instrument, like a violin.
Baka; a sort of dwarf monstrosity employed by Sorcerers for magical purposes (Legendary).
Bonda; the buttocks.
Cachimbo; a tube in terra cotta or wood inserted into the clay pipe smoked by peasants.
Gongolo; a species of myriapod.
Gris-Gris; ornithological term to describe a bird of prey.
Gombo; an edible plant *(hibiscus esculentus).*
Marabout; term denoting a pigmentary colour.
Samba; a dance term.
Tanga; a sort of loin-cloth used to cover the male or female sexual organs.
Yam; an edible root *(Dioscorca data).*
Zombi; a person whose apparent death has been provoked by a magician and whom he will bring back to disincarnate life as an automaton. (Legendary.)

We would emphasize that this summary and restricted vocabulary is merely given here by way of example, since it would be inappropriate to extend its scope, as that is not our purpose. Nevertheless, it will be found to be nearly identical with that published by Renato Mendoça in his book called "A influença Africana no portugues do Brasil" published at Rio Janeiro in 1934. The same vocables are used in the same sense in the Portuguese of Brazil. They bear witness to the African survivals in this country just as the thousands of words collected by Fernando Ortiz in his great work, *Glosario d'afro negrismos* afford proof of the influence of African phonetics on the Spanish of Cuba. But it is above all in the field of religious or superstitious beliefs that this proof is most abundant in American circles. It is obviously more or less marked according to the demographic importance of the Negro group. In Haiti, for example, where the Voodoo cult has a great number of adherents among the popular and peasant masses the whole Voodoo Olympia borrows its vocabulary from African dialects. It may be said that Dahomey, Nigeria and Congo have dispensed the sacred language of Voodoo in the same way that Rome dispensed Latin to Roman and Apostolic Catholicism. It is enough to indicate that the priestly body of this cult — *hougans, bocors* (priests), *mambos* (priestesses) *ougenikons, ounsis* (hierarchic dignitaries of the cult), the cosmogony and the deities, *Legba, Ogou, Damballa, Ouedo, Shango, Linglesou,* (Olympic deities) *ounfo* (altar) *asen,* (sceptre); *tambours, ve-ve,* (symbolic signs), in short, all the morphology of Voodoo derives from that West African coast. This however, has not prevented it from undergoing the influence of Roman Catholicism, whose light prevails in the Haitian community. Obviously, following a contact between the two cults over many centuries, the result has been a syncretism of popular beliefs which gives its unique tone to the religion of the Haitian masses. This is where the process of acculturation takes place, under which two cultures in contact interpenetrate each other to a point at which the exchange gives the resulting product an appearance of interpretative novelty. The subtlety of the operation in the present case consists in the transposition of the Catholic deities into the African mould and the consequent accommodation is revealed by the two-fold piety of the faithful to both cults by a curious harmonisation of the parts. The same phenomenon is found in different aspects in the Negro communities in the Protestant countries of America. In ceremonies known as *revivals* the Holy Ghost is often incarnated in the person of the faithful in the course of religious gatherings where to the sound of hymns marked by the rhythmic clapping of hands or stamping of feet a sort of collective trance descends upon part of the congregation, which shouts and dances (the shouters) in the enthusiasm of ecstatic transports. Such a spectacle leaves no doubt in the mind of the ethnographer, who sees in it the trade mark of a sublimated African influence.

For the rest, this influence becomes crucial in the case of small Negro bush communities, whose contacts with the colonists from the European mainland have been few and brief and who have retained a certain age-old independence. They have earned the right to preserve unchanged the tribal physiognomy of the African countries. The manners and customs of the Saramaca, the Awka, the Boni and the Djuka of Dutch Guiana, are of this kind. These tribes who inhabit the dense sub-equatorial forest of the region have stoutly defended the right to live in their own way under Treaties made between themselves and the Dutch Government, following long and bloody revolts against colonial oppression. They have in the course of time kept intact the way of life of their ancestors led into slavery from across the Atlantic. So much so that at the present moment they serve as controls, in laboratory terms, of the acculturation of their racial brothers placed elsewhere in the same Hemisphere under other conditions among people of Western culture, and of the original stock in the African countries. But even among them the same folk themes exist that are found in Cuba, Haiti, Jamaica or the United States.

The African presence moreover asserts itself in many other aspects of American life.

It would be wrong to pass over in silence the introduction into our diet of spices like pepper and pimento, which are proper to African cooking and which season the insipidity of food prepared in European fashion. Moreover, one should not forget the very marked propensity towards peasant polygamy which is customary in some societies in the Antilles. In Haiti this feature of manners derives from ancestral habitudes, thanks to which the peasant provides himself with helpers for work in the fields by the proliferation of natural children. He multiplies the homes which are so many starting points for the formation and recruitment of those temporary and occasional mutual aid associations, known as *combite,* by which he assembles the necessary labour for his farming operations, in return for similar action to help his collaborators. It certainly seems that these customs are an African legacy.

It has also been noted that farming implements in the Haitian economy in its peasant form have retained the type of hoe and bush-hook knife which sociology classes as the signs of obsolete technique, and which are usual in West Africa.

Be that as it may, Africa, on this side of the Atlantic, as elsewhere, has inspired a prodigious flowering of the plastic arts which has overwhelmed the modern world like a revelation. Is it not true that painting and sculpture have found in African realism a fertile source of renewal and freshness? Is it not true that music has seized upon the emotive power of the Negro soul to express in the blues and the spirituals all the unplumbed depths of human suffering?

Is it not true that by these means the Negro has made himself the messenger of another gospel, that of patience and hope?

Then, if by chance, you need to galvanise your flagging energies, if you thirst after the movements proper to the call of an ardent and tumultuous life, there is Jazz to offer you the magic enchantment of its polyphonic orchestration and the sorcery of its power of evocation. It is Negro.

Was it then a freak of chance or had the moment arrived for a man to appear, Gilberto Freyre, Brazilian sociologist and philosopher, an enthusiast for study and truth, who in a magnificent book *Casa Grande e Senzala*[1], dared to proclaim in this twentieth century what his community owed to the Negro. Here are the words in which he pays tribute to the contribution of the African to the formation of the Brazilian;

"Every Brazilian" he writes "even if he is light skinned and has fair hair, bears in his soul (and if not in his soul on his body; quite a number of people in Brazil have the Mongolian mark) the shadow or the mark of the native or the Negro. Of the Negro particularly on the seaboard, from Maragnan to Rio Grande in the South and in the State of Mines. The influence of the African is direct or vague and remote. In our way of expressing tenderness, in our excessive mimicry, in our Catholicism which is a delight of the senses, in our way of walking and talking, in the songs which cradled our childhood, in short in all the sincere expressions of our life, the Negro influence is patent."

This courageous profession of faith is singularly moving in a universe which still resounds with the echoes of racial hatred, where the human value of the Negro is still disputed by the imbecile fanaticism of retarded racists. It links up with the curious observation of C. G. Jung reported by Hermann von Keyserling in his famous work, "The Psycho-analysis of America";

"The first thing which attracted my attention among the Americans", said Jung "was the influence of the Negro, an obviously psychological influence regardless of any mixture of blood."

The expression of emotions among Americans and particularly their laugh cannot be better studied anywhere than in the society columns of the American newspapers; the inimitable Roosevelt laugh is found in its primitive form among American Negroes. That special disjointed walk, that swaying of the hips, which one observes so often among the Americans, are of Negro origin. American music derives its principal inspiration from the Negro; their dancing is Negro dancing, the expression of religious emotion, the Revival meetings, the Holy Rollers and other abnormalities undergo a strong Negro influence and the celebrated American ingenuousness in its charming forms as well as in its less agreeable, may well be compared with the childishness of the Negro."

And Keyserling, taking up the theme to analyse its content in depth, concluded with the following remark:

> "There is therefore nothing paradoxical on my part in foreseeing that the greatest cultural achievements of America may very well be due to her sons of Negro race."

If, twenty years after this prophecy was made, it is still unfulfilled, nothing has changed its basis.

"The future is in God's hands."

Note
1. Translated into French under the Title 'Maîtres et Eselaves' published by Gallimard.

The Social Framework

Elsa Goveia

The Caribbean that I mean to speak about today is not the whole of the area bordering on the Caribbean sea. It is in fact the West Indies and the Guyanas, and I have chosen to speak about that area because it is my area of particular interest and also because it has a common history which does not include the other areas of the Caribbean around the Caribbean Sea.

The whole history of this particular set of Caribbean countries now emerging to independence has been a history of colonialism and this is very important for an understanding of their society today. They have always been dependent societies attached to a wider grouping with a ruling metropolis outside the area of the Caribbean. This colonial status has been reflected in political dependence, in economic dependence, in social dependence and in cultural dependence: Cuba has a strongly Spanish culture; the French West Indies have now become the overseas departments of metropolitan France — an indication of how far they have accepted integration into the metropolis; and then the British islands in the West Indies have a predominantly British culture, though some of them, having changed hands between Europeans in the course of their history, don't have an entirely British culture in the way that Cuba, which has always been Spanish, has a Spanish culture.

The colonial status of these islands in the West Indies is reflected, very sharply, to take another instance, in their language which usually follows the language of the metropolitan power. There are partial exceptions, in the Creole language, or languages, that are spoken in the West Indies; but these exceptions apply only to small or socially uninfluential groups of speakers. The speakers of standard European languages in the West Indies usually follow the usage of the metropolitan country; and speech and thought in terms of speech are so important that this has left a stamp of metropolitanism on the West Indies which still remains even though some of these territories are becoming wholly independent of their metropolitan governments. It appears to me that even after the colonial link has been broken this is going to be one of the most important areas of metropolitan influence. I think that there is a connection between this fact and the fact that so many West Indian writers live abroad rather than in the West Indies, but that's a point which no doubt others here will wish to dwell on more than I can, at the moment.

In the West Indies we have then, colonial societies in some cases just emerging into independence and we have a great heritage of metropolitan influence over the social and cultural activities of the West Indian territories. This metropolitan influence has not been exclusive in the West Indies. It has been accompanied by a very important heterogeneous variety of culture. In areas which were French and Spanish, for instance, we have Roman Catholicism as the official religion, but also Afro-West Indian cult groups only partly influenced by European ideas of religion, and with a very considerable African element in their religious activities. These cult groups usually belong to the lower classes in the community who do not conform as completely to the metropolitan influence as the more educated members.

The same thing is true of language. Language in the West Indies is a double-edged sword. It is European on the one hand and it is West Indian Creole on the other so that you have in addition to the English, or French, or Spanish that is spoken, a polyglot language made up of words, in many cases taken from European languages, on a structure, a linguistic structure that is not European, and in this way you have in fact a complete dichotomy between the way in which many people speak and think in the West Indies, and the official language which is set by the attachment to a metropolitan power.

In the West Indies, therefore, and in the Guyanas you have a very complex situation created by the inter-locking of two different sets of cultural behaviour, two different sets of social behaviour. In the one instance there is the metropolitan pattern which is particularly strong among the upper classes, and in the other case, there is a Creole culture which is born in the West Indies and which contains non-European forms in large numbers. The important thing I think about this contrast of two cultures is that it has divided the West Indies rather than helping to unite them. The division within each territory is compounded by a long-standing division across territories. The West Indies have very little communication, for instance, with Cuba or the rest of the Caribbean; and this is not just because a lot of West Indians are unsympathetic to Fidel Castro. It has been the case for most of our history that we have tended to be more apart than we are together. The great feeling is always to look outside of the West Indies, to look to the metropolitan country rather than to other West Indian territories for sources of inspiration, and this again is a state of being in the West Indies which has not ended with independence. We can see from the break-up of the West Indian Federation, for instance, the great force of divisive elements in the Caribbean, even among colonies which belong to the same metropolis and which might be expected, as a result, to have at least more in common than they have with their foreign neighbours. Quite often we have no idea in the islands themselves what happens elsewhere in the West Indies, and it is only within fairly recent times that a consciousness of the West Indies as a whole has begun to grow, particularly among the people who regard themselves as intellectuals.

But to return to the division within territories. The West Indies is an area which has a common culture in the sense that there are resemblances which carry over from one culture to another, but a common culture which is divisive in its effect. This is reflected in the fact that the European language belongs to the upper class while the Creole language belongs to the lower class; that Roman Catholicism and conventional Protestantism belong to the upper class whereas cult groups belong to the lower classes. This great internal division of culture is repeated in relation to many other subjects besides religion and language though these are obviously two of the most important as far as the West Indies is concerned. The division of culture between different sections of the West Indian population also relates to such things as attitudes to land holding, the way of arranging kinship, and marriage ties. In the lower class, as is well known, marriage is the exception rather than the rule and most of the children born in the West Indies are illegitimate in the eyes of the law. This is a pattern which cuts the lower classes off from the rest of the community which practices a conventional Christian type of marriage. But it is worthwhile noticing, I think, that although there is this sharp division between the different parts of the community, there are, nevertheless, ways in which the relationship of these different cultural elements tend to overlap. For instance, lots of middle class men (not middle class women) have "outside" children, as we call them. That is, children not of their own marriages but children who are illegitimately begotten. These "outside" children do have a place, although it is an inferior place, in the relation between the father and all of his children, and in this way the monogamous marriage pattern of the ostensibly Christian West

Indian upper class is very significantly modified by the conditions of West Indian life and by the cultural heterogeneity of the West Indies. If one wanted, it would be possible to go through a long list of cultural items in which there is a distinct difference between the culture of the upper classes and the culture of the lower classes in the West Indies, and in fact this has been so marked, in the British territories at least, that M. G. Smith has argued that these territories constitute what he calls a plural society; that is a society that is held together by economic reasons and by force and not by any common culture or common set of values, shared by the population as a whole.

Now I don't agree with Mike Smith's interpretation of the West Indies on this particular point because it seems to me on the basis of my own historical work that the West Indies in the past have had an integration which has transcended internal divisions, and the very division between the classes is in fact part of the rationale, part of the integrating organisation of the society in which the different classes live differently. I have tried to point out elsewhere[1] that this integrating factor which affects the society as a whole, is the acceptance of the inferiority of Negroes to whites. Now this is a very important element, it seems to me, of the whole society of the West Indies and one which continues to be significant up to the present day, though it is no longer so all-pervading as it was in the era of slavery in which I was particularly interested. Under the slave system the Negroes and the free people of colour, as they were called, were shut out of the political system by the whites who controlled it and who were supported in their control of the political system by their connections to an overseas metropolis. The importance of the overseas metropolis was partly in providing the resources of support which were needed to keep the society in being, since it included large majorities of blacks who were subordinated to a smaller minority of whites and who could not have been kept in this position of subordination without the intervention, at least on some occasions, of the use of force in defence of the vested interest in the West Indian society. Although, force was always needed in the last resort, what I have found in my work on the Leeward Islands is that it was needed only as a last resort; it was not the typical way of preserving the society over the years. It was the way which was used when the society was threatened from within by slave revolts which undoubtedly occurred with quite considerable frequency in the West Indies during this period of the 18th century, but which nevertheless involved in most cases only a minority of the slaves. The majority of the slaves on the whole tended to acquiesce in their condition as subordinates of the small minority of whites, and to help this acquiescence to become more internalised the whites insisted throughout the period of slavery on the inferiority of the Negro groups in the society, interpreting this inferiority once slavery had become well established as an inferiority of race not just of social position. This is what has been inherited in the West Indies from the period of their slave history.

Now, in my view, the belief although this has not been established by research in all of the West Indies, the belief that the blacker you are the more inferior you are and the whiter you are the more superior you are, has not by any means died out in the West Indies. It is still there in the West Indies and it is one of the elements which still integrate the West Indian society, though it is obviously to the disadvantage of the great majority of the West Indian population. This divisive kind of integration is shared by all of the groups in the West Indies in spite of the fact that they belong to different cultural sections of the community. If one looks at these differences of culture, it then becomes clear that they fit into and are made intelligible by, the larger integration on the basis of a racial inequality. They belong to a universe in which it is the accepted thing that the upper class should be people of white or of lighter complexions as the lower classes should be people of dark complexions, and this is not simply a matter of the society being held in this position by force. We no longer have, in many cases in the West Indies, the force of a metropolitan power to hold the society in this particular state of equilibrium and yet, nevertheless, we have a position in the West Indies in which the social structure inherited from the colonial power does in fact survive, though some sections of the society are now beginning, naturally enough, to react against it.

Now the cultural heterogeneity of the West Indies is a feature of the racial heterogeneity of the West Indies, but it is also a feature of the social heterogeneity of the West Indies which makes it right for the upper classes to behave in ways in which the lower classes are not expected to behave. This relationship of dominance of a light skinned minority over the black majority is still one of the leading aims of the West Indian social system, at least as I understand it. But the interesting thing about the West Indies at the moment, though it was not so in the slave past, is that this social division is now accompanied by a political system which rests on a basis of support for the policies of the government, not merely by the light-skinned upper classes, but also by the black masses who now have universal adult suffrage which enables them in theory, at any rate, to influence what is done by the government in the West Indies. This is a political factor which is of great significance in relation both to the society and to its culture because it means that the political system contradicts the social system in fundamental ways.

The political system of the West Indies has in fact allowed the black population to assume the most important, the superior role, in the choice of the governments which are to rule these islands, and in this choice the white population has very little influence because in most cases it is less than 5 per cent of the total population of these islands. And even the brown middle class has relatively little influence except where the parties are very evenly balanced, because they are only about 20 per cent or so of the population. The predominant 70 per cent and over, in most cases in the West Indies, is provided by a Negro population which now has one man one vote as the basis of its political system.

I have been talking chiefly about the territories in which there is a history of plantation slavery and where the population is divided into white and brown and black. But this is not the only kind of cultural and racial heterogeneity which affects the West Indian territories. In Guyana and in Trinidad in particular, there are large Indian populations which have their own cultural traditions separate from those of the Creole society into which they were introduced as indentured labourers. And in these areas, as in Surinam, we have a situation in which the social structure is dictated by the heritage of the past — that is by plantation slavery—and follows the line of superior white, middle brown and inferior black. But it is a situation which is not only within this particular system of relationships, it also includes the Indian population (which in most cases is still predominantly agricultural) and the smaller, much smaller minorities of Chinese and Lebanese and European whites; so that the whole of the West Indian pattern of interrelations of white and brown and black is complicated in these cases by the introduction of subsidiary groups which have to be fitted into some relationship with the system, and I think it is rather interesting to look at the way in which these groups get themselves fitted into the system when they come to the West Indies and make the West Indies their home.

In the case of the Indians they are fitted into the social structure in the lowest rung because this is where the society tends to place its agricultural labourers. And of course, since Indians are dark skinned people, though not as dark as the Negroes, they are regarded as fitting into the same social structure based on colour which affects the working of the whole society. It is relatively easy to regard Indians as being simply another kind of Negro, though this is not the way in which the Negro tends to regard the Indian. But in the West Indies there are also waves of movement by which some Indian people have become members of the middle class and have become assimilated to the brown middle section of the community, fitting easily into the system of coloured classes in the West Indies because they have the same sort of skin colour as the people already in the middle class.

But when we come to the smaller groups, to the European-born whites who migrate into the West Indies, when we come to such minority groups as the Chinese we find that again, the way of fitting them into the social structure is determined by the use of the inferior/superior criterion which applies to the Creole groups in the society. The Chinese, for instance, were fitted in after they had left agriculture for business, fitted in as middle class groups and have gradually moved to the top of the middle class in those areas where they have settled in considerable numbers. From the point of view of judging the attachment of the West Indian to the inferiority/superiority rating of colour groups we find that the Chinese were among the first of the coloured groups in the West Indies to be admitted to work in banks, and in airways offices for example. When the pressure on the banks and airlines became too great to resist, they picked, in other words, the people who in physical appearance, in their having light skins and so called good hair, were closest to the leading group, the white group in the community. In the same way, immigrant whites from Europe tend to get fitted in to the middle class and its upper reaches and into the upper class of the West Indies. This pattern of colour classing means that everybody in the West Indies tends to be ranked on a superiority/inferiority basis which includes the ethnic factor as one of the most important factors in the ratings.

In addition to the ethnic factor there is also the factor of acquisition of wealth and this is one of the ways in which one sees that the West Indian society is responding to other criteria besides that of skin colour, or racial origin, which has been so very important in the past. In the West Indies and in the Guyanas the great importance attached to colour is equalled only perhaps by the importance attached to wealth. Yet we must bear in mind that these two criteria still tend to coincide to a considerable extent, because the dark skinned are generally the most numerous and the most poor. The area of employment opportunities in the West Indies has been very much influenced by the availability of education to the mass of the people, and even today when some of the governments in the West Indies talk about providing free secondary schooling for the whole of the population, there is a very important inequality of opportunity which tends to limit the groups which start at the bottom of the society and try to rise by means of their own merits and achievements.

The whole of the West Indies then is an area in which the way of classing people is by measuring them in racial origins against, an inferior/superior rule, and in the same way by measuring them against richer/poorer rule, and we find that these two sets of measurement tend in many cases to coincide. The people who have the lowest status on account of their racial origin have also the least wealth in the community, and the least opportunity for acquiring more wealth than they have. And conversely, the group which gets the highest rating socially is that which has also the greatest wealth and the lighter complexion. It is not surprising therefore, in view of this very strong, very entrenched interest in racial inequality that there should arise constant conflicts between the survival of the social structure in the West Indies and the new political system which has been introduced in the West Indies largely during the present century. The politics tend to put an emphasis on the virtue of numbers, because the more people there are the more votes you can get from them and this of course, is fully appreciated by the politicians; whereas when we consider the social structure, it is usually the case that the smaller the group, the higher its social status, and the larger the group the lower its social status.

Now this is the framework within which Caribbean artists have to operate, and it seems to me that they have a vested interest in ensuring that the system of race and of wealth classification in the West Indies should be abandoned at the earliest possible time. I am not suggesting that the writers need to be politicians though I believe that some of them are. But the fact is that unless the writer throws his weight on the side of the democratisation of West Indian society he is unlikely ever to be able to find a way of living in his own society. The only way that the writer can hope to earn his living in the West Indies is by helping to create a society that gives more money to more people, more education to more people, and a greater degree of respect to the people who make up the majority of the population, so that while they are thinking about being West Indian and what it means, the writers will not be scared off by problems arising from the fact that they belong to a society in which the majority has a very hard, and a very uncomfortable place.

Now the writers of the West Indies have been profoundly influenced by the political changes which took place in the West Indies during the 1930s and 1940s and which culminated, in the case of Jamaica, Trinidad, Guyana and Barbados, in independence during the 1960s. It was only after the riots of the 1930s had led to a democratisation of the political system in the West Indies that the society as a whole began to turn inwards and to look to itself for the basis of its political system, for the basis of its social system, for the basis of its cultural system. In the islands and in the Guyanas, we find that it is at this time, with the society beginning to look inwards to see what was wrong with its own organisation that the writers, and indeed other kinds of artists suddenly found their voice. They had been silent, or almost silent, for a long time and we suddenly find a flowering ardent West Indian culture which seems to be tied to the sudden change which was taking place in the West Indian's conception of himself. And the artists and writers have tended to make this conception more real for the small groups which take an interest in their work by utilising in their writing, the Creole dialect, by making their stories, stories about the West Indies and the way in which the West Indian society is organised, and also by giving centrality to people of dark complexion, helping to establish that the fact of blackness is not a fact of inferiority. In the West Indies and in the Guyanas the great movement forward in the arts which has taken place between the 1930s and the 1960s has led to the emergence of a group of people who share common ideas of the way in which the West Indies should develop. These ideas are the exact reverse of the inferiority/superiority rankings which have in the past helped to integrate the West Indian society. The people who now want to identify themselves with the West Indies, who want to be understood as West Indians, have in fact in many cases, the idea that one of the conditions under which they will consent to remain in the West Indian society is the condition that West Indian society should change from the old form and that it should change fundamentally from the old form that it had taken. And even if painters, as some of ours seem to do, tend to think in terms of abstract art rather than in terms of painting which can be socially influential, nevertheless I think each artist, each writer in the West Indies has got to make his own choice about his commitments on this question of the future of West Indian society and the future of West Indian culture.

The artist cannot afford to isolate himself from the question of how the future is to be formed and what its content is to be. And because this is so, and because this concern with the future is shared by many West Indians, particularly West Indians who are of that much maligned group, the intellectuals, the real impact of the new changing intellectual group in the West Indies is going to be of great importance both for the livelihood of artists and for the growth of West Indian society. Until we have made a choice between the conflicting elements of which our society is composed at present, between the inferiority/superiority ranking according to race and wealth, and the equality which is implied by the slogan of one man one vote, until we have made up our minds about that particular choice, we are not going to be able, it seems to me, to be sufficiently sure of ourselves, of our own identity, to produce art or writing or any of the other creative forms of activity including, if I may say so, the activity of teaching both in schools and in universities. Until we have made this choice we are not going to be in a position to be really creative as individuals because our energies are going to be absorbed by the terrible job of working from two completely different sets of premises; from the inferiority/superiority premise on the one hand, and from the one man one vote premise on the other. We cannot, it seems to me, expect West Indian society to continue in an integrated form unless this choice is made and unless it is made quickly. The problem is one of urgency because until this choice is made the whole energy of West Indian society is going to be absorbed by the conflict of directly opposed integrating factors, the particularism and the ascription of race and wealth on the one hand and the universalist, the democratic ideas of one man one vote on the other. And until we make a decision about the way in which we want the future to be built it is not going to be possible to find enough creative energy in the West Indies to produce the new culture which we need.

It has been a matter of some importance that within the last 20 years the elements of integration have been growing in the West Indies in the cultural field. For instance, in the middle class appreciation of calypsoes and in the new prestige given to folk songs and folk dances in the West Indies. But this is only a beginning. It has to be much more consciously done in future, and it has to be much more consciously done as a choice about the way in which we want the West Indian society and the West Indian culture to grow.

Note
1. Elsa V. Goveia, *Slave Society in the British Leeward Islands at the End of the Eighteenth Century* (New Haven, CT: Yale University Press, 1965).

Caribbean Man in Space and Time[1]

Edward Kamau Brathwaite

archipelago: fragments: a geological plate being crushed by the pacific's curve, cracking open yucatan; the arctic/north american monolith: hence cuba, hispaniola, puerto rico: continental outriders and the dust of the bahamas. atlantic africa pushing up the beaches of our eastern seawards

the history reflects the pressure and passage of lava, storm, stone, earthquake, crack, coral: their rise and fall of landscapes: destructions, lost memories: atlantis, atahualpa, ashanti: creations: fragments

it would be better to begin with Caribbean man: crouched: legitimate bastard: against space: dwarf, clenched fist of time

the unity is submarine

breathing air, the societies were successively amerindian, european, creole. the amerindian several; the european various; the creole plural

subsistent plantation maroon

multilingual multi-ethnic many ancestored

fragments

the unity is submarine

breathing air, our problem is how to study the fragments/whole

Part One
THE OUTER PLANTATION

I. Caribbean Studies

This is an exercise of enormous difficulty. Not because of the quantity of material involved (heavily financed directed research would take care of this), but because its success will be limited by the scholar's aboriginal concept and perception of wholes. Most people in the post-mediaeval world deal almost instinctively with fragments/specializations. The historian, especially, will periodise his material. There will be general periods: pre-columbian, slavery etc; there will be century blocks; and more specific dates e.g. 1492-1500; 1838-1844 etc. There will also be limitations on territorial treatment (Henri Bangou, *La Guadeloupe*: 3 vols., Paris, 1962, 1963; Douglas Hall, *Five of the Leewards*; Carib. U. Press, Barbados, 1971), or enterprise (L. J. Ragatz, *The fall of the planter class*: NY 1928; W. Westergaard, *The Dutch West India Company*: NY 1917; C. H. Haring, *The buccaneers in the West Indies in the 17th century*: NY 1910).

The major thrust of Caribbean historiography has been in this mode and has been the predominant tendency since the beginning of written study of the area. (See Elsa Goveia, *A study on the historiography of the British West Indies to the end of the 19th century:* Mexico 1956; Lambros Comitas, *Caribbeana 1900-1965*, U. of Washington Press 1968). It reflects, basically, the European political subdivision of the region; the influence of European empirical scholarship, the role of the gentleman-scholar; the interest of North America since 1900 in individual Caribbean territories for specific strategic/economic reasons; and the absence, until 1937, of locally based university institutions primarily concerned with Caribbean studies.

But even before the work of the Institute of Social and Economic Research at the U.W.I. and the Institute of Caribbean Studies at Puerto Rico (the ISER's journal, *Social and Economic Studies* began publication in 1953; the ICS's *Caribbean Studies* in 1960) important works of an inter-Caribbean orientation began to appear: Guerra y Sanchez, *Azucar y poblacion en las antillas* (Habana 1927); Noel Deerr, *History of sugar*, 2 vols (London 1949). In 1938, C. L. R. James' *Black Jacobins*, a study of the Haitian revolution under Toussaint, was published; and in 1944, Eric Williams' doctoral thesis, *Capitalism and slavery* (N. Carolina Press) appeared. What is interesting and significant about these four works is that they were concerned with the central aspect of the Caribbean experience up to that time: the presence of sugar as a prime factor of Caribbean (as opposed to island/fragment) industry, trade, international politics and socio-cultural formation. In a way, they were built upon the solid but more static empirical work of Ragatz, Debien,[2] Pares,[3] among others; but their subject matter immediately resolved them from the 'pebble' or single territory complex, into remarkable essays in comparative synthesis which moved towards a definition of 'Caribbean' that had not been present before, Guerra y Sanchez, by comparing the production and attitude to sugar in British Protestant Barbados and Hispanic Catholic Cuba, not only provided us with suggestive illustration of the difference in British and Spanish mercantilism, seen from the local/staple end, but indicated the presence of differing psycho-social Caribbeans in the two islands. Deerr's comprehensive work outlined the presence of a comprehensive Caribbean, sharing certain essential conditions which made sugar (and itself) possible. James and Williams, coming at a period of acute political self-consciousness in the area, used their awareness of local reality as a basis for anti-colonial scholarship: Williams illustrating that it was international economics, not paternalistic humanitarianism that made and unmade the slave system, while James made the case that the repression/control forces of this same international economic system could be (and had been) defeated and brought to the point of compromise by its international proletariat. The way had been cleared for the concept of 'plantation' in Caribbean scholarship.

II. Plantation Studies

Historians of slavery have always been familiar with the plantation; it is their main unit of study; but the conceptualization of the Caribbean (or a significant part of it) as plantation, comes out of the work, first of social anthropologists, then of economists dealing with the Caribbean contribution and reaction to mercantilism. In 1957 the Research Institute for the Study of Man (Columbia University, NY), held a seminar on plantation systems in the western hemisphere, their contention being that there was by then enough work and interest in the field to warrant such an enterprise.[4] Plantations were defined as tropical territorial units set up by colonizing Europeans for mineral or crop exploitation, and the nexus and network of production was designated a plantation system. There was a differentiation of these into island and mainland (where they were to be distinguished from haciendas), and between British and Spanish in the kind of economic attitude and emphasis outlined by Guerra y Sanchez in *Azucar y poblacion*. At the same time, the social anthropologists conceived of the tropical plantation as an area within which a culturation process was taking place, leading to what was designated a mestizo culture in the hispanic/hacienda area, based largely on Amerindians; and a mulatto culture in the plantation area, where large numbers of African ex-slaves were to be found.[5]

In 1966[6] Lloyd Best began to articulate his 'Model of pure plantation economy'[7] in which the plantation was posited as exploited hinterland to the industrial metropole, bound more or less permanently, structurally and functionally, to this relationship. In 1972 George Beckford published *Persistent Poverty* (OUP/ISER) in which this model was applied to a wide-ranging discussion of under-development generally, but with specific reference to the Caribbean plantation. The only criticism that can (and has) been made of this formulation is the obvious one: that it does not include and account for non-plantation areas of the Caribbean/Third World. Would an island like Carriacou, for instance, fit the model? Or, as Mathews[8] asks, would Puerto Rico in the 17th and Haiti in the 19th century? The answer of course is that we now need a study relating marginal economic areas of the Caribbean to the plantation. We can also point out that these marginal areas, although not 'plantation', fit into the wider model of underdevelopment as 'maroon economies.'[9]

III. Comment

Plantation system studies, therefore, tell us a great deal about how the Caribbean came to be exploited and why; and in a very real sense, define the region in these terms, even though this is not a conscious intention. The mainstream of cultural continuity in the Caribbean derives from the functional requirements of the plantation society, past and present, with an overlay of cultural particulars stemming from old and recent centres of cultural diffusion, adapted to local situations.'[10] The plantation model, in other words, is in itself a product of the plantation and runs the hazard of becoming as much tool as tomb of the system that it seeks to understand and transform.

Let me re-state the position. History in pursuing a continuous wall as its domain, in consolidating national or local political and economic self-interest, becomes the servant of a material vision of time. As such it has not realised criteria to assess the subtle discontinuities which point to the originality of man as a civilisation-making animal who can alter the architectural complex of an age. Such an alteration or dialectic of alteration would seem to me the cornerstone for a philosophy of history in the Third World of the Caribbean. It would bring into play the inspiration for new criteria within the dead-end of economic and political institutions. It would alert us to the duality that is characteristic of calendars of fate associated with dead time as the spectral irony and archaeology of the muse.[11]

This commentary is necessary at this stage for several reasons, all connected with our joined endeavour to perceive/define Caribbean reality. The irony and ambiguity of all our action/thought must constantly be kept in mind. The plantation, as we observed earlier, does not contain all that is planted. Therefore it is essential that our concepts and models, when made and applied, should be applied not only to the outer field of reality, but to our inscapes equally; that not only academics but artists and other kinds of intellectuals should have access to them for test of sense. Second, we must remember that models appear at the abstract zone of our spectrum/continuum; that if they do not change, the reality they seek to 'explain' nevertheless changes around them (cf. the concept of 'plural society' in 1955 and now),[12] and that in the final analysis, the model/system must contain *or live with* people. Indeed we may fairly confidently assert that the conception of Caribbean societies in our literature reflects very much what we should expect from the criticisms levelled at the plantation in the literature: instability, plurality/ambivalence, dependence. What we have to keep in mind, as we proceed with our examination, is that this social reality may be as much figment as fragment: result of our apprehension of reality; that the pessimistic/plantation view of Caribbean society, to put it another way, may very well not be the last word on Caribbean society.

IV. Societies within the system: main characteristics
1. Instability

    i.   loss/absence of aboriginal base
    ii. heavy and long-run in-migration (xvi-xix centuries) followed by significant
    iii. inter- and out-migration, resulting in
    iv. heterogeneous populations (ethnic and nationally aligned)
    v.   largely 'unorthodox' (i.e. un-metropolitan) family structures, under pressure from (i) and (iii) and
    vi. massive inequalities in land/man, man/resource and political arrangements, leading to
    vii. rigid stratification of (in)equalities resulting in
    viii. drop-out, samfie or bongo strategies, which in a more significantly general way, lead to

2. Pluralism

The rigid classificatory orders (culture, class, colour, money, status) set up as the result of colonialism and slavery, developed into caste-like structures mainly because of the massive importation of African slaves and Asiatic labour between the xvii and xix centuries. These peoples brought with them into the region a non-European culture which under the extensive and multiform conditions of the plantation, developed into a kind of negative pole to the white European orientated patterns of the elite, reacting with these to create a *creole* personality. But this 'creole', as a result, no doubt, of its origin and manner/circumstances of evolution, did not become a single/whole norm; but itself a product of the fragmentation syndrome of the entire region, divided itself into multivariate orientations, reflecting its complex ancestry. Caribbean creole society may therefore be seen as reacting to an electro/magnetic norm, producing euro-creole, afro-creole, indo-creole or sino-creole characteristics, so that it is truly possible to produce, in our parts, a white *or* black mulatto. This is the phenomenon of cultural pluralism: an interculturative process still faced with the ultimate possibilities of (1) *homogeneity* (when all orientations at last accept a solid and functional core of norms), (2) *federation* (when some or all of the various groups agree to live separately under the flags of their separate cultural grandfathers, but within a mutually agreed-on polity) or (3) *plural equilibrium* (a norm-troika situation).

The literature on this subject is now quite extensive.[13] The notion of cultural orientation and of creolization/pluralism as process rather than discovered structure is treated in Hoetink, and my own *The development of creole society in Jamaica 1770-1820*[14] as well as *Contradictory Omens*.[15] There is an interesting difference between this 'process' approach and M. G. Smith's original formulation (1955/61)[16] in which a situation was outlined where competing/alternative institutions/attitudes exist side by side, related to a 'whole' only through the superordinate control of the economic and governmental ruling system,[17] and taking little account of historical change.

3. Dependency syndrome

The structural/functional instability of the society, the ambiguities introduced into it through its plural framework, and the persistent poverty and low status of the overwhelming majority of its numbers, led/leads, according to most of those who have written on this, to social and individual disnomia: dependence, imitation, aggression, lack of initiative, the quashie complex: inhibiting growth, change and the realization of identity. It is, as I observed earlier, what one would expect, given the inherited concept of exploitation and destitution.

Part Two
THE INNER PLANTATION

But it is in the area of cultural life and expression that the scholarship of the Caribbean has so far been most wanting. This deficiency is a product and result of our outer plantation emphasis, the concern with our constitutional and economic relationship with the metropoles, and our reaction for/against the norms and styles of the (former) masters. We have therefore, most of us, been involved with little more than 'creole' versions of the imposed plantation. Hence the burden of (historiographic) scholarship has been with constitutional and political history; with war, trade, the plantation (aspects of mercantilism); race relations, social forms and problems (hacienda, plantation, urban). At the same time, there has been very little study of the institutions which support our political, commercial and social activity; measures of adaptation (if imported); transformations due to time and circumstance; effectiveness in terms of 'efficiency' and in terms of how far/how much the various social groups are/were able to express themselves through them. Even the family, too intimate, I should have thought, for this kind of thing, has been conceived as an 'institution,' given an abstract/functional treatment and reduced to statistics, or (at least in the anglophone Caribbean) 'investigated' (impetus Simey) because of the utilitarian needs of Social Development and Welfare, or fertility concern agencies; and it is only recently that education (perhaps the key to the entire developmental process, and perhaps only because of Common-wealth Caribbean pessimism over the outcome of the first years of constitutional independence) has come under close academic scrutiny; and this still largely confined to institutional/statistical effects rather than with content/curriculum research and its relationship to the embodying culture.[18]

It is therefore to the body of work connected with what I call here, 'The inner plantation,' that I wish to address myself during the remainder of this paper. Here we are concerned with cores and kernels; resistant local forms; roots, stumps, survival rhythms; growing points. . .

I. Areas of Research

1. Creolization

I have already, in Part One of this paper, pointed to the intercultural process we call creolization and noted the possibility of describing it in terms not of a 1:1 give and take act of gift or exchange, resulting in a new or altered product, but as a process, resulting in subtle and multiform orientations from or *towards* ancestral originals. In this way, Caribbean culture can be seen in terms of a dialectic of development taking place within a seamless guise or continuum of space and time; a model which allows for blood flow, fluctuations, the half-look, the look both/several ways; which allows for and contains the ambiguous, and rounds the sharp edges off the dichotomy. What we need now are specific histories of the process. European settlement, for instance, instead of being seen in terms of static political description as in, say, C. S. S. Higham's *The development of the Leeward Islands under the Restoration* (Cambridge U. P. 1921), would now provide a (clear) picture of the ancestral culture, and indicate how this in persons, families and institutions, was adapted to the Caribbean environment of land, ideology and other people. In this way we would be able to test Hoetink's hypothesis[19] that it is at the point of impact/origin that plural society sets up its characteristic dominant/subdominant segmented pattern and proceeds from there on a fairly predictable course, to a point of crisis/termination: eventual homogeneity or permanent plurality. All the ethnic groups which make up Caribbean society could be studied in this manner, moving through the period of settlement, through slavery and the post-emancipation period and the arrival of new ethnic immigrants, into the more recent phenomenon of vicarious culture contact through tourist, book, magazine, film, television: a process which is particularly interesting since here we find an increasing reaction to external stimulus from the segmented orders as a whole.

2. Creole institutions

These may be divided into two main groups: those derived from the European or initiating segment of the society (legislatures, courts of law, police systems, the 'established' Christian churches, press/mass media, banks, commercial organizations), and those peculiar to the inner plantation: friendly societies and co-ops that reveal themselves in susu, gyap, landship (Barbados), la rose (St. Lucia) and the spectrum of religious organizations from pentecostal and revival, right through to shango, vodun and cumfa.

Once again we observe that it is the outer plantation that has received most attention from scholars, especially those elements of it that have been most successful in the mercantilist sense, or have been found most useful in the area of control. Hence there has been a great deal written on the Navigation laws, on the legislatures of the various territories and their role in conflict or agreement with the metropoles.[20] But legislatures and law courts as local institutions have received little or no attention.[21] Similarly there have been church histories recording, essentially, the missionary or administrative success of the various denominations of the area; but no study of a particular church in a particular community like, say, Malcolm J. Calley's descriptive analysis of West Indian Pentecostal sects in England.[22] On the commercial and finance management aspect of mercantilism, there has been surprisingly little historical treatment: Lillian Penson on the Colonial Agents,[23] Douglas Hall on the West India Committee,[24] Girod's studies of the Hecquet family in St. Domingue,[25] Pares' *A West India fortune*[26], the Craton/Walvin study of Worthy Park.[27] Similarly I know of no work on the press since Cundall's brief survey of Jamaican printers prior to 1820[28] and a contribution to the history of journalism in Guadeloupe by Lenis Blanche.[29] For the inner plantation, the more dramatic aspects of cultural expression have caught eye and ear, especially in the religious area of most intense culture focus, and there have been a number of quite impressive studies on Afro-Caribbean religious expression and belief.[30] What we still need is a history of the progress (or not) from an ancestral base (African, E. Indian), to the present position in the creole continuum of these religious and connected systems, and an account of the *secularization* of sub-dominant religious forms generally in the Caribbean.

3. Creole/oral archives

With this, we reach the heart of research into the life/meaning of the inner plantation. Our weakness/failing as scholars is that we have been, on the whole, too (and surprisingly) concerned with abstractions rather than with people: putting the cart before the horse. This, I suppose, is another inheritance from the metropole, where the 'people' spade work has already been done as part of the steady evolution towards national identities, and where colonies, except for those visitors who bothered, were little more than abstractions/producers anyway. But this is only a fragment of this reality. If we penetrate to the inner metropole we find wonder, we find Labat, Mocquet, the indefatigable Raleigh, Defoe, Shakespeare, and the myth of El Dorado: exploitation converted to dream and image. For us, on the plantation, there should have been a similar atomic beginning: ourselves, the networks of us: relation to landscape, accumulation of language and experience. The novelists have written and there is a long history of song. But scholarship has given us little since the Herskovitses, Ortiz, Price-Mars, Bascom and Simpson.

We have had Oscar Lewis' *La vida*,[31] Sidney Mintz' *Worker in the cane*,[32] M.G. Smith's *Dark Puritan*,[33] V.S. Naipaul's *The loss of El Dorado*.[34] These are important contributions to Caribbean sociocultural history but are not themselves — nor were they intended to be — systematic social histories. These are still painfully absent. Cundall[35] in Jamaica between 1900 and 1920 made a start but there has been no line of succession: constitutional and now political and economic studies supervening. We have had no one of the vision of say, Gilberto Freyre to boast of. The books in English have sometimes made concessions by including a chapter of social history, especially for the slave period; and recent wide-ranging surveys by Gordon Lewis,[36] David Lowenthal,[37] Crassweller[38] among others, have brought us, in a way, up to date. But there has been no full-scale follow-up, for instance, to Pares *West India fortune,* on the one hand, or to Margaret Katzin's 'The Jamaican country higgler'[39] on the other; although the work of Handler[40] on Barbados and Girod for Haiti, in their different ways looks promising; and the recent interest in the study of carnival/calypso/steelband in Trinidad is for me a most welcome sign.[41]

But as a *central concern*, we can state that there has really been no systematic study of Caribbean culture and cultural expression, outside the period of slavery,[42] and certainly no history of it in terms of 'plantation' or the multiform creolization outlined above. This is because our culture history (essentially of the inner plantation) has had no 'archive' to work from. The archive of course is there, all around us: in the speech and actions of us. But until a major oral recording project can be undertaken; and until we begin to give thought to the techniques of collecting information from 'live' informants[43] (and these, I think, should be our major research priority for the 1970s), we will get nowhere with our attempts to connect, establish links, test for continuities within our plural framework. This is why we must develop a discipline of social arts to work along with (and sometimes run counter to) the social sciences. This is why our concept of scholarship must include the creative arts; why there must be more collaboration than there is at present between historians and social scientists; and between these and socio-linguists, ethnomusicologists and ethnobotanists; why we must continue to study the religion(s) of the interplantation. In this connection, it might be useful for Caribbean scholars to take a look at the work going on in Africa converting oral ambience into book: for example, G.S. Vere, *A history of the Abaluyia of Western Kenya*; B.A. Ogot, *History of the Southern Luo*.[44]

4. The Word

a' remember, one day a' find some lilies an' a' plant de lilies-dem in a row an' one Sunday mornin' when a' wake all de lilies blow. Seven lilies an' is seven a dem blow... An' a' leave an' go down in de gully bottom to go an' pick up some coconut an' when a' go a' see a cotton tree an' a' jus fell right down at de cotton tree root. An' is dere a' take now. Well a' don't heat anything. Twentyone days a' dont heat—anything. Twentyone days a' dont heat. In de nights in de cotton tree comin' like it hollow an' I hinside there. An' you have some Africans you understan'? Well dose tombs aroun' de tree light up wid cyandles an' I resting now put my hand dis way an' sleepin' an' a' honly hear a little voice come to me an' dem talkin' to me but dose tings is spirit talkin' to me an' dem speakin' to me now an' say 'Now is a little nice little chil' an' you gwine get you right up now in de African worl' because you' brains — you will take someting. So derefore we gwine to teach you something...' A man name Man Parker 'ave a dance in Dalvey a Hafrican dance an' a' went there — leave mi' mudder in de night to look on de dance an' when a' go dere a' see everybody was dancin' an' a' stan' up an' fol' mi' han' like dis an' a' feel mi' whole body like it is growin' growin' an' a' see a girl jump from away an' jus hol' mi' in mi' neck an' a' drop an' after a' drop now a' fain' a' jus' gone an' a' started to dance ...[45]

5. Autobiography of the family

R.T. Smith comes close to the point and orientation of this paper when he notes in *The Negro family in British Guiana*:

> Much confusion about the nature of lower-class family life in the West Indies has arisen as a result of taking verbal statements from members of the middle-class, or even of the lower-class, too much at their face value, and regarding them as statements of fact rather than as symbolic statements of a state of inter-group relationship.
>
> It is a part of the mythology of the West Indies that the lower-class Negro is immoral and promiscuous, and that his family life is 'loose' and 'disorganized', and unless it is clearly recognized that such myths are an integral part of the system of relationships between various groups, reflecting value judgements inherent in their status rankings, then serious bias may be introduced into objective study.[46]

Despite Smith's caveat, no study — at least in the anglophone Caribbean — has been undertaken and published, which attempts to examine the autonomous reality of the West Indian family, be it upper, middle or lower class; white, brown or black, chinese or amer/indian. There have, of course, been generalizations about families: mainly lower class black[47] and (east) indian;[48] and within this, there have been statistical/census studies[49] and mating pattern/fertility studies[50] basically concerned with, or the off-shoots of the 1930s colonial concern with the Caribbean 'crisis' of poverty/disnomia/overpopulation.[51] Even when as in Smith, for example, or Edith Clarke,[52] the centre and concern of the study has been local, the scholars involved have not been able to perceive the qualitative difference between inner and outer plantation. Clarke, for instance, for all her native sympathy, never allows her subjects to speak for themselves; so that, like Smith, she unwittingly makes an (educated) distinction between 'statements of fact' and 'symbolic statement' — thus vitiating the very spirit of Creole language/experience.[53]

This is why I have juxtaposed the quotation from Smith (above) with the tape-transcript from a Jamaican Kumina Queen. This authentic inner plantation statement, it will be observed, attains the quality of poetry. It is my contention that it *is* poetry. But it is at the same time a statement of fact — as St. Paul's account of the road to Damascus is a fact. Among the folk, life was and is lived in accordance with this kind of symbolic vision/expression.[54] And not the life of Saul/Queenie only, but the accretions around that life/experience: Queenie's husband, her children, her family, her kin, her dependents, her followers. In West Kingston, for instance, this reality and language represents a truly creole cultural unit, interacting with other groups and through them, with the society as a whole. And it is my understanding that the kind of familial and interpersonal units we find there do not always or necessarily conform to our inherited expectations, and that if this is so, we shall have to restructure our models.

II. Caribbean Models

I do not propose, however, model making at this point. But it should at least be clear that a great deal of our primary work in the 70s will be towards re-examining our two main working ideographs: the plural society and the plantation model. To do this we shall have to add oral archival resources to our inherited scribal ones. With regard to the plural model, we shall have to introduce *process* as well as structure, and open ourselves to the inputs of race, creolization and americanization, in ways that we have not attempted before. We shall also have to bear in mind the possibility that the resolution of this process may, but will not necessarily, be socio-cultural homogeneity.[55] Our new models should leave us open to the possibility of permanent co-existent plurality.[56]

With regard to the plantation model, we shall have to allow for interaction of unit structures: plantation/hinterland vs. metropole; but we shall also have to introduce the concept of inter-structure; that is, the interaction between inner and outer plantation, inner and outer metropole, and the lateral and diagonal relationships between these, With this kind of multi-dimensional model, our assumptions about 'traditional' and 'modern', and certainly the usual dialectical assumption that there is a natural progression from 'traditional' to 'modern'[57] may well have to be modified.

Finally, in the seventies, our research will have to equip us to more precisely observe, account for, and assess *agents of change*: the changes (material, spiritual and electronic) in the inner and outer metropoles; and the processes of change within and between the inner and outer plantation. And we shall have to try to describe these specifically/totally: as socio/national phenomena, as regional phenomena, and as hemispheric occurrences.

Towards this, there are several procedures. My own inclination is to establish a base in the inner plantation and proceed outwards: connection with the inner metropole, with the ancestors, with the outer plantation, and with the neglected maroons.

III

The unit is submarine.

Notes
1. Paper presented to the Association of Caribbean Universities and Research Institutes' Conference on 'Caribbean Man and his Environment' at UWI, Cave Hill, Barbados, January 1973.
2. G. Debien, *Une Plantation de Saint-Domingue* (Cairo, Egypt: L'institut Français d'Archéologie Orientale du Caire, 1941).
3. Richard Pares, *War and Trade in the West Indies* (Oxford: Routledge, 1926).
4. See, Pan American Union, 'Foreword,' in *Plantation Systems of the New World* (Washington, DC: Columbia University, Research Institute for the Study of Man, 1959).
5. See, for example, Charles Wagley, 'Plantation America: A Culture Sphere,' in *Caribbean Studies: A Symposium*, ed. Rubin (Seattle: University of Washington Press, 1960).
6. 'Current Development Strategy and Economic Integration in the Caribbean,' in *Caribbean Integration*, ed. Lewis and Matthews (San Juan: Institute of Caribbean Studies, University of Puerto Rico, 1967), 58–76.
7. *SES*, 17:3 (1958).
8. See Thomas Matthews, 'Los Studios de la Historia Economica del Caribe,' presented at the XXX1X Congress of Americanists in Lima, Peru, August 1970, and submitted to the Caribbean Universities Conference, 15.
9. Kari Levitt, 'The Old Mercantilism and the New,' *SES* XIX:4 (1970); Norman Girvan, 'Multinational Corporations and Dependent Underdevelopment in Mineral-export Economies,' *SES* XIX:4 (1970).
10. Vera Rubin, 'Social Perspectives in Caribbean Research,' in *Caribbean Studies*, already cited, 121.
11. Wilson Harris, *History, Fable and Myth in the Caribbean and Guianas* (Georgetown, Guyana: Natural History and Arts Council, 1970), 32.
12. See M.G. Smith's, *A Framework for the Caribbean Studies* (Kingston: University College of the West Indies, 1955) and the concerns of the 1973 Conference which, in a sense, was our first major re-assessment since Smith wrote.
13. See, for example, the bibliography in H. Hoetink, *Caribbean Race Relations* (London: Oxford University Press, 1957) being a translation and shortened version of De gespleten samenleving in

het Caribisch gebied (Assen 1962) and Leo A. Despres, *Cultural Pluralism and Nationalist Politics in British Guiana* (Chicago: Rand McNally, 1967).
14. Oxford, 1971.
15. Savacou Publications, Mona, 1974.
16. See M.G. Smith, *The Plural Society in the British West Indies* (Berkeley: University of California Press, 1965).
17. See for example, Smith, *Plural Society*, 175.
18. See, as an example, some recent studies in *SES*: Manley XII:1 (1963); Lewis XII:3 (1964); Tropp XIV:1 (1965); Roberts XIV:1 (1965); Bacchus XV:1 (1966), XVI:2 (1967), XVI:4 (1967), XVII:2 (1968), XVIII:3 (1969); Schwartzbaum & Cross XIX:3 (1970).
19. *Caribbean Race Relations*, 98, 109, 133–4.
20. See the status reports for Historical Studies presented by Woodville Marshall and Rene Acheen to the Caribbean Universities' Conference.
21. See Keith Patchett's, Status Report presented to the Conference.
22. Malcolm J.C. Calley, *God's People* (London: Oxford University Press, 1965).
23. Lillian Penson, *The Colonial Agents of the British West Indies* (London: University of London Press, 1924).
24. Douglas Hall, *A Brief History of the West India Committee* (Barbados: Ginn, 1971).
25. Francois Girod, *Une Fortune Colonial sous l'Ancien Regime: La Famille Hecquet a Saint-Domingue, 1724-1796* (Besançon: University of Besançon, 1970); *Une Famille Parisienne a St Domingue: Les Hecquet-de-wailly-duval et Leger, 1724-1796* (Besançon: University of Besançon, 1969).
26. London, 1950.
27. Michael Craton and James Walvin, *A Jamaican Plantation: The History of Worthy Park, 1670-1970* (London: W.H. Allen, 1970).
28. Frank Cundall, *The Press and Printers of Jamaica prior to 1820* (Worcester, Mass.: American Antiquarian Society, 1916); *A History of Printing in Jamaica from 1717 to 1834* (Kingston: Institute of Jamaica, 1935).
29. Lenis Blanche, *Contribution à l'Histoire de la Presse a la Guadeloupe* (Basseterre: Imprimerie Catholique, 1935).
30. See, among others, Bascom (1950), Metraux (1959), Simpson (1965/1970), Moore (1953), Herskovits (1937, 1941, 1947, and 1954), Barrett (1974).
31. New York, 1965.
32. Yale University Press, 1960.
33. UWI (Mona), 1963.
34. London, 1970.
35. Cundall's instinct was towards biography and socio-cultural history. Biographical Annals of Jamaica: A Brief History of the Colony Arranged as a Guide to the Jamaica Portrait Gallery... (Kingston, 1904); *Historic Jamaica* (London: West India Committee, 1915).
36. Gordon Lewis, *The Growth of the Modern West Indies* (London: Monthly Review Press, 1968).
37. David Lowenthal, *West Indian Societies* (London: Oxford University Press, 1972).
38. Robert D. Crassweller, *The Caribbean Community* (London: Pall Mall Press, 1972), 14–34.
39. *SES* VIII:4 (1959): 421–35.
40. Jerome Handler has conducted a massive socio-anthropological study of slavery in Barbados in historical perspective, and has already published, ancillary to this, *A Guide to Source Materials for the Study of Barbados History, 1627-1834* (Carbondale, IL: Southern Illinois University Press, 1971); 'Aspects of Slave Life in Barbados; Music and Its Cultural Content,' *Caribbean Studies* 11:4 (Jan. 1972): 5–46; 'An Archaeological Investigation of the Domestic Life of Plantation Slaves in Barbados,' *Journal of the Barbados Museum and Historical Society* 34, no. 2 (May 1972): 64–72; 'The History of Arrowroot and the Origin of Peasantries in the British West Indies,' *Journal of Caribbean History* 2 (May 1971): 46–93; among others.
41. See J.D. Elder, *Evolution of the Traditional Calypso in Trinidad and Tobago*... PhD thesis, University of Pennsylvania, 1966; Ann Arbor microfilm text, 1970; Errol Hill, *The Trinidad Carnival*... (Austin, TX: University of Texas Press, 1972). There has also been 'The Bertie Marshall Story' (steelband) in *Tapia*; Will Simmonds, 'The Story of the Steel Band,' *West Indian World* (Sept. 29, Oct. 6, Oct. 20, Oct. 27, Nov. 3, 1972); Gordon Rohlehr's 'Forty Years of Calypso,' *Tapia* (Sept. 3, Sept. 17, Oct. 8, 1972).
42. An exception/attempt for the Anglophone Caribbean is Ivy Baxter, *The Arts of an Island: The*

Development of the Culture and of the Folk and Creative Arts in Jamaica, 1494–1962 (Metuchen, NJ: Scarecrow Press, 1970).

43. Reference might be made to Jan Vansina, *De la Tradition Orale*, (Tervuren: Musée Royale de l'Afrique Centrale, 1961); Philip Curtin's, 'Field Techniques for the Collection and Processing of Oral Data,' *Journal of African History*, 1X:3 (1968); and the Introduction to B.A. Ogot, *History of the Southern Luo* (Nairobi, 1967).
44. Both published by the East African Publishing House, Nairobi, 1967.
45. Tape transcript of conversation with Queenie (Mrs Kennedy) speaking with Monica Schuler and Maureen Warner. A study of certain aspects of this tape, by Maureen Warner, appears in *Savacou* 11/12.
46. R.T. Smith, *The Negro Family in British Guiana* (London: Routledge & Paul, 1956), 259.
47. Blake (1961), Clarke (1957), Cumper (1958), Greenfield (1959), Henric (1965: for Guadeloupe), Henriques (1953), Kreiselman (1958: for Martiqique), Smith, M.G. (1962); Comhaire-Sylvain (1958), and Hubert de Roncerey (1969) for Haiti.
48. Davids (1964), Jayawardena (1960, 1962, 1963), Klass (1961), Schwartz (1965), Smith, R.T. (1959), Speckmann (1965).
49. See the work, in the Anglophone Caribbean, cf George Roberts, *The Population of Jamaica* (Cambridge: Cambridge University Press, 1957), and Abbott, et al. in *SES*.
50. In *SES*: Ibberson, V:1 (1956), Cumper, XV:3 (1966), Byrne, XV:4 (1966; Bouvier and Macisco, XVII:1 (1968), Weller, XVII:3 (1969), Ebanks, XVIII:4 (1969), Otterbein, XIII:2 (1964), Wag, XX:2 (1971).
51. See T.S. Simey, *Welfare and Planning in the West Indies* (Oxford: Clarendon Press, 1946); Basil Matthews, *Crisis of the West Indian Family* (Port-of-Spain, Trinidad: University College of the West Indies, 1953); Judith Blake, *Family Instability and Reproductive Behavior in Jamaica* (NY: Milbank Memorial Fund, 1955). The titles of some of the latter's work are revealing: 'Family Size in the 1960's – a Baffling Fad?' (1967); 'Are Babies Consumer Durables?' (1968), both for the Urban Research Institute, California. See also Dora Ibberson, 'A Note on the Relationship Between Illegitimacy and the Birthrate,' *SES* V:1 (1956): 93–99.
52. Edith Clarke, *My Mother Who Fathered Me* (London: G. Allen & Unwin, 1957).
53. I am thinking especially of the appendix, 'The Death and Burial of Mrs Malcolm,' 217–27 of the 1966 edition.
54. See, for instance, E.E. Evans-Pritchard, *Nuer Religion* (Oxford: Clarendon Press, 1956).
55. See Hoetink, 106.
56. This is explored more fully in *Contradictory Omens*.
57. For a recent brilliant example of this assumption, see Walter Rodney, *How Europe Under-Developed Africa* (London and Dar-es-Salaam: Bogle L'Ouverture Publications, 1972).

Retentions and Survivals

Sidney W. Mintz and Richard Price

If African-American cultures do in fact share such an integral dynamism, and if, as we shall argue, their social systems have been highly responsive to changing social conditions, one must maintain a skeptical attitude toward claims that many contemporary social or cultural forms represent direct continuities from the African homelands. Over the past several decades, historical research has reduced the number of convincing cases of formal continuities, but has hinted at new levels of continuity—levels which may eventually tell us a great deal more about the actual development of African-American cultures. Students of the African-American heritage have witnessed a gradual shift from the analysis of isolated cultural elements viewed largely from the outside, to the analysis of systems or patterns in their social context. Students of creole languages, for example, increasingly have located the unique aspects of these languages on the syntactic (or discourse) level, rather than simply on the lexical level; and analogous arguments have been proposed for such diverse things as art forms and onomastics.[1]

These shifting perspectives are well illustrated by the history of studies of Suriname Maroon woodcarving. Traditionally, scholars considered this to be the prototypical "African art in the Americas";[2] an art historian discussing this art among the Saramaka has noted that the "arabesques in openwork...even-sided flat bands, and...brass studs to enhance curvilinearity" strikingly recall eighteenth-century Akan work.[3] Yet recent ethnohistorical field research strongly suggests that this distinctive art form was forged in the Guianas and is largely a nineteenth-century development. It has also demonstrated that many of the most striking formal similarities with West African art are quite recent innovations.[4] More generally, such research urges upon us a reorientation of our focus, from trying to explain similarities of form considered in isolation to comparing broad aesthetic ideas, the implicit "grammatical" principles which generate these forms. The very real formal similarities between the art of the Maroons and that of some West African peoples are not, then, mere evidence of static "retentions" or "survivals," but rather products of independent development and innovation, within historically related and overlapping sets of broad aesthetic ideas. The wood-carving of the Maroons, like their naming, cicatrization, and other aesthetic systems, then appears to be highly creative and to be "African" more in terms of deep-level cultural rules or principles than in terms of formal continuities: in short, a highly adaptive subsystem, responsive to the changing social environments of the artists and critics who continue to carry it forward.

We keep in mind that, in art as in much else, the relationships between individual artist and group are likely to be complex and subtle. To what extent art is produced and modified in a context of freedom of expression, and to what extent group and individual creator are bound by conservative values, must be specified separately for each society and, often, for each art medium or genre. We can assume that West African artistic expression varied to some degree from one society to another, while the opportunity for individual creativeness or innovativeness probably varied with the social function of the particular art form. Presumably much the same has been the case with African-American art. Given the social circumstances of its beginnings, however, we choose to suppose that a high degree of freedom for variation may have been institutionalized in many art forms at the outset. In order to make the most possible sense of how these forms evolved in African-American societies, it will be necessary both to learn all we can of those initial situations, and to pursue our study of art and other African-American cultural manifestations in their social contexts,[5] and not purely as delineations of changing or conservative forms.

Recent historical research on Afro-America also has taught us some of the dangers of extrapolating backward to Africa in the realm of *social* forms. We may mention but one obvious example drawn from our own work. Saramaka men, who now commonly have two wives each, turn out upon careful investigation to be far more "polygynous" (one might say "African-looking," in Herskovits's terms) today than were their ancestors two centuries ago, due to changing institutions in the wider society, with newly evolved patterns of wage labor and the skewed local sex ratios such patterns have created.[6] It seems likely that systems of social relations are generally even more highly responsive to changing environmental conditions than are cultural systems. As in the cultural realm, however, we would suggest that delving below the surface of social forms to get at the value systems and cognitive orientations that underlie and accompany them may reveal long-term continuities of another kind.

In calling for more subtle, in-depth research, we do not mean to deny the existence of direct "survivals" or "retentions" in Afro-America, or that careful investigation of the specific reasons for their continued persistence will help us better to understand the formative years of African-American history. We might cite two brief examples. The ultimate "ordeal," the equivalent of the highest court in Saramaka today, is in the hands of a small cult group in a single village; its techniques, which include thrusting a medicated feather through the tongue of the accused to determine guilt or innocence, seem traceable directly to the eighteenth-century Kingdom of Benin.[7] In this case, it seems likely that a specific cluster of ritual knowledge was carried to Suriname during the earliest years of slavery by a single specialist, and that the tradition (which is attested to in eighteenth-century Saramaka[8]) was perpetuated in much the same way as we describe for our hypothetical "twin birth" ritual. In contrast, divination with a coffin—the interrogation of the spirit of the deceased (in which the movements of the bearers of the corpse are "controlled" by the spirit, anxious to reveal the cause of death)—provides a different sort of example. It was a widespread practice in West and Central Africa as part of funeral rites, and we find it again in widely separated parts of colonial Afro-America—from Jamaica to Dominica to Suriname.[9] Unlike the Saramaka ordeal, which involves a highly specialized body of knowledge from a particular society that nevertheless served a function recognized as crucial in many West and Central African societies, divination with the corpse was probably familiar to most of the first transported slaves. These two particular continuities, even viewed thus summarily, can be seen to illustrate somewhat different processes in the development of African-American cultures. Careful consideration of other such real historical continuities almost certainly will help us to understand some of the choices open to early African-Americans, as well as the later course their cultures took.

We wish to consider, in equally sketchy fashion, two other cases of continuity, partly in order to emphasize the relationship between continuity of culture and continuity of personnel, partly to enlarge the range of cases of such continuities, and to expose the complexity involved in their study. Following Emancipation in the British West Indies (1834–1838), free Africans were imported to a number of British colonies, including Trinidad, in the hope of expanding agricultural settlement and of supplying additional labor to the planters. In a twenty-year period (1841–1861), Trinidad received 6,581 *free* Africans;[10] between 1834 and 1867, that island received a total of 8,854 *liberated* Africans, taken off slavers headed for Cuba or Brazil by British cruisers.[11] A large number of different African cultural groups were represented by these migrations, including Ibo, Temne, Wolof, Yoruba, Ashanti, Fulani, and Mandingo peoples.[12]

In a tantalizingly brief but intriguing account, Carr described a "rada" (Dahomean) community outside Port-of-Spain, founded by one Robert Antoine (Aboyevi Zāhwenu) about fifteen years after his arrival in Trinidad. Antoine acquired a small property by purchase in 1868, where he settled with his common-law wife and son. By the time of his death in 1899, his house and compound had become a center for migrant Dahomeans, many of whom had previously settled nearby: "during the ceremonial occasions of those early days it is said that so large were the gatherings at the compound that there was hardly room in which to accommodate the people."[13]

Antoine initiated and maintained a substantial portion of the Dahomean ceremonial calendar at his compound. It is significant that those who emigrated at the same time to Trinidad had included a trained *hubonõ* or high priest, and two male *vodũnsi* (cult initiates), and all three of these men actively perpetuated traditional ceremonies. It may be of equal interest that the gods who are celebrated by this group often carry saints' names, typical of African-American religious groupings in Catholic countries elsewhere, as in Brazil, Cuba, and Haiti. Carr asked his informants how the African deities acquired Christian names and was told that they had "always" had them. The idea that such names had been attached to the African godheads after contact with missionaries in Africa was rejected by the elderly compound member with whom Carr spoke. Thus we have no information as to how or when such names were in fact acquired.

It is not our intent here to examine in detail the correspondences and divergences between the religious expressions of this group and those typical of nineteenth-century Dahomey. But we must note that this case reveals both substantial continuity—as in calendrical allocation of ceremonies, gods' names, priestly roles, sacrifice, possession, etc.—and substantial modification, both by syncretism (for instance, the attachment of saints' names, which we believe to have occurred in Trinidad itself) and in terms of the sociology of the new setting. No male *vodũnsis* have appeared since the deaths of Alokasu and Kunu, who accompanied Antoine from Africa. The *Kututo* ceremony for the dead, which is held in November, is now linked to a Catholic mass for the souls in Purgatory. Five deities, who formerly possessed native African migrants, have not reappeared since the deaths of these men. Some shrines have vanished. Even in small ways, change reveals itself. The *Sakpata* shrine, still maintained in the compound, once had at its head a euphorbia plant, supposedly in accord with African tradition. But a child's eyesight was damaged by the milky fluid of the plant some years ago, whereupon it was replaced with a dragonblood plant (*Dracaena* spp.).

Even without a thorough comparative examination, it should be clear that the sociocultural religious system of the homeland did not survive intact and unchanged in the new context—and, of course, it would be quite extraordinary if it had. Doubtless more significant is the fact that Antoine was able to count on the services of three trained religious specialists when he initiated the ceremonial calendar a century ago. While we cannot weigh the importance of the disappearance of male *vodũnsis*, we think it defensible to assume that it would have affected the forms and functions of the ceremonial calendar today.

A final example may be drawn from the literature on Afro-Cuban religion. While it differs in many ways from that provided above, it shares with the Trinidadian case a relative recency of implantation of African custom in the New World setting. The slave trade to Cuba ended about 1865, though it seems certain that additional slaves were imported during several years immediately following. Curtin has estimated that twelve thousand slaves were imported in 1865, but calls this "guesswork," and suggests that he has picked a relatively high figure because he supposes that the trade continued briefly thereafter.[14] Materials on the ethnic origins of Cuban slaves during the last stages of the trade are unsatisfactory; the trade was illegal, and manifests of slave ships, or other information of the sort available for, say, Saint-Domingue at an earlier period, are lacking. Nonetheless, it is certain that substantial numbers of Yoruba were imported, and the Afro-Cuban religious and linguistic materials suggest as much. Having carried out field investigations both among the Yoruba of Ife, Nigeria, and the Lucumí of Matanzas, Cuba, Bascom and Montero de Bascom were able to document continuities of certain kinds in divinatory practices, including the 256 permutations resulting from the casting of a sixteen-unit, two-part divinatory necklace. Though important changes in the materials employed, in the terminology of explanation, and in the pronunciation of terms have occurred, "Both the names and the order of the double figures ... check exactly with those recorded for the Yoruba by Epega, Aderoju, Frobenius, Monteil, and Dennett, for Dahomey by Bertho and Maupoil, and for the Ewe by Spieth."[15] The Afro-Cuban data are particularly convincing because the various elements in divinatory practices are clearly separable, but occur in both Nigeria and Cuba in such intimate interrelationship that diffusion from Africa to the New World cannot be questioned seriously.

These two cases reveal both continuity and change. The Afro-Cuban case makes clear that a relatively complex portion of culture can be carried substantially intact from one locus to another. Though certain substitutions of material (e.g. coconut disks for kola nuts) occur and are obvious enough, migrant diviners needed only to have around them persons from the same or a related society where such divination was practiced to have been able to ply their skills. The Afro-Cuban divinatory practices, however, both show continuities with more than one West African culture and suggest that other groups besides the Yoruba contributed to the forms assumed by older materials in the Cuban context. The Trinidadian case does not demonstrate any obvious intermixture of original African forms, even though there was considerable change in the new setting over time. The Cuban case suggests that the African materials diffused from overseas originated with persons who were members of different groups, even though very solid continuities with past practice are demonstrable.

Two obvious features of these cases require mention. First, both of the emigrations in question, relative to certain others, occurred fairly recently. Second, in one case the migrants were free or freedmen, and, in the other, slavery had ended only about twenty-five years after the last migration. In both of these regards, the Trinidadian and Cuban examples differ substantially from most other examples of African continuities. In a general way, it can be claimed that both the strength of the continuities and their relative lack of modification probably are related to recency of migration and to the presence (in Trinidad) or nearness (in Cuba) of freedom. Such assertions do not explain away the many other cases of such continuities, often maintained in the face of great oppression and imposed disorder, nor can we deal adequately here with the whole issue of illegal slave trading, as it must have influenced the whole panorama of continuities in the New World. But overall, direct formal continuities from Africa are more the exception than the rule in any African-American culture, even in those such as Saramaka, which have been most isolated.[16]

Notes

1. See, for example, Richard Price and Sally Price, '*Kammbá:* The Ethnohistory of an Afro-American Art,' *Antropologica* 32 (1972): 3–27; idem, 'Saramaka Onomastics: An Afro-American Naming System,' *Ethnology* 11 (1972): 341–67; Sally Price and Richard Price, *Afro-American Arts of the Suriname Rain Forest* (Berkeley and Los Angeles: University of California Press, 1980).
2. Philip J.C. Dark, *Bush Negro Art: An African Art in the Americas* (London: Tiranti, 1954); J.L. Volders, *Bouwkunst in Suriname: Driehonderd Jaren Nationale Architectuur* (Hilversum: G. van Saane, 1966).
3. Robert F. Thompson, 'From Africa,' *Yale Alumni Magazine* 34 (1970): 18.
4. Jean Hurault, *Africains de Guyane: La Vie Matérielle et l'Art des Noirs Réfugiés de Guyane* (The Hague: Mouton, 1970); Richard Price, 'Saramaka Woodcarving: the Development of an Afro-American Art,' *Man* 5 (1970): 363–78; idem, 'The Guiana Maroons: Changing Perspectives in "Bush Negro" Studies,' *Caribbean Studies* 11(4) (1972): 82–105; Price and Price, *Afro-American Arts*.
5. See, for instance, John F. Szwed, 'Afro-American Musical Adaptations,' in *Afro-American Anthropology*, ed. N. Whitten and J. Szwed (New York: Free Press, 1970), 219–28; Sally Price, *Co-Wives and Calabashes* (Ann Arbor: University of Michigan Press, 1984).
6. Richard Price, 'Saramaka Emigration and Marriage: A Case Study of Social Change,' *Southwestern Journal of Anthropology* 26 (1970): 157–89; idem, *Saramaka Social Structure*.
7. Gerhard Lindblom, *Afrikanische Relikte und Indianische Entlehnungen in der Kultur der Busch-Neger Surinams* (Göteborg: Elanders Boktryckeri Aktiebolag, 1924), 92–93; John Barbot, 'A Description of the Coasts of North and South-Guinea,' in *A Collection of Voyages and Travels* 5, ed. Awnsham Churchill (London, 1732), 373.
8. C.L. Schumann, Saramaccanisch Deutsches Wörter-Buch,' in *Die Sprache der Saramakkaneger in Surinam*, ed. Hugo Schuchardt, Verhandelingen der Koninklijke Akademie van Wetenschappen te Amsterdam 14 (1914): 46–116. s.v. *kangra*.
9. Charles Leslie, A *New History of Jamaica* (London: J. Hodges, 1740), 308–9; Thomas Atwood, *The History of the Island of Dominica* (London: J. Johnson, 1791), 268–69; F. Staehelin, *Die Mission der Brüdergemeine in Suriname und Berbice im achtzehnten Jahrhundert* (Herrnhut: Vereins für Brüdergeschichte in Kommission der Unitätsbuchhandlung in Gnadau, 1913–19, 3(2): 55.
10. Wood, *Trinidad*, 80.
11. K.O. Laurence, *Immigration into the West Indies in the 19th Century* (London: Caribbean Universities Press, 1971), 14.
12. Wood, *Trinidad*, 240–41.
13. Andrew Carr, 'A Rada Community in Trinidad,' *Caribbean Quarterly* 3(1) (1953): 40.
14. Curtin, *Atlantic Slave Trade*, 40, 43.
15. William R. Bascom, 'Two Forms of Afro-Cuban Divination,' in *Acculturation in the Americas*, ed. Sol Tax (Chicago: University of Chicago Press, 1952), 172–73; see also Montero de Bascom, 'Influencias Africanas en la Cultura Cubana,' *Ciencias Sociales* 5 (1954): 98–102.
16. A large but uneven literature deals with African survivals and retentions in the New World. Pioneering works include Herskovits, *Myth of the Negro Past*, and selected essays dating back to 1930 by the same author; see Melville J. Herskovits, *The New World Negro* (Bloomington: Indiana University Press, 1966) and Arthur Ramos, *Las Culturas Negras en el Nuevo Mundo* (Mexico: Fondo de Cultura Económica, 1943). Bastide's *Les Amériques Noires* is available in English translation as *African Civilisations in the New World* (New York: Harper and Row, 1971). A useful debate about survivals and retentions is to be found in *Caribbean Studies: A Symposium*, ed. V. Rubin (Seattle: University of Washington Press, 1957), where M.G. Smith exchanges views with George E. Simpson and Peter B. Hammond (34–53).

The "Creolisation" of Indian Women in Trinidad[1]

Patricia Mohammed

Introduction

"Creolisation" is a troublesome but useful term. Troublesome because there are so many interpretations of the word; useful because it confronts the issues related to ethnicity and ethnic relations in a multi-racial society. It is a daring, perhaps even an offensive word to use in reference to Indian women in Trinidad, for it was used popularly to refer to those women who mixed or consorted with people of African descent, especially men – Indian women who changed their eating and dress habits and who adopted non-Indian social customs. But this perhaps draws on a more popular interpretation of the term. A derivative of the word "Creole", used in Trinidad to refer to descendants of African slaves to distinguish them from indentured Indian immigrants, "creolisation" was viewed as synonymous with the absorption of Black culture at the expense of one's own – a process referred to as "acculturation". Anyone appreciative of the history of the relations between the two majority ethnic groups in this society – Blacks and Indians – understands immediately the anathema which greets the suggestion of acculturation, especially from the Indian population.

The term creolisation, however, has a vastly richer meaning that that suggested above, and it is in the more expansive framework of the concept that I want to discuss the changing status of Indian women in the post-independence period in Trinidad and Tobago. I am drawing first on the original Spanish sense of the word, from *criollo,* which meant born in and committed to the area of living. In Trinidad and Tobago we have been accustomed to using it in this sense – for instance, when we refer to French or Spanish Creoles. Creole societies emerge in the context of a colonial arrangement with a metropolitan power, so that there is the additional dimension of an internal reaction against external metropolitan pressures. There is, simultaneously, a process of internal adjustments taking place between the cultures interacting in the society. This is a more reciprocal relationship between cultures, an "intermixture and enrichment, each to each", as it has been formulated by Kamau Brathwaite[2] – or, in other words, interculturation as opposed to acculturation. Included in the latter process is also the acceptance of the values inherent in Creole society – in this instance, its preoccupation with class and colour. My discussion is focused on these ongoing and dynamic processes – acculturation, commitment to one's country of birth, reactions against external cultures and interculturation.

There, however, are two other concerns though which are central to any consideration of movement and cultural change in society: first, the impact and influence of political movements on attitudes and practices among competing ethnic groups; and second, the effect of "modernisation" on the competing cultures.

Where and how do Indian women fit into this matrix of cultural change? How do they contribute to the process and how are they affected by it? That they comprise a significant proportion of the population is a demographic fact worth noting. In the 1980 census of the population, Indian women accounted for 39.6 per cent of the total female population of Trinidad and Tobago, while women of African descent comprised 39.9 per cent. They therefore account for just under one-quarter of the total population of the country. It is also important to recognise that Indian is not synonymous with Hindu: in fact, in 1980 Hindu women comprised 24 per cent of the total female population, while Muslim women comprised six per cent, Presbyterians four per cent and other Christians just under six per cent. Although Hindu women predominate, there are subtle differences to be found between Indian women of different religions, differences which transcend their ethnic similarity.[3]

The Pre-Independence Period

We need to start at the very beginning. Post-independence changes are clearly meaningless if they are not matched against the pre-independence era. From all accounts, Indian women's introduction into the new society was dramatic to say the least and made for the rather paradoxical situation in which the first Indian female immigrants found themselves in the new society – a paradoxical situation of being at the same time more free yet less free. First of all, consider the sexual imbalance between Indian males and females that existed for the entire period of indenture 1845–917, and well into the post-indenture period. Between 1881 and 1891 there were 2,117 males to every 1,000 females. Not given to celibacy, Indian men found the situation unsatisfactory. Planters were also concerned about accretions to their labour supply, especially when it seemed that the system of indenture would be discontinued. Thus, efforts to increase female immigration resulted in a ratio of 1,354 males to every 1,000 females by 1911. Despite these efforts, at no time during the indentureship system did the number of females equal that of the number of males imported into the colony. By 1931, there was still an imbalanced ratio of 1,135 men to 1,000 women.

Second, consider the type of woman who was indentured. Rhoda Reddock has suggested that those women who came would have already been a more independent breed; it is calculated that two-thirds of the women who were recruited were either single, widows who would have been forbidden to remarry in India, women who had separated from or been abandoned by their husbands or other women of "easy virtue".[4] Though more conclusive research is needed, the fact remains that under new and more promising conditions, the Indian woman could challenge her former role in India. She was now in the enviable position of being a scarce and valuable resource. She was also, like her male counterpart, a wage earner on the estate.

These two factors obviously created conditions for a more independent and less passive role for Indian women. This, however, was more easily said than done. Indian men could no longer rely on the rules, which entrenched patriarchy in India in both Hindu and Muslim families. On the estate they could not make recourse to the rules governing Hindu life, as the doctrines of karma and dharma, while glorifying womanhood, also placed femininity in a passive role as chattel to masculinity, ensuring female subservience and passivity. Indian men in Trinidad violently coerced their women into submission. Bridget Brereton notes that between 1872 and 1900, 87 murders of Indian women occurred, of which 65 were wife murders.[5] This legacy of institutionalised violence persisted and appears to have been one of the features of the relations between Indian men and women when they were married, such as those typified in the cruel and dehumanised relationship between Pa and Ma in Tola Trace in 1905 in Harold Sonny Ladoo's *No Pain Like this Body*.[6]

Yet in the face of this kind of coercion, it is believed that Indian women were the keepers of the culture, establishing in the new society as many of the traditions and cultural practices of the motherland. It is strangely ironic that Indian women would voluntarily recreate a pattern of life which would be restricting and oppressive to them. We need to ask, as sociologist Kim Johnson has done, if Indian women sought independence in the first place, then who was it from? His explanation appears to me to be a logical one. He suggests that, like Indian men, Indian women clung to their remembered culture as the only solace and strength: there was nothing in the new culture which replaced the old. It was possible, proposes Johnson, that Indian women were not "struggling for chimeric independence but for an altered balance of power within the family",[7] a balance which was altered in their favour.

Certainly neither Indian men nor women attempted at first to become integrated or even familiar with the new society. Loyalties were first to India, to which they hoped to return some day. They lived culturally apart from the rest of the "Creole" society. Geographical and occupational separation, combined with mutual contempt and misunderstanding, kept the various races apart. For their part, Blacks, who had internalised the values of Creole society had contempt for this group of immigrants who spoke "barbarous" languages, dressed differently, and worked for cheaper wages than they did. Indians, on the other hand, regarded the Blacks as untouchables and polluted as they ate the flesh of pigs and cattle and engaged in occupations which they considered ritually impure. Despite the scarcity of Indian women, sexual relations between Indian men and African or Creole women were extremely rare. Twenty-six years after Indian indenture had begun, the Protector of Immigrants could note that there "was not a single instance of an indentured immigrant who cohabits with one of the negro race".[8]

The last 30 years of the nineteenth century marked a turning point in Indian integration into the wider island community. The sugar market became depressed, more and more Indians were still being introduced and improved technology in the sugar industry lessened the availability of jobs in the factories. Indians sought jobs that were formerly held by Africans. In addition, Crown lands were being sold to them instead of repatriation to India. They began to recreate Indian villages on these settlements – something they were unable to do under conditions on the estates.

This movement out of the estates into little villages, and the knowledge that they would no longer be returning to Mother India must clearly have had an impact on the way in which Indians began to relate to the wider non-Indian community. Certainly, the movement out of cloistered estates and housing settlements and intermixing as a result of job diversification led to greater contact between the Indians and non-Indians. While our sociologists may have been less observant on the subject of acculturation, as early as 1939, some calypsonians had begun to notice and comment on the changes which were taking place among, at least, some Indian women.

In 1939, in a calypso entitled *Marajh Daughter,* Invader sang:

> I want everybody to realise
> I want a nice Indian girl that is creolise
> I don't want no parata or dhal water
> I want my potato and cassava

Gordon Rohlehr comments, and accurately so, that this calypso does not provide a true portrait of the Indian woman, revealing instead the rejection of Indian women's culture.[9] We can also deduce though, that there must have been a growing tendency on the part of Indian women to become "creolised" in order for this calypsonian to begin to comment, in less than complimentary fashion, on the phenomenon. By the 1940s, however, we see more conclusive evidence of cultural change among Indian women. Killer, leader of the Young Brigade, commented:

> ... But I notice there is no Indian again
> Since the women and them taking Creole name
> Long ago was Sumintra, Ramnawalia ...
> But now is Emily, Jean and Dinah ...
>
> Long ago you hadn't a chance
> To meet an Indian girl in a dance
> But nowadays it is big confusion
> Big fighting in the road for their Yankee man
> And see them in the market they ain't making joke
> Pushing down nigger people to buy dey poke
> And see them in the dances in Port of Spain
> They wouldn't watch if you call an Indian name[10]

Reference to the Yankee men in this calypso is very significant. The expansion of employment opportunities on the American bases provided an option for some Indian women to find jobs and also mix with men who were thought, perhaps especially by their parents, to be more acceptable than men of African descent But movement out of the rural villages and socialising with non-Indian men created gaps between the expectations of the older generation of Indians and their daughters.

From 1957–1958, Morton Klass carried out anthropological fieldwork in Amity, a fictional name for an existing Indian village in Trinidad. If we view this village as generally but not entirely representative of Indian attitudes and lifestyles in other parts of Trinidad, especially rural Trinidad where Indians were largely concentrated, a brief look at some aspects of its social organisation is very revealing of the prevailing condition and status of Indian women in the society at the time. Klass subtitled his research, "A study of cultural persistence", and this is precisely what he found.[11]

Kinship relations were still as binding and observed. In fact, Klass was struck by what he termed the "East Indian capacity for indefinite extension of kinship" and by the important observance of the rules and regulations that governed kin relations.

A major concession had been made in the area of marriage. Boys and girls were now introduced to each other before the marriage and had a right to veto the proposed match. While a boy was considered of marriageable age from the time he was 16 until around 30, and even over 30 he was still very eligible, the Indian girl was really only marriageable between the ages of 15 and 17. An unmarried girl over age 18 became a serious problem for the father if not a disgrace to the entire family – no one wished to have an unmarried daughter in the house. Apart from being an economic liability, it was feared that she would lose her virginity or become pregnant before she could be married or, worse yet, consort with the dreaded polluted race of Black men bringing utter shame and disgrace on the family. Indian men used the notion of an untrammelled female sexuality as another rationale for the close vigilance of Indian girls and women. On this Klass noted "It is a generally held assumption in the village that no female has any capacity to resist sexual advances. Only the continually watchful eyes of her family can protect her." This clearly had the effect of restricting the freedom which Indian women could otherwise have had, but it also had the contradictory effect of allotting them a vibrant women's culture based on the freedom of female libido, a factor which perhaps, despite their subservient and passive role, undoubtedly made for greater female self-confidence. The ritual of *lawa* in the *maticore* ceremony before the Hindu marriage is illustrative of this point. In this ceremony there is a frank and ribald sharing and enjoyment between older women with the younger ones, of the joys or otherwise of the sexual experience. In addition, the bride (and separately the groom) is anointed with a mixture of yogurt and tumeric to prepare their bodies for the first nights of their sexual union. I speculate that on such bases Indian women were geared for better adjustment to the mixed and multi-racial society when they attained greater freedoms in the society of Trinidad in the decades that followed.

Restrictions had been imposed before marriage to ensure their purity while they were schooled in the art of pleasing their menfolk. This schooling clearly did not entail education outside the home and by this time only a small proportion of Indian women – mainly those who had been converted to Christianity – had had access to any formal schooling. For many young Indian brides in both the Hindu and Muslim households, marriage represented simply a changing of the guards. The bride was now under the protection of a new extended household in which other oppressive conditions were the norm – while the *doolaha* or bridegroom could expect to be served by his new *doolahin* in addition to his mother. The new *doolahin* was expected to shoulder the full burden of the household chores, with greater acceptance into the new family only coming with the birth of her first child. She was also expected to display ample evidence of her fertility by producing many sons, another activity which ensured her total domestication and restricted her involvement in any activity in the wider society. It was not uncommon, for instance, to find Indian women in the rural areas at the age of 21 already with five or six children. Jack Harewood has found that the level of fertility in Trinidad and Tobago's women of Indian descent was for a long time appreciably higher than that of non-Indian women as a group, and more specifically than that of women of African descent – so much so, that in the analysis of fertility in this society, demographers often separated the rest of the female population from women of Indian descent. Between 1946 and 1960, the completed fertility of Indian women was still in the vicinity of 40 per cent to 50 per cent higher than that of women of African descent.[12]

While this unfolding picture for Indian women can be generalised across Indian women of different religions, there were subtle differences between Hindu and Muslim women and women converted to Christianity. For instance, in Amity, Klass noted that the Muslim young people, being in the minority, exhibited some indication of a sense of alienation from the community. Two young Muslim girls who had become converted to Presbyterianism professed a certain distance from the community in terms of its "backwardness" and the "ignorance of its inhabitants". And in Amity, between those who had been converted to Christianity and those who had not, there was a feeling of mutual contempt. Clearly, the process of creolisation whether acknowledged or not, had started. The Indian population had begun to embrace the values inherent in Creole society.

Although we have begun to see qualitative changes in the relationship of Indians to the wider community, on the political front, if conditions under the period of indentureship ensured separatism between the dominant cultures and a certain degree of hostility, other features which emerged in the society up to the period of independence also kept much of this distance alive. These data are highly schematised and so omits much of the detail of the underlying political struggle between the two dominant cultures. But it is interesting to note that the period of decolonisation in Trinidad and Tobago did not also coincide with a growing nationalist consciousness among the majority of peoples of Indian descent. Selwyn Ryan notes for instance, that between 1919 and 1939, the bulk of the Indian population did not identify with the nationalist movement,[13] while Marianne Ramesar makes the point that the development of a group consciousness among Indians during the period 1921 to 1946 in fact contributed to friction with other groups developing similar nationalism. In addition, the movement to self government and the coming to power of the Peoples National Movement (PNM) was characterised by differences and rifts among the Indian community itself, and certainly not wholehearted support for a party which they felt would take advantage of them when in power.¹⁴ Apart from a few urbanised Muslims and Christian Indians, the Hindu population was largely anti-PNM.

Evidence of Indian integration, though limited, could be seen in the greater occupational diversification among the Indian population. Although the Tyson report shows that in 1931 only a small percentage of Indians comprised the non-agricultural work force in Trinidad, we see evidence of both male and female inroads into various professions. There is no question that there is a clear predominance of Indian men over Indian women in the gainfully occupied work force – for instance, of the 637 men and women recorded under the category, professions, only 72 were women and these were all teachers. In fact, women comprised 29.2 per cent of the total work force of Indians and, of this, 25 per cent were in the lowest paid, lowest status jobs, and were either agricultural labourers or domestic servants.¹⁵

Despite their increasing integration of one sort or another in the wider community, actual racial intermixing was very limited. A crude indicator of the degree of intermixing with non-Indians is seen in the following figures. In 1911 there were 1.47 mixed Indians to every 100 unmixed Indians. In 1921 this figure had increased to 1.87 per 100 unmixed Indians and, by 1946, to 4.29. On the other hand, intermixing in the urban areas was greater for the 1946 census calculated at a rate of 21.37 Indian Creoles per 100 unmixed Indians in the main city of Port-of-Spain.¹⁶ This leads one to conclude that another factor that contributed to the gap between the two major cultures was the geographical separation from each other.

When greater integration into the community developed for Indian men and especially Indian women, it came in through educational and employment opportunities away from the home or family farm. Initially, education was mainly for boys. It was thought unwise to educate girls. In Seepersad Naipaul's *Adventures of Gurudeva* (written in the 1940s) we see some of the reasons why. Gurudeva is impatient with his new child bride Ratni's proclivity to answer back and seeks advice from his father Jaimungal:

> Gurudeva: I have not patience with her. She is rude and crude and gives me back-answers.
> Jaimungal: I know that. But she is only a woman and will ever be foolish, no matter what you do: but you must keep your temper, for you can read and write, and know good from bad…But she – well to her letters are like dirt.¹⁷

Indian women had not been given early opportunity of the rudimentary education system available then. In 1899, after 30 years of Canadian missionary schooling, girls comprised only 28 per cent of total enrolment in primary schools and were mainly kept at home to do domestic chores. Even where and when the Canadian missionaries educated them, this was initially meant to prepare them to make good wives for the converted Indian men who had become teachers in the Presbyterian schools. Illiteracy rates were relatively high compared to the rest of the population. A look at the proportions of females of various ethnic groups in Trinidad and Tobago who were illiterate according to the 1946 census gives a very good idea of the extent of the problem. 65.7 per cent of Indian females ten years and older were illiterate, compared with 10.1 percent for women of African descent, 3.4 per cent for women of European descent and 8.3 per cent for women of Chinese descent.¹⁸ By the 1950s there was an organised attempt to catch up with the rest of the population and by this time too it had become more acceptable to educate daughters as well as sons. The Indian Centenary Review of 1945, for instance, includes entries of 16 women in professions or business and, of those, one Gladys Ramsaran was a barrister. It is again significant that these women were all Christians and most came from families that had attained professional status a generation before.[19] The Muslim and Hindu communities opened their own schools or expanded existing facilities to include secondary education. With the easier acceptance of education offered by the Presbyterians, very soon the effects could be seen on the female Indian population.

Given their delayed entry into the education system, it is interesting to note the effects of these development among Indian girls five years before independence. In 1957, Vera Rubin and Marisa Zavalloni carried out a survey among a relatively large sample of secondary school students on their aspirations in the developing society of Trinidad and Tobago. In correlating university orientation with expectations of becoming full-time housewives, they found that only 17 per cent of the Indian girls compared with 50 per cent of the White girls intended to make home a post-career focal point. The researchers concluded from other indicators as well that, whereas higher education had become a normative expectation for middle- and upper-class girls as preparation for marriage, for Indian girls, securing an education entailed greater sacrifice and more of a break with their culture and consequently was seen as a channel to a career and personal independence rather than as preparation for a housewife's role.

It is again ironic, or on the other hand, perhaps perfectly understandable and inevitable, that in a culture which has suppressed women for so long, Indian women would readily embrace opportunities to engage with the rest of the society. Consider, for example, the aspirations of one Indian girl in Rubin and Zavalloni's study:

> I will go in for the Legislative Council Elections.
> If I am successful I can then help the people of my country
> most of all whether I am the Minister of Health or not,
> though I would be extremely happy if I am the Minister of
> Health or Education.[20]

To my knowledge, there were no Indian women involved in politics at the time. Even within this striving for individual expression and ambition, one sees evidence of those qualities that characterised the traditions expected of Indian women in the society. As another young Indian girl writes:

> I want to be a doctor, yet everything is against me ... I get no real encouragement. They think it is foolish that a girl should sacrifice so many years to study and then at the end of it she'll get married. And even if I decide to go ahead with this idea there is the very real difficulty of finding fees. My father has four children to provide for, two of them are boys who really need a good start in life.[21]

This epitomises the role which Indian women were expected to perform in the Indian community. They were keepers of the culture, they were passive and submissive, they were expected to sacrifice their own ambitions for the benefit of their brothers and husbands. Despite all of this, we can see that some Indian women had begun to commit themselves to goals which identified with the national interest. These aspirations are dear indications, though, that at least some Indian women had begun to become integrated into the Creole society and outside the arena of their erstwhile-restricted domain.

The Post-Independence Years

Independence itself meant very little to most Indians. An interview with a woman who had had the experience of a rural Indian girl, who had come from a small village and had won a scholarship to a prestige grammar school in Port-of-Spain, was insightful: she said quite frankly, that for most of the Indians she knew, independence appeared to be another victory for the Blacks.

Despite indifference from some Indians, guarded participation from others and outright support from few, certain values had become common to the various ethnic groups in the larger society, especially to people of African and Indian descent. One of these was the importance of education as a means of attaining social mobility. Developments in various areas of the economy and society were to benefit all groups even if they benefited some more than others. Developments in the education system and economic expansion in the post-independence period in fact accelerated the integration of Indian women into Creole society.

The rapid expansion in the provision of free secondary education for both rural and urban Trinidad and Tobago was clearly important for Indians, a large percentage of whom still lived in rural Trinidad. For instance, of the total Hindu population in 1960, 68.3 per cent lived in rural districts. The introduction of the Common Entrance Examination, which offered equal chances to boys as well as girls, created major differences in the attitudes to the education of girls and in attitudes to their later employment out of the home. The establishment of the Junior Secondary and Senior Comprehensive school systems later on also contributed to changing attitudes and practices between young people of different ethnic groups, perhaps through contact with each other at earlier ages. And free university education, albeit limited in its offering, also became available to the local population.

The second factor which was of major importance was the opening up and expansion of the cash economy in the 1960s and 1970s. New developments in the economy, especially from the 1970s, which made available jobs in the various sectors – commercial, petroleum and other industrial and public sectors – also involved a greater geographical shifting and displacement in the Indian female population. Indian women began to enter the Public Service as well and mix with the Black men and women who predominated in the public sector. Many Indian women joined the teaching profession, a profession in which they were encouraged as it was regarded as an extension of their nurturing role. Indian women who had had access to a university education began to move into other professions, with the legal profession proving to be one of the most attractive. The main outcome of all of this were the changes which began to occur in the traditional Indian family setting. In the shift to a greater consumer economy, the women's wage or salary earning contribution was now being viewed as important.

Changes, which occurred in the Indian family in the post-independence period, appear to be more sudden than they in fact were as these were evolving over the last few decades. Certainly the extended family network had become eroded over time and replaced by the nuclear family. Researchers and other insightful observers now freely commented on the somewhat oppressive nature of the extended Indian family, despite the glorified notions of support and security which it purported to offer. Pariag's extended family network dominated by a rich uncle in Earl Lovelace's *The Dragon Can't Dance* illustrates the relations of economic dependence which ensured kin allegiances.[22] Some research has revealed a shift to more nuclear-type families among Indians in urban settings – for instance, in San Fernando in 1980, 88 per cent of Indian families were nuclear; in Arouca and El Dorado 48 per cent and 44 per cent of the families were extended and these were based primarily on economic cooperation.[23]

A study on social and cultural change in the Indian community of El Dorado from 1960–1980 is also useful. Sharmatee Sieunarine finds this Indian community not at all homogeneous either by religion or by generational attitudes and practices. With regard to the question of marriage, most of the older women she interviewed between the ages of 50 and 60 indicated that they were married by the age of 12. One woman recounted that she had never seen her husband before the wedding and she only knew she was going to be married on the Sunday when on Thursday her mother took her to town to buy some new clothes. The situation had changed drastically by the 1980s. There was a significant decrease in arranged marriages, and the unmarried girls above 20 felt and said there was no disgrace attached to being unmarried at that age.[24]

Where changes have occurred though, some of them have shown a startling shift for only a few decades. For instance, Jack Harewood has measured a remarkable reduction in the Crude Birth Rate among Indians, from 45.9 per cent to 29.1 per cent from 1960 to 1970. This appreciable decline among the Indian population was due in part to the greater availability and accepted use of contraceptive practices, lower fertility among more educated women and later and deferred childbearing among women who also deferred their age of marriage. It might be pointed out here that despite many changes in mating and fertility practices of Indian women, there is still little acceptance for unmarried pregnancies, especially for women resident in their parents' homes.

At some point we need, however, to differentiate between creolisation and modernisation. In the post-independence era the two are necessarily linked. Creolisation has been interpreted to mean a commitment – political and social – to the new society, as well as physical engagement with the society so that the existent cultures are mixed and enriched in the process; modernisation is taken to mean the intrusion of the external and metropolitan. V.S. Naipaul in *The Middle Passage* is incisive on this: modernity in Trinidad means more than the trappings-air-conditioned bars and supermarkets, night clubs and restaurants, "It means a constant willingness to change, a readiness to accept anything which films, magazines and comic strips appear to indicate as American."[25]

Modernisation and petroleum revenues have been the major democratising agents in the society in the last twenty years or so. The creolisation process becomes interlocked with modernisation as new values are formed and shared between and among the various groups.

To speak of the "creolised" Indian woman at present is to employ both concepts at the same time. If we compare some of the obvious changes in the pre-independence and post-independence periods the picture is a more vivid one.

For instance, the staple diet of Indian women or the meals they prepare in Indian households can no longer be said to be comprised of a traditional cuisine but includes many other "Creole" dishes as well as the more modern North-American fast food. Certainly one wonders also whether the objection to pork and beef is still as strong.

It is very uncommon to see even older Indian women wearing their *ohrnis* – the traditional muslin cover which it was incumbent on them to wear as a form of respect – in the presence of menfolk or the public. In fact, like the *sari*, the *ohrni* and forms of Indian dress have become traditional wear for religious or ceremonial functions. Among younger Indian girls I can detect little difference in their trendy style of dress from women of other ethnic groups. Similar findings, but always with exceptions for age, class and location, can be stated for linguistic patterns, musical preferences and leisure-time activities.

To gauge the extent to which there have been changes among Indian women, I thought a useful exercise would be to assess my theory against the views of some younger women of Indian descent who were born in and are products of the post-independence era. I asked fourth and fifth-form girls from two secondary schools, one school predominantly Indian and the other mixed, to write short essays on growing up in the multi-racial society of Trinidad and Tobago. The responses were encouraging yet troubling. The early paradox which Indian women faced had now been replaced by other paradoxes and in the more complicated society today by a series of growing contradictions.

One Indian girl of 14 writes:

> As an Indian girl I feel fairly well adjusted to being in a multi-racial society. I don't consider myself as being superior to anyone else. Although at times I tend to feel a bit inferior when I hear people say "look a coolie", but I don't let this keep me down. Being an Indian has given me a fairly good opportunity to break the tradition that my grandmother and mother followed. I mean I don't have to quit school at an early age for the purpose of learning to handle a household so that I can get matched for marriage. But quite differently, I can pursue a career ahead of me. I think having a career is important because then I would be less dependent on a man.[26]

This independence of thought and action is a source of conflict between many younger and older women as this youngster's predicament tells us:

> Anytime I get into a quarrel with my mother, she gets into a rage and says its time for me to get married...anytime I want to go somewhere, for example to the cinema or a bazaar, my mother has to bring up some "nancy" story and say that when she was my age, she never wanted to go anywhere or she never quarrelled with her parents. I know I can't cook, but I try and then at that moment my mother begins her "nancy" stories again, and says that when she was my age she already knew how to cook, wash and take care of a house. She totally hates to see me talking to a boy in person or talking to him on the phone...then and there she starts to talk about marriage again. While I am on the topic of marriage she says she doesn't mind who I marry as long as he's rich, has a good job, does not smoke or drink and is not a Muslim.

Young Indian girls today are also keenly aware of the conflicts in male/female relationships which have arisen from greater female autonomy, but it seems that they are also ready to deal with these situations. Another young girl writes:

> A lot of Indian women today are working women. The Indian men, however, do not like the idea of this because they like to be the superior one. I think that people expect too much from an Indian woman and that they have a lot of changes to make in their lives. Indian women have to have the right to their say!

Conclusions

It has obviously not been possible to deal with every factor or every qualification in presenting these arguments for the creolisation of Indian women in Trinidad and Tobago. In fact, I know I have run the risks of over-generalisations and over-simplifications. I would like, however, in summarising my conclusions to incorporate some observations about the present trend which this process has taken.

My first conclusion is that there has been a tremendous shift in the status of Indian women in this society from their early introduction to the present time. The stereotype of Indian woman as primarily keeper of the culture, sacrificial and passive, can no longer apply to all Indian women. They have become more integrated into the society, a process accelerated in the post-independence era by the increased opportunities available to them in education and employment out of the home. Indian women who embraced Christianity fairly early were among the first to become creolised, but there is a distinct and growing trend for women of the Hindu and Muslim faiths to assert their presence in the society.

The second conclusion I would draw attention to is that contemporary creolisation has been a selective one. While it has involved a necessary degree of interculturation, there is also a qualitative change. Indian women's affirmation of their national identity does not automatically mean a negation of ethnic or religious identity. On the one hand, there is a greater political "national" consciousness among both Indian men and women. This is, perhaps, especially evident in political events over the last decade of the twentieth century–although it is clear that women are grossly under-represented in national politics. But a growing confidence in national assertiveness, encouraged by an Indo-Trinidadian prime minister governing the society for the first time, has also reinforced a confidence in ethnic and religious identity. This might explain, for example, the recent attention being paid by the more fundamentalist Hindu groups to the roles expected of Hindu women in this society. Even those Indian women and men who do not subscribe to the Hindu faith, or blindly follow the path of ethnic politics, are reluctant to relinquish the source of their cultural strength. And rightfully so, for it is not clear that the answer to the ethnic problems of plural societies is that of cultural homogenisation.

Finally, what has this meant for Indian women themselves? A process of change, which was in my view, inevitable, has created a number of severe contradictions for Indian women today in their relationships with the rest of the society.

Accustomed to the stereotype of the passive and submissive female role, Indian men have reacted to the growing confidence of Indian women in confused and sometimes violent fashion. This violence is not always manifested physically but can take the form of vicious, degrading or obscene insults slung at Indian women who choose to be friendly with men outside their ethnic group. Without fail, all of my interviewees repeated the theme "Indian men are traumatised by the new and assertive Indian woman they are now seeing," Several felt that the phenomenon of a relatively large proportion of professional Indian women, who were unmarried today, was a result of their increasing outspokenness and assertiveness. The reasons for this reaction on the part of Indian males certainly need to be researched to complete this picture.

Several respondents also hinted at the uneasy relationship which existed between Indian women and women of other ethnic groups in the society. They suggested that this was due to their growing assertiveness in the professions, in an area in which they were historically lagging compared to non-Indian men and women. I cannot claim to substantiate any of these statements, as they can only be subjective and impressionistic at the moment. They reveal, nonetheless, the new contradictions and paradoxes faced by Indian women who have become "creolised".

One can only be optimistic about change which creates possibilities for developing the potential of a group or a sex. I think that the qualities traditionally ascribed to Indian women are being turned in the direction of becoming virtues. Indian women have not become embittered by their history, thus subservience becomes discipline, submissiveness, passion and sacrifice, diligence. Wedded with intelligence, these virtues have only served to propel those Indian women who are prepared to challenge the imposed limits fast forward into a rewarding future.

Notes
1. This paper was originally published in Selwyn Ryan, ed., *Trinidad and Tobago: The Independence Experience 1962-1987* (St Augustine: ISER, 1988). The changes to this original paper have been deliberately few, although my own work on the area of gender relations in the Indian community has grown substantially in the last 20 years in both scope and depth. On rereading, I feel convinced that it captures a sentiment and component of creolisation, which, if I were to adjust, would not convey the mood, or the moment which the paper expresses at this time. After one decade, I also still agree with most of what I wrote as a younger, more callow scholar.
2. Kamau Brathwaite, *Contradictory Omens, Savacou Publications*. Monograph 4. Mona, 1985.
3. *Census of the Population of Trinidad and Tobago, 1980* (Port of Spain: Central Statistical Office, 1982).
4. Rhoda Reddock, 'Women Labour and Struggle in 20th Century Trinidad and Tobago 1898–1960,' PhD Thesis, ISS, The Hague, 1984.
5. Bridget Brereton, *Race Relations in Colonial Trinidad, 1870-1900* (Cambridge: Cambridge University Press, 1979).

6. Harold Sonny Ladoo, *No Pain Like This Body* (London: Heinemann, 1972).
7. Kim Nicholas Johnson, 'Considerations on Indian Sexuality,' paper presented to the Third Conference on East Indians, 29 August–4 September 1984, University of the West Indies, St Augustine, Trinidad.
8. Bridget Brereton, *Race Relations in Colonial Trinidad, 1870–1900* (Cambridge: Cambridge University Press, 1979).
9. Gordon Rohlehr, 'Images of Men and Women in the Calypsoes of the 1930s on the Sociology of Food Acquisition in the Context of Survivalism,' in *Gender in Caribbean Development*, ed. Patricia Mohammed and Catherine Shepherd (Trinidad and Tobago: Women and Development Studies, 1988), 232–306.
10. Raymond Quevedo, *Atilla's Kaiso* (Trinidad and Tobago: Extra Mural Department, University of the West Indies, 1983), 88.
11. Morton Klass, *East Indians in Trinidad: A Study of Cultural Persistence* (New York: Columbia University Press, 1961).
12. Jack Harewood, *The Population of Trinidad and Tobago*, CICRED Series (St Augustine: ISER, 1975).
13. Selwyn Ryan, *Race and Nationalism in Trinidad and Tobago* (Kingston: ISER, UWI, 1974).
14. Marianne Ramesar, 'The Integration of Indian Settlers in Trinidad after the Indenture Period,' *Caribbean Issues* 11, 3 (December 1976): 52–70.
15. Tyson Report, 1938–1939 (London: HMSO, 1939).
16. *Census of the Population of Trinidad and Tobago, 1946* (Port-of-Spain: Central Statistical Office, 1948).
17. Seepersad Naipaul, *The Adventures of Gurudeva and Other Stories* (London: Andre Deutsch, 1976), 33.
18. Patricia Mohammed, 'Women and Education in Trinidad and Tobago, 1938–1980,' MSc Thesis, Department of Sociology, UWI, St Augustine, 1987.
19. Jeremy Poynting, 'East Indian Women in the Caribbean: Experience and Voice,' in *India in the Caribbean*, ed. D. Dabydeen and B. Samaroo (London: Hansib Publishing, 1987), 231–63.
20. Vera Rubin and Marisa Zavalloni, *We Wish to be Looked Upon* (New York: Teacher's College Press, 1969), 89.
21. Ibid, 91.
22. Earl Lovelace, *The Dragon Can't Dance* (London Heinemann, 1972).
23. Adita Mohandaye Maharaj, 'The Changing Pattern of the East Indian Family in Trinidad,' Caribbean Studies Thesis, University of the West Indies, St Augustine, (n.d.).
24. Sharmatee Sieunarine, 'The Social and Cultural Change in the East Indian Community of El Dorado in 1960–1980,' Caribbean Studies Thesis, UWI, St Augustine, (n.d.).
25. V.S. Naipaul, *The Middle Passage* (London: Penguin Books, 1962), 48.
26. This and subsequent quotes were taken from essays written by fifth-form students of the San Juan Senior Comprehensive School. I would like to thank Vasanti Boochoon, a teacher of this school who carried out this exercise for me when writing this paper.

Reputation and Respectability:
A Suggestion for Caribbean Ethnology

Peter Wilson

It is no exaggeration to say of ethnographical work in the Caribbean that it has virtually equated social with domestic organisation. A good illustration of this is the volume entitled *Caribbean social organization* (Mintz 1961) in which all the articles discuss aspects of domestic organisation. Although this pre-occupation dates from the 1930's and early 1940's, notably with the work of Simey, Herskovits, Henriques and Frazier (in the United States), the present period of study dates from the years 1956–7 'when the first systematic studies of West Indian family systems were published by R.T. Smith on Guyanese Negroes and by Edith Clarke on Jamaica respectively' (M.G. Smith 1966: x, and see Mintz 1961: 529). Mintz has further observed that most of these studies are 'functionalist' and that they 'have put the weight of analysis on the relationships between domestic organization and characteristics of the wider contemporary society' (1960: 593), such that a major consequence has been that 'few studies have taken full account of the importance of informal groupings lacking any institutional articulation' (Mintz in press). M.G. Smith, in criticising R.T. Smith's work has specifically pointed out that the latter 'dismisses the internal differentiation of these villagers as irrelevant to his analysis' and that he ignores the internal differentiation of communities (1966: xii). It is to this matter of 'informal grouping' and 'internal differentiation' that I wish to direct particular attention. I suggest that a recognition of the moral and social values revolving around the ideas of 'reputation' and 'respectability' will illuminate both matters and might lead to a more sensitive appreciation of the social organisation of a major sector of Caribbean societies.

Now, my argument is, I admit, based on rather scant data and is culled piecemeal from many sources describing many societies which can be considered quite diverse, depending on the vantage point from which they are viewed. This disregard of the functionalist shibboleth: 'everything in its matrix' should not be taken too seriously for all the material I use was written by anthropologists, which gives the expression of the data a certain amount of comparability. It is also an implication of my thesis that, despite the differences among societies of the Caribbean, there is a functional equivalence of the moral values discussed here and their role in social organisation. Lastly, the consequence of this presentation is that the argument can and should be tested by further fieldwork; and this, when all is said and done, is a good reason for theory.

Community as Social System

R.T. Smith writes of the Guyanese villages that he studied: 'There is a value system differentiated with respect to the social sub system...a moral system within a moral system so to speak' (R.T. Smith 1956: 149). He goes on to say, however, that we cannot study these moral sentiments because 'they are held by individuals' and are 'presumably homologous with the social value system, being its individually internalised personality counterpart.' He does observe, nevertheless, that this value system may derive 'directly from the processes of interaction in the system itself' (1956: 150). Here, at least, R.T. and M.G. Smith are in agreement, for the latter notes that 'the primacy of social factors and relations in the differentiation of rural communities simply reflects the fact that communities are essentially social units constituted in terms of social relations' (M.G. Smith 1965: 185). Yet apart from these general suggestions, and with the notable exception of Jayawardena's (1963) work among East Indians of British Guiana there has been virtually no explicit exploration of the principles of social relations which might serve to structure the moral and social system of a community. Yet there is evidence that these do exist, just as, equally, there is evidence that the ethnographers have missed their meaning and significance. I will now try to suggest some of these principles and their significance for a moral and social system, by extrapolating from the major ethnographical reports.

Almost every ethnographical report from the Caribbean makes mention of a 'double standard' of sexual morality. Males are esteemed for their virility and are granted a freedom which they are expected to exploit. Females are, ideally, constrained in their sexual activities before and after marriage, and are expected to observe these constraints and other allied modes of behaviour (such as modesty and obedience). (See, for example, for Jamaica, Clarke 1957: 81, 91, 96; Davenport 1961: 426; for Andros Island see Otterbein 1966: 67; for British Guiana (now Guyana) see R.T. Smith 1956: 144, 141; for Carriacou see M.G. Smith 1962 ch. 5 and 6; for Puerto Rico see Landy 1959: 67; Manners 1956: 147; Lewis 1966: 427; Scheele 1956: 441; for Martinique see Horowitz 1967: 64–5; for Haiti see Bastien 1961: 498.) This distinction of sexual morality has also been noted in the major context of ethnographical investigation, the domestic structure, wherein males are often described as being 'marginal' and where kinship and household (social structure?) are considered female centred and matrifocal (e.g. R.T. Smith 1956: 142, 223). However it is one thing to suggest that males are marginal to the household but quite another thing to imply their marginality to society in general, and some of the discussion of Caribbean peasant economics seems almost to go this far.

Manhood

Let us take this separation of male and female and examine first the ways in which male morality is perhaps the centre of a rational system of values. Thus, as often as it is mentioned that males are permitted and expected to be sexually active it is also mentioned that men must be virile, and that their virility is especially manifested by their sexual activities and their fathering of children. Virility or masculinity is the most highly valued quality that a man can possess. This value has been most detailed for Puerto Rican society where it also appears to have been made most explicit among the people themselves. The quality is termed *macho*, and the complex of attitudes, expectancies and performance, *machismo*.

In Puerto Rico 'beginning about the time when they start to toddle, boys are taught that aggressiveness is male ... this emphasis on maleness is strongly marked. The word for male, *macho* is used freely. From infancy on the boy learns that he must be *muy macho*' (Mintz 1956: 384). Manners observes that 'a boy's masculinity is frequently exhorted and tested in feats of strength, sometimes in intellectual and mechanical skills, in his capacity to hold his liquor and in his ability to defend his and his family's honor' (1956: 147). And Scheele concludes that 'So much emphasis is placed on this [machismo] that one might say a man's life is pervaded by a cult of *machismo*' (1956: 436). *Machismo* is then that quality evidenced in sexual prowess, made manifest in the conquest of many women and the ability to father children, readiness to fight, particularly in response to a challenge usually offered in the form of an insult, in drinking and in any form of activity culturally defined as the prerogative of males.

There seems little doubt of the centrality of *machismo* in Puerto Rican values and the question now arises as to whether a comparable value is in evidence for other, non-Spanish societies of the

Caribbean? There being no explicit statement on the matter we must rely on clues to suggest the hypothesis. The fundamental feature of *machismo* is sexual virility evidenced by fatherhood. R.T. Smith writes of Guyanese Negroes: 'For a man to have children all about is a matter of pride rather than shame, for it proves he is a "man", strong and virile' (1956: 141). In Jamaica 'the proof of a man's maleness is the impregnation of a woman' (Clarke 1957: 96) and, notably in the lower class community of Sugartown, 'men enjoyed talking about their sexual prowess, the number of children they had fathered and the number of their conquests, referring with especial pride to any relationship with a virgin' (1957: 91). In Andros Island, in the Bahamas, Otterbein reports: 'In order to attain adult status a man must have premarital as well as extramarital sex relations' (Otterbein 1966: 67). If he does not he is thought to be a 'sissy' or homosexual and this innate sexuality of the male is noted in the saying 'boys are like dogs'.[1] In Martinique fathers impress on their sons 'expectations of their masculinity' (Horowitz 1967: 64). In Haiti the situation is less clearly defined, but Bastien mentions an ideal—'the successful "woman's man" is enviously and approvingly called *gasô*, manly; *bô kòk*, a good rooster or *cho* hot' (Bastien 1961: 498).[2] I suggest that the 'virility' aspect of the *machismo* complex can be found in certain strata of Caribbean societies other than Puerto Rico. Moreover, there are hints that other aspects of the complex are also present.

As already noted, a 'man' is one who responds aggressively to any challenge to his manhood, and such challenges are often issued in the form of stylised insults. Unfortunately it appears as if there are no adequate reports of fighting except for Jayawardena's (1963) study of East Indians in British Guiana. But in this study he mentions that the chief way in which to insult and shame a man (and thereby challenge him) is to suggest he has been cuckolded and that his wife is promiscuous (1963: 83).[3] Such insults are not only a reflection of the expectancy of fidelity and modesty in wives; for a man who is unable to keep his wife satisfied cannot be considered *macho* and whoever lures his wife away is more *macho*. Similar expectancies among spouses are reported throughout the Caribbean—husbands are expected to be unfaithful to some extent, and wives are expected to be faithful and modest (see Otterbein 1966: 68; Clarke 1957: 90 though Clarke notes that middle class Jamaican husbands are expected to remain faithful; R. T. Smith 1956: 114, 180; Horowitz 1967: 56; and Bastien 1961: 498). Another facet of this complex for which evidence is provided in the Caribbean is the strong attachment of a man to his mother and the fact that an equally serious insult is an aspersion of one's mother. Clarke mentions for example that 'there is nothing worse that can be said of a man or woman than that they "would even curse their mother"' (1957: 159) while the close tie between mother and son is mentioned constantly. It is, of course, dangerous to push a point too far, but I would suggest that the seriousness with which insults to one's mother are considered is related to the presence of a value system centring on 'virility'.

Reputation and Status

In fact, *machismo* is part of a value system or complex—it is, as it were, cocooned in a broader concept for which the commonly accepted term is 'honour'. As might be expected, the most explicit notice of these values has been made in Puerto Rico. Here, *machismo* is both an absolute and relative measure of a man's worth or *dignidad*. *Dignidad* is, in a sense, what accrues to a man as a result of his masculine activities and in Puerto Rico 'it is one of the most important values on the island. Anyone can have *dignidad*—a bootblack or a bank president ...When a person's evaluation is that he has played his role successfully, he has this important characteristic of *dignidad*' (Scheele 1956: 431). *Dignidad* demands recognition, however, and recognition is accorded through stylised forms of behaviour, or etiquette. Thus a man is obliged to observe etiquette and to demand it, for if he is not shown his due, in the recognised and meaningful way, his worth is challenged, and he is insulted.

Thus performance and expectation of this 'etiquette' are together summed up, in Puerto Rico, in the concept of *'respeto'*. Lauria has defined *respeto* as follows: a 'proper attention to the requisites of the ceremonial order of behaviour and to the moral aspects of human activities' (1964: 55). It then becomes the image of one's self as a man which is confirmed by the opinions and reactions of others with whom one lives. 'The man who is indeed *de respeto*, possessing *dignidad,* or who is truly *macho*, who is *serio*, taking the moral and ceremonial order seriously, and *cumplidor,* who complies with the obligations of proper inter-personal treatment, is the *hombre complete*, the integral or complete man' (Lauria 1964: 56). Holding to these values means that there are standards by which social relations are governed, as is clearly instanced in Mintz's discussion of relations between workers and employers on a Puerto Rican sugar plantation (Mintz 1956: 369). There are ideals towards which men aspire and by which they may be evaluated relatively or according to absolute cultural standards. The relative importance of activities which are culturally valued may vary considerably— in one society or in one social class, drinking may count more as a mark of manhood than fighting. But again, my concern here is not so much to analyse these values as to ask whether or not there is evidence for their existence in Caribbean societies. I have established their presence in Puerto Rico and noted their importance and my main task is to hypothesise for other, particularly English-speaking, societies of the Caribbean.

R.T. Smith makes one comment about Guyanese Negroes which virtually sums up what I have noted for Puerto Rico. He writes: 'There is a pre-occupation with trying to preserve a good reputation which results in extreme sensitivity to insult and leads to a great deal of litigation concerning this' (1956: 218). In Jamaica we learn that a man whose wife does not show him 'proper decorum [cf. *'falta de respeto'* in Puerto Rico] was not only commiserated, but blamed for having married her' (Clarke 1957: 91). In Puerto Rico part of a man's *respeto* depends on his ability to provide for his wife and children and a similar ideal is noted in both Guyana and Jamaica and Andros Island, together with the related imperative that a man should provide a house for his wife. Clarke even mentions the proud boasting of a man whose wife did no work, thereby publicising his reputation as a provider (1957: 78). And on Andros Island a man can only expect his wife to be faithful if he provides financial support (Otterbein 1966: 70). Reputation attaches not only to sexual and marital matters, though these perhaps are the most important, but also to proficiency in all male activities and to fulfilment of obligations attached thereto. Throughout the Caribbean, male migration in search of jobs is extensive and this migration is attended by many adventures (which are mostly sexual). Thus the well travelled man with many stories to tell adds to his reputation, especially if his exploits can be verified in some way. So, on Andros Island for example a man's adventures or his travels, particularly in the United States, are a favourite topic of conversation in the bars. In British Guiana the young men of the village leave to work in the bauxite mines and when they return, their smart clothes, their swagger, their generosity are not only attractions to the girls, they are also assertions of a man's own accomplishments and his reputation (R.T. Smith 1956: 137).

As we have suggested for the Puerto Rican notion of *respeto*, reputation is both a cumulation of personal worth and an assemblage of signs of that worth. The matter of these signs, although the subject of extensive investigation in American culture (Goffman 1959), has barely been noted in the Caribbean. And when it has been noted, it has clearly not been understood (except perhaps by Lauria). Smith remarks that when the young men come back from the bauxite mines in British Guiana they are 'easily distinguishable with their berets, sun glasses, long coats and narrow bottom trousers' (1956: 137) and he also comments on their ostentatious spending. These, I suggest, are signs of manhood and reputation.[4]

Reputation and Names

Clearly these 'signs' of reputation have important economic consequences. But I wish to postpone discussion of these and take up another facet of the notion of reputation, which is also both a sign and an integral part of the values expressed. I refer to naming practices, though, as with everything else, one must caution against inferring too much from too little evidence. There seem to be three factors of interest—that a name is a male property, that nicknames are used extensively and that considerable (though varying) attention is given to the bestowal of titles. But all three aspects seem clearly related to matters of social status.

Again, R.T. Smith states most clearly the connexion we are trying to establish. He writes: 'By the time the child has reached school age, its father has generally been established, and his name, in the form of the child's surname, is entered in the school register in all but a very few cases. The importance of this cannot be stressed too much, for we must never lose sight of the emphasis which is placed on paternity, and the fact that the social norm is for every individual to have a father figure' (1956: 133). What we must also bear in mind is that a child bearing its father's name is evidence of the latter's virility. In Jamaica 'the name' indicates the patrifilial tie as opposed to 'the blood' which indicates the matrifilial relationship (Clarke 1957: 48). Similarly on Andros Island 'the majority of outside children use their putative father's surname' (Otterbein 1966: 76). In Martinique 'illegitimacy is not normally disadvantageous' and I surmise that all children, with a few exceptions, will be known by their fathers' name (Horowitz 1967: 56). A similar situation exists in St Lucia (Crowley 1957) and Carriacou (M.G. Smith 1962: 92–3). In all cases it seems to me that the association of the name with the father is indicative *inter alia* of the centrality of a man's reputation in the social value system.

The extensive use of nicknames is noted by all the authors mentioned above, and again, it stands out clearly that one of the functions of such nicknaming is the indication of status. They are used particularly among or between persons of implicit equality—on Andros Island chiefly among siblings for example (Otterbein 1966: 118); in Jamaica 'pet names' are used between a mother and her children in particular, but the use of nicknames among males also is evident. Yet another variation occurs in Carriacou where 'church' names are kept secret for fear of *obeah* and a person is generally known by his or her 'house name' (Smith 1962). What we do not have, however, is evidence of the use of nicknames similar to that noted for Puerto Rico. Thus Lauria observes: 'Many Puerto Ricans have two nicknames: one, the *apodo* or *sobrenombre* serves as an alternate or sometimes the only name by which a person is addressed, the other, the *mal nombre,* is wounding and derogatory, unless the situation in which it is used is otherwise carefully defined' (Lauria 1964: 58). This use of nicknames is related particularly to the dialogue of insults or *relajo,* a relatively stylised pattern of conduct by which a man's manhood and reputation is insulted and he is often thereby challenged to affirm it. Here, the only evidence of the existence of this pattern of behaviour in the Caribbean outside of Puerto Rico seems to be among East Indians in British Guiana (Jayawardena 1963), while I have witnessed this in Providencia, though I have not published a report of it.

The third aspect of naming, the use of 'titles', is one that is fairly widely reported, though again usually without any comment. In the most normal sense the word title is used to denote a person's surname (which as we have seen is taken from the father). As significant is the fact that on Andros Island for example a woman takes as her title on marriage the 'first name' of her husband (Otterbein 1966: 117). In Jamaica a woman who is legally married and thereby enjoys higher status uses the title 'Mistress' to distinguish her from a 'friend', a 'keeper', or 'Miss So-and-So' and the same is reported for British Guiana (Clarke 1957: ch. 3; R.T. Smith 1956: 180). But it is the bestowal and appropriation of euphemistic titles by males that is of chief interest. Again they are not reported but one is for example familiar with the use of aristocratic titles by West Indian musicians and, among East Indians in British Guiana, Jayawardena mentions that 'people pay each other exaggerated deference with such terms of address as Captain or Cap, Skipper or Skip, Chief, Big Boy, Boss, Sadhu, Uncle etc.' (1963: 74). I can report that similar titles were used in Providencia as well as King, Earl, Duke, Lord, Count and Champ. Such titles suggest to me that they may be used as a means of indicating some sort of status position or some sort of fulfilment of status and reputation requirements. Insofar as they denote especial pre-eminence in activities such as hustling, smuggling, gambling, sports, music and love-making, these titles are particularly significant because the activities overlap, or undermine some of the values and rules of the total societal system. I will return to this point later.

The Economics of Reputation

At the moment, I wish to return to a question raised earlier, the economic implications of the value complex of reputation, especially as these are raised in the signs by which reputation is manifest.

The predominant attitude taken by ethnographers to the economic attitudes and behaviour of the Caribbean lower class is exemplified, once again, in R.T. Smith's observation of Guyanese Negroes. He says: 'Despite the limited range of commodities available in rural Guiana shops one does encounter *seemingly anomalous* situations. For example, persons with a low standard of living will buy relatively expensive commodities such as "Ovaltine" in a very small shop in Perseverance. This seems to be *symptomatic of the lack of concern with* "economizing" or showing planned selectivity in purchasing ...' (Smith 1956: 41, my emphasis). A similar emphasis on ostentatious expenditure has already been noted for Andros Island, while Edith Clarke writes of the pattern of expenditure in lower class Sugartown that it was 'a few weeks with money to spend in the taverns and at the gaming tables followed by a few weeks of enforced idleness and dependence on the charity of strangers' (Clarke 1957: 188) and in middle class Orange Grove the mark of status is to keep a servant, no matter what the husband's income (1957: 150). It would appear that this spending pattern is not only symptomatic of a lack of concern with economising, a peculiarly ethnocentric judgement, but it is symptomatic of a concern for reputation. Money is but a means to the procurement of the signs of accomplishment. Making a lot of money is a sign that one possesses certain skills and spending it in certain ways permits one to demonstrate other skills. Money itself is meaningless, and so too is economising. The so-called 'high status' elite of the (undifferentiated?) village of August Town was drawn together by parties which were 'occasions for status display and lavish consumption' (Smith 1956: 209). When adolescents leave home in Jamaica to find work and cannot find it they are reluctant to come back as this means admitting failure—'We are told, you should only go back when you can do so with good clothes on your back, a spare suit or so, and money in your pockets to treat the home folk' (Clarke 1957: 173). The same appears to be true of unskilled East Indian labourers whose expenditure pattern is characterised as 'hedonistic' (Jayawardena 1963: 47–8). Similar examples can be cited for every Caribbean society and they force one to the same conclusion.[5] The way money is spent—the fact that it is *spent*—is related to the basic complex of values dominating the lives and social relations of 'lower class' Caribbean society. Beyond this there may indeed be correlations with other factors such as 'disproportionate expenditure on luxuries to insecurity of employment and fluctuating income' (Jayawardena 1963: 48) but that does not help us to understand the 'why' of the disproportionate expenditure.

Womanhood

Thus far I have attempted to establish the existence of a value complex of 'reputation' according to which social relations are governed. This has notably emphasised males and almost left females out of account. It has however been noted that, with respect to sexual morality, ideals of femininity complementary to ideals of masculinity do exist in the Caribbean. Women are more or less confined to the house as soon as they reach puberty, in many instances they are chaperoned to social events, and they are expected to be modest and obedient. On marriage they are ideally expected to be virgins, and after marriage to remain faithful to their husbands. But whereas male values do seem to be expressed and confirmed, albeit to varying extents, in actual behaviour, the ideals of femininity would seem rarely to be met in practice. In fact one could almost say that ideals of 'womanhood' in some societies of the Caribbean are quite contradictory. In Sugartown, Jamaica 'not only is sexual activity regarded as natural: it is unnatural not to have a child and no woman who had not proved that she can bear one is likely to find a man to be responsible for her since "no man is going to propose marriage to such a woman"' (Clarke 1957: 95). On Andros Island although a virgin is the most desirable marriage partner, 'what a man wants is a girl who has not been promiscuous' (Otterbein 1966: 42) and the fiction of virginity is pursued throughout the marriage ceremony. To say the least, there is some disparity between the expectations and the reality of female chastity. This disparity becomes a little less puzzling when it is noted that throughout the Caribbean the most frequent form of marital union is common law marriage rather than legal marriage, and that the latter is most often entered into when the partners are past childbearing (M.G. Smith 1966: xxxiv; R.T. Smith 1956: 168). If this is so, then clearly the pre-marital requirements of a man's reputation that he marry a virgin, or the extra-marital requirement that his wife remain faithful become redundant or non-applicable. He has not publicly invested his reputation or honour in her if she is a 'concubine', 'sweetheart', 'friend', or 'common-law wife', which means she is relatively free to engage in relations with other men and her 'keeper' does not thereby lose his reputation. It can in fact be argued that in some cases loss of honour can, through the infidelity of a wife, be regained by fighting the wife's seducer. But the problem that now presents itself is that while the value complex of reputation may indeed be basic, it might not be unique. There is also the possibility of distinct, though overlapping, value complexes, one for men and another for women. And since the crux of the matter seems to lie in the meaning of marriage, *legal* marriage, which is an institution of the total society, the matter of the relationship between the 'internal' value system (reputation) and the 'external' system is also raised (these terms are Homans's (1950)).[6] It is to these questions that we now turn.

Respectability

Caribbean ethnographers frequently allude to an ideal of 'respectability'. In particular, marriage is said to confer respectability on partners (cf. R.T. Smith 1956: 180–1; Clarke 1957: 75) and to indicate a higher class status. At the same time marriage is described by R.T. Smith as being 'in conformity with the ideals of the whole society' (1956: 180) and by marriage is understood a union recorded by civil and/or Church authorities (Davenport 1961: 427). And as already noted, in Jamaica at least, persons marry rather late in life after having several children, and after marriage 'a man stops wandering about the country and settles down' (Clarke 1957: 84).

We can, I think, generalise from these few facts as follows: marriage is a legal institution and a religious institution; it is older people who get married, often after they have had their children. Marriage also confers respectability, so respectability is a degree of approximation to standards of the external, legal society and is mostly incurred by older people. As is also pointed out in all the sources, marriage at an earlier age is often economically difficult, but in cases where persons are married at a young age we can infer a certain degree of economic security, and thence respectability.

I have hypothesised that respectability is a value derived from conformity to the ideals of the total society or the legal society. Marriage is the chief way in which respectability is affirmed, but the other important matter is the Church, the only institution which is part of the legal society, which is present in villages, and in which villagers can participate in an official capacity. However the officials and congregation of a village church are predominantly older persons, married persons and females—'respectable' people. Nor is it uncommon, in the case of some of the older males to find that, prior to their marriage and/or their entry into the church, they enjoyed 'infamous' reputations as great studs, drinkers, fighters and gamblers. It is in many instances the most profligate who become the most active proselytisers and preachers. In a sense then, the status of preacher often denotes a status of greatest reputation and respectability, the former adding power to the latter. In this instance we have the point of overlap between the value systems. A further point to be made derives from the fact that women participate most extensively in the value complex denoted by 'respectability'. Davenport, for example says of Jamaican women that they are regarded as the 'carriers of respectability' (1961: 430) which we can now understand as meaning upholders of the legal morality based on the Church. I would like to tie this in with the frequently observed fact that women, as distinct from men, are bound in with an active network of kinship relations. Men it has been noted are, in general, marginal to the household and to the family, but women constantly involve themselves in the norms and expectations that derive from their activity among a network of relatives, a factor that derives chiefly from the constancy of the tie between a mother and her children (cf. Davenport 1961: 442; R.T. Smith 1956: 55–6, 152; Clarke 1957: 173). To have children, to look after them, to look after a kinswoman's children and then to be looked after by one's children or by other kin—these are the expectancies of a woman and the things she values, and they coincide with the values of the legal society, with 'respectability'.

Women then always subscribe to a value system based on respectability and only partially, perhaps reluctantly, to a value system based on 'reputation'. Men, on the other hand, are completely involved in a value system based on 'reputation' but with age and social maturity, measured by economic security, marriage and so forth, move into a value and status system based upon respectability.

Consequences
The Pitch of Social Relations

'Reputation' and 'respectability' are of course closely connected at all times and this juxtaposition has certain consequences which do not seem to have been fully understood (though I hasten to add that what follows is but suggestion, not affirmation). As noted, reputation is the key to a social system based on interaction within a community, the internal system, whereas respectability stems from the legal society or the external system. Following R.T. Smith, Jayawardena has emphasised the equality of status persisting between members of a given community and he has brilliantly analysed the various ways and means by which this equality is challenged, resolved and maintained, how it governs the conduct of critical relations in the community. Other writers have observed in passing the constant claims made by people to equality, to the 'fact' that 'we is all one family'. Jayawardena's analysis of 'eye pass' disputes and the concept of 'mati' or equality, although describing East Indians, seems so reminiscent of the insults, the quarrels and the *respeto* of Puerto Rico, and of my own experiences among Negroes and mixed people of Providencia, that I feel fairly sure that much of what he says is more widely applicable. Yet there is a sense in which I think the emphasis of Jayawardena's analysis is misplaced. He argues that the 'eye pass' disputes and the invocation of the concept of 'mati' exemplify the equality of the persons involved, for a 'claim to superior prestige made by a person who belongs in all respects to the group frustrates the expectations of his fellows and undermines the solidarity of the group as a whole' (1963: 71). But in many of the cases presented by Jayawardena the status of the antagonists, in terms of their reputations, is different. The dispute arises, for example in case 1 and case 2, when a man of inferior reputation claims equality, in the form of a challenge which must be met in order to preserve the *status quo* of *inequality* of status. In case 1 the challenger falsely claims equality on the basis of 'respectability'.[7] The concept of 'mati', or equality, seems more to be a concept of propriety, comparable to *respeto*. But as such it encapsulates a complex of values which marks off the community or persons within the community from 'outsiders'. Thus all those who subscribe to this value complex (*reputation, respeto,* 'mati') are equals *vis-à-vis* outsiders, but very markedly differentiated among themselves, though possibly according to criteria ' trivial' to outsiders. In the sense that these values and their associated behaviours and symbols are common to a stratum of a total society, then it can be thought of as homogeneous, and this is the position taken by R.T. Smith (1956: 223). But he, and those who have followed him, have also stopped there with the result that much of what is meaningful to the people being studied is left out of account, and this can be summed up in the differentiation occasioned by the fine gradations of reputation. Since reputation depends, above all, upon small group, face to face interaction it represents a value that cuts off groups from each other. On the other hand, respectability is a value complex with a somewhat more absolute standard of measurement, to which reputation can contribute, as when a respectable occupation or activity is carried out with 'style'.

I have just suggested that the value system based on reputation depends on small groups and face to face interaction. This then brings me to a consideration of the possible structural attributes of this value system as reflected in the nature of social groupings.

Social Groupings

There are two forms of social grouping that have been distinguished in the Caribbean. One, the household, has been the major, if not the only, subject of analysis while the other, the community, has hardly been analysed at all. Some attention has been given to forms of kinship network, but, as kindreds, these have barely approximated to social groupings. I do not wish to say anything about the household, but rather to direct some attention to the community. It has been argued time and again that, in the Caribbean, there is a 'weak sense of community cohesion and local communities are but loosely organized' (Wagley 1960: 8); that 'many research workers in Caribbean societies have been struck by the relative absence of community-based activity in daily life' (Mintz 1966: 932–3). The same writer then goes on to point out 'such institutional centers as the church, the school, the social club and the political party office are likely to be entirely absent or at least very unimportant in rural community social life'. Yet, in spite of this non-community aspect of communities, most ethnographers have carried out their research in communities, which one assumes are not figments of their imagination. Once again there seems to be evidence of certain preconceptions about communities among ethnographers, as suggested in Mintz's summary above. A community, in their eyes, seems to be a co-residential population with political and ritual 'solidarity' and reducible to a structure of institutions, rather than social relations. But throughout the Caribbean, the church, the school and the political party are institutions *external* to the village and not therefore organically a part of the social system of the village. Frequently their personnel are alien, and certainly their rules are.

Bearing in mind that the social system can be based on social interaction, and accepting that the codes and values governing that interaction are based on 'reputation', we can perhaps infer features of the structure of those social relations. 'Reputation' is a complex of values which reflects the congruence of the way a man views himself and the way he is viewed by others. It relies upon the existence of peer groups—males of approximately equal life situations and life chances. I have elsewhere suggested the term 'crews' for these Caribbean peer groups (Wilson 1967). These peer groups are premised on already established proximity, whether it be co-residence or co-employment, but they are not centred on the household and most ethnographies note that, for males, and even married males, the house is little more than a dormitory. Males are very mobile, especially during the early years of their lives, but this mobility does not isolate them from meaningful social contexts by which they achieve an identity as persons. The social structure in which they operate is, as it were, carried around with them, for peer groups can be formed wherever and whenever peers gather together. Thus the community contains these units, but does not necessarily bound them, though I would suggest a distinction whereby they are bounded.

A man is likely to be a member of two types of groups; the first will be residential and be based on his community of birth and/or adolescence and the second will be based on the place where he finds work. There may well be situations in which his residential crew differentiates itself from crews of other communities—similar to the way in which peer groups harden into gangs controlling ghetto blocks (cf. Brown 1965). Crews centre not upon institutional meeting places but upon bars, rum shops, front room stores, cotton or palm trees or a corner. They play dominoes, cards or checkers, they drink in a ritual fashion, they argue, they sing, they boast, brag and fight. They may also work together and they certainly influence each other. More research needs to be done on the way in which the composition of a crew changes and the ways in which facets of manhood are differently emphasised, but I would suggest that groupings of this nature are the more significant for males. For females, whose value system is based on 'respectability', kinship networks and the household would appear to be the principal social matrices within which they act out their relationships. But there is some evidence that among co-residents and within kinship networks there are female peer groups (cf. Clarke 1957: 105; Otterbein 1966: 121). Females, it has been noted, seem far more active at an earlier age than males in church activities, and they are joined by married males and older persons. Even though a church building may not be present in a village, 'meetings' may still be held in homes, or persons may go to another village to worship and participate in church activities. I wonder then if it would not be reasonable to suggest that at a certain level of social significance, a congregation would not be an important social grouping. This is most clearly suggested for Haiti, where the various *vodun* shrines include members from different villages, and where the congregations both overlap in membership and co-operate in certain activities not all of which are religious (Bastien 1961: 495; Métraux 1959). This possibility gains further relevance when we realise that religious and politico-religious cults have proved one of the most successful ways of mobilising segments of Caribbean populations.

Rather than dismiss the residential community as a unit of no sociological importance, I think we should accept its undoubted existence but learn to analyse it more in terms of the way it is viewed by its inhabitants. For males it is a reference point within which function constituent operational social units. For females it is somewhat more of an organic unit, there being some sort of structural continuity based on kinship between the household, the family and the village. Through the conjunction of values of kinship and religion there is some continuity in the female value system as it is lived out in interpersonal social relations and as it is idealised in the total society.

This contrasts with the marked, though by no means complete discontinuity between the male value system expressed in inter-personal relations and the value system of the 'total' or 'legal' society.

Morality Against the Law

In Puerto Rico observers have pointed out the prevalent indulgence in illegal activities such as the lottery and numbers (*bolita*), drinking illegally distilled rum ('bushy' in most Caribbean societies), living in consensual unions, fighting and so on (Mintz 1956: 364). In studies of European peasantry (e.g. Pitt-Rivers 1961) similar activities and proclivities are noted and those who are most proficient become folk heroes enjoying great 'reputations'—bandits and smugglers for example. A similar though not necessarily identical feature seems to be characteristic of Caribbean societies. It is surely not accidental that the very activities most central to the achievement and maintenance of manhood and reputation are those proclaimed illegal by the total society (gambling, smuggling, fighting or readiness to fight, banditry, embezzlement and bribery, for example). In fact, in its most general sense a reputation is gained according to the degree to which a man is proficient in undermining, disobeying or circumventing the legal system of the society.[8] But because this is so it does not make it any the less valid as a sociological reality. It is then according as a reputation is fulfilled, and as the chances for a man to enter into the 'legal' status system are increased that he can become 'respectable'. But very importantly it must be emphasised that the value system based on 'reputation' is a *positive* one and the only realistic one for the persons involved. For it allows of the attainment of individual identity and social relatedness through activities and behaviour accessible to these people. A young Caribbean 'peasant' cannot become 'respectable' in part because he cannot participate economically or politically in the total societal system within which 'respectability' is the chief value. He is not literate and thus cannot enter the bureaucracy or the political or legal hierarchy. He is unskilled and hence cannot begin to climb the economic status ladder to achieve an income that will permit him to assume the signs of respectability. But at the same time he is politically, legally and economically under the rule of the total society, and those who impress this rule on him are alien—of a different 'class' and/or a different race and/or a different nationality. From this situation arise the circumventions, the misunderstandings, and the real differences reflected in conduct and values.

Conclusion

A number of studies of European and to a lesser extent Middle American peasantry have drawn attention to the importance of the value complex centring on an ideal of manhood and guarded by codes of honour and shame (see the most important of these studies, Peristiany 1966). In this article I have enquired whether and to what extent a similar complex of values is to be found in the Caribbean. I must stress the word similar, for I do not want to imply that identical values may exist. Many and subtle are the differences of values even among European societies, and between European and Middle American societies, while Oscar Lewis has noted a difference of emphasis on *machismo* between Mexican and Puerto Rican people (Lewis 1966: xxvii). Differences have also been noted between rural and urban expressions of *machismo* (cf. Rivière 1967: 582, note 17). But what little evidence there is for the Caribbean, and it must be stressed that the 'evidence' consists almost entirely of passing references to factors considered incidental by the authors, does suggest that it might be worthwhile to look more deliberately for such values.

Even the evidence adduced clearly indicates considerable variation of content and expression between different societies of the Caribbean. The values with which we have here been concerned are most explicit in Spanish-speaking Puerto Rico and I have tried to see mainly if there are any clues in writings about the English-speaking West Indies. It might be useful to postulate Puerto Rico as representing the extreme end of a continuum or alternatively to construct an overall conceptual framework involving the Caribbean somewhat along the lines suggested by Geertz in his analysis of Balinese village structure (1959). Here I would envisage the presence of a number of principles of organisation and values, but with differing degrees of emphasis in different societies.

Finally, in citing Jayawardena's work among East Indians in British Guiana and accounts of American urban Negroes, I have implicitly suggested that the phenomenon I have been considering is not bounded by race or geography, or culture for that matter. Nor is it a matter of urban or rural differences. Rather these populations share in common such factors as an isolation from the total, politically constituted society, albeit an isolation expressed in different ways. But this isolation is at the same time dependent upon specific conditions of social, political, legal and economic relatedness. The consequences of these conditions are somewhat of the nature tentatively outlined above.

However it is not my aim in this article to attempt weighty conclusions and profound insights. I wish merely to call attention to certain neglected possibilities that might lead to further research and increase our understanding of Caribbean social organisation.

Notes

My thanks to my students with whom I discussed these possibilities. This article is also a response to, and a product of, discussion and dispute with Professor Sidney Mintz, of Yale University, to whom I owe a permanent intellectual debt.

1. This characterisation of male nature is reminiscent of the characterisation of Puerto Rican males as inherently evil or *malicias*, who can do nothing to inhibit their innate sexuality (see Landy 1959).
2. In a review of Otterbein, Freilich notes that the term 'hot boy' is used in the Bahamas (1967, 239).
3. This is exactly the substance of the most inflammatory insults as reported in Spanish cultures (Pitt-Rivers 1966, 46–8; Lewis 1965, 27; Rivière 1967, 574).
4. Although I am consciously avoiding detailed comparison with non-Caribbean cultures it is apposite here to draw attention to the comparability of urban American Negro culture and its moral values. Thus, apropos of the Guyanese Negro's signs of reputation and manhood, Charles Keil observes of the urban American Negro: 'Prettiness (wavy hair, manicured nails, frilly shirts, flashy jackets), plus strength, tender but tough, this is the style that many Negro women find irresistible' (1966, 27). And in a source that makes explicit for the Harlem Negro so many of the inferences we are drawing for the Caribbean, Claude Brown describes the slickest hustler on the street: 'Mr Jimmy changed cars every year, dressed up with shining shoes every day of the week, always had plenty of money, always had a pretty woman with him, and kept his hair slicked back' (1965, 70). Throughout the book there are instances of the behaviour we are describing, and in many places, Brown comes close to generalising in the sense of this article. In Chapter 10 for example he has an extensive discussion of 'reputation' and its importance. He also sums up honour: 'You don't mess with a man's money: you don't mess with a man's woman: you don't mess with a man's family or his manhood – these were a man's principles' (1965, 266).
5. I should note here that at least one Jamaican community, 'Rocky Roads,' is said to emphasise hoarding and accumulation rather than expenditure. However, this seems, even by the ethnographers' opinion to be an anomalous village (Cohen 1954, 110).
6. Many writers have noted the distinction between the internal and external system, but no term seems really satisfactory. What I mean when I variously use external/internal system, societal, total society or legal society is the politically constituted society governed according to law and procedures uniform throughout the society, imposed by force, and usually originating from England, France, Holland, or the United States – even with present day 'independence'.
7. Pitt-Rivers (1966, 31) writes that 'A man is answerable for his honour only to his social equals, that is to say, to those with whom he can *conceptually* compete' (my emphasis). Within the limits of this conceptualisation, then, there must be considerable differentiation – some men have greater/lesser reputations than others, but all affirm the common criteria that make up reputation.
8. Crowley makes a most interesting observation which is also significant to my argument when he notes that in St Lucia nicknames are used to circumvent the outside system of government and that,

since no one in St Lucia is confused, the practice must conform to some sort of rationale meaningful to the society (Crowley 1957, 90).

References

Bastien, R. 1961. Haitian Rural Family Organization. *Social Econ. Stud*. 10:478–510.
Brown, C. 1965. *Manchild in the Promised Land*. New York: New American Library.
Clarke, E. 1957. *My Mother Who Fathered Me*. London: Allen & Unwin.
Cohen, Y.A. 1954. The Social Organization of a Selected Community in Jamaica. *Social Econ. Stud*. 2:104–33.
Crowley, D. Naming Customs in St Lucia. *Social Econ. Stud*. 5:37–42.
Davenport, W. 1961. The Family System of Jamaica. *Social Econ. Stud*. 10:420–54.
Freilich, M. 1967. Review of Otterbein, K. The Andros Islanders. *Am. Anthrop*. 69:239.
Geertz, C. 1959. Form and variation in Balinese village structure. *Am. Anthrop*. 61:991–1012.
Goffman, E. 1959. *The Presentation of Self in Everyday Life*. New York: Doubleday Anchor.
Homans, G. 1950. *The Human Group*. New York: Harcourt, Brace & World.
Horowitz, M. 1967. *Morne-Paysan: Peasant Village in Martinique*. New York: Holt, Rinehart & Winston.
Jayawardena, C. 1963. *Conflict and Solidarity in a Guianese Plantation* (Lond. Sch. Econ. Monogr. Social Anthrop. 25). London: Athlone Press.
Keil, C. 1966. *Urban Blues*. Chicago: University of Chicago Press.
Landy, D. 1959. *Tropical Childhood: Cultural Transmission and Learning in a Puerto Rican Village*. Chapel Hill: University of North Carolina Press.
Lauria, A. 1964. 'Respeto,' 'Relajo' and Interpersonal Relations in Puerto Rico. *Anthrop. Quart*. 37:53–67.
Lewis, O. 1966. *La Vida*. New York: Random House.
Manners, R. 1956. Tabara: Subcultures of a Tobacco and Mixed Crop Municipality. In *The People of Puerto Rico*, ed. J. Steward. Urbana: University of Illinois Press.
Métraux, A. 1959. *Voodoo in Haiti*. New York: Oxford University Press.
Mintz, S. 1956. Canamelar: The Subculture of a Rural Sugar Plantation Proletariat. In *The people of Puerto Rico*, ed. J. Steward. Urbana: University of Illinois Press.
———. 1960. The House and Yard Among Three Caribbean Peasantries. *Actes VI Congr. Int. Sci. Anthrop. Ethnol*, 591–6.
———. 1961. A Final Note. In *Caribbean Social Organization. Social Econ. Stud*. 10:528–35.
———. 1966. The Caribbean as a Socio-Cultural Area. *J. Wld Hist*. 9:912–37.
———. In press. The Caribbean. *Int. J. Social Sci*.
Otterbein, K. 1966. *The Andros Islanders*. Lawrence: University of Kansas Publications.
Peristiany, J., ed. 1966. *Honor and Shame: Values in Mediterranean Society*. Chicago: University of Chicago Press.
Pitt-Rivers, J. 1961. *People of the Sierra*. Chicago: University of Chicago Press.
———. 1966. Honor and Social Status. In *Honor and Shame*, ed. J. Peristiany. Chicago: University of Chicago Press.
Rivière, P. 1967. The Honour of Sanchez. *Man* (N.S.) 2:569–81.
Scheele, R. 1956. The Prominent Families of Puerto Rico. In *The People of Puerto Rico*, ed. J. Steward. Urbana: Univ. of Illinois Press.
Smith, M. 1962. *Kinship and Community in Carriacou*. New Haven: Yale University Press.
———. 1965. Community Organization in Rural Jamaica. In *The Plural Society in the British West Indies*. Berkeley, Los Angeles: University of California Press.
———. 1966. Introduction. In *My Wother Who Fathered Me* [by] Edith Clarke. London: Allen & Unwin.
Smith, R.T. 1956. *The Negro Family in British Guiana: Family Structure and Social Status in the Villages*. London: Routledge & Kegan Paul.
Wagley, C. 1960. Plantation America: A Culture Sphere. In *Caribbean Studies: A Symposium*, ed. Vera Rubin. Seattle: University of Washington Press.
Wilson, P. 1967. Caribbean Crews: Some Unconsidered Aspects of Social Structure. Unpublished paper.

That Event, This Memory:
Notes on the Anthropology of African Diasporas in the New World[1]
David Scott

> It was the Atlantic this side of the island, a wild-eyed, marauding sea the color of slate, deep, full of dangerous currents, lined with row upon row of barrier reefs, and with a sound like that of the combined voices of the drowned raised in a loud unceasing lament—all those, the nine million and more it is said, who in their enforced exile, their Diaspora, had gone down between this point and the homeland lying out of sight to the east. This sea mourned them. Aggrieved, outraged, unappeased, it hurled itself upon each of the reefs in turn and then upon the shingle beach, sending up the spume in an angry froth which the wind took and drove in like smoke over the land. Great boulders that had roared down from Westminster centuries ago stood scattered in the surf; these, sculpted into fantastical shapes by the wind and water, might have been gravestones placed there to commemorate those millions of the drowned.
>
> Paule Marshall, The Chosen Place, the Timeless People

Between Old World and New, Past and Present

In this unforgettable passage, Paule Marshall evokes the relation between the past and the present of the African diaspora, between the historical trauma of an inaugural event and our collective memory of it. In this essay, I am going to concern myself with a certain way of reading this relation, a way that I believe has been a central element in the identity of the anthropology of peoples of African descent in the New World. And a way that, I also believe, is mistaken.

This anthropology has—from its formal inception in the work of Melville J. Herskovits in the late 1920s down to its current elaboration in the work of such contemporary Afro-Americanists and Afro-Caribbeanists as Sidney Mintz and Richard Price—turned in a very profound way around a narrative of "continuities," continuities between the Old World and the New, between the past and the present. The reasons for the privilege and the persistence of such a narrative in the archive of this anthropology are not so hard to come by. After all, it is well enough known that the African presence in the New World began with a sharp and irreversible severance in the holds of slave ships crossing the Middle Passage and in historically unprecedented circumstances of social disordering and social reordering on the colonial slave plantations. Not surprisingly, anthropology manifests a deep, humanist inclination toward a story about continuities and embraces the earnest task of demonstrating the integrity and the intactness of the old in the new, and of the past in the present, of these societies. Nor, likewise, should it be surprising that in the plotting of this narrative of continuities, the two figures of "Africa" and "slavery" have come to form its generative and constitutive points of reference.

Obviously, this story about continuities is not confined within the disciplinary parameters of anthropology. It is a story that has in a variety of ways structured our own "imagined community," our own narratives of identity and tradition. For this reason it would be possible (not to say pertinent) to speak here of at least two historically interconnected yet distinct and analytically separable registers. One is anthropological, strictly speaking, inasmuch as it has to do with the properly disciplinary construction of a distinctive theoretical object, namely, "the New World Negro" (to give it its inaugural name) and the conceptual apparatus employed to identify and represent it. The other is, we might say, extra-anthropological, being transdisciplinary, sometimes positively antidisciplinary, and having rather to do with the varying cultural-political discourses of identity and tradition produced by peoples of African descent in the New World, in the course of our own practices and struggles.[2]

These registers of knowledge-producing cultural practice are of course not identical, but what is noteworthy is that even in nonanthropological discourse, anthropology, taken as the (self-described) "science of culture," is often seen as crucial in providing the authoritative vocabulary in terms of which the claims of difference are established. Anthropology—and for quite definite historical reasons, American cultural anthropology more specifically—has often been taken as providing what we might call the foundational discourse for the cultural politics of identity among peoples of African descent in the New World.[3] Certainly this has been the case at least since Franz Boas's famous commencement address at Atlanta University in 1906 ("The Outlook for the American Negro"), given at the invitation of W. E. B. Du Bois.[4] And it was to become more clearly and more decisively the case with the seminal work of Herskovits two decades later.

I want to inquire here into the specifically disciplinary side of this concern with continuity. I can see that in leaving the "native" texts (so to call them) aside my exercise can only be a partial one. I accept that. But if anthropology, in its capacity as the science of culture, has been able to claim for itself, or have claimed for it, the role of a higher or more foundational authority in the matter of cultural difference, then there is an initial labor of internal, disciplinary interrogation to be carried out, a prior critical accounting for the kind of theoretical object this anthropology establishes and circulates in its authoritative texts on the cultural practices of peoples of African descent in the New World.[5]

First, I shall briefly outline the thesis advanced by one recent contribution to this anthropology, Richard Price's *First-Time: The Historical Vision of an Afro-American People*. In outlining Price's thesis, I will not only emphasize some of the conceptual premises of his argument about a past in which slavery forms the single most important referent but will also inquire into the ideological assumptions of the specifically anthropological problem established through it. To do so will lead me to an inquiry into its links with the inaugural problematic of the "New World Negro" formulated by Herskovits, in whose work it is Africa rather than slavery that forms the single most important referent. I shall seek to argue that in the discursive or narrative economy of this anthropological problematic, *slavery* and *"Africa"* function as virtually interchangeable terms, or, to put it another way, that slavery in the work of Price comes to perform the same rhetorical-conceptual labor as Africa in the work of Herskovits. Both turn on a distinctive attempt to place the "cultures" of the ex-African/ex-slave in relation to what we might call an authentic past, that is, an anthropologically identifiable, ethnologically recoverable, and textually re-presentable past. And what is particularly revealing is that both Price and Herskovits seek to exemplify their arguments about the pasts and cultures of peoples of African descent in the New World on the basis of the study of the same New World peoples, the Saramaka of Suriname.[6]

Though my disagreements will be evident, my reason for adopting the strategy I do is not primarily to criticize either Price or Herskovits. Nor, more importantly, is it my aim to dispense with the trope of continuities as such, or with either (or both) of those profoundly generative and resonant figures—Africa and slavery—through which this description of continuity has been theoretically constructed. As I have already suggested, this pronounced discourse of continuity in the work of Afro-Americanists and Afro-Caribbeanists is in part the measure of the sympathetically affirmative character of the anthropology of peoples of African descent in the New World, the singular mark, one might say, of its strong humanism. My intention, rather, is to indicate what seem to me to be some of the limits of this conception as presently constructed in the authoritative discourse of anthropology; to suggest how inquiring into the formation of conceptual objects such as "the New World Negro" can be of importance in assessing theoretical strategies; and to sketch in something of the outline of an alternative strategy for retaining the concern with continuities in a way theoretically more fruitful to historical and anthropological, or at least to a cultural-critical, inquiry.

First-Time

"There was a day in time when the last eyes to see Christ were closed forever." With this arresting and allusive quotation from Jorge Luis Borges as an epigraph, Richard Price, perhaps the leading anthropologist of the Saramaka of the Suriname rain forest, opens his much-acclaimed ethnography, *First-Time: The Historical Vision of an Afro-American People*. *First-Time* is undoubtedly an ethnography of the first importance. It has indeed, and more than once, been cited as an example of what the best experimentation in contemporary ethnographic writing is all about.[7] Perhaps this is so. Certainly it is true that in this novel work, Price has involved us to an admirable degree in the conditions of the negotiation of his fieldwork, in some of its ethical and epistemological dilemmas. But be that as it may, it is not, strictly speaking, as an exemplary ethnographic text that I shall consider this work of Price's. Or rather, I shall be concerned with the textual strategies it employs only in relation to the substantive argument they support. For to my mind Price's book is important precisely because its textual strategy appears to offer a novel approach to a distinctive anthropological problem, and it is really the seeming nature of this problem that interests me.

Price's opening epigraph is the first and most important clue to the overall structure of his concern: the question of a living collective consciousness of the past in the African diaspora. He writes in the evocative opening lines of this work:

> In a sacred grove beside the river of Dangogo, shaded by equatorial trees, stands a weathered shrine to the Old-Time People (*Amonenge*), those ancestors who "heard the guns of war." Whenever there is a collective crisis in the region—should the rains refuse to come on time or an epidemic sweep the river—it is to this shrine that Saramakas repair. As libations of sugarcane beer moisten the earth beneath the newly raised flags, the Old-Time People are one by one invoked—their names spoken (or played on the *apinti* drum), their deeds recounted, their foibles recalled, and the drums/dances/songs that they once loved performed to give them special pleasure. (5)

The Saramaka, a New World people today numbering roughly twenty thousand, are descendants of Africans sold into slavery in Dutch Guiana (today's Suriname) in the late seventeenth and early eighteenth centuries. These ancestors, however, the "Old-Time People," escaped into the forested hinterland and established there "maroon"[8] communities fiercely independent of the coastal colonial slave plantation system (see Price, *The Guiana Maroons* and *To Slay the Hydra*). And they, along with neighboring maroon communities such as the Djuka, the Aluku, and the Kwinti, have to this day remained a distinct and more or less precariously autonomous people. If the story of the coming of Africans to the New World—their capture, their deracination, their enslavement—is told as tragedy (as among modern historians it most often is), then its most compelling heroes are these maroons.[9] Theirs must be the most remarkable instance of sustained collective resistance in the history of New World colonial slavery. African slaves escaping the clutches of the colonial plantation early enough to avoid European cultural influence, and in large enough numbers to establish independent communities in the new soil of the Americas: no other New World people seem more to exemplify the moment of transit between the Old World and the New, between the past and the present.

Price opens his argument in *First-Time* with the statement of what he takes to be an essential conceptual paradox: whereas thousands of individual Saramakas, he says, must actually have "heard the guns of war," that is, must actually have lived during the time of the colonial war against the Saramakas (between the 1680s and the Peace of 1762), the names of only a small fraction of these ancestors are today invoked at the shrine to the Old-Time People. Therefore, Price maintains, history (by which he means the "consciousness" of a specifiable past) is clearly "selective." And the uniqueness of *First-Time*, he suggests:

> lies in its taking seriously the selection that is made by those people who gather at this shrine. It is about those people and those long-ago events that Saramakas today choose to think about, talk about and act upon; but it is also about the ways that Saramakas transform the general past (everything that happened) into the significant past, their history. This book is an attempt to communicate something of the Saramakas' own special vision of their formative years.

And Price does, with consummate care and an evident ethnographic generosity, communicate to us something of this special vision of the Saramaka. As we read of the legendary Fankia who "heard the guns of war" and who conveyed to her people how they should henceforth speak with the Old Time People, we feel the force of a profound and demanding past and see how, for the Saramaka, Fankia instantiates an inaugural site of historical authority. But as we shall see, Price's book is actually more than this attempt to convey to us the flavor of the historical vision of the Saramaka. In fact, it attempts to corroborate that vision, to put before us evidence from contemporary colonial sources that are supposed to confirm that the events of which his Saramaka informants speak were an historical actuality, that they really happened. Indeed it is the slippage between this desire on the one hand to share with us the "special vision" of the Saramakas and the desire on the other to confirm the historical truth of what the Saramaka tell that forms the central tension of *First-Time*, and this makes it an exemplary instance of that kind of (I think unsatisfactory) anthropological problematic that sees its task as one of representing authentic pasts.

First-time knowledge, knowledge, that is, of that inaugural era of struggle against the Dutch colonial army, is crucial to Saramaka culture and collective identity. It is knowledge that marks out for them a temporal and even a spatial break, a threshold of exile and slavery beyond which they passed only with the most sustained sacrifice, and that must now be held up for generations to come as a constant danger, the ever-present possibility of a return that must, at all costs, be prevented.[10] As a result, first-time knowledge is distinguished, for example, from knowledge of the more recent past by what Price calls "its overwhelming inherent power" (*First-Time* 6). And for this reason it is an area of local knowledge that is "singularly circumscribed, restricted, and guarded" (6). It is a knowledge that, as Price informs us, requires special handling (because such knowledge, Saramaka people say, can "kill"); special occasions of utterance (e.g., "cock's crow," the hour or two just before dawn); and specialist keepers (individual Saramakas who, for one reason or another, become renowned as repositories of Saramaka historical knowledge).

Moreover, first-time knowledge is knowledge that requires special discursive forms of utterance. Interestingly, the Saramaka have no Great Narrative of their origins, the kind of single, interconnected story that, passing through discernible and successive phases of beginning, middle, and end, brings us from that day to this. Rather, first-time knowledge is embedded in a variety of other, disparate sorts of discursive or rhetorical forms: as Price describes them, they include "genealogical nuggets," personal epithets, commemorative place-names, proverbs, songs, etc. And this knowledge is preeminently a knowledge of "events." For Saramakas, Price maintains, it is the "event" that constitutes the "very stuff of history." He writes:

> In the present book, my unit of analysis is the event. Taking fragments (often a mere phrase) from many different men, comparing them, discussing them with others, challenging them against rival accounts, and eventually holding them up against contemporary written evidence, I try to develop a picture of what the most knowledgeable Saramakas know, and why they know and preserve it. (*First-Time* 25)

Now in the development of this "picture of what the most knowledgeable Saramakas know," Price adopts a unique and compelling strategy of ethnographic representation. The substantive portion of the text of *First-Time* is divided into two parts occupying the upper and lower halves of each page, running like simultaneous "channels" of narrative. In the upper channel, we read Saramaka accounts of a specific "event"; in the lower, a commentary on these events. These commentaries, Price maintains, are intended to serve at least three functions. The first two—regarding the intelligibility of the accounts to those uninitiated in Saramaka discourse and the special meaning each has for the individual Saramaka informant uttering it—are fairly straightforward and need not concern us here. The third function, however, is conceptually the most interesting and indeed the most crucial for the point of Price's argument: it serves to introduce "information from contemporary written sources—chronology, geography, and other facts" in order to "work toward a picture of 'what really happened' against which we can measure and grasp the complex processes of selection used by Saramakas in regard to their distant past" (*First-Time* 39).

Such, briefly sketched, is the bold and innovative ethnographic strategy of *First-Time*. It tells a powerful story about continuities between the present and a past called slavery. I shall suggest, however, that it is really only a plausible strategy insofar as we accept the conceptual premise (i.e., that pasts are preservable and representable) and the ideological assumption (i.e., that the special task of an anthropology of peoples of the African diaspora consists in providing the apparatus for corroborating pasts) that organize the theoretical object it seeks to elaborate.

There is in Price's argument a notable ambiguity that turns on what one might call the agenda of historical understanding, on what is believed to be at stake in understanding a people's consciousness of its past. Price tells us that Saramaka discourse about their past, about plantation slavery and their struggle against it, is a "selective" one and that what is selected is of significance to the structure of expectations operating in the present. However, this selective, constructed past is not so much examined to reveal the reasons for particular selections as to show the verifiable actuality of the content of Saramaka statements about it. For Price, the really important problem thrown up by the selective character of Saramaka discourse about the past is not the economy of significance in which selections operate. Though Price does indicate the ideological character of first-time knowledge, he does not do so by way of opening access to a formal discussion in this register. Referential accuracy is his principal concern, so the anthropological problem that presents itself to us is not, as it might have been, that of mapping or describing the ways in which the past is ideologically produced and used by the Saramaka in the construction of authoritative cultural traditions and distinctive identities, the variable ways these constructions are negotiated, become conventions, are subverted, are redescribed, and so on, but rather that of determining how far what is selected actually happened, how far it is indeed an accurate representation of what really was.

Such a conceptual strategy must then logically presuppose the availability of an historical/

interpretive apparatus that can identify and represent "what really happened" in the Saramaka past, independent of Saramaka accounts of it; it must do so in order to provide historical representations that can be employed as a sort of authoritative baseline against which to measure the accuracy of their own memory of it. In Price's text this historical apparatus consists of the archive of Dutch colonial documents about the period in question. This archive, it follows, is not so much to be "read," that is, to be interrogated as a discursive density, an irreducible configuration of colonial politics and ideological textualization, but to verify Saramaka statements about certain events. To point this out is not to impugn the use of archival material in anthropological research but rather to differ with what appears to be Price's view, namely, that both the oral testimony of his Saramaka informants and the written texts of the Dutch colonizers are culturally different, yet conceptually uncomplicated, ways of re-presenting the past in the present.[11]

Price's conception of historical consciousness, then, is not a very coherent one. However, the epistemological issues of how to adequately know the Saramaka past and what kind of evidence would serve to substantiate it are less intrinsically interesting to me here than the question of the ideological assumptions that serve to secure the seeming authority of such anthropological arguments regarding it. In my reading, this is where the important stakes lie. And these ideological assumptions have to do with the kind of anthropological object that the Afro-American or the Afro-Caribbean (or anyway the New World Negro) has historically been constructed as. I would argue that at least one of the pervasive ideological assumptions through which this theoretical object has been constructed is that peoples of African descent in the New World require something like anthropology, a science of culture, to provide them with the foundational guarantee of an authentic past.

Price wants to demonstrate conclusively that an Afro-American people does indeed have an accurate memory of past events. But why, we might ask, does this need to be demonstrated in the first place? What are the ideological conditions that motivate it? Or, to put it another way: What are the sources that give special significance to the bold subtitle of Price's ethnography—"the historical vision of an Afro-American People"? For what is implicit in its inclusive claim is that this "historical vision" of the Saramaka that is about to be described to us, is, in some way, to be taken as illustrative of the historical vision of Afro-American people as such. The Saramaka, in short, are a sort of anthropological metonym; they are to be understood as providing the exemplary arena in which to argue out certain anthropological claims about a discursive domain called Afro-America. And here, I think, is the first thing to notice about the ideological structure of *First-Time*: its place within the genealogy of a specific anthropological problem, that is, the problem of the African in the New World.

First-Time is a compelling piece of ethnography, in part because it seems a nearly conclusive rebuttal of that old anthropological notion regarding the supposed "timelessness" of primitive peoples, their lack of "historical consciousness." *First-Time*, like Renato Rosaldo's *Ilongot Headhunting*, presents the case that this is nothing but an anthropological (or, if you like, western) prejudice; Price more or less explicitly says so.[12] I suggest, however, that much of the seeming power of Price's argument derives from another source, that is, its more local agenda, its concern to put to rest the prominent notion that peoples of African descent in the New World suffer from "pastlessness."[13] Curiously enough, while explicit expression of this agenda is suppressed in the body of *First-Time* itself, it becomes the subject of a small, almost unnoticed essay on "Caribbean historical consciousness"[14] published soon after. In this essay, Price takes as his target what he calls the "denial of history" to the New World descendants of Africans—the "vanguard for those people to whom history has too often been denied" ("An Absence of Ruins?" 24). A number of West Indian writers—most notably, V. S. Naipaul, Orlando Patterson, and Derek Walcott—are singled out for sharp criticism. These writers, in Price's estimate of them, are complicit in the argument (a "bourgeois illusion, a function of our [?] own ethnocentrism") that "Caribbean peoples suffer from a profound lack of historical consciousness, that they know (and care) almost nothing about their own complex and often unhappy pasts" (25). And a bit later he tells us, "[t]he strongest evidence I could muster against the notion of a pastless Afro-Caribbean is undoubtedly contained in *First-Time*. That book lays bare a vision of the past with overwhelming relevance to present-day Saramakas" (27).

I do not want to enter here into the interesting question of Price's reading (or misreading, as I think it is) of the historical imaginary of West Indian literature. That I will leave to others.[15] My concern is only to indicate something of the ideological location of *First-Time*. On the basis of the verification of an authentic consciousness of a past in which slavery forms the generative referential moment, it sets itself against the pervasive assumption of the "pastlessness" of peoples of African descent in the New World. The Saramaka—uniquely situated as they are—are the exemplary stage upon which both this problem of the pasts of Afro-American diasporas and its anthropological resolution can be set out in sharpest relief. The following question then poses itself: What are the historical sources of this idea that the theoretical problem posed by the existence of peoples of African descent in the New World consists in corroborating their past? I want now to turn my attention to this.

The Anthropological Problem of "the New World Negro"

The anthropological problem of peoples of African descent in the New World is more a problem constituted by American cultural anthropology than by British social anthropology, and it bears the distinctive marks of that determinate origin. If British social anthropology has been criticized (often justly) for its relation to the British Empire and to the sources, structures, and representations of colonial rule, American cultural anthropology has had the good fortune to appear in a much less unsavory light. Perhaps with reason. For Franz Boas (the leading figure in the founding of professional American anthropology) not only opened the way for a concept of "culture" according to which each people's practices were to be taken on their own terms but was himself an outspoken critic of racial and ethnic discrimination (see Boas, "Outlook"; Stocking, "Anthropology"; and Hyatt). This distinction, however, should not obscure the necessity of inquiring into the ideological determinants of the discourse of American cultural anthropology. The question to be addressed here is not the often-repeated (if nevertheless important) one regarding the dearth of adequate anthropological research on Afro-American culture (see Willis; Szwed) but rather that of how the object itself, Afro-America, came to be constituted in the texts of this cultural discourse.

Richard Price is not the first American anthropologist to study the Saramaka. Nor is he the first to envision that the Saramaka offer, in some way, the key to the anthropological problem of the African in the New World. He is preceded on both counts by Melville J. Herskovits.[16] A student of Franz Boas (and much influenced by him in this regard) Herskovits, perhaps more than anyone, helped to establish the "New World Negro" as a positive anthropological problem, that is to say, as a visible and distinctive problem of "history" and "culture."[17]

Herskovits's contribution to the formation of an anthropology of the "New World Negro" is inseparable from two other debates. One is the wider discourse that constructed the Negro as a *social* problem of a certain kind, and the other is that discussion of the conceptual categories of the nascent "science of culture" that formulated the New World Negro as a *theoretical* problem of a certain kind. Though it is impossible to delineate here the full historical complexity of these social and ideological preconditions, it is necessary to point to at least some aspects that were crucial to the conceptual problematic into which Herskovits inserted himself.

In its social and ideological aspects, the "Negro Question" in the pre-First World War years of this century had to do with whether the Negro could be considered a candidate for full social and moral citizenship in the American body-politic.[18] Could the Negro become assimilated to the values and ethos of American society? Or was there something distinctive about the Negro that either precluded, or at any rate seriously qualified, assimilation? In one way or another, this question of the Negro's ambiguous identity turned on the idea, pervasive at the turn of the century, that Negroes were a people with no consequential past and therefore a people with no distinctive contribution to Civilization, no Culture in the Arnoldian sense. This idea was itself linked to two other images: the image of slavery as an institution that had completely erased the African identities of the slaves and the image of Africa as itself a dark and savage place (see Fredrickson). Framed as it was by an evolutionary tradition presided over by Herbert Spencer (Stocking, "Franz Boas"), much of the social-science thinking of this period accepted these assumptions and images. Certainly these questions formed part of the ideological atmosphere in which the professional discipline of modern American anthropology emerged; indeed it could be said that these questions were part of the ideological horizon on which the new anthropology defined itself and the distinctive labor of its seminal concept: culture.

Between the late 1880s and the turn of the century, Boas had set about what we might call a strategy of skeptical interrogation (see Krupat) of the two existing "branches" of anthropology, the "biological" and the "psychological." In so doing, he demonstrated the unpersuasiveness of their arguments (regarding, on the one hand, the question of the mental ability of different races and, on the other, the historical reconstruction of the stages of the social development of "mankind"), as well as the ideological overdetermination of their claims for the superiority of the West. This skeptical interrogation would have a number of strong conceptual effects: among them, the displacement of "race" as the explanatory key to difference; the antihierarchical revaluation of this difference as "culture"; and the reconfiguring of the "science" of anthropology around the historical and ethnographic study of particular, that is, "cultural," instances of difference.

Most pertinent to our concern with the conceptual preconditions of the anthropology of "the New World Negro," these cultural instances, Boas argued, have to be analytically understood in terms of the psychological and historical integration of "elements" into "wholes." Cultures are distinctive (and therefore valid) by virtue of the growth of an inner unity (a "style" or "ethos") composed of traits transmitted or diffused historically from place to place or group to group. The culture of any tribe, Boas maintained, "no matter how primitive it may be, can be fully explained only when we take into consideration its inner growth as well as its relation to the culture of its near and distant neighbors and the effect that they may have exerted" ("Principles" 278). Not only were all cultures valid—the European no more than the African—but they each bore a distinctive relation to the pasts from which they were derived. In view of this (for its time) quite radical reformulation of the question of difference, it is not surprising that Boas responded to the contemporary racist image of black culture by attempting to place it in a certain proximity to an anthropologically rehabilitated representation of its African past. For it followed from Boas's conception of "cultural" difference that any appreciation of Afro-America would have to consider "its relation to the culture of its near and distant neighbors." This is, in fact, what Boas attempted to demonstrate at Atlanta University in 1906 when he "reminded" his audience of black graduates of the past cultural "achievements" of their African forebears ("Outlook").

What is most notable about Boas's remarks about black culture, however, is not only their authoritative force, but the fact that they stopped short of claiming any essential "Africanness" for Afro-American culture. For Boas, the culture of "the New World Negro" is not set in a direct, continuous relation to the ethnohistorical African past he authoritatively evokes. The "genius" or geist of Afro-Americans, that feature which gave to their varied practices the "wholeness" or "integrity" that Boas claimed for "culture," is not traced in some (analytically salient) way to this evoked Africa. Rather, this ethnologically rehabilitated Africa supports a past that belongs to the Negro only as a potential source of inspiration, something toward which such young Afro-American intellectuals as Boas was himself addressing in Atlanta might confidently cast a nostalgic backward glance even as they tackled the hard (and as Boas no doubt believed, real) work of racial uplift. This attitude reflects perhaps the cautious, assimilationist tenor of cultivated politics, both white and black, in liberal America in the prewar years—the confidence in "the marvelous power of amalgamation of our nation," as Boas ("Principles" 202) put it. For it was indeed a politically delicate issue; to have asserted the distinctiveness of Afro-Americans at a time when difference was still argued out in racial terms would have provided grist for the mill of racist segregationists, for whom blacks were so different as to be unassimilable. Yet Boas's ethnological evocation of Africa was in its way a profoundly significant moment, and it is not hard to see the cause of Du Bois's enthusiasm; for here, in the white anthropologist's statement, was the enigmatic sign of our racial memory, the metaphorical Ethiopia and Egypt of the recently published *Souls of Black Folk* ("The shadow of a mighty Negro past flits through the tale of Ethiopia the Shadowy and of Egypt the Sphinx" [3]), given a tangible, that is to say, a scientific grounding and guarantee.

The conditions of the relation between Boasian "culture" and Afro-America changed considerably after the First World War, so that anthropology would more precisely specify this illusive grounding (i.e., Africa) and so address more boldly, more declaratively, the question of the scientific guarantee of Afro-American race-pride. There were at least two kinds of reasons for this change, one having to do with conditions of race ideology that saw the advent of a "new" Negro (see Locke) and the other with developments in what George Stocking (*Ethnographic Sensibility* 210) has referred to as the "classic" period of modern American anthropology.

Over the course of the war years, the political conditions of race ideology (as indeed of much else about the texture of social life in the United States) altered so that "talented tenth" assimilationism was increasingly brought into question by a more vigorous, more uncompromising cultural nationalism (Huggins, *Voices*). One consequence of this was that across a range of contemporary Afro-American ideological positions—from the working-class disciples of Marcus Garvey to the intellectual organizers of Pan-Africanism and the artists and literati of the Harlem Renaissance—peoples of African descent were themselves reclaiming, in various inflections, a past called Africa, and placing it in the foreground of their assertions of cultural identity and community.[19] I think something of this widespread mood is heard in the Harlem essayist and bibliophile Arthur Schomburg's contribution to Alain Locke's *The New Negro*. Schomburg, who opens his remarkable essay, "The Negro Digs Up his Past," by suggesting that Afro-Americans could not embrace the Emersonian idea that in America it "is unnecessary to have a past," closes with the rousing assertion that though the Negro has been maligned as "a man without a history because he has been considered a man without a worthy culture," he was now seeing "himself against a reclaimed background, in a perspective that will give pride and self-respect ample scope, and make history yield for him the same values that the treasured past of any people affords" (Schomburg 237).

And yet, at least by that very measure which the well-informed Schomburg himself invoked—the evidence of African ethnology—this background was still vague, undefined. As the late Nathan Huggins put it in his brilliant discussion of the cultural politics of 1920s Harlem: "All seemed to know, or sense, that Africa should mean something to the race; there should be some race memory that tied black men together; [however,] ambiguity and doubt always left the question unresolved" (*Harlem Renaissance* 80–81).

The ideological space into which Melville Herskovits entered, having taken his degree with Boas at Columbia University in 1923, was characterized by a complex of positions in which the past and its signal figure, Africa, played a critical role in articulating a positive relation to being somehow both distinctively Negro and American. Certainly in these altered ideological circumstances, the question "How could Afro-American race-pride be placed on a scientific footing?" must have appeared to a Boas-trained student like Herskovits (who himself had many prominent friends in the Harlem community[20]) to demand a different, or at least a less equivocal, answer than the one given it by Boas two decades before. And certainly, too, the discipline's emerging scientific self-consciousness in these years made such an answer seem possible.

For by the middle 1920s the professionalization of American anthropology had begun to lend to its practitioners an air of intellectual confidence and scientific authority. After all, the discipline could now boast its own "laboratory"[21] (as was powerfully demonstrated by Margaret Mead's South Seas research), and, in the various approaches of Mead, Ruth Benedict, and Robert Redfield, it employed an increasingly streamlined and sophisticated methodological apparatus. However, the development during this period that is particularly pertinent to our concern with the formation of an anthropology of the New World Negro is the elaboration of the concept of "acculturation." Adumbrated in Boas's idea of the historical dissemination and integration of cultural elements,[22] acculturation by the late 1920s and early 1930s was acquiring a conceptual distinctiveness and scholarly appeal. As programmatically outlined by Redfield, Ralph Linton, and Herskovits in their memorandum for the Social Science Research Council, the concept was sharply distinguished from such other related concepts in the Boasian lexicon as "culture-change," "assimilation," and "diffusion"; it was given a definitional precision and methodological rigor that it was lacking hitherto. The study of acculturation was to be oriented around the careful identification of "traits," and the problem of their selection, their determination, and their integration into other patterns. This identification and classification of traits was further to be combined with an investigation of the "psychological mechanisms" of selection and integration.

This view retained the inaugural Boasian idea of culture as constituted of essential, quantifiable elements or units integrated into a psychologically meaningful whole that was unproblematically representable in ethnographic texts. It also added to that base a more positivist program of inquiry: a methodological apparatus for systematically identifying and classifying these traits, for tracing their authentic origins and sources, and for conceptualizing the way they fit into an essential cultural totality. So conceived, the anthropology of acculturation was scientifically more credible. Moreover, if Boasian anthropology still retained (as indeed it did in an even more urgent way than before the war) the socially conscious conviction that its science could have the practical humanist effect of inspiring Afro-Americans with race-pride, this could now arguably be accomplished in less speculative, more empirically sound terms. Herskovits's seminal contribution to the anthropology of the New World Negro, I suggest, may be read as an attempt to demonstrate how the Negro could indeed be both distinctively Negro and American, and to do so in the context of a new, more assured, science of culture (see Jackson).

In the early 1920s, Herskovits still held the assimilationist view, common enough among white American liberals, that the Negro was not culturally distinct, but was indeed as American as anyone else: "the same pattern, only a different shade!" as he famously put it in his contribution to *The New Negro* ("The Negro's Americanism" 353). Even as late as 1927 he could speak of Afro-Americans as a people "of the most diverse racial stock, yet living the life of white Americans" ("Acculturation" 224). But by the end of this momentous decade of black cultural expression, Herskovits, deeply influenced by the vocal and assertive wave of black consciousness, completely reversed this position, and began to outline the ideas he would become best known for.[23] On the basis of a number of ethnographic studies (of which *Life in a Haitian Valley* [1937] is perhaps the best loved), and works of conceptual refiguration (of which *The Myth of the Negro Past* [1941] is doubtless the best known), which together constitute the cornerstone of an anthropology of African diasporas in the New World, Herskovits set out to demonstrate that not only was the New World Negro culturally distinct, but that this distinctiveness was owed precisely to an authentic African heritage.

Significantly, the first place to which Herskovits went in this undertaking to uncover the distinctive Africanness of Afro-American culture was to the then Dutch colony of Suriname, visiting (with his wife, Frances) in the summers of 1928 and 1929. Sketching retrospectively the path of their successive concerns as they wrote *Rebel Destiny: Among the Bush Negroes of Dutch Guiana*, their popular description of 1920s Saramaka life, the Herskovitses wrote:

> It began in 1923 with the inquiry into Negro-white crossing in the United States. As this work progressed it became evident that the problem demanded more knowledge of the sources of the slaves who compose the Negro ancestry of the American Negroes than was available. This knowledge, which historical documents do not give us, was, therefore, to be sought in a comparison of Negro cultures in the New World and Africa. (viii–ix)

On this conception—one in which an understanding of contemporary cultural practice requires a knowledge of its authentic sources—the North American Negro (in terms of whom the problem as such was formulated) remained something of an enigma. It therefore became necessary, or so it seemed, to go elsewhere in search of the sources of the North American Negro. Already in the early 1930s, then, Herskovits was constructing the metonymic narrative that would join Afro-America into a whole differentiated by a measurable proximity to Africa.

In their study of Dutch Suriname, the Herskovitses adopted the comparative strategy of studying both the Saramaka of the hinterland and the town Surinamese of Paranaraibo, the capital. Their assumptions are obvious. The Surinamese of the town, by virtue of their long association with European culture, were less likely to have retained as many of the traits of Africa as the Saramaka in the "bush." And indeed the Herskovitses found that the critical difference between the bush and the town is that "the bush is Africa of the seventeenth century" (x). Putting it more sharply, they write:

> The importance of the Bush Negroes for the student of Negro cultures, then, is that they live and think today as did their ancestors who established themselves in this bush, which is to say that they live and think much as did the Negroes who were brought to other parts of the New World, and who became the ancestors of the New World Negroes of the present day. (xii)

By 1930, soon after Herskovits's return from Suriname, he elaborated what he called a "scale of intensity of Africanisms," on the basis of which he argued the possibility of measuring the degree and the extent to which the Negro in the New World had actually retained elements of African culture.

> It is quite possible on the basis of our present knowledge to make a kind of chart indicating the extent to which the descendants of Africans brought to the New World have retained Africanisms in their cultural behavior. If we consider the intensity of African cultural elements in the various regions north of Brazil...we may say that after Africa itself it is the Bush Negroes of Suriname who exhibit a civilization which is the most African....Next to them, on our scale, would be placed their Negro neighbors on the coastal plains of the Guianas, who, in spite of centuries of close association with the whites, have retained an amazing amount of their aboriginal African traditions, many of which are combined in curious fashion with the traditions of the dominant group. (149)

And so on, until: "Finally, we should come to a group where, to all intents and purposes, there is nothing of the African tradition left, and which consists of people of varying degrees of Negroid physical type, who only differ from their white neighbors in the fact that they have more pigmentation in their skins" (150). From the Bush Negroes of Suriname at one end of the "scale of intensity of Africanisms" to North American blacks at the other, Herskovits was reconstructing the precise extent to which the New World Negro had retained the Old in the New, the past in the present.

This, I think it is fair to say, is the inaugural moment of a lasting anthropological problematic. The New World Negro had been ideologically constituted by a dominant and racist nineteenth century discourse as a figure with neither a determinate past nor, its supposed corollary, a distinctive culture. And by the mid-1920s, black counterdiscourses were, in the articulation of a radical identity-politics, making impressive and unignorable claims for an active African heritage. Therefore, on the conceptual terrain established by the categories of Boasian culture, the task presented to the new anthropology was to show in as scientifically conclusive a way as possible that the New World Negro did in fact have both a determinate past and a distinctive culture. Since Africa was assumed to be the authentic cultural origin of the Negro diaspora, Herskovits set out to demonstrate, by an effort of corroboration, the remnants of that past in the cultural traits of contemporary Negro societies. The Saramaka, then, seemed to provide the unique possibility of demonstrating this.

Richard Price, it is true, is not concerned with cultural retentions as such. He is not trying to show that there are authentic traits of a past called Africa still around in the New World.[24] The anthropological conception of culture had in the meantime drifted away from the hard, positivist ground of traits towards the more semiotic field of symbols and "consciousness,"[25] and ideological conditions after the 1960s no longer required (or at least not in the same way as in the early decades of this century) that the New World Negro be placed in direct proximity to a rehabilitated figure of Africa. Rather, Price wants to show that there is an authentic "memory" or "consciousness" of a past called slavery. But it is not hard to see that in spite of this apparent difference, both Herskovits and Price share a fundamental assumption regarding the history and culture of peoples of African descent in the New World, namely, that their history and culture has to be anthropologically argued out in terms of a notion of an authentic past (whatever its name, whatever its modality) persisting in the present and that this persisting past, moreover, can be conclusively demonstrated on the ethnographic example of an exemplary case, the Saramaka of Suriname, a people supposedly closest in proximity to that past.

Between That Event and This Memory: Tradition

I would like to propose that we attempt to change this anthropological problematic altogether, this sustained preoccupation with the corroboration or verification of authentic pasts. The issue has nothing to do with erasing either of the figures of Africa or slavery (or even the resonant narrative of continuity that embodies them) from the anthropology of peoples of African descent in the New

World. Rather, what I propose is their theoretical relocation; between that event (Africa or slavery) and this memory there spreads a complex discursive field we may usefully call "tradition."[26] By tradition I have in mind a differentiated field of discourse whose unity, such as it is, resides not in anthropologically authenticated traces, but in its being constructed around a distinctive group of tropes or figures, which together perform quite specific kinds of rhetorical labor.

The first and most obvious of tradition's labors is to secure connections among a past, a present, and a future. In the theoretical field occupied by the work of Herskovits and Price, the figures of Africa and slavery circulate as authentic presences, which anthropology is supposed to make legible in the practices or consciousnesses of the descendants of Africans and slaves. The project I commend would be concerned with the following kinds of questions: What are the varying ways in which Africa and slavery are employed by New World peoples of African descent in the narrative construction of relations among pasts, presents, and futures? What, in each case, are the salient features with which these figures are inscribed? What is the rhetorical or, if you like, ideological, work that they are made to perform in the varied instances and occasions in which they are brought into play? For example, the "first-time" of Rastafarians in Jamaica (and Rastafarians do speak of "first-time"), like that of the Saramakas, turns on the central figure of slavery; but it is likely to be inscribed with a different set of ideological investments, reflecting its own specific historical and political conditions. What would be at stake here is less whether one can measure the extent to which this disaporan community of Rastafarians retains an accurate memory of any verifiable preemancipation event than the ways in which this figure, slavery (and those figures metaphorically and metonymically connected to it), enables (or prevents) establishment of positions in a cultural and political field.

Cultural traditions, however, are not only authored; they are authorized. They not only make intelligible; they make legitimate. The second of tradition's labors therefore has to do with securing what we might call a distinctive community of adherents. What space do Africa and slavery occupy in the political economy of local discourse? To what kinds of authority do they make their appeal? From what kinds of audience do they seek their support? What are the conditions—discursive and nondiscursive—of reception that facilitate their persuasiveness? Take, for example, the uses of the figure of Africa by Arthur Schomburg (the bibliophile) and Marcus Garvey (the mass leader), or again, its uses in the verses of a Calypsonian, on the one hand, and the political rhetoric of a Michael Manley, on the other. The point is that this figure can have different political uses, different modes of authorization, can address itself to a variety of audiences—and yet at the same time belong to a distinctive tradition insofar as a single figure is being employed in the construction of a relation between pasts and presents.

The third of tradition's labors is to link narratives of the past to narratives of identity. This is of course because tradition seeks not only to make the past intelligible and legitimate but also to instruct, that is to say, to actively cultivate the virtues it valorizes. How are the figures of Africa and Slavery employed in the fashioning of specific virtues, in the cultivation of specific dispositions, specific modes of address, specific styles—of dress, of speech, of song, of the body's movements; how, in other words, do these figures participate in those techniques by means of which the construction of appropriate bodies and selves are effected?

It seems to me that these kinds of questions enable us to ask theoretically more interesting questions about pasts in the present. It might be noted too that they are not, on the one hand, essentialist, inasmuch as they do not presuppose the full or partial presence of an Africa or slavery that needs only to pass through the interpretive grid of anthropology to be recognized and appreciated as such. Nor, on the other hand, are they antiessentialist, inasmuch as they do not assert that there is no actual continuity between Africa or slavery and the present, that these are merely empty signifiers. These questions in fact do not seek to make any claims whatsoever regarding the ultimate ontological status of Africa and slavery in the present of the cultures of the New World and therefore do not see the theoretical task of anthropological inquiry as trying either to accurately represent the proximity between the present and the past or to deny it. At the same time, these questions affirm that peoples of African descent in the New World do make of Africa and slavery a profound presence in their cultural worlds, and seek rather to describe the tradition of discourse in which they participate, the local network of power and knowledge in which they are employed, and the kinds of identities they serve to fashion.

Notes

Versions of this paper have been read at the University of California, Santa Cruz; Northeastern University, Boston; and Rice University, Houston. I have benefited from the comments offered on each of these occasions. I am especially grateful to Elizabeth Eames for her searching criticism of an earlier draft and to Herman Gray, in conversations with whom many of the ideas expressed here were discussed.

1. These, of course, may be either popular or scholarly, but this distinction may be bracketed for my purposes in this essay.
2. There is a contemporary story, in many ways a counterhegemonic story, according to which anthropology is central to undoing the hegemonic master narrative of the West. In this story, anthropology, as the discourse of culture, is counterposed to Philosophy, the adjudicative discourse of Reason. It is thus seen as a potential way of empowering Other rationalities – i.e., culture(s) – against Reason (or at least, Reason as a distinctive kind of cultural knowledge, that of the West since the Enlightenment). But it is perhaps not sufficiently appreciated how in so doing 'culture' itself can be made to simply replace Reason as new authentic foundation, the ground, so to put it, for another ontology.
3. The text of this lecture is reproduced in Boas ('Outlook'). Its effect on the young Du Bois is now well known. In a famous passage in the preface to his *Black Folk, Then and Now* (1939), he wrote: 'Franz Boas came to Atlanta University where I was teaching history in 1906 and said to a graduating class: You need not be ashamed of your African past; and then he recounted the history of the black kingdoms south of the Sahara for a thousand years. I was too astonished to speak. All of this I had never heard and I came then and afterwards to realize how...silence and neglect...can let truth utterly disappear or...be unconsciously distorted' (vii).
4. The distinction is, I think, an important one to insist on. For note that what anthropology constructs is a theoretical object, not a cultural identity (except insofar as anthropology has now become crucial to the cultural identity of the West [see McGrane]). Another possible task might be to inquire into the ways in which the anthropological object gets appropriated by peoples of African descent in the New World for their various purposes.
5. In a recent comment on anthropological theory, Arjun Appadurai has made the instructive point that anthropology has not sufficiently problematized the relation between place and theory (356–61). This is a point I wish both to endorse and elaborate.
6. In the course of a discussion of the possible ways open to a postmodernist anthropology, James Clifford has written of *First-Time* that it 'is evidence of the fact that acute political and epistemological self-consciousness need not lead to ethnographic self-absorption, or to the conclusion that it is impossible to know anything certain about other people' (7). See also Marcus and Fischer.
7. 'The English word maroon,' writes Price (in one of the unpaginated pages), 'derived from the Spanish *cimarron*, a term originally used in Hispaniola to refer to domestic cattle that had taken to the hills; by the early 1500s, it had come to be used in plantation colonies throughout the Americas to designate slaves who successfully escaped from captivity.'
8. For a discussion of the tropic emplotment of historical reconstruction, see White.
9. This is like 'the time of the Japanese' of the Ilongot of the Philippines studied by Rosaldo in 'Doing Oral History' and *Ilongot Headhunting*. Rosaldo, in a more nuanced and theoretically self-reflexive way, shares some of the same faulty concepts.

10. It is part of Price's concern to caution us against the uncritical imposition of Western assumptions about history (supposedly the idea of history as, quintessentially, written documents) and to encourage us to a closer and more careful attention to the distinctive local (and very often oral) ways of re-presenting the past in the present. Notwithstanding the fact that the idea that the authorized version of the past is the written one is not in itself a western idea (witness for example the Sinhalas' conception of their Great Chronicle, the *Mahavamsa*), this doubt is a worthy one and the advice useful.
11. Note the epigraphs taken from Robert H. Lowie and A.R. Radcliffe-Brown that open the second chapter, 'Of Speakers/To Readers.'
12. Part of the problem with Price's argument is that there is a conflation of these two related but distinguishable registers, 'timelessness' and 'pastlessness.' 'Timelessness' has to do with the primitive's supposed lack of historical depth; 'pastlessness,' with the black's supposed lack of a significant past.
13. The essay was entitled 'An Absence of Ruins?' the allusion being to (and critical of) Orlando Patterson's 1967 novel, *An Absence of Ruins*.
14. For some considerations of the West Indian writer's relation to history, see variously, Baugh, Walcott, Brathwaite, and McWatt.
15. In point of fact, Herskovits himself was preceded by Morton C. Kahn (1931). Kahn was a student of 'public measures as applied to tropical disease' (*Djuka* xvii). While he had visited the 'South American tropics' in 1922, 1923, and 1925, visits which 'took me to the border of the Bush Negro countries,' his first visit to the Djuka was undertaken in 1927, 'under the auspices of Dr. Clark Wissler of the Museum of Natural History, [and] with the financial aid of Mr Myron I. Granger' (xviii). On a second 'expedition,' in 1928, he was accompanied by Herskovits.
16. See Jackson; I am greatly indebted to this very thoughtful essay. For a recent appreciative reflection on Herskovits, see Fernandez.
17. Indeed this had been the central issue since the end of the Civil War. For a discussion of the debates about the status of Afro-Americans in the post-Reconstruction period, see Meier.
18. In fact, Afro-Americans had earlier developed consciousness of Africa. See, for example Edwin Redkey's study of nineteenth century back-to-Africa movements, *Black Exodus*.
19. Among them were W.E.B. Du Bois, Alain Locke, James Weldon Johnson, and Zora Neale Hurston. Indeed one recent commentator would refer to him as an 'honorary New Negro'; he was one of only three white contributors to Alain Locke's *The New Negro* (see Lewis 116).
20. I borrow this phrase from George Stocking (*Ethnographic Sensibility* 209); but see, for example, Herskovits's use of it ('Acculturation' 217; and 'Negro' 147).
21. As Herskovits ('Acculturation') points out, the 'peculiarly American' term 'acculturation' is 'not of recent development,' but had been used by such prominent American ethnologists as W.J. Powell in the latter part of the nineteenth century. See Stocking's argument ('Franz Boas,' 212) that the evolutionist use of it differed greatly from Boas's.
22. Herskovits himself suggests a direct link between his new ideas and the rise of 'the New Negro' (see 'Negro' 151).
23. He has indeed been critical of just this idea of Herskovits's. See Price ('Saramaka Woodcarving') and Mintz and Price.
24. Or more precisely, the other side of the Boasian conception of culture, which, stressing 'pattern,' 'style,' 'ethos,' had more or less displaced 'traits.' As Stocking expressed it: 'On the one hand, culture was simply an accidental accretion of individual elements. On the other, culture—despite Boas' renunciation of organic growth—was at the same time an integrated spiritual totality that somehow conditioned the form of its elements' ('Franz Boas,' 214).
25. See Asad for an instructive deliberation on the concept of 'tradition' in relation to Islam.

Works Cited

Appadurai, Arjun. 1986. Theory in Anthropology: Center and Periphery. *Comparative Studies in Society and History* 26, no. 2:356–61.

Asad, Talal. 1986. *The Idea of an Anthropology of Islam*. Occasional Papers Series. Washington D.C.: Center for Contemporary Arab Studies.

Baugh, Edward. 1978. *Derek Walcott: Memory as Vision: Another Life*. London: Longman.

———. 1977. The West Indian Writer and His Quarrel with History. *Tapia* 20 February.

Boas, Franz. 1974. The Outlook for the American Negro. *The Shaping of American Anthropology 1883–1911: A Franz Boas Reader*, ed. George W. Stocking, Jr. New York: Basic.

———. 1974. The Principles of Ethnological Classification. *The Shaping of American Anthropology 1883–1911: A Franz Boas Reader*, ed. George W. Stocking, Jr. New York: Basic.

Borges, Jorge. 1984. *Twenty Four Conversations with Borges*, trans. Nicomedes Suarez Arauz, Willis Barnestone, and Noemi Escandell. New York: Grove Press.

Brathwaite, Edward. 1974. Timehri. *Is Massa Day Done?* Ed. Orde Coombs. New York: Anchor.

Clifford, James. 1986. Introduction: Partial Truths. In *Writing Culture: The Poetics and Politics of Ethnography*, ed. James Clifford and George Marcus. Berkeley: University of California Press.

Du Bois, W.E.B. 1939. *Black Folk, Then and Now: An Essay in the History and Sociology of the Negro Race.* New York; Henry Holt.

———. 1989. *The Souls of Black Folk.* 1903. New York: Bantam Books.

Fernandez, James. W. 1990. Tolerance in a Repugnant World and Other Dilemmas in the Cultural Relativism of Melville J. Herskovits. *Moral Relativism*, ed. Alan Page Fiske. Special issue of *Ethos* 18, no. 2:140–64.

Fredrickson, George M. 1971. *The Black Image in the White Mind: The Debate of Afro-American Character and Destiny, 1817–1914.* New York: Harper.

Herskovits, Melville J. 1972. Acculturation and the American Negro. *Southwestern Political and Social Science Quarterly* 8, no. 3:211–24.

———. 1941. *The Myth of the Negro Past.* New York: Beacon.

———. 1930. The Negro in the New World: The Statement of a Problem. *American Anthropologist* (ns), no. 32:145–55.

———. n.d. The Negro's Americanism. Locke 353–60.

———. 1971. *On Life in a Haitian Valley*, 1937. New York: Anchor.

Herskovits, Melville, and Frances Herskovits. 1971. *Rebel Destiny: Among the Bush Negroes of Dutch Guiana*, 1934. New York: Books for Libraries Press.

Huggins, Nathan. 1979. *Harlem Renaissance.* New York: Oxford UP.

———, ed. 1976. *Voices from the Harlem Renaissance.* New York: Oxford UP.

Hyatt, Marshall. 1985. Franz Boas and the Struggle for Black Equality: The Dynamics of Ethnicity. *Perspectives in American History* ns, no. 2:269–95.

Jackson, Walter. 1986. Melville Herskovits and the Search for Afro-American Culture. In *Malinowski, Rivers, Benedict and Others*, ed. George W. Stocking, Jr. Vol. 4 of *History of Anthropology*, ed. Stocking. 7 vols. to date. Madison: University of Wisconsin Press.

Kahn, Morton C. 1931. *Djuka: The Bush Negroes of Dutch Guiana.* New York: Viking.

Kruput, Arnold. 1988. Anthropology in the Ironic Mode: The Work of Franz Boas. *Social Text* 19/20 (Fall): 105–18.

Lewis, David Levering. 1979. *When Harlem was in Vogue.* New York: Oxford UP.

Locke, Alain, ed. 1925. *The New Negro.* New York: Atheneum.

McGrane, Bernard. 1989. *Beyond Anthropology: Society and the Other.* New York: Columbia UP.

McWatt, Mark. 1982. The Preoccupation with the Past in West Indian Literature. *Caribbean Quarterly* 28.1–2:12–19.

Marcus, George E., and Michael M. J. Fischer. 1986. *Anthropology as Cultural Critique: An Experimental Moment in the Human Sciences.* Chicago: University of Chicago Press.

Meier, August. 1963. *Negro Thought in America, 1880–1915.* Ann Arbor: University of Michigan Press.

Mintz, Sidney W., and Richard Price. 1976. *An Anthropological Approach to the Afro-American Past: A Caribbean Perspective.* Philadelphia: Institute for the Study of Human Issues.

Price, Richard. 1985. An Absence of Ruins?: Seeking Caribbean Historical Consciousness. *Caribbean Review* 14, no .3:24–29, 45.

———. 1983. *First-Time: The Historical Vision of an Afro-American People.* Baltimore: Johns Hopkins UP.

———. 1976. *The Guiana Maroons: A Historical and Bibliographical Introduction.* Baltimore: Johns Hopkins UP.

———. 1970. Saramaka Woodcarving: The Development of an Afroamerican Art. *Man* 5, no. 3: 363–78.

———. 1983. *To Slay the Hydra: Dutch Colonial Perspectives on the Saramaka Wars.* Ann Arbor: Karoma Publishers.

Redfield, Robert, Ralph Linton, and Melville J. Herskovits. 1936. Memorandum for the Study of Acculturation. *American Anthropologist* ns, no. 38:149–52.

Redkey, Edwin S. 1969. *Black Exodus: Black Nationalist and Back-to-Africa Movements, 1890–1910*. New Haven: Yale UP.
Rosaldo, Renato. 1980. Doing Oral History. *Social Analysis* 4:89–99.
———. 1980. *Ilongot Headhunting, 1883–1974*. Stanford: Stanford UP.
Schomburg, Arthur. n.d. The Negro Digs up His Past. Locke 231–37.
Stocking, George W., Jr. 1979. Anthropology as *Kulturkampf*: Science and Politics in the Career of Franz Boas. *The Uses of Anthropology*, ed. Walter Goldschmidt. Washington DC: American Anthropological Association.
———. 1989. The Ethnographic Sensibility of the 1920s and the Dualism of the Anthropological Tradition. In *Romantic Motives: Essays on Anthropological Sensibility*, ed. George W. Stocking Jr. Vol. 6 of *History of Anthropology*, ed. Stocking. 7 vols. to date. Madison: University of Wisconsin Press.
———. 1968. Franz Boas and the Culture Concept in Historical Perspective. *Race, Culture, and Evolution: Essays in the History of Anthropology*. Chicago; University of Chicago Press.
Szwed, John F. 1974. An American Anthropological Dilemma: The Politics of Afro-American Culture. In *Reinventing Anthropology*, ed. Dell Hymes. New York: Vintage.
Walcott, Derek. 1974. The Muse of History. In *Is Massa Day Done?* Ed. Orde Coombs. New York: Anchor.
White, Hayden. 1978. Interpretation in History. In *Tropics of Discourse: Essays in Cultural Criticism*. Baltimore: Johns Hopkins UP.
Willis, William. 1970. Anthropology and Negroes on the Southern Colonial Frontier. In *The Black Experience in America: Selected Essays*, ed. James C. Curtis and Lewis L. Gould. Austin: University of Texas Press.

Creolization and Nation-Building in the Hispanic Caribbean

Antonio Benítez-Rojo

Using the word *criollo*, 'creole' in English, in discourse concerning the Spanish Caribbean is hardly new. People have been writing uninterruptedly on it since the sixteenth century, when what we presently call the Caribbean was nothing but a dispersed collection of towns and small plantations in the islands of Cuba, Hispaniola, Puerto Rico, and Jamaica, and a few port-towns on the mainland like Veracruz, Nombre de Dios and Cartagena, all of them linked by the Spanish fleets. At that time the term *criollo* was applied to people of European or African origins born in any of those places. Eventually the adjective *criollo* was applied in the Americas to many things, including flora, fauna and cultural expressions.

'Plantation' is also an old word in the Hispanic Caribbean. The first sugar plantations were started up in Hispaniola around the second decade of the sixteenth century. Both Bartolomé de las Casas and Gonzalo Fernández de Oviedo tell in their respective histories of the sprouting up of sugar-mills, offering at the same time some interesting data about the industry's beginning. In any case, the Spanish Crown very soon sponsored the development of sugar plantations with loans, debt moratoria, tax exemptions, machinery, technical advice and, above all, authorization for an increase of African slave importation to guarantee their functioning. Regarding the other colonies in the Caribbean that followed the Hispaniola's example, thirty mills are spoken of in Jamaica in 1523, and ten in Puerto Rico. It is also known that toward the second half of the sixteenth century exports from Cuba reached an annual average of 460 tons.[1] Around 1550, with the plantation practice then generalized, the number of slaves in the Antilles exceeded by far that of the white population, a demographic reality that left an indelible mark on the islands' societies and cultures.

Concerning creole rhythms and performances, we have it that in 1573 the Town Government of Havana ordered that all of the free Negroes should be incorporated, with their songs and dances, into the festivals with which Corpus Christi was celebrated. These songs and dances were not totally African nor totally European: they were arrays of cultural fragments in state of creolization, fragments in flux, fragments momentarily put together here and there by different performers according to their desires, interests and capabilities. Even at that early stage, it is not possible to complete a thorough inventory of the many types of creole dances that coexisted then in the Hispanic Caribbean; nor is it possible to find the name of a founding dance, a mother dance, a particular performance that we can invest with the notion of origins. The only thing we can recover from the past is a fractured series of names, such as: *gayumba, zambapalo, retambo, paracumbé, cachumba, yeyé, zarambeque, gurrumbé, chacona, zarabanda, guineo, calinga, chica, yuka, chuchumbé* and many others.[2] It is interesting to note that those early creole dances reached Spain in the last quarter of the sixteenth century and were commented on by Cervantes, Lope de Vega, Quevedo and other Golden-Age writers. Their popularity was so great that the Spanish Inquisition censured them more than once for being indecent.

If I mention these cases, it is only to note that the plantation system, as well as the Creole rhythms and performances, had already provoked important comment in the distant past.

Well, then, what relation do I find between the Caribbean plantation and the phenomenon of creolization? Naturally, first of all, a relation of cause and effect; without the one we would not have the other. But what do I understand by creolization? I will begin by saying that to my way of thinking none of our cultural manifestations is creolized, but is, rather, in a state of creolization. I think that creolization does not transform literature or music or language into a synthesis or anything that could be taken in essentialist terms; furthermore, it does not even lead these expressions into a predictable state of creolization. For me, creolization is a term with which we attempt to explain the unstable states that Caribbean cultural artifacts, continuously transformed by a series of performers, present over time; for me this is not a process – a word that implies forward movement – but a broken series of recurrences, of happenings, whose only law is change. Where does this instability come from? I think that this is the product of the transatlantic plantation system, whose presence covers the map of world history's contingencies, through the great changes in economic discourse to the vast collisions of races and cultures that humankind has seen. This system, in its slow explosion, threw out millions and millions of cultural fragments in the direction of the Caribbean basin; fragments of diverse kinds that, in their endless fall-out, come together in an instant to form a dance step, a linguistic trope, the line of a poem, and afterwards they repel each other to re-form and pull apart once more, and so on. I think that in the coming together and pulling apart of the innumerable fragments that circulate through the Caribbean sociocultural space many kinds of forces are at work. To begin with there is an assortment of competing desires; not simple desires but complex ones which we can relate to anthropological terms like retention, resistance, assimilation, acculturation, enculturation, and so forth. Those desires, of course, are energized in the individual by a variety of interests that respond to several types of needs, that is, social needs, sexual needs, political needs, religious needs, etc. For example, let's take the case of enculturation, which is the process of cultural transmission. In eighteenth-century Africa the initiation curriculum consisted of a whole set of cultural values, tribal religion, myths, philosophy, history, rituals, and other knowledge. This knowledge's purpose was to guarantee the growth of individuals as tribal members and the thorough comprehension of their way of life during passage from pre-puberty to post-puberty.[3] However, since initiation practices were not possible in the Caribbean plantation, those in charge of a child's education, generally the child's mother, had to chose – and choosing involves desire – what fragments of the old culture were to be transmitted. And not only that: the child would learn from her about plantation life; that is, a new kind of knowledge that was to act as a survival kit.

But then we have the fact that, coexisting with such deliberate things as desires and interests, there is chance, unpredictability. For example, both the First and Second World Wars – unforeseeable events – played a part in the coming to the fore of African components of Caribbean culture and literature, such as Claude McKay's and Marcus Garvey's works and, later on, the emergence of Aimé Césaire's *Négritude* movement. In my country, Cuba, the arrival of the radio, the victrola, the recording industry and the cinema – also unpredictable events – contributed to the popularity of the son, the rumba, and the conga in the decade of the 1920s. Before then, this kind of music existed only among the Negro population and was not accepted as anything like a national music. The victrola and the radio made it possible for the compositions, songs and rhythms of black people to be listened and danced to in white peoples' homes. Something similar happened in movie houses, since it was customary then to show silent films with live music, and later, with the arrival of talking pictures, with a musical variety show. Because of these new developments, black people found an unexpected place of coexistence with whites within popular music, a unique space where instead of being marginalized they were recognized and acclaimed; furthermore, they were sought after and paid well for playing at private parties, theatres, dance halls and night clubs.[4] Now, once these rhythms had been internalized by the majority of Cubans, they in turn contributed to the formation of what was known then as Afro-Cuban culture. In sum, the phenomenon resulting from the interplay of all of these deliberate and unpredictable factors, of this endless give and take, is what years ago Fernando Ortiz called transculturation and today we call creolization.[5]

In any case, as a result of those competing desires and unpredictable events, the early creole dances that we mentioned either served their purpose and disappeared from the social stage – its fragments back again in the cultural flow – or were gradually transformed into different dances. For example, we know for certain that the creole dance called *yuka*, uprooted from the Congo, was transformed by a series of Cuban performers into the dance called rumba. However, we know nothing about the destiny of the dances called *gayumba* and *gurrumbé*, although some of their fragments — let's say, a particular combination of beats or steps – might be playing some kind of role in some present dance.

Now, if we look at this phenomenon in a horizontal way, it will be easy to understand its nation-building potential. I will begin by acknowledging a type of early Hispanic Caribbean culture that I will identify as '*criollo* culture'.[6] A culture that, if it does indeed express a wish to differentiate itself from things Spanish, yet manifests itself before the formation of a national culture. Therefore, all the creole dances with funny names that I have mentioned belong to this type of culture. In general, *criollo* culture first began to appear roughly between 1575 and 1625 in different cities and towns. Their principal agents of dissemination were the *criollos*, both whites and blacks, particularly those of the second and third generations. In its formation several factors, of a geographic, demographic, socio-economic, ethnological and political nature, play a role. In any case, the fact that I wish to stress is that in its final stage of development, upon the appearance of alliances between the localities within a given socio-economic region, *criollo* culture goes from being an exclusively local system to one that has a regional character. This regionalization ought not to be seen as a synthesis of local cultures, but rather – I repeat – as an alliance within which there prevail cultural artifacts that were first assembled in different localities.

Toward the end of the eighteenth century, when a national feeling emerged throughout the Spanish colonies, the Creole population that lived in those regions began to feel itself to be Cuban, Dominican or Puerto Rican, though without giving up certain cultural traits that it had acquired as much in the region as in the locality in which it lived. Thus, today, a Cuban or a Puerto Rican feels himself or herself to be precisely such, but, at the same time, he or she keeps certain characteristics of the region and even of the locality in which he or she grew up. From this we can infer that any national culture is a very complex system of competing differences, and so the scheme that I am putting forth should be taken only as something pointing toward a discussion much more serious in both depth and breadth.

For example, to go into detail a little, one must keep in mind that in the formation of *criollo* culture there enter components in state of creolization that have been originally brought by the colonizer, such as the Spanish language, the Catholic religion and the epistemes of medieval and renaissance Spain; components taken from indigenous cultures – of great utility to the conquistadores during their process of adapting to the land – such as things relative to the local flora, fauna, agriculture, minerals, food, lodging, and artifacts unknown in Europe, like *bohíos*, hammocks and canoes;

African components brought by the different captive peoples, such as beliefs, myths, rhythms, dances, oral literature, pantomimes, forms of association, and a predilection for certain foods like plantains, root vegetables and rice. On the other hand, it is also important to consider several differentiating factors arising in the colonial world, such as ethnicity, class, gender, age, place of residence, education, and occupation.

Now, let's see how this scheme worked out in the case of Cuba. In around 1550 the population of Cuba living in towns amounted to 3,300: 1,500 Spaniards, 1,000 Indians and 800 slaves.[7] This means that, given the scant number of European women who traveled to the island in those years, the first generation of *criollos* was characterized by its ethnic pluralism. Diego de Sarmiento, Cuba's bishop, testified to this when he says that he baptized many mestizo and mulatto children. In any case, the population of Cuba had quintupled by the beginning of the seventeenth century, oscillating between 15,000 and 20,000 inhabitants, more than half of whom lived in Havana. At that time there were two cities and seven towns in the island, distributed in two socio-economic regions; in the west Havana, Guanabacoa, Sancti Spiritus, Trinidad and El Cayo; in the east, Santiago de Cuba, El Cobre, Baracoa, Bayamo and Puerto Principe (now Camagüey).[8]

The western region was controlled by Havana, the residence of the governor and the bishop, and the only port authorized for trade with Seville. The city had begun to grow rapidly after 1543. In that year it was decided that the two fleets making the transatlantic crossing (one from Veracruz, the other from Cartagena and Nombre de Dios), should unite in its excellent bay to undertake the annual return trip in a single convoy. Given that the fleets' stay lasted three or four months, Havana had a guaranteed 'tourist season' every year, having to provide lodging, food and entertainment to no fewer than five thousand people, an exhorbitant number for those times. Naturally, the new commercial situation increased the risk of pirate attacks, since the fleets were loaded with precious metals extracted on the continent. Thus, the city began to convert itself into a strong point, its fortresses constructed with slave labour. At the same time, in addition to exporting tobacco, hides and wood, Havana began to export sugar in growing quantities, which sealed its fate as a sugaring and slaveholding city. Nonetheless, given that the Spanish law allowed the slaves to buy their freedom, the number of free Negroes began to grow slowly but perceptibly. Toward the end of the sixteenth century the first African *cabildos* sprang up, which were associations of a cultural nature that brought together blacks according to what part of Africa they came from. These *cabildos* elected their "kings" and "queens," and they had their meetings and cultural activities in their own houses and lands.[9] Later on, the participation of the blacks of Havana and its environs would be extended to the festivity of the *Día de Reyes,* the Epiphany, where the slaves enjoyed a day of freedom to celebrate their dances and pantomimes in the streets of the city, even dressing in their particularized folk costumes.[10] At the end of the seventeenth century a hermitage dedicated to the Virgin of Regla was built on the other side of the bay, which would prove to have great cultural importance: the image would begin to be adored simultaneously as a Catholic virgin and as the *orisha* Yemaya – Olokun, lady of the sea in the Yoruba pantheon and a key figure in Cuban *santería;* very soon she was elevated to Havana's patron saint.[11] In addition to the Yoruba influence, the *criollo* culture of the region was influenced by other African cultures, in particular those brought by slaves from the Congo and from the Calabar coast. Nevertheless, African traditions were never well received by the colonial power. For example, in 1687 it was prohibited for slaves to attend certain *cabildos* in places outside the city's wall, and they were told to celebrate their dances and songs in the city's streets and before the call to prayer; violaters of this ordinance would receive two hundred lashes in public.[12] In fact, the African presence in Havana was always regulated by the power structure. It is possible to document through the course of more than three hundred years an entire historical record of prohibitions, persecutions and even confiscations of musical instruments. The city, as I said, was the cradle of the plantation system, and even the *criollo* producers would remain at the mercy of the royal monopolies in things related to export commerce as well as to the importation of slaves.

The social and economic development of the eastern region was different from Havana's. This difference was motivated by the absence of free trade, since the eastern producers, kept from exporting anything via any port than Havana, had to pay for costly shippings and run many risks along the bad roads that went between the two regions. Naturally, this situation made it inevitable that, in violation of Spanish laws, the eastern *criollos* would take up contraband. With the gold from the mines and rivers exhausted, the region's economy transformed itself from one based on mining to a livestock-raising one, specializing in the export of hides through French, English and Dutch merchants. Keep in mind that in that period leather was as useful as plastic is today; many objects were partially or totally made of leather, from boots to wineskins, from furniture to saddles and belts. Furthermore, the jerked beef, lard and bacon derived from the killing of livestock were sold at a good price to the merchants of the powers that rivalled Spain, since at that time they hadn't acquired colonies of their own in the region in which their ships might get provisions. In any case, both in livestock raising and in its continuous intercourse with foreign ships, this region was drifting apart from Havana. Also, in the western part of the neighbouring island of Hispaniola there existed a similar situation with respect to Santo Domingo, the only port authorized for commerce. So that the inhabitants of the western part (now Haiti) also developed an economy based on livestock intended for contraband trade. Given the closeness of the two islands – the crossing over the Windward Passage could be made in one night – the *criollos* of one region and the other became one big family with common interests, such as free trade, and with very similar local and regional cultures. In fact, we can speak of a Windward Passage culture that included the northwest part of Jamaica before this island was invaded by the English. What merchandise did the towns acquire through their smuggling? Everything that the commercial monopoly made inaccessible to the *criollos*, either because of its high price or its scarcity in Spain: fabrics, porcelain, metal objects, firearms, even furniture and hats, but above all slaves brought directly from Africa. Thus, in a few years, the population of these isolated lands began to dress in a singular manner, combining the fabrics and fashions of England, France and Holland; at the same time there were, covering their tables, tablecloths from Holland, English plates and pitchers, and French knives. What did they read? Hispaniola's chronicles speak of "heretical" bibles and all sorts of forbidden books translated into Spanish by Jews in Flanders. At the same time, the customs were more flexible, and every time that a merchant ship arrived, fairs and festivals were organized. But perhaps the most important difference from Havana had the slave as its centre. Given that the production of sugar and the construction of fortresses required a forced labour discipline, racial tensions in the Havana area were much sharper than in the eastern region, whose livestock-growing economy made it so that many slaves lived under a patriarchal slave system. Thus, the Negro was here a much more important acculturating agent than in Havana, since he could make mixed marriages more easily and his presence within *criollo* society was considerably more active. I think that all of these cohesive factors influenced the eastern region's becoming organized culturally earlier and its having a higher degree of creolization than Havana's.[13]

Now I'll give some examples of cultural artifacts, still in a state of creolization, that went beyond their regional boundaries and joined the system of Cuba's national culture. The first religious image made in Cuba (1610) owes its existence to the artisans of Havana; it was St Bárbara's, who was taken up quickly by people of Yoruba origins as a representation of Shango, a noted male *orisha* in the Yoruba pantheon. It should come as no surprise that St Bárbara, a woman, has been identified with Shango, the essence of masculinity. Keep in mind that St Bárbara's image is represented by the attributes of a red cloak (Shango's colour), a gold crown (according to Yoruba tradition, Shango was king of Oyo), a golden chalice in one hand and a sword in the other (Shango likes wine and is a warlike *orisha*); furthermore, St Bárbara, patron saint of artillerymen and protectress of explosions and lightning, presented a parallel to Shango, the lord of fire, lightning and thunder. This case provides an excellent example of creolization. First, we can imagine one or more Yoruba persons staring at St Bárbara's image and establishing its symbolic likeness to Shango, an action that involves desire; then we can think of one of those persons – whom I prefer to call a performer – placing on its Yoruba altar a printed image of St Barbara; then, immediately after, we have the emergence of *santería*: that is, the coming together of a Yoruba *orisha* and a Catholic saint thanks to the phenomenon of creolization.

Now I'll mention two examples related to food. The first one is a national dish called *moros y cristianos* (Moors and Christians). It consists of rice, originally brought from Spain, and black beans, which were brought to Havana from Mexico, possibly in the eighteenth century. The second one are corn tamales, also imported from Mexico although havanized – if you allow me the word – in being filled with pork.

As far as popular theatre is concerned, the Negroes' pantomimes assumed great importance in Havana thanks to the festival of the *Día de Reyes,* January 6, when the city slaves were allowed to perform in the city's streets and squares. The best known of them was the dance of "killing the snake," a sacrificial pantomime of Bantu origins in which the slaves danced and sang in Spanish around an artificial snake and finally simulated the killing of the animal.[14] Various snake-killing songs have been collected, and one of them, anonymously composed in the seventeenth century, inspired Nicolás Guillén to write his well-known poem "Sensemayá." Another snake-killing song, collected by Fernando Ortiz, plays a crucial role in Alejo Carpentier's novel *Concierto barroco* (Baroque Concert). Furthermore, several of these snake-killing songs were selected by José Lezama Lima as part of his *Antología de la poesía cubana;* that is, they transcended its local boundaries and joined Cuba's national literature.

Coming from Cuba's eastern region we have numerous examples. I'll mention just a few. The first *criollo* dish is called *ajiaco*, a kind of *pot-pourri* composed of cassava, sweet potato, pumpkin, corn, chili, *malanga* (indigenous components); pork and jerked beef (European components); plantain and yam (African components). This dish, which was already popular in the sixteenth century, provides an excellent example of creolization.[15] There is another dish called *congrí*, which is basically rice and kidney beans with bacon. It disembarked on the docks of Santiago de Cuba at the turn of the eighteenth century; it came with the refugees of the Haitian Revolution and later on was creolized in Cuba. It managed to keep much of its French name, originally *congo riz*. The same French refugees also brought their Creole music with them, particularly a rhythmic cell that we call *cinquillo* in Cuba. This syncopated sequence of five beats eventually got into the Cuban country dance and later on gave shape to what we call the habañera beat: ta-ta-tat/tata.[16]

But then, of course, the most important contribution of the eastern part of the island is the cult of the Virgin of la Caridad, a Catholic–Yoruba cult that simultaneously locates in the virgin the images of Our Lady and the *orisha* Oshun. According to local tradition, the virgin's dark-skinned image appeared at the beginning of the seventeenth century to three men, two white and one black, known as the three Juans. Her prominence grew steadily through the centuries and, in

1916, a group of distinguished Negro veterans of the War with Spain (1895–98) asked the Pope to designate her as Cuba's patron saint. The Pope granted this request immediately, perhaps not knowing that to many Cubans the Virgin of la Caridad was the Oshun of *santería*.[17] So, in the 1920s, while the so-called black music was making its impact on other cultural forms, *santería* legitimized itself along with Catholicism as a national religion, having an influence also on music, painting, dance, theatre, literature, and even on language – for example, words of African origin like *chébere, ashé, mayombe, bembé, ebbó, ekobio, babalawo, asere, íreme, orisha, monina, bilongo, nganga,* and many others, started to be used during those years. Why was her cult so successful? Because the Virgin protectress of the three Juans was a symbol, an icon, that carried a desire for ethnic integration within the space of the nation. Needless to say, what fuelled the phenomenon of creolization here was the existence of this common social desire. Eventually, as I said, the dark-skinned Virgin of la Caridad would turn out to be the patron saint of Cuba, displacing a white-skinned madonna from the Havana area; she would contribute decisively to the Cuban nation's integration in many ways, particularly during the wars against Spanish rule, and after independence she would appear in a kind of patriotic installation along with the Cuban flag, the coat of arms, the images of the founding fathers, the map of the island and the national anthem; moreover, she is still is and ever will be in a state of creolization.

Notes

1. Eric Williams, *From Columbus to Castro: The History of the Caribbean* (New York: Harper & Row, 1970), 27.
2. On early Creole dances, see Fernando Ortiz, *La Africanía de la Música Folklórica de Cuba* (Havana: Ministerio de Education, 1950); also Alejo Carpentier, *La Música en Cuba* (Mexico City: Fondo de Culture Económica, 1946), translated as *Music in Cuba*, tr. Alan West-Durán, ed. and intro. Timothy Brennan (Minneapolis and London: Cultural Studies of the Americas 5, University of Minnesota Press, 2001).
3. For a comprehensive definition of enculturation, see *Encyclopedia Britannica* (1990), vol. 18:2; vol 24:725.
4. On the impact of the victrola and the radio in Cuba, see Cristóbal Diaz Ayala. *Música Cubana: Del Areíto a la Nueva Trova* (Miami: Ediciones Universal, 1993).
5. See Fernando Ortiz, *Contrapunteo Cubano del Tabaco y el Azúcar* (Havana: Jesús Montero, 1940).
6. On *criollo* culture, see Antonio Benítez-Rojo, 'La Cultura Criolla en Cuba,' *Actual: Revista de la Direction General de Cultura de la Universidad de los Andes* 30 (1955).
7. Leví Marrero, *Cuba, Economía y Sociedad*, vol. 2 (Madrid: Playor, 1973), 325.
8. Marrero, *Cuba, Economía y Sociedad*, 35–40.
9. On Afro-Cuban *cabildos*, see Fernando Ortiz, *Los Cabildos Afrocubanos* (Havana: Universal, 1921).
10. Fernando Ortiz, *La Fiesta Afrocubana del "Día de Reves"* (Havana: El Siglo XX, 1925).
11. On the *orisha* Yemaya, see Lydia Cabrera, *Yemayá y Ochún* (Miami: Chicherekú, 1980).
12. Marrero, *Cuba, Economía y Sociedad*, 175.
13. Antonio Benítez–Rojo, 'From the Plantation to the Plantation,' in *The Repeating Island: The Caribbean and the Postmodern Perspective*, ed. Benitez-Rojo, tr. James E. Maraniss (Durham, NC and London: Duke UP, 1992/rev. ed. 1996), 33–81.
14. On the dance of 'killing the snake,' see Fernando Ortiz, *La Fiesta Afrocubana del "Día de Reyes."*
15. On the *ajiaco*, see Fernando Ortiz, 'Los Factores Humanos de la Cubanidad,' *Revista Bimestre Cubana* 45, no. 2 (1940).
16. On the *cinquillo*, see Alejo Carpentier, *La Música en Cuba*.
17. For extensive historical information about the Virgin of la Caridad, see Olga Portuondo Zúñiga, *La Virgen de la Caridad del Cobre: Simbolo de Cubanía* (Santiago de Cuba: Editorial Oriente, 1995).

Works Cited

Benítez–Rojo, Antonio. 1955. La Cultura Criolla en Cuba. *Actual: Revista de la Dirección General de Cultura de la Universidad de los Andes* 30.

———. *The Repeating Island: The Caribbean and the Postmodern Perspective*, trans. James Maraniss, *La Isla Que se Repite: El Caribe y la Perspectiva Posmoderna*, 1989, trans. 1992. Durham NC & London: Duke UP, 1996.

Cabrera, Lydia. 1980. *Yemayá y Ochún*. Miami: Chicherekú.

Carpentier, Alejo. 1974. *Concierto Barroco*. Mexico City: Siglo Veintiuno Editores.

———. 2001. *La Música en Cuba* (Mexico City: Fondo de Cultura Económica, 1946). *Music in Cuba*, trans. Alan West–Durán, ed. and intro. Timothy Brennan. Minneapolis and London: Cultural Studies of the Americas 5, University of Minnesota Press.

Diáz Ayala, Cristóbal. 1993. *Música Cubana: Del Areíto a la Nueva Trova*. Miami: Ediciones Universal.

Lezama Lima, José, ed. 1965. *Antología de la Poesía Cubana*. Havana: Consejo Nacional de Cultura.

Marrero, Leví. 1973. *Cuba, Economía y Sociedad*. Madrid: Playor.

Ortiz, Fernando. 1950. *La Africanía de la Música Folklórica de Cuba*. Havana: Ministerio de Educación.

———. 1921. *Los Cabildos Afrocubanos*. Havana: Universal.

———. 1940. *Contrapunteo Cubano del Tabaco y el Azúcar*. Havana: Jesús Montero.

———. 1940. Los Factores Humanos de la Cubanidad. *Revista Bimestre Cubana* 45, no. 2.

———. 1925. *La Fiesta Afrocubana del "Día de Reyes."* Havana: El Siglo XX.

Portuondo Zúñiga, Olga. 1995. *La Virgen de la Caridad del Cobre: Símbolo de Cubanía*. Santiago de Cuba: Editorial Oriente.

Williams, Eric. 1970. *From Columbus to Castro: The History of the Caribbean*. New York: Harper & Row.

Culture, Color and Politics

Michel-Rolph Trouillot

Both witnesses and participants found it easy to describe the so-called Revolution of 1946 as a victory of "black power" over *mulâtre* domination (e.g., Bonhomme 1946; 1957; Collectif Paroles 1976). Similarly, the Duvalier regimes, especially that of the father, have often been referred to as black power regimes. Yet the label is misleading. In both cases, though color was an idiom of politics, the members of rival groups could not be immediately identified solely on the basis of their phenotype. There were dark-skinned individuals both for and against Estimé, and light-skinned individuals both for and against the two Duvaliers. Further, the grievances expressed in 1946 were not aimed simply at color prejudice; some called for a sweeping reevaluation of the social and cultural practices and values that typified Haitian urban life.

Part of the difficulty in dealing with color and politics in Haiti is that while the "color question" cannot be separated from Western cultural influence and a worldwide hierarchy of races, religions, and cultures, at the same time it cannot be reduced to a mere avatar of Western prejudices. Indeed, few Haitian practices and beliefs can be considered derivatively Western. In the social perception and use of somatic differences, as in most domains, the cultural influence of the West is constantly being challenged, even if only partially by local practices, beliefs, and values.

A second difficulty stems from the fact that in Haiti conflict between color-cum-social categories does not simply reflect an opposition between social classes, however defined: the dominant classes are not composed exclusively of light-skinned individuals; nor do all such individuals belong to those classes. A third difficulty is the widespread disapproval of discourses and practices that hint at institutional discrimination on the basis of color—or "race"—alone. Models of discrimination on the basis of appearance, drawn from the experiences of South Africa or the United States, lose their meaning in Haiti because the social postulates on which they are based (and which are, in turn, maintained by discrimination) simply do not apply. Neither do traditional models of racial conflict. There are no bomb threats for moving into the "wrong" neighborhood, no graffiti slurs on school walls, no lynchings, no street wars. Haiti never had a "color riot," let alone a "race riot."

An underlying proposition of this chapter is that the beliefs and practices that Haitian urbanites refer to as the "color question" do not operate in a social vacuum, to the exclusion of all else. Instead color-cum-social categories operate in various spheres of urban life as part of different strategies of competition and struggle. They materialize most vividly in the familial alliances typical of certain urban classes and they are often a favored idiom of politics. But they also function as referents for sociocultural oppositions outside of the immediate political arena. It is this complexity that explains the fact that references to the "color question" could bestow upon Estimé, in 1946, and Duvalier, in 1957, the legitimacy they then claimed for themselves. To discover the roots of this legitimacy, which François Duvalier inherited from Estimé, we must first turn to the international hierarchy of races, colors, religions, and cultures, and to the ambivalent response of the Haitian elites to the cultural domination of the West.

THE "COLOR" COMPLEX

Those who persist in claiming that the West is *merely* capitalist will have difficulty acknowledging that the international division of labor is paired with a hierarchy of races, colors, religions, and cultures whose complexity cannot be reduced to labor-market segmentation. Ethnocentrism preceded the creation of a European proletariat, let alone an international one. It is fair to say that ethnic identity even foreshadowed the advent of class-based societies. The comparison between "us" and "them" implies, among other evaluative criteria, the existence of what H. Hoetink (1967) called a somatic norm-image, a physical ideal of beauty. All things being equal, "we" are always more attractive than "they."[1] At the very least, we are closer to what human beings really should look like.

But things are not always equal. Because of the differential accumulation of technology, as well as the institutionalization of a combative posture that marked the evolution of Mediterranean peoples well before the rise of capitalism, what came to be called the "West" gave itself a distinct identity. The West defined itself, so to speak, in the course of a history punctuated by internal and external conquests, a history engaged almost from the start in a legitimizing discourse. These conquests and this discourse preceded the north-south social fissure of the Mediterranean from which Europe, as we now know it, was born. Aristotle had already formulated the hypothesis, echoed in fifteenth-century Spain, that some men were inferior and therefore fated to be slaves. Diodorus Siculus found the Ethiopians "primitive," and from Pliny the Elder's imagination sprang monstrous subhumans in the heart of black Africa—men without mouths, noses, voices, or eyes, unspeakably ugly monsters.

No doubt other cultures developed similar themes of exclusion of the Other. But as I said earlier, all things were not equal, for the accounts that have come down to us are those of Diodorus and Pliny, along with those of myriads of Westerners, from the Renaissance to the present. I would thus hesitate to argue that capitalism alone allowed Europe to spread and systematize an unflattering image of others. At any rate, that spread and that systematization brought qualitative changes in the European social perception of somatic differences. If ethnocentrism was ever naive, it certainly stopped being so after the systematic demeaning of the cultures of the Other used to justify colonial conquests and plantation slavery. This new threshold required in turn the European vision to be just as systematically imposed on the dominated peoples themselves. By the 1620s, Africans and Amerindians of the Antilles and the Atlantic coast of the American mainland had to be aware of their differential status on the European-imposed scale, just as Asian immigrants were to find out in the 1850s that European preconceptions of their failures and worth had accompanied them to the New World (Du Tertre 1667; Gage [1648] 1958; Trollope [1859] 1985).

All this is to say—and it is of extreme importance—that the phenomenon described in Haiti in rather sibylline terms as the "color question" is etched within the framework of an international hierarchy that was formalized well before Haitian independence. A female member of the Haitian bourgeoisie conveniently reaffirmed this age-old context when she told anthropologist Micheline Labelle "If they marry a *noir*, people will say that the children are horrible, and since color prejudice is international, if they are sent abroad to study they will have problems" (cited in Labelle 1976: 35).

Saint-Domingue, and then Haiti, thus inherited a differential evaluation of races, colors, religions, and cultures. This evaluation included an aesthetic in which blackness was found at the bottom of the scale. To pretend that this aesthetic has disappeared is ludicrous: photos of recent beauty contests or the sight of advertising posters confirm its continued existence. Admittedly, aesthetic evaluations vary according to the socio-economic class and phenotype of those who judge, and the results are sometimes surprising to foreigners (Labelle 1976, 1978). Generally speaking "white," for example, is *not* considered to be the most pleasing color. Social evaluations of phenotypes in Haiti are nonetheless generally *Western dominated* and, other things being equal, beyond a certain degree of increased melanin, these evaluations imply a denigration of blackness.

But here again, other things are rarely equal. Thus the reader who is unfamiliar with Haiti must be immediately cautioned lest he or she takes the preceding to imply that Haitian color prejudice is simply a toned-down version of Western racism. As Sidney Mintz (1984: 299) has lucidly written, "North American ideas about what 'color' someone is are far more hindrance than help in understanding Haiti." Nor am I certain that a European perception would be more useful.[2] To start with, Haitian "color" categories refer to many more aspects of phenotype than skin color alone, even when their etymology seems to indicate an exclusively epidermic referent. Epidermic shade remains crucial, but skin texture and depth of skin tone, hair color and appearance, and facial features also figure in any categorization. Thus two individuals who seem to be the same "color" can be classed in different categories because of other somatic criteria. Color thus functions as a dividing line, negatively delimiting a field of possible categories. In other words, it would be much easier for two Haitians to agree that X could *not* be considered *noir* because he is too "light," or that Y could *not* be considered *mulâtre* because he is too "dark," than to agree on the category (which is not always intermediate) in which to place X or Y. The color line that separates *clairs* (including subgroups such as *mulâtres, griffes, grimauds,* and *mulâtres bruns*) from the *noirs* (including the more or less dark epidermic shades and various types of hair) is the most important among a number of somatic boundaries that operate together. Color never operates alone, even in the perception of physical difference.

More importantly, color categories embrace characteristics that go far beyond the perceived phenotype into the field of social relations. These can include income, social origin, level of formal education, customary behavior, ties of kinship or marriage, and other characteristics. And different combinations of these social traits can move a person from one category to a more or less proximate one. Thus terms such as *mulâtre* and *noir* do not simply mean—and sometimes do not mean at all— "mulatto" or "black" in the American sense. The kind of social discrimination that operates in Haiti is not exclusively based on physical features, even when phenotype plays a role in the application and description of this discrimination. For example, up until very recently some people were discouraged from frequenting certain clubs because they were "too *noir*," although others, visibly darker, could enter. In short, Haitian color categories refer not only to skin color and other somatic features, but to a large range of sociocultural attributes that do not have a somatic referent.

The reshaping of these categories—a process that has been going on at least since independence— has been facilitated by the growth of beliefs and practices in which Western influence figures but does not go uncontested. If it is important to note that Haitian color prejudice relates to a Western-dominated hierarchy of races, colors, religions, and cultures, it is equally crucial to note that very few Haitians, even among the elites, ever accepted that hierarchy as a "true" depiction of their reality. In any case, the urban elites, the most Westernized part of the population, never gained such full control of the cultural terrain that they could impose a pre-packaged Western view on the rest of the population.

THE CULTURAL GUERRILLA WAR

We saw in chapter 2 the limits of the dualist view that treats Haitian society as if it consisted of two separate parts. I have also suggested that the physical to-and-fro of the peasantry from the hinterland to the urban trenches meant that it has come to occupy part of the urban social and cultural terrain. That terrain does not simply mirror the political scene. Nor is it a mere reflection of economic structures: while the economic and political divisions may be reminiscent of trench warfare, the cultural relations between the classes are more reminiscent of a guerrilla war. The peasantry is not the master of this space—or never for long—but it penetrates it deeply and harasses the enemy, while remaining ready to retreat at any point. It does not dictate the dominant cultural codes, but those who impose them must take its values into accounts. For example, there is no aspect of Haitian economic and political life that explains why the Jaegerhubers, a commercial family of German origin firmly ensconced within the bourgeoisie, should have invested a considerable amount of time at the beginning of this century in transcribing peasant songs. It is true that their interest in musical folklore had Wagnerian overtones, but their sympathetic view of the peasant tradition cannot be explained without reference to Haiti's cultural dynamics. The history of urban arts, of painting and music—as well as of religion, language, and the organization of kinship networks—all indicate the existence within civil society of another order of relationships alongside the dominant one. The peasantry cannot be said to be victorious in the cultural sphere, but it has an implicitly acknowledged presence there, to a degree as yet unmatched in the political and economic arenas.

Of course, even in this cultural domain the peasantry does not have the last word. Just as peasant practices filter into the city, the dominant culture's hostility to many of these practices filters back to the peasantry, subtly adding to its isolation by repeatedly stressing its inferiority.[3] Thus the cultural distance between town and countryside lies as much in the social assessment of practices and beliefs as in their actual distribution. A significant number of peasant practices that are publicly spurned by the elites are still nurtured privately among all urban classes. More importantly, even when practices vary—as of course they do—they often take root in the same underlying values. The crux of the matter is that these underlying values are differently acknowledged, and carry a different symbolic weight in different class presentations.

Religion provides a good example of these similarities and differences. In the half-century of incubation that followed independence, what is commonly referred to as Vodoun by nonpractitioners emerged as the religion of the majority, a distinctly Haitian complex of philosophical tenets, religious beliefs, and ritual practices. But while the masses publicly cherished these practices and beliefs, which they never considered antithetic to Catholicism, the urbanites always professed an exclusive adherence to orthodox Christianity, even though, to different degrees, they shared religious beliefs rooted in the same African-dominated cosmology and took part in similar rituals. Elite distortion of Catholic (and today Protestant) theology and liturgy ended only when and where the influence of Vodoun on their "Christian" practice was publicly identifiable. Short of that, substantial tenets of the same philosophy and a number of the same basic beliefs are held by most Haitians.

Language offers another example. Most linguists have stopped calling Haiti bilingual. They speak instead of a diglossic situation, in which a bilingual minority imposes one language as the language of power. This analysis is a positive intellectual development but may still fall short of the truth. Two languages do indeed coexist in Haiti: French and Haitian. The Haitian (Creole) language probably arose during slavery and solidified during the first half-century of independence. All Haitians speak Haitian as their native language: only a few of the most educated urbanites are native bilingual. The majority of French speakers (less than 8 percent of the total population) reach varying degrees of competence through the school system. Thus the linguistic dichotomy does not appear at the level of communication, or even in an unqualified preference for French: any Haitian is capable of communicating anything to any other Haitian in Haitian, and the most francophile urbanites often prefer to use Haitian in situations where everyone is competent in French.[4] Rather, the dichotomy resides in the power attached to certain forms of communication, most of which include the use of French; in the fact that mere knowledge of French gives differential access to power; in the prestige attached to that language; and in the fact that this prestige is nationwide—even the peasantry believes in it to some extent. The political consequence is that the exclusive use of French in the nation's official discourse appears "natural." In point of fact, the elites have never bothered to make that exclusivity official: French became Haiti's official language during the U.S. occupation through a constitution that Franklin D. Roosevelt later claimed to have written personally. By then, French exclusivity in the spheres of power was threatened by English rather than by the Haitian language, and legitimization was seen by many as reinforcing not just French, but the entire French/Creole complex, set in contradistinction to English.

In its own way, the example of language hints at the complexity of Haitian cultural traditions and struggles, and at the cultural ambivalence of the Haitian elites. Because these elites inherited some of the ambiguities of the French colonists' sense of identity (see chapter 1), and because the peasantry consistently preserved its claim to the cultural arena, the dominant classes never succeeded in imposing Western cultural domination on the people. It is even more startling that they may never have entirely wished to do so. Haitian writers have rarely presented the West as a sociocultural ideal *in toto*, even though they clearly saw France, Germany, Holland, and the United States—more or less in that order—as imitable superiors in specific domains. But even those specific achievements did not imply the innate superiority of the "whites," inasmuch as many Haitian literati genuinely believed in the perfectibility of all human groups—the ultimate primacy of culture over nature. Within that framework, the recognition of Western achievements did not carry with it the need to reject all indigenous practices. Thus while the Haitian elites placed French literature on a pedestal, they reserved for themselves the right to speak the native language, to sing Creole songs, to write of the beauty of the peasant woman in verses patterned after what they perceived as the latest Parisian literary style. While they held foreign—especially French—diplomas in high esteem, they continuously decried the lack of natural and human warmth in the Western countries they visited. While they proudly adopted European manners, they also engaged proudly in many indigenous practices that they judged worthy of their time and attention. This in turn meant that the peasantry—and many customs or features that the elites' imagination associated with that peasantry, including "blackness" — were often ennobled in words, even if kept at safe distance in practice. It also meant that the Western-dominated hierarchy of races, colors, religions, and cultures was never swallowed whole, never accepted without modification.

Understandably, then, *mulâtrisme* as an ideology of *mulâtre* power, has always been on the defensive in Haiti, in part because it could always be accused of being a version of Western racism. Its most diehard proponents—who often looked, sounded, or acted more "Western" than other Haitians—rarely dared to claim exclusive social and political rights for any group of Haitians identified on the basis of "color," however defined. Light-skinned politicians and intellectuals consistently denied any trace of color prejudice. Even an immigrant like Joseph Saint-Rémy could write: "I belong to no caste, to no sect ..." (Nicholls 1979: 94). In public, at least, they professed varying degrees of paternalistic "respect" for the black peasantry and many of its cultural traditions—Vodoun being for a long time the major exception. Early *mulâtre* claims to political control were therefore not based on assertions of inherited superiority but on the allegedly greater contribution made by their light-skinned ancestors in the forging of the Haitian nation.

The impossibility of publicly advocating color prejudice in Haiti in face-to-face debates was furthered by the history of Haiti itself—or by the elites' perception of that history. More for them perhaps than for the common folk, the Haitian revolution was and remains the final symbol of the regeneration of the entire "black race" from the abyss imposed by slavery (Nicholls 1979). The revolutionary war was a war against the "whites," and independence in 1804 a victory over colonialism, slavery, *and* white supremacy. Further, the relentless ostracism imposed on the black republic during the nineteenth century reinforced, among Haitian urbanites, a sense of racial identity that included *all* blacks. For instance, Pétion's *mulâtre*-dominated government did not abrogate Dessalines' law that gave near automatic citizenship to any black person landing on Haitian soil. Similarly, Pétion and Boyer both tried to help anti-slavery forces throughout the Americas as much as they could. Disagreements about the state notwithstanding, from the war of independence to the present the nation has always conceived of itself as a "black" community. This racial sense imposed severe limits on the expression of *mulâtre* ideology.

Demographics reinforced these limits, especially after 1843, when it became clear that power would have to be shared with a minority of dark-skinned individuals. The use of color rhetoric by black politicians since Toussaint Louverture had taught light-skinned leaders that it was politically dangerous to be either pro-white or anti-black in Haiti. If some light-skinned individuals did claim a privileged right to govern, they made it clear that this right proceeded in part from the blackness they shared with the rest of the population. Whether or not they were sincere is hard to tell, and probably beside the point. The important fact is that a combination of historical, cultural, and demographic factors made it impossible for them to claim political legitimacy if they excluded all positive references to blackness.

Given that there has never been a public discourse denigrating blackness in independent Haiti, some authors have concluded that color prejudice as such does not exist and that the "color question" is nothing more than "metaphysical sophistry" (e.g., Lamartinière 1976). I have already suggested that, contrary to such assertions, color is indeed salient in Haiti, if only because of the Western influence on sociocultural ratings, including aesthetic evaluations. The next three sections will show how color materializes in the play of familial and class alliances among the urban population.

THE BIOLOGICAL REPRODUCTION OF COLOR

Consider the demographic data for Saint-Domingue at the start of the slave uprising in 1791. How does it happen that there are so many people in Haiti who are still light enough to be considered *clairs* or *mulâtres*? The answer to this question unequivocally proves that color is salient when there are social choices.[5] For however much one plays with the figures, they do not agree with the statistical probabilities of demography or physical anthropology. The conclusion is obvious: it is just as impossible to explain the survival of light-skinned people in Haiti by genetic coincidence as it is to explain the survival of a black minority in the United States without reference to the (social) segregation of biological reproduction.

In 1789, Saint-Domingue had around 500,000 blacks, 27,500 free *gens de couleur,* and about 31,000 whites. Although in absolute terms the war of independence killed a greater number of blacks (Auguste and Auguste 1985), it affected the other two groups to a proportionately greater degree because they were so much smaller. The slaves' victories reduced the white presence to a negligible number and also sharply reduced the number of individuals of mixed descent, many of whom left the country for other islands or for the United States (particularly Louisiana, Maryland, and Pennsylvania). Thus Haiti became independent with a tiny white population (probably less than 1 percent) and a small mulatto minority (5 percent at most). Under these conditions, the laws of biological reproduction cannot explain the survival of this minority, which should have collapsed under the weight of a darker majority.

And that weight was substantial. Indeed, the epidermic line separating *clairs* and *noirs* itself shifted because of the preponderance of the darker tones: darker and darker people began to be included within the group of *clairs,* almost by default, so that a large number of individuals who are considered *mulâtres* today would have flunked the exam, on somatic grounds, at the end of the last century. But the *clair/noir* divide does not disappear under the weight of genetics; instead the main somatic boundary continues to shift. It is the elasticity and resilience of this boundary—the fact that it always allows for the isolation of a category of people called *clairs*—that bears witness to the social reality of color. It is the very survival of such categories and subcategories, all with increasingly fluid somatic referents, that shows the preeminence of social over biological reproduction.[6] The *clairs* of Haiti reproduced themselves essentially "from the inside" (that is, with no significant alliances with white outsiders), with the most *mulâtre* families (those that best combined light skin, valued facial and hair characteristics, *and* economic and social success) leading the way. In addition, the *mulâtre* sector of the Haitian elites has practiced an endogamous policy, marrying its sons to its daughters whenever possible. This choice can only be explained in terms of color prejudice, because class relations do not lend themselves to the same divisions. This is, moreover, the dilemma that (traditional) Marxist analysis of the *noirisme/mulâtrisme* duo refuses to confront. Either the color question is an immediate reflection of class relations—and then it would have no autonomy, for *the entire dominant class would be clair and all the clairs would be of the dominant class* (which is obviously false, and very close to the Denis-Duvalier 1938 thesis)—or color prejudice is relatively autonomous with regard to economic structures, and this autonomy must be taken into account.

THE SOCIAL REPRODUCTION OF COLOR

Color divisions do not simply replicate socioeconomic classes, or even income groups. In fact, the "color line" (the key boundary between *noirs* and *clairs*) and the boundary between poor and rich have both been moving since independence, each in its own direction. As mentioned before, somatic boundaries have moved to include darker and darker epidermic shades among the *clairs*. At the same time, fewer and fewer *clairs* are found among the underprivileged classes. Jean-Jacques Acau, the nineteenth-century leader of a private rural army that once controlled parts of the South and repeatedly challenged Port-au-Prince's central power, is credited with the famous saying "Nèg rich se milat; milat pòv se nèg" ("The rich black is a mulatto; the poor mulatto is a black").[7] But we must face the facts. Today there are many black-skinned individuals among the rich—or at least many more than before—but few light-skinned individuals among the very poor. We are far from the time when Candler (1842: 55) met, among the peasantry, a poor mulatto woman whose prejudice seemed to him more virulent than that of her urban counterparts.[8] Let me suggest that the movement of those two lines, color and income, is connected—and that it is through this dual movement that the reproduction of a social stratum perceived as *clair* fits within the reproduction of the dominant urban strata.

Jean Price-Mars, the dean of Haitian ethnology, provides the example that I shall use as a point of departure. Around 1870 in Cap-Haïtien, on the same street where Anténor Firmin, a young *black-skinned* intellectual, lived with his aunt, there also lived "a pretty young girl, a *mulâtresse brune*, Mlle. Marie Louise Salnave, also known as Rosa. [She was the daughter of the president who was executed in January 1870.] She lived with her mother, brothers, and sisters....The two young people, Anténor and Rosa, fell in love and promised to marry. But on both sides of the two families, the parents, it seems, opposed the marriage" (Price-Mars n.d.: 119). The reasons were unclear, but wags hinted that the heart of the matter was that the Salnave family, which was light-skinned, believed that the union was a mismatch. At any rate, in 1876 Rosa Salnave married a *clair*. In 1878 Rosa's husband died. Three years later, she took Anténor Firmin as her second husband.

Price-Mars (n.d.: 119–127) refers to numerous alliances between *noir* and *mulâtre* families of Cap-Haïtien and to the imposing number of prominent *noirs* of the North in order to suggest that color prejudice was not at work in the region and therefore cannot explain Anténor's first rejection. I accept Price-Mars' description of these alliances, but I would like to suggest that they prove the opposite thesis. What these alliances suggest, and what Anténor's and Rosa's marriage indicates, is that even in Cap-Haïtien, not just any *noir* could marry a *mulâtre*.

Price-Mars' analysis falls short in the secondary role that it attributes to what I call "social direction," that is, the path that an individual is perceived to be taking up or down the social ladder. Assuming that social positions are never fully guaranteed in complex societies, that they must be gained or maintained and can always be lost, I would suggest that individuals are always in motion on that ladder, however minimally. Society judges this continuous movement positively or negatively, and "social direction" is the result of that judgment. It is a measure of the social distance between what is thought to be known of an individual's origin and what is thought to be known of his or her future. It is a value-loaded perception of a projected distance. Individual time matters a great deal in that light.

In the case of Salnave and Firmin, we can see how individual time mattered. To be sure, between 1870 and 1881 the actors' phenotypes had not changed: the individuals were the same, only older. But it is surprising that an ethnologist makes so little of the fact that this was a second marriage for Salnave. Her social direction was no longer on the ascent. On the other side of the somatic boundary—that is, on the Firmin side—there had been a rise in social standing and, more importantly, the promise of a future that might even end in the presidency. Price-Mars admits that between the young intellectual of 1870 and the man who married the *claire* daughter of a former president lay the difference of time and social promotion. In other words, by 1881 Firmin was one of the very few *noirs* who could enter what Price-Mars calls the clique "of patricians, who, because of their position of wealth, or what so appeared, occupied the summit of the social hierarchy" (Price-Mars n.d.: 126).

Price-Mars' references to cross-color marriages among the northern elites takes on their full meaning once couched in these terms. It was not that the North did not know color prejudice but that the aristocracy that had sprung from Christophe's secessionist kingdom had produced an extraordinary number of *noirs* who could marry *mulâtres* if their hearts so desired. I am prepared to concede that if this aristocracy had reproduced itself across the entire country, and if the promotion of urban blacks like Firmin had been more widespread, color prejudice would perhaps have disappeared. Socioeconomic status would have achieved the upper hand in what Lévi-Straussian anthropology pompously calls "wife exchange." But Christophe's kingdom did not extend across the entire country and the alliance it produced between the *noir* and *mulâtre* landed aristocracies did not operate on the national level, where the prejudice itself was regenerated. Moreover, the original northern alliance across the epidermic line was based on the accumulation of land. Yet we have seen that Pétion, Boyer, Hérard, and their successors, squeezed by the peasantry, abandoned land accumulation in favor of an exploitative system centered around the customhouses. The feudal dream in which a *noir* aristocracy would have equal footing with its *mulâtre* counterparts crumbled with this choice.

In other words, even though color has never functioned alone, it has had an independent social value, even in the North. It is a commodity in the game of inter- and intra-class alliances. It has an exchange value, which can be and is calculated, even if that value is much lower in the North than in the West (e.g., Jacmel) or the South (e.g., Jérémie). Color is always part of what Price-Mars (n.d.:

126) delicately refers to as the "particularities of the social condition" in Haiti. And as a particularity of an individual's social condition, color plays a role in the reproduction of the social groups to which the individual belongs.

Historian Jean Fouchard (1972) reminds us that a number of families in the Haitian elites have a *noir* branch and a *mulâtre* branch, while other families move from the *noir* to the *mulâtre* pole of intellectual and political factions, and vice versa. This is true, even though it is difficult to find *noir* branches among the families who have traditionally been at the very top of the economic ladder. But what no one has ever emphasized is the socioeconomic exchange governing these passages or alternations. Here, I would submit—as a working hypothesis that must be further developed—that the passage from the *noir* side to the *mulâtre* side is often coupled with socioeconomic promotion. Conversely, the passage from the *clair* side to the *noir* side is often an indication of demotion. Demotions and promotions crosscut one another, because the respective social directions of bride and groom usually cancel each other out, with the darker partner being, most often, the one on the rise. Thus the couple as such neither rises nor falls—it becomes. The results of the exchange are confirmed only one or two generations later.

I will take a classic case. A young woman who can be placed in the *clair* category works as a salesgirl in a store or as a secretary in public administration. Her limited education betrays her lower-middle-class origins, but she spends much more money on clothes than her darker colleagues. What she guarantees by her dress, her discretion, and the places she frequents is in the end a social investment—her color. She will probably not marry into the top layer of the *mulâtre* elite, because the *mulâtre* aristocracy is endogamous. But she will try to marry "up," to marry a businessman, a professional, a well-placed public servant, preferably also a *clair*. Chances are, however, that the desired *clairs* will tend to think twice about a legal union with her, since they are playing the same game. Hence it is most likely that the young lady will marry within the *noir* group. But not any *noir* will do. First, the groom will probably have one of the few phenotypes somatically valued in spite of dark complexion (e.g., *bon noir, noir fin, marabout*). More important, his social direction will be unambiguously upward.

In short, the light-skinned bride contributes epidermic capital while her darker husband brings a diploma, savings, or the promise of a successful future, together with a reasonably acceptable somatic package. Social direction being a projection into the future, the promise may never materialize. Further, even if the projection is correct, the results will not be immediately apparent. Once more, the couple as such does not rise, or barely. It will not be admitted into the *crème de la crème:* people will "forget" to invite them to certain birthday or tennis parties. But their children, already lighter than their father, will freely associate with those who match their status, family income, and perceived phenotype. Increasingly, they will gravitate around individuals a shade lighter than themselves. The children are the ones who will enter smaller and smaller circles inaccessible to both parents: they are the ones who have a chance of becoming *mulâtres* of a kind. And their own children—if they marry a *clair*—will become part of an endogamous circle, pushing the somatic boundaries a little further in the direction of darker shades, but in doing so continuing to guarantee the domination of color.

THE REPRODUCTION OF COLOR AND CLASS

If we reverse the genders and place a male on the *clair* side of the exchange, we need make only small modifications to our scenario—he would need a higher level of formal education than his female counterpart, a professional diploma, a successful military career, or the label of "intellectual."[9]

Numerous *p'tits mulâtres de province* have bartered their skin color for security. Not for their own security, perhaps (because they do not enter *ipso facto* into the most exclusive circles), but for the security of their children—or, to be more exact, for the security of their names.

For color prejudice weighed on the progeny very early. Jonathan Brown reports the case of a *mulâtresse* who rejected one of the best catches of Boyer's republic on the basis of his color. The young lady insisted, with arrogant frankness, that she herself cared little about the pigmentation of her suitor. "But to have children blacker than herself, *petits enfants griffes,* how horrible!" (Brown [1837] 1971, 2: 284). And as the main somatic divide moved to include darker skins among the *clairs,* this emphasis on the progeny increased.

And here is where the exchange is deceptive: it does not operate immediately but over the span of generations. In the to-and-fro of the exchange, many are the *clair* families that have a *noir* skeleton in the closet. And while these families have made it their duty to exhibit this skeleton if necessary to prove their blackness, in the meantime the reproduction of prejudice continues along on its merry way. Mothers know this—they who so strictly control those whom their sons and (especially) their daughters associate with. It is a matter of reducing the field in such a way that the exchange can involve only the trade-off between social promotion and phenotype, the other possibilities having been eliminated by restricted association. Numerous common expressions jovially but discreetly exchanged among close friends and relatives register the trade-off. The darker partner is said to be "putting some milk into his/her coffee," or simply "improving the race." The lighter one is said to be aware of his/her own game (in Haitian, "Se li ki konnen zafè li"). Yet the returns are not necessarily collected during the timespan of the marriage, but later on, even generations later. Thus the display of wealth and influence, or the schema of economic structures, never reflect color cleavages in the short run. At any given moment the exchange guarantees a discrepancy between the economic and political domains and socio-epidermic classifications. But the very fact that the exchange continues, and that most urbanites participate in it—within their own restricted pool—maintains the pernicious impression of "an aristocracy of the skin" that all the involved parties believe in. The phrase attributed to Acau can now be modified: a rich black *becomes* a mulatto, a poor mulatto *becomes* black.

COLOR AND POLITICS

The ambiguity inherent in the practices described above have made color prejudice a choice subject for dark politicians. While they could not easily point to institutionalized discriminatory practices in Haiti, such as those of the United States or South Africa, they had no need to prove the existence of an epidermal elite because everyone believed it existed. Predominantly *mulâtre* clubs, schools, neighborhoods, and political cliques existed, even though legally everyone had access to them and even though a small number of *noirs* were found there. Over time, this perception of an epidermal elite, whose income, education, and social status remained inaccessible to the majority and which treated that majority with arrogant indifference, created extraordinary resentment among urban *noirs,* particularly those of the middle classes. This resentment, which reached its height in 1946, reinforced the twentieth-century version of *noirisme*.

Ironically, the *noiriste* theory of power finds its direct origins in the political ideology espoused by many mulattoes from the 1780s to the 1830s. It boils down to an epidermic quota: the representatives of the largest color group should have "natural" access to power. This is an argument whose origins can be traced to certain pre-independence mulattoes, such as Vincent Ogé, but slavery and colonial rule limited its impact. After independence, Beaubrun Ardouin, writer, politician, and *mulâtre* ideologue, took up with renewed enthusiasm Ogé's argument that the mulattoes and their descendants had a natural right to rule Haiti by virtue of their origins—because the blacks came from Africa and the whites from Europe.

The *noiriste* theory of power is one more version of this argument of "natural" legitimacy. The crucial difference is that in the mouths of politicians perceived as darker than their opponents, in a context where color matters—even if in the rather labyrinthine manner described here—the argument could both refer and appeal to much larger segments of the citizenry. As such, *noirisme* has always been an extremely potent discourse in Haiti, and it is likely to remain so as long as the perception of an "aristocracy of the skin" remains. An embryonic *noirisme* was already visible in Louverture's polemical use of the "color question" against Rigaud in the late 1790s. *Noiriste* arguments appeared in 1843 in the fight against Boyer, then less subtly in the 1860s with the Parti National, whose slogan was, significantly, "The greatest good for the greatest number." There was no doubt in this context to whom the "greatest number" referred.

Whereas *noirisme* tends to make explicit references to skin color, *mulâtrisme* avoids them at all cost. After independence, light-skinned politicians systematically denied the existence of color prejudice. Once they had established the *mulâtre*-controlled form of "government by understudy," they removed most references to color from their political discourse. To be sure, they first tried, in vain, to associate Saint-Domingue mulattoes with the leadership of the Haitian revolution; but once that strategy failed, *mulâtrisme* capitalized on the illusion of competence. The theory was encapsulated by the middle of the nineteenth century in the slogan of Edmond Paul, a dark-skinned theoretician of the Parti Libéral: "Le pouvoir aux plus capables" ("Power to the most competent"). One can trace the roots of that slogan in the writings of many *mulâtres* in the immediate aftermath of independence.

The reference to competence gave a distinct advantage to the *clairs,* especially in the nineteenth century. Just as everyone knew to whom the "greatest number" referred, so they knew who claimed to be "most capable." As a group, the *clairs* had clear economic and educational advantages since before independence: they could indeed define what it meant to be "capable." But the reference to competence allowed them to claim power for themselves while deflecting accusations of discrimination. Competence was a commodity supposedly available to everyone, an objective toward which the *noirs* themselves aimed. In contradistinction, phenotypical resemblance to the majority was not an ideal, even for *noir* leaders. Indeed, a majority of the *noiriste* ideologues had light-skinned wives, light-skinned progeny, or at the very least progeny lighter than themselves.[10]

The competition between *noir* and *mulâtre* factions for control of the state apparatus never took on the appearance of an all-out color war. The "most capable," like the "greatest number" or other expressions of this type, functioned as a polite code behind which everyone recognized the "color question," without it being explicitly formulated and detailed. In fact, *noiriste* political factions never got rid of their own mulattoes. The most recent example of this is François Duvalier, but President Salomon also put the presence of "his" *mulâtres* in the state apparatus to good use (Gaillard 1984: 47, 142–146). *Mulâtre* political factions in turn almost always included black intellectuals and military men. Edmond Paul and Anténor Firmin, the most coherent theoreticians of the Parti Libéral (the *mulâtre* party *par excellence*) had black skins. Nord Alexis, a powerful general who sold his support to the highest bidding *mulâtristes,* was also black. Even in 1946, when the electoral battle clearly took on the aspect of a color struggle, the rivals of the *noiriste* candidate, Dumarsais Estimé, were all black skinned (Bonhomme 1957).

Contrary, therefore, to the interplay of family alliances, the appeal to color in the field of politics did not need a concrete somatic referent. Anténor Firmin asserted that, in the electoral campaign of 1879, *mulâtres* of Cap-Haïtien campaigned against him, a dark-skinned liberal allied to a *mulâtre* party, by arguing that he was "a *mulâtre* as light-skinned as a white" (Firmin, cited in Price-Mars n.d.: 117). Price-Mars doubted the veracity of this report, which reflects negatively on his native province, but one cannot doubt that similar tactics were used in the North, both in the nineteenth century and at other times, as well as in other places.[11] Light-skinned Sylvain Salnave sent his nephew into areas of the northern countryside where he himself was not known to campaign against the "yellow people." Early supporters of François Duvalier report that in 1957, Duvalier's opponent, Louis Déjoie, was described as being "very light-skinned," "almost white," in several areas of the Artibonite Valley, about 100 miles north of Port-au-Prince, where the masses of voters had never seen him. The game went on intermittently, the *mulâtres* making reference to their competence, which was more apparent than real, the *noirs* to their "natural" representativeness, which was just as much a matter of appearance.

But appearances mattered, if only because of the conflicting associations they engendered. The *mulâtres*' praise of the virtues of "competence" and "civilization," as well as their palpable somatic preference, linked them vaguely with a more sympathetic view of the West. Yet that linkage was denied by the *mulâtres* themselves whenever it seemed to displace the association between Haiti and blackness, or the fundamental values that permeated the cultural terrain. That, more than the personal shame of being taken for blatant racists, was what had kept the *mulâtres* on the defensive after independence. The U.S. occupation and the presidency of Elie Lescot removed this defensive attitude, sharpening the conflict and putting it in terms that convinced a majority of urbanites that Haiti's political and cultural future was at stake.

THE COLOR OF THE OCCUPATION

The United States' desire to create an American-style middle class in urban Haiti during the occupation remained unfulfilled. But the harassment of small landowners, the building of new roads, and the administrative and political centralization carried out by the Marines swelled the ranks of the peasants, artisans, students, and professionals who found their way to the coastal cities, and especially to Port-au-Prince. Between 1915 and 1945, an ever increasing number of newcomers rushed into the already limited space within which the ultimate battle for power was traditionally fought.

The *noirs* who surged into this urban arena did not always believe themselves destined to occupy its lowest rungs. Dark-skinned residents of Port-au-Prince were becoming increasingly qualified for public service, although their qualifications did not—as they had not for numerous *mulâtres* before them—go beyond the secondary school Baccalauréat. Since 1804, if not before, a minority of black businesspeople, intellectuals, professionals, and politicians had carved for themselves a niche in the structure of urban life. In the latter part of the century they were joined by the inheritors of the more open system of public education developed under Salomon. In the 1880s, Salomon, whose grandfather had been one of the few black magistrates of the Louverture regime, explicitly tried to give to a significant number of blacks what public education under Pétion had given to many light-skinned families—the hereditary privilege of academic competence. Competence doubtless varied from Grandpapa's primary school education to the prodigy grandson's European diploma, but its genealogical transmission occurred among a large segment of the population. Together, the descendants of the pre-1804 black professionals, the relatively recent elites created by Salomon, and the newcomers fleeing the decline of the provincial pyramids formed a new intellectual majority in the capital. The time was gone when economist Edmond Paul, himself a member of a dark elite family, could exclaim in all sincerity, "Le pouvoir aux plus capables," with the conviction that the "most capable" were also the lightest. Sometime before the end of the occupation, the reference to competence ceased to be to the exclusive advantage of the *mulâtre* minority.

But now that the "greatest number" also had their own "most capable," the *mulâtres*, who had been the previous winners in the war of rhetoric, suddenly changed the rules of the game. They abruptly revealed themselves to be less than conciliatory. They denied most of the newcomers the intellectual and political recognition they had been hoping for, the "elite" membership traditionally allowed to successful *noirs*. Naked color prejudice now supplanted the rule of the most capable, behind which it had been conveniently hidden.

Infractions of the law of the most capable preceded the occupation. The very existence of color prejudice and its mode of operation implied that, given equal levels of competence, the perception of "color," if not the exact degree of pigmentation, worked to the disadvantage of the *noir*. But U.S. racism added its institutional systematism to Haitian colorist favoritism. The Marines witnessed the successive installation of five *clair* presidents, three of whom were undeniably *mulâtres*. The U.S. "advisers," who in fact ran many government services, openly showed their preference for light-skinned officials, without considering the elaborate etiquette that the Haitian "aristocrats of the skin" had patiently refined for a century. The visibility of the *mulâtres* grew—as did their arrogance. These political precedents portended a battle of new dimensions, particularly since the occupation had affected the ideological landscape at least as profoundly as it had changed the rules of political competition.

THE INDIGENISTE MOVEMENT

I have already mentioned that in spite of color prejudice, Haitian national identity implied a positive identification with the black race. Martiniquan writer Aimé Césaire put it quite simply: it was in Haiti that *négritude* first appeared. However, this nationalist posture was always circumscribed by the intellectual and emotional attachment of the elites to the West, and to France in particular. These elites preferred Latin cultures and ways to Anglo-Saxon technocentrism and lack of polish: it was French literature that supplied them with their thematic and formal models. But they also valued what they saw as the achievements of northern Europe and the United States. In their view, there were no superior races, but there were superior cultures (Lewis 1983: 317). And since those cultures were European (or European derivatives), whiteness evoked a certain *savoir-faire* as well as a certain *savoir-vivre*.

The U.S. occupation, in different degrees and for different reasons, called each of these propositions into question. *Savoir-vivre* was the first to go. North Americans were not *sans-manière* ("without manners") in the sense that the elites would say this of the peasants, implying perfectibility. Instead they had crude manners, being by choice *de grossiers personnages*. *Savoir-faire* was more tenacious, but the occupation did not bring the spectacular changes in technology and material life for which many in the elites had been secretly hoping.

As the occupation forced a redefinition of whiteness, it also questioned its nemesis, blackness. The strong identification with blackness and the nationalist posture that cemented the ideological world of the elites could only be seen in the light of the slave revolution and independence. The nation stood for blackness because its black forefathers had fought for freedom *and* won over the best European army of the time. Indeed, this victory had been the sole empirical reference point of Haitian nationalist discourse. By the 1920s, however, the daily presence of the Marines had brought into question contemporary Haitians' claims that they shared their ancestors' courage and nobility (Danache 1950).

The pre-1915 Haitian elites had never held to any ideological proposition with fanatical conviction—except perhaps the association of the 1804 revolution with the regeneration of the black race. Ambiguity was their forte. But by undermining many tenets of the elites' vision of themselves and others, the occupation revealed inconsistencies inherent in that vision that they had conveniently ignored. More important, in questioning political independence—the proof of 1804—the occupation undermined the basis of the delicate edifice that these contradictory propositions constituted. The times called for a redefinition (Mintz 1984: 263–288), or at least for a reshaping, of the old categories within a more coherent whole. It is this reformulation that various intellectuals, loosely referred to by later writers as the *mouvement indigéniste,* tried to supply.

In 1928, the publication of Jean Price-Mars' book *Ainsi parla l'oncle* (Price-Mars 1983) launched the Haitian *indigéniste* movement. A series of attempts by *noir* and *clair* intellectuals to mount a wide-ranging reevaluation of the national culture followed Price-Mars' work. These writers criticized the elites' tendency to imitate the West and to ignore peasant culture. They emphasized the need to study the peasantry, to make an inventory of its practices, and to take into account the African roots of Haitian culture. The *indigénistes'* critique suggested that the elites' political failure stemmed in part from their contempt of Haitian popular culture, an argument at times quite explicit in Price-Mars' other writings (Antoine 1981; M.-R. Trouillot 1986b). But *indigénisme* as such had no political program and regrouped intellectuals of different political persuasions, including a few socialists.

This cultural nationalism can be distinguished therefore from *noirisme,* a strictly political ideology rooted in claims of "natural" legitimacy and calling for a color quota within the state apparatus. *Indigénisme* overlaps with *négritude,* but the scope of *négritude* is much wider. Whereas the range of *noirisme* is limited to relations of state power (and thus essentially to the urban arena), and *indigénisme* aims for the national arena, *négritude* theoretically aims for the world space in which the unequal evaluation of peoples, religions, and cultures originates.

These distinctions are important inasmuch as they continuously influenced political alignments among the elites. Since the nineteenth century, numerous *clairs* and other supporters of *mulâtre* political factions forcefully argued for the equality of all human races in the international arena while maintaining the colorist status quo in their own country (Firmin 1885; Price 1900; Nicholls 1979). By the same token, Jean Price-Mars, the founder of *indigénisme,* never endorsed *noiriste* politics; more, he publicly disassociated himself from *noirisme* during François Duvalier's regime, no small sign of intellectual integrity and personal courage (Antoine 1981).

Mass political symbolism, however, proceeds by association rather than by an intellectual exercise in classification. Haitian *mulâtrisme* had always been susceptible to the charge of duplicating white racism, even though, as we have seen, it was no mere derivative of Western values. It had survived the association with the West, in part because of another association equally potent among the elites: that of whiteness and *savoir-faire.* I have suggested that the practices of the U.S. occupiers raised questions about the Haitians' views of whiteness. The *indigéniste* movement provided new answers: no culture was superior, either in *savoir-faire* or *savoir-vivre.* Thus the most Westernized Haitians were not necessarily the best Haitians, nor the most useful to the country. These answers were not immediately "political." But in challenging the superiority of "white cultures" in the midst of the occupation, the *indigéniste* movement dealt a major blow to the rationale behind the claims to "competence."

THE 1946 DIFFERENCE

The *indigéniste* reevaluation of the cultural roots and tendencies of the nation opened the political field for the proponents of "legitimacy," the self-proclaimed advocates of the "greatest number." They could now insist on the associations implicit in the nineteenth-century world view, conveniently ignored by previous generations. And those associations themselves had become more powerful once *négritude* and *indigénisme* gave *noirisme* a new critical mass. If most of the *indigéniste* writers were not *noiristes*, most *noiristes* were *indigénistes* with an eye on the worldwide *négritude* movement. Thus, although *noirisme* itself was not in fact as popular in the political field as it now appears in retrospect, it had all the right cultural associations. By 1938, some *noiriste* intellectuals associated with the *Griots* group (which included a number of self-trained ethnologists and historians, among whom was François Duvalier) started to think of political strategies based upon these associations (Denis and Duvalier 1938). By 1945, President Lescot's growing unpopularity made it possible for most *noiriste* factions to call on such associations.

Lescot (1941–46) not only pursued the U.S. practice of systematically placing light-skinned individuals in the top echelons of the public service, but he also extended color favoritism to all levels of the administration without the slightest bow to the rule of perceived competence. In so doing, he repeatedly violated tradition. By 1945, for the first time in Haitian history, the distribution of power had become explicitly colorist. By then also—and again for the first time in Haitian history—a *mulâtre* regime was being accused of incompetence and judged guilty by a majority of urbanites. To add insult to injury, Lescot took many stands against the national culture, notably by facilitating an "anti-superstition campaign" that the Catholic church organized against Vodoun in 1941–42.

By 1945–46 these flagrant violations of political tradition and cultural tolerance, carried out in the midst of the intellectual reaction to the effects of the occupation, allowed a group of politicians to intermix *noirisme*, *indigénisme* and *négritude* in the perception of most urbanites. Anti-*mulâtre* resentment was at its height among the *noir* intellectuals and politicians, among students, and among the urban masses. At the same time, a majority of the population in the cities and towns was supportive of any attempt to restore national and cultural dignity, especially since the U.S. Marines had displayed to the Haitians, in their own country, the crassest dimensions of international racism. The most vocal among the *noiriste* intellectuals and politicians found themselves at the intersection of the three movements. Being from the masses, they said, they were its most "authentic" representatives, alone capable of ushering in the "new order" (Bonhomme 1946, 1957). Hadn't Lescot's government shown that a class of men born with silver spoons in their mouths would do anything to maintain their privileges? For the *authentiques*, the most vocal of the 1946 *noiristes*, cultural reevaluation and the regaining of national dignity, like the end of arbitrariness, required a change of "class" within the state apparatus.

Naiveté or Machiavellianism? Probably a little of both. The various associations put forward by the *authentiques* had been made implicitly by many urbanites since the nineteenth century, and it is possible that some of the 1946 leaders saw them as irrevocably intertwined. The fact remains that people who might not have supported the *authentiques* in other circumstances took their side in the battle against Lescot. The fusion of *noirisme*, *indigénisme*, and *négritude*—facilitated by the general indignation over Lescot's practices and the reevaluation of the nation in the light of the occupation—created an ideological tidal wave unprecedented in Haitian history, which imposed the presidency of Dumarsais Estimé.

Today it is easy to see that the *noiriste* retaliation against *mulâtre* power also hid a trap. But in re-reading contemporary accounts (e.g., Dorsinville 1972; Collectif Paroles 1976; Pierre 1987), we realize that in 1946, as would also be true in 1957, *noirisme* was perceived as the only viable political alternative by the vast majority of the middle classes. The very terms of urban political debate wold not allow the question of color to be set aside. As a privileged witness confirms:

> I told you: I was a *"noiriste."* And I will add that whoever in my social class in Haiti, after Lescot, under Lescot, whoever was not a *noiriste* would have been scum. ... They forced upon us a culture of contempt. To this culture of contempt, we opposed our resistance and our hate. ... (Dorsinville 1985:21).

> All the ministers, all the important administrative posts, all the embassies were in the hands of *mulâtres,* the administrative offices of subcontracting companies were full of light-skinned girls ... (Dorsinville 1972: 130–31).

> They ran the country as they would have run a plantation. And me, living there, the fruit of a certain culture, of a certain education, being conscious of my identity, I would not have been *noiriste? Merde!* (Dorsinville 1985: 21).

It must be understood how much this *merde* was shared among the middle classes, how it had profound repercussions for the thousands of intellectuals, artisans, small shopowners, well-to-do peasants, commodity *spéculateurs,* and vast segments of the lumpen masses. Moreover, this bitterness still resonates, because Duvalierism could not resolve either the color question or the more or less subtle forms of cultural and social domination. Nevertheless, in 1946 this general resentment against the *mulâtre* faction of the elites gave Estimé a political mandate of rare dimensions in Haitian history—as it would also give Duvalier, in 1957, the benefit of the doubt.

Estimé did little with his mandate. He enjoyed unlimited support in the first years of his presidency, but his popularity declined precipitously. His attempt to get re-elected facilitated the army's takeover. The same three-man junta that had ensured the transition from Lescot to Estimé announced new elections. Colonel Paul Magloire, once more the junta strongman, quickly became a presidential candidate. He won the 1950 elections—the first in which all adult males could vote directly for president—almost without electoral opposition.

The *authentiques* experienced Magloire's presidency (1950–56) as a frustrating interim. And, in many respects, this period was indeed a parenthesis, a reprieve in the denouement of the crisis. But for those who had lived through 1946, the frustration could be traced back to Estimé himself. The president had not been the *"mulâtre-eater"* his enemies had feared and his supporters had hoped. He had, of course, applied "color mathematics," giving an extraordinary number of *noirs* access to government positions. But he did not have a program that distinguished him from his predecessors (Collectif Paroles 1976), and the *authentiques* found his reforms limited (Bonhomme 1957: 13). Their frustration increased with Magloire, whom they saw as the very negation of the 1946 revolution, a reign of *"noirs* without color" at the service of the *mulâtre* bourgeoisie (Bonhomme 1957: 40). When the bourgeoisie itself seemed ready to abandon Magloire, when the church and commercial interests opposed his attempts to illegally prolong his term, it became necessary for the *authentiques* to find themselves a crown prince, an heir who would close the parentheses and carry on the uncompleted work of Estimé, who had since died in exile.

Only now have we begun to learn the appalling details of the maneuvering that permitted François Duvalier to surface as the Estimist representative in the 1957 elections.[12] The fact remains that this was Duvalier's most difficult campaign. Once he had won the support—or silence—of the most prominent Estimists, he inherited a political mantle and an apparatus that had solid support among lower level army officers and intellectuals. Above all, he inherited a vision of Haitian society which, vague and poorly defined as it was, presupposed continuity in change, the desire to complete an unfinished "revolution." If the reevaluation of the black race was legitimate, if the reevaluation of national culture and the restoration of national dignity was legitimate, then *noirisme* was legitimate. And if *noirisme* was legitimate, then Duvalier was legitimate. We now know that those syllogisms were profoundly incorrect; but once more, political symbolism proceeds by association; it feeds on analogies rather than on logic.

Victory was not easy, however. Duvalier's arguments were not remarkable, his personal image was rather dull. But though his campaign took time to get off the ground, by February 1957, he was considered a serious contender by those who had dismissed him a few months earlier. From then on, he campaigned seriously (Duvalier 1966b; Célestin 1958a, 1958b, 1959). By April he had mastered all the right analogies and had begun to take full advantage of his opponents' symbolic and tactical mistakes. More important, with the help of *noiriste* army officers, he virtually forced all the other dark-skinned candidates out of the race—a process of elimination that left him in a head-to-head contest with *mulâtre* Louis Déjoie on election day. Finally, the election itself was fraudulent: Duvalier won some districts with more votes than the actual number of residents.

Thus Duvalier ultimately owed his power to the army, which supervised the voting process and exercised a veto over the presidency. In fact, the army dominated the long transition from Magloire to Duvalier, shaped the climate for the presidential campaign, and paved the way for totalitarianism. I will return to the crucial role of this institution when I detail the context of the transition in the next chapter. The point is that, in spite of the fraud and the superficial character of the campaign, there is no evidence to indicate that Duvalier would not have won in regular elections. The dream of 1946 carried him, and it was a dream that embodied a century and a half of urban and rural frustration—frustration that the new middle classes that had arisen from the occupation, the self-proclaimed representatives of the masses in the state apparatus, decided to end once and for all.

Notes
1. In any given society, the somatic norm-image is likely to vary according to class and ethnic origins. In the extreme cases of societies with multiple ethnic mixtures, such as Venezuela, Colombia, or Brazil, the category as defined by Hoetink could even turn out to be inoperative. But this is not the case in Haiti.
2. Indeed, foreign observers tend to make major mistakes in specifying the 'color' of specific Haitians. One counts, among the most important gaffes, Leyburn's (1941, 316) classification of President Salnave as 'dark' and, more recently, Ferguson's (1987, 72) branding of Simone Duvalier (François' wife) as a 'mulatto'!
3. The Haitian school of ethnology, oriented toward folklore, has not touched on the complex relationship between culture and power. Only recently have a few works of cultural anthropology, published abroad, begun to sketch out paths of inquiry in this area (Amer and Coulanges 1974; Bebel-Gisler and Hurbon 1975; Hurbon 1979).
4. The preferred uses of Haitian varies with age, gender, and the context of communication among the elites, but there are social penalties for using French at the 'wrong' time, just as there are penalties for the improper use of Haitian by French-competent speakers.
5. I thank Czerny Brasuell and Michel Acacia, who forced me to deal with this question.
6. One cannot make reference to the continued immigration of whites and *mulâtres* to explain the

survival of persons considered *'clairs.'* White and *mulâtre* immigration certainly played a role, but it was more social than biological.
7. Candler, during his visit of 1838–40, noted that 'a large number among the class of *mulâtre* citizens residing in the capital were immigrants from the United States' (Candler 1842, 165). Later, white and light-skinned newcomers had different points of origin: Cuba, the Dominican Republic, France, the British West Indies, Austria, Corsica, Sicily, Syria, Lebanon, Germany, and especially Martinique and Guadeloupe. Many adapted quickly and formed prominent 'Haitian' families (Aubin 1910). But the in-flow was too slow for this immigration alone to maintain the biological reproduction of a *clair group*. In addition, the migratory flow was not in one direction. The long regimes of Soulouque (1847–59) and of Salomon (1879–88), for instance, which were dominated by *noirs*, forced numerous *mulâtres* to leave the country.
8. Maxime Raybaud, who lived in Haiti during Acau's lifetime, gives a detailed version of the origins of this saying. It seems that during a demonstration Acau demanded that *all* the mulattoes be expropriated. A disapproving murmur came from the crowd, in which there were mulattoes in rags. Acau replied, 'Oh! *These* are blacks!' Then, says Raybaud, 'a black of about thirty years of age, who worked as a laborer in a rum plant, stepped forth and said to the crowd: Acau is right, because the Virgin said, "Nèque rich qui connait lit et écri, cila mulâtre, mulâtre pauve qui pas connait li ni écri, cila nèque."' [The rich black who knows how to read and write is a mulatto, the poor mulatto who does not know how to read or write is a black.] This black was named Joseph, and from that day on he called himself *Brother Joseph*. With a white kerchief on his head, dressed in a white shirt which gripped a pair of white pants, he walked, candle in hand, among Acau's troops, [repeating]: 'The rich black who knows how to read and write is a mulatto, etc.' (d'Alaux 1856, 112–13). Note the association of 'reading' and 'writing' to wealth and skin color in this early version of the saying.
9. The disappearance of poor mulattoes might also explain the double semantic twist in the term *mulâtre*, which has come to include darker and darker people but also to increasingly exclude individuals at the bottom of the social ladder. Today in the countryside there is a tendency to call a very light-skinned peasant *ti rouj, ti blan*, or simply *hlan* (literally little red one, little white one, white) rather than *milat*. The same is done in the city for an artisan, a laborer, or a member of the lumpenproletariat.
10. Jacqueline Gautier and Evelyne Trouillot have both suggested to me that the assimilation of the Western-dominated aesthetic is stronger among Haitian males than among Haitian women, at least in the *petite bourgeoisie*. In other words, my example reversing the genders might not be completely justified. It is possible that the interiorization of the *mulâtre* aesthetic is more general among males, and that the emphasis on social promotion through the offspring is more systematic among women. Cultural anthropologists have yet to systematically study relations of alliance and kinship in urban Haiti and their influence on class reproduction.
11. The vast majority of political leaders who have consistently or temporarily utilized *noiriste* rhetoric have themselves chosen to have *clair* progeny, or at the very least, progeny more *clair* than they themselves. Salomon married a Frenchwoman; Estimé and François Duvalier married women less dark than themselves; Jean-Claude Duvalier had a child with a *mulâtresse* before he married Michèle Bennett, a *clair* though not a wealthy *mulâtresse*, as often claimed in the international press.
12. Price-Mars knew well that color prejudice could decide a candidate's lot. As a *noir*, he did not use it, and this speaks well of him (Antoine 1981, 190–91), but the maneuver was possible and it usually worked. There were others who seemed much more qualified to be Estimé's heir, either because of their greater ideological allegiance to *noiriste* dogma, their greater partisan loyalty to Estimé, or their political preparation. According to Col. Pressoir Pierre, a personal friend of Duvalier, his success was due mainly to a palace coup, as it were, that took place within the ranks of the ex-president's supporters after Estimé's death in exile. Some young officers (among them Pierre), profiting from support given by Estimé's widow, tipped the balance in favor of Papa Doc (Pierre 1987). It has also been said that Duvalier made a pact with several Estimist leaders, promising them that he would pass power on to them after his term was over.

References
Antoine, Jacques Carmeleau. 1981. *Jean Price-Mars and Haiti*. Washington, DC: Three Continents Press.
Auguste, Claude B., and Marcel B. Auguste. 1985. *L'Expedition Leclerc, 1801–1803*. Port-au-Prince: Imprimerie Henri Deschamps.

Bonhomme, Colbert. 1946. *Les Origines et les Leçons d'une* Révolution *Profonde et Pacifique*. Port-au-Prince: Imprimerie de l'Etat.
———. 1957. *Révolution et Contre-Révolution en Haiti, de 1946 à 1957*. Port-au-Prince: Imprimerie de l'Etat.
Brown, Jonathan. 1971. *The History and Present Condition of St Domingo*. Rept. ed. London: Frank Cass. First published 1837 by William Marshall and Company.
Candler, John. 1842. *Brief Notices of Hayti: With Its Conditions, Resources and Prospects*. London: Thomas Ward & Co.
Célestin, Clément.1958a. *Compilations pour l'Histoire, Vol. 1. Les Gouvernements Provisoires, 6 décembre 1956 au 25 mai 1957*. Port-au-Prince: Imprimerie N.A. Théodore.
———. 1958b. *Compilations pour l'Histoire, Vol. 2*. Port-au-Prince: Imprimerie N.A. Théodore.
———. 1959. *Compilations pour l'Histoire, Vol. 3. Conseil Militaire de* Gouvernement. Port-au-Prince: Imprimerie N.A. Théodore.
Collectif Paroles. 1976. *1946–1976, Trente ans de Pouvoir Noir en Haïti*. La Salle, Canada: Collectif Paroles.
Danache, B[ertomieux]. 1950. *Le Président Dartiguenave et les Américains*. Port-au-Prince: Imprimerie de l'Etat.
Denis, Lorimer, and F. Duvalier. 1938. *Le Problème des Classes a Travers l'Histoire d'Haïti*. Port-au-Prince.
Duvalier, Francois. 1966. *Ouvres Essentielles: La Marche à la Présidence*. Vol. 2. Port-au-Prince: Presses Nationales d'Haïti.
Dorsinville, Roger. 1972. 1946 ou le Délire Opportuniste. *Nouvelle Optique* 6:117–40.
Dorsinville, Roger. 1985. Dans le Fauteuil de l'Histoire. Interview with Michel Adam and Edgard Th. Gousse. *Etincelles* 1, no. 10:18–21.
Du Tertre, Jean-Baptiste. 1667. *Histoire Générale des Antilles Habiteés par les Français*. Paris: Th. Jolly.
Firmin, Anténor. 1885. *De l'Egalité des Races Humaines*. Paris.
Fouchard, Jean. 1972. *Les Marrons de la Liberté*. Paris: L'Ecole. Trans. A. Faulkner Watts. 1981. *The Haitian Maroons: Liberty or Death*. New York: Blyden Press.
Gage, Thomas. 1958. *Thomas Gage's Travels in the New World*. Intro. J. Eric Thompson. Norman: University of Oklahoma Press.
Gaillard, Roger. 1974–1984. *Les Blancs Debarquent*. 5 vols. Port-au-Prince: Presses Nationales, Imprimerie Le Natal.
Hoetink, Harry. 1967. *The Two Variants in Caribbean Race Relations*. London: Oxford University Press.
Labelle, Micheline. 1976. Témoignages sur la Question de Couleur. *Lankansiel* 5:25–43.
———. 1978. *Idéologie de Couleur et Classes Socials en Haiti*. Montreal: Les Presses de l'Université de Montréal.
Lamartinière, Jacqueline. 1976. *Le Noirisme*. Paris: MHL.
Lewis, Gordon. 1983. *Main Currents in Caribbean Thought*. Baltimore and London: Johns Hopkins University Press.
Mintz, Sidney. 1984. *Caribbean Transformations*. Baltimore and London: John Hopkins University Press.
Nicholls, David. 1979. *From Dessalines to Duvalier: Race, Colour and National Independence in Haiti*. Cambridge: Cambridge University Press.
Pierre, Pressoir. 1987. *Témoignages: 1946–1976, l'Espérance Déçue*. Port-au-Prince: Imprimerie Henri Deschamps.
Price, Hannibal. 1900. *De la Réhabilitation de la Race Noire par la République d'Haïti*. Port-au-Prince.
Price-Mars, Jean. 1983. *So Spoke the Uncle*. Washington, DC: Three Continents Press.
———. n.d. *Anténor Firmin*. Port-au-Prince: Imprimerie Séminaire Adventiste.
Rolph-Trouillot, Michel. 1986. Review of *So Spoke the Uncle* by J. Price-Mars. *Research in African Literatures* 17, no. 4:596–97.
Trollope, Anthony. 1985. *The West Indies and the Spanish Main*. Gloucester: Alan Sutton.

West Indian Society 150 Years after Abolition:
A Re-Examination of Some Classic Theories[1]
Lloyd Best

A MISPLACED REGION

The Caribbean is a misplaced region. That is its first distinguishing feature. Latin America, in contrast, is hopelessly misnamed, as is the Far East. Mr Nehru was once asked what he thought would happen there. 'Far from where?' he replied. Latin America is another of these Eurocentric conceptions but it is less a Latin than an American civilisation whether in Bolivia, Paraguay, Peru, Guatemala or even Mexico. It is an American civilisation with a Spanish garland.

The Caribbean entered world society as a result of a search for the Pacific by way of the Atlantic, an attempt to find the sunrise in the sunset, if you like. Long distance trade in the Mediterranean was trying to go around the Saladin's roadblock as Celso Furtado has reminded us. Going West, Columbus took island for mainland and even thought he had found the Khans. But in spite of the hopes and the dreams of the Admiral of the Fleet, the Caribbean has remained resolutely island. The islands are therefore not North America; they are not South America; and not Central America either. Trinidad's northern Archipelago is no more than ten kilometres from Venezuela and I doubt that we even know it exists, conflicts over marine oil and fishing rights notwithstanding.

The Caribbean is clearly a case apart. When I went to Allende's Chile in their fall of 1972, it was only shortly after Fidel Castro had been there. 'What did you think of our modern Enriquillo?' I kept on asking.

'*Bueno,* Fidel is a good boy; *pero un poco más tropical para nosotros.*' A little too tropical for them, indeed. It was sheer illusion on the part of the Ché Guevara and Fidel Castro to think that they could export a Caribbean revolution to American America. It was almost as arrogant as those Europeans who believe that in 500 short years they have Latinised and civilised the Aztecs and the Incas. Fidel's most fertile ground is not there but right here in the Indies.

American America is an entirely different world from the Latin Mediterranean. It is different even from European America in Argentina, Southern Brazil and North America. And the Caribbean is something else again. The islands are marked by an imported Afro-Asian population in America operating European institutions. This absence of roots and ruins does have its limitations. But it also provides us with corresponding opportunities. There exists a definite psychology of rootlessness but it would be a mistake to take that for any simple floating condition. The whole culture is anchored in institutional arrangements requiring us, therefore, to scrutinise the other characteristics.

PLANTATION ECONOMY

The second distinguishing feature of the region is the all-pervasiveness of what the historians first described as 'plantation economy'. The expositors have made a great deal of this concept in the contemporary literature. Here we need to dwell on just a few characteristics germane to the current discussion.

We know that the plantation economy has its moorings in external dependence. It relies on the outside world for its enterprise, for its management, for its organisation. Necessarily, the surplus generated by production accrues to venturers outside the region. Even in modern times, there has been a vast gap between the domestic product and what is retained at home as national income. This we all know and it is extremely important. What, however, is crucial at this moment is that this type of dependence limits the options for adjustment when there is crisis. Partly because the entrepreneurs and the risk takers live outside, and partly because the social and political structures are rigid, the adjustment to crisis is not through intrinsic development such as technological or organisational change. Rather it is expansionist, evasive, escapist even. You do not attempt to burst the bonds of your integument, if we may borrow a phrase from Marx; you do not innovate and reorganise your ways of doing and thinking; you go around instead by moving the same old operation to somewhere else. Or you carry the same old attitudes into other lines of production where natural conditions offer you easy options.

It was the whole matrix into which the society and its politics were cast which dictated this pattern of adjustment to economic crisis in terms of falling productivity, rising costs and declining markets. I am, of course, ruthlessly simplifying the story. But the theory of business management which underlies our work on plantation economy is meant deliberately to focus this mode of adjustment. Rather than introduce new techniques on given land, planters under the extreme conditions of slavery would instead engross the plantation by acquiring more land or new land.

The sugar industry expands by the identical type of adjustment. It shifts terrain. The industry moves from North East Brazil to Barbados, Antigua, St Kitts, Martinique and the Virgin Islands. As soil exhaustion and declining profitability set in, it moves to Jamaica and then to Saint Domingue, right up to Trinidad and Cuba in the nineteenth century. When the West Indians become high cost producers, technological developments do not bring long-run costs down; the industry expands to embrace East India. What makes this possible is not just that the market is outside; that is the least of the apostles. What makes that adjustment almost mandatory is that the enterprise is uncommitted to the environment. Moreover, the surplus necessary to facilitate new commitments elsewhere by the entrepreneurship conveniently accrues outside. It accrues in the hands of the metropolitan merchant venturers.

So the adjustment is by a widening rather than a deepening. The corollary of this is that the economic system employs more labour per unit of output as well as per unit of land. You do not train or equip existing labour to raise its skills or its productivity. Instead, you bring more bodies in at existing levels of skill and productivity. Thus engrossment, shifting of terrain and induction of additional labour are all of a piece in the theory of plantation economy. In terms of the business management involved, account needs also to be taken of overwork and underfeeding as means of adjustment, meant to increase the milkable surplus in times of crisis. But the full theory of plantation management, rich as it is, is not the issue here on this occasion.

Important here is not the economics but the sociology. New populations are being repeatedly introduced through this pattern of expansionist adjustment. This describes a highly turbulent demographic situation. The facts about the economics are intriguing, concerned with the international divison of labour and the international distribution of income. There is a full theory of growth and development. But it is the demography which must now detain us, since that is what complicates the crucial question as to what social cleavages and what political conflicts came to be characteristic of the West Indian environment since the abolition of slavery.

We need not begin with any simple, one-dimensional model of cowboys and indians. In the Caribbean we have both social stratification and social fragmentation, at one and the same time and of equal importance. The nineteenth-century Western European mind simply refuses to entertain it. But there is no law which requires us to choose between class and race and colour and religion as causes of cleavage. We can and do have all of them at once. In any given situation, we do have to rank them and to determine, in Mao Tse Tung's terminology, which is primary and which secondary contradiction. But the answer is not pre-ordained by nineteenth-century Marxist political sociology or indeed by any other given 'bible'.

FRAGMENTED SOCIETY

The economics suggests to me that there may be three types of cleavage and contradiction which we need to acknowledge in the West Indies and the Caribbean. I suspect that the primary cleavage opposes the residentiary groups, on the one hand, to plantation groups on the other. By the residentiary groups, I mean those involved in the kind of activity which predated the hegemony of the large sugar plantation. Before 1640 these were small peasant settler-farmers; later they were on the whole Maroons until the slave system broke up in the middle of the nineteenth century. Of course, these settlers produced mainly for export. The colonies needed foreign exchange in order to pay for their food and material imports and to defray the capital costs of establishment. They were not, however, export-specialised in the sense that exporting and earning foreign exchange were their very reason for existence.

In the nature of the case, this contradiction was for a long time disguised by that other contradiction between plantation *staff* on the one hand – the management elites – and the plantation *inmates* on the other – the multitude of the subjugated slave population. Neither staff members nor inmates were substantially settlers in any important sense. The one had no interest in settlement; the other had no means to achieve it. Psychologically and culturally, the whole of the order was absentee. At the same time, the long-run options open to the slave population tilted the latter's commitment towards a settler interest even if the short-run possibilities generated enormous ambiguity.

The third contradiction in the traditional social system of the Caribbean emerges from the two wings of plantation existence. Amongst the staff, four categories of members are to be distinguished. First of all, there are the lords proprietors who enjoy the proprietary patents and draw their share of the surplus in rent. Secondly, there are the merchant venturers who are the entrepreneurs of the economic system and are well placed to extract their share of the surplus in the form of venture profit. The theory of income distribution of plantation economy shows that the location which the merchants enjoy at the source of imported supplies and at the destination of exports is crucial. Absenteeism confers on them two advantages. Firstly, they can increase their share of the product by taking part of it as head office charges on imports and exports. Secondly, they can switch their investible funds to new terrain whenever profit opportunities dictate that option.

The merchants and the lords proprietors are, therefore, manifestly in a somewhat different position from the planters, and, indeed, from the attorneys involved in the day-to-day management. There rages a running battle between them over the distribution and sharing of surplus. Eric Williams and Douglas Hall have both noted that there was little love lost between them until deteriorating business conditions drove them together very late in the eighteenth century. But even under conditions of collaboration – jointly to urge the case for imperial preference – the attorneys and the planters have markedly different options from those of the lords proprietors and the merchants. In spite of themselves, the former are saddled with some sort of implicit settler interest. In times of crisis, idle capacity takes the form of unemployed labour. They are, therefore, obliged to realise their surplus not in terms of foreign exchange earned in the metropolitan market but in terms of an output of domestic services and even goods available and consumable only within the colonial economy. Here, therefore, is a potent source of conflict amongst the management interests of the plantation economy.

Amongst the inmates equally, there exists a developing cleavage. Edward Kamau Brathwaite has singled out 'domestic slaves, female slaves with white lovers, slaves in contact with missionaries, traders or sailors, skilled slaves anxious to deploy their skills, and above all, urban slaves in contact with the "wider" life'. Doubtless there are powerful forces driving the inmates together; but we cannot always assume that they constitute a single united interest. Depending on issue and situation, the differences in their ambiguities are exceedingly potent. To explain their political behaviour we have no choice but to trace their careers. What we cannot do is to deduce it *a priori* from any given theoretical dissertation. We certainly cannot conclude that there emerges a conflict between the bourgeoisie and the proletariat.

There has never existed any bourgeoisie in the Caribbean. For one thing, there have been no *bourgs* in the region. The *bourgs* and the *faubourgs* which grew up outside the medieval manor and produced St Michel and St Germain, involved a specific cultural and social response to the revival of long-distance trade between the Mediterranean and the maritime countries of Western Europe. Pirenne has carefully established the particular context. The mere ownership of property outside of these cultural conditions does not automatically reproduce a bourgeois conspiracy or a capitalist ethic. Capitalism has arisen from a set of property relations cast in the mould of a given society and culture, blessed or cursed by its own psychology, its own history, its own sense of past and present and future. It, therefore, does not make much sense to me to assume that the mere transposition of European enterprise and European capital into India or Bolivia or the West Indies under widely different cultural, social and psychological conditions, can have produced the capitalist world system that is so highly touted in the literature today.

There does, of course, exist a set of common denominators. But, equally, there exists a set of differentiating factors. It stands to reason that the capitalist world system is a congeries of different hybrid cultures, each resulting differently from penetration by Atlantic enterprise, capital and management into very varied initial conditions. It is sheer arrogance to assume that all of these differing initial conditions have been summarily remade in one individual image. It is sheer ignorance to sweep so many explosive differences under the convenient carpet terminology of 'underdeveloped, Third-World systems'. The so-called problems of underdevelopment in the Caribbean and elsewhere are not problems of underdevelopment at all. They are the consequences of structures and cultures forged by the particular relationships of history but systematically misunderstood in the context of the one-dimensional, nineteenth-century Atlantic analytic paradigm.

The other way of understanding and unravelling the problem of viable development is simply to trace the actual career of these social and cultural systems. From this point of vantage, we are faced in the Caribbean, as we have seen, with first, a historically misplaced region; secondly, a plantation economy; thirdly, a social system both stratified, and fragmented and marked by several levels of conflict, cleavage and contradiction.

PLURAL CULTURE

There is a fourth feature of Caribbean society which needs to be adduced in a factually-based assessment of the region's viability. The factor in question is plural culture which, however, is distinct from M.G. Smith's 'Plural Society'.[2] Here we perceive in culture a dimension separate from that of social order. Cleavages attributable to social differences such as race, colour, religion, economic class, occupation and income level are enhanced by an additional factor. That factor is national, or more properly, ethnic tradition. In other words, what is being evoked is the ancestral aspect of social identity. It is the unconscious element in the consciousness of self and of group. It is more a Freudian than a Marxian dimension, though Marx was clearly groping for it in his attempt to establish ideology as a property inherent in mere being. This ancestral element in the make-up of identity is to be distinguished from what we may call the existential element in the consciousness of self. The latter describes a much more current and, therefore, much more concrete aspect of existence.

It follows that plural culture describes not a given state but a dynamic process of the social system. In the Caribbean this has been true in two separate ways. First of all, the demographic turbulence which is inherent in the patterns of business management and economic adjustment has entailed a repeated in-migration or import of new ethnic formations. In time, it comes to entail a steady outmigration and export of populations with ethnic biases that in important ways govern feedback, but to explore this point here would be too much of a complication.

The pluralisation of culture resulting from demographic instability has been most pronounced in such territories as Trinidad, Guyana, Suriname and Cuba where the plantation emerged as a late developer. The abolition or the diminution of the slave trade, followed by the emancipation of the slaves, had led to a widening of the catchment for plantation labour. The heterogeneity of the population, therefore, took on a higher visibility. But the ethnic diversity had, of course, always been present in the transfer to America of huge multitudes of African servants drawn from different culture areas and put to serve an elite of European managers that was in itself surprisingly heterogeneous. What has happened is that the fact of wide diversity has been masked by historical interpretations which emphasise race and class as against ethnic identification, in response to the dominant paradigm of the North Atlantic.

This first dynamic element in the plural culture of the Caribbean derives, then, from the movement of people. As the sugar economy expands or adjusts, we might say that there is a corresponding movement on the external margin of the population. This is a widening or expansionist tendency, at least in the conditions of the Golden Age. (When gall and wormwood come, the same tendency shows up of course from the negative aspect, i.e. by way of contradiction.) The second dynamic element involves a deepening or an intrinsic tendency. You might say it represents a movement on the internal frontier of population. It is on this second aspect that most of West Indian social theory has focused.

Theorists such as Lloyd Braithwaite and Raymond Smith have tended to perceive interaction of the initially separate ethnic strands as ultimately yielding ground to an overriding pattern of social stratification. In other words, they have emphasised the existential element in social identity under conditions where the lines of interest dividing the managerial elites from the labouring inmates sometimes achieved a caste-like separation. By contrast, other theorists such as M.G. Smith, Leo Despres and Harry Hoetink have tended to stress the ancestral element of group identity thereby projecting an enduring political dissensus.[3]

The view taken here is that both these tendencies represent valid options on first approximation. The historical outcome of the cultural interaction is in no way determinate. As in every concrete situation, it depends on the particular interventions achieved by policy and, therefore, to some extent on the clarity, realism and the relevance attained by theoretical and historical interpretation. From that point of view, stratification theory may or may not have been more helpful than pluralist theory but not because it has been more optimistic or less pessimistic about social dissensus and political violence in Caribbean society. If it has been more powerful, it has been because it has captured more of the ambiguities and the contradictions in the interactions which have been playing themselves out on the internal margin of the Caribbean populations.

From this point of view, the work which perhaps comes closest to capturing and distilling the process of adaptation between initially competing ethnicities in the Caribbean is a work of profound contemplation put out by Edward Kamau Brathwaite under the title *Contradictory Omens*. The focus lies on the many-sidedness of the adjustment pattern by processes formal and informal, conscious and unconscious, involving capitulation as much as confrontation. *Contradictory Omens* improves on the vital distinction offered by Sylvia Wynter between creolisation and indigenisation but it effects this improvement by the device of regarding the two as one single process enjoying, however, a dual aspect.

Here Kamau Brathwaite postulates a colonial arrangement. The society is multi-racial but organised for the benefit of a minority of European origin.

'Creole society' is the result therefore of a complex situation where a colonial polity reacts, as a whole, to external metropolitan pressures and at the same time to internal adjustments made necessary by the juxtaposition of a master and labour, white and non-white, Europe and colony, European and African (mulatto Creole), European and Amerindian (mestizo Creole), in a culturally heterogeneous relationship.[4]

In this process of adaptation, one face presents 'the process of absorption of one culture by another'. This is acculturation. In Sylvia Wynter's meaning, it is simply 'creolisation'. Wynter's other concept, that of 'indigenisation' is equated with 'inter-culturation'. This is the second face to the process of adaptation. It presents 'a more reciprocal activity, a process of intermixture and enrichment, each to each'.[5]

The view of this lecture is that this interpretation could profitably be extended to uncover yet a third face to the process of Caribbean adaptation. It is a face which was somewhat subsumed in Wynter's extremely suggestive if not wholly completed notion of indigenisation. If we allowed it, this third face would acknowledge a deliberate and necessary involvement in insurgency against the process of acculturation. It would recognise a necessary affirmation of selfhood and, therefore, an unyielding if not unflinching resolve to pursue the paths of the subordinated culture by creating sundry repositories of the ancestral or ethnic tradition. This third face might appropriately be termed 'anti-culturation'. In the nature of the case, the activity is insurgent and subversive; it is necessarily illegitimate and, therefore, underground, devious and correspondingly eclectic. The balance of institutional power in both the slave society and the colonial condition – particularly in business and the economy as in government and administration – dictates both an attitude of negation and a concentration in those cultural areas where formal institutions cannot easily penetrate: in the arts, in sport, family life and in folk religion.

It is precisely the placing of this absolute necessity to indulge a cultural insurgency against the background of an institutional powerlessness which made West Indian society the tinderbox it has been throughout its post-Columbus history, as the Moyne Commission noted when reporting the disturbances in the English-speaking islands during the turbulent 1930s. What is more, the combination also explains the tremendous ambivalence in the chosen techniques and methods of subversion, to such a degree that limitation and self-censorship were transformed into some of the most potent forms of cultural insurgency. The plain fact is that, in the particular context, adaption through acculturation, certainly the strategem of calculated acculturation was often the most effective and, therefore, the most menacing form of anti-culturation if only because its end result was to establish the fitness for freedom, in the coloniser's terms, of the subjugated ethnic groups, what Norman Manley used repeatedly to term 'our fitness to rule'.

A methodological problem, therefore, exists here, as much for historians and social scientists as for men of affairs and action. It arises from the fact that the dynamics of plural culture within the specific framework of Caribbean colonial institutions, as distinct from the dynamics of plural culture within, say, North American post-1776 or even pre-1776 colonial institutions, is a process with many nuances. It is a process which cannot be easily fitted into the single-plane, one-dimensional paradigm of social movement which has come to capture the Western (though not so much the non-Western) mind ever since the nineteenth century triumph of materialist political philosophy both in the west of the West and the east of the West.

In the Caribbean, as in so many parts of the 'capitalist world system', there has been no simple historic confrontation of classes. The field has not been so ruthlessly ordered as in eighteenth-century England. The Industrial Revolution precipitated the whole of English society over a veritable cliff of history and took the whole of the Atlantic civilisation along, in the process harnessing huge multitudes of proletarianised labour to the treadmill of urban life, from morning until night, for twelve or fifteen hours a day, six days a week, for a lifetime, from childhood to early and final retirement. The factory environs were so encompassing of proletarian personality that there could be no contradiction between the Freudian and the Marxian dimensions of political psychology. The only surviving contradiction was that which threatened a final and definitive resolution of conflict between capitalist and worker. It was, at least, a plausible hypothesis even if one ultimately devastated by ethnic ambiguity and new national tradition. The workers of the world still believed in 'proud' England and in France and in Bingen-on-the-Rhine. Up to this day they can be persuaded to fight for commissar and king. And yet, capital and labour can be said to have a deep-seated sense of being pitted one against the other in mortal combat.

In the Caribbean, class ambivalence has been for much longer the dominant theme of the system. What has engaged the popular imagination as carrying the seeds of a fight to the finish has always been the jarring clash of ethnic tradition, particularly the clash of Africa and Europe in America. In the nature of the case, the surrounding conditions of economy and society in the region have never permitted a fight to the finish to be anything but an idle daydream. In Saint Domingue and again in Cuba, attempts have been made – from opposite sides – at genocide and at definitive extermination. In the end, the people of the Caribbean came to realise that they had nothing in the world to save but their chains.

The process of creolisation has been marked by upward and downward cycles, both around a trend of inescapable inter-culturation and around a changing pattern of anti-culturation. As Kamau Brathwaite points out, there has been a necessary acculturation of all ethnic groups from Africa, Asia or Europe to their new Caribbean environment. But there has also been an acculturation of black norms to white norms as well as inter-culturation between white norms and black norms. With virtually all the islands save Jamaica and Barbados perpetually in what Williams has called 'a state of betweenity', certain necessary overlapping contexts developed, to use Wilson Harris's felicitous phrase. Overlaps developed as much in relation to what have been regarded as the British, French, Dutch or Hispanic versions of white or European norms as on the relation established between these elite norms and the different African and later Asian ethnic traditions.

The process of creolisation, therefore, has been marked by changes of pace, changes in acceleration, changes in specific ethnic content and changes in specific ethnic proportions. And nowhere, not even in Haiti, has the framework of intercourse been so irretrievably fixed as to anchor the process in viable civic order. There have, therefore, been, in an important sense, as we shall see later on, important changes of social direction, changes brought about by revolutionary or at least fundamental developments, instanced as much from above as below. The Haitian revolution, following on the American and the French revolutions, was one such instance. Emancipation, following on abolition of the slave trade, was another. The post-war accession of Cuba (1959), Santo Domingo (1961) and many of the islands (post-1962) to a new kind of political independence, following on the post-war break up of the Atlantic empire, marks another such watershed in the political record of the island region.

AFRO-SAXON PERSONALITY

It has been a most bewildering movement of modern history. Fortunately, the record of events is so compressed in both historical time and geographical space that it, nevertheless, yields a wide range of extremely graphic concepts which capture its essence. From that point of view, the notion of the Afro-Saxon personality is nothing short of transcendental. In the limiting case of its arithmetic, it describes a mimic-man, an African slave in a bowler hat, manifestly fit to rule on account of his Oxbridge training and Oxford accent. The Afro-Saxon personality, therefore, captures all the absurdity of the Caribbean condition. But as Raymond Smith has remarked, its potency lies precisely in its irony. For when 'Afro-Saxon' translates itself into algebra and becomes a model which embraces the mulatto, the dougla and, indeed, every caricature of the Caribbean hybrid, it suddenly ceases to be absurd and becomes instead that paradigm which discovers the enormous power of generality and simplification and, by cutting through the dense foliage of cultural adjustments, exposes the core of our dilemma with a brutal directness.

This concept of Afro-Saxon personality is not at all loaded. It points clinically to the two basic cultural traditions which have created a mid-Atlantic civilisation, responding out of America to both Africa and Europe, hopelessly torn between two lovers. In the West Indies the European component is Saxon only because England in that case was the source of the European tradition. But the algebra holds good for the whole of the region. And yet, clinical as it is, or perhaps because it is clinical, the concept provokes a vast resentment at different levels.

The Afro-Creole resents it because there is an implicit ranking of the two traditions. Kamau Brathwaite's two mothers – Africa and Europe – are not on par in the initial founding conditions. There exists a hierarchy in which acculturation takes precedence over cultural insurgency. What is more, the great number of ethnic formations involved in the process of creolisation means that there are several different streams of insurgents, all of which are also subject to ranking. As the ethnic catchment widens over time, the later insurgents are forced to adapt not only to the dominant or great 'Saxon' tradition; they are also obliged to adapt to earlier versions of the little 'Afro' tradition.

It is in this sense that there is no such thing as an Indo-Saxon or a Sino-Saxon. The Indians and the Chinese resent having had to adapt to the metropolitan culture which dominated formal existence in the Caribbean; but they resent that less than having had to adapt to the creolised versions of that culture with which they had been endowed by the prior interaction between the African and the European mother traditions. What we have, therefore, is Afro-Saxon but Indo and Sino-Creole. And precisely because acculturation enjoys a higher status than anti-culturation, the Afro-Saxon enjoys a higher ranking than any breed or variant of Creole.

Here again there seem to be some interesting oddities of historical interpretation. It is in precisely those parts of the West Indies where the ambiguities of the creolisation process have been easiest to discern that the apparently simpler models of social stratification have tended to emerge. Lloyd Braithwaite and Raymond Smith have dealt in evidence from the new lands, which after abolition imported comparatively larger amounts of plantation labour, thereby widening their catchment of ethnic traditions. We refer here particularly to Trinidad and Guyana. On the other hand, M.G. Smith made his field observations in Jamaica and Grenada (Carriacou). The latter are the older, more settled and more mature of the colonies, not so marked by demographic turbulence (other than outmigration). They have experienced a much longer process of acculturation, which has come to mask the myriad cross-currents. Yet, it is within the latter context that the plural hypothesis has been most cogently advanced, which is certainly a paradox worth unravelling. To do so, we have only to agree that the obsession with insurgent activity in the form of independent affirmation of ancestral tradition by multiple cultural fragments is itself the evidence for the all-pervasiveness of the tradition according to which the Euro is ranked higher and the Afro (and therefore the Creole) lower in the scale of values.

The theorists of stratification have simply followed through the logic of the creolisation process. They acknowledge that what divides Creole society is a cleavage between those who had been more enmeshed in the process of acculturation from those who had been less enmeshed. In practical terms, the line of cleavage is no more indistinct than that which has forced Marxian and Marxist theory to invent the notion of 'the bourgeoisification of the proletariat'. It is no point denying that although there undoubtedly were uncompromising Maroons at both ends of the spectrum, virtually the whole of the population, in different degrees at different times, has been ambiguously and ambivalently caught up in acculturation as well as insurgency though, inevitably, with different results, depending, as it were, on group and individual life chances.

Where these theorists may have engendered misunderstanding if not confusion was in omitting to concede to the pluralists that Caribbean stratification did not (so much) rank capitalists and workers or the middle and the lower classes. The very notion of middle class in the Caribbean is absurd, since the Ricardian economic model on which class theory is based simply does not apply, there being no history of landlords, capitalists and workers. Even if, therefore, we were to approach the problem by this route, we would have to settle for two classes: upper and lower. But in any event, stratification would rank them only incidentally. What it does rank centrally are ancestral traditions, thereby uncovering specifically Caribbean cleavages and, therefore, providing clues to political parties which may appear to be 'race' parties or 'class' parties but which are really ethnic parties which resolutely exclude race and class kin parading different ethnicity or culture. In other words, in the Caribbean, ethnicity is the vital basis of class, if, for a moment, we were to accept that conventional way of conceptualising the problem. (And it is sometimes useful to be deliberately acculturated to that metropolitan tradition for the simple reason that the act of doing so is an act of identification with the 'little' as against the 'great' metropolitan tradition, thereby constituting an act of insurgency.)

Ethnicity is certainly the most fissionable issue in the region – even in so-called communist Cuba, where Fidel Castro's Africa policy cries out for a domestic explanation as distinct from the facile Atlantic perception of a 'Soviet surrogate pressed into action'. There exists no issue so bearing on the primordial as does ethnicity, none so likely to torpedo civil order and trigger violence. Raymond Smith had a penetrating insight into the matter. In his book, *British Guiana*, he seemed to be hinting that the ultimate source of the violent confrontation then developing in that country might not at all be Dr Jagan's advocacy of 'alien ideology'.[6]

Dr Smith seemed to be saying that the problem lay instead in the accession to political office, under the terms of adult suffrage then current, of a majority group which, against the background of Creole cultural expectation, was infinitely less fit to rule than Mr Burnham's Demerara minority. Here, indeed, was a brilliant insight. The evidence suggests that even Dr Jagan regarded and regards, in a curious kind of way, Mr Burnham as the man most fit to rule Guyana, in terms of the cultural skills the latter undoubtedly commands in the world of the North Atlantic. Perhaps Dr Jagan's communism, which is extremely otherworldly, and enjoys little or no vital life in the practical world of his political constituency, is largely another act of identification with the 'little tradition' of the North Atlantic and therefore a symbolic act of anti-culturation.

It is, therefore, unfortunate that Dr Smith's insight was not systematically pursued to its logical conclusion. It could provide clues to the working of the political system further afield in the Caribbean than British Guiana. The processes of land acquisition, escape to the city, churching and schooling, as well as the whole thrust towards 'fitness to rule' evident in later days of slave society and which have been described by Elsa Goveia, and which increasingly featured in post-emancipation society as described by a growing number of historians including Sewell, Hall, Wood, Eisner, Brereton and Marshall, have undoubtedly provided a basis for political division of Caribbean society even while developing a central Creole civilisation and Afro-Saxon culture.[7] It should not have to be repeated that here alone in this social history, before and after abolition, can we find the clues to our present day political prospects.

DOCTOR POLITICS

We must now turn to the political underpinnings of Caribbean society. The fifth and final feature of Caribbean society is the prevalence of what I have described in the Trinidad and Tobago context as 'doctor politics'.[8] In terms of the political algebra of the region, we are focusing here on the all-pervasive caudillo figures, the 'maximum leaders', who are called upon to play a transcendental role. To my mind, the continuing domination of the Caribbean political system by these single individuals is a much more important phenomenon than the emergence, in recent years, of so-called ideological diversity.

Left or Right, communist or capitalist, these strong figures arise to cross the frontiers of ideology and language and constitutional arrangement. In spite of the rich variety of window dressing, there may well be a cord which binds Gomez, Machado, Jiminez, Batista, Trujillo, Duvalier, Munoz Marin, Bustamante, Manley Senior, Bradshaw, Williams, Burnham, Jagan, Bird, *et al.*, into a single political tradition. If there is any merit in this hypothesis, we cannot simply be satisfied with the view that there is something askew with Caribbean man or with Caribbean political leaders. We cannot accept the facile political assertion that in Georgetown and Kingston, Havana, Santo Domingo and Port au Prince, there has been an over-endowment of king-sized political ambition. Rather, we must pose the question whether there might not be certain common underlying conditions which explain the recurrence of doctor politics almost everywhere in the region, even if we are forced to distinguish, as this observer has done elsewhere, between public school, grammar school, Sunday school and army school doctors.

No, the evidence suggests that you have large political ambitions in every part of the world. What we also have in the Caribbean is a new and unsettled social order and a plural culture. The perpetual movement of labour from diverse ethnic catchments has inevitably left behind community structures that are palpably weak. In this context, the political system is desperately short of the means of organisation. It is hard put to distil intelligence and to canvass opinion. It encounters extreme difficulty in elaborating community plans and in establishing machinery for collective action. The result is that crisis mobilisation tends to become a necessary substitute for long-term organisation. Leadership, therefore, emerges less as instrument and more as symbol. In the context, the theatre of political authority assumes more than usual meaning and the most enduringly charismatic candidates are necessarily those who add instrumental capacity to theatrical command.

This highly personalised and, therefore, centralised mode of political leadership is dictated equally by the corollary of weak community structures; which is to say, by external dependence or, in the extreme case, external domination. The Caribbean has been one of the most complete illustrations of the pure case of what Singham has described as a 'subordinate political system', not merely dependent on or dominated by the external world but actually deriving its legitimacy from an imperial centre.[9] Whether government was the military government established at acquisition through cession or conquest, or the planter governments which emerged in the eighteenth century to speak for the interest of the management elites, or indeed, the Crown colony governments deliberately instituted in the West Indies during the nineteenth century to govern from outside and above, political authority in the Caribbean has traditionally been devoid of any base in valid community support. In that context, even where such community support does appear, the choice of leadership tends to be disciplined by the demands of external negotiation. This is perhaps another way of saying that, quite apart from its subordinacy to metropolitan government under conditions of actual colonialism or informal supervision, the primacy of external transactions in the plantation economy, reinforced by the exceeding external exposure of small island states, exercises a definite impact on leadership patterns. Even in comparatively self-sufficient states, policy has shown a tendency to become bi-partisan and authority to become 'imperial', the better to admit expeditious and consistent central decision. This tendency is redoubled in the Caribbean. Doctor politics, whatever else it may mirror, must also be clinically regarded as one practical response to peculiar conditions.

There is another sense in which the personalisation of power is best taken as a response to the demands of external negotiation. In this case, what is at issue is not policy foreign to country but policy foreign to party. Cleavages, we have urged, are mainly ethnic and ancestral rather than existential. Parties, therefore, like leaders, are more symbolic in their substance than they are instrumental. They exist more for what they are and what they stand for than for what they do or are able to achieve. Their importance to the difficult task of mobilisation in a fragmented political community is much greater than it is in that of managing the affairs of the state. They are typically more adept at electioneering and campaigning than they are at government and administration. This also is a self-perpetuating condition. The lack of experience of responsibility provides a context congenial to the breeding of irresponsibility and, therefore, a continuing predominance of symbol over instrument. So, the whole of the polity poses a greater challenge by far to political management than could ever be posed by the sum of its parts.

Some of the corollaries here should be made explicit. We have implied that the political managers who tend to be selected are only incidentally those whose skills are addressed to the requirements of government. This is what sets up pressures, by what seems to be an invisible hand, to create informal structures parallel to and, therefore, subversive of the formal agencies of state and society. It helps to explain cases where appointed houses and nominated members are called upon to play a disproportionate part in relation to elected houses and elected members; where handpicked task forces replace bona fide functionaries of the Civil Service and where the processes of informing and instructing the executive by validly elected parliamentary representatives are replaced by *ad hoc* and semi-formal consultations and similar assemblies, all invariably distinguished for being instruments of controlled participation by the chief executive.

Such an authority and a responsibility then devolves on the maximum leader that even if he were genuinely polyvalent he would still not be able to cope with the impossible burden. The only choice left is now to invent a superhuman leader, larger than life. This explains in part the developing delusions of caudillo or charismatic politics, *The Autumn of the Patriarch*, to borrow the title of Gabriel Garcia Marquez' magnificent novel about Caribbean dictatorship.

The syndrome is once more self-perpetuating. In the context, all informal alignment and formal voting, whether legislative, municipal, cantonal or other, necessarily becomes uncompromisingly presidential. The electors cannot but opt for the man or against the man. There is no other issue of policy, programme or plan; nothing else matters but the maximum leader. It follows that the supporting cast become less and less likely to be the standardbearers of expertise. Institutional incapacity then becomes institutionalised for good, and all processes need to become progressively more informal if any tasks at all are to be accomplished. The ultimate absurdity is achieved when the process is pushed so far that the political system becomes locked into a world of total delusion, with a universally lionised leader who not only does not but need not deliver anything save chaos but whose survival in the transcendental role must be made to persist even after his death. The cost of returning to reality is even more prohibitive than that of continuing to inhabit the world of sustained and deliberate delusion.

The contemporary Caribbean is not without examples of this situation, a factor which will need to be carefully weighed in assessing its viability. It is worth repeating that this factor is likely to be much more potent than the development of so-called ideological diversity. But it also enjoys relevance to a field much wider than the Caribbean. The thesis here is that this mode of politics does not arise by accident but arises from a disjunction of structure in society and culture. It is, therefore, to be wondered how much real difference exists between the so-called underdeveloped countries marked by the ascendancy of personal power and the so-called developed ones featured more and more by a brand of politics centred on charismatic iron leaders. What is there to be discerned about the underlying structures in these metropolitan societies? Might it not be that the politics as well as the economics of underdevelopment can be achieved at any level of machine technology and income? If so, we are obliged to pose the question as to whether those Atlantic countries whose structures have been highly specialised in the domination of empire can be much better placed than those which have been specialised at the other end of the tandem – in subordination to empire – but which have been summarily cut loose in the few heady years since India broke away in 1947.

VIABILITY?

Misplaced region, plantation economy, fragmented society, plural culture and doctor politics, all revolving around the Afro-Saxon personality: these are some of the elements of a theory of Caribbean society. They set out some of the main ingredients with which to embark on a more valid historical interpretation of the region's viability. They offer a background against which to evaluate what might be the critical events and what the crucial moments. In this latter regard, the accession to new forms of freedom which, as we have noted, began with the Cuban revolution, was advanced by the fall of Trujillo and was then pursued through the independence of Jamaica as the first of a series of similar developments in the Dutch and British territories, marks a manifest watershed in the evolution of the record.

What it marks is the culmination of a process the start of which might be dated, in the case of the West Indies, from about the middle 1880s when the walls of Crown colony government were breached in Jamaica with the turn to representative government and with that, the opening of the gate to more responsible forms of government. On the way to adult suffrage and full self-government, in Kingston in 1944 and then in Port of Spain in 1946 and in most other capitals thereafter, the first ever general elections in 1925 to the Legislative Council in Trinidad (not Tobago), the model Crown colony, represents another important date following on the Wood Commission. By acknowledging that government needed to be anchored in the home community, the elections, limited as was the franchise, constituted a definite attack on the subordinate political system, unleashing repercussions that we may still be experiencing.

In other terms, the Caribbean did not begin in the year 1982 with the grandiose announcement of the Caribbean Basin Initiative. Nor did it begin in 1917, which opened the possibility of the current 'ideological diversification'. It did not even begin with emancipation in the middle nineteenth century, which in importance stands on a par with independence in the middle twentieth century. If the latter put an end to colonialism, the former put an end to slavery. Both events vastly changed the options. Indeed they both altered the ranking of priorities in the creolisation process, in the terms which we have already discussed. Emancipation, paradoxically, increased the premium on strategic acculturation. It definitely enhanced the prospect of successfully beating the system by capitulating to it. Independence, however, made that strategy completely obsolete. In contrast, it emphasised the value of cultural insurgence. No longer was it necessary to establish a fitness to rule, in the terms of the coloniser. The problem of the succession, therefore, expressed itself not in the affirmation of the Creole condition but in asserting a certain distance and a careful difference from it. While emancipation strengthened centripetal forces, independence released centrifugal ones. The pluralists were right but it was not simply that metropolitan might and power withdrew and left a vacuum in plural society, but that the contradictions of the plural culture were an autonomous source of confusion.

It ought not at all to be surprising that independence legitimated 'black power' all over the West Indies. In a society bred to dependence on metropolitan fashion, the legitimation first required the long hot summers of civil rights agitation in the United States of America, with all of its international news coverage and its television images. And yet, as Gordon Rohlehr has insisted, the assertion of an insurgent position fed not on imported but on internal sources of anxiety. This lecturer suspects that we have not yet been privileged to live to the very end of the story. Certainly, the escalation of an otherwise puzzling violence in Jamaica during the second half of the 1970s is very much a sequel.

The orthodox interpretation of the last days of Michael Manley's People's National Party administration adduces an ideological confrontation between conservative, North American backed, liberal democracy, espousing Caribbean basin capitalism, on the one hand, and on the other, a radicalising, communist and Castro-supported social democracy, on the way to socialism. This, however, is little more than mindless Mickey Mouse rhetoric, with little grounding in the world of empirical facts. Neither capitalism nor socialism has enjoyed any footing in Jamaica. All the evidence suggests that Norman Manley introduced merely the symbolism of socialism as part of the entirely valid strategy of capitulation when the PNP was formed under the distinguished patronage of Sir Stafford Cripps. The moment socialism arose as a policy option, it was summarily abandoned and the three celebrated Hs (Hill, Hart, Henry) were expelled from the ranks of the party. They were sidelined for the very good reason that the modalities of socialist reconstruction, with its emphasis on nationalisation and co-operatives and procedures that emerged from the Western European experience, do not respond to the perceptions which Jamaicans and West Indians have of necessary collective action. Norman Manley was wise enough to appreciate that it would be sheer folly to turn the sugar industry over to co-operatives owned and run by the workers. He probably sensed that what was needed was a form of 'morning sport', that is to say, an ancestral reference in collaborative endeavour, known and understood by the population and, therefore, capable of inciting them to work together for the general good in the existential situation of the contemporary Indies. In the context, he had no such practical proposals on offer. The intellectuals in his milieu had failed to distil and to deliver any kind of praxis relevant to the region. The whole basis of their legitimacy lay in their ability to master bookish concepts in the coloniser's idiom. The founder of the PNP died still a sane and serious man, capable of more than token sacrifices. He died in search of another vision, one based on a different moral insight into his own and Jamaica's particular condition.

Such a vision would offer an alternative to the orthodox interpretation of the sequel to Norman Manley, which played itself out in terms of the hopes and the disappointments of the critical 1970s. It would notice that the two traditions formed by the creolisation process had been pushed by events into a certain polarisation. The alignments had been there all along, separating those who had been more fully caught up in the idiom of the coloniser from those less fully or only minimally so involved. On the whole, Mr Bustamante and the Jamaica Labour Party represented the latter. The constituency included both white and black, both the very rich and the very poor, mainly people beyond the portals of schooling and feeling less pressure or less need to acculturate to the dominant tradition. Norman Manley and the PNP represented the other constituency, drawn mainly from the middle or intermediate ranks of society, intermediate by colour, occupation and income but above all, most torn by the ambiguities of option. It is precisely the ambivalence of this group which prevented any inflexible polarisation and rendered possible several times over the alternation in office of the two political parties. What may have triggered the polarisation and the hardening of position was the change in the ranking of the two traditions brought on by the advent of independence.

The PNP had come to office in 1972 not merely on the normal swing of the pendulum. More significantly, its leadership had also understood how – in the new dispensation – black power had become not only fashionable but potent, even explosive. The language, the style, the conceptualisation and the historic intentions of the Maroon had suddenly come of age, particularly in its Rastafarian version which had somehow discovered, in its reggae and ganja culture, the software of an international significance. All the campaign resources of the PNP were assiduously addressed to the capture of this constituency which, by 1976, delivered a colossal landslide victory in the general elections.

The contradiction lay in the fact that the PNP at its core was, in conventional terms, the party most fit to rule while its leader, more perhaps than any figure in the entire West Indies, was regionally regarded as having the most complete command of the relevant idiom. Michael Manley had 'emerged from the appropriate stable; he was a thoroughbred of West Indian culture; he looked right, spoke right and was right'. That is how one distinguished commentator from the University of the West Indies once put it in a private interview with this lecturer. The view was universally shared in the Caribbean.

It seems to follow that the origins of the subsequent crisis must have been in the fact that the black power revival was led by a group the premises of which had always been more or less the negation of cultural insurgency. The conflict moreover was more than symbolic. In instrumental terms, it expressed itself in a total incapacity of the PNP government to devise practical policies responding to the perceptions and the capacities of the people it was leading. The relevance of the whole pattern of leadership formation in Jamaica (and the West Indies) was subjected to the test of practicality by a hugely legitimated administration, vastly supported and enjoying every opportunity to transform the society. The resulting programme of action can only be described as tragically amateur.

When the cadres of the party needed to address the complex realities of the Jamaican economy, they could nowhere find the rigour and the resolve to abandon symbolic rhetoric. Destabilisation was ritually adduced as a major factor, coupled with the constraints of the old international economic order and capitalist wickedness. Little or no attempt was made to locate the crisis in the currents of the domestic cultural tradition and to situate the exceptional violence of the response in autonomous frustrations having little to do with Cold War politics. To the end, the PNP intellectuals continued to respect the dominance of the great tradition. By far the smaller part of the story is that many of them physically retreated to other countries and situations. The larger part lies in an all-pervasive psychological retreat from reality into a world of endless declamation, particularly by those who remained at the centre. There was not even a serious fight over the leadership of the movement, even though doctor politics was delivering encompassing chaos.

This failure to adduce an algebra capable of making sense of contemporary developments has not affected Jamaica alone or even Jamaica principally. The other explosive illustration of the bankruptcy of the conventional paradigm comes from the record of events in Trinidad and Tobago. In that country, one party will have remained in office for thirty unbroken years, if it arrives safely at 1986. The orthodox explanation adduces the magical properties of the founder of the ruling party, the incompetence of the opposition, the backwardness of the population, the flood of petro-dollars, the failure to found a socialist party and every manner of escapist analysis except one that locates the functioning of the system in the context of the inherited ethnic structures. The consequence here too has been the survival of doctor politics in its most absurd incarnation. The country had become so locked into worship of the virtue of the maximum leader that on his disappearance the only possible candidate for the succession was the minimum leader.

I am happy to be able to say here and now that, fully two clear years before the succession, we were able to provide an exact account of the subsequent scenario. Needless to say, we are not by this revelation aiming to ascribe or attribute the gift of prophecy. What we are pointing to is an aid to judgment, which in the case of Trinidad and Tobago is to be found by acknowledging that there is a framework of some nine ethnicities which explain much of the apparently absurd life of the political system and its constituent parties. We have elsewhere attempted to elaborate the features of this framework. What we insist on here, by way of closure, is that there can be no substitute for independent thinking. More than fifteen years ago, this lecturer made the case for independent thought as the major ingredient in Caribbean freedom. He offers no apology for today's restatement of the case in a different version.

Notes

1. This is a drastically revised and shortened version of the public lecture originally delivered at the University of Hull.
2. M.G. Smith, *The Plural Society in the British West Indies* (Berkeley: University of California Press, 1965).
3. See, for example, Lloyd Braithwaite, 'Race Relations and the Industrialization in the Caribbean,' in Industrialization and Race Relations, ed. G. Hunter (London: Oxford University Press, 1965); Raymond Smith, 'Social Stratification, Cultural Pluralism and Integration in West Indian Societies,' in *Caribbean Integration*, ed. S. Lewis and T.G. Mathews (Rio Piedras, 1967); M.G. Smith, op. cit.; Leo Depres, *Cultural Pluralism and Nationalist Politics in British Guyana* (Chicago: Rand McNally, 1967); Hermannus Hoetink, *The Two Variants in Caribbean Race Relations* (London: Oxford University Press, 1967).
4. E.K. Brathwaite, *Contradictory Omens* (Mona, Jamaica: Savacou Publications, 1974), 10–11.
5. Sylvia Wynter, 'Jonkonnu in Jamaica: Towards the Interpretation of Folk Dance as a Cultural Process,' *Jamaica Journal*, June 1970, 34–48. On 'inter-culturation,' see Brathwaite, 52–55.
6. Raymond Smith, *British Guiana* (London: Oxford University Press, 1962).
7. Elsa Goveia, *Slave Society in the British Leeward Islands at the End of the Eighteenth Century* (New Haven: Yale University Press, 1965); Donald Wood, *Trinidad in Transition: The Years After Slavery* (London: Oxford University Press, 1968); Gisela Eisner, *Jamaica 1830-1930: A Study in Economic Growth* (Manchester: Manchester University Press, 1961); Douglas G. Hall, *Free Jamaica, 1838-1865: An Economic History* (New Haven: Yale University Press, 1959); William Grant Sewell, *The Ordeal of Free Labour in the West Indies* (New York, 1861); Bridget Brereton, *Race Relations in Colonial Trinidad, 1870-1900* (Cambridge: Cambridge University Press, 1979); Woodville K. Marshall, 'Notes on Peasant Development in the West Indies since 1838,' *Social and Economic Studies,* vol. 17, (1968): 252–63. Also by Woodville Marshall 'Aspects of the Development of the Peasants,' *Caribbean Quarterly,* vol. 1 and no. 1, 1972; 'A Review of Historical Writing on the Commonwealth Caribbean since 1940,' *Social and Economic Studies*, vol. 2 and no. 3, 1975.
8. On 'doctor politics,' *Trinidad Express*, 31 May 1969 and early issues of *Tapia*.
9. A.W. Singham, *The Hero and the Crowd in a Colonial Polity* (New Haven: Yale University Press, 1968).

Cultural Identity and the Arts –
New Horizons for Caribbean Social Sciences?

Rex Nettleford

The Historical Dimension

The organic relationship between cultural identity and artistic creation has long been known to be a significant phenomenon in the shaping of modern Caribbean society. The Hispanic wing of that fragmented disparate family of rocks and mainland out-posts recently designated the 'Caribbean Basin' on the agenda of hegemonic geopolitics, has long recognised the importance of arts and culture in forging their national and cultural identities, possibly because they broke with their historical imperial master much earlier than the Afro-Saxon wing of the region. Francophone Caribbean, with the exception of Haiti, remains politically the ward of its mother country but culturally yearns for its Caribbean reality following on that now historic return to his native country by the artist armed with the reassurance of negritude as well-spring for poetic expression and political consciousness.[1]

The West Indies, alias Anglophone Caribbean and also known as the Commonwealth Caribbean (this part of the region still carries a plurality of designation, matching the internal plurality of self-perceptions) came only recently to political independence. Its pedigree in the struggle for freedom and rehumanisation on the part of the majority of the population, however, dates back almost to the beginning of the era of Caribbean history that followed on the fateful encounter of the Old Worlds of Europe and Africa on the one hand with the ancient civilisations of the Americas on the other. The stage was therefore set very early for the quest for self-definition in what came to be a-historically labelled the New World. It was not 'new' to the indigenous peoples, many of whom disappeared after the contact with the *newcomers*. It was 'new' to the strangers comprising conquerors and vanquished, torturers and victims, enslavers and enslaved. The opposition of one category of inhabitants to another compounded the issue of identity within the context of political and cultural power play. Cultural identity was therefore a part of the genesis and the subsequent nurturing of an entire hemisphere. In this sense the contemporary United States and Latin America are no different from the Caribbean. Only that as part of the hemisphere the Caribbean of necessity approached the issue from the specificity of its own experience; and it is that specificity that has fed the creative vision, artistic sensibility and aesthetic energy of the region.

It is significant that the topic 'Cultural Identity and the Arts' should have been seen as a legitimate item on the agenda of a Conference on 'New Perspectives in Caribbean Studies' organised by Vera Rubin in 1984 to discover, articulate and define new and/or appropriate frameworks of Caribbean studies following on a quarter of a century and more of conscious observation, analysis and projection of the region's political, social and economic dynamic and potential.[2] The initiative speaks to a reality of Caribbean existence which forces out of many who have been trained in the hallowed, if still insecure, tradition of scientific non-normative social sciences, recognition of the fact that the arts, as products of the creative imagination, are as fundamental to the understanding of human society as are national income and GNP statistics, voter opinion scientifically polled and quantified, economic integration formulae, technology transfer options, and development theories encased in often different and opposing imported ideological frameworks.

No less attention must be paid to finding the pertinent, appropriate analytical tools or methodological devices to get to the heart of the region's cultural dynamics so that the Caribbean's contemporary life and projected future can benefit from the fruits of such acts of intelligence which describe the nature of artistic activity as they do scientific/intellectual activity. The two forms of creativity were never mutually exclusive as M.G. Smith who was poet before he was sociologist and Kamau Brathwaite who remains both poet and historian would affirm.[3] One could hazard the guess that the social sciences in the Caribbean would benefit considerably if more of its practitioners were better informed by the arts of the imagination, not least among which is numbered the study of the history of the region. The economist Arthur Lewis brought welcome insights to the issue of West Indian culture and identity in a characteristically provocative article published in the Law Journal.[4] The call by Wilson Harris,[5] as visiting artist to the UWI many years ago, spoke eloquently to the need for greater correspondence between intellectual activity and the arts of the imagination in support of his theory of the essential unity of man, with the Caribbean man as archetype – being a synthesis of ancestral Amerindian, African and European sensibilities.

The inclusion of the subject in a social science seminar admits, then, the centrality of the artist *qua* artist to modern Caribbean development in particular and generally to the shaping of new societies in their quest for new designs for social living – a quest which follows on the shifts of bases of power from colonialism to independence, from the orderly and predictable world of imperial domination to the post-colonial order threatening disintegration and disorder. If the study of the Rastafarian movement is considered proper for a social science faculty as part of the received intellectual concerns about cargo cults, redemption ethic and the like, it is no less appropriate for the faculty to engage in serious content analysis of the lyrics of Bob Marley as a guide to a fuller grasp of ghetto values, urban concerns and preoccupations among the marginalised poor. Social commentary by the calypsonians of the society's reaction to national policies, capitalism gone mad, political authority, or the self-importance of the native inheritors of the colonial power is a form of action – expressed through art – that addresses problems of self-definition and gives critical clues about a people's perceptions of themselves. These in turn can inform public policy and often do so more appropriately than the decisions arbitrarily taken for the people by political directorates and their planning advisers or the answers cleverly crafted by informants in response to cleverly crafted survey questionnaires of field researchers. Such scientific devices are useful and necessary in a modern state, but the other devices usually associated with artistic discovery and sometimes shared by anthropologists are no less so.

One or two Commonwealth Caribbean founding fathers (in the political sense) understood the centrality of the artist to the self-government ideal and sought to appropriate the work of artists without denying to artistic action its own inner logic and consistency. Even in post-revolutionary Cuba where the ethos of the new dispensation reputedly gave to the artist everything within the revolution while denying him all outside of it, the artist has managed to flourish independently sometimes with more traces of 'bourgeois' culture than the guardians of the revolution would care to admit. In the English-speaking Caribbean, the independence of the artist went hand in hand with notions of democratic freedoms. Therefore Norman Manley of Jamaica had, in his political credo, a central place for the unfettered exercise of the creative imagination, the sort of process in which artists are involved. He saw nation-building itself not only as an act of intelligence but also as the work of an artist giving form to substance and grappling with the reality of human experience to take everyday existence to higher levels of civilised expression (the nation, democracy, civilisation).[6]

He even declared (informally) George Campbell the poet of Jamaica's self-government 'revolution' as Nicolas Guillen was to become for Cuba's transformation. However the nature of art does not always depend for its flourishing on such patronage. The common people whose music, dance, theatre and oral literature rank them among the greatest of artists in the region, are able to continue in their myriad acts of creativity under all sorts of adverse conditions. More than that, they provide individual talents with a vital source of energy, thus giving to the region groups of creative artists in a wide range of artistic activity that has served to promise the Caribbean (or individual parts of it) greater cultural certitude, sense of form and sense of purpose.

Foremost among such artists have been the writers – literate, healthily schizophrenic, insightful, and truly among the first to explain formally the Caribbean to itself, whether in the printed poem, novel or short story. George Lamming, a virtual dean of the corps, made early claims for the primacy of the writer as animateur, philosopher and guide to West Indian civilisation. The creative musician, choreographer, painter, sculptor were to follow in the writer's wake, some of them helped not a little by the improved technologies of communication, especially the electronic media and recording industry as well as the aeroplane facilitating the travel of artists and artworks within the Caribbean to Caribbean Festivals of Art (Carifestas) and outside the region on commercial or government-to-government cultural exchange tours.[7]

The Arts and Caribbean Social Reality

The notion that all art is mediated by social reality is not a monopoly of the Marxist intellectual tradition which has been presented as an option in the region's earnest search for solutions. Rather it is borne out by the facts of the Caribbean literary creative impulse. This is so whether the declared aim of this or that writer is to be a *writer* rather than a *Caribbean* writer or to belong primarily to a 'tradition of the writer's craft; a tradition that overrides ethnic and social distinctions'.[8] The truth is that none of these writers has been able to ignore the real-life issues of history (Caribbean history), race, colonialism, the plantation, neo-colonialism, social change, identity (national and cultural), linguistic loyalty to Europe's imposed standards of life and the awesome hold such standards have even on artists who are rebelling. Nor can they ignore Africa-in-the-Americas, the crucible in which much of what is artistically and culturally *Caribbean* was forged over four centuries of creolisation.

Somehow it is understood that Mother Europe needs fewer carbon copies of Shakespeare, Molière, Conrad, or Marlowe; Brahms, Beethoven or Mahler; Picasso, Van Gogh or Renoir; Petipa, Balanchine or Bournonville. She would rather settle for the original impulse of foreign artists encouraged to enrich her soil. Walcott and Naipaul are of interest to the North Atlantic precisely because they are not only good writers but writers with something unique to say about the human condition; and where they come from and how they were socialised and bred just happen to give that something a special pitch and tone of importance and relevance to a North Atlantic world, itself in search of new patterns and new designs for its continuing existence. The pretence that it is otherwise, is part of the self-parody of Caribbean artists playing others instead of being themselves.

Novels, poems, short stories, literary criticism, and plays are indeed laced with 'Caribbean pre-occupations even if notions of the writer's tradition', 'mainstream literature', or the 'humanist tradition' are considered the more desirable (and respectable) ends of artistic creation transcending, presumably, the insularity of regions or the provincialism of race and ethnic considerations. What a closer look at Caribbean artistic creation serving cultural identity may indeed demonstrate is that the so-called 'writer's tradition' *et al* is likely to be the richer for the textured and specific contributions by Caribbean artistic infusions.

The names of George Lamming, Wilson Harris, Jean Rhys, John Hearne, Derek Walcott and V.S. Naipaul – all creatures of the colonial Caribbean – have gained fairly widespread recognition in the North Atlantic. However, studies of serious world literature would also be the poorer without the names of Edward Kamau Brathwaite, Victor Reid, Martin Carter, Andrew Salkey and Samuel Selvon, to name but a few. The vigour of the creolised indigenous Caribbean languages must in any case determine their own criteria of judgement for artistic excellence and universal verities, and so the lyrics of the calypsonians and reggae artists (Marley's 'Redemption Song', Jimmy Cliff's 'Many Rivers to Cross' do address universal verities in poetry), the verse of Louise Bennett, as well as the utterances of latter-day Jamaican dub poets,[9] to whom writing down is secondary to oral-rendering, all challenge the arbiters of Caribbean artistic legitimacy to new perceptions of reality in the region.

Many of the world's great artists 'steal' as a matter of course from the past, if for no other reason than the past offers mankind many of the greatest that is tried and tested in the profession of art.[10] Even in this, many a Caribbean artist has a problem. For the past from which they choose to steal does not often include their own Caribbean past either in its intensely creolised (native-born, native-bred) sense or in respect of that part of the past which spells Africa. On the other hand, that part which spells Europe, from the ancient Mediterranean to 19th century England and its extension into Anglo-Saxon contemporary United States, all have ready and willing imitators. Furthermore latecomers India, China and Lebanon are yet to count in any deep cultural sense to those who consider themselves to possess greater *Caribbean* ancestral pedigree – what with the conflict between the earlier arrivants to the Caribbean yet to be resolved.

It may well be remembered that at least one major Caribbean artist has volunteered a justification for the neglect on the basis that there is no Caribbean history, since history is about achievement and achievement has to do with creating.[11] Having created nothing, the region has achieved nothing. In effect, the place is in the long run incapable of development, cultural identity or any meaningful growth. V.S. Naipaul's 'castrated metaphor', to use Lamming's deliciously wicked phrase, need not be seen as anything more than a rhetorical excess spat out at a society that admittedly denies too many of its citizens a sense of place and purpose. Naipaul, for all his frustrations, is nonetheless a 'creation' of that very society, and a brilliant one at that. The myth he articulated persists, however, in pockets of cynicism and cultural perversity.

Happily it is being exploded by the active creative power and brilliance of not only writers but also painters, sculptors, dancers and musicians all over the region. The creators of the Cuban *son, mambo* and *rhumba,* the devastatingly observant calypsonians of Trinidad and the Eastern Caribbean, the Rastafarian-inspired reggae composers from urban ghettos of Kingston have all 'stolen' from the past – their own past. They draw naturally on the wealth of that past ancestral certitude and wisdom to create for the modern Caribbean still in search of itself. They entertain no inhibiting doubts about the pedigree of their own history both in the Caribbean and before the severance of forefathers from far-off homelands. Although they are conscious of the brutality of suffering in that history, they are no less aware of the achievement in terms of creative acts by their forbears-in-exile, whether in the devising of new tongues to communicate with each other, in shaping the right music, movement patterns and belief-systems into ordered rituals of worship, or in the creation of operational frameworks for daily living despite every well planned effort to keep the majority population barely ahead of the beasts. Without being academic historian or sociologist of history, the Caribbean's popular artist, like some of his prestigious writer-colleagues, effectively uses the facts of history, in all their essence, both to interpret modern Caribbean society and to inform contemporary Caribbean life. A past without achievement could not have done any of this, unless of course such acts of the creative imagination and intellect as described are not seen as genuine acts of achievement.

The evidence, indeed, demonstrates that the Caribbean with its record of creative acts can help to determine a mainstream culture rather than be expected merely to enter one that is predetermined by the cultural norms forged and recorded (i.e. in written or notated form) over centuries in the nations that conquered, colonised and conditioned subject peoples like those who still inhabit the Caribbean. In overcoming the consequences of such conditioning, as a function of cultural identity or self-definition, the artists from among such peoples need to speak to each other *within* the region rather than continue to communicate through a connexion hooked up in London, Madrid, Paris or of late New York. If a Lamming once had to discover himself in London and an Aime Cesaire needed Paris to see the light, it has long become critical to examine and take seriously the discoveries on homeground. Derek Walcott (for all his latter-day New England encounters)[12] and, to a certain extent, Edward K. Brathwaite represent something of the new breed. In addition the return home (physically and mentally) of Lamming and others is important to the grasp of the import of the issue of identity through artistic creation and cultural action. The Alejo Carpentiers and Nicolas Guillens stand out as homegrown icons not only for post-revolutionary Cuba but for an emerging culturally coherent Caribbean as well. The popular artists of the ilk of The Mighty Sparrow of Trinidad or of Jimmy Cliff and the late Bob Marley of Jamaica have had no problems being homegrown *Caribbean* artists, secure as they have been in the knowledge that the wider world beyond the North Atlantic does provide profitable and appreciative markets for their work. They were, all three, 'heroes' at home before they were recognised abroad – in direct contrast to most of the earlier Caribbean writers who sought legitimacy and recognition, if not identity, from the metropolitan centres of the North. The increased cultural awareness among Anglophone Caribbean people following on the transfer of imperial power to the region has facilitated greater access to legitimacy and recognition at home on criteria rooted in Caribbean reality. From this, 'schools' of painters, sculptors, choreographers, playwrights, and poets as well as creative intellectuals have benefitted not a little since the late 1950s.

The remarkable impact of Caribbean artist-musicians on the wider world with seemingly minimal concessions to the cultural dictates of the Establishment prejudices of Western civilisation throws into sharp relief questions about the market for, and the nature of, Caribbean writing. Could it be that writing as an art carries with it greater burdens of alienation than do other artforms? Publishing and printing facilities are admittedly either still rare or expensive in the region, yet more exist now than before and in any case the difficulties of publishing abroad while writing from homebase have been largely overcome.

The question of 'the market' cannot however be ignored. Who does the Caribbean writer really write for? Does he write for the Caribbean readership still growing but yet to offer that critical mass which brings profits? Is he addressing the more affluent North American suburban class or the intelligentsia now in the throes of discovering a Walcott and a Naipaul? Does he write for the British literati with a long tradition of playing patron to sibling talents from the outposts of Empire? Furthermore, what of the new governing elites of the developing world, many of whom are admittedly blasé before they are civilised? Better still, does the Caribbean writer write for the proverbial homogenised world devoid of class, ethnic, or cultural particularities? Or does he write for himself? Many of the performing artists, because their art needs an immediate audience, do sing, dance and act for their own people first, and for others secondarily. Can the literary arts, then, be regarded as the most appropriate for people who have been brought up in a strongly oral tradition against which has been counterpoised the scribal writ as part of a colonial conditioning?

Richard Dwyer[13] felt no fear of contradiction when he wrote that 'all of them [meaning Caribbean writers] know that to want to *write* at all is to claim citizenship in a world elsewhere'. Can this be true, fair or reasonable in the contemporary world of the Caribbean which has conceded the necessity of Gutenberg and is even now in fear of the penetrative power of the aural and visual fare offered by the electronic media through television, video and radio? The choreographer, the music composer, the painter, the sculptor are all constantly bombarded with reminders of the superiority of European classical dance-theatre, of Beethoven's 'unsurpassable' symphonies, of the rightness of perspective and use of colour in a Titian or a Rembrandt, and of the perfection of Greek statuary. These artists are no less vulnerable than the writer threatened with being an alien in his own Caribbean homeland. Even the 'rootsy' popular artist must come to terms with a Michael Jackson or a Lionel Richie, to name just two of the 'pop' influences of the 1980s that have demonstrated the all-pervasive power of American satellite transmission.

The Caribbean is now challenged to fall back on the inner reserves of its own historical experience and cultural dynamic in order to exist on its own terms, which is partly what cultural identity is about.[14] The experience is indeed instructive in such fields as music, dance, painting and sculpture as well as in many of the artistic expressions associated with religious rituals, masquerade and Carnival.[15] A great many, if not most, of the artists in these fields have been drawn largely from the unlettered commonfolk – the people from below who are traditionally marginalised and denigrated. Not even the educated writer-exiles have been able to escape the reality of Caribbean roots long after the fertiliser from the metropole has drenched their soil. All of this says something about:

- the arts (their role and function),
- other cultural indices (such as religion, kinship),
- value-systems at work in the society,
- identity (personal and collective),
- attitudes to political authority,
- the nature of economic activity, and
- the interaction between all these elements in Caribbean life.

Such were the 'issues' that prompted the authorship of *Caribbean Cultural Identity – the Case of Jamaica* with a sub-text which addressed cultural action and social change.[16] So persistent is the urgency of this factor of the arts interacting with social reality and social change in dealing with cultural identity that a published account of the first 21 years of Jamaica's National Dance Theatre Company forced the author to place the story precisely within the context of 'cultural self-definition and artistic discovery'.[17] The role and function of artistic expression, in this case the dance, as a tool of cultural resistance dating back to slavery and continuing through colonial (Crown Colony) rule to the contemporary contradictions in Independence, is covered in the volume. An examination of all this takes place within the context of the social mediation of creative artistic expression, the history of marginalisation in the region of all such expressions forged by the people from below, the employment of survival-skills by those very same people resisting oppression and the history of 'suffering' and outcome of the phenomenon of severance from ancestral hearths. The further examination of the creative work, organisation, management, leadership structures, and policy-options open to the NDTC in terms of its own continuity, takes the book outside the genre of 'artist memoir' and attempts to relate the reality of certain deep social forces to what is produced through the arts of the imagination.

That such an approach could be anathema to the 'pure artist' as much as it is to the insecure social scientist who is overly jealous about the 'scientific' integrity of his 'discipline', there is little doubt. Yet, Caribbean social phenomena of which collective and individual creative artistic experience are prominently a part, remain refractory to mono-dimensional approaches to their analysis and explanation. Whether 'empirical' or 'intuitive' (both value-loaded terms in themselves), serious observation of such phenomena leads both 'observing' artist and 'researching' social scientist to some of the most challenging issues facing the generators of new, or the manipulators of old knowledge in the Western world of scholarship. Coming to grips with Caribbean reality is in no way helped by exaggerated claims to 'scientific' pedigree by often the most subjective of social science scholars coupled with parallel claims by those who are arch-sceptics about the dominance of 'science' in the Western intellectual tradition.

The wider world is even now abandoning such polarisation of knowledge and its generation in the service of humankind, and regards the resolution of the 'conflict' as vital to Man's secure entry into the Third Millenium. The subordination of the human sciences (including most branches of the social sciences) to the physical sciences is nowadays courageously questioned as to the validity of such ranking. One academic (out of an American university's Philosophy department) has reportedly argued that 'it is the physical sciences that depend on the human for their heuristic currency and that they need to be brought under the larger constraints of social existence if, together, they are to achieve their fullest philosophical potential'.[18]

This follows on the questions long raised by others about the nature of science and the limits to its claims to objectivity, prediction and the capacity to find perfect solutions for human problems. Within the social sciences themselves there are already signs of increasing openness, even a sense of daring, in the admission by economists into their equation of some of the variables that would be otherwise regarded as alien and unquantifiable imponderables for which there need be no accounting. Structural adjustment 'with a human face', human resource development taking a central place in national development strategies, and public policy oriented towards social-cost concerns, are now major 'issues' for many an economist working in the developing world.[19] This, one might add, does no known irreparable harm to the integrity of the work pursued by committed econometricians or empiricists whose place in the pantheon of academe's authorities is assured, precisely because the work they do is critical to genuine understanding.

Moreover, so is that of others who use other tools of investigation and analysis and focus on other themes both evident and emergent. The region, and the wider world for that matter, may well be now ready for yet more genuinely seminal work in the social sciences of the order of what it received in the 1950s from the cultural pluralism and stratification debate as well as from the studies, analyses and incipient theoretical constructs of the New World Group addressing up to the late 1960s, Caribbean economic integration.[20]

The call into question by the Rastafarians of some of the fundamental premises on which Caribbean society was built and seemed content to reside remains a current of such revolutionary force and viability that the most sceptical of scholars have been forced to grapple with their thought and vision if not actually to enlist as adherents of their Faith.[21] That the 'philosophy and opinions' of Marcus Garvey, the movement's major icon, should now be granted the relevance these have long had for Caribbean development and being, is another sign of the Caribbean social scientist's growing, if belated, expansion of his intellectual horizons.[22]

Such new horizons promise to Caribbean social science greater texture and the internal richness matching the complexity of the real world beyond the UWI's campuses and equal to the still valid claims that the social sciences are part of the vanguard of problem-solving for a Caribbean rich in people-resources.

This challenging gift of humanity, for all its awesome dimensions, is anxiously awaiting mobilisation, not only for the rationalisation of the material resources which are admittedly limited (though very much in place), but also for the achievement of full mastery over the conceptualisation of approaches to the shaping of a Caribbean social order, recently inherited.

Paradigms, Models and Themes

The experience surrounding the nature, scope and function of creative artistic activity impacting on Caribbean self-definition may be seen as paradigm for the study and understanding of the development process in terms of both the region's actual dynamics and its potential for discovering some of the likely solutions to key problems. The assumption is that the 'bottom-line' for all that goes by the name of 'development' is creativity; and that creativity, though concentrated operationally in the realm of artistic action, is by no means solely restricted to that area of human activity. Indeed, the shaping of a society, the building of a nation, the planning and consolidation of a revolution, and the devising of institutional and operational frameworks in response to social and economic change, all place a heavy charge on the creative intellect and the creative imagination.

The creativity in state craft expressed, for example, by the fledgling United States, when it abolished the monarchy and devised a complex, cumbersome, but workable federal system, is of an order of invention no less desirable in the post-colonial Caribbean. The same can be said of the innovative impulse that drove the Soviet Union to radical transformation of much that had been Czarist Russia before 1917. The Cuban experiment is yet to achieve the pedigree of antiquity but her attempts at a new post-colonial society in 20th century Caribbean are also part of the creative process shared by artists and nation-builders alike. The manipulation of symbols by artists and creative politicians admittedly have much in common but the symbols in each other's grasp are different and of their own particular kind. This is not an argument for imitation, as many Caribbean Reaganauts, Keynesians, Westministerites, or doctrinaire Marxist-Leninists would have it. It is an argument, instead, for the mandatory independent exercise of the creative imagination and intellect in the region's approach to statecraft and societal formation, as is demanded of the artist turning out a piece of creative writing, a musical score, a dance, a piece of sculpture, a painting, some utensil or other from the potter's wheel, or a yarn of fabric from the spinning wheel.

Much of this has taken place within the framework of historical realities in the Caribbean experience. The framework of history linked to existential realities suggests a number of approaches to the study of Caribbean life. These are not without their pitfalls since historical determinism, like all other theoretical constructs and models, leave out variables that may be critical to a fuller understanding of the phenomena with which one is grappling. Models are by definition selective with respect to what is in and what is out. Suffice it to say that the study of the region without a sense of history is like a body without a nervous system. Neither artist nor academic can function adequately in the region without that sense of history or the importance of that history to the existential realities of contemporary Caribbean life. The artist, whether by intuition or on the basis of conscious study, is able to respond to the socio-cultural phenomena mediated by historical/existential reality and in so doing throws added light on the inner dynamics of Caribbean and, by extension, human society.

Out of this have emerged other constructs or frameworks within and through which investigation and analysis of Caribbean life and society have been conducted. Socio-cultural and psycho-cultural analyses may indeed draw on hypotheses of psychic inheritance rooted in the unbroken experience of dependency starting with chattel slavery and continuing with mother-sibling colonial relationships and the consequences of psychic and cultural conditioning. The resultant oppressive marginalisation of the mass of the population has produced among the tools of survival strategies of cultural resistance. These have manifested themselves largely in the exercise of the creative imagination to produce oral literature, Creole languages, original music, dances, and ritual worship. The study of such products, as a function of resistance against denigration and oppression (social, economic, political and cultural), merit a priority place on the agenda of Caribbean Studies in the foreseeable future. The work already being done in conventional literature, history, cultural anthropology plus the actual 'texts' of artistic creations (as in creative writing, critical essays, musical compositions, dances, paintings, sculpture, pottery etc.) are the substantive aids to the task; but the multi-disciplinary methods of ferreting form and meaning out of Caribbean social phenomena now need to be transformed from the realm of rhetoric to effective action. New areas of investigative concern need to be discovered, though such labels as mass communication, socio-linguistics, ethnomusicology, psycho-history are gaining currency in the highly absorptive Caribbean.

Much of this may not lend itself to the quantification techniques of behavioural science. However, it does not rule out an important place for the measurement of (*a*) the marginalisation, in demographic and economic terms, of the mass of the population and (*b*) the correlation between those numbers and a headcount of those who create works of art that speak definitively to the society's perception of itself. It will take more than tabulated figures, however, to explain why the innovation in steel pan music came from the unlettered yards of Port-of-Spain, the *mambos* and *rhumbas* from the ritual-derived recreations of the Cuban poor or why the invention of reggae took place in the 'government-yards' of Trench Town, and not among the social elite uptown. Even when the literate, born to or absorbed by education into that elite, write their novels, plays and poems, they dare not ignore the people from below and often use the rich experience of those people as a source of energy for their art. There are, however, other aspects of the arts which respond to scientific measurement. The arts as a source of income and employment is such an area. Any serious work of that kind would no doubt be welcomed as policy options for Caribbean decision-makers who have been exposed to UNESCO's recommendations citing 'cultural tourism' as a policy-tool in development strategy. Many Caribbean countries are aware of the importance of creative artistic skills to the field of advertising especially where free-enterprise corporate economic competition is being encouraged.

Book illustrating also needs artistic skills and would appeal to those who see education and mass communication (especially through television) as pivotal to the region's growth and development. Designs for cottage industries intended both for domestic use and export, prompt many politicians to take the arts seriously. There are politicians who focus on the entertainment value of the performing arts in particular, whether those arts are used in bread-and-circus fashion as sop to a restive populace, or mobilised to project a good 'image' of the country abroad, or treated as investment to attract much needed hard currency. There are also those who see the arts as genuine outlets for the human creativity deemed essential to a civilised society. The arts and the notion of cultural identity do admittedly defy analytical tools or an academic vision which is anchored in economic determinism.

Caribbean Marxists sometimes have difficulties coming to terms with the high visibility and seemingly forceful dynamic of superstructure (which is what the arts of the imagination are deemed to be) in a situation where the material base characterised by economic deprivation (unemployment, bad housing, inadequate supply of basic food) carry an undoubted sense of urgency. How does one deal with the notion that the Caribbean peoples have had their creative imagination and intellect to themselves and have used them as means of production to survive and to take themselves beyond survival? Ghetto progeny like the Mighty Sparrow, the late Bob Marley and hundreds before them challenge any doctrinaire hold Caribbean scholars may wish to have on an exclusive economic determinist approach to explaining social reality. Capitalist interpretations of that reality do not take the Caribbean much further either. A lopsided society inherited with all the institutionalised injustices against the mass of the population, needs collective social action to facilitate the unleashing of individual creative energy that free enterprise philosophy purports to be able to do. The legal expropriation of the slave property of the Caribbean planters by none other than the British Government in passing the Slave Abolition Act of 1834 points to the ironies of Caribbean history.

To this day Caribbean governments have had to take the initiative in securing for the mass of the population minimal protection against the viler consequences of *laissez-faire* economics though not against the political liberalism which is its hand-maiden. The private sector is often the engine of development in name only. In fact though many Caribbean artists imitate the 19th century liberal traditions of Europe which guaranteed the right for them to starve in a turret or voluntarily to pawn their talents to a private patron, they need the legitimation of their society in terms of guaranteed gainful employment, guaranteed markets for the goods produced by artists, and fair returns in income – material and psychic – for the talents they exercise, so as to escape alienation and anomie.

There is room, then, for both the scientific, empirical quantification methods of approach to the study of the arts in Caribbean society and the discursive, reflective, and intuitive devices reinforced by boldness of speculation and the application of what some sceptics would call poetic insights. In dealing with the socio-cultural phenomena of the region it may turn out that these different approaches are not mutually exclusive. Rather, a closer look at the phenomena in the field may produce methodological insights for further sharpening of tools of analysis. The sophistication of intellect and the sharpness of the imagination are both needed to help in such investigations. Acquaintance with the creative process as it applies in artistic production is not necessarily a hindrance, and can often be of tremendous help, to the academic investigator armed with his hopes of scientific observation and value-free rigorous analysis. The proverbial 'hunch' is admitted by natural scientists who do not have the inanimate elements they experiment with talking back at them. How much more, then, must social scientists, historians and students of the Humanities be dependent on that 'third eye' in dealing with the human factor in all their investigations into the human condition!

Certain thematic concerns will continue to invite greater focus than others and give clues to methodologies, theoretical constructs, new paradigms etc. *Creolisation,* as the substance of social and cultural formation, becomes a Caribbean concern subsuming such time-worn preoccupations as transculturation and acculturation. The indigenising process in the Caribbean would claim to have clues to that organic, symbiotic interaction between peoples and cultures in their separate encounters. Played out in the context of economic exploitation and political domination the process gets triggered by elements of violence, resistance, counter-resistance, psychological conditioning and the countless unquantifiable ill-determined variables which defy the determinism of frameworks forged out of different and alien social and historical conditions.

Addressing creolisation brings the student of Caribbean affairs closer to the deep social forces as well as the complex, contradictory and dialectical reality of Caribbean life. The arts as impulse, consequence and occasion of the creative process at once complement and challenge the much discussed and sometimes discredited cultural pluralism of early Caribbean sociological analysis. As an agent of social cohesion cutting across class and colour barriers, the arts have been used as manifesto in meeting the negative aspects of cultural pluralism. Privileged Whites and aspiring Browns dance the dances and sing the songs that are the inventions of the Black underclass. Outsider Indians and Chinese beat pan, jump Carnival and sing calypsos and the Blacks have come to dance Indian dances and play Indian music in Trinidad and Guyana and even in Jamaica where latecomer groups are in a minority. There is, however, a continuing 'struggle' between the notions of high art (usually that which comes from Europe) and low art (that which comes from the descendants of Africans or others of the Caribbean 'folk' class), between the Little Tradition and the Great Tradition, between 'fine art' and 'folklore'; and this confirms the persistence of the pluralist commitment on the part of many Caribbean people - in sensibility if not in rigid social structures.

The phenomenon of *cultural pluralism* is not by any means dead and the attempt to relegate it to a spatial-temporal habitat in 18th and early 19th century Caribbean is to under-estimate the persistence of plantation structures and attitudes through sheer resilence and adaptability. Not even post-revolutionary Cuba can ignore the fact of this persistence as much of her artistic manifestations imply. The debate between the 'pluralists' and the 'stratificationists' may indeed turn out to be purely academic in the light of contemporary Caribbean realities. The primacy of *power* in affecting what social cohesion there is in the face of subterranean cultural exclusivities, may have indeed changed in degree but not altogether in kind. 'Black', 'Brown' and 'White' have long ceased to be exclusively epidermal. Rather, they signify 'culture' in many places and situations, whatever may be the ease of mobility of individuals shunting between classes and hurdling race categories.

A *social psychology of race* in the Caribbean here becomes another thematic imperative. It is intuited by many an artist but is often neglected by academics which may find the variable too difficult to measure in their quest for conceptual tidiness and methodological rigour. It is certainly ignored by political ideologies from both the Right and the Left which may find the phenomenon disruptive of established categories of identification. Without being racist, the Caribbean artist knows that his protagonists, besides being proletarian, bourgeois or petitbourgeois, are also likely to be denigrated Africans-in-exile, outsider ex-indentured Indian or Chinese, or privileged Whites burdened with the anguish and anxieties of an historically-determined sense of superiority which invites resentment, combat, guilt or cynicism. Therefore it is possible to play one thing or the other or everything together without the advantage or encumbrance of kin or skin. The hope of a Caribbean person is presumably rooted in a synthesis of contradictory elements in the dialectical reality of Caribbean life. This chaotic state of affairs is admittedly an ideal subject for the creative artist rather than for the solemn academic or the doctrinaire politician armed with his manifesto for changing the region come what may.

The relationship between *cultural policy, identity and mass communication* is another theme of extreme urgency in a region which is bombarded by the might of media technology. There are definite benefits – undoubtedly, the world-wide popularity of reggae artists and of Afro-Latin music must be attributed in large measure to the region's access to technology. That access carries with it a price which is paid in the satellisation of Caribbean artistic culture or the weakening of artistic products through instant penetration via the media.

The 'media' must not be restricted to the electronic though that, admittedly, is the most visible and the one with the greatest impact on the non-scribal mass population. The print media have long influenced the Caribbean's cultural identity through books authored by artists of the North Atlantic or by West Indians writing for a North Atlantic market and with metropolitan eyes and feeling, as well as through newspapers owned, controlled and operated by Caribbean persons of a decidedly Eurocentric bias. A place for serious research into who owns, who controls, who writes for the media is now proving a matter of urgency – not to speak of the need for on-going content analysis of programmes, headcounts on television and radio sets, assessment of access by Caribbean artists to these media, determination of the ratio of locally produced programmes to imported fare, and analyses of media-policy emphases with respect to arts and culture both on the part of Caribbean governments and private media houses in the region. The entire region is a ready-made gift for open discussion, bold speculation and myths. In this there has been no shortage of volunteers especially in the area of popular journalism.

Finally, the arts themselves invite serious study in their own right, especially in the way they operate in the Caribbean. Psychological categories place them in a position of priority on the societal growth continuum of imitation, adaptation/adjustment, creativity. The view that Caribbean society has been trapped by colonialism into an adaptation/adjustment stasis after barely abandoning imitation usually proceeds to the notion that the only breakthrough to independence is through a creativity which can manifest itself not only in artistic production but also in political revolution and strategies of fundamental social transformation. This hypothesis invites some serious testing especially since there is evidence of the vigorous co-existence of imitation, adaptation/adjustment and creativity in the region at the moment with the dominant mode shifting according to the set of circumstances being dealt with.

Another area of investigation and analysis directly related to the arts and cultural identity would be the cycle of artistic creative action based on the symbolic relationship between the ancestral/traditional mode of cultural expression, the contemporary and popular mode and the classic(al) mode which depends for its continuing vitality on the other two as it does on the conscious application of individual genius to the creative process. It seems that all societies, *to be societies,* should have the capability of activating all three modes of artistic/cultural expression. Further empirical and comparative study of societies in terms of this may indeed help to explode the persistent myth that all things classical (and therefore good) come from Europe and only the folk and ephemeral 'pop' material, as primary products, can come from places like the Caribbean. That the arts of the Caribbean linked to the question of cultural identity have been able in their actual manifestations to explode this myth is still to be acknowledged by the Caribbean itself. Having convinced itself that it has created something, the region may begin to believe that it does have a history and an existential reality worth taking seriously.

Those Caribbean scholars, economic planners and pragmatic politicians or self-acclaimed citizens of the world who see questions about the arts and cultural identity as psychic heresies against Western rationalism, humanism and practical commonsense, need to be reminded of the dismissal of notions of equality, liberty and fraternity as 'metaphysical nonsenses' when they emerged out of Continental European revolutionary zeal at the end of the 18th century. Those 'nonsenses' were to feed the impulse of revolutionary change in the Americas and are part of the Caribbean heritage. The aspirations they engendered were to serve as stimuli for many who would regard themselves as 'progressive' in the region. Concerns about identity and its achievement through the creative imagination can indeed lead to a fantasy-filled romanticism. However, excellence of the products from the artists themselves and a tradition of intellectual sensitivity in dealing with the phenomena that are the stuff of artistic creation can also save the region from self-indulgence, chauvinism and another kind of distortion of itself.

Notes

1. See Aimé Césaire's, *Cahier d'un Retour au Pay Natal* (Paris: Présence Africaine, 1966). *Cahier* was regarded as a 'lyrical autobiography' by many critics. It was written in 1939 before Césaire's return to Martinique. Raymond E. Betts, *The Ideology of Blackness* (Mass.: DC Heath & Co., 1971) wrote that what all agree on is the power of the language, the rich images it evokes, the Caribbean world it discovers, the tenacity with which it clings to the native land wracked by colonialism, 103. Both Césaire and his poet/philosopher colleague, Leopold Senghor, were to become active politicians in Martinique and Senegal respectively.
2. This was the final conference mounted by the late Dr Vera Rubin, founder of the New York-based Research Institute for the Study of Man (RISM) on 'New Perspectives on Caribbean Studies: Towards the 21st Century and Prospects for Caribbean Basin Integration' at Hunter College, New York from 28 August to 1 September 1984. The Conference was sponsored by RISM in collaboration with the City University of New York (CUNY), where this paper was first presented.
3. M.G. Smith who has taught at UWI, UCLA, Kings College, London and Yale University is known for his seminal work on cultural pluralism in the Caribbean and for his studies in West Africa. He also belongs to the early cultural movement that flourished alongside the self-government movement in Jamaica. Edward Kamau Brathwaite who was Professor of Cultural History in the UWI (Mona), has published work on the history of Jamaican plantation society and is the author of internationally acclaimed books of poetry, winning the regional Commonwealth Literary Prize from the Commonwealth Institute, London, in 1986. His *History and Society* course sought to integrate historical and socio-cultural studies into one degree programme.
4. Arthur Lewis, 'Striving To be West Indian,' *West Indian Law Journal* (Council of Legal Education) 6, no. 1, May 1962.
5. Wilson Harris, 'History, Fable and Myth in the Caribbean and Guianas,' *Caribbean Quarterly* 16, no. 2 (June 1970): 98–122.
6. Rex Nettleford, *Manley and the New Jamaica* (Kingston: Longman Caribbean, 1971), 98–122.
7. Caribbean-wide festivals of arts date back to 1952 when a 'meeting' of Caribbean artists was held in Puerto Rico exposing performing artists from all over the Caribbean to each other for the first time. The Festival marking the launching of the West Indies Federation in 1958 was another such important occasion though restricted to artists in the Anglophone Caribbean. Not until 1972 did the more recent set of festivals (Carifesta) begin with the first in Guyana, the second in Jamaica (1976), the third in Cuba (1978) and the fourth in Barbados (1981). A fifth scheduled to be held in Jamaica 1988 was first postponed to 1989 and then finally cancelled following on the ravages of Hurricane Gilbert. Trinidad and Tobago hosted Carifesta V in 1992. Popular entertainers have long made international tours to Europe and North America but these have increased in frequency and intensity since the 1970s. Reggae superstars Bob Marley, Jimmy Cliff, Peter Tosh are well known in all continents of the world. Tourist promotion tours have featured entertainers. Dance companies from Jamaica, Cuba and Trinidad and Tobago have toured extensively. The Cuban companies have toured parts of Latin America and Eastern Europe. The Jamaican National Dance Theatre Company has toured the Soviet Union, the United Kingdom, West Germany, Australia, Finland, USA, Canada, Mexico, Venezuela, Cuba and the Commonweatlh Caribbean. The Trinidad Theatre Workshop under Derek Walcott toured the USA and the Caribbean while the Jamaican Folk Singers led by Olive Lewin has visited Argentina, the UK and the USA. An exhibition of Jamaican art in 1984 toured

the USA under the curatorship of the Smithsonian Institution and displays of Trinidad and Tobago costumes have been mounted in many cities of the North Atlantic, accompanying a variety group directed by Aubrey Adams ('Ambalaika').
8. Richard Dwyer, 'Caribbean Textuality,' *Caribbean Review* xi, no. 4, Fall 1982.
9. Mervyn Morris, 'People's Speech: Some Dub Poets,' *Race Today* 14, no. 5 (1983): 150–57.
10. In an interview in the Trinidad *Express* (14 March 1982) Derek Walcott reportedly said, 'Empires are smart enough to steal from the people they conquer. They steal the best things, and the people who have been conquered should have enough sense to steal back'. See Dwyer (op. cit). 'Stealing' as an artist's stock in trade is acknowledged by a great American Modern Dance choreographer who in an interview at age 90 was reported as saying '. . . I steal. But I only steal from the best…usually the past'. See Martha Graham in *Ballet International*, March 1984.
11. Vidia Naipaul's much quoted and controversial paragraph from *The Middle Passage* (Hammondsworth: Penguin 1969) is a point of departure in a discussion of West Indian writing by Mohr (*See* Eugene V. Mohr's, 'The Pleasures of West Indian Writing: An Introduction to the Literature,' *Caribbean Review* xi, no. 2, [1982]:13). The actual quote is, 'History is built around achievement and creation; and nothing was created in the West Indies'. Professor Kenneth Ramchand of UWI (St Augustine) in introducing Naipaul at a Public Lecture held in Port of Spain on Friday, February 7, 1992 insisted that the (in)famous Naipaul statement referred to the desolation by the colonial powers rather than to any inability of the Caribbean people themselves to create and achieve.
12. Derek Walcott's recognition beyond his native Caribbean has been reinforced by his connection with the Boston literati and his longstanding friendship with the late Robert Lowell (see his article 'On Robert Lowell' *New York Review of Books* xxxi, no. 3 (March 1984): 25–30.
13. Richard Dwyer, 'Caribbean Textuality,' 12.
14. John Nunley and Judith Bettelheim, *Caribbean Festival Arts* (Seattle: University of Washington Press in association with St Louis Museum, Missouri, 1988.)
15. See Nunley and Bettelheim, *Caribbean Festival Arts*. The Prologue was written by Robert Farris Thompson and the epilogue by Rex Nettleford, who was also Special Consultant to the project. Significant research and writing on Caribbean Festival Arts and their social significance have been done over the past two decades by such people as Errol Hill, Sheila Barnett and Cheryl Ryman, Abner Cohen, Everton Pryce, Monica Schuler. See *Caribbean Festival Arts*, especially 214.
16. Rex Nettleford, *Caribbean Cultural Identity – The Case of Jamaica* (Kingston: Institute of Jamaica and UCLA 1978).
17. Rex Nettleford, *Dance Jamaica – Cultural Definition and Artistic Discovery: The National Dance Theatre Company of Jamaica*, (New York: Grove Press, 1985). See chapter on 'Cultural Resistance….'
18. See Joseph Margolis, *Texts Without Referents – Reconciling Science and Narrative*, (Oxford: Basil Blackwell, 1980); also Robert Scott Root Bernstein, 'Creative Process as a Unifying Theme of Human Cultures,' *Daedalus*, Summer 1984, 184ff; also C.P. Snow, *The Two Cultures: And a Second Look* (Cambridge: CUP, 1959); also Frederick Turner, 'Escape from Modern Technology and the Future of the Imagination,' *Harper's Magazine*, November 1984, 45–55.
19. See Derrick Boyd, 'The Impact of Adjustment Policies on Vulnerable Groups: The Case of Jamaica 1973–1985,' in *Adjustment With a Human Face II: Ten Country Case Studies* (A Study by UNICEF), ed. Giovanni Andrea Cornia, Richard Jolly, Frances Stewart (Oxford: Clarendon Press, 1988); also Khadija Haq and Unar Kirdar, eds., *Managing Development* Islamabad, North-South Roundtable, 1988, being papers prepared for the Budapest Roundtable on Managing Human Development, September 6–9, 1987.
20. The relevant works in the cultural pluralism debate are M.G. Smith's, *The Plural Society in the British West Indies* (Berkeley: University of California Press, 1965); R.T. Smith, 'Social Stratification Cultural Pluralism, and Integration in West Indian Societies,' in *Caribbean Integration*, ed. S. Lewis and T. Matthews (Rio Piedras, Puerto Rico: Institute of Caribbean Studies, 1961) and Lloyd Brathwaite, 'Social Stratification and Cultural Pluralism,' in *Annals of the New York Academy of Sciences* Vol. 83, (1960): 816–36. These studies have since served as a point of departure for several other studies of Caribbean society. The New World Group comprised a number of academics (largely economists) working out of the Faculty of Social Sciences of the UWI, Mona, Jamaica in the 1960s. Their focus on Caribbean economic integration was fitting response to the failure of the political federation (1958–61) and a natural, and probably non-self-conscious, response to the challenges of Independence fast approaching on the entire region. Among the major scholars identified with the movement

were Havelock Brewster, C.Y. Thomas, George Beckford, Lloyd Best and Alister McIntyre. A slightly younger generation carrying names like Norman Girvan, Compton Bourne was to emerge in the 1970s with work of Caribbean-wide significance in such areas as Bauxite, Central Banking, and Science and Technology Policy Studies.

21. See Smith, et al., *Report on the Rastafarians in Kingston, Jamaica*, (Kingston: Institute of Social and Economic Research [ISER], 1960). This survey was co-ordinated by Arthur Lewis (then Principal of the UCWI). It not only informed public policy and helped to change negative attitudes towards the Rastafarian movement but also excited further and sustained interest in the study of the movement and its place in Caribbean social and cultural development. Earlier work had been done on the yet embryonic movement by George Easton Simpson of Oberlin College, Ohio, as part of his general interest in the nature and function of religious cults in the Caribbean region. In the late 1960s many from the student body at Mona were to become active members of the movement which spread to such other territories as Antigua, Dominica, St Lucia and later to Barbados, Trinidad and Tobago and the British Virgin Islands. It was considered as part of the all-pervasive Black Power Movement which manifested itself in the support given by many of the young to the 1968 'Rodney riots' following the banning of the UWI History lecturer Walter Rodney, a Guyanese by birth, from Jamaica where the Mona campus is located.

22. This echoes the views expressed by Rupert Lewis, a Reader in the Department of Government, UWI (Mona) on the occasion of the launching of the volume of essays: Rupert and Maureen Lewis, eds., *Garvey, Africa, Europe and the Americas* (Kingston: Institute of Social and Economic Research, 1986). Rupert Lewis is also the author of a later book – *Marcus Garvey 'Anti Colonial Champion'* (London: Karia Press, 1987). The political philosophy of Garvey has been investigated by Tony Martin operating out of the United States. The impressive and almost complete documentation of Garvey's writing and utterances is edited in several massive volumes by the Jamaican scholar Robert Hill, who also works out of the USA (UCLA) but who did begin his work on documentation in his studies for the Master's degree at the University of the West Indies in the Faculty of Social Sciences, at Mona, Jamaica.

A Dialogue:
Nation Language and Poetics of Creolization
Kamau Brathwaite and Edouard Glissant

PART I

Brathwaite:
Because of putting the point of departure for this discussion in the scope of the *nation language*, I will try to explain what it is like. In the first place, it expresses the experiences of an oppressed people always criticized and put down by the establishment because of its status. *Nation language* is not taught in the schools; it is not regarded as a respectable version of speech and literature. The only place where you can hear it publicly in the English-speaking Caribbean is on the radio, in advertisements and songs. That means that it is, semi-officially at least, recognized now; that it is possible to reach the mass of the people through this means. It can also be heard in the theater because in drama it is necessary to bring forward the language of the people. This area of experience and expression has always been with us as our main resource. The tragedy is that this main resource, as so many other things, have been marginalized.

Let me give you some examples of what it sounds like. When people say something like: "Let eyewater kiss the light of your lashes," now, "eyewater" means "tears" and the light of your lashes is describing the effect that the tears have on the lashes of your eyes. In standard-English we say, "I see your eyes glisten as you cry" or something similar. The "eyewater" itself comes as a translation from Kwa, from the Akan languages, in a way that there is no particular verb for "cry." An adjective is being used as a verb and transforms syntax, in itself interesting, but which we have not yet been able to standardize.

Another example is: "Mek dumplin bom your belly." Here we are using a lot of explosives. "Mek" for "make," and "dumplin" which is a food that we eat pounding and making it into a tight ball. If "dumplin" boms your belly it means that this is going to hit your stomach and hit with a force, create a force within you, to give you some kind of gravity. There is also a lovely old proverb: "Fowl nyam cockroach in the court of kings." Again "nyam" comes from West Africa, "nyam" is the verb for "to eat" in many African languages, transferred to the Caribbean where it is used in the same way. But it is also given this decorative form showing that the English court of kings is an alien concept in juxtaposition to an African type of expression. Another example is, "Cricket sound creep like stars." It means there is the sound of crickets (cicada) creeping in the grass and it is moving in this slow manner in and like the night.

Nation language is not 'dialect' or pidgin or 'vernacular' though it is perhaps based on these elements; but unlike 'dialect,' as we use that term in the Caribbean, with its implication of broken or sub-standard or stupid, ignorant, not important, marginal, *nation language* implies a tongue-cosmos in its own right; a language-energy which since it carries the memory and 'luggage' of the ancestors, carries the enriching wisdom (reverberation) of pro/verb and italics and nomenclature, where the name of the thing is the same or part of its sound, of its song, of its depth. Above all, *nation language* with all its resources ancient and modern (demonic, demotic, magically surreal, vodouniste) looks always to the future of the nation/language/culture. Lamming's Fola, Miss Queenie's kumina, EKB's limbo, Bob Antoni's *Divina Trace*, Toni Morrison's *Beloved*, Julian Hunte's *Swim around Barbados* (Sea doan have no back door; Full belly na fraid a wind; God doan love ugly; She delight in the fritter of de finger-dem). It is part of our people's expression but one which has not been allowed to become a central part of our official culture. We struggle with it, we selfconsciously use it in many cases or submerge it altogether.

I want to give you an example from my own self of how difficult it was to achieve this concept of reality. I was born in Barbados, which is a very small coral island, the most easterly of all the Caribbean islands. The Caribbean is now a tourist destination, an arch of 2,000 miles, a lovely arch of some 2,000 islands for the matter, stretching from the tip of Florida right along to the South American coast. Its tips are a sunken range of mountains which a million years ago angled a great eastward spiral from the Americas, from the Rockies to the Cordillera of Central America and into the awesome Andes. We are at right angles to this, and because we were at right angles we were weaker, more subject to the pressures of the sliding curve of movement. And so we collapsed into the ocean, creating a catastrophe of sunken memory and leaving only the sunken tips of these volcanic memories, the islands of the Caribbean. It is my impression that even now, a million years later, we still hear the echo of that catastrophe, and much of our work relates to that memory. We somehow lost the sense of the mainland, the sense of wholeness and we became holes in the ocean. People who were on their way to Atlantis in the Atlantic ocean were now stranded like blind turtles in that sea.

Of course, growing up in that little island of Barbados, I was aware of this only dimly. I walked along the beach, all day, growing up, throwing pebbles into the ocean and hearing the sound of that sea, that mighty ocean, that sense of distance in a very small island of only 144 square miles; my sense of space and distance, therefore, had to come from the ocean and the sky. I had the sense that somewhere out there was the genesis of the Caribbean; somewhere out there was the answer to what I hoped to be able to create as an artist, a genesis which is really where all art begins.

As I was walking along that beach I recognized that the history that I had inherited did not permit me to inherit any natural genesis. It permitted me to inherit a sense of genocide, which is quite different from genesis, fundamentally the opposite, because the people that inherited that landscape picking up the echo of that catastrophe had been exterminated by the Spanish, by the conquistadores of Columbus: within thirty years, some thirty million people died. So that when the Caribbean was inherited by what has been called the New World, the modern world, we had no original native ancestors. We had, instead, an imposed language, an imposed politics, an imposed culture which did not permit me, walking along the beach in Barbados, let's say in 1960, on the eve of independence, to have a natural inherited sense of genesis.

I very much yearned, therefore, to write the beginnings of the Caribbean. Unless I could write the beginnings of the natural geopsychic Caribbean there was no way that I could begin with my own poetry. So I skidded my pebbles into the ocean, blooming our islands moving in my imagination like whales on the horizon. But I could not write the poem of genesis because I had no model nor sense of the natural history in our archipelago. When I tried to write that genesis I stumbled upon intrusive models from prejudice, from literature, from school. Instead of writing about 2,000 miles of islands I could only write about a little pool at my feet, influenced by John Keats, "Ode to the pool, o lonely pool in the mighty ocean." Or if I attempted the genesis in another way, there was the intrusion of mighty Milton, tones which did not permit me to capture the essence of our history. It did not permit me to capture that catastrophe which I spoke about. The iambic pentameter which is what we had inherited as colonials and which has been consecrated in our schools gave me things like "I wandered lonely as a ... on hills ... daffodils ... or parting day ..." and it gave me wonderful Milton and Shakespeare.

But the hurricane which cuts into the Caribbean every year does not howl in pentameters. And for the slave-girl whose back is harshed by the whip of the slave-master when she shrieks in pain there is no English metric. Unless I could find something that sounded like some native fossil, there was nothing I could write about except pools and so on.

So I pitched my pebbles into the pool and was still unable to get anywhere. Until from stones skidding on the water, I had for the first time one visual sense; that if God had created the Caribbean, he would have used a pebble, not an anvil or discobolus, and each made him, at last, a Caribbean god. He was not going to use a brush or canvas or Sixtine Chapel ceiling, like Michelangelo, or a thunderstorm like Thor or Baldur or Richard Strauss; he would have used a pebble, and each skidding of a stone on the water would have created an island, and so I had Cuba, Santo Domingo, Puerto Rico, the Virgins, the Saints, Antigua, Montserrat, Martinique, Trinidad, Barbados. As the stone skidded on water it even created the curve with its inertia and that is the curved shape of the Caribbean.

But I still found that that stone did not really skid, in my mind, to the rhythm of my song. Until I discovered that the skid of the stone, that pointilliste syncopation, that unexpected movement of stone on water, that even the way it looks like a little curve makes it very similar to the face of what we had created in the Caribbean, what we call a steelpan, I could not write the poem. One of the original inventions of the 20th-century, the steelpan, is basically the music of Trinidad. And with that sense of butterfly, Anansi, steelpan, calypso, it occurred to me that I did have available –although the schools had not permitted me to acknowledge it– an ancient and very modern song which would correlate to the skidding of the stone on the water and which could make it possible for me to write that simple genesis of the Caribbean. If I could relate the sound of the skidding stone, it would be possible for me to find my own expression. I would not only be able to write the first chapter of the genesis, but I might be able to initiate myself into the poetry of the Caribbean. And so this poem, which is the heart of my concept of *nation language* because I could relate the skidding stone to the song of the calypso, freed me of Milton and the pentameter and Michelangelo and anybody else. It celebrates the rhythms of our own people permitting to enter in the experience that the rhythms correspond to. It is very important to recognize that every rhythm, every metaphor, everything that is native is a silent symbol for something which is much deeper, much more native, which as you begin to relate to it leads you to the future of its written reality.

And so I started writing: "The stone had skidded arc'd and bloomed into islands, Cuba and San Domingo, Jamaica, Puerto Rico, Grenada, Guadeloupe, Bonaire." That is how the simple poem began, that is the skidding stone. But in fact, the poem, although it might appear like that on the page, there is much more to it than only scripture because *nation language* is essentially a holistic experience. *Nation language* is an experience which is connected at the same time to visual and audible experience. *Nation language* has to have movement in it. You attempt in a sense to reduce or to atomize the essence in a single vocable. That is the essence of nation language. To be able to create a total picture of experience through a simple sound. This poem is not to be said at all, but to be sung. So it sounds like this, the first poem that I wrote:

> The stone had skidded arc'd and bloomed into islands:
> > Cuba and San Domingo
> > Jamaica and Puerto Rico
> > Grenada Guadeloupe Bonaire

curved stone hissed into reef
wave teeth fanged into clay
white splash flashed into spray
Bathsheba Montego Bay
bloom of the arcing summers...

Glissant:

It was very interesting what Brathwaite discussed. I see some differences, however, in relationship with my own situation. First of all, in my country Martinique there is a Creole language. It existed in Trinidad and Jamaica and Barbados with an anglophone variant, but there it vanished. In Martinique we still have a Creole language which is francophone because, in the seventeenth century, the French occupied Martinique, as well as San Lucia and Dominica. On these islands the same Creole is spoken as in Martinique. But people from Martinique call the San Lucians English and the people from Santa Lucia call the Martinicans French, although speaking the same Creole. When I meet with my friend Derek Walcott, we speak Creole because it is easier.

There is a definition that Creole is a composite-language with elements taken from two different master-languages. That means that Creole in Martinique, Haiti, Guadeloupe, San Lucia or Dominica is made from a French lexicon. Saying it more precisely, it is *not* the French language, it is the language from the Normandie and Bretagne, the language spoken by sailors and other immigrants. The syntax is a kind of syntax of various languages from Africa's West Coast. Creole, hence, is really a composite-language and also a language of compromise between the ancient slaves and the ancient masters. The genius of our people is to have made of this compromise a real language.

In general, you can distinguish this Creole from pidgin or from a dialect. Pidgin or a dialect are made from one language, but you do not find this specific mixture of Western lexicon and African syntax elsewhere, only in the Caribbean. In my opinion, it is not just interbreeding, or métissage. You cannot predict its results, *creolization* is unpredictable. And that is a main point I have to make here. In the Caribbean the composition and the cultural compromise are unpredictable.

I was impressed when I heard Brathwaite speaking about the Caribbean. Because from my point of view, if you would make a parallel between the Caribbean and the ancient Mediterranean, you can find that the ancient and old Mediterranean is a sea that concentrates, that forces you into the unity of being. You can see that all the monotheist religions were born around the Mediterranean. It is there that the philosophy of the "l'un," of the unity, of the one was born. And if you look at the Caribbean, you find that it is a sea that diffracts. It does not concentrate but diffracts. You do not have the sea and the lands around, but the sea and the lands are inside. This is something my friends in Paris do not understand. They asked me: "Can you live in such a small country?" They think that I feel locked up because Martinique is a small island. But that is not true because Martinique is not a concentrating world. I can spend six years there without going anywhere because the genius of the country is diffracting, to imagine something that occurs elsewhere. This is the *poetics* of what I call *creolization*, a composite, unpredictable, multi-lingual.

When I wrote *Le discours antillais* (1981), selectively translated as *Caribbean Discourse* (1989) into English, young writers in Martinique, well-known in the area, took the topics from my work for developing a theory on "créolité." They published it as a book, *Eloge de la Créolité* (1989) in Paris, referring all the time to the *Le discours antillais* as its source and root. As they gave me the manuscript, I told them to go ahead. But when the book was published, I told them that I did not agree with the theory of créolité. Because for me, *creolization* is a process which diffracts, I do not pretend to propose something as a model for humanity as Western cultures have done for us. We are in a process of *creolization*. We are no definition of being Creole. That makes a big difference.

There is a concept I am fighting for in relation with filiation and legitimation in the Western cultures. They have developed a concept of transparence of mankind that all women and men in the world fit in. Some of them are near to the model and some are far from it. The problem of this concept is that all people must correspond with its model. But I have another point. In the struggle of decolonization the concept of the right for difference has been very strong. But this is not enough. I want the right for opacity. It means that it is not necessary for me to understand what I am. I can surprise myself, do things, work, and so on. When I mentioned this concept of opacity for the first time, six years ago, everybody said: "How can you live with something or somebody you do not understand!" But I think that this point of view is a trap. The first meaning of "comprendre" is already significant. Because "comprendre" means "prendre" and maybe strangle. This is a typical Western scientific attitude. Countries and cultures such as the West Indians do not provide a model for humanity. I do not think that we are only finding a genesis in the West Indies, a genesis of our culture, but we are returning to the narrative, we are conquering a future. That can be a little different from what Brathwaite said but, in general, I totally agree with what he said.

Brathwaite:

Although I have met Glissant several times, this is the first time we have ever exchanged opinions. I am grateful for that because, as he said and I confirm, we share so many ideas. All those concepts of future, transparence and opacity. Of course, I do put it in a different way, coming from the English-speaking Caribbean and he from a francophone area. But what is exciting for me is that we do share this common base, which in a sense is another aspect of *nation language*. Although we have been separated by distance, by language and by the politics of the metropole, we are still communicating in this interconnected way. I agree with the point of not using parallels. I used to talk about Western cultures as being missilic, and Glissant made all the movements of a missile. The other culture, the culture of the *nation language*, is the capsule, the thing that is carried by the missile as it goes out into the space. The capsule holds its self-containing life forces whose paradigm is not cutting his legs off but self-containment, what he called opacity, the plea for privacy. It is therefore an assertion of non-conquest, a culture that is not concerned with acquiring or grandizing other peoples' languages or other peoples' possessions. It is a dream and an idea, but I think that increasingly we have to say it, and to say it as loudly as possible.

Glissant:

It is interesting to think in this context about the concept of landcape, so often applied to as a model of humanity. I use to give a quotation from a work by a German researcher, Ernst Robert Curtius, *The European Literature and the Latin Middle Ages*. Curtius states that all the parameters of European literature have one topic as an ideal landscape, the meadow and the source. According to him, the parameters and the prosody of all European literatures have this topic as a common ground. I realize that this is different for the Caribbean. All the literatures in our area speak about jungle, earthquake or storm. You said the same, Brathwaite, speaking about the skidding stone on the sea! In the great European literature, landscape is a decor, a frame. When a poet or novelist describes the landscape, he may do that marvelously. I like the landscape in Balzac's *Le lys dans la Vallée*. And there are many other examples, but it is always a decor. It is not an intra-part. In our literatures, landscape is not a decor but a character of its own.

We have two variants of the landscape. First as we came by sea, the Middle Passage, to the islands, and there we imagined the sea, as Kamau said. And, besides that, we were in the period of slavery. When you say slavery, there are maroons who went to the forest, to the mountains, to be free. Thus, our ideas of freedom, of liberty, are connected to the mountains and the sea. And between these two extremes we have to manage freedom, between the mountains and the sea.

These ideas of freedom are a very important condition for us. For instance, when Fidel Castro was in the opposition, he could have gone to Havana and live in town. But he went to the Sierra Maestra. On the one hand, that was politically stupid, because Batista's soldiers were there waiting for him. And of 120 persons only twelve got into the Sierra Maestra. On the other, it was incredibly typical for a maroon to be in the Sierra Maestra; it was a West Indian act. The relation with the landscape came from a long history. Maybe he did not know it, but the symbolism of this act was very strong.

It is clear that our relation to the landscape is something you cannot imagine when you do not have these kind of images in mind. When I was in Martinique, I could observe it on the houses. You have the crest. Traditionally all the masters' houses were on the crest, because there is more fresh air. And all the slaves' houses were further down. It is not only the air but also when there is a cyclone, all the earth goes down on the houses of the poor. And now you see the Martinicans conquering the crest, sociologically a very interesting point. This relation means that not only because of becoming rich and buying a house your status is changing. More important is the relation to the landscape which changes; *you* change. I would not call that a model for humanity, but rather a kind of being in the world.

Brathwaite:

I would like to add to that. Our landscape is much more violent, constantly changing by sunlight, by heat, by earthquake, by storm. In a sense, one has to go back to a former situation to describe that landscape. Let me give you the example of my own poem "Flutes." Until 1988 I lived in the hills in Jamaica, in a place called Irish Town, and there was a trunk of bamboo. Every year I became closer to it. So finally I wrote a poem that I regard as the poem of the bamboo, "Flutes." And the relationship between me and that trunk of bamboo was very close until 1988, when hurricane Gilbert transformed that place of golden bamboo into a grim, dark, catastrophic place twice as high as my house. Everything that had been related to bamboo became dark and cataclistic. The tenure of my poetry altered, it was as if my whole soul had been dumped into this kind of dirt. This is a very strong relationship you will find in the works of many Caribbean artists.

From light and glittering, soft and hopeful, the poetry became very dark and landsliding. Since then, it converted into a kind of prose, as the only way to relate to that particular disaster. But as Glissant said, it is impossible to make a model out of it. Because a model of 1986 becomes a different model in 1988. And now the bamboo has started to push back its way again at the landslide and soon we will have a Creole landscape, one that is born dark and catastrophic and, at the same time, still hopefull and green. I will have to balance between that. Only after there are enough expressions of such experiences, the critic begins pointing out a common denominator; it is what they call theory. But the expressions of these experiences precede that theory. A Caribbean artist cannot begin with a theory, with a model; he always has to begin with his or her relationship to what *is there*.

Glissant:

This is very important! Take for instance our relationship with Latin America. In the sixteenth century, the Caribbean Sea was called "The sea of Peru." And Peru is on the other side of the continent. Hence, it was called that way because in those times you had to pass the Caribbean Sea to get there. There were no other routes for the conquerors. I think we have a point here. There are a lot of Americas: North America, South America, Central America and the West Indies or Caribbean. This question of not having a filiation, not having a link to origins, is the same for all the Americas. Except maybe for the Amerindians, the only ones that can pretend to this kind of genesis. However, as I studied the cultures and theology of the Mesoamericans, I found a very interesting concept of genesis and filiation. It begins without any link because of its system of cyclical periods of 52 years. So there is a hole! You will never find that in a Greek myth nor in the Christian religion which start directly from the genesis. And if you have a hole, you decide that Methusalem lived 900 years, or that Noah lived 700 years. You have to do that to have a legitimation to conquer. In the Mesoamerican cultures you do not find the same preoccupation, nor is there such a link in African cultures. You have filiation not by legitimation but by adoption. This is the creolization that is working all around the world and what I call the *Poétique de la Relation* (1990).

Brathwaite:

It is interesting that Glissant is speaking about Martinique as a part of Latin America. There is no way that Jamaica and Barbados, or Antigua and St. Kitts, have ever dreamt of Latin America. They do not even know what the word means. Our concept of history of the world is very AfroSaxon and Protestant, as the products of a very weird and materialistic English society. So that we grew up in a Caribbean which only knew London or Australia or Canada, anything vital to the British empire. But everything that was Caribbean, we were almost forbidden to engage with. Our own music, our own language expressions, the language that we had created over the years, and above all the isolation from the rest of the Caribbean.

Let me give you an example. If I would have lived on the island of San Lucia, in the year 1400, and wanted to visit Glissant in Martinique, I could go to the Morne above Castries, send a signal to him or his uncle, by a mirror or smoke-signal, to say to him: I am coming over that afternoon in a canoe. And we could plow into the waves at the right time and would no doubt safely arrive on the beach. Today, if I wish to get to Glissant from San Lucia to Martinique, all I have to do is to take an ocean-liner from San Lucia to London, from London across the channel to Calais and then take a French liner. Even the telephone goes that way. That is the distance, that is part of the problem. It is not only linguistic or political; it is part of a whole communication compartmentalization (compartMENTALization) system. And it is particularly so for the English-speaking Caribbean. In the case of the French islands, they have remained linked to Europe so that they have an outlet to the world; they are, in a sense, part of France. Although even that might be a difficult position. The metropole never conceived us as worthy of education. It had to be, in a sense, illegitimate. We taught ourselves, which was extraordinary. The teacher could not teach us what we wanted to be taught, so our parents urged that the school allow us to teach ourselves. And also to take the examination which was still publicly there. In teaching ourselves we discovered Harlem and we discovered T.S. Eliot. And in discovering T.S. Eliot we discovered a modern voice in poetry. Without that we would have been bumped into the English pentameter, into the English romantics, you know, the Swinburne attitude. At school I never came into contact with a man called Nicolás Guillén; I did not know that Brazil had slaves, that Brazil was a plantation society similar to ours; I did not know that Africa existed as a great place either, although Barbados is the most easterly of the Caribbean islands and on a misty day we can imagine the coast of Guinea.

In the discovery of Harlem we saw the modern voice in poetry connected with the music, the relation of music and word in Louis Armstrong or Duke Ellington for instance. It was the whole release of art as expressed into music-word-dance. In other words, we realized that some of us could sing. Some of us were singing even in another country; even though we had been made to understand that singing was not good for us. The calypso was forbidden in Barbados then. Parents would be very upset if you sung the calypso, it would never be heard on radio. People regarded it as devil's music, expressed only by a certain unimaginable kind of person. And certainly not in Barbados at all, but in another island.

In teaching, though, this concept of opacity, transparency and future is always misleading. I am working in the Department of History, but I am a poet and operate as such. So if the students come expecting to hear about history, and economic history above that, you will not hear that from me. I have not done research in the archives looking for political and economic history. My research always arises from the metaphors I discover in my poetry. Only now we are discovering the submerged areas of the Caribbean, the lives of the people and the institutions they have provided for themselves over this long period of slavery and colonization. An institution like "Landship," a self-help organization in Barbados, for instance, inspires me and includes the old notion of "susu," or "coumbite," as you can find in Guadeloupe and Haiti.

When I came to write my poem "The Cabin," which is based upon a slave cabin in Jamaica, I was able to describe the cabin because I could see it. But when I came to open the door of the cabin, I realized that I did not know what was in there, nor did I know the people inside. The only cabin that I knew at that stage was Harriet Beecher Stowe's *Uncle Tom's Cabin* (1855). Therefore, as a historian, I had to do that necessary research to discover what the Jamaican slaves were doing at that time, what they were called and what kind of mental and physical furniture would be within their world. That is the kind of research that I do. Each time it has come from a metaphor, from a poem which was unresolved because of ignorance. Any attempt to discover something about the Caribbean has been based first of all upon an imaginative leap into the unknown, and then into a historical, archival effort to understand and define that. And I would say that that is the same anywhere in the world, except that our resources are so rich and so untapped, so untamed even, that it is necessarily done.

Therefore, this multidisciplinary approach is essential in the Caribbean. Everything you approach has a multiplicity of connotations, of overtones, of implications on many levels. I learnt this quite by accident. I studied history at the University of Cambridge, where I had to choose between literature and history. I decided to do history because I felt it would be more difficult, since literature was already with me. Having left Cambridge, I escaped as I hoped from history for many years. Living on the island of San Lucia, in a way hiding in the island of San Lucia, I was discovered by an historian, an academic from the University of the West Indies. He found it a disgrace for a historian, a Cambridge-man as he called it, to be out in the woods like that. And they engineered my return to Jamaica which is about twenty years ago now. There is no need to say that the academics, my professional colleagues, hardly speak to me in the Department of History. They do not understand how this thing works but have now accepted that it works. And thanks to our efforts, cultural and social history is now becoming central at the University of the West Indies. Everybody is now dealing with social and cultural history.

It is very important, even as academics, to have your own biography, your own autobiography, to know how you reach that conclusion out of your own experience. And that is what I always intend to do. We are not separating word from essence. For us the word and the world remain contiguous. Whereas in many other disciplines and in many other societies, since the Renaissance, the word and the world have been growing further apart. I am still 'discovering' the Caribbean. So I do not have any sense of 'inventing' anything. If anything the Caribbean is 'inventing' me! It is the Caribbean that has impinged on me more and more seriously as I have toiled in that area. And I have to use words like toil, you see, because our colonial history —of course— is similar to yours, but our colonialism has been done by the British, anglophone and Protestant. They cut us off from the rest of the Caribbean.

Glissant:

My experience comes from the plantation where I was born. My father was a kind of foreman and went from place to place. So I got to know quite well all aspects of the cultures from Martinique.

In my childhood I heard the Creole-tales and music in the country side. That is why I feel the need to intellectualize all these experiences instead of turning back to the essence. This is a difference with some of my fellow writers in Martinique, young writers of today who live in towns and who do not know plantation life. So I have a tendency to consider a kind of whole being in the world, to emphasize not only the essence —I do not like this word—but also the intellectual comprehension of things. Half and half. Maybe I am pre-Socratic, certainly not Heideggerian. I have a great feeling for the pre-Socratics. Because I do not think that it is since the Renaissance that men have been separated from the word. It is since Socrates and Plato. Maybe the pre-Socratics were black people in their mind. They were not from the Western culture. They were something else that has been lost. Maybe we have to try to find again what it was.

The other question is that listening to Brathwaite I was thinking about the francophone West Indies. We had the best and the worst part. The best because we had access to knowledge, but without this kind of attitude there is in the English-speaking or Spanish-speaking West Indies. I was always amazed (working at the Unesco) by the conflicts between my friends from Jamaica and Trinidad and Barbados and Santo Domingo and Cuba. There always was a conflict. There was a Trinidadian lady, very intelligent, saying: "Trinidad is an Atlantic power." And I said, "What are you talking about, what is that?" And the English-speaking West Indians saying: "You from Cuba try to colonize us." And the other saying, etc. But these points of discussion are obsolete for me. Maybe we have the opportunity to be close to the Latin Americans and close to the anglophones and do a kind of league.

So, we from the francophone West Indies had access to knowledge which was good. The bad thing is that it meant to be assimilated. English colonization is certainly bad, because an Englishman cannot consider a Trinidadian or a Barbadian as a really English citizen. But doing that, in a way, the Englishman respects the other culture. He does not do anything in favor of that culture, but he does not touch it either, he does not contaminate it. When I went to Dominica, it was incredible what I saw. The English have done nothing; not a road, not a house, nothing at all. The French in Martinique provided roads, electricity, telephones, but we were contaminated in our minds because of this assimilation by the French culture. So that the English- and the Spanish-speaking in the West Indies are closer to their "essence," let's say, to the relation with themselves, than the francophones.

I remember something the Cubans told me a long time ago. I was discussing with some leaders in Cuba, and at that time they had only one word in their mind: América Latina. And I answered them, okay, América Latina, but you are West Indian. And if you are not West Indian, your Latin America-being is false, not real but rhetorical. And I remember that they did not understand what I was saying. For them, at that time, the West Indies was nothing. And it took them fifteen years to understand that they could not be Latin American without being West Indians. At the end of the discussion, they told me something amazing by saying: "You from Martinique and Guadeloupe are the more accurate in mind, because you are the most fragile and threatened." And it seems to me that *that* is the real point of the situation in the West Indies regarding the francophones, anglophones or hispanophones. My conclusion is that we do not do enough to converge. Maybe this will happen by the strength of history.

Brathwaite:

Well, the first thing to converge would be political. The British West Indies have planned a political union for a long time, but never included the French or Spanish in their vision. I think, that that would have to be the first point. The other one would be cultural congresses and breaking down that communication barrier of the languages making sure that children at school speak all the languages of the Caribbean. We lack a unifying language which would make communication at all levels much more easy. This should coincide with a common political structure. I would hardly ever meet Glissant in the Caribbean. There is no relationship between the University of the West Indies and the ones in Martinique and Guadeloupe. From time to time we send our students over and have exchanges, but these are very half-hearted. And on your own, you cannot do it. You would burn up all your energy, you would create a crusade. And I doubt that it would have any follow-up as long as the structures remain so seriously separated.

Of course, we have a natural link, Africa. Whenever we meet at festivals or anywhere else, we recognize this "sameness" in many aspects. But it has not been used as an unifying force, because Africa in the Caribbean still is something you do not speak about. There are two reasons for that. The good one is that we do not know anything about Africa. That is the good one. The bad one is that when we speak about Africa, the other ethnic groups in the Caribbean are protesting against blowing the whistle! For instance, the game of cricket, that great game that we have. Our captain said a few years ago that we had won a certain series, thanks to the excellent play of a young 'African' [African-looking] (Caribbean) guy on the team. People never forgave him. And as he went after several years to Guyana where 70% of the population is from Indian heritage, he was booed. Because of that declaration. So Africa cannot be used as a unifying force. Maybe the Amerindians would be a better base, but there again, our ignorance of Amerindians is even greater than that of Africa. Our ignorance of the past is frightening.

Glissant:

This might be true but, in my opinion, the difficulty is that we are prisoners, prisoners of our own conception of identity. I think that particularly Western culture put this in us. Identity, as a conception, has developed in Western cultures in order to conquer the world. We have to define another conception of identity, not with this conception of the roots which excludes the other by war, or conquest, or intolerance. I say this because I have the personal experience of political struggles in my own country as well as of the vision of political struggles in other countries, like Algeria for instance. And each time I saw this intolerance, I realized that the result would not be what we expected. That one more time intolerance, racism, anti-feminism, religious fundamentalism or anti-fundamentalism would come up. We have to try to define another kind of identity, not this sectoral rooting, but a relationship through a network.

In Latin America and in the West Indies you have a series of contradictory levels. You have the nation building which is contradictory with the class struggle, and you have the class struggle with the nation building as the definition of collective and communal identity. You have five or six different ethnic communities and when you try to build a nation, one community can say that you do that on *their* shoulders. So you have all these contradictions, especially in Latin America. But how can we live in community while we are still making propaganda for the idea that the human being only finds his identity in his roots. Take myself, for instance. I come from a plantation, I know that. But that is not all of me. My identity is not only the cabin where I was born, the cane-field where I grew up. I know that, it is within me. As a person, I do not need to go back to it all the time. We only need to do that as a collective. Because they cut that out of our memory. We have to recuperate this history. If West Indians and Latin Americans do not try to do that, they will be crushed by outside forces. Be it as it may, this is not the way to change the mind of mankind; rooted identity constructions are not enough. According to my concept of the *poetics of creolization* we have to fight against all mono-something. If I defend my maternal language Creole, it is not on the basis of mono-language. I defend my own language, because I think that if my language vanishes, something of mankind's imagination will perish. And I do not only think of my language. Each year a language dies in Africa and that is unbelievable. One of the policies in the conquest of time is to fight against mono-something, mono-lingualism, mono-conception of nation-state or the concept of race, etc. And if we fight for that question of multiplicity and have a chance to succeed in this life, then we will succeed in other lives after us. This concept of multiplicity is not opposed to the concept of unity. I think even that the more you consider multiplicity, the more you have a chance to realize unity. That is my first point. The second is that evidently political, military or economic power is on the side of the identity concept I denounce. But history is unpredictable. You do not know if in twenty or ten years the economy here in the United States or in Japan will not fall! You do not know what will happen! If somebody, one year ago, would have said that the Soviet Empire was about to fall, you would have laughed and found it impossible. It is not possible to say what will happen in worldwide relations, nor possible to count on concrete actions on this respect.

Brathwaite:

Your concerns seem to be remarkably political and intellectual. You made the point that a nation state can fall. I would make another point. In fact, I was interested in what I consider divergence of the concerns of the poetry which can subvert the nation state from within, I hope. If it cannot, what are we doing sitting here anyway. Because it means that we are being completely futile if we do not have any Utopian dream, if we do not really and fundamentally believe that a nation state is part of us and that we can influence it in some way. So it depends on our definition of the nation state, how we conceive this strange functional apparatus. Do we have any nation state, can we change it as intellectuals or poets? I would say that if we can change I am willing to read poetry. And poetry that has a very strong rhythmic impact. In my case, rhythm becomes much more noticed when you have significant poetry, when there is syncopation and caesura and so on.

In all Caribbean work you will find that the rhythm responds as closely as possible to that remarkable rhythm of the landscape. A real hopscotch of landscape. It creates a rhythm you have to live with, which you observe and see, which you dream about. Then the very abrupt changing of seasons would be another rhythm, and also of course the rhythm of the people themselves. How they walk, how they talk in the market-place, the sudden violence followed by laughter, the constant sign of a carcass in the streets. And the carcass has the signal of a butterfly. These are rhythms which are very much part of our lives, because the butterfly is sucking some of that blood that is creating a sign of loveliness about that destination. Then you have a form which counterpoints two conflicts. And it seems to me that the nation state might be the cow, the nation state might be that carcass. And the creation of the sign should be us, in some way a signal of the possibility of metamorphosis.

Glissant:

So here we are back at the beginning of this discussion on *nation language* and its tongue-cosmos and rhythms. All music born in the West Indies, the gospels, the blues, the beguines, the calinda, were born from silence. Because it was forbidden to speak aloud and to sing. It was born from silence and in silence. One of the common cultural points of music in all the plantation areas of the Americas was the necessity to sing without being heard by somebody else, by the master or another person. The art of silence is fundamental in this kind of music. And when the music explodes in sounds, it remains in these explosions, this kind of art of silence. It gives the syncope of this music. And, therefore, these political and intellectual concerns are in the same way incorporated in its rhythms, with their "unpredictable pointilliste syncopation and unexpected movement," as Brathwaite explained and in what I call our *poetics of creolization*.

Caribbean Aesthetics

Of the Marvellous Realism of the Haitians

Jacques Stephen Alexis

It is with emotion that I salute, in the name of Haitian writers and artists, our brothers and sisters of the Negro world who are attending this First Congress of Negro Writers Artists and Intellectuals. It is not only the Haitian writers and artists, but the whole Haitian press, all the intellect of Haiti who have been keenly interested by this historic meeting between men of culture of Negro origin. Following the weekly *Reflets d'Haïti,* which was the first in our country to speak of the Congress and to popularise the idea the whole of the Haitian press has, for weeks, been running a campaign, studying the question and discussing and criticising the form of Haitian participation. The Haitian press, daily and periodical, as well as most of our intellectuals, deplored the fact that thoughts were not directed towards constituting a large delegation *which* would reflect the choice of our intellectuals themselves. The discussion was valuable, because it gave us this delegation, which is representative in more than one respect. In spite of everything, in spite of the discussion, in spite of the clearly expressed desire to proceed in the manner previously laid down, it must be said that conditions were such that there was no time for an organisation to be created to take in hand the formation of the delegation and the financing of the voyage. The intellectuals of Haiti wanted a big campaign to popularise the guiding ideas and objects of the Congress to be organised on the national scale, both in the capital and the provinces. They wanted it to be explained to large layers of the population how important it was for the people of Haiti to fight their battles shoulder to shoulder with the brother peoples of the Negro world, as well as with all the others. They wanted the whole intellectual life of Haiti, without any exclusion to be represented by the best of its writers, by its novelists, by its poets, by its theatre folk, by its journalists, by its ethnologists, by its painters, by its sculptors, by its musicians, by its singers, by its dancers, so that, on their return to Haiti they could explain to their respective circles what intellectuals of Negro origin are doing, and how they judge Haitian efforts. Finally they wanted it to be the obol of each Haitian which financed the voyage of their delegates. That in the end the Government had to finance the voyage of this delegation, incomplete perhaps, but very representative of important sectors, a delegation with which, moreover, I co-operate in the most fraternal spirit, that the Government, as I say, assumed this responsibility, demonstrates the interest which Haitian intellectuals have taken in this Congress. Numerous and important meetings and discussions have taken place this year about the themes of the Congress; as well as to clarify the situation and tasks of Haitian Culture in relation to the culture of other brother peoples. Thus, since I had occasion to be in Paris at the time when this Congress was being held, numerous Haitian writers and artists have delegated to me the signal honour of presenting the views which are dominant among us about what should be the orientation of Haitian literature and art, in the light of the origins, history, geography and struggles of our people. The Paper which I am presenting is largely a personal work, but it has been widely discussed and approved by numerous Haitian writers and artists. I must particularly thank the Groupe Folklorique Simidor, certain members of the Foyer des Arts Plastiques and the Theatre d'Haiti and its Troupe d'Acteurs Populaires for their collaboration in certain sections of this Paper. I must also thank all the Haitian writers, and intellectuals, who by their critical contributions or their methodological considerations enabled me to improve this work. It is because the great mass of Haitian creators produce in a realistic way, a realistic way which, it is well understood, is proper to them, that we have thought it useful to bring to light what makes it necessary for us to have a Haitian art which is national in its form of expression, and at the same time human and universal in its aesthetic content. That is the origin of these Prolegomena to a Manifesto on the Marvellous Realism of the Haitians.

Before I go on to present this Paper, allow me, from the bottom of my heart, to thank the great Review of intellectuals of Negro origin, *Présence Africaine,* thanks to which this Congress has met. We cannot be accused of Negro particularism, so long as the culture of the Negro peoples, like those peoples themselves, is still the victim, of the racism, the denigration and paternalism of a certain West which is still nostalgic for a vanished past, but this fact also calls upon us to define our propositions clearly, clinging closely to the realities on which they are based. Thus I can tell you that all the conscious and militant intellectuals of the Republic of Haiti desire and believe in the cultural brotherhood in arms of the Negro peoples of the World, against the background of the brotherhood in struggle of all the peoples of Earth.

PROLEGOMENA TO A MANIFESTO ON THE MARVELLOUS REALISM OF THE HAITIANS

1. Introduction

All the intellectuals of our time feel themselves more or less confusedly at one with Man and at one among themselves. Among them, those who are most conscious and most far-seeing about the mission of Art are convinced that their action in dispersed order is an impediment to the impetus of a conscious and radiant art truly at the service of man. It seems to them that it is not enough to sustain each other in specific instances, as, for example, when the freedom of the artist is threatened, but that the fire of criticism must be brought to bear upon aesthetic itself. That is what explains this meeting of Negro intellectuals for example.

In this century, when men are already travelling at the speed of sound, when ideas cross the frontiers without a passport, this century of the greatest discovery of energy of all time, —a discovery which permits so many liberations, so many leaps forward, which even yesterday were still inconceivable,—this century which has set on foot the final eradication of injustice and exploitation, this century, in which all races, all peoples, all countries, are impetuously launched upon the conquest of an ultimately humane standard of living, this century, in which equality and progress are the order of the day, it is natural that the fundamental content of works of art should tend to embrace the whole of the problems which face men everywhere. In consequence, there is to-day an inevitable meeting of the art of all peoples on the level of aesthetic content; love of the real, of nature and of life, love of liberty, justice and truth, love of man above all, in other words, a new humanism.

It is true that in all times the artist has been a witness to the life of the city; he has reproduced its essential types and scenes, its manners, customs, beliefs and morals, he has sung its beauties, its struggles and its dramas, the artist has been a professor of the ideal, of courage, an educator of the public, a singer of hopes and dreams, in antithesis to the hardships and ugliness of the moment. One could have said that the artist was an Aeolian harp, vibrating with every breath; naturally, that is no longer enough. It is not a question of merely bearing witness to the ideal and explaining it, it is a question of transforming the world, each one, naturally, working within the sphere which is proper to him. It is a question of aiding the blossoming of that which is coming to birth and developing, it is a question of aiding the liquidation of that which is perishing, that which is an impediment to the impetus of man. The artist must take sides, he must be a militant.

It is therefore useful that, going beyond their individual consciousness of their mission and their tasks, that, all together and freely, the progressive artists of a country, the only ones in whom the whole people recognises itself, should compare and collate their points of view on the current tasks of national art, in the light of the history of their people, its traditions, its manifest tendencies, its tastes, hopes and dreams, its certainties and its combats. It is useful that *a general programme of work* should be set on foot, simple and concrete, linked at once with national artistic traditions, with the new values which are coming to birth, with the future, and with men everywhere. It is true that this programme will have to be worked out in detail, in relation to specific forms of creation; but it is important that, in the first place, the needs of the whole of national art should be defined overall, for the art of writing, for the scenic arts, for the plastic arts for music, as well as for the other disciplines.

The object of these Prelogomena is not to give an answer which purports to be complete and final, but merely to stimulate discussion and to contribute to the clarification of the general programme of work in the light of the most obvious current realities and of the prospects. This Paper is therefore only a sketch, a preliminary clearing of the ground, and not a true Manifesto, which would call for fuller discussion. Since everything shows that there is a manner proper to the Haitians in art, that there is at the present time a School of New Realism peculiar to the Haitians, a school which is trying to find itself, and which is gradually taking shape, a school which is beginning to be called the School of Marvellous Realism, this Paper, presented before the intellectuals of brother Negro peoples, might, thanks to the contributions of all, hasten the establishment of this Haitian School on clear fundamental bases.

2. Haitian Culture

It is known that, at the beginning of the sixteenth century, a few years after the discovery by Columbus and the invasion of the Conquistadors, only a very small part was left of the Taino Indian people of Haiti, the Chemes people. In effect, after the heroic struggles of Anacaona the Great, the Golden Flower, poetess, musician, choreographer, and ballerina of talent, as well as a resolute political leader, those of Caonabo and other Cacique Indians, his people had been decimated and reduced to slavery in the gold mines. They perished in mass as a result of bad treatment, the hard labour to which they were unaccustomed, the collective suicide to which, in despair they abandoned themselves, and of diseases imported by the Spaniards. The Chemes people and the local culture which was their expression, had ceased to exist; it was a culture expressed in technique which was already advanced (open hearth pottery, goldsmiths' work, agriculture in dispersed mounds, production of cassava and Indian corn, brewing mabi beer, etc.) a culture which also expressed itself in an animist religion (a Pantheon of gods, called Xemes, an individualised clergy of butio-priests, specific ceremonies, etc.) expressing itself in a music, songs and dances performed by specialised artists, samba, wall-paintings, sculpture in stones, and tin-glazed china of the majolica type, as in Mexico, etc.

As the craze for gold grew incessantly worse, the Spaniards introduced the Negro Slave Trade to replace the failing Indian slaves. The first revolts took place, and under the leadership of a Cacique Indian, the great and noble Cacique Henri, Indians and Negroes took up arms, and took refuge in our Bahoruco, in the neighbourhood of our lakes and high hills clad with pine forests. There they victoriously defended themselves to such an extent that the Spaniards had to sign a peace with them.

It was there that the revolted Indians and Negroes, these "Marrons" as they were called, —-perhaps the word originally designated the Negro-Indian halfcaste, the zambo—achieved the Taino-African cultural syncretism, the reality of which we shall illustrate later by present day examples. It was natural that in the "yucuyaguas", the villages of the rebels, there should be a fusion of the techniques of production, of the songs and dances, of the plastic arts, and of the Pantheons of these two animist populations. Long after the epic of the Cacique of Liberty, the Bahoruco remained a refuge for Negro slaves and the remnants of the Chemes population. Moreover, it is known that, during the great revolution of slaves in the XVII century, orgainsed under the leadership of the Negro Padrejean, the zambo half-castes were an important element.

With the invasion of the French buccaneers and freebooters, France was going to provide herself with a colony, a colony which was also going to become a customer for the "ebony trade". Haitian culture became progressively individualised at the same time as the Haitian nation, in the interior of the San Domingo slave society. In the course of a long historical ripening, during which the residue of the autochthonous Chemes population intermingled in San Domingo with the multiple African elements decanted by the slave trade (Mandingo, Bambara, Ibo, Fulah, Arada, Congo, etc.) and also with some European elements (principally French and Spanish) Haitian culture gradually took shape, based on the decisive African contribution, until Independence Day, 1st. January, 1804, after which the Haitian nation, and its culture in the process of formation were to pursue an autonomous development. The Negro known as "bossale", that is, recently introduced into the colony whatever his origin, gradually merged into the community of Negroes known as "Creoles", that is, born in the country. These "Creole" Negroes tended gradually to unify the mosaic of cultural elements of diverse origin which they had received. They made themselves a language (the speech of the Creole Negroes, the Creole speech), common songs and dances, a common music, tales, legends and an oral literature which naturally reflected the incredible diversity of the contribution. Its originality and wealth were all the greater for that, and I all the contributions mingled well; since, with the exception of the French and Western contribution they all reflected societies at approximately the same stage of historical deveopment. These contributions were fused in the workshops of the slaves, with such rapidity that even religion was unified and became the reflection of conditions of existence proper to all the slaves of the colony, taking into account the long survival of ideological superstructures, notwithstanding the disappearance of the basis which conditioned them. Once independence was conquered and a comparative freedom of movement throughout the country was secured, fusion was to become even more rapid against the background of a country where nearly everything had to be reconstructed, since the War of Liberation had called for the destruction of the whole product of the sweat of the former slaves, all the wealth of this small country which absorbed half the external trade of France. The fact of this "scorched earth" war must not be forgotten, for it explains a number of the delays which the country has experienced, and, in particular, the slowness with which works of culture of universal value have emerged during the first steps of this nation, which has achieved the incredible feat of winning its independence at the very moment when the predatory powers were beginning to launch themselves upon the conquest of the less developed countries.

What is a culture, in fact, if not, on a general level, the product of that tendency which impels men to organise the elements of their knowledge of the universe, and of the society in which they live, to organise them collectively, in relation to the past and the present, and to re-compose an image of them which is vaster than the apparent one, an image which is projected in their psychism, in their acts, in their comportment and in all their productions? One can say, then, from what has gone before, that primitive communities even when they are very slightly developed or organised, have a culture albeit a local culture.

When societies enter upon the process of forming a people or a nation, culture becomes something more complex, richer and more varied. One might say that in this case culture is a community of psychism, of tastes, of tendencies, of concepts, which expresses itself in all fields of human activity, a community formed by history, more or less clearly defined, more or less stable, a community resulting from a psychic heritage, and exteriorising itself by works of beauty and reason, in variable relation with the development of the productive forces and the social relationships of the society which produces it. If the society in question is still imperfectly unified within its own territory, one can speak of the culture of a people (the culture of Ancient Greece or Ancient Egypt, for example) and also of national culture when it is the expression of a real nation in the course of formation or already formed (Haitian or German culture, for example.)

It would nevertheless be a good thing to delve a little more deeply into the reality which is concealed by this word culture, so as to have a lively conception of the phenomenon. Frequently, in effect, one includes in the patrimony of a national culture, works produced long before one could regard the existence of the nation in formation as an accomplished fact. We therefore see that, when we speak of national culture we assume the long cultural continuity of a territory which is to-day occupied by an individualised nation, notwithstanding the different social structures and stages of development of productive forces which have succeeded each other there. Works of culture have, in effect, a very long life, much more extensive repercussions than the society which has conditioned them, or than the tendencies of the spirit of the men who were contemporary with these works. As a result of this, culture is a fact which embraces the whole life of a people, from the beginning of its formation, its gradual constitution, down to its modern organisation; culture is an incessant happening, whose origins are lost in the darkness of time, and whose prospects fade away into the mists of the future.

This indicates how narrow we consider the views of those who reduce culture to a few works of art and literature of universal value and scope, without paying attention to the sense of the true, the beautiful and the human which has not yet been translated into works which are familiar to the whole world; very often these conceptions of beauty are neglected of set purpose. It is true that a culture exteriorises itself by means of a body of works of witness, which exemplifies the culture in question in the eyes of all men, but it is not by means of such works alone that a people demonstrates the originality and general humanity of its cultural contribution. We shall remain faithful, pending further proof, to the formula under which the people, taken in the mass, are the sole source of all live culture; they are, in some sort, its basis, the foundation from which the contributions of men of culture rebound; it must be added that very often, these individual projections of a national sense of beauty react to such an extent on the base which has conditioned them that this base itself is modified. Sometimes cultural works are markedly in advance of the culture of which they form part. The opposition which some people tend to establish between the forms contributed by men of culture, and the forms contributed collectively by the masses, derives from an absurd cataloguing logic which wants to set up arbitrary watertight compartments. Even when an artist tries to justify the originality of his contribution by a theory of his own invention, the consciousness of that artist is a social consciousness, a consciousness which is collective as much as individual, and which revives, often without realising it, popular forms, rhythms and symbolisms, sometimes quite recent, sometimes already old, sometimes very remote. For us the culture of a community is a primary fact, although the production of universal works of art —a secondary fact—always reacts on the culture in question, impels it forward, and demonstrates its autonomy. We must therefore look at the whole of the manifestations of our activity as a people which bears witness to Haitian cultural autonomy; and not only a part of its manifestations, the works of witness which are regarded as universal by a great part of mankind. Otherwise, without daring to pronounce the word, one is constrained to contemplate the existence of superior and inferior cultures, and in this way one justifies the manifest tendency towards cultural imperialism on the part of those States who make a desperate effort to stifle the cultural contributions of other peoples.

It is beyond dispute that some contemporary peoples have contributed more works than others; it is also true that cultures reflect, in varying measure, the development of the productive power of the community, but who, on this basis, would dare to assert that the sculpture of Praxiteles is inferior to that of the last hundred years? And yet Praxiteles lived in a slave society, where the productive powers were little developed. For us a work of culture is a whole which bears witness for human beings, and it is absurd to believe, for instance, that a culture which has contributed ten thousand known and recognised works is superior to a culture which has only contributed a hundred. Cultures necessarily include the positive and the negative, and whatever may be the people under consideration, it is always struggling to show its true visage, through inhuman social structures and unfavourable circumstances. The cultures of all peoples are sisters of different ages, but still sisters.

These, then, are the bases on which we judge the culture of our country. Haitian culture is a national culture, that of a well individualised nation, although it still has a long way to go, and we know it. But we also know that it is a great and beautiful culture, like the Haitian people, great and fine, although they live in a small territory. It will be through efforts and struggles that we shall travel the long road that lies ahead of us, but the Haitian writers, artists and intellectuals have confidence in their culture and in their people.

3. *The constituent contributions to Haitian culture*

From the foregoing historical summaries, we can recognise that the constituent contributions to Haitian culture were three in number:

1. The Taino Chemes Indian contribution,
2. The African contribution,
3. The Western, and more particularly, French contribution.

The Taino contribution to Haitian culture is often minimised; this is a mistake. The first cultural field in which one can see the Taino Chemes contribution to Haitian culture is that of technique. Everyone knows that the type of the Haitian rural dwelling is definitely in the style of the Chemes ajoupa; the technique of making pottery, that of weaving cotton hammocks, that of making cakes of manioc, called cassavas, that of building the canoes called boumbas, that of brewing mabi beer, and various other techniques in current use, come to us direct from the Indians.

The second field in which Indian influence is found is the Voodoo religion. It is a known fact that many of the instruments of cult of this religion are often of Indian origin, such as the consecrated stones, the attributes of the loas, certain ritual jugs (the govi) ; statues of the Xemes, Indian gods, are sometimes even buried under the consecrated altars of certain Voodoo gods. Even more, it seems that syncretism applied to these gods themselves (the Mistress of the Water, the Siren, the red Simbis, Sobo Naqui Dahomey, etc.). Spanish iconography on the Tainos leads us to think that the "kandales" worn by our little kings in the popular carnivals of to-day are of Chemes origin, just as the dances performed by these carnival Kings convey the impression that these successors of the famous Ostro, king of the "Brillant de Soleil" band of Bel-Air, dance in a style of Indian inspiration.

Some ethnographers think that the "Rara" rural festivities are of Indian origin, and even that the "ve-ve", symbols of the Voodoo gods, drawn on the ground in the course of the ceremonies, are also taken from the Chemes (this fact is disputed by others). It may also be thought that the technique, mainly linear, or the Chemes plastic arts (bas-reliefs of the Zim Basin, for example) is found again in the style of many reredoses of existing Voodoo altars. It is an important task for us to seek the heritage of the children of Anacaona, the Golden Flower, and the Cacique Henri in Haitian culture. It is encouraging to see our specialists directing their attention to these researches, which are very important for a clear understanding of our past and our present, and thus of our future. It is striking to find the fidelity which the mass of Haitian people display towards the Chemes Indians ; thus, in the Carnival, which often translates the profound ego of peoples, the processions are traditionally led by flocks of people dressed up as Indians and bearing the names of the great Caciques. Moreover, a comparative study of the various types of majolica faience in use throughout the Gulf of Mexico and the various islands of the Antilles at that period, opens up great possibilities of obtaining information: in addition, a systematic study of the regions of the Orinoco Delta and the Guineas, where the Chemes originated, and where some populations of Taino origin still live, would make it possible to throw a good deal of light on the Ciboney phases and the various Taino phases.

At the same time, the contribution which has played the largest part in constituting Haitian culture, is the African contribution. Whatever field of the creative activity of the Haitian people one looks at, one finds the indelible imprint of the Negro. Whether it is a question of oral literature, of our legends, of our chanted tales, or the extraordinary romancero of Bouqui and Malice, whether it is a question of music or dance, of plastic arts or religion, the African kinship leaps to the mind. It is true that all these works have the Haitian colour, they are proper to us, they reflect the country we live in, as well as our epic history, and they cannot be super-imposed on those of this or that Negro people, but they have an unmistakable Negro family likeness.

The West, and particularly France, has also left its mark upon us. Just as we cannot overlook the influence of the French Revolution on the Haitian Revolution of 1804, so we cannot forget that France has shared in a positive manner in the constitution of our Haitian culture.

We are indebted to France for the essential part of our Creole language, which, if it is of African kinship through its semantics, contains only a small percentage of words derived from the Chemes speech, the African dialects or Spanish. That can be understood, since, the African dialects being different from each other, the French words in use in the slave workshops were a convenient means of communication between the slaves themselves and with the French colonists. It would be a very idealistic attitude to imagine that the French vocabulary could be communicated without at the same time transmitting, in whatever degree, ways of thought and conception. In our opinion, based on discussions which have been going on among us now for nearly thirty years, Creole is a real language, and not merely a patois. Far more, Creole is a flexible and perfected instrument which allows all the present day reality of Haiti to be taken into account. Suppose someone had the idea, for example, of forbidding the use in Haiti of any other language except the official language of French, well then, over the whole extent of the territory, production and economic life, like social life, would be immediately and irretrievably paralysed and one would no longer be able to speak of a Haitian community or a Haitian nation, it would be the Tower of Babel. There is, then, a collective unifying factor in Haiti, the Haitian Creole language, of African semantics, although mainly of French vocabulary.

That is not all. It is, in effect, inconceivable that the French colonists should have lived more than 150 years in Haiti without influencing in other spheres the Negro slaves with whom they were in social relations. Not only did the French transmit to our fathers many usages which are current in our countryside, but they gave them artistic forms which have been assimilated by our people so as to be expressed in a manner which is specifically Haitian. The minuet, the Haitian square dance of to-day, lullabies, folk songs, the fabulous nature of certain stories, and a whole treasury, which, in spite of its air of kinship with its French counterpart, can no longer be claimed as French. Haitian music in certain of its most authentically Haitian forms of expression, our national dance, the mérengué, for example, has been influenced by French music of the XVII and XVIII centuries. The Voodoo religion is the product of a cultural syncretism with the catholicism imported by the French, the Catholic saints being to some extent confounded, particularly in iconography, with the Voodoo Loas, and other gods being even regarded as purely white (Le Damoiseau Blanc, for example). From this one can judge how important the imprint has been.

Still more, if Cap-Français, to-day Cap Haitien, at the period when the luxurious and enormously wealthy French colonists lived there, was known as "the Paris of San Domingo", if, for example plays and operas originally performed in Paris were put on there, if concerts were given there, all that was bound to be transmitted to a number of Haitians. Haitian men of letters and of culture have not only kept the taste for French art and literature, but they have also adopted its forms. It is true that in their capacity of "bourgeois" creators, if I may say so, at the outset they copied these forms mechanically, while often infusing into them a Haitian content. From this was born that literary and artistic stream, French in language and expression, which was gradually to become Haitianised, down to its very forms, to give us the Haitian art and literature of to-day. We cannot reject the fine things which have been done by Madiou, Beaubrun Ardouin, Ignace Nau, Oswald Durand, Massillon Coicou, Pétion Jérome, and so many others, without denying values which cannot be explained without the context of Haiti, which are Haitian above all. France has bequeathed to our ruling classes the French language, but she has also bequeathed it to Haitian creators who were, to some extent, linked with the people, lovers of Haitian culture and its popular forms of expression. Such is the origin of the work of these great witnesses, which is expressed in forms inherited at once from France and from Haiti.

In conclusion, it would be fair to add that Spain has given us more than just a few words in our vocabulary. The rebellious troops of Jean-François, of Biassou, of Toussaint-Louverture did not fight shoulder to shoulder with Spanish soldiers for the liberation of their territtory, Haiti did not constitute one and the same country with the Spanish part for tens of years, without this having an influence on Haitian culture. Down to the present, Spain continues her influence through intermediaries, through the intervention of Cuba and the Dominican Republic where hundreds of thousands of Haitian workers are engaged permanently or seasonally. Lastly, we should say that the Polish and German soldiers of Napoleon's troops who crossed over to the Haitian Army of Independence and were subsequently adopted as true and faithful sons of the Haitian people have also transmitted something to us. Even to-day, their descendants are concentrated in the South (at Fonds-des-Blancs, for example) and the North-West (Bombardopolis.)

All these contributions, of an incredible diversity, have been intermingled to form a single body, and, if the African element has dominated all the others, Haitian culture has, none the less, a singular originality which justifies great hopes for the future.

4. Special Incidences in Haitian National Culture

It is commonly said in certain Haitian circles, that there are in practice, two cultures which co-exist in Haiti. The ruling classes are French in language and culture, and the masses, the overwhelming majority of whom are analphabetic, are Haitian in culture, that is to say, strongly Africanised. These views, which are currently expressed among us by assimilationists, the parrots of culture, who want to make Haiti into "a cultural province of France" are naturally false, in the sense that they do not penetrate beyond the outward appearance of things. It is certain that, in any country, there is a different incidence of national culture according to social classes, that is, what some people call bourgeois culture and proletarian culture, within the framework of the same national culture. All the ruling classes of the world are to-day attacked by that malady which is called "cosmopolitanism". It is certain that our ruling classes are more smitten with French history and literature than with Haitian history and literature, it is certain that they sing all the fashionable popular songs, dance all the maxixes, all the Lambeth Walks, that they spend their holidays in Normandy, on the Côte d'Azur, in Florida or New York, and know little about the countryside or the interior of the country. It is true to say that the ruling classes have never been more careless, more scornful of the past, present and future of their country, but, in spite of all, one cannot say that they do not share in the national Haitian culture.

We would say that the Haitian ruling classes are of Haitian bourgeois culture, under their superficial veneer of French culture and cosmopolitanism. All the personal, political, artistic, religious, sentimental and social reactions of these people correspond to the particular semi-feudal and pre-capitalist structure of Haiti. Furthermore, they love and react intensely to the national music, from early childhood they learn, if only from their domestics, the tales, legends and oral literature of Haiti, they take part in the bands of the popular carnival, very often they are as much animist and voodooist as the people, in a word, they react generally in the same way as other Haitians.

These verbose theories on Haiti, as a "cultural province" of France, were naturally bound to excite violent reactions. Haitian intellectuals, artists and writers, in the face of this, have reacted by promulgating diametrically opposed theories. Often in their good will and their great loyalty towards Haitian realities, they have exaggerated and fallen into a cultural nationalism: a populism, which has not always been of the highest quality, but on the whole, their action has been, and continues to be, beneficial. Divested of a certain "Negroism", a certain populism, this indigenist trend in art and literature is a dynamic thing, and profitable to Haitian culture. At the same time, we must also say that all these glosses and all this gloating over an alleged "Negroness" are dangerous in this sense, that they conceal the reality of the cultural autonomy of the Haitian people, and the need for solidarity with all men, with the peoples of Negro origin also, that goes without saying.

We do not think that Haitian culture is an off-shoot, a province of French culture, it is something quite proper to our own soil and to the sons of that soil. Popular forms and symbolisms must be the basis on which we must build up our cultural production, having regard to the future, in the West and in Africa, of forms which have already long been Haitian, which Haiti has renovated.

The novel, poetry, the theatre, music, the forms of the plastic arts, have, at least in Haiti, a double heritage, which is at once Western and African, that is to say, they are Haitian syntheses. If assimilationists in the old days mechanically copied the Western and French modes and forms, that is not the fault of French culture; moreover, by the renovated use made of them by Marcelin, Hibbert, Lhérisson and Roumain in the field of the novel, by Oswald Durand, Louis Diaquoi, Isnard Vieux, Roussan Camille, Morisseau-Leroy, Émile Roumer, Jean Brierre and René Depestre in poetry, Justin Elie, Occide Jeanty and Ludovic Lamothe in music, and so many other creators in all forms of art, we are the heirs of a whole treasure which we must impel forward, so that it may reflect, in form as well as in content, the true visage of our people, their problems, their hopes and their struggles.

5. The Permanence of Cultural Contributions

If the ruling classes of Haiti, often at one with a certain racist imperialism, wish to deny the African cultural heritage, it must be said that the masses of our people, headed by the intellectuals of the advance guard, claim their quality as Negroes, and the permanence of the African cultural heritage. Without evasion they recognise the kinship of their culture with that of their cousins and brothers of African origin.

It is certain that all peoples who trace their origins to Africa show a permanence of cultural features which it would be obvious bad faith not to recognise: the masses of Negroes transplanted into America, and who have become nations or national minorities, and the Africans of today share in this permanence. Another indisputable fact is that the works which spring from countries of Negro origin are more immediately felt, more deeply penetrated, by men of Negro origin. Numerous are the Haitian musical rhythms which resemble certain African rhythms, sometimes to the point of being mistaken for them: the Haitian Voodoo, the Brazilian Macumba, the Cuban Santeria, have manifestations which are not merely akin, but which irresistibly attract the spirit towards certain similar religious manifestations which are proper to Africa. The Haitian or Cuban popular tale, not only in its fabular form, but in the way of telling it, is near to the African tales. One could multiply examples.

This permanence of cultural features (whether it is African or Western) is least stable and least lasting when the internal economic and historical realities of the country under consideration cause it to develop differently from other peoples with related cultures. Constant geographic conditions, trade and social relations are also important for the long durability of inherited cultural features. This permanence of cultural features always becomes enfeebled in the long run in an individualised nation. At the same time, this cultural cousinship, these elements of culture, will not disappear without leaving traces in a national culture situated far from the region from whence it is derived. In effect, nations are subject to other cultural influences, those of other nations which live in the same geographical zone as them, where relations and trade are frequent. Moreover, very often in the world of to-day, the nations of the same geographic zone have an internal economic and historical reality which is neighbouring, if not parallel.

6. Zonal Cultural Confluence

When one thinks, for example, that round the Caribbean Sea and the Gulf of Mexico, a real Mediterranean of Central America, the different nations who live there have known in the past similar conditions of settlement and migration, that these migrations are still going on, that the semi-feudal and pre-capitalist stage is common to them all, and that the same economic and political dependence is their lot, one cannot be astonished at the fact that they experience a confluence of their diverse national cultures. Certain reactions of these peoples towards realities, their habits of social life, their sentimental reactions sometimes show a striking resemblance, often even their art has analogous tendencies, not merely in content, but also, to some extent, in the form of expression. Moreover, the history of the Latin American peoples, the way in which they helped each other to conquer their respective independence, the aid given by Dessalines and Pétion to the Mexican General Mina, to Miranda, to Bolivar, the Haitian volunteers who shed their blood in the Latin American lands, all that creates a brotherhood which is favourable to cultural confluence. That leads us to the conviction that our efforts cannot be dissociated, and it is certain that we must pay attention to all the cultural movements of the Dominican Republic, Porto-Rico, Mexico, Panama, Venezuela, etc.

Furthermore, zonal cultural confluence is not peculiar to Central and Latin America, but all the nations of Western Europe seem to have embarked on a process of the inter-penetration of diverse national cultures, and in all the great regions of the globe one finds the same phenomenon. In Western Europe the schools of art, music, literature, fashion in dress, customs, technique, science, and many other spheres influence each other, and even the vocabulary of the language is becoming loaded with words borrowed from neighbouring countries. In the same way, looking at the Slavonic nations of Central Europe, at Asia Minor and North Africa, South-East Asia, North Asia and Negro Africa, we may well ask in face of this confluence of national cultures by zones if we are not witnessing in the world to-day the beginnings of the constitution of zonal cultures, which, at a higher stage, will crown the national cultures.

7. "Culture"—"Human Culture"

In the same way, people often speak of "Culture" or "Human Culture". In spite of the interested use which is made of this term to justify a number of aims which have nothing to do with culture, imperialistic aims, aims of rapine and trusteeship, we think it useful to preserve this term, to characterise the actual fact, the tendency towards the constitution of a cultural community of all men. It is true that this is merely a question of a factor which is only vaguely distinguished up to now, but this factor is steadily emerging and taking shape. "Culture" or "Human Culture" is in fact the product of a selection, of a critical choice by the consciousness of progressive men between everything that is most positive, most valid and most dynamic in the various existing national cultures. The new humanism for which hundreds of millions of men in the world are struggling seems to us to be exactly the nucleus of that culture of the future, proper to all men. The constitution of this human culture will not proceed without battles, and it is good and profitable that this nucleus, the new humanism of to-day, should be incessantly verified, discussed and called in question in all its provisional aspects. That is to say that the spirit of self-sufficiency, the spirit of chauvinism in relation to the problems of culture, is not only opposed to progress but is daily breached by the reality which is piling up before our eyes the first signs of this culture of the future, proper to all men. We Haitians do not think it is complacency to say that for our part, our people will have contributed and are contributing to it, certainly with the few works of value which they have produced for the joy and happiness of men, with their art, and their art of living, but also with the humanism of Toussaint-Louverture, that of Jean-Jacques Dessalines, like that of Jean-Jacques Acaàu.

We do not see why, in the light of all that has gone before, the son of any people, of any culture existing on earth, should have an inferiority complex towards this or that other culture, unless he wishes to deny to other men the qualities and possibilities which he attributes to himself. In recent centuries the West has found itself at the head of the movement of humanity in the production of universal works of culture, we recognise that willingly, but what do a few centuries represent in relation to the long millenniums of culture which there have been in the past, and, with still more reason, in relation to the future which awaits us all? The moment has come to raise our black hands in the debate, alongside all the fraternal hands, yellow, white or red. Temporary difficulties still exist in the world of to-day, there are many oppressions, many injustices, against which all men of heart must struggle, but already it is possible to say that we are orienting ourselves towards a harmonious concert of national cultures. The spirit breathes everywhere, and no race, no area of the world has a monopoly of culture; the realities of the modern world prove that.

8. The Historical Quarrel between Realism and Formalism

It is our reasoned opinion that, as a general rule, for Haitians as for our Negro brothers, since we are dealing with them to-day, art is fundamentally linked to life. We are dreamers, yes, but infinite realists, even if indisputable, inevitable and even natural shades of opinion exist between us. Art for us is essentially linked to practical life; before the collectors arrived in Africa, the craftsman was a decorator of useful objects, ritual or otherwise, the griot was the poet of the people... In the same way, the Central and Latin American people, whose cultures seem to be in confluence to-day, have nearly always produced works which were, in general, linked to the real. It is true that on the morrow of their respective independence, these peoples have nearly all known phases of imitation, particularly of France, but nothing lasting has come out of them. Everything notable and valid which has been done in their literature has proceeded from realism. Haitian art was realistic long before the *Revue Indigène*. It was a furious battle which the Haitian companions of the spiritual gained, a long time ago, over the scanty partisans of "pure art".

We are convinced that the tendency which consists in launching oneself into intellectualist and cosmopolitan experiments, experiments which have no link with the history of one's country, no contact with the native soil, no solidarity with the man of our time and his combats, this tendency towards "pure art", to unbridled liberty in lieu and instead of a sense of human liberation; this tendency to licence, is only the doing of a small fringe of artists, linked to the decadent social classes, the expression of the real pederasts of culture. Unfortunately, some of these people exist in every country. It is true that, throughout the history of culture, there has been a swing of the pendulum between these two poles, Realism and Formalism, depending whether the ruling classes were dynamic or decadent, but the essential part of the production of all great artists has taken the side of realism, of the humanism of their time, and of the national expression, in spite of the caprices of "the wishes of society" or in other words, the market for culture. It is true that the disciples of licence could point to ancestors and forerunners, and, more, that some great artists have been subjected to negative influences, have committed venial sins, have attached too much importance to the formal side, but they were only ultimately great because their work remained globally realist and humanist. In conclusion, one may say that if the humanist and realist trend has formed a powerful stream, a permanent stream which traverses and illuminates the whole history of art, the formalist trend has never been anything except a recessive manifestation. This continuous school, which traverses history, that of a realism, sometimes ingenuous, sometimes naturalistic, sometimes mystic, sometimes humanist, often dynamic, national and social, has reached its zenith in our day, and shows itself in the aspect of a neo-humanist, national and social, if not popular realism. It is true that this school had to find itself and is still finding itself, through exaggerations, mistakes and false steps —moreover, we strongly claim for it the right to make mistakes, that is, the right to seek the truth through efforts and struggle—but this school exists in our time as a living thing, indisputable. In art, as in every other field, we are always continuing the work of our ancestors and our heroes, which is why we must resolutely reject the play of words, sounds, colours, lines or masses. Whatever consciousness a true artist may have of his time, of society, and of humanism, he sterilises himself for ever as a creator of joy, beauty and courage in daily life and of hope in the destinies of men, if he gives himself up to mere artistic juggling, to aesthetic pederasty.

Let there be no mistake, the realism which dominates our time does not forbid that art should be a matter of delight ; on the contrary. But just as a man of sense would not refuse to enjoy good cooking on the pretext that eating is a mere biological necessity, just as there exists good cooking which satisfies the requirements of a sound diet, social realism does not ask anyone to swallow "artistic earth-worms". What realism wants is that art and literature should not forget their purpose; to produce healthy and life-giving nourishment for the spirit and heart of man, a nourishment which will at the same time satisfy his good taste. Art and literature have their vices, like sexuality and gastronomy, the pleasure of drinking and the right to repose.

Social realism has joined forces with revolutionary romanticism. In effect, if classicism is understood to be, as it has so often been made, a dogmatism, an academism preaching the eternity of the laws of beauty and the necessary adoption of the old organons, denying that beauty is a continuous creation, then we relegate that classicism to the lumber room of retrograde ideologies. We do not for that reason reject the classicism which created the great works that we know, which bear witness for the men of their time, which bear witness to the great aspiration towards dignity, happiness and justice, and to the liberation-aspiration which is eternal. That classicism is, at bottom, nothing but a synonym of joy for numerous generations to come. Romanticism has been, in nearly all countries, in spite of childish ailments, an authentically revolutionary movement in relation to a classicism frozen in its ideas of beauty. Romanticism is revolutionary in the sense that it understands that nothing is eternal, that artistic forms are born, live, grow old and die, that one can always surpass the grandiose achievements of the past by actualising man in his social surroundings and in the nature in which he lives, by throwing a more lively light on to the contradictory character of human consciousness, by giving a larger place to lyricism and dreams. This does not mean that one must therefore fall into an anarchy of form, into the outright negation of everything which the past has created in the way of forms. What is form, except the vehicle which makes it possible to convey the content, to communicate it? In other terms, the only rules which forms must obey are that they should correspond to the content, that they should be beautiful, pleasing, digestible and enchanting.

Since one people's taste and feeling for forms is not valid for another people, the forms in a national culture must, before anything else, correspond to the character and tendencies of the people in question.

The forms must, before anything else, be capable of stirring the people for whom the work of art is designed. Forms which were accepted in a people's past are not necessarily, therefore, the only garment which suits the present facts. There is in all national cultures a veritable treasure of original popular forms, which are still little used by professional artists; it is clear that these can adapt, according to their own personality, these forms, taking into account, naturally, the traditions of the past, or even creating entirely new forms which respect the national spirit. It is a glorious mission for creators who are partisans of a living social realism and a popular aesthetic, to draw upon this treasure, which is constantly being enriched by the people, and which is disdained by less clear-sighted artists.

9. *The Haitian View of the Traditional Organons*

In the light of our present national reality we do not think in Haiti that the artistic styles and modes which have flourished in the West, and which are used by our creators, and are, moreover, precious for culture everywhere, are complete and perfect. The Haitian people, like other peoples of Negro origin, for example, has a very personal vision of the reality that can be felt, of the movement and rhythm of life. For a Haitian, musical harmony is not solely Western harmony, the perfect chord is not that of Bach; his conception of glissando, of vibrato, of musical syncope is original, his technique of singing laughs at the rules of singing in the Italian style; one could say the same thing for all artistic styles and modes. We think ourselves capable, within the framework of our national traditions, in a style which is our own, of renovating these forms and modes created by the West. We certainly have too much sense of the national to wish to impose on others what is proper to us, but there is a certain Western outlook upon beauty, in judging what is proper to us, which we often find intolerable, and which leaves a taste of cultural imperialism. There is beauty in all men, and all cultures are capable of renewing beauty in the eyes of all men. It seems that the weight of the traditional laws of art-forms still weighs heavy upon the Westernised spirit. There are barely a handful of advanced men who conceive the possibility of a progressive evolution of the organons, an evolution nevertheless insensible, which might, in the long run, bring about a decisive transformation of the canons. Everything in us rebels against such an artistic reformism, although our impetuousness does not in any way mean that we reject in principle the dynamic contribution of the past, whatever may be its origin. It is impossible that all the means of the past should be adequate for the messages of the present; we must resolutely rejuvenate the ancient organons, discover them and rediscover them, if not invent them, according to the outlook of our people, naturally. How can the men of the twentieth century fail to realise that art forms have barely entered upon their adolescence? All the masterpieces of the past whose harmony enchants us will be as nothing beside what is still to be born. In our view new beauties can only be born on condition that we say "No" to the organons whose *spirit* we have inherited; in effect these old organons also had to inherit from older ones, which themselves in turn had denied their forerunners; the movement is continuous.

It seems to us, in effect, that Haitian art, like the art of other peoples of Negro origin, is greatly differentiated from the Western art which has enriched us. Order, beauty, logic and controlled sensitiveness, we have received all that, but we intend to surpass it. Haitian art, in effect, presents the real, with its accompaniment of the strange and fantastic, of dreams and half light, of the mysterious and the marvellous; beauty of form is not in any of its fields an accepted premise, a primary purpose, but Haitian art achieves it from all angles of approach, even that of the said ugliness. The West of Graeco-Latin descent too often tends to intellectualisation, to idealisation, to the creation of perfect canons, to the logical unity of the elements of feeling, to a pre-established harmony, whereas our art tends towards the most exact sensual representation of reality, towards creative intuition, character, power of expression. This art does not shrink from deformity, from shocks, from violent contrast, from antithesis as a means of stimulating emotion and aesthetic investigation, and, astonishing result, it achieves a new balance, more contrasted, a composition equally harmonious in its contradictions, a wholly internal grace, born of singularity and antithesis.

It seems to us that Haitian art, like that of its African cousins, is profoundly realistic, notwithstanding that it is indissolubly linked to the myth, the symbol; the stylized, the heraldic, even the hieratic. Stripping down, the search for the characteristic sonorous, plastic or verbal feature, goes very well with accumulation and richness. Each element is stripped down to its very essence, but these elements together may constitute a formidable accumulation. This art demonstrates the falseness of the theories of those who would reject the marvellous on the pretext of realist purpose, claiming that the marvellous is solely the expression of primitive societies. The truth is that these drily and pretendedly realistic works miss their mark and do not touch certain peoples. Down with this analytical and reasoning realism which does not touch the masses! Up with a living realism, linked to the magic of the Universe, a realism which stirs not only the mind, but also the heart and the whole network of the nerves.

Haitian art seems to be looking for the type, but the way in which it deals with its types is *actual*, in the Latin sense of the word, *actualis*, that which acts, so actual that all particularised subjects can be found in it. This art is that of the characteristic moments of life, but it summarizes the real in its entirety. Imagination reigns there as mistress and re-fashions the world after its own guise, and yet you will not find there a single superfluous element, a single detail which has not its practical underlying reality, immediately intelligible to the mass of men for whom it exists. Even the arabesque, the symmetry, the heraldic, the totemic, far from being abstract, have a direct link with everyday life. The result is unique; violence, interlacing rhythms, ingenuousness, exuberance, sharpness of tone, aggressiveness of line, luxuriance of spirals, the pathos of the vibrato, savage joy in words, the dolorous lyricism of melody, the exaltation and voluptuousness of colour, dissonance and syncope, the sense of movement, the splendour and sobriety of design, ornamentation both intricate and clear at the same time, lavishness and taste of composition — zoomorphic elements asymmetrically assembled, confronted, to terminate in a flower, a human sentiment, a genuine thrill, concrete, harsh, and even shameless images, poignant reversions, monotone percussions, and from the midst of all that, surges Man, labouring for his destiny and his happiness.

This teeming art defies all the rules, and embodies them all; it is all the contradiction, all the vibration, of the life which enters into it. One sole criterion is valid for judging it; does it throw light upon man and his destiny, his day-to-day problems, his optimistic combats and his enfranchisements? The miracle is that, in contrast with the intellectualist constructions of a certain decadent West, its cold-blooded surrealistic researches, its analytical games, Haitian art, like that of peoples of Negro origin, leads always to man, to the fight for hope and not to free art and the ivory tower. It was in this sense that most of us perfectly understood what our beloved Aimé Césaire meant when he said "Blood is a powerful voodoo! ..." Blood, yes, but all the blood; in other words, we would never be the disciples of a narrow particularism which would divide the world into water-tight compartments of antagonistic races and categories.

10. Towards a dynamic integration of the Marvellous; Marvellous Realism

The art and literature of several peoples of Negro origin, like those of many countries of the Antilles and Central and Latin America, have frequently given the example of the possible dynamic integration of the Marvellous in realism. It does not seem to us fair to think that the fascination, originality, and singular attractions of the aesthetic forms proper to countries of Negro origin are inexplicable, or that they are the result of chance, or the attraction of novelty, or a question of fashion. It is true that all peoples, whoever they may be, are endowed with feeling as well as with reason, but let us remember the saying that "the people who have no more legends are condemned to perish of cold", and let us objectively recognise the fact that modern life with its stern rates of production, with its concentration of great masses of men into industrial armies, caught up in the frenzy of Taylorism, with its inadequate leisure, and its context of mechanized life, hampers and slows down the production of legends and a living folk lore. By way of contrast, the under-developed populations of the world who have still quite recently had to live in contact with Nature, have for centuries been compelled particularly to sharpen their eyes, their hearing, their sense of touch. The peoples among whom industrial life is most highly developed, have, for their part, used their senses to a lesser extent during the last few centuries, since material civilisation has saved them a great deal of effort; that has been the price of industrial mechanization, certain regrettable consequences of which everyone recognizes. The under-developed populations of the world, on their, part, know a blend of mechanical civilisation and "natural" life, so to speak, and it is beyond dispute that they have feelings of special liveliness. The problems which they have to face, the low standard of living, unemployment, poverty, hunger and illness are also problems which it is important to liquidate, and we do not overlook this.

These specially lively feelings give these peoples artistic possibilities which should be used. From there it is only a step to conceiving that the Haitian, for instance, does not seek to grasp the whole of sensible reality, but what strikes him, what threatens him, what in Nature particularly touches and stirs his emotions. From another angle, since reality is not intelligible in all its aspects to the members of under-developed communities, he naturally transposes his conceptions of relativity and of the marvellous in to his vision of everyday reality. A bird in rapid flight is, above all, a pair of wings, a woman giving suck impresses by her round and heavy breasts, a wild beast is essentially a footfall and a roar, the body responds naturally to music without following a pre-ordained plan, in contrast to other men who exercise a constant restraint over their bodies in order to conform to the social usages of polite society. To demonstrate the peculiar, and sometimes paradoxical, sensitivity of the Haitian, for example, we would cite the fact that in our Voodoo religion a man possessed will sometimes take a red hot iron in his hands without burning them and lick it; he climbs trees with agility, even if he is an old man, he succeeds in dancing for several days and nights on end, he chews and swallows glass... Quite apart from any mystic conception of the world, in the light of numerous observed facts, there are many values which should be revised by science. Can one, in effect, strip a human being of all his antecedents, of all the unconditioned reflexes born of the conditioned reflexes transmitted by heredity? A human being cannot be the son of no man, the past and history cannot be denied; the Haitian, and, through him, his culture, is the legatee of an inheritance of reactions of behaviour and habitude anterior to his hundred and fifty years of independence ; he is still, to a large extent, heir of cultural elements derived from distant Africa. The Haitian has an air, a family likeness, internal as much as external, which makes him resemble on many planes his other brothers in the world of Negro origin. That, moreover, is why we are here at this Congress.

It is because they recognize that their people express their whole consciousness of reality by the use of the Marvellous, that Haitian writers and artists have become aware of the formal problem of its use. Behind the imaginary characters of the romancero of Bouqui and Malice, it is a faithful picture of the conditions of rural life which the Haitian story-teller executes, it is its beauties and its ugliness, and struggles, the drama of the oppressors and the oppressed which he brings on to their stage. In his working songs, for among us work is unthinkable without music, or without songs in which all the workers take part, —in his working songs the Voodoo gods of the Haitian are nothing but an aspiration towards the ownership of the land on which he works, an aspiration towards the rain which feeds the harvest, an aspiration towards abundant bread, an aspiration to get rid of the maladies which afflict him, an aspiration towards betterment in every sphere. Even the religious songs and dances are transparent symbols in which they beg the gods for the solution of a specific problem; there are, moreover, peasant gods, soldier gods, politician gods, powerful gods and exploited gods, gods who are unhappy in love, infirm gods, one-legged gods, blind gods, dumb gods, rapacious gods and gods who are simple, kind and helpful, poets and laughers. When they are mariners, our people also include the width of the horizon, the murmuring of the waves, the drama of the seas, in the form of Agouet Arroyo, the Loa of the Ocean, they hymn the Diamond Siren, "the Sun Queen", as they sometimes say, but nothing more actual, nothing more truthful, nothing more living than all these entities. How could we be unconscious to the extent of refusing to use all that in the service of realizing specific and actualized struggles? That is what made the poet and playwright Morisseau-Leroy write as follows in a recent article;

> "We are again living through a renaissance of the Haitian song. We see flourishing again forms of expression, both rich and original, as in the times when dithyrambic or satyric, lyric or bucolic couplets flowed from the lips of a people whose temper and humour were proof against all misery... From one end of the Republic to another nephews and uncles, nieces and aunts are singing or humming in cadence... And if Agoue T'Arroyo does not afford that rude class of workers enough protection against shipwreck, the official social institutions of the Republic have hardly done better in that direction. It is therefore gratuituously that in their songs they invoke the gods and the chiefs... I want before everything to emphasize that if reality in its local aspect, as in its universal aspect, escapes those who have been led astray by a certain humanism, the popular bards, the "composes" remain, in my view, the sole masters of Haitian poetry, the only ones capable of making us sing and dance together in the unavowed and common conviction that the people are safe and sound."

What, then, is the Marvellous, except the imagery in which a people wraps its experience, reflects its conception of the world and of life, its faith, its hope, its confidence in man, in a great justice, and the explanation which it finds for the forces antagonistic to progress? It is true that the Marvellous implies ingenuousness and empiricism, if not mysticism, but it has been proved that something else can be bound up with it. When the great painter Wilson Bigaud painted a picture called "The Earthly Paradise" he made full use of the Marvellous, but has the painter not expressed the way in which the Haitian people conceives a time of happiness? Look at all those fruits which accumulate in bunches on the canvas, those dense masses of colour, all those splendid animals, tranquil and fraternal, including the wild beasts, is it not the cosmic dream of abundance and fraternity of a people still suffering from hunger and deprivation? When in his play "Rara" Morisseau-Leroy shows a man dying for his right to a feast day in the drabness of his working days, paralytics who get up and dance, mutes who begin to sing when, after the death of heroes, people recount that they are traversing the region, when ghosts are seen, no-one is mistaken, no-one gives it a mystical significance, but everyone sees in it an incitement to the fight for happiness. Naturally, one must always do better, and the combatants, of the advance guard of Haitian culture recognize the need resolutely to transcend whatever is irrational, mystic and animist in their national patrimony, but they do not think that that is an insoluble problem. They will reject the animist garment which conceals the realist nucleus, the dynamics of their culture, a nucleus charged with good sense, life and humanism, they will put on its feet again what is too often walking on its head, but they will never deny that cultural tradition, which is a great and fine thing, the only one which they possess as their own. Just as there is no question of any people denying religious art or works influenced by a mystical conception of life, Haitian men of culture will be able in a dynamic, positive and scientific way, a way of social realism, to combine the whole human protest against the harsh realities of life, all the emotion, the long cry of struggle, distress and hope which are contained in the works and forms transmitted to them by the past.

Social realism, conscious of the imperatives of history, preaches an art human in its content, but resolutely national in its form. This means that the pseudo "world citizens" of culture, the true cosmopolitans, the true expatriates, have nothing to do with the man of our time, nothing to do with progress, and therefore nothing to do with culture. If all human races and all nations are equal and sisters, they have none the less their own traditions, their own temperament and forms which are more likely to touch them. If Art were not national in its form, how could the citizens of a country set about recognizing the perfumes and the climates which they love, so as truly to relive the works of beauty which are offered to them, and to find in them their share of dreams and of courage? The result would be that the people in question would find it difficult to take part in the forward movement of mankind towards liberation, since that art and that literature, essential elements in realization as much as in delight, would have no hold upon their feelings.

Haitian artists made use of the Marvellous in a dynamic sense before they realized that they were creating a Marvellous Realism. We became gradually conscious of the fact. Creating realism meant that the Haitian artists were setting about speaking the same language as their people. The Marvellous Realism of the Haitians is thus an integral part of Social Realism, and in its Haitian form it follows the same preoccupations. The treasury of tales and legends, all the musical, choreographic and plastic symbolism, all the forms of Haitian popular art are there to help the nation in solving its problems and in accomplishing the tasks which lie before it. The Western genres and organons bequeathed to us must be resolutely transformed in a national sense, and everything in a work of art must stir those feelings which are peculiar to the Haitians, sons of three races and an infinity of cultures.

To sum up, the objects of Marvellous Realism are:

1. To sing the beauties of the Haitian motherland, its greatness as well as its wretchedness, with the sense of the magnificent prospects which are opened up by the struggles of its people and their solidarity with all men, and in this way to attain the human, the universal and the profound truth of life;
2. To reject all art which has no real and social content;
3. To find the forms of expression proper to its own people, those which correspond to their psychology, while employing in a renovated and widened form, the universal models, naturally in accordance with the personality of each creator.
4. To have a clear consciousness of specific and concrete current problems and the real dramas which confront the masses, with the purpose of touching and cultivating more deeply, and of carrying the people with them in their struggles.

In relation to particular forms of art, there are many aspects which need to be made clearer, but only a detailed discussion would enable us to come nearer to the truth. It is not an easy task to progress along the road of this kind of realism, and there are many gropings and many errors ahead of us, but we shall know how to profit even by our mistakes, to reach as soon as possible what is already taking shape before our eyes. Work will settle all the rest.

11. The current problems of Haitian culture

We have said that Haiti faces a serious problem, caused by its bilingualism. This bilingualism would not be a problem if it were not for an element which throws everything out, namely a percentage of analphabetics in excess of 85%. If Haitian literature has not produced very much, that is because of analphabetism, which limits the literary market and is hardly an encouragement to Haitian writers who find it very difficult, and with a few exceptions, impossible to live by their art. For this very reason Haitian writers are compelled to look to the public service, and not only can they devote little time to their art, but their freedom of expression is singularly limited in the atmosphere of a country where the public service is, as a matter of history, a partisan question. The gravest problem is that no true communication is possible between the Haitian people and those of its sons who are valid creators and who honour and shed lustre upon its culture. Our position is clear on this point; the fight for the greatness of Haitian literature is inseparable from the struggle to launch a real campaign, on a large scale and State organized, to end analphabetism. A writer who did not appreciate this historic task of ending analphabetism in Haiti, a writer who did not appreciate the practical necessity of taking part in a great and powerful fighting organization to induce the people and the government to devote a substantial part of our resources to this work, would not only be neglecting his duties as a patriot, but also his mission as a writer and a clerk.

We consider that there are two languages which could give literary expression to the living reality of Haiti, namely Creole and French. Creole for us is at the stage which French had achieved in relation to Latin during the Middle Ages. French was then the language of the people, Latin the language of men of letters and learning. At that period, it was difficult to foretell which language would emerge victorious in the future, the vernacular or the Latin language; the objective conditions of France resulted in French developing and enriching itself and in Latin becoming bastardized, turning into kitchen Latin, falling into disuse, and finally disappearing (as also in Italy). At the present moment, although Creole is the language of the overwhelming mass of the population, we should not like to prophesy about the future, because the conditions of modern life are not those of the Middle Ages, but we must nevertheless take up a practical attitude until such time as French and Creole have liquidated their historic quarrel in Haiti. We think in effect that it is our duty to teach the Haitian people to read in their mother tongue of Creole, and that we should not perpetuate the folly which has, for a hundred and fifty years, ruined all efforts at public education, namely obstinately trying to teach illiterates to read in a language which, in spite of its cousinship, is foreign to them. Certainly we are in favour of teaching French at all stages as a privileged language, but Creole should be the basis, at any rate in the primary and rural schools. In this way we should avoid the hazard of seeing those who are supposed to have been cured of analphabetism by French, rapidly reverting to functional analphabetics, as commonly happens. We also think that, after French, a privileged place in teaching should be given to Spanish, having regard to the Latin American complex to which we belong, as well as to the fact that hundreds of thousands of Haitians speak this language.

On the literary plane, we think that both languages, French and Creole, should be used in conjunction, instead of a half-way language, French in its grammatical form, and Creole in its presentation, thanks to the use of an archaic French, which is now obsolete. It will not be a half-way language which is victorious in Haiti, it will be either French or Creole, and, moreover, in the distant future, the victorious language will be consequential upon our relations with other neighbouring States of the Antilles and of Latin America. We do not regard as Don Quixotes those Haitian writers who are beginning to publish works in Creole; this question is inseparable from the campaign against analphabetism, and we need texts in Creole straight away, in order to make this campaign successful. We should also think about translating into Creole the works of all worth-while Haitian writers and of all the Haitian classics. With regard to the movement for a Creole language theatre, which has been developing for some years, this is of immense importance in bringing culture home to all levels of the population.

In the field of the plastic arts we are delighted with the immense interest which is being taken all over the world in Haitian painting almost on a par with Mexican painting. We are happy to see that in all competitions for painting organized in Central America, Haitian painting is always to be found among the first places if it does not actually win the major prizes, but at the same time we are aware of a danger which is threatening the Haitian plastic arts. What happened a few years ago to our sculpture, which was so promising, is now threatening our painting. In fact the Haitian market for the plastic arts is largely a foreign market, a North American market, and in the same way that many of our sculptors allowed themselves to be corrupted by the love of certain North American tourists for the picturesque and the wild and produced works which no longer had any real Haitian quality, the beginnings of the same disease may be diagnosed among our painters. It is important that some voices should be raised in opposition to this commercialisation, but we should also contemplate ways of fighting for an extension of the national market for the plastic arts. At the same time we should present our works in Europe, as well as in other parts of the world which are showing an interest in the successors of Hector Hippolyte, the brilliant Pleiad of whom Wilson Bigaud, Dieudonné Cedor, Louverture Poisson and Philome Obin are the leaders. We hope that a profoundly national and realistic spirit may serve as our loadstone, a loadstone which has led us and continues to lead us towards great successes.

While the menace which threatens our plastic art applies equally to our singing and folk dancing, always in relation to the steadily increasing flow of tourists from North America, it is not so important in connexion with our music. While we recognize the influence upon our music of Cuban and Dominican music, this is most frequently merely the return of what we have ourselves exported, and moreover it is not necessary to be unduly perturbed about these influences, since the cultural heritage of the Cuban and Dominican composers is not fundamentally different from our own. That does not mean to say that we should not be very concerned faithfully to express our national reality in music. What principally disturbs us is the falling off of interest in chamber music and symphonic music among us. There are not many parts of the world where the occupation of composer is a profitable one. We must however study the problem in all its aspects, in order to make sure that we have in our midst many successors to Justin Elie, Occide Jeanty and Ludovic Lamothe.

Conclusions.

And now the moment has come for us to turn to our brothers of Negro origin and tell them how much we have need of them to fulfil our tasks. How many tasks there are ahead of us in our respective countries! Co-operation and mutual aid are essential for us; we all contemplate that this First Congress should be followed by many others so that we may constantly compare, in the spirit of amity and fraternity, what we are accomplishing. May we be permitted to express a wish? It is desirable that there should be a permanent organization which would help us to make the best of our co-operation; there should be, at least in every country concerned, a National Committee of Intellectuals of Negro origin and that an effective International Liaison Committee of Intellectuals of Negro origin should between Congresses co-ordinate the different manifestations of co-operation and solidarity of the various National Committees. Perhaps in each of our important towns there should also be Local Committees responsible for publicising and applying any decisions. However only the Working Commissions of this Congress can consider this proposal in detail, and so, in the name of the Haitian Intellectuals, Writers and Artists, I extend fraternal greetings to all our brothers and sisters, from different countries, met together to work in unison in a determined spirit of fraternity and solidarity.

"Preface" and "Afrocubanism"

Alejo Carpentier

Preface

Orphaned by conquest of its indigenous artistic traditions, impoverished in its popular art forms, slighted by its colonial architects, especially when compared to other Latin American nations, the island of Cuba, on the other hand, has powerfully created a distinctive music that has long enjoyed extraordinary success abroad. The worldwide popularity achieved by Cuban dances since 1928 was nothing new for the island. Earlier, Cuban *contradanzas* had garnered similar accolades by European and American audiences under such diverse names as *habaneras, danzas habaneras, tangos habaneras, americanas,* and so on, creating genres that were widely cultivated in France, Spain, Mexico, and Venezuela. Our research has encountered creole *guarachas* from the eighteenth century with rhythms that remain popular today. Many of the percussion instruments that have recently enriched the percussion sections of all dance orchestras, such as the *claves,* were commonly used in seventeenth-century Havana. By the end of the sixteenth century, there were *conjuntos típicos* [folk ensembles] in Santiago, and their *sones* were sung in Cuba for more than two hundred years.

What this reveals is that at every moment of its history, Cuba elaborated a sonorous and lively folklore of surprising vitality, receiving, meshing, and transforming diverse contributions, all of which led to the creation of new and clearly defined genres. We should not forget that, at the same time, other types of musical activity arose, considerably in advance of other intellectual manifestations. Even before Cuba had its first theater or its first newspaper, there was a notable and learned composer such as Esteban Salas in the cathedral of Santiago. We discovered extremely important work after prolonged searching and after many assurances that the work had been lost forever; until now, most music scholars and writers on Latin America are unaware of Salas's work. At the end of the eighteenth century, the names of Haydn, Pergolesi, Paisiello, Grétry, Monsigny, were honored in Havana. As a maritime crossroads, Havana had hosted French companies en route to New Orleans that performed an extraordinarily advanced repertoire for the Americas of that time. Before the mid-nineteenth century, Cuba could boast of a symphonist and composer such as Saumell, who clearly had conceptually defined what later would be called musical nationalism. Espadero and Villate were famous in Europe. Ignacio Cervantes, with his *Danzas,* exercised a definite influence over many musicians of the New Continent.

We make no claim, of course, to exaggerate the universal significance of Cuban music, or the place it should be assigned in the panorama of the world's music. But the study of its development within a specific context, that is, the presence of different ethnicities and their percentage of the population, bring forth a series of exceedingly interesting problems. If we take these factors into account, we observe that they are closely analogous to those similar aspects that a researcher might encounter in other countries of the continent. They contribute to explaining the mechanisms by which certain cultures of the New World are formed. Given these concerns, we have tried to situate the musical events in their historical milieu without losing sight of social, economic, and demographic factors. The study of the census, for example, with its proportion of whites, mulattoes, and blacks, of freed slaves and slaves, has always been necessary to comprehend certain characteristics in the evolution of musical culture and folklore in a country that has endured so many and diverse immigrations.

For the same reason we have tried to create, along with our central theme, a schematic study of the music of other Antillean islands—in particular Haiti—whose slave-led revolution unexpectedly brought to Cuba a number of rhythms and genres, altering certain aspects of its folklore. This method has convinced us that there is much that American musicology stands to gain in studying the music of the continent by *geographic zones* subject to the same ethnic influences, to the same migrations of rhythms and oral traditions, *rather than by region or country*.

This work has been written almost entirely with primary documents. Given the shallowness or lack of seriousness in the few books on Cuba's musical history,[1] I felt obligated to return to primary sources of information. There were early warning signs that a number of generally accepted claims made in the work of even solid foreign scholars, misled by their credulity, had been the result of the most ingenuous fantasy. Moreover, almost all the published work focused on certain particular or anecdotal aspects, influenced by the private sympathies or personal aesthetics of the writer, and in no way attempted to offer an overall vision of the development of the island's music from the onset of colonization.

Given this we embarked upon the patient scrutiny of cathedral archives — principally of Santiago and Havana — of capitulary records of churches and city halls, of parish closets (with brilliant results in Santiago, but none in Santa María del Rosario), of manuscript documents, private libraries, individual collections, and the shelves of secondhand bookstores, thoroughly inspecting the newspapers, gazettes, and magazines of the colonial period. In many cases we had to do research helter-skelter, looking for facts in texts that dealt with anything but music (histories of tobacco and coffee, judicial decrees and military ordinances, or political essays). Needless to say, in the course of our labors we have had to wade through many more texts than appear in our bibliography, and we have more than once stumbled upon the all-too-familiar obstacles that so often dishearten the Latin American researcher: libraries in disarray, the lack of card catalogs, incomplete collections, mutilated books, and so on. We do not even mention the collectors that behaved like dogs in the manger. Luckily, we have been providentially favored by the discovery of several scores whose absence would have reduced this book to being a mere chronicle.

On the other hand, we have counted on a cooperation to which we can never be sufficiently grateful: that of Monsignor Arteaga, archbishop of Havana, who furnished us with credentials to go through the archives of the diocese; of Father Fidel Ruiz, parish priest of the cathedral of Santiago, who allowed us to copy the scores of Esteban Salas and Juan París — which we discovered in an old forgotten piece of furniture; of Doctor José Antonio Ramos, assistant director of the National Library, and of Mr. Villanueva, bookseller at the same institution, as well as the librarians of the Sociedad Económica de Amigos del País, so highly conscious of their professional mission. Finally, we should give thanks to Natalio Galán, who worked several months with us transcribing some of Salas's scores, especially those so damaged by time.

This history of Cuban music, the first to be written, does not pretend to have exhausted the subject. Much will be added when scientists undertake the study of the continent's music and its African roots. The examination of certain colonial newspapers buried in unused private libraries could enrich the documentation of Havana musical life during the first years of the nineteenth century. We still have not chanced upon Antonio Raffelin's first or second symphony, which should be retrievable in some North American library. The letters between Gottschalk and Espadero contain much that still needs to be revealed ...

But a first book on this subject must conserve a sense of proportion, lest it result in the lack of global vision that has characterized the majority of texts written in Cuba about its music up to now. Accordingly, we have refrained from using certain documents that might have been offered as good research finds, especially when their secondary nature might have obscured the main themes of our narrative. We also left aside the noble area of revolutionary music — more of historical than artistic interest—since we decided that figures such as Perucho Figueredo, for example, author of the Cuban national anthem, ought to be the subject of a different type of research, more closely linked to the patriotic reproduction of iconographic documents or manuscripts. On the other hand, we abstained from lengthy personal comments at the margin of events, believing that basic information should be the main goal of this work, undertaken on almost virgin soil, and whose principal documentary sources are nothing more than the manuscripts or the references lost in ledgers and colonial newspaper collections. We believe that the general thrust of the study traces the continuous development of Cuban music and its culture from the beginning. Thus, with an opening panoramic vision obtained in this first general overview, we then proceed to study individual cases and fill the lacunae that are still found in the life of Saumell, for example, or to detail the activities of a Raffelin in France, Spain, and the United States. Nevertheless, with this book, we think we have set in place —for other researchers and for ourselves — the necessary point of departure.

Note

1. One exception must be made: the well-documented study by Edwin Tolón and Jorge Antonio González, *Óperas Cubanas y Sus Autores*.

Afro-Cubanism

Sánchez de Fuentes's repugnance in admitting the presence of black rhythms in Cuban music can be understood as a reflection of a general outlook during the first years of the republic. Years had transpired since blacks were no longer slaves. However, in a newly conceived country that aspired to bring itself up to date with the cultural currents of the day, the authentically black cultural experience — that is, those deeply rooted and surviving African elements that remained in a pure state — was looked upon with disgust, as a kind of barbaric holdover from the past, and could only be tolerated as a necessary evil. In 1913, the traditional *comparsas* were prohibited. The religious festivities of blacks were prohibited. Undeniably, certain ritual crimes, committed by witch doctors, justified police persecution against the practices of the *babalawos* [Santeria priests]. Some street fighting between enemy *ñáñigo groups* had also logically generated repressive measures. But it should not be believed that these deeds were so frequent, nor that they reached the magnitude of the common crimes committed. It had been a long time since knife-wielders like Manuel Cañamazo, Manita en el suelo, or the black man Sucumbento were the terror of neighborhoods outside the city limits. Furthermore, if so many blacks were loitering among hoodlums with a drum on their belly, much of the blame rested with whites, who always relegated them to a marginal existence, offering them the worst jobs, except when they wanted votes, in which case they appealed to their baser qualities. The kind of politicking that went on during the first years of the republic did nothing to improve the social or cultural condition of blacks; indeed, it fueled their vices as long as blacks were useful for political ends. All these factors contributed to the attitude held by well-heeled men of mistrusting all matters black, and since they were not inclined to ask difficult questions, they did not notice that high on the scaffolds, in the heat of the foundries, under the sun of the rock quarries, or in the coachman's seat, an entire sea of humanity was on the move, a people who conserved their poetic and musical traditions, quite worthy of being studied.

Of course, these traditions offered a wide spectrum in their purity of preservation. As Ramos put it so aptly:

> In the New World, the relationships between blacks and whites brought as a corollary the subordination of one to the other, segregation and separation, and all the subsequent racial and cultural conflict (at times, acute) this subordination implied. This segregation caused the almost total disappearance, in some cases, of primitive institutions. When an individual is separated from his cultural group and placed in contact with other groups and cultures, he tends, in the second or third generation, to forget the primitive cultures and to assimilate the new cultures he has come in contact with.

This process of transculturation has happened several times in previous centuries. The *"Son de la Má' Teodora"* constitutes the most typical sixteenth-century example of this. For an Ulpiano Estrada, a Brindis de Salas, black Creoles of several generations, little was left in the nineteenth century of the primitive cultures of their grandfathers. Only an instinct survived — in this case a rhythmic instinct — of these black musicians and composers who contributed to the evolution of Cuban music in its first phase, without changing the form or the existing melodic sources. Nothing differentiated "the black Malibrán woman," married to an officer of the Spanish army, from any other Cuban woman of her time, except the color of her skin. This explains why so many blacks made "white music" during the nineteenth century, refusing to play the roles of "black professors," while the whites — a Bartolomé José Crespo, a Guerrero — were the ones who dressed up as blacks.

But it must not be forgotten that while the transculturation process had completed itself for certain generations, the slave ships kept bringing, with a horrendous regularity, their cargo of "ebony flesh." Thousands upon thousands of slaves kept swelling the workforces of Cuba's plantations, reinitiating a cycle of adaptation whose earlier phases were fixed in the Cuban vernacular: *bozales,* when they arrived from Africa and spoke only in their dialects; *ladinos* when they began to speak in Spanish; *criollos,* the offspring of the ladinos; and *reyoyos,* the children of the criollos. With free slaves or those recently emancipated, the process of transculturation took place swiftly, since contact with the outside world was immediate. But in the slave barracks it was infinitely slower, because knowledge of white culture was gleaned from what the slave could observe at a distance, when there was a party in the master's house. The slave was told to dance his native dances, because it was considered important for the preservation of his health. The slave traders had learned this much earlier than the landowners. However, there were limitations. In 1839, a circular by General Ezpeleta established that, "the slaves in the countryside should be allowed to dance their native dances known as 'with drums,' on holidays, under the vigilance of their overseers, without blacks from any other farm being present." That is, if the slaves from one farm were, in their majority, from one tribe or nation, they would not have the slightest opportunity to have contact with a neighboring workforce of different ethnic origins. The varying conservation or dilution of African traditions derives from this history, and holds true even today among Cuban blacks. Certain old men, born in captivity, remember legends and songs from Africa with extraordinary precision. The black man Yamba, more than a hundred years old, whom I met at a farm in the remote countryside, spoke just like blacks in the work of Bartolomé José Crespo, without knowing any other type of dance than what he had seen in the slave barracks as a child. Those same dances are long gone, a tradition the black university student is unaware of, equally true for the mulatto musician of a Havana swing orchestra. After severing the umbilical cord of the slave trade, Cuban blacks lost their contact with Africa, conserving an ever hazier memory of their ancestral traditions. When the *comparsas* were allowed to function again, about ten years ago [1937], they no longer had the same power; they had gained much as moving spectacle, as luxurious theater, in abundance of instruments; but they had lost authenticity. There are not many performers today who are capable of making the array of *batá* drums speak. And yet, their musical awareness is incomparably vaster than that of their grandfathers.

This might explain why certain arcane aspects of black music have taken so long to interest more "serious" composers, more directly drawn to what they immediately heard: the rhythms and singing of the *comparsas,* incorporated into the *contradanzas* in the last phase of their evolution. There was more. Much more. Without mentioning groups from long ago, like Nuestra Señora de los Remedios, founded by free blacks in Havana in 1598, nor the petition for land to establish *cabildos,* which figure in the town records of eighteenth-century Santiago, in 1796 there was already a Cabildo de Congos Reales, under the name of one of the Three Kings, Saint Melchior. The increasing black population, together with a proportionately greater manumission of slaves, made these groups proliferate. Essentially, the *cabildos* were "mutual aid societies," which prevented the ex-slave from being buried in a common grave. The following *cabildos* appeared: Arará, Apapá, Apapá Chiquito, Mandinga, Oro, Lucumí, Carabalí Ungrí, Nación Mina Popó de la Costa de Oro, Arará tres ojos, and so on. The blacks from Calabar created secret *ñáñigo* societies, whose first activities date from around 1835, when the Acabatón society appeared in Regla. Although the *cabildos* composed of offspring of the "nations"—blacks from different regions/ethnicities — endured to our times, *ñañiguismo* spread throughout Cuban society, because it had a more inclusive notion of membership. They admitted people of all races and walks of life into their ranks, as long as they observed the established rules. (Chinese, Creoles, even Spaniards were affiliated with *ñañiguismo*.) Their initiation ceremonies and the true brotherhood of those who belonged made *ñañiguismo* a true popular masonry. Around 1914, in Havana, Regla, Guanabacoa, and Matanzas, there were fifty-seven *juegos* [groups] of *ñañigos*. Currently, even though *ñañiguismo* has lost a lot of its strength because of the previously described transculturation process, various groups still remain, strict guardians of the language and the ritual.

If the black *cabildos* were mutual aid societies, they also specified, when legally registered, that they were created for "recreational and leisurely pursuits." This authorized them to hold dances and form *comparsas* for Three Kings Day [January 6] or, after the abolition of slavery, for carnival. In different periods the *comparsas* paraded through the streets of Havana, sporting vivid names: *El gavilán, Los congos libres, El alacrán chiquito, La culebra, El pájaro lindo, Mandinga Moro Rizo, Mandinga Moro Azul, Los moros, Los peludos.* [The hawk, The free congos, The small scorpion, The snake, The pretty bird, Mandinga curly Moor, Mandinga blue Moor, The Moors, The hairy ones]. The *comparsas*, more than just a marching rhythmic collective, were like an itinerant ballet. They had their "themes." A spider or a snake, represented by a huge figure held on high by an expert dancer, served as the focal point for dancing and singing. The *comparsa* members would "kill the spider" or "kill the snake."

"Mamita, mamita, yen, yen, yen:
que me mata la culebra, yen, yen, yen.   (the snake's gonna kill me,)
Mírale los ojo   (Look at its eyes, they seem like fire
que parecen candela;
mírale lo diente, que parece filé   look at its teeth
(alfileres)"   they seem like needles
"Mentira, mi negra, yen, yen, yen;   It's a lie, my black woman,)
son juego e mi tierra, yen, yen, yen."   (they are the game of my soil,)

As Ramos observed referring to similar dances seen in Brazil, those figures that used to (and still do) inspire the name of certain *comparsas* undoubtedly represent a totemic survival. In the snake dance, Fernando Ortiz sees an offshoot of a Dahomey snake cult that still persists in Haiti, where a serpent of forged steel appears on all voodoo altars. As for the violent and bloody strife between *ñañigo* groups in the nineteenth century, Vivó maintains that they reflect old intertribal rivalries from Africa. The initiation ceremony of the *ñañigos*, which we have witnessed many times, is truly a collective spectacle, in which episodes of the same legend are mimed, danced, and sung with slight variations. Something of old funeral rites has stayed embedded in them. A government edict in 1792 prohibited that "blacks could conduct or allow others to conduct, to the *cabildos* the cadavers of blacks, in order to sing or cry as is customary in their native land." Years later, the bishop Trespalacios insisted on the point. As for the festivities with magic — a different issue altogether — their main objective continues to be a believer's possession, so thoroughly studied by Jacques Roumain in his *Le sacrifice du Tambour Assohtor*. In the commonly accepted notion, the possession by a saint or divinity in the black pantheon is syncretically represented almost always by a Catholic image. This is currently referred to in Cuba as *"bajar al santo"* [to make the saint descend] or *"subirse el santo"* [to make the saint come up through you]. But let us not linger here on matters amply dealt with by specialists in the field.

Musically, the matter is very complex. Because to say "African music" is the same as saying "medieval knights." As Ortiz has pointed out, "in studying Afro-Cuban music one has to distinguish between music descended from Dahomey, or the Yoruba, or the Carabalí and Conga." Unfortunately, a scientific work of notation, compilation, comparison, rhythmic and modal study, with its ensuing classifications, still has not been undertaken, because the task, admittedly so, is beyond the scope of one individual. In the first place, if one does not have informants who are intelligent and trustworthy, it is impossible to find out when and where a religious ceremony or a profane drumming session will be held. In the second place, because the true ñáñigos — that is, the most interesting ones — ascertained on many occasions, are opposed to having their musical rituals notated or taped, since they view these acts as a profanation of their secrets. In the third place, a researcher's interest quickly awakens the greed among people who do not know any better, who then scheme up some kind of charade in exchange for a few coins. Fernando Ortiz, appealing to a heroic sense of patience, is the person who has most deeply researched these matters. But he is not a musician, nor does he claim to be, and for different reasons he has been bereft of the best collaborators that he could have had in his musical research.

Let us rely, then, on certain authoritative conclusions drawn by Ortiz:

> The river peoples of the Niger, particularly the Yorubas and the Nagós, in Cuba known as *lucumís,* brought, along with their complex religious beliefs, drums, songs, and dances of their ancient rites that still resonate intact under the skies of the Americas imploring favors from their African divinities. Dahomeyan music, or of the *dajomés,* as in Cuba they have been referred to with true phonetic propriety, is almost identical to that of their neighbors, the *arará,* and both have been maintained, sheltered by *lucumí rites.* We know that the Yoruba pantheon spread among the bordering towns, especially toward the north, penetrating Dahomey and its coastal area, in the ancient Ardrá or Arará region, absorbed more than a century earlier by that very powerful kingdom. For this reason, among blacks of this region one finds an advanced theological and liturgical syncretism, and the chants, drum beats, and instruments have intermingled, where similar deities are invoked under different names. This allows us to infer, if we know beforehand the religious nomenclature of these peoples, whether a chant is Dahomeyan or Yoruba, according to the language of the prayer or name of the god being propitiated. It is easy to deduce that a chant to Shangó (deity of lightning), is from the *lucumís,* and one for Ebioso (also an igneous god) is from Dahomey or the *dajomés.* Ñañiguismo has an unmistakable musical personality; its naked simplicity sustains *carabalí* music in Cuba.

And Ortiz adds in another work:

> Here, at the core of our people, there is still much music of *bantú* or *conga* origin in the dances of our peasants; we have *gangá* music, from which the primitive rumba is derived; some bits of *arará* or *dajomé* music, called voodoo in Haiti, which here tends to mix in with *lucumí* music; and, finally, best-conserved and varied of Cuba's African music, the religious liturgy of the Yoruba.

Lucumí and *ñáñigo* music generally has melodies that are ample, noble, slow in contrast with the dynamism of the percussion. It is sung by the faithful, in unison or in octaves. In all of the hymns one observes an antiphonal form: a soloist and a chorus or two semichoruses, the second repeating the phrases of the first. "In Yoruba religious chants the antiphonal soloist initiates or raises the chant to a pleasing level, and the chorus, called the *ankori,* responds in the same tone as the soloist" (Ortiz). This liturgy comprises, among others, songs to Elegguá, overseer of all roads; to Ogún, blacksmith and inventor of the anvil, represented by the image of Saint Peter; to Ochosi, god of hunting and warriors (Saint Norbert); to Babalú-Ayé (Saint Lazarus); to Yemayá, goddess of the sea and cosmic mother; to Obatalá, to Ochún, to Changó, to Oyá … It is extremely rare to find a theme of these chants that begins on the dominant note. The elimination of the leading note is so frequent that when a popular composer wants to impart an "African air" to a melody, by instinct he suppresses or alters the seventh note. Quite frequently the hymns are based on pentatonic scales without semitones. But the use of these ranges is capricious, without obeying the rules. We will not speak of modes or particular characteristics of one or another kind of music, since the scarcity of scientifically established documents makes any analysis pointless.

As for percussion, it is simply prodigious. The Afro-Cuban drums compose an entire arsenal: the *ñáñigos*, tensed with strings and wedges, one-sided, played with two hands, designated generically with the name of *encomos*, although the family includes, as Israel Castellanos points out, the *bencomo*, the *cosilleremá*, the *llaibillembi* and the *boncó enchemillá*; the *batá* drums, "bimembraned, played on both sides, with a wooden hourglass shape, closed, permanently taut with a rope-like skin" (Ortiz), which are called, as we have seen, *okónkolo* (the smallest), *itótele* (the medium-sized one), and *iyá* (the largest), which is "the mother of the drums." In addition, one must mention the *tumba* and the *tahona*, used for profane and sacred functions. To these are usually added, although not as a rule, the *cajón*, the *marímbula*, the *güiro*, the *econes*, or the little iron bells without tongues, and the *claves*. Also used are two types of *marugas*: the one that consists of two tin cones, welded at the base and filled with little stones (what is called in other Antillean isles the *chá-chá*), and the one that consists of a cone made of laced fibers, filled with seeds or *mates*, which is shaken from the top down, and held by a ring fixed at its vertex (one of the many kinds of basket rattles known by certain indigenous peoples of the Americas).

Notice that Afro-Cuban music dispenses with any melody-making instruments. Pure singing over percussion. On the other hand, in the ceremonial rituals — the *ñáñigo* initiation, for example, or those of Santeria — one does not observe the slightest watering down of a way of singing that remains true to old African customs. Blacks who pride themselves on knowing ancestral hymns and traditions are unaware of hybrid genres, analogous to the windward *fulía*, for example, and that the *décima* derived from the *romance* — in Cuba part of the cultural patrimony of white peasants — alternated with sung and instrumental passages of purely African technique. There are cases where the *batá* drums, aided by their rich tuning and the virtuosity of their performers, play entire solo passages, eliminating the voices. Once, at a Santeria party in Regla, we heard the drummers play a "march" and a "wail" of considerable duration, which were true pieces, complete, balanced, developed within the tempo, evolving from fundamental rhythmic cells. In many cases, this prime beat flowers into a *rhythmic mode*. Really, how can we properly speak of rhythm when faced with a true phrase, composed of notes and groups of notes, that outpaces all metrical limits before acquiring a rhythmic function through sheer repetition? When this happens — and it does so frequently — we are in the presence of a rhythmic mode, with its own accents that have nothing to do with accepted notions of a strong or weak beat. The player stresses this note or another, not for scansional reasons, but because the traditional expression of the *rhythmic mode* demands it. It is not mere happenstance that blacks say that "they make the drums speak"! Now consider the disconcerting effect of movement, of internal palpitations given off by the simultaneous pacings of various rhythmic modes, which end up establishing mysterious relationships among themselves, conserving, however, a certain independence, and you will have a remote idea of the kind of bewitching effect produced by certain expressions of the *batá* drums!

On the other hand, we must not forget that in certain kinds of ceremonies the chants respond to very diverse uses and emotions. If the practice of "making the saint descend" is accompanied by a monotonous chant whose purpose is to engender an obsession, a fixed idea conducive to an ecstatic state; conversely, in the *ñáñigo* celebrations, for example, there are so many different chants and phases that accompany an intricate initiation ceremony. A true mystery play, the *juego* includes, in this case, antiphonal hymns, dances by *diablitos* [little devils], prayers for the dead, marches, processionals, and an invocation to the sun, as well as recitations of formulas "in native tongue," measured out on the skin of the drum. It is pointless to go on about the rich sonorities of these types of folkloric expression.

In 1925, Amadeo Roldán began to consciously exploit this wondrous wellspring of rhythms and melodies. However, a phenomenon prevalent in all Afro-Cuban symphonic output bears pointing out: bereft of scientific work where they can study the modal and rhythmic laws governing black music, the Cuban composer works with materials haphazardly chanced upon at a ceremony that he has personally witnessed, without really knowing the rich textures of this sonorous treasure. Although *ñáñigo* music is a branch of the *carabalí* tree, it is easy to note that, along with its basic percussion, it is unaware of the music's origins. This allows us to differentiate between what is *ñáñigo* and what is *carabalí,* an almost imperceptible difference if compared to the dissimilarities between certain expressions of Yoruba music from *lucumí* or *conga* music. Under apparent similarities, each one of these musics possesses its own sound environment, rules, ways of being. Without having to subscribe to the role of cultured composer as ethnographer when approaching the primitive soul and his music, we see how, in the work of Roldán, as well as in that of a García Caturla — when they compose girded by the document in hand — all of the elements of that vast sonority of the Afro-Cuban realm are all mixed together. And thus we find, side by side, the *lucumí* hymn, the tune of a *bembé,* the *ñáñigo* invocation, as well as an array of percussion — from the regular and symmetrical that accompanies the dance of the *diablito* or *írime,* to the complex percussion of the Yoruba drums.

The Afro-Cuban music movement initiated by some composers provoked a violent reaction from those opposed to anything black. *Guajiro* music was pitted against Afro-Cuban music, the former purveyed as representative of white music, more noble, melodic, pure. However, those who claimed to utilize *guajiro* music in larger-scale works were surprised that after a first score nothing else was left to be done. And this for an unforeseen reason: the *guajiro* sings his *décimas* with the accompaniment of the *tiple* [treble guitar], but he does not invent anything new musically.

This unique fact is explainable: when he sings, the *guajiro's* poetic invention is fitted to a traditional melodic pattern, whose roots are steeped in the tradition of the Spanish *romance* [ballad], brought to the island by the first colonizers. When the Cuban *guajiro* sings, he sticks to the inherited melody with utmost fidelity. Throughout the Cuban nineteenth century, the popular printing presses flooded the towns and villages with reams and reams of *décimas* "to be sung accompanied by the tiple." But all of those volumes did not include a single bar of music. Why? The reason is simple: if it is true that the *guajiro* was inclined to renovate the lyrics to his songs, learning the words of others, or relying on his own inspiration, he made no pretense of introducing the slightest variety in terms of the tune. The *décimas* offered had to adjust to a model known by all. Quite the poet, the *guajiro* is no musician. He does not create melodies. Throughout the island, he sings his *décimas* over ten or twelve fixed patterns, all similar to one another, whose original sources can be found in any old anthology of ballads from Extremadura [Spain]. (The Venezuelan poet and folklorist Juan Liscano made the same observation when studying certain popular expressions of his country, quite rich in poetic content, but always the same musically.) The same thing happens with the *zapateo.* There is no such thing as different *zapateos.* There is only one, always the same, which returned after eighty years, like a classical quote, in the works of popular Cuban composers:

Anckermann, Marín, Varona, and so on. (Formerly, there was another type of *zapateo* that has disappeared without a trace, and it is harmonized, in published works of last century, in pure Haydnesque style.) At times, and what recently occurred with "La guantanamera," is an example, a *guajiro* singer seems to have invented a new melody. But let us not fall for the ploy. It is simply a reappearance of the ballad, whose song was conserved by those in the interior. And as for the much-heralded "total Cubanness" of the *guajira* melody, we should not have too many illusions. The *guajira* melody of Cuba is identical to that of the Venezuelan *galerón*. (The only difference between the two genres is in the type and number of verses employed.) The only thing that imbues any élan to this static folklore is the virtuosity of the performer or the inventive verve of the singer. But felicitous moments do not a tradition make. Furthermore, the song of the Cuban *guajiro* seems to have lost the luster of its grace, praised a hundred years ago by the Countess of Merlin. There is an evident impoverishment of material.

This explains why scores such as *Suite cubana* by Mario Valdés Costa (a prematurely deceased composer) or the *Capricho* for piano and orchestra by Hubert de Blanck, based on *guajiro* themes, exhausted the possibilities of a folklore after the first attempt. In mixed-blood and black music, on the other hand, if the interest in the lyrics seems scant, the sonic material is incredibly rich. This is why attempts to create a work of national expression always return, sooner or later, to Afro-Cuban and mestizo genres or rhythms.

"What is Art?"

C.L.R. James

I have made great claims for cricket. As firmly as I am able and as is here possible, I have integrated it in the historical movement of the times. The question remains: What is it? Is it mere entertainment or is it an art? Mr Neville Cardus (whose work deserves a critical study) is here most illuminating, not as subject but as object. He will ask: "Why do we deny the art of a cricketer, and rank it lower than a vocalist's or a fiddler's? If anybody tells me that R.H. Spooner did not compel a pleasure as aesthetic as any compelled by the most cultivated Italian tenor that ever lived I will write him down a purist and an ass." He says the same in more than one place. More than any sententious declaration, all his work is eloquent with the aesthetic appeal of cricket. Yet he can write in his autobiography: "I do not believe that anything fine in music or in anything else can be understood or truly felt by the crowd." Into this he goes at length and puts the seal on it with: "I don't believe in the contemporary idea of taking the arts to the people: let them seek and work for them." He himself notes that Neville Cardus, the writer on cricket, often introduces music into his cricket writing. Never once has Neville Cardus, the music critic, introduced cricket into his writing on music. He finds this "a curious point". It is much more than a point, it is not curious. Cardus is a victim of that categorization and specialization, that division of the human personality, which is the greatest curse of our time. Cricket has suffered, but not only cricket. The aestheticians have scorned to take notice of popular sports and games—to their own detriment. The aridity and confusion of which they so mournfully complain will continue until they include organized games and the people who watch them as an integral part of their data. Sir Donald Bradman's technical accomplishments are not on the same plane as those of Yehudi Menuhin. Sir John Gielgud in three hours can express adventures and shades in human personality which are not approached in three years of Denis Compton at the wicket. Yet cricket is an art, not a bastard or a poor relation, but a full member of the community.

The approach must be direct. Too long has it been impressionistic or apologetic, timid or defiant, always ready to take refuge in the mysticism of metaphor. It is a game and we have to compare it with other games. It is an art and we have to compare it with other arts.

Cricket is first and foremost a dramatic spectacle. It belongs with the theatre, ballet, opera and the dance.

In a superficial sense all games are dramatic. Two men boxing or running a race can exhibit skill, courage, endurance and sharp changes of fortune; can evoke hope and fear. They can even harrow the soul with laughter and tears, pity and terror. The state of the city, the nation or the world can invest a sporting event with dramatic intensity such as is reached in few theatres. When the democrat Joe Louis fought the Nazi Schmelling the bout became a focus of approaching world conflict. On the last morning of the 1953 Oval Test, when it was clear than England would win a rubber against Australia after twenty years, the nation stopped work to witness the consummation.

These possibilities cricket shares with other games in a greater or lesser degree. Its quality as drama is more specific. It is so organized that at all times it is compelled to reproduce the central action which characterizes all good drama from the days of the Greeks to our own: two individuals are pitted against each other in a conflict that is strictly personal but no less strictly representative of a social group. One individual batsman faces one individual bowler. But each represents his side. The personal achievement may be of the utmost competence or brilliance. Its ultimate value is whether it assists the side to victory or staves off defeat. This has nothing to do with morals. It is the organizational structure on which the whole spectacle is built. The dramatist, the novelist, the choreographer, must strive to make his individual character symbolical of a larger whole. He may or may not succeed. The runner in a relay race must take the plus or minus that his partner or partners give him. The soccer forward and the goalkeeper may at certain rare moments find themselves sole representatives of their sides. Even the baseball-batter, who most nearly approaches this particular aspect of cricket, may and often does find himself after a fine hit standing on one of the bases, where he is now dependent upon others. The batsman facing the ball does not merely represent his side. For that moment, to all intents and purposes, he is his side. This fundamental relation of the One and the Many, Individual and Social, Individual and Universal, leader and followers, representative and ranks, the part and the whole, is structurally imposed on the players of cricket. What other sports, games and arts have to aim at, the players are given to start with, they cannot depart from it. Thus the game is founded upon a dramatic, a human, relation which is universally recognized as the most objectively pervasive and psychologically stimulating in life and therefore in that artificial representation of it which is drama.

The second major consideration in all dramatic spectacles is the relation between event (or, if you prefer, contingency) and design, episode and continuity, diversity in unity, the battle and the campaign, the part and the whole. Here also cricket is structurally perfect. The total spectacle consists and must consist of a series of individual, isolated episodes, each in itself completely self-contained. Each has its beginning, the ball bowled; its middle, the stroke played; its end, runs, no runs, dismissal. Within the fluctuating interests of the rise or fall of the game as a whole, there is this unending series of events, each single one fraught with immense possibilities of expectation and realization. Here again the dramatist or movie director has to strive. In the very finest of soccer matches the ball for long periods is in places where it is impossible to expect any definite alteration in the relative position of the two sides. In lawn tennis the duration of the rally is entirely dependent upon the subjective skill of the players. In baseball alone does the encounter between the two representative protagonists approach the definitiveness of the individual series of episodes in cricket which together constitute the whole.

The structural enforcement of the fundamental appeals which all dramatic spectacle must have is of incalculable value to the spectator. The glorious uncertainty of the game is not anarchy. It would not be glorious if it were not so firmly anchored in the certainties which must attend all successful drama. That is why cricket is perhaps the only game in which the end result (except where national or local pride is at stake) is not of great importance. Appreciation of cricket has little to do with the end, and less still with what are called "the finer points" of the game. What matters in cricket, as in all the arts, is not finer points but what everyone with some knowledge of the elements can see and feel. It is only within such a rigid structural frame that the individuality so characteristic of cricket can flourish. Two batsmen are in at the same time. Thus the position of representatives of the side, though strictly independent, is interchangeable. In baseball one batter bats at a time. The isolated events of which both games consist is in baseball rigidly limited. The batter is allowed choice of three balls. He must hit the third or he is out. If he hits he must run. The batter's place in the batting order is fixed—it cannot be changed. The pitcher must pitch until he is taken off and when he is taken off he is finished for that game. (The Americans obviously prefer it that way.) In cricket the bowler bowls six balls (or eight). He can then be taken off and can be brought on again. He can bowl at the other end. The batting order is interchangeable. Thus while the principle of an individual representing the side at any given moment is maintained, the utmost possible change of personnel compatible with order is allowed. We tend to take these things for granted or not to notice them at all. In what other dramatic spectacle can they be found built-in? The greatness of the great batsman is not so much in his own skill as that he sets in motion all the immense possibilities that are contained in the game as structurally organized.

Cricket, of course, does not allow that representation or suggestion of specific relations as can be done by a play or even by ballet and dance. The players are always players trafficking in the elemental human activities, qualities and emotions—attack, defence, courage, gallantry, steadfastness, grandeur, ruse. This is no drawback. Punch and Judy, Swan Lake, pantomime, are even less particularized than cricket. They depend for their effect upon the technical skill and creative force with which their exponents make the ancient patterns live for their contemporaries. Some of the best beloved and finest music is created out of just such elemental sensations. We never grow out of them, of the need to renew them. Any art which by accident or design gets too far from them finds that it has to return or wither. They are the very stuff of human life. It is of this stuff that the drama of cricket is composed.

If the drama is very limited in range and intricacy there are advantages. These need not be called compensating, but they should not be ignored. The long hours (which so irritates those who crave continuous excitement), the measured ritualism and the varied and intensive physical activity which take place within it, these strip the players of conventional aspects, and human personality is on view long enough and in sufficiently varied form to register itself indelibly. I mention only a few—the lithe grace and elegance of Kardar leading his team on to the field; the unending flow of linear rhythm by which Evans accommodated himself to returns from the field; the dignity which radiates from every motion of Frank Worrell; the magnificence and magnanimity of Keith Miller. There are movie stars, world-famous and rightly so, who mumble words and go through motions which neither they nor their audience care very much about. Their appeal is themselves, how they walk, how they move, how they do anything or nothing, so long as they are themselves and their particular quality shines through. Here a Keith Miller met a Clark Gable on equal terms.

The dramatic content of cricket I have purposely pitched low—I am concerned not with degree but kind. In addition to being a dramatic, cricket is also a visual art. This I do not pitch low at all. The whole issue will be settled here.

The aestheticians of painting, especially the modern ones, are the great advocates of "significant form", the movement of the line, the relations of colour and tone. Of these critics, the most consistent, the clearest (and the most widely accepted), that I know is the late Mr Bernhard Berenson. Over sixty years ago in his studies of the Italian Renaissance painters he expounded his aesthetic with refreshing clarity. The merely accurate representation of an object, the blind imitation of nature, was not art, not even if that object was what would commonly be agreed upon as beautiful, for example a beautiful woman. There was another category of painter superior to the first. Such a one would not actually reproduce the object as it was. Being a man of vision and imagination, the object would stimulate in him impulses, thoughts, memories visually creative. These he would fuse into a whole and the result would be not so much the object as the totality of the visual image which the object had evoked in a superior mind. That too, Mr Berenson excluded from the category of true art (and was by no means isolated in doing so): mere reproduction of objects, whether actually in existence or the product of the sublimest imaginations, was "literature" or "illustration". What then was the truly artistic? The truly artistic was a quality that existed in its own right, irrespective of the object represented. It was the line, the curve, its movement, the drama it embodied as painting, the linear design, the painterly tones and values taken as a whole: this constituted the specific quality of visual art. Mr Berenson did not rank colour very high; the head of a statue (with its human expression) he could usually dispense with. It was the form as such which was significant.

Mr Berenson was not at all cloudy or mystifying. He distinguished two qualities which could be said to constitute the significance of the form in its most emphatic manifestation.

The first he called "tactile values". The idea of tactile values could be most clearly grasped by observing the manner in which truly great artists rendered the nude human body. They so posed their figures, they manipulated, arranged, shortened, lengthened, foreshortened, they so articulated the movements of the joints that they stimulated the tactile consciousness of the viewer, his specially artistic sense. This significance in the form gave a higher coefficient of reality to the object represented. Not that such a painting looked more real, made the object more lifelike. That was not Mr Berenson's point. Significant form makes the painting life-giving, life-enhancing, *to the viewer*. Significant form, or "decoration", to use his significant personal term, sets off physical processes in the spectator which give to him a far greater sense of the objective reality before him than would a literal representation, however accurate. Mr Berenson does not deny that an interesting subject skilfully presented in human terms can be interesting as illustration. He does not deny that such illustration can enhance significant form. But it is the form that matters. Mr John Berger of the *New Statesman*, ardent propagandist of socialist realism in art, claims that what is really significant in Michelangelo is his bounding line. The abstract artists get rid of the object altogether and represent only the abstract form, the line and relations of line. If I understand Mr Berger aright he claims that all the great representational paintings of the past live and have lived only to the degree that their form is significant—that, however, is merely to repeat Mr Berenson.

The second characteristic of significant form in Mr Berenson's aesthetic is the sense of "movement".

We have so far been wandering in chambers where as cricketers we are not usually guests. Fortunately, the aesthetic vision now focuses on territory not too far distant from ours. In his analysis of "movement" Mr Berenson discussed the artistic possibilities and limitations of an athletic event, a wrestling match. His exposition seems designed for cricket and cricketers, and therefore must be reproduced in full:

> Although a wrestling match may, in fact, contain many genuinely artistic elements, our enjoyment of it can never be quite artistic: we are prevented from completely realizing it not only by our dramatic interest in the game, but also, granting the possibility of being devoid of dramatic interest, by the succession of movements being too rapid for us to realize each completely, and too fatiguing, even if realizable. Now if a way could be found of conveying to us the realization of movements without the confusion and the fatigue of the actuality, we should be getting out of the wrestlers more than they themselves can give us—the heightening of vitality which comes to us whenever we keenly realize life, such as the actuality itself would give us, *plus* the greater effectiveness of the heightening brought about by the clearer, intenser and less fatiguing realization. This is precisely what the artist who succeeds in representing movement achieves: making us realize it as we never can actually, he gives us a heightened sense of capacity,

and whatever is in the actuality enjoyable, he allows us to enjoy at our leisure. In words already familiar to us, he *extracts the significance of movements,* just as, in rendering tactile values, the artist extracts the corporal significance of objects. His task is, however, far more difficult, although less indispensable: it is not enough that he should extract the values of what at any given moment is an actuality, as is an object, but what at no moment really is—namely, movement. He can accomplish his task in only one way, and that is by so rendering the one particular movement that we shall be able to realize all other movements that the same figure may make. "He is grappling with his enemy now," I say of my wrestler. "What a pleasure to be able to realize in my own muscles, on my own chest, with my own arms and legs, the life that is in him as he is making his supreme effort! What a pleasure, as I look away from the representation, to realize in the same manner, how after the contest his muscles will relax, and the rest trickle like a refreshing stream through his nerves!" All this I shall be made to enjoy by the artist who, in representing any one movement, can give me the logical sequence of visible strain and pressure in the parts and muscles.

Now here all of us, cricketers and aesthetics, are on familiar ground. I submit that cricket does in fact contain genuinely artistic elements, infinitely surpassing those to be found in wrestling matches. In fact it can be said to comprise most of those to be found in all other games.

I submit further that the abiding charm of cricket is that the game has been so organized that the realization of movement is completely conveyed despite the confusion and fatigue of actuality.

I submit finally that without the intervention of any artist the spectator at cricket extracts the significance of movement and of tactile values. He experiences the heightened sense of capacity. Furthermore, however the purely human element, the literature, the illustration, in cricket may enhance the purely artistic appeal, the significant form at its most unadulterated is permanently present. It is known, expected, recognized and enjoyed by tens of thousands of spectators. Cricketers call it style.

From the beginning of the modern game this quality of style has been abstracted and established in its own right, irrespective of results, human element, dramatic element, anything whatever except itself. It is, if you will, pure decoration. Thus we read of a player a hundred years ago that he was elegance, all elegance, fit to play before the Queen in her parlour. We read of another that he was not equal to W.G. except in style, where he surpassed The Champion. In *Wisden* of 1891 A.G. Steel, a great player, a great judge of the game and, like so many of those days, an excellent writer, leaves no loophole through which form can escape into literature:

> The last-named batsman, when the bowling was very accurate, was a slow scorer, but always a treat to watch. If the present generation of stone-wall cricketers, such as Scotton, Hall, Barlow, A. Bannerman, nay even Shrewsbury, possessed such beautiful ease of style the tens of thousands that used to frequent the beautiful Australian ground would still flock there, instead of the hundred or two patient gazers on feats of Job-like patience that now attend them.

In 1926 H.L. Collins batted five hours for forty runs to save the Manchester Test and Richard Binns wrote a long essay to testify among much else that Collins was never dull because of his beautiful style. There is debate about style. Steel's definition clears away much cumbersome litter about left shoulder forward and straight bat: "no flourish, but the maximum of power with the minimum of exertion". If the free-swinging off-drive off the front foot has been challenged by the angular jerk through the covers off the back foot, this last is not at all alien to the generation which has experienced Cubism in posters and newspapers advertisements.

We are accustomed in cricket to speak of beauty. The critics of art are contemptuous of the word. Let us leave it aside and speak of the style that is common of the manifold motions of the great players, or most of them. There are few picture galleries in the world which effectively reproduce a fraction of them—I am sticking to form and eschewing literature and illustration. These motions are not caught and permanently fixed for us to make repeated visits to them. They are repeated often enough to become a permanent possession of the spectator which he can renew at will. And having held our own with the visitor from the higher spheres, I propose to take the offensive.

And first I meet Mr Berenson on his own ground, so to speak. Here is John Arlott, whose written description of cricket matches I prefer to all others, describing the bowling action of Maurice Tate.

> You would hardly have called Maurice Tate's physique graceful, yet his bowling action remains—and not only for me—as lovely a piece of movement as even cricket has ever produced. He had strong, but sloping shoulders; a deep chest, fairly long arms and—essential to the pace bowler—broad feet to take the jolt of the delivery stride and wide hips to cushion it. His run-in, eight accelerating and lengthening strides, had a hint of scramble about it at the beginning, but by the eighth stride and well before his final leap, it seemed as if his limbs were gathered together in one glorious wheeling unity. He hoisted his left arm until it was pointing straight upwards, while his right hand, holding the ball, seemed to counter-poise it at the opposite pole. Meanwhile, his body, edge-wise on to the batsman, had swung its weight back on to the right foot: his back curved so that, from the other end, you might see the side of his head jutting out, as it were, from behind his left arm. Then his bowling arm came over and his body turned; he released the ball at the top of his arm-swing, with a full flick of the wrist, and then plunged through, body bending into that earth-tearing, final stride and pulling away to the off side.
>
> All these things the textbook will tell you to do: yet no one has ever achieved so perfectly a co-ordination and exploitation of wrist, shoulders, waist, legs and feet as Maurice Tate did. It was as if bowling had been implanted in him at birth, and came out—as the great arts come out—after due digestion, at the peak of greatness which is not created—but only confirmed—by instruction.

Because most people think always of batting when they think of cricket as a visual art another description of a bowler in action will help to correct the unbalance.

> From two walking paces Lindwall glides into the thirteen running strides which have set the world a model for rhythmic gathering of momentum for speed-giving power. Watching him approach the wicket, Sir Pelham Warner was moved to murmur one word, "Poetry!"
>
> The poetry of motion assumes dramatic overtones in the last couple of strides. A high-lifted left elbow leads Lindwall to the line. The metal plate on his right toe-cap drags through the turf and across the bowling crease as his prancing left foot thrusts directly ahead of it, to land beyond the popping crease. This side-on stretch brings every ounce of his thirteen stone into play as his muscular body tows his arm over for the final fling that shakes his shirtsleeve out of its fold. In two more strides his wheeling follow-through has taken him well to the side of the pitch. Never had plunging force and science formed so deadly an alliance.

We may note in passing that the technique of watching critically, i.e. with a conception of all the factors that have contributed to the result, can be as highly developed and needs as many years of training in cricket as in the arts. But I do not want to emphasize that here.

What is to be emphasized is that whereas in the fine arts the image of tactile values and movement, however effective, however magnificent, is permanent, fixed, in cricket the spectator sees the image constantly re-created, and whether he is a cultivated spectator or not, has standards which he carries with him always. He can re-create them at will. He can go to see a game hoping and expecting to see the image re-created or even extended. You can stop an automobile to watch a casual game and see a batsman, for ever to be unknown, cutting in a manner that recalls the greatest exponents of one of the most difficult movements in cricket. Sometimes it is a total performance branching out in many directions by a single player who stamps all he does with the hallmark of an individual style—a century by Hutton or Compton or Sobers. It can be and often is a particular image—Hammond's drive through the covers. The image can be a single stroke, made on a certain day, which has been seen and never forgotten. There are some of these the writer has carried in his consciousness for over forty years, some in fact longer, as it is described in the first page of this book. On the business of setting off physical processes and evoking a sense of movement in the spectator, followers of Mr Berenson's classification would do well to investigate the responses of cricket spectators. The theory may be thereby enriched, or may be seen to need enrichment. To the eye of a cricketer it seems pretty thin.

It may seem that I am squeezing every drop out of a quite casual illustration extracted from Mr Berenson's more comprehensive argument. That is not so. Any acquaintances with his work will find that he lavishes his most enthusiastic praise on *Hercules Strangling Antaeus* by Pollaiuolo, and the same artist's *David Striding Over the Head of the Slain Goliath*. In more than one place *The Gods Shooting [arrows] at a Mark* and the *Hercules Struggling With a Lion,* drawings by Michelangelo, are shown to be for him the ultimate yet reached in the presentation of tactile values and sense of movement, with the consequent life-giving and life-enhancing stimulation of the spectator. Mr Berenson, in the books I have mentioned, nowhere analyses this momentous fact: the enormous role that elemental physical action plays in the visual arts throughout the centuries, at least until our own. Why should he believe that Michelangelo's projected painting of the soldiers surprised when bathing would have produced the greatest masterpiece of figure art in modern times? I have been suggesting an answer by implication in describing what W.G. brought from pre-Victorian England to the modern age. I shall now state it plainly.

If we stick to cricket it is not because of any chauvinism. The analysis will apply to all games. After a thorough study of bull-fighting in Spain, Ernest Haas, the famous photographer, does not ignore the violence, the blood, the hovering presence of death, the illustration. Aided by his camera, his conclusion is: "The bull fight is pure art. The spectacle is all motion. ... Motion, the perfection of motion, is what the people come to see. They come hoping that this bull-fight will produce the perfect flow of motion." Another name for the perfect flow of motion is style, or, if you will, significant form.

Let us examine this motion, or, as Mr Berenson calls it, movement. Where the motive and directing force rests with the single human being, an immense variety of physical motion is embraced within four categories. A human being places himself physically in some relation of contact or avoidance (or both) with another human being, with an animal, an inanimate object, or two or more of these. He may extend the reach and force of his arms or feet with a tool or device of some kind. He propels a missile. He runs, skips, jumps, dives, to attain some objective which he has set himself or others have set for him. In sport there is not much else that he can do and in our world human beings are on view for artistic enjoyment only on the field of sport or on the entertainment stage. In sport cricket leads the field. The motions of a batter in baseball, a player of lawn tennis, hockey, golf, all their motions added together do not attain the sum of a batsman's. The batsman can shape to hit practically round the points of the compass. He can play a dead bat, pat for a single, drive along the ground; he can skim the infielders; he can lift over their heads; he can clear the boundary. He can cut square with all the force of his wrists, arms and shoulders, or cut late with a touch as delicate as a feather. He can hit to long-leg with all his force or simply deflect with a single motion. He can do most of these off the front foot or the back. Many of them he can do with no or little departure from his original stance. The articulation of his limbs is often enough quite visible, as in the use of the wrists when cutting or hooking. What is not visible is received in the tactile consciousness of thousands who have themselves for years practised the same motion and know each muscle that is involved in each stroke. And all this infinite variety is from one base, stable and fixed, so that each motion in its constituent parts can be observed in its detail and in its entirety from start to finish.

The batsman propels a missile with a tool. The bowler does the same unaided. Within the narrow territory legally allowed to him there is, as Mr Arlott on Tate has shown, a surprising variety of appeal. He may bowl a slow curve or fast or medium, or he may at his pleasure use each in turn. There have been many bowlers whose methods of delivery has seemed to spectators the perfection of form, irrespective of the fate which befell the balls bowled. Here, far more than in batting, the repetition conveys the realization of movement despite the actuality. Confusion is excluded by the very structure of the game.

As for the fieldsmen, there is no limit whatever to their possibilities of running, diving, leaping, falling forward, backwards, sideways, with all their energies concentrated on a specific objective, the whole completely realizable by the alert spectator. The spontaneous outburst of thousands at a fierce hook or a dazzling slip-catch, the ripple of recognition at a long-awaited leg-glance, are as genuine and deeply felt expressions of artistic emotion as any I know.

You will have noted that the four works of art chosen by Mr Berenson to illustrate movement all deal with some physical action of the athletic kind. Mr Berenson calls the physical process of response mystical. There I refuse to go along any further, not even for the purpose of discussion. The mystical is the last refuge, if refuge it is. Cricket, in fact any ball game, to the visual image adds the sense of physical co-ordination, of harmonious action, of timing. The visual image of a diving fieldsman is a frame for his rhythmic contact with the flying ball. Here two art forms meet.

I believe that the examination of the stroke, the brilliant piece of fielding, will take us through mysticism to far more fundamental considerations than mere life-enhancing. We respond to physical action or vivid representation of it, dead or alive, because we are made that way. For unknown centuries survival for us, like all other animals, depended upon competent and effective physical activity. This played its part in developing the brain. The particular nature which became ours did not rest satisfied with this. If it had it could never have become human. The use of the hand, the extension of its powers by the tool, the production of a missile at some objective and the accompanying refinements of the mechanics of judgment, these marked us off from the animals. Language may have come at the same time. The evolution may have been slow or rapid. The end result was a new species which preserved the continuity of its characteristics and its way of life. Sputnik can be seen as no more than a missile made and projected through tools by the developed hand.

Similarly the eye for the line which is today one of the marks of ultimate aesthetic refinement is not new. It is old. The artists of the caves of Altamira had it. So did the bushmen. They had it to such a degree that they could reproduce it or, rather represent it with unsurpassed force. Admitting this, Mr Berenson confines the qualities of this primitive art to animal energy and an exasperated vitality. That, even if true, is totally subordinate to the fact that among these primitive people the sense of form existed to the degree that it could be consciously and repeatedly reproduced. It is not a gift of high civilization, the last achievement of the noble minds. It is exactly the opposite. The use of sculpture and design among primitive peoples indicates that the significance of the form is a common possession. Children have it. There is no need to adduce further evidence for the presupposition that the faculty or faculties by which we recognize significant form in elemental physical action is native to us, a part of the process by which we have become and remain human. It is neither more nor less mystical than any other of our faculties of apprehension. Neither do I see an "exasperated vitality" in the work of the primitive artists. The impression I get is that the line was an integral part of co-ordinated physical activity, functional perhaps, but highly refined in that upon it food or immediate self-preservation might depend.

Innate faculty though it might be, the progress of civilization can leave it unused, suppress its use, can remove us from the circumstances in which it is associated with animal energy. Developing civilization can surround us with circumstances and conditions in which our original faculties are debased or refined, made more simple or more complicated. They may seem to disappear altogether. They remain part of our human endowment. The basic motions of cricket represent physical action which has been the basis not only of primitive but of civilized life for countless centuries. In work and in play they were the motions by which men lived and without which they would perish. The Industrial Revolution transformed our existence. Our fundamental characteristics as human beings it did not and could not alter. The bushmen reproduced in one medium not merely animals but the line, the curve, the movement. It supplied in the form they needed a vision of the life they lived. The Hambledon men who made modern cricket did the same. The bushmen's motive was perhaps religious, Hambledon's entertainment. One form was fixed, the other had to be constantly re-created. The contrasts can be multiplied. That will not affect the underlying identity. Each fed the need to satisfy the visual artistic sense. The emphasis on style in cricket proves that without a shadow of a doubt; whether the impulse was literature and the artistic quality the result, or vice-versa, does not matter. If the Hambledon form was infinitely more complicated it rose out of a more complicated society, the result of a long historical development. Satisfying the same needs as bushmen and Hambledon, the industrial age took over cricket and made it into what it has become. The whole tortured history of modern Spain explains why it is in the cruelty of the bull-ring that they seek the perfect flow of motion. That flow, however, men since they have been men have always sought and always will. It is an unspeakable impertinence to arrogate the term "fine art" to one small section of this quest and declare it to be culture. Luckily, the people refuse to be bothered. This does not alter the gross falsification of history and the perversion of values which is the result.

Lucian's Solon tells what the Olympic Games meant to the Greeks. The human drama, the literature, was as important to them as to us. No less so was the line, the curve, the movement of the athletes which inspired one of the greatest artistic creations we have ever known—Greek sculpture. To this day certain statues baffle the experts: are they statues of Apollo or are they statues of athletes? The games and sculpture were "good" arts and popular. The newly fledged democracy found them insufficient. The contrast between life under an ancient landed aristocracy and an ancient democratic regime was enormous. It can be guessed at by what the democracy actually achieved. The democracy did not neglect the games or sculpture. To the contrary. The birth of democracy saw the birth of individualism in sculpture. Immense new passions and immense new forces had been released. New relations between the individual and society, between individual and individual, launched life on new, exciting and dangerous ways. Out of this came the tragic drama. After a long look at how the creation of the Hambledon men became the cornerstone of Victorian education and entertainment, I can no longer accept that Peisistratus encouraged the dramatic festival as a means of satisfying or appeasing or distracting the urban masses on their way to democracy. That would be equivalent to saying that the rulers of Victorian England encouraged cricket to satisfy or appease or distract the urban masses on their way to democracy. The Victorian experience with cricket suggests a line of investigation on the alert for signs both more subtle and more tortuous. It may be fruitful to investigate whether Peisistratus and his fellow rulers did not need the drama for themselves before it became a national festival. That at any rate is what happened to the Victorians.

The elements which were transformed into Greek drama may have existed in primitive form, quite apart from religious ceremonial—there is even a tradition that peasants played primitive dramas. However that may be, the newly fledged Greek democrat found his need for a fuller existence fulfilled in the tragic drama. He had no spate of books to give him distilled, concentrated and ordered views of life. The old myths no longer sufficed. The drama recast them to satisfy the expanded personality. The end of democracy is a more complete existence. Voting and political parties are only a means. The expanded personality and needs of the Victorian aspiring to democracy did not need drama. The stage, books, newspapers, were part of his inheritance. The production of these for democracy had already begun. What he needed was the further expansion of his aesthetic sense. Print had long made church walls and public monuments obsolescent as a means of social communication. Photography would complete the rout of painting and sculpture, promoting them upstairs. The need was filled by organized games.

Cricket was fortunate in that for their own purposes the British ruling classes took it over and endowed it with money and prestige. On it men of gifts which would have been remarkable in any sphere expended their powers—the late C.B. Fry was a notable example. Yet even he submitted to the prevailing aesthetic categories and circumscribed cricket as a "physical" fine art. There is no need so to limit it. It is limited in variety of range, of subject-matter. It cannot express the emotions of an age on the nature of the last judgment or the wiping out of a population by bombing. It must repeat. But what it repeats is the original stuff out of which everything visually or otherwise artistic is quarried. The popular democracy of Greece, sitting for days in the sun watching *The Oresteia*, the popular democracy of our day, sitting similarly, watching Miller and Lindwall bowl to Hutton and Compton—each in its own way grasps at a more complete human existence. We may some day be able to answer Tolstoy's exasperated and exasperating question: What is art?—but only when we learn to integrate our vision of Walcott on the back foot through the covers with the outstretched arm of the Olympic Apollo.

History, Fable and Myth in the Caribbean and Guianas

Wilson Harris

It occurred to me as I contemplated this series of talks entitled 'History, Fable and Myth' that it may prove illuminating to look first of all at J. Thomas' rebuttal of the nineteenth-century historian Froude in his book *Froudacity*. *Froudacity* was first published in 1889 and has been reprinted by New Beacon Books in 1969. It is not my intention to review *Froudacity* at this time but rather to highlight the crux of the dispute between Froude and Thomas as I believe this will help to make clear the kind of historical stasis which has afflicted the Caribbean I would suggest for many generations.

The crux of the dispute between Froude and Thomas appears to me to have been set forth by C.L.R. James in his introduction to the 1969 republication of *Froudacity*.

In that introduction James quotes Froude as follows:

> In Egypt or India or one knows not where, accident or natural development quickened into life our moral and intellectual faculties; and these faculties have grown into what we now experience, not in the freedom in which the modern takes delight, but under the sharp rule of the strong over the weak, the wise over the unwise.

James then goes on to say that Thomas now 'has him [Froude] in the historical prison in which he had placed himself, and he [Thomas] overwhelms the great historian.' This overwhelming rebuttal, as James sees it, springs from Thomas' insight into a controlling law of history in contradistinction to Froude's emphasis on the dicey, accidental character of nature and society. In fact James sums it up in this way: 'What is important is not the difference in tone and temper of the two writers. It is that Thomas bases himself on a sense of history which he defines as a controlling *law*. And if you have no sense of historical law, then anything is what you choose to make it, and history almost automatically becomes not only nonsense, i.e. has no sense but is usually a defence of property and privilege, which is exactly what Froude has made of it.'

The question nevertheless arises – Does Thomas' stress on Law – as C.L.R. James implies – dispense with Froude?

In order to answer this let us look first of all a little more closely at Froude's position and after that come back to Thomas.

As I read Froude I am reminded of a certain dilemma which was put brilliantly by Darwin in his *Descent of Man*. Darwin begins by speaking of the horns of certain beetles then he moves on to look at crests and knobs on other creatures.

> The extraordinary size of the horns, and their widely different structure in closely allied forms, indicate that they have been formed for some important purpose: but their excessive variability in the males of the same species leads to the inference that this purpose cannot be of a definite nature. The horns do not show marks of friction, as if used for ordinary work. Some authors suppose that as the males wander much more than the females, they require horns as a defence against their enemies; but in many cases the horns do not seem well adapted for

defence... The most obvious conjecture is that they are used by the males for fighting together; but they have never been observed to fight, nor could Mr Bates, after a careful examination of numerous species, find any sufficient evidence in their mutilated or broken condition of their having been thus used...The conclusion which best agrees with the fact of the horns having been so immensely yet not so fixedly developed – as shown by their extreme variability in the same species and by their extreme diversity in closely allied species – is that they have been acquired as ornaments. This view will at first appear extremely improbable; but we shall hereafter find with many animals, standing much higher in the scale, namely fishes, amphibians, reptiles and birds, that various kinds of crests, knobs and horns have been developed apparently for this sole purpose.

This ornamental stasis with implications that point to the wasteland – to excess baggage from cradle to grave – depicts rather ironically but accurately Froude's relationship to property as something so sovereign, so accidental, so fortuitous, it serves to eclipse all sensibility. Such an eclipse of sensibility may well be an omen of an age in which, not long before, the person had been property (slave property). And this area of eclipse of sensibility held Froude unwittingly, I would imagine, in its toils – in its historical prison. Indeed it is in this way, in terms of sovereign object or prison – eclipse of the person in slave property – eclipse of the resources of sensibility – that I find myself re-reading James' remark (rereading it with a different slant, in a different way, I must confess) that history makes non-sense or no-sense, non-sensibility or no-sensibility.

Froude's defence of property – property implying both flesh-and-blood (in the fetish of the slave) as well as inanimate conviction (the world of things) – was a historical prison and Froude – as prisoner of his age – may well have taken a malicious and pessimistic view of nature and society. The world of objects, the world of achievement for him – in its ornamental stasis – was fortuitous, dicey (and therefore fundamentally precarious, fundamentally inclined to be wasteful or purposeless) and the human person was an object to be measured, validated, pronounced fit or unfit in an economic ruling context. Froude therefore could see no merit in change. He prized stability as so fortuitous, so accidental that any society which 'worked', which held itself together in some shape or form should be safe-guarded against change. In this context, Anglo-West Indian Society of the nineteenth century appeared to him to 'work', to hold itself together. Froude distrusted change since in his estimation everything was so dicey, so fortuitously consolidated that change, in fact, was likely to rob it of any conservative historical shape it already possessed.

All of Froude's biases and aberrations in his reports on the Caribbean sprang, I would suggest, from this central dilemma. A dilemma we have not yet solved and which presses in on us – in the late twentieth century – in many forms. It resides at the heart of economic fascism wherever this is practised. Rhodesia and South Africa are glaring examples.

And now I would like to return to Thomas. When C.L.R. James says with brilliant polemic that Thomas overwhelmed the great historian Froude I take it he means that Thomas broke out of Froude's prison of history by visualizing a law in contradistinction to a philosophy of fortuitous achievement, dicey establishment, realm of accident.

But (with all due respect to C.L.R. James) we must ask ourselves – Did Thomas really achieve such a breakthrough? The answer to this may well lie in the way Thomas wrestled with the law in terms of the existing magistracy of his day and in terms of various Governors of Trinidad and other nineteenth-century figures.

It is here that – beyond a shadow of doubt – the unwitting irony of Thomas' book is laid bare. For the scale of *Froudacity* upon which Thomas measures his magistrates and governors is consistent with a comedy of manners. In that comedy of manners the law consolidates itself – as a just instrument – around noble or benevolent figures which include Chief Justice Reeves of

Barbados, certain good and conscientious Governors of Trinidad and Gordon of Khartoum. On the other hand it consolidates itself into a bad instrument around bad magistrates, Governors etc. Because of these fluctuations in Thomas' comedy of manners the law comes into close *rapport* with Froude's ornament and ironically reinforces fortuitous idols on the side of heaven or on the side of hell.

According to Thomas, had such-and-such a Governor remained things might have been different. Had such-and-such a Governor never arrived things likewise might have been different. In the same token in the twentieth century had Kennedy not been assassinated things might have been different in the United States. In short, Thomas' wrestle with the Law would seem to consolidate a fortuitous destiny or ornament of history.

In support of what I have been saying let us look at the implications in these key passages in Thomas' *Froudacity*.

It is almost superfluous to repeat that the skin-discriminating policy induced as regards the coloured subjects of the Queen since the abolition of slavery did not, and could not, operate when coloured and white stood on the same high level as slave owners and ruling potentates in the colony.

Thomas expands on this in the following:

> History, as against the hard and fast White-master and Black-slave theory so recklessly invented and confidently built upon by Mr Froude, would show incontestably – (a) that for upwards of 200 years before the Negro Emancipation in 1838, there had never existed in one of those then British colonies…any prohibition whatsoever, on the ground of race or colour, against the owning of slaves by any free person possessing the necessary means, and desirous of doing so; (b) that as a consequence of this non-restriction, numbers of blacks, half-breeds, and other non-Europeans, besides such of them as had become possessed of their 'property' by inheritance, availed themselves of this virtual license, and in course of time constituted a very considerable proportion of the slave-holding section of those communities; (c) that these dusky plantation owners enjoyed and used in every possible sense the identical rights and privileges which were enjoyed and used by their pure-blooded Caucasian brother-slave-owners. The above statements are attested by written documents, oral traditions, and better still perhaps, by the living presence in those islands of numerous lineal representatives of those once opulent and flourishing non-European planter-families.

According to Thomas, therefore, it would appear that with the decline of capital 'slave-property' – with the decline of investment in human persons owned by blacks and whites alike – a hard and fast White-master and Black-slave-substitute theory came into force. This theory high-lighted pigmentation differences as never before as part and parcel of the ornament of society to which the law conformed. In short, the whole society remained an economic commodity though this time a new sophistication, pigmentation, came into force.

Thomas is not an apologist for slavery – in fact he indicts slavery with great passion – but the trap into which he falls is in most ways identical to the stasis (the stasis of ornament, of property as accident, as fortuitous establishment or comedy of manners) to which Froude conforms. Froude and Thomas, in this respect, were children of the nineteenth century and neither possessed the genius to penetrate intuitively or otherwise the ironic trap of the ornament, of the prison of the wasteland.

Clearly Thomas failed to deepen the ornament of his age in such a way that unpredictable intuitive resources would affect the *prison* of the object and therefore the *person* of the object. *Prison* and *person* had become locked together as uniform property and both Thomas and Froude played on this synonymous condition in their individual comedy of manners. This meant, in fact, that Thomas – passionate as he felt about objects of injustice – could not supply a figurative meaning beyond the condition he deplored.

It is my view therefore that Thomas does not really overwhelm Froude. The duel which they fought is nevertheless a very instructive one in pointing up the historical stasis which afflicts the West Indian sensibility and which may only be breached in complex creative perspectives for which the historical convention would appear to possess no criteria. Oddly enough James ends his introduction to *Froudacity* with a quotation from Merleau-Ponty which helps to make the view I have been expressing more clear: 'The act of the artist or philosopher is free, but not motiveless. Their freedom ... consists in appropriating a *de facto* situation by endowing it with a figurative meaning beyond its real one.'

In this connection we must note that both Thomas and Froude shared a common suspicion of Haitian vodun and other primitive manifestations which signified for them a 'relapse into obeahism, devil-worship and children-eating'. Therefore they consolidated an intellectual censorship of significant vestiges of the subconscious imagination which they needed to explore if they were to begin to apprehend a figurative meaning beyond the real or apparently real world.

It is my intention to concentrate in some degree on those vestiges as part and parcel of the arts of the imagination. In this respect I believe the possibility exists for us to become involved in perspectives of renascence which can bring into play a figurative meaning beyond an apparently real world or prison of history.

I want to make as clear as I can that a cleavage exists in my opinion between the historical convention in the Caribbean and Guianas and the arts of the imagination. I believe a philosophy of history may well lie buried in the arts of the imagination. Needless to say I have no racial biases and whether my emphasis falls on limbo or vodun, on Carib bush-baby omens, on Arawak zemi, on Latin, English inheritances – in fact within and beyond these emphases – my concern is with epic stratagems available to Caribbean man in the dilemmas of history which surround him.

There are two kinds of myths related to Africa in the Caribbean and Guianas. One kind seems fairly direct, the other has clearly undergone metamorphosis. In fact even the direct kind of myth has suffered a 'sea-change' of some proportions. In an original sense, therefore, these myths which reflect an African link in the Caribbean are also part and parcel of a native West Indian imagination and therefore stand, in some important ways I feel, in curious *rapport* with vestiges of Amerindian fable[1] and legend.

Let us start with a myth stemming from Africa which has undergone metamorphosis. The one which I have in mind is called limbo. The limbo dance is a well known feature in the Carnival life of the West Indies today though it is still subject to intellectual censorship as I shall explain as I go along in this paper. The limbo dancer moves under a bar which is gradually lowered until a mere slit of space, it seems, remains through which with spreadeagled limbs he passes like a spider.

Limbo was born, it is said, on the slave ships of the Middle Passage. There was so little space that the slaves contorted themselves into human spiders. Limbo, therefore, as Edward Brathwaite, the distinguished Barbadian-born poet, has pointed out is related to anancy or spider fables. If I may now quote from *Islands*, the last book in his trilogy –

> drum stick knock
> and the darkness is over me
> knees spread wide
> and the water is hiding me
> *limbo*
> *limbo like me*

But there is something else in the limbo–anancy syndrome which, as far as I am aware, is overlooked though intuitively immersed perhaps in Edward Brathwaite's poems, and that is the curious dislocation of a chain of miles reflected in the dance so that a re-trace of the Middle Passage from Africa to the Americas and the West Indies is not to be equated with a uniform sum. Not only has the journey from the Old World to the new varied with each century and each method of transport but needs to be re-activated in the imagination as a limbo perspective when one dwells on the Middle Passage: a limbo gateway between Africa and the Caribbean.

In fact here, I feel, we begin to put our finger on something which is close to the inner universality of Caribbean man. Those waves of migration which have hit the shores of the Americas – North, Central and South – century after century have, at various times, possessed the stamp of the spider metamorphosis, in the refugee flying from Europe or in the indentured East Indian and Chinese from Asia.

Limbo then reflects a certain kind of gateway to or threshold of a new world and the dislocation of a chain of miles. It is – in some ways – the archetypal sea-change stemming from Old Worlds and it is legitimate, I feel, to pun on limbo as a kind of shared phantom limb which has become a subconscious variable in West Indian theatre. The emergence of formal West Indian theatre was preceded, I suggest, by that phantom limb which manifested itself on Boxing Day after Christmas when the ban on the 'rowdy' bands (as they were called) was lifted for the festive season.

I recall performances I witnessed as a boy in Georgetown, British Guiana, in the early 1930s. Some of the performers danced on high stilts like elongated limbs while others performed spreadeagled on the ground. In this way limbo spider and stilted pole of the gods were related to the drums like grassroots and branches of lightning to the sound of thunder.

Sometimes it was an atavistic spectacle and it is well known that these bands were suspected by the law of subversive political stratagems. But it is clear that the dance had no political or propaganda motives though, as with any folk manifestation, it could be manipulated by demagogues. The whole situation is complex and it is interesting to note that Rex Nettleford in an article entitled 'The Dance as an Art Form – Its Place in the West Indies' (which appears in *Caribbean Quarterly*, March–June 1968) has this to say: 'Of all the arts, dance is probably the most neglected. The art form continues to elude many of the most intuitive in an audience, including the critics.'

It has taken us a couple of generations to begin – just *begin* – to perceive, in this phenomenon, an activation of subconscious and sleeping resources in the phantom limb of dismembered slave and god. An activation which possesses a nucleus of great promise – of far-reaching new poetic synthesis.

For limbo (one cannot emphasize this too much) is not the total recall of an African past since that African past in terms of tribal sovereignty or sovereignties was modified or traumatically eclipsed with the Middle Passage and with generations of change that followed. Limbo was rather the renascence of a new corpus of sensibility that could translate and accommodate African and other legacies within a new architecture of cultures. For example, the theme of the phantom limb – the re-assembly of dismembered man or god – possesses archetypal resonances that embrace Egyptian Osiris, the resurrected Christ, and the many-armed deity of India.

In this context it is interesting to note that limbo – which emerged as a novel re-assembly out of the stigmata of the Middle Passage – is related to Haitian vodun in the sense that Haitian vodun (though possessing a direct link with African vodun which I shall describe later on) also seeks to accommodate new Catholic features in its constitution of the muse.

It is my view – a deeply considered one – that this ground of accommodation, this art of creative coexistence – pointing away from apartheid and ghetto fixations – is of the utmost importance and native to the Caribbean, perhaps to the Americas as a whole. It is still, in most respects, a latent syndrome and we need to look not only at limbo or vodun but at Amerindian horizons as well –

shamanistic and rain-making vestiges and the dancing bush-baby legends of the ancient Caribs which began to haunt them as they crouched over their campfires under the Spanish yoke.

Insufficient attention has been paid to such phenomena and the original native capacity these implied as omens of rebirth. Many historians have been intent on indicting the Old World of Europe by exposing a uniform pattern of imperialism in the New World of the Americas. Thus they conscripted the West Indies into a mere adjunct of imperialism and overlooked a subtle and far-reaching renascence. In a sense therefore the new historian – though his stance is an admirable one in debunking imperialism – has ironically extended and reinforced old colonial prejudices which censored the limbo imagination as a 'rowdy' manifestation and overlooked the complex metaphorical gateway it constitutes in *rapport* with Amerindian omen.

Later on I intend to explore the Amerindian gateways between cultures which began obscurely and painfully to witness (long before limbo or vodun or the Middle Passage) to a native suffering community steeped in caveats of conquest. At this point I shall merely indicate that these gateways exist as part and parcel of an original West Indian architecture which it is still possible to create if we look deep into the rubble of the past, and that these Amerindian features enhance the limbo assembly with which we are now engaged – the spider syndrome and phantom limb of the gods arising in Negro fable and legend.

I used the word 'architecture' a moment or two ago because I believe this is a valid approach to a gateway society as well as to a community which is involved in an original re-constitution or re-creation of variables of myth and legend in the wake of stages of conquest.

First of all the limbo dance becomes the human gateway which dislocates (and therefore begins to free itself from) a uniform chain of miles across the Atlantic. This dislocation or interior space serves therefore as a corrective to a uniform cloak or documentary stasis of imperialism. The journey across the Atlantic for the forebears of West Indian man involved a new kind of space – inarticulate as this new 'spatial' character was at the time – and not simply an unbroken schedule of miles in a log book. Once we perceive this inner corrective to historical documentary and protest literature which sees the West Indies as utterly deprived, or gutted by exploitation, we begin to participate in the genuine possibilities of original change available to a people severely disadvantaged (it is true) at a certain point in time.

The limbo dance therefore implies, I believe, a profound art of compensation which seeks to re-play a dismemberment of tribes (note again the high stilted legs of some of the performers and the spider-anancy masks of others running close to the ground) and to invoke at the same time a curious psychic re-assembly of the parts of the dead god or gods. And that re-assembly which issued from a state of cramp to articulate a new growth – and to point to the necessity for a new kind of drama, novel and poem – is a creative phenomenon of the first importance in the imagination of a people violated by economic fates.

One cannot over-emphasize, I believe, how original this phenomenon was. So original it aroused both incomprehension and suspicion in the intellectual and legal administrations of the land (I am thinking in particular of the first half of the twentieth century though one can, needless to say, go much farther back). What is bitterly ironic – as I have already indicated – is that present day historians in the second half of the twentieth century, militant and critical of imperialism as they are, have fallen victim, in another sense, to the very imperialism they appear to denounce. They have no criteria for arts of originality springing out of an age of limbo and the history they write is without an inner time. This historical refusal to see – this consolidation of an incomprehension of the past – may well be at the heart of the Terrified Consciousness which a most significant critic to emerge in the West Indies at this time, Kenneth Ramchand, analyses brilliantly in his essay in the *Journal of Commonwealth Literature* (West Indies number) July 1969 (published by Heinemann and the University of Leeds). One point which Kenneth Ramchand did not stress in his essay – but which is implicit in what he calls the 'nightmare' in Jean Rhys' novel *Wide Sargasso Sea* – is that Antoinette is mad Bertha in *Jane Eyre* and that Jean Rhys, intuitively rather than intentionally, is attempting to compensate a historical portrait of the West Indian creole – to bridge the gap, as it were, between an outer frame and an inner desolation. It is this that sharpens the pathos of her novel and makes for that terrified consciousness which Ramchand sees now as a universal heritage.

It is this cleavage between a statistical frame and the inner portrait of reality that makes for unwitting irony in the so-called new emancipated writer and Gerald Moore in his new book, *The Chosen Tongue* (published by Longmans, 1969), brings it into sharp focus when he states –

> Both M.G. Smith, the Jamaican anthropologist, and V.S. Naipaul appear to believe that the West Indies possesses no genuine inner cohesion whatever and no internal source of power. Having no common interests to cement them, the inhabitants of the area can be held together only by external force. Professor Elsa Goveia reaches an opposite but equally depressing conclusion. She argues that the West Indies had one integrating factor historically, and this has been 'the acceptance of the inferiority of Negroes to the Whites'.

In this context it is illuminating to recall that Froude was doing on behalf of imperialism what many contemporary historians are doing in a protest against imperialism. Namely he, too, set out to demonstrate that the West Indies had no creative potential. His view sprang out of the arrogance of the nineteenth century civilized European whereas theirs would appear to spring out of what Martin Carter, the distinguished Guyanese poet, calls the 'self-contempt' of the exploited, formerly indentured or enslaved, West Indian. Such a dead-end of history in which nineteenth-century imperialist and twentieth-century anti-imperialist come into agreement is material for a theatre of the absurd.

I believe that the limbo imagination of the folk involved a crucial inner re-creative response to the violations of slavery and indenture and conquest, and needed its critical or historical correlative, its critical or historical advocacy. This was not forthcoming since the historical instruments of the past clustered around an act of censorship and of suspicion of folk-obscurity as well as originality, and that inbuilt arrogance or suspicion continues to motivate a certain order of critical writing in the West Indies today.

Capitalism and Slavery (a brilliant and impressive formal thesis of research written when he was at Oxford by Eric Williams, who became Prime Minister of Trinidad) would seem to be the model British West Indian historians have elected. And I must now draw to your attention something which, I believe, confirms my view of the inbuilt censor in West Indian historical convention. Professor Elsa Goveia regards Dr Williams as 'the most influential writer on West Indian history to emerge from the West Indies during the present century'. Yet in an article entitled 'New Shibboleths For Old' (appearing in *New Beacon Reviews*, Collection 1, 1968) she has this to say of his recent work –

> In spite of all Dr Williams' protestations about the need for cultivating a West Indian inspiration, in spite even of his own authorship of *A History of the People of Trinidad and Tobago*, can the reader be expected to draw any other conclusion than that a West Indian subject-matter is somehow worthless? Dr Williams cannot have it both ways. If he ignores or devalues writers because they write about the West Indies rather than about other subjects, then he is perpetuating the very attitudes of mind which have in the past led to the neglect of West Indian studies which he himself constantly condemns. The combination of omissions and hasty dogmatism which mars his present book will not remedy the unhappy conditions which have for so long retarded the development of our understanding of 'the unique antecedents of the people of the West Indies'.

This I fear is lamentably true. Until the gap is visualized, understood and begins to close, the West Indian historian and anthropologist will continue to reinforce a high-level psychological censorship of the creative imagination and to consolidate a foreboding about the risks involved in every free election of spirits.

As such the very institutions of the day will become increasingly rigged by fear and misgiving, and political deterioration is the inevitable corollary. And this indicates to me that in the absence of a historical correlative to the arts of the dispossessed, some kind of new critical writing in depth needs to emerge to bridge the gap between history and art. Denis Williams stated the dilemma very effectively in 'Image and Idea in the Arts of Guyana' (The Edgar Mittelholzer Memorial Lectures, second series, January 1969, published by the National History and Arts Council of Guyana). I now quote –

> Yet the first fact of the Caribbean situation is the fact of miscegenation, of mongrelism. What are the cultural implications of this mongrel condition? It is important to have experienced the homogeneity, richness, the integrity of the racially thoroughbred cultures of the Old World in order properly to take the force of this question. It is important if only as a means of discriminating between our condition and theirs, of assessing the nature and status of our mongrel culture when contrasted with the cultures of the thoroughbred, of realising the nature and function of the ancestor as he determines our cultural destiny. For we are all shaped by our past; the imperatives of a contemporary culture are predominantly those of a relationship to this past. Yet in the Caribbean and in Guyana we think and behave as though we have no past, no history, no culture. And where we do come to take notice of our history it is often in the light of biases adopted from one thoroughbred culture or another, of the Old World. We permit ourselves the luxury, for one thing, of racial dialectics in our interpretation of Caribbean and Guyanese history and culture. In the light of what we are this is a destructive thing to do, since at best it perpetuates what we might call a filialistic dependence on the cultures of our several racial origins, while simultaneously inhibiting us from facing up to the facts of what we uniquely are.

I would now like to resume the earlier thread of my argument in the dance of the folk – the human limbo or gateway of the gods – which was disregarded or incomprehensible to an intellectual and legal and historical convention. I had begun to point out that, first of all, the limbo dance becomes the human gateway which dislocates (and therefore begins to free itself from) a uniform chain of miles. In this context I also suggested that the gateway complex is also the psychic assembly or re-assembly of the muse of a people. This brings me now to my second point about limbo, namely, that it shares its phantom limb with Haitian vodun across an English/French divide of Caribbean cultures. This is a matter of great interest, I believe, because Haitian vodun is more directly descended from African myth and yet – like limbo which is a metamorphosis or new spatial character born of the Middle Passage – it is also intent on a curious re-assembly of the god or gods. Therefore I ask myself – is vodun a necessary continuation of a matrix of association which had not fulfilled itself in the Old World of Africa? If so that fulfilment would be in itself not an imitation of the past – much as it is indebted to the past – but a new and daring creative conception in itself.

If Haitian vodun is a creative fulfilment of African vodun one must ask oneself where do the similarities and differences lie. The basic feature they hold in common lies in 'possession trances' – trance features, I may add, which are not the case with limbo.

Pierre Verger in an essay appearing in *Spirit Mediumship and Society in Africa* (published by Routledge and Kegan Paul, 1969) writes –

> Possession trances occur regularly among the Nago-Yoruba and Fon people of Dahomey during rites for orisha and vodun...They are the culmination of an elaborate ritual sequence. Seen from the participant's point of view, such trances are the reincarnations of family deities in the

bodies of their descendants – reincarnations which have taken place in response to the offerings, prayers, and wishes of their worshippers.

In a footnote to his essay he defines orisha and vodun as: 'The general names given by the Yoruba and Dahomean people respectively to the deities worshipped by them. They are generally considered to be the very remote ancestors who dealt during their lifetime with some force of nature, and who can still do so on behalf of their worshippers.'

Pierre Verger has been speaking here of African vodun. I would like now to give my definition of Haitian vodun which appears in *Tradition, The Writer and Society* (New Beacon Publications, 1967) as this will help me, in parenthesis, to unravel certain similarities and differences in African and Haitian vodun and to look back afresh at the significance of the human limbo gateway.

Haitian vodun or voodoo is a highly condensed feature of inspiration and hallucination within which 'space' itself becomes the sole expression and recollection of the dance – as if 'space' is the character of the dance – since the celebrants themselves are soon turned into 'objects' – into an architecture of movement like 'deathless' flesh, wood or stone. And such deathless flesh, wood or stone (symbolic of the dance of creation) subsists – in the very protean reality of space – on its own losses (symbolic decapitation of wood, symbolic truncation of stone) so that the very void of sensation in which the dancer begins to move, like an authentic spectre or structure of fiction, makes him or her insensible to all conventional props of habit and responsive only to a grain of frailty or light support.

Remember at the outset the dancer regards himself or herself as one in full command of two legs, a pair of arms, until, possessed by the muse of contraction, he or she dances into a posture wherein one leg is drawn up into the womb of space. He stands like a rising pole upheld by earth and sky or like a tree which walks in its shadow or like a one-legged bird which joins itself to its sleeping reflection in a pool. All conventional memory is erased and yet in this trance of overlapping spheres or reflection a primordial or deeper function of memory begins to exercise itself within the bloodstream of space.

Haitian vodun is one of the surviving primitive dances of sacrifice, which, in courting a subconscious community, sees its own performance in transgressive terms – that is, with and through the eyes of 'space': with and through the sculpture of sleeping things which the dancer himself actually expresses and becomes. For in fact the dancer moves in a trance and the interior mode of the drama is exteriorized into a medium inseparable from his trance and invocation. He is a dramatic agent of subconsciousness. The life from within and the life from without now truly overlap. That is the intention of the dance, the riddle of the dancer.

The importance which resides in all this, I suggest, is remarkable. For if the trance were a purely subjective thing – without action or movement – some would label it fantasy. But since it exteriorizes itself, it becomes an intense drama of images in space, which may assume elastic limbs and proportions or shrink into a dense current of reflection on the floor. For what emerges are the relics of a primordial fiction where the images of space are seen as in an abstract painting. That such a drama has indeed a close bearing on the language of fiction, on the language of art, seems to me incontestable. The community the writer shares with the primordial dancer is, as it were, the complementary halves of a broken stage. For the territory upon which the poet visualizes a drama of consciousness is a slow revelation or unravelling of obscurity – revelation or illumination within oneself; whereas the territory of the dancer remains actually obscure to him within his trance whatever revelation or illumination his limbs may articulate in their involuntary theme. The 'vision' of the poet (when one comprehends it from the opposite pole of 'dance') possesses a 'spatial' logic or 'convertible' property of the imagination. Herein lies the essential humility of a certain kind of self-consciousness within which occurs *the partial erasure, if nothing more, of the habitual boundaries of prejudice.*

I have quoted rather extensively here from my previous essay because I think this may help us to see in rapport with Pierre Verger's definition of African vodun that while the trance similarity is clear, the functions have begun to differ. Haitian vodun – like West Indian and Guianese/Brazilian limbo – may well point to sleeping possibilities of drama and horizons of poetry, epic and novel, sculpture and painting – in short to a language of variables in art which would have a profoundly evolutionary cultural and philosophical significance for Caribbean man. Such new resources (if I may diverge for a brief moment and speak as someone whose chosen tongue is English) are not foreign to English poetry except in the sense that these may be closer to the 'metaphysical poets' – to a range and potency of association in which nothing is ultimately alien – of which Eliot speaks in his famous essay on 'dissociation of sensibility'.

Such a variable emphasis is outside the boundaries of intention in African vodun which is a conservative medium or cloak of ancestors. The gulf therefore between an inbuilt uniform censor and the imagination of a new art which exists in the British West Indies, in particular, is absent in Africa. African vodun is a school of ancestors: it is very conservative. Something of this conservative focus remains very strongly in Haitian vodun but there is an absorption of new elements which breaks the tribal monolith of the past and re-assembles an inter-tribal or cross-cultural community of families.

The term *loa,* for example, which means *spirit* or *deity* is of Bantu origin – not Yoruba or Dahomean, the tribal homes (some say) of vodun. Furthermore (I now quote from Harold Courlander's *Vodun in Haitian Culture* published by the Institute for Cross-Cultural Research, Washington):

> The various cults encompassed by the term Vodoun in its larger sense are not easy to set down diagramatically because of different degrees of blending and absorption in different regions of Haiti. Had the old cults or 'nations' remained independent of one another, as they probably were in early days, they probably would have included the following: Arada (Dahomey or Fon), Anago (Yoruba), Mahi, Ibo, Kanga, Congo (including Moundongue, Solongo, Bumba, etc., or these elements also might have maintained independence), and Petro (a cult in the African pattern that appears to have originated in Haiti). In certain parts of Haiti one still finds Ibo, Congo, and Nago cults that have resisted absorption, but this pattern does not hold for most of the country...There has been intrusion of Catholic practices and doctrine into Vodoun. Many of the *Loa* are identified with Catholic saints.

Elsewhere Courlander has this to say – 'Vodoun has perhaps the same meaning to some Haitian leaders as astrology to some leaders in India.'

All in all – while it is true that the role of Haitian vodun or vodoun is part and parcel of a prophetic and esoteric perspective in the Haitian body politic – the strict collective traditional sanction which belongs to Africa has varied in a manner comparable in some degree to the cleavage we have noted between history and art in the British West Indies.

I could not help noting this passage in Courlander's essay –

> The question of Vodoun's influence in politics in earlier days is blurred or distorted for a variety of reasons. European writers sometimes were unaware of Vodoun as a genuine religious pattern common to the entire nation, and, as we have noted, frequently delighted in depicting the superstitious character of the people. Haitian historians of the past were sensitive to the charge that the country was overrun with pagan rites, and they largely avoided mention of Vodoun. Little on the subject is likely to be found in government archives for much the same reason.

It is my assumption, in the light of all the foregoing, that a certain rapport exists between Haitian Vodun and West Indian limbo which suggests an epic potential or syndrome of variables.

That epic potential, I believe, may supply the nerve-end of authority which is lacking at the moment in the conventional stance of history.

But we need to examine this with the greatest care in order to assess and appreciate the risks involved.

In the first place the limbo imagination of the West Indies possesses no formal or collective sanction as in an old Tribal World. Therefore the gateway complex between cultures implies a new catholic unpredictable threshold which places a far greater emphasis on the integrity of the individual imagination. And it is here that we see, beyond a shadow of doubt, the necessity for the re-visionary, profoundly courageous, open-spirited and receptive artist of conscience whose evolution out of the folk as poet, novelist, painter is a symbol of risk, a symbol of inner integrity.

With African vodun – as we have seen – the integrity of the tribal person was one with a system which was conservative and traditional. There was no breath of subversion – no cleavage in the collective. History and art were one medium.

With Guyanese/West Indian limbo that cleavage is a fact and the rise of the imaginative arts has occurred in the face of long-held intellectual and legal suspicion. Therefore the rise of the poet or artist incurs a gamble of the soul which is symbolized in the West Indian trickster (the spider or anancy configuration). It is this element of tricksterdom that creates an individual and personal risk absolutely foreign to the conventional sanction of an Old Tribal World: a risk which identifies him (the artist) with the submerged authority of dispossessed peoples but requires of him, in the same token, alchemic resources to conceal, as well as elaborate, a far-reaching order of the imagination which, being suspect, could draw down upon him a crushing burden of censorship in economic or political terms. He stands therefore at the heart of the lie of community and the truth of community. And it is here, I believe, in this trickster gateway – this gamble of the soul – that there emerges the hope for a profoundly compassionate society committed to freedom within a creative scale.

I would like to re-emphasize the roles of 'epic' and 'trickster'. The epic of limbo holds out a range of variables – variables of community in the cross-cultural tie of dispossessed tribes or families – variables of art in a consciousness of links between poetry and drama, image and novel, architecture and sculpture and painting – which need to be explored in the Caribbean complex situation of apparent 'historylessness'. And furthermore in the Americas as a whole, it would seem to me that the apparent void of history which haunts the black man may never be compensated until an act of imagination opens gateways between civilizations, between technological and spiritual apprehensions, between racial possessions and dispossessions in the way the *Aeneid* may stand symbolically as one of the first epics of migration and re-settlement beyond the pale of an ancient world. Limbo and vodun are variables of an underworld imagination – variables of phantom limb and void and a nucleus of stratagems in which limb is a legitimate pun on limbo, void on vodun.

The trickster of limbo holds out a caveat we must reckon with in our present unstable situation. It is the caveat of conscience and points to the necessity for a free imagination which is at risk on behalf of a truth that is no longer given in the collective medium of the tribe. The emergence of original works of art is consistent with – and the inevitable corollary of – an evolution of folk limbo into symbols of inner cunning and authority which reflect a long duress of the imagination.

Note
1. Fable and myth are employed as variables of the imagination in this essay.

The Love Axe (I):
Developing a Caribbean Aesthetic 1962–1974

Edward Kamau Brathwaite

If you are the big tree
We are the small axe
Sharpened to cut you down
Ready to cut you down

Bob Marley and the Wailers
Burnin' (1973)

ONE
Roots and Marches

I

Exiles

Paule Marshall's novel, *The Chosen Place, the Timeless People* (New York, 1969) has, in a most interesting way, served as the signal and signpost for a profound revolution in West Indian consciousness.[1] No novel has since, so far, gone "further" than it. In fact, since 1969, there has been something of a dearth in West Indian prose fiction.[2] George Lamming has returned, after a ten year silence, to his negative treatment of philosophical colonialism in two recent novels: *Water With Berries* (1971) and *Natives of My Person* (1972). V. S. Naipaul continues the exploration of alienation from *The Mimic Men* (1967) into *In a Free State* (1971). Austin Clarke has produced a short masterwork in "Griff,"[3] but this, in many ways, is a culmination of the theme of exile within the content of "social realism."[4] Indeed, there are signs that in "Griff," Clarke, sensing the approach of technical cul de sac, is turning, perhaps, to a surrealist style, already present in Lindsay (Eseoghene) Barrett's *Song for Mumu* (1967), Naipaul's "A Flag on the Island"[5] and more recently in Wilson Harris' *Black Marsden* (1972). And while one would not wish to deny the continuing importance of, richness, and enriching quality of this literature of the Caribbean, one must also recognize that nearly all our major novelists continue to live, as they have done since the 1950s and early 1960s, abroad; and so they are increasingly cut off from the metaphorical and stylistic explosions that are even now taking place at home.

Caribbean: Haiti and Cuba

The signs of our new local creativity can be quickly recited. What is interesting is that several events and movements, at one time invisible, unrecognized, ignored (though they were there all the time) are slowly revealing their significance, connections and continuity with what we can now call the folk or alternative tradition in our part of the world.

The first major event was unquestionably the revolution in Cuba under Fidel Castro. Not since the revolution in Haiti in 1792, had a West Indian territory gained world significance *and* local integrity through the courage of opposing, and defeating, the jaguarnauts of Western mercantilism. In both cases, the success of the revolution was based upon a reliance on native resources; a recognition, transformation and utilization of those resources in a way that illuminated and expanded them from West Indian island to Caribbean matrix and from this to a resonant contribution to the aspirations and ideas of the entire family of nations. Cuba, then, as Haiti had done before, recalled us from isolation to Caribbean responsibility, and though at first our various establishments tried to prohibit our contact, they could not effectively censor our listening and understanding. And by the middle sixties, Cuba had become an ideal for most of the progressive thinkers in the Caribbean; why look abroad when the pride and practice of revolutionary change was *indeed* at home? The voice of C. L. R. James (see for instance *The Black Jacobins*[6] and its appendix "From Toussaint L'Ouverture to Fidel Castro") was especially important at this time. So too was the voice of the historian Elsa Goveia (see especially *A Study on the Historiography of the British West Indies*),[7] though hers is a case of statements and presences slowly revealing themselves to the mass, under the beneficent influence of "consciousness."

Caribbean Intellectuals

What I'm saying is that counterpointing the great movement of exile of the 'fifties and 'sixties and contiguous with the more dramatic assertions from Cuba, there were, in the anglophone Caribbean, two very articulate voices, neither of which immediately influenced our artists because their existing work for a long time remained either unrecognized or unknown. Although, for instance, *The Black Jacobins* has been read by some, at least, of the more radical "left," it had remained out of print between the date of its first publication (1938), and 1963, when James took the opportunity to add that critically important appendix. Goveia's *Historiography* has been available since 1956, but it was published in Mexico, as a scholarly edition, and therefore has remained underground and invisible to all but a few specialists in West Indian history until the thrust toward Westindianization which is reflected in the Arts curriculum of the University of the West Indies (UWI) toward the end of the 'sixties. Since then, an increasing number of undergraduates and research students have been exposed to this quiet, profoundly critical mind that has been able to suggest, without rancour or bias, that the European intellectual tradition (with honourable exceptions) warped itself in the colonies and therefore unfitted itself for more than exploitation of the Third World because it allowed itself to become debased in its attempt to justify slavery and racism, or was unable or unwilling (after the damage had been done in the 18th century) to re-examine itself in the light of its own native liberal (and revolutionary) tradition in the period that followed.

What Goveia also implied — and it is what Eric Williams states most brilliantly and forcefully in *Capitalism and Slavery*[8] and what our novelists of exile are/were on the verge of articulating (and I'm thinking especially of Lamming's *Natives* and *Berries*) — was that this humanistic debility, infecting first the extremities, as Bryan Edwards had noted in his *History*,[9] has most surely corrupted the metropole itself. Hence, its capacity to "rule," for cooperation rather than exploitation, has to be seriously questioned. This was, in fact, done at Bandung (1955) and has continued throughout the former and neo-colonial world ever since.

2

Anti- and Neo-colonialism

Ideological Cuba, then; the academic voices of James, Goveia, Williams; the increasingly consciously West Indian University of the West Indies: these are some of the founding factors of the New Movement. But communication/education was slow and poorly adapted to our needs, and so the effect of the forces honoured above was not immediately articulate: their yeast-like influence far far slower than what we felt we needed for our daily bread. But communication/education is one of the final tools and agencies of the establishment; so it was fortunate that two at least of our academics, James and Williams, were also (or also became) anti-colonial politicians. Their work and ideas were thus able, like sudden sparks, to leap the gap of print and reach the people. Williams, in fact, between 1954, when he began his "University of Woodford Square" lectures, and 1960 when embattled with the United States over the possession and use (as Federal capital) of our own soil (Chaguaramas), he led the March in the Rain and symbolically burned the Seven Deadly Sins of Colonialism, was seen and hailed throughout the region as the leader of anti-imperialist militance: reaching on the one hand to Castro in Cuba and on the other to the more culturally oriented but equally intransigent anti-colonialist politics of Negritude, developing under Aimé Césaire in Martinique. But as it turned out, the United States was not prepared to allow *fidelismo* to go beyond Cuba. A deal was struck with Williams and the nascent Federation of the West Indies over Chaguaramas, and Césaire's Negritude proved too metropolitan a product and reaction to bear effective praxis in the islands. In 1953, Cheddi Jagan's Marxist/native government in Guyana, with its crucial Afro/Asian political alliance, was suspended "by a characteristic act of Churchillian gunboat diplomacy," and the following year "overthrown," in Gordon Lewis' words, "under a thin guise of constitutionalism."[10] In 1962, the Federation of the West Indies broke up. Jou'vert and not Massa Day, was done, and the second great migration of our talent from the region began. True, we'd been left with universal adult suffrage, and this had taken us into our various independences and, certainly, especially in Jamaica, there was a certain spirit and expression of nationalism. But our "actions" had been mainly "international" gestures: anti-establishment, anti-colonial: not popular, people-based, certainly not native. Césaire remained untranslated, Goveia unread, James expatriate, expelled from his position of influence by Williams, whose "Doctor Politics" now became a local style. Jagan became involved in Cold War politics without Castro's courageous luck and infrastructural advantages. The Federation turned out to be a dream of London. Somewhere along the line we'd forgotten Garvey, our grassroot selves, the insurrection of the 1930s.

3

Rodney

But the native movement had persisted, underground and stubborn, so that when Walter Rodney, at the Mona campus of the University of the West Indies, suddenly, in October, 1968, galvanized students and "sufferers" into a movement of protest against the downpression of Pharaoh and demanded a return to the Promised Land of Africa *and* Marxist socialism, the (now black) establishment was taken by surprise and could only respond with road-block and riot police. Rodney was excluded from Jamaica, and students protesting against this act were baton-charged and tear-bombed, the University ringed with steel for weeks. But the links—artistic and intellectual—with the *people* (essential for the (re)-assertion of any local tradition) had been (re)-established. Rodney's *The Groundings With My Brothers* (1969) written in exile, became an "invisible" best-seller, a kind of, as the sound-systems chanted it, *duppy conqueror,* to be followed by a literal explosion of grassroots artistic/intellectual activity in: *Bongoman, Ital, Rasta Voice, Abeng, Revolutionary Poems, Pivot, Moko, Tapia* (in Trinidad), *Ratoon* (in Guyana) and later *Manjak* (in Barbados); Marina Maxwell's Yard Theatre and "Towards a Revolution in The Arts,"[11] the occupation of the Creative Arts Centre by a group of students; finally, Malcolm, Rasta, and Lloyd Reckord's production of Genet's *The Blacks* (in which, in fact, many students had acted; and so on to the February Revolution (1970) in Trinidad, with its moment of military confrontation and martial law.

In all cases, as before, the establishment "triumphed." But the native gains were nevertheless significant, and although there was repression and censorship, the revolution was at least converted into reform with, perhaps for the first time, the Great or Elite Tradition attempting to come into some contact with its Little or Folk Tradition. This was because, perhaps for the first time in our history, our native protest movements had a considerable measure of organization, and their artistic/literary output was large and significant. So that after the violence, the anger and confusion, there was still something important and permanent to which many could relate. It was in this way, I think, that the Establishment as well as the government was influenced by the Revolution.

4

Bongo-Man

Bongo-Man: Journal of African Youth, edited and largely written by Rupert Lewis, then a student in the Department of Government at the University of the West Indies at Mona, and now a lecturer in that Department with a M.Sc. (Master of Science) thesis on Marcus Garvey to his credit, began to appear in December 1968, as a direct response to the Rodney crisis and ran for about six issues until October, 1969, when *Abeng* took over. Its contents reflect Lewis' scholarly, literary and political interests and provide a fairly accurate picture of the kind of focus that Rodney had provided at the University among the youth. There were reprints from Garvey, Walter Domingo, George Padmore and Frantz Fanon, an editorial on the University's betrayal of Rodney, C.L.R. James on "Walter Rodney and Caribbean Misrule," and four pieces by Rodney himself, three of which were to appear later in *Groundings*. There was also C.Y. Thomas on Guyana, Amy Jacques Garvey, Trevor Munroe's "Black Power as a Political Strategy in Jamaica," Bongo Rupert's own "Marcus Garvey and the Damned," and several attacks (probably also by Lewis but unsigned) on the University's dismissal of Thomas (see above), the distinguished Guyanese economist and colleague of Rodney, and its repressive attitude toward students, especially those oriented towards Rastafari. The artistic side of this production, however, is disappointing. There were contributions from Rasta poets: Ras Dizzy, Bongo Jerry, Mortimo Planno and by others (Timothy Callender, Pat Lewis, Daryll Crosskill) moving toward Rastafari, but none of these is given enough space to develop a point, and there is no critical or socio-cultural work like, say, Garth White's "Rudie o Rudie," which appeared in *Impact*,[12] to indicate how the artists were in fact relating to the Revolution, although all the artists represented in *Bongo-Man* were in fact socially and intellectually very active and influential. Ras Dizzy was (and is) a poet, painter, journalist and philosopher who has issued innumerable mimeographed broadsides in his own idiosyncratic style, in addition to four books of poetry/prose meditation and comment. Bongo Jerry is a young Rasta leader and poet who during the *Bongo-Man/Abeng* period was presenting poems like "The Youth," "Black Mother," and most importantly, "Mabrak"[13] (with drum chorus, the style coming out of Rastafarian *grounnation*) to audiences at the

Yard Theatre and Rastafari celebrations. Mortimo Planno, Rasta leader, poet, actor and philosopher was one of the blessed four who was invited by the Jamaica government to take part in a mission to Africa, following the favourable reception of the University's report on the Rastafari in 1960.[14] It was Planno again who, when all else had failed, on the occasion of the late Haile Selassie's visit to Jamaica in 1966, took over from the police and the Establishment and controlled the vast amazing crowd assembled at Palisadoes Airport—it had burst all boundaries and had surrounded the Emperor's plane even before he had left the aircraft—so that H.I.M. could at last descend the steps onto Jamaican soil.

"Black Culturalism"

Bongo-Man didn't reflect much of this, perhaps because it didn't have time to develop; there were only, as I've said, six issues. But there was also a conflict within *Bongo-Man* (which becomes clearer in *Abeng*) between those who were willing to tolerate and even encourage what Trevor Munroe called "black culturalism" and those (like Munroe) who saw it as a possible distraction and division:

> If the statements of the politicians so far are trying to press on us a confusion between authority and power, a confusion between the presence of black officials and the occupation of black sufferers of their environment in a way which benefits themselves, then because of the extremeness of the psychological oppression of this kind of society one is getting an equally antithetical reaction, and this reaction finds its expression [in] what I call *Black Culturalism*. This means quite simply that people who have become in recent times conscious of the extent to which the society through violent means has whitened them, are now beginning through equally extreme measures to re-Africanize themselves, to discover a culture from which they were torn violently. Now this [is] necessary, I would argue; it is good, I would also argue, but it has several dangers. The men who grow their hair long, who don't cut it, the women who cut down their hair, the men who wear dashikis and don't talk to anybody else except those who do the same are reacting to the totality of psychological oppression by negating it, by denying it in their own personal modes of behaviour. *But the danger in this kind of activity is that it confuses personal emancipation with collective liberation.* We must understand this because the danger in personal, culturalist activity is that it divides black sufferers on the basis of their ability to adopt the superficialities in very many cases of a contrary way of proceeding than that to which the society has inculcated us. The danger is clear, because if the business of oppression is collective, if it does not discriminate as between black people who are in a dominated position in the economy and society, then equally the business of liberation (if it must succeed) has not, cannot rely on being a personal act alone, but has to make itself collective in the same way that the business of oppression is.[15]

One can see the danger that Comrade Munroe is worried about, especially when he perceives the mere move back to blackness as a superficial fad and therefore something selfish and individualistic. But Munroe, I think, underestimated the real deep instinct for Africa which our people carried in themselves, and mistook the dashiki and the afro for divisive fashions, when in fact they were/are the awakenings to a new style, a real alternative aesthetic possibility, creating not a sense of individuation, as "press hair" does, but of the very collective solidarity that he calls for. And with the style and the new-found confidence, went the desire to know more: hence the popularity of Rodney's lectures in African history, the formulation of an Afro Women's Study Group after the scandals of headmistresses in certain secondary schools turning girls away because they dared enter the precincts in their afros, and the reverberations of the "Africa Night" held at Mary Seacole Hall (Mona Campus) in November, 1968. This was the first time that our students had been exposed in any serious way to African art, music, dress, poetry. I can still remember the effect, for instance, of my reading from Okot p'Bitek's *Song of Lawino*:

> They cook their hair
> With hot iron
> And pull it hard
> So that it may grow long.
> Then they rope the hair
> On wooden pens
> Like a billy goat
> Brought for the sacrifice
> Struggling to free itself.
>
> They fry their hair
> In boiling oil
> As if it were locusts,
> And the hair sizzles
> It cries aloud in sharp pain
> As it is rolled and stretched.[16]

It led for one thing, to a widening abandonment of pressed hair. But there was another point, made by a student reviewer:

> At this point in our history, the question that concerns us most is the matter of identity. Our writers point always to the dislocation of the West Indian and his attendant problems; the intellectuals involve themselves in defining what our "position should be", and the common black-white discussion is clearly part of the same problem. As a matter of fact the entire problem can be resolved to black-white Africa-Europe, without much simplification. And what is significant is that we have been carrying out this examination of ourselves in a cultural situation which is predominantly Europe and scarcely Africa. Even our literature and history courses at UWI fail to provide enough which is relevant to the West Indies directly or to Africa.[17]

"Black culturalism," therefore, far from dividing, was strengthening the movement and providing it with a sense of style and spiritual value—an aesthetic.

5

The Creative Arts Centre

The crunch came when in February, 1970, The Creative Arts Centre was occupied by a group of students demanding the Westindianization of the cultural events at the Centre and greater student participation in and control of its administration. Here at last, you might say, was our Sir George William, our Cornell, perhaps our Kent State—for there were rumours, throughout most of the occupation (February-April, 1970) that the police were going to be asked to intervene. And there *was* that element, that feeling of identity with what was going on abroad. One very militant even cried out that we should seize the Computer Centre, and there was the general feeling that though Babylon had ringed us round with steel during the Rodney crisis this, at least/last, was our own internal affair—an issue between I-an-I and the Administration (Menagement)[18] over *participation*.

This, in fact, was the key issue since the *volte face* of the University over Rodney[19] and the removal, after this, of some of our finest lecturers: C.Y. Thomas, Ken Post, Pat Emmanuel, Bill Riviere, among others. Students felt they were not getting a fair share in the running of the University, and some of the more "conscious" lecturers felt so too. They insisted that the University was, in fact, being run by an oligarchy and that all those outside this carpeted cadre had no say whatever. But there was also an ideological issue connected with this: the psychological Westindianization of the University. The point was dramatized by Lucille Edwards, then Secretary of the Guild of

Undergraduates and soon to be one of the "occupators" of the Creative Arts Centre,[20] when she refused to perform the role, traditional to her office, of carrying the train of the Chancellor's robe in the annual procession of students. A meeting of the Guild Council (3 February 1970) supported the sister "on the ground that this ceremonial practice is neither relevant or necessary, and that it tends to perpetuate a tradition to which West Indians no longer subscribe."[21] Nineteen days after this, on Sunday, 22 February 1970, the students occupied the Creative Arts Centre.

The Liberal Tradition

The occupation is crucial since it testified to the beginning of our post-colonial definition, or, aesthetics. George Lamming, artist in residence at the "green academy" as he called it in 1955, had said that his first impression of undergraduates was that they seemed to him to have been "on holiday since birth."[22] But our art, perhaps, had flourished in this heady atmosphere, for this was the Renaissance period of the University with names and talents like Derek Walcott, Rex Nettleford, Slade Hopkinson, Garth St. Omer, Erroll Hill, Mary Brathwaite, Carol Dawes, Barbara and Ancille Gloudon, Stan Irons, Archie Hudson-Phillips—and all these on a campus of only 200.

> ...this was the era of Walcott, the poet, painter, dramatist, and sometime student; and the medical undergraduate who was also athlete, debator, orator, photographer, horticulturist, was not entirely unique.... The extraordinary fact would have been if this constellation of talents had not produced something fine and exciting in the performing arts. And as they moved through a repertoire ranging from Sophocles to Tennessee Williams, the University players demonstrated the levels of creative professionalism possible in student theatre.

This was the time, too, when the Dean of the Faculty of Arts could tell the Freshmen class of 1954/55:

> The pursuit of learning is "not a race in which the competitors jockey for the best place, it is not even an argument or a symposium; it is a conversation." The scholar does not "preach" and the teacher does not "instruct" — the voices which make up the conversation are not the assertive voices of the world of power or politics. And the value of the conversation does not depend on any dogmas which might emerge but on the quality of mind which evolves in the participants. I like this idea of "conversation" (taking the word in a pretty wide sense, of course—Oakeshott, you will notice includes conversation with oneself)—I like it for two reasons. First of all, as I have suggested, it implies that the pursuit of learning is urbane, civilized, tentative—that it belongs to a world of tolerance which is threatened on all sides nowadays. The pursuit of learning in a university is not basically a search for remedies for the ills of the outside world. It is not a search for a faith of any kind. These things may come into the university "conversation" but if they provide its only or its main driving force then the university becomes a technical college or a seminary.[23]

> The undergraduate belongs to one of the few remaining leisured classes.... Leisured, not in the sense of allowing your mind to lie fallow, but leisured in the sense that you have time to explore, however fragmentarily, the world of the mind. You are not passive—yet you are not *committed*.[24]

Demonstration, under this ruling concept, could be then little more than "excursions into the world" in the liberal/humanitarian tradition of Anglican dissent, and concerned with "international" issues. Hence the Sharpeville marches of March/April 1960, when Busta and Hugh Shearer "joined the University speakers on the platform at Victoria Pier to cry out against injustice, racial hatred and so on."[25]

But the student involvement in the pro-Federation campaign in 1961 was a quite different and a less ecumenical excursion, since it had come nearer home. With Rodney, public student demonstration was prohibited, and so the implosions occurred: The Creative Arts Centre (1970), Barclays Bank (1971), Trevor Munroe and the Campus Workers Strike (1972). The artist/intellectual was no longer a leisurely green academic; whether he was committed or not, he was in a situation of engagement, in which the emerging values of the folk (workers, Calibans, blacks, students, women, the colonized) were coming into increasing contact with the Establishment and demanding a re/formation of values.

6

Towards a New Value System

The aesthetic issues involved in the occupation of the Centre were brilliantly expressed at this time, in their very different ways, by Ras Dizzy the poet and by Sylvia Wynter, novelist, critic, literary historian and lecturer in Spanish at the University (Mona).

> Rastafarian poet and artist Ras Dizzy has protest against the critix on Rastafarians painting made by Dr. Roy Marshall, V.C. of the U.W.I, in addressing the Art Exhibition opened at the Jamaica Government Institute a few days ago by Roy Marshall. The poet said that the V.C. of the U.W.I. should reconsider his criticism that Rastafarian artists only paint about Africa and of only strange things. Ras Dizzy said that Dr. Marshall should remember piece of his work he sold to him. Titled Jamaican Market Woman which have nothing to do with another land — The poet said althow moust scientist professors lecturiors, and the interloctuals buys abstrockt and creative painting — he had always hanour the realistic work of the Rastafarians whenever a piece is seen — Ras Dizzy said he is at present holding some of his realistic work for who wants to chanels them. The best realistic painter in the island Ras Dizzy said is Ras Daniel. And that no artist has yet seen to run against Daniels work excepting Ras Dizzy. And no one to run against Ras Dizzys work other than Ras Daniel. And Watson in Denham Town third. Ras Dizzy said that a psychological fight is recently set up against Rastafarians painters and writers since a certain sector of people belonging to the top of the society was awaiting the obsence of the unparciall editor of the Gleaner who is Mr. T. Sealy to replace a biasminded one.[26]

But it was Sylvia Wynter who put the issue into aesthetic perspective when she wrote:

> The conflict between *high standards* or *new standards* is not the *either/or dichotomy* that it appears to be. It is a matter of emphasis. High standards achieved by established civilizations are all part of the cultural heritage of the Caribbean people. It is this multiplicity of heritage that promises the creation of a new culture, a new civilization. All the great cultural advances of man have come from cross-fertilization of cultures. The *high standards* achieved by a Greek play, a Chinese poem, an Indian song, the Japanese theatre, an African Benin head are all relevant to our present experience.
>
> To deny any of these is to maim a part of ourselves. To reject any one is to reject a part of ourselves. Yet, to insist as we have hitherto done on any one part—i.e., the European—to the total exclusion of *any* or *all* of the others, is to humiliate and exile a part of ourselves. And is paradoxically, to betray, through distortion, even that part which we accept—i.e., European—since we presume to pass off a part of mankind's experience, however rich and vivid, as the whole of it, as the total sum of its possibilities and potentiality. To understand West Indian history we must turn to the history of Africa, Asia, of the indigenous peoples of the American Continent, Europe.
>
> We cannot accept the Greek play, and reject the African Benin head—or even worse, pay it a lip service acceptance. Nor can we emphasize the African Benin head and leave out the Greek play, the Chinese poem. Yet even when we accept the high standards of all of them, we cannot remain frozen in their achieved beauty. To borrow a fine phrase of the Chancellor at the recent University

graduation exercise, one should keep relics but one should not allow them to degenerate into ruins.[27]

In an earlier article, "Issues Behind Creative Arts Centre,"[28] Miss Wynter had outlined a whole series of instances in which events of West Indian interest (and importance) had been denied *hospes* at the Centre, and from this she developed two points, both of them relevent to our discussion:

1. that the Centre's refusal to take part in the Jamaica Festival (drama section) could be, and was, taken to imply overt contempt by "better off groups" for the "masses," and that this "overt contempt for the masses has been interpreted by the students as an overt contempt for being black"

and

2. that the University had opted to act, "not [as] a *catalyst* for change in our society, but rather as a powerful new Establishment, determined to protect its innumerable fringe benefits, and its privileged academic status quo."

"In the prevailing atmosphere," she continued, "an atmosphere for which we are all responsible,"

> to be young and generous and unable to accept injustice is to find oneself either gradually conforming with cynicism, or losing oneself in the ugly wasteland of professional and sterile protest. To be caught between these two attitudes is to live in anguish. The lucky ones, "the silent majority," remain unaware and unawakened and acquiesce in any system. But they do not build a society. They merely prop it up.
>
> *For myself I can say that my feeling of alienation, of not in any way belonging has been complete and profound. My efforts to "belong" have left me more alienated than ever.*[29]

Negation and the Collective Vision

This is a bitter confession for anyone, not least of all for a sensitive committed artist who had returned home to help build the new society. It gives significance to Martin Carter's "All are involved, all are *consumed*"[30] and Gordon Rohlehr's comment that:

> Carter burned out in five years into the sad blue "Poems of Shape and Motion" (*Kyk-Over-Al*, Vol. 6, No. 20, 1955), whose doubt was much more movingly shaped into poetry than his earlier oratorical commitment. The weight of compassion, life and time which those poems contain, tells me clearly as anything, how our lives will from generation to generation be denuded slowly into grief, tiredness and silence. In twenty years, if spared by ganja, soul, cacapool rum and the widening barbarity of our politics, most of today's youth will be respectable citizens, without illusions, and terribly afraid of tomorrow's children, whose ears they will try to fill with fables of the swinging seventies.[31]

To me this (simply?) means that our new native art, our own home-blood aesthetics will have its devastations and disfigurements. But this is saying little more than that like all "whole" cultural expressions, it must be rounded, complex, paradoxical, uncertain, despairing at times, tragic and ironic as well as optimistic. But never negative.

Not negative because the aesthetic expectations of an emerging culture cannot be that in the same way that a growing child or planet or constellation cannot be. So that although we may lose the *individuals*, we cannot lose the individual contribution to the *collective vision* of our now revealing selves. For there is too much complexity of history to understand, of cultures to understand, of local tree and bird and places to know, of local language to command. There might be slavery, yes: but liberation also; it might be schistosomiasis, dungle, the kiss of alcohol: but nevertheless growth:

process out of that: a constant transformation. So that my own aesthetic formulation for ourselves begins with rhythm: survival rhythm, emancipation rhythm, transfiguration rhythm; and how the one, the ego, comes to this, comes out of this, relates to this and us and others.

I therefore return to Sylvia Wynter and find her, despite the conflict of alienation, really speaking not for herself alone, but for the lonely occupators of the Centre. She has internalized the emotion of the mind that drove them there to make that stand and symbol:

> The University for 21 years now the apex, or the supposed apex of our educational system, cannot now wash its hand of the kind of human material put out by the schools, or even the homes. The product of those schools have been taught by an increasing number of graduates turned out from the University. The degree of thistlesness or figness in the products turned out from the schools, depends to some extent on us. Wherever there is a failure in the system, it is partly our failure. After all, WE ARE THE SYSTEM.
>
> We cannot then, with Olympian detachment "reveal" figures proving the failure of any part of the educational system, without admitting our partial responsibility for this failure. Yet, if we continue to believe as the Chancellor does, that our role is merely to receive fig trees and help them grow into figs, then we can continue to indulge in this expert buck-passing which has characterized recent "revelation." But if we believe in a dynamic process —i.e., that we put out the teachers who help to create the products they send to us, then we accept that the buck stops right here.
>
> More than that, we would be prepared to challenge the Chancellor's statement, and to say that in this age of technological miracles, the only possible role for this most expensive piece of equipment, put down in a poor society, is the role of transforming thistles into figs or vice versa; or failing that, to devise ways and means by which thistles will be far more useful and valuable — than those much over rated figs, which I for one, have at all times found unpalatable.[32]

This (new) sense of responsibility and inter-relatedness is what I would note as fundamental to any definition of our aesthetic. But our definitions cannot evolve out of a vacuum — wishing cannot make us be. We must therefore work to discover ourselves, to excavate from memory, if necessary. Then we must sort out, categorize, store, define and then begin the process of education, re-definition, rediscovery and re-assessment.

7

Sylvia Wynter

Sylvia Wynter[33] was born of Jamaican parents in Cuba, and was educated in Jamaica, London and Madrid. She has therefore, for a start, a wider than usual (for the West Indies) cultural and experiential background. But although the first phase of her adult life was spent in the European metropoles, she retained, like most West Indian (expatriate) writers, a very clear sense of the folk (*The Hills of Hebron*, 1962). She had also, as early as this first phase, already formulated a model of the ideal West Indian literary prose-form: a kind of picaresque prose-poem, rooted in the "physicality" of the West Indian dialect: and the concern of the West Indian writer should be with the anonymous mass of our people — those who have "absolutely no documented history at all:"[34]

> [We must] stop competing with the Europeans and go down into the tremendous unexamined force which is breaking at home but which we find it difficult to find a form for, [knowing] that if we can catch it authentically enough and honestly enough it will be of universal [significance because] it will be the true story of a people.[35]

Miss Wynter herself has not yet been able to capture that "form," but like Derek Walcott, I think she now feels that it is in drama that the possibility lies, and her increasingly successful experiments from *The House and Land of Mrs. Alba* (c.1963?) and *Ballad for a Rebellion* (1965) through to *Rockstone Anancy* (1970) and the jonkonnu play for JBC television (1973) suggest that she is slowly internalizing her ideas. And although she has not yet, either, been able to celebrate or discern this "form" in any other creative writer, her contribution has been invaluable in a number of important ways which I shall attempt briefly to enumerate.

On her return to Jamaica, where she took up a teaching post (in Spanish) with the University of the West Indies, her concerns were at first chiefly academic: a long look at *Lady Nugent's Journal* (1967),[36] and a study of Bernardo de Balbuena, a 16th century poet/abbot of Jamaica (1967/70).[37] But there was also her "Reflections on West Indian Writing and Criticism" (1968/69).[38]

"Reflections"

This piece is one of our great critical landmarks: a major *essai* into literary *ideas,* and the first to be written *in* the West Indies.[39] Miss Wynter's point of departure here is three other University-based works: Wayne Brown's "The Novelist in an Unsettled Culture"; W.I. Carr's "Roger Mais — Design for a Legend"; and *The Islands in Between: Essays in West Indian Literature,* edited by Louis James.[40]

But Miss Wynter's concern here was not so much with her disagreements with what her colleagues wrote, as with the meaning of her disagreements with them. And the meaning of her disagreement with them has to do with the University of the West Indies and its (lack of) contribution to our culture on the very issues that Rodney and the occupators of the Creative Arts Centre had been (and would be) concerned about. What she finds is that the critics she examines, working out of a "branch plant industry of a metropolitan system," be they Englishmen or West Indians, almost all failed to understand — or at any rate, discuss with any reason or resonance — the true nature of West Indian creative writing: its separation from its source.

> West Indian books have a function in West Indian society. West Indian writers have none ....
> When the creative instinct is stifled or driven into exiles, the critical faculty can survive only as maggots do — feeding on the decaying corpse of that which gives it a brief predatory life.[41]

These rather harsh words can be explained (away) by recognizing that Miss Wynter, not too long returned herself from a long period abroad, was still feeling sympathy for the predicament of our "exile." But it is too anti-colonial and simple to claim, as she goes on to do, that just as the Communist commissars send their dissident writers to prison, so do the Western "market commissars by inducing writers to find outlet and function only at the metropolitan centre, [send] them into exile."[42] The exile of our writers is, after all, as much our responsibility as the metropole's — at least it must be conceived as such if we are to speak responsibly of *our own* culture. It is not until the crisis of the Creative Arts Centre that Miss Wynter seems to have come to recognize this.

But what makes "Reflections" important is its attack on a "West Indian" academic criticism coming out of an "impure" English university tradition. The brilliant myth of Europe held by James, Carr, Brown, Morris and Naipaul causes them to misapprehend, for one thing, the presence of Africa in our society and so to misinterpret the role of Caliban, the native of it. For it is assumed, Miss Wynter claims, that natives are natives and not men. Men is something the natives grow into. And that which makes men grow, distinguishing them from natives, is "culture" — European culture. Hence the separation of art from life, in these critics, and Naipaul's notion that "nothing was created in the West Indies." What we have to recognize, Miss Wynter counters, is that *failure,* not "nothing," is the residual element of all West Indian societies and that it is this, not the "triumph of the human spirit," that the West Indian novel is about. It is from this perception that we can begin to appreciate the "daily revolution" of the Caribbean sufferer and artist; it is from this mud of deprivation that we can begin to appreciate Caliban's devices of defence/attack until Prospero is at least forced into dialogue. It is from the necessary dialogue (interculturation of Great and Little traditions) that "culture" comes, has meaning — as, she observes, E.R. Braithwaite demonstrates in *To Sir With Love*. His black Prospero refuses to accept that the East End (Caliban) school children should be excluded "from all the props of [his] humanity" and his struggle for this "comes from his own memory and still present experiences...of the [Caribbean] torment."[43]

Miss Wynter's indictment against the academic critics is that unlike the creative writers they write about, they are unable to make these links between traditions of the oppressor and the oppressed. "These are [therefore] for me essentially 'acquiescent' critics — critics who reflect and parallel the inauthenticity of the university and its society."

Two months before the publication date of this article, Walter Rodney had been cashiered from the University of the West Indies. This event, I can only suppose, must have made a deep impression on Miss Wynter. By the time of the second University crisis (in March, 1970), she had started to move into the second phase of her development: a consideration of folk, rather than colonial, culture.

Jonkonnu

"Jonkonnu in Jamaica: Towards the Interpretation of Folk Dance as a Cultural Process,"[44] which appeared in June 1970, is a masterwork by any standard. It no doubt came, partly at least, out of the debates current at the time over the significance to our cultural life of the work being produced by the National Dance Theatre Company of Jamaica (NTDC) under Rex Nettleford.[45] But for Sylvia Wynter such debates — and I'm not even sure whether she was involved in them — would have been marginal to what was now her major preoccupation: the development of an image/ikon/event with and through which she could symbolize the folk: in a way similar to how Marina Maxwell and Errol Hill, for instance, had conceived of Carnival in Trinidad.[46] Indeed, Jonkonnu, as Miss Wynter herself points out in this study, is (or rather was) Jamaica's carnival: West African custom brought over with the slaves, given permission to surface publicly at Easter and Christmas, but never, as in Trinidad, receiving the support and active participation of the brown and upper classes and so marginalized even before the end of slavery under missionary pressure and because the establishment itself had come to have good reason to distrust it, since it was so often used as mask not only of god but of rebellion.

"Jonkonnu" is really a study in creolization: an extension of Miss Wynter's notion (in "Reflections") that there should be dialogue between Prospero and Caliban; and to realize this piece, she has assembled and interpreted an impressive corpus of historical detail. The African mask in Jamaica is slowly transformed in form and meaning under the pressure of slavery and becomes a paradigm of adaptation/survival, through which means the slave comes into authentic possession of the landscape and so can be taken as the true reflector of local values and (art)-forms. But "local" is now, for Miss Wynter, no longer a stampen ground — "what remains" of the conflict between imperator and colonial; alienated product of mercantilist waste. She has moved from Marxist overtones and citations, to African culture; so that in *Rockstone Anancy*, the musical play she wrote for the annual and now traditional Jamaican pantomime at the end of 1970, we find her struggling clumsily but bravely with huge African mask/gods and startling (?) her public with the idea that Anansi the spider is (also) a god.

When in Trinidad in February of that same year, the militant marchers occupied the Roman Catholic Cathedral of Port-of-Spain and declared that GOD IS BLACK, the two Revolutions had, if briefly, been joined.

Tapia

The print holding the strain in Trinidad at this time was *Tapia*, started by Lloyd Best at the Tapia Group in October, 1969. *Tapia,* like *Abeng,* is an expression of the reformed/radicalized New World Group founded by Best, in 1963, as a way of getting Caribbean intellectuals *in* the West Indies (in effect at U.G. and UWI) to discuss the problem of Caribbean (un)-identity and underdevelopment *and what we could do about it.* From the beginning, Best's New World was an optimistic solutions-oriented programme, calling on a wide range of talents and providing an impressive portfolio of exploration: definition: concern. The foundation for all our future work of nativization: political, economic, educational and cultural: went on in the New World Group sessions that started in Georgetown in 1963, moved (with Best) to Mona (1964-66). But what the Rodney and CAC Revolutions revealed, was that crucial as this activity may have been, it was/had become increasingly confined, on the one hand, to academia, with no or little interchange with the yout' of the society (the term is used here to connote not an age-group, but growing-points) especially those post-Independence consciousnesses (sufferer, Rasta, black, Marxist, guerrilla) becoming increasingly disaffected with our continuing condition of poverty and powerlessness; and on the other, that there was a continuing (traditional) gap between our artists and our academics, new and old. The gap, which still persists, is very much to be deplored, especially when one is aware of the high quality of criticism possible from George Beckford (of his comments on the NDTC), Bobby Hill and Trevor Munroe (or their interventions during seminars at the Creative Arts Centre on Walcott's *In a Fine Castle* 1970, and Barry Reckord's *In the Beautiful Caribbean,* 1972).

Best's re-formation of New World (Trinidad) into Tapia (1968) was an answer to these perceived divergencies.[47] Tapia House was designed to create a new kind of base for the discussion of and self-education into Caribbean problems. Set in the peculiarly fragmented/developing urban/plantation context of Trinidad, Best saw the role of his new group as essentially integrative. He recognized, for instance, that the charismatic/nationalist politics of Eric Williams had failed, after 1962, because it was based on the dictatorship of the PNM (a default "dictatorship"; there was no integrative opposition) because there was no vision of how we should plan our economy (starting with control of resources); no idea of how the people could participate in their own government; but above all, he recognized that the fragmentation of the society stemmed from over-individuation (materialist ethos), from lack of native education, lack of native institutions (or failure to recognize and use them); from a multi-racial ethic that was sterile because imposed (structural/fortress) and lacking in movement (interculturation). Best's practical programme of solution was based upon the establishment, federated from Tapia House, of a series of Tapia cells, governed by local and central assemblies and linked by visits and the *Tapia* newspaper. In this way the older New World concept of study and self-education was given an immediate and wider provenance; and from the beginning (and certainly until 1972/73 when *Tapia* becomes increasingly and more directly involved in "conventional" politics), the artist/intellectual was given as much prominence and encouragement as the academic and political thinkers. If therefore it can be said that Rodney was the first of our modern native intellectuals to introduce a new dynamic for change into our plantation society, linking academic and yout', Lloyd Best represents that essential receptivity or dynamo which now attempts to use and integrate this light and energy and fashion forward out of it. And in the same way that Sylvia Wynter emerged to supply the aesthetic links and rationale for what was happening in Jamaica (the First Revolution), so Gordon Rohlehr has emerged (mainly from the pages of *Tapia*) as the leading explorator of the even more complex (and native) aesthetic demanded by the Second Revolution.

9

Gordon Rohlehr

Like most of us from in the colonial tradition, Gordon Rohlehr (b. Guyana, 1942) began with a "liberal" outlook — he may well have heard Professor Croston's lectures (above). He went to the metropole (Birmingham University) to do his Ph.D. (he chose Conrad, he says, because the Pole was an "outsider"), and his first literary critiques reflect the *academics* that Sylvia Wynter had come to dislike: "Predestination, frustration and symbolic darkness in Naipaul's *A House for Mr. Biswas* (1964), *Crusoe and the Establishment* (1968?), "Character and Rebellion in *A House for Mr. Biswas*" (1969). The first "break" came in 1967/68 at CAM[48] in London and developed in the period 1968/69 with considerations against negativism in Naipaul, Walcott's *Gulf* and the novels of Garth St. Omer. These are counterpointed with a eulogy on Don Drummond, the "mad" Jamaican trombonist who died in May, 1967. Here, for the first time, Rohlehr makes a link between dispossession and the creativity of the blues: sKa, rock steady, Billie Holiday, Rastafari; and links these, in turn, with the poetry of Martin Carter, Derek Walcott and Edward Brathwaite, all "articulate as exponents of the Blues."[49] From here he went to a more detailed report on the Jamaican situation ("Sans humanite," 1969), beginning his report with the significant rising figures of crime and violence, and the complementary rising Government and police repression:

> Between 1962 and 1963 there were 66 murders in Jamaica, 7,274 cases of wounding, also 238 sexual offences, as compared with 111 murders, 9,125 cases of wounding and 351 sexual offences between 1966 and 1967. ...[50]

> In February (1966), the Government began bull-dozing the shanties along Marcus Garvey Drive without making any provision for the displaced black people. Later, it was Paine Avenue and Industrial Terrace. Altogether about 3,000 people lost their homes. They were called "squatters."

> Some of the dispossessed, rightly interpreting the symbolism, of the Government's action, pitched camp among the graves of May Pen Cemetery.[51]

The "sounds" of this are in Don Drummond's trombone, in the rock-steadies and rudie riddims which followed, and in the poetry which also came out of this context.[52] And so it was on to the Sabina Park riot and tear-gassing (also described by Orlando Patterson)[53] and the Rodney crisis which Rohlehr, more than most of us, saw in its total socio-political context of pressure and underdevelopment:

> In fact the violence of October 1968 was the direct aftermath of a series of strikes in Kingston in the months immediately before. The firemen, policemen, telephone company workers, workers in Water and Sewage all were on strike. The opposition party held a march in September at which the army and police were in attendance with their guns. Shearer himself cut short a trip to the U.S. in an attempt to alleviate the crisis. He was glad when the Rodney affair occurred. It diverted the attention of the people from the crucial issues of social and economic hardship, which had involved them. It postponed the moment of reckoning. But best of all, it provided him with an easy scapegoat, whose timely slaughter would wipe away the government's own sins of omission and commission. Thus, it was necessary for Shearer to stress that it was "the foreign students" who were misleading innocent and gullible Jamaicans. And of course, Seaga played a nice second

fiddle when he spoke of the need for a Jamaica University, because too many West Indians were emasculating Jamaican manhood.[54]

After this, it was Trinidad and the February Revolution, with Rohlehr himself in the thick of it.[55] For creative correlation and surrogate, he turned increasingly to a study, first of the "The Calypso as Rebellion" (1970), "Calypso and Politics" (1971), and then to a full-blooded study of the history of calypso as such.[56] From this, he could now confidently set up his aesthetic link, started in "Sparrow and the Language of Calypso" (1967) and "Jamaica Blues" (1970) between "folk" forms and "art" forms, thus paralleling the development of Sylvia Wynter in "Jonkonnu."

TWO
Beginnings

1

But the Establishment's battle was already lost. By 1972 there was Omo Ajini, Yoruba, Kairi, Dem Two, Anthony Hinkson and the Barbados Writers Workshop, the Centre Universitaire at Guadeloupe's Poul'bois Group, Bruce St. John, Iouanaloa activity in St. Lucia, Alliouagana in Montserrat, The Dreads in Dominica, Shake Keane's *Nancitori*, Derek Walcott's *Ti Jean and His Brothers*, the NDTC's *Kumina*. There had been the ACLALS Conference, the great *Savacou* debate, all culminating in the miracle of Carifesta in Guyana.[57] And in Jamaica coming out of the Rodney Revolution, like *Bongo-Man* and *Abeng*, there was Marina Maxwell's Yard Theatre.

Yard Theatre

Yard was revolutionary in that everything about it not simply rejected/ignored the notions of traditional/colonial Euro-American theatre, *it provided a viable and creative alternative*. There was no house, no building. The theatre was as its name said: a yard: in a yard: 12 Princess Alice Drive, August Town, Mona: transferred from time to time to other (people's) yards. There was therefore no "fixity"; no "audience," for one thing in the traditional sense; no gate, no entrance fee, no foyer, no box office, no boxes; therefore no dress-up, no gossip between acts: no drinks, no clinks, no place where the privilege of those who could afford to pay could be displayed; no profit (and we hoped: but wrong) no loss. Instead, there was simply those who came: invitation, rumour and, most important, those of the neighbourhood, the street/community; those passing by who could see with the knowledge of ears: as in their own yards. And since there was no pay, no privilege, no fixed seats, there was no social stratification; instead, there was this democracy of witness and, as we shall see later, a democracy of participation, since in the small space available in the yard, actor=singer=dancer was also often audience: watching with the "audience" his brothers and sisters "perform"; and the "audience" (small, tight, democraded) becoming increasingly *consumed* into the pressure of their involvement.

And because it was a theatre of unconventional structure (*process*, in fact, not structure): no walls, no "audience," there was an instinctive subterranean flow towards "unconventional" dramatic content and presentation — in addition, that is to the Omowale's own revolutionary ideas. *Play Man* (1968), *Consciousness I* (1969), *Rights of Passage* (1970), *One Love* (1971), the Harambee experiment (1972)[58] and the ill-fated *Persistent Plantations* (1973):[59] all conceived of art as a seamless garment: no curtain into scenes or acts, no "change of scenery," no "lights" but what there was: star, gas, kerosene; no distinction of performers, poets, dancers, singers, etc. (though there were these). It was, as she insisted, "total theatre," not to be scene again (in Jamaica) until Serumaga's Uganda

Players brought *Renga Moi* and *Amarykitti* in 1973 and 1974 respectively, which in turn influenced, in certain important respects (rhythm, choreography of voices, symbolization), Carol Dawes' production of Dennis Scott's *Echo in the Bone* (1974) and her adaptation of Soyinka's *Bacchae of Euripides* (1975). What these "plays" all have in common is that they are really *sound poems*,[60] with central and radiating metaphors of poetry extended into movement, gesture, mime, taking us all, as through the tips of fingers, into the audience and from them back to us: cross-rhythm: free flow: reverberation.

A brief description of the first yard production will help to make the point: though the collaborativeness of the effort, the improvisation from work into idea into action, have for the time being to remain submerged.

2

Consciousness I (one/i) is about violence and oppression in the Rodney/Vietnam period and about the survival riddims of the Mothers of the Third World against this. As the witness/participants take their places (chair, box, stone, earth, wall, railing, tree-stump, foot), the cat-cry of police sirens is mimicked and then beaten down by the sound of Pharoah Sanders/Alice Coltrane or Immamu Baraka's Jihad with Sonny Murray. This is amplified through our soul-system {August Town: slave village, free settlement, Bedward's one foundation) is a place of sound-grenades: louder and louder: it might be heavy reggae dub: until it seems the audience or congregation cannot bear it anymore and the only reality: peace out of black: is the stars above the loom: dry water whale: of Long Mountain with its memories of poems. Then sudden silence: star bright star beat: and the first drum beat: Rasta *funde* and repeaters: Pat Lewis and Bongo Jerry's bredren ... .

> Then the flame: naked starlight: but yellow, richer with a hint of smoke, nearer, thicker of the earth, blacker, butterer: the flambeaux: processing of the Mothers faces symbolically scarred with paint: with yellows reds and blues ...

> Then rhythm change: the heart-beat bass drum and the voice of human chant: raw spiralling male, coming out of the chalkpits of the valley, returning thunder to the bloomed and dynamited dry-river gullies: Hope, Papine, Tavern, Hermitage. And the processing of men: for Marina: priest poets: robed *okyeames:* bearing the chained afflicted, sacrificial burden of the Sufferer: dead god: enslaved christos: fragmented tiger of the emerging world. On a tree trunk: crossroad: Ogun's stump of wood, altar of the dead: imprisoned flesh with its leaven of sound: yeast of all song: place him and the lips lids leaves: rustle: begins. ...

3

The Literature of the Yard

Now, with the insight and help of sisters like Maureen Warner Lewis,[61] Dell Lewis, Lucille Mathurin-Mair[62] and Erna Brodber,[63] to select only four, new seeing tools emerge. Speaking at a recent seminar at Mona, Dell Lewis, graduate research scholar into "the literature of the yard," demonstrated an inter-disciplinary instinct which some of us have been demanding/hoping for for years. And not only did she employ the concept of yard, she beautifully, I thought, wedded it to culture-concepts of "missile" whole and "impure" transfers, circle/target, already referred to in this study.

The idea of using the yard as a critical/aesthetic model to help with our consideration of West Indian literature begins, I suppose, with my analyses of Roger Mais' novel, *Brother Man* (1954) in

"Jazz and the West Indian Novel," "Brother Mais" and the unpublished "Houses."[64] But it is Dell Lewis who has articulated the clear, positive, truly native/continental mode:

> We think in terms of the Eskimo *igloos*, the Red Indian tents, the Bedouins, the Indians, the Chinese .... But for the purposes of our study, I find that we have to relate directly to Africa and I have had to work out a sort of system whereby we see the transplant of the African compound to our...situation and what has happened in the process .... Whether the yard has come across whole of [whether] the concept of the yard has been tampered with, and how that relates to present West Indian life ...a nd how the present-day thinkers and critics and writers look at it ... .[65]

Or, as she went on to formulate it,

> ... the minute you have confrontations between people within a boundary, you have a yard.[66]

The recognition that we are at last experiencing an *aesthetic*, rather than the more limited critical mind in action, may be seen in this discussion of Orlando Patterson's *Children of Sisyphus* (1964): Patterson's novel is set in the Kingston slums, the dungle.

> ... I classify that as a yard, [novel] because the people find themselves drawn there together — these are of the Rastafarian faith — but they find themselves there based on a common belief that a ship would come to take them back to Africa. ... So they all kept themselves together to await this day. In this case, the boundary that keeps them together is not man-made, the boundary is not "natural"... it is a *psychological* boundary; it is their beliefs which keep them together as a group to await something; and it also shows [the] element of hope they have ...
>
> Another centre in the same book is the *balm yard*. There is this girl who runs away from the dungle, as she puts it, "trying to find a better life" and she goes up into another area and she becomes part of the balm yard life, in that she becomes a convert — and even more than that, she becomes directly connected to the Shepherd.
>
> In this case, the boundary is a cactus fence. The cactus reminds us of the desert right away — it is symbolic of the aridity and the harshness of desert climates and it is a comment on the type of life the people are experiencing .... But whereas we might believe that the cactus fence is put there to keep *in* the inmates, I really think that it is put there to keep *out* [non-believers]; because there is an element of secrecy and community there and unless you believe, they are not willing to admit you into [the] community, because [of] the [possibility] of ridicule. ...[67]

What the sister is achieving here is a cool reference and use of a wide range of information (human geography, African culture, Caribbean sociology) and applying it accurately and relevantly to our interests and concerns, *from a base which* we all share. Her insights into our novels, have a universal/particularity and an ease of expression, which the Establishment critics often lack, concerned as they are with "literary" rather than human/communal relationships. What I'm getting at is that at last, the daughters of the Revolution are providing us with a way of seeing=thinking/feeling=saying; so that we are beginning to possess a literary criticism not of description (of parts, of features) but of *explanation*.

> What we are really dealing with, you know, is the breakdown of the concept of the circle [result of slavery] transplantation .... Sometimes I relate it to the religious imagery of Christ as the Shepherd. You see, what used to happen is that a circle of stones would be put up; there would be one little space left; and when evening comes, the shepherd would drag the sheep in and then he stands at the door. There is no door on a hinge, as such, just an opening; so the person in charge has to put himself in this space as the door, when night comes, to protect the sheep. I relate the [traditional] African compound to that: in that the head of the household had his hut near to the [entrance] and there was only one entry into the place: no back door. So the transplant to our

present-day situation now, is that for one thing, *the fence is not wholesome* [my italics]. If you think of Mais' *Hills:* it is "a buck-tooth, broken-down, leaning over fence" [paraphrasing from memory] ... and the back of the yard leads down into a gully; and people can just come in at any point in the fence, although there is a gate, "a broken-down, white-washed, gate ..."[68]

4

End - paper

This is as far as we will go for the moment. I have not, in this paper, attempted to give a "history" of West Indian writing, far less of its criticism, and I have clearly singled out certain "names" for certain reasons. The image of the broken-down but open gate, indicates the fragility and initiatory character of my piece. But we must recognize that our literature began on the slave plantation with imitation Euro-writing by Europeans and white Creoles[69] on the one hand, and the often unremembered sound-poems, stories and religious litanies of the slaves, on the other;[70] that after slavery (c. 1838-1938) we entered the slough of colonial despond when very little creative work was produced among the literate and the existent folk culture was attacked/submerged, even by our more fortunate (?) selves. The anti-colonial consciousness of the period from 1900 produced our first authentic novels and witnessed the beginning of native newspaper work and publishing.[71] The period of national consciousness marked by the publication in 1949/50 of V. S. Reid's novel, *New Day*, saw what is now regarded as the "Renaissance" of West Indian writing, with over 100 novels appearing in print between 1950 and 1965. But most of this talent was in exile, and as political independence approached in the early and mid-sixties, we discovered a contradiction between our expatriate artistic selves and the local existential reality. Orlando Patterson's *The Children of Sisyphus* (1964) and *An Absence of Ruins* (1966) were perhaps the most portentous omens of this.[72] The dichotomy took us into post-colonial blues when we seemed, especially after the break-up of the Federation of the West Indies, to be heroless and leaderless. The result, in the late sixties, was the implosion of people and thought I have described.

This implosion (1968-1972) brought us, in a sense, to our senses. Our people's revolutions created/caused some new hard thinking among our intellectuals/radicals who in turn affected the Establishment. The people's explosions also affected our artists, throwing up a whole new "school" of natively conscious poets and singers ("folk art," "self-taught artists," "sufferers' art," etc.), who, for the first time in our history, found it possible to be seen and heard on a more or less *permanent and serious basis* because of the presence of the well organized sub-establishment of people-oriented forces (*Abeng, Tapia,* Yard, Yoruba, etc.) I've placed at the base of this study. These have in turn influenced/infiltrated the Establishment mass media. Finally, in response to the entire Revolution and chiefly, perhaps, out of the need to explain to self and others what was taking place, there emerged the creative critics: Lewis, Wynter, Rohlehr, Maxwell, Best: who are no longer concerned with colonial despair, with our having "nothing", our "exile"; but with a total roots-directed (re-) definition of ourselves: an aesthetic: word, act, vision, value system.

5

The results are still tentative, the divorce between our politics and our art, our people and our preachers, still very painful, the race between achievement and chaos still very much on. But the gate is there, broken but open

> and as the drums, now live, led by a real kumina master, began to mutter in the darkness, the inexplicable transformation of structure began. It was as if, as audience, we were being drawn by a great vortex into the movement of the stage: no longer stage: but lighted pool and island
>
> and as a harsh shiver of voices slowly breathed: agitation of water out of the tide of drums: i want to know-o, i want to know-o: it was as if we had been spoken to from some deep involuntary sounding
>
> and all this while the bodies moving: circles of inexorable progress through song through sound through thunder: torso flung back from pelvis: the feet shuffling freely forward: then flung back towards the music: wave upon wave of dancers: diagonal entrances and exits: clash: warrick stick: weave: clash: warrick stick: divide and interweave: and the entranced singers crying deep from the psyche of our hounforts, riding blindly on the horses of their sound

And it was fitting that all this should have been rejected a few weeks later by some English critic in his box at Sadlers Wells, where the group went — where else — to culminate the tenth year of their founding — colon colon semi/colonie ... Here, so far from Carifesta, their art became "religious frenzy ... evoked by rhythmic drum ... expressed through groups of stamping and gyrating dancers ..."

> o tacky toussaint hannibal ...
>
> it was not in "the" tradition, it was not of "the" tradition, where were the structures here? They had eroded and obscured the boundaries of form: colonial and capital to rahtid
>
> as we in georgetown knew rising to meet them with the sound of rainfall in our ears: applause acknowledging this little victory so very near our tears.[73]

Notes
1. For a discussion of this see my review of *The Chosen Place, the Timeless People* ('Rehabilitations') in *Bim* 51 (July–Dec, 1970): 174–84 or in *Caribbean Studies* (CS) vol. 10, no. 2 (July 1970): 125–34.
2. For the position at the end of the '60s, see my 'West Indian Prose Fiction in the Sixties,' *Black World* (September 1971): 15–29.
3. *Savacou* 9/10 (1974): 40–54.
4. The theme of exile in the West Indian novel is treated in my 'Sir Galahad and the Islands,' *Bim* 25 (July–December 1957): 8–16 and, briefly, in Kenneth Ramchand's *West Indian Narrative* (London, 1966), 224–26.
5. In *A Flag on the Island* (London, 1967).
6. James's history of the revolution in St Dominque was first published in New York in 1938. 'From Toussaint L'Ouverture to Fidel Castro' is included (391–418) in the Vintage Books edition, New York, 1963.
7. Elsa Goveia, (b. Guyana) was a Professor of West Indian History at the University of the West Indies, who began teaching in the late '50s. When she started teaching, she was regarded as one of the finest historians in the region. Her books include *Slave Society in the British Leeward Islands at the End of the Eighteenth Century* (New Haven, 1965), *West Indian Slave Laws of the 18th Century* (Bridgetown: Caribbean Universities Press, 1970), and *A Study on the Historiography of the British West Indies to the End of the Nineteenth Century* (Mexico City: Instituto Panamericano de Geografia e Historia, 1956).
8. University of North Carolina Press, 1944.
9. See Bryan Edwards, *The History, Civil and Commercial, of the British Colonies in the West Indies* (London, 1793), 1801 ed., vol. 2, 433: '... for it has been well and eloquently said, that whenever the liberties of Great Britain be devoted [sic.], it is probable her dissolution will not begin in the centre: [but] *she will feel subjection, like the coldness of death,* creeping upon her from her extremities.' (Italics in text.)
10. Gordon Lewis, *The Growth of the Modern West Indies* (London, 1968), 270.
11. See *Savacou* 2 (September 1970), 19–32.
12. *Impact* was one of the many mimeographed student publications (others were *Rising Star* and *Scope*)

that proliferated during this period. White's article appeared in *Impact* vol. 2, no. 2 (1966) and was reprinted in *Caribbean Quarterly* vol. 13, no. 3 (September 1967).
13. These three poems appear in an important (if small) selection of Jerry's work to be found in *Savacou* 3/4 (1970/71): 12–17.
14. The Rastafari (Rastas), a bearded often 'dreadlocked' group of several thousand now, first appeared in Jamaica in 1930 soon after the coronation. Most scholars agree, 'their designation is a combination of Ras Tafari, son of Ras Makonen of Harar, as Emperor Haile Selassie I, King of Kings and Lord of Lords, Conquering Lion of the tribe of Judah. The group, usually described as 'messianic,' is connected to the Garvey Movement which preceded it in that it reveres Garvey as the prophet who announced that a new age would begin when a king should arise out of Africa. The Rastas recognized Selassie as this king and nominated him divine, the returned Messiah, the black living Christ and declared it their intention and destiny to be reunited with the Father in Ethiopia. As a result of this unorthodox – indeed heretical – conviction, the Rastas were ostracized by the more conventional mass of the population (see Roger Mais' novel, *Brother Man*, for instance); though at the same time, and much more dramatically, they cut themselves off from conventional society (which they designated 'Babylon'), even unto refusing employment or fraternization. Rasta in fact became a state within the state, although there was never one Rasta body but separate camps and settlements, some passive, some militant, some more political than others, etc., but all united in the worship of the Emperor, the rejection of Babylon, the determination to return to 'Ityopia,' the life of poverty, a Coptic form of service with the increasing use of drums and 'African' chants, the smoking of the 'weed' (ganja) and the concept of the sacred head and hair. It was not long before there were open clashes between Rasta and the public, between Rasta and the police, and things reached a virtual state of emergency in 1959 when a group of Rastas was accused of conspiring to mount a military operation (with outside help) to capture Jamaica as a prelude to returning to Africa. It was in this explosive atmosphere that the then Vice-Chancellor of the UWI, Sir Arthur Lewis, proposed to the Jamaica government that a team of West Indian scholars should study and report on the Movement, since it was felt in some liberal/academic quarters that the Rastafari were as much sinned against as sinning. *The Report on the Rastafari Movement in Kingston, Jamaica,* by the sociologist M.G. Smith, historian Roy Augier, and the artist and Extra-Mural tutor, Rex Nettleford, appeared in 1960 – a date which marks, in the view of many, a revision of public attitude to Rastafari and a consequent 'toning down' of Rastafari aggression toward Babylon. But Rasta has remained a positive and intransigent force, constantly growing and adapting until now, in the '70s, its influence is being felt in the arts (especially painting, people's music, drumming) but above all in the life-style of the youth not only in Jamaica but increasingly throughout the Caribbean and into the more northern areas (New York and London) of the Caribbean diaspora. Rasta hair, Rasta language and speaking-style is very much in vogue, and the Rasta value system (worship, meditation, poverty, moral rectitude, purity of body, mind and spirit, righteousness and above all a positive African and an equally positive anti-European, anti-colonial, anti-imperial, anti-mercantilist attitude and philosophy) has started most definitely to influence West Indian artists and intellectuals in their search for nativism and self-identity.
15. Trevor Munroe, 'Black Power as a Political Strategy in Jamaica,' *Bongo-Man* (June, 1969): 7–8.
16. Okot p'Bitek, *Song of Lawino* (Nairobi: East African Publishing Company, 1966), 59.
17. *Scope*, December, 1968, 8.
18. Man (the singular} in Rasta parlance, refers to the elect, the favoured, Men (the plural) to Babylon. In the poem 'Mabrak,' Bongo Jerry writes:
Save the YOUNG
from the language that MEN teach
the doctrine Pope preach
skin bleach.
HOW ELSE...MAN must use MEN language to carry dis message
(*Savacou* 3/4, 15)
*Men*agement therefore, is a term of the above for *man*agement. In fact, all references to the sacred Rasta self are in the singular and are expressed as 'I'. No other personal pronoun is used. A Rasta would not say 'Come to me' but 'Come to I' and instead of 'we', he uses 'I an I'.
19. When the news of Rodney's exclusion from Jamaica broke and the protesting students had run into police tear-gas and batons and Government and media spokesmen had started blaming the University for the consequent rioting of down-town sufferers, etc., and threatened to take us over or close us down, etc, the Vice Chancellor came out strongly for the independence of the University,

the right of the student/academic to protest, etc. But within hours of the Prime Minister's statement to Parliament on the 'evidence' of Rodney's subversive activities, the UWI Administration shut up and at a meeting of the entire University body, advised all of us to desist from further protest and return to normalcy. The University has not been the same since. For perhaps the best account of this crisis and its consequences, see Norman Girvan, 'After Rodney – The Politics of Student Protest in Jamaica,' *New World Quarterly* (NWQ) vol. 4, no. 3 (1968): 59–68.
20. Sister Icille, as now known, (is and has married a Rasta and teaches, with her husband, the large school of Rasta children who live on Mona Common. Her Caribbean Studies project for the UWI (1974) describes this. She was also one of the leading actors in the 'consciousness-making' production of *The Blacks* referred earlier. Born in Barbados, Icille contributes to our arts/ideas started with Elton Mottley's Black Night (now Yoruba House) group there. She also played an important part in Marina Maxwell's *Consciousness-I* (1969).
21. *Scope*, no. 3 (March 1970): 3.
22. See Lucille Mathurin-Mair, 'The Student and the University's Civilising Role,' *Caribbean Quarterly* (CQ), vol. 15. nos. 2 & 3 (June–September 1969): 9.
23. Professor A.K. Croston, 'The Concept of a University,' *Pelican Annual*, 1955, 22–23.
24. Ibid.
25. Mathurin-Mair, 14.
26. Ras Dizzy, *Scope*, no. 3 (March, 1970): 9.
27. Sylvia Wynter, 'New Standards or High Standards . . .,' *Sunday Gleaner*, 15 March 1970.
28. *Sunday Gleaner*, 8 March 1970.
29. Ibid., *my* italics.
30.
>   This I have learnt:
>   to-day a speck
>   to-morrow a hero
>   hero or monster
>   you are consumed!
>
>   Like a jig
>   shakes the loom,
>   Like a web
>   is spun the pattern
>   all are involved!
>   all are consumed!

Martin Carter, 'You are Involved,' *Poems of* Resistance (London: Lawrence and Wishart, 1954), 18; *Poems of* Resistance (Georgetown: University of Guyana, 1964), 18.
31. Gordon Rohlehr, 'West Indian Poetry: Some Problems of Assessment,' *Tapia*, 29 August 1971; reprinted *in Bim* 55 (1972): 144.
32. Sylvia Wynter, 'A question of Standards. . .,' *Sunday Gleaner*, 29 May 1970.
33. Or Sylvia Wynter Carew, as wife of the Guyanese novelist, Jan Carew. In this study, I use her maiden name since this is the one she usually uses as a writer.
34. BBC, *Caribbean Voices*, 8 June 1958.
35. Sylvia Wynter in a BBC discussion on West Indian writing with other London-based West Indian writers, 24 May 1956. My transcription from tape.
36. *Jamaica Journal* (JJ) (December 1967): 23–34.
37. *JJ* (September 1969): 3–12; (December 1969): 17–26; (March 1970): 11–19; (September 1970): 6–15.
38. *JJ* (December 1969): 22–32; (March 1969): 26–42. The *Jamaica Journal,* started in 1967, has not only, until recently, been responsible for the publication of much of Miss Wynter's work, it has, with its illustrations, photographs and art work imaginatively set out, been one of the most important expressors of Jamaican culture since political independence.
39. Before this was Lamming's 'A Way of Seeing,' 56–85 of *The Pleasures of Exile* (1960) and Wilson Harris, *Tradition and the West Indian Novel*, a lecture to the West Indian Students Centre, London, in 1964, and published by the Centre in 1965 with an Introduction by C.L.R. James. It is included in *Tradition the Writer and Society* (London & Port of Spain: New Beacon Publications, 1967), a collection of Harris's critical essays. There is also of course James's own *Mariners, Renegades and Castaways: The Story of Herman Melville and the World We Live In* (New York, 1953).
40. Brown's piece, 'The Novelist in an Unsettled Culture,' appeared in *Impact* (1968), Carr's in CQ 13:1 (1967). *The Islands in Between* was published by the Oxford University Press, London, 1968.

41. Wynter, 'Reflections,' *JJ* (December 1968): 25–26.
42. Ibid., 26.
43. Ibid., 32.
44. *JJ* (June 1970): 34–48.
45. The most positive and thought-provoking contribution to this debate came from George Beckford at a seminar on the dance-part of a series on the creative arts held at Mona in 1965. A transcript of Beckford's intervention appears as 'Reflections on the National Dance Theatre Company' in the NDTC's *Newsletter* for 1965 and is included as one of the appendices in my originally full-length treatment of this paper. The contribution of other social scientists (Girvan, Bobby Hill, Trevor Munroe) to the cultural discussion of the period is also referred to in the original.
46. See Marina Maxwell, 'Towards a Revolution in the Arts,' *Savacou* 2 (1970): 21, 28–30; and Errol Hill, *The Trinidad Carnival: Mandate for a National Theatre*, University of Texas Press, 1972.
47. Ivar Oxaal, who has already given us studies of James and Williams, *Black Intellectuals Come to Power* (1968), and one of the February Revolution in Trinidad, *Race and Revolutionary Consciousness: A Documentary Interpretation of the 1970 Black Power in Trinidad* (1971), has recently published a study of Best.
48. The Caribbean Artists Movement (CAM), founded in London in 1965 by Andrew Salkey, John La Rose and myself, with Aubrey Williams and Orlando Patterson in on the original planning committee, was a kind of writers and artists co-operative. The idea was the West Indian writers/artists in the metropole (the 'exiles') should get to know each other (the isolation was quite remarkable at the time), get to know each other's work and talk about it informally among ourselves ('small group sessions'), and through lecture-discussions-readings, exhibitions, touch our West Indian and wider audience, which came to include host-country critics, editors and publishers. Annual conferences were held – in addition, that is, to our monthly public meetings – and there was a mimeographed *Newsletter* (1966–68). The Movement has now more or less been absorbed into other interests in London and has not really prospered in the West Indies, though Yard (Mona) and Kairi (Port of Spain) were active spin-offs by CAM members. *Savacou*, however, started 1970, remains the journal of the Movement. See Edward Brathwaite. *CQ*, 14: 1 & 2 (1968): 57–59; Anne Walmsley, *Bim* 46 (1968): 80–83 and *Bim* 48 (1969): 233–36.
49. Gordon Rohlehr, 'Jamaica Blues,' *Cipriani Labour College News*, June 1970, 38.
50. Rohlehr, 'Sans Humanite,' *Moko*, 25 April 1969, 4.
51. Ibid., 3.
52. Rohlehr deals with this in 'Jamaica Blues,' loc. cit.; 'Islands,' *CQ*, 16:4 (Dec, 1970): 29–35; another review of *Islands* (1969), in *Caribbean Studies* 10:4 (June, 1971): 173–202, which he had wanted called 'Blues and Rebellion'; 'West Indian Poetry; Some Problems of Assessment,' loc. cit., which is the classic discussion of the subject; and a review of the first Jamaican feature film, *The Harder They Come*, in *Tapia*, 17 June 1973.
53. See Orlando Patterson, 'The Ritual of Cricket,' *JJ* (March 1969): 22–25.
54. Rohlehr, 'Sans Humanite,' *Moko*, 9 May 1969.
55. See for instance 'White Fridays in Trinidad,' *Savacou* 3/4 (1970/72): 18–24; *Tapia*, 3 September, 17 September, and 8 October 1972.
56. See 'Forty Years of Calypso' based upon the texts of 25 half-hour broadcasts he gave on the subject during 1972.
57. There is as yet no cultural history of our lives, but most of the forces/influences mentioned in the text have been noticed in our underground presses and sometimes in the liberal establishment ones like the Caribbean Council of Churches' *Contact*. In my fuller treatment of this subject, which I hope will one day appear as a book, I included sections on the Association of Commonwealth Literary and Language Societies' (ACLALS) Conference at Mona (1971) with its confrontation: academics and gorillas, and I gave my view of the debate, again between academics and gorillas, that arose out of the publication of the 'too black' anthology of new writing in the Caribbean (*Savacou* 3/4: 1970/71) which I edited. Eight articles in the Barbados *Advocate-News* (16 October –3 December 1972) contain my reaction to Carifesta '72, which I regard as one of the most important events to have happened in the Caribbean since Emancipation.
58. A play (*Black Destiny*) written and mounted by Frank Hasfal, one of the authors of *One Love* (1971), a Rasta/sufferer collection of poetry and prose which, like its publishers, Bogle L'Ouverture, also came out of the Rodney crisis. According to Marina, the play attempted to 'synthesise Rasta belief and the puberty rites of the Ashanti in symbolic statement' (*In Work-Yard*, unpub., 1974).
59. This was to have been Marina's most ambitious production (this time for Lloyd Reckford's National Theatre Trust). In addition to her usual focus of poets-actors-dancers, a group of Zambian artists, and

the musical/culture group, the Light of Saba, under Cadric 'Im' Brooks, himself one of the founders of The Mystic Revelation of Rastafari, and students and staff from the Jamaica School of Art among the large and very varied/talented cast. (One of the principles of Yard is/was the bringing together of 'schooled' and 'unschooled' artists: the elite and mass.) Unfortunately, the proprietor of the Garden Theatre suddenly felt, a few hours to opening, that he couldn't really take all those sufferers and drums, and closed the premises, according to report, on a technicality.

60. See 'The African Presence in Caribbean Literature,' *Daedalus* (Spring 1974): 73–109.
61. Maureen Warner Lewis is the founder of Omo Ajini, a group which presents African (mainly Yoruba) songs and dances found in the West Indies (mainly Trinidad and Tobago, Ms Lewis's chief area of study) and author of an important interview/study of Mrs Kennedy, a *kumina* queen in West Kingston. She has been on a year's study leave (1974–75) to Ife, continuing work on her study of the socio-linguistic connections between Trinidad and Nigerian Yoruba. She is now wife of Rupert Lewis of *Abeng/Bongo-Man*.
62. Lucille Mathurin-Mair has recently presented an important PhD dissertation, *A Historical Study of Women in Jamaica from 1655 to 1844*, Mona, 1974 from which has already come *The Rebel Woman in the British West Indies During the Period of Slavery* (Kingston: Institute of Jamaica, 1975).
63. Erna Brodber will, in my view, emerge as one of the most important conceptual thinkers of the 1970s. She is a social psychologist in the Department of Sociology, UWI, and has already published a seminal article, 'Social Psychology in the English-Speaking Caribbean – a Bibliography and Some Comments,' *Social and Economic Studies*, vol. 23, no. 3 (September 1974): 398–417, in which she illustrates certain crucial and necessary differences in methodological approach between metropolitan authorities on social thought, and the Caribbean efforts. It is an important contribution to the definition of our aesthetic. Her study of yards in Kingston will carry us a stage further, but what to me is most exciting is her major project, the tape recording of the experience throughout Jamaica, of citizens over the age of 70.
64. 'Jazz and the West Indian Novel,' *Bim* 44 (January–June 1967): 275–84; *Bim* 45 (July–December 1967): 39–51; *Bim* 46 (January–June 1968): 115–26. The section on Mais is in *Bim* 46. 'Brother Mais' appears definitively in *Tapia* (27 October 1974): 6–8, with an earlier version as Introduction to the Heinemann Educational Books reprint of *Brother Man* (1974).
65. Transcript from tape of 'History, Society and Ideas Seminar,' UWI, Mona, April, 1975. Dell was speaking, without notes, informally, so please don't expect the precision/formality of the prepared statement.
66. Ibid.
67. Ibid.
68. Ibid.
69. There was an exception – who else – a free black of Spanish Town, Jamaica, named Francis Williams (b. 1700) who wrote Ovidian odes – in Latin – and who, it is said, was sent to Cambridge University to study Classics and mathematics as an 'experiment,' though my own research has so far unearthed no record of Williams at the English seat of learning. One of his odes, however, was preserved for posterity by Edward Long, the planter historian, who on pages 475–85 of Vol. 2 of his *History of Jamaica* (1774) tried to hold Francis and his works up to ridicule. But Locksley Lindo (*Savacou* 1 [1970]: 75–80) argues that not only was Williams' Latin much better than Long allowed (or knew) but that even in the density of the mimicked-form, the free Negro in the slave world was able to make his stand.
70. Anglophone West Indian (written) literature during the period of slavery has been discussed by O.R. Dathorne in *Caribbean Narrative* (London, 1966), 3–4, *Caribbean Verse* (London, 1967), 2–3; Arthur Drayton in 'West Indian Consciousness in West Indian Verse: A Historical Perspective,' *Journal of Commonwealth Literature*, No. 9, (July 1970): 66–82 and 87, and in my 'Creative Literature During the Period of Slavery,' *Savacou* (1970): 46–73. The recognition of our literature as inclusive of the oral tradition of the slaves and our descendents occurs in 'The African Presence in Caribbean Literature,' cited in note 60.
71. Some aspects of this early nationalist period are treated in Kenneth Ramchand, *The West Indian Novel and Its Background* (London, 1970).
72. For my account of this developing dichotomy, see 'Sir Galahad and the Islands' (1957) cited in note 4; 'Roots,' *Bim* 37 (1963); 'West Indian Prose Fiction in the Sixties,' *Black World* (September 1971).
73. A variation of my description of the NDTC's kumina performance at Carifesta '72, which first appeared in the Barbados *Advocate-News*, 19 November 1972.

Articulating a Caribbean Aesthetic: The Revolution of Self-Perception

Gordon Rohlehr

During the period of slavery in the Caribbean, the "selves" of master and slaves, white and black, were prescribed by the rigidities of slavery and the plantation system. These were really imposed selves, hardened by the fact that the system endured for over three centuries and was thorough in its methods, most of which were directed towards the restriction of human potential and the reduction of people to tools, objects.

The limits within which Caribbean people lived were visible in every area of life; in the economics of primitive capitalism, which shackled the fragile island economies to that of the metropole; in the class stratification which resulted from the economic system, and was reinforced by the factor of race; by the various slave codes or laws, which anticipated the psychology of the modern concentration camp by several centuries. But the limits within which Caribbean people lived were most clearly visible in the need which the dominant race, class and civilization felt, to create and perpetuate stereotypes, systems of coercion (laws), and propaganda which reinforced stereotypes (education), both during and after slavery.

There is no doubt that much was destroyed, much lost or obliterated. Many minds were shattered, most accepted and adapted to the limits which had been placed on human potential. Hence we have the role-playing Black, the jive-ass Black, the Uncle Tom stereotype, and the dozens of other well-known stereotypes which have existed since slavery and have gone through several cycles of permutation since Emancipation. Du Bois in several of his works, Ellison in *Invisible Man*, Edward Brathwaite in *Rights of Passage*, have all dealt with the phenomenon of the enduring stereotype. Frantz Fanon has given it psycho-philosophical definition in his now seminal testament *Black Skin White Masks*.

The "revolution of self-perception" really began with the inner resistance of the slaves to the self imposed on them by the plantation system and slavery. In its most fundamental form it was the refusal to be a thing, an object, a tool, mere chattel: the *negation of a process of reification*.

The positive aspect of this revolution involved *the constant affirmation of the validity of the submerged self* the self – to borrow Edward Kamau Brathwaite's phrase – in maroonage; the marooned, submerged and often subversive self. This *self-in-maroonage* was affirmed in infinite ways:

a. Rebellion and constant resistance on the plantation (suicide, malingering, rioting, the Haitian Revolution, Cannes Brulées, etc)

b. The preservation of religions with an African base, or the adaptation of these under pressure of the plantation system/structure during slavery. After Emancipation several religions existed in face of constant harassment from the Law and pressure from the Established Churches. The anthropological work on Afro-Caribbean religions is beginning to constitute an important body of literature. Off-hand, I can list a number of concerns which have emerged from the study of these religions.

1. The continuity of West African heritages in the Caribbean. Factors instrumental in such continuity have been the isolation of some communities; the inadequacy of the education system; the fact that during the post-emancipation period communities of "liberated Africans" who had never been enslaved, were settled in various islands (Trinidad, e.g.)

2. The notion of a continuum stretching between religions with the greatest "African" content and those with the greatest "European" content. Donald Hogg in *Jamaica Religions: A Study in Variations* advances this thesis for Jamaica. Continuum theory allows for overlapping, syncretism, conflict and consensus, and leads to a notion of religion as lived process within the framework of a total society, rather than as static, fixed structures.

3. The syncretic blending of West African and European proletarian heritages, in religions such as Zion Revival, Pukkumina, Rastafarianism in Jamaica, the Spiritual Baptists or Shouters in Trinidad. Vodun in Haiti reveals another dimension of syncretism, including a post-Medieval Catholicism and a Dahomean cosmology in a single seamless theological system.

4. The relationship between religion and social institutions, such as communities and political parties. The cult/sect and charismatic or authoritarian political leadership. The cult/sect as an exploitable reservoir of popular lumpen -proletarian faith and emotion.

These are some of the concerns which have emerged from the study of Afro-Caribbean religions. That these religions are capable of leading scholars to such fundamental questions is the surest testimony of their vital and vibrant existence as the ground of being for large numbers of Caribbean people. It is also the clearest evidence of the survival of the *self-in-maroonage* after so many years of hostile laws, education, economic suppression and the cultural contempt of the white, brown and black servitors of the establishment.

c. The survival of folktales, proverbs, rhetoric, patterns of performance, and the capacity to create style, are further evidence of the continued existence of the self-in-maroonage. If the original folktale has almost disappeared, the capacity for storytelling has not. Hence the storytelling tradition is maintained in The Calypso, Paul Keens-Douglas, Abdul Malik, Brathwaite's *The Arrivants,* and a growing corpus of short stories and anecdotes, which exactly parallels what has been taking place in the Afro-American tradition.

If the original propensity for proverbs and aphorisms has been modified, a tradition of moralizing still exists, and is evident in the weighty didactic element in some reggae and a few calypsoes; the desire to instruct through art.

The revolution of self-perception, then, is process, is ongoing *self-affirmation* which, in the face of the unchanging rigidity of oppression generally means self-assertion. In asking what that revolution means today we are in fact attempting to assess the quality of our self-affirmation in all the areas of our conscious living. These include:

a. Politics and the on-going class struggle.

b. Literature and that constant, complex exploration of the no-longer-submerged inner self; the no-longer-marooned personality.

c. Music – Blues, Jazz, Gospel, Calypso, Funk, Reggae – and the life-styles, both sacred and secular, which sustain the music. Hence we shall have to ask ourselves what is the meaning of our capacity for celebration, dance, carnival on the one hand, and the trauma, agony and constant struggle which celebration masks. For our music, whether created by 'Trane, Sanders, 'Tosh, Marley, Chalkdust, Black Stalin or Bird, is connected with the phenomenon of survival. Sometimes as with 'Trane, it seeks to energize and humanize a city of stone and steel. Sometimes as with Chalkdust, Valentino, Marley and 'Tosh it cries out against, attacks and erodes a stone-deaf politics which, like the old plantation system it has succeeded, still regards people as things, objects, tools.

The body of my paper will be an outline of some of the trends in West Indian literature in English, which together constitute part of the on-going revolution of self-perception. For purposes of convenience I have arbitrarily divided my time-period into three interlocking phases: 1920–1950, 1950–1960 and 1960 to the present.

1920–1950

The twenties was the period of Garvey, Claude McKay and the Harlem Renaissance, to whose political and literary aspects both of these outstanding Jamaicans contributed. The thirties saw C.L.R. James's *Minty Alley*, his play *Toussaint L'Ouverture* (1936). The novels of Portuguese author Alfred Mendes *(Pitch Lake, Black Fauns)* and the short stories of Seepersad Naipaul *Gurudeva and Other Tales* indicated the multi-ethnic nature of the Trinidad experience. The forties were a period of steady growth in which regional periodicals such as Frank Collymore's *Bim* and A.J. Seymour's *Kyk-Over-Al* emerged. Louise Bennett, whose creative acceptance and dramatization of the language of the Jamaican people was in itself a revolution, had begun to write her poems in the late thirties, and had by 1950 become an artist whose work was known throughout the archipelago and in Panama. One of her contributions to West Indian letters was to establish the fact that the little people had not only a voice, but a way of seeing, placing and reducing the world of their social superiors.[1]

The Calypso emerged during this period from the traditional structures of *kalinda* and *sans humanité picong*[2] to a flexible medium capable of accommodating narrative, social and political protest, scatological humour, and celebration. An entire and virtually unexplored body of oral literature exists in the Calypso. It is a literature which has intimately reflected social change, and can provide the scholar with a documentary of the changing attitudes of grassroots Trinidad.

The literature of this period was being accompanied by serious inquiry into the roots and heritage of the people of the African diaspora. There had already been the substantial work of Edward Wilmot Blyden. In America this work was to be built upon and augmented by W.E.B. DuBois. The impulse to understand, explore and vindicate an African heritage was politicized by Garvey, whose *Philosophy and Opinions* (1923) is one of the few Afro-Caribbean publications which have survived the rigid censorship of that period.

Equally remarkable was Norman Cameron's *The Evolution of the Negro*[3] (1929). Cameron was a Guyanese student of mathematics at Cambridge, whose vocation to teach in Liberia impelled him to find out all he could about that country. This awakened in him an appetite to know more about Africa itself, particularly in the pre-European period: he read all the collected works of all the early travellers. He augmented these with French translations of Arab and Moorish documents. He developed a keen interest in African art and sculpture which led him to those museums in England which house artifacts stolen from Africa during the scramble. Thirty years before Basil Davidson's now famous *Old Africa Rediscovered* Cameron had already posited the link between Egypt, the Western Sudan and Africa south of the equator. He had already refuted the then current notions that excellence in African sculpture in bronze, iron and gold was the result of European influence.

He was interested in other things besides. In Chapter 11 on the Mali Empire he showed an interest in oral traditions such as the drum and elephant horn orchestras; the praise songs and use of poetry for the recording of oral history. He felt that our poets and playwrights ought to be interested in such things and wrote poetry and didactic plays himself, in some of which he consciously sought to include an "African" presence and ethos. Forty years later in Edward Brathwaite's *Masks* (1968), there at last emerged a Caribbean poet who could give impressive shape to identifiably West African oral traditions: the drum, atumpan, mmenson, the idea of masks, as well as the history, old ceremonies, dances and aspects of Akan cosmology.

Cameron, in his introduction, anticipated the criticism that there was nothing worth studying in African history. He also anticipated the now current accusation that to be seriously concerned with the African past is to be atavistic or nostalgic. *The Evolution of the Negro* was based on the idea that the past should explored as part of one's duty to oneself. One doesn't free oneself from the trauma of history by forgetting the past. One needed, instead, to accept past struggle as the basis for a self-confidence necessary for facing the present and creating a future. Thus, besides the descriptions of the pre-European kingdoms of Africa, Cameron dealt with the effects of contact with Europeans, slave life on the plantations and the Abolition of Slavery and emergence of the Afro-Caribbean person.

If his reading suggested the destructive nature of slavery, his vision was directed towards what was or would become possible if Afro-Guyanese people were to discover their roots. Thus *The Evolution of the Negro* sought to define these roots. Cameron spent some time describing the layout of villages as well as social institutions, laws, aspects of local government in Africa. He was interested in things such as cloth designs and hair styles, things which did not reenter popular black consciousness until the 1960's.

Cameron's book, which went into two volumes (1929 & 1934), was about History as continuity, and the historian as healer, bridger of hiatuses in our knowledge and consciousness. But the conscious or unconscious aim of education in the English-speaking Caribbean was to divorce the Caribbean person from issues and concerns of central relevance to his knowledge of self and milieu. Thus Cameron's profound and scholarly work, self-published and distributed, reached only a few people, went out of print to resurface in 1970 when it was reprinted in America. Unlike many other such reprints, it hasn't appeared on the shelves of Caribbean bookstores. Garvey's vision, too, remained in the borders of our consciousness and was for years beyond the reach of our curricula.

This is essentially what we are up against, then, a *tradition of discontinuity* by which our most crucial perceptions and discoveries are relegated to the margins of consciousness. *The Black Jacobins* (1938) C.L.R. James' great study of the Haitian revolution, took twenty-two years to be republished (1962). George Padmore is still a name. Sylvester Williams remote, despite Owen Mathurin's fairly recent publication. Robert Love is virtually unknown. F.E.M. Hercules has scarcely been heard about. This is probably why an era which produced work such as Garvey's, Cameron's and the early work of Eric Williams, should have produced artists who were generally little more than excellent observers of the surface of actions and recorders of manners.

The creative sensibility of the period was largely divorced from the creative thought of the period. One of the obvious reasons for this was the fact that Caribbean people were not in control of their political destinies, or of their economies. This point had been made over and over again in the polemics of the 1930's and 1940's. It resurfaced in the various discussions about the possibility of a West Indian Federation. One of the most interesting blueprints for a federation was A.P. Maloney's *After England We* (1949) which examined the potential and the limitations of the region as a whole, and envisioned a multi-lingual federation, and the emergence of a "cosmic race". Maloney was one of a family of distinguished Trinidad scholars, resident in the United States.

1950–1960

The period of 1950–1960 saw the evolution of a substantial body of literature. Mais, Lamming, Selvon, Salkey, Carew, Hearne, Mittelholzer, Harris, Reid, Carter, Walcott, V.S Naipaul, Keane, Roach and Brathwaite all emerged in this decade. Dennis Williams and Edward Brathwaite lived in Africa during this period, as had Peter Blackman (*My Song Is For All Men*). Reid, without having actually lived there had written in *The Leopard* an imaginatively impressive novel, set in Kenya. The theme of African continuity or conversely of divorce from Africa appeared in the poetry of Roach and Walcott, while Brathwaite was writing plays for Akan school children, and had by 1962 already given shape to the first half of *Masks*. Dennis Williams *Other Leopards* (1963) explored the split sensibility of the Caribbean *omowale* and left his schizophrenic hero in a desert, almost stripped of his old self, and savouring possibilities of growth in an inscrutable future.

The writers of this decade had a better opportunity to draw on a body of emerging thought and scholarship than had those of the generation before. In anthropology alone, for example, there was the work Melville and Frances Herskovits, George Eaton Simpson, M.G. Smith, Raymond Smith, Andrew Pearse and Daniel Crowley. Afro-Caribbean folklore, religions, folkways, folktales, rhetoric and patterns of performance suddenly became "visible", and we find Edward Brathwaite in an early essay; "Sir Galahad and The Islands" (BIM, 1957) suggesting that in these discoveries lay the basis for a new and alternative aesthetic.[4] We also find him writing reviews of West Indian literature while in Ghana, suggesting, as Cameron had done earlier, that a knowledge of African oral traditions would help Afro-Caribbean writers in defining and using their own still vibrant oral traditions.[5] He was in addition, a contributor to radio programmes in Ghana, and as an education officer, part of the new thrust towards the indigenization of education there, in that early post-Independence period.

In history, the impact of Eric Williams's *Capitalism and Slavery* began to be felt on the Mona Campus of the University of the West Indies. Elsa Goveia's *A Study on the Historiography of the British West Indies* provided those who were interested with a means of locating most of the current notions about the history and potential of Caribbean peoples in their historical context. George Lamming read and was deeply influenced by the ideas of C.L.R. James.

Horizons widened during this decade. Lamming's "The Negro Writer and His World", (1956)[6] for example, moved far beyond the normal stereotyped discussion, to suggest the complex situation of the Black as diasporan, as twentieth century man, and as one who had to refashion both for himself and the benefit of the Other, that image which the Other had imposed on him, The artist is seen as rebel, as adamic refashioner of word and world, as lonely descender into private hell, and as illuminator of social and political reality. Lamming, who had read Richard Wright's *Black Boy* years before, was aware of himself as one of an international group of New World writers who were involved in a process of transforming the historic stereotypes which had been imposed on Black people, by speaking from within the self-in-maroonage. Significantly, "The Negro Writer and his

World", was a conference paper read at the First International Conference of Negro Writers, held in Paris in 1956. James Baldwin also attended that conference, and provides a perceptive account of that crucial period in one of his essays.

1960 to Present

Janheinz Jahn in *Muntu* (1958) had helped lift Afro-Caribbean literature out of its solitude and to locate it – often erroneously – in a wide Pan-Africanist context which had existed before in the dreams of a handful of scholars. His main concern was the literature of the Francophone Caribbean. Gabriel Coulthard's *Race and Colour in Caribbean Literature* (1962) began for the Anglophone Caribbean the crucial business of comparative Caribbean literature. As we have seen, this was taking place while the writers themselves were, through exile, in the process of widening their horizons and deepening dimensions.

The Pan-African context, however, was but one of the possible contexts within which the literature of the diaspora could be placed. V.S. Naipaul was an outsider to such a context. His position of outsider/insider enabled him to mock it, caricature it, critically analyze it. Never for one moment could he be fully part of it, however much of it was part of him. For "seepage" from the world of Creoledom was viewed by him as violation and chaos.[7] Naipaul, after a decade of wrestling with the problems confronting the *Asiatic* presence in a post-colonial society where the Afro-Creole presence was only just beginning to be defined and accepted as such, wrote *The Mimic Men*. In this novel he posits that the violations of history have impaired both the public and the private selves; both what I have termed *the imposed self and the self-in-maroonage*. Because of this each ethnic group is seen as festering in its separate cell; while the public forum of school, parliament or business provides them with no real possibility, no common ground for dialogue. "Mimicry" in that novel is more than simple copying of other people's stuff. It is the result of the attenuation and destruction of will through historical process, the loss of the capacity for choice and the possibility of self-hood and because of these things, the openness of the psyche's shell to every chance, opinion, fashion and style, and the replacement of willed choice by role-playing.

Derek Walcott could not be satisfactorily placed in a Pan-African context either. His stance, which he eventually defined as "mulatto"[8] was one of Janus-faced ambivalence which could at one and the same time theoretically reject and accept both Africa and Europe in the Caribbean. Lamming, indeed, notes ambivalence as one of the major aspects of the Caribbean sensibility, particularly when it faces the dilemma of affirming an 'African' presence.[9] Walcott's seminal work seems always to grow out of this ambivalence. He has called it "making creative use of schizophrenia." In practice, this has meant the display of considerable strength in the affirmation of a European presence in the Caribbean sensibility and a considerable bitterness in confronting the resurgence of an African one.[10]

Just as Naipaul is able to deny the validity of the inner self-in-maroonage, Walcott is, in "The Muse of History" able to reject all the manifestations of this inner self – the drums, music style, rhetoric, religion, symbolism, etc. – as the basis for a new aesthetic. The difference between the outsider/insider position of the "Asiatic" and the "schizophrenic" position of the "mulatto" is that the latter is generally forced to affirm whatever he denies. Hence Walcott accepts the drums, music, style rhetoric, folklore, dance and so forth as a viable basis for the construction of a New World drama, and has recently included in his poetry some of the very elements for which he has roundly abused a host of unnamed other Caribbean poets.

Wilson Harris could not be fitted into a Pan-African context. He started with the notion of the Caribbean and New World sensibility as "the latent ground of old and new personalities" – a meeting place of the crumbling old world and the unborn new one. In the unnamed, untamed, osmotic heartland of this New World – aptly symbolized by the virgin forests, black inland rivers, and extensive savannahs of Guyana – all primal cosmologies, mythologies, dreams of civilization and conquest meet, intersect, echo or parallel each other, creating tension conflict, and at the same time infinite possibility. Yet the vessels within which these cosmologies meet are an odd collection of rum guzzlers, murderers, delirious pork-nockers, money-lenders, whores, cattle-ranchers, rustlers, land-surveyors, and psychotics from the coast of "domesticity and lights," who find themselves like white America's newest Thoreau, Jim Jones, in the Guyana forest of the night. There, all these people find nothing but themselves; the self stripped of its social, ethnic or economic prop; and the result of such encounter is disintegration and the possibility of transformation through lived ordeal.

Harris's preoccupation with inner quest and cosmic issues had its base in a very particular sense and knowledge of the Guyanese political scenario. There, more than anywhere else in the English-speaking Caribbean, was the visible evidence of that plural, schismatic society, which the sociologists were trying to define in the sixties.[11] There is no doubt that the break-up of the PPP and with it the African and East Indian coalition in Guyana (1954–57) is partially responsible for the themes of Harris's first four novels *Palace of the Peacock, The Far Journey of Oudin, The Whole Armour* and *The Secret Ladder* (1961–65). In these novels – the first two in particular – history is ordeal, a legacy of bitterness and guilt. It has maimed the psyches of both colonizer and colonized, and established brutal authoritarian and materialist patterns, not only in Euro/Afro-Creole society but also within the world of the indentured East Indian peasantry and their descendants. The ghost of this legacy of guilt, materialism, brutality and psychic crippledom cannot be laid by amnesia or evasion, but by confrontation and atonement, and since the crippledom exists within the psyche and has been maintained by ex-colonial peoples long after the physical withdrawal of the colonizers, then confrontation and atonement have to occur within the psyche.

Where Naipaul's people remain paralyzed before their crippledom, and Walcott, faced with the maimed remains of history at one point advocates amnesia, Harris like the Hindus or the Buddhists, involves the psyche in terrible and agonizing Kharmic processes, in which the intolerable burden of history has to be borne and worn because it is our own burden. Time has to be imaginatively re-entered and relived until one becomes worthy of reprieve or movement beyond. The price of becoming a person in the sense that Harris understands personhood requires a *movement through history* then *movement beyond history*; a gradual peeling off of the old personality, a divestment of the props of colour, status, race, power and authority. Walcott eventually adopts a similar position in his play *Dream on Monkey Mountain* which owes much conceptually to Harris.

By the mid-sixties, then, the Pan-African paradigm had proven inadequate in the face of the multi-faceted complexity of the total Caribbean experience. It was qualified by the notion of an ethnically plural and culturally diverse archipelago; by the idea of a mulatto heritage in which European and African elements are blended; and by the notion of an emerging indigenized Caribbean tradition which was flexible, complex and had grown, or was growing out of the confrontation, competition, intersection and collapse of several peoples, life-styles and cultures over a process of time and under pressure from a rigid, authoritarian and exploitative system.

If Harris's work suggests the interior dimensions of this shift in perception, Lamming's *Of Age and Innocence* was the first serious attempt to deal with its political aspect. Coming in the wake of the collapse of multi-ethnic politics in Guyana, this novel reveals the deep sense of schism running through West Indian society, as well as the desperate or resolute hope of unity in an open and ominous future. Secrecy and communion constitute the opposite poles of this novel. True political liberation can only be based on open dialogue, shared experience and communion both within and between ethnic groups; and communion requires trust, absolute candour and honesty between the leadership and the people on the one hand, and between the different ethnic groups in a culturally diverse society.

But these qualities of openness, trust and candour have never been permitted existence in a colonial situation such as the one described earlier in this paper. Thus secrecy and mistrust permeate the relationship between Africans and Indians, the major ethnic groups in *Of Age and Innocence*, and become the catalyst for the tragic divisions which occur towards the end of the novel. If *In the Castle of My Skin*(1953) ended with a perception of the complexity of the African heritage, and an emerging vision of the spiritual and emotional oneness of the Black experience, *Of Age and Innocence* ends with the more complex vision of a multi-ethnic society in which the African heritage is only one of the many heritages competing for visibility and political presence, and Pan-Africanism a source of strength or a prop only to one segment of the population. *Of Age and Innocence* also ends with the embryonic dream of the younger generation; a dream – like Martin Luther King's – of openness, graciousness, cultural exchange in a world where there are no secrets, only a sharing of modes of living and seeing. It is the single hopeful possibility Lamming permits in a horizon of omen and smouldering catastrophe.

The intolerable wrestle between dream and reality has intensified since the mid-sixties. Far from achieving dialogue and communion among the oppressed, Caribbean societies have deepened the divisions of class and race. Central to this development was the Black Power movement in America, which forty years after Garvey reopened the questions about the self-perception, economic position, and real presence of Black people in America. These questions had to be reopened; and viewed positively, the profound reassessment of the situation of Black people in the diaspora has led to a deepening of consciousness both in America and the Caribbean. There are far more people who are aware of their history and of the continuity of struggle, survival and creativity. While the system still seeks to marginalize Black people in general, there are far more people at every level of life who are articulate, resolute and conscious. There is far more publishing being done, more to read.

But it is also true to say that in places such as Trinidad and Guyana, the situation which Lamming explored in *Of Age and Innocence* still obtains. In those two countries, the two major races view each other as competitors and thus view each assertion of racial presence by the other, as a threat to self-hood. The masses of both African and Indians remain exploitable, divided and open to manipulation by politicians who because of the deepening of ethnic consciousness, have had for the last twenty years to project themselves as charismatic, ethnic culture heroes. Elsewhere in the Caribbean, politicians have even manipulated the religions of the oppressed, drawing on the fervour of the cult for political support which at points reaches fanaticism. This is true of Jamaica and Guyana and was true of Grenada and of course Haiti.

What one is dealing with in the 1970's then, is no longer the denial of racial presence to Afro-Caribbean people, but the exploitation of awakened racial consciousness by Black political leaders. So that the deepening of consciousness which could be a strength has ironically become the basis of fresh exploitation. Attempts to transcend racial and class divisions have taken the form of (a) verbal nationalism (b) a renewal of Marxist/Leninist ideology. The struggle for both of these ideals is just beginning, and promises to be long, paradoxical and bitter. Nationalism, for example, can easily become traditional insularity, which renders the region as a whole even more vulnerable in the world. Marxism/Leninism is, so far, advocated in a rigid and doctrinaire fashion, which seems to me to ignore the multi-faceted complexity of the Caribbean situation. It isn't surprising that in both Trinidad and Guyana, the cleavages along racial lines have remained and been most pronounced even in parties which have proclaimed a universalist Marxist ideology.

Since the mid-sixties various "directions" have been evident in the literature. Edward Kamau Brathwaite's trilogy *The Arrivants* (1967-1969) has been the mature fruit of an intense and richly various enquiry into the meaning of the African presence in the Caribbean and the Americas. One of his most important contributions has been his ceaseless experimentation with form, and his ability to use models drawn from the basic folk, folk-urban and proletarian forms of Black people of the diaspora, and on the continent of Africa.[12]

What has happened in Jamaica since then has resulted in an entirely different sort of poetry, best seen in his collection *Black + Blues* (1976). There, the poetry emerges out of the bleak mood which succeeded the assassination of the Black Power and Civil Rights movement in America and its collapse in the Caribbean. It constantly asks questions about the connection between Revolution and consciousness. In "Glass", for example, the poet posits that Revolution must be based on spiritual continuity with past revolutionary effort. But Blacks have inherited a tradition of discontinuity which, as Brathwaite had already illustrated in *Rights of Passage*, forces them to alternate between creative action and role-playing, revolutionary consciousness and the minstrel dance of death. How does one, beginning as colonials have had to begin, break the circle or repression/reprisal/retribution/revolution/repression? What creative action brings the necessary release from this wheel?

Brathwaite asks these questions with respect to a society which is half-urban and half-primal, facing the full stress of modern life with very few visible resources. Under pressure this world begins to prophesy; to create song, legend, myth and dread omen out of the materials of everyday horror. Black people caught in the system, whether they jive in Harlem ("Glass"), or sharpen their ratchet knives in Kingston ("Springblade", "Starvation") become representative of all subjugated peoples, disoriented since the break-up of the Roman Empire and the formation of Western European civilizations. The Caribbean diaspora is placed in a long and vast historical context which has seen movement of peoples, disorientation, the extermination of millions of primal peoples in the Americas by the bearers of a superior technology of warfare, the confrontation of the materialistic West with the kingdoms of spirit in India, Africa and meso-America; the elevation of Western materialism into skyscraper, rocket, spaceship and mushroom cloud, until today the West predicts its own destruction, sees each new invention as an omen of catastrophe (*Future Shock, The Greening of America, Silent Spring*) and longs for its now abolished sense of wonder, the reinstatement of its dead gods.

Brathwaite's problem becomes that of the entire New World sensibility; that of locating his ex-primordial peoples in this context of movement, disequilibrium and destruction. It is Walcott's problem, that of Lamming's last two novels (*Water with Berries* and *Natives of My Person,* that of Carpentier, (*The Lost Steps, Explosion in a Cathedral*), Harris and Fuentes (*Terra Nostra*). It involves a profound reassessment of the meaning of European history, which Brathwaite had already begun in some of his earlier poems, (e.g., "Heretic," "Judas of Barcelona" in *Other Exiles*).

The two sets of possibilities represented by Harris's *Palace of the Peacock* and Naipaul's *The Mimic Men* now become the poles between which our self-perception swings. On the one hand there is the possibility of rebuilding the lost kingdoms of the spirit whose ruins remain as reminders of who we were. How we are to do this becomes the basis of fresh debate. Is Tom's transformation into Ogun still possible? Can Makak really return to the green beginnings? Will Donne ever attain the palace of the peacock or Mohammed be purged by the refining fire of spirit? Naipaul's constant answer to this has been a resolute NO.

Brathwaite, with all his hopes for revolutionary transformation, has grave doubts. On the one hand the ruined city man has created roots and prophecy, and his rumble of consciousness moves like an earthquake under the frail structures of "our mindless architects." But on the other hand, the city man is a victim who sees "vistas of rot only." Each new generation is "a new generation of clogged gutters," and constantly betrays its lightning flashes of intuitive vision: "the flash of dark into which I have carved no holy place." ("Caliban").

So that if *The Arrivants* moved with the faith of spiritual dialectic towards an equilibrium of negation and affirmation, void and structured form, silence and widening circle of sound, *Black + Blues*, constitutes a veritable *de profundis* of catastrophe. The landscape is more dreary the manscape more ravaged. The result in terms of form is directness and plainness of statement on the one hand, and a restless unfocussed turbulence on the other. There is a greater intellectual width and depth and a burning intensity of inner search.

Fierceness and bleakness of vision are characteristic of the 1970's. Our poets at home have become furiously driven men. Walcott, Carter, Brathwaite, McNeill, Scott, Roach or Questel all share this "driven" quality, which is a direct response to the quality of chaos which exists in the contemporary Caribbean. One has travelled a considerable distance from the simple vision of the thirties and forties. The revolution of self-perception has always been taking place; and it continues, grows increasingly more complex and multi-faceted. It embraces now both the notion of ethnic heritages and their competition and confrontation in the contemporary post-independence Caribbean. It involves the relentless class struggle, and the survival of the structures and instruments of exploitation and repression. It hovers between the alternatives of adamic renewal or return, and existentialist sense of void. It challenges conventional notions of history and is part of a vast worldwide movement to relocate the submerged cultures of the devastated in the kingdom of human and humane achievement.

Notes

1. Gordon Rohlehr, 'The Folk in Caribbean Literature,' *Tapia* vol. 2 nos. 11 and 12 (December 17 and 24, 1973).
2. Gordon Rohlehr, 'Forty Years of Calypso,' *Tapia* vol. 2 nos. 1, 2 and 3 (September 1972).
3. N. Cameron, *The Evolution of the Negro* (Westport, Connecticut: Greenwood Press, 1970), originally published in 1926 and 1934, in Georgetown, Guyana.
4. Gordon Rohlehr, 'The Creative Writer and Society,' *Kaie*, (Guyana) no. 11, (August 1973): 48–77.
5. Edward Brathwaite, 'Review of *Voices from Ghana*,' *Bim* 30 (January–June 1960): 88–90.
6. George Lamming, 'The Negro Writer and His World,' *Caribbean Quarterly* vol. 5 no. 2 (February 1958).
7. Gordon Rohlehr, 'Predestination, Frustration and Symbolic Darkness in Naipaul's *A House for Mr Biswas*,' *Caribbean Quarterly* vol. X, no. 1 (1964): 3–11; also Gordon Rohlehr, 'The Ironic Approach,' in *Modern Black* Novelists (Englewood Cliffs, NJ: Prentice Hall, 1971), 162–76.
8. Derek Walcott, 'What the Twilight Says: An Overture,' Introduction to *Dream on Monkey Mountain and Other Plays* (New York: Farrar, Straus & Giroux, 1970); 'The Muse of History,' in *Is Massa Day Dead*? Ed. Coombs O (Anchor, New York: Doubleday, 1974).
9. George Lamming, 'Caribbean Literature: the Black Rock of Africa,' in *African Forum* vol. 1, no. 4 (Spring 1966): 32–52.
10. Derek Walcott previously cited. For my comments on this aspect of Walcott's work see: Gordon Rohlehr, 'My Strangled City,' *Caliban* vol. 3, no. 1, (Fall/Winter 1976): 50–122.
11. M.G. Smith, *The Plural Society in the British West Indies* (Berkeley: The University of California Press, 1965).
12. For a full-length study of Brathwaite's *Arrivants*, see Gordon Rohlehr, *Pathfinder: Black Awakening in The Arrivants of Edward Kamau Brathwaite* (Port-of-Spain, 1981).

The Battle for Space

Rex Nettleford

Creative artists, intellectuals, cultural agents in the Caribbean are today particularly concerned with what I have come to call the battle for space. The phenomenon turns on just about everything that informs the struggle to make sense of Caribbean existence whether one views this from the point of politics, economics, social development or cultural dynamics.

I am reminded of this matter of space by the Caribbean's own ancestral resort to maronnage – retreats into safe psychic sanctums calling on inner reserves beyond the reach of external violators. The Indian seers saw the phenomenon in marvellously dialectical terms.

'As far, indeed, as the vast space outside, extends the space within the heart. Within it, indeed, are contained both heaven and earth, fire and wind, sun and moon, lightning and the stars, both what one possesses here and what one does not possess – all is contained in SPACE.'[1]

The concept of inner and outer space conjures up in the mind of the Caribbean person a number of ideas about his existential reality. Centuries of marginalisation will have placed him on the periphery of existence, taunting him to great expense of energy in a bid to enter a 'mainstream' not of his making, rather than attributing to him, as human being, the capacity for participating in the determination of that mainstream. The dichotomy between his inner space and outer space is a function of his alienation, his balkanised consciousness, of a disparateness of elements which go to make the human whole, of an impotence that renders him all but totally out of control of his own destiny. The all-pervasive nature of this marginalisation – the denial to the individual man and woman of the harmonisation of inner and outer space – is manifest in myriad and mutually reinforcing but dichotomous and discrete phenomena in social relationships. These phenomena are variously described as master/slave, management/labour, bourgeois/low culture, superordinate/subordinate.

Happily, none of these 'relationships' is static since human nature (still to be fathomed and understood in its entirety) gives to social interaction a certain dynamic, known in some quarters as dialectical. This opens up to the marginalised opportunities for spatial options that would otherwise be denied. In the Caribbean world where colonial dependency, superordinate/subordinate, powerful/powerless categories determined social reality from its modern beginnings dating back at least four centuries, such dialectical relationships have been central to human existence as a matter of course. The ensuing battle for space, in both an elemental and physical sense, constitutes, then, the *force vitale* of a still groping society. To this day the phenomenon of numerical majorities functioning as cultural and power minorities persists in the Commonwealth or Anglophone Caribbean[2] despite the disappearance of the British Raj, the coming of the one-man-one-vote principle, and the strident rhetoric aspiring to participatory democracy.

Modern Indian experience shares some of this contradiction. Except that the ancestral reality of an India that antedates the coming of the British Raj suggests quicker and more effective liberation out of colonial space. I view the strong cultural renaissance of contemporary India in its philosophical, intellectual and artistic assertive vitality not only as the recovery of its inner space but as the necessary condition for the occupation of that outer space demanded by the fact of post-colonialism, the imperatives of development and entry into the 21st century seen as the fulfilment of Western science and technology. More important I see the recovery of inner space by ancestral civilisations like those of India and part of Black Africa as the necessary control over the awesome and dynamic process of harmonisation of inner space discovered and outer space to be effectively occupied. The strength and certitude of ancestral centres of psychic and cultural power have a logical priority for the grasp of and command over the wonders of high tech modernity. The story of the Green Revolution and the science and technology capability of India are the pride of all the Third World. However, I make bold to say that Rajiv Gandhi and his fervent thrust into modernity could make no sense without the ancestral wisdom of Tagore.

We in the contemporary Caribbean can make no sense in our craving after Western-type prosperity without the ancestral wisdom of our people honed in half a millenium of unique historical experience characterised by severance (uprooting from ancestral lands), suffering and survival. Each of these states of experience defines some sense of space or other. The severance was from Africa (in its violent uprooting with all the consequences of such involuntary uprooting), from Europe (peaceful and benign for the most part but with the supporting mechanisms of that sense of power and superior military and industrial technology), and later from India and China (admittedly without the traumas of physical enforcement but with the anguish of economic dispossession and psychic displacement).

The suffering was in turn an abuse of human space – in terms of deprivation of human beings of that sense of self or of society. The slave suffered on the one hand from social death and natal alienation.[3] On the other he was deprived of that universal claim to that one last area of the psyche that is deemed to be inviolable.

Free will, the capacity for rational choice, moral responsibility or natural rights have existed, however, under constant threat of obliteration whether under slavery, indentureship, class oppression or colonialism. The exploitation of man by man proceeds by various means (physical torture, social control, psychological conditioning) but with the same effect – the abuse or denial of personal space. This was a normal feature of Caribbean life under slavery and colonialism and continues, albeit in modified and subtle form(s), in Independence with the new perpetrators to be found among the native governors, the mimic men, and/or the neo-colonial superpowers brought in as allies in pursuit of hegemonic control of geographical spheres.

The US penetration of the Caribbean Basin by way of political, military, intellectual, economic and telecommunications means in a latter-day version of the age-old attack on the space of the Caribbean people is likely to perpetuate the 'suffering' of dependency and powerlessness. *Power* in its elemental sense has less to do with the possession of so many nuclear warheads and ballistic missiles and more to do with the capacity to generate the knowledge that underlies the production of those very warheads and missiles. The capacity to make definitions about oneself and to follow through with action on the basis of those definitions is the substance of power. It expressed the capability for integration of inner space, conceived as the capacity to generate knowledge and to create, and outer space perceived as the follow-through to action on the basis of such thought, knowledge and creativity.

The Caribbean people are in search of that power now. Something called Independence has recently come to the Anglophone section of the region comprising some 15 countries.[4] It is decked out in national flags, anthems and symbols (from flowers to heroes). However, the actual redistribution, relocation and determining of who should administer power among the native (and foreign) contenders for that power remains a fact of life. The battle for space continues – between the mass of the population and an oligarchic few who would wish to freeze their current occupation of political and economic space into timeless legitimacy. In addition, the battle is also between the region as a whole (in its self-perception as a member of the Third World) and the powerful North Atlantic complex which has realigned itself into the omnipotent OECD group of countries, the World Bank or the IMF. With such monumental power concentrated in outer space, Caribbean countries have had to fall back on themselves, their self-reliance, their innate self-confidence, their logically prioritised area of 'inner space'.

In this there are lessons to be learnt from the experience within the society itself which has a tradition of slaves, colonials, the working class, and the poor retreating into their inner space as strategy of demarginalisation. Oriental philosophy is supposed to attribute to mind and imagination, creative power. But it is the phenomenon of marginalisation in the experience and existential reality of the Occidental Caribbean that has done exactly this. One, however, takes note of the journey to Oriental transcendental meditation by the alienated in the developed Western world.

In the Caribbean, mind and imagination – creative intellect and artistic creation – have been major ingredients in the Caribbean's battle for space in the first place and in the other, in the region's efforts to 're-integrate' self and society into an organic totality by the harmonisation of inner and outer space. We in the Caribbean have not built pyramids, pillars, cathedrals, amphitheatres, opera houses etc that are the wonders of the world, but we have more creative artists per square inch than is probably good for us. In addition we have created and are creating mental structures which are intended to be the basis of that self-confidence, that sense of place, purpose and power without which there can be no integration of inner and outer space. Music, dance, religious expression, language, literature, appropriate designs for social living are the structural products of the Caribbean's creative impulse. They serve as guarantees of inner space meeting outer space in a dynamic existence that turns on creative rather than disintegrative tension.

This phenomenon is best described by the phrase inward stretch outward reach, neither of which activity is possible without a sense of space. The battle for space in the Caribbean has found its fiercest expression in the indigenising process of a society that is wholly the creature of colonial transplantation and the impulse of commercial profit. For most of that existence the battle has found most cogent form in the struggle of the African presence to claim a place of centrality in the Caribbean ethos. The Eurocentricity of mainstream Caribbean life for all this time is the problematique of cultural development. The very notion of Eurocentricity is a spatial concept. Its manifestations in concrete terms are in the primacy of systems of law, constitutional frameworks, education, dress, diet, language, religion, kinship patterns, artistic manifestations, politics, economics and technology. The European imperial raj displaced from their ancestral space the subject peoples brought there. There are, however, residual areas of inviolability left to the human being, however total the attempt at displacement by domination, fear or psychological conditioning, might have been.

The Caribbean has long found these areas of inviolability to lie in the exercise of the mind and the creative imagination. These became the sacred groves, the caves of the heart, the inner landscapes, the metaphors of actual living which form the very essence of culture. The Caribbean is in every sense a cultural expression. Three particular areas spring to mind. They are language, religion and the creative arts. They circumscribe the inner spaces beyond the reach of oppressors; they constitute the 'innate structures' that are the monopoly of no one race, no one civilisation, no one world power. Consciousness of the existence and power of such innate structures provide the wings to liberation rather than for retreat into myth.

On language, one's cosmology can be expressed in one's own language without resort to the master's tongue. Even when the master's tongue continues to spell scribal legitimacy, the lexicon is utilised but transmuted by the force of native syntax, tone and significations as well as rhythm. The Caribbean is today a rich laboratory of Creole languages – 'creole' in the proper sense of native-born and native-bred and not in the sense of an aberration of a dialect to the norm of a Standard tongue[5]. The very code-switching, so normal to Caribbean people in the liberal use of creole for appropriate circumstances transformed to the lingua franca as the occasion demands (sometimes in one sentence), is a sign of the capacity to master the flow between inner and outer space on one level. English may be the lingua franca in the Anglophone Caribbean for the dialogue with outer space (read the wider world, 'mainstream Western culture') but Jamaica Talk and patois are the languages of everyday living. Dutch, Spanish and French in the rest of the region may govern but it is srnan tonga, papiamento, patois etc, that rule. When the 'governors' of outer space and the 'rulers' of inner space are truly integrated, linguistic wholeness will be achieved. The integration does not come only by the replacement of one or the other. It comes as much by the acceptance of linguistic pluralism rooted in mutual respect for the legitimacy, inner logic and consistency of each. Until that comes, and it has not yet come in the Caribbean, the battle for space continues.

It continues no less in the field of religion in which the Caribbean has never been short of expressions. In the battle for space between Europe and Africa on foreign soil, syncretised expressions have emerged as synthesis for survival among the mass of the population. To go *beyond survival* is to achieve reintegration of inner and outer space into organic totality. In effect these syncretised forms which are relegated to the world of marginalised life (subculture) must now battle for place and purpose with orthodox Christianity. The tyranny of distance between 'subculture' religion and 'high culture' Christianity continues to be defied by the inward stretch and outward reach of a group like the Rastafarians.[6] By a skilful reinterpretation of the Old Testament, the group has invented a cosmology consonant with the Black man's search for dignity and identity in a space (the Western world) which has for centuries defined itself in terms of the inherent superiority of the Caucasoid races and the corresponding inferiority of inhabitants of elsewhere especially the Dark Continent. The spatial liberation from down under, or from periphery to centre (I-and-I), challenges some basic tenets of the Christian belief system which confines divinity to an historical figure and attributes to Man the affliction of Original Sin to be redeemed by the Crucified One. To the Rastafarians any Original Sin that was committed was committed *against* the Black man and not *by* him. He holds himself subject to no such self-humiliation and protects his self-dignity ferociously. He is in fact divine. *All* men are divine and with a piece of God within, the basis is provided for genuine equality among all men, for universal brotherhood. Outer space is reintegrated with inner space by the claim of divinity. All men are created equal, *are* equal. This is the only true basis for any design for civilised social living. No pyramid, temple, edifice of grandeur can be more wondrous than this which safeguards and celebrates the magnificence of the greatest structure of all structures – the human being. The human body in Rastafarian parlance is termed 'the structure'.

One's body is, after all, one's own. It belongs to no one else and what it creates out of its mind and imagination, is a source of power. The arts of the imagination and the system of thought provide the routes to independence, to spatial definitiveness and on one's own terms.

It is in this sense that music and dance provide the Caribbean with two of the most effective weapons in the battle for space. Sound and movement are the life-making abstractions beyond the reach of external domination. A Government bans the lyrics of a song. It can never really ban the tune. If lyrics are bawdy and subversive, the tune is the tune – deceptively harmless! Limitless options in the permutations of sound values suggest a command over the use of space. The calypso of Trinidad, the rhumba of Cuba, the reggae of Jamaica have jumped out of the specificity of their geographical environments, from the carnival tents of Port of Spain, the mambo temples of Havana and the anguished urban ghettoes of Kingston, into the universality of popular music all over the globe, appealing to the young on all continents and from different cultural backgrounds. This conquest of outer space serves to demarginalise the Caribbean in the way that the sitar has demarginalised India in the world of 'serious' music. Ravi Shankar, Bob Marley, the Mighty Sparrow belong to the world, not to their native lands anymore.

As with music, so with dance. The oppressed of the Caribbean have always danced. Coupled with music and performed in the context of religious ritual, the dance assumed elemental proportions affording contemporary use of the creative imagination and as invaluable sources of energy in the continuing battle for space. Caribbean dance-theatre becomes a means of revitalisation, of integrating inner and outer space in the sense that it is seen to serve as route to self-confidence that underpins the creation of one's own destiny in modern life. Dance-theatre draws on such energies for definition and further discovery. It is to the rituals, the songs and stories, the legends, the history, contemporary social life, the rhythm, the sounds, the physical landscape, the ambience of existence that Caribbean dance-theatre turns for impulse and growth. In carving designs in space (which is what dance does through time and in rhythm) Caribbean dance-theatre enters the traditional battle for space by seeking to contribute to bringing the African presence to the centre of the Caribbean ethos. This in itself implies transformative powers of dance bringing an entire society to terms with itself, interpreting an entire society to itself and challenging an historically dependent entity to originality and self-definition in terms of its own realities.

The African continuities are here critical; their transcultutation into creolised Caribbean forms no less so. The centrality of the Earth, of sculpted moulded form as against the attenuated linearity of European art-dance is emphasised, but even in this the battle for space persists. European classical ballet is projected as the Standard and all other forms, dialects of it. One Black American artistic director once insisted that even a stripper is a better stripper for having studied European classical ballet. Caribbean dance-theatre responding to the reality of the African presence must be conscious of the suppleness of the spine, the arched back, the 'groundedness' of the body in motion, the setting up of different rhythms simultaneously in axial comfort. From the simple walk to the most vigorous of contortions the control of small areas of space with the implosion of energy in the inner space gives to Caribbean dance-forms its own kinesthetic quality.

The carriage of the arms still seen in everyday life throughout the region puts energy in the elbows – bearing weight on the head, resting akimbo in repose – and has no counterpart in the 'port de bras' of academic European classical ballet. The giving into Mother Earth the source of all life, the rotation or contraction-release of the pelvis another source of all life, the extension of the body by the use of masks to suggest power through space – such are the elements that persist in the rituals, African-derived, in the Caribbean. They are quite properly the source of our dance-theatre.[7]

Thus are the belief systems of ancestor worship, of life as a cycle of those dead, living and yet unborn, of the divine powers or spirits that mount the devotees in ritual to be acted or danced out as if to link the inner with the outer space, the imagined with the real, the body with the spirit. Caribbean dance-theatre draws on the strength of such ancestral forces to inform contemporary life. Rituals are not transposed from natural habitats: that's anthropology. They are instead distilled to transform contemporary life into altered states of consciousness to offer the Caribbean being a sense of place and purpose.

Is that asking too much of the dance? Perhaps! However, as instrument of integration between worlds of inner and outer space, of spiritual psychic experience and physical reality it offers an excellent environment for self-fulfilment. Empirical evidence is in support of this claim. The physical environment itself is a source of energy. 'The arms, like other parts of the body must be able to describe the curve of mountains, of swans and the shapes of Gothic cathedrals, skyscrapers, and pine trees piercing the winter sky have found correspondences in dance attitudes.'[8]

For the wider contemporary society in search of itself, the dance is as good as any to instil self-discipline, for the pursuit of individual self-fulfilment but through co-ordinated social action as the villagers in their circles at wakes, in ring-games, or other such occasions did and still do. For modern participatory democracy it teaches valuable lessons about the powerlessness of the powerful, of excellence and achievement through orchestral management. The choreographer (leader) is nothing more than a conductor. The dancer (as instrument of expression) is also part of the creative process. One can destroy a line of poetry that doesn't work. One cannot destroy a dancer.

None of this rules out the challenge for the East Indian variable in the continuing creolisation of Caribbean culture, especially in Trinidad and Guyana where the matter of numbers cannot continue to be ignored. Despite the transformation of many men and women of East Indian ancestry into *Caribbean* men and women with sensibilities honed in the crucible of the traditional Euro-African battle for space, one is aware of the force of more recent reconnexions with Mother India as well as with the creolised Caribbean Indian forms which must find their place in a textured Caribbean ethos sooner rather than later. The subliminal battle for space between the creolised Afro-Caribbean and the late-comer East Indian Caribbean is second only to the major battle between Europe and Africa on foreign soil. The products may be different, the process is the same. We have much to teach each other therefore and the area of the arts is probably the best mediator.

What an excellent road to cognition for the young! The integration of mind and body, of imagination and intellect, of the expressive (outer space) with the internal feeling and understanding of a theme, a musical phrase, a situation (inner space). Dance in Education is a serious thrust by many Caribbean educators in the formation of the next generation, though North Atlantic Physical Education Studies in Polytechnics of the United Kingdom persist with a vengeance. The battle for space continues. The learning of Jamaican history through the music and dance festival of Jonkonnu brought from West Africa with correspondences from English mumming brought from Britain is still at the 'project' stage in Jamaican dance education.[9] However, the hope continues that schools will adopt such projects like one in the Orisha tradition in Shango into their curricula soon enough and provide for the next generation a viable alternative to the penetrative powers of American television by satellite, and televangelists.

Above all, the creative arts in general can help to clarify categories of viewing human achievements in the world or re-define those categories which have subtly served to perpetuate the deprivation of the Third World peoples of their space and the opportunity to integrate inner and outer space. The truth is that while we can speak of economic underdevelopment, it is ill-advised to speak as glibly of cultural underdevelopment. In the field of culture there is no 'developing world'.

Yet a new international cultural order must be on the agenda especially for the developed world. The quite indefensible categorisation of the world of the arts into 'classical' meaning Europe's excellences, and the rest (usually ethnic), into high and low culture, with high up north and low down south, must be changed. All civilisations are endowed with the cycle of mutually reinforcing modes of artistic expression which I have elsewhere described as ancestral/traditional, contemporary/popular and classic. This is the story of all civilisations worth their salt. The spaces occupied by the different modes of expression are not mutually exclusive. Rather, they inhere within the experience of the same people over time and their cyclical existence confirms the dynamic process of integrating the different worlds of human experience which makes man the textured resourceful organism that he is – the victor rather than the vanquished in the battle for space.

Notes

1. *Chandogya Upanisad* VIII, 1, 3, (transl. Vedic Experience) quoted in main programme-brochure of International Seminar on Inner and Outer space, India International Centre, New Delhi.
2. The majority of the populations of the Commonwealth Caribbean are people of African ancestry with the exception of Guyana where some 53 per cent of the population are of Indian heritage. The rule applies equally since the Eurocentric value system determines the ethos and Indians are expected to become 'West Indians' in order to 'belong' to Guyana.
3. See H. Orlando Patterson's excellent study of slavery entitled *Slavery and Social Death: A Comparative Study* (Washington DC: Howard University Press, 1982).
4. The following Anglophone Caribbean countries are independent: Antigua/Barbuda, Bahamas, Barbados, Belize, Dominica, Grenada, Guyana, Jamaica, St Kitts/Nevis, St Lucia, St Vincent, Trinidad/Tobago while Anguilla, British Virgin Islands, the Cayman Islands and the Turks/Caicos Islands remain British colonies.
5. The region is rich in 'creole languages' created over the past four centuries following on the encounters between migrants from the Old Worlds (Europe and Africa mainly and later in Asia). See notes 2 and 3 to the essay, 'The Caribbean: Crossroads of the Americas'.
6. For further reading on the Rastafarians of Jamaica, see M.G. Smith, F.R. Augier, and R. Nettleford, *The Rastafari Movement in Kingston, Jamaica* (Kingston; ISER, 1960); Leonard Barrett, *The Rastafarians* (London: Heinemann, 1977); 'Rastafari,' *Caribbean Quarterly* vol. 26, no. 4, 1980.
7. See my *Dance Jamaica: Cultural Definition and Artistic Discovery* (New York: Grove Press, 1985).
8. Rex Nettleford, 176–7.
9. See Shelia Barnett's, 'Jonkonnu and the Creolisation Process in Jamaica: A Study in Cultural Dynamics,' unpublished Master's Thesis, 1977.

Gender and Sexuality

Afterword:
"Beyond Miranda's Meanings:
Un/Silencing the 'Demonic Ground' of Caliban's 'Woman'"[1]

Sylvia Wynter

The point of departure of this *After/Word* is to explore a central distinction that emerges as the dynamic linking sub-text of this, the first collection of critical essays written by Caribbean women. This distinction is that between Luce Irigaray's purely Western assumption of a universal category, "woman", whose "silenced" ground is the condition of what she defines as an equally universally applicable, "patriarchal discourse," and the dually Western and post-Western editorial position of a projected 'womanist/feminist' critical approach as the unifying definition of the essays that constitute the anthology. The term *'womanist/feminist,'* with the qualifying attribute "womanist" borrowed from the Afro-American feminist Alice Walker, reveals the presence of a contradiction, which, whilst central to the situational frame of reference of both Afro-American and Caribbean women writers/critics, is necessarily absent from the situational frame of reference of both Western-European and Euroamerican women writers. Thus whilst at the level of the major text these essays are projected within the system of inference-making of the discourse of Feminism, at the level of the sub-text which both haunts and calls in question the presuppositions of the major text, the very attempt to redefine the term *feminist* with the qualifier "womanist," expresses the paradoxical relation of Sameness and Difference which the writers of these essays, as members of the Caribbean women intelligentsia, bear to their Western European and Euroamerican peers. This dual relation is expressed by both editors if not precisely in these terms. Thus if for Boyce Davies, the term *womanist* necessarily qualifies *feminism*, for Elaine Savory Fido, the unique positional situation of Caribbean women writers/critics, as expressed in their writings, is that of a *cross-roads*, that is, one in which they experience themselves as placed at a crossroad of three variables. These are, on the one hand, the variable of sex-gender, as well as of class, both of which they share with their European/Euroamerican counterparts—*class* in that many members of both intelligentsia groups are still one generation away from our non-middleclass origins, even where this is numerically truer of the intelligentsia of the still, until very recently, colonized Caribbean—and, on the other, the variable of "race" which of course strongly demarcates the situation of the Caribbean women intelligentsia, whether Black or White from that of their Western/Euroamerican counterparts.

I want to argue in this After/Word, from its projected "demonic ground" outside of our present governing system of meaning, or theory/ontology in de Nicolas' sense of the word[2] that it is precisely the variable "race" which imposes upon these essays the contradictory dualism by which the writers both work within the "regime of truth" of the discourse of feminism, at the same time as they make use of this still essentially Western discourse to point towards the epochal threshold of a new post-modern and post-Western mode of cognitive inquiry; one which goes beyond the limits of our present "human sciences," to constitute itself as a new science of human "forms of life."[3]

The German scholar Hans Blumenberg, in exploring the parallel epochal threshold which led from the European Middle Ages to the emergence of the modern world *pari passu* with the advent of Renaissance humanism and the Copernican Revolution, widens the concept of Thomas Kuhn's theory of "scientific revolutions." This theory, he argues, which describes "the breakdown of dominant systems as a result of their immanent rigorism," and the "downfall" of "the pedantic disposition of every school-like mode of thought" (with both breakdown and downfall leading "with fateful inevitability" to the "self-uncovering of the *marginal* inconsistencies from which doubt and opposition break into the consolidated field") can be capable "of generalization to a high level in relation to historical phenomena;"[4] and therefore to the shift/mutation of one age or epoch and its related, in Foucault's terms, episteme,[5] to the other. And the central point I want to make in this After/Word is that the contradiction inserted into the consolidated field of meanings of the ostensibly "universal" theory of feminism by the variable "*race*," and explicitly expressed by the qualifiers of "womanist" and "cross-roads situation," of these essays points toward the emergent "downfall" of our present "school like mode of thought" and its system of "positive knowledge" inherited from the nineteenth century and from the Industrial epoch of which it was the enabling mode of rationality and participatory epistemology[6]; and that it does this in the same way as feminist theory itself had earlier, inserted the contradiction of the variable *gender* into the ostensibly "universal" theories of Liberal Humanism and Marxism-Leninism.[7]

Because these theories and their related "universalisms" had been erected on the apriori self-description of the human on the model of a "natural organism" [as the inversion of the Euro-Christian "image of God"], the variable "race" was/is constituted as an "object of knowledge" able to function in the system of symbolic representations (Levi-Strauss' "totemic schema," Marlene Philip's system of images as the human analogue of "the D.N.A. molecules at the heart of all life") as a central topos of our present system of meaning and its regulatory behavioral mechanism. For as such a *topos*, "race," functions to signify a system-specific mode of causality, that is, the causality of a "materialistic substrate" which not only acts so as to place genetically determined constraints on human behaviors, but also, above all, to *prescribe* a teleology—that is, to imply that "ends," now no-longer, after the full-fledged secularization of the European Enlightenment, set by the most remote watchmaker of Gods, are still extra-humanly set for the human by *nature*, in our case, by the constraints of nature and/or of history.[8] Thus, if, for Freud, as Irigaray dissects with respect to the variable of "sexual difference," biology was destiny, with the functioning of the "anatomical model" being described by Freud in a manner which prescribes behaviors,—"It seems" Irigaray writes, speaking ironically in Freud's voice, "[...] you take the term *masculine* to connote *active*, the term *feminine* to connote "passive" and it is true that a relation of the kind exists for "the male sex cell is actively mobile and searches out the female one, and the latter, the ovum, is immobile and waits passively"... And I, Freud, have to tell you that the behavior of the *elementary* sexual organisms is indeed a model for the conduct of sexual individuals during intercourse. My way of envisaging ... these ..."things" would therefore imply that the psychic is *prescribed by* the *anatomical* according to a *mimetic order*, with anatomical science imposing *the truth of its model* upon psychological *behavior*",[9]—the variable of *race/racial* difference is, since the sixteenth century, even more primarily destiny. For with Western Europe's post-medieval, expansion into the New World, (and earlier into Africa), and with its epochal shift out of primarily *religious* systems of legitimation, and behaviour—regulation, her peoples' expropriation of the land/living space of the New World peoples was to be based on the secular concept of the "non-rational" inferior, "*nature*" of the peoples to be expropriated and governed;[10] that is, of an ostensible difference in "natural" substance which, for the first time in history was no longer *primarily* encoded in the male/female gender division as it had been hitherto in the symbolic template of all traditional and religiously based human orders, but now in the cultural-physiognomic variations between the dominant expanding European civilization and the non-Western peoples that, encountering, it would now stigmatize as "natives." In other words, with the shift to the secular, the primary code of difference now became that between "men" and "natives," with the traditional "male" and "female" distinctions now coming to play a secondary—if none the less powerful—reinforcing role within the system of symbolic representations, Levi-Strauss's totemic schemas[11], by means of which, as governing charters of meaning, all human orders are "altruistically" integrated.[12]

Nowhere in this mutational shift from the primacy of the *anatomical* model of sexual difference as the referential model of *mimetic* ordering, to that of the *physiognomic* model of racial/ *cultural* difference, more powerfully enacted than in Shakespeare's play *The Tempest*, one of the foundational endowing[13] texts both of Western Europe's dazzling rise to global hegemony, and, at the level of human "life", in general, of the mutation from primarily religiously defined modes of human being to the first, partly secularizing ones. Whilst on the other hand, both mutations, each as the condition of the other, are nowhere more clearly put into play than in the relations between Miranda the daughter of Prospero, and Caliban, the once original owner of the island now enslaved by Prospero as a function of the latter's expropriation of the island. That is, in the relations of enforced dominance and subordination between Miranda, though "female", and Caliban, though "male"; relations in which *sex-gender attributes* are not longer the primary index of "deferent" difference[14], and in which the discourse that erects itself is no longer primarily "patriarchal", but rather "monarchical" in its Western-European, essentially post-Christian, post-religious definition. Therefore, in whose context of behaviour-regulatory inferential system of meanings, as the essential condition of the mutation to the secular, Caliban, as an incarnation of a new category of the human, that of the subordinated "irrational" and "savage"[15] *native* is now constituted as the lack of the "rational" Prospero, and the now capable-of-rationality-Miranda, by the Otherness of his/its *physiognomic* "monster" difference, a difference which now takes the *coding* role of sexual-anatomical difference, with the latter now made into a mimetic parallel effect of the former, and as such a member of the *set* of differences of which the former has now become the primary "totemic operator."[16]

Correspondingly, as the play reveals, with this ontological and epistemological mutation effected in the sixteenth century, the new physiognomic model of "race", (or, in the terms of Elsa Goveiá, the Caribbean historian, used in a critical 1970 essay on the integrative principles of Caribbean societies, the "ascription of race"),[17] was to begin that ongoing transformative meaning process by which it would come to function, within our contemporary, behaviour-regulatory theoretical models and systems of meaning, to provide, parallely to the earlier traditional sex-gender models of *anatomical* difference of truly "patriarchal" orders, the grounding "mimetic model" or totemic operator which now *primarily* describes/prescribes at the multiple levels of the global order, analogical behavioural relations of dominance/subordination activity/passivity, theory-givers/theory-takers[18] between human populations/geographical races, cultures, and societal groups, i.e. ethnic, class, gender, sexual-preference, etc. The "mimetic model" or totemic operator therefore, which legitimates these relations in now *purely secular* terms, as relations ostensibly pre-ordained by the extra-human ends set by, firstly, in the narrative schema/story of the monarchical discourse of civic humanism (as enacted in *the Tempest*) by an allegedly universally applicable "natural law"[19], and later in the Malthusian-Darwinian-Haeckelian, narrative schema of a monist discourse of "social naturalism" or "biological idealism"[20], by, allegedly, evolutionary biology. Thus, if in the first schema of "civic humanism," the model of *physiognomic* difference was still attached to the model of religio-cultural difference – with the New World peoples and African slaves defined as "pagan sacrificers of other humans and as idolatious "cannibals"[21], in the second, the now purely *physiognomic* difference came to provide a *somatic* mode of difference which would function from the early nineteenth century onwards as the *primary* "totemic operator" of the principle of Sameness and Difference about which our present global, and now purely secular order, auto-regulates its socio-systemic hierarchies, including those of gender, class, sexual preference, culture—including, therefore, the processes central to literary scholarship itself and to its normative system of interpretative readings, which have been defined by Cary Nelson as that of "literary idealization" by means of which, in Euro-American "humanism" processes of literary transcendence (i.e. literature as "one of the finer things on earth" one which "exhibits at once a powerful realism about the human condition and a visionary synthesis of its highest ambitions") are attached "to the experience of only one race, one sex, a restricted set of class fractions within a few national cultures." With the experiences of most of the world's peoples "having to be, rule-governedly, within the parameters of the 'play'[22] of its interpretative readings," and regulatory system of meanings, "obliterated"[23]; as the experiences of the physiognomic Other, the "natives", and in their most "primal" form *niggers*. The systemic "obliteration" is central, therefore to the imperative which impels the counter-readings of these essays.

It is in this context that we can begin to approach the significance both of this collection of essays themselves as essays projected both from the hitherto "silenced" vantage point of the obliterated "experiences of most of the world's peoples" and from the vantage point of gender, that is of a Miranda now speaking in her own intelligentsia name—instead of in the name of her monarchical father, and of *The Tempest's* Miranda's speech to Caliban; that we can grasp the significance of her legitimated expropriation of the right to endow his purposes—when he did not "savage" know "his own meanings"—with "words that made them known," her expropriation then of what Marlene Phillips defines as "image-making power." And here, we begin to pose in this context a new question, the question not of the absence of Caliban's legitimate father as posed by Aimé Césaire and commented on by Clarisse Zimra in her essay on Francophone Caribbean women writers, nor even the question posed by Zimra herself, that of the "silent presence of a mother not yet fully understood" which carries with it the implicit project of "discarding the logos of the Father," and of replacing it instead with "the Silent Song of the Mother," but a new question related to a new project. This question is that of the most significant absence of all, that of Caliban's Woman, of Caliban's physiognomically complementary mate. For nowhere in Shakespeare's play, and in its system of image-making, one which would be foundational to the emergence of the first form of a secular world system, our present Western world system, does Caliban's mate appear as an alternative sexual-erotic model of desire; as an alternative source of an alternative system of meanings. Rather there, on the New World island, as the only woman, Miranda and her mode of physiognomic being, defined by the philogenically "idealized" features of straight hair and thin lips is canonized as the "rational" object of desire; as the potential genitrix of a superior mode of human "life," that of "good natures" as contrasted with the ontologically absent potential genitrix—Caliban's mate—of another population of human, i.e., of a "vile race" "capable of all ill," which "any print of goodness will not take," a "race" then extra-humanly condemned by a particular mode of Original Sin which "deservedly" confines them to a "rock," thereby empowering the "race" of Miranda to expropriate the island, and to reduce Caliban to a labor-machine as the new "massa damnata"[24] of purely sensory nature—"He does make our fire,/fetch in our wood, and serve in offices/that profit us"[25]. And since the empirical relation of rational humans to purely sensory nature humans, and its related physiognomic-cultural model of difference/deference will now serve retrospectively, as the *mimetic model* of an order whose intra-group societal hierarchical structures have been preordained by an allegedly universally functioning code of natural law,[26] the "desire" of the 'lower class' sailors Stephano and Trinculo can also only be *for* Miranda, with their *optimal* "desire" also transferred from their own "lower class" mates, to her. Hence the non-desire of Caliban for his own mate, for Caliban's "woman", is, as Maryse Condé brilliantly suggests, in another context, a founding function of the "social pyramid"[27] of the global order that will be put in place following upon the 1492 arrival of Columbus in the Caribbean; a function then of its integrating behaviour-regulatory system of meanings and "semantic closure principle."

In this first phase of Western Europe's expansion into the Americas, Caliban, as both the Arawak and African "forced" labor needed by the mutation in the land/labor ratio which followed[28], and given the existence of rapidly available fresh supplies provided by the expanding slave trade in "negroes" out of the Europe-Africa-New World triangular traffic, had no need/desire for the procreation of his own "kind", since such a mode of "desire" would only be functional in the very much later stages for the master-population group's purpose, as the only secularly-theoretically "idealized" purpose which now mattered.

Hence the empirical logic of the absence from the play's character system of Caliban's woman, for its erecting of its plot upon the "ground" not only of her absence, but also of the absence of Caliban's endogenous desire for her, of any longing. All his desire instead is "soldered" on[29] to Miranda as the only symbolically canonized potential genitrix. Hence his first act of overt rebellion is his attempt to "people this isle with Caliban's"; his attempt to copulate with her. However, this rebellious possibility is not to be—for if the absence of Caliban's woman is a central function of the play's foundational ontology in which Caliban "images" the human as pure sensory nature and as appetite uncurbed by reason, whilst Prospero and the prince, Fernando, "image" the human possessed of a rational nature and therefore able to curb their lustful appetites, (with the ship's Boatswain and the sailors Stephano and Trinculo, lower down the scale between the two), then the metaphysically imperative elimination of the *potential* progeny of Caliban, must rule-governedly bar him from any access to Miranda as the potential genitrix of a "race" which, as the beneficiaries of both rational and sensory natures bequeathed them by Nature, must necessarily behave so as to effect the "ends" ostensibly implicit this differential legacy; that is, must ensure the stable dominance of the "race" of good natures over the "vile race" of Caliban's purely sensory nature, if the now secularizing behaviour—regulatory system of meaning, and its related "semantic closure principle" is to be stably replicated.

The absence of Caliban's woman is therefore an ontological absence, that is, one central to the new secularizing behaviour-regulatory narrative schema, or in Clarisse Zimra's term, mode of "story-telling"[30], by means of which the secular Laity of feudal-Christian Europe displaced the theological spirit/flesh motivational opposition[31] and replaced it with its own first secularly constituted "humanist" motivational opposition in history. That is, the rational/sensory opposition between a projected redeemed "race" of "gentes humaniores" as the bearers of a rational nature able to master their own sensory nature at the same time as they mastered—and mistressed—the "vile race" dys-elected by Nature to be bearers of a purely sensory nature, and the new secular *massa damnata* of the "vile race" themselves.[32]

To put it in more directly political terms, the absence of Caliban's woman, is an absence which is functional to the new secularizing schema by which the peoples of Western Europe legitimated their global expansion as well as their expropriation and/their marginalization of all the other population-groups of the globe, including, partially, some of their own national groupings such as, for example, the Irish.[33] Yet it was with this same secularizing narrative schema that they were also to effect that far-reaching mutation, in which they were to displace, not only their own *religious* version of the narrative schemas of good and evil and their modes of "story-telling",—that is, their own religious version of the behaviour-motivational schemas/stories, by means of whose opiate-inducing signifying meaning systems which function to trigger the neuro-chemical processes of what Danielli defines as the internal reward system of the brain[34] and to induce and regulate the collective set of "altruistic" behaviours by means of which each human model of being and related human orders are stably brought into, and maintained in, being—but *all* other religious versions to the marginally private, rather than centrally public, spheres of human existence.[35] And, if the latter schemas, religious and/or mythological, together with their projection of a transcendentally ordered behaviour-regulatory definition of good and evil, had hitherto functioned to stabilize and guarantee all human "forms of life", the new narrative schema, powerfully re-enacted in the plot-line of *The Tempest*, was to initiate the first form of a secularly projected definition of Good and Evil, and therefore of a secularly guaranteed and stabilized "form of life" or human order, now dynamically brought in to being by the collective behaviours motivated and induced by its (the schema's) oppositional categories of secular "good" (as rational nature incarnated in Prospero and Miranda) and of secular "evil" (as pure sensory nature outside of the control of rational nature incarnated in Caliban when his own "master, his own man.")[36] In other words, in this epochal threshold shift to the secular, the physiognomic (and cultural) difference between the populations groups of Prospero/Miranda and that of Caliban is now made to function, totemically, as a new, so to speak infra-scendental[37] oppositional principle of good and evil which is ostensibly as extra-humanly ordained (by Natural Law), as, before, the Spirit/Flesh opposition had been ostensibly pre-ordained by supernatural decree—rather than as, in both cases ordained by the imperative of the respective narrative schemas, and the "semantic closure of principle" of their respective behaviour regulatory systems of meanings.[38]

It is within this latter "real" imperative that the absence of Caliban's woman as Caliban's sexual reproductive mate functions to ontologically negate their progeny/population group, forcing this group to serve as the allegorical incarnation of "pure" sensory nature; that is, the group for whom the image of Caliban stands, i.e., the original owners/occupiers of the New World lands, the American-Indians, now displaced empirically and metaphysically reduced, by the new regulatory system of meanings, to a "native" savage Human Other status now central to the functioning of the first secularizing behaviour - regulatory schema or motivational apparatus in human history. Whilst with the rapid decimation of the indigenous Arawaks of the Caribbean Islands, Africans bought and sold as "trade goods" were now made to fill the same slot in the behaviour regulatory schema, as they were made to fill a parallel slot in the system of forced labor. As such they too, as Caliban's women, are reduced to having no will or desire that has not been prescribed by Prospero/Miranda in the name of the existential interest of the population-group for whom the "images" of Prospero/Miranda, stand. Given that the idealization/negation of both groups is effected precisely by the dominant group's imposition of its own mode of volition and desire (one *necessarily* generated from the *raison d'etre* of its group—existential interests) upon the dominated; as well as by its stable enculturating of the latter by means of its theoretical models (epistemes) and aesthetic fields, generated from its increasingly hegemonic and secularizing systems of meanings. In consequence if, before the sixteenth century, what Irigaray terms as *"patriarchal discourse"* had erected itself on the "silenced ground" of women, from then on, the new primarily silenced ground (which at the same time now enables the partial liberation of Miranda's hitherto stifled speech), would be that of the majority population-groups of the globe—all signified now as the "natives" (Caliban's) to the "men" of Prospero and Fernando, with Miranda becoming both a co-participant, if to a lesser *derived* extent, in the power and privileges generated by the empirical supremacy of her own population; and as well, the beneficiary of a mode of privilege unique to her, that of being the metaphysically invested and "idealized" object of desire for all classes (Stephano and Trinculo) and all population-groups (Caliban)[39].

This therefore is the dimension of the contradictory relation of Sameness and Difference, of orthodoxy and heresy which these Caribbean critical essays must necessarily, if still only partially, inscribe, and do inscribe with respect to the theory/discourse of feminism, (as the latest and last variant of the Prospero/Miranda ostensibly "universally" applicable meaning and discourse-complex); the relation of *sameness and difference* which is expressed in the diacritical term *"womanist"*. And if we are to understand the necessity for such an *other* term (projected both from the perspective of Black American women (U.S.) and from that of the "native" women intelligentsia of the newly independent Caribbean ex-slave polities,) as a term which, whilst developing a fully articulated theoretical/interpretative reading model of its own, nevertheless, serves, diacritically to draw attention to the insufficiency of all existing theoretical interpretative models, both to "voice" the hitherto silenced ground of the experience of "native" Caribbean women and Black American women as the ground of Caliban's woman, and to de-code the system of meanings of that other discourse, beyond Irigaray's patriarchal one, which has imposed this mode of silence for some five centuries, as well as to make thinkable the possibility of a new "model" projected from a new "native" standpoint, we shall need to translate the variable "race", which now functions as the intra-feminist marker of difference, impelling the dually "gender/beyond gender" readings of these essays, out of the epistemic 'vrai'[40] of our present order of "positive knowledge"[41], its consolidated field of meanings and order-replicating hermeneutics. Correspondingly, since this order/field is transformative, generated from our present purely secular definition of the human on the model of a natural organism, with, in consequence this organism's "ends" therefore being ostensibly set extra-humanly, by "nature", i.e. Haeckel's monism, neo-classical economics Natural Scarcity, Marx's "materialist" imperative of the "mode of production", Feminism's … bio-anatomical "universal" identity[42], we shall need to move beyond this founding definition, not merely to *another* alternative one, non-consciously put in place as our present definition, but rather to a frame of reference which parallels the "demonic models" posited by physicists who seek to conceive of a vantage point outside the space-time orientation of the humuncular observer. This would be, in our case, in the context of our specific socio-human realities, a "demonic model" outside the "consolidated field" of our present mode of being/feeling/knowing, as well as of the multiple discourses, their regulatory systems of meaning and interpretative "readings", through which alone these modes, as varying expressions of human "life," including ours, can effect their respective autopeosis *as such* specific modes of being. The possibility of such a vantage point, we argue, towards which the diacritical term "womanist" (i.e. these readings as both gender, and not-gender readings, as both Caribbean/Black nationalist and not-Caribbean/Black nationalist, Marxian and not-Marxian readings)[43] point, can only be projected from a "demonic model" generated, parallely to the vantage point/demonic model with which the laity-intelligentsia of Western Europe effected the first rupture of humans with their/our supernaturally guaranteed narrative schemas of origin,[44] from the situational "ground" or slot of Caliban's woman, and therefore of her systemic behaviour regulatory role or function as the ontological "native/nigger", within the motivational apparatus by means of which our present model of being/definition-of-the-human is given dynamic "material" existence, rather than from merely the vantage point of her/our gender, racial, class or cultural being.[45] In other words, if the laity intelligentsia of Western Europe effected a mutation by calling in question its own role as the ontological Other of "natural fallen flesh" to the theologically idealized, post-baptismal Spirit, (and as such incapable of attaining to any knowledge of, and mastery over, either the physical processes of nature or its own social reality, except such knowledge was mediated by the then hegemonic Scholastic *theological* interpretative model,) and by calling this role in question so as to clear the ground for its own self-assertion which would express itself both in the political reasons-of-state humanism (enacted in *The Tempest*), as well as in the putting in place of the *Studia Humanitatis* (i.e. as the self-study of "natural man"), and in the laying of the basis for the rise of the natural sciences,[46] it is by a parallel calling in question of our *'native'*, and more ultimately, nigger women's role as the embodiment to varying degrees of an ostensible "primal" human nature. As well, challenging our role as a new 'lay' intelligentsia ostensibly unable to know and therefore to master our present sociosystemic reality, (including the reality of our "existential weightlessness" as an always "intellectually indentured"[47] intelligentsia), except as mediated by the theoretical models generated from the vantage point of the "normal" intelligentsia, clears the ground for a new self-assertion. This time, as one which brings together the human and natural sciences in a new projected science of the human able to constitute *demonic models* of congition *outside* what Lemuel Johnson calls, in one of the essays in this collection, the always non-arbitrary pre-prescribed, "designs of the measuring rod" in whose parameters both our present hegemonic interpretative and anti-interpretative models are transformatively generated; one able in fact to take these designs of the measuring rod and their "privileged texts" as the object of our now conscious rather than reactive processes of cognition[48]. In effect, rather than only voicing the "native" woman's hitherto silenced voice[49] we shall ask: What is the systemic function of her own silencing, both as women and, more totally, as "native" women? Of what mode of speech is that absence of speech both as women (masculinist discourse) and as 'native' women (feminist discourse) as imperative function?

The larger issue then is of the ontological difference and of our *human* and *"native"* human subordination, hitherto non-conscious, to the governing behaviour-regulatory codes of symbolic "life" and "death." It is an issue which calls for a second self-assertion able to respond to the new metaphysical imperative, not now of altering nature, but of altering our systems of meanings, and their privileged texts, and, therefore, of abolishing Elsa Goveia's ascriptions of "race" and "wealth" (whose *particularisms* work to contradict the *universalism* of one-(wo)man,-one-vote), as well as those other ascriptions of the same totemic set which function to the same effect, i.e. culture, through the mechanism of literary scholarship's "idealized" (Cary Nelson) canonism,[50] religion, an allegedly "natural" erotic preference[51] as well as that of gender. The issue then of a second epistemological mutation—based on the new metaphysical imperative of the now conscious alterability of our governing codes, their modes of ontological difference and their rule-governedly generated behaviour-regulatory meanings, together with their always non-arbitrary "designs"[52] of interpretative readings—one able to complete the *partial* epistemological mutation of the first which ushered in our modern age as well as that first process of the non-conscious secularization of human modes/models of being, of whose order-maintaining discourses, the doubly silenced "ground" of Caliban's "native" woman, was a central meaning-coherence function; and of whose *incomplete epistemological mutation*, both the gender hierarchy of the ostensible equality of our symbolic contract, as well as of the "hard and uncomfortable life" of the, since the 1960's, now politically empowered Caribbean black and poor majority as noted by, and finely imaged in, Christine Craig's complex figure *Crow*, as both young woman metaphysically invested as the negative of normative object-desire, and old woman/Carrion bird with the garbage dump as food for both), as well as then, of the "hard and uncomfortable" life of all those who inhabit the global archipelagoes of hunger in the midst of a new technologically produced surfeit of global abundance,[53] are an imperative effect and consequence.⁵⁴ That is, the paradoxical effect of that first, incomplete, and now objectified, secularizing epistemological mutation:

> "There are phases of objectivation" Blumenberg wrote, "that loose themselves from their original motivation (*the science and technology of the later phases of the modern age provide* a stupendous example of this); and to bring them back to their human function, to subject them again to man's (the human's) purposes in relation to the world, *requires* an unavoidable counter-exertion. The medieval system ended in such a phase of objectification that has become autonomous, of hardening that is insulated from what is human. What is here called 'self-assertion' is the counter-move of retrieving the lost motives, of a new concentration on man's (human) self-interest."⁵⁵

The appeal of the Abeng is therefore to the larger issue of retrieving the lost motives of our "native" human self-interest, and, increasingly degraded in our planetary environment, of our human self-interest. This issue, which clearly calls for a second counter-exertion, has been initiated, in its first transitional phase by these diacritically "womanist" essays as the counter exertion of a "native women" intelligentsia, who, by refusing the "water-with berries" strategy sets, of all our present hegemonic, theoretical models in their "pure" forms, based on their isolated "isms", has enabled the move, however preliminary, on to the "demonic" and now unsilencing trans-"isms" ground of Caliban's woman. This terrain, when fully occupied, will be that of a new science of human discourse, of human "life" beyond the "master discourse" of our governing" privileged text", and its sub/versions. Beyond Miranda's meanings.

Notes

1. Editors' note: This is the first section of a much longer manuscript which could not be included here in its entirety, generated, in part, by our request for this afterword.
2. See A.T. de Nicolas, 'Notes on the Biology of Religion,' *Journal of Social and Biological Structures* 3, no. 2 (April 1980): 225.
3. I have put forward this proposal in two earlier essays, but most fully in the second. See Wynter, 'On Disenchanting Discourse: Minority Literature and Beyond,' *Cultural Critique, The Nature and Context of Minority Discourse* 11, no. 7, Fall 1987.
4. See Hans Blumenberg, *The Legitimacy of the Modern Age* (Cambridge, Mass.: M.I.T. Press, 1983).
5. See Michel Foucault, *The Order of Things: An Archaeology of the Human Sciences* (New York: Vintage Books, 1973).
6. For the concept of 'participatory epistemology' see Francisco Varela, *Principles of Biological Autonomy* (New York: North Holland Series in General Systems Research, 1979).
7. At the theoretical level 'feminist' theory developed on the basis of its rupture with the purely economic and class-based theory of Marxism, thereby calling into question both the 'universalisms' of Marxian Proletarian identity and of the Liberal humanist 'figure of man.'
8. See Blumenberg, where he discusses the function of Darwinian thought in this articulation of the concept of ends set by nature and by evolution.
9. See her *Speculum of the Other Woman* (Ithaca: Cornell University Press, 1985), 15.
10. See Anthony Pagden, *The Fall of Natural Man: The American Indian and the Origins of Comparative Ethnology* (Cambridge, England: Cambridge UP, 1982).
11. See Levi-Strauss, C. *Totemism* (Harmondsworth: Penguin, 1969).
12. See J.F. Danielli, 'Altruism: The Opium of the People,' *Journal of Social and Biological Structures* 3, no. 2 (April 1980): 87–94.
13. See D. Halliburton, 'Endowment, Enablement, Entitlement: Toward a Theory of Constitution,' in *Literature and the Question of Philosophy*, ed. A.J. Cascari (Baltimore: Johns Hopkins University Press, 1986) where he develops this concept of 'endowment.'
14. A play on the Deridean concept of 'difference' where the temporal dimension is replaced by the stratifying/status dimension, making use of the concept of 'deferent' behaviour which functions to inscribe difference, and to constitute 'higher' and 'lower' ranking.
15. See in this respect, the book by Jacob Pandian, *Anthropology and the Western Tradition: Towards an Authentic Anthropology* (Prospect Heights, Illinois: Waveland Press Inc., 1985).

16. See for an excellent analysis of this concept, the book by Claude Jenkins, *The Social Theory of Claude Levi-Strauss* (London: The MacMillan Press Ltd., 1979).
17. See her essay, 'The Social Framework,' in *Savacou*, Kingston, Jamaica, 1970.
18. The analogy here is to the always *deferent* relation of the wife-taker category to that of the wife-giver category.
19. See Anthony Pagden, op. cit. for an analysis of this intellectual process which was to lay the basis of today's concept of 'international' law.
20. See my discussion of this concept/discourse which is founding to our present order of knowledge in the Cultural Critique essay already cited.
21. See Pagden, op. cit.
22. The reference here is to the 'freeplay' concept of the deconstructionists. As is clear, our counter concept is that the parameters of interpretation are always set, in the last analysis, by what we develop later as the mode of ontological difference and its related code of symbolic 'life' and 'death.'
23. See Cary Nelson, 'Against English: Theory and the Limits of the Discipline in Profession,' 1987, M.L.A. Publication.
24. The analogy here is to the Christian theological concept of the non-elect by predestination.
25. See William Shakespeare, *The Tempest*, ed. R. Langbaum, (New York: Signet Classic, 1964).
26. This code, developed from Aquinas' formulation of an ontological natural law able to be detached from its Christological base, will be central to the later mutation to the secular orders of things.
27. See her book, *La Parole des Femmes: Essais sur Les Romancieres des Antilles des Langues Françaises* (Paris: Harmattan, 1979).
28. Europe's expropriation of the lands of the Americas initiated a land/labor ratio of a new unprecedented extent. Both the encomienda and hacienda and the plantation institution were the answer to this vast 'enclosure system' by which the category of 'native labor' and 'native being' came into existence.
29. See the essay by Arnold Davidson where he quotes Freud's point about the plasticity of the 'sexual instinct' and how it can be easily 'soldered' on to specific objects of desire. See his essay, 'How to do the History of Psychoanalysis: A Reading of Freud's *Three Essays On The Theory of Sexuality in Critical Inquiry*,' 13:2 Winter 1987.
30. See the illuminating point made by Clarisse Zimra in her essay in this collection.
31. The proposal here is that the Spirit/Flesh opposition of medieval Europe functioned as the motivational mechanism of desire/aversion by means of which the secular laity were made desirous of attaining to being only through the baptismal model of medieval Christianity. See Walter Ullman's book, *Medieval Foundations of Renaissance Humanism* (Ithaca, New York: Cornell University Press, 1977).
32. The roots of contemporary racism are sited in this system of speculative thought that would be 'materialized' in the *encomienda* and the *plantation* systems, since these institutions were to be based on this new secular post-Christian mode of legitimation.
33. Recent work by political scientists have begun to focus on the parallels between the discourses by means of which the New World Indians were expropriated and those by which the Cromwellian conquest and partial occupation of Ireland were also legitimated i.e., by the projection of a 'by nature difference' between the dominant and the subordinated population groups.
34. In this respect see the original and illuminating essay by James F Danielli, 'Altruism and the Internal Reward System or The Opium of the People,' *Journal of Social and Biological Structures*, 1980, 3.
35. Even where in the case of the Ayatollah Khomeini, and Islamic fundamentalism this might seem not to be so, the religious tenets of Islam are now a *function* of a religious-nationalist ideology adapted from the West's process of secularization.
36. This then legitimates his subordination to 'rational nature' incarnated in Prospero.
37. Coined on the model of transcendental, but this time, although also extra-humanly, but from below.
38. The concept of a 'semantic closure principle' is borrowed from the biologist Howard Pattee's description of the integrative functioning of the cell. The proposal is that human orders *should* function according to analogous principles. See Howard H. Pattee, 'Clues from Molecular Symbol Systems,' *Signed and Spoken Language: Biological Constraints on Linguistic Forms*, ed. U. Bellugi and M. Studdert-Kennedy (Berlin: Verlag Chemie, 1980), 261–74, and 'Laws and Constraints, Symbols and Languages,' in *Towards a Theoretical Biology*, ed. C.H. Waddington (Edinburgh: University of Edinburgh Press, 1972), 248–58.

39. The sailors' dream too, is to be king on the island and to marry Miranda.
40. The term is used by Foucault in his talk, *The Order of Discourse* given in December 1970 and published as an Appendix of the *Archaeology of Knowledge*, trans. A.M. Sheridan-Smith (New York: Harper and Row, 1972). Here Foucault notes that Mendel's findings about genetic heredity were not hearable at first because they were not within the '*vrai*' of the discipline at the time.
41. In *The Order of Things*, Foucault points out that because 'Man' is an object of 'positive knowledge' in Western culture, he cannot be an 'object of science.'
42. 'Women' can only be co-identified as a universal *political* category on the paradoxical basis of their/our shared bio-anatomical identity.
43. The force of the term *womanist* lies in its revelation of a perspective which can only *be partially* defined by any of the definitions of our present hegemonic theoretical models.
44. With respect to the functioning of the narrative of origins in human orders, including the 'evolutionary' narrative of origin of our own which also functions as 'replacement material for genesis,' see Glyn Isaacs, 'Aspects of Human Evolution,' *Evolution From Molecules to Men*, ed. D.S. Bendall (Cambridge, New York: CUP, 1983), 509–43.
45. The contradiction here is between 'cultural nationalism' i.e., the imperative to revalue one's gender, class, culture and to constitute one's literary counter-canon, and the scientific question. What is the function of the 'obliteration' of these multiple perspectives? What role does this play in the stable bringing into being of our present human order?
46. See Walter Ullman, op. cit. and Hans Blumenberg, op. cit. as well, as Kurt Hubner, *The Critique of Scientific Reason* (Chicago: The University of Chicago Press, 1983), for the linkage of the rise of the natural sciences to the overall secularizing movement of humanism.
47. The term is Henry Louis Gates's, and is central to the range of his work. See for example, his use of a variant of this term ('interpretative indenture') in his essay, 'Authority (White) Power and the (Black) critic,'*Cultural Critique*, no. 7 (Fall 1987): 19–46.
48. That is, cognition outside of the parameters prescribed by our participatory epistemology (See Francisco Vorela, op. cit.) or the World View, integrative of all orders, including our own.
49. In a paper given as a panel presentation at the recent 1988 March West Coast Political Science Conference, Kathy Ferguson of the University of Hawaii pointed to the contradiction, for feminist deconstructionists, between' the imperative of a fixed gender identity able to facilitate a unifying identity from which to 'voice' their presence, and the deconstructionist program to deconstruct gender's oppositional categories.
50. The attack on the master canon, and the thrust to devise new canons by hitherto marginalized intelligentsia groups allow us to speak of canonism, as one of the ordering '*isms*'.
51. The stigmatization of homoerotic preference, plays a key role in the projection of the idea of 'natural' preference, which is founding to the inferential logic of the discourse of economics.
52. Again the point here is that interpretative readings occur within parameters set by the governing code, and are never arbitrary, even if the governing codes are.
53. The problem that faces the world is one of distribution. But if as we argue, economic distribution is a function, in the last instance of the *integration* of our present order, then the contradiction between the global surpluses of food enabled by the Green Revolution and the spread of massive world hunger reported by world agencies is an effect, not of an economic imperative, but of an order-maintaining one, i.e., of the imperative of its 'altruistic' integration.
54. In *The Tempest*, Caliban accuses Prospero of having given him 'water with berries' and stroked him when the latter arrived, thereby getting Caliban to show where the streams and food sources on the island were. The proposal is that all theoretical models function both as 'knowledge' and as the water-with berries strategy sets of specific groups. I have developed this more fully in a paper – *Why We Cannot Save Ourselves in a Woman's Manner: Towards a Caribbean World View*, to be presented at the First Conference of Caribbean Women Writers and Scholars, and hosted by the *Black Studies Dept.* at Wellesley College.
55. The proposal here is since all the *isms* constitute a totemic system or set, the attempt to abolish any of these as an isolated ism is everywhere a 'strategy set' of the specific group for whom, as in the case of Duvalierism for the new Haitian black middle class, the abolition of a specific *ism* will be empowering. See with respect to feminism, Moraga and Anzaldua, op. cit.

"What's Identity Got to do with It?"
Rethinking Identity in Light of the *Mati* Work in Suriname

Gloria Wekker

> *At minimum, all social construction approaches adopt the view that physically identical sexual acts may have varying social significance and subjective meaning depending on how they are defined and understood in different cultures and historical periods. Because a sexual act does not carry with it a universal social meaning, it follows that* the relationship between sexual acts and sexual identities is not a fixed one, *and it is projected from the observer's time and place to others at great peril.*
>
> —Vance 1989:18, emphasis mine

The concept of "homosexual identity" plays a privileged and tenacious part in discussions about homosexual behavior (cf. D'Emilio 1984; Vance 1989; De Cecco and Elia 1993). The concept is used as a particularly powerful mediator of gay and lesbian behaviors. Sometimes these discussions are limited to the Western world, but the concept is also, apparently without much hesitation, used in cross-cultural contexts. Even though in constructionist approaches the relationship between sexual acts and sexual identities is thought to be variable, scholars often do not question the notion of homosexual (or homoerotic) identity in itself nor its ubiquitousness (cf. Vance's statement quoted above; Newton and Walton 1984; Lewin 1995). Whether "homosexual identity" is conceived of as an essentialist category, with biological and physiological influences preceding cultural ones and setting limits on the latter, or as a constructionist concept privileging social and cultural experiences, it is striking that a concept used with such frequency in the literature is not subjected to more reflection. However the concept is conceived, it apparently speaks to deeply ingrained, ethnopsychological notions in Western subjects that the core of our being, our essence, the privileged site in which the truth about ourselves and our social relationships is to be found, corresponds to something that we call (homo-)sexual identity (Foucault 1981; Kulick 1995). What has generally been lacking is an exploration of the implication and embeddedness of "identity" in hegemonic, Western thought, even if in feminist and "queer" versions. While it is not my intention here to give a thorough "reading" of the history of this concept in either Western folk wisdom or in various disciplinary domains, I think it generally will be agreed upon that "identity" carries heavy connotations of stasis, "core, unitary character," that which is immutable about a person, whether this core is ascribed to inborn or to learned characteristics (Geertz 1984; Weedon 1987; Kondo 1990). It will be my contention in this article that students of sexuality should problematize the notion of "identity" in order to avoid circuitous reasoning and premature closure.

By way of focusing on a widespread institution among Creole[1] working-class women in Paramaribo, Suriname, called the *mati* work, I want to present a differently conceived sexual configuration that does not posit a fixed notion of "sexual identity." Mati, although by no means a monolithic category, are women who engage in sexual relationships with men and with women, either simultaneously or consecutively, and who conceive of their sexual acts in terms of behavior. In focusing on female mati, I embark on a much overdue project in a Caribbean context: "to theorize from the point of view and contexts of marginalized women not in terms of victim status or an essentialized identity but in terms that push us to place women's agency, their subjectivities and collective consciousness, at the center of our understandings of power and resistance" (Alexander 1991:148).

First, I will describe the mati work within its historical and sociocultural setting, and I will consider how this "unruly sexuality" relates to dominant, heterosexual patterns in the same context. Second, I want to defend the claim that conceptualizing homosocial bonding and homoerotic behavior among women in this Third World context as "identity" inscribes and reproduces hegemonic Western analytical categories. Third, and more generally, I will address the question of how to proceed fruitfully in theorizing homoerotic behavior cross-culturally, without radically distorting emic realities. It is vital to put the genesis of "homosexual identity under capitalism" (D'Emilio 1984) into cultural and historical perspective as just one possible configuration among many, without universal validity. Thinking about homosexuality should start from the realization that "homosexualities"[2] cross-culturally have in common sexual acts between same-gendered people, but these acts are also and importantly different and contextually conceived in multiple ways.

The Mati Work

I was alerted to the mati work by the literature while doing research for my master's thesis in the early 1980s. The institution is first mentioned in 1912, when a high Dutch government official, Schimmelpenninck van der Oye, on a fact-finding mission concerning the health situation of the population in the colony of Suriname, deplores the widespread occurrence of the "sexual communion between women, the *mati play*" (Ambacht 1912). Another observer in the 1930s remarks upon the fact that "the unusual relationships among women in Suriname...were not dependent on social rank, intellectual development, race or country of origin" (Comvalius 1935). In the course of this century, several studies—mostly by men, occasionally by white women— have dealt with "the unusual relationships between women" (Herskovits 1936; Buschkens 1974; Janssens and van Wetering 1985; van Lier 1986). My curiosity about the phenomenon was piqued by these descriptions, and I decided to devote my doctoral research to the mati work.

From January 1990 through July 1991, I explored how working-class Creole women construct themselves sexually in Paramaribo, Suriname.[3] As a black sociocultural anthropologist, born in Suriname and trained in the Netherlands and the United States, my interest in local constructions of subjectivity, gender, and sexuality clearly bespeaks issues in my own situated life (Wekker 1992b). In the course of my sexually coming-of-age in Amsterdam, the Netherlands, during the seventies, I noticed that there were at least two models available to me on how to be a woman who loved other women. There was a dominant model, mostly engaged in by white, middle-class women, in which the rhetoric of "political choice," feminist chauvinism, conformity between partners along a number of dimensions, including socioeconomic status and age, and predominantly childlessness, played central parts. And there was a subjugated model, of which I discerned merely the contours at the time but which I later learned to identify as the mati work. The latter was lived by working-class Afro-Surinamese women, who often differed greatly in age from their women partners, typically had children, and apparently maintained their ties with men, either as husbands, lovers, friends, or sons. My awareness of these two models, which did not seem to come together on any shared ground, made me increasingly aware of the situatedness and sociocultural construction of my own

(Eurocentric) sexuality and its axioms, which I had taken for granted. When at a later stage I chose to occupy various sexual sites that are distinguished within a Western universe, it became clear that significant amounts of mental, psychological, and social work were necessary, both within myself and within the predominantly middle-class (white and black) circles in which I moved to obtain any kind of credibility for those choices. My periodically returning structural malaise in applying Western sexual labels (hetero-, homo-, and bisexuality) to myself while failing to "identify" with them was a major impetus to engage in this particular research. As Reinharz, among others, has noted "in feminist research 'the problem' frequently is a blend of an intellectual question and a personal trouble" (1992:258).

Most of the authors, who have dealt with the mati work, locate its emergence at the beginning of this century, when men were frequently absent from the city due to migrant labor as gold diggers and balata bleeders in the interior of Suriname. Ironically, these authors explain the widespread occurrence of the mati work among women by the absence of men, either in a strict numerical sense or in a psychological or emotional sense. I have interpreted Creole working-class women's sexual behaviors by focusing on the accounts women themselves give of them, while locating them within an African-American diasporic framework. It should be clear that when talking about the mati work, I am not referring to a recent or a marginal phenomenon. In contradistinction to the periodization most students of the mati work give, I have argued that there is no good reason to assume that it was not already present from, possibly, the time of the Middle Passage and the beginning of the colony in the seventeenth century. Although it is, of course, impossible to obtain reliable quantitative data on the occurrence of the mati work in Paramaribo in the past or today, it is clear for those who have eyes to see (the symbolic behaviors) and ears to hear (the powerful, metaphorical language mati speak to each other) that it is widespread in the working class. I have suggested that three out of four working-class Creole women will be engaged in it at some point in their lives. There is no significant stigma attached to the mati work in a working-class environment. The longevity, tenacity, and vitality of the mati work are striking, given the fact that I first "saw" the mati work in Amsterdam—after large communities of Surinamese had migrated to the metropolis at the time of independence (1975)—without being fully cognizant of what it was I saw.

Although there is a comparable, yet less institutionalized, less visible, and less widely accepted, phenomenon also called mati work among Creole men, in this contribution I will focus exclusively on Creole, working-class women. While some mati, especially older women who have borne and raised their children, do not have sex with men anymore, other, younger mati have a variety of arrangements with men, such as marriage, concubinage, or a visiting relationship. Women's relationships with women mostly take the form of visiting relationships, although a minority of female partners with their children shares a household. These varied arrangements are made possible by the circumstance that most Creole working-class women own or rent their own houses and are single heads of households. Mati thus form part of and actually continually "cross over" in a dual sexual system, which comprises an opposite-gendered and a same-gendered arena. I will come back to this sexual system in more detail later.

I Am a Gold Coin

The most frequent response working-class women gave me when I asked them to name a proverb that most closely expressed how they saw themselves, was "I am a gold coin." Creole culture, like other Black cultures in the diaspora, abounds with verbal arts: *odo* (proverbs), riddles, stories, word games, and songs. Blacks formulated odo during slavery as a running commentary on their everyday experience, and many odo bespeak a woman's everyday reality (Wekker 1997). "I am a gold coin" is a clipped version of an odo, used by insiders who often only need the first three or four words to understand what is being referred to. The entire odo goes like this: *"Mi na gowt' monni, m'e waka na alasma anu, ma mi n'e las' mi waarde"* ("I am a gold coin, I pass through all hands, but I do not lose my value"). It expresses with precision, yet characteristic indirection, some important features of the (sexual) universe Creole working-class women inhabit. An analysis of the odo gives important insights into this universe, while it simultaneously contradicts some of the most frequent, hegemonic explanations of social and gender patterns in the Caribbean.

The entire odo points to working-class women's adherence to a value structure in which middle-class values like legal marriage, monogamy, the heterosexual contract, one man fathering all one's children are designated as irrelevant to their reality. In effect, working-class women (whether exclusively involved with men, women, or both) are saying: It does not matter how many relationships I have had, whether with men or with women. What counts is how I carry myself through life, as a mother, with dignity, (self-) respect, and savvy, all of which characterize a *dyaya uma* (a mature woman, who knows how to take care of business). This autonomous set of values, found in the working class, runs counter to such a concept as "the lower-class value stretch" (Rodman 1971), which implies that working-class black people stretch middle-class values like monogamy and marriage, until their own practices can be said to fall within middle-class parameters.

My (African-American) understanding of the mati work and the alternative value structure in which it is embedded also flies in the face of Wilson's "respectability and reputation" paradigm (1969). Wilson stipulates that Afro-Caribbean working-class women are the bearers and perpetuators of inegalitarian, Eurocentric "respectability" due to their closer association with the master class during slavery as concubines and domestic slaves. Afro-Caribbean men, on the other hand, are said to subscribe to the egalitarian value system of "reputation," an indigenous counterculture based on the ethos of equality and rooted in personal as opposed to social worth. As I have shown elsewhere, Creole women participate fully in the local reputation system through their leadership roles in Winti, spirit possession, prophecy and healing, the significance and desirability of motherhood, their oral skills, and their entrepreneurial, political, and organizational roles (Wekker 1992b, 1997). Creole women have been and are central to cultures rooted in the tradition of slave resistance, which emerged in response to colonialism and the plantation system and which continued later in opposition to hegemonic, middle-class value patterns. My understanding of the frequency and openness of the phenomenon builds on West African heritage, the "grammatical principles" (Mintz and Price 1992) surrounding selfhood, gender, and sexuality, which Surinamese slaves elaborated upon under a specific constellation of historical, demographic, and cultural-political circumstances (Wekker 1992b). In addition, there are strong reasons to believe that slave women in other parts of the Caribbean developed comparable forms of relating to each other (Lorde 1983; Silvera 1992), pointing to the resiliency of the West African cultural heritage.

On a final note, the odo flatly denies the heterosexist representations of Caribbean women, encapsulated in the concept most widely used (and abused) to explain Caribbean family patterns and gender relations: matrifocality. The gendered sexual images that can be culled from the prolific literature on matrifocality is that men are sexually hyperactive, high performers, while women wait around patiently and pitifully for the hunter to bestow his favors upon them. So far, it has apparently been extremely difficult for (mostly male, heterosexual?) anthropologists to conceive that women did not wait around but took responsibility for orchestrating their own sexual pleasures.

Multiplicitous Subjectivities

Analyzing the parts of the odo "I am a gold coin," we first find an identification with *gold*. By inserting this adjective, women indicate that they consider themselves inherently worthy and valuable, which is symbolized by the allusion to the most desirable, durable, and precious good available in Surinamese society. Furthermore, gold is wanted to adorn and placate instantiations of the multiplicitous self as it is envisioned within the framework of the Afro-Surinamese Winti folk religion. Unlike the Western version of the subject as "unitary, authentic, bounded, static, trans-situational" (Geertz 1984), the self in an Afro-Surinamese working-class universe is conceptualized as multiplicitous, malleable, dynamic, contextually salient. Winti builds deeply upon West African "grammatical principles" (Mintz and Price 1992) and pervades virtually all aspects of life, from before birth to beyond death. Within this framework there is a relatively egalitarian gender ideology, in which both men and women are thought to be composed of male and female *winti*, gods. Also, importantly, both men and women are deemed to be full sexual subjects, with their own desires and own possibilities to act on these desires. Sexual fulfillment per se is considered important, healthy, and joyous, while the gender of one's object choice is regarded as less important. The following quote comes from an eighty-four-year-old mati, Misi Juliette Cummings, a retired market woman, who has had a variety of relationships with men in her life. She bore twelve children, seven of whom are alive today. The "apples of her eye," throughout her long life, were definitely women:

> "*Mi, noit' mi ben wan' trow, ef' mek' verbontu nanga man*[4] [I never wanted to marry or "be in association with a man"]. *Mi yeye no ben wan' de ondro man* [My "soul"/ "I" did not want to be under a man]. Some women are like that. I am somebody who was not *hebzuchtig* [greedy] on a man, *mi yeye ben wan' de nanga umasma* [my "soul," "I," wanted to be with women]. It is your "soul" that makes you so. It is more equal when you are with a woman; the same rights you have, I have too. (Wekker 1992b:284)

In this quote Misi Juliette demonstrates some of the different instantiations of "I": in referring to herself she talks about *mi* (I) and *mi yeye* (my "soul'/I) wanting to be with women. *Yeye* refers to a decisive component of "I," made up of a male and a female God, both of which accompany the individual from birth (Wekker 1992b). An emic explanation of the mati work takes into account that one of the Gods, making up the *yeye*, is a male God, an Apuku, who desires women. This God, who is strong and jealous, cannot bear to see his child, the woman, involved on a long-term basis with a real flesh-and-blood male. Thus a mati is conceptualized as a woman, part of whose "I" desires and is sexually active with other women. Since the "I" is conceived as multiple and open, it is not necessary to claim a "truest, most authentic kernel of the self," a fixed "identity" that is attracted to other women. Rather, mati work is seen as a particularly pleasing and joyous activity, not as an identity. Linguistically, this conceptualization of sex as behavior is apparent in the phrase mati use to describe themselves. When pressed about the issue, as I often did in my role of "outsider within" (Hill Collins 1990) asking most impertinent, direct questions, they would say: *M'e mati*, using a verb ("I mati"), instead of: *"Mi na wan mati"* ("I am a mati").

A Dual Sexual System

In a further analysis of the odo "I am a gold coin" the identification with a coin is striking. First, this elicits the obvious connotation of a coin, passing from hand to hand, with its counterpart of women going from one relationship to the next, "trying to find their happiness," as they themselves explain. The analogy between money and women having multiple relationships is made without attaching negative value to it, as the third part of the odo—"but I do not lose my value"—shows.

But there is a second, relatively hidden, meaning to the allusion to money. Far from sovereignly imagining oneself above money, it is the standard by which women measure the seriousness of intent of their male partners: women envision a relatively straightforward exchange relationship between sex and money in their connections with men. As one woman told me, when she was describing an imaginary but, in her eyes, most undesirable and ludicrous outcome of such a cross-gender connection: *"A kon sidon na mi tapu, dan e n'e tya mi sensi kon ... dan m'e law"* ("Then he comes, sits down in my house and doesn't bring me my money, then I must be crazy") (Wekker 1992b:178).

The transactional nature of opposite-gender relationships is by no means an exclusively Afro-Surinamese phenomenon. It is a connection found in divergent urban working-class settings, such as nineteenth- and early twentieth-century white New York (Peiss 1984, 1986), contemporary white American (Rubin 1976), African-American (Liebow 1967; Stack 1974), Nairobian (Nelson 1979), and Jamaican working-class cultures (Harrison 1988). It has, furthermore, been found in white middle-class settings that women tend to make more "pragmatic" choices regarding their mates, "knowing...that economic security is more important than passion" (Peplau and Gordon 1985:264). Working-class women, both mati and women who are exclusively involved with men, by their own accounts, need men to make them children in a system where the epitome of womanhood is motherhood, and they need men's financial contributions to keep their households afloat (Wekker 1992b). Demonstrating one's fertility, by having a large *bere* (literally, belly: children and grandchildren) used to be important to both men and women in a working-class culture that leaves few other avenues for distinguishing oneself. Younger women, in general, do not want to raise large families anymore, but motherhood remains vital. In accounting for their relationships with men, some women, who are embedded in the Afro-Surinamese Winti religion, argue that it is unhealthy for your "insides" not to have sexual communion with men at least once in a while. This argument, again, needs to be understood in the framework of an outlook on subjectivity, embedded within Winti, that stresses the importance of balancing the multiple aspects of the self; male and female "instantiations" of the person need to be satisfied and kept in harmony.

In their relationships with women, mati deploy money in a much less direct way. Although female lovers do exchange money and help each other cope financially, this aspect of the relationship is embedded in a rich flow of reciprocal obligations, which include the sharing of everyday concerns, the raising of children, nurturing, emotional support, and sexual pleasure. Money, as an exchange object for sex, thus plays an independent and outspoken role in relationships with men, but it is part of a more elaborate, a "thicker" stream of exchanges and reciprocal obligations in relationships with women. In fact, the term *work* in mati work implies that there are mutual obligations involved between two female partners. Mati contrast mati work with another modality they call *didon gewoon*, i.e., "just lying down"/"sleeping around," a sexual connection that does not imply rights and obligations toward another woman. *Didon gewoon* is not part of an ongoing relationship but marks an unencumbered, incidental sexual encounter. The rights and obligations in mati work generally involve the (social, psychological, economic) activities that are needed to help one's partner weather life. This may be by going to the doctor with her when she is ill, helping her finance a "crown" year celebration (when she reaches an important, five-yearly birthday), or, as the younger partner in the relationship, by showing one's mati the appropriate, respectful behavior. Most important, mati have sexual obligations toward each other: when one partner feels sexual desire, the other is obliged to satisfy her. It is generally agreed by mati that when a woman's desire is consistently denied by her partner, she may go and seek sexual pleasures with someone else. This may very well spell the demise of the relationship, since few women will tolerate it when their partner openly engages in sex with another woman.

During my research period, I asked several women to reflect on what some of the differences were between being in a sexual relationship with a man or with a woman. My landlady Misi Juliette, the eighty-four-year-old market woman, often explained to me that, "I really did not mind much, when that man [Dorus, the man she had five children with] went to visit other women. Frankly, I often thought: Well, it is better that he goes and harasses them instead of me. I also didn't mind when Coba, her mati, lay down with a man. If she could find a little money with him, why not? But if she slept with another woman, now that was different business!! I did not tolerate it."

In this and other conversations we had, it was abundantly clear that the intensity of Juliette's feelings was entirely focused on Coba, not Dorus, and that jealousy was channeled toward Coba's encounters with other women, not men. It made the socially constructed nature of such "natural" feelings as jealousy vividly clear to me.

The following quote from Lydia de Vrede, a thirty-seven-year-old nurse's aide, mother of five, who is currently married to the father of her last two children, helps to further illustrate these differences:

> I see it like this: love between two women is stronger than between a man and a woman. Maybe emancipated women will tell a man what they like in the bedroom, or tell him: do this or do that! But to satisfy that man, most women will pretend that they have come. But with a woman, you know what you like sexually and so does she, *dus a san' kan law yu ede zodanig, a kan tya' yu go na Kolera* [so the thing can make you so crazy, it may carry you into a mental hospital]. (Wekker, 1992b:283)

Before she was married, Lydia had several relationships with women, but given the jealous nature of her husband, she presently misses having a female lover but finds it impossible to accommodate a woman in her situation.[5] The quote reveals the existence of a dual sexual system, in which different power dynamics between partners obtain. There is an opposite-gendered arena in which masculine values and men are hegemonic. This arena within the working class is fed by an array of societal forces and influences, including inegalitarian middle-class gender arrangements and values, government regulations producing inequalities between men and women in the area of, among others, income,[6] and media and educational institutions transmitting homogenizing, normative, nuclear family contents. Men, because of their stronger economic positions and because they mostly do not carry the exclusive or main financial burden of having to bring up children, have more free-floating capital. As elsewhere in the Caribbean, we find in Suriname an overall picture of a dually segmented labor market, where men are found in the heavier and more profitable sectors of the formal and informal economy, working under better conditions and with higher salaries; women, on the other hand, work in the softer sectors of the economy, for the government, where wages are notoriously low, and in the informal sector (Tjoa 1990; Wekker 1992b). It is through their economically stronger position, however tenuous it may in itself be at times, that men get the upper hand in defining the proceedings of opposite-gender sexual encounters. Within this opposite-gender exchange system, women have less room to maneuver, and even less so within a steadily declining economy and following the adoption of Structural Adjustment Programs. The following account by forty-three-year-old Mildred Jozefzoon, a hairdresser and mother of four children, illustrates some features of her visiting relationship with Johnny Samuel, who is the father of three of her children and who lives with another woman:

> I get 100 or 125 Surinamese guilders from him, a week.[7] Mostly he comes around 11:30 a.m. and needs to be out of my house by 1:00 p.m. He wants it to be quick-quick. The way I feel about

it is that somebody has come to take something away from me and then he leaves. I feel misused, taken in, even though he gives me the money. It goes like this: he takes off his shirt and his trousers, lies down on my bed. Then he wants me to come lie down beside him. Sometimes I sabotage the whole business by being agonizingly slow in taking off my clothes. Sometimes I say I don't feel like it. Then he says: I will make you feel like it. What can I do? He wants it so often and I need the money. (Wekker 1992b:224)

Pertinent in this segment of the sexual system is also that women tend to see each other as competitors for men's favors, and they do not exchange sexual information. Women consistently report an unfavorably skewed sex ratio, i.e., that the number of women far exceeds the number of men, yet what seems more likely to be the case is that the number of men whom women consider *eligible*—i.e., economically viable partners—is rather limited. Yet women still refuse, to varying degrees, to give up their subject status and agency. By elaborating on the concept of *kamraprekti*, chamber (i.e., sexual) obligations, women, whether they are in a permanent or in a more incidental relationship with a man, assert their own standards of fairness concerning the exchange of sexual favors for money; from unfavorable positions women try to adjust and manage the unequal balance of economic power with men (Wekker 1992b).

In the other domain of the dual sexual system, the same-gendered one, women are able to define what their sexual and emotional pleasures are. Life in society as a whole, but most markedly in the working class, is constituted along distinctly homosocial lines; men spend most of their time with other men, while women, whether they mati or not, are more likely to share time, work, attention, nurturing and, possibly, sexual encounters with other women. Since most women spend the greater part of their time in the company of other women, this means that there is no marked difference in the daily, social environments of mati and women who are sexually active only with men. On the contrary, working-class women, regardless of the gender of their sexual partners, frequently mingle and share the same environments. Among older mati we find relationships that have sometimes lasted thirty, forty, or more years. They raise their children together, share everyday concerns and ritual obligations and celebrations: *"Let' anu e was' krukt' anu"* ("the right hand washes the left"), is how older women typically conceive of their bonds with their mati. Traditionally, older women who were in a mati relationship used to wear dresses made out of the same material, *parweri*, but nowadays that is seen less often. Among younger mati there is a lively, sexual culture enacted at parties at people's homes and at *Winti Prey*, outdoor ritual gatherings in the framework of the Winti religion. Flirting and seeking each other out by linguistic, symbolic, and behavioral means have been made into an art form in this universe. By all accounts, sex with women is an important feature of women's lives, and they talk about it, often indirectly and metaphorically, but with obvious gusto (Wekker 1992a,b). One such narrative, which illustrates the joy inherent in sex with women, is told by Milly Pinas, a fifty-six-year-old street sweeper, mother of three children:

I had this lady that I was really infatuated with, Ingrid. She had a steady relationship with Lucia and I was living with a man at the time. One Saturday afternoon, I took the bus to her place, bringing a bag of groceries and some ice-cold beers. She was expecting her lover that afternoon, too, however, so she told me to lock the door from the outside and climb through a window. Pretty soon we were upstairs in bed. We were "stealing," so it had to be fast work. We were almost hitting, when pam-pam-pam, who comes knocking at the door? I was not afraid, I wanted to go on, but Ingrid was shaking. She jumped from the bedroom window unto her neighbor's roof. It turns out that Lucia had a spare key to the house, so she came upstairs. I was sitting on the bed, wearing only a black slip. She said: "Good afternoon." I said: "good afternoon to you, too." Ingrid stayed outside, did not dare to come in. Lucia had been after me for a long time, so we hit on each other right away. (Wekker 1992b:275)

Women friends actively exchange sexual information and young girls are often initiated into the mati world by older women, sometimes explicitly in the form of an apprentice relationship (Wekker 1992a,b). Women often structure their relationships erotically into a "male" and a "female" role, with the male role having more prerogatives, just as in the world out there. These sexual roles are not carved in stone, however, and many women can and do change roles, either in the same relationship or in another one. Economically, mati relationships are more egalitarian than those between men and women. I have also concluded that sexually and emotionally they are more satisfying to many women than their cross-gendered relationships.

If the foregoing analysis of a dual sexual system in the Afro-Surinamese working-class, namely an opposite-gendered and a same-gendered arena, holds any validity, it is to be expected that there will be "leakage" between these two domains. There is considerable overlap in the personnel moving from one part of the system to the other, notably in the persons of mati, and it thus should not be surprising that several features of sexual culture, in the form of shared practices, are held in common in both parts of the system. The importance of motherhood; the polarization of roles within relationships, in a "male" and a "female" counterpart with accompanying role expectations; the existence of patterns of jealousy and violence between partners; the existence of sometimes wide age gaps between partners; and the underlying cosmology as it pertains to personhood and sexual being are all part of mati culture as well as of opposite-gender sexual arrangements. Thus the notion that the same-gendered arena proceeds according to a specific set of ideas, rules, and practices, which is totally distinct and insulated from what takes place in the opposite-gendered domain, cannot be held up.

While it is true that in many Western gay and lesbian sexual arrangements elements of dominant heterosexual culture are evoked, the point I am making here is a different one. From an emic point of view, mati and women exclusively involved with men have more in common with each other than is different between them. Being sexually active and fulfilled is more important than the object of one's passion. Mati are not singled out or stigmatized in a working-class environment nor do they feel the necessity to fight for their liberation or to "come out." Thus to the extent that I have stressed the differences between mati and women relating to men only, I may paradoxically and involuntarily have been highlighting the pernicious tendency of Western, bounded, fixed categories to insert and reproduce themselves in radically different constructions of being a (sexual) person.

What's Identity Got to Do with It?

It is clear that within this Afro-Surinamese working-class setting, there is a radically different conceptualization of personhood and same-gender desire than is customarily the case within a Western frame of reference. I will first briefly address the latter configuration. The troubled Western relationship with homosexuality, naturalized, compartmentalized, medicalized, consecutively made into sin and into the "deepest, truest" expression of the self, of one's identity, is historically and culturally embedded (Foucault 1981; De Cecco and Elia 1993). Whether a homosexual identity is understood as the pure sediment of biological or physiological processes, or whether some kind of interaction between the biological and the cultural is envisioned, or whether primacy is given to sociocultural experiences, the notion of a sexual identity in itself carries deep strands of permanency, stability, fixity, and near-impermeability to change. Furthermore, the mere existence of a sexual identity is usually taken for granted. The static nature of sexual identity is in line with the ways personhood in general is envisioned within a Western universe. Despite much evidence to the contrary, this culture stubbornly persists in the fictive notion that a person has a stable "core" character (Shweder and Bourne 1984):"a bounded, unique, more or less integrated motivational and cognitive universe...organized in a distinctive whole and set contrastively...against other such wholes" (Geertz 1984:126).

It is noteworthy that in most Indo-European languages there is only one way to make statements about the self: the personal pronoun "I." This particular understanding of a person as a bounded, fixed, rational, and self-determining agent is produced and reproduced in and by modern political, legal, social, and aesthetic discourses. Subjectivity has, until recently, implicitly been envisaged along masculine lines, thus leaving femininity no conceptual space but the nonmasculine; femininity is not just different, but in a hierarchically subordinate position to the masculine (Weedon 1987; Haraway 1991). While male sexuality is seen as aggressive and potent, female sexuality is conceptualized as passive and weak, needing to be awakened by a stronger force. Furthermore, one is either heterosexual or homosexual, with bisexuality muddying these clear waters. Dichotomous, either/or, hierarchical thinking characterizes this system.

A Creole universe is characterized by additive, inclusive, both/and thinking (cf. Hill Collins 1990). A person is conceived of as multiple, malleable, dynamic, and possessing male and female elements. Furthermore, all persons are inherently conceived of as sexual beings. A linguistic reflection and construction of this multiple, dynamic conceptualization of personhood is that in Sranantongo, the local creole, there are infinite possibilities to refer to "I" (Wekker 1992b). It is possible to talk about the self in masculine and in feminine terms, in singular and in plural forms, and in terms of third person constructions, regardless of the gender of the speaker. All of these different terms refer to different instantiations of "I."

A human being in this universe is understood to be made up of human and "godly" elements. From conception until death, a person is "carried" and protected by winti, gods. These gods are very near to a person's experience, and they are conceptualized like human beings, possessing the same virtues and vices. A person who is carried by Mama Aisa, the Uppergoddess of the Earth, for example, likes beautiful clothes and jewelry and is caring and nurturing. Both men and women can be carried by Aisa. Some characteristics of a person, such as those that she gets from the gods who accompany her throughout her life, or traits inherited from a biological parent, are seen as permanent, while others are temporary and contextually realized.

Women who engage in the mati work are, as we have seen, thought to be carried by a strong, male god, an Apuku, who is jealous of his "child," the woman, engaging in permanent sexual relationships with flesh-and-blood males. The Apuku is believed to be so strong and demanding that his child will have difficulty relating to men and will be more attracted to other women. An emic explanation of the mati work does not claim a core homosexual identity; rather, the behavior is conceived of as engagement in a pleasant activity, desired and instigated by one particular instantiation of the "I." It is the Apuku who is sexually attracted to women, and there is no emic reason to privilege this instantiation of the "I" above others by making him the decisive, "truest" element of the self. Likewise, when women state that it is good for your "insides" to have sex with men at least once in a while, they are building on an understanding of multiplicitous personhood that temporarily privileges a female instantiation of "I," which desires a man.

It is in keeping with the multiplicity of the "I" that a multiplicitous sexual repertoire was realized in the Creole working-class. There is no significant stigma attached to parts of this repertoire. Girls growing up in Creole working-class neighborhoods are confronted with different sexual choices and engaging in one variety—e.g., the same-gendered one—does not expose the girl to disapproval nor does it predispose her to stay in that part of the sexual system forever. Thus we see women who are alternately or simultaneously active in either part of the system. There are clear economic coordinates associated with their behavior (Wekker 1992b). Conceiving of same-gender sexual behavior embodied in the mati work in terms of "identity" inscribes and reproduces Western thought categories with their legacy of dichotomy, hierarchy, and permanency, thus distorting a phenomenon that is emically experienced in quite different terms.

Theorizing Same-Gender Sexual Behavior Cross-Culturally

Finally, what does all of this mean in light of our ongoing efforts to theorize same-gender sexual behavior cross-culturally? First of all, I hope to have made a case for the critical investigation and bracketing of the concept "homosexual identity." The deeply essentialist strand it often unwittingly introduces hampers rather than facilitates our understanding of the behavior we are trying to understand cross-culturally.

In the second place, emic constructions and explanations of same-gender sexual behavior need to be taken seriously. There is no reason to assume that the Western folk knowledge about sex, which has been elevated into academic knowledge (cf. Lutz 1985), should have any more validity than folk knowledge anywhere else. Feminist anthropology has proven not to be immune against problems that have haunted the discipline from its inception: the exclusion, erasure, or negation of the subjectivity and the critical agency of the colonized, especially women (cf. Mohanty 1991; Harrison 1993).

Third, the cross-cultural study of same-gender sexual behavior should proceed from the realization that "homosexualities" are multiple and manifold, realized in different contexts and charged with different meanings. Clearly, there are some institutional domains within every society that seem crucial in understanding the local constructions of the phenomenon—such as notions of personhood, gender systems—in their ideological and practical dimensions and their crosscutting ties with other domains, such as the economy and religion. It is misleading and self-defeating to talk of same-gender sexual behavior as one single, cross-cultural institution. The use of seemingly innocuous concepts, such as "homosexual identity," contributes to the export of Western categories of thought.

Finally, if in participant observation it is the person of the researcher that serves as the most central and sensitive instrument of research, it behooves those of us who do (cross-cultural) sex research to be transparent, accountable, and reflective about our own sexualities (cf. Kulick and Willson 1995). Awareness of the situatedness and sociocultural construction of our own sexuality and about the different modalities in which we engage with others are only some of the minimal requirements we ought to place on ourselves.

Notes

1. Creoles, the second largest population group in Suriname, are the descendants of slaves and are a mainly urban group. I will alternately call them Creoles, the local designation, and Afro-Surinamese. They distinguish themselves culturally, psychologically, and ethnically and are recognized by others to be distinct from other blacks, Maroons. The latter are the descendants of fugitive slaves who fled the plantations starting in the beginning of the seventeenth century.
2. In the rest of this article I will, sometimes at great and laborious length, avoid speaking of hetero-, homo-, and bisexuality. Because of their embeddedness within radically specific theological, medical, and social discourses, these concepts cast a distorted light on the phenomena I want to analyze here. As I have argued elsewhere (Wekker 1993), the mati work differs from bisexuality in sociohistorical background and embeddedness and in emic understanding.
3. This fieldwork was made possible through grants of the Inter-American Foundation (Washington, DC) and the Institute of American Cultures (UCLA).

4. *Mek' verbontu nanga man,* to make an association with a man, can be used in two ways: (1) It refers to a ritual oath a man and a woman may take not to have other sexual partners. If people do not keep this oath, it is believed that punishment, in the form of sickness or death, will follow. Women also can take this oath together. (2) It refers to the institution, initiated by the Evangelical Brethren Society during slavery when slaves were not allowed to marry, that men and women state publicly in church that they will be faithful to each other.
5. This particular husband's reaction is not the only imaginable one, nor, I would say, the most typical. Working-class men, who are also embedded within Winti and share its weltanschauung, display a variety of reactions toward their wives or lovers engaging in relationships with women. If they, too, understand the need of the woman's "I" to be with other women, many men know and accept it.
6. Functioning as an economic safety net, the government is the largest employer in Suriname, employing about 45% of the total labor force. Of the female labor force (an estimated 40% of the total), 67% work for the government, mostly as cleaners, streetsweepers, and lower office personnel, thus in the lowest salary scales (Tjoa 1990). Furthermore, due to the flagrantly invalid, patriarchal notion that men are heads of households and that women earn merely additional income and have a breadwinner at home, women earn consistently less than men for the same labor.
7. Price index middle of 1991. Since then, inflation has risen rapidly.

References

Alexander, Jacqui. 1991. 'Redrafting Morality: The Postcolonial State and the Sexual Offences Bill of Trinidad and Tobago.' In *Third World Women and the Politics of Feminism,* ed. Chandra Mohanty, Ann Russo, and Lourdes Torres, 133–52. Bloomington: Indiana University Press.
Ambacht. 1912. *Het Ambacht in Suriname.* Rapport van de Commissie Benoemd bij Goevernementsresolutie van 13 januarie 1910, No. 13. Paramaribo.
Buschkens, Willem. 1974. *The Family System of the Paramaribo Creoles.* Verhan-delingen van het Koninklijk Instituut voor Taal-, Land-, en Volkenkunde, no. 71. Gravenhage: Martinus Nijhoff.
Comvalius, Th. 1935. Het Surinaamsch Negerlied: De Banja en de Doe. In *West-Indische Gids* 17:213–20.
De Cecco, John and John Elia. 1993. A Critique and Synthesis of Biological Essentialism and Social Constructionist Views of Sexuality and Gender. In *If You Seduce a Straight Person, Can You make them Gay? Issues in Biological Essentialism and Social Constructionism in Gay and Lesbian Identities,* ed. John De Cecco and John Elia, 1–26. New York: The Haworth Press.
D' Emilio, John. 1984. Capitalism and Gay Identity. In *Powers of Desire: The Politics of Sexuality,* ed. Anne Snitow, Christine Stansell, and Sharon Thompson, 100–13. London: Virago.
Foucault, Michel. 1981. *The History of Sexuality. Vol. 1, An Introduction.* Harmondsworth: Pelican.
Geertz, Clifford. 1984. From the Native's Point of View: On the Nature of Anthropological Understanding. In *Culture Theory: Essays on Mind, Self, and Emotion,* ed. Richard A. Shweder and Robert A. LeVine, 123–36. Cambridge: Cambridge University Press.
Haraway, Donna J. 1991. *Simians, Cyborgs, and Women: The Reinvention of Nature.* London: Free Association Books.
Harrison, Faye. 1988. Women in Jamaica's Informal Economy: Insights from a Kingston Slum. *Nieuwe West-Indische Gids* 62 (3 & 4): 103–28.
———. 1993. Writing against the Grain: Cultural Politics of Difference in the Work of Alice Walker. *Critique of Anthropology* 13 (4): 401–27.
Herskovits, Melville J. and Frances Herskovits. 1936. *Suriname Folk-Lore.* New York: Columbia University Press.
Hill Collins, Patricia. 1990. *Black Feminist Thought: Knowledge, Consciousness, and the Politics of Empowerment.* London: Harper Collins Academic.
Janssens, Mari-José and Wilhelmina van Wetering. 1985. Mati en Lesbiennes, Homoseksualiteit, en Etnische Identiteit bij Creools-Surinaamse Vrouwen in Nederland. *Sociologische Gids* 54 (6):394–415.
Kondo, Dorinne. 1990. *Crafting Selves: Power, Gender, and Discourses of Identity in a Japanese Workplace.* Chicago: University of Chicago Press.
Kulick, Don. 1995. Introduction: The Sexual Life of Anthropologists: Erotic Subjectivity and Ethnographic Work. In *Taboo: Sex, Identity, and Erotic Subjectivity in Anthropological Fieldwork,* ed. Don Kulick and Margaret Willson, 1–28. London: Routledge.
———. and Margaret Willson, eds. 1995. *Taboo: Sex, Identity, and Erotic Subjectivity in Anthropological Fieldwork.* London: Routledge.
Lewin, Ellen. 1995. Writing Lesbian Ethnography. In *Women Writing Culture,* ed. Ruth Behar and Deborah

Gordon, 322–35. Berkeley: University of California Press.
Liebow, Elliot. 1967. *Tally's Corner: A Study of Negro Streetcorner Men*. Boston: Little, Brown.
Lorde, Audre. 1983. *Zami: A New Spelling of My Name*. New York: The Crossing Press.
Lutz, Catherine. 1985. Ethnopsychology Compared to What? Explaining Behavior and Consciousness among the Ifaluk. In *Person, Self and Experience: Exploring Pacific Ethnopsychologies*, ed. Geoffrey White and John Kirkpatrick, 35–79. Berkeley: University of California Press.
Mintz, Sidney and Richard Price. 1992. *The Birth of African-American Culture: An Anthropological Perspective*. Boston: Beacon Press.
Mohanty, Chandra Talpade. 1991. Under Western Eyes: Feminist Scholarship and Colonial Discourses. In *Third World Women and the Politics of Feminism*, ed. Chandra Mohanty, Ann Russo, and Lourdes Torres, 51–80. Chicago: University of Chicago Press.
Nelson, N. 1979. How Women and Men Get By: The Sexual Division of Labour in the Informal Sector of a Nairobi Squatter Settlement. In *Casual Work and Poverty in Third World Cities*, ed. R. Bromley and C. Gerry, 283–302. Chichester, NY: John Wiley.
Newton, Esther and Shirley Walton. 1984. The Misunderstanding: Toward a More Precise Sexual Vocabulary. In *Pleasure and Danger: Exploring Female Sexuality*, ed. Carol Vance, 242–50. Boston: Routledge and Kegan Paul.
Peiss, Kathy. 1984. 'Charity Girls' and City Pleasures: Historical Notes on Working-Class Sexuality, 1880–1920. In *Powers of Desire: The Politics of Sexuality*, ed. Ann Snitow, Christine Stansell, and Sharon Thompson, 74–87. London: Virago.
———. 1986. *Cheap Amusements: Working Women and Leisure in Turn-of-the-Century New York*. Philadelphia: Temple University Press.
Peplau, Letitia and Stephen Gordon. 1985. Women and Men in Love: Gender Differences in Close Heterosexual Relationships. In *Women, Gender, and Social Psychology*, ed. Virginia E. O'Leary, et al. Hillsdale: Lawrence Erlbaum Associates.
Reinharz, Shulamit. 1992. *Feminist Methods in Social Research*. Oxford: Oxford University Press.
Rodman, Hyman. 1971. *Lower-Class Families: The Culture of Poverty in Negro Trinidad*. London: Oxford University Press.
Rubin, Lillian. 1976. *Worlds of Pain: Life in the Working-Class Family*. New York: Basic Books.
Shweder, Richard and Edmund Bourne. 1984. Does the Concept of the Person Vary Cross-Culturally? In *Culture Theory: Essays on Mind, Self, and Emotion*, ed. Richard A. Shweder and Robert A. LeVine. Cambridge: Cambridge University Press.
Silvera, Makeda. 1992. Man Royals and Sodomites: Some Thoughts on the Invisibility of Afro-Caribbean Lesbians. *Feminist Studies* 18 (3): 521–32.
Stack, Carol. 1974. *All Our Kin*. New York: Harper and Row.
Tjoa, Twie. 1990. *Vrouw Zijn in Suriname: Inleiding in het Kader van de Vierde Lustrumviering van de Vereniging van Medici in Suriname*. Paramaribo: ms.
Vance, Carole. 1989. Social Construction Theory: Problems in the History of Sexuality. In *Homosexuality, Which Homosexuality?* Ed. Dennis Altman et al., 13–34. Amsterdam: An Dekker/Schorer.
Van Lier, Rudolf. 1986. *Tropische Tribaden: Een Verhandeling over Homoseksualiteit en Homoseksuele Vrouwen in Suriname*. Dordrecht: Foris Publications.
Weedon, Chris. 1987. *Feminist Practice and Poststructuralist Theory*. Oxford: Basil Blackwell.
Wekker, Gloria. 1992a. 'Girl, It's Boobies You're Getting, No?' Creole Women in Suriname and Erotic Relationships with Children and Adolescents: Some Impressions. *Paidika: The Journal of Paedophilia* 2 (4): 43–48.
———. 1992b. I Am Gold Money (I Pass Through All Hands, But I Do Not Lose My Value): The Construction of Selves, Gender, and Sexualities in a Female, Working-Class, Afro-Surinamese Setting. Ph.D. diss., University of California, Los Angeles.
———. 1993. Mati-ism and Black Lesbianism: Two Idealtypical Expressions of Female Homosexuality in Black Communities of the Diaspora. *Journal of Homosexuality* 24 (3/4): 145–58.
———. 1997. One Finger Does not Drink Okra Soup: Afro-Surinamese Women and Critical Agency. In *Feminist Genealogies, Colonial Legacies, Democratic Futures*, ed. M. Jacqui Alexander and Chandra Mohanty, 330–52. London: Routledge.
Wilson, Peter. 1969. Reputation and Respectability: A Suggestion for Caribbean Ethnology. *Man* (n.s.) 4 (1): 70–84.

Uses of the Erotic: The Erotic as Power[1]

Audre Lorde

There are many kinds of power, used and unused, acknowledged or otherwise. The erotic is a resource within each of us that lies in a deeply female and spiritual plane, firmly rooted in the power of our unexpressed or unrecognized feeling. In order to perpetuate itself, every oppression must corrupt or distort those various sources of power within the culture of the oppressed that can provide energy for change. For women, this has meant a suppression of the erotic as a considered source of power and information within our lives.

We have been taught to suspect this resource, vilified, abused, and devalued within western society. On the one hand, the superficially erotic has been encouraged as a sign of female inferiority; on the other hand, women have been made to suffer and to feel both contemptible and suspect by virtue of its existence.

It is a short step from there to the false belief that only by the suppression of the erotic within our lives and consciousness can women be truly strong. But that strength is illusory, for it is fashioned within the context of male models of power.

As women, we have come to distrust that power which rises from our deepest and nonrational knowledge. We have been warned against it all our lives by the male world, which values this depth of feeling enough to keep women around in order to exercise it in the service of men, but which fears this same depth too much to examine the possibilities of it within themselves. So women are maintained at a distant/inferior position to be psychically milked, much the same way ants maintain colonies of aphids to provide a life-giving substance for their masters.

But the erotic offers a well of replenishing and provocative force to the woman who does not fear its revelation, nor succumb to the belief that sensation is enough.

The erotic has often been misnamed by men and used against women. It has been made into the confused, the trivial, the psychotic, the plasticized sensation. For this reason, we have often turned away from the exploration and consideration of the erotic as a source of power and information, confusing it with its opposite, the pornographic. But pornography is a direct denial of the power of the erotic, for it represents the suppression of true feeling. Pornography emphasizes sensation without feeling.

The erotic is a measure between the beginnings of our sense of self and the chaos of our strongest feelings. It is an internal sense of satisfaction to which, once we have experienced it, we know we can aspire. For having experienced the fullness of this depth of feeling and recognizing its power, in honor and self-respect we can require no less of ourselves.

It is never easy to demand the most from ourselves, from our lives, from our work. To encourage excellence is to go beyond the encouraged mediocrity of our society is to encourage excellence. But giving in to the fear of feeling and working to capacity is a luxury only the unintentional can afford, and the unintentional are those who do not wish to guide their own destinies.

This internal requirement toward excellence which we learn from the erotic must not be misconstrued as demanding the impossible from ourselves nor from others. Such a demand incapacitates everyone in the process. For the erotic is not a question only of what we do; it is a question of how acutely and fully we can feel in the doing. Once we know the extent to which we are capable of feeling that sense of satisfaction and completion, we can then observe which of our various life endeavors bring us closest to that fullness.

The aim of each thing which we do is to make our lives and the lives of our children richer and more possible. Within the celebration of the erotic in all our endeavors, my work becomes a conscious decision – a longed-for bed which I enter gratefully and from which I rise up empowered.

Of course, women so empowered are dangerous. So we are taught to separate the erotic demand from most vital areas of our lives other than sex. And the lack of concern for the erotic root and satisfactions of our work is felt in our disaffection from so much of what we do. For instance, how often do we truly love our work even at its most difficult?

The principal horror of any system which defines the good in terms of profit rather than in terms of human need, or which defines human need to the exclusion of the psychic and emotional components of that need – the principal horror of such a system is that it robs our work of its erotic value, its erotic power and life appeal and fulfillment. Such a system reduces work to a travesty of necessities, a duty by which we earn bread or oblivion for ourselves and those we love. But this is tantamount to blinding a painter and then telling her to improve her work, and to enjoy the act of painting. It is not only next to impossible, it is also profoundly cruel.

As women, we need to examine the ways in which our world can be truly different. I am speaking here of the necessity for reassessing the quality of all the aspects of our lives and of our work, and of how we move toward and through them.

The very word *erotic* comes from the Greek word *eros*, the personification of love in all its aspects – born of Chaos, and personifying creative power and harmony. When I speak of the erotic, then, I speak of it as an assertion of the lifeforce of women; of that creative energy empowered, the knowledge and use of which we are now reclaiming in our language, our history, our dancing, our loving, our work, our lives.

There are frequent attempts to equate pornography and eroticism, two diametrically opposed uses of the sexual. Because of these attempts, it has become fashionable to separate the spiritual (psychic and emotional) from the political, to see them as contradictory or antithetical. "What do you mean, a poetic revolutionary, a meditating gunrunner?" In the same way, we have attempted to separate the spiritual and the erotic, thereby reducing the spiritual to a world of flattened affect, a world of the ascetic who aspires to feel nothing. But nothing is farther from the truth. For the ascetic position is one of the highest fear, the gravest immobility. The severe abstinence of the ascetic becomes the ruling obsession. And it is one not of self-discipline but of self-abnegation.

The dichotomy between the spiritual and the political is also false, resulting from an incomplete attention to our erotic knowledge. For the bridge which connects them is formed by the erotic – the sensual – those physical, emotional, and psychic expressions of what is deepest and strongest and richest within each of us, being shared: the passions of love, in its deepest meanings.

Beyond the superficial, the considered phrase, "It feels right to me," acknowledges the strength of the erotic into a true knowledge, for what that means is the first and most powerful guiding light toward any understanding. And understanding is a handmaiden which can only wait upon, or clarify, that knowledge, deeply born. The erotic is the nurturer or nursemaid of all our deepest knowledge.

The erotic functions for me in several ways, and the first is in providing the power which comes from sharing deeply any pursuit with another person. The sharing of joy, whether physical, emotional, psychic, or intellectual, forms a bridge between the sharers which can be the basis for understanding much of what is not shared between them, and lessens the threat of their difference.

Another important way in which the erotic connection functions is the open and fearless underlining of my capacity for joy. In the way my body stretches to music and opens into response, hearkening to its deepest rhythms, so every level upon which I sense also opens to the erotically satisfying experience, whether it is dancing, building a bookcase, writing a poem, examining an idea.

That self-connection shared is a measure of the joy which I know myself to be capable of feeling, a reminder of my capacity for feeling. And that deep and irreplaceable knowledge of my capacity for joy comes to demand from all of my life that it be lived within the knowledge that such satisfaction is possible, and does not have to be called *marriage,* nor *god,* nor *an afterlife.*

This is one reason why the erotic is so feared, and so often relegated to the bedroom alone, when it is recognized at all. For once we begin to feel deeply all the aspects of our lives, we begin to demand from ourselves and from our life-pursuits that they feel in accordance with that joy which we know ourselves to be capable of. Our erotic knowledge empowers us, becomes a lens through which we scrutinize all aspects of our existence, forcing us to evaluate those aspects honestly in terms of their relative meaning within our lives. And this is a grave responsibility, projected from within each of us, not to settle for the convenient, the shoddy, the conventionally expected, nor the merely safe.

During World War II, we bought sealed plastic packets of white, uncolored margarine, with a tiny, intense pellet of yellow coloring perched like a topaz just inside the clear skin of the bag. We would leave the margarine out for a while to soften, and then we would pinch the little pellet to break it inside the bag, releasing the rich yellowness into the soft pale mass of margarine. Then taking it carefully between our fingers, we would knead it gently back and forth, over and over, until the color had spread throughout the whole pound bag of margarine, thoroughly coloring it.

I find the erotic such a kernel within myself. When released from its intense and constrained pellet, it flows through and colors my life with a kind of energy that heightens and sensitizes and strengthens all my experience.

We have been raised to fear the *yes* within ourselves, our deepest cravings. But, once recognized, those which do not enhance our future lose their power and can be altered. The fear of our desires keeps them suspect and indiscriminately powerful, for to suppress any truth is to give it strength beyond endurance. The fear that we cannot grow beyond whatever distortions we may find within ourselves keeps us docile and loyal and obedient, externally defined, and leads us to accept many facets of our oppression as women.

When we live outside ourselves, and by that I mean on external directives only rather than from our internal knowledge and needs, when we live away from those erotic guides from within ourselves, then our lives are limited by external and alien forms, and we conform to the needs of a structure that is not based on human need, let alone an individual's. But when we begin to live from within outward, in touch with the power of the erotic within ourselves, and allowing that power to inform and illuminate our actions upon the world around us, then we begin to be responsible to ourselves in the deepest sense. For as we begin to recognize our deepest feelings, we begin to give up, of necessity, being satisfied with suffering and self-negation, and with the numbness which so often seems like their only alternative in our society. Our acts against oppression become integral with self, motivated and empowered from within.

In touch with the erotic, I become less willing to accept powerlessness, or those other supplied states of being which are not native to me, such as resignation, despair, self-effacement, depression, self-denial.

And yes, there is a hierarchy. There is a difference between painting a back fence and writing a poem, but only one of quantity. And there is, for me, no difference between writing a good poem and moving into sunlight against the body of a woman I love.

This brings me to the last consideration of the erotic. To share the power of each other's feelings is different from using another's feelings as we would use a kleenex. When we look the other way from our experience, erotic or otherwise, we use rather than share the feelings of those others who participate in the experience with us. And use without consent of the used is abuse.

In order to be utilized, our erotic feelings must be recognized. The need for sharing deep feeling is a human need. But within the european-american tradition, this need is satisfied by certain proscribed erotic comings-together. These occasions are almost always characterized by a simultaneous looking away, a pretense of calling them something else, whether a religion, a fit, mob violence, or even playing doctor. And this misnaming of the need and the deed give rise to that distortion which results in pornography and obscenity – the abuse of feeling.

When we look away from the importance of the erotic in the development and sustenance of our power, or when we look away from ourselves as we satisfy our erotic needs in concert with others, we use each other as objects of satisfaction rather than share our joy in the satisfying, rather than make connection with our similarities and our differences. To refuse to be conscious of what we are feeling at any time, however comfortable that might seem, is to deny a large part of the experience, and to allow ourselves to be reduced to the pornographic, the abused, and the absurd.

The erotic cannot be felt secondhand. As a Black lesbian feminist, I have a particular feeling, knowledge, and understanding for those sisters with whom I have danced hard, played, or even fought. This deep participation has often been the forerunner for joint concerted actions not possible before.

But this erotic charge is not easily shared by women who continue to operate under an exclusively european-american male tradition. I know it was not available to me when I was trying to adapt my consciousness to this mode of living and sensation.

Only now, I find more and more women-identified women brave enough to risk sharing the erotic's electrical charge without having to look away, and without distorting the enormously powerful and creative nature of that exchange. Recognizing the power of the erotic within our lives can give us the energy to pursue genuine change within our world, rather than merely settling for a shift of characters in the same weary drama.

For not only do we touch our most profoundly creative source, but we do that which is female and self-affirming in the face of a racist, patriarchal, and anti-erotic society.

Note
1. Paper delivered at the Fourth Berkshire Conference on the History of Women, Mount Holyoke College, August 25, 1978. Published as a pamphlet by Out & Out Books (available from The Crossing Press).

Theorizing Sexual Relations in the Caribbean:
Prostitution and the Problem of the "Exotic"
Kamala Kempadoo

Introduction

In social, historical and anthropological studies, prostitution stands as a prism through which the social organization of sexuality can be viewed. Since the 1970s such studies have been profoundly shaped by radical feminist theorizing in which prostitution has been theoretically located as a universal expression of violence to women and as the quintessence of patriarchal dominance and female sexual subordination.[1] Nevertheless, other feminist approaches have indicated that there is no straightforward correlation between patriarchy and prostitution (Truong 1990; Shrage 1994; Kempadoo 1996; Lim 1998). Rather, it is argued, entrance into prostitution or other forms of sexual relations, and the contexts and conditions in which these sexual activities take place, vary according to local, regional and international relations of power along gendered, economic, national and ethnic divides.[2] The reduction of sexual relations to a gendered dynamic is thus seen to be inadequate to theorize the various histories, experiences and everyday realities of the organization and exploitation of sexuality around the world.

In this chapter I further this argument through an examination of the construction of prostitution in Caribbean colonial and post-colonial societies. Central here is an exploration of how the exoticization of the cultural "other" through Caribbean history has contributed to the construction of the prostitute and to the shaping of sexual relations. Prostitution can be seen through this history not simply as a way in which women's bodies, sexuality and labour were acted upon, exploited or strategically employed under patriarchal domination, but also as an articulation of racialized relations of power and resistance[3] at both local and global levels. Some of this complexity is illustrated here through historical and anthropological studies of the colonial Caribbean. In the second part of this paper I investigate the articulation of exoticism in the post-colonial tourism industry, drawing on an analysis of postings to an Internet website by sex tourists to the Caribbean in the 1990s.

The tracing of a history of prostitution through the discourse of exoticism is not an attempt to dismiss the relevance of masculine control of female sexuality as a crucial factor in the construction of prostitution and other sexual relations. Rather, this analysis seeks to emphasize the ways in which colonial and global relations of power and ruling have contributed to the process. As Parker, Barbarosa and Aggleton summarize the state of the study of sexuality at the turn of the twenty-first century, "One key challenge confronting sexuality research has thus emerged as the urgent need to rethink the effects of colonialism and neo-colonialism" (2000, 9). In this way, this essay can best be read as an attempt to *complicate* existing feminist theorizing of prostitution, rather than to offer an alternative framework.

Historicizing Colonial Sexuality

The Caribbean region has been richly studied, interpreted and reread for the ways in which notions of race and ethnicity have constituted the cultural, social and political identity of its peoples and nations, and the elaboration of this focus with a critical gender analysis has produced a substantial body of work that describes and theorizes Caribbean women's lives and experiences.[4] To more fully apprehend the intersectionality of racialized, sexualized processes and relations of power in the Caribbean, the theoretical notion of exoticism is of interest, for it captures the simultaneous romanticization and oppression and exploitation of the racial, ethnic or cultural other, and has been defined as part of the practice and ideology of earlier colonial and imperialist projects (Said 1979; Alloula 1986; Kabbani 1988; Rousseau and Porter 1990a; Hentsch 1992; Lewis 1996; Yeğenoğlu 1998; di Leonardo 1998).

Exoticism has been most commonly identified in the context of orientalism – the broader lens through which Europe viewed "the East" during the eighteenth and nineteenth centuries – although is not confined to the western European cultural response to that part of the world nor to that historical period only. As an approach to the non-Western world, it is associated with the legitimation of European conquest, control and domination, as well as with escapist fantasies and vicarious enjoyment of sex and violence by European literary intellectuals and artists: In a contemporary reflection on this particular period in Europe, Rousseau and Porter write:

> The invention of the "exotic" evidently satisfied needs amongst a European and, later, an Atlantic, civilization which, as it progressively explored and dominated the entire globe with its guns and sails, increasingly assumed the right to define human values and conduct in their highest expression. Other, cultures, other creeds, were not merely different, not even merely lower, but positively – even objectively – strange. It was not merely the remoteness of geographical distance in a world where miles counted for much, but the ineluctable sense that all their mental processes and logical deductions were equally as alien. Labeling the anthropological Other as exotic legitimated treating the peoples of the "third world" as fit to he despised – destroyed even, or at least doomed, like the Tasmanian aborigines, to extinction – while concurrently also constituting them as projections of Western fantasies, (1990a, 6–7).

Exoticism valorized peoples and cultures that were different and remote, concomitantly imposing a status of inferiority upon them. "The Orient" was captured as the epitome of the exotic: a strange and unfamiliar world, both fascinating and terrifying, inviting to the curious explorer yet threatening to all the standards of civilization upheld in Europe, seductive in its paradise-like, unblemished "virgin" state, yet bestial in its perceived barbaric, cannibalistic moments. The eroticization of women of these different cultures was integral to this movement, whereby their sexuality was defined as highly attractive and fascinating, yet related to the natural primitiveness and lower order of the other cultural group. According to Porter, exotic lands and peoples provided Europeans with "paradigms of the erotic". Away from the repressive sexual mores of western Europe, strange cultures, and particularly the women in them, became sites where sex "was neither penalized, nor pathologized nor exclusively procreative" (Rousseau and Porter 1990b, 118). Womanhood among the colonized came to represent uninhibited, unbridled sensuality and sexual pleasure for the colonizer. Asian female sexuality signified temptation, eroticism, pleasure and danger – veiled mysteries to be possessed and controlled within western Europe's expansionist project – and theorists of orientalism have pointed out that it was the harem of Persia, courtesan arrangements in India and Japan, *devadasis* (temple girls) of India, *ronggeng* (dancing girls) of Indonesia and polygamous lifestyles that were seized upon by Western travellers, traders, photographers and crusaders to illustrate and perpetuate myths of the exotic other (Alloula

1986; Kabbani 1988; Yeğenoğlu 1998). Exoticism in its various expressions brought legitimacy to Western rule; it is distinguished from other racisms by fostering the illusion of an admiration for and attraction to the other while simultaneously enacting murder, rape, genocide and enslavement.

Di Leonardo's elaborate study of American exoticism points out that the discourse was not tied simply to direct colonial rule that proceeded from western Europe, but also to those imperial projects through which the United States began to assert its dominance in world affairs. Exoticism, she notes, appeared most prominently at the end of the eighteenth and turn of the nineteenth centuries, bringing "a sense of psychic healing and therapeutic personal integration" to the elite at a time also marked by "recurrent crises of masculinity and American state actions against 'primitives' both at home and abroad" (di Leonardo 1998, 159–60). It was:

> a period of the consolidation of capitalist industrialization, of a bloody war against a significantly European immigrant labor force, and of federal abandonment of reconstruction in the South and the establishment there of a white reign of terror against black Americans…It was as well the end of the war of expropriation against Native Americans…the heyday of American imperialist expansion into the Caribbean, Latin America, and the Pacific; and the period of an ongoing Victorian woman movement still twenty-seven years short of the achievement of female voting rights and tinged by racist and classist response to short-lived post-Civil War black male suffrage. (di Leonardo 1998, 4)

While exoticism is most often identified as a white masculine discourse, it has been pointed out that it was also mediated through the white imperial feminine imagination, although the subjectivities, positions and roles of white women have not been much explored in studies of colonial or post-colonial societies (Hall 1995). Nevertheless, we are reminded that women cannot be overlooked in the production of an orientalist or exoticist discourse. In Reina Lewis's study of nineteenth-century feminist writings she argues that it is necessary to examine all the contradictory positions inherent in imperialism, to "'disentangle' the ways in which representations of an orientalized Other simultaneously undercut and contribute to Orientalist ideas and policies" (1996, 26). Regarding women writers during the nineteenth century she notes:

> As agents socialized in an age of everyday imperialism it would have been impossible for the subjects of this study to be unaware of, or influenced by, imperial discourse – even if they couched their relationship to it as oppositional. That some of the key writers of the twentieth-century feminist literary canon, like Brontë and Eliot, couched their demands for female emancipation precisely through the Orientalizing of a structural other requires even more our willingness to include the conditions and discourses of imperial difference in our analysis of the work. (1996, 29)

Writers such as Lewis open the door to thinking about how white/European women participated in the construction of the gendered other – feminine and masculine – in imperialist and colonial projects. The analyses suggest that it is not simply overt "racist" white women's behaviour and ideologies that can be seen to reproduce the imperial gaze and conditions, but that many women were complexly located in relations of domination and ruling.

The Caribbean has not escaped exoticization. Colonialism, with its attendant systems of slavery and indentured labour, also produced ideologies of the exotic, and few women in the colonies were not subject to an eroticizing, sexualizing gaze. While black African women were defined by Europeans as "slaves by nature" and as passive, downtrodden, subservient, resigned workers, they were also perceived as sexually promiscuous, "cruel and negligent as a mother, fickle as a wife" and immoral (Bush 1990). A prevailing view of black women under Caribbean slavery as naturally "hot constitution'd" and sensuous in an animal-like way, lacking all the qualities that defined "decent" womanhood or women of "purity of blood", has been consistently noted by various scholars

(Morrissey 1989; Bush 1990; Kutzinski 1993; Reddock 1994). The sexual imagery, leaning on associations between black womanhood and natural earthy instincts, licentiousness, immorality and pathology, was often painted to arouse disgust and abhorrence for purposes of maintaining slavery by the plantocracy or, alternatively, to illustrate the abolitionists' cause by pointing out how slavery degraded the lives of Africans. It did not, however, deter European male pursuit of sexual intercourse with black women or their fascination, delight and pleasure with the black female body. Henriques concludes that, the planters "became adept at attributing their own promiscuity to the inherent licentiousness of the Negro" and to the "debauchery" of slave women (1965, 195). The region came to be represented in European imaginations "as a land of sexual opportunity for young European males", and black women – enslaved or free – were defined as the sexual property of white men (Morrissey 1989, 147).

Perceptions of black women as sexual and erotic objects were consolidated in various ways. Researchers on slave-trade activities in the seventeenth century, for example, have noted the predominance of young girls and boys in the slave-ship crews' "property", as well as emotional attachments of slave-ship captains and officers to young African women during the middle-passage voyage, leading them to conclude that particular women, girls and boys were targeted as sexual slaves or servants (Bush 1990; Postma 1990). Thus even before arrival in the colonies, African women were objectified as sexualized beings in the eyes and minds of the traders. Romanticized descriptions of African women as "ebony queens" and "sable beauties" can also be found in documents of European travellers, traders and plantation owners, and were later echoed in nineteenth-century art, poetry and literature (Bush 1990, 17).[5] This specific appreciation of black femininity, while popular among Europeans, was not parallelled to the same extent in the United States, yet had a profound impact on notions of eroticism and beauty in Europe and Europeanized Caribbean colonies.[6] Nevertheless, throughout the Americas women of mixed descent were in general perceived more favourably by the European elite than "pure" African women, a view that has barely diminished in post-colonial societies. If white womanhood represented the pinnacle of femininity, couched in assumptions of fairness, purity, frailty and domesticity, and black womanhood the total opposite because of its presumed closeness to nature, dark skin, masculine physique and unbridled sexuality, the combination of western Europe and Africa produced notions of the "light-skinned" woman who could almost pass for white yet retained a tinge of colour, as well as a hint of the wantonness and uninhibited sexuality of exotic cultures. The "coloured" woman was then often described as possessing "a great physical attraction for the European" (Henriques 1965, 110), and observations such as the following echoed this sentiment:

> Physically, the typical fille de couleur may certainly he classed, as white creole writers have not hesitated to class her, with the "most beautiful women of the human race". She has inherited not only the finer bodily characteristics of either parent race, but a something else belonging originally to neither, and created by special climatic and physical conditions – a grace, a suppleness of form, a delicacy of extremities...a satiny smoothness and fruit-tint of skin – solely West Indian.
> (Henriques 1974, 110)

Rogers's three-volume study of race and sex also documents in rich detail various views of the colonial elite and European male travellers during the eighteenth and nineteenth centuries in the Dutch, Spanish, English and French Caribbean, illustrating the trend of exoticization of "mixed-race" women in the region. Remarked a surgeon in the Dominican Republic, for example:

> When among the populations of the Antilles we first notice these remarkable metis, whose olive skins, elegant and slender figures, fine straight profiles and regular features remind us of the inhabitants of Madras or Pondicherry (India) we ask ourselves in wonder while looking at their

long eyes, full of strange and gentle melancholy and at the black rich silky gleaming hair, curling in abundance over the temples and falling in profusion over the neck – to what human race can belong this singular variety...(Rogers 1972, 146)

Interestingly, a commonality in the perceptions, desires and passions of European men for women in the East and West is lodged in this particular image. The mixed-race woman in the West Indies is likened to mixed-race women from "the East" – in this instance, India. Women from both parts of the globe, in the eyes of the surgeon, constituted a particular "race" – remarkable and decidedly different, other, strange – constituted by a brown complexion, silky, loose-curling hair and facial features and a physical build that approximated the European ideal. The surgeon's comments reflect not only a fascination with slim, "olives"-skinned women but also elements of an orientalist ideology through its equation of Indian women with exotica – not simply a racialization of non-Western peoples, but again a delight in European male minds with foreign, "exotic" others. Historical records left by men living in or visiting the colonies confirm descriptions of these women as frequent objects of sexual desires and passions, enacted far away from the everyday confines and repressions of European society and the dominant sexual morality (Bush 1990). The "high brown", "mulatto", "morena", "metis" or light-skinned Caribbean woman remained highly desirable and attractive to European men.

Much post-colonial theory has designated orientalism and exoticism as a Western approach or "textual attitude" that includes dreams, images and vocabularies about the "other". "Orientalism," writes Yeğenoğlu. "refers to the production of a systematic knowledge and to the site of the unconscious – desires and fantasies" (1998, 23). This discourse is not, however, without material and embodied dimensions, and thus is defined not only as authorizing colonial and imperial domination for economic and political purposes, but as articulations of social relations, institutions and everyday practices. Exoticism thus is visible not only in ideologies and perceptions, but also in embodied relations, and in the Caribbean under colonialism was most evidently lodged in, and visible through, prostitution and other non-romantic sexual arrangements.

Sex in Caribbean history is inextricably tied to the power and control exerted by European colonizers over a black population, at a time when western European nations sought to find new resources for the accumulation of capital and new sites upon which to establish empire, and the enslavement of Africans was integral to the consolidation of racial power in the Americas. Beckles points out that slavery meant "not only the compulsory extraction of labor from the Blacks but also, in theory at least, slave owners' right to total sexual access to slaves" (1989b, 141). White slave-owners made ample use of this "right": rape and sexual abuse were commonplace, and concubinage and prostitution quickly became an institutional part of Caribbean societies. "In time," writes Henriques, "no European male in the Caribbean, who could afford it, was without his colored mistress, either a freedwoman or slave" (1965, 195). Bush (1990), Morrissey (1989) and Henriques (1965) also point out that this power was exerted not only by the colonial elite and planter class but, because of the existing racial hegemony of white over black, extended to include white men of lower classes. Even European bondservants, who stood at the margins of white society in a position almost comparable to that of slave, were seen to have "augmented the process of their masters" through engaging in clandestine sexual affairs with slave women as a result of the privilege that their whiteness conferred upon them (Henriques 1965, 201).

Racialized dimensions of sexuality under slavery were, however, not uniform, with the category of women "of mixed race" – the mulatto, "mustee" or "coloured" woman – being considered particularly exotic. This social category, which itself arose from the exercise of power over black slave women, was, however, legally and ideologically placed outside of white society, representing to Europeans racial impurity and moral, racial and social degradation, constituting an "unnatural transgression of the rules of social propriety" (Kutzinski 1993, 75). The mulatto woman (*la mulata*) represented the erotic and sexually desirable yet was outcast and pathologized and emerged during slavery as the symbol of the prostitute – the sexually available yet socially despised body – the eroticized other, the trope of the exotic.

Within the context of slavery, prostitution was lodged at the nexus of at least two areas of women's existence: as an extension of sexual relations (forced or otherwise) with white men and as an income-generating activity for both slave and "free coloured" women. Beckles notes about Barbadian society in the early 1800s that slave women were frequently hired out by white and free coloured families as "nannies, nurses, cooks, washerwomen, hucksters, seamstresses" yet "the general expectation of individuals who hired female labor under whatever pretense, was that sexual benefits were included" (1989b, 143). Concubines often served as both mistresses and housekeepers and were sometimes hired out by their owners to sexually service other men "as a convenient way of obtaining cash" (p. 142). Furthermore, in times of economic slump on plantations (particularly in British colonies), when blacks, both men and women, were expected to provide for themselves or to bring in wages through work outside the plantation, "the number of slave women placed on the urban market as prostitutes by sugar planters would rapidly increase", and in the towns "masters and mistresses would frequently send out female slaves as prostitutes for ships' crew" (pp. 142–43). Reddock reports that in Trinidad, "For the most part women were hired out as domestic slaves, field labourers, as concubines, to temporary male European settlers, or were made to work as petty traders or prostitutes handing over most of their earning to their masters" (1994, 20). Black women's manual and sexual labour was, in effect, "pimped" by the slaveholders. Beckles suggests that white women were not exempt from this position of pimp, as they "may have owned and managed as much as 25 percent of Caribbean slaves, with a greater concentration of ownership in towns" and many "made a thriving business from the rental of black and colored women for sexual services in the port towns" (1999, 168, 65). Geggus (1996) furthermore remarks upon the numerous cases mentioned in historical records of slave women in the French Caribbean who, besides their marketing activities, were able to profit financially from selling their own or their daughters' sexual labour. Morrissey (1989) concludes that in the early nineteenth century in the British Caribbean, domestics who worked in taverns and inns in the towns also served as prostitutes.

Colonial sexual relations – forced or otherwise – often produced children, yet in the absence of marriage and formal recognition of the child by the white father, the child took on the condition of the mother and was defined as part of either the slave population or the free coloured class. Sex during slavery thus was a way in which the labouring classes and slaves were reproduced. Abraham-Van der Mark points out that "concubinage gave them [Jewish men in nineteenth-century Curaçao] the benefits of a category of children which, if necessary, provided labor but could not make any legal demands and were excluded from inheritance" (1993, 46). Moreover, mulattos were more highly valued in slave markets, and children of black slave women and white slave-owners could bring in a higher income than children of black parents. Beckles argues that in this respect, the sexual servant or prostitute was particularly valuable to the slave-owner, for "unlike other female slaves, she could generate three income flows: from labor, prostitution and reproduction" (1989b, 144).

The period immediately following slavery in the Caribbean has been characterized as a time when women established autonomy of work away from the plantations and where gendered relations were transformed under changing relations of production.[7] Waged labour for women took on greater importance, with European middle-class patriarchal family ideologies gaining primacy, yet many areas of "women's work" that had been established under slavery continued. Domestic service, marketing and prostitution continued to be constituted as black and "coloured" women's activities. Henriques also notes that "emancipation did not fundamentally alter the patterns of sexuality which had been established under slavery. Women might no longer be bound to masters but the 'white bias' in the society still facilitated illicit sexual relations between white and colored" (1965, 203). While there is a paucity of research from which to draw from for this period in Caribbean history about black and brown women's lives, Kerr's study on female housekeepers of lodgings in Jamaica concurs with Henriques's observations. She notes that the women – who were predominantly mulatto – "turned their weaknesses into strength by capitalizing upon white men's sexual desire for them. Their lodging houses became places 'flocked to' mainly by white males who sought sexual services from women of color. The housekeepers diversified their services so that they not only increased their incomes but eventually became women of importance" (1995, 210). However, the significance of racialized hierarchies and identities within the sex trade, the new constraints and possibilities for women in the labour markets, and the changes in demand for sex work remain under-explored and require far more attention than has been given by historians.

Almost completely hidden from view is the story of sexual relations between white or European women and black men. Apart from conventional understandings that white women were positioned as the symbols of moral purity and ideal domesticity in Caribbean colonial society and required protection by white men, Beckles proposes that during slavery, because children took on the condition of the mother and the male planters' interest was to reproduce the slave population and not the group of free people of colour, black male sexual access to white women had to be blocked so that "the progeny of black males were not lost to the slave gangs" (1999, 69). Black men, he states, "faced punishments such as castration, dismemberment, and execution for having sexual relations with white women, who in turn were socially disgraced and ostracized" (p. 68). Nevertheless, he indicates that sexual relations between white women and black men "were not as uncommon as generally suggested" (p. 62).

Such claims, while perhaps hinting at some dimensions of the sexual relations between white women and black men and emphasizing the ways in which white male patriarchy and the plantation economy shaped white women's behaviour and roles, nevertheless seem overly deterministic and fail to allow for explorations into the constructions of white female or black male sexuality and sexual agency under colonial relations. So while in this history much emphasis has been placed upon the ways in which black women were considered important by the planter class for "breeding" slave populations, little has been done to examine the ways in which the flip side of such policies encouraged the construction of the black male "stud" as an important impregnator of women, and how this informed ideas about black male sexuality in the Caribbean.

Alternatively, the characterization of European women as morally corrupt and degraded through interactions with black men and women has left little space for the interrogation of white women's sexual agency and desire in the context of colonial relations of ruling, although some recent attention has been given to the more general construction of white womanhood in Caribbean colonial societies (Hall 1995; Beckles 1999; Campbell 2001). These lacunae in Caribbean historiography leave a void in our understandings of colonial sexualities.

Despite this paucity of historical studies about the significance of racialized, sexualized subjects in the post-slavery context, the introduction of indentured workers from India in countries such as Trinidad, Guyana, Suriname and Jamaica signals another social group that was subject to an eroticizing gaze. While stereotypes of a "docile, insipid, tractable shadow of a being with no mind, personality or significance of her own" has dominated Caribbean understandings of Indian womanhood (Cumber Dance 1993, 21; Poynting 1987; Espinet 1993; Moore 1999), an orientalist representation of her – as a highly sexual being and a temptress – follows close behind. Reddock (1985a), Mangru (1987) and Shepherd (1995) observe that in discussions about the recruitment of female labour from India in the indentureship programme, British colonial government officials held that many of the female immigrants were prostitutes, social outcasts and women who had abandoned marriage and domesticity, all of whom were considered to "have gone astray", to be "prone to immoral conduct", to exercise a "corrupting influence" on "respectable" women, or liable to be tempted into "abnormal sexual behavior by single men with money". In the eyes of officialdom then, the women were highly sexual, of dubious character and well outside the boundaries of "decent" colonial womanhood. Reddock notes that the skewed perception of Indian womanhood held by the British reinforced patriarchal tendencies within the Indian community, locating the women not only as immoral, but as corrupted sexual servants to non-Indian men.[8] Often labelled and categorized as lewd and lascivious, working-class Indian women were cast as evil, corrupting elements who disrupted dominant notions of decency and proper family values. Indian men were complicitous in upholding certain sexualized notions of Indo-Caribbean womanhood. However, while Indian men may have deplored and vilified working women, an exoticist discourse that celebrated non-white female sexuality – while inscribing it with racial and gender inferiority – was performed through black male lyrics in the post-indentureship period.[9] Gordon Rohlehr's analysis of Trinidadian calypsos in the 1930s to 1950s (1988) notes that among the various racialized and gendered images, Indian women gained attention as exotic temptresses but were also classified as "unattainable" – of being guarded and hidden away from men – as the classic trope of Oriental mystique. Equally pervasive was the image of Indo-Trinidadian women as "street girls" working for "Yankee dollars" that emerged through these popular songs. Shalini Puri's analysis of texts of two black male calypso singers – Mighty Killer and Lord Superior, popular in 1952 and 1958 respectively – indicates that the songs vividly conjured up an image of Indian women as exclusively sexual actors – prostitutes – who worked for the American military troops stationed in Trinidad during the Second World War (Puri 1993; Reddock 1998a).

Exoticism was thus both an attitude and a set of practices visited upon the Caribbean by Europeans during slavery and in its aftermath, constituting the "brown-skinned" colonized and enslaved woman, as well as the lands she inhabited, as sites for sexual pleasure and fantasy as well as exploitation, enslavement and violence. Constructed through the domination of the Caribbean by western Europe and consolidated through slavery, it can be argued that this history has had profound implications, both within the Caribbean itself and between the region and neocolonial centres of power. In the remaining part of this essay I explore dimensions of the continued legacy of exoticism, in which tourism plays an increasingly important role.

Exoticism in the Twentieth Century

The shift from a discourse that was primarily articulated through the white European, masculine, colonial consciousness to one that is embedded in the imaginations and desires of the colonized man has been a subject of interrogation and discussion by anti-colonial Third World intellectuals. This discourse has been explored through black American perspectives (hooks 1993; West 1993) and lightly touched upon in Caribbean gender analyses (Mohammed 1998; Lewis 1998). It is my argument here that besides the profound influence that colonialism has had on notions of the superiority of whiteness (including white femininity) among the colonized, it has also imparted a legacy of exoticization of the cultural other and the brown woman. Both were infused into new relations of power and privilege structured through anti-colonial and nationalist struggles for political independence that appeared on the Caribbean landscape in the twentieth century. One encounters attitudes and ideas within the Caribbean itself that reflect both a racialization of sexual desire as well as an exoticization of cultural difference, much of which revolve around the brown female body and identity. In Cuba, for example, the *mulata* was considered exotic not only by foreign men, but by male Cuban writers, artists and poets, who also "enshrined the erotic image of Cuba's *mulatas*" during the nineteenth and early twentieth centuries (Schwartz 1997, 86; Kutzinski 1993). In Curaçao, sex with a light-skinned women from the Spanish-speaking Caribbean or Latin America has been considered highly attractive and desirable among local men. A popular image that dominated on the island during the twentieth century identified women from the Dominican Republic as specially trained and groomed to provide sexual pleasure to men, and thus particularly suited to sex work. Haitian women, however, were located by this population as "too black" and "unhygienic" for sexual encounters (Lagro and Plotkin 1990). The exotic "Sandom" image in the minds of Curaçaoan men in this particular instance combined with colonial state policies during the 1930s and 1940s to attract large numbers of migrant workers from surrounding countries – for work in the oil-refining industry, to provide a base for the US and Dutch naval fleets, and simultaneously to protect local womanhood from the "coarse" sexualities of the sailors and other migrant workers. Foreign, culturally other women in this scenario were legalized to work on the island as prostitutes and domestics. The national, cultural and ethnic differences of foreign women were coded as sexually desirable but inferior to notions of proper femininity, and those who provided erotic, sexual services became relegated to marginalized, informal – and heavily policed – sectors of society.

Similar notions of the exotic, erotic other have been recorded in research on prostitution in Suriname and Guyana, where "light-skinned" Latin American, Brazilian and Spanish-speaking Caribbean women have been positioned as migrant workers in the sex trade, and thus highly exploitable and highly vulnerable in relationship to the resident population, yet defined as "hyper-sexual" by local dominant gender ideologies (Kane 1993; Antonius-Smits et al. 1999; Red Thread 1999). In Haiti male sexual preference for the lighter-skinned, silky-haired Dominicans is cited as part of a "culture of exoticism" that includes beliefs that Spanish is "the language of love" and that women from the Dominican Republic are more "professional" and attractive in sex work and preferable over Haitian women (Chanel 1994, 14). Equations of the cultural other with notions of the erotic can be seen to continue beyond the Western male imagination, and also to dominate contemporary Caribbean male perceptions and appreciations of sensuality and sexuality.[10]

Expressions of exoticism run through Caribbean history, constructed under slavery and Europan colonialism, pulsing though American constructions of nation and coursing through masculinist national ideologies and practices in the post-colonial societies. This view reasserts itself through the new forms of Western economic and cultural imperialism, inscribed in the tourism industry. Promoted by the United Nations since the 1960s as a strategy to participate in the global economy, tourism was adopted by Caribbean governments at different times as a way to diversify their economies, to overcome economic crises that threatened to cripple the small nation-states and to acquire foreign exchange. The largest tourism market in the 1990s was North America, and in second place was Europe, with France, the United Kingdom and Germany taking the lead. The industry accounts for approximately 25 per cent of all formal employment in the region and is generally seen to be one of the fastest-growing sectors in the twenty-first century. Tourism represents one of the few ways in which small island nations can compete in the global economy. Using the estimate that for every person in formal employment in tourism there is at least one other engaged in informal activities in the industry, it is predicted that tourism in the Caribbean will continue to be an important source of livelihood for its working peoples (*Travel Industry* 1997; Patullo 1996).

Caribbean tourism hinges on the exploitation of a number of the region's resources, particularly its year-round sunny conditions and beaches, but also its tropical rainforests and coral reefs, as well as its music, such as reggae and calypso, its cuisine and other cultural symbols such as carnival. It offers a variety of packages, including golf vacations, weddings and honeymoons, dive trips and eco-tours, its sole *raison d'être* to provide pleasure to the visitor. Caribbean women and men in this sector work for meagre wages in jobs such as barman, waitress, cook, cleaner, maid, gardener and entertainer. Male and female labour and energies constitute a part of the package that is paid for and consumed by the tourist during the period in which she or he seeks to relax and enjoy – in the leisure time the tourist has set aside to recuperate and restore the mind and body in order to maintain a healthy and productive working life on return home (Crick 1989; Walvin 1992; Kinnaird and Hall 1994). Caribbean sexuality also constitutes a critical resource within this panorama, and it is in arrangements and representations of this aspect of the tourism industry that new articulations of exoticism are evident. An examination of Internet representations of sex in the Caribbean, drawn from a website that allows people to exchange experiences and views about commercial and other types of sex around the world, illustrates some dimensions of contemporary exoticism.

Exoticism and Tourism

In the eighty-three letters written about the Caribbean that were publicly posted on a "World Sex Guide" website between November 1994 and July 1999, over one-third explicitly related racial and cultural difference to sexual desirability.[11] For the authors of these letters, a hierarchy of attractiveness associated with notions of race and culture emerged. Comments about Puerto Rican Latinas, Cubanas, Dominican "mulattos" and "light-skinned" Caribbean women tended to prevail and to be highly positive.[12] Some of the recurring ideas about the erotic, hyper-sexual "nature" of the Caribbean and its women were represented as follows:

> I decided I wanted to go on vacation, but with that decision, there were two things I had to consider: first, that I didn't have a lot of money to spend on such things, two, that availability of sex was VERY important!!...the Caribbean made sense.[13]

> A guy with enough hard currency can have the time of his life in what is probably the most romantic city in the world with, in my humble opinion, the most dropdead gorgeous sultry tanned beauties in the hemisphere.[14] [Written about Havana, Cuba.]

> The DR has wonderful possibilities. Prostitution jives fairly well with the culture. Dominican women are beautiful, prices are excellent, and you have a fair chance of being treated well...I find that watching a fine brown-sugar Dominican teenager take off her clothes and shake her ass like only Dominican chics can does wonders for clearing your mind and getting up your guts (not to mention you [sic] cock) for the bargaining process.[15]

> The whole island is a brothel, possibly the cheapest one in the world.[16] [Written about Cuba.]

> You can live like a king, complete with harem, on less than $500/week. I did.[17] [Written about Cuba.]

Latinized, Spanish-speaking Caribbean cultures and "brown" femininities are often represented in the letters as sexually attractive and available to the men. As one tourist clearly described this,

> Since I prefer Latinas and brunettes, for me Cuba is the closest thing to paradise I think I'll ever see. It's heavenly because many of these young Cubanas are "available".

Or as others write,

> Aruba is the place where you go to get the knockout of your life. The Ladies are all from Colombia and Venezuela.[18]

> For $100 per night...one can find a gorgeous, light skinned and young latina to spend the night with.[19] [Written about the Dominican Republic]

Promotional materials for tourism to the Caribbean have appropriated the image of the brown-skinned sexy Caribbean woman to seduce and entice potential clients. As Dagenais points out, popular representations of Caribbean women "portray them as sexual objects and publicity drops; the tourist industry presents them as sensual mulattoes with endless free time to enjoy the beaches and, of course, the (male) visitors" (1993, 83). There are, however, some exceptions to this generalized pattern, with a few authors on the sex-tourist website expressing a specific appreciation for black women.

> By far the best place for sex in Jamaica is Negril. Sex is available and cheap, and for those of us who prefer black women, I can't think of anywhere that comes close.[20]

There are also comments that denigrate blackness (sometimes associated with Haitian nationality):

> I know beauty is in the eye of the beholder, but most of these women are truly not great lookers ... This is not to say that there were not some attractive women available – but they are in the minority. In terms of race, most are black – about 70% – while the rest are more Latino looking – There were actually a number of nights that I went back to my hotel room alone because none of the women appealed to me (this would never happen in Brazil or Thailand!) ... these are without a doubt some of the butt ugliest women I have ever come across. Unbelievably ugly. Most are Haitian and are old (at least in hooker years) and heavy.[21] [Written about the Dominican Republic]

These patterns that position the brown-skinned woman as more desirable than the black woman in the contemporary tourism industry do not seem to contradict the earlier-described European-American and Caribbean notions of the exotic. However, they are reinforced by a comparison with sexual relations in the North (the United States in particular) and the sensuality of the white (female) body, where a delight in *sexy, mixed-race, mulata, sultry, tanned, Latin, brown-sugar* Caribbean women contrasts with representations of white femininity and sexuality as staid, cold, impersonal or mundane:

> Let's start out with a pleasant introduction to Latin sex ... Unlike [massage] places in the US of this nature, it is not a rip-off, they aim to please.[22] [Written about the Dominican Republic]

> I went in and noticed that most of the girls were not Puerto Rican. Most looked like rejects out of an American (NY, LA, Dallas) strip bar. The show was pathetic ... Immediately some lady from New York came up. She was too ugly... As soon as she left a hot Puerto Rican girl came up with large breasts and a nice body...[23] (Written about Puerto Rico.]

> Another very noticeable thing was how friendly all the girls were. There was none of that "hard ass" attitude so commonly seen here in the States ... Being with these girls was a thoroughly pleasant experience. [Written about the Dominican Republic]

> I love it here the table's [sic] are turned and the women were chasing me around. New York women are cold as fish, in comparison.[24] [Written about Cuba.]

> Be warned: eurochicks will want a real romance from you, with all the related mind trips, they consider intercourse a mere byproduct of that ... As usual, you will have to pay for their drinks and stay up late speaking about psychology and their childhood to get some, the day before you leave, once. [Written about Aruba.]

Cabezas notes that "Dominican women reported that foreigners construct them, both sexually and racially, in opposition to European women ...White skin is devalued because it is connected to civility, or feminist discourse, and is thus less sexual" (1999, 111). The exotic is sexier than femininity or sex in white post-industrial "developed" societies, and is thought to be found in the still natural backwards, untamed world. The contemporary tourist industry enables the men to dabble in their exoticizing sexual fantasies while away from home.

In addition, many of the men described the women in the Caribbean as "non-professional". They write that many, most or all of the sex workers are "not real hookers" but that they participate in prostitution because of financial need and lack of other economic opportunities. However, even though the authors stated that the women are in sex work because of financial need, the letters indicate that the men believe the women genuinely enjoy all types of sex with them, and that the women are particularly good at what they do:

> None of these are real hookers – most are part time girls who like sex and want to make some money for clothes and...[25] [Written about Cuba.]

> Just how good are they sexually speaking? Pretty damn good for the most part...No dead fish here...They really are very uninhibited...[Written about the Dominican Republic]

> Basically Marcia (not her real name) is not a real hooker, but a very attractive and horny girl who likes to make a bit of extra money (much needed in Jamaica). In return, if you treat her right, she'll give you a great time with no hassle. There's plenty of village girls like this around Negril and Montego Bays these days. [Written about Jamaica.]

> You never get the feeling that they are after your money, and they don't have a [sic] attitude of a whore ... These chics have so much class its hard to believe they are prostitutes.[26] [Written about the Dominican Republic.)

The highly sexualized image of Caribbean women held by sex-tourists about Caribbean women, explain O'Connell Davidson and Sanchez Taylor, rests on assumptions "that local girls 'are really hot for it' " and the women's "highest ambition is to be the object of a Western man's desire" – that, after all, the women "are doing what just comes naturally" to them (1999, 47). They are not, in the minds of the men, prostitutes who are having sex for money, but are perceived to be poor women who genuinely enjoy the sex. The idea that the women are naturally sexy and desire to have sex with much older men for pleasure enables the tourists to deny any exploitative aspects of their relationship with the Caribbean. Indeed many tourists rationalize their visits to the Caribbean for sex as a way to benefit poor, oppressed women; twenty-two letters in our sample presented some aspect of this idea. As one writer put it,

> I much rather sponsor a Cuban family by renting a room in their house than giving the money directly to the Cuban government ... I much rather give my money to a suffering Cuban ...[27]

Furthermore, the idea that women in the Caribbean are hyper-sexual creatures who are not professional prostitutes often results in the tourists presenting their encounters with the women as "romances" or "love":

> These women are not whores by choice, nor are they doing it just to buy jewelry. Because they are average women caught in circumstances beyond their control it is all that much easier to fall for them. [Written about Cuba.]

> We spent the day together, Life was good! My American buddy just about married the girl he was with ... Pamela took me to the airport early in the morning ... She cried ... I felt like shit. I wish I could have brought her home with me ... If you are going to Santo Domingo be prepared to fall in love with these women. I'm going back again ... [Written about the Dominican Republic]

> Girls are incredibly sexy and behave like real girlfriends.[28] [Written about Cuba.]

> Is she ever hot though! They just don't come that way back home ... I'm in love. I'm pretty convinced she is too ... (Written about Cuba.]

Constructing prostitution in poor countries as something that comes naturally to the local inhabitants, as romance or as a way to "help" women and their families masks the inequalities of power that are involved, and allows the sex-tourist to perceive of himself as benevolent and desirable. Tourism in the Caribbean at the end of the twentieth century appears to confirm exoticizing tendencies present in the region since the sixteenth century. However, new global hegemonies, which rest upon an increasing economic gap between post-industrial capitalist centres and peripheral areas that provide cheap labour, natural resources and playgrounds for the rich, can been seen to extend its scope. Western European and North American women are increasingly participants in a form of tourism that involves exoticization of the local population. As a male tourist explains:

> There are tons of beautiful German (80%), Italian, and French women from 18 to 50 who are willing to pay for sex and affection!!! believe it or not. I saw many 9 and 10 [good-looking] twenty year old girls paying for it!! One had to see it to believe it. There seems to be a fantasy thing with German (both men and women) to find the darkest (and sometimes no [sic] so pretty) locals and pay to be with them. There was a German girl next door to me that had about 10 guys in a week. She lookes [sic] like Demi (Bruce Willis' wife, but younger) ...[29] (Written about the Dominican Republic]

Such observations are not widely found on sex-tourist websites that traffic in fantasies and tales by men about women. Nevertheless, female sex tourism in the Caribbean has been noticed, researched and commented upon since the 1960s and is a growing spectacle in countries such as Barbados, Jamaica, the Dominican Republic, the Dutch Antilles and Belize. O'Connell Davidson and Sanchez Taylor note about this trend, "As Others, local men are viewed as beings possessed of a powerful and indiscriminate sexuality that they cannot control, and this explains their eagerness for sex with tourist women" (1999, 40). Specific to this trend is not brown sensuality and feminine eroticism, but an image that secures the young Caribbean man as the "Black stud" (Phillips 1999). The darker the man is, the more sexually attractive he is considered, with some being explicitly rejected for not being "black enough". Blackness is equated with "well-defined muscles", dreadlocked hair and "skin darkened almost blue-black" – characteristics that signal an African ancestry brimming with "an untamed, primitive nature and exotic appeal" (Phillips 1999, 187). It is an image that harks back to older notions in both European and US culture of the black African man as an embodiment of insatiable sexual appetite and uncontrollable lust, with a penis size to match. Albuquerque remarks that this image of black male sexuality and body also stirs the passions of some female tourists to the Caribbean, causing them to "literally get off the plane single mindedly embarked on the holy grail (the search for the big bamboo)" (1998, 88).

Similar to the ways in which some male tourists perceive sex in the Caribbean to be "not really prostitution", so too do tourist women often define their sexual encounters with black men as "romance".[30] In their study of sexual relationships between female tourists and Jamaican men, Pruitt and La Font (1995) define many of the sexual relationships as such. Likewise Ragsdale and Anders (1998) describe the relationship between some women tourists to Ambergris Cay, in Belize, and Belizean men as a form of *makoibi* – a "love sickness" in Belizean Creole – which the authors compare in intensity to a first love. Nevertheless, it has been pointed out that while "romance relationships between tourist women and local men serve to transform traditional gender roles across cultural boundaries" and may contribute to "[b]reaking taboos and challenging tradition", it has been acknowledged that the relationships end up "recapitulating the patriarchal structure of tourism" or "reproducing much of what is challenged" (Pruitt and La Font 1995, 436–38). The relationships can also be seen to be reproducing long-standing racist stereotypes of black male sexuality. O'Connell Davidson furthermore points out that the ambiguities inscribed in informal tourism-related prostitution allow for a form of self-deception, "so that even when the women tell themselves that they can only have sex in the context of romantic intimacy, they are not disbarred from sexually exploiting local men and boys in poor countries they visit" (1998, 183).

Many male sex-tourists express the view that in their home countries women enjoy excessive power, through which traditional male authority is undermined (O'Connell Davidson and Sanchez Taylor 1999; Cabezas 1999). In the Caribbean they are able to fully reaffirm their masculinity through sexual relations based on their racialized and cultural economic power. Simultaneously, black Caribbean masculinity becomes the ground upon which European and North American women experiment with or expand their gender identities. While they retain a sexualized femininity, it is commonplace among women tourists to exercise control over (local) men. The black man is required to be the sexually aggressive and dominant partner, allowing the tourist woman to combine economic power and authority with traditional Western notions of femininity as sexually submissive and subordinate. It would appear that in such scenarios, exoticized Caribbean masculinity and femininity and male and female bodies become a platform for reshaping and redefining Western identity and power – "a stage for First World gendered performances" (Kempadoo 1999a). O'Connell Davidson and Sanchez Taylor (1999) also note that the sexual encounter enables the tourist to attain a sense of control over her or his sexuality while reassuring himself or herself of racial and/or cultural privilege. Caribbean men and women alike are constructed in tourist imaginations as racialized sexual subjects/objects – the hyper-sexual black male "stud" and the "hot" mulatto or black woman – whose main roles are to service and please the visitor. Taking into account both racializing and gendered structures of power and domination reveals some of the contradictory positions that women and men from post-industrial centres hold in relation to the eroticized, exoticized other – both female and male.

Conclusion

Sexuality – the ways in which it is organized, expressed, enjoyed and exploited – has not been a focus for many Caribbean scholars, for while the region has a long-standing international reputation for being a sex haven, and Caribbean women and men have both been the objects as well as the subjects in writing the sexual script in the Caribbean, it remains an undervalued area within social research. Nevertheless, drawing from the few studies available, I have argued here that the subject of Caribbean sexuality requires investigations that address the intersectionality and simultaneity of gendered and racialized relations of power. Privileging one axis of power serves to elide other important social relations and dynamics. The notion of exoticism as a discourse that romanticizes and eroticizes black and brown bodies and subjectivities in the Caribbean, yet also reinforces exploitative and oppressive regimes, offers a possibility. Prostitution becomes one of the prisms through which we can witness the naked performance of exoticism – its lusts and desires as well as its violence and oppressions. In tracing exoticism through the history of prostitution in the Caribbean, this essay offers a glimpse at the configurations and reconfigurations that have taken place over time around sexuality. However, it also makes visible areas that could use further exploration. In particular this essay points to a broader need for Caribbean scholarship to uncover histories of black male sexuality as well as the construction of white Caribbean women's identities, desires and sexualities in relationship to histories of empire. It also points to some of the other silences that have shaped sexualities, raising questions about how relations of domination and power around not just gender but also race and ethnicity have in the past infused sexual relations – and continue to today. Most importantly for a post-colonial society, it poses the question of how we can proceed with theorizing our own sexual heritages and desires. Sex, it would seem, still requires much thought.

Notes

1. For classical radical feminist definitions of prostitution, see Barry 1984, Jeffreys 1997.
2. For an overview of these studies, see Kempadoo 2001.
3. Because of the scope of this work, the element of resistance is not explored in this essay. However, resistances of racially sexualized subjects have been noted elsewhere. See, for example, Kempadoo 1996, 1999b and Barnes 2000. Nevertheless, it remains an area for further investigation in both historical and contemporary contexts.
4. See for example. Mathurin 1974, Beckles 1989b, Bush 1990, Reddock 1994, and Peake and Trotz 1999, and essays in the edited volumes on women and gender in the Caribbean by Mohammed and Shepherd (1988), Shepherd, Brereton and Bailey (1995), López Springfield (1997), Barrow (1998b), and Kanhai (1999). Far less attention, however, has been paid to the experiences and lives of men in the Caribbean from a critical race/gender framework, although the works of Frantz Fanon, Errol Miller, Barrington Chevannes and Linden Lewis have provided invaluable insights into the social and psychological constitution of racialized Caribbean masculinity.
5. Baudelaire's 'Black Venus' and other poetry inspired by his mistress of colour, the bust *Venus Africaine* sculpted by Cordier in 1851 and Picasso's *Olympia* of 1901 all belong to the tradition of Europe's exoticization of African women (Nederveen Pieterse 1990, 182).
6. In di Leonardo's account of exoticism in the United States, the Chicago World's Columbian Exposition in 1893 exemplifies how nineteenth-century 'America' viewed and defined the 'other', with certain groups of women marked as particularly exotic. 'In the common orientalist parlance, Asian and Middle Eastern women were largely apprehended as embodiments of exotic beauty and sexuality...Black women, however, were frequently portrayed as offensively ugly and frighteningly savage' 1998, 7. White women, on the other hand, though coming 'close to slipping into the category of "otherness" reserved for "savages" and "exotics" in the perceptions of the exposition's male architects, were redeemed from this category "through their capacity to serve as mothers of civilization"' (p. 8). In the Caribbean, both black and brown women were sexualized through the eyes of the colonizer.
7. See, for example, Brereton 1999, Shepherd 1995 and Reddock 1994.
8. Mohammed Orfry, CO 571/4 WI22518 (1916), quoted in Reddock (1985a. 84).
9. Although most of the studies on the period after indentureship concern Trinidad, it is reasonable to assume that similar images were constructed in other parts of the region, given the parallels in histories of Indians in the Caribbean.
10. The complexity of colour and sexual desirability in the post-colonial Caribbean societies remains a contested subject. Noting the shift around beauty ideals in the Caribbean during the 1960s,

Henriques, citing research by Errol Miller, points out that attractiveness was no longer seen as constituted by white femininity, but rather 'the beautiful girl has Caucasian features and is Fair or Clear in color,' but that 'the paradox of the situation is that even the most vehement of Black Power leaders in both the Caribbean and the United States tend to have white wives' (1974, 113). This is not unlike trends I encountered in my earlier research in Curaçao (Kempadoo 1996). Barnes (1997) and Mohammed (2000a, 2000b) have also both grappled with this complexity, exploring aspects of the ideologies of 'whitening-up' and 'browning' that cohabit with notions of sexual desirability.

11. <http://www.paranoia.com/faq/prostitution>; <http://www.worldsexguide.com/world/cuba/index.htm>. These letters described tourist experiences in the Caribbean countries of Aruba, Cuba, Curaçao, Dominican Republic, Jamaica, Puerto Rico and Suriname. In most cases the authors did not identify their home countries, but several authors indicated that they lived in Chicago, Los Angeles, Miami, New York, Nevada, Texas, Canada, Germany, England, the Netherlands or the United States in general.
12. It should be kept in mind that these images combine with actual prostitution activities in which the women's sexual labour is criminalized and their lives are subject to intense harassment by police and government authorities, coercion and force by men seeking to make a monetary profit from their exoticized bodies and exploitation for the satisfaction of tourist's desires. See Kempadoo 1999b for case studies and rich descriptions of the conditions of the sex trade in various Caribbean locations.
13. 11 February 1996, <http://www.paranoia.com/faq/prostitution/BocaChica.txt.html>.
14. 11 June 1997, <http://www.paranoia.com/faq/prostitution/Havana.txt.html>.
15. 20 October 1997, <http://www.paranoia.com/faq/prostitution/dr_expert.txt.html>.
16. 4 March 1996, <http://www.paranoia.com/faq/prostitution/cuba_bits.txt.html>.
17. 16 April 1996, <http://www.paranoia.com/faq/prostitution/dr_travel.txt.html>.
18. October 1996, <http://www.paranoia.com/faq/prostitution/aruba_general. txt.html>.
19. 20 January 1997, <http://www.paranoia.com/faq/prostitution/dr_travel.txt.html>.
20. 6 May 1997, <http://www.paranoia.com/faq/prostitution/Negril.txt.html>.
21. 5 September 1996. <http://www.paranoia.com/faq/prostitution/dr_travel2.txt.html>.
22. 11 March 1997, <http://www.paranoia.com/faq/prostitution/Santo-Domingo.txt.html>.
23. 7 March 1997, <http://www.paranoia.com/faq/prostitution/Puerto-Rico.txt.html>.
24. n.d., <http://www.paranoia.com/faq/prostitution/Guanabo.txt.html>.
25. 28 March 1997, <http://www.paranoia.com/faq/prostitution/Havana.txt.html>.
26. 27 June 1995, <http://www.paranoia.com/faq/prostitution/dr_travel.txt.html>.
27. 2 July 1995, <http://www.paranoia.com/faq/prostitution/cuba_faq.txt.html>.
28. 26 July 1998, <http://www.worldsexguide.com/world/cuba/index.htm>.
29. 19 March 1997, <http://www.paranoia.com/faq/prostitution/drbits.txt.html>.
30. Perhaps the best-known illustration of the eroticized relationship between North American women travellers and Caribbean men can be found in Terry MacMillan's novel *How Stella Got Her Groove Back*. MacMillan's account has also spurred the notion that 'love' can be found by women vacationers to the Caribbean. As one young woman writes under the heading 'Want What Stella Had!': 'My girlfriend and I are planning a JAMAICAN getaway in July/August, but don't know where to go. We want a place that's suitable for two 25 year-old (single) best friends...We're looking for our groove with the hope of getting it back like Stella did!' (22 December 1999, <http://www.jamaicatravel.com/cgi-bin/mboard/jamaica/thread.cgi?361,0>l. In a more reflective mode. Gearing (1995) – a white American woman – offers one of the more honest accounts of doing anthropological fieldwork as a doctoral student and marrying one of her 'native' informants.

References

Abraham-Van der mark, Eva. 1993. Marriage and Concubinage among the Sephardic Merchant Elite of Curaçao. In *Women and Change in the Caribbean*, ed. Janet Momsen, 38–49. Kingston, Jamaica: Ian Randle Publishers.

Albuquerque, Klaus, ed. 1998. Sex, Beach Boys, and Female Tourists in the Caribbean. *Sexuality and Culture* 2, no. 1:87–112.

Alloula, Malek. 1986. *The Colonial Harem*. Minneapolis: University of Minnesota Press.

Antonius-Smits, Christle C.F. 1999. Gold and Commercial Sex: Exploring the Link Between Small-Scale Gold Mining and Commercial Sex in the Rainforest of Suriname. In *Sun, Sex and Gold: Tourism and*

Sex Work in the Caribbean, ed. Kamala Kempadoo, 237–59. Lanham, Md.: Rowman and Littlefield.
Beckles, Hilary. 1989. *Natural Rebels: A Social History of Enslaved Black Women in Barbados*. London: Zed Books.
———. 1999. *Centering Woman: Gender Discourses in Caribbean Slave Society*. Kingston, Jamaica: Ian Randle Publishers.
Bush, Barbara. 1990. *Slave Women in Caribbean Society, 1650–1838*. Kingston, Jamaica: Heinemann.
Cabezas, Amalia L. 1999. Women's Work is Never Done: Sex Tourism in Sosua, the Dominican Republic. In *Sun, Sex and Gold: Tourism and Sex Work in the Caribbean*, ed. Kamala Kempadoo, 263–90. Lanham, Md.: Rowman and Littlefield.
Campbell, John. 2001. Single White Female...Reconsidering the Dialectic of White Women, Power and Sugar Management on Eighteenth Century British West Indian Caribbean Sugar Estates. Paper presented at the seminar, Conversations with Gender 5, University of the West Indies, Mona, Jamaica, 22 February.
Chanel, Ives Marie. 1994. Haitian and Dominican Women in the Sex Trade. *CAFRA News* 8:13–14.
Crick, Malcolm. 1989. Representations of International Tourism in the Social Sciences: Sun, Sex, Sights, Savings and Servility. *Annual Review of Anthropology* 18:307–44.
Cumber Dance, Daryl. 1993. Matriarchs, Doves and Nymphos: Prevalent Images of Black, Indian and White Women in Caribbean Literature. *Studies in Literary Imagination* 26, no. 2:21–31.
Dagenais, Huguette. 1993. Women in Guadeloupe: The Paradoxes of Reality. In *Women and Change in the Caribbean*, ed. Janet Momsen, 83–108. Kingston, Jamaica: Ian Randle Publishers.
Di Leonardo, Micaela. 1998. *Exotics at Home: Anthropologies, Others, American Modernity*. Chicago: University of Chicago Press.
Espinet, Ramabai. 1993. Representation and the Indo-Caribbean Woman in Trinidad and Tobago. In *Indo-Caribbean Resistance*, ed. Frank Birbalsingh, 42–61. Toronto: TSAR.
Geggus, David P. 1996. Slave and Free Colored Women in Saint Domingue. In *More Than Chattel: Black Women and Slavery in the Americas*, ed. David Barry Gaspar and Darlene Clark Hine, 259–78. Bloomington: Indiana University Press.
Hall, Catherine. 1995. Gender Politics and Imperial Politics: Rethinking the Histories of Empire. In *Engendering History: Caribbean Women in Historical Perspective*, ed. Verene Shepherd, Bridget Brereton and Barbara Bailey, 48–59. Kingston, Jamaica: Ian Randle Publishers.
Henriques, Fernando. 1965. *Prostitution in Europe and the Americas*. New York: Citadel Press.
———. 1974. *Children of Caliban: Miscegenation*. London: Secker and Warburg.
Hentsch, Thierry. 1992. *Imagining the Middle East*. Montreal: Black Rose Books.
Hooks, Bell. 1993. Dreaming Ourselves Dark and Deep: Black Beauty. In *Sisters of the Yam: Black Women and Self-Recovery*, 79–98. Boston: South End Press.
Kabbani, Rana. 1988. *Europe's Myths of Orient: Devise and Rule*. London: Pandora Press.
Kane, Stephanie C. 1993. Prostitution and the Military: Planning AIDS Intervention in Belize. *Social Science and Medicine* 36, no. 7:965–79.
Kempadoo, Kamala. 1996. Prostitution, Marginality and Empowerment: Caribbean Women in the Sex Trade. *Beyond Law* 5, no. 14:69–84.
———. 1999. Continuities and Change: Five Centuries of Prostitution in the Caribbean. In *Sun, Sex and Gold: Tourism and Sex Work in the Caribbean*, ed. Kamala Kempadoo, 263–90. Lanham, Md.: Rowman and Littlefield.
Kerr, Paulette A. 1995. Victims or Strategists? Female Lodging-house Keepers in Jamaica. In *Engendering History: Caribbean Women in Historical Perspective*, ed. Verene Shepherd, Bridget Brereton and Barbara Bailey, 197–212. Kingston, Jamaica: Ian Randle Publishers.
Kinnaird, Vivian, and Derek Hall, eds. 1994. *Tourism: A Gender Analysis*. Chichester, UK: Wiley.
Kutzinski, Vera M. 1993. *Sugar's Secrets: Race and the Erotics of Cuban Nationalism*. Charlottesville: University Press of Virginia.
Lagro, Monique, and Donna Plotkin. 1990. *The Suitcase Traders in the Free Zone of Curaçao*. Port of Spain, Trinidad: Economic Commission for Latin America and the Caribbean, Subregional Headquarters for the Caribbean.
Lewis, Linden. 1998. Masculinity and the Dance of the Dragon: Reading Lovelace Discursively. *Feminist Review*, no. 59:164–85.
Lewis, Reina. 1996. *Gendering Orientalism: Race, Femininity and Representation*. New York: Routledge.

Lim, Lin Lean, ed. 1998. *The Sex Sector: The Economic and Social Bases of Prostitution in Southeast Asia*. Geneva: International Labour Office.

Mangru, Basdeo. 1987. The Sex-Ratio Disparity and Its Consequences under the Indenture in British Guiana. In *India in the Caribbean*, ed. David Dabydeen and Brinsley Samaroo, 211–30. London: Hansib.

Mohammed, Patricia. 1998. Towards Indigenous Feminist Theorizing in the Caribbean. *Feminist Review*, no. 59:6–33.

Moore, Robert J. 1999. Colonial Images of Blacks and Indians in Nineteenth Century Guyana. In *The Colonial Caribbean in Transition: Essays on Postemancipation Social and Cultural History*, ed. Bridget Brereton and Kevin A. Yelvington, 126–58. Kingston, Jamaica: University of the West Indies Press.

Morrisey, Marietta. 1989. *Slave Women in the New World: Gender Stratification in the Caribbean*. Lawrence, Kansas: University Press of Kansas.

O'Connell Davidson, Julia. 1998. *Prostitution, Power and Freedom*. London: Polity.

O'Connell Davidson, Julia, and Jacqueline Sanchez Taylor. 1999. Fantasy Islands: Exploring the Demand for Sex Tourism. In *Sun, Sex and Gold: Tourism and Sex Work in the Caribbean*, ed. Kamala Kempadoo, 263–90. Lanham, Md.: Rowman and Littlefield.

Parker, Richard, Regina Maria Barbarosa and Peter Aggleton. 2000. Framing the Sexual Subject. Introduction to *Framing the Sexual Subject: The Politics of Gender, Sexuality and Power*, 1–25. Berkeley: University of California Press.

Patullo, Polly. 1996. *Last Resorts: The Cost of Tourism in the Caribbean*. Kingston, Jamaica: Ian Randle Publishers.

Phillips, Joan L. 1999. Tourism-Oriented Prostitution in Barbados: The Case of the Beach Boy and the White Female Tourist. In *Sun, Sex and Gold: Tourism and Sex Work in the Caribbean*, ed. Kamala Kempadoo, 263–90. Lanham, Md.: Rowman and Littlefield.

Postma, Johannes Menne. 1990. *The Dutch in the Atlantic Slave Trade, 1600–1815*. Cambridge: Cambridge University Press.

Poynting, Jeremy. 1987. East Indian Women in the Caribbean: Experience and Voice. In *India in the Caribbean*, ed. David Dabydeen and Brinsley Samaroo, 231–63. London: Hansib.

Pruitt, Deborah, and Suzanne La Font. 1995. For Love and Money: Romance Tourism in Jamaica. *Annals of Tourism Research* 22, no. 2:422–40.

Puri, Shalini. 1993. East Indian/West Indian: Discourses of Race and Place in Trinidad. Typescript.

Ragsdale, Kathleen, and Jessica Tomiko Anders. 1998. The Muchachas of Orange Walk Town and Sex Work in Belize. Typescript.

Red Thread Women's Development Programme. 1999. 'Givin' Lil Bit fuh Lil Bit': Women and Sex Work in Guyana. In *Sun, Sex and Gold: Tourism and Sex Work in the Caribbean*, ed. Kamala Kempadoo, 263–90. Lanham, Md.: Rowman and Littlefield.

Reddock, Rhoda. 1985. Freedom Denied: Indian Women and Indentureship in Trinidad and Tobago, 1845–1917. *Economic and Political Weekly* 20, no. 43:79–87.

———. 1994. *Women, Labour and Politics in Trinidad and Tobago: A History*. London: Zed Books.

———. 1998. Contestations over National Culture in Trinidad and Tobago: Considerations of Ethnicity, Class and Gender. In *Caribbean Portraits: Essays on Gender Ideologies and Identities*, ed. Christine Barrow, 414–35. Kingston, Jamaica: Ian Randle Publishers.

Rogers, J.A. 1972. *The New World*. Vol. 2 of Sex and Race. New York: Helga M. Rogers.

Rohlehr, Gordon. 1988. Images of Men and Women in 1930s Calypsoes: The Sociology of Food Acquisition in a Context of Survivalism. In *Gender in Caribbean Development: Papers Presented at the Inaugural Seminar of the University of the West Indies Women and Development Studies Project*, ed. Patricia Mohammed and Catherine Shepherd, 232–306. St Augustine, Trinidad: Women in Development Studies Project, University of the West Indies.

Rousseau, G.S., and Roy Porter, eds. 1990. *Exoticism in the Enlightenment*. Manchester: Manchester University Press.

Said, Edward W. 1979. *Orientalism*. New York: Vintage Books.

Schwartz, Rosalie. 1997. *Pleasure Island: Tourism and Temptation in Cuba*. Lincoln: University of Nebraska Press.

Shepherd, Verene. 1995. Gender, Migration and Settlement: The Indentureship and Post-Indentureship Experience of Indian Females in Jamaica, 1845–1943. In *Engendering History: Caribbean Women in*

Historical Perspective, ed. Verene Shepherd, Bridget Brereton and Barbara Bailey, 233–57. Kingston, Jamaica: Ian Randle Publishers.

Shrage, Laurie. 1994. *Moral Dilemmas of Feminism: Prostitution, Adultery and Abortion*. New York: Routledge.

Travel Industry World Yearbook, 1996–7. 1997. New York: Child and Waters.

Truong, Thanh-Dam. 1990. *Sex, Money and Morality: The Political Economy of Prostitution and Tourism in South East Asia*. London: Zed Books.

Walvin, James. 1992. Selling the Sun: Tourism and Material Consumption. *Revista/Review Interamericana* 22, no. 1–2:208–25.

West, Cornel. 1993. Black Sexuality: The Taboo Subject. In *Race Matters*, 81–91. Boston: Beacon Press.

Yeğenoğlu, Meyda. 1998. *Colonial Fantasies: Towards a Feminist Reading of Orientalism*. Cambridge: Cambridge University Press.

In the Night

Jamaica Kincaid

In the night, way into the middle of the night, when the night isn't divided like a sweet drink into little sips, when there is no just before midnight, midnight, or just after midnight, when the night is round in some places, flat in some places, and in some places like a deep hole, blue at the edge, black inside, the night-soil men come.

They come and go, walking on the damp ground in straw shoes. Their feet in the straw shoes make a scratchy sound. They say nothing.

The night-soil men can see a bird walking in trees. It isn't a bird. It is a woman who has removed her skin and is on her way to drink the blood of her secret enemies. It is a woman who has left her skin in a corner of a house made out of wood. It is a woman who is reasonable and admires honeybees in the hibiscus. It is a woman who, as a joke, brays like a donkey when he is thirsty.

There is the sound of a cricket, there is the sound of a church bell, there is the sound of this house creaking, that house creaking, and the other house creaking as they settle into the ground. There is the sound of a radio in the distance—a fisherman listening to merengue music. There is the sound of a man groaning in his sleep; there is the sound of a woman disgusted at the man groaning. There is the sound of the man stabbing the woman, the sound of her blood as it hits the floor, the sound of Mr. Straffee, the undertaker, taking her body away. There is the sound of her spirit back from the dead, looking at the man who used to groan; he is running a fever forever. There is the sound of a woman writing a letter; there is the sound of her pen nib on the white writing paper; there is the sound of the kerosene lamp dimming; there is the sound of her head aching.

The rain falls on the tin roofs, on the leaves in the trees, on the stones in the yard, on sand, on the ground. The night is wet in some places, warm in some places.

There is Mr. Gishard, standing under a cedar tree which is in full bloom, wearing that nice white suit, which is as fresh as the day he was buried in it. The white suit came from England in a brown package: "To: Mr. John Gishard," and so on and so on. Mr. Gishard is standing under the tree, wearing his nice suit and holding a glass full of rum in his hand—the same glass full of rum that he had in his hand shortly before he died—and looking at the house in which he used to live. The people who now live in the house walk through the door backward when they see Mr. Gishard standing under the tree, wearing his nice white suit. Mr. Gishard misses his accordion; you can tell by the way he keeps tapping his foot.

***

In my dream I can hear a baby being born. I can see its face, a pointy little face—so nice. I can see its hands—so nice, again. Its eyes are closed. It's breathing, the little baby. It's breathing. It's bleating, the little baby. It's bleating. The baby and I are now walking to pasture. The baby is eating green grass with its soft and pink lips. My mother is shaking me by the shoulders. My mother says, "Little Miss, Little Miss." I say to my mother, "But it's still night." My mother says, "Yes, but you have wet your bed again." And my mother, who is still young, and still beautiful, and still has pink lips, removes my wet nightgown, removes my wet sheets from my bed. My mother can change everything. In my dream I am in the night.

"What are the lights in the mountains?"
"The lights in the mountains? Oh, it's a jablesse."
"A jablesse! But why? What's a jablesse?"

"It's a person who can turn into anything. But you can tell they aren't real because of their eyes. Their eyes shine like lamps, so bright that you can't look. That's how you can tell it's a jablesse. They like to go up in the mountains and gallivant. Take good care when you see a beautiful woman. A jablesse always tries to look like a beautiful woman."

***

No one has ever said to me, "My father, a night-soil man, is very nice and very kind. When he passes a dog, he gives a pat and not a kick. He likes all the parts of a fish but especially the head. He goes to church quite regularly and is always glad when the minister calls out, 'A Mighty Fortress Is Our God,' his favorite hymn. He would like to wear pink shirts and pink pants but knows that this color isn't very becoming to a man, so instead he wears navy blue and brown, colors he does not like at all. He met my mother on what masquerades as a bus around here, a long time ago, and he still likes to whistle. Once, while running to catch a bus, he fell and broke his ankle and had to spend a week in hospital. This made him miserable, but he cheered up quite a bit when he saw my mother and me, standing over his white cot, holding bunches of yellow roses and smiling down at him. Then he said, 'Oh, my. Oh, my.' What he likes to do most, my father the night-soil man, is to sit on a big stone under a mahogany tree and watch small children playing play-cricket while he eats the intestines of animals stuffed with blood and rice and drinks ginger beer. He has told me this many times: 'My dear, what I like to do most,' and so on. He is always reading botany books and knows a lot about rubber plantations and rubber trees; but this is an interest I can't explain, since the only rubber tree he has ever seen is a specially raised one in the botanic gardens. He sees to it that my school shoes fit comfortably. I love my father the night-soil man. My mother loves my father the night-soil man. Everybody loves him and waves to him whenever they see him. He is very handsome, you know, and I have seen women look at him twice. On special days he wears a brown felt hat, which he orders from England, and brown leather shoes, which he also orders from England. On ordinary days he goes barehead. When he calls me, I say, 'Yes, sir.' On my mother's birthday he always buys her some nice cloth for a new dress as a present. He makes us happy, my father the night-soil man, and has promised that one day he will take us to see something he has read about called the circus."

***

In the night, the flowers close up and thicken. The hibiscus flowers, the flamboyant flowers, the bachelor's buttons, the irises, the marigolds, the whitehead-bush flowers, the lilies, the flowers on the daggerbush, the flowers on the turtleberry bush, the flowers on the soursop tree, the flowers on the sugar-apple tree, the flowers on the mango tree, the flowers on the guava tree, the flowers on the cedar tree, the flowers on the stinking-toe tree, the flowers on the dumps tree, the flowers on the papaw tree, the flowers everywhere close up and thicken. The flowers are vexed.

Someone is making a basket, someone is making a girl a dress or a boy a shirt, someone is making her husband a soup with cassava so that he can take it to the cane field tomorrow, someone is making his wife a beautiful mahogany chest, someone is sprinkling a colorless powder outside a closed door so that someone else's child will be stillborn, someone is praying that a bad child who is living prosperously abroad will be good and send a package filled with new clothes, someone is sleeping.

***

Now I am a girl, but one day I will marry a woman—a red-skin woman with black bramblebush hair and brown eyes, who wears skirts that are so big I can easily bury my head in them. I would like to marry this woman and live with her in a mud hut near the sea. In the mud hut will be two chairs and one table, a lamp that burns kerosene, a medicine chest, a pot, one bed, two pillows, two sheets, one looking glass, two cups, two saucers, two dinner plates, two forks, two drinking-water glasses, one china pot, two fishing strings, two straw hats to ward the hot sun off our heads, two trunks for things we have very little use for, one basket, one book of plain paper, one box filled with twelve crayons of different colors, one loaf of bread wrapped in a piece of brown paper, one coal pot, one picture of two women standing on a jetty, one picture of the same two women embracing, one picture of the same two women waving goodbye, one box of matches. Every day this red-skin woman and I will eat bread and milk for breakfast, hide in bushes and throw hardened cow dung at people we don't like, climb coconut trees, pick coconuts, eat and drink the food and water from the coconuts we have picked, throw stones in the sea, put on John Bull masks and frighten defenseless little children on their way home from school, go fishing and catch only our favorite fishes to roast and have for dinner, steal green figs to eat for dinner with the roast fish. Every day we would do this. Every night I would sing this woman a song; the words I don't know yet, but the tune is in my head. This woman I would like to marry knows many things, but to me she will only tell about things that would never dream of making me cry; and every night, over and over, she will tell me something that begins, "Before you were born." I will marry a woman like this, and every night, every night, I will be completely happy.

Caribbean Religions and Spiritualities

Introduction to *Creole Religions of the Caribbean:*
An Introduction from Vodou and Santería to Obeah and Espiritismo

Margarite Fernández Olmos and
Lizabeth Paravisini-Gebert

> What piece of our soil was not saturated with secret African influences?
> —Lydia Cabrera, *Yemayá y Ochún*

Luis is a young man who works in the stockroom of a tourist café in Havana. An inventory reveals five boxes of missing supplies and, despite his claims of innocence, the police consider him a suspect. In his distress, he seeks Marín, his spiritual godfather or *padrino*, a lifelong friend whose spiritual work in Santería, Regla de Palo, and Espiritismo follows the practices of his African ancestors. Marín summons the spirit of Ma Pancha, an African slave with whom he has communicated on previous occasions. Marín sits before a home altar that contains, among other things, the statues of the Catholic saints San Juan Bosco and Santa Bárbara, and a glass of water. Uncorking a bottle of strong cane liquor, he pours a drink into a dry gourd, lights a homemade cigar, and chants a verse, calling upon her spirit to respond "in the name of Jesus Christ and of Papá Changó." At this point Ma Pancha greets them in broken Spanish through Marín's voice with "Good morning, how are my children here on this earth?" and is informed of the problem. Stating that Luis's boss is responsible for the theft, Ma Pancha counsels the men to gather the bark of certain types of trees "to open the eyes of the police" and suggests that Marín prepare a *macuto* or magical pouch, and dedicate it to Ochosi, the deity of forests and herbs, patron of those with problems involving the law, to protect Luis and convince the authorities of his innocence. The macuto is assembled with the name of the guilty party placed inside and set at the base of a nganga or spiritual cauldron.

Paulette, a middle-aged Haitian woman living in Coral Gables, Miami, has been married to a lawyer and former politician for many years. When she discovers that her husband is having an affair with his young secretary, a friend suggests she speak with Denizé, a houngan, or Vodou priest who does spiritual readings using cards for divination. During the reading Paulette discovers that her tutelary *lwa* is Erzulie, spirit of femininity and sensuality, and Denizé advises her to make efforts to become more attractive to her husband. He recommends a purifying bath of white flowers, powdered egg shells, and perfume, during which Paulette would be released from all negativity. Afterwards, she is to leave the flowers at a crossroads. He instructs Paulette to cleanse her house with water composed of the same ingredients as the bath, adding a bit of honey. She is to make an offering to Erzulie of sweet fruit and honey to be placed on her home altar. After the reading, Denizé prepares a small bottle of perfume for Paulette to bring her *chans*, or luck. In it he had inserted a small plant (wont) believed to have the power to open paths for the achievement of goals.

Desmond and Earl, young Jamaicans living in Toronto, have engaged in a series of robberies involving small suburban banks. They are assiduous clients of an Obeahman, from whom they seek the ritual cleansings and massages they believe will protect them from arrest and punishment. When they kill a young woman during a robbery, their Obeahman alerts the police to their possible involvement. Surveillance equipment is installed in his consultation room, and when his clients return—this time seeking protection that will allow them to return to Jamaica, where the woman's duppy or spirit will not follow them to do them harm—their sessions are recorded and the evidence leads to their arrest. The case against them centers on the admissibility of the evidence, an issue that itself revolves around the confidentiality—or sacredness—of the communications, or "confessions," between the Obeahman and his client. The sanctity of their interactions is rejected by the courts on the basis of Obeah being a healing practice and not a religion, and the two are convicted of robbery and murder.

These tales—based on the actual experiences of people living in the Caribbean and its Diaspora—speak to the continuing power of the Afro-Caribbean spiritual traditions that have sustained the peoples of the region for centuries. *Creole Religions of the Caribbean* is intended as a comprehensive introduction to the creolized, African-based religions that developed in the Caribbean in the wake of European colonization. It seeks to show how Caribbean peoples fashioned a heterogeneous system of belief out of the cacophony of practices and traditions that came forcibly together in colonial society: the various religious and healing traditions represented by the extensive slave population brought to the New World through the Middle Passage; Spanish, French, and Portuguese variants of Catholicism; the myriad strands of Protestantism brought to the English and Dutch colonies; and remnants of Amerindian animistic practices.

These creolized religious systems, developed in secrecy, were frequently outlawed by the colonizers because they posed a challenge to official Christian practices and were believed to be associated with magic and sorcery. They nonetheless allowed the most oppressed sectors of colonial Caribbean societies to manifest their spirituality, express cultural and political practices suppressed by colonial force, and protect the health of the community. These complex systems developed in symbiotic relationships to the social, linguistic, religious, and natural environments of the various islands of the Caribbean, taking their form and characteristics from the subtle blends and clashes between different cultural, political, and spiritual practices. This book traces the historical-cultural origins of the major Creole religions and spiritual practices of the region—Vodou, Santería, Obeah, Espiritismo—and describes their current-day expression in the Caribbean and its Diaspora.[1]

Caribbean Creole religions developed as the result of cultural contact. The complex dynamics of encounters, adaptations, assimilation, and syncretism that we refer to as creolization are emblematic of the vibrant nature of Diaspora cultures. They led to the development of a complex system of religious and healing practices that allowed enslaved African communities that had already suffered devastating cultural loss to preserve a sense of group and personal identity. Having lost the connection between the spirits and Africa during the Middle Passage, they strove to adapt their spiritual environment to suit their new Caribbean space. The flexibility, eclecticism, and malleability of African religions allowed practitioners to adapt to their new environments, drawing spiritual power from wherever it originated. More than simply a strategy for survival, this dynamic, conscious, syncretic process demonstrates an appreciation for the intrinsic value of creativity, growth, and change as well as for the spiritual potential of other belief systems.

Transculturation, a term coined by Cuban anthropologist Fernando Ortiz to describe the ceaseless creation of new cultures, was intended to counterbalance the notion of *acculturation*, the term in vogue among anthropologists during the 1940s. Ortiz understood the notion of acculturation as one that interpreted the development of Caribbean cultures as the one-way imposition of the culture of the dominant or conquering nation on the conquered societies, an imposition that devalued and eventually supplanted the conquered cultures. Believing that colonization had initiated instead a creative, ongoing process of appropriation, revision, and survival leading to the mutual transformation of two or more pre-existing cultures into a new one, Ortiz posited the notion of transculturation as a more accurate rendering of the processes that produced contemporary Caribbean cultures.

Religious practices were at the very center of the processes of transculturation. "Throughout the diaspora, African religions provided important cultural resources for not only reconstructing ethnic ties and social relations that had been disrupted by slavery, but also for forging new collective identities, institutions and belief systems which partook of the cultures of diverse African peoples to meet the daunting challenges of new and oppressive social contexts" (Gregory 1999: 12). The metaphor for the process of transculturation used by Fernando Ortiz is the ajiaco, a delicious soup made with very diverse ingredients, in which the broth that stays at the bottom represents an integrated nationality, the product of synthesis. This metaphor has found an echo throughout the Caribbean region, finding its counterpart in the Dominican sancocho and the West Indian callaloo. However, although rich in metaphoric power, neither the ajiaco nor the callaloo are ideal formulas. They have been challenged by Caribbean scholars and critics for failing to do full justice to the "undissolved ingredients" represented by the magical, life-affirming elements of Afro-Caribbean religions. Cuban art critic Gerardo Mosquera, for example, has argued that "beside the broth of synthesis, there are bones, gristle, and hard seeds that never fully dissolve, even after they have contributed their substance to the broth. These undissolved ingredients are the survivals and recreations of African traditions within religious-cultural complexes" (1992: 30).

Creolization

Creolization—that is, the malleability and mutability of various beliefs and practices as they adapt to new understandings of class, race, gender, power, labor, and sexuality—is one of the most significant phenomena in Caribbean religious history. Given the subtle negotiations necessary for the survival of the cultural practices of the enslaved and colonized in the highly hierarchical colonial societies of the Caribbean, the resulting religious systems are fundamentally complex, pluralistic, and integrationist. In our approach to the creolized religious systems that developed in the region in the wake of colonization, we seek to avoid essentialist definitions of religious experience, opting instead for a practice- or experience-based presentation and analysis, rooted in particular historical circumstances. Although the Creole religions vary in their origins, beliefs, and rituals, all of them demonstrate the complexities and the creative resourcefulness of the creolization process.

The term *creole* was first used in the Americas to refer to native-born persons of European ancestry and evolved from a geographical to an ethnic label: New World enslaved Africans were distinguished from African-born contemporaries by the label *criollos*. Hoetink notes the multiple contemporary nuances of the term:[2]

> I take the word *creole* to mean the opposite of foreign. Thus *creole culture* refers to those aspects of culture that evolved or were adapted in the Western Hemisphere and became part of a New World society's distinctive heritage. In Latin America, the term *criollo*, when used in reference to people, was originally reserved for native whites. In the Hispanic Caribbean nowadays, it often includes all those born and bred in a particular society. Elsewhere, as in Suriname, the term may be used to denote long-established population groups, such as the Afro-Americans, as opposed to more recent immigration groups (Hoetink 1985: 82).

Melville Herskovits challenged prevailing assumptions regarding the survival of African influences in the New World in his *The Myth of the Negro Past* (1941), demonstrating in great detail that African culture has survived and indeed thrived. In the 1970s, Edward Kamau Brathwaite in his essay "The African Presence in Caribbean Literature" and in *Folk Cultures of the Slaves in Jamaica*, claimed that the Middle Passage "was not, as is popularly assumed, a traumatic, destructive experience, separating the blacks from Africa, disconnecting their sense of history and tradition, but a pathway or channel between this tradition and what is being evolved, on new soil, in the Caribbean" (E. Brathwaite 1974: 5).

Creolization thus describes the ongoing and ever-changing process (not the static result) of new forms born or developed from the interaction of peoples and forces due to "adaptive pressures omnipresent and irresistible" in the Americas (Buisseret, "Introduction" 2000: 7). The concept of Creole and creolization has been extended to other "transplanted" categories of interchange: from linguistic speech variations (*Créole*, for example, refers to the national language of Haiti, developed as a result of Old and New World contact) and literary to a wide range of cultural contexts—religious, musical, curative, and culinary (Mintz and Price 1985: 6–7). "There is, then, a vast range of examples of the Creolizing process, even without taking into account such areas of human activity as art, law, material culture, military organization, politics, or social structures" (Buisseret, "Introduction" 2000: 12).

Anthropologists, historians, literary and social critics continue to expand the linguistic application of the term creolization to that of metaphor for a wide and diverse cross-cultural and transnational phenomena. Aisha Khan's essay in *Creolization: History, Ethnography, Theory* describes our conception of the term as defined above and throughout this book as a "means of revealing the successful and creative agency of subaltern or deterritorialized peoples, and the subversiveness inhering in creolization, which contradicts earlier notions of cultural dissolution and disorganization" and considers it among several definitions used in creolist scholarship.[3] The editor of Creolization, Charles Stewart, acknowledges that the term "'creole' has itself creolized, which is what happens to all productive words with long histories."[4]

> [T]he concept of creolization is at once fascinating, fertile and potentially confusing. Those who approach it from one or another of the disciplinary approaches or literary currents ... or with the normative meaning from a particular historical period in mind, are in for some surprises should they encounter it outside their own familiar territory (3).

According to Silvio Torres-Saillant in *An Intellectual History of the Caribbean*, in the late 1980s the focus on postcolonial cultural studies and globalizing theoretical approaches in European and North American intellectual circles elicited globalized paradigms from Caribbeanists: "Perhaps sensing that the focus of Third World thought production had shifted away from their region, Caribbeanists gradually came to give in to the new academic world order. Thus marginalized, they began to assert the relevance of their studies by highlighting their link to the larger, grander, and more 'theoretical' postcolonial field" (43). The manner in which they secured their intellectual legitimacy, however, is problematic for Torres-Saillant: Caribbeanists relied on the pillars of Western tradition as they did prior to the rise of anticolonialism in the region, reaffirming the "centrality of Western critical theory" (44).[5] One example he cites among many is Antonio Benítez Rojo, who examined the notion of creolization utilizing the Western scientific branch of physics known as Chaos Theory in his influential work, *The Repeating Island: The Caribbean and the Postmodern Perspective* (1989), which describes creolization by means of three fundamental principles: plantation, rhythm, and performance.

> [C]reolization is not merely a process (a word that implies forward movement) but a discontinuous series of recurrences, of happenings, whose sole law is change. Where does this instability come from? It is the product of the plantation (the big bang of the Caribbean universe), whose slow explosion throughout modern history threw out billions and billions of cultural fragments in all directions—fragments of diverse kinds that, in their endless voyage, come together in an instant to form a dance step, a linguistic trope, the line of a poem, and afterward repel each other to re-form and pull apart once more, and so on (1998: 55).[6]

Cultural *bricolage*, from the French meaning to improvise with whatever is at hand—a concept introduced by French structural anthropologist Claude Lévi-Strauss in *The Savage Mind* (1966) to describe a form of being in the world—is another Western model used to describe the creolization process. "Creolization can be seen enacted through *bricolage* as the art of the disparate and fragmentary; the art of adopting and adapting multiple concrete fragments or artifacts as well as elements of imaginative, ideological, cultural, social or religious practices, experiences, and beliefs" (Knepper 73). Wendy Knepper notes, however, that while Lévi-Strauss's use of the term *bricolage* may be politically neutral, the application of the word to describe the creolization process in the Caribbean is evasive; there cultural *bricolage* was an uneven process, highly politicized, involving "selective, coerced, forced, and violent intermixtures in addition to spontaneous meldings, subversive appropriations, and processes of adaptation. The creolist appropriation of this structuralist term could be seen as instituting a kind of white-washing of *bricolage* rather than consciously embracing the ambivalent cultural and sociopolitical etymology of *bricolage* within the Caribbean" (73).

The concept of creolization has thus expanded to become synonymous with hybridity, syncretism, multicultural, *créolité, métissage, mestizaje,* postcolonial and diasporic.[7] In an age of mass migrations and globalization, creolization is employed to reframe notions of past and present transnational and diasporan cultures and communities. In the French West Indies, for example, the concept of *créolite* was formulated by authors Jean Bernabé, Patrick Chamoiseau and Raphael Confiant in their *Eloge de la créolité* (In Praise of Creoleness, 1989) wherein creole identity is based on a multi-ethnic and multi-lingual Caribbean culture; it is also a response to the African-identified model of *négritude* and its defiant affirmation of black anticolonial identity.

Martinican author Edouard Glissant contributes to the discourse on cultural creolization by expanding the multiple metaphors of the creolization process and the language of creole cultural identity. Responding to the notion of *créolité*, Glissant presented his influential concept of *antillanité* (Caribbeanness) creating a postcolonial "Archipelic" view: a creole identity which is highly flexible and adaptable and "traces the path from an ontological model of being to an historically and geographically situated, hence changeable, existence" (Schwieger Hiepko 244). Indeed Glissant speaks of the "archipelagoization" of the Caribbean in its interaction with Africa and the United States, and of the world.

> Europe is being "archipelagoized" in its turn and is splitting into regions. Florida is in the process of changing completely in response to its Cuban and Caribbean populations. It seems to me that these new dimensions of existence escape national realities which are trying to resist the forces of archipelagoization. ...We must accustom our minds to these new world structures, in which the relationship between the center and the periphery will be completely different. Everything will be central and everything will be peripheral (2000).

Creolization as a concept can never be neutral; its very semantic origins force us to confront issues of power, race and history. Stephan Palmié questions the "proliferating mangroves of metaphors" of Caribbean/Creolization rhetoric beyond linguistic applications to other "kinds of discourses on 'culture,' local or global", creating a transglobal identity that may be empirically and theoretically ill advised (2006: 443, 434). Although scholars and critics are always eager for new analytical and descriptive tropes, more specificity in the construction of indigenously Caribbean analytical and political projects could avoid an imaginary reinvention of the region: "It is difficult to understand how—other than by retrospectively constructing a 'Caribbean' of the (nonregionalist) anthropological imagination—we could ever have regarded the region as a 'prototype' (in both temporal and evolutionary senses) of an allegedly global postmodern condition" (443). Palmié offers the example of Ulf Hannerz's 1987 article "The World in Creolisation," regarded by Palmié as an essay that establishes a "creolization paradigm" in which Hannerz claims "we are all being creolised" yet does not recur to a "single intellectual (or social scientist) from the Caribbean" (443). The expediency of using creolization as a conceptual tool will undoubtedly continue to be controversial and problematic. For Torres-Saillant, such authors as Glissant and Benítez-Rojo, while contributing impressive organizing metaphors that capture the complexity of Caribbean history and culture at a discursive level, fail, in his estimation, to take into account the region's extratextual reality nor the "trauma of our catastrophic history... postcolonial studies have seldom shed meaningful new light on historical, cultural, or political dynamics in the region" (238).

Syncretism

In current theories of globalization, creole and creolization are often mentioned as synonyms of hybridity and syncretism. "All these terms, currently used in positive senses to describe the resilience, creativity, and inevitability of cultural mixture, had extremely pejorative meanings in the past. In the cases of syncretism and hybridity, various writers have examined these pasts and reappropriated the terms through a positive reevaluation of the political significance of mixture" (Stewart 2007: 4).The strategies of religious syncretism—the active transformation through renegotiation, reorganization, and redefinition of clashing belief systems—are consistent with the creolization process.

In *African Civilizations in the New World,* Roger Bastide differentiated between various categories of religious syncretism in the Caribbean, among them morphological or mosaic syncretism based on the juxtaposition and coexistence of African-derived elements and Catholic symbols—the Vodou *pé,* or altars, with stones, wax candles, crosses, the statues of saints, and pots containing souls of the dead, for example—and institutional syncretism, which combines prescribed religious observances by reconciling Christian and African liturgical calendars (1971: 154–156). The most common, however, is syncretism by correspondence, or what Leslie Desmangles calls a "symbiosis by identity," through which an African deity and a Catholic saint became one on the basis of mythical or symbolic similarities.[8]

Syncretism has been a polemical term for centuries. In the seventeenth century it was used to defend "true" religion against heresy and referred to the "illegitimate reconciliation of opposing theological views" (Droogers 1989: 9). The term was later applied by scholars to the early forms of Christianity that were perceived to be syncretic as well, and was later broadened to apply to all religions when a review of religious history revealed syncretic elements at the foundation of all major religions. However, syncretism is not a value-free concept. The identification of Creole religions as "syncretic" is problematical and disparaging: a Eurocentric bias limits the definition to non-European religions, negating their full legitimacy. Creole religions are frequently identified with and "legitimized" by accentuating their Roman Catholic elements, for example, but are not always afforded an equivalent status.

The term "syncretism" first appeared in Plutarch's *Moralia* in reference to the behavior of the Cretan peoples who "mixed together," came to accord, or closed ranks when confronted by a mutual enemy; it was later used to describe an integration of two or more separate beliefs into a new religion. Thus, from its origins, the term presupposes encounter and confrontation between systems: "Syncretism is in the first place *contested* religious interpenetration" (Droogers 1989: 20).[9] Though all definitions of syncretism are thorny, Michael Pye recognizes the term's dynamism when he describes it as "the temporary ambiguous coexistence of elements from diverse religions and other contexts within a coherent religious pattern" and considers that the process should be understood as "a natural moving aspect of major religious traditions...a part of the dynamics of religion which works its way along in the ongoing transplantation of these religious traditions from one cultural context to another whether geographically or in time" (1971: 92). However, despite the existence of historical interactions, borrowings, and modifications based on contact and context that have occurred among all the major religions, the rhetorical division between so-called *pure* faiths and *illicit* or "contaminated" syncretic belief systems persists, often mentioned with the related concepts of "hybridization and creolization as a means of portraying the dynamics of global social developments" (Stewart 1999: 40). Syncretism in the Creole context is not the description of a static condition or result but of a dynamic process. Roman Catholic missionaries adopted a policy of "guided syncretism" during the conquest of the Americas and the colonial period, tolerating the existence of a polytheistic idolatry that could be identified with Catholic saints and considering it a necessary evil—a transitional state that would eventually lead the conquered peoples to the "true" faith and the elimination of such beliefs. However, the policy never fully realized its goals. The old gods refused to disappear (and still do).[10]

Whether to avoid further oppression in a type of "defensive syncretism"[11] or to gain legitimacy, the conquered peoples embraced Christian forms but with new meanings they themselves had refashioned, at times appropriating them as tools of resistance.[12] According to Mosquera, syncretism should designate "something that corresponds more to the concept of 'appropriation,' in the sense of taking over for one's own use and on one's own initiative the diverse and even the hegemonic or imposed elements, in contrast to assuming an attitude of passive eclecticism or synthesis," strategies that he claims are clearer now thanks to the evolution of a "postmodern" contemporary consciousness (1996: 227). The stress on syncretism and such terms as "syncretic cults" emphasizes the "accessory syncretic elements to the detriment of the essence: the truly effective evolutions of African religions in America" (Mosquera 1992: 30).

In an interesting example of the historical revision of the definition of cultural and religious "legitimacy," Stephen Palmié notes in "Against Syncretism: 'Africanizing' and 'Cubanizing' Discourses in North American òrìsà Worship," that the American Yoruba movement created in the United States in the 1960s, also known as Yoruba-Reversionism or Oyotunji-Movement, has attempted to purge all European elements from Cuban and Cuban-American Santería/Regla de Ocha in order to regain a more "pure" form of worship and cultural "legitimacy." The re-Africanization of "syncretistically adulterated" Cuban beliefs and practices "runs counter to an understanding of 'tradition' still at the very heart of North American variants of Afro-Cuban religious practices" (77). A movement to eliminate any vestiges of European religions from Santería and other Creole religions, led by so-called "African revisionists," and return to a more "pure" and "authentic" African-centered religion has led to African-centered movements in Cuba as well where some advocate for a "religión Yoruba" to replace Regla de Ocha/Santería.

For Andrew Apter, religious syncretism is yet another form of empowerment, another modality of revision and popular resistance:

> The syncretic revision of dominant discourses sought to transform the authority that these discourses upheld...the power and violence mobilized by slave revolts and revolution were built into the logic of New World syncretism itself. The Catholicism of Vodou, Candomblé and Santería was not an ecumenical screen, hiding the worship of African deities from official persecution. It was the religion of the masters, revised, transformed, and appropriated by slaves to harness its power within their universes of discourse. In this way the slaves took possession of Catholicism and thereby repossessed themselves as active spiritual subjects. (1991: 254)[13] And, according to Laura E. Pérez in "Hybrid Spiritualities and Chicana Altar-Based Art," U.S. Latina/o artists and intellectuals in the fields of religion and visual arts are radically redefining the understanding of religious and cultural syncretism beyond the Eurocentric notion "that vestiges of the precolonial survive as largely incoherent fragments within the engulfing colonial culture" and replacing it with the realization that globalization has restructured religious beliefs and practices and given birth to "altogether new forms" (344-345).

Shared Characteristics of Creole Religions

Despite notable differences among African-based Caribbean Creole practices, a general overview of the Creole religions reveals that they share a number of fundamental features.[14]

1. The first of these is their characteristic combination of monotheism and polytheism. At the center of all Afro-Caribbean religions is a belief in a unique Supreme Being—creator of the universe. This belief is complemented by belief in a pantheon of deities (*orishas, loas,* and the like) who are emanations of the Creator and who serve as intermediaries between mankind and the supreme god.

2. These religious practices are also linked by a cult of dead ancestors and/or deceased members of the religious community who watch over and influence events from beyond.

3. In addition, Creole religions share a belief in an active, supernatural, mysterious power that can be invested in objects (mineral, vegetable, animals, humans); this force is not intrinsic to the objects themselves.

4. This belief is in turn linked to animistic beliefs in other spirits (often found in nature), beyond the divinities and the ancestors, who can also be contacted and who can exert a positive or negative influence over a person's life. Plants and trees, for example, have a will and a soul, as do all things under the sun.

5. Afro-Caribbean religions are centered on the principle of contact or mediation between humans and the spirit world, which is achieved through such numerous and complex rituals as divinatory practices, initiation, sacrifice, spiritual possession, and healings.[15]

6. These contacts are mediated by a central symbol or focus, a fundament or philosophical foundation that serves as the dynamic organizing principle of spiritual worship: the sacred stones (*otanes*) of the Afro-Cuban Regla de Ocha and the *nganga* cauldron and sign tracings of Regla de Palo, the sacred Ekué drum of the Abakuá Secret Society, and the *poto-mitan* of the Vodou ritual space (the *hounfort*). These and other consecrated objects are not merely the symbols of the gods but are the material receptacles of divine power. The image of Catholic saints and the crucifix may appear to dominate altars or shrines, but, as William Bascom has noted regarding the Afro-Cuban religions, the stones, blood, and herbs of ritual

offerings and sacrifice contain the "secrets" and are the real focus of religious power (1950, 1972).

7. Central to religious ceremonies of Creole Religions is music and dance: sound has the power to transmit action. Consecrated drums and the polyrhythmic percussion they produce, along with clapping, the spoken or sung word in repeated chants and dance (rhythms and dance are coded to the identities of the gods that are summoned in ceremonies and rituals), produce an altered focus of consciousness that beckons the supernatural entities and communicates between worlds.[16]

8. Music and dance are also instrumental in strengthening the conscious sense of community and an institutionalized regrouping of Africans and their descendants, and transference of African "space" into houses, temples, or rooms. More than simply religious groups, ritual communities re-create the type of family ties and obligations to the deities and to each other that would have existed in Africa.

9. The re-creation relies on religious leaders responsible for the care of the religious space, sacred objects, and ritual implements and the general spiritual care of the community, who represent "the depository of maximum mystical and initiatory powers and liturgical knowledge. The cult priest [priestess] distributes or 'plants' power by initiating novices and infusing them with the power of which he is the depository" (Dos Santos and Dos Santos 1984: 77). There is no central authority in Creole religions, however; worship is individualized and community-based. Devotees are members of a religion, but not of a specific institutionalized church.

10. In Caribbean Creole religions, spiritual power is internalized and mobilized in human beings who become, through the experience of possession, "a real live altar in which the presence of the supernatural beings can be invoked."[17] In possession, the deities—orishas, loas—manifest themselves through the bodies of the initiated.[18] "During the experience of possession, the entire religious system, its theogony and mythology, are relived. Each participant is the protagonist of a ritualistic activity, in which Black historic, psychological, ethnic, and cosmic life is renewed" (Dos Santos and Dos Santos 1984: 78). Ritual dramatizes myth and promotes the magic that responds to life's problems.[19]

11. The practice of magic in the form of spells, conjurations, and ethno-magical medicine-healing; given its complexity it deserves a more extensive examination here.

Magic, Witchcraft and Healing

The logic, structure and "technology" of magic in Creole religions follow the principles described by Sir James Frazer in his classic text *The Golden Bough (1922)*: "homeopathic" or "imitative" magic following the law of similarity in which like produces like and an effect resembles its cause so that one can produce any effect by imitating it (a photograph or doll in the likeness of a person one wishes to influence); and "contagious" magic which follows the law of contact, namely, that things which have once been in contact continue to act upon each other at a distance, a "magical sympathy" that exists between a person and any severed portion of his or her person (human remains or dirt from a grave invested with the power of the deceased, for example). Anyone gaining possession of human hair, nails, or other portions of the body may work his or her will upon the person from whom they were obtained, at any distance.[20]

In *Spiritual Merchants: Religion, Magic and Commerce,* Carolyn Morrow Long uses the generic word charm to designate "any object, substance, or combination thereof believed to be capable of influencing physical, mental, and spiritual health; manipulation personal relationships and the actions of others; and invoking the aid of the deities, the dead, and the abstract concept of 'luck'" (xvi). Although the objects themselves may be commonplace and ordinary, faith and belief invest them with their true "power".

> More important than the magical principles of imitation and contact is the spiritual presence that governs the charm. In the African traditional religions, European folk Christianity and popular magic, and the African-based New World belief systems, charms are often believed either to be endowed with an indwelling spirit or to enable the user to contact and direct an external spirit. An African deity, God the Father, Jesus, the Holy Ghost, one of the saints, a folk hero, or the dead might be summoned through the use of charms. In African American hoodoo practice the religious concept of an indwelling spirit has sometimes been lost, and the user may believe that the charm itself performs the desired act. The principles of imitative and contagious magic, plus the spiritual presence behind the charm, work to achieve the intention of the charm user through choice of ingredients, charm type, and related ritual actions (xvii-xviii).

Bastide notes that Europeans brought their own varieties of medieval magic with them to the New World, often in the form of witches and magicians who were no longer burned at the stake but rather deported to the new Western territories. (Recall that the major phase of the European witch trials coincided with the colonization of the Americas and that the *Malleus Maleficarum,* the handbook for witch-hunters and Inquisitors throughout late Medieval Europe, was published in 1487, five years before Columbus's voyage.) "Of greatest importance was the folk Christianity and popular magic practiced by many Europeans of the sixteenth through the nineteenth centuries. Characterized by veneration of the saints as minor deities, belief in spirits, and the use of sacramental objects as charms, folk Christianity was remarkably similar to the traditional religions of Africa. European popular magic and healing were also compatible with African magical and medicinal practices" (Morrow Long 9).

European magic retained the advantage, however, of representing the practices of the ruling class and was perceived to be superior in one major aspect: it guaranteed European hegemony, while African magic had not prevented enslavement. "This is why, though they never rejected any of their own African practices which proved effective, the black population would reinforce the unsuccessful one with some European formula" in a process referred to as "magical accumulation" which serves to strengthen the operative force of a given spell or remedy (Bastide 1971: 16). He also observes, "It remains to be said that, while Negroes may borrow European magic to strengthen their own spells, the reverse is also true. Europeans tend to regard Negro magic as more effective, because of its 'weird' character and the old colonial terrors which it inspired" (161). According to Eugene Genovese:

> Magic, in the widest sense of the word, as Frazer, Tylor, and other pioneer anthropologists taught, is a false science with an erroneous idea of cause and effect, but it is akin to science nonetheless in its appeal to human devices for control of the world....For peasantries magic, however petty many of its applications, has served the vital social function of providing some defense, no matter how futile in the end, against the natural disasters and forces beyond their control. (1976: 230–231)

Magic is typically associated with the religions and cultures of pre-Modern societies. That notion, however, is contested by scholars who have noted the interconnectedness of cultures created by world economic systems and link the practices of magic and witchcraft in the Americas to modernity and to the Western colonial and anticolonial processes. In *Wizards & Scientists: Explorations in Afro-Cuban Modernity & Tradition* Palmié's argues for the "modernity" of Afro-Cuban religious and cultural adaptation to the transatlantic experience, establishing that the modern structures of power in the transition from the colonial period to the modern were located not only in the New World of colonial power, but within the very structure of religion itself. Both, he claims, are linked to Western rationality, emerging out of the relations of inequality and oppression in colonization that created modernity's achievements, and citing Swiss anthropologist Alfred Métraux's 1972 statement, "It is too often forgotten…that Voodoo, for all of its African heritage, belongs to the modern world and is part of our own civilization" (2002: 57). Magic and witchcraft have been linked to forms of political and cultural resistance but also, as in Raquel Romberg's *Witchcraft and Welfare: Spiritual Capital and the Business of Magic in Modern Puerto Rico,* to the consumerism and the global flow of products and ideas in a postcapitalist world where brujos become "spiritual entrepreneurs" providing for the spiritual, emotional and at times economic needs of their clients (2003: 14).

Religious and cultural development follows many paths; a true understanding of magic and its place in a society requires an appreciation of cultural context, as we will observe in the chapters following. A complex and thorny issue, magic can be used a form of resistance or retaliation, a means of redressing issues within a group, of defining self with regards to others, or a mode of gaining a sense of security and empowerment.[21] On some level, magical thinking is common to all societies, but magic as a religious and spiritual practice is a category that is perhaps the most misunderstood, maligned, feared, and sensationalized of all identified with African derived religions. Value-laden assumptions have been assigned to the category and definitions of "miracles" and "magico-religious" practices as well as their legitimacy and authenticity; indictments of superstation and witchcraft are common.

Of course, the expression "magico-religious" itself is problematic, usually assigned to the religions and the spiritual practices of the "Other" that the modern Western world consider archaic. Where does one draw the line between magic and religion? A straightforward definition can be found in Keith Thomas's *Religion and the Decline of Magic*: "If magic is to be defined as the employment of ineffective techniques to allay anxiety when effective ones are not available, then we must recognize that no society will ever be free from it" (667). It is a question that Yvonne P. Chireau also examines in *Black Magic: Religion and the African American Conjuring Tradition,* a book concerning:

> The creations that black people have woven into their quest for spiritual empowerment and meaning. It is about magic, as that term refers to the beliefs and actions by which human beings interact with an invisible reality. But it is also about religion, which may be defined as a viable system of ideas and activities by which humans mediate the sacred realm. In some African American spiritual traditions, ideas about magic and religious practice can enclose identical experiences…Individuals may utilize the thetoric of miracle to characterize this kind of spiritual efficacy, or they may adopt a lexicon that is associated with magic. Or they may choose both. A fixed dichotomy between these ideas is not always apparent. It is clear, then, that we are dealing with contested notions of belief. (2-3).

Diasporan Religions and Religion in the Diaspora

The "diasporan religions," a term coined by Joseph Murphy,[22] share significant traits but perhaps the most characteristic is their dynamism. The globalization process has created an "intense intra-Caribbean circulation of ritual specialists—a free-flow of *espiritistas, santeros, brujos* [witches or sorcerers]…These encounters and the availability of ritual commodities from distant parts of the world yield incomparable opportunities for mutual learning and exchange....These interactions have broadened the pool of saints, deities, and spirits" (Romberg 2005: 141-142).

In the 2001 edition of Karen McCarthy's ground breaking ethnography *Mama Lola: A Vodou Priestess in Brooklyn* we learn that cultural pluralism and transnational contacts have expanded religious options for Alourdes, the Haitian mambo whose story is the focus of the book. In addition to Haitian Vodou, Aloudes has added Santería and was initiated into the religion by a friend who was born in Puerto Rico and lives in Oakland, California, where she hopes that "bringing Vodou and Santeria together can help reduce the tensions between the Latino and black populations in Oakland" (399). Mama Lola observed the similarities between the two religions in rituals and when asked why, if they are, in her words, "almost the same thing," Mama Lola would go through the expense and responsibility of adding Santería to her religious practices, her response demonstrates a practical and religious intent: she wants to add more spirits to insure protection for herself, her family and her support network, living and deceased. "I do it because my grandmother ... she used to travel to Cuba ... in her trade. That's how she get it. Now, I got Yemaya too" (400).

The religious and cultural influence of the Creole religions of the Caribbean and its diaspora has broadened its reach: to the African American and US Latino population, and, interestingly, to the artists and writers of those communities who have demonstrated an affinity with and been inspired by the Creole spiritual traditions, an issue we will discuss further in subsequent chapters. Orishas and loas have claimed such spiritual daughters in the African American feminist spirituality movement as writer, performer and ritual priestess Luisah Teish in the Bay area of California, an initiated elder in the Ifa/Orisha tradition of the West African Diaspora and a devotee of Damballah Hwedo, the Haitian Rainbow Serpent, under the guidance of Mama Lola. In *African American Folk Healing*, Stephanie Y. Mitchem observes that Teish "like many African-Americans who are searching for religious meaning, draws from multiple African traditions to construct and define a spiritual tradition" (124)

> For some, then, African religions reconcile seemingly disparate parts of the self—culturally, religiously, and socially. Part of the attraction is what theologian Joseph Murphy describes as "the reciprocity between community and spirit." For some, there is a sense of belonging and coming home. In a way, the participant constructs his or her core identity. (125)

One woman Mitchem interviewed who was disillusioned with Roman Catholicism and found a spiritual home in Santería claimed, "Thank God for the Cubans who saved it for us" (125).[23]

Mexican-American muralists, writers, and poets have combined Creole spirituality with Native American and European influences in their art and their lives. Hailing from the Rio Grande Valley of South Texas, the acclaimed Chicana[24] author and cultural theorist Gloria Anzaldúa—who helped transform contemporary Chicana and border theories and whose works appear in class syllabi throughout the country in courses on contemporary American women writers, Chicana/o and Latina/o literature, among others—considered herself a spiritual activist and daughter of Yemayá and included the orisha in her spiritual pantheon, according to AnaLouise Keating, editor of *The Gloria Anzaldúa Reader*.[25] In her influential work *Borderlands/La Frontera: The New Mestiza*, Anzaldúa crosses bridges and borders with illuminating analyses surrounding gender, class, racial and ethnic identity.

In the bilingual opening poem of the first chapter of *Borderlands*, "The Homeland, Aztlán/El otro México" the author invokes Yemayá's name with that of the Catholic Virgen of Guadalupe, the patron saint of Mexico. Both spirits guide the inhabitants of the borderlands, "transgressors, aliens—whether they possess documents or not, whether they're Chicanos, Indians or Blacks" who populate the US-Mexican border, an area Anzaldúa refers to as a third country or "border culture" (3).

> [...]
> But the skin of the earth is seamless.
> The sea cannot be fenced,
> *el mar* does not stop at borders.
> To show the white man what she thought of his arrogance,
> *Yemayá* blew that wire fence down.
> [...]

Anzaldúa's invoked Yemayá in the years prior to her death in 2004 to summon the orisha, her "ocean mother," as protector spirit in the final years of the poet's life and we will see the artistic and spiritual significance of a "spirited identity" in our discussion of Creole religions and Mexican Americans.

The chapters that follow will seek to elucidate how the various elements described above manifest themselves in the specific systems of belief and practice of the major Creole religions of the Caribbean and its Diaspora, as well as their influence on US Latino cultures in contact with Creole diasporic cultures. As we trace the histories and characteristic elements we will seek to illustrate how, although at times severely restricted, controlled, penalized, ostracized, and devalued by the dominant cultures of the respective countries, they constitute practices of resistance that devotees have succeeded in maintaining for centuries, contesting the racialized inequalities in their societies, defining and shaping the everyday lives of individuals and communities. As such the Creole religions are at the very center of the process of transculturation that has defined Creole societies.

Notes

1. The spelling of Vodou (also Voodoo, Vodoun, and Vaudon) is, like many other terms of African origin used to describe various practices and beliefs, a constant source of debate among scholars and believers. The text reflects our preferences; citations naturally maintain the individual preference of those cited.
2. See *Creolization: History, Ethnography, Theory* 'Introduction' for an excellent historical overview of the use of the term (1–25). In the same volume, 'Creole Colonial Spanish America' by Jorge Cañizares-Esguerra examines the political use of the term by Latin Americans who contrasted their creole status as a tactic against Spanish 'Peninsulars' in the struggle for independence (26–45).
3. Aisha Khan, 'Creolization Moments' (237–38).
4. Stewart 2007: 5.
5. For an interesting discussion on the global preoccupations of Caribbean authors and the issue of postcolonial cultural identity, see 'Myth and Revolution in the Caribbean Postmodern' by Patricia Krüs in *Cultural Identity and Postmodern Writing* (149–67).
6. Torres Saillant notes that when Benítez Rojo was questioned during a lecture at Syracuse University in 2001 by Puerto Rican author Mayra Santos-Febres as to why he relied on Chaos Theory, 'given the availability of similar paradigms in the cosmology of Santería in his own native Cuban culture, he immediately agreed with her and proceeded to explain his choice in terms of what he thought would be preferred in the US academy' 87.
7. *Créolité*, as we note in our discussion, is a French Antillean literary term for Creole identity. *Métissage* (French) and *mestizaje* (Spanish) both relate to mixture of race and/or culture.
8. Desmangles (1992: 172). In 'Trans-Caribbean Identity and the Fictional World of Mayra Montero,' Fernández Olmos argues for yet another category of religious syncretism, exemplified by the *Gagá* cult in the Dominican Republic. Gagá is a Vodou-derived practice brought by emigrating Haitian sugarcane workers to the Dominican Republic, where it was transformed and reinterpreted by local

folk practices and beliefs. It is 'an interesting example of nontraditional Caribbean syncretism: instead of a hybridity between the European and the colonized, Gagá exemplifies a secondary type of syncretism, one between (ex) colonized peoples' (1997: 273).
9. '[T]he concept of syncretism has been used in many different ways since Plutarch wrote the history of the Cretans. During the period of expansion of European colonialism, for instance, when ethnography was deployed to describe colonized peoples, syncretism defined a stage of evolution (progress), serving to explain the ways "uncivilized" societies "assimilated" more "advanced" cultures... [W]e propose a reinscription of the contact between, for example, European and African symbolic systems in syncretic articulations, not as contradictory but as *antagonistic,* i.e., in relations which are animated by the partial presence of the other within the self, such that the differential identity of each term is at once enabled and prevented from full constitution. These relations, which, depending on the configurations of power in contingent historical conditions, may or may not crystallize into oppositionalities, exist both horizontally (in equivalential alignments among diverse groups united in struggle, as in the Cretan example) as well as vertically (in dominant/subaltern confrontations, as in colonialism). Antagonistic relations, then, indicate the limits of absolutist conceptions of culture based upon a closed system of unalloyed, hetero-topic differences, and thereby expand the logics of struggle' (Becquer and Gatti 1991: 70–72).
10. Patrick Bellegarde-Smith believes that syncretic process in Haitian Vodou deviates from that of other 'Neo-African' religious expressions in the Americas for historical reasons: 'Vodou is a heteroclite compendium of many African cults "rendered" in a Haitian historical and sociological context. It appears perhaps as the most creolized of African-derived systems in the Americas. It's liturgical language is Haitian(Creole), not Fon, Ewe, Yoruba, or Lingala. Cut off from the source of "fresh" Africans, paradoxically because of its early independence, and abandoned to itself, Vodou has become the least "pure" of the new religions, neither Nago or Kongo, yet African in its essence. Early contacts with islamicized Africans—and these had transformed Islam—had long ended. Government- and church-sponsored endemic persecutions tended to reinforce the conflation between *lwa*/orisha and Roman Catholic saints, but these functional equivalencies remained tenuous. Deities, after all, are cosmic energy, archetypes, and moral principles. Saints, however, are dead (white) people whose edifying life stories remain in darkness for almost all Haitians.... few of the adepts [have] any knowledge of the lives of the saints whose images they revere as representations of their gods. The saints have disembodied spirits, as the person who is 'mounted' by the spirit does in the ritual. Each *lwa*/orisha has multiple aspects, represented by *different* saints (unconnected to each other in time and space), a situation so complicated that only one with the patience of a saint could hope to unravel it, but they would not succeed. Camouflage was *one* consideration' (62–63).
11. In *Voice of the Leopard: African Secret Societies and Cuba,* Ivor L. Miller notes that the nineteenth century Afro-Cuban religious leader Andrés Petit introduced the Christian crucifix into the Abakuá lodges to meet a need at that historical moment – defend the practices from official repression. This 'illustrates the intentional fusion of distinct practices by innovators with a community-based tradition, who are often criticized by the traditionalists... Church purists have consistently characterized non-Christian practices as "syncretic," therefore false. The various traditions emerging from this activity evidence why traditions like Abakuá, Santería (Ocha), and Palo Mayombe cannot be contained within a ritual recipe book, because their ceremonies are never stagnant reproductions, but ritual theater and artistic enterprises that develop according to the mastery of those present' (116).
12. For a discussion of legitimacy and religious syncretism in Latin America, as well as power and empowerment via the articulation of syncretic elements, see Benavides (1995).
13. In his study of the Abakuá Society in Cuba, David H. Brown (2003) notes that, although Creole sycretisms are typically believed to result from the encounter of African and Catholic belief systems, those interpretations preclude individual idiosyncratic agency in the creation of religious cultural meaning and the significant influence of popular and mass culture in the transformation of religious symbols. Altars serve as an excellent example: 'Abakuá objects and signifying practices, no less than those of any other group, are produced as the ongoing outcomes of struggles and exceed the "results" of any imagined initial "encounter" of "Europe" and "Africa"....Altars are examples of "synthetic" knowledge production and aesthetic creativity par excellence, assemblages from fragments or streams of multiple cultures as opposed to direct representation of nature' (6).

14. Based primarily on Castellanos and Castellanos, *Cultura afrocubana* (1992, 3: 16–18). Just as the insights regarding the creolization process described above have crossed the boundaries of the geographic region – Brazil and other Latin American countries, and even such US cities as New York and Miami reveal the type of cultural amalgamation characteristic of the region – it should be noted that Creole religious beliefs have gone beyond geographic, racial, and class boundaries as well. Their devotees are found throughout South America –including areas of Brazil with Italian, Polish, and German immigrants and in countries like Uruguay and Argentina with an insignificant number of persons of African descent – and in the United States outside the Cuban and Latino communities (Barnes 1989: 10).
15. See Cros Sandoval (1995), and Fernández Olmos and Paravisini-Gebert (2001).
16. Juana Elbein Dos Santos and Deoscoredes M. Dos Santos (1984: 78).
17. African-derived practices are often described in the scholarly literature as 'spiritist' religions due to the element of possession of followers by the spirits. In this book only Espiritismo is referred to as 'Spiritism' or spiritist, as identified in the Caribbean. Of course, to some degree all religions that believe in the spirits can be identified as spiritist; the Christian Pentecostal rituals that attempt to achieve a direct experience of possession by the Holy Ghost are one example of a Christian spiritist practice, albeit one with a more 'mainstream' spirit.
18. Spirit possession exists throughout the world in one form or another and can be defined as an 'altered state of consciousness indigenously interpreted in terms of the influence of an alien spirit' (Crapanzano and Garrison 1977: Introduction, 7).
19. Joan D. Koss has written of the creativity of Caribbean cult rituals and the 'transformation of the mundane through the use of possession-trance' (1979: 376). When ritual participants are possessed by the *dramatis personae* of a particular belief system, rather than follow the limited stereotypical patterns associated with the supernatural character incarnated, numerous variations (the multiple avatars of the *orisha* and the *loa*, for example, and the portrayal of the more typical spirit guides in *Espiritismo*) allow for individual variation of their characterization in possession. A successful cult leader, she claims, must be flexible and creative in combining meaning and aesthetics to the cult ritual 'performance.' Koss cites Métraux (1972: 64), who describes the ideal *hungan* as 'at one and the same time priest, healer, soothsayer, exorcizer, organizer of public entertainment and choirmaster.'

    Ritual as a creative forum is most clearly seen, in my opinion, in these cult cases. Two important attributes of cult activity provide for this condition: first, cult rituals, as distinct from those of most established religions, attract their participants through the offer of direct contact with supernatural beings. Even though this contact may be achieved initially only through a third party, the cult adept, priest, or spirit medium, there is a process of democratization of the 'power' to communicate with the supernatural world which is both ideal and actual – that is, that any believer can become an adept, even though not all develop sufficient powers to do so. Second, cult ideologies in the Caribbean are, in terms of their basic patterns, deceptively simple. They consist of good and bad *loa*, *orisha*, spirits or powers who 'work' according to the dictates of their human communicants but can as often manifest their own characterological attributes to disturb the behavior of those who lack the knowledge and power to deal with them. Those who become adepts and can organize their own groups acquire their leadership status by successfully dealing with the multiple, variable expressions of the personal disturbances of their followers. Their manipulative techniques of divining, healing, and advice-giving cannot possibly respond to set and detailed formulas, pedantically derived by arduous interpretation over years of discussion. To be a successful cult leader or adept, creative ability is requisite (376–77).
20. Following in the path of Edward Tylor, one of the earliest anthropologists who developed an evolutionary theory of religion in his *Primitive Culture* (1871), Frazer's work was influential in its time, viewing magic as part of a progressive development of societies on the developmental path to religion and ultimately to science. However, Frazer's unilinear evolutionary approach, his clear bias against religion, and his ethnocentric methods and use of ethnographic sources have been criticized and are viewed as problematic today and of little value to scholars of religion.
21. Magic is also a means to a political and social end, as we see in the Haitian Revolution that famously began with a Vodou ceremony and a solemn oath or pact to gain liberation. African slaves were convinced that they would overcome their French oppressors due to the power afforded them by

Vodou's ritual magic and the protection they would receive from the African deities, the *loas*. The belief that persons can assume an animal form to escape the bullets of the enemy, lycanthropy, a type of metamorphosis or magico-ecstatic transformation accomplished through the use of ritual possession, ointments or charms. 'El propósito del Pacto Solemne que figura en *El reino de este mundo* de Carpentier es precisamente poner a los esclavos bajo la protección de las divinidades africanas. . . En general los hechos relacionados con el vodú se saben ya que hasta ahora lo mencionado en la obra de Carpentier se realiza cada día en las campañas de Haíti; quiero hablar del poder licantrópico, de personas que no pueden ser alcanzadas por las ballas etc. Todo esto es moneda corriente hoy día en Haíti.' (Personal correspondence with Haitian Joseph Pierre-Antoine.) In 'Romantic Voodoo: Obeah and British Culture, 1797–1807,' Alan Richardson describes a similar role of Obeah in slave revolts in the British West Indies regarding oaths of secrecy and fetishes that promised invulnerability. Yvonne P. Chireau observes that spiritual oaths were administered by priests and other appointed religious functionaries for various motives. In the well-known historical event, the New York Conspiracy of 1712, an insurrection of a diverse group of 'American-born blacks, native American Indians (or mestizos), and Africans of the "Nations of Caramantee and Pappa,"' the participants had sworn an oath and used an enchanted powder to ensure their invulnerability, 'The conspirators were bound together by the act, having sealed a covenant between themselves and the invisible forces of the supernatural world.' Nearly all were apprehended, tried, condemned and executed (61).

22. *Working the Spirit: Ceremonies of the African Diaspora* 6–7. See our *Sacred Possessions: Vodou, Santería, Obeah, and the Caribbean* (1997) 3.
23. Also if interest in the area of African American expressions of religious pluralism, globalization and sexual diversity is Monica A. Coleman, *Making a Way Out of No Way: A Womanist Theology*. Minneapolis: Fortress Press, 2008.
24. Some Mexican-Americans refer to themselves as Chicano/a, usually considered a more politically-identified term, popularized as a result of the Mexican-American social justice movements of the 1960s.
25. Duke University Press, 2009. Also see Gloria Anzaldúa, *Interviews* (*Entrevistas*), ed. AnaLouise Keating. New York: Routledge, 2000.

Bibliography

Anzaldúa, Gloria. *Borderlands: The New Mestiza (La frontera)*. San Francisco: Aunt Lute, 1987.
———. *Interviews (Entrevistas)*, ed. AnaLouise Keating. New York: Routledge, 2000.
Apter, Andrew. 'Herskovits's Heritage: Rethinking Syncretism in the African Diaspora.' *Diaspora: A Journal of Transnational Studies* 1.3 (1991): 235–60.
Barnes, Sandra T., ed. *Africa's Ogun: Old World and New*. Bloomington: Indiana University Press, 1989.
Bascom, William R. 'The Focus of Cuban Santeria.' *Southwest Journal of Anthropology* 6, no.1 (1950): 64–68.
———. *Shango in the New World*. Austin: African and Afro-American Research Institute, University of Texas at Austin, 1972.
Bastide, Roger. *African Civilizations in the New World*. Trans. Peter Green. London: C. Hurst and Company, 1971.
Becquer, Marcos, and Jose Gatti. Elements of Vogue. *Third Text* 16, no.17 (winter 1991): 65–81.
Bellegarde-Smith, Patrick, ed. *Fragments of Bone: Neo-African Religions in a New World*. Urbana: University of Illinois Press, 2005.
Benavides, Gustavo. Syncretism and Legitimacy in Latin American Religion. In *Enigmatic Powers: Syncretism with African and Indigenous Peoples' Religions among Latinos*, ed. Anthony M. Stevens and Andrés I. Pérez y Mena. New York: Bildner Center for Western Hemisphere Studies, 1995, 19–46.
Benítez Rojo, Antonio. *The Repeating Island: The Caribbean and the Postmodern Perspective*, trans. James E. Maraniss. Durham: Duke University Press, 1996.
Brathwaite, Edward. *Folk Cultures of the Slaves in Jamaica*. London: New Beacon Books, 1970. Reprint 1974.
Brown, David Hilary. Garden in the Machine: Afro-Cuban Sacred Art and Performance in Urban New Jersey and New York. Vols. 1 and 2. Ph.D. dissertation, Yale University, 1989.

———. *The Light Inside: Abakuá Society Arts and Cuban Cultural History*. Washington: Smithsonian, 2003.
Brown, Karen McCarthy. *Mama Lola: A Vodou Priestess in Brooklyn*. Berkeley: University of California Press, 1991.
Buisseret, David, and Steven G. Reinhardt, eds. *Creolization in the Americas*, intro. David Buisseret. College Station, Texas: University of Texas Press, 2000.
Cañizares-Esguerra, Jorge. 'Creole Colonial Spanish America.' In *Creolization: History, Ethnography, Theory*, 26–45.
Castellanos, Jorge, and Isabel Castellanos. *Cultura Afrocubana 1 (El negro en Cuba, 1492–1944)*. Miami: Ediciones Universal, 1988.
———. *Cultura Afrocubana 3 (Las religiones y las Lenguas)*. Miami: Ediciones Universal, 1992.
Chireau, Yvonne P. *Black Magic: Religion and the African American Conjuring Tradition*. Berkeley: University of California Press, 2003.
Coleman, Monica A. *Making a Way Out of No Way: A Womanist Theology*. Minneapolis: Fortress Press, 2008.
Crapanzano, Vincent, and Vivian Garrison, eds. *Case Studies in Spirit Possession*. New York: John Wiley, 1977.
Cros Sandoval, Mercedes. 'Afro-Cuban Religion in Perspective.' In *Enigmatic Powers: Syncretism with African and Indigenous Peoples' Religions among Latinos*, ed. Anthony M. Stevens and Andrés I. Pérez y Mena. New York: Bildner Center for Western Hemisphere Studies, 1995, 81–98
Desmangles, Leslie G. *The Faces of the Gods: Vodou and Roman Catholicism in Haiti*. Chapel Hill: University of North Carolina Press, 1992.
Droogers, André. 'Syncretism: The Problem of Definition, the Definition of a Problem.' In *Dialogue and Syncretism: An Interdisciplinary Approach*, ed. Jerald Gort et al. Grand Rapids, Michigan: William B. Eerdmans, 1989, 7–25.
Fernández Olmos, Margarite, and Lizabeth Paravisini-Gebert, eds. *Healing Cultures: Art and Religion as Curative Practices in the Caribbean and Its Diaspora*. New York: Palgrave–St Martin's Press, 2001.
———. *Sacred Possessions: Vodou, Santería, Obeah, and the Caribbean*. New Brunswick: Rutgers University Press, 1997.
Frazer, Sir James George. *The Golden Bough*. Abridged ed. New York: St Martin's Press, 1966. (Unabridged edition published 1936).
Genovese, Eugene D. *Roll, Jordan, Roll: The World the Slaves Made*. New York: Vintage Books, 1976.
Glissant, Edwouard. 'The Cultural "Creolization" of the World: Interview with Edouard Glissant.' *Label France* 38 (January 2000).
Gregory, Steven. *Santería in New York City: A Study in Cultural Resistance*. New York: Garland, 1999.
Herskovits, Melville. *The Myth of the Negro Past*. Boston: Beacon Press, 1958 [1941].
Hoetink, H. '"Race" and Color in the Caribbean.' In *Caribbean Contours*, ed. Sidney W. Mintz and Sally Price. Baltimore: John Hopkins University Press, 1985, 55–84.
Khan, Aisha. 'Creolization Moments.' In *Creolization: History, Ethnography, Theory*. 237–53.
Knepper, Wendy. 'Colonization, Creolization, and Globalization: The Art and Ruses of Bricolage.' *Small Axe* 21, no. 3 (2006): 70–86.
Koss, Joan D. 'Artistic Expression and Creative Process in Caribbean Possession Cult Rituals.' In *The Visual Arts: Graphic and Plastic*, ed. Justine M. Cordwell. The Hague: Mouton, 1979.
Krüs, Patricia. 'Myth and Revolution in the Caribbean Postmodern." In *Cultural Identity and Postmodern Writing*,' ed. Theo Dhaen and Pieter Vermeulen, 149–67.
Métraux, Alfred. *Voodoo in Haiti*, trans. Hugo Charteris. New York: Schocken, 1972.
Miller, Ivor L. *Voice of the Leopard: African Secret Societies and Cuba*. Jackson: University Press of Mississippi, 2009.
Mintz, Sidney W., and Sally Price, eds. *Caribbean Contours*. Baltimore: John Hopkins University Press, 1985.
Mitchem, Stephanie Y. *African American Folk Healing*. New York: New York University Press, 2007.
Morrow Long, Carolyn. *Spiritual Merchants: Religion, Magic and Commerce*. Knoxville: The University of Tennessee Press, 2001.
Mosquera, Gerardo. 'Africa in the Art of Latin America.' *Art Journal* 5, no. 4 (Winter 1992): 30–38.
Murphy, Joseph M. 'Lydia Cabrera and *la Regla de Ocha* in the United States.' In *En Torno a Lydia Cabrera*, ed. Isabel Castellanos and Josefina Inclán. Miami: Ediciones Universal, 1987, 246–54.
———. *Santería: African Spirits in America*. Boston: Beacon Press, 1993.

———. *Working the Spirit: Ceremonies of the African Diaspora*. Boston: Beacon Press, 1994.

Palmié, Stephan. 'Against Syncretism: "Africanizing" and "Cubanizing" Discourses in North American òrìsà Worship.' In *Counterworks: Managing Diverse Knowledge*, ed. Richard Fardon. London: Routledge, 1995, 73–104.

———. 'Creolization and its Discontents.' *Annual Review of Anthropology* 35 (2006): 433–56.

———. 'Ecué's Atlantic: An Essay in Methodology.' *Journal of Religion in Africa* 37, no. 2 (2007): 275–315.

———. 'Ethnogenetic Processes and Cultural Transfer in Caribbean Slave Populations.' In *Slavery in the Americas*.Wolfgang Binder, ed. Würzburg: Königshauser & Neumann, 1993, 337–64.

———. *Wizards & Scientists: Explorations in Afro-Cuban Modernity & Tradition*. Durham: Duke University Press, 2002.

Pérez, Laura E. *Chicana Art: The Politics of Spiritual and Aesthetic Altarities*. Durham, NC: Duke University Press, 2007.

Pye, Michael. 'Syncretism and Ambiguity.' *Numen* 18 (1971): 83–93.

Richardson, Alan. 'Romantic Voodoo: Obeah and British Culture, 1797–1807.' In *Sacred Possessions: Vodou, Santería, Obeah, and the Caribbean*, ed. Margarite Fernández Olmos and Lizabeth Paravisini-Gebert. New Brunswick: Rutgers University Press, 1997, 171–94.

Romberg, Raquel. 'Glocal Spirituality: Consumerism and Heritage in a Puerto Rican Afro-Latin Folk Religion.' In *Contemporary Caribbean Cultures and Societies in a Global Context*, ed. Franklin W. Knight and Teresita Martínez-Vergne. Chapel Hill: The University of North Carolina Press, 2005, 131–55.

———. *Witchcraft and Welfare: Spiritual Capital and the Business of Magic in Modern Puerto Rico*. Austin: University of Texas Press, 2003.

Schwieger Hiepko, Andrea. 'Creolization as a Poetics of Culture: Édouard Glissant's "Archipelic" Thinking.' In *A Pepper-Pot of Cultures: Aspects of Creolization in the Caribbean*, ed. Gordon Collier and Ulrich Fleischmann. Amsterdam-New York: (Matatu [Journal] 27–28.) Rodopi, 2003, 237–59.

Stewart, Charles. Ed. and 'Introduction.' *Creolization: History, Ethnography, Theory*. Walnut Creek, CA: Left Coast Press, 2007.

Thomas, Keith. *Religion and the Decline of Magic*. New York: Charles Scribner's Sons, 1971.

Torres-Saillant, Silvio. *An Intellectual History of the Caribbean*. New York: Palgrave Macmillan, 2006.

Tylor, Edward Burnett. *Primitive Culture: Researches into the Development of Mythology, Philosophy, Religion, Art, and Custom*. London: J. Murray, 1871.

The Spirit of the Thing:
Religious Thought and Social/Historical Memory
Patrick Bellegarde-Smith

When speaking of African religions and the philosophical thought that has derived from them, one asserts prima facie their existence. One also reveals a concern for what may be perceived as an elitist framework, though it need not be. This is particularly true of *religions initiatiques*. The paradox is more apparent than real. Though the blueprints for understanding life, worlds, and universes range beyond complex rituals and the *pronunciamentos* of mere adepts, the stories told by them are nonetheless helpful narratives in a larger discourse. The importance of popular beliefs does not belie the awesome training and esoteric knowledge, *konesans*, of priests and other mystics. Between the one and the other lies a complicated relationship, *une courroie de transmission*, in which mentalities are forged and active memory created. As a *houngan asogwe*, I become aware of the necessity to explore both themes and ontological domains in the Haitian religious corpus.

In the cauldron, one finds dozens of West and West Central African belief systems, together with a *few* assimilated and unassimilated Islamic and European religious ideas. The world that is revealed out of amalgamated and creolized fragments is distant from that world expressed in western mentalities. In fact, it challenges it. In this approach to subject-matter phenomena, one undertakes a "paradigm shift" that augurs well for the possibility of massive societal transformations, provided international conditions lend themselves to it. My point of departure is to observe a people as if it mattered, respecting a tradition, not by way of contrast with the (western) known world but as a culture sui generis, based on its own premises. Some religious systems transcend religion to become spiritual disciplines and encompass collective experience in diverse realms in science and the humanities. Translated in societal terms, one may argue that if a broad swath of the Haitian population participated in *res publica*, the "public thing," a transformative democracy could ensue, anchored in a paradigm shift in which societal organization is attuned to thought. Modeling would thus come from a cultural capital produced by the *culture de base*.

J.G.A. Pollock argued that "'since so large a part of men's consciousness of environment and time is gained through consciousness of the frame of social relationships that they inhabit, the conceptualization of tradition is an important source of their images of society, time, and history. The importance of these visibly transcend the political; we are looking at one of the origins of a distinctly human awareness.'"[1]

Contextual History and the Local Universe

The engagement of Vodou in Haitian temporal affairs and history has been constant. The many revolts of the enslaved were efforts toward freedom and liberation writ large, from within an ethos that, at the outset, had incorporated similar elements from diverse African ethnicities. That could have occurred only under conditions established in colonialism. As with the Haitian (Creole) language, the Vodou religion brought solace, courage, and theoretical explanations to persons, two-thirds or three-fourths of whom were born in Africa at the time of the Haitian Revolution of 1791. Language and religion provided common idioms in which uprisings took root, flourished, and prospered. These were the building blocks of nationality. These primary cultural elements were a *lieu de rencontre,* the meeting ground common to all Haitians, all of whom had ancestry on the African continent.

All Haitians recognized the "moment," the official start of the revolution, as August 14, 1791. The Vodou ceremony held on that date at Bois Caiman, in the Morne Rouge district in northern Haiti, became a *lieu de mémoire* agreed upon by all.[2] Early chieftains and post-Independence leaders seemed well versed in their ancestral religion, some as *houngan, manbo,* or *bòkò*. The population at large were actors in a psychopolitical drama in which there could only be two outcomes: death or freedom. And death was freedom.[3] As with mythical figures in Africa, generals of the insurgency could become deities in their own right.[4] This belief system and these religious practices were embraced by slaves and *affranchis,* blacks and *mulâtres, citadins* and peasants, rich and poor.[5]

Once ensconced in power, however, the general/presidents, fearful of the demonstrated power of the religion, outlawed it to preserve their own hold on power, or to appease (European) world public opinion. Most co-opted or tried to co-opt Vodou, but they practiced in secrecy what they did not preach. Oral history reveals that all Haitian chiefs of state knew the religion well and that their extended families had a *hounfò* (temple) on ancestral lands to which they retreated at crucial times. Oral history asserts further that a *différend* between Toussaint Louverture and André Rigaud, in which about fifteen thousand *mulâtres* died in 1799, had started three generations earlier in Dahomey.[6]

Found in most *hounfò* and *wogatwa* (personal and family altars), the national flag found its meaning in esoterism. The dark blue symbolizes cosmic energy, particularly in the form of the "female" deity, Ezili Dantò, which represents maternal love and collective welfare. The dark red represents Ogou Feray, the iron will necessary in warfare. The national banner, as leitmotiv, shall reappear later in this chapter.

Early Haitian state institutions seemed to want to parallel those created elsewhere in other Maroon settlements, in the *palenques* and *quilombos,* the proto-African communities in the Caribbean basin and Latin America. This occurred, typically, in regions where Africans did not hold formal or ultimate authority, as in Cuba, Suriname, Jamaica, or Brazil.[7] The new chief of state, Emperor Jean-Jacques I (Dessalines) and his Council of State, seemed to want to re-create a form of benign despotism in dialogue with harsh, lived colonial reality and familiar patterns of thought. The emperor did not usher in a nobility in a pattern reminiscent of West Africa and sought, by executive fiat, to erase distinctions of class and color, landmarks of the colonial order. The panoply of Dessalines's iconography illustrated the point. The "Father" of the nation preserved the memory of long-dead Arawak/Taino Amerindians by giving back to Saint Domingue its old name, "Hayti." Other acts similarly alarmed the incipient bourgeoisie, Haiti's westernizers.[8]

The struggle was about differing conceptions of the world. Dichotomous assumptions framing the western spirit—black or white, good or bad, civilized or primitive, Christianity or satanism, the French or Haitian language—were not shared by many Haitians, which stymied a more encompassing vision in which rules were on a sliding scale, reality and survival brooked compromises, morality was situational, and people understood themselves always as a part of a linguistic, religious, sexual, and racial continuum.

Jean-Jacques Dessalines, the father of the Haitian nation (*père de la patrie*), was assassinated in an act of patricide/regicide in October 1806.

The overlapping categories of class and color were reasserted with a vengeance after 1806. Official historiography relates the birth of the Haitian bicolor flag as the union between the blacks and the browns, the slaves and the freedmen, against the white *colon,* a necessary condition for victory. This interpretation of the creation of the Haitian flag on May 18, 1803, does not contradict the first but complements it by emphasizing the complex levels of hidden meanings, even if these were to be found "contradictory," so dear to traditional African metaphysical thought. The operating principle here is less dualism than thesis, antithesis, and synthesis, represented by the numeral 3, the sum is greater than the parts. This is illustrated by the concept Marasa Dosu/Dosa, the twins and the child that follows.[9] And God, after all, is not unadulterated goodness but embodies the worst characteristics within *itself* as well. But the westernizers in Haiti were victorious, and the new dominant culture ostensibly rejected traits and remnants of an African past, with fracas. Halfheartedly, they pursued efforts at "civilizing" the blacks, anticipating later French colonial cultural policies of assimilation and christianization as the road to salvation.[10] An independent Maroon society, they argued, would be recolonized, and Haitian survival depended on the adoption of European culture. It remained to be seen if that culture would be Latin or Anglo-Saxon.[11] At the same time, Europeans described Haitian social policy as "apish mimicry."[12] Meanwhile, *national* institutions, particularly those in the provinces, remained essentially the same, evolving apart and away from the superimposed structures of the predatory state, eventually leading to conditions resembling South African apartheid.

Language and religion nonetheless remained the bond and the "glue" between social classes, while increasingly repressive measures in defense of the status quo and economic exploitation insured the "success" of the western model in Haiti. The paradigm shift that might have taken hold after the revolution could never be, in view of the array of forces present on the national scene.[13] Internationally, Haiti was isolated, ostracized, and marginalized. And as a condition for its inclusion into the economic world order, the country would have to join the orthodoxy of the (European) nineteenth century, starting in the 1860s.[14] Today, Haiti is no longer isolated, but it is still marginalized.

A Brazilian saying serves us well at this juncture: "The country grows when the government is asleep." Amended to fit Haitian societal patterns, one might say that national institutions do best when state structures are the weakest.[15] Between the late 1790s and the 1860s, worldwide ostracism, a weak state, endemic uprisings, and rural isolation led to seventy years of unimpeded growth for Vodou. Language and religion had entered a constructive phase. That armature would become the foundation upon which rested a nationality, if not a national identity. In point of fact, in the prevailing anarchy, where strong regional currents prevailed, provincial centers competed with Port-au-Prince, and possibilities existed that would disappear in the 1920s under American aegis and reappear only in the 1980s, to again disappear under American aegis soon thereafter.[16] All things considered, a strong government and disinterested elites might have taught what they preached, the universality of the French language and Christianity, as occurred elsewhere in the Caribbean and Latin America, with Spanish or English, and variants of Catholicism and Protestantism, in the postemancipation period.[17]

Even the Concordat signed between Haiti and the Holy See in 1860, regularizing the role of the Roman Catholic church, revealed the angst of elites thirsting for recognition: Haiti, it was said, could not be a land subjected to missionary work. It was already Christian. The framework adopted was that of parishes, not missions. Vodou was bad Catholicism, "un catholicisme mal digéré," much as Haitian (Creole) was corrupt French, as it passed through the gullet of Negroes.[18] Mere reforms would suffice. By the middle of the nineteenth century, a neocolonial order was imposed through renewed contacts between Haiti and the outside world. Never wishing for autarchy, Haiti nonetheless was in no position to dictate terms to the United States or Western Europe.[19]

The constitutional models, the state apparatus, social classes and elitist structures, the educational system, written literature and social thought, and the ideologies of the fledging state were all patterned after western and especially French ideals. A large peasantry rebelled at critical moments of the country's history. "Modernizing" governments were unwittingly whittling down the economic and financial preeminence of Haitian commercial elites to benefit expatriate elites.[20]

The Piquet Uprising of 1844 (the "Armée Souffrante"), the endemic Caco rebellions in the north, and the armed insurrection against the American military presence at the turn of the twentieth century came from the provinces. Vodou was always well represented in the leadership of these movements, yet alone in the ranks.[21] The *projet de société*, the societal blueprint implied by these revolts, was articulated from within a national though subaltern ethos, dismissed as inarticulate by most scholarly authorities. The nation was at war with the state.[22]

The movement that rid Haiti of the Duvalierist dynasty (1957–86) originated in the provinces, notably in Cap Haitien and Gonaives and in the slums of the capital. It was nurtured in two noncompeting, not mutually exclusive, fluid, and complementary popular structures, the *hounfò* and the *ti-legliz,* the Vodou temples and the Catholic base communities established in the wake of liberation theology. The *hounfò* had been the repository of resistance to cultural oppression over the course of several centuries. The *ti-legliz,* despite its populist moorings, reflected also the social consciousness of lower clergy from the petite bourgeoisie. Scholarship found it easier to speak of the role of liberation theology, largely because of ideological reasons. Most foreign scholars (if they are "pro"-Haitian), might actually find it distasteful to address the role of Vodou in political development, especially as socioeconomic development is equated with westernization.[23]

The Constitution of 1987 responded to some of the popular *desiderata* but eschewed thoughts of widespread reform that might imply a paradigm shift. The constituents erred on the side of caution. Social peace, it was felt, involved establishing a delicate balance between the needs of the many social classes in the wake of the trauma of the Duvalier era, on the one hand, and an awareness of what the paramount power, the United States, would allow, on the other hand. In the first instance, neither the upper nor the middle classes nor the praetorian army would want to relinquish their powers as arbiters, or the power to define Haiti culturally. In the second instance, not to embarrass the country, "ne pas faire honte au pays" (away from western models of governance) became an unspoken consideration. However, under pressure, they enshrined what amounted to the decriminalization of the national religion and confirmed Haitian as one of two official languages. These small steps had implications, and the country elected its first popular government in the nation's history with President Jean-Bertrand Aristide in December 1990.

Contextual Universe and Local Culture

The Haitian nationality developed from a base that evolved, foremostly, from the compendium of not identical but similar elements and systems rooted in the peoples of West and West Central Africa. One adopted or adapted what was necessary from the French slave owner and his culture. Even the *mulâtre* was raised by his or her mother, always a black woman, whether he or she was a slave or an *affranchi*. The cultural impact of France was real, but it need not be overstated, since it was based on the power deficit in which Haitians were the losers. The overwhelming number of erstwhile Haitians had been born in Africa, not in the Americas, at the time of Independence in 1804. With a ratio of about one white for every fifteen persons of color, what had been the possibility of rapid westernization under the circumstances? Then ensued sixty years of enforced isolation. Haitian national culture became countercultural in opposition to the dominant culture of the country's elites, though in actuality they shared much sub rosa. Majoritarian culture was the population's principal ally in sociopolitical and economic resistance, a *foyer de résistance*. The pattern was established much earlier, during the colonial period, but became a sort of permanent *marronnage*. The expression is judicious. According to popular culture, Haiti still belongs to the long-dead Amerindians, and Haitians return to Afrik-Ginen upon death, a metaphorical land perhaps, but home to gods, ancestors, and the newly departed nonetheless. One implication remains the acceptance of the rootedness of Haitian culture in distant lands, of historical and sociological linkages from which an individual might draw strength and a nation its ethos.[24]

Traditional and neotraditional thought connects religious interpretations to social organization in fairly "intact" societies. But no society is intact any longer; all are subject to the vagaries of a turbulent world in which a few win and most lose. The losers find ways to negotiate their surrender. Creolization embodies that process, and that process is more likely to use synthesis than the misplaced concept of syncretism. These are mangled cultures, far from being intact. Obvious illustrations might be the relative success of Irish or Koreans in the United States as contrasted with African Americans. Social thought, religious systems, and society form, by definitional necessity, a coherent whole that does not, as a matter of course, reject adaptations of ethnic groups with rough parity. This applies to colonial situations as well, except that the power differential between a small group of colonists at the helm and a large subaltern population is critical. In a real sense, all were colonists in Haiti, whether Africans or Europeans. But power creates its own set of imperatives to which we remain sensitive.

In much the same way as one speaks of Buddhist or Islamic societies, one speaks of Vodouist society, based on autochthonous and autonomous philosophical and scientific systems.[25] The specificity of the Haitian universe, and by extension the systems from which it derived, established its distinctiveness vis-à-vis "world" religions and the world powers that derived their ontological assumptions from these religions. Janheinz Jahn wrote, "philosophy, theology, politics, social theory, land law, medicine, psychology, birth and burial, all find themselves logically concentrated in a system so tight that to subtract one item from the whole is to paralyze the structure of the whole."[26] As an illustration, "American" democracy arises from instruments peculiar to a social history rooted in a Western European ethos, and none other. The concept of "Haitian" democracy could not resemble its American counterpart, yet both might be democratic in some profound sense, with safeguards against the abuse of power by the powerful against the weak.

The philosophical dimension and scientific understanding are of concern to the *houngan* and the manbo, and these show parallels with other "natural" religions, such as Japanese Shinto and Native American beliefs. One notes that these religions still dominate the human landscape in their profusion and by their age. The broad concepts that are at the root of the Haitian system do not illustrate concepts of morality so much as interaction writ large, scientific principles, and a certain "coolness" from the part of the spirit world. In these humanistic, "earthbound" religions, the human person is never far from the center of interest:

—Humans create gods in their image by anthropomorphizing cosmic energy.
—There are no messiahs: only you stand at the center.
—The objective for each life is to master both the forces of good and the forces of evil.

—Heaven and hell do not exist, except for that which you create.
—The evil one launches into a sea of anger, vengeance, or indifference, someday returns to port and to you.
—Understanding is achieved through effort; power is achieved through sacrifice.

"Sacrifice" would seem to be essential to the human condition, in its multifarious aspects. In a dog-eat-dog world, one may have to eat a few dogs, or perhaps make propriation through self-denial, the offering of flowers, fruit, some fowl, and maybe a quadruped. Life, like art, is not always pretty.[27] Blood coursing through a body represents the presence of life, indeed its essence, and dreams in the sleep state of an abundant flow of blood are positive emanations to be cherished in such cultures.[28] One sacrifices by surrendering.

—All things are related and one; coincidences are not a part of the script.
—Everything is poison; nothing is poison.
—Nature is and must be revered. The energy fields that course through it are the divine work of deities.

As one might expect, deities were created by some supreme entity, *bondie* or *gran mèt,* and are cosmic energy, a "chip of the ol' block," within a monotheistic and somewhat "deist" construct. These energy flows house within themselves oppositional forces that maintain a seemingly precarious but creative balance.

—Deities are knowable fragments of an unknowable God.
—There is no devil, there is no Satan, but there is evil.
—When you look into the mirror, the image that beams backs at you is the image of God.
—Polarity: opposites subsist within each entity.
—God is neutral, neither good or bad, but "cool."

And as expected, the impersonal supreme entity, which at times is collapsed with the impersonal idea, "chance," is seldom directly addressed:

—*Bondie* (God) is immaterial in every sense of the word.

The most relevant interaction finds expression in negotiated spaces, the intimate interstices, the broad collective boulevards inhabited by humans, ancestors, and deities. The latter two, ancestors and deities, exercise functions relinquished by Gran Mèt; the former, humans, occupy a considerable place as embodied spirits. Humankind is at the crossroads of the enterprise. Let the negotiations begin.[29]

—When I dance, my ancestors dance with/through me.
—The favorite child carries the heaviest burden.
—Imbued with wisdom, ancestors legislate.
—Konesans (esoteric knowledge) is simplicity itself, yet complex.

The world we inhabit, sight unseen, responds to certain imperatives or laws, responsive to dialoguing entities in constant and perpetual motion. The human presence looms large in the scheme of things, the subject of its own liberation through free will, with inordinate personal powers *inside* a communitarian "idea." In this context, the law (*loi*) and the *lwa* (deities) are not immune to change or unmovable in the flux of situational ethics. One speaks always of conscious energy fields.

—Balance and equilibrium must always be maintained. "Rhythm is to force what consciousness is to idea."[30]

The spheres and the realms being structural analogues, harmony is sought. And how does one "tap" into the wisdom of the universe?

—Divination: the future is knowable as tendencies, since time wraps around itself.

But much remains hidden in *religions initiatiques*. At once democratic and elitist, the search for variegated truths remains arduous and intensively personal. The one certainty, perhaps, suggests a primordial connection between entities and beings. The astronomer Carl Sagan reached similar conclusions when he wrote:

> All life on earth is the same life. There are superficial differences that, understandably, seem important to us. But down deep at the heart of life, we are, all of us—redwoods and nematodes, viruses and eagles, slime molds and humans—almost identical. We are all expressions of the interaction of proteins and nucleic acids. This insight of modern biology has important implications for our concern for the environment, for our reverence for life. Every one of those other organisms—plants, animals, and microbes—is our cousin, co-evolved over billions of years of tortuous evolution from a common, microscopic and most humble ancestor. [They] have as a distinguished and ancient an ancestral line as we do.[31]

Call and Response: Theorems of Liberation

The historical formations of diasporic peoples of primary African descent is diverse. These histories responded to politics, policies, and demographic imbalances as existed between the ruler and the ruled. The framework, however, remained the same everywhere.[32] The western world assumed its cultural and racial superiority, a refrain adopted by culturally miscegenated elites, born of the interaction and functioning as a middle ground. It is in that context that considerations of power, class, color, racism, colonialism, and christianization are always a part of the discourse.[33] Equally, in this context, the psychological phenomenon of collective self-esteem (not to speak of self-hatred) remains a factor in colonized societies rendered *minoritaire* by the system in place. In colonialism, we find the closest illustration of European theonomy. These factors, however, are usually absent from conventional scholarly analyses. There were many daily compromises and wholesale subterfuge on the part of displaced persons *mal dans leur peau* (ill at ease in their skins), from dislocated and disparaged cultures in a new location. The space created by the struggle for survival was the arena where creolization was the credible response.

In the impetus to formally christianize enslaved Africans (and Native Americans) as further justification for their enslavement, certain empires fared "worse" than others. The Portuguese, Spanish, and French empires were less "successful" than the English, Dutch, Danish, and U.S. empires. Through the Roman Catholic church, ten thousand saints would shield African deities, but rituals and basic tenets continued a preordained course.[34] And indeed, syncretism cannot occur outside a far-ranging discussion about power, survival, and oppression. At one level, all religions are syncretic, though this is seldom argued in reference to Judaism, Christianity, and Islam. One finds it disturbingly easy to do so with African-derived religions and languages, rendering the thoughts of nations somewhat unoriginal. I prefer terms such as "creolization," which infers a struggle between uneven forces, or Roger Bastide's term, "the interpenetration of civilizations," to syncretism. The idea of *magie* comes into play as well. Whites were and are seen as having powerful magic, and Christianity, by extension, is "it." American Protestantism shows greater magic than

French Catholicism because of U.S. secular power. Haitians "serve the spirits." All spirits.[35] One might want to divorce what appears to be a ploy in order to continue forbidden practices, from genuine adaptations of foreign phrases and specific items in belief. Natural religions tend to recognize the value of all spiritual systems. Additionally, they have shown extraordinary flexibility as they move from place to place, occupying different spaces, a condition described by a Haitian anthropologist as the apanage of "living," as distinct from preserved religions.[36] "Religions," wrote Roger Bastide, "had to seek out, in the social structures imposed on them, 'niches' where they could establish themselves and develop. ... This called for radical transformations of religious life itself. The superstructures that had formally connected family, village, and tribe had to be linked with new substructures."[37]

The most important test concerning syncretism, however, resides with the piecemeal or wholesale transformations of theologies, cosmogonies, and cosmology. I find little evidence of such profound shifts.[38] The one important element atrophied, perhaps because of the presence of Christianity, is the fairly universal element of reincarnation, now virtually absent from the Haitian scene.[39]

Vodou is a heteroclite compendium of many African cults "rendered" in a Haitian historical and sociological context. It appears perhaps as the most creolized of African-derived systems in the Americas. Its liturgical language is Haitian (Creole), not Fon, Ewe, Yoruba, or Lingala. Cut off from the source of "fresh" Africans, paradoxically because of its early independence, and abandoned to itself, Vodou has become the least "pure" of the new religions, neither Nago or Kongo, yet African in its essence. Early contacts with islamicized Africans—and these had transformed Islam—had long ended.[40] Government- and church-sponsored endemic persecutions tended to reenforce the conflation between *lwa*/orisha and Roman Catholic saints, but these functional equivalencies remained tenuous. Deities, after all, are cosmic energy, archetypes, and moral principles. Saints, however, are dead (white) people whose edifying life stories remain in darkness for almost all Haitians.

In view of the hardships and the persecutions, it was indeed helpful to cloak the *lwa* in the garb of saints whose vestments were the proper color, or whose chromolithographs carried the proper implement. The slave owners had transformed the West African liturgical calendars away from their moorings. November 1 and 2 being All Saints' and All Souls' Day, the entire month of November is dedicated to the Gede, the family of the *lwa* of death, cemeteries, bawdiness, life, and children.

Lithographs carry within their fringed borders unintended meanings and triggers, such as the snakes at the feet of Saint Patrick (Danbala Wedo), or Saint Gérard (Bawon Samdi) dressed in black, carrying a hand cross. But in Haiti, Dandaba Wedo—whose female principle is Ayida Wedo—can be Saint Patrick, Jesus, Moses, or Aaron (the head of the Cohanim, the priestly caste in Judaism). Still in Haiti, Legba can be Saint Anthony or Jesus. In Brazil, Exu/Legba can be transformed into Satan, since his color is black and red—the black devil and the red flames of hell. Shango/Xango, a very macho deity, in Cuba is Saint Barbara; in Brazil he is Saint Jerome. Saint Anthony is Ogum in Brazil, Legba in Haiti. Ogou Feray, in Haiti, is Saint James the Elder or Saint George. Saint Barbara is Yansan/Oya in Brazil but Shango in Cuba. The Haitian Oya, Gran Brijit, is Saint Brigit that carries a skull in her hands. And the complications continue, with few of the adepts having any knowledge of the lives of the saints whose images they revere as representations of their gods. The saints have embodied disembodied spirits, as the person who is "mounted" by the spirit does in the ritual. Each *lwa*/orisha has multiple aspects, represented by *different* saints (unconnected to each other in time and space), a situation so complicated that only one with the patience of a saint could hope to unravel it, but they would not succeed. Camouflage was *one* consideration.

Might we conclude that populations of primary African descent were hopelessly confused and that, indeed, their beliefs are *un Catholicisme indigeste,* an undigested Catholicism? By borrowing from the Catholic pantheon instead of from Hinduism, Vodou might have acquired some respectability. Are neo-African religious expressions in the Americas largely derivative? If so, of what? Applied in this sense, syncretism would acquire an uncharitable mien.[41] In a (western) secular world, respect for paganism and other cultural expressions is found wanting. Conversely, their acceptance by mainstream societies in the West would indicate a sea change against quiet and smug affirmations of western dominance in all areas, fields, and domains. Typically, the West questions itself from *within;* the rest of us do so in regard to the West. There are good reasons for this, as we have seen.

The slave owners feared their slaves' traditions not because they believed in them (although some did) but because of the revolutionary potential of elements that united persons of a same ethnic group or from diverse groups. Often as an afterthought, wholesale conversions to Christianity attempted to forge a new reality and a docile and compliant slave. In Haiti, christianized slaves commanded a higher price at the auction block. They had been "housebroken" and were called "creoles" as distinct from "bossales."[42] That the Haitian Revolution was so complete and so overwhelmingly popular among the enslaved in its fifteen years (1791–1806) may show that the situation was untenable and that most Haitians did not share in the dominant (and nonmajoritarian) ideology.

The coat-of-arms of the Republic of Haiti, drawn by President Alexandre Pétion, brought together esoteric African traditions, freemasonry, French esotericism, and the *bonnet phrygien* of revolutionary France atop the Royal Palm. That palm, the tree of life, represents the *lwa* Ayizan; the *poto mitan,* center post of the *hounfò,* is the vertical axis that transpierces the horizontal plane. It is the graphic representation of the crossroads, Legba's domain, the metaphysical and temporal axes in which the Haitian (and West African) universe plays itself out. Ayizan protects from evil and is said to have been (together with Ogou Feray) Dessalines's primary spirit protector. These interpretations retain their secrets to most non-Haitians, much as the ceremonial enthroning of President Aristide did in February 1991.[43]

In 1997, thirteen Haitian scholars from multiple disciplinary backgrounds met at the University of California, Santa Barbara. They concluded a colloquium on Haitian Vodou by creating the Congress of Santa Barbara (KOSANBA); their views were set forth in the Declaration of the Congress:

> The presence, role, and importance of Vodou in Haitian history, society, and culture are unarguable and recognizably a part of the national ethos. The impact of the religion qua spiritual and intellectual discipline on popular national institutions, human and gender relations, the family, the plastic arts, philosophy and ethics, oral and written literature, language, popular and sacred music, science and technology, and the healing arts is undisputable. It is the belief of the Congress that Vodou plays and shall play a major role in the grand scheme of Haitian development and in the socio-economic, political, and cultural arenas. Development, when real and successful, always comes from the modernization of ancestral traditions, anchored in the rich cultural expressions of a people.[44]

KOSANBA saw the engine of development as internal, not external. So is it with democracy, which, furthermore, benefits from too much popular participation rather than too little. Foreign structures that are superimposed do not easily take root nor thrive well in non-native soils. Much as with syncretism and the view of Caribbean societies as largely derivative, development specialists may hold the viewpoint that Haitian salvation lies with massive foreign assistance. In other words, development would come from the same sources that rendered Haiti helpless in the first instance and saw the development of underdevelopment. The use of the drum does not preclude playing the accordion or the violin. But for most Haitians, identity was revealed in forms of cultural resistance in which creativity and some control can be exercised. This implies the rejection of the paradigm found extant in the dominant discourse, though not the wholesale rejection of specific features because these make sense or because they are inevitable. The West has much to contribute. The paradox is more apparent than real, though for the colonized, this remains a schizophrenogenic world.[45]

As civil rights harked back to situations established by the liberal state responding to particular histories, these rights bespoke of the primacy of the individual qua individual and of individualism as a subset of liberalism. In some nonwestern systems of governance, the ontological assumptions may posit different positions without necessarily sacrificing the person (as distinct from the individual), or without jeopardizing democratic principles. Framing thought as it is framed by it, language is but a pale reflection of rich interiors given largely by a spiritual discipline and a dimension that itself constitutes a worldview. Vodou is a metalanguage, a superstructure that gives definitions to worlds in the closed universe each people creates for itself. It is architectonic.

Democracy acquires meanings largely unknown in the West. As process rather than an end-state, in Haiti it is realized when state structures are "Africanized" rather than Europeanized, as the law mandates, allowing at last for the recognition of critical cultural constructs that have defined Haiti for nearly five centuries. The state might then mirror the nation. Then the country will be in measure to develop, grow, progress, and mature. The absence of political freedom, the persecution of a majoritarian religion, and the denigration of national language each played a part in silencing the voice. The fact that under the circumstances, some chose to assimilate to western values when faced with a "hopeless" situation does not justify these policies. To make available opportunities for "advancement" in a process *controlled from above* is antidemocratic and, in this case, racist and paternalistic.

The Haitian narrative is pregnant with possibilities that may remain at the level of unrealized potential for the reasons described earlier. In her Nobel lecture in 1993, a daughter of the African Diaspora, Toni Morrison, spoke of collectivities and persons attached to a narrative:

Narrative is radical, creating us at the very moment it is being created. We will not blame you if your reach exceeds your grasp; if love so ignites your words they go down in flames and no thing is left but their scald. Or if, with the reticence of a surgeon's hands, your words suture only the places where blood might flow. We know you can never do it properly—once and for all. Passion is never enough; neither is skill. But try.

I take these words and these worlds most seriously. Spoken through an elder, these seem to erupt from the fount of ancestral wisdom. "Imbued by wisdom, ancestors legislate."

Notes

1. Quoted in Brenda Gayle Plummer, *Haiti and the Great Powers* (Baton Rouge: Louisiana State University Press, 1988), 15. The head of the Vatican Congregation for the Doctrine of the Faith, Joseph Cardinal Ratzinger, said that on doctrinal matters, 'truth' is not arrived at by the majority; it flows from the top. In Haitian Vodou, in contradistinction to Dahomean Vodou, common people 'create' the religion, though levels do exist among adepts based on cosmic/mystical awareness and initiations. See also Patrick Bellegarde-Smith, 'Renewed Traditions: Contrapuntal Voices in Haitian Social Organization,' in *Imagining Home: Class, Culture, and Nationalism in the African Diaspora*, ed. Sidney W. Lemelle and Robin D.G. Kelley (London: Routledge/Verso, 1994), 85–92; Patrick Bellegarde-Smith, 'Eddies in the Stream: Issues for Haitian History and Historiography,' in *Historia y Sociedad* 8 (1995–96): 31–49; and Patrick Bellegarde-Smith, 'Resisting Freedom: Cultural Factors in Democracy – The Case for Haiti,'

in *Haiti Renewed: Political and Economic Prospects*, ed. Robert I. Rotberg (Washington, DC: Brookings Institution, 1997), 27–46.
2. The Haitian government declared the site of Bois Caiman a *haut lieu de l'histoire* on July 13, 1998. This made it a protected sanctuary. Earlier that month, Protestant missionaries were arrested there for trying to 'exorcize' Satan and Boukman from Haiti.
3. One is reminded of a line in an African American hymn that served as Martin Luther King Jr.'s epitaph: 'Free at last, thank God almighty, I am free at last.'
4. General Jean-Jacques Dessalines, in his red coat, becomes a deity in the Petwo rite of Haitian Vodou. See Lilas Desquiron, *Les Racines du Vodou* (Port-au-Prince: Editions le Natal, 1990), 136, 140–41.
5. The conceptual worldview of Vodou is pervasive among most Haitians and throughout all classes. Oftentimes, a specific family member 'does what needs to be done' for his or her extended family. Elite Haitians often see or subscribe to Vodou for its magical properties, while the lower classes take a broader view of the religion as spiritual discipline.
6. Chiefs of state used Vodou as 'insurance,' to assuage friends and to placate enemies.
7. Jean Fouchard, *The Haitian Maroons: Liberty or Death*, trans. A. Faulkner Watts (1972; reprint, New York: Blyden, 1981).
8. The *mulâtres affranchis* wished to inherit plantations abandoned by their putative fathers; Dessalines resisted. A number of the measures he took on behalf of the former slaves were held against him by Haiti's westernizers.
9. West African thought is not rooted typically in Manichean dichotomies. At the level of individual behavior, one finds a process of situational ethics, where choice is predicated on context. See Karen McCarthy Brown, *Mama Lola: A Vodou Priestess in Brooklyn* (Berkeley: University of California Press, 1991).
10. The assimilationist impulse erupted full-blown during France's 'second empire,' after the loss of Saint-Domingue/Haiti. See Patrick Bellegarde-Smith, *In the Shadow of Powers: Dantès Bellegarde in Haitian Social Thought* (Atlantic Highlands, NJ: Humanities Press, 1985), 11–12, 48–53, 109.
11. Dantès Bellegarde, *Dessalines a Parlé* (Port-au-Prince: Société d'éditions et de Librairie, 1948), 180; Auguste Viatte, *Histoire Litteraire de l'Amérique Française* (Paris: Presses Universitaires de France, 1954), 424–27.
12. Ghislain Gouraige, *La Diaspora d'Haiti et l'Afrique* (Ottawa: Naaman, 1974), 102.
13. The risks were simply too great to bear. The social philosopher Dantès Bellegarde, the quasi-official ideologue of the state in the 1930s, asked not so rhetorically, 'What would become of a Dahomean islet in the heart of the Americas?' Dantès Bellegarde, *Haiti et ses Problèmes* (Montreal: Valiquette, 1941), 17.
14. Haiti reintegrated the world in a number of far-reaching events, notably, the Concordat signed between Haiti and the Vatican in 1860, US recognition in 1862, and various measures instituted by the Salomon government between 1879 and 1888, such as joining the Universal Postal Union and the telegraph. See Brenda Gayle Plummer, *Haiti and the United States: The Psychological Moment* (Athens: University of Georgia Press, 1992), 63.
15. This has been the thrust of my published work since 1974. See Patrick Bellegarde-Smith, 'Haiti: Perspectives of Foreign Policy; An Essay on the International Relations of a Small State,' *Caribbean Quarterly* (September–December 1974): 21–39. See also Michel-Rolph Trouillot, *Haiti: State against Nation* (New York: Monthly Review Press, 1990). He makes a similar argument to mine but stops shy of advocating the neo-African-derived cultural system for Haiti.
16. For the earlier period, see Sidney W. Mintz, preface to *The Haitian People*, by James G. Leyburn (New Haven, Conn.: Yale University Press, 1966), v–xxxvi.
17. Haiti is arguably the epitome of a creolized culture in that the violent clash between French culture, as one side of the equation, and a plethora of West and West Central African cultures, as the other side, resulted in a genuinely authocthonous Haitian culture rooted in struggle and a national identity cemented by language and religion. Elsewhere the colonial languages were made universal by neocolonial elites, and Christianity was and is a greater factor.
18. There are diverse and contradictory explanations concerning the rise of the Haitian language. There is some logic in admitting that a largely French vocabulary was superimposed on West African linguistic structures. After all, at independence, as many as three-quarters of all Haitians had been born in Africa, and one presumes that they had not forgotten everything.
19. See Alex Dupuy, *Haiti in the World Economy: Class, Race, and Underdevelopment since 1700* (Boulder, Colo.: Westview Press, 1988).
20. See Brenda Gayle Plummer, *Haiti and the Great Powers, 1902–1915* (Baton Rouge: Louisiana State University Press, 1988), 41–66.

21. See Jean-Marie Jan, *Collecta III* (Port-au-Prince: Editions Henri Deschamps, 1955), 340–44. For a similar integration of traditional priests in a Marxist movement, see David Lan, *Guns and Rains: Guerrillas and Spirit Mediums in Zimbabwe* (Berkeley: University of California Press, 1985).
22. Trouillot, *Haiti*; Gérard Barthelemy, *Le Pays en Dehors* (Port-au-Prince: Le Natal, 1989).
23. See Anne Greene, *The Catholic Church in Haiti: Political and Social Change* (Lansing: Michigan State University Press, 1993).
24. An interesting Haitian version of the *Juif errant*, the yearning of religious Jews for a homeland long disappeared. Though very much rooted in Haitian soil, Haitians speak nonetheless of a metaphorical motherland, a version of both hell and heaven.
25. See Patrick Bellegarde-Smith, *Haiti: The Breached Citadel* (Boulder, Colo.: Westview Press, 1990), 9–19; and Wade Davis, *The Serpent and the Rainbow* (New York: Warrior Books, 1985), 72–73.
26. Janheinz Jahn, *Muntu: The New African Culture* (New York: Grove Press, 1961), 97.
27. If the temple in Jerusalem is rebuilt, one may have to resume animal sacrifice. See Lawrence Wright, 'Forcing the End,' *New Yorker*, July 20, 1998, 42–53.
28. Conversations with the Haitian psychologist Viviane Nicolas, over 20 years.
29. See the significant anthropological work by Karen McCarthy Brown, especially *Mama Lola*.
30. George E. Carter, 'Traditional African Social Thought,' in *Pan Africanism Reconsidered*, ed. American Society of African Culture (Berkeley: University of California Press, 1962), 254–66.
31. A passage from Carl Sagan, in a short piece for *Parade* magazine in 1984.
32. See Frantz Fanon, *Black Skins, White Masks* (New York: Grove Press, 1967); and Aimé Césaire, *Discourse on Colonialism* (New York: Monthly Review Press, 1972).
33. See Roger Bastide, 'Color, Racism, and Christianity,' in *Color and Race*, ed. John Hope Franklin (Boston: Houghton Mifflin, 1968), 34–49; and Fouchard, *Haitian Maroons*, 208.
34. See the chart of deities and saints in the appendix.
35. In monoreligious areas, naming the religion is quite unnecessary. The existence of several religions demands, as it were, that they be differentiated and better specification achieved. However, in traditional systems, one is usually content to appropriate features of the dominant cult that may allow one to survive and continue one's belief that all beliefs are 'appropriate.' 'Vodun/Vodou' does not refer to the Haitian religion primarily. The preferred response of an adept (who will also define him- or herself as a good Catholic) to an inquiry is to say, 'I serve the spirits.'
36. See Michel S. Laguerre, *Voodoo Heritage* (Beverly Hills, Calif.: Sage Publications, 1980), 22.
37. Roger Bastide, *The African Religions of Brazil: Toward a Sociology of the Interpenetration of Civilizations* (Baltimore: Johns Hopkins University Press, 1978), 58.
38. Based on my conversations with priests in Haiti, Cuba, Brazil, Canada, and the United States over two decades.
39. A culturally significant point arises with Tibetan Buddhism: will the next Dalai Lama be found in the West or be a Tibetan, now that China is expected to interfere in the process?
40. See the impressive work of LeGrace Benson, especially 'How the Houngan Uses the Light from Distant Stars,' *Journal of Haitian Studies* 7 no.1 (2001): 106–35.
41. One will never be able to eliminate racism as a factor, historically. Its corollary is a modicum of self-hatred. The works of Fanon, Bastide, and a number of other scholars in the field of black psychology make this clear. For a somewhat different position, see Leslie Desmangles, *The Faces of the Gods* (Chapel Hill: University of North Carolina Press, 1991).
42. Desquiron, *Racines de Vodou*, 103–4. Desquiron supports the position of Moreau de Saint-Méry, *Descriptions*...vol. 2 (Philadelphia: n.p., 1797), 56. Creole slaves believed that Christian baptism gave them superiority over slaves in Africa. Desquiron also cites Roger Bastide, who argues that Africans adopted certain features (elements of magic) to become stronger than the whites, seeing European cultures as 'a technique for social mobility' (*African Religions*, 94).
43. In moments rife with symbolism, Aristide took the presidential oath in the Haitian language and received the sash of his office from an elderly *manbo*, who was not identified publicly as such. Later, at the Notre Dame basilica, greetings between Aristide and priests at the inaugural Te Diem were familiar to Vodouisants and freemasons. Aristide was deposed in a coup in February 1991, returned to power in October 1994, and deposed once more in February 2004.
44. From the 'Deklarasyon Kongrè Santa Barbara' (Declaration of the Congress of Santa Barbara), a part of the by-laws of KOSANBA.
45. Besides the work and life of Frantz Fanon, see also the Tunisian Albert Memmi, *Portrait du Colonisé Précédé du Portrait du Colonisateur* (Paris: Editions Buchet/Chastel, 1957); and O. Mannoni, *Psychologie de la Colonisation* (Paris: Editions du Seuil, 1950).

Healing the Nation:
Rastafari Exorcism of the Ideology of Racism in Jamaica

Barry Chevannes

In a recent and timely article Joop van Kessel and André Droogers have criticised the failure of development theory in Latin America to view religion as anything but the irrelevant remnant of an outmoded past destined to disappear or be relegated to the private sphere of life with the transition of the countries of the region to modernization (1988). This failure, according to the authors, explains the wider failure to produce any substantial result in the region over the last forty years of application. Development processes, they argue, cannot succeed in Latin America if identity is neglected, and since religion is an integral part of Latin American identity, the need to integrate the anthropology of religion into development sociology becomes clear.

The problem, unfortunately, has been a far more generalised and broader one. In many quarters of development studies religious movements as a constituent part of social movements for change are still an undeveloped field, despite the importance of religion in the so-called developing world; despite, also, the richness of anthropological literature on the subject, particularly in Asia and Africa. But it is not just religion which development theory has ignored up to now, and with results similar to Latin America, but the broader area of life we know as culture. Fortunately, there seems to be a growing awareness of this shortcoming. In a series of public lectures a few years ago at the Institute of Social Studies on the theme of culture and development, Professor van Nieuwenhuijze declared:

> It is high time...to inquire, no doubt belatedly, into the significance of culture or civilization for the notion and practice of development. Clearly this cannot be a one-eyed inquiry, in the sense that one would look, as has occasionally been done without result, into socio-cultural constraints hampering otherwise good economic development policies in particular settings. There is need to account for the significance of the cultural frame of reference at both ends of the given international — read, intercultural — transaction concerned with development. (1984: 4).

More recently Stavenhagen (1986) has entered a plea for ethnicity to be incorporated within the purview of development theory.

Still, as van Ufford and Schoffeleers remind us (1988:4—6), the problem was also as much the making of anthropology, given its evolution into a discipline focusing almost blindly on culture to the exclusion of poverty and underdevelopment.

Thus, the obligation to continue the discussion resting as much with development theory as with anthropology, this paper explores the case of a religious movement whose contribution to the solution of what must be one of the most debilitating features of colonial underdevelopment, namely racism, has been a decisive factor in the development of Jamaican nationalism. By keeping alive the issue of identity and forcing it on national consciousness, the Rastafari movement has helped to expose and by so doing overturn certain assumptions of the ideology of racism, particularly among the middle classes.

To be a bit more specific, at the risk of appearing somewhat dramatic, this is what the before picture looked like in the Jamaica of the 1940s:

> In training and in outlook these middle classes are European. They retain little or no trace of their African origin except the colour of their skin. Some have been educated at Oxford, the Sorbonne, Madrid. They are coloured Europeans, in dress,...in tastes, in opinions and in aspirations.[1]

And in the early 1950s:

> The coloured person in the West Indies represents a unique phenomenon in the hybrid world. He is generally almost entirely ignorant of African culture and despises what little he does know as being primitive and connected with the undesirable, that is the black.... For such individuals there is a conscious ideal of self-identification with the European or Englishman (Henriques, 1953: 52—53).

The after picture, from quantitative research carried out among middle class tertiary students in the early 1980s, now looks like this:

> Africans, that is black Jamaicans, emerged as the most accepted of all groups on all categories of the Social Distance Scale, and also as the group towards which the most favourable attitudes were expressed on the Attitudes to Minorities Scale. Such a finding suggests that the low esteem he enjoyed from others is now a thing of the past...Since the largest group in the sample was of mixed origin, it is not only the pure African alone who accepts himself, his blackness, his kinky hair, but the figures strongly suggest that Black is now indeed both beautiful and desirable generally (Richardson, 1983: 158).

Wondering, but without examining, what might have brought about this change, Richardson mentions the Black Power movement and the fact of Independence. My argument is simply that **the main credit for this change belongs to the Rastafari.** Because Rastafari membership is still relatively small,[2] its contribution is often overlooked. But the story also has wider relevance. Blacks are lowest on the totem pole in virtually every non-black country of the world. Thus, while the case of the Rastafari may well enrich our understanding of the role of identity in development, it also has direct implications for black identity in other parts of the world, including Latin America itself where religion rather than race is the main focal point.

Class and Race

Before introducing the Rastafari, a brief word on the class structure of Jamaica is necessary. Henriques, in the work cited above, drew the sketch of a three-tiered triangle representing a lower, a middle and an upper class, and correlating with colour ranging from black to coloured to white, respectively. There has never been any doubt among Caribbean social scientists that race and skin colour figure prominently in the stratification systems of the Caribbean. The question is what are their relative roles. Is stratification based on class or on race and colour, or both? If class, then we are dealing with an open system, in which there are broadly shared values; if race, with a system of ethnic segmentation, one prone to ethnic violence. The divisions on the issue have been mainly between functionalism and pluralism.

M.G. Smith, adapting the economic model of pluralism developed by J.S. Furnivall, has argued that Caribbean societies are plural societies, comprising different racial segments within the same polities, with each having its own distinct and separate cultural practices and norms (1965). They are brought together only by the market place, and held together by the political system. Thus, in a country like Jamaica, race is closely identified with culture.

Smith's model of pluralism has triggered considerable debate which has continued into the present.[3] Lloyd Braithwaite, from a functionalist perspective, argued that Trinidadian society was integrated by a universally shared system of values, among them the ascriptive norms by which skin colour was associated with privilege, the closer to white the more of it, the closer to black the less (1955).

Most scholars accept the applicability of pluralism to Caribbean society up to the end of slavery, but reject it as no longer a useful model for understanding the dynamics of the modern societies of the region. Race and colour remain as attitudinal remnants of the colonial past. Though 80% of Jamaica's population, for example, are of African descent, 15% of mixed African-European and the rest European and other white ethnic minorities, the fact is that upward social mobility by blacks is changing the complexion of the middle classes. In a recent effort aimed at reconciling both paradigms, however, Mills (1988) makes use of the Gramscian concept of hegemony to argue that while Caribbean societies are stratified by class, nevertheless race functions as ruling ideology. Concerned though he also was to answer widely expressed criticism that Marxism, by its one-sided focus on class, has no comprehensive answer to the realities of the Caribbean, he has in fact touched upon the issue which I believe to be central in any explanation of the rise of the Rastafari, namely, racism as an ideology.

Ideology of Racism

The following brief sketch of racism as ideology provides an indication of its scope. I focus on the Black population, for it was primarily aimed at subordinating them.[4] The main thing to understand is that racial ideology always presents itself as a cognitive system of binary opposites. All the qualities singled out for devaluation in the racially different group are the opposites of qualities which provide the subject group with a positive self-evaluation. Racism and ethnocentrism are always packaged as "they" and "we".

Skin Colour: white vs. black

In European culture, white is a symbol of purity and goodness, its opposite, black, a symbol of impurity and evil. By calling Africans "black" and themselves "white",[5] Europeans set the stage whereupon the enslavement and subsequent subordination of Africans could be elevated to the level of mythology. Thus, one common explanation of the racial difference was that the "darker" races were the children of Ham, that son of Noah who was struck with a curse for having looked on his father's nakedness. Both in the United States and throughout the Caribbean may be found stories of creation which offer explanations as to why some men are white, others black.[6] While the tongue-in-cheek humour of many of them suggests that they are not accorded mythological status, they are nevertheless significant in that the common theme running through them all is that blackness is a mistake, due either to error on God's part or weakness and sin on man's part.

The concepts of "white" being pretty and "black" being ugly went effectively unchallenged until the emergence of Marcus Garvey in the 1920s. Even so, these usages are not uncommon today.

The incongruity of black Christians praying that God wash them "white as snow", was not merely an ecological but a religious one as well, for, as the prophet Alexander Bedward saw it, even the skin colour of blacks was to be transformed into white following ascent to heaven.[7] And no wonder, if Jesus and his angels were themselves white.

Body Norms: handsome vs. ugly

Skin colour represented only one aspect of the phenotypical differences between whites and blacks, the remaining ones being hair quality (fine vs. coarse, straight vs. spiralled), nose shape (straight vs. flat, narrow vs. wide) and lip size (thin vs. thick). These qualities also contributed to defining who was beautiful, who ugly. A common practice among mothers was the pinching of children's noses to make them straight and thin.

Character: moral vs. immoral

Orlando Patterson tells us that **Quashee**, the Twi day-name for males born on Sunday, was used by whites to personify their stereotype of the African slaves as deceitful, lying, capricious and lazy (1967: 174—81). Applying Merton's concept of the "self-fulfilling prophecy", he argues that the slaves responded "by either appearing to, or actually internalizing" these stereotypes (p. 180). After slavery, and certainly into the twentieth century, the term "Quashee" shed its connotation of deceitful and acquired instead that of stupid or foolish. It was more hurtful to call one Quashee than to call one stupid, since an element of race still clung to the usage.

Quashee was not the only proper noun to be used as stereotypes. Two others **Kofi**, the day-name for males born on Friday, and **Bongo**, the name of one of the Congo tribes and of a religious cult appearing among the Maroons, were also used to mean stupid or uncouth.

No doubt, the misuse of these day-names was partly responsible for their gradual disuse and the preference for Biblical and Anglo-Saxon names.

Another "failing of character" which became ideological was the accusation by whites that blacks were sexually irresponsible. Ironically, the proof of irresponsibility was not the large coloured population of the island, but "illegitimate births". There were two issues here. One was the failure to enter into the legal institution of marriage, and the other was what some sociologists have referred to as "serial polygamy". The former was a target of theological teaching of the Protestant Missionaries on holiness, as Robotham shows (forthcoming):

> Not the study of the scriptures and the demonstrated understanding of them; not good works nor religious revelation were the decisive factors, but the acceptance of certain social institutions as superior and others as inferior and the adherence to the superior system — this was the critical factor in "living holy" and entering into and sustaining a "church connection" (p. 83).

During the late 1930s and the 1940s, a group of upper-middle class women, at one time led by the wife of the colonial Governor, used to stage mass marriages.

"Serial polygamy" referred to the series of consensual, or common law, unions which many people enter during their first fifteen years of cohabitation, resulting in a complex system of half-brothers and half-sisters. Many women therefore bear children for different genitors, while many men sire children of different mothers, often complicating the situation by their failure either to acknowledge or to bear paternal responsibility. Naturally, these forms of male and female "irresponsibility" have through the decades been placed at the root of crime, lawlessness and immorality.

Though the pattern of mating has not changed since emancipation, according to Roberts and Sinclair (1980), the institution of marriage, which is the mating form used by whites, although they too practise what could be called "serial polygamy" except that it is legal,[8] is one way of acquiring social respectability. Common-law unions, once the spouses pass thirty-five or forty years of age, thus tend to end in marriage at some point.

The Motherland: Africa vs. Europe

Racist arguments about the savagery and lack of civilization of Africa are now too well known to need any exposition here.[9] They were very common in Jamaica, where the ideology seemed to have taken root much more among those exposed to the higher levels of the education system, for there is much evidence to show that among the uneducated masses Africa was always cherished as the land of the forefathers.[10]

As Africa was the land of darkness and savagery, so was Europe generally and England in particular the land of light and civilization. England became for every school child up to the time of Independence in 1962 the "Mother country".

Culture: Savagery vs. Civilization

Not surprisingly, many of the more important aspects of Jamaican folk culture were the object of ideological denigration. The folk religion, in all its variants, was described by one of Jamaica's leading intellectuals of the 1920s and 1930s as **the mud**, which he contrasted with **the gold**. The mud was that tradition of African superstition and savagery, with its wild drumming, dancing, spirit possession and polytheism, in which the ignorant masses were mired; the gold the tradition of real religion, with its Easter morning pealing of bells, word of the one true God and studied reflection (Delisser, 1913). To the missionaries and Christian preachers themselves Afro-Jamaican religion was the work of the Devil himself. Christianity, of which they were the bearers, was the work of God.

While not all Blacks were stuck in the mud, all Blacks, except the relatively few who acquired a certain level of education, spoke "bad" English. In rural Jamaica "good" English was the speech of the local elite, the school teachers, the justice of the peace, the sanitary inspector, and so on. Nothing less was expected of them. Such people using the dialect were thought to be common and lacking in "ambition". "Good" English was thus the speech of the upwardly mobile, "bad" English the speech of the uneducated and ignorant.

Using culture in the narrow sense of the fine arts, whites also inflated their own culture and claimed racial superiority over blacks.

I have spent some time illustrating the ways in which racism entrenched itself in Jamaica in the cognitive life of the people, because it is my view that the impact of the Rastafari is to be sought here rather than elsewhere. Naturally, to make out a claim for Jamaica as a special case is not only absurd, but makes questionable the suggestion which I make at the end of the paper that there is much about Rastafari that may have significance for other countries. For racist and ethnocentric ideology has been the experience of colonialism, of Romans over English, English over Irish, Japanese over Chinese. Racism against the Africans is unquestionably, however, the most extreme. Thus, my main aim so far is to illustrate the varied ways in which that ideology was propounded and in some measure internalised, in order to contextualise what I argue constituted the *raison d'être* of the Rastafari movement.

I say "in some measure", because behind the studied propagation of white racist ideology always lurked the fear of threat to white racist superordination. The country had experienced more slave revolts and plots than any other colony in the hemisphere, hosted the only maroon settlement which forced the British into treaty, had brought slavery to an end in 1834 with the greatest revolt in its history, had witnessed the suppression of a rebellion in which peasants rallied and slew on the basis of colour in 1865, and the overawing of a popular religious movement, whose leader had agitated for the overthrow of whites in 1895. Now on the eve of the appearance of Rastafari it was about to face the black nationalism of Marcus Garvey.

Marcus Garvey

Marcus Garvey was not the first black nationalist in Jamaican history, but he was the first to have fired the imagination of the masses on a grand and dramatic scale. He led the largest social movement among American blacks prior to the civil rights movement led by Martin Luther King Jr., and led the largest ever international black movement. The fact that Blacks in Africa and the Americas were inspired to become his followers indicated that theirs was a common experience. In fact, Garvey later revealed that what fired his imagination to uplift his race was finding the Blacks of central America in the same position he had left them in Jamaica. Garvey had an impact far greater than his own organization, the Universal Negro Improvement Association (UNIA), or his actual teachings, far-reaching though these were. Just the fact that he was such a great man of itself did much to change the self-perception of blacks.[11]

Linking the degrading conditions of blacks, which he found everywhere he went throughout the hemisphere, with their lack of power, Garvey set himself the task of building a power base through which, and only through which, blacks could command the respect of the world. To this end, his first step was the formation of the Universal Negro Improvement Association (UNIA). But at the same time keenly aware that blacks were themselves partly to blame, owing to their lack of consciousness and low self-esteem, he also set himself the task of educating the race. Thus Garveyism was both a political and an ideological movement, whose points of focus may be summarised as follows:

Political Achievements
1. Founding of local economic enterprises, such as factories.
2. The launching of the Black Star Shipping Line, to foster and develop international pan-African trade.
3. Campaigning for the decolonization of Africa, under the slogan "Africa for the Africans at home and abroad".
4. Launching a back-to-Africa movement to encourage skilled and professional blacks to return and contribute to the development of Africa.
5. Publication of an organ through which to spread the ideas of race consciousness.

Ideological Teachings
1. The black race constituted one nationality, whose native land was Africa. "Garveyism was Pan-Africanism at the level of popular mass organization to confront the ideology of racism."[12]
2. As the seat of many early civilizations, Africa played a role in the development of world culture.
3. By its survival of European enslavement, where other races have been wiped out, the black race has revealed its inner endowment.
4. The past achievements of the race and its survival are sources of pride and self-confidence. They are also the sign of its present and future possibilities.
5. All races are equal. The present subjugation of blacks is transient; as transient, for example, as the past enslavement of the English by the Romans.
6. Self-reliance is the only way forward to gain the respect of other nations.

These activities and ideas were in their time revolutionary. The UNIA boasted of an eleven million membership at the height of Garvey's popularity in the early 1920s, scattered throughout the Americas and Africa. In French West Africa it became a capital offence to read Garvey's paper, **The Negro World.** In the United States the FBI, bent on crushing his movement, arrested Garvey on the trumped up charge of using the mail to defraud. Sentenced to prison, Garvey was deported to his native Jamaica, where he lost little time in entering the political life of the country. Forced to attend to the declining fortunes of the UNIA, he left Jamaica for England, where he died in 1940.

By his intense concentration on the black man, Garvey was mainly responsible for the attention which increasingly larger numbers of Jamaicans began to pay to events in Africa.[13] The coronation of Ras Tafari in Ethiopia in November 1930 was one which the founders of the Rastafari movement interpreted as the fulfilment of prophecy. Before reaching the peak of his career Garvey was already a hero to the Jamaican masses, in both the common and mythological senses of the word. Myths had developed about what he said and did, making him superhuman.[14] Thus, it was alleged, in one of his many speeches he had prophesied that one was to come after him greater than himself and that the people should look to Africa when a King would be crowned for their redemption. As if to strengthen their belief, Tafari, as Haile Selassie, took several titles of religious significance: "King of Kings and Lord of Lords", "Light of the World", and, claiming descent from the Solomonic line, "Conquering Lion of the tribe of Judah".

Leonard Howell, Joseph Hibbert and Archibald Dunkley, all three of whom were returned migrants, Robert Hinds and Brother Napier — were among the earliest to start preaching that Prince Tafari was God. But they went further and transposed the Biblical metaphor of the children of Israel in captivity, from which Christianised blacks had always found inspiration and hope, into the reality itself. Black people were the true Israel and Ras Tafari the returned messiah come to deliver his people. Christ, they preached, was and had always been black. He was the real King of the black race; therefore blacks owed no allegiance to King George. Thus was the Rastafari movement born.

The movement took root mainly in the city of Kingston among the marginalised stratum of the working class, peasants uprooted by social conditions in the countryside and blocked from external migration.[15] Right up to the end of the 1960s this was the stratum most drawn to the faith.

Rastafari Beliefs

Rastafari beliefs and practices have developed over the years and it seems best to summarise them in this way. I identify three phases of growth up to the present time, each covering approximately two decades.

In the first two decades, the 1930s and 1940s, beliefs centred on the identity of God, as set out above. Propagating the faith took the form of street meetings. Each preacher established his own "King of Kings" mission, which was attended by those converted at the public meetings. Ritual practices varied from mission to mission, but included baptism, fasting and celebration of special anniversaries, such as the coronation, and the cultivation of head and facial hair according to the Nazarite vow as set out in the Book of Leviticus.

The second two decades, the 1950s and 1960s, were marked by agitation for repatriation and by the rise to ascendancy throughout the movement of a radical trend which became known as the Dreadlocks. As I shall be dealing more fully with the most important of the repatriation episodes, it should suffice to make two observations. First, this demand to return to Africa had been institutionalised as a part of Rastafari ideology by the early founders, following fast on the heels of Garvey's Back-to-Africa movement, but except for one episode in August 1934, they carried out no mass action towards this goal. According to the concept blacks are Africans, or rather Ethiopians, for Ethiopia was the name of the continent before the white man renamed it; Africans, or "Ethiopians", were seized and transported to the Americas against their will; hence Repatriation, or return to the motherland. But Repatriation is a divinely ordained act, depending on the will and action of God, not on man. It is different from migration. In that August 1934 episode, it was alleged, they expected the sea to part, just as in the time of Moses, but this time only for those with a beard.

The second observation is that mass agitation for repatriation when it did take place, in 1958 and again in 1959—1960, came against the background of increased external migration to Britain and increased attention by old Garveyites to the possibilities for migration to Liberia and other West African countries. In fact, through the Ethiopian World Federation Haile Selassie made a land grant at Sheshamane in Ethiopia for the settlement of blacks, in token of appreciation for their support during the anti-fascist invasion of his country. The gift aroused great interest, particularly among the Rastafari, when a Federation official visited Jamaica in 1955 and made the announcement. Scholars who argue that the movement is essentially millenarian need to exercise caution, for only thrice in the six decades (1934, 1958 and 1959) did the dream of the millenium result in mass millenarian activity. The growth and impact of Rastafari have not been dependent on the dream of the millenium.

The Dreadlocks emerged in the course of overturning the authority of the older generation, whom they judged to be too compromising towards the society. They were more separatist, symbolising their ideological stance in their spectacular hair style. To the older generation the scissors and razor had been taboo; to the Dreadlocks the scissors, the razor and the comb.

Other beliefs and practices institutionalised by the Dreadlocks were:

1. sacralisation of ganja (marijuana) as a sacrament;
2. development of an argot, focused on the concept of the personal pronoun I;
3. symbolic identification of the status quo with the concept **Babylon;**
4. ritual ascendancy over women;
5. extension of the concept of God as man to include man as also God.

Many of these beliefs and practices are the results of idealisation of beliefs and practices already present within the culture of the folk, but carried to extremes. Such, for instance is the God-man concept, which derives from folk belief in the immanence of God; such also the sacred ritualisation of female subordination, which has precedence in social and cultural life.[16] But in other instances, deliberately and consciously they identified with traditions which were vilified under racist ideology. For example, the Dreadlocks appropriated the names associated with stupidity. One which soon became, and which still remains, a title of respect was **Bongo.** The name **Nati,** referring to hair quality, is another.

The last two decades, the 1970s and 1980s have been marked by three far-reaching developments. The first was the use of reggae music as the medium of expression of Rastafari sentiments, and the mutual identity of the two; second, the internationalisation of the movement, due to the impact of reggae, to migration and racism in the metropoles of both the northern and southern hemispheres. These have been well documented.[17] Third, but not yet fully studied, is the triumphant entry of Rastafari into the middle classes. With this last we come to the central point of this paper.

As our "before" picture presented at the beginning would have made clear, the middle classes, made up predominantly of the coloured population, were far from immune to the ideology of racism. In his analysis of class consciousness in the period leading up to the 1938 labour rebellion, Ken Post explains:

> Race was also a very important factor in the consciousness of the lower middle class. Along with their collars and ties a light brown skin and 'good' hair and features were the marks of their superior status, and were among the criteria for getting a job. But race was not only important to the lower stratum; it was crucial for the entire middle class (1978: 103).

But the symbols of social mobility were not the only concern of the middle classes, Post further explains. They "tended to reproduce quite faithfully the ideas of their betters. Indeed,...it was the special task of many of them to develop and propagate those ideas, since clergymen, teachers, journalists and others were concerned specifically with cognitive practice" (p. 101). In other words, white colonial society had produced the intellectuals on whom it could rely for its apologia.

To view the middle classes from this point of view alone would be one-sided. As Phillips explains, in the pre-war years there had emerged among the middle classes a nationalist movement split between those with a "Jamaican" and those with a " 'Pan-African tendency' focussed on a wider set of Pan-Nationalist concerns" (1988: 106). The latter, it is clear, were motivated by the racial contradiction, and would have been influenced by Garveyite and pre-Garveyite black nationalism. For the former — the larger and more influential — their nationalism derived from other contradictions, such as the control by the colonial government of "education and other matters vital to the middle class" (Post, 1978: 103).

Middle class nationalism, led by the "Jamaican" tendency, soon crystallised in the formation of the People's National Party (PNP) in 1938, whose demand for self-government, strengthened by the labour rebellion and meeting objectives of the British government, led to a process of gradual decolonization which culminated in independence in 1962. According to Munroe (1972), the main problem facing the upper middle class, which led this process, was how to secure control of the country without the arousal of the masses. Though the thesis overestimates the independent political potential of the working class and underestimates the significance of the black nationalist wing in the national movement,[18] it aptly identifies the process as "constitutional decolonization", and explains its results as the "growth and consolidation of middle class dominance" over political life (p. 75) and a constitution patterned off the British.

In effect, therefore, the independence movement avoided the issue of race. Thus, the nationalism which Norris found among the educated in Jamaica on the eve of political Independence lay "in the confidence that Jamaica can successfully build a miniature Britain, America or a European-type state" (Norris, 1962: 72) rather than build on the "cultural traditions or creative spirit of the Jamaican people" (p. 88).

Still, there was hope — the Rastafari:

> While the conformist is still over-deferential to the white stranger, the Rastafarian expresses his defiance by abusing him publicly. While the conformist still looks on a white man as a source of financial assistance and few would hesitate to beg from him if the opportunity offered, the Rastafarian prefers to live in appalling squalor, but does not beg. (Norris, p. 98).

She found Rastafari to be "an instinctive kind of nationalism and an instinctive search for dignity and naturalness as far removed from race hatred as straightforward national consciousness is removed from hatred of other nations", notwithstanding its being a "crank" philosophy (p. 99). In other words, by electing to lead a life based on the affirmation of being black, without at the same time being racist, the Rastafari have seized hold of one of the main springs of national development, namely a sense of national identity. In this respect, they represented, for Norris, not so much a signpost leading the way to Rastafari, as a symbol of the harmony between the reality of being black and the consciousness of and confidence in that reality.

This point must not be glossed over. Some commentators accuse Rastafari of being a form of "reverse racism", sometimes comparing it to the Black Muslims. Nothing could be further from the truth. As Father Owens observes, this judgment derives from a failure to grasp the essence of a doctrine which not only "effectively negates the white racism pervading the society, but which also strives to overcome the logical premises which make any type of racism possible" (Owens, 1976: 57). Most other Whites who have studied the Rastafari would share that view. This gives the Rastafari a humanism with potential lessons for other groups and peoples.

Rastafari exorcism of the ideology of racism among the middle classes and inspiring of a more wholesome sense of identity began in the period of the Dreadlocks, with a millenarian episode which, not surprisingly blown out of all proportion, had the effect of treating the Rastafari seriously for the first time and of beginning a process of self-examination. Ken Post describes Jamaica as an open society prone to external influences. Understandably, therefore, the impact on the middle classes was in no small measure facilitated and enhanced by the rapid acquisition of independence by African nations and equal status with other sovereign states of the world. But while external processes made the middle classes better listeners, the Rastafari forced them to think, and to choose.

On New Year's day 1959, Fidel Castro entered Havana in triumph. The event made a great impact throughout the Caribbean and the rest of the hemisphere. Later that same year, one Reverend Claudius Henry, leader of a group of Rastafari, proclaimed October 25 to be "decision day" when Israel's scattered children would return to Africa.[19] Undaunted by the failure of this prophecy, but less open to the public, Henry quietly began planning for repatriation, when a police raiding party swooped down on his headquarters and seized an arms cache and two letters. The arms included two or three firearms and several rounds of ammunition, dynamite, machetes and clubs. The letters, addressed to Castro, informed him that as they were about to depart for Africa they wished to hand over the country to him. Henry was charged with treason felony: intent to intimidate and overawe Her Majesty's Government and to invite in a foreign power. As if that was not enough, weeks later news broke that members of Henry's church were involved in guerrilla operations in the Red Hills area above Kingston, and that two British soldiers were killed in an operation against them. A manhunt soon resulted in the capture of a four-man squad which included Henry's son, Ronald. These they charged with the murder of a police infiltrator whom they had buried near their training ground in the hills.

The effect was electrifying, especially among the middle classes. Not since the Morant Bay rebellion in 1865 had a group of Jamaicans taken up arms against the state. As if that was not enough, here was a group of people who wore their contempt of society by their hair and even facial expressions. It was time to put a stop to the lunacy that was Rastafari. The police were not slow to take their cue from the general public, as a wave of intimidation, shaving of locks, arrests, beating and imprisonment, descended on all Rastafari, in unprecedented scale and scope.

Acting wisely, a small group of Rastafari led by Mortimo Planno approached the University with the suggestion that a carefully documented and publicised study of their movement would go a long way in convincing the society that Rastafari was essentially peaceful. It was a brilliant stroke, for the University, then an affiliate of the University of London and headed by W. Arthur Lewis, was already making great headway in challenging the pro-British, anti-Jamaican orientation of the middle classes, by an already deserved reputation for scholarship and excellence, especially in the field of tropical medicine. The sanction of such an institution would not be lost on the real sources of influence and power.

The urgency of the situation led Lewis to assign three of his finest scholars, all Caribbean, to carry out the investigation. The result after two weeks of intense field work was *The Rastafari Movement in Kingston, Jamaica* by M.G. Smith, Roy Augier and Rex Nettleford, which Lewis presented to the Government. Sketching in brief outline the beliefs, the historical course and structure of the movement, the scholars gave an analysis which exposed the appallingly bad social conditions and poverty in the midst of which Rastafari was the only hope to large numbers of people. After careful study, the Government seized upon one of the several recommendations, that a mission be sent to Africa to explore the possibilities for migration there, and acted swiftly. The Mission, which included three Dreadlocks, set off early in 1961, and after visits to Sierra Leone, Liberia, Ghana, Nigeria and Ethiopia, it returned to present a majority and a minority (Rastafari) report, both of which were published and hotly debated in the press.

Predictably, initial middle class reaction was very hostile. Some felt betrayed by the sympathetic tone of the University study, while many objected to the Mission as a waste of taxpayers' money. But coming from the University, and backed by a popular Government, both Report and Mission made it quite respectable for middle-class persons to show sympathy towards the Rastafari. This was something new. Roger Mais, the way artists often see ahead of their times, had a decade earlier portrayed Rasta in heroic terms in his novel *Brother Man*. Now, however, the University initiative was to mark the beginning of an entirely new stage in the development of the society. No scholar has understood this better than Nettleford and no title conveys more the essence of a book's content than does his *Mirror, Mirror* (1970). With the issue of national identity confronting Jamaicans at independence in 1962, history was kind to the country by providing three events in the course of the sixties, three lessons for those who wished to learn: the Henry crisis and its aftermath (Report and Mission), the Visit of Haile Selassie in 1966 and the Black Power Movement in 1968—69. Different events but the same question, the same search. Assessing the "lessons from the sixties", Nettleford noted "trends which are irreversible", notably the fact that "the established order, despite its misgivings about race consciousness, dares no longer to see itself psychologically as an adjunct of Great Britain" (1970: 221). But we jump too far ahead.

To be brief, the three-day visit of Emperor Haile Selassie remains unparalleled for the extraordinary level of popular enthusiasm, crowd size and tolerance towards the Rastas.

> He cried as he stood on the steps of an aircraft of Ethiopian Airlines which had brought him from Trinidad and Tobago to Jamaica and surveyed the vast and uncontrollable crowd which had gathered at the Palisadoes Airport to greet him. The tears welled up in his eyes and rolled down his face. It...was an emotional welcome.
>
> Because from Wednesday night people had gathered at the Palisadoes from all parts of Jamaica, coming on foot, in cars, in drays, in carts, in hired busses, on bicycles and by every means of transport that can be imagined, and there never has been in the whole history of Jamaica such a spontaneous, heart-warming and sincere welcome to any person, whether visiting monarch, visiting V.I.P. or returning leader of any Jamaican party.
>
> Of the welcome His Imperial Majesty said later that he was overwhelmed and deeply moved. It demonstrated, he said, the close ties and affection which bind the people of Jamaica to Africa and Ethiopia ...
>
> And the enthusiasm was too much for mere authority. The police were surrounded by the tide of it all ... The result: all the prearranged ceremony went by the way ... The emperor was in

fact hurried in nervous haste to the Governor-General's car to make his triumphant entry into Kingston, ... and to start what must have been the biggest traffic snarl in the history of the city...

The cries were everywhere: "The day has come. God is with us. Let we touch the hem of His garment."

As the Governor-General's car moved off, people continued to mill around it and to place themselves in its way, some shouting, "Remember me. Prepare a place for me in thy kingdom" (Owens: 1976: 250—52).

Later in the official state receptions, first with Government and then with Royal guest as hosts, for the first time middle and upper-middle class elites actually came face to face with the Dreadlocks. Indeed, it was said to be the in-thing to be seen on friendly and familiar terms with them. Police action against them was muted for the three days, and they made no attempt to conceal their smoking of ganja. The treatment of the Dreadlocks during Selassie's state visit amounted to unofficial legitimization of the movement.

The Black power movement in Jamaica was the work of the Guyanese Lecturer in African History at the University in 1968, Walter Rodney. Rodney formally launched a Black power group on the campus and, more importantly, took his expertise *extra muros* among the Rastafari, including the Claudius Henry group, whose leader had just been paroled from a ten-year prison sentence for treason felony. The Government, which had had him under surveillance, took advantage of his departure abroad to attend a Black writers conference in Canada, to ban him from re-entry as a dangerous subversive. A protest march by University students against the action triggered several hours of rioting and arson by unemployed youths throughout the city. At several roadblocks which the youths set up, the only white and coloured people let through without damage to their cars or injury to their persons were those recognized for their work on behalf of black people.

The "Rodney riot", as the event became known, had its causes in grave economic and social conditions. Industrialisation by development saw unemployment double from 13% at the beginning to 25% at the close of the sixties, while all around were the signs of growing affluence. The riot once again did violence to middle class consciousness by raising the question of racial identity. But this time, thought found expression in action, as a group of intellectuals formed the "Abeng" movement, so called from the horn used by the Jamaican maroons, and began the publication of a weekly by the same name. Abeng ran for only six or seven months in 1969, but, apart from the dissemination of radical black nationalist ideas its significance is to be found in the organic link it sought to establish, in the Rodney tradition, between the middle and working classes. It became a partisan voice of the poor.

But the middle class University-based intellectuals, learning from Rodney, understood that Rastafari critique of the society was already creating changes in the consciousness of the masses. Thus, although many individual Rastafari became active participants in the Abeng group and contributors and distributors of the weekly, it was the adoption of the linguistic symbolism developed by the Dreadlocks, and by then part of urban street culture, which more than anything else proved that the country was indeed in a new stage. The use of words such as *grounding, Babylon, beast, men* was a regular feature of the newspaper,20 and of the vocabulary of intellectuals, especially at the University. Rodney, for instance, titled his reflections on the whole experience, *Groundings with my Brothers*.[21] By 1971, amid speculation about the date of election, the then Prime Minister reminded an audience: "Only one man can call a general election, and that man is *I man*."

That election, when it finally came in February 1972, saw the use of other Rastafari symbolisms.

Understanding the positive symbol which Africa had become largely through the impact of the Rastafari, both incumbent Prime Minister, Hugh Shearer, and Leader of the Opposition, Michael Manley, made widely publicised trips to the Motherland the year before. Each visited Ethiopia and received gifts from the Emperor. Manley's gift, however, was a rod, which in the traditional semiology of the folk represented spiritual power, a tradition the Rastafari, with their brightly painted multi-coloured rods, had continued.

Coincidentally, there were many allegations of corruptions against the Government, so that when Manley, popularly known to his followers as "Joshua", in exploiting this produced the "rod of correction" which Haile Selassie had given him, he set loose very powerful emotions.

Thousands of Jamaicans came to believe that the Rod was imbued with supernatural powers, and everywhere he appeared people wanted to touch this potent source of power, a few ascribing to it healing properties.[22]

Understanding quite well the potency of the symbolism, Edward Seaga[23] then claimed to have found the real rod, which was nothing more than a "stick of detention". The PNP, however, did not fall for the humour of the campaign, as many middle class persons treated it. Instead they responded by publishing a full page ad refuting the claim and in a carefully staged moment at a public meeting Manley dramatically reasserted possession of it by producing a box out of which he took it and held it aloft.

Commenting on the episode, Adam Kuper remarks:

> One cannot dismiss this sort of thing as merely symbolic or as cynical vote-mongering. The historical depreciation of blackness and African-ness in Jamaica was achieved by the manipulation of symbols, and these symbolic gestures help to liberate people from ingrained feelings of inadequacy and impotence ... Symbolic reversals of the traditional value system have helped to undermine the whole traditional structure of deference. It is true that these things are merely symbolic as opposed to the continued inequalities in Jamaica. But this does not mean that the politicians are being cynical. It would take a very cool man to disrupt these attitudes while deliberately calculating to maintain the established system of privilege. (1976: 106–71).

There can be no doubting the role of the Rastafari in this reversal of values, an achievement accomplished without effecting any large scale conversion of the population. Its methodology, if one may call it that, is one of *symbolic* confrontation, and on many fronts, hair, language, dress and several other modes we have been unable to detail in this essay.

Kuper puts it another way. Rejecting the class and race models of Jamaican society, including the plural society model, as being rigid models out of alignment with actual reality, and substituting the folk model of status used by Jamaicans, with an ambiguity and a variability that he argues correspond more to real life, Kuper diagnoses the Jamaican political system as fairly healthy, impervious to any threat of division based on either race or class. Thus, he argues, black nationalism does not provide any basis on which to change the system. Where then does he consign the Rastafari?

'Rastas' and 'rich whites' do not make up Jamaica, except for television crews. But they provide useful reference points for the self-definition, by contrast, of the 'ordinary Jamaican' (p. 99).

That "ordinary Jamaican" swept Manley into power in an election in which 60% of the new People's National Party voters and 44% of Jamaican Labour Party voters who switched to the PNP identified positively with the rod (Carl Stone, 1974: 26). Although the rod was a symbol rather than the cause of their identification with Manley's vision of correcting the ills of the society, Stone's figures showed that identification with the Rastafari movement was proportionately greater than with the rod.

Responses to Rastafari Movement and to the Rod of Correction

	% Sympathetic and Supporting Rastafari	% Indifferent to Rastafari	% Hostile
New PNP Voters	68	18	14
New JLP Voters	38	12	50
JLP Voters who switched to PNP	36	31	33
Consistent JLP Voters	35	25	40

	% Positively identifying with Rod	% Indifferent and unaware	% Cynical and hostile
New PNP voters	60	18	22
New JLP voters	12	29	59
JLP voters who switched to PNP	44	37	19
Consistent JLP voters	12	49	39

Source: Stone (1974), pp. 26 and 27.

More new voters (68% PNP and 38% JLP) expressed sympathy towards the Rastafari than expressed identification with the rod (60% PNP and 12% JLP). The new voters were mainly the youths who had reached the voting age of twenty-one between the 1967 and the 1972 elections.

Not only the working class youths, but the middle classes as well were now defining themselves closer to the Rasta than to the white reference point. A fascinating development was the appearance and growth of the Twelve Tribes of Israel, a Rastafari organization formed late in the 1960s, which, according to van Dijk, has become a haven for middle-class Rastas, allowing them to preserve liberal middle-class values, such as much greater equality between the sexes than among other Rastas groups. For example, women "may speak as often and with as much authority as the male representatives" and "are considered to be equal in all respects but the male comes first, just as in the Bible" (van Dijk, 1988: 11). Also, there is freedom for those who prefer not to grow the beard or wear dreadlocks, and freedom for women to wear pants — a licence which is taboo among the Dreadlocks.

Not all middle-class Rastafari belong to the Twelve Tribes. There are lawyers, journalists, lecturers, doctors and other professionals who have been professing the consciousness of Rastafari but are not members of the Twelve Tribes. Twelve Tribes, however, is itself symbolic of the kind of "shift in consciousness"[24] that has been forced upon the Jamaican middle-class by the Rastafari movement. This does not mean that the middle-class is becoming Rasta. Far from it. But it does signify a tendency to identify more with the African reference point than with the European.

One of the most important aspects of Jamaican culture which facilitated the change has been popular music. Originating in the ghettos of Kingston, reggae rose to become a national music form whose popularity made the political parties use it in their campaigns. Sections of the middle-classes used to deplore what they considered its artless monotony. But when reggae made it internationally, beginning with the song which made the first break-through on the English charts, Desmond Dekker's **Poor me, Israelite,** through to the genius of Bob Marley and the Wailers, Peter Tosh, Jimmy Cliff and a veritable constellation of stars, all shining the light of Rastafari, international approval silenced all middle-class criticism and opened the way for even greater identification. The name people in the rest of the world associate most with Jamaica is Bob Marley.

The appropriation of Rastafari argot by the intelligentsia which began with the Abeng movement proved not to have been a mere transient fashion but to have signalled a profound and lasting change. In a recent paper, Velma Pollard traces the use of certain Rastafari words of philosophical import in the works of two of the country's major poets, Dennis Scott and Lorna Goodison, to convey a sense of black identity. "[T]he culture of Rastafari," she observes, "has moved like yeast through the Jamaican society infusing all these expressions with its power" (1989: 18).

Conclusion

As an ideology racism was internalised by black Jamaicans at both folk and middle-class levels of the society. For the middle-class in particular it was important for upward mobility. Their role in society also made them serve as the reproducers of anti-black African and pro-white European ideas. Rastafari emerged in the 1930s among the marginalised urban population as an ideological antidote. By forcing on the country, especially the middle classes, whose dominance over social and political life was consolidated during the period leading up to Independence, a re-examination of its identity, the movement helped to achieve a readjustment to the reality of being black. External factors (such as African independence) and other internal (such as the short-lived Black Power movement) helped to bring this about, but there is no denying the major role played by the Rastas.

To be sure, Rastafari remains a small fraction of the population of two million people. Its impact is therefore assessed not by counting the number of adherents, but by discovering its symbolic role. This the late Edna Manley, wife of Norman, the man most identified with Jamaican nationalism, and mother of incumbent Prime Minister (for the second time) Michael, understood very clearly when in the last dated entry of her diaries she revealed that in the 1950s she was yet to understand the Rastafari, but that when she did, what struck her more was not the belief in Haile Selassie but "the identification with a Black God".

All the white imagery that consciously and unconsciously had found its creative expression in the white Christs all over Europe — all over the world — carried there with the Christian religion, couldn't mean the truth to the black people of the Caribbean or black America, and this was true not only in the case of the poor masses but also to the intelligent thinking youth of the middle class (1989: 291).

All this has not meant the end of racism as ideology in Jamaica. Derek Gordon in research carried out in 1983 found light-skinned persons moving up the social ladder more quickly than blacks and remaining there in larger proportion (1988: 277). But whereas this was accepted reality in the 1940s, the middle class no longer accepts this.

During the incumbency of Prime Minister Seaga in the 1980s an often-voiced complaint was that the Government relied too heavily on foreign and local white consultants and advisers. When therefore the new Manley administration announced the appointment of some local white advisers in March 1989, it sparked a public controversy. Many blacks were of the view that appointments revealed yet again a lack of confidence in the ability of blacks, at a time when they manifested equal if not greater competence and loyalty to the country. So hot was the issue that **The Jamaica Record,** run by a black entrepreneur, devoted two Sunday issues to the debate. In his contribution, Nettleford observed:

> Some feel that the deliberate and conscious defocusing of social and economic issues away from the reality of the Black imperative in development is not the least among the causes of past failures (1989: 4).

As with Latin America, so also with the Caribbean, it is being suggested, development policies have failed because they ignore the issue of identity, in this case black. Which is to say, assuming the argument to be true, that they will continue to fail to the extent that they ignore the issue.

This leads me to a final suggestion. Norman Girvan (1988) argues that the integration of European migrant labour into the industrialising economies of Latin America in the nineteenth and twentieth centuries took place on a basis of a racial segmentation of the labour force into "non-competing" groups. White workers were assigned the role of supplying skilled, Indians and Blacks the role of supplying cheap and unskilled, manpower. Thus, in the lowland temperate regions where European migrants settled, Blacks were relegated to *minifundios* in the agricultural sector and to the marginalised low-paying occupations of the city. Indians fared similarly.

This process was both reinforced by an ideology of racism, and in turn reinforced it. Since it benefited both white labour and white owners of capital it was characterized by a powerful alliance of attitudes and actions within the white community as a whole in relation to non-whites. Therefore it introduced a deep and abiding cleavage along racial lines so far as the development of a true "proletarian" consciousness, from the standpoint of the relations of production, was concerned (1988: 17).

The white proletariat of Latin America is therefore itself a carrier of the ideology of racism. Girvan does not say to what extent Blacks and Indians have internalised the sense of inferiority, but is quite clear that it was natural that black nationalism and *indigenismo* were responses to the specific historical and contemporary conditions of the respective peoples of Latin America.

This makes the identity question in Latin America somewhat more complex. While it is true that religion plays a major role in it, the fact that "the struggles of white proletarians and other exploited white groups lacked a racial dimension" (Girvan, p. 20) makes their struggles that less effective and complete. Blacks in Latin America, therefore, could learn from the experience of Jamaica and the Rastafari movement, not necessarily in adopting the religion but in learning from its methodology of ideological transformation through symbolic confrontation.

Notes

1. Eric Williams, *The Negro in the Caribbean* (Washington: Panaf Publications, 1942), 60, quoted in Trevor Munroe (1972, 181–82).
2. There are no figures of membership. Rastafari is still not included in census takes. One 'guesstimate' was 70,000–80,000 in the early 1970s.
3. See, for example, Vera Rubin, ed., *Social and Cultural Pluralism* (Seattle: University of Washington, 1962), which is a collection of the views of some of the most prominent Caribbean anthropologists and sociologists. See also, H.I. McKenzie, 'The Plural Society Debate,' *Social and Economic Studies*, volume 16, 1967. Recently Smith has been involved in an on-going controversy with Don Robotham in the pages of *Social and Economic Studies*, volumes 29, 32 and 33.
4. Throughout the history of slavery Jamaica had the highest incidence of revolts and plots against the system. The successful Haitian revolt led by Toussaint L'Ouverture was thought possible in Jamaica, and for a hundred years after Emancipation in 1838, whites lived in mortal fear of a black uprising.
5. Donald Woods (Cry Freedom) had the South African judge ask Steve Biko why they called themselves black when they really were brown. Biko retorted, 'Why do you call yourselves white when you are really pink?' 'Precisely,' said His Honour.
6. See Zora Hurston, *Mules and Men* (Bloomington and London: Indiana University Press, 1978) and Daryl C. Dance, *Folklore from Contemporary Jamaicans* (Knoxville: University of Tennessee Press, 1985).
7. Martha Beckwith, *Black Roadways: A Study of Jamaican Folk Life* (Chapel Hill: University of North Carolina Press, 1929), 172–73.
8. See M.G. Smith (1965), who shows that divorce and remarrying is a norm among the Jamaican whites.

9. See Herskovits' summary of them in his *Myth of the Negro Past* (New York: Harper, 1941).
10. The historians tell us that many slaves resorted to suicide, believing that they would return to Africa on death. In my own research I found positive concepts of Africa that survived in the families of orientation of informants born in the early decades of this century. See my Social and Ideological Origins of the Rastafari Movement in Jamaica (forthcoming).
11. Among the many works written about Garvey and/or the UNIA, see E.D. Cronon, *Black Moses* (Madison: University of Wisconsin Press, 1955); Robert Hill, ed., *The Marcus Garvey and Universal Negro Improvement Association Papers*, Volume I–III (Berkeley: University of California Press, 1983–85); Rupert Lewis, *Marcus Garvey: Anti-colonial Champion* (London: Karia Press, 1987); Rupert Lewis and Maureen Warner-Lewis, eds., *Garvey: Africa, Europe, the Americas* (Kingston: Institute of Social and Economic Research, 1986); Rupert Lewis and Patrick Bryan, eds., *Garvey: His Work and Impact* (Kingston: University of the West Indies, 1988); Tony Martin, *Race First: The Ideological and Organizational Struggles of Marcus Garvey and the Universal Negro Improvement Association* (Westport, Connecticut: Greenwood Press, 1976).
12. Horace Campbell, 'Garveyism, Pan-Africanism and African Liberation in the Twentieth Century,' in *Garvey: His Work and Impact*, ed. Rupert Lewis and Patrick Bryan (Kingston: University of the West Indies, 1988), 168.
13. Mainly, but not solely. Post correctly notes the role which 'the refocusing of consciousness outside the island onto the ancient African kingdom of Ethiopia' (1978, 161) played, and traces the effect of Ethiopianism on that consciousness.
14. See Barry Chevannes, 'Garvey Myths among the Jamaican People,' in *Garvey: His Work and Impact*, ed. Rupert Lewis and Patrick Bryan (Kingston: University of the West Indies, 1988).
15. This process is traced in my *Social Origins of the Rastafari Movement* (Kingston: Institute of Social and Economic Research, 1978).
16. In the article, 'The Phallus and the Outcast: The Symbolism of the Dreadlocks in Jamaica,' I attempt to show that ritual and ideological dominance over women was a necessary sequel of their ideological and symbolic break with the society.
17. On reggae music and Rastafari, see Sebastian Clarke, *Jah Music* (London: Heinemann, 1980), Stephen Davis, *Reggae Bloodlines* (Norwell: Anchor, 1977) and Timothy White, *Catch a Fire* (Austin: Holt, Rinehart & Winston, 1983); on Rastafari overseas, see Horace Campbell, *Rasta and Resistance* (Hertford: Hansib, 1985). A number of publications have been put out on the Rastafari in Britain, among them E. Cashmore, *Rastaman* (Crow's Nest, Austarlia: Allen & Unwin, 1979), Peter Clarke, *Black Paradise* (Aquarian, 1986), Len Garrison, *Black Youth* (ACERP, 1979) and D. Hebdige, *Reggae, Rastas and Rudies* (University of Birmingham, 1975). For a study based in Rotterdam, see P. Buiks, *Surinamse Jongere op de Krauskade* (van Loghun Slaaterus, 1981).
18. For example, in 1948 the House of Representatives unanimously passed a resolution calling on the Government to aid the Back-to-African movement; between March and May 1954 the Opposition PNP pressed for Government to invite Haile Selassie; and in November 1954, Government hosted a state visit from President Tubman of Liberia.
19. For a fuller presentation of his activities see my "Repairer of the Breach", in Frances Henry (editor), Ethnicities in the Americas (The Hague: Mouton, 1976).
20. The derivation of Babylon and Beast is Biblical. See the Book of Revelation. Man refers to a person of integrity and authenticity. Rastas refer to themselves as I man, and to another person as di man. Men is the opposite of man. For a brief explanation of Rasta talk, see Owens (1970), 64–68.
21. (London: Bogle-L'Ouverture, 1969).
22. Olive Senior, *The Message is Change: A Perspective of the 1972 General Election* (Kingston: Kingston Publishers Limited, 1972), quoted in Adam Kuper (1976), 105.
23. Seaga studied folk religion in West Kingston, which he represented in Parliament.
24. To borrow a phrase of Ken Post.

Bibliography

Braithwaite, Lloyd. 'Social Stratification in Trinidad: An Analysis.' *Social and Economic Studies* 2 (2–3), 1953.

Delisser, H.G. *Twentieth Century Jamaica*. Kingston: Jamaica Times, 1913.

van Dijk, Frank Jan. 'The Twelve Tribe of Israel: Rasta and the Middle-Class.' *New West Indian Guide* 62(1–2), 1988.

Girvan, Norman. 'The Political Economy of Race in the Americas.' In *Garvey: His Work and Impact*. Edited by Rupert Lewis and Patrick Bryan. Kingston: University of the West Indies, 1988.

Gordon, Derek. 'Race, Class and Social Mobility in Jamaica.' In *Garvey: His Work and Impact*. Edited by Rupert Lewis and Patrick Bryan. Kingston: University of the West Indies, 1988.

Henriques, Fernando. *Family and Colour in Jamaica*. London: Eyre & Spottiswoode, 1952.

van Kessel, Joop and André Droogers. 'Secular Views and Sacred Vision: Sociology of Development and the Significance of Religion in Latin America.' In *Religion and Development: Towards an Integrated Approach*. Edited by Philip Quarles van Ufford and Matthew Schoffeleers. Amsterdam, Free University Press, 1988.

Kuper, Adam. *Changing Jamaica*. London & Boston: Routledge & Kegan Paul, 1976.

Manley, Rachel, ed. *Edna Manley: The Diaries*. London: Andre Deutsch, 1989.

Mills, Charles. 'Race and Class: Conflicting or Reconcilable Paradigms?' *Social and Economic Studies* 36, no. 2, 1987.

Munroe, Trevor. *The Politics of Constitutional Decolonization: Jamaica 1944–62*. Kingston: Institute of Social and Economic Research, 1972.

Nettleford, Rex. *Mirror, Mirror: Identity, Race and Protest In Jamaica*. Kingston: Collins-Sangster, 1970.

——. 'This Matter of Melanin: Calling a Spade a Spade.' *The Jamaican Record*, Sunday, March 19, 1989.

van Nieuwenhuijze, C.A.O. 'Development Regardless of Culture?' In *Development Regardless of Culture?* Edited by C.A.O. van Nieuwenhuijze. Leiden: E. J. Brill, 1984.

Norris, Katrin. *Jamaica: The Search for an Identity*. Institute of Race Relations; London: Oxford University Press, 1962.

Owens, Joseph. *Dread: The Rastafarians of Jamaica*. Kingston: Sangster, 1976.

Patterson, H. Orlando. *The Sociology of Slavery*. London: MacGibbon & Kee, 1967.

Phillips, Peter. 'Race, Class and Nationalism: A Perspective on Twentieth Century Social Movements in Jamaica.' *Social and Economic Studies* 37, no. 3, 1988.

Pollard, Velma. 'Dread Talk – The Speech of Rastafari in Modern Jamaican Poetry.' Paper presented at ACLALS Silver Jubilee Conference, University of Kent, Canterbury, August 24–31, 1989.

Post, K.W.J. *Arise Ye Starvelings: The Jamaica Labour Rebellion of 1938 and its Aftermath*. The Hague, Boston and London: Nijhoff, 1978.

Quarles van Ufford, Philip and Matthew Schoffeleers, eds. *Religion and Development: Towards an Integrated Approach*. Amsterdam: Free University Press, 1988.

Richardson, Mary F. 'Out of Many, One People – Aspiration or Reality?: An Examination of the Attitudes to the Various Racial and Ethnic Groups within the Jamaican Society.' *Social and Economic Studies* 32, no. 3, 1983.

Roberts, George and Sonja Sinclair. *Women in Jamaica: Patterns of Reproduction and Fertility*. New York: KTO Press, 1978.

Robotham, Don. *Ethics and Ethnicity*. University of the West Indies.

Smith, M.G. *The Plural Society of the British West Indies*. Berkeley, University of California Press, 1965.

Stavenhagen, Rodolfo. 'Ethnodevelopment: A neglected dimension in development thinking.' In *Development Studies: Critique and Renewal*. Edited by R. Apthorpe and A. Krahl. Leiden: E. J. Brill, 1986.

Stone, Carl. *Electoral Behaviour and Public Opinion in Jamaica*. Kingston: Institute of Social and Economic Research, 1974.

Ritual in Diaspora:
Pedagogy and Practice Among Hindus and Muslims in Trinidad
Aisha Khan

Diasporic Consciousness and Religious Ritual

The subject of religious ritual is certainly one that has had its share, some might say more than its share, of scholarly and popular attention. Thousands of pages have been committed to analyzing religious rituals—their form, function, and meaning—from various parts of the world, over centuries, and by various kinds of observers, including social scientists, religious scholars, and practitioners. South Asian rituals are not only no exception to this abiding fascination, they arguably have been central to the development of contemporary academic analyses of rituals. Given the amount of preceding, and ongoing, work in this area, and all the possible directions in which one might train one's lens, my interest here is directed toward just one dimension of ritual practice. This dimension has to do with the degree of dynamism in ritual practice, the ways in which this dynamism is interpreted both by practitioners and external observers, and thus its ethnographic significance. When we consider the persistence of rituals over time among local communities, it becomes clear that even when these communities have become permanently settled, certain cultural practices, such as religious rituals, can remain characterized in terms of arrival, newness, rupture, loss, and uncertainty. In other words, in diasporic contexts, such as those of the Indo-Caribbean, a consciousness of diaspora can shape fundamental, ostensibly timeless and fixed practices that define a community's identity.

As many scholars have noted, religious rituals have long been characterized as representing cultural convention, stability, and timelessness; anthropologist Peter van der Veer (1996: 144) reminds us that still prevalent is the "formal point of view," where rituals are "characterized by conventionality, condensation, and repetition." When viewed as unchanging and thus static, ritual is seen to represent "tradition" and the symbolic moral framework or charter of a society, which ostensibly needs to remain constant in order to hold the society together. Yet when viewed as contextually responsive and fluid in addition to representing conventionality and repetition, rituals become a different kind of object of analysis. In joining the scholarship that approaches ritual in terms of responsiveness and fluidity, what I hope to underscore in this chapter is that, as a multilayered phenomenon, religious rituals among Hindus and Muslims in Trinidad—one of two islands that comprise the Republic of Trinidad and Tobago—employ repetition and conventionality, but do so as part of ideological projects rather than always or necessarily in terms of customary tradition, and that, at the same time, dynamism and contingency are key aspects of Hindus' and Muslims' ritual practices. In the Indo-Caribbean diaspora as a whole, and in Indo-Trinidad in particular, we can see that context, ideology, dynamism, and conventionality in ritual practice are linked and mediated through two powerful cultural motifs: *betrayal*, or "being fooled," and *exegesis*, access to and creation of knowledge through explanation or interpretation.

The material on which my discussion rests involves the ways Hindu and Muslim Indo-Trinidadians understand the importance of gaining religious knowledge by means of ritual and what the meaning and explanations of ritual and religious knowledge should be. Rather than examining specific rites, my interest here is in how people talk about and assess religious practice as a kind of metanarrative. Thus, I do not offer a description or study of religious content per se. What I would like to argue, at its broadest, is that we look at the concept of ritual as suggesting more than it defines, as guiding rather than cementing. In being more suggestive than definitive, rituals can offer a more ethnographically effective frame for understanding the shifting contexts in which local practitioners find themselves, particularly those who comprise diasporic communities. In short, ritual practice and diasporic consciousness are always in a mutually defining dialogue with each other.

A diaspora is a particular kind of historical experience, with far-reaching implications for cultural forms and social relationships. That is to say, the very fact of uprootedness has shaped the sense of self of entire communities; a consciousness emerges among members of a community that memorializes its displacement in everyday discourse and practice. This diasporic consciousness takes different forms of memorialization over time, in part because the historical conditions in which it is meaningful change over time, and in part because the discourses and practices in which it is expressed also change over time. Nonetheless, as varied as the theme of memorializing displacement may be, given different historical moments and cultural expressions, what remains a key constant is a community's emphasis on its awareness of its outsider-foreign origins, the struggle in local contexts to overcome the stigma with which outsider-foreign origins contend, and the eventual victories over local forms of social inequality that this stigma takes. Given these specifications we are able to understand that certain populations are diasporic. In other words, all peoples throughout human history have experienced migration in some form, and all cultural forms have undergone transformation over time—but only some populations have become communities based in large part on a shared ideology of deterritorialization that actively has inspired their culture and cultural production. The difference between "diaspora" and "migration" is not simply about retaining a feeling of belonging to a homeland or the creation over time of communities symbolically connected to ancestral origins. It is also about consciously interpreting one's culture as indelibly marked for all time by the experience of being uprooted. As such, diaspora represents among Indo-Caribbeans a monumental rupture in self-determination.

If a community's diasporic consciousness is necessarily always in a mutually defining dialogue with the historical conditions in which the community finds itself and with the cultural expressions it manifests, then it stands to reason that diasporic consciousness also shapes and is shaped by religious ritual, which is one form of discourse and practice that is part of a community's history and culture. A community's sense of self, and consciousness about how that self has been constituted historically and culturally, will both influence and reflect its core institutions, like that of religion and its rituals. Despite assumptions that religious rituals are ostensibly stable and timeless charters, which renders them impervious to, for example, the impact of practitioners' forms of consciousness about their identity, rituals are, rather, *presented* as stable and timeless charters by practitioners, as well as at the same time *interpreted* to the contrary (as being responsive to change). These presentations and interpretations of ritual work in concert with the community's particular consciousness about its identity; that is, they are in accord with how this consciousness informs ideas about the ways its identity is, or should be, defined and demonstrated. As I noted above and explore further below, two powerful motifs in Indo-Caribbean consciousness of self are betrayal, or "being fooled," as the local parlance expresses it, and exegesis, access to and creation of knowledge through explanation or interpretation. Both of these themes are expressed discursively, as narratives about awareness, struggle, and victory. They are also registered in ritual, as the means of gaining knowledge and conveying, through the "lectures," or sermons, of ritual specialists and the interpretation of religious rites, what the meaning and significance of ritual and religious knowledge should be, in its work as identity marker among Indo-Caribbeans. In a sense, rituals are constant commentaries on the condition and state of diaspora, and diasporic consciousness is always and necessarily a constitutive element of ritual practice and interpretation. Together they give rise to ritual's emphasis on overcoming disfranchisement through self-teaching: memorializations that assert Indo-Caribbean identity and thus force of presence in the region—thereby defying their historical marginality as uprooted, extraneous persons.

Constituted by the mutually defining dialogue between a community's (1) diasporic consciousness about its identity (tempered by historical and cultural transformations) and (2) the cultural expressions that represent that identity, religious ritual among diasporic Hindu and Muslim Indo-Caribbeans has become in the New World a site of instruction; religious ritual is not simply an anchor to the past but also preparation for the future. As such, ritual is ideological as well as "cultural"; it is fluid as well as stable; it represents the projection of "tradition" as well as the propulsion of "modernity."

Fooled into Submission

The Indo-Caribbean, which is part of the greater nineteenth-century South Asian diaspora to the Americas, is distinguished by the one and a half century presence of "East Indian," as they are still known, immigrants to the Caribbean region from India. Beginning in 1838 to what was then British Guiana (today Guyana), and then in 1845 to Trinidad (now the Republic of Trinidad and Tobago), almost half a million Indians arrived in the region as "bound coolies," indentured laborers contracted by the British labor scheme to bolster sugar production on their colonial plantations after the emancipation of enslaved Africans (or, by that time, Afro-Caribbeans). Today in Trinidad in particular, as in the Indo-Caribbean more generally, memories, and memorializing, of this movement are encapsulated in the powerful metaphor of betrayal, of being fooled. There are several elements to this metaphor of betrayal. One is being fooled into becoming indentured labor emigrants in the first place. The foundational moment for subsequent anxieties about being fooled is the initial luring away from home that indenture contracts may have represented to would-be immigrants gathered in the exit depots of Calcutta and Madras, and as they certainly represent among Indo-Caribbean peoples today.

Another element is being fooled into grossly subordinate positions as colonial subjects—as "coolie labor"—and then as ambivalently national citizens. From the perspective of the political, economic, and cultural authority exercised by colonial and postindependence governmental structures, Indo-Trinidadians were imagined as implicitly or overtly loyal to "Mother India" and therefore only uncertainly dependable and trustworthy in terms of their allegiance to colony and country. As a geographically and socially marginalized population for much of the indenture period, which officially ended in the Republic only in 1917, and well into the twentieth century, Indo-Trinidadians have been concentrated within grassroots communities where few opportunities for upward social mobility have been available. Most notable among these mobility opportunities was formal education, widespread access to which Indo-Trinidadians did not enjoy until the second quarter of the twentieth century, when Hindus and Muslims began to build their own schools. Until that time the only reliable educational opportunity came from attending Presbyterian schools, called Canadian Mission schools, whose missionaries first arrived in Trinidad from Canada in 1868. As late as 1946, however, census reports showed that over half (51 percent) of the Indo-Trinidadian population remained illiterate (see, for example, Singh 1996).

A final element in the metaphor of betrayal is being fooled in the sense of the difficulty Indo-Trinidadians see themselves as having experienced in successfully extricating themselves from their subordinate position. Reliance on local social institutions for support, from which historically they were kept apart, has been an exercise in tenacity, inventiveness, and alternative strategies. For example, Indo-Trinidadians' initially cautious embrace of Canadian Mission schools was represented by Euro-colonial and middle-class "colored" (Afro-Caribbean) sectors of the society, and well into the postindependence period, as indicative of Indian recalcitrance to assimilate and their general backward lack of appreciation of literacy and self-improvement. It was, however, indicative of indentured immigrants' reluctance to shed their religious heritage and accept Presbyterianism to the exclusion of Hinduism and Islam, which were, and remain, cornerstones of their identification of themselves as a particular community. Once they realized (and it took less than a generation) that they could "convert" to Presbyterianism, and thereby take advantage of the educational and employment opportunities (primarily in Presbyterian schools) such conversion offered, without necessarily eschewing their Hindu and Muslim worldviews and customs, Indo-Trinidadians shrewdly took advantage of this opportunity. Many, of course, became devout and exclusive Christians; many others practice, inclusively, heterodox forms of worship. Other examples of tenacity, inventiveness, and alternative strategies include Indo-Trinidadians' mid-twentieth century organizing and funding of Hindu and Muslim primary and secondary schools, and their continuous, energetic political participation (at times anticolonial or straightforwardly counter-hegemonic, and at other times not necessarily so), which preceded mid-twentieth century independence struggles and remain emblematic of their national presence today. Part of their diasporic consciousness, then, is an acute awareness of not simply the universal exigencies of life but the specific configuration of colonial hierarchies. As much as Indo-Trinidadians today may engage in a rhetoric of resignation about the circumstances of their New World diaspora (as many have said to me with a shrug, "wha' yuh go' do? That is how it was, we ent [didn't] know"), or of self-congratulations (for being the rescuers of empire after emancipation left the sugar plantations without local [read free] labor, and for overcoming the odds and enjoying significant upward social mobility), there is often at the same time an undercurrent of indignation, or at least an ironic appreciation of the workings of social inequality structured according to ethnic, religious, citizenship, rural/urban, and labor hierarchies. Built into diasporic consciousness, then, is a particular form of agency: a motivated and purposive engagement with power and authority.

Rituals, Agency, and Resistance in Context

At least three broad historical processes provided the conditions for the development of ritual practice and interpretation among Indo-Trinidadian Hindus and Muslims. First, founding generation indentured laborers "kept up we religion," as contemporary Indo-Trinidadians phrase it, often by covert means, taking unauthorized leaves from the estates to meet with fellow Hindus or Muslims and worship together. By the 1880s, as a means of curbing labor unrest, colonial policy enforced laws governing the movement of indentured laborers off their assigned estates. In addition to legalized punishments were controls in the form of contemptuous ridiculing of traditional forms of authority, commonly in the form of charges of chicanery and superstition rather than moral rectitude and divinely-inspired insight. The diaspora narratives that memorialize clandestine religious activities work to countermand the legacy of pejorative images of Indians as ignorant and pliable. In a conversation I had with Mr. Zayn, an older head imam (Muslim religious leader) and community elder who was born and raised in southern Trinidad, he spoke of his father, an indentured immigrant who arrived in Trinidad in the early twentieth century. A learned man, his father traveled among sugar estates surreptitiously in the night, in order to spread knowledge of Islam among fellow indentured and no longer indentured Indians. I heard virtually identical narratives from Hindus about their forebearers, as well. These kinds of activities were clearly forms of cultural resistance to plantation authority, surely strengthening the bonds and the resolve among immigrants.

The second of these broad historical processes was in plain view by the mid-1930s. Well underway was the consolidation of Hindu and Muslim identities among Indo-Trinidadians. For one thing, religio-cultural organizations, notably the Sanatan Dharma Maha Sabha (founded in 1932) and the Anjuman Sunnat-ul Jamaat (founded around 1931), that still represent Hindus and Muslims, respectively, were becoming increasingly institutionalized. They showed a growing investment in promoting certain doctrines of orthodoxy, as well as authorizing the pandits (Hindu religious leaders) and imams (Muslim religious leaders) that represented those doctrines. For another, a more formalized role for pandits and imams as community and religious leaders was developing. The overall effect of these processes was the attempt, in part in the spirit of teaching and learning to foster knowledge, to formalize and codify both Hindu and Islamic doctrine out of multiple and sometimes divergent traditions and pedagogies. This formalization and codification has at its discursive center the problem of "culture": the cultural heritage of India and its place in Caribbean contexts. In Indo-Trinidadians' parlance, "traditional," or "long time," or "grassroots" modes of understanding either hinder progress toward modernity or propel one forward, empowering one's group with forceful—plentiful and correct—knowledge of selected traditions, which were, for the most part, taken from religious practice.

Finally, compounding the processes of plantation-based strategies of resistance and organizational codification of religious belief and practice was the postindependence period's formation of Trinidadian political culture and party politics. Gaining independence in 1962, the Republic established parliamentary democracy based in part on universal suffrage and government distribution of patronage, in the form of resources and opportunities, on the basis of voting constituencies that are grouped according to ethno-cultural identities. These are tacitly understood to be "racially" constituted, and "culturally" represented primarily by "religious" diagnostic emblems. In Trinidad's self-proclaimed "rainbow" diversity of 40.3 percent Indo-Trinidadian, 39.6 percent Afro-Trinidadian, 18.4 percent Mixed, 0.5 percent Chinese/Syrian/Lebanese, 0.6 percent white/Caucasian, and 0.6 percent not stated (according to the national census) (Central Statistical Office 1990), Indo-Trinidadian and Afro-Trinidadian are the two salient politico-cultural entities. While Indo-Trinidadian Christians (Protestants and Catholics) are not defined as a political constituency in their own right, Hindus and Muslims, 24 percent and 6 percent of the total population, respectively (Central Statistical Office 1990), tend to be distinguished both from each other and from the entire Indo-Trinidadian population in political terms; that is, as distinct groups to be recognized and courted by the state. Thus, in sum, groups vie for state patronage in part within a discourse of deservedness based on "difference," or cultural alterity defined primarily by boundaries that are established through the practice of tradition and heritage.

Dimensions of Ritual Practice, and Ways of Knowing Them

There are numerous dimensions of ritual practice among Indo-Trinidadians. Many considerations (one might say variables) are pertinent to any discussion of Hindu and Muslim rituals in the Caribbean diaspora. Among the most important of these dimensions are the key interlocutors whose cultural practices, worldviews, and insistent interpretations shape ritual content. First are the different generations of Hindus and Muslims. Although now almost one hundred and seventy years after their initial arrival to the region, and thus constituting several generations, the most significant distinction among generations in terms of religious issues is between "older heads," as it is expressed locally, and "younger people." Older heads tend to be "grassroots," that is, poor or working class. Older heads symbolize a particular kind of religious and cultural authenticity and authority that celebrates forebearers who tenaciously struggled to keep their "traditional" worldview as a means of stabilizing a profoundly uncertain environment. At the same time, this kind of authenticity confronts other, "modern" notions of authenticity, underscoring the contradictory aspects of Indo-Trinidadians' past, both venerable and inglorious. Younger generations tend to be associated with modernity, largely through having experienced some degree of upward social mobility, primarily through greater access to formal education, both secular and religious. Yet "traditional" and "modern" do not simply denote past and present among Indo-Trinidadians. Each is itself a metaphor containing its own internal layers of meaning: authenticity can derive from traditions made genuine by being rooted in the pure and original India-based culture of indentured fore-bearers, or it can evoke spuriousness through a backwardness derived from those very same roots simply interpreted differently; authenticity can derive from traditions made genuine by being freed from the same roots, this time interpreted as untutored, ad hoc, contextually contingent beliefs and practices, and enlightened by rigorous formal training, or it can evoke a dangerous distancing from tradition toward a culturally diluted no-man's land of Westernized religious and cultural ambiguity.

Also an important part of the Indo-Trinidadian population are Christians, both Protestant and Catholic (about 3 percent of the total population). More numerous, Indo-Trinidadian Protestants in turn can be divided into old and new communities, in the sense of established congregations, such as the Presbyterians, and more recent (since about the 1970s)—and growing—congregations of evangelicals and Pentecostals. There are, as well, Afro-Trinidadian Muslims, who share certain Islamic philosophical and theological precepts with Indo-Trinidadian Muslims while they at the same time engage in debates over other doctrines and practices. Out of these multiple layers emerge discourses, at times incendiary, about what ritual practice should be and how it should be interpreted, what form of authenticity should be represented and what the distinctions between "religious" and "cultural" authenticity might be, and even whether or not rituals should be performed at all—that is, questions about whether they are atavistic and antimodern.

In addition to the material forces of social hierarchy and political culture in which rituals are performed, the cultural themes of betrayal and its recuperation through exegesis shape rituals' dynamic quality. Stories of betrayal are allegorical narratives that symbolize a dramatic reference point among Indo-Trinidadians that represents vulnerability through ignorance. I have heard many dozens of betrayal narratives from Indo-Trinidadians. The general contours of the narratives, which are both apocryphal and historical, emphasize Indians' deception, being tricked into overseas indenture in "Chinidad" (*chini* is *sugar* in Hindi/Urdu), where they were to sift sugar, perceived as an easy task, for an inordinately high daily wage. The following story encapsulates nicely the betrayal theme. It was told to me a few years ago by Vishnu, who although only in his mid-thirties at the time, considers this story as much a part of his identity as an Indo-Trinidadian as it was to the man three generations earlier, to whom the story refers. As Vishnu recounted, "Ninety-nine-point-nine percent of Indians tell the same story. They came [to the Caribbean] with a willing mind, but they were fooled into thinking they'd find a pot of gold there. Because that's the way the white people told them. My great-grandfather's parents in India sent him to the grocery store to get sugar. On his way to the shop, the people [indenture recruiters] came up and they told him, he was a young boy, 'Come on this ship, there's lots of candies there, so much things to eat.' The next thing you know, he was in Trinidad. He grow up on the cane plantation. Then the time came to give people [time-expired laborers] parcels of land [Crown lands in lieu of return passage fare or a lump sum] ... So that's how he ended up down there [in Trinidad]." Whereas in Vishnu's version the protagonist is a child, the majority of the narratives feature an adult—amenable, diligent, and gullible—who is led down an unknown path with false promises and left to fend precariously in unfamiliar and disfranchising, hierarchical societies such as those of the Caribbean.

Both Indo-Trinidadian Hindus and Muslims rely on rituals as a key diagnostic emblem. They refer to rituals as "a prayers" or as a "function" (which are interchangeable). The most common rituals among Hindus are the *puja*, the *yagya*, and the *sat sangh*. Pujas and yagyas are devotional forms of worship focused on one or more deities; in a sat sangh the focus is on the epic Ramayana. Among Indo-Trinidadian Muslims the most common "functions" are the *maulood sherif* (Quranic reading), the *haqika* (pledging oneself to Allah), and calendrical commemorations such as *Eid ul-Fitr* (feast breaking fast of Ramadan) and *Milad ul-Nabi* (the birthday of the Prophet Mohammed).

In considering the recuperation of betrayal through exegesis (or access to and creation of knowledge), I join the multilayered approach to ritual school of thought specifically in distinguishing two important elements of Indo-Trinidadian Hindu and Muslim ritual practice: the rites themselves, including actions/movements, objects, sacred recitations (which as I noted at the outset I do not address in this chapter), and the sermons, *kuttha* among Hindus and *kutbah* among Muslims—or, as they are locally referred to, "lectures"—which are in essence tutorials that accompany the vast majority of ritual "functions" or "a prayers." Pandits and imams not only make rituals dynamic in the ways lectures register contemporary issues, but in the ways their debates about the diagnostic emblems of identity politics keep even the rites from being simply repetitive and conventional—even as practitioners strive to maintain their form as such. As I observed earlier, repetition, stability, and conventionality of rites not only must be distinguished from other elements of a given ritual, they also need to be understood as ideological projects of practitioners who are invested in demonstrating the timelessness of those rites, desires that always occur in conjunction with larger political, social, and cultural contexts.

By underscoring the distinction of these two prime elements of Hindu and Muslim rituals among Indo-Trinidadians (and the Indo-Caribbean in general), I am arguing against the idea, one that still remains influential in scholarly and popular discussion, that rituals are not geared toward intellectual pursuits, that they convey their messages through dramatic performance rather than through intellectual presentation. I would like to suggest instead that, at least in historically shifting and precarious environments of Indo-Caribbean diasporic communities, rituals are performances very much about intellectual pursuits and mental faculties, specifically the creation and apprehension of knowledge—as information and its interpretation. In other words, it is memories of movement, the conditions of movement, and the contexts of the changing present that shape the form and substance of ritual practice among Hindu and Muslim Indo-Trinidadians. Among these communities, religious rituals engage Indo-Trinidadian subordination by constituting the force by which being fooled/being foolish is countermanded. Rituals serve *simultaneously* (1) as tethers to heritage (which conforms to still-conventional scholarly and popular interpretations of ritual), though these tethers are constantly debated, and (2) as agentive exercises that prepare people for an improved future—specifically in terms of tutorials: self-edification lessons that both challenge and rectify social subordination through the attainment of certain forms of (religious) knowledge.

When Indo-Trinidadian Hindus speak about a heritage of "tradition," it is in a variety of contexts and often with a number of different referents. Two dimensions in particular are salient. One is the Great Tradition of Sanatan Dharm, which, even if at one level is understood to be located in India, transcends time and place as religious patrimony. The other dimension is an ancient cultural lifeway and worldview perceived as deeply rooted in place and time and thus able to provide the means to heal the ruptures of diaspora. The Great Tradition falls under the aegis of "lectures"; cultural roots are associated with older head, hence grassroots, pandits, both valorizing them and raising the issue of their being anachronisms in the current modern, middle-class moment of formally trained, younger generation pandits. Of course, participants in rituals as well as other community members weigh in on these evaluations in everyday conversations.

The pandit, older head or younger generation, has a double mission. This mission involves him being both a conduit of devotions to the deities and blessings to the devotees and a source of wisdom and tutelage both to his *chelas* (godchildren) and community of devotees. As one older head, Deo, told me about a prayers, "the people are mostly interested in the *text* being read and the pandit can provide it for the people." Yet in a conversation I had in my field site in Trinidad with Selwyn, a teenage boy, about the yagya his household had recently sponsored, he remarked that older head pandits often lack sufficient breadth of scriptural knowledge—"what we can comprehend *these* days." Among the most important capabilities among people *"these* days" is the ability to distinguish between the literal interpretations of text and metaphor and allegory. A younger-generation pandit offered me an example:

> The Gita is not a scripture, like the Ramayana. It is a philosophy, it goes to a higher level. Philosophy is not religion. Religion tells you how you should live in your religion. The Gita tells you there is a God…And that God could be anything … People don't understand that. For we have come from a grassroots background. So when you sit down and you read the Gita, that God has a thousand arms and a thousand eyes … they [devotees] say you crazy! But now you interpret it. It mean that God can see everything, it doesn't literally mean something.

Here, then, where "a prayers" constitutes a pedagogical arena, learning what the correct rites are, their sequence, and their meaning, as well as the philosophical messages of the sacred texts (authorized by the pandit) increases cultural knowledge, where being informed about the subcontinental motherland shores up the boundaries delineating religious and "racial" groups—that is, making oneself and one's group, in a sense, palpable, "real" in political terms. Another informant, Frank, put this very thoughtfully one evening when we were talking about the importance of Hindu rituals: "you must know where you coming from," he said. "To know how the religions were formed and how the people were living in India while English people were taking over. All we really know since we know ourselves here [in Trinidad] is how the English carrying on." For Frank, and many others, ritual participation is both the continuity of history and the awareness of historical change. And it is the connection between ritual and scripture that is at the heart of this relationship, and which forms of knowledge and expertise should have precedence, one based on "traditional ways," or one based on synchronicity with "modern" progress.

In contrast to Indo-Trinidadian Hindus' call for philosophical as opposed to literal interpretations, Indo-Trinidadian Muslims focus their attention on "pure" practices shorn of "cultural innovations." What constitutes purity and authenticity, however, are matters of serious scrutiny and are expressed in ritual. Embodied in the personas and practices of imams and other religious leadership, "functions"/"a prayers" are arenas of discourse and debates about correct religious knowledge, the definition and place of authentic cultural traditions in religious practice, and the implications these have for a Muslim identity that contends with an ambivalent relationship to ancestral India and ambiguous ties to Hindu kin and neighbors. As among Indo-Trinidadian Hindus, the effort to *know* sufficiently as well as correctly is a means to an end, rather than a final objective. That is, these efforts are always in dialogue with attempts to counteract the betrayal that renders them vulnerable, in sites still perceived as uncertain and under social conditions that still define them, in some important ways, notably in terms of local political culture, in terms of their foreign otherness as diasporic communities.

Let me briefly illustrate with the example of maulood sherifs. While they have always been integral to Indo-Trinidadian Muslim identity construction, one of my informants, Akeela, explained to me that today maulood sherifs are even more common because "people are hearing more about it through lectures." "People get smarter now," her sister added. In the effort to encourage jamaat (congregation) members and wider community residents to consistently attend and sponsor functions, hosts as well as imams (and a small but growing number of *maulanas*, or Islamic scholars) often remind participants why "a prayers" are imperative. At one annual household maulood sherif I attended, the masjid president gave the opening address, which included his statement that, "we have all attended today in order to honor a dear neighbor's invitation, to honor Allah, and to gain knowledge." At another I attended some time later, an honored guest invited to give an address asked rhetorically, "what is the purpose of this function today? To socialize in Islamic society and atmosphere ... [and] to get education." Edification includes gaining greater familiarity with laws or scripture, Arabic script, correct enactment and understanding of rites, or related text-based knowledge.

Because Islam presupposes, at least ideally, a coherence that renders actual or possible variations in practice a matter of discussion on the part of clerics, lay practitioners, and scholars, "correct models" are subject to debates about interpreting the significance and modes of practices that belong to Islamic tradition (see, for example, Asad 1986, 1993). Embedded in these debates, and in the interpretations themselves, are relations of power (among groups and individuals) that shape the shifting hierarchies of value that designate, over varying periods of time, particular interpretations as being correct and as what must prevail. Counseling against blindly following religious traditions, my neighbor Dolly explained: "Just because you see your parents doing it [Muslim rites], maybe you don't know *why* or *what* it is ... You can't just stay home again [any more]. You have to go out and look for it [knowledge about correct practice]. Who going to teach you [at] home?" Her older head neighbor Leila agreed: "even at my age we can still learn, as people will laugh at us in the masjid [mosque] and say, 'she is so old and hasn't learned the right thing?'" At still another maulood sherif I attended, the guest maulana urged in his address that, "unless we are educated and taught how to educate others, we are lost in a dark world. And we must save ourselves from corrupted doctrines coming into our religion and unnecessary arguments among ourselves. As the Prophet says, 'knowledge isn't compulsory, but to *seek* knowledge is compulsory.'" This guardianship of the correct, so to speak, is not to establish purity for purity's sake (simply for its iconic value) but to withstand inappropriate acts and beliefs whose untutored or improperly tutored "folk" versions maintained in diaspora from the subcontinent, or influences from Hinduism, can derail true Muslim practice. These folk Islamic or "Hinduized" practices are discredited as "innovations," characterized as "cultural" and "traditional," and traced according to their accretion through social and cultural influences rather than through demonstration by or dictum of the Prophet Mohammed.

Among the most common practices that foment ideological divisions among Indo-Trinidadian Muslims occur in ritual: saying prayers over food, celebrating the Prophet's birthday and *meeraj* (ascension to Heaven), singing *qaseedas* during rituals, and standing for the *tazeem* (praise sung for the Prophet Mohammed). An Indo-Trinidadian Muslim man said to me, "way back in the fifties and sixties I just thought I was a Muslim, because I was *born* in a Muslim family ... The practices in my environment, though, were different from what I later read ... We had in the past, and we still have, a lot of practices that we got from our foreparents in India. We are grateful to them for keeping up Islam, but people are not trying to *learn* more. They are just *listening* to what is said ... They go to functions and sit, but don't *educate* themselves." At the heart of the distinction between the legitimacy of customary or traditional religious practice and tutored religious practice guided by religious authority is the high value placed on self-conscious, achieved knowledge—in essence, doing something correctly and understanding its significance.

At one maulood sherif I attended, a woman present praised the officiating imam: "you must talk proper, make the sermon *meaningful*." The quest for meaning may be heightened for individuals as they comprehend religiously charged moments in the Islamic calendar. One informant explained that Ramadan is a time when she is "always learning something *new*, whether it is a *sura*, a lesson, or whatsoever. She "soaks up the lectures" given during this period's numerous functions and tries to take time out every day to read; her bed is always "covered with books the whole month." As community residents invoke the idea of "meaning" in their reflections on an individual's attitude in undertaking rituals and on the nature of religious practice, *meaning* becomes both reified and a master symbol. In local usage, *meaning* encompasses distinct referents; in doing so it articulates these referents into what is familiar religious discourse. At another maulood sherif where I was present, the imam included in his remarks, "[it] is only when we get together like this [that] we can get the message. Our weakness is [lack of] knowledge, knowledge of Islam, and how to run our lives. Today a person talks [in order] to use you with *iklas*, in Arabic, ulterior motives. Trying to trick you. And it is only by practice [that] you can perfect your *salaat* [worship]." In the imam's comment, "meaning" addresses the theme of being fooled; here, worldly knowledge (not succumbing to trickery) and religious knowledge (perfecting salaat) enhance each other. Through group edification—"get together like this"—such as that which occurs during ritual functions, "meaning" ameliorates gaps, slippages that are threatening in both sacred and secular terms.

It is gaps like these that imams must fill as they work on the precision of their craft. The performances of older head imams and their "traditional" ways as they serve their jamaats are particularly susceptible to charges of engaging in practices that seem too much like meaningless, going through the motions (as many see it) ritual, and thus too Hindu-influenced, too India-derived, and therefore too innovative with mixed cultural, as opposed to purely religious, traditions. Imam Rahman, an older head "reformist" imam, as he identified himself, explained that:

> *traditional* practices are different from the handed-down practices of the Prophet ... *Traditional* means practices of old...But the reforms were found through *research*, like [in] the Hadith ... We don't make *naj* [prayers] over *sirni* [ritual sweets]. We question putting food for the dead, the dead cannot eat ... and this was never done in the days of the Prophet. This was brought in as a innovation from India...a Hindu relic.

In the sense of being both a tie to ancestral heritage and a restraint on contemporary transformation (and therefore an authenticating medium), rituals are culturally stabilizing performances, reminding practitioners of their identity through connection with the past. They are, at the same time, however, culturally transforming tutorials, emphasizing identity through connections with the present. As sites where diacritic emblems are reproduced, rituals clarify the ambiguities of both heterodoxy (the local array of religious possibilities) and syncretism (when those possibilities converge into other, new, and debated, forms). They do this by repetition of certain rites, thereby establishing or fortifying boundaries between what is appropriate and what is incorrect. But rituals involve greater agency than mere reiteration, in their emphasis on the exegesis, and leadership, of the pandit and imam. In Hindu and Muslim rituals, therefore, there is a good deal of emphasis on correct performance. Participants make an effort to eschew spontaneity and innovation. As Peter van der Veer (1996: 144) observes, in Hindu ritual (and I would add in Muslim ritual), "despite all the evidence of change and consistency, the performers try their hardest to exclude creative innovation." Referred to as "lectures" by Indo-Trinidadian practitioners, the sermons that most Hindu and Muslim rituals highlight, however, are discursive spaces where formal continuity and creative innovation meet. While the issue of correct performance is always present, appreciation of the meaning and significance of performance is taught by the messenger (pandit or imam as learned authority) rather than simply through the medium (the rites). Different generations of leadership claim authority not simply through carrying out the rites, but through their ability to guide practitioners intellectually. Their claims reflect competing interpretations of Indo-Trinidadian cultural history and religious identity.

By teaching about religion, rituals augment educational opportunities more readily available to the socially privileged, but they also instruct in the way "religion" ought to be constituted, and why. Through the guidance of religious leadership and their lectures, a number of potential inadequacies can be alleviated: alienation from one's culture, underdeveloped piety, subordinate class position, or general naivete—a lack of sophistication and worldliness, and hence inability to assume the mantle of Western modernity. The multilayered dimensions within a given ritual, then, are always in dialectical tension.

In order to be effective, "a prayers" or "functions" must be seen as pure, in the sense of credibly sacred (indubitably "religion") and credibly authentic (indubitably "correct"). Yet at the same time, even if practitioners work to reinforce repetitiveness and conventionality, rituals still respond to the rhythm of political ideology and social striving. The performance of rituals must distinguish and announce distinctly Hindu and Muslim identities within a daily reality where rituals are "the busy intersections" where many distinct social processes converge (Rosaldo 1989). For Indo-Trinidadian Hindus and Muslims, rituals are intended to be revelatory and transformative as much as they are meant to reiterate and confirm. Thus they are sites of dynamism, not simply stasis, and can pedagogically rescue participants from the mental and material deprivations of diaspora's betrayal.

Conclusion

This chapter has told two distinguishable but articulated stories, one of diaspora and one of religious ritual. Its aim has been to argue five points. One is that as a way of understanding community identity and culture, "diaspora" must be understood as a particular kind of historical experience, one that has far-reaching implications for cultural forms and social relationships, and that necessarily involves a particular consciousness about the experience of migration on the part of those who constitute these communities, such as Indo-Trinidadians—one that both marks the very act of uprooting as shaping their sense of self and that memorializes displacement in everyday discourse and practice. Secondly, like all forms of consciousness, diasporic consciousness exists as a part of, and thus is responsive to, the changing historical and cultural contexts of Indo-Trinidadian life. My third point is that, like all discourses and practices, a community's religious rituals occur within these same contexts, making them also subject to the vicissitudes of history and culture, so that rather than ritual lying outside of these forces and pressures and thereby allegedly remaining stable, timeless, and the epitome of fixed "tradition," Indo-Trinidadian Hindu and Muslim rituals are context contingent, and their putative constancy is actually a matter of ideological projects emerging from the current moment. Fourth, these ideological projects are informed by modes of marking (defining and interpreting) Indo-Trinidadian identity which are a part of diasporic consciousness and are manifest in rituals as participants work to assert themselves politically and culturally by means of self-edification through competing forms of authorized knowledge. My final point is that the interplay of diasporic consciousness and ritual occurs at the nexus where identity, ideology, and cultural practice meet, intertwining diasporic consciousness and religious ritual together.

What does their connection tell us? Diaspora represents among Indo-Caribbeans monumental rupture in their self-determination. If we probe the discursive dimensions of diaspora—how it is envisioned and talked about among members of diasporic communities—rather than solely relying on it as an externally imposed (and, often, one-size-fits-all) analytical category, we get a clear idea of the agency that diaspora entails. By understanding diaspora as a dynamic phenomenon we are better able to understand the dynamism of cultural practices like religious ritual among diasporic communities. A key cultural practice in most communities and societies, religious ritual has been conventionally approached by both scholars and practitioners alike as static rather than dynamic and, linked to this idea of stasis, best characterized as dramatic performances rather than involving shifting consciousness and intellectual reflection. In the historically uneasy (in both senses: difficult and insecure) Caribbean environments with which Indian indentured immigrants and their diasporic progeny had to contend and make the best of, rituals are precisely about dynamism: agency and resistance through engagement with colonial and postindependence structures of social inequality. This engagement takes the form of *exegesis*, the creation and grasp of knowledge, conveyed through rituals. Although debated in terms of their respective degree of authority, Indo-Trinidadian Hindu and Muslim exegeses consistently evoke the theme of *being fooled*, challenging the forms of subordination that accompany, or are caused by, betrayal and marginalization. Among Indo-Trinidadian Hindus and Muslims, rituals are, in part, intellectual exercises that promote ideologies about the value of unchanging heritage that rituals are meant to demonstrate. At the same time, rituals are also intellectual exercises that acknowledge and actively engage the past, present, and future conditions of everyday life and well-being in this diasporic community.

Acknowledgments

I would like to thank Rhacel Parreñas and Lok Siu for inviting me to contribute to this volume and for their helpful editorial comments. This chapter is based on material taken from my book, *Callaloo Nation: Metaphors of Race and Religious Identity among South Asians in Trinidad* (Khan 2004). All names of individuals appearing herein are pseudonyms. A version of this chapter appears in *Cultural Dynamics* (in press, 2007).

References

Asad, Talal. 1986. The Idea for an Anthropology of Islam. March. Occasional Paper Series. Center for Contemporary Arab Studies, Georgetown University, Washington, DC.
———. 1993. *Genealogies of Religion*. Baltimore: Johns Hopkins University Press.
Central Statistical Office, Republic of Trinidad and Tobago. 1990. *Demographic Report*.
Khan, Aisha. 2004. *Callaloo Nation: Metaphors of Race and Religious Identity among South Asians in Trinidad*. Durham: Duke University Press.
Rosaldo, Renato. 1989. *Culture and Truth*. Boston: Beacon.
Singh, Kelvin. 1996. Conflict and Collaboration: Tradition and Modernizing Indo-Trinidadian Elites (1917–56). *New West Indian Guide* 70(3–4): 229–53.
van der Veer, Peter. 1996. Authenticity and Authority in Surinamese Hindu Ritual. In *Across the Dark Waters*, ed. David Dabydeen and Brinsley Samaroo. London: Macmilian, 131–46.

Visitation:
The Legacy of African-Derived Religions in Jamaica
Dianne M. Stewart

There are at the present time many herbalists in the Caribbean and South America, and the evidence of their influence is found in the United States wherever there is a heavy concentration of Afro-Americans. Every island of the Caribbean is a veritable pharmacological garden in which there can be found every type of herb and root sufficient for the healing of the nation. One only needs to spend a day with an old woman to be impressed by the assortment of weeds necessary for each ailment liable to occur.[1]

An Ancient Remedy for a Postmodern Age

The sociopolitical focus in Rastafari theology might be well paired with the healing focus in Kumina. Kumina is perhaps the most misunderstood African-Jamaican religious tradition, in part because Kumina practitioners produce no liturgical or theological literature pertaining to their beliefs and practices.[2] It is also misunderstood because it is conspicuously African-oriented and therefore stereotyped by the dominant society. As attested to by Kumina devotees, the weight of such social condemnation is felt via Christian anti-African ideas.[3]

The scholarship on Kumina is also insufficient. Kumina is dynamic and with each generation contributes something novel to its inherited past. My exploration of Kumina, then, is informed by its expressions in contemporary Jamaica with relevant insights from the existing literature on the subject. My research with Kumina communities took place over six months (two visits in 1995 and 1996) in the parishes of St. Thomas and St. Catherine. During my second research trip to Jamaica, in November 1996 I was fortunate enough to have an audience with Jamaica's former prime minister and leader of the opposition, Edward Seaga. Seaga, whose advanced training in sociology was truncated by his professional entry into politics, is nonetheless one of the most important researchers in the study of Revival Zion and Kumina. Seaga's contribution, however, has not been significantly felt, for most of his twenty-plus years of research materials may be found in Jamaican institutions awaiting scholarly interrogation and analysis.

During the course of the interview, Seaga expressed deep disappointment regarding the superficial studies of Jamaican religion that have informed the teaching and works of professional scholars and performance artists who replicate Kumina dances on stage. Since the 1960s Seaga had introduced a number of native Jamaican scholars to Revival Zion and Kumina practitioners with the hope that they would continue his legacy of research and, even more, publish substantially in the area. More than thirty-five years have passed since the publication of Seaga's noted article "Revival Cults in Jamaica," yet the scholarship on Jamaica's African-derived religions remains insufficient. When compared with the publications generated by a growing scholarly interest in the African-derived religions of Haiti. Cuba, and Brazil, we find the literature on African-derived Jamaican religions inadequate, as scholars base much of their interpretations upon unsubstantiated or inconclusive data.

One factor contributing to the emphasis on African-derived religions in Haiti, Cuba, and Brazil is the conspicuous and central appearance of African deities in those traditions. Esu or Ellegua; Ogou or Ogun; Sango; Yemoja, Yemanja, or Yemaya; Oya; and Obatala are only some examples of divinities which can be found in Yoruba and Vodun religious practices in West Africa as well as in Haiti, Cuba, and Brazil. Although Jamaican Kumina emphasizes continuity between the visible and invisible domains of the human and ancestral world, practitioners claim to worship one Deity, whom they call Zambi or King Zambi.[4]

Consequently, the African character of Jamaican religions is often depicted as less salient than that of Vodun in Haiti or of Yoruba derivatives in Cuba and Brazil. Perhaps the preoccupation with origins and nature in the study of African and African diasporic religions has encouraged the proliferation of scholarship on diasporic traditions that have identifiable parent cultures in Africa. While Haitian Vodun has been traced to its Dahomean, Yoruba, and Kongo sources; Cuban Yoruba and Santeria to their continental Yoruba and Kongo sources: and Brazilian Candomblé and Umbanda to Yoruba and Congo sources; on the whole, African-derived Jamaican religious traditions offer less tangible evidence of direct continuity with parent cultures in Africa.

Furthermore, when we speak of African-derived religions in Jamaica, we are not referring to one or two widespread popular religions with markable beginnings and discernible trajectories of growth, transformation, or cross-fertilization. On the contrary, we are referring primarily to traditions with ambiguous origins, unpredictable evolutionary patterns, and, at times, regional significance. As discussed in previous chapters, Obeah, Myal, and the Native Baptists emerged as islandwide traditions in Jamaica during the period of African enslavement; Kumina and Revival Zion traditions emerged, respectively, during the 1840s and 1860s.

Following the interpretation of Leonard Barrett, until recently, scholars held that Kumina was also a tradition practiced by enslaved Africans in Jamaica. However, Monica Schuler's research on African indentured labor in Jamaica between 1841 and 1865 and Bilby and Bunseki's field research on Kumina firmly establish it as a BaKongo-based religious practice that was introduced into eastern Jamaica by African indentured laborers just a few years after the abolition of slavery. Some studies have documented another tradition, Convince, which has been recorded as a spirit possession ritual practiced mostly by the Maroons and eastern Jamaicans.[5] More work is needed in this area, however, if we are to understand its history and evolution in Jamaica.

Some other African-derived religiocultural traditions are Jonkunnu or Burru, Gumbay, Ananse, Ettu, Tambu, Gerreh, Dinki Mini, Ni-Nite, Brukin' Party, and Zella.[6] Regional retentions have also been documented on the western end of the island in the Abeokuta village in the parish of Westmoreland, which derived its name from Abeokuta in Nigeria, as the community was able to retain fragments of Yoruba language and culture.[7]

In my view, one of the greatest challenges facing researchers is that of understanding and explaining how these diverse deposits of African religious cultures in Jamaica relate to Africa and to one another. With regard to Kumina, some would argue that it is not a religion but a dance or an ancestral "cult." I would argue, though, that Kumina is a religion inasmuch as it is a coherent system of belief, religious ritual, and spiritual practice structured upon the metaphysical principles and cultural norms of classical African societies. As Bilby and Bunseki write, "Kumina is indeed an African form of dance, but it is a great deal more than this. It is a religion, a worldview, and a living cultural preserve."[8]

Most of the research on Kumina is descriptive and derivative. Among scholars, there is a tendency to treat Kumina with some interpretive distance by focusing on its outward expressions of dance, song, drumming, and so on. For example, Rex Nettleford, founder and former director of Jamaica's National Dance Theater Company (NDTC), has emphasized the ritual dance component of Kumina both in his scholarship[9] and in the dance compositions performed by the NDTC. Joseph Moore has written about the songs and dances in Kumina ceremonies.[10] During the 1970s, Maureen Warner-Lewis undertook a deeper study of Kumina through the personality and religious lore of Imogene Kennedy, a Kumina queen from St. Catherine.[11] And in a more recent essay, "The Ancestral Factor in Jamaica's African Religions," Warner-Lewis makes a fitting attempt to identify African retentions in a wide array of Jamaican religiocultural traditions with specific African continental institutions. She also observes reciprocal patterns of influence in these traditions since the period of African enslavement. With regard to Kumina, Warner-Lewis discusses one of the interpretive tasks facing researchers if we are to deepen our understanding and appreciation of Kumina as an institution of knowledge, meaning, and contemporary relevance in Jamaican society. She maintains that we "need to ascertain what values [the Ancestors] hold for the present generations who invoke [them]."[12] Olive Lewin's treatment of Kumina is also a significant contribution of recent years.[13]

The truth is that most accounts of Kumina do not include enough detailed information about Kumina as an institution, including its theological and social significance to practitioners and to the larger Jamaican society. The earliest accounts of Kumina, by Zora Neale Hurston in the 1930s[14] and Madeline Kerr in the 1950s,[15] were informed by primary field research. Nevertheless, the experiences described in their works were based upon shallow appearances at a limited number of Kumina ceremonies. The most comprehensive study on Kumina as a structured religious institution was written by Kenneth Bilby in collaboration with Fu-Kiau Bunseki in 1978 as an unpublished master's thesis at the University of the West Indies (now published in *Les Cahiers du Cedaf*). The definitive import of their study is demonstrated by the unprecedented scope and depth of their research among a number of Kumina communities in Jamaica. Through attending ceremonies and intensive interviews, they collected a database of oral histories, folk stories, songs, and linguistic glosses. Thus, they offer a more developed portfolio of Kumina—one that contextualizes Kumina as a product of history, culture, and social transformation.[16]

As a system of ritual practice, Kumina is often described as an insular ancestral cult which places little, if any, significance upon analyzing and responding to social oppression. In one of her articles, Warner-Lewis compares Kumina with historic and contemporary Jamaican religious traditions, remarking:

Myalism, the Native Baptist movement, Bedwardism, and Rastafarianism all belong in one set of Afro-Jamaican religions which consciously aim to demolish the politico-economic evils of their age, whether slavery, colonialism, or neocolonialism. On the other hand, on the face of it, the ancestor cults adopt a neutral position vis-à-vis socio-economic conditions. With the exception of Convince, they appear to survive more out of a sense of clan identity and to foster feelings of spiritual fellowship within communities. Through them, communal history is relived in possessions, dreams, shared communions of food, and the immortalization of individuals and groups through song. But with time, the link between the living and ancestors at greater generational depth must become attenuated.[17]

Warner-Lewis suggests that the ancestral focus in Kumina is cultural and distinct from the kind of political consciousness fostered by other African-Jamaican religions such as Rastafari, Revival Zion, and Myal, which were explored in earlier chapters. My own research among Kumina practitioners is more consistent with Bilby and Bunseki's depiction of Kumina as a complex and cogently nuanced expression of religious ideas and ritual that govern the lives of adherents as they negotiate experiences that promote or compromise human potential for health (and general well-being) productivity, and fulfillment. For example, Bilby and Bunseki maintain:

Kumina can neither be reduced to a quaint survival nor dismissed as a fantasy of Africa reenacted. It is a vibrant and fully living African-based religion. Those who belong to the "Bongo Nation" and practice Kumina really *do* consider themselves Africans, regardless of what others might wish to believe about them. Their African identity and consciousness are not designed; they are rooted in the still-remembered historical experience of nineteenth-century African immigrants who adapted their cultural pasts to the new surroundings in which they found themselves, and passed the product on to their children and their children's children. The end-result is that mere exists today in eastern Jamaica, and particularly St. Thomas, a social and economic network of "Africans"—people who belong to a bona fide "subculture" based on an African-derived religion, ideology, and language.[18]

In identifying some of the limitations of former studies, I do not intend to trivialize the meaningful contributions that Warner-Lewis, Kerr, Hurston, Barrett, Moore, and others have made to the body of research on Kumina. Collectively, these scholars were the pioneers in documenting the ritual content, language, and structure of Kumina as a religiocultural institution. The challenge before scholars today is to expand the understanding of the historical evolution and social significance of this 150-year-old cultural preserve in Jamaica.

The only credible way of deepening our understanding of Kumina, as an oral-based transgenerational tradition, is through more intensive field research on practicing Kumina communities. My field research among Kumina communities in the parishes of St. Thomas and St. Catherine introduced me to a Jamaican worldview steeped in forms of African consciousness that I had only previously associated with Rastafari culture. I came to understand the saliency of Africa for Kumina communities during six months of attending Kumina ceremonies, interviewing practitioners, and collecting songs and lexicons.

It is important to acknowledge that the scope of my research involved a limited number of communities and, therefore, precludes any precise comparative analysis, which will be required in the end for a definitive commentary on Kumina spirituality and cosmology. With this in mind, I attempt here to portray Kumina as I encountered it in the narratives, songs, rituals, and visible-invisible loci of the practicing communities. And I will do so sequentially, following the order in which I was permitted access to the essential components of Kumina identity. First, which people comprise the Kumina community? And what unifies them as a people with a shared past and a common destiny? Second, what is Kumina as religious practice? What is the purpose and significance of the various Kumina ceremonies to practitioners and non-practitioners?

The Kumina people are self-identified "Africans." They do not refer to themselves as Black, Jamaican, Afro-Jamaican, or even African Jamaican. They conceive of their African identity exponentially. They are simultaneously ethnic Africans[19] and Pan-Africans, thereby presenting themselves to be Africans ethnically, racially, culturally, and more specifically, spiritually. If we are to hear and understand what Kumina Africans intend by this assertion of identity, we must be willing to surrender, or at least suspend, postmodern critiques that render diasporic ethnocultural and racial identifications with Africa essentialist, romantic, and therefore inauthentic and contrived.

The African identity claims of people eight generations removed from ancestors who were born and buried on the continent of Africa disclose that Africanness has always signified something symbolic, intangible, and even inaccessible to many descendants of enslaved Africans in the

Caribbean and the Americas. Yet it has also taken on a very specific meaning in the Caribbean and the Americas, one with which, at the end of the day, continental Africans must also identify—that is, Africanness, as an identity, is a consequence of the rise of the modem West. Europe's Africanization of distinct ethnic communities such as the Igbo, Yoruba, Fon, Mende, Asante, Hausa, and so on was essential to the proliferation of the racist ideological justifications for the transatlantic slave trade. Thus for many of the Igbo, Yoruba, Fon, Mende, Asante, Hausa, and so on, who became shipmates on slave vessels, African identity soon replaced or existed alongside ethnic identity in contexts of exile from family, clan, civilization, and ancestral homeland. For a significant number of diasporic Africans, "Africa" has been an all-encompassing symbol of the inaccessible ancestral homeland and the preservation or rearticulation of African continental institutions and worldviews in spite of slavery, Western cultural dominance, and their devastating impact on African diasporic cultures.[20]

For Kumina Africans, Africa (that intangible, inaccessible something) is also awesome and sacred, indeed something transcendent and deserving of reverence. And thus, in Kumina anthropology, we find clues for understanding why Kumina Africans do not experience the kind of ambivalence many diasporic Africans (especially those persuaded by postmodern critiques of essentialism) experience regarding their African heritage. Kumina devotees do not subscribe to a universal theological anthropology like that expressed by the Christian doctrines of original sin and universal redemption. They believe that each human being is essentially who she is due to the unique combination of her *kanuba* (spirit), *deebu* (blood), and *beezie* (flesh). The *kanuba* shapes the human personality and is patrilineally derived. The *beezie,* on the other hand, is matrilineally derived, and the *deebu* can be derived from either side. Some Kumina practitioners maintain strict taboos regarding these three components of their human makeup.

The *kanuba, deebu,* and *beezie* are the umbilical cord unifying the individual with his specific *nkuyu* (Ancestors) and unifying the larger community with the entire ancestral community.[21] The Ancestors are the departed who achieve spiritual status as members of the Divine Community and as Nzambi's messengers in the invisible world domain. They acquire power and use it to assist their living descendants in the visible world domain. Kumina devotees are in constant communication with Ancestors who validate and replenish their steadfast identification with Africa.

In Kumina anthropology, African identity is restored and epitomized in the transcendent yet accessible ancestral community. Through spirit manifestation and other devotional rituals, Kumina Africans constantly strengthen the metaphysical continuity between the living and the dead, the visible and the invisible, the Bongo[22] nation and the Bongo Ancestors. With the assistance of the Ancestors, Kumina devotees configure a space for accessing and applying African ideas and values to the concrete tasks and challenges they confront in the visible dimension of life. Pan-African theologian Josiah Young asserts that this process of reconciliation and empowerment has been an important aspect of African North American religiosity as well. In describing the underpinnings of his approach to theology, he writes:

Those values that intrigue me most may be characterized as the communication between the living and the dead—a spirituality reappropriated in Pan-African theology today. I suspect that within certain cultures, namely those inherited by today's Gullahs, such communication was established through the liminality of ritual. Liminality has to do with the suspension of the prevailing sacred space, where a people discover, in the kinetic fervor of religious feeling, genuine liberation. Here social distinctions are eschewed in favor of a spiritual, transcendent state, in which devotees experience the intensification of community, and revel in their most heartfelt commitments.[23]

There is in Kumina a "heartfelt commitment" to African identity and its multivocal expressions in the oral cultural traditions, ceremonial possession rituals, and other acts of devotion. At the core of Kumina culture is a collective memory, grief, and indignation regarding African people's capture, exile, enslavement, and oppression by Whites or "the White supremacists," as one informant constantly remarked. All of the Kumina practitioners I interviewed identified their heritage in Jamaica with the period of African enslavement. Moreover, in each community, there were several elders and leaders who could give accounts of ancestral journeys from "Africa" to Jamaica, with specific details about the brutalities suffered on the slave ships and the hardships endured both during slavery and after Emancipation. One such narrative was recounted by Uncle P,[24] the sixty-seven-year-old grandson of a late Kumina queen in Port Morant, St. Thomas:

Mi say, di White man, him wicked! Him tek fi wi ancestor-dem pon di ship an mek dem suffa. My grandmodda was rape[d] 'on di slave ship. Dem tek har, a fourteen-year-ole pickney, an rape har!. ... So di blood, it mix up because she get pregnant, and dem neva help har wan bit (di White people I mean). . . . We no truss dem because dem wicked. But you cyaan blame di chile. . . .a no har fault har fahdda White. We African a wan people.[25]

One's immediate reaction to Uncle P's story might be suspicion, for when we do the math, it could not possibly be the case that his grandmother was born before the abolition of slavery in the British Caribbean, let alone before the abolition of the slave trade in 1807, However, studies of the slave trade and the abolitionist movement in Britain show how and when the rape could have taken place. Monica Schuler's research on African emigration to Jamaica provides insight into this puzzling dimension of Kumina memory.

Schuler's study documents that 8,000 "recaptive [West and Central] Africans"[26] were sent to Jamaica from St. Helena and Sierra Leone between 1841 and 1865. Says Schuler, "Two categories of Africans arrived in Jamaica in numbers unanticipated by authorities—children orphaned by the slave trade, and Africans of all ages landed in Jamaica from Cuba-bound slave ships captured by the British navy in the Caribbean."[27]

The British navy rescued Africans from Portuguese-Brazilian and Spanish-Cuban slave ships throughout the 1860s. It is possible that Uncle P's grandmother was raped on a ship en route to Brazil or Cuba during the late 1860s before the British navy arrested its crew and rescued the Africans from their impending captivity as slaves. She could have survived to pass down her story to her children and grandchildren or to other members of her community, who helped to preserve the memory of her violation.

Ultimately, the rape narrative is the collective property of Kumina Africans, who are now bearers of their ancestral legacy in Jamaica. Uncle P's "grandmother" is the archetypal victim of sexual exploitation, a dehumanizing rite of passage experienced by African females throughout the Middle Passage and slavery. Members of the Kumina community, today apparently unaware of the unique sequence of events that led to their foreparents' arrival in Jamaica only *after* official emancipation, actually situate themselves within the broader collective history of African experience in pre-emancipation Jamaica and function then as retainers of national memory. For example, Edward (Kamau) Brathwaite cites an archetypal lynching story from a taped interview with one of the most celebrated and publicized Kumina queens, Imogene Kennedy. Kennedy described the lynching of African people on a cotton tree in Port Morant, St. Thomas:

[I]s not dey-one came, is a whole heap-a-dem come 'ere in de slavery...because take for instant Morant Bay. ... when dey came here ... you 'ave a cotton tree out dere ... what de buil' a gas station now ... dat dey *use to heng people* ... an' you husban' leave an come ... after you ... an' dey heng you;

you husban' come to look fuh you ... dey d'win de same ... you children come out in de slavery time ... but dose time it was still de African-dem...you understan'... ? Well dey hang dem out there, because at de las' time since I been here, an' when dey gwine to cut down dat cotton tree to buil' de gas station, it lick dung about four to five men ... kill dem.[28]

In relating her version of countless African lynchings in Port Morant, Kennedy establishes that many Africans apart from her BaKongo Ancestors came to Jamaica as slaves. Thus, her report of these brutal executions concerns Africans both within and outside of her personal ancestral lineage, reflecting an inclusive and Pan-Africanist understanding of African community. Accordingly, we gain insight into the Pan-African motif as a probable recent development in contemporary Kumina culture for, as late as 1978, Bilby and Bunseki documented a strong consciousness and assertion of BaKongo ethnic identity among Kumina practitioners. "Like their ancestors," they write:

> many present-day "Africans" in eastern Jamaica maintain the concept of tribal affiliation, if not an actual genealogical map behind it. Individuals may assert, for example, that they are descended primarily from the Muyanji or Munchundi tribes ... Present-day descendants of the nineteenth-century Central African immigrants continue, in the tradition of their forebears, to set themselves apart—at least in theory—from the Afro-Jamaican majority surrounding them.[29]

At the time that I collected information from Kumina adherents in 1996, I observed a spirit of Pan-African unity in the attitudes of Kumina Africans toward nonpracticing Jamaican Blacks. They uniformly embraced nonpractitioners as kinfolk and held that any person of African descent from any cultural or geographic location has a right to claim allegiance to the Bongo Ancestors and a space in the Kumina-practicing Bongo nation. When I pressed informants to explain exactly what they mean by referring to themselves and the Ancestors as "Bongo," they often responded that Bongo is the African tribal or national place of origin. One informant, a Kumina queen well respected by fellow practitioners for her upkeep of the culture, also described the Ancestors as "Kongo" and explained that "Bongo" and "Kongo" are interchangeable names for the specific African lineage claimed by the Kumina community. The Kumina community's extension of membership in the Bongo nation to Blacks in the wider society synchronizes its particular sense of ethnic affiliation and its universal, Pan-African affinity with all Jamaican Blacks.

The depth of African identity consciousness in Kumina culture can also be assessed in the practitioners' perceptions of Whites. Kumina practitioners view Whites as culturally and spiritually Other. "White people can't hear the drum," said one Kumina queen when I asked if they are allowed to join Kumina bands. Another Kumina queen responded by asking of me, "How can White supremacists ask the Bongo Ancestors for help?"[30] Imogene Kennedy stressed the importance of speaking the "African language" in communicating with the Ancestors and responded, "Whites don't know the language or the rhythm of the dance. They can't talk to the Ancestors." Kumina practitioners are convinced that White supremacy is the dominant factor in African people's chronic suffering worldwide. They remain suspicious of Whites and blatantly critical of White religiocultural traditions. Even more telling of the anti-White ideological tendency in Kumina is the affirmative responses received when I asked those same informants if Indians and Chinese people are welcome to join Kumina bands (as Jamaica has a small Asian population). Kennedy responded that Asians could participate if they want because they are colored.[31]

The deep-seated African consciousness exhibited by Kumina devotees is generated as well by the community's resistance to and contempt for White supremacy and White oppressors. Their distrust of Whites is derived from the lessons taught by oral tradition. I take exception to Warner-Lewis's characterization of Kumina as lacking in social consciousness when compared with Rastafari. I would argue that the memory of the violence and violation that their Ancestors endured during the late nineteenth century, when they were literally released from slave ships and accorded free status, has actually served to engender a type of pro-African consciousness among practitioners that Rastafari adherents would embrace. With each generation, recycled stories about their Ancestors' exploitation and confinement on the plantations, despicable wages, harassment, and intimidation had to have reinforced the Kumina community's collective suspicion that the White person is an altogether different type of human being with a greater potential to harm Africans than to bring about any authentic liberation.

One informant (with the initials BH) attempted to recount the dreadful conditions under which Central Africans were brought to Jamaica. Her vague account was slightly incoherent, difficult to follow, and virtually indecipherable until I discovered documentation that corroborated the pieces of her memory that remained intact. A portion of our dialogue is translated below:

> BH They would tell them to join the line or they wouldn't get help. They really didn't have a choice.
> DS What line?
> BH They had to join the force and fight the war for the White man or stay slave.
> DS Where did this happen?
> BH Back in Africa.[32]

Our conversation took place within a larger discussion about the British navy rescuing Africans from slave ships, as I was attempting to discern if contemporary Kumina practitioners have retained any oral traditions about the specific details of their ancestors' extended Middle Passage from Sierra Leone and St. Helena to Jamaica under the indentured labor program. B.H. did not confirm or deny any of the information I shared with her about the conditions of her ancestors' passage to Jamaica during the postemancipation period. She immediately began talking about Africans having to "join the line." B.H.'s story always intrigued me but I did not know how to contextualize it. I initially assumed that when she discussed "the White man" she was possibly referring to colonial officers. I had also presumed that when she said the exchange occurred in Africa, she meant Central Africa. My conjecture was that she could have been describing Central African encounters with colonial officials or missionaries in the region. I was to discover some months later that B.H.'s story presented a fraction of the exchanges that took place between recaptured Africans and British government representatives ("the White man") in Africa, as she stated, but she meant Sierra Leone and not Central Africa. In her study of African immigration to Jamaica during the postemancipation period, Monica Schuler notes:

> By 1844 forced emigration of recently arrived recaptives from the Freetown Queen's Yard was an idea whose time had obviously come. In February the Colonial Secretary dispatched instructions to the Sierra Leone governor to offer recaptives the choice of immigrating to the West Indies or remaining in Sierra Leone without government assistance formerly offered. An older option, which had always existed for men—that of enlisting in the West India Regiments—remained. In reality the new dispensation read, "emigrate, enlist, or fend for yourself." The instructions made no exceptions for children.[33]

Schuler's research lends support to B.H.'s faded recollection and to the community's record of "the White man's" ill treatment of recaptive Africans. B.H.'s account suggests that the "older option" of military enlistment also noted by Schuler was not interpreted as a humane option by recaptive Africans. Schuler provides even further evidence for why this was so:

Newly-liberated Africans had never before exhibited any interest in emigrating to the West Indies and were prone to take to the bush when emigration recruiters approached their villages. Recruiting in the Queen's Yard [Sierra Leone], therefore, was not simply a matter of inviting people to travel to the West Indies. ...The standard practice was to isolate new arrivals from all except West India Regiment and plantation recruiters, and in some cases recaptives were detained in the Queen's Yard for one to three months awaiting the arrival of an emigrant ship.[34]

Faced with the options of "no help," "joining the line," or immigration to the Caribbean, recaptive Africans were forced to accept emigration. They never chose it. They had endured the hardships of torture and unsanitary conditions on slave ships and were rescued only to confront three basic options: abandonment in still a foreign country (Sierra Leone), the extended Middle Passage to the Caribbean as indentured laborers, or, for males, enlistment in the West India Regiments. It was unlikely that they would settle on boarding another ship under the direction of White men to labor in a country thousands of miles away. The oral traditions, songs, and rituals of the Kumina culture in Jamaica suggest that the only ships recaptured Africans desired to board were those that would take them back to their original birthplaces. Those ships never materialized and so they found ways to resurrect traditions from home in their new settlements in Jamaica.

Kumina narratives disclose a collection of experiences that have been extensively shaped by the sea. Their inclusive sense of shared peoplehood with all Jamaicans of African descent is salient in individual and communal identity formation. However, their sense of a shared situation of oppression with those in the Asian Jamaican minority who would participate in Kumina culture also points to an inclusive principle in the community's assessment of social oppression and to an acknowledgment of their extended Middle Passage as a context for identity formation and group solidarity. According to Schuler, the Central Africans who settled in St. Thomas displayed many levels of identification and group affiliations with all Africans, shipmates, all Central Africans in the parish of St. Thomas, Central African subethnic groups, and fellow villagers.[35] Ship records indicate that East Indians sailed to Jamaica as indentured laborers with Africans from depot stations in St. Helena.[36] The shared shipmate experience of transportation to Jamaica and subsequent experiences of working side-by-side on the plantation estates apparently shaped the Kumina community's perception of their Asian neighbors and their acceptance of those who have expressed interest in Kumina practices and ceremonies.

Through stories like Uncle P's, Kennedy's, and B.H.'s. Kumina Africans acknowledge the historical struggles of the Ancestors who withstood centuries of brutal violence in the African-Jamaican experience. They feel existentially connected to the ancestral narratives in that they too encounter violence, censorship, and religiocultural persecution in a Jamaican society that has absorbed the colonial Western Christian perception of African religions as pathological and uncivilized. Kumina practitioners are well aware of the battles they must fight on so many fronts if they are to protect themselves against cultural genocide.

More than anything else, Kumina ancestral narratives emphasize the indefinite quality of African suffering. For a community devoted to ancestral legacies, it is not surprising that the stories told reach back to the period of African enslavement, which is considered by many diasporic Africans to be the genesis of their collective oppression. The experiences of abuse, exploitation, social discrimination, and persecution recounted time and time again by narrators like Uncle P, Kennedy, and B.H. may well be orally recorded historical accounts of the conditions to which African indentured laborers (who were the actual carriers of Kumina culture to Jamaica) were subjected during their voyages from Africa to Jamaica and thereafter as exploited laborers in a post-emancipation plantation economy. Bilby and Bunseki's study contains testimonies in which Kumina informants actually do liken the experience of indentured labor to slave labor.[37]

Having said something about the heritage and identity of Kumina practitioners, I turn now to healing practices, the dimension of Kumina religiosity that appears to be most significant for practitioners and nonpractitioners alike. Healing and the sharing of healing remedies are constant activities in the daily journeys of Kumina practitioners. Although Kumina ceremonies, which are called by the same name (Kumina), are held to mark the significance of births and deaths, to express gratitude to the Ancestors, and to commemorate past struggles and achievements of the African Ancestors in Jamaican history, most of the Kumina ceremonies I attended were held for one or more sick persons. Kumina leaders, who are almost always female, are regularly sought out by the sick and troubled for their expert knowledge of therapeutic plants and access to ancestral power. When a person experiences grave misfortune, in terms of physical or psychological illness or any other personal problem, a Kumina queen may organize a ceremony at the request of the client or based upon her own assessment of the problem.

According to Kennedy:

> Wi do [Kumina] all di while in di smalla country [St. Thomas], Wi jus tek di drum an wi gwan play. Who fi teach one annoda teach off di drum. An yuh have di ole people who will sid dung wid yuh an gwan home wid yuh. ... But hear mi a tell yuh someting, mi no get no whole heap a teachment from nobody but di creator and my spirit dem who teach me.[38]

Kennedy also describes essential facets of Kumina religious practice that allow for healing, transformation, and equilibrium, through ritual sacrifice and food offerings, as well as possession trance and mediumship.

> In di African world when yuh gwine buil a sacrifice yuh use a ram goat, yuh use fowl, *malavu* which is rum ... an when I making it now di yard full! People from all bout, people from foreign, people from all bout Jamaica, is here—cause mi mek it at watch night ... when yuh gwine go buil a duty [ritual offering] now, yuh use bread, yuh use rice, rum, yuh get everyting dat yuh know dat yuh can travel unda; kyangle—peace an love; prosperity—blue an white. ... Suppose yuh sick an yuh wan to buil someting as a tanksgiving or a uplifting or a deliverance yuh use blue an white, an yuh talk to yuh messenja ... the Ancestors; dem tell yuh everyting.[39]

I had the opportunity to spend considerable time with one Kumina queen, with the initials HB, in Port Morant, St. Thomas, and observed her prepare for what she called a "double Kumina." "This is a serious work we have to do tomorrow night" were her words to the members of her bands, "and we have to start preparing from now."[40] HB delegated tasks to all in her group, and the community went to work. While I will not provide a detailed account of the rich experiences I had accompanying HB and her entourage into the mountains to gather the necessary plants and, later, attending the actual ceremony where an adult woman and a young man were treated for physical and psychological ailments, I will summarize my observations.

My most surprising discovery, which supports the claim that Kumina is actually a way of life steeped in religious traditions, was that collecting medicinal plants is a *religious* activity of supplication, libation, and absolute reverence for the natural elements in creation, the invisible forces that pervade the elements, and the person or persons seeking help. On the day before the Kumina, I witnessed six members of the bands gather leaves from a wide assortment of plants, trees, and bushes. Some healing plants had to be extracted from the sands of shallow springs; others came from the huge limbs of pimento trees; and still others were gathered from the cracks of stony paths. The thread of consistency that for me characterized the exercise as religious ritual was the formulaic prayer and libation offered by every collector before picking each plant. For example, one prayer was recited as follows:

> Good morning, whosoever lives here, we come asking for health and protection. We come in peace; and we take life so as to give life to [the person for whom the medicinal plant is sought is named in full]. We seek not to destroy but to bless and uplift so that love and goodness will be spread throughout the nation. We ask for your help in this work. Let it be done.[41]

After the prayer, a libation of white rum is always poured onto the root of the plant or the stem of the leaf at the point of breakage. Kumina practitioners gave two reasons for doing this: the first was that rum has medicinal properties that, along with the prayer, help to wake up the sleeping plants; and second, rum is the sacrifice that must be offered to the Ancestors who might be buried directly below the trees and plants from which leaves are removed. This is done as a sign of respect for the sacred space occupied by the Ancestors. They also hold that leaves must be gathered with precision and care; they cannot be picked hastily, nor can they be carelessly discarded. Kumina practitioners retain oral traditions about the significance of the local geography to their oppressed Ancestors, to whom they refer as enslaved. They treat particular streams, rocks, bushes, and mountainous hiding spaces as shrines that provided safe haven for their African Ancestors when they were escaping from plantation slavery. They often recount stories of oppression and the emancipation provided by the natural surroundings as they travel along the same paths in search of therapeutic plants for their clients.

After about three hours of collecting plants, the party returned to the compound where HB used the leaves to prepare both liquid prescriptions and healing beds for her clients. On the following night, the Kumina began at 6:00 P.M. and was not officially completed until 6:00 A.M. the next morning. Through ritual acts of animal sacrifice, singing, drumming, and (Myal) spirit manifestation, the Kumina bands summoned the assistance of the Ancestors in restoring health and vitality to the sick clients. I had the opportunity to ask the clients how they felt after the Kumina. Both clients acknowledged that they were very satisfied with the results of the Kumina and confessed that they would not hesitate to seek out Kumina as a remedy for their troubles in the future.

The ongoing work of healing is one of Kumina's practical contributions to the larger society. Despite the popular culture's disdain toward Kumina practitioners, they are regularly consulted by nonpractitioners for solutions to their daily problems. In this regard, Kumina's contributions to Jamaican society, even today, appear to be indispensable.

Kumina was introduced to Jamaica only after Emancipation; yet, for years, scholars erroneously associated its Jamaican origins with the period of African enslavement.[42] Barrett identified Kumina with Akan culture, linguistically tracing the term to two Twi words: *akom* (the state of being possessed) and *ana* (relationship or ancestor).[43] Barrett opined that the Maroons, who were mostly of Asante heritage, introduced Kumina to the wider Jamaican society. In *Soul Force*, Barrett writes, "It is our intention here to show that myalism was the legitimate survival of the traditional religion of Africa and that myal and the Jamaican Cumina religion therefore are one and the same phenomenon."[44] Comparing Charles Leslie's eighteenth-century observation of Pawpaw/Popo religious ideas with Melville Herskovits's research on Dahomean ancestral veneration, Orlando Patterson traces Kumina to a Dahomean origin.[45] Although his work precedes Schuler's research establishing Kumina's Kongo roots, Patterson's argument is unpersuasively (though understandably) supported by generic comparisons between Kumina and a Dahomean ceremony, comparisons which could probably be made between Kumina and any African religious tradition.

The chief issue giving rise to these and other misinterpretations of Kumina is the significance of Myal to Kumina adherents. Scholars have assumed that since Myal's eighteenth-century origins during the period of African enslavement are incontestable, then Kumina too was manifest during the same period. However, Kumina's regional appearance in eastern Jamaica, especially in the parish of St. Thomas, is consistent with the importation patterns pertaining to Central African indentured laborers in the same region. Second, Kumina oral tradition includes references to geographical locations and cultural traditions from the Central African region. Third, the most convincing evidence of Kumina's Kongo origin is linguistic. Kumina adherents have retained a significant vocabulary of Kikongo words. Bilby and Bunseki collected lexicons from a number of Kumina bands and found Kikongo cognates for nearly all of the words. Many of the Kumina songs are also unintelligible to native African Jamaicans because they are sung in a Kikongo-based language.[46] Today, Kumina practitioners call their ancestral language "African"; they also call the songs "African"; they also call the songs "African or "country" songs—country being perhaps a reference to the African *country* of origin.

Another linguistic indication of Kumina's Kongolese African cultural location is the peculiar term *bands,* which serves to qualify a single Kumina or Revival band as well as multiple bands. *Bands* is used for both the singular and plural noun forms and so practitioners speak of a Kumina bands as well as Kumina bands. As a native Jamaican, I have always been perplexed by its appearance in the Kumina lexicon, In the past, I took it for granted that *bands* was an English term for it was commonly used to discuss groups of catechists, prayer circles, traveling singers, as well as rebels and criminals. I was never satisfied with this explanation, however, because syntactically the term is idiosyncratic in the grammar structures of the Jamaican Creole and English languages.

Specifically, in English, it is grammatically incorrect to use the term *bands* to describe a singular group, while in Jamaican Creole it is grammatically incorrect to use the term *bands* to describe either a single group or multiple groups. The plural form for nouns in Jamaican Creole is not realized by placing "s" at the end of a noun (as in English) but by placing the term *dem* after the noun. To illustrate the point most precisely, the plural form of the word band in Jamaican Creole would be *band-dem* or to take another example, the word *group* would become *group-dem* in the plural form.

Additionally, I noticed that Kumina practitioners would exaggerate the pronunciation of the vowels so that the vowel "a" sounded more like a long version of the term "ah" in English, while they de-emphasized the "d" at the end of the term. In other words, I heard the term *baahnz* rather than *bands,* which would have a slightly less stressed ah sound and a harder d sound (bahnd) in Jamaican Creole. So why all this fuss around bands, baahnz, and bahnd? I suspect that "bands" is actually a Central African cognate. When I was introduced to the Central African terms *mbanza* (house), and *inabanza* (possessor or head of the home), I heard the words spoken by a native Congolese.[47] I immediately recalled the Kumina term *baahnz,* for the pronunciation sounded exactly the same to me. As I inquired further about possible meanings for the term, I became convinced that "bands" (baahnz) is a bantu-derived term with parallel meanings in the Jamaican and Congo contexts. Most ethnic groups from Central Africa associate the term *mbanza* with primarily the household and town. There may be a difference in emphasis depending on the group. For example, with the creation of the Kongo kingdom, the term *mbanza* took on political significance as it became associated with the seat of power or the capital, and so one would hear *Mbanza Kongo*. In more remote areas of the kingdom and among neighboring cultural groups like the Luba in eastern and central Congo, *mbanza* is associated with the central position the wife has in the home. *Mbanza* was not necessarily associated with a centralized government but with the home. Even more intriguing to me is how the presence of and roles assigned to women in the home are what qualifies a home as *mbanza* and the female as the possessor (*ina*) of that home. In other words, a bachelor is not an *inabanza* for a bachelor's lifestyle may be random and inconsistent while a woman's presence and stature in the home give it stability, structure, and purpose.

The political and gender carryovers are obvious. Kumina female leaders hold the title of queen, connoting official governing power as in the Central African case of associating the term *mbanza* with the Kongo capital. *Modda* (mother) is also another title affectionately bestowed upon Kumina queens; however, I would argue that the mother/queen tides hold deeper meanings, connecting their status and role as ruler, head, decision maker, possessor with that of the *inabanza* in Central African households. And no doubt, the Kumina queen is central to the establishment, definition, and security of the *baahnz* in Jamaica. She is also a possessor of Myal secrets, leading many scholars to ponder the peculiar association between Myal and Kumina.

In Kumina rituals, the term *Myal* is used to describe the most powerful manifestations of ancestral visitations. Myal is the highest state of mystical encounter between the Ancestors and humans, for when a medium "catches" Myal, the best opportunities for healing, fellowship, and reconciliation become available to the community. Thus the goal of any authentic[48] Kumina is to achieve Myal possession.

As noted by Kennedy: "Afta yuh in di trance dere and dem [the Ancestors] give yuh di prayers, yuh got di Myal, den now, yuh can know what yuh about. Because yuh suppose to get di African prayers, and den di bailo [Kumina songs and chants uttered in Jamaican Creole] and den di country [African language/songs]."[49] Myal possession may manifest in any devotee and is not reserved for the Kumina queen; however, as is typical in religions where possession trance is salient, some devotees appear more susceptible to possession trance and mediumship than others.

During an interview with Maureen Warner-Lewis (1970s) Kennedy described Myal as a somatic experience of aggressive intercourse with a possessing agent:

> when de *m*yal gwine *tek* you now
> you' whole body becomes
> like it *col'*
> see?
> and *you feel*
> you' *feet* dem *draw*
> an' you *neck* yah—
> sometime you' *neck*
> fe away back yah *so*___
> Myal is de *ting* dey call a *spirit*
> where you' head '*pin* roun' an' you
> *drop* an' you' '*kin* pupalick 'pon you *neck*
> you see?
> Dat a *myal spirit*
> Dat a bongo myal spirit
> which all de *hol' African* dem—
> de dead *African* dem dem *come* roun'
> an' dem *lick* you all a' you' *headside*
> an' *ride* you 'pon you' *neck* an' you *drop*.
> You see?
> Dat dere mean to say *myal hol'* you now.[50]

Commenting on Myal as a mode of knowledge acquisition and fellowship, Kennedy asserted more recently:

> Myal is a spirit dat yuh get when yuh de pon di mada clay...barefoot! Dat is a spirit dat yuh got. An dem give yuh dat. Dat a when di old time people dem dead, dem gwine pass it on to yuh ... an when dem lick yuh wid dat, yuh gwine haf fi tell someting. Di first ting yuh know, yuh haf fi know how fi sing de African prayers...When dem pass it on to yuh now, dem suppose to giv yuh someting dat when anybody aks yuh, yuh can tell dem something...The first ting dat I get in mi African traveling is di prayers, di Our Father prayers in di African language. Yuh get di prayers and yuh get di bailo [Creole songs] to match it. Cause afta yuh say yuh prayers, yuh hafi sing, cause yuh kinda chant di messenja.[51]

The marriage between one of the oldest and one of the youngest African-derived religions in Jamaica might not be so perplexing if we situate this obscurity within our broader discussion of the Kongo antecedents of African-Jamaican religious cultures. In chapter 1, we considered the Kikongo term *mwela (miela,* plural), an apposite cognate for the term *myal*. We may do the same with regard to the term *kumina,* which Bunseki interprets as a derivative of the Kikongo noun *lusakumunu* (blessing) or its verb form *sakumuna* (to bless), which is only used in a spiritual context. There is also the term *sakumunwa* (to be blessed). Even more interesting is how Bunseki speaks of the link between *mwela/miela* and *lusakumunu,* for through *miela* (the energy of the elders and Ancestors primarily and of all entities in the cosmos) comes *lusakumunu:*

A specific ritual will be done, and when the ritual is completed, you will be blessed. And this is a specific secret ritual, in the sense that specific words have to be used. There are songs involved and specific people who can speak during this ritual, specialists who are trained to do the ritual. Through sakumuna, the person receives the living energy of the ancestors. In the process, it is a ritual made between the living community, priest, person/s seeking to overcome a problem, and the ancestors and the cosmic world.[52]

Building upon Bunseki's remarks, I interpret Jamaican Myal and Kumina as symbiotic ritual processes that facilitate the distribution of cosmic energy for life-enhancing purposes. In the pre-emancipation period, African initiates eventually referred to this religious composite as Myal, while post-emancipation BaKongo laborers, who no doubt came into contact with Myalists during their settlement period (1840s–1860s), qualified their collection of rituals with the term Kumina. Bunseki's notation that religious specialists are empowered to sing and speak specific words during the ritual is no different from the eighteenth-, nineteenth- and early-twentieth-century testimonies about the secret practices and undecipherable songs and chants associated with Myal specialists and Bilby's late-twentieth-century discovery of "myal sing" in St. Elizabeth Gumbay Play rituals.[53] Kennedy also alludes to this esoteric ritual proficiency among Kumina queens when she describes the African prayers, the bailo (creole songs), as well as the country (African songs) that one must master in order to "chant di messenja." To be sure, many African religious cultures across ethnic societies would have fostered similar practices and rituals. My supposition though is that both Myal and Kumina, no matter which other religious cultures they have absorbed over time, are cognate religious institutions that bear the indelible signature of Kongo religious culture.

It would be misleading if I did not say for the record that my participant observation experiences tainted my interpretive location such that I could not resist inferring a link between eighteenth century Myal and twentieth-century Kumina. I had read numerous descriptions of Myal before doing any fieldwork in Jamaica and, due to the racist tone of much of the descriptive literature, did not expect to find something "familiar" in the ceremonies I planned to attend. To my surprise, in the very first Kumina ceremony I attended, I felt transported back to the eighteenth century, almost as if the observers from that period were narrating the events unfolding before me. As I observed, I heard the missionaries and planters describing the Myal rituals of their time. Even those behaviors that were derisively and inaccurately portrayed as unbridled licentiousness or disingenuous performances were evident in the ceremonies I attended. Recalling this dimension of my research, the similarities were abundant then and continued to emerge as I read current ethnographic details from the research of scholars such as Kenneth Bilby and Maureen Warner-Lewis. For example, several Kumina devotees achieved Myal possession at the double Kumina healing ceremony discussed above. One young woman who went into Myal immediately reached for one of the sick clients for whom the Kumina was organized. Upon her touch, he fell unconscious to the ground and remained so for several hours while practitioners attended to his head and body. The client's healing included elaborate processions to ancestral burial grounds, while both the client and the healers were under the influence of the ancestral spirits; the client had to be carried in his unconscious state to each site. He did not regain consciousness until the climax of the ceremony had passed.[54] Such loss and revival of consciousness in the healing process was perhaps that component of Myal healing rituals during the period of enslavement winch White observers often belittled as a feigned exhibition of death and resurrection. This was the ritual practice emphasized by William fames Gardner when he wrote of Myal in 1842:

> Its first mode of development was as a branch of Obeah practice. The Obeah man introduced a dance called Myal dance, and formed a secret society, the members of which were to be made invulnerable, or if they died, life was to be restored. Belief in this miracle was secured by trick. A mixture was given in rum, of a character which presently induced sleep so profound, as by the uninitiated and alarmed, to be mistaken for death. After this had been administered to someone chosen for the purpose, the Myal dance began, and presently the victim staggered and fell, to all appearance dead. Mystic charms were then used; the body was rubbed with some infusion; and in process of time, the narcotic having lost its power, the subject of the experiment rose up as one restored to life.[55]

In the Kumina ceremony I attended, the sequence of events renders it highly unlikely that the young man was given any substance to induce his state of unconsciousness or restored consciousness. What appears more likely is that this Kongo-based healing procedure was only fortified in what became Kumina culture, as a result of the encounter between BaKong immigrants and African Jamaicans of Myal persuasion during the nineteenth-century.

The history of African-derived religions in Jamaica is, in the end, the reconstitution of Myal religiosity in Jamaica from slavery to the present. Myal has claimed a definitive place of authority in each of the African-Jamaican religious traditions, demonstrating its theological, spiritual, and political resilience. Within this spiritual orientation, I see indispensable resources for an African-centered, womanist theology of the cross which contests the traditional Euro-missionary theologies of the cross that were preached to Africans as the good news afforded them through their captivity.

African-Derived Religions in Jamaica: Toward an African-Centered, Womanist Theology of the Cross

In the first chapter I described six features of African-derived religions which index reconstitutions of African religious traditions in the Caribbean and the Americas. These features deserve reiteration as the backdrop for my construction of an African-centered, womanist theology of the cross. I have discussed above how a Divine Community (communotheism), divination and herbalism, ancestral veneration, food offerings and animal sacrifice, possession trance, and neutral mystical power are universal orthodox components of African spirituality and ritual practice. And I have attempted to identify these features in the variegated expressions of African-derived religions in Jamaican history.

As a religious symbol, the cross is not the exclusive property of Christianity. It is one of the oldest religiocultural icons in Africa. The cross symbolizes the holistic spiritual and philosophical orientation regarding the visible-invisible sacred cosmos, which is normative for many classical African societies. It represents abounding theories of complementarity, opposition, and integration. The African (BaKongo) cross, with its surplus of meaning, also holds significance for practitioners of African religious cultures in Jamaica. I suspect that by the time enslaved Africans began to hear the gospel preached as well as missionary reflections on the cross, the African cross was influential enough to subvert the perceived metasignificance of the Euro-missionary cross as they considered their situations as humans in bondage by capture or by birth. For example, Obeah oath rituals, which scholars maintain were enacted before every African rebellion, might very well have been influenced by classical Kongo cosmology, which uses the cross as its icon.

Moreover, in conversation with the womanist theological tradition, I see in Kumina and other African-derived religions important resources for constructing an African-centered theology of the cross that promotes the holistic liberation of Black women and Black communities. Taking seriously Delores Williams's argument that the Christian cross has been used to convince Black women that bearing crosses of constructed suffering and surrogacy is a Christian virtue,[56] I want to suggest some ways in which women's experiences in the Kumina religion point to another type of cross-bearing that might enhance African-Jamaican struggles to come to terms with the role of the Divine in human suffering.

Several African studies scholars have identified salient meanings in the Kongo Yowa cross that are pertinent to this discussion. For example, Wyatt MacGaffey's examination of the Kongo cross coheres with the theological meanings of both women's pragmatic focus upon problem solving in the Kumina religion and the pre-Emancipation African practice of taking Obeah oaths in preparation for revolts. According to MacGaffey:

The simplest ritual space is a Greek cross [+] marked on the ground, as for oath-taking. One line represents the boundary; the other is ambivalently both the path leading across the boundary, as to the cemetery; *and* the vertical path of power linking "the above" with "the below." This relationship, in turn is polyvalent, since it refers to God and [humanity], God and the dead, and the living and the dead. The person taking the oath stands upon the cross, situating himself between life and death, and invokes the judgement of God and the dead upon himself.[57]

The cross is a fundamental symbol of religious life in classical Kongo civilization. Although we cannot be certain that this particular cosmological orientation informed the specific Obeah oaths that were taken during the period of Jamaican enslavement, MacGaffey's explication of the Kongo cross offers a view into the type of religious orientation that endowed ritual oath taking with sacrosanct meaning in the classical African societies from which enslaved Africans in Jamaica may have inherited such rituals. On the other hand, given that Kumina is a Kongo tradition, it could be argued that there is a specific connection between the Kongo religious orientation, symbolized by the cross as described by MacGaffey, and current Kumina rituals in Jamaica.[58] As such, Kongo cosmology is essential in determining the theological meaning of the African-derived religious practices of Kumina women.

The notion of incarnation, for example, may be applied to the shared religious orientation of BaKongo groups and their Kumina descendants. However, incarnation is not a christocentric doctrine in Kongo religious culture. Incarnation, in this context, points to the concrete embodiment of a Divinity or Ancestor for the benefit of the human community. This happens repeatedly in countless African religions and, as I have already discussed, in Jamaican Myal, Revival Zion, and Kumina. Robert Farris Thompson's reflections on Kongo theological anthropology of ancestorhood and reincarnation provide a backdrop for contextualizing what I call the Kongo "cross of incarnation," as evident in the Kongo spirituality of Jamaican Kumina devotees:

This Kongo "sign of the cross" has nothing to do with the crucifixion of the Son of God, yet its meaning overlaps the Christian vision. Traditional Bakongo believed in a Supreme Deity, Nzambi Mpungu, and they had their own notions of the indestructibility of the soul: "Bakongo believe and hold it true that [a person's] life has no end, that it constitutes a cycle. The sun, in its rising and setting, is a sign of this cycle, and death is merely a transition in the process of change." The Kongo *yowa* cross does not signify the crucifixion of Jesus for the salvation of [humanity,] it signifies the equally compelling vision of the circular motion of human souls about the circumference of its intersecting lines. The Kongo cross refers to the everlasting continuity of *all* righteous men and women.[59]

Here Thompson not only describes the place of the Ancestors and the human life cycle in Kongo cosmology, but he also correctly perceives that the Kongo sign of the cross does not signify the death of Jesus Christ. To be sure, the Yowa cross does not signify the death of any member of the Divine Community. With further analysis, it is evident that the Yowa cross counteracts death by mediating extended life, connection, and metaphysical continuity across the visible-invisible world domains. Thus the Yowa cross might be compared with what happens with the birth of Jesus Christ as embodied Deity rather than with the death of Christ.[60]

Yet, while the incarnation may be valid for Christians in terms of its christological focus, it is important to remember that, for BaKongo groups and other devotees of African-derived religions in Jamaica, the incarnation is the recurring event of embodied Deity/Ancestor made manifest in possession trance. From my study of Black religious formation, in several African diasporic contexts, I hold that the incarnational emphasis in African-derived religions provided a theological strainer, if you will, an aesthetic and discriminating theological device through which a majority of enslaved Africans filtered Christian symbols and religious ideas. Consequently, what emerged in both African-derived religions and the Black North American Christian traditions was an emphasis on the spirit (pneumatology).[61]

On Jamaican soil, the pneumatocentric dynamic is configured as spirit messengers within the Revival Zion tradition. In Kumina, Myal ancestral possession dramatizes the sign of the cross as the crossroads where the invisible meets the visible. This encoding of the cross through dance movements and ritual placement of objects at strategic points around a center pole facilitates a process of collaboration among the inhabitants of the visible and invisible world domains. Both world domains then are represented in the image of the cross. The vertical pole, marking the invisible domain, is physically represented by the center pole in Kumina ceremonies and signifies the sky and the locus of disembodied life.[62] The horizontal pole marks the visible domain, encapsulating the earth and embodied life. The point of penetration, the crossroads, symbolizes the event of incarnation.

Incarnations manifest as the disembodied living (Ancestors) unite with the embodied living (humans). Such an integrative and complementary show of divine power is the basis for a valuation of the body as an indispensable spiritual medium. This type of embodied spirituality can be observed in Black churches as spirit manifestation, despite the tendency in some churches to embrace popular dualistic Christian notions of the soul as good/sacred and the body as bad/profane.[63] Furthermore, this spirituality is the basis for a holistic anthropology which renders all people—females, males, elders, minors, the able, and the disabled—potential hosts of divine power, that is, participants in the event of incarnation. The African-derived religions of Jamaica testify through the body that health and well-being are restored when the embodied living and the disembodied living demonstrate their relational interaction, especially in its most concentrated expression, Myal. I suspect that this is the rationale for why Revival Zionists would testify to holding a Kumina when they are confronted with the gravest problems. They do not resort directly to Christ, for the power to restore temporal well-being is not derived from soteriological beliefs about Jesus' death but from African beliefs about recurring incarnation as the locus of life-sustaining power.

The exception, however, is the African-centered Rastafari tradition where incarnation is especially important because of its christological focus. As already discussed in chapter 3, Rastas view Haile Selassie as the incarnation of God—the Black messiah/Jesus Christ—and proclaim the divinity of all African people. In Rastafari theological anthropology, Black people are manifestations of the true God—the African God of Abraham, David, and Jesus. But Rastafari does not embrace Lutheran notions of cross-bearing. Indeed the Rastafari understanding of evil and *sufferation* as a concrete disruption of the temporal life to be enjoyed is much more consistent with Myal notions that evil offenses are acts against society and must be eradicated in this world.[64] Bob Marley's denouncement of the "preacher man's" theology illustrates how Rastafari Christology is most informed by Hebrew scriptural depictions of a political messiah who will not take up the cross per se but will lead the divine war against oppression and exile. Collectively, his songs dispute colonial missionary theology and profess the Rastafari belief in radical human agency and divine inspiration in the struggle for sociopolitical liberation.[65]

Rastas contend that divine incarnation in Africans inspires them toward sociopolitical resistance against oppression. Thus, the Rastafari notion of incarnation is congruent with that of the Kumina community in that it is explicitly related to practical, temporal experiences within the human community and eschews theologies of temporal suffering and subsequent eschatological reward.[66] Rastafari incarnational theology, however, reflects the intense Pan-Africanist political ideology that undergirds the religion's piety, doctrines, and praxes. Kumina's incarnational theology is subversive and therefore politically astute despite the tradition's nurturance of a subterranean Pan-Africanist ideology that is often overlooked or unrecognized by scholars because it is only subtly or conditionally expressed to outsiders.

Kumina's Kongo-based incarnational spirituality also underscores the point that, in spite of the resurrection, the cross becomes central in Christian theology because of the suffering and death of God. In Kumina and other African-derived religions, the cross is significant because it represents divine or ancestral incarnation for the concrete purpose of restoring health and wholeness within the community. This theology of the cross can never be related to the endurance of suffering as it is in Christian theology because it is based upon a religious view of life that is committed to the immediate alleviation of suffering.

By way of comparison, Kelly Brown Douglas speculatively suggests that enslaved Africans in North America made connections between what I call the classical African cross (of incarnation) and the Christian cross (of the crucified-and-resurrected Jesus). She posits this connection by alluding to the parallels between the stress on intimacy between the living and the dead in African religion and the intimacy between enslaved Africans and the crucified-and-resurrected Jesus in the context of exile from Africa and bondage in America.[67] I find this analysis intriguing and dialectically provocative as both a problematic and a resolve in the debate on Africanisms in Black religion (a problematic) and the lack of attention to Africanisms in Black theology (a resolve).[68] I differ with Douglas, however, in that I see no evidence that the crucified-and-resurrected Jesus (i.e., the Christian cross), interpreted through the matrix of the African cross (intimacy between the living and the dead), is most salient in forging the bond between enslaved Africans and Christ. The evidence suggests to me that the two crosses are actually oppositional if not antithetical while the African cross (of incarnation) and the Christian notion of incarnation are more compatible and infer reflection on pneumatology as a theological priority over reflection on Christology in African-derived religions that incorporate christianisms and in the sanctified Black churches that have linkages to the ring shout and hush harbor practices of enslaved Africans.[69] Delores Williams's discussion of the continuities between the Christian notion of incarnation and the African incarnational cross would seem to indicate the need for such a shift in black/womanist theological discourse: "The angel Gabriel tells [Mary], 'The Holy Spirit will come upon you, and the power of the Most High will overshadow you; therefore the child to be born will be called holy, the Son of God' (Luke 1:36). Translated in terms of African-American heritage from traditional African religions, one can say, 'The Spirit mounted Mary.' The word was first made flesh in Mary's body."[70]

In short, the resurrection of the deceased Jesus is less (if at all) compatible with the African cross than is the incarnation of God in Jesus via Mary's body.[71] The extant data on African American Christian formation support the position that some enslaved Africans forged intimate bonds with Jesus and Jesus' cross not because of their reverence for and intercourse with their Ancestors but because of the obvious parallels between their undeserved and unjust suffering and that of Jesus. The testimonies of enslaved converts to Christianity in Jamaica that were examined in chapter 3 are but a few examples.[72]

The suffering Christ in African American Christianity, prominent though it is, did not eclipse the African cross of divine incarnation. This normative feature of African religion survived in black North American Christianity as Black Christians found ways to reconcile it with the dominating Christian cross of divine death and resurrection. For example, in many traditional black churches a prevalent sermonic motif is the death and resurrection of Jesus the Christ (the Christian cross), yet another established religious practice in these same churches is spirit possession (the African cross of divine incarnation). The implications of the survival of the African cross within Black religious experience are not inconsequential for the sanctified and charismatic Black Christian traditions of North America, and they deserve further attention in the works of Black and womanist theologians.

Comparative studies of incarnational spirituality in Black Christian and African-derived traditions might prove most useful in combating sexism, due to the prominence of women as mediums for Divine manifestations and as significant leaders in African-derived religions. Again Williams is instructive on this point as she challenges Black male theologians to incorporate more female-inclusive sources in their works. Williams specifically proposes that shifting from a christological-soteriological to an incarnational focus on the cross is more productive in addressing sexism within the Christian tradition:

The critique of atonement views by womanist theology invites black [male] liberation theologians to begin serious conversations with black females about the black Christians' understanding of atonement in light of African-American women's experience of oppression. Perhaps such a conversation can begin with the *incarnation and the cross*. By removing their sexist lens, black theologians can see that though incarnation is traditionally associated with the self-disclosure of God in Jesus Christ, incarnation also involves *God's self-disclosure in a woman:* Mary.[73]

Thus Williams suggests that if we are willing to view divine disclosure through Mary's body, we are compelled to raise questions about the essential meaning of the cross and resurrection to Christian faith and teaching. To begin with the incarnation in Mary's body indicates that the resurrection is no longer proof of divine disclosure and positions Mary, a woman, at the center of revelation. I would argue, though, that the Kumina approach to incarnation and the cross emphasizes the connection between women and divine revelation and offers even more promising antisexist symbols and concrete practices for a liberating and inclusive understanding of revelation, not only because women's bodies are hosts of the incarnation but also because any number of divine personalities manifested in human form are female. Furthermore, at the most elemental level, the incarnational focus in the Kumina tradition is a protest against any glorification of female suffering.

For example, because women are the keepers of the Kumina culture and of its esoteric meaning and religious rituals, Kumina queens are rendered unwavering respect within their communities for their multiple roles as psychologist, doctor, priest, and judge. Kumina queens take on tremendous responsibility for managing and facilitating harmony and well-being in their communities as they serve people from diverse backgrounds and regions of the country. One must demonstrate a peculiar sensibility pertaining to both the visible and invisible world domains to ascend to the rank of Kumina queen.

The female leadership in Kumina is well established. Women are not symbolic figureheads; they are active participants along with other women and men in the worshiping community. Women are visible in Kumina because the community's faith testimony is dramatized through their bodies. Theirs is a carnal rather than ideational testimony, which is experienced in the community's spiritual embrace of sensuality in prepossession dance, in the rhythms of drums, in the hyperbolized circular motion of bodies,[74] in the hands that sacrifice and anoint, and in the hands that rub medicines on the bodies of the sick and troubled. These are all aspects of embodied testimony from which one can derive important resources for womanist theological reflection. Indeed, Kumina's ritual focus on possession trance invites the womanist theologian to investigate the meaning of revelation, incarnation, and the cross in African-derived religions and underscores existing womanist/feminist critiques of those doctrines in the Western Christian tradition. Thus Kumina women's embodied spirituality emerges as a source for a theological interpretation of the cross as a fixation upon temporal well-being in Kumina and other African-derived religions.

In saying this, I actually see alternative approaches to human suffering, liberation, and revelation in the religious practices of Kumina tradition, which can address formidable concerns of both feminist and womanist theologies. Although Mary Daly writes from a White North American perspective, her scrutiny of traditional Christology is relevant to issues of oppression, survival, and liberation in womanist theology and corresponds with the religious practices of women in African-derived religions such as Kumina, Orisha/Yoruba, Vodun, and Candomblé. Daly contests the Christian teaching that the redemptive revelation of God occurred as a specific and unique, unrepeatable historical event. She contends that the idea that Jesus, a first-century Jewish man, was the Incarnation of God and therefore is the redemptive Christ, coupled with sexist Christological doctrines, is undeniably detrimental to women's liberation. Daly also opposes the tendency in Christian theology to hail Jesus, the sacrificial scapegoat, as a role model that women should emulate.[75]

Along similar lines, Delores Williams critiques traditional atonement theories as oppressive for Black women, who have been taught to ritually identify their surrogate experiences of sacrifice and suffering with Jesus' redemptive death on the cross. Although Williams turns away from the cross and toward Jesus' ministry for affirming examples of redemptive living, her critique of the cross and reconstruction of redemption does not address the problem of special revelation. Womanist theologians across the board have neglected to engage this doctrine, even when their evaluations of normative Christian traditions would logically necessitate a rejection of special revelation. For example, in one of her early essays on womanist Christology. Jacquelyn Grant is scathingly critical of the colonial missionary project. Nevertheless, she does not make the obvious link between the missionary enterprise and the doctrine of special revelation when she writes, "In the area of foreign missions...conversion to Christianity implicitly meant deculturalization and acceptance of the western value system on the part of Asians, Africans, and Latin Americans. Upon conversion, one had to withdraw from indigenous ways of imaging the divine reality."[76]

Through her prose and fiction, Alice Walker, who coined the term *womanist* in 1983, undoubtedly suggests that any thorough womanist treatment of Black female oppression must entail a critical assessment of Christianity as a tool of colonialism that has sponsored the centuries-long demonization of African and other non-Christian religious cultures. Walker, who is not a professional theologian, has been more forthright than any womanist theologian in addressing this theological problem on multiple levels in her works.[77] It may be that Christian systematic theological reflection is too much an exercise of apologetics to encourage this type of deconstruction. A comparative theological approach on the other hand would allow womanist theologians to examine non-Christian religious traditions as resources for theological reflection. For example, with regard to special revelation, Kumina women's spirituality of recurring incarnation offers a corrective to this theological conundrum as it implies an understanding of divine revelation that is expansive and inclusive. Devotees experience this in both tangible and symbolic ways.

In Kumina culture, God is African, the Ancestors are African, and they belong to the spirituality of Africa and the African diaspora. In the words of Imogene Kennedy: "Kumina, is just direc African kulcha, yuh know—di African kulcha. But yuh see, in dem tradition, dey say Kumina. Yuh understand? but di direc ting is African kulcha. Kumina now, dem jus put di Kumina but is African, is dy-rec African kulcha, cause wi a African children."[78]

In Kumina ceremonies, Kumina devotees do not venerate the same deities and ancestors as those venerated in the White Christian tradition, and they do not have to engage in exercises of hermeneutical gymnastics to convince themselves that Christ is *really* Black and not White or that women can be hosts of divine power. In other words, Kumina provides an alternative approach to divine power for women like Celie in *The Color Purple,* who cannot reimagine God without whiteness or maleness because, as Celie says, "[H]e been there so long, he don't want to budge."[79]

The presence of African-derived religions in the Americas and the Caribbean demonstrates that some religious communities resisted Euro-Christian domination and the cooptation of their images of the Divine under the ubiquitous image of Jesus Christ as the only valid divine revelation. Kumina women's religious experience, then, contests Christian exclusivism, especially in terms of the doctrine of special revelation.[80] This is crucial for women of African descent because generations of European Christian authorities found justification in the doctrine of special revelation to support their exclusion of women from positions of leadership and authority in Christian churches and to anchor their condemnation of non-Christian religions, which do not recognize Jesus as the redemptive revelation of God.

The Christian perspective that the doctrine of special revelation necessitates the condemnation of African-derived religions and religious practices has also become normative for many African

American and Caribbean Christians, who have uncritically accepted traditional European and Euro-American standards for evaluating Black religious experience. This condemnation intensifies the poverty and exploitation of female practitioners of African-derived religions because they are Black and female and because they partake in repressed religions that lack the cultural capital required for uncensored expression, progressive development, and public approval. This type of anti-Africanness or devaluation of African-derived religions is another facet of Black women's anthropological impoverishment.

Practitioners of African-derived religions, such as Kumina, Yoruba/Orisha, and Vodun, do not conceive of humans as being in need of any special redemption or salvation from some intrinsic depraved condition. They understand the human experience as susceptible to chaos, misfortune, disease, and ill will, and their religions are oriented toward identifying and overcoming the specific problems that compromise human fulfillment, well-being, and abundant life.

Cross-bearing is a Kumina ritual practice that validates women's bodies as capable of representing the Divine and exposes divine incarnation as a recurring event in human experience. And yet the "cross-bearing" women of the Kumina community serve as only one of many examples where women are reinforcing classical African ideas that affirm the value of meaningful life on earth. Taken as a whole, their spirituality directly challenges prevailing Christian beliefs that are oppressive to women of African descent while institutionalizing praxes of female empowerment and authority within the structures of African-derived religions.

In African-derived religions, the theology of the cross is a theology of the eternal manifestation of incarnation and can be understood as an emancipatory theology as it relates to the restoration of well-being (social, personal, spiritual, physical, material, political, and so on). This theology then invalidates the endurance of suffering as a spiritual quality favored by the Divine Community and stresses instead the Divine Community's role in addressing suffering. The political imperatives in Kumina and Revival Zion are not as explicitly stated as they are in Rastafari. However, it is instructive to recall the Myal/Native Baptist heritage of Revival Zion, which nurtured a political practice of militancy during the period of enslavement, contributing significantly to emancipation in the British West Indies.

In addition, the Paul Bogle Rebellion of 1865 is a pivotal event that may demonstrate, in the long run, a militant political strain in Kumina and Revival Zion. It might also prove to be a historical moment of intense collaboration among Native Baptists, Zionists, and Kumina communities. The socioeconomic context of the rebellion—increased labor exploitation in the face of growing economic decline—was mirrored in other parishes in the island. Yet the rebellion occurred after two decades of the receptive/liberated African indentured-labor program in Jamaica. The year 1865 basically marked the final stage of more than twenty years of BaKongo (Central African) resettlement in Jamaica. The rebellion occurred four years after the end of the Great Revival, which gave birth to Revival Zion, a novel form of traditional African Myalism, and Native Baptist Christian Myalism. The rebellion also occurred in the parish of St. Thomas where most BaKongo (Kumina practitioners) worked as indentured laborers.[81] Monica Schiller maintains. "The voice of revival, because it partook of the Myal tradition, could also be revolutionary," as militant literature pertaining to the social oppression of the "Sons and Daughters of Africa" and their "day of deliverance" emerged from Revival circles in western Jamaica.[82] Schuler concludes, however, that the Native Baptist and Revival Zion traditions provided religious inspiration for the Bogle rebellion without the involvement of BaKongo Kumina practitioners. Schuler describes the social context in St. Thomas as one where the Black creole population and BaKongo African indentured laborers had different responses to the changing economy. BaKongo indentured laborers, whose livelihoods depended upon maintaining positions on the estates where they worked, were less likely to take part in a revolt that would jeopardize job security. Although Schuler admits that at least one BaKongo African was involved with the Bogle Rebellion, she notes that there are still a number of oral narratives that tell of African immigrants who, although they were not involved, were implicated as insurgents and brutally punished in the aftermath of the revolt.[83]

Today, Kumina practitioners have a strong attachment to the Bogle Rebellion and claim Paul Bogle as an Ancestor with whom they interact.[84] Kumina bands also commemorate the event with yearly celebrations in Morant Bay. It is possible that the Bogle Rebellion might have been (or might have provided) the context for a cross-fertilization and collaboration among Native Baptists, Revival Zionists, and Kumina practitioners. Is it plausible that Myal was introduced to Kumina during religious meetings that gave inspiration to the up-risers?

It will take more research before any conclusive statements can be made about the relationship between the Bogle Rebellion and the Revival Zion and Kumina religious traditions. What can be acknowledged now, however, is the pledge of solidarity that occurs among practitioners of the Revival Zion, Kumina, and Rasta religions. This was constantly affirmed during my field research in Jamaica. As one Zionist, Sister BT, said in response to my question about how she, as a Zionist, feels about Rastafari, "[D]en dem a no Zion too! Ahll a we a wan!"[85] Similarly, on another occasion, just before I was leaving the island to return to the United States, a Kumina informant told me about an important meeting that was to occur between some "Rasta bredren" and her Kumina bands. The meeting was called to discuss socioeconomic issues in the aftermath of the dosing of one of Jamaica's national banks. Many Jamaicans, especially the poor, lost money in the process and had not been compensated. The agenda for the meeting was to organize protest groups and to plan strategies for collecting the money that was "robbed from the people." She went on to relate the plight of African Jamaicans to that of Africans on the continent and proclaimed that if Nelson Mandela called for an army of protesters for the struggle in South Africa, she could fill two airplanes with people ready to fight.[86]

The potential for sociopolitical praxis is so strong in the Kumina tradition because of its approach to human fulfillment and well-being and its explicit memory of African oppression in Jamaica. Since all of life is integrated and complementary, well-being is threatened if any aspect of life is jeopardized. In Kumina culture, there is no moral tension between the spiritual and the political. It might well be the case that some of the ripest ears for a Caribbean theology of liberation are to be found not only among the valiant male populations of Rastafari groups but also among female devotees across the Kumina communities.

The female voice is prevalent in Kumina leadership and appears to have been more prevalent in Zion traditions that met in balmyards as opposed to church structures.[87] For reasons not altogether known, women have by and large secured the posts of authority in Kumina. Unlike the Rastafari, who are suspicious of women's power. Kumina institutionalizes (1) the nurturing of Black female agency; (2) the empowerment of Black women as official leaders and teachers of their religious traditions; and (3) divine revelation via incarnation in female bodies as a recurring event. Support for female authority is evident in other African religious cultures of the Caribbean and the Americas as well.[88]

African religious practitioners in Jamaica's past and present appear to experience the incarnated Ancestors/spirit messengers/African political messiah (Haile Selassie) as a liminal gateway where humans meet divine emancipatory power. For Kumina devotees, the significance of the Ancestors is especially felt in the sign of the cross and is respected by their Revival Zion compatriots. Ancestral visitation through Myal possession forges a spiritual connection between present-day practitioners of Kumina and the enslaved Africans whose indigenous Pan-African religion was Myal. The diverse expressions of African-derived religions in Jamaica show that the Ancestors,[89] incarnation, and the cross of alleviated suffering are the center of African-Jamaican spirituality, *not* Jesus and Christology.

I think it is important at this juncture to emphasize that this spiritual orientation (the African sign of the cross) carries tremendous weight in shaping the cultural, psychological, and political dispositions of African religious practitioners across multiple traditions and social contexts. I imagine the crossroads as an apposite theological concept, layered with meanings from which African and African-Caribbean/American scholars may extrapolate resources for constructive theologies of liberation. The Yoruba and Vodun traditions have a wealth of material on this subject, including textual, iconic, and performative resources. Both traditions honor Esu-Elegba (also known as Eshu, Elegba, Legba, or Ellegua), the manifestation of the Divine as the guardian of the crossroads. Esu-Elegba is said to "open and close doors." He is the Deity who opens the doors of communication between humans and all other manifestations of divinity. Esu is the messenger of the deities. He is also the cunning trickster who, along with the Akan Ananse, became reconstituted in the personalities of Brer Rabbit[90] and Anancy the Spider.[91] This archetypal trickster Deity, the source of communication between the invisible and the visible, is the cross-bearer. Thus, when practitioners of Yoruba-based religions open ceremonies, they salute and pour libation first for Esu-Elegbara to petition for Orisha blessings in the form of divine possession—the crossroads (+).

Having examined the prominent sites and scenes of African people's religious journey in Jamaica, I pause at what I consider to be the crossroads between the social scientific documentation of African religious traditions in Jamaica and the history of theological commentary on African-Jamaican religious experience to interrogate the problems and concerns that will have impact upon my own theological prescriptions in the final chapter. One issue is the persistence of anthropological poverty in the African-Jamaican experience and its impact upon the multiple expressions of African-derived religions. Consequently, in the following sections, I aim to critically evaluate Jamaica's African religious inheritance with a focus upon external factors that have obscured our present understanding of this inheritance, invalidated its life-giving focus, discounted its integrity as a legitimate cultural contribution to Caribbean civilization, and exacerbated the multidimensional impoverishment of African practitioners. It is my view that the Afrophobic and anti-African perspectives, so deeply embedded within the Jamaican intellectual and popular imaginations, have cast a wide shadow over the range of conversations among theological scholars. Only by traversing this ideological crossroads can we attempt to engage in theological discourse that is critical, constructive, and prophetic in Jamaica and in the wider Caribbean.

African-Jamaican Religious Traditions: Ambiguous Sources, Sources of Ambiguity

African-Jamaican religions have managed to come through fires of persecution and condemnation. They are survivors of colonial Christian anti-Africanness and Afrophobia.[92] However, African-derived religions have been bruised and burned by manifestations of anti-Africanness, first in European missionary Christianity and later in the anti-Africanness of African-Jamaican Christianity.[93]

Within Jamaica, the context of enslavement and Christian evangelism compelled African religions to operate underground, clandestinely beyond the inspection of the White gaze. Yet with each opportunity for social toleration, Myalists emerged with their agenda, appropriating and adapting Christian sources to suit their moral imperatives and religious predilections. Myalists were selective appropriators and independent interpreters of Christian sources. For Native Baptists, John the Baptist was more appealing to the Myal personality than was Jesus. In John, Africans saw an archetypal forest or water priest, empowered by the Creator Deity[94] to consecrate Jesus' mission. As Chevannes notes:

The Africans took rapidly and in large numbers to the new religion, but in doing so absorbed it into the Myal framework. African water rituals resurfaced in Christian baptism and missionaries had to wage theological battle to convince the people that John the Baptist was not greater than Jesus and should not be worshipped.[95]

William Wedenoja adds: "Myalist syncretisms, such as use of the Bible for protection from spirits and a pantheon of Christian figures—John the Baptist, the disciples, prophets, and angels—who replaced African gods in name but not in form or function, were incorporated into Revival."[96]

For Myalists, the Christian Bible was a symbolic text with infinite hermeneutical potential. African-Jamaican appropriations of biblical symbols offer concrete examples to validate Paul Ricoeur's assertion that texts have a surplus of meaning.[97] In honoring John the Baptist as the (biblically legitimate) priest of the water deities, they were honoring and preserving classical African theological beliefs and practices. The Native Baptist (Myal) affinity for John the Baptist was probably inspired by a Pan-African understanding that the natural elements (water, air, earth, fire) are invested with spiritual/mystical power.

The personality of John the Baptist has not lost significance for contemporary Revivalists and Kumina devotees. During my research among the two groups, several informants made reference to John the Baptist as an anointed prophet and spirit messenger. The centrality of John the Baptist in these traditions is evidence that the Native Baptist (Myal) religion is the progenitor of the Revival Zion religion.

Monica Schuler's persuasive analysis of the transformative moments in Myal evolution and the rich interaction between Myal traditions and Kumina is also pertinent. Her interpretation of African-Jamaican religious formation punctuates my view that the encounter between African-derived religions (Obeah and Myal) and Christianity was in large part an exercise in an African-oriented hermeneutics giving birth to more African-centered religions (Rasta and Revival Zion). Schuler writes:

Myalists extracted and emphasized two central elements of the Baptist faith—the inspiration of the Holy Spirit, and baptism, in the manner of John the Baptist, by immersion—because they seemed to correspond with beliefs or symbols already familiar to them. Some members actually referred to their church as John the Baptist's Church. The leaders developed a technique for attaining possession by the Holy Spirit and "dreams" experienced in this state were crucial to a candidate's acceptance for baptism. Without them they could not be born again, "either by water or the Spirit." The Myalist emphasis on ritual immersion by water may be understood better by a comparison with beliefs of twentieth-century Kumina adherents (descendants of nineteenth-century Central African immigrants) concerning baptism. Kumina members profess a special attachment to Baptists and Revivalists who practice baptism by immersion in the river because the river is the house of African spirits who they believe protect Baptists and Revivalists as they do Kumina devotees. In addition, Kumina members deliberately seek Christian baptism for their children because the ritual is believed to provide the protection of a powerful spirit—the one the Christians call the Holy Spirit. The Afro-Jamaican religious tradition, then, has consistently reinterpreted Christianity in African, not European, cultural terms.[98]

The ambiguity surrounding the multiple expressions of African-derived religions in Jamaica is directly related to their subjugated and marginal status in Jamaican history. We know most about Rastafari because it has a received tradition of literature and songs (organic theology and hymns). In addition, since the 1990s, Rastas have garnered wider sympathy and even social acceptance from a number of Christian compatriots.

Kumina and Revival Zion. however, are oral-based traditions. They are yet to be accepted by the wider Christian community as legitimate sacred traditions. Thus most Jamaicans have an investment in remaining culturally distant from Kumina and Revival Zion traditions. Indeed too many are more culturally distant from their native religions, Kumina and Revival Zion, than they are from the imported religions and theologies of White North American Christian fundamentalists—Jimmy Swaggart, Oral Roberts, Jim Bakker, and the like.[99]

In the end, even with all of the unsolved puzzles pertaining to the intersecting roads among the African-derived religions in Jamaica, after worshiping with and interviewing the Revival Zionists, Kumina practitioners, and Rastas, I can assert without hesitation that these religious communities share a collective consciousness of the African-Jamaican struggle against anthropological poverty (the censoring and vilification of things and peoples African) in the forms of Afrophobia and anti-Africanness.[100] They also demonstrate religious sympathy and solidarity for the spiritual values and cultural and political consciousness represented in varied configurations within each tradition. Their ethical principle of religious solidarity is derived from shared theological assumptions about divine power, humanity, and human destiny. More than anything, the Rastas, Revival Zionists, and Kumina practitioners together recover and re-member subjugated knowledges derived from the collective African-Jamaican struggle to ensure freedom and well-being through religious autonomy and spiritual agency. Together these traditions present a strong case for continued reflection upon the meaning of Africa in the African diaspora. Suppose, for instance, we said that in the past we had no convincing reason to introduce the category "African religion" in the continental context, due to religious distinctions that can dearly be drawn along ethnic, clan, or regional lines. However, a study of African-Jamaican religions shows that, in the African diaspora. Black religious formation within the acculturating rubric of Pan-Africanization introduces a new logic for outlining composite features of what we may call denominations of African religion or African-derived religion in the Jamaican context. Over the centuries, the apparently slippery and elastic margins of the various traditions, as they have encountered and traded resources within their informal institutional structures, have actually served to protect them from the policing structures of the colonial state, proving the resiliency of the Obeah-Myal religious framework as a tool of subversion even into the twenty-first century.

Externally Imposed Anthropological Poverty: The Stigmatization, Marginalization, and Exoticization of Practitioners of African-Derived Religious Traditions

The thing with any tradition is how it is used. If you use it for good you will get good; if you use it for evil you will get evil.[101]

Before proceeding any further, I must give a description of the *obeahman*. He is the agent *incarnate* of Satan. The *Simon Magnus* of these good gospel days; the embodiment of all that is wicked, immoral and deceptious. You may easily at times distinguish him by his sinister look, and *slouching* gait. An obeahman seldom looks anyone in the face. Generally he is a dirty looking fellow with a sore foot. ... The obeahman is to be feared in the system of poisoning which he carries on. He is well versed in all the vegetable poisons of the island.[102]

The Obeah practitioner, Revival Zionist, Kumina practitioner, and Rasta remember, represent, and are often represented among anthropologically impoverished African Jamaicans who have been divested of land, heritage, language, religious/cultural significance, and the material profit of their labor. Most Jamaicans are of African descent and poor (the legacy of African enslavement and colonialism). In the past, Third World theologians have identified fundamental oppressions that compromise human beauty, dignity, and agency as created by God. As a group, they have decried the manifestations of racism, sexism, colonialism, and classism in the Christian church and in Christian theology. They denounce these social sins as un-Christian abominations before God.

In the Caribbean there is racism, sexism, heterosexism, neocolonialism, classism, and anti-Africanness. Within the African diasporic context, anti-Africanness is not reducible to racism but inclusive of it. Anti-Africanness and Afrophobia concern not only the reality of discrimination against those who have been racialized as Black but the hatred and negation of the origin and heritage of the "Black race." Anti-Africanness is a moral problem for any theology of the African diaspora because it contributes to the multifaceted manifestations of poverty in African diasporic communities.

Historically, practitioners of African-derived religions have been doubly jeopardized when it comes to economic impoverishment and social immobility. It is not accidental that Haiti, the first Black republic in the Western Hemisphere (1801), is today the poorest, stricken with one affliction after another— oppressive regimes, militarism, AIDS, imperialism, and so on. It must also be remembered that Africans in Haiti wrested political control of the island from the French under the leadership of Vodun priests and by the inspiration of Vodun culture. As Western Europe evolved into a Christian civilization, Haiti, by the time of the revolution, had become a Vodun civilization equipped to manage the takeover of the island. In no other place has African religion adopted the character and disposition of a people whose ancestral surname is Exile. Haiti could achieve this as a result of its revolution. Not only was it a successful revolution, it happened early in the exilic period when a critical mass of Africans in the colony demonstrated a collective memory of their continental heritages. And so African culture saturated the horizon of what Haitian culture would become over two centuries and, within the boundaries of sovereignty allotted for rebels, Vodun came to resemble its broken and raging populace, its fierce and unrelenting exiles wrestling with modernity with little more than the tools of slaves.

Put another way, Haiti is poorest because its population is most conspicuously African not solely in terms of culture but also religion. The European and American powers punished Haiti for its show of African determinism. Haiti was immediately isolated from the global economy,[103] and its Vodun civilization has been targeted for derision and condemnation ever since.[104] The Haitian story is the quintessential story of anthropological poverty in the African diaspora. Mveng's notion of anthropological poverty, as depriving Africans of both what they possess and who they are, is well punctuated by René Depestre's reflections on the crisis in Caribbean identity. Depestre asks:

In what way will [Black people] of the Caribbean come to terms with [themselves,] convert [themselves] to what [they are,] find [their] true [selves] in society and in history?...men and women have not yet been able to recover their social character[,] their profound personality, their humanity and beauty which colonization has alienated. Literature and the arts, just as science and education do not meet the immediate and future needs of our people. Our cultures continue to grow to the rhythm of western neocolonialism and lack the possibility of advancing in accordance with their own internal dynamism. With the sole exception of Cuba, the development of our nations is not conceived in terms of a decolonization of the alienating structures of the past. Our islands are victims of malnutrition, underemployment, illiteracy, intellectual underemployment and cultural hibernation.[105]

Most practitioners of African-oriented religions are poor. Their wealth is religiocultural, internally derived, and precapitalistic. Kumina and Revival Zion practitioners are especially impotent when it comes to navigating globalization and its market-driven culture that sustains socioeconomic stratification in Jamaican society. Within Rastafari, however, some individuals have been able to do just this through their involvement with the music industry. All the same, the two parishes most noted for their retention of African cultural traditions, St. Mary and St. Thomas, are also the poorest in the island.

The personal experience of interviewing Imogene Kennedy, for example, led me to raise ethical questions about the dispossessed woman in what might be called "performance" Kumina and the discrepancy between Kumina women's symbolic cultural wealth and their socioeconomic impoverishment within Jamaican society. In 1996, Kennedy was residing in the parish of St. Catherine in a small, squalid, dilapidated three-room shack. Kennedy was the subject of two significant articles on Jamaican Kumina, numerous taped interviews, and several video documentaries.[106] She was also responsible for introducing Edward Seaga, Jamaica's former prime minister, to the lore, music, and esoteric beliefs of Kumina culture.

During several conversations, Kennedy took pride in discussing her conversion from Revivalism to Kumina, which took place in the hollow base of a silk cotton tree when she was a young girl growing up in the parish of St. Thomas. There, for twenty-one days, the *Nkuyu* (Ancestors) taught her the "African" language and lore of Kumina. Kennedy reported that, during his tenure as Jamaica's first chief minister (1950s), Alexander Bustamante sponsored her relocation from Dalvey, St. Thomas to Kingston after her drums had been destroyed by local police during a Kumina ceremony.[107] "Jamaica treat African people-dem bad.... Dem treat we bad, man," Kennedy complained in a frail voice.[108] Confronted at once with the paradox of her prestige and deprivation, it was obvious that the decades of struggle against religious and cultural annihilation had taken their toll on her body and spirit. As she approached seventy, her pronounced impoverishment belied her public reputation as the famous "Miss Queenie," whom the Jamaican political leadership had displayed so proudly at government-sponsored Kumina competitions, presidential inaugurations, international "folk dance" competitions, National Heritage Weeks, and Devon House's[109] Friday night entertainment spots.[110]

Kennedy, with virtually no material possessions, had prize possessions— trophies, certificates, ribbons, and awards—to document her long journey as a Kumina exhibitionist. The quintessential symbol of the ironic joke Jamaica had played on her was her certificate of the Order of Distinction, which she received under Edward Seaga's administration on January 8, 1983. The Order of Distinction is one of the highest honors annually bestowed upon select Jamaican citizens for their distinguished service to the nation.[111] The point made is not one of discredit. One could argue that Kennedy deserved the honor after bringing visibility to a tradition that was subjugated and rendered invisible by the wider Jamaican society. For several centuries, the exotic mystique commonly associated with the tradition of exhibiting African peoples (especially women's bodies) and African religious cultures has no doubt facilitated the visibility of the marginalized and the colonized among large populations through museum displays, international world fairs, and the performing arts.[112] A womanist assessment of power, gender, and religion, however, contests the exhibition of African religious cultures through women's bodies.

Womanist theological method involves multidimensional analysis of oppression, religiocultural analysis, a sociopolitical analysis of wholeness, and bifocal analysis.[113] Each of these provides an important basis from which to critique performance Kumina as a colonial script that manufactures a reified notion of African religion in popular Jamaican thought. The collective work of womanist theologians suggests that womanist analysis of religion seeks to understand it as a product of culture. Thus, womanists insist that consistent critique of sociocultural traditions is a necessary task when attempting to analyze Black women's multidimensional oppression.

Because womanist theology is concerned about the liberation of Black communities, the principle of wholeness ensures that womanist sociopolitical analysis considers communal dynamics, but not at the expense of Black women's liberation. Wholeness compels womanist theologians to critically examine and respond to specific manifestations of oppression in a given Black community without prioritizing one manifestation over another. Furthermore, womanist theologians are bifocally critical of both external oppressive forces in the dominant society and internal oppression perpetuated within Black communities.

This womanist leaning toward intersectional analysis renders performance Kumina a complicated site of Caribbean cultural production that obscures Kumina's complex African religious foundations and women's mastery of its philosophical, theological and pharmacological system of thought and communl care. When *Kumina* and other African cultural practices are showcased in invented contexts of entertainment and cultural enrichment, their dignity and sanctity are compromised for an exotic visibility and cheap public recognition,[114] It is in this role, and this role only, that *Kumina* queens have found widespread yet compromised visibility in the larger society, which customarily seeks cultural and theological distance from much of what they represent. The festival venue in which Kumina is performed as a dance provides no opportunity for national reflection on Kumina's contribution to the making of African-Jamaican civilization.

Maureen Warner-Lewis, one of the first scholars to interview Kennedy, penned her thoughts about the underestimated resilience of the Kumina tradition, which has survived within a wider culture of hostility, and its import to reshaping the colonized consciousness of the Jamaican people. According to Warner-Lewis:

> [G]roups like Miss Queenie's kumina "bands" attempt to preserve a sense of historical continuity through spiritual and cultural means. At every kumina dance, each time an ancestral *nkuyu* possesses a devotee, this continuity is re-enacted. One wonders at the sense of purpose that could be unleashed in the West Indian people, if either through spiritual or secular means, or both, a sense of participation in a long historical process could be fostered. Despite its comparatively short existence in Jamaica, it is a miracle that kumina continues to flourish. It represents even more of a miracle of positive survival when one considers that this religion lives on, in the face of its non-visibility for so many in the total society, or indifference on the part of some, or scorn and disparagement from others. It is in fact a credit to the persistence of that traditional African awareness of the past as symbolized through the ancestors.[115]

The principal role of government organizations and initiatives in establishing performance Kumina as a permanent fixture of postindependence Jamaican nationhood cannot go unnoticed. No government official can take more credit for the evolution of a national agenda to recognize Jamaica's African cultural inheritance than former prime minister, Edward Seaga. Stemming in part from his ethnographic research on African-Jamaican religious cultures, Seaga's direct interest in exposing and celebrating Kumina and Revival Zion distinguishes him from other Jamaican heads of state.

Although Seaga is credited for bringing some legitimacy to Kumina and Revival Zion in the eyes of Jamaican Christians, his emphasis upon promoting African religious traditions as staged public ceremonies has reinforced the trivialization of African-based religions as "folk culture." Thus, despite their periodic appearances before the Jamaican public, African-derived religions remain peripheral in the Jamaican collective consciousness where status is given to Christianity as a national religion and as the foundation of respectable culture. Seaga's contribution to African religious communities then is limited by the very contradictions in his approach to them. Entertaining performances of African religious practices in staged competitions, coupled with the distribution of champion ribbons and certificates, are, in the end, dramatic displays of Jamaican social stratification and colonialist consciousness. The negligible economic compensation offered to performers especially suggests that the Jamaican government's reductionist treatment of African-derived religion is no less than a recolonization of an imagined and symbolic "Africa," one that must be viewed as self-imposed if it is to be overcome in the future.

In his capacity as prime minister, Seaga missed a considerable opportunity to shape Jamaica's demonstration of national solidarity with practitioners of African-derived religions. A more productive initiative could entail the future investment of government funds and intellectual resources within African-based communities toward the development of local religious and cultural projects. This might prove to be much more valuable than performance-oriented initiatives of the past in promoting sustainable formalization and institutionalization of African-derived religious cultures in Jamaica.

Moreover, it could stimulate a respectful interest in and engagement with African-derived religious cultures like Kumina among the wider Jamaican citizenry. The Kumina queens I interviewed in 1996 lamented their plight as poor people with no resources to institutionalize and monitor the preservation of their culture. They have dreams of building Kumina schools where the "African" language can be taught systematically to each generation. They also expressed the desire to hold formal sessions on Kumina herbalism, spirituality, and theology.[116]

Government agencies such as the African Caribbean Institute of Jamaica and the Jamaica Cultural Development Commission have worked tirelessly to document and expose Kumina and other African-Jamaican cultural traditions, yet little has been done to support the formal institutionalization of African-derived religions in their local contexts. Only when this takes place can outsiders encounter Kumina and other religious traditions in their natural environment, where practitioners, especially women, maintain authority and credibility in transmitting knowledge about their traditions to the general public. Through deeper exchanges between Kumina practitioners and the outside world, we might discover that Kumina religious thought can, as Warner-Lewis suggests, "unleash" "a sense of purpose" and "foster" "a sense of participation in a long historical process" within the collective body of Jamaicans.

To the average Jamaican Christian, encountering Kumina culture outside of contrived settings would be a reach knowing that the repercussions for identifying with things and peoples African are still unbearable, even with 170 years of distance from enslavement. Thus, most Jamaicans would exempt themselves from Banbury's remark that [s]uperstition, the belief in magic, witchcraft, the active intervention of ghostly or diabolic forces in the world of nature and the lives of men is surprisingly strong [in Jamaica]. It is of African origin but goes up the social scale much farther than one would expect."[117] African Jamaicans have learned the hard way that African religion and culture are incompatible with social status. Yet. while they publicly opt for the latter, the onset of crises or insurmountable tragedy sends many Jamaicans "down" the social scale to privately seek effective remedies from the former.

The African Religious Heritage: The Permanent Scapegoat for Evil and Pathology?

To many the word "religion" suggests, at first, something pertaining to the sacred, pious, or good life. Most would like to think that religion and evil are mutually exclusive, yet so much evil is committed by humans in the name of religion—*all* religions. Among the religions of the world, African religions and their diasporic derivatives have become the permanent scapegoat for evil and pathology. One would be hard-pressed to find sympathetic depictions of African-derived religions in Christian literature and lore or in popular Western culture from the period of African enslavement to the present day. Instead, one discovers the unmitigated vilification of Vodun, that is, "Voodoo," Yoruba, Kumina, and other African-derived religions in the Caribbean and the Americas. The stories about human sacrifice, cannibalism, zombification, sticking pins in dolls, and the like[118] have had definitive authority in rendering African-derived practitioners powerless to call the names of their deities; incapable of identifying the ideals, gifts, and life-sustaining potential within their traditions; and often defenseless against the condemnation of the worlds in which they find themselves.

Furthermore, the exoticization and mystification of the "evil" associated with African-derived religions induces Afrophobia, the most intense fear of and disdain for anything produced on the "dark" and "savage" continent. Indeed I have discussed in earlier chapters the African belief in mystical power, its omnipresence, and its moral and immoral appropriations by humans. Mystical power is *potentially* injurious. The enduring question is: why should *mystical* power be more feared and contested than *concrete* power? Aware of this mystical baggage of evil that attends the very word *Africa,* I have attempted to present African-derived religions from the starring point that they are life-giving traditions that nurture hospitable relations, life over disease and extinction, and the pursuit of freedom.

Perhaps I have betrayed the common expectation that the study of African-derived religions necessarily discloses something sinister and intolerable. The African-centered perspective finds nothing sinister or intolerable about Africans rebelling against those who kidnap, torture, and enslave them, nor does if see anything sinister about the movement of ancestral spirits and deities among African people in response to their petitions for help and protection.

Joseph Murphy also refuses to whet the general public's insatiable appetite for the antipathetic presentation of African religions. In his publication *Working the Spirit: Ceremonies of the African Diaspora,* Murphy prefaces his study with the following commentary:

> One of the highest hurdles to overcome in interpreting diasporan traditions to outsiders is the deep-seated popular image of them as "voodoo," malign "black magic." Hundreds of books and scores of films have portrayed the spirituality of millions of people of African descent as crazed, depraved, or demonic manipulations of gullible and irrational people. These images have their origin in the French colonial reaction to the revolt of Haitian slaves whose motive in liberating themselves from grinding and brutal enslavement was thought to rest in *vaudoux*. The success of the Haitian revolution sent shock waves through the white world that are still being felt today. I think that the relegation of "voodoo" to the horror genre reflects mass America's real horror of independent black power. If voodoo was powerful enough to free the slaves, might it not free their descendants?[119]

We should not think that Murphy is overstating the point. If Hesketh Bell's remarks about Haiti, almost a century after the Haitian Revolution, reflect the sentiments of his White contemporaries, we see how White people's commitment to anti-Africanness was harnessed into an ideology and, even worse, a presupposition. Bell writes:

> The [Haitian] monarchy did not last long, and was soon replaced by a republic; tumults and bloodshed were of constant recurrence. The negroes, jealous of the mulattoes, massacred or banished all the latter, and up to the present moment this beautiful island is constantly the scene of revolution and bloodshed, and the Haytians are frequently being called on to pay heavy indemnities to foreign traders and others for the damage done to their property in these constantly recurring riots. As may be expected civilization among the lower classes of Haytians is not very advanced, especially in the interior, where the authority of the Government is even less than nominal. Dreadful accounts reach us of thousands of negroes having gone back to a perfectly savage life in the woods, going about stark naked, and having replaced the Christian religion by Voodooism and fetish worship. Cases of cannibalism have even been reported, and nowhere in the West Indies has Obeah a more tenacious hold over high and low than in Hayti. Such a shocking state of affairs cannot be allowed to continue long, and covetous eyes are cast towards Hayti by more than one of the great powers.[120]

Bell's disdain for Haiti was indeed shared by Whites throughout the Americas, the Caribbean, and Europe. And Murphy is right: such disdain was and continues to be sparked by White people's "horror of independent black power." As demonstrated by Bell's comment, Whites have interpreted African religious and political power as a threat to international security. Thus Bell suggests Euro-imperialism (the forces of the "great powers") as the appropriate antidote for Haiti's "irreligion" and "barbarism." Against this established White portrait of Haiti and Vodun (or "Voodoo," which became the generic term for African-derived religions in the Caribbean and the Americas), we should not be shocked by Murphy's confession:

> Whenever I present this liberating view of diasporan traditions I will be reminded that there are genuine practices of malign sorcery within them. Yet I have grown tired of answering calls to present the less-salutary dimensions of diasporan spirituality in the interests of "balance." I take it for granted that peoples of African descent are as venal as anyone else, and charlatans and spiritual sadists might be readily located among them. I see my task in presenting the traditions to outsiders as practitioners might wish them to be presented, concentrating on the spiritual depth and beauty that practitioners find. As this spirituality is almost never reported by outsiders, this book may be a corrective toward a "balanced" view.[121]

The ultimate tragedy is that, as a general rule, African-Caribbean populations, having come under the influence of White Christian culture, perpetuate Afrophobic and anti-African ideas and attitudes regarding African-derived religious traditions. For example, in 1984 the African-Caribbean Institute of Jamaica sponsored a televised presentation of a Kumina ceremony in celebration of Jamaica's annual Heritage Week. During a taped interview (September 1996) the organizer of the program, Hazel Ramsay, recalled the general public's response to the presentation:

> We presented everything on the television. The drumming and the spirit possession and even the chicken sacrifice. I don't think I have recovered, after all these years, from the onslaught of negative responses we received after the program aired. People said we were an embarrassment—that we were promoting devil worship and heathenism. The Jamaican people were not ready to receive their own heritage—the very spirituality of people who live just beyond their own back yards.... It was devastating to experience.[122]

During formal interviews and informal conversations with Jamaican studies scholars, the theme of Black anti-Africanness constantly surfaces as an obstacle.[123] In fact, I believe that I was able to secure an audience with Edward Seaga due to familial connections. When sitting before him, he questioned me quite aggressively, attempting to understand my purpose in undertaking research on African-derived religions, especially as a theological student. He assumed that I approached the subject with a confessional Christian bias and that my aim was to discredit the traditions from that Afrophobic location. Even White researchers have noted the pejorative views that Blacks hold about African religion and culture. For example, Laura Tanna conducted research on Jamaican folk songs and stories in eight parishes in the island. She recalled, "The Nago people, Yoruba descendants, lived in the village of Abeokuta in Westmoreland and were *one of the few* enclaves of immigrants who took pride in preserving their African culture."[124] Tanna, a White North American, also recounted an incident involving a man in Abeokuta, Jamaica, who was present when his compatriot agreed to sing folk songs and tell folk stories while being taped. "[J]ust as we were about to set up the tape recorder," Tanna writes, "the second farmer began to complain loudly about Whites exploiting the people and coming to make them look like monkeys."[125]

While Black anti-Africanness is alive and well in Jamaica, the truth is that it is Euro-derived. It did not emerge from practitioners of African religions but from the legacy of White Christian culture in Jamaica. The terminology used by contemporary Jamaicans to categorize Kumina practitioners, Revival Zionists, and Obeah practitioners is not African-derived. Rather, it was scripted into Jamaican cultural narratives by White traders, missionaries, and enslavers.

A critical evaluation of the extension of this Eurocentric, Afrophobic, and anti-African consciousness to diasporic Black thought and behavior in the Caribbean and the Americas invites one to consider which evil is worse: the nebulous mystical evil of the African antisocializer[126] or the concretized evil— enslavement, torture, murder, neocolonialism, and so on—historically perpetrated against Africans by Europeans. Somehow, the evil committed against African peoples by White missionaries, enslavers, and colonial authorities has been rationalized as a justified means to the righteous end of Christianizing African heathens and has managed to evade the notorious reputation automatically associated with Obeah and Kumina. White Christian evil appears less hazardous than African Obeah evil.

It is important to critique the intentional manipulation of human dependency upon religious ideas and beliefs as a dimension of human behavior in all religious systems. African religions, like all religions, offer their leaders opportunities to capitalize on the beliefs, fears, and anxieties of their adherents. However, African religions are often scapegoated as predisposed toward the abuse of power when compared with Christianity, where the evils committed by White Christians and their sustained impact on diasporic Africans are ignored,[127] justified, or excused as anomalous acts of morally corrupt individuals. For example, from the idea's inception, invested parties could not discuss the prospect of transporting indentured laborers to the British West Indies without somehow linking it to anti-African sentiments about African religion and culture. In deliberating on the pros and cons of endorsing the plan, Lord John Russell, the British secretary of state for the colonies, concluded:

> [T]he establishment of a regular intercourse between Africa and the West Indies, will tend greatly, not only to the prosperity of the British West Indian possessions, but likewise to the civilisation of Africa. A new epoch has arrived for the African race. We have in the West Indies 800,000 Negroes, of whom perhaps three fourths are Christians in the enjoyment of practical freedom, of means of education and of physical comfort to a very high degree. There is no reason to suppose that their advances in wealth, knowledge and religious improvements may not be in proportion to the most hopeful anticipations. Nothing like this state of Society exists among the African race elsewhere. In Heyti there is a very low standard of government and Civilisation; in Cuba, in Brazil, and in the United States, slavery; in Africa, slavery, human sacrifices and the most degrading superstitions.[128]

African exposure to Euro-Christian culture emerges time and again in Jamaican history as the end that always justifies the means. In the case of indentured African laborers, the means were so treacherous and degrading it is no small wonder that Kumina culture is one of the most expressive memory sites of African enslavement in Jamaica.

The very fact that Myal is of marginal significance to the average Jamaican is evidence of the intentional demonization of African-derived religions in Jamaican culture. Why is it the case that, outside of the Revival Zion, Kumina, Gumbay, and Jonkunnu traditions, most Jamaicans are unfamiliar with the term *Myal*, let alone its roots and legacy in Jamaican culture? Yet every Jamaican knows very well the infamous name and legacy of Obeah. Where Myal was adopted, sheltered, and respected, it is known today by name and personality— in isolated regions across the island. However, Myal, the tradition historically noted (even by Whites) to counteract malicious uses of mystical power, has lost its name and positive influence in the broader contemporary Jamaican culture. Myal, the heartbeat and blood flow of Jamaica's African-derived religious traditions, is anonymous. This is why a scholar such as Edward (Kamau) Brathwaite, in seeking to nullify the Eurocentric conception of African-derived religions in Jamaican culture, focuses on a redefinition of Obeah. Obeah, with all of its negative associations, has come to signify any expression of African-derived religion in Jamaica, especially divination and herbalism. Although Jamaican Christians are repeatedly helped or healed by "Obeah" practitioners, they consult them in desperation, momentarily suspending their pejorative views about Obeah. At the end of the day, those same Jamaicans usually remain committed to anti-African ideas that stigmatize and denigrate the integrity of that which they call Obeah. Thus writes Brathwaite:

> According to [Matthew] Lewis [a nineteenth-century White Jamaican proprietor], however, it was difficult to know if the slaves had any real religious beliefs or practices, since the only external sign of a priest was the obeah man. Lewis was perhaps nearer than he knew to the truth about his slaves' religious beliefs and practices, but he did not understand the function of the obeah man, since he was associated in the Jamaican/European mind with superstition, witchcraft and poison. But in African and Caribbean folk practice, where religion had not been externalized and institutionalized as in Europe, the obeah man was doctor [and] philosopher as well as priest.[129]

The Myal movement, which appeared in 1842, just a few years after Emancipation, has also been used to reinforce the antipathetic interpretation of Obeah. As discussed in chapter 1, I found no pre-emancipation descriptions of Myal independent of Obeah, and so firsthand accounts of Myalism as an independent tradition date back to this postslavery period. The 1842 outbreak was the most public expression of Myal, for before that time, Myalists and Obeah practitioners clandestinely combined their expertise to resist enslavement by any necessary means.

According to contemporary sources, some Myal groups of the 1840s had come under Christian influence (or at least publicly presented themselves in this manner), proclaiming that they were doing God's work and that they were clearing[130] the land for Jesus' return.[131] In many cases, Myal rituals interrupted plantation work, and aggravated proprietors had Myal organizers arrested. The missionaries also tried to suppress the movement but were met with vehement resistance. Hope Waddell, a Presbyterian missionary, confronted Myal resistance directly when he attempted to eradicate Myal activities on the Blue Hole estate. After he accused women in the movement of madness, enraged members retorted, "They are not mad. They have the spirit. You must be mad yourself, and had best go away. Let the women go on, we don't want you. Who brought you here? What do you want with us?"[132]

Monica Schuler duly notes that one of the strongest African tenets of this Myal movement was its insistence that evil made manifest necessitated a concrete human response. Myalists viewed evil as an "offense not against God but against society."[133] This African orientation toward evil[134] is significant, for it explains the "this-world" focus upon well-being and human fulfillment in each manifestation of African-derived Jamaican religions. Obeah, Myal, Native Baptist, Kumina, Revival Zion, and Rastafari all seek to combat disease, misfortune, dislocation, and *sufferation* by promoting well-being and reconciliation through practical, concrete means: divination, herbalism, armed resistance, animal sacrifice, ancestral possession, clearing rituals, and so on.

Because Africans generally believe that peculiar manifestations of misfortune can result from malicious assertions of mystical power, when economic decline and a large number of unexpected deaths struck the northern parishes of Trelawny and St. James, Myalists were summoned to cleanse the troubled estates of "Obeah." If it is true that the malicious assertion of mystical powers was the root cause of even some of the region's problems, according to my reinterpretation of Obeah outlined in chapter 1, the Myalists of this 1842 movement were actually combating the evil manipulation of Obeah, that is, *obeye* (neutral mystical power).[135] This interpretation contests the uniformly accepted notion that Myal and Obeah were contentious during slavery and especially during the 1842 Myal movement.[136] The equation of Obeah with immoral agency—including the 1842 context where Myalists proclaimed war against "Obeah"—is inconsistent with African people's beneficent use of Obeah/*obeye* to rebel against slavery, to procure remedies and antidotes for illnesses, and to secure protection against misfortune. By 1842, the automatic association of Obeah with immoral agency was deeply entrenched in White Jamaican popular culture. Apparently the ancient African association of moral agency with the human will as opposed to mystical power had lost saliency in the African-Jamaican community as Myalists declared open war against "Obeah." In ancient Akan societies, the struggle between good and evil was a struggle between good and ill human will, between persons who accessed *obeye* for beneficent ends (*obirifo/okomfo*) and those who accessed *obeye* for malevolent ends (*obayifo*).[137] Thornton identifies a similar ethical orientation among Central Africans, whose "theology did not usually envision evil as the provenance of specific supernatural beings, which were entirely evil, such as Christian theology of the Devil did. Rather, the African concept was more inclined to see the evil in the actions of people with wicked intentions enlisting some of the supernatural world in their projects."[138]

In light of the foregoing analysis, I am of the same mind as Braithwaite in his attempt to bring hermeneutical authenticity to a neutral interpretation of Obeah. Obeah, in its most comprehensive usage, represents African-derived religious traditions in Jamaica and as such needs to be redeemed from its criminal reputation. Obeah should be associated with the life-affirming spirituality, values, and goals of African-derived religions, as they have unfolded in Jamaica and must be reconceptualized to cohere with its legacy in ancient Akan, Kongo, and other African religious cultures because that legacy has also been established in diasporic manifestations of Obeah. Jamaican Obeah, like its Akan parent, *obeye,* is energy. In truth, Obeah is a scientific principle that is not foreign to any of us. We rely on this principle daily in our implementation of the various technologies that enhance our lives and facilitate our productivity. Yet, we also know that technology can be used to exploit and destroy life. A tangible comparison might be helpful at this juncture. We could conceive of a charged battery as one particular construal of the Obeah principle. As stored-up energy, a battery could be expended to supply electric current to a computer or a smoke detector. It may also be used to charge a stun gun, which could then be accessed as a weapon of self-defense (good intentions) or as a weapon of attack to disable a victim (negative intentions). When conceived in this sense, it is only in its application—the context in which, intentions with which, and means by which Obeah is deployed— that moral agency can be determined to be good or bad with reference to Obeah.

African studies research has probed the cultural determinants of power and agency within classical and contemporary African societies.[139] The diasporic presence of Obeah, Conjure, Hoodoo, and other African-derived traditions suggests that classical African conceptions of power and agency continue to permeate not only contemporary African communities but also African-American and Caribbean societies. As discussed above, power (as neutral) offered enslaved Africans avenues and vehicles for negotiating physical, emotional, psychological, and spatial confinement; static and monotonous work regimens; and sheer powerlessness over their bodies and social liberties. Enslaved Africans were inclined then to use mystical power to transform their lives in any number of concrete ways, including revolts and acts of sabotage against the slave regime. In comparing Western and African conceptions of power, Ivan Karp offers insight into why these systems of power and agency, with their transformative warrants, have been so resilient and salient in the lives of enslaved Africans in the Caribbean and the Americas. According to Karp:

> A different view of power is exhibited in African societies than in Western social science. The stress in Africa is not on the element of control but on the more dynamic aspect of energy and the capacity to use it. ... African ideas of power ... have to do with engaging power and creating or at least containing the world. They may allow for the possibility of transformations in a way that Western social science concepts of power do not.[140]

Obeah then is only one of the many approaches to transformative power in what might be called the African cosmos that captured the imagination and agency of countless enslaved Africans in the Caribbean and the Americas and continues to do so for many of their descendants today.

Anti-Africanness, Duplicity, and the Aesthetic Meaning of Masking

As a prolegomenon to my treatment of the theoretical and theological implications of African-based religions in Jamaica for Black religious studies, it seems appropriate to offer some closing thoughts about the transmission of anti-African values from Euro-Christianity to Afro-Christianity. Anti-Africanness, as I have defined it, is not the critique or modification of things African but the negation and denigration of things African, simply because they are African.

I am both intrigued and perplexed by the potent legacy of African religions in Jamaica and other Caribbean islands. I am intrigued because of the resilience of African people, who developed clever devices for disguising, protecting, and preserving their religions in response to the lethal measures taken by the planters and missionaries to exterminate their remnants in the Caribbean. I remain perplexed, however, by the cognitive dissonance in the attitudes of Caribbean peoples toward the African roots of their religious cultures. Very rarely does one find Caribbean people who feel comfortable accepting and appreciating their African heritage. As discussed above, Black anti-Africanness, or what I call a negative distance[141] from Africa, is a very real cultural attitude in the Caribbean, a consequence of the rise of the modern West. Black anti-Africanness has the effect of alienating and marginalizing the minority of Caribbean people who do not experience cognitive dissonance in relation to their actual daily religious habits, but who genuinely embrace and appreciate the traditions of their African ancestors. This is true not only in Jamaica but across the entire inhabited archipelago.

Stephen Glazier's 1984 publication on his study of the Spiritual Baptists in Trinidad offers broader insight into this negative distance between Caribbean peoples and their African heritage:

> Many Baptist leaders, in their quest for respectability, have tried to downplay African elements within the faith. Several Curepe informants, commenting on the published accounts of Herskovits

and Simpson, complained that the accounts do not make their religion appear "as other faiths" (by which they meant London Baptists, Presbyterians, Anglicans, and so on). One leader who was extremely anxious that my book should "set things right," was very careful lest I visit churches with [Yoruba Orisha] Shango connections and get the "wrong impression." Ironically, his own church had Shango connections, and so he did not take me there.[142]

Glazier further observes, "[m]ost Shango leaders have Spiritual Baptist affiliations, while many Spiritual Baptists do not have Shango affiliations."[143] As in Jamaica, it is generally apparent in Trinidad that the most identifiably African religious practitioners are the least respected and accepted in "official" cultural scripts, both elitist and nonelitist. It is to the Shangoist's or Orisha[144] devotee's advantage to be open to alternative Christian traditions, for the Orisha devotee, or any representative of traditional African religion, must align herself with socially valued traditions if African traditions are to persist transgenerationally. I have noted above that African religions were traditionally dynamic and penetrable by cross-cultural encounters. However, the predicament of enslavement and the threats of African cultural extinction that pervaded the slave experience left Africans no choice but to open themselves even to undesired change and the opportunities for transgenerational survival that attended the most legitimate forms of Eurocentric religion and culture.

The representatives of African cultural traditions are not unaware of their pariah status in their wider cultures, and perhaps this is why defensive forms of Black nationalist consciousness continue to surface as nemeses of Afrophobic legacies in Black religion and culture. For example, Stephen Glazier's research indicates that, in some Shango services, African spirits are suspicious of attempts to mitigate or supplement African rituals with Christian ones:

> Sometimes Shango leaders conduct prayer meetings themselves. Most of the time, however, they ask the Baptist leader associated with that church to perform them. When a leader performs his own prayer meetings, he is in what one Baptist leader described as a "most discomfortable" position—he is a celebrant in two religious traditions at the same time. This is thought to be dangerous because at a later date the African powers might question his "sincerity."[145]

Some may understand these contradictions and cognitive dissonances as an indigenous and unavoidable dimension of African diasporic history and experience, which was poignantly articulated by W. E. B. Du Bois in his "double consciousness" or "twoness" theory.[146] I concur, but would argue that anti-Africanness is a persistent factor in our cultures of contradiction. And so, as long as African diasporic religiosity continues to compose variations on the dominant themes in continental religions, it might be helpful to understand the distinct diasporic flavor of African-Caribbean religious traditions like Obeah, Kumina, Orisha (Shango), and Vodun, not as truncated from their continental African roots but as illustrations of positive distance from Africa, marked by the consequences of exile, new types of cultural contacts, and the flow of innovations ignited by such encounters.

In view of the duplicity that deeply characterizes the consciousness of the Caribbean people, especially in the arena of negotiating Christianity and their African religious heritage, we might also examine this phenomenon from a slightly different and less tragic angle than that of double consciousness. I have already discussed how in contemporary Jamaica the official Christian populace scorns and fears Obeah and Kumina practitioners by day but respects and consults them by night. Ironically, such behavior, outlandish though it is, authenticates African religiosity as actual and necessary for the survival and well-being of Jamaican people. I would even dare to suggest that such inclinations are inspired by deeply embedded sensibilities for the beauty and the grotesque in things African. I am tempted to interpret these sensibilities as spiritual impulses. Camerounian philosopher and theologian Eboussi Boulaga identifies these types of human inclinations as "esthetic." His perspective is useful for understanding the penchant for things African that is consciously and unconsciously harbored within so many Black people throughout the diaspora. Boulaga maintains:

> One of the great events of our experience, and perhaps of our age is the advent of esthetic human beings. Their fashion of attaching to the past, to traditions, is neither dogmatic nor rationalistic. They have no intention of worshipping what their fathers venerated nor of burning it at the stake either. They are not concerned about choice between the thesis of the unsurpassable wisdom of the ancients and the Ancestor, and the antithesis of the antiquated imbecility of these same ancients or Ancestor. Their minds are elsewhere. For them, traditions are treasures of forms and models, and the most durable of them are styles that cannot be reproduced without fakery, but which ever inspire and enchant, which lend more zest to the present, our present, and more assurance to our own quest for the beauty that abides. For these styles procure for us the necessary space and distance to play our own game, ephemeral but unique. They refer us to the irreducibility of sensation, of the sense of situation. This sense is the presence of the human being to the simultaneous totality, momentary and epochal, of things and beings—a totality that is the explosion of the origin, revealing human beings to themselves as a total part of the world.[147]

If Boulaga is correct, the African diasporic pursuit of things African may very well be an aesthetic quest to find freedom, meaning, security, and authenticity in an unfamiliar, yet familiar, past. And yet, given the devastating impact of slavery and Euro-Christianity upon African religions and cultures, such pursuit is akin to getting dressed in a completely dark room with the hope that, when exposed to the light, all of the clothing colors and styles will be well coordinated.

Two proverbs often uttered by Jamaicans bring home the initial point: "If yu wa-an good yu nuose ha fi run,"[148] and "Everything that glitters is not Gold." As African Jamaicans began to subscribe to the "glittering" official church doctrine and orthodox forms of Christian piety, they began to lose something as well. Lost was a connection to significant African-derived religions, the memory of the historical meanings and value of surviving African religious forms, the freedom and cultural legitimacy to affirm African religious traditions as worthy and beneficial for personal and communal health, and an awareness that some African values and practices continue to be expressed under the performance masks of Black Christian and quasi-Christian rituals. Boulaga's insights help us to see, however, that these performance masks are aesthetic conveyers of "epochal," "momentary," or even spontaneous experiences, which combat tragedy, exile, and dislocation in the African diasporic personality as they reconnect the performers with their African heritage time and time again.

Notes

1. Barrett. *Soul Force*, 87.
2. Some Kumina songs have been recorded by researchers over the years.
3. On my first Kumina site visit. I stopped at a home where a neighborly looking woman was sitting on the front porch. I asked her for directions to the home of my intended informant. The woman responded by waving her hand at me and saying that she wanted nothing to do with those "devil people" who lived up the road. She pointed to the left with a suspicious look on her face. Later, some time after I had developed a relationship with my informant. I told her about the incident. She smiled and responded that the woman's husband is a Jehovah's Witness minister who condemns Kumina culture any time he has a public platform to do so. Ironically, one day he became very ill and sent his son to my informant to snoop around and see if anyone would prescribe some natural medicine for his malady (as Western medicine had proved to be ineffective). My

informant wasted no time: she cured the man that very day, yet he continues to condemn Kumina and Kumina practitioners. These types of incidents—of stigmatization and condemnation from Christians—were repeatedly confirmed by Kumina and Revival Zion practitioners.

4. This deity is Nzambi in Central African Kongo culture. See Simon Bockie. *Death and the Invisible Powers*, 108.
5. Donald Hogg, "The Convince Cult in Jamaica," *Papers in Caribbean Anthropology* 58 (New Haven, CT: Yale University Publications in Anthropology, 1960); Chevannes, *Rastafari and Other African-Caribbean Worldviews*, 19. Chevannes specifically associates the practice of Convince with the parish of St. Mary in Jamaica, The year 1867 is sometimes mentioned as the official termination date for the indentured labor program.
6. For a developed discussion of these traditions, see Ivy Baxter, The *Arts of an island*; also see Patterson, Sociology *of Slavery*, 231–259.
7. See Laura Tanna, *Jamaican Folk Tales and Oral Histories* (Kingston: Institute of Jamaica Publications, 1984), for insight into the music, song, and folklore of these traditions and cultures.
8. Kenneth Bilby and Fu-Kiau Bunseki. "Kumina: A Kongo-based Tradition in the New World" (Brussels: Les Cahiers du Cedaf, 8 (1983): 1.
9. Rex Nettleford, *Inward Stretch. Outward Reach: A Voice from the Caribbean* (London: Macmillan, 1993). See chapter entitled "Cultural Resistance in Caribbean Society: Dance and Survival." 91–115.
10. Joseph Moore. "Religion of Jamaican Negroes: A Study of Afro-American Acculturation" (Ann Arbor: University Microfilm Publication 7053, Doctoral Dissertation Series, 1953).
11. Female Kumina leaders are often given the titles queen and/or mother. Maureen Warner-Lewis. "The Nkuyu: Spirit Messengers of the Kumina" (Kingston, Jamaica: Savacou, 1977).
12. Maureen Warner-Lewis. "The Ancestral Factor in Jamaica's African Religions," in *African Creative Expressions of the Divine*, ed. Kortright Davis and Elias Fara-jaje Jones (Washington. DC: Howard University School of Divinity, 1991), 74.
13. Olive Lewin, *Rock It Come Over; The Folk Music of Jamaica* (Barbados: University of the West Indies Press, 2000), 215–303.
14. Zora Neale Hurston, *Voodoo Cods; An Inquiry into Native Myths and Magic in Jamaica and Haiti* (London: Dent, 1939), and *Tell My Horse* (Berkeley, CA: Turtle Island for the Netzahualcoyotl Historical Society. 1983).
15. Kerr, *Personality and Conflict in Jamaica.*
16. Bilby and Bunseki, "Kumina: A Kongo-based Tradition in the New World," 2.
17. Warner-Lewis, "The Ancestral Factor in Jamaica's African Religions," 74.
18. Bilby and Bunseki, "Kumina: A Kongo-based Tradition in the New World," 3.
19. In 1978, Bilby and Bunseki discovered a pervasive awareness of cultural continuity with BaKongo culture among Kumina practitioners. See Bilby and Bunseki, "Kumina: A Kongo-based Tradition in the New World," esp. 11–13.
20. See Appiah, *In My Father's House,* for a discussion of Europe's construction of Africa. While I agree with Appiah's critical assessment of the European construction of "Africa," he misperceives the problem of exile from Africa and African diasporic responses to that problem. Appiah does not give enough credit to the reasons that many people in today's African diaspora hold tenaciously to less than "factual" ideas about Africa, nor does he give proper consideration to the religious meaning of the symbol "Africa" for Africans in the diaspora. Compare with V. Mudimbe, *The Idea of Africa* (Bloomington: Indiana University Press. 1994).
21. Moore, "Religion of Jamaican Negroes: A Study of Afro-Jamaican Acculturation," 115–117.
22. Bongo, 1 was told by several informants, is the actual name of the African ancestral homeland and the ethnic identity of the Kumina Ancestors.
23. Josiah Young, "God's Path and Pan-Africa," in *Black Theology: A Documentary History*, vol. 2: 1980–1992, ed. Wilmore and Cone (Maryknoll, NY: Orbis, 1993). 22.
24. Some informants chose to be represented by pseudonyms or initials to protect their identities.
25. Uncle P, interview with author, Port Morant, St. Thomas, Jamaica, September 19, 1996.
26. Schuler employs the term *recaptives* "to describe recent African arrivals in St. Helena or Sierra Leone who still resided in reception depots." Some of the recent arrivals came from intercepted slave ships en route from Africa to Cuba. See "*Alas, Alas, Kongo*," 5.
27. Monica Schuler, " 'Yerri, Yerri, Koongo': A Social History of Liberated African Immigration into Jamaica, 1841–1867" (Ph.D. diss., University of Wisconsin, Madison, 1977). 138.

28. Edward Brathwaite, "Kumina: The Spirit of African Survival in Jamaica," *Jamaica Journal* 42 (1978): 47.
29. Bilby and Bunseki. "Kumina: A Kongo-based Tradition in the New World," 11.
30. Maureen Smith and Hortense Bailey, personal communication, Port Morant, St. Thomas, Jamaica, November 9, 1996. A Kumina group is referred to as a "bands." In 1969, Seaga noted that Revival groups also used the term self-referentially. See "Revival Cults in Jamaica," 6.
31. Imogene Kennedy, interview with author, St, Catherine. Jamaica, October 7. 1996.
32. Translated from audio-recorded material, Port Morant, St. Thomas, Jamaica. October 23. 1996.
33. Schuler, " 'Yerri. Yerri, Koongo.'" 74.
34. Ibid., 75.
35. Ibid., 175.
36. Ibid., 78. 183.
37. Billy and Bunseki, "Kumina: A Kongo-based Tradition in the New World," 17–21.
38. Imogene Kennedy, interview with author, St. Catherine, Jamaica, October 17. 1996.
39. Ibid.
40. Cited from field notes. Port Morant, St. Thomas, Jamaica, October 10, 1996.
41. Cited from audio-recorded material. Port Morant, St. Thomas, Jamaica, October 10. 1996.
42. Monica Schuler could not be more correct in her contention that "[m]ost social studies of English- and French-speaking Caribbean societies, preoccupied with the persistence of certain African cultures, have tended to assume, until recently, that they must be retentions from the slave period. Sufficient evidence exists to show that this is an incomplete explanation, however. Besides Jamaica, other territories that received African indentured laborers in the nineteenth century, such as Trinidad, Grenada, and Martinique have recognizable Yoruba or Central African cultures. The same late arrival, large numbers, and group cohesiveness that conditioned their survival in Jamaica account for the preservation of these cultures elsewhere." Schuler also identifies some scholars who have miscontextualized Kumina within the period of enslavement. See *"Alas, Alas, Kongo."* 9.
43. Barrett, *Soul Force*, 69.
44. Ibid., 68.
45. Patterson, *Sociology' of Slavery*, 201. See the broader context of Patterson's interpretation of Leslie and Herskovits in chapter 1.
46. I also collected lexicons and songs similar to the ones included in Bilby and Bunseki's article "Kumina: A Kongo-based Tradition in the New World."
47. I am thankful to Dr. Kalala Ngalamulume for taking the time to discuss these terms with me.
48. I use this qualifier to distinguish between Kuminas that are exhibited on stage at national celebrations, competitions, and other public appearances as demonstrations of Jamaica's "African heritage" and those organized within the legitimate boundaries and authority of Kumina communities. I understand the former to be in-authentic and by and large exploitative.
49. Imogene Kennedy, interview with author. St. Catherine, Jamaica, October 17, 1996.
50. Original emphases. Warner-Lewis, "The Nkuyu: Spirit Messengers of the Kumina," 59–60.
51. Imogene Kennedy, interview with author, St. Catherine. Jamaica, October 17, 1996.
52. Fu Kiau Bunseki, interview with author, Atlanta, GA, April 23, 2004.
53. Two important details from an early twentieth-century description are germane to this discussion. Martha Beckwith describes the Pukkumerian tradition as a derivation of Revival Zion and Obeah, noting that they "hold their meetings near a graveyard, and it is to the ghosts of their own membership that they appeal when spirits are summoned to a meeting 'They jump and dance and sing and talk in a secret language because the spirits do not talk our language.'" See Martha Beckwith, *Black Roadways*, 176–177. In chapter 1 of this text, I include Bilby's discussion of the importance of the graveyard in Gumbay Play/Myal rituals. Carrying sick victims to ancestral burying grounds and communing with their spirits at the burial sites were also essential in the Kumina ceremonies I attended.
54. I was convinced of the authenticity of events as they unfolded, in part because the young man's mother had requested the Kumina to correct what appeared to be a psychological affliction of her son. The young man cooperated but seemed unprepared for what was to happen. When one of the young women caught Myal, the young man began to laugh hysterically. Within seconds he had collapsed on the ground in an unconscious state. At first. I thought he was dead, but

later learned that his collapse into unconsciousness was the work of the Ancestors which was necessary for the healing process.
55. Gardner, *History of Jamaica*, 192.
56. Delores Williams, *Sisters in the Wilderness* (Maryknoll, NY: Orbis, 1993).
57. From unpublished work cited by Thompson, *Flash off the Spirit*, 108.
58. The contemporary Kumina community maintains a memory of oath-taking rituals which is tangential to this discussion. According to Kumina oral tradition, the oaths were followed even after Emancipation. Several practitioners gave accounts of the "sacred oath" that was sealed before the Paul Bogle Rebellion of 1865. which occurred in the parish of St. Thomas, the home of (Kongo-based) Kumina. It is not clear whether the oath was taken based upon the authority of the Bible, or whether Obeah rituals were involved, or both.
59. Thompson, *Flash of the Spirit*, 108. Thompson cites from John Janzen and Wyatt MacGaffey, *An Anthology of Kongo Religion: Primary Texts from Lower Zaire* (Lawrence: University of Kansas Press, 1974), 34.
60. Although it might be tempting to interpret the resurrection of Jesus Christ as coherent with the cross of recurring incarnation in Kongo traditions, the enfleshing of the Divine within the human corpus is absent in the resurrection, and thus I make a clear distinction between the two.
61. Zora Neale Hurston's research on the sanctified (Pentecostal) church in the early twentieth century documents that the sign of the cross as incarnated spirit/Divinity has also dominated the religiosity of Blacks who accepted Christianity in the United States. Hurston argues that there is a definite connection between the phenomenon of spirit possession in the sanctified church and in African-derived religions like Vodun, See her *The Sanctified Church*, 79–107. Aiso see Herskovits, *Myth of the Negro Past*.
62. I use the term *disembodied life/living* to refer to the "living dead" or the Ancestors. This domain of the Ancestors, which is under the earth, is known as *Kalunga* in Kongo cosmology. "Through its icon, the cross, the Kongo Cosomogram shows the Kalunga where the "invisible" vertical pole sinks beneath the "visible" horizontal pole. *Kalunga* is reconceived among BaKongo Kumina descendants in Jamaica as the Atlantic Ocean. See Thompson. *Flash of the Spirit*, 109; Schuler, "Alas, Alas, Kongo," 95.
63. I submit that this was not the intention of St. Augustine, who conceptualized the soul and body as hierarchically created by an ultimate good God. In Augustine's anthropology nothing about human nature is actually bad or evil because everything has its source in God's goodness. Augustine appraised the soul as good and the body not as bad, but as a lesser good when compared to the soul.
64. See Schuler, 182–183 for a fuller discussion of her argument.
65. See especially Robert Marley, "Get Up, Stand Up" (Burnin' Island Records, 1973).
66. This has been a defining characteristic of Rastology since the beginning of the movement and continues to distinguish the Rastafari ethos from local Jamaican expressions of Christianity.
67. Douglas, *The Black Christ*, 22–29.
68. In other words, although I do not support her conclusions on this matter, the connections that Douglas makes between classical African spirituality and Black North American Christianity is an important move in Black and womanist theological discourse. In this way she takes steps toward addressing the apparent lack of interest among far too many Black and womanist theologians in the African religious heritage and its significance to Black religious formation in North America.
69. The ringshout and other hush harbor practices were aspects of slave religion whereby possession trance and other forms of ecstatic religious expression, consistent with features of African religion, were nurtured and expressed within concealed spaces away from and outside the purview of White authority. See Raboteau, *Slave Religion*.
70. Williams, *Sisters in the Wilderness*, 168.
71. ee note 60 above.
72. ee also Raboteau, *Slave Religion*, and Clifton H. Johnson, ed., *Cod Struck Me Dead: Voices of Ex-Slaves* (Cleveland: Pilgrim, 1993) for similar testimonies among North American African captives. Although several contemporary constructive African Christologies have imaged Jesus as ancestor par excellence, I am not persuaded that, in the context of slavery, Africans, who were introduced to Jesus Christ as God, would have reinterpreted this perhaps intriguing and inviting yet exotic White Christian deity as an ancestor. Ancestorhood in classical African religions concerns the family unit— its ethical codes, taboos, and protocol, generativity in the family lineage, and the

continuity of life, along with the acquisition and assertion of knowledge (wisdom), onto-logical status, and power. An analysis of the complex theology of ancestorhood falls most appropriately within the rubric of theological anthropology, for ancestors are departed family members whose names are remembered, and invisible presences felt through ritual acts of veneration and through the sacramental experiences of mundane living: eating, harvesting crops, giving birth, fishing, hunting, fighting wars, curing diseases, and so on.

73. Emphases added. Williams, *Sisters in the Wilderness*, 168.
74. Consistent with BaKongo cosmology, in Kumina ceremonies, circular motion represents the continuity of life. This motion is hyperbolized as devotees make simultaneous circular motions with multiple parts of their bodies. This is done as they move around the center pole and drummers move in the same direction and configuration of the sun (a counterclockwise circle) and as they spin around on their feet intermittently within that circle.
75. See Mary Daly, *Beyond God the Father* (Boston: Beacon Press. 1970), 75–81.
76. Jacquelyn Grant, "Womanist Theology: Black Women's Experiences as a Source for Doing Theology, with Special Reference to Christology," in *Black Theology, A Documentary History*, Vol. 2: 1980–1992, ed. Wilmore and Cone, 273.
77. Besides *In Search of Our Mothers' Gardens*, see, for example, Walker's *The Color Purple* (New York: Pocket, 1982); and Walker, *Anything We Love Can Be Saved: A Writer's Activism* (New York: Random House. 1997).
78. Imogene Kennedy, interview with author, St. Catherine, Jamaica, October 17, 1996.
79. Walker. *The Color Purple*. 204.
80. JoAnne Terrell examines the theme of Christian exclusivism more closely than many other womanist theologiants in her text *Power in the Blood? The Cross in the African American Experience* (Maryknoll, NY: Orbis, 1998).
81. This is not to say that there were no other expressions of protest against the rising socioeconomic problems. For example, there were strikes on several other sugar estates in 1863 and 1864, See Campbell, *Rasta and Resistance*, 34.
82. Schuler. " 'Yerri, Yerri. Koongo': A Social History of Liberated African Immigration into Jamaica, 1841–1867," 105.
83. Ibid., 105–110.
84. I have slides of a "duty" (shrine) of four colossal statues of Marcus Garvey, Paul Bogle, Nanny, and Cudjoe, which are on Imogene Kennedy's front lawn. Kennedy built the duty in the early 1990s at the instruction of the Ancestors, "They must be remembered" is what she reported to me during a personal interview, St. Catherine, Jamaica, October 25, 1996.
85. Interview with author, Yallahs, St. Thomas, October 20. 1996. Translation: Rastafari and Zion affirm the same values and principles. We are all one.
86. Paraphrased from research journal, November 4, 1996.
87. See Barrett, The *Sun and the Drum*; Kerr, *Personality and Conflict in Jamaica*, 114–136.
88. See Karen Brown, *Mama Lola: A Vodou Priestess in Brooklyn* (Berkeley: University of California Press, 1991), 156–157, 189–190. 220–221.
89. Josiah Young makes this argument for the African North American context in his assertion that the Ancestors were the norm of enslaved Africans' religion. Young refutes James Cone's claim that Jesus was the norm of enslaved Africans' religion. See Young, *A Pan-African Theology*, 106–116.
90. See Linda Gloss and Clay Gloss. eds., *Jump Up and Say! A Collection of Black Storytelling* (New York: Simon and Schuster, 1995).
91. 91 See Daryl Dance, *Folklore from Contemporary Jamaicans* (Knoxville: University of Tennessee Press, 1985).
92. See Robert Marley, "Survival," *Songs of Freedom* (Island Records. 1979).
93. Contemporary manifestations of anti-Africanness are discussed and responded to in a publication of the Caribbean Conference of Churches: Burton Sankeralli, ed., *At the Crossroads: African Caribbean Religion and Christianity* (Trinidad and Tobago: Caribbean Conference of Churches, 1995).
94. The Creator Deity is known as Onyame or Nyankpong among the Akan, Olodumare in Yoruba culture, Chukwu in Igbo culture—to name a few.
95. Chevannes, *Rastafari and Other African-Caribbean Worldviews*. 8–9. Also see Waddell, a contemporary of the movement, in *Twenty-nine Years in the West Indies and Central Africa*, 190ff.
96. Wedenoja, "The Origins of Revival, a Creole Religion in Jamaica," 106.

97. Paul Ricoeur, *Interpretation Theory: Discourse and the Surplus of Meaning* (Fort Worth: Texas Christian University Press. 1976).
98. Schuler, *"Alas, Alas, Kongo,"* 36.
99. North American fundamentalist religion has won mass numbers of converts among the Jamaican people. Jamaicans have access to their televised sermons through both local and cable network television. Lewin Williams raises this issue as a moral problem to be addressed by Caribbean theology. See *Caribbean Theology* (New York: Lang, 1994), 14–18, 24–27.
100. I saw countless examples of fellowship, affirmation, and support among the three groups. In addition, the three communities share the same beliefs about a variety of religious practices. The Zionists and Kumina devotees use the coconut, fresh water, and rum For the same purposes in their religious rituals. Rastas, Revivalists, and Kumina practitioners shun the use of salt in food prepared for ritual and in some cases even in nonritual dietary consumption. Monica Schuler persuasively identifies the taboo against salt with the nineteenth-century BaKongo immigrant belief that salt intake would prevent them from flying back to Africa. See *"Alas, Alas, Kongo."* 93–96. Compare with Chevannes, *Rastafari: Roots and Ideology*, 34–35. Chevannes convincingly argues that the persistence of the taboo against salt in the Kumina, Revival, and Rastafari religions is a symbol of African resistance to European culture.
101. Homer Lobban, pastor of Mount Zion Baptist Church of Holiness, interview with author, Yallahs, St, Thomas, Jamaica, October 19, 1996.
102. Banbury, *Jamaica Superstitions, or. The Obeah Book: A Complete Treatise of the* Absurdities *Believed in by the People of the Island*, 7.
103. For an extensive treatment of this issue, see Paul Farmer, *The Uses of Haiti* (Monroe, ME: Common Courage, 1994).
104. For a thorough treatment of this subject, see Laguerre, *Voodoo and Politics in Haiti*. Also see Sidney Mintz's introduction to Métraux, *Voodoo in Haiti*, 1–14, Eric Williams cites the derisive commentaries forwarded by Thomas Carlyle in 1849 and by J. A. Froude in 1887 with regard to Haiti's sovereignty as a Black nation in *British Historians and the West Indies*, 82, 182–183.
105. Réné Depestre, "Problems of Identity for the Black Man in Caribbean Literatures." *Caribbean Quarterly* 19, no. 3 (September 1973): 51.
106. The African Caribbean Institute of Jamaica (ACIJ) has sponsored and supported numerous research projects on Kennedy. Over the years, the ACIJ has acquired a significant collection of materials on Kennedy and the Kumina tradition. Also see Maureen Warner-Lewis, "The Nkuyu: Spirit Messengers of the Kumina," Savacou Publications Pamphlet No. 3, 1977; and Edward Brathwaite, "The Spirit of African Survival in Jamaica," *Jamaica Journal* 42 (1978), 44–63.
107. See Edward Seaga, "Revival Cults in Jamaica," *Jamaica Journal*, 3/2 (1969), 5. "Revivalist groups are not forbidden by any Statutory Law but Cultists sometimes infringe the Night Noises Prevention Law of 1911 and die so called Obeah Law of 1898,—die latter defines the consultation with practitioners of Obeah and the publication and distribution of any material 'calculated to promote the superstition of Obeah.' " According to my informants in both the *Kumina* and Revival Zion traditions, these laws were brutally enforced until Edward Seaga "cut the ribbon" and "gave the license" for them to practice their religions without molestation from the Jamaican police.
108. Imogene Kennedy, interview with author, St. Catherine, Jamaica, October 17, 1996.
109. Devon House is a historic colonial local attraction, located in the heart of Kingston, which sponsors a number of social and cultural activities.
110. Edward Seaga described the Friday night Kumina and Revival Zion performances to me as venues for "cultural expression." Edward Seaga, interview with author, Kingston, Jamaica, November 3, 1996.
111. By way of comparison, the Jamaica Order of Distinction catalogue lists as corecipients for the Order of Distinction: Charles Hyatt, actor, broadcaster, and producer (August 6, 1980); Lt. Col. Ian Jameson, commanding officer, Third Battalion, Jamaica Regiment (August 5, 1974); Dr. Horace Keane, dental surgeon and past president, Jamaica Dental Association (August 1, 1978); Arthur Jones, marine pilot, superintendent of pilotage. Port Authority, Kingston (August 6, 1980). Imogene Kennedy is listed as a "folklorist" and is honored "for services in the development of African heritage." See Chancery of the Order Distinction. *The Order of Distinction* (Kingston, Jamaica: Chancery of the O.D., 1988), 35–36, 87–123.
112. For a thorough treatment of the ethics, politics, and controversy surrounding the exhibition of cultures in a global context see Ivan Karp and Stephen D. Lavine, eds., *Exhibiting Cultures:*

The Poetics and Politics of Museum Display (Washington, DC: Smithsonian Institute Press, 1991). Also see Rachel Adams, *Sideshow U.S.A: Freaks and the American Cultural Imagination* (Chicago: University of Chicago Press, 2001).
113. See Kelly Brown Douglas. "Womanist Theology: What Is Its Relationship to Black Theology?", in *Black Theology; A Documentary History*, Vol. 2: 1980–1992, ed. Wilmore and Cone, 290–299.
114. This is exactly what happened at Jamaica's October 1996 Caribbean Heritagefest, where a number of African religiocultural dances were performed. The organizers introduced each tradition with sketchy references to their historical background. To say the least, the dances were misunderstood by a crowd that was alienated by time and memory from their significance as religious worship. I witnessed several people gawking and laughing at the presenters. This subject is thoroughly treated from a global perspective in Karp and Lavine. eds.. *Exhibiting Cultures*. Also see Edward Brathwaite's critique of the performance of Jamaican culture in Brathwaite, "Kumina: The Spirit of African Survival in Jamaica."
115. Warner-Lewis, "The Nkuyu: Spirit Messengers of the Kumina," 77.
116. Fieldnotes, Port Morant, St. Thomas, Jamaica, September 23, 1996 and October 5, 1996, Yallahs, St. Thomas, Jamaica, October 17, 1996 and November 3, 1996.
117. Cited by Cassidy, *Jamaica Talk*, 240–241. Leonard Barrett offers insight into this issue in the following passage: "There are few Jamaican elites now alive who can truthfully say that their lives have never been affected in some way by [folk healers]. A particular individual might not have had personal contact with them, but if pressed hard enough he generally admits that either his parents or some of his relatives have been cured or helped in some way by an African practitioner. The writer recalls quite vividly a medical doctor and graduate of a prestigious British university, who, on learning of the author's plan to study the healer, Mother Rita, declared with all sincerity 'the woman saved my life!' He then proceeded to tell die story. As a small boy his older sister (age five) died of vomiting sickness and following her death, he too came down with the illness. The family became greatly alarmed because all the professional treatment that was available had not saved his sister's life. His father, a school teacher and a catechist in the mission church, could not openly associate himself with the folk specialists in the community, but his maternal uncle was a believer in the folk tradition and his mother was also very sympathetic to them. This uncle prevailed upon the father to consult Mother Rita. He finally decided, and under much secrecy he went for consultation. One bottle of medicine was all that was necessary. The doctor in question is convinced that it was through the work of this folk healer that his life was saved. Numerous stories of this type could be told among Jamaican elites but few are as honest as the doctor in acknowledging these experiences." See Barrett, "The Portrait of a Jamaican Healer: African Medical Lore in the Caribbean," 7.
118. For thorough documentation of these ideas, see Métraux, *Voodoo in Haiti;* Williams, *Voodoos and Obeahs*.
119. Murphy, *Working the Spirit*, x.
120. Bell. *Obeah: Witchcraft in the West Indies*, 58.
121. Murphy, *Working the Spirit*, x.
122. Hazel Ramsay, interview with author, Kingston, Jamaica, September 29, 1996.
123. The problem was raised during conversations with Rex Nettleford, Olive Lewin, Barry Chevannes, and Edward Seaga.
124. Italics mine. Tanna, *Jamaican Folk Tales and Oral Histories*, 6.
125. Ibid., 12.
126. I elect to construct a distinct term to signify a person who uses mystical power for antisocial purposes. I prefer *antisocializer* because I find terms such as "witch," "sorcerer," "magician," and related compounds or derivations inadequate to describe the person who manipulates mystical power for antisocial purposes. Although the latter terms are widely used across religious studies to describe this phenomenon in a variety of settings, they have been overused to describe African religion and religious practices. Indeed they have also been erroneously maligned within Western Christian discourse with reference to pre-Christian European traditions.
127. This is especially true in White academic theology—a moral and prophetic vocation which calls on the theologian to expose and denounce evil. For centuries White theologians in Europe and America wrote about God, Christ, human destiny, salvation, sin, evil, and justice in most cases without even mentioning the slave trade and African enslavement.
128. Cited by Schuler, *"Alas, Alas. Kongo,"* 4.

129. Edward Brathwaite, *Folk Culture of the Slaves in Jamaica* (London: New Beacon, 1981), 9–10.
130. "Cutting and clearing destruction," that is, discovering and eradicating evil, is one of the chief foci of contemporary Revival Zion religiosity.
131. Waddell, *Twenty-nine Yean*, 188.
132. Ibid., 190–192.
133. Schuler, *"Alas, Alas, Kongo,"* 36.
134. See J. Omosade Awolalu, "Sin and Its Removal in African Traditional Religion," *Journal of the American Academy of Religion* 44, no. 2 (1976): 275–287. Awolalu argues that the African response to evil is immediate and concrete. When confronted with evil, Africans exorcise it through concrete ritual acts and attempt to restore harmony and well-being.
135. See chapter I for a full discussion.
136. This is the interpretation endorsed by every scholarly study of Obeah and Myal that I have read. Schuler, Chevannes, Barrett, Patterson, and others opt for this interpretation even after acknowledging the significance of Obeah in the African pursuit of liberation from slavery, as well as the role of the Obeah practitioner in exorcising evil and restoring health.
137. See chapter I for a full discussion of Obeah. Another puzzling dimension of this scapegoating of African traditions as innately evil or negative is the use of the term *Nkuyu* by Kumina devotees themselves to refer to the Ancestors. Given traditional KiKongo terms for the living dead, the legitimate term for Ancestors (residents of Mpemba or the Community of the Dead) is *Bakuyu*, while *Nkuyu* specifically refers to a living dead who has been exiled from Mpemba. The *Bankuyu* (plural form of *Nkuyu*) "are evil dead who in their lifetime in this world were engaged in negative acts...adultery, murder, theft, and all other major crimes." This development among BaKongo descendants is worth more study. Perhaps semantic nuances in terminology by region might account for the variation. However the survival of the negative term for the living dead *(Nkuyu)* and the apparent absence of the term for revered Ancestors *(Bakuyu)* among Kumina devotees in Jamaica is intriguing. See Bockie, *Death and the Invisible Powers: The World of Kongo Belief*, 131.
138. John Thornton, "Religious and Ceremonial life in the Kongo and Mbundu Areas, 1500–1700," 81. Thomton's comparison of European and African conceptions of "witchcraft" demonstrates the contrasting views even more poignantly on 81–82.
139. See, for example W. Arens and Ivan Karp, *Creativity and Power: Cosmology and Action in African Societies*. (Washington, D.C.: Smithsonian Institution Press, 1989).
140. Ivan Karp, "African Systems of Thought," in *Africa*, ed. P. O'Meara and P. Martin (Bloomington: Indiana University Press. 1986), 199–212.
141. I use the terms *negative distance* and *positive distance* to capture the different attitudes or responses of diasporic Africans to continental Africa. The neutral factor in the diasporic African experience is "distance" (from continental Africa). What is interesting and important to note are the positive and negative ways in which Blacks in the Caribbean and the Americas understand and interpret their "distance" from continental Africa. See 186 where I conclude that African-Caribbean religious traditions are examples of positive distance from continental Africa.
142. Stephen Glazier, *Marchin' the Pilgrims Home: Leadership and Decision-Making in an Afro-Caribbean Faith* (Westport, CT: Greenwood, 1984), 122.
143. Ibid.
144. Since the late 1980s, the tradition formerly known as Shango in Trinidad has been renamed "Orisha" by devotees, taking the name that signifies die collective Yoruba divinities. Like Glazier, after five years of research in the island (1998–2003), I have encountered deeply entrenched anti-African and Afrophobic attitudes among the wider Christian Trinidadian population with regard to the Orisha tradition.
145. Glazier, *Marchin' the Pilgrims Home*, 133.
146. W. E. B. Du Bois, *Souls of Black Folk* (New York: Bantam, 1989), 3.
147. Eboussi Boulaga, *Christianity without Fetishes*. 205. Cited by Josiah Young, *A Pan-African Theology*, 117.
148. This particular aphorism is indigenous to black Jamaicans and in English translates as "If you want something good your nose has to run." In pursuing any desired end, one must sacrifice something to achieve that end. In the case of Jamaican farmers expecting a good harvest, they have to work not only in the sun but also in the rain, which often brings on the discomforts of the common cold.

Diaspora

Thinking the Diaspora: Home-Thoughts from Abroad

Stuart Hall

The occasion for this lecture was the fiftieth anniversary of the founding of the University of the West Indies (UWI). Nineteen forty-eight was also, as it happens, the year of the arrival at Tilbury Docks in the UK of the SS *Empire Windrush,* the troopship, with its cargo of West Indian volunteers, returning from home-leave in the Caribbean, together with a small company of civilian migrants. This event signified the start of postwar Caribbean migration to Britain and stands symbolically as the birth date of the Afro-Caribbean postwar black diaspora. Its anniversary in 1998 was celebrated as symbolizing "the irresistible rise of multi-racial Britain".[1]

Migration has been a constant motif of the Caribbean story. But the *Windrush* initiated a new phase of diaspora formation whose legacy is the black Caribbean settlements in the UK. The purpose here is not to offer a historical account of the evolution of this diaspora – though its troubled history deserves to be better known in the Caribbean, even, one (dare one suggest) more systematically studied. The fate of Caribbean people living in the UK, the US or Canada is no more 'external' to Caribbean history than the Empire was 'external' to the so-called domestic history of Britain, though that is indeed how contemporary historiography constructs them. At all events, the question of diaspora is posed here primarily because of the light that it throws on the complexities, not simply of building, but of imagining Caribbean nationhood and identity, in an era of intensifying globalization.

Nations, Benedict Anderson suggests, are not only sovereign political entities but "imagined communities".[2] Thirty years after independence, how are Caribbean nations imagined? This question is central, not only to their peoples but to the arts and culture they produce, where some 'imagined subject' is always in play. Where do their boundaries begin and end, when regionally each is culturally and historically so closely related to its neighbours, and so many live thousands of miles from 'home'? How do we imagine their relation to 'home', the nature of their 'belongingness'? And how are we to think of national identity and 'belongingness' in the Caribbean in the light of this diaspora experience?

The black settlements in Britain are not totally separated from their roots in the Caribbean. Mary Chamberlain's *Narratives of Exile and Return,* with its life histories of Barbadian migrants to the UK, emphasizes how strong the links remain.[3] As is common to most transnational communities, the extended family – as network and site of memory – is the critical conduit between the two locations. Barbadians, she suggests, have kept alive in exile a strong sense of what 'home' is like and tried to maintain a Barbadian 'cultural identity'. This picture is confirmed by research amongst Caribbean migrants in general in the UK that suggests that, amongst the so-called ethnic minorities in Britain, what we might call 'associational identification' with the cultures of origin remains strong, even into the second and third generation, though the places of origin are no longer the only source of identification.[4] The strength of the umbilical tie is also reflected in the growing numbers of retired Caribbean returnees. Chamberlain's judgement is that "A determination to construct autonomous Barbadian identities in Britain…if current trends continue, is likely to be enhanced rather than diminished by time."[5]

However, it would be wrong to see these trends as singular or unambiguous. In the diaspora situation, identities become multiple. Alongside an associative connection with a particular island 'home' there are other centripetal forces: there is the West-Indianness that they share with other West Indian migrants. (George Lamming once remarked that his [and, incidentally, my] generation became 'West Indian', not in the Caribbean but in London!) There are the similarities with other so-called ethnic minority populations, emergent 'black British' identities, the identification with the localities of settlement, also the symbolic re-identifications with 'African' and more recently with 'African-American' cultures – all jostling for place alongside, say, their 'Barbadianness'.

Mary Chamberlain's interviewees also speak eloquently of how difficult many returnees find reconnecting with the societies of their birth. Many miss the cosmopolitan rhythms of life to which they have become acclimatized. Many feel that 'home' has changed beyond all recognition. In turn, they are seen as having had the natural and spontaneous chains of connection disturbed by their diasporic experiences. They are happy to be home. But history has somehow irrevocably intervened.

This is the familiar, deeply modern, sense of dis-location, which – it increasingly appears – we do not have to travel far to experience. Perhaps we are all, in modern times – after the Fall, so to speak – what the philosopher, Heidegger, called 'Umheuimlicheit' – literally, 'not-at-home'. As Iain Chambers eloquently expresses it:

> We can never go home, return to the primal scene, to the forgotten moment of our beginnings and 'authenticity', for there is always something else between. We cannot return to a bygone unity, for we can only know the past, memory, the unconscious through its effects, that is when it is brought into language and from there embark on an (interminable) analysis. In front of the 'forest of signs' (Baudelaire) we find ourselves always at the crossroads, holding our stories and memories ('secularized reliques', as Benjamin, the collector, describes them) while scanning the constellation full of tension that lies before us, seeking the language, the style, that will dominate movement and give it form. Perhaps it is more a question of seeking to be at home here, in the only time and context we have… .[6]

What light, then, does the diaspora experience throw on issues of cultural identity in the Caribbean? Since this is a conceptual and epistemological, as well as an empirical, question, what does the diaspora experience do to our models of cultural identity? How are we to conceptualize or imagine identity, difference and belongingness, after diaspora? Since 'cultural identity' carries so many overtones of essential unity, primordial oneness, indivisibility and sameness, how are we to 'think' identities inscribed within relations of power and constructed across difference, and disjuncture?

Essentially, it is assumed that cultural identity is fixed by birth, part of nature, imprinted through kinship and lineage in the genes, constitutive of our innermost selves. It is impermeable to something as 'worldly', secular and superficial as temporarily moving one's place of residence. Poverty, underdevelopment, the lack of opportunities – the legacies of Empire everywhere – may force people to migrate, bringing about the scattering – the dispersal. But each dissemination carries with it the promise of the redemptive return.

This powerful interpretation of the concept of 'diaspora' is the one most familiar to Caribbean people. It has become part of our newly constructed collective sense of self and deeply written in as the subtext in nationalist histories. It is modelled on the modern history of the Jewish people (from whom the term 'diaspora' was first derived), whose fate in the Holocaust – one of the few world-historical events comparable in barbarity to that of modern slavery – is well known. More significant, however, for the Caribbean is the Old Testament version of the story. There we find the analogue, critical to our history, of 'the chosen people', taken away by violence into slavery in 'Egypt'; their 'suffering' at the hands of 'Babylon'; the leadership of Moses, followed by the Great Exodus – "movement of Jah People" – out of bondage and the return to the Promised Land. This is ur-source of that great New World narrative of freedom, hope and redemption which is repeated again and again throughout slavery – the Exodus and the 'Freedom Ride'. It has provided every black New World liberatory discourse with its governing metaphor. Many believe this Old Testament narrative to be much more powerful for the popular imaginary of New World black people than the so-called Christmas story. (Indeed, in the very week in which this lecture was first delivered at the UWI Cave Hill campus, the *Barbados Advocate* – looking forward to independence celebrations – attached the honorific titles of 'Moses' and 'Aaron' to the 'founding fathers' of Barbadian independence, Errol Barrow and Cameron Tudor!)

In this metaphor, history – which is open to freedom because it is contingent – is represented as teleological and redemptive: circling back to the restoration of its originary moment, healing all rupture, repairing every violent breach through this return. This hope has become, for Caribbean people, condensed into a sort of foundational myth. It is, by any standards, a great vision. Its power – even in the modern world – to move mountains can never be underestimated.

It is, of course, a closed conception of 'tribe', diaspora and homeland. To have a cultural identity in this sense is to be primordially in touch with an unchanging essential core, which is timeless, binding future and present to past in an unbroken line. This umbilical cord is what we call 'tradition', the test of which is its truth to its origins, its self-presence to itself, its 'authenticity'. It is of course, a myth – with all the real power that our governing myths carry to shape our imaginaries, influence our actions, give meaning to our lives and make sense of our history.

Foundational myths are, by definition, transhistorical: not only outside history, but fundamentally a-historical. They are anachronistic and have the structure of a double inscription. Their redemptive power lies in the future, which is yet to come. But they work by ascribing what they predict will happen to their description of what has already happened, of what it was like in the beginning. History, however, like Time's arrow, is, if not linear, then successive. The narrative structure of myths is cyclical. But within history, their meaning is often transformed. It is, after all, precisely this exclusive conception of 'homeland' that led the Serbs to refuse to share their territory – as they have done for centuries – with their Muslim neighbours in Bosnia and justified ethnic cleansing in Kosovo. It is a version of this conception of the Jewish diaspora, and its prophesied 'return' to Israel, that is the source of Israel's quarrel with its Middle Eastern neighbours, for which the Palestinian people have paid so dearly and, paradoxically, by expulsion from what is also, after all, their homeland.

Here, then, is the paradox. Now, our troubles begin. A people cannot live without hope. But there is a problem when we take our metaphors too literally. Questions of cultural identity in diasporas cannot be 'thought' in this way.[7] They have proved so troubling and perplexing for Caribbean people precisely because, with us, identity is irredeemably a historical question. Our societies are composed, not of one, but of many peoples. Their origins are not singular but diverse. Those to whom the land originally belonged have long since, largely, perished – decimated by hard labour and disease. The land cannot be 'sacred' because it was 'violated' – not empty but emptied. Everyone who is here originally belonged somewhere else. Far from being continuous with our pasts, our relation to that history is marked by the most horrendous, violent, abrupt, ruptural breaks. Instead of the slowly evolving pact of civil association so central to the liberal discourse of

Western modernity, our 'civil association' was inaugurated by an act of imperial will. What we now call the Caribbean was reborn in and through violence. The pathway to our modernity is marked out by conquest, expropriation, genocide, slavery, the plantation system and the long tutelage of colonial dependency. No wonder in van der Straet's famous engraving of Europe encountering America (c. 1600), Amerigo Vespucci is the commanding male figure, surrounded by the insignia of power, science, knowledge and religion: and 'America' is, as often, allegorized as a woman, naked, in a hammock, surrounded by the emblems of an – as yet unviolated – exotic landscape.[8]

Our peoples have their roots in – or, more accurately, can trace their 'routes' from – the four corners of the globe, from Europe, Africa, Asia, forced together in the fourth corner is the 'primal scene' of the New World. Their 'routes' are anything but 'pure'. The great majorities are 'African' in descent – but, as Shakespeare would have said, "north-by-north-west". We know this term 'Africa' is, in any event, a modern construction, referring to a variety of peoples, tribes, cultures and languages whose principal common point of origin lay in the confluence of the slave trade. In the Caribbean, 'Africa' has since been joined by the East Indians and the Chinese: indenture enters alongside slavery. The distinctiveness of our culture is manifestly the outcome of the most complex interweaving and fusion in the furnace of colonial society, of different African, Asian and European cultural elements.

This hybrid outcome can no longer be easily disaggregated into its original 'authentic' elements. The fear that, somehow, this makes Caribbean culture nothing but a simulacrum or cheap imitation of the cultures of the colonizers need not detain us, for this is so obviously not the case. But the cultural logic at work here is manifestly a 'creolizing' or transcultural one, as Mary Louise Pratt uses the term, following in the tradition of some of the best cultural theoretical writing of the region.[9] Through transculturation "subordinated or marginal groups select and invent from materials transmitted to them by a dominant metropolitan culture". It is a process of the 'contact zone', a term that invokes "the spatial and temporal co-presence of subjects previously separated by geographic and historical disjunctures...whose trajectories now intersect". This perspective is dialogic since it is as interested in how the colonized produce the colonizer as the other way around: the "co-presence, interaction, interlocking of understandings and practices, often [in the Caribbean case, we must say always] within radically asymmetrical relations of power".[10] It is the disjunctive logic that colonization and Western modernity introduced into the world and its entry into history constituted the world after 1492 as a profoundly unequal but 'global' enterprise and made Caribbean people what David Scott has recently described as "conscripts of modernity".[11]

In the early 1990s, I made a television series, called *Redemption Song*, for BBC2 about the different cultural tributaries within Caribbean culture.[12] In the visits I made in connection with the series, what amazed me was the presence of the same basic trace elements (similarity), together with the ways these had been uniquely combined into different configurations in each place (difference). I felt 'Africa' closest to the surface in Haiti and Jamaica. And yet, the way the African gods had been synthesized with Christian saints in the complex universe of Haitian vodoun is a particular mix only to be found in the Caribbean and Latin America – though there are analogues wherever comparable syncretisms emerged in the wake of colonization. The style of Haitian painting often described as 'primitive' is in fact the most complex rendering- in visionary terms – of this religious 'double-consciousness'. The distinguished Haitian painter whom we filmed – Andre Pierre – said a prayer to both Christian and vodoun gods before he commenced work. Like the Jamaican painter, Brother Everald Brown, Pierre saw painting as essentially a visionary and 'spiritual' task. He sang us the 'story' of his canvas – white-robed, tie-headed black 'saints' and travellers crossing The River – as he painted.

I felt close to France in both Haiti and Martinique, but to different Frances: in Haiti, the 'France' of the Old Empire, which the Haitian Revolution (the explosive fusion of African slave resistance and French Republican traditions in the demand for liberty under Toussaint L'Ouverture) brought to its knees; in Martinique, the 'France' of the New Empire – of Republicanism, Gaullism, Parisian 'chic' crossed by the transgressions of black 'style' and the complex affiliations to 'Frenchness' of Fanon and Césaire. In Barbados, as expected, I felt closer to England, and its understated social discipline – as one once did, occasionally, but feels no longer in Jamaica. Nevertheless, the distinctive habits, customs and social etiquette of Barbados are so clearly a translation, through African slavery, of that small-scale, intimate plantation culture that refigured the Barbadian landscape. In Trinidad, above all, the complex traditions of 'the East' in 'the West' – of Indian Carnival Queens, roti stalls on the savannah and Diwali candles glittering in the San Fernando darkness, and the distinctively Spanish Catholic rhythm of sin-contrition-and-absolution (Shrove Tuesday's masque followed by Ash Wednesday mass) that is so close to the Trinidadian character. Everywhere, hybridity, *différance*.

The closed conception of diaspora rests on a binary conception of difference. It is founded on the construction of an exclusionary frontier and depends on the construction of an 'Other' and a fixed opposition between inside and outside. But the syncretized configurations of Caribbean cultural identity require Derrida's notion of *différance* – differences that do not work through binaries, veiled boundaries that do not finally separate but double up as *places de passage,* and meanings that are positional and relational, always on the slide along a spectrum without end or beginning. Difference, we know, is essential to meaning, and meaning is critical for culture. But in a profoundly counter-intuitive move, modern linguistics after Saussure insists that meaning cannot be finally fixed. There is always the inevitable 'slippage' of meaning in the open semiosis of a culture, as that which seems fixed continues to be dialogically reappropriated. The fantasy of a final meaning remains haunted by 'lack' or 'excess', but is never graspable in the plenitude of its presence to itself. As Bakhtin and Volosinov argued,

> The social multiaccentuality of the ideological sign is a very crucial aspect ... it is thanks to this intersecting of accents that a sign maintains its vitality and dynamism and the capacity for further development. A sign which has been withdrawn from the pressures of the social struggle ... inevitably loses its force, degenerating into allegory and becoming the object not of a live social intelligibility but of philological Comprehension.[13]

In this conception, the binary poles of 'sense' and 'nonsense' are constantly undermined by the more open-ended and fluid process of 'making sense in translation'.

This cultural 'logic' has been described by Kobena Mercer as a "diasporic aesthetic".

> Across a whole range of cultural forms there is a powerful syncretic dynamic which critically appropriates elements from the master-codes of the dominant cultures and creolizes them, disarticulating given signs and re-articulating their symbolic meaning otherwise. The subversive force of this hybridizing tendency is most apparent at the level of language itself [including visual language] where creoles, patois and Black English decentre, destabilize and carnivalize the linguistic domination of 'English' – the nation-language of master-discourse – through strategic inflections, reaccentuations and other performative moves in semantic, syntactic and lexical codes.[14]

Caribbean culture is essentially driven by a diasporic aesthetic. In anthropological terms, its cultures are irretrievably 'impure'. This impurity, so often constructed as burden and loss, is itself a necessary condition of their modernity. As the novelist Salman Rushdie once observed, "hybridity, impurity, intermingling, the transformation that comes of new and unexpected combinations of human beings, cultures, ideas, politics, movies, songs" is "how newness enters the world".[15] This is not to suggest that the different elements in a syncretic formation stand in a relation of equality to one another. They are always differently inscribed by relations of power – above all the relations of dependency and subordination sustained by colonialism itself. The independence and postcolonial moments, in which these imperial histories remain actively reworked, are therefore necessarily moments of cultural struggle, of revision and re-appropriation. However, this reconfiguration cannot be represented as a 'going back to where we were before' since, as Chambers reminds us, "there is always something else between".[16] This "something else between" is what makes the Caribbean itself, pre-eminently, the case of a modern diaspora.

The relationship between Caribbean cultures and their diasporas cannot therefore be adequately conceptualized in terms of origin to copy, primary source to pale reflection. It has to be understood as one diaspora to another. Here, the national frame is not very helpful. Nation states impose rigid frontiers within which cultures are expected to flourish. That was the primary relationship between sovereign national polities and their 'imagined communities' in the era of European nation state dominance. It was also the frame adopted by the nationalist and nation-building politics after independence. The question is whether it still provides a useful framework for understanding the cultural exchanges between the black diasporas.

Globalization, of course, is not a new phenomenon. Its history is coterminous with the era of European exploration, conquest and the formation of the capitalist world-market. The earlier phases of this so-called global history were held together by the tension between these conflicting poles – the heterogeneity of the global market and the centripetal force of the nation state – constituting between them one of the fundamental rhythms of early capitalist world systems.[17] The Caribbean was one of its key scenarios, across which the stabilization of the European nation-state system was fought through and accomplished in a series of imperial settlements. The apogee of imperialism at the end of the nineteenth century, two world wars and the national independence and decolonizing movements of the twentieth century marked the zenith, and the terminal point, of this phase.

It is now rapidly drawing to a close. Global developments above and below the level of the nation state have undermined the nation's reach and scope of manoeuvre, and with that the scale and comprehensiveness – the panoptic assumptions – of its 'imaginary'. In any event, cultures have always refused to be so perfectly corralled within the national boundaries. They transgress political limits. Caribbean culture, in particular, has not been well served by the national frame. The imposition of national frontiers within the imperial system fragmented the region into separate and estranged national and linguistic entities from which it has never recovered. The alternative frame of "The Black Atlantic", proposed by Paul Gilroy, is a powerful counter-narrative to the discursive insertion of the Caribbean into European national stories, bringing to the surface the lateral exchanges and 'family resemblances' across the region as a whole which a nationalist history obscures.[18]

The new, post-1970s phase of globalization is, of course, still deeply rooted in the structured disparities of wealth and power. But its forms, however uneven, are more 'global' in their operation, planetary in perspective, with transnational corporate interests, the deregulation of world markets and the global flow of capital, technologies and communication systems transcending and side-lining the old nation-state framework. This new 'transnational' phase of the system has its cultural 'centre' everywhere and nowhere. It is becoming 'decentred'. This does not mean that it lacks power, or indeed that nation states have no role in it. But that role has been in many respects subordinated to larger global systemic operations. The rise of supra-national formations, such as the European Union, is testimony to the ongoing erosion of national sovereignty. The undoubted hegemonic position of the USA in this system is related, not to its nation-state status but to its global and neo-imperial role and ambitions.

It is therefore important to see this diasporic perspective on culture as subversive of traditional nation-oriented cultural models. Like other globalizing processes cultural globalization is deterritorializing in its effects. Its space-time condensations, driven by new technologies, loosen the tie between culture and 'place'. Glaring disjunctures of time and space are abruptly convened, without obliterating their differential rhythms and times. Cultures, of course, have their 'locations'. But it is no longer easy to say where they originate. What we can chart is more akin to a process of repetition-with-difference, or reciprocity-without-beginning. In this perspective, black British identities are not just a pale reflection of a 'true' Caribbeanness of origin, which is destined to be progressively weakened. They are the outcome of their own relatively autonomous formation. However, the logic that governs them involves the same processes of transplantation, syncretization and diaspora-ization that once produced Caribbean identities, only now operating in a different space and time frame, a different chronotope – in the time of *différance*.

Thus dancehall music and subculture in Britain was, of course, inspired by and takes much of its style and attitude from the dancehall music and subculture of Jamaica. But it now has its own variant black British forms, and its own indigenous locations. The recent 'dancehall' film, *Babymother,* is 'authentically' located in the mixed-race inner-city zone of Harlesden, in the streets and clubs, the recording studios and live venues, the street life and danger-zones of North London.[19] The three ragga girls, its heroines, shop for their exotic outfits in another suburb of London, Southall, which is familiarly known as Little India. These *différances* are not without real effects. Unlike the classic representations of dancehall elsewhere, this film charts the struggles of three girls to become ragga dancehall DJs – thereby bringing the vexed issue of sexual politics in Jamaican popular culture dead centre to the narrative, where other versions are still hiding it away behind a cultural nationalist screen. Isaac Julien's documentary film, *The Darker Side of Black,* has three locations – Kingston, New York and London. Perhaps it is this relative 'freedom of place' that enables him to confront the deep homophobia common to the different variants of gangsta rap without collapsing into the degraded language of 'the innate violence of the black posses' that now disfigures British Sunday journalism.

Dancehall is now an indigenized diasporic musical form – one of several black musics winning the hearts and souls of some white London 'wannabe' kids (that is 'wannabe black'!), who speak a mean mixture of Trench Town patois, New York hip-hop and estuary English and for whom 'black style' simply is the symbolic equivalent of modern street credibility. (Of course, they are not the only garden-variety of British youth. There are also the skin-heads, swastika-tattooed denizens of abandoned white suburbs such as Eltham, who also practise their violent manoeuvres 'globally' at international football matches, five of whom stabbed the black teenager, Stephen Lawrence to death at a South London bus stop, simply because he dared to change buses in their 'territory'.)[20] What is now known as jungle music in London is another 'original' crossover (there have been many since British versions of ska, black soul, two-tone and 'roots' reggae) between Jamaican dub, Atlantic Avenue hip-hop and gangsta rap and white techno (as *bangra* and tabla-and-bass are crossover musics between rap, techno and the Indian classical tradition).

In the vernacular cosmopolitan exchanges that allow 'Third' and 'First' World popular musical traditions to fertilize one another, and which have constructed a symbolic space where so-called advanced electronic technology meets the so-called primitive rhythms – where Harlesden becomes Trench Town – there is no traceable origin left, except along a circuitous and discontinuous chain of connections. The proliferation and dissemination of new hybrid and syncretic musical forms can no longer be captured in the centre/periphery model or based simply on some nostalgic and exoticized notion of the recovery of ancient rhythms. It is the story of the production of culture, of new and thoroughly modern diaspora musics – of course, drawing on the materials and forms of many fragmented musical traditions.

Their modernity needs, above all, to be emphasized. In 1998, the Institute for the International Visual Arts and the Whitechapel Gallery organized the first major retrospective of the work of a major Caribbean visual artist, Aubrey Williams (1926–90). Williams was born and worked for many years as an agricultural officer in Guyana. He subsequently lived and painted, at different stages of his career, in England, Guyana, Jamaica and the USA. His paintings embrace a variety of twentieth century styles, from the figurative and the iconographic to abstraction. His major work demonstrates a wide variety of formal influences and inspirational sources – Guyanese myths, artefacts and landscapes, pre-Columbian and Mayan motifs, wildlife, birds and animal figures, Mexican muralism, the symphonies of Shostakovitch, and the abstract-expressionist forms characteristic of postwar British and European modernism. His paintings defy characterization, as simply either Caribbean or British. These vibrant, explosively colourful canvases, with their cosmic shapes and the indistinct traces of forms and figures faintly but suggestively embedded in the abstract surfaces, clearly belong to, but have never been officially recognized as part of, the essential story of 'British modernism'. No doubt his flirtation with European music and abstraction, in some minds, qualified his credentials as a 'Caribbean' painter. Yet, it is the two impulses working together, his translation position between two worlds, several aesthetics, many languages, that establish him as an outstanding, original and formidably modern artist.

In the catalogue produced for the Williams retrospective, the art critic, Guy Brett comments:

> Of course, the subtlety of the matter – the complexity of the history that has yet to be written – is that Aubrey Williams' work would have to be considered in three different contexts: that of Guyana, that of the Guyanese and West Indian diaspora in Britain, and that of British society. These contexts would have to be considered to a degree separately, and in their complicated inter-relationships, affected by the realities of power. And all would have to be adjusted in relation to Williams' own desire to be simply a modern, contemporary artist, the equal of any other. At one moment he could say, 'I haven't wasted a lot of energy on this roots business...I've paid attention to a hundred different things ... why must I isolate one philosophy?'; at another, 'the crux of the matter inherent in my work since I was a boy has been the human predicament, specifically with regard to the Guyanese situation'.[21]

What, then, about all those efforts to reconstruct Caribbean identities by going back to its originary sources? Were these struggles of cultural recovery useless? Far from it. The reworking of Africa in the Caribbean weave has been the most powerful and subversive element in our cultural politics in the twentieth century. And its capacity to disrupt the post-independence nationalist 'settlement' is certainly not over. But this is not primarily because we are connected to our African past and heritage by an unbreakable chain across which some singular African culture has flowed unchanged down the generations, but because of how we have gone about producing 'Africa' again, within the Caribbean narrative. At every juncture – think of Garveyism, Hibbert, Rastafarianism, the new urban popular culture – it has been a matter of interpreting 'Africa', rereading 'Africa', of what 'Africa' could mean to us now, after diaspora.

Anthropologically, this question has often been approached in terms of 'survivals'. The signs and traces of that presence are, of course, everywhere. 'Africa' lives, not only in the retention of African words and syntactic structures in language or rhythmic patterns in music but in the way African speech forms have permanently disrupted, inflected and subverted the way Caribbean people speak, the way they appropriated 'English', the master tongue. It 'lives' in the way every Caribbean Christian congregation, familiar with every line of the Moody and Sankey hymnal, nonetheless drag and elongate the pace of "Onward Christian Soldiers" back down to a more grounded body-rhythm and vocal register. Africa is alive and well in the diaspora. But it is neither the Africa of those territories, now obscured by the postcolonial map maker, from which slaves were snatched for transportation nor the Africa of today, which is at least four or five different 'continents' rolled into one, its forms of subsistence destroyed, its peoples structurally adjusted into a devastating modern poverty.[22] The 'Africa' that is alive and well in this part of the world is what Africa has become in the New World, in the violent vortex of colonial syncretism, reforged in the furnace of the colonial cook-pot.

Equally significant, then, is the way this 'Africa' provides resources for survival today, alternative histories to those imposed by colonial rule and the raw materials for reworking in new and distinctive cultural patterns and forms. In this perspective, 'survivals' in their original form are massively outweighed by the process of cultural translation. As Sarat Maharaj reminds us:

> Translation, as Derrida puts it, is quite unlike buying, selling, swapping – however much it has been conventionally pictured in those terms. It is not a matter of shipping over juicy chunks of meaning from one side of the language barrier to the other – as with fast-food packs at an over-the-counter take away outfit. Meaning is not a readymade, portable thing that can be 'carried over' the divide. The translator is obliged to construct meaning in the source language and then to figure and fashion it a second time round in the materials of the language into which he or she is rendering it. The translator's loyalties are thus divided and split. He or she has to be faithful to the syntax, feel and structure of the source language and faithful to those of the language of translation ...We face a double writing, what might be described as a 'perfidious fidelity'...We are drawn into Derrida's 'Babel effect'.[23]

In fact, every significant social movement and every creative development of the arts in the Caribbean in this century has begun with or included this translation-moment of the re-encounter with Afro-Caribbean traditions. The reason is not that Africa is a fixed anthropological point of reference – the hyphenated reference already marks the diasporizing process at work, the way 'Africa' was appropriated into and transformed by the plantation systems of the New World. The reason is that 'Africa' is the signifier, the metaphor, for that dimension of our society and history that has been massively suppressed, systematically dishonoured and endlessly disavowed, and that, despite all that has happened, remains so. This dimension is what Frantz Fanon called "the fact of blackness".[24] Race remains, in spite of everything, the guilty secret, the hidden code, the unspeakable trauma, in the Caribbean. It is 'Africa' that has made it 'speakable', as a social and cultural condition of our existence.

In the Caribbean cultural formation, white, European, Western, colonizing traces were always positioned as the ascendant element, the voiced aspect: the black, 'African', enslaved and colonized traces, of which there were many, were always unvoiced, subterranean, and subversive, governed by a different 'logic', always positioned through subordination or marginalization. Identities formed within the matrix of colonial meanings were constructed so as to foreclose and disavow engagement with the real histories of our society or its cultural 'routes'. The huge efforts made, over many years, not only by academic scholars but by cultural practitioners themselves, to piece together these fragmentary, often illegal, 'routes to the present' and to reconstruct their unspoken genealogies, are the necessary historical groundwork required to make sense of the interpretive matrix and self-images of our culture and to make the invisible visible. That is, the 'work' of translation that the African signifier performs, and the work of 'perfidious fidelity' that Caribbean artists in this post-nationalist moment are required to undertake.

The struggles to rediscover the African 'routes' within the complex configurations of Caribbean culture, and to speak through that prism the ruptures of transportation, slavery, colonization, exploitation and racialization, produced the only successful 'revolution' in the anglophone Caribbean in this century – the so-called cultural revolution of the 1960s – and the making of the black Caribbean subject. In Jamaica, for example, its traces are still to be found in a thousand unexamined places – in religious congregations of all sorts, formal and irregular; in the marginalized voices of popular street preachers and prophets, many of them declared insane; in folk stories and oral narrative forms; in ceremonial occasions and rites of passage; in the new language, music and rhythm of urban popular culture as well as in political and intellectual traditions – in Garveyism, Ethiopianism, revivalism and Rastafarianism. The latter, as we know, looked back to that mythic space, 'Ethiopia', where black kings ruled for a thousand years, the site of a Christian congregation hundreds of years before the Christianization of western Europe. But, as a social movement, it was actually born, as we know, in that fateful but unlocatable 'place' closer to home where Garvey's return met Revd Hibbert's preaching and Bedward's delusive fantasies, leading to the retreat to and the forced dispersal from Pinnacle. It was destined for that wider politicized space where it could speak for those – if the phrase is forgiven – 'dispossessed by independence'!

Like all these movements, Rastafarianism represented itself as a 'return'. But what it 'returned' us to was ourselves. In doing so, it produced 'Africa again' – in the diaspora. Rastafarianism drew on many 'lost sources' from the past. But its relevance was grounded in the extraordinarily contemporary practice of reading the Bible through its subversive tradition, through its unorthodoxies, its apocrypha: by reading against the grain, upside-down, turning the text against itself. The 'Babylon' of which it spoke, where its people were still 'suffering', was not in Egypt but in Kingston – and later, as the name was syntagmatically extended to include the Metropolitan Police, in Brixton, Handsworth, Moss Side and Notting Hill. Rastafarianism played a critical role in the modern movement that made Jamaica and other Caribbean societies, for the first time, and irrecoverably, 'black'. In a further translation, this strange doctrine and discourse 'saved' the young black souls of second-generation Caribbean migrants in British cities in the 1960s and 1970s, and gave them pride and self-understanding. In Frantz Fanon's terms, it decolonized minds.

At the same time, it is worth recalling the awkward fact that the 'naturalization' of the descriptive term 'black' for the whole of the Caribbean, or the equivalent, 'Afro-Caribbean' for all West Indian migrants abroad, performs its own kind of silencing in our new transnational world. The young Trinidadian artist, Steve Ouditt, has lived and worked in the USA, England and what he describes as the 'Sucrotopia' of Trinidad. He describes himself as "a post-independence American/English educated Christian Indian Trinidadian West Indian Creole male artist", whose work – in written and installation form – "navigates the difficult terrain between the visual and the verbal". He addresses this issue head-on in one of his recent pieces for his online diary, "Enigma of Survival".

> Afro-Caribbean is the blanket term for any Caribbean in England. For real. It is as real as when many well-educated people here say to me, 'You are from the Caribbean, how come, you are nor even black, you look Asian'... I do believe that the term 'Afro-Caribbean' is a British naming and perhaps it is supposed to represent the image of the majority of West Indian migrants who came here in the post-war period. And it is used to mark and remember in their past the politics and horrors of slavery, the European classification of Africans as ultrainferior. The fragmentation and loss of 'culture' but with desires to negotiate a new 'Afroness' in this diasporic site...In this specificity I can deal with 'Afro-Caribbean'... but not when it is used as the privileged index of horror to settle and centre all other subaltern Caribbean historiographies under an Afrophilia of the Caribbean here in Britain ... Trinidad has had a history of indentureship of Indians in labour camp apartheid for as long as it has had 'organized' slavery ...[25]

What these examples suggest is that culture is not just a voyage of rediscovery, a return journey. It is not an 'archeology'. Culture is a production. It has its raw materials, its resources, its 'work-of-production'. It depends on a knowledge of tradition as "the changing same" and an effective set of genealogies.[26] But what this 'detour through its pasts' does is to enable us, through culture, to produce ourselves anew, as new kinds of subjects. It is therefore not a question of what our traditions make of us so much as what we make of our traditions. Paradoxically, our cultural identities, in any finished form, lie ahead of us. We are always in the process of cultural formation. Culture is not a matter of ontology, of being, but of becoming.

In its present, hectic and accentuated forms, globalization is busily disentangling and subverting further its own inherited essentializing and homogenizing cultural models, undoing the limits and, in the process, unravelling the darkness of the West's own 'Enlightenment'. Identities thought of as settled and stable are coming to grief on the rocks of a proliferating differentiation. Across the globe, the processes of so-called free and forced migrations are changing the composition, diversifying the cultures and pluralizing the cultural identities of the older dominant nation states, the old imperial powers, and, indeed, of the globe itself.[27] The unregulated flows of peoples and cultures is as broad and as unstoppable as the sponsored flows of capital and technology. The former inaugurate a new process of 'minoritization' within the old metropolitan societies whose cultural homogeneity has long been silently assumed. But these 'minorities' are not effectively ghettoized; they do not long remain enclave settlements. They engage the dominant culture along a very broad front. They belong, in fact, to a transnational movement, and their connections are multiple and lateral. They mark the end of a 'modernity' defined exclusively in Western terms.

In fact, there are two, opposed processes at work in contemporary forms of globalization, which is itself a fundamentally contradictory process. There are the dominant forces of cultural homogenization, by which, because of its ascendancy in the cultural marketplace and its domination of capital, technological and cultural 'flows', Western culture, more specifically, American culture, threatens to overwhelm all comers, imposing a homogenizing cultural sameness – what has been called the 'McDonald-ization' or 'Nike-ization' of everything. Its effects are to be seen across the world, including the popular life of the Caribbean. But right alongside that are processes that are slowly and subtly decentring Western models, leading to a dissemination of cultural difference across the globe.

These 'other' tendencies do not (yet) have the power, frontally, to confront and repel the former head-on. But they do have the capacity, everywhere, to subvert and 'translate', to negotiate and indigenize the global cultural onslaught on weaker cultures. And since the new global consumer markets depend precisely on their becoming 'localized' to be effective, there is certain leverage in what may appear at first to be merely 'local'. These days, the 'merely' local and the global are locked together; not because the latter is the local working-through of essentially global effects, but because each is the condition of existence of the other. Once 'modernity' was transmitted from a single centre. Today, it has no such centre. 'Modernities' are everywhere; but they have taken on a vernacular accentuation. The fate and fortunes of the simplest and poorest farmer in the most remote corner of the world depends on the unregulated shifts of the global market – and, for that reason, he or she is now an essential element part of every global calculation. Politicians know the poor will not be cut out of, or defined out of, this 'modernity'. They are not prepared to be immured forever in an immutable 'tradition'. They are determined to construct their own kinds of 'vernacular modernities', and these are the signifiers of a new kind of transnational, even postnational, transcultural consciousness.

This 'narrative' has no guaranteed happy ending. Many in the old nation states, who are deeply attached to the purer forms of national self-understanding, are literally driven crazy by their erosion. They feel their whole universe threatened by change, and coming down about their ears. 'Cultural difference' of a rigid, ethnicized and unnegotiable kind, has taken the place of sexual miscegenation as the primal postcolonial fantasy. A racially driven 'fundamentalism' has surfaced in all these Western European and North American societies, a new kind of defensive and racialized nationalism. Prejudice, injustice, discrimination and violence towards 'the Other', based on this hypostasized 'cultural difference', has come to take its place – what Sarat Maharaj has called a sort of "spook look-alike of apartheid" – alongside the older racisms, founded on skin-colour and physiological difference – giving rise in response to a 'politics of recognition', alongside the struggles against racism and for social justice.

These developments may at first seem remote from the concerns of new emerging nations and cultures of the 'periphery'. But as we suggested, the old centre-periphery, nation-nationalist-culture model is exactly what is breaking down. Emerging cultures that feel threatened by the forces of globalization, diversity and hybridization, or that have failed in the project of modernization, may feel tempted to close down around their nationalist inscriptions and construct defensive walls. The alternative is not to cling to closed, unitary, homogenous models of 'cultural belonging' but to embrace the wider processes – the play of similarity and difference – that are transforming culture worldwide. This is the path of 'diaspora', which is the pathway of a modern people and a modern culture. This may look, at first, just like – but is really very different from – the old 'internationalism' of European modernism. Jean Fisher has argued that, until recently,

> Internationalism has always referred exclusively to a European-European diasporan axis of political, military and economic affiliations... This entrenched and dominant axis creates, in Mosquera's words, 'zones of silence' elsewhere, making it difficult for lateral communications and other affiliations to take place. Araeen and Oguibe remind us that the present initiative [to define a new internationalism in the arts and culture] is only the most recent in a history of such attempts at cross-cultural dialogue which have been erased from 'established narrations of cultural practice in Britain [and which failed] to overwhelm the deep-seated and firm structures which we interrogate' (Oguibe).[28]

What we have in mind here is something quite different – that 'other' kind of modernity that led C. L. R. James to remark of Caribbean people, "Those people who are in western civilization, who have grown up in it, but made to feel and themselves feeling they are outside it, have a unique insight into their society."[29]

Acknowledgment

This lecture was first given as part of the celebrations of the fiftieth anniversary of the founding of the University of the West Indies (UWI) held at the Cave Hill campus, Barbados, in November 1998.

Notes
1. This is the subtitle of the volume, *Windrush,* by Mike Phillips and Trevor Phillips (London: HarperCollins, 1998) that accompanied the BBC TV series.
2. Benedict Anderson, *Imagined Communities* (London: Verso, 1991).
3. Mary Chamberlain, *Narratives of Exile and Return* (Houndsmill: Macmillan, 1998).
4. See T. Modood, R. Berthoud, et al., *Ethnic Minorities in Britain* (London: Policy Studies Institute, 1997).
5. Chamberlain, *Narratives,* 132.

6. Iain Chambers, *Border Dialogues: Journeys in Post-Modernity* (London: Routledge, 1990), 104.
7. See Stuart Hall, 'Cultural Identity and Diaspora,' in *Identity: Community, Culture, Difference*, ed. Jonathan Rutherford (London: Lawrence and Wishart, 1990); and S. Hall and P. duGay, eds., *Questions of Cultural Identity* (London: Sage, 1997), 222–37.
8. See Stuart Hall, 'The West and the Rest: Discourse and Power,' in *Formations of Modernity* (Cambridge: Polity Press and The Open University, 1994), 274–320.
9. Mary Louise Pratt, *Imperial Eyes: Travel Writing and Transculturation* (London: Routledge, 1992). See, *inter alia*, Fernando Ortiz, *Cuban Counterpoint: Tobacco and Sugar* (New York: A.A. Knopf, 1947); Edouard Glissant, *Le Discours Antillais* (Paris: Editions du Seuil, 1981); Edward Kamau Brathwaite, *The Development of Creole Society in Jamaica, 1770–1820* (Oxford: Oxford University Press. 1971).
10. Pratt, *Imperial Eyes*, 6–7.
11. David Scott, 'Conscripts of Modernity' (unpublished paper).
12. *Redemption Song*. Seven programmes made with Barraclough and Carey for BBC2 and transmitted 1989–90.
13. M. Bakhtin and V.N. Volosinov, *Marxism and the Philosophy of Language* (New York and London: Seminar Press, 1973).
14. Kobena Mercer, 'Diaspora Culture and the Dialogic Imagination,' in *Welcome to the Jungle: New Positions in Black Cultural Studies* (London: Routledge, 1994), 63–64.
15. Salman Rushdie, *Imaginary Homelands* (London: Granta Books, 1990), 394.
16. Chambers, *Border Dialogues*, 104.
17. Immanuel Wallerstein, 'The National and the Universal,' in *Culture, Globalization and the World System*, ed. A. King (London: Macmillan, 1991), 91–106.
18. Paul Gilroy, *The Black Atlantic* (London: Verso, 1993).
19. *Babymother* was released in London, the USA and Jamaica in 1998. It was directed by Julian Henriques, the son of a distinguished Jamaican anthropologist who lives in London and produced by his wife and partner, Parminder Vir, who is from the Punjab. They met, needless to say, from these two poles of Empire, in London.
20. The official inquiry chaired by Sir William Macpherson into the death of Stephen Lawrence, convened after five years only as a result of the heroic efforts of his parents, Doreen and Neville Lawrence and a small group of block supporters, was a public event and a cause célèbre in 1998, and a turning point in British race relations. It resulted in the judge finding the Metropolitan Police guilty of 'institutional racism.' See Sir William Macpherson of Cluny, *The Stephen Lawrence Inquiry Report*, Cmnd. 4262–1 (1999).
21. Guy Brett, 'A Tragic Excitement,' in *Aubrey Williams* (London: Institute for the International Visual Arts and Whitechapel Gallery, 1998), 24.
22. See David Scott, 'That Event, This Memory: Notes on the Anthropology of African Diasporas in the New World.' *Diaspora* 1, no. 3 (1991): 261–84.
23. Sarat Maharaj, 'Perfidious Fidelity,' in *Global Visions: Towards a New Internationalism in the Visual Arts*, ed. Jean Fisher (London: Institute of the International Visual Arts, 1994), 31. The reference is to Jacques Derrida, 'Des Tours des Babel,' in *Difference in Translation* (Ithaca: Cornell University Press, 1985).
24. The title of one of the most important chapters in Frantz Fanon, *Black Skin, White Masks* (London: Pluto Press, 1986).
25. Steve Ouditt, 'Enigma of Survival,' in *Annotations 4: Creole-in-Site*, ed. Gilane Tanadros (London: Institute of the International Visual Arts, 1998), 8–9.
26. For 'tradition as the changing same,' see Gilroy, *The Black Atlantic*.
27. See, for example, Arjun Appadurai, *Modernity at Large* (Minneapolis: University of Minnesota Press, 1996).
28. Jean Fisher, 'Editor's Note,' in *Global Visions: Towards a New Internationalism in the Visual Arts*, ed. J. Fisher (London: Institute for the International Visual Arts, 1994), xii.
29. C.L.R. James, 'Africans and Afro-Caribbeans: A Personal View,' *Ten 8*, no. 16.

The Diasporic Mo(ve)ment:
Indentureship and Indo-Caribbean Identity

Sean Lokaisingh-Meighoo

The argument of this chapter will unfold in four scenes. Each scene will lead into the next, and new concepts will be encountered within each scene. I think it necessary to follow my argument in this way if the many layers of the story I want to tell are to be appreciated. Of course, there are themes that will recur throughout, and some sort of narrative that will hold it all together. My argument is organized around the concept of what I will call the diasporic mo(ve)ment—that historical point of rupture between diaspora and home, which pins but does not fix diasporic identity in both time and space. So although this paper is about the significance of Indian indentureship in the Caribbean, there are many interrelated problems, both specific and general, ethno-historical and theoretical, that must be met along the way—the constitution of Indo-Caribbean identity, the meaning of diaspora, and even the very workings of identity.

The first act, as such, will deal with the concept of diaspora in two scenes. In starting with a discussion of diaspora as a style rather than an identity itself, I want to suggest right away that diaspora is neither an intra- nor an extra-cultural concept. That is, the concept of diaspora cannot be theorized without reference to specific cultural identities, and yet, diaspora always escapes any such reference. The meaning of diaspora does not lie either fully inside or fully outside specific cultural identities, but may only be approached through the ongoing articulation of these identities. This, then, explains the first of my chapter's excesses: in discussing Indo-Caribbean identity, we must always consider its relationship with Afro-Caribbean and other diasporic identities. And let me also spell out a corollary here, that my discussion of indentureship in this chapter offers important insights not only into Indo-Caribbean identity but into the intercultural politics of diaspora.

The second act will move on to address indentureship in particular, again in two scenes. Revisiting some of the key characters introduced in the first act, I want to further suggest that not only must any discussion of cultural identity grapple with the challenge of cultural difference, but that moreover, this challenge of cultural difference must itself grapple with its own limits. The theoretical discourse of difference has certainly proven invaluable in dislodging nationalist and fundamentalist claims based on notions of absolute identity. However, this discourse itself runs the risk of falling into an equally absolute notion of difference, an unrelenting relativism that prohibits any critical discussion of the relationships that bring together different nations, religions, and cultures. The final part of the chapter, on the comparison between indentureship and slavery within Indo-Caribbean studies, then, will attempt to confront this renewed problem of cultural identity and difference.

Yet I still have not explained the second of the excesses: my brief discussion of Indo-Caribbean religion is buried within a largely theoretical treatment of diasporic identity. But this is only apparently the case. Let us not forget, after all, that the concept of diaspora, the organizing theme of this chapter, is itself a religious one, appropriated from the Jewish tradition of textual exegesis and oral transmission. However, anyone at all acquainted with current cultural politics knows that diaspora is not "just" a religious concept anymore. But what a more critical consideration of the diaspora concept would question is that it ever was "just" a religious one, and that the religious ever has been so distinct from the secular. Rather, diaspora indicates that the religious and the secular are always already mutually implied and that the notion of religion as a discrete social practice is itself an invention of modem secularism. The implication of religion with other social practices is perhaps especially evident in the Caribbean, where issues of identity and difference along with themes of captivity and redemption seem to inform all areas of life. But let me suggest here that this relation between the religious and the secular is not at all unique to the Caribbean. What the study of Caribbean religion and culture suggests, as such, is that the object of religious studies in general must not be limited to "just" the religious, at least not in its conventional sense. And likewise, what the concept of diaspora in particular gestures toward is the importance of religious studies in the critical understanding of not only modern Caribbean but modern world culture.

DIASPORA AS STYLE

Diaspora is not the objective result of dispersal through any and all sorts of migration from an already constituted cultural center, as much as a cultural process of the articulation of both this center and its dispersal. That is, home itself is produced only through diaspora. Thus, the naturalness of diaspora as well as home must be brought into reckoning with their artificiality. This dialectical relationship between diaspora and home is radically unstable and fraught with all those tensions that so characteristically exist between those living in diaspora and those living at home. In many circumstances, communication between those in diaspora and those at home may seem to be strained beyond the possibility of mutual recognition. However, the relationship between diaspora and home must be maintained, for not only is home always present in the articulation of diaspora, but diaspora is always present in the articulation of home. As is often the case indeed, the more tenuous the bond between diaspora and home, the more tenacious is its claim. Now, this is not to say that no other sense of home may be produced besides that of the diasporic process. However, for those engaged in the formation of diasporic identities, the familiarity of home is recognized only through this cultural process.

Diasporic culture must be theoretically approached, then, as a *style* of identity formation rather than a specific cultural identity. The articulation of diasporic identities works through the popular cultural processes of recognition and repetition, substitution and subversion. The concept of style has been most carefully theorized by Dick Hebdige in *Subculture: The Meaning of Style* (1993). In analyzing the race politics and aesthetic practices of the British postwar working-class youth subcultures of reggae, rock, and punk, Hebdige offers a reading of style as "signifying practice" (117–27). Drawing from the theoretical work in semiotics of the Tel Quel group including Julia Kristeva and Roland Barthes, Hebdige argues against "the simple notion of reading as the revelation of a fixed number of concealed meanings...in favour of the idea of *polysemy* whereby each text is seen to generate a potentially infinite range of meanings" (117, his emphasis). The meaning of style, as such, is approached in "the *process* of meaning-construction rather than [in] the final product" (118, his emphasis). Hebdige further argues that this concept of style as signifying practice allows for a "rethink[ing] in a more subtle and complex way the relations not only between marginal and mainstream cultural formations but between the various subcultural styles themselves" (120). Thus, while Hebdige does not attend to the theoretical concept of diaspora in his study of black and white

British youth subcultures, his theoretical work on style may be stretched here to accommodate the concept of diaspora.

This theorization of diaspora as style or signifying practice has some important and interrelated implications. While the concept of diaspora is highly developed in certain cultural traditions and in particular the Jewish tradition, diaspora as cultural process is not culturally specific—that is, peculiar to certain "ethnic" groups. Rather, as a set of creative practices, this style of identity formation is always receptive to collaboration and innovation, even in the process of the articulation of specific cultural identities. It is in this sense that diaspora is neither an intra- nor an extra-cultural concept, neither inside nor outside specific cultural identities, but is rather a cultural style through which specific identities are formed.

As such, diaspora cannot be said to be a new cultural form. Rather, diaspora constitutes an old and even traditional style of historically conceptualizing new and ever-changing circumstances. In some cultural contexts, including the formation of African-American, South Asian, Afro-Caribbean, and Indo-Caribbean identities, the current proliferation of cultural practices associated with the articulation of these diasporic identities is certainly a remarkably recent phenomenon. Yet even in these contexts, these practices are historically related to those much older cultural practices that articulated various versions of what may be called proto-diasporic African and Indian identities. At the same time, this current proliferation of diasporic identities is also a matter of style, for the concept of diaspora is certainly subject to trends of popularity. The widespread currency of the term itself in its varied cultural contexts indicates precisely its present fashionability in aesthetic, political, and academic practices alike.

As diaspora constitutes a particular cultural style, then, there surely exist other styles or sets of signifying practices. Popularly circulating in current cultural politics are a number of salient styles of identity formation, including those of First Nations and Latin American cultural identities, not to mention other formations in current cultural politics organized around gender and sexual, as well as national and religious, identities. Certainly, these cultural styles are not impervious to each other, and they freely infiltrate one another. Yet each of these styles as a particular set of signifying practices articulates different meanings. First Nations cultural identities are articulated through a sense of nativeness, aboriginality, or indigeneity and connection to the environment. In contrast, diasporic cultural identities are marked by a sense of exile and often alienation from the land of residence. Meanwhile, Latin American cultural identities selectively incorporate these concerns of First Nations indigeneity and diasporic alienation through the articulation of *mestizaje,* or cultural mixing. Each of these cultural styles carries certain sets of meanings as much as it works through certain sets of practices. Diaspora, as such, constitutes a particularly meaningful though currently popular style of identity formation.

THE DIASPORIC MO(VE)MENT

The theorization of diaspora as style may be extended, then, to the ontological level—that is, the level of meaning. Diasporic identities are marked by ontological significance for those who are engaged in the creative practices of their articulation. Certainly, one of the most basic though important points of Hebdige's semiotic approach to style is his insistence on the meaning of style. As he emphatically puts it, "Style in subculture is...pregnant with significance" (1993: 18). Similarly, the formation of diasporic identities involves the work of meaning as much as a play on meaning. Diaspora works through the subversion as well as the substantiation of identities. "Substance" therefore, is inscribed within the concept of diaspora as "style." Simply put, diaspora means something to "diasporics."

In working toward the particular meaning of diaspora, then, the work of C.L.R. James, Cornel West, and Paul Gilroy on what may be called black modernity has been most constructive for me in thinking through diaspora as ontology. For much like modernity, diaspora is based on an acute sense of *historical rupture*. And yet it is conceptually different from modernity, or at least Eurocentric modernity, in a significant way. My counter-position of diaspora and modernity as styles of identity formation in this section is primarily informed by this work on black modernity. Although of these theorists only Gilroy deals specifically with the concept of diaspora as well as that of modernity, it is important to realize that James, West, and Gilroy have all written during the period when the concept of diaspora was taken up by Caribbean, American, and British national citizens in identifying themselves culturally as diasporic Africans. While James wrote early in this period, when the concept of diaspora as adopted from Jewish tradition was just beginning to gain currency among pan-African advocates, West and Gilroy have written more recently, when the diaspora concept was being extended further by cultural communities other than the African diaspora. Of course, we are still in this historical period that is marked by the proliferation of diasporic identities.

In his appendix to the second edition of *The Black Jacobins,* "From Toussaint L'Ouverture to Fidel Castro" (1963), James inaugurates this work on black modernity in a brief though succinct argument:

> When three centuries ago the slaves came to the West Indies, they entered directly into the large-scale agriculture of the sugar plantation, which was a modem system. It further required that the slaves live together in a social relation far closer than any proletariat of the time. The cane when reaped had to be rapidly transported to what was factory production. The product was shipped abroad for sale. Even the cloth the slaves wore and the food they ate was imported. The Negroes, therefore, from the very start lived a life that was in its essence a modern life. That is their history—as far as I have been able to discover, a unique history. (392)

For James, then, modernity is constituted by the international economic system, in which the African slaves were central in terms of both production and consumption from its early beginnings. As such, James suggests that the African slaves on the Caribbean plantations, not the European capitalists or even the workers, were the first fully fledged moderns. James's theorization of modernity, then, is significantly different from and yet very relevant to my own, for I maintain that his revision of Eurocentric modernity is itself a prerogative of diasporic identity.

West also only briefly addresses black modernity in discussing his commitment to what he calls "prophetic criticism" in his preface to *Keeping Faith* (1993). West places this "prophetic vision and practice ... at the core of [his] intellectual vocation and existential engagement" (x). Citing Du Bois's notion of double-consciousness, he posits that prophetic criticism draws from both Euro-American modernity and New World African modernity. He describes this New World African modernity as "what we get when Africans in the Americas...remake and recreate themselves into a distinctly *new* people" (xii-xiii, his emphasis). Recalling yet significantly revising the argument of James, West asserts, "If modernity is measured in terms of newness and novelty, innovation and improvisation—and not simply in terms of science, technology, markets, bureaucracies and nation-states—then New World African modernity is more thoroughly *modern* than any American novel, painting, dance or even skyscraper" (xiii, his emphasis). In further considering the relationship between these multiple modernities, West argues, "New World African modernity radically interrogates and creatively appropriates Euro-American modernity by examining how 'race' and 'Africa'—themselves modem European constructs—yield insights and blindnesses, springboards and roadblocks for our understanding of multi-various and multileveled modernities" (xii).

While West does not particularly address the concept of diaspora, he does deal with migration, the attendant concerns with temporality and spatiality, and the concept of home. Arguing that "[t]he fundamental theme of New World African modernity is neither integration nor separation but rather migration and emigration" (xiii), West explains that "[i]n the space-time of New World African modernity, to hope is to conceive of possible movement, to despair is to feel ossified, petrified, closed in" (xiv). He describes the search for home as historically exemplified in the Garveyite movement as the "wedding of black misery in America to transnational mobility to Africa, forging a sense of possible momentum and motion for a temporal people with few spatial options" (xiii–xiv). West's own discussion in the preface to his book is occasioned by his marriage and incorporation into a prominent Ethiopian family, raising for him "urgent issues of inheritance and rootlessness, tradition and homelessness" (x). Questioning his urge to leave America and live in Ethiopia, "the land of New World African modern fantasies of 'home'" (xv), he rhetorically asks, "Is this the urge of an émigré, an expatriate or an exile?" (x). Furthermore, embodying the dialectics of diasporic identity, West's prefatory essay is itself divided by the three headings "In Ethiopia," "In America," and lastly, "At Home."

It is Gilroy who most thoroughly deals with both black modernity and the concept of diaspora in his remarkable book *The Black Atlantic* (1993). In this work, he theorizes historical black thought on as well as current vernacular and literary cultures of modernity, also employing, like West, Du Bois's notion of double consciousness. Drawing from the work of Zygmunt Bauman, he posits the Black Atlantic diaspora as "a distinctive counterculture of modernity" (36). But Gilroy is most concerned with the relationship between modernity and diaspora in dealing with current black cultural politics. Arguing that "integral" to modernity is the "decentred and inescapably plural nature of modern subjectivity and identity" (46, 48), he further claims that postmodernity is thus "foreshadowed, or prefigured, in the lineaments of modernity itself" (42). In addressing black discourse, Gilroy critiques what he calls "Africentrism" and more specifically the sustained ideological opposition between the modern and the traditional in "Africentric" politics. He argues that the "Africentric movement appears to rely upon a linear idea of time that is enclosed at each end by the grand narrative of African advancement" in which "the duration of a black civilisation anterior to modernity is invoked" (190). Those who subscribe to Africentrism claim a "ready access to and command of tradition—sometimes ancient, always anti-modern" through which "Africa is retained as one special measure [of] authenticity" (191). Gilroy seeks to unsettle this easy acceptance of tradition as the "antithesis" (187) of modernity, "outside of the erratic flows of history" (191).

In this project, Gilroy takes up "the undertheorized idea of diaspora" (6). In doing so, he rejects the theoretical symbolization of diaspora "as the fragmentary opposite of some imputed racial essence" in "the unhappy polar opposition between a squeamish, nationalist essentialism and a sceptical, saturnalian pluralism" (95, 102). Rather, he claims that the cultural history of the Black Atlantic "explodes the dualistic structure which puts Africa, authenticity, purity, and origin in crude opposition to the Americas, hybridity, creolisation, and rootlessness" (199). Gilroy works toward an understanding of the concept of diaspora in tracing the attempts of black intellectuals to rewrite modernity;

> Du Bois, Douglass, Wright and the rest shared a sense that the modern world was fragmented along axes constituted by racial conflict and could accommodate non-synchronous, heterocultural modes of social life in close proximity. Their conceptions of modernity were periodised differently. They were founded on the catastrophic rupture of the middle passage rather than the dream of revolutionary transformation. (197)

Commenting on what may be called this diasporic revision of modernity in which James also participated, Gilroy suggests that "[t]he idea of diaspora might itself be understood as a response to these promptings—a utopian eruption of space into the linear temporal order of modem black politics which enforces the obligation that space and time must be considered relationally in their interarticulation with racialised being" (198). In his project, then, Gilroy proposes "to integrate the *spatial* focus on the diaspora idea...with the diaspora temporality and historicity, memory and narrativity that are the articulating principles of the black political countercultures that grew inside modernity in a distinctive relationship of antagonistic indebtedness" (191, his emphasis). His work aims to "reckon with the tension between temporalities [in black political culture] that leads intellectuals to try to press original African time into the service of their attempts to come to terms with diaspora space" (196–97). As such, Gilroy arguing that "[d]iaspora time is not, it would seem, African [as in Africentric] time" (196), theoretically articulates and politically commits himself to "[t]he desire to bring a new historicity into black political culture" (190).

In his discussion of diaspora and modernity, Gilroy's work has most obviously stimulated my own approach to the concept of diaspora, whether or not our theoretical treatments are fully compatible. I begin with the postulation that diasporic identity is articulated through the experience of historical rupture. Yet modern identity is also based on a sense of historical rupture. Thus, diaspora and modernity are conceptually different though ambivalently related. In theorizing the relationship between the historical rupture of diaspora and then of modernity, then, the concept of history itself must be problematized through the critical consideration of *temporality* and *spatiality*.

Modern identity is based on rupture, and this historical sense of rupture is temporal. Thus, modernity is not based on the material fact of social or technological progress, but it is rather this belief in progress that characterizes modem identity. Modernity is articulated through the assertion of the newness of current times, not in any banal sense of novelty but in a profound sense of a distinct order of newness. The modern is thus cleaved from the traditional. This cleavage is marked by a specific point in time. Regardless of any disagreement over which point in time this actually was, the significant feature of modernity is that the split between the traditional and the modern is identified within a linear temporal history. The traditional in this sense as well as the modern, then, are the dialectical products of modernity. The traditional is constructed as the very nemesis of the modern, the anti-modern.

The concept of tradition, however, may be used to undermine modernity. Tradition may be revived not as the anti-modern but as an irruption into the modern through which the separation between the modern and the traditional is problematized. Tradition is commonly used in this subversive sense in diasporic politics as well as in other styles of cultural politics, such as the First Nations movement, and other forms of politics that similarly challenge modernity, such as environmentalism.

Postmodernity, then, constitutes another production of modernity. Postmodernity certainly problematizes the modern notion of progress as it signifies that modernity is not the end of history. Yet in claiming a break not only with the traditional but also with the modern itself, the postmodern is thoroughly modern precisely in that this historical break is temporalized. Thus, the logic of modernity as characterized by the linear temporality of history is not negated as much as multiplied, if not arithmetically then exponentially, in the logic of postmodernity.

Now, like modern identity, diasporic identity is based on rupture, but the concept of history and thus the meaning of historical rupture differ significantly between these identities. Whereas the concept of history in modernity is strictly temporal, history in diaspora includes the senses of both temporality *and* spatiality. Diaspora is thus articulated through the experience of temporal *and* spatial rupture. The traumatic significance of this rupture is condensed into a specific historical point—*the diasporic mo(ve)ment*—both a moment in time and a movement in space. This is the point that pins but does not fix, like a thumbtack on a corkboard, that perpetually unstable dialectical structure of diasporic identity. Every diasporic identity hinges upon such a mo(ve)ment. For the Jewish diaspora, the Dispersion marks this mo(ve)ment, while for the African diaspora, the Middle Passage marks it. The significance of these foundational events does not lie in their historicity as such, but is rather approached through their condensation into particular historical points, both temporal and spatial. This diasporic mo(ve)ment marks the split between diaspora and home. Now, while the concept of history in diaspora is both temporal and spatial, there is a characteristic emphasis on the latter dimension of spatiality within diasporic cultural practices.

Although the historical rupture of diaspora is thus significantly different from that of modernity, then, diasporic and modern identities are ontologically related. Certainly, the spatial dimension of diaspora is emphasized at least partly as a direct challenge to the linear temporal history of modernity. Diasporic history displaces modernist history, or rather more appropriately, diasporic history *places* modernist history. The claim to universality of modernity is challenged by diaspora in that diasporic history relativizes the linear temporal history of Eurocentric modernity. Diasporic identity introduces another history—a counter-history—into modern identity. Or rather again, as modern identity is not necessarily ontologically or chronologically prior to diasporic identity, diaspora and modernity provide counter-histories to each other.

As previously noted, West and Gilroy in comparison to James have written on diaspora during the recent period, in which diasporic identity was being claimed by various cultural communities other than the diasporic African community. The relationship between these various diasporic identities must also be critically addressed. James, in his diasporic revision of modernity, comments on the "unique history" of the "Negro" slaves (1963: 392). Similarly, West notes that prophetic criticism is "primarily based on a distinctly black tragic sense of life" (1993: x). Considering these claims of what may be interpreted as cultural specificity, then, the appropriateness of the work of James, West, and Gilroy on black modernity for my theorization of diaspora as ontology, which is not specific to the African cultural context, might well be questioned.

This issue of the relationship between diasporic communities, however, has not only recently become central to the cultural politics of diaspora. The appropriation of the very concept of diaspora from the Jewish tradition by pan-African advocates has already necessitated a primary attention to this issue. Gilroy explicitly attends to this appropriation, calling for the collaboration between black and Jewish thinkers in particular and providing an argument for "the intercultural history of the diaspora concept" (1993: 211) that effectively addresses the issue of cultural specificity. Repudiating the "pointless and utterly immoral wrangle over which communities have experienced the most ineffable forms of degradation" (212), Gilroy emphatically states:

> I want to resist the idea that the Holocaust is merely another instance of genocide. I accept arguments for its uniqueness. However, I do not want the recognition of that uniqueness to be an obstacle to better understanding of the complicity of rationality and ethnocidal terror to which this book is dedicated. This is a difficult line on which to balance but it should be possible, and enriching, to discuss these histories together. (213)

Similarly then, while the particularity of African slavery must be appreciated, this recognition must not limit the use of the black tradition in understanding the intercultural politics of diaspora. As such, the work on black modernity by James and West as well as by Gilroy constitutes a significant theoretical intervention into diasporic cultural politics in its broadest sense, not only black political discourse.

As there are indeed many diasporic identities besides African identity circulating in current cultural politics, there are certainly many diasporic histories challenging the linear temporal history of Eurocentric modernity. However, these various histories do not necessarily undermine each other, for their spatialization allows for the relative placing of all of them. Diasporic histories, as such, are *concurrent*. Furthermore, the articulation of diasporic identities challenges Eurocentric modernity precisely in its placing of modernist history as also concurrent with diasporic histories. The postmodernist break with the modern is at least partly a response to the entry of these diasporic identities into modernist political discourse. Of course, the success of postmodernism in grappling with the challenge of diaspora, as well as other such significant interventions into modernity as feminism and queer politics, is debatable.

However, this diasporic dimension of spatiality may seem to imply that these various diasporic histories are *parallel*—that is, that they never meet and are thus discrete. I argue that this is the most urgent problematic within the articulation of diaspora itself. The relative placing of diasporic histories suggests that diasporic identities coexist independently alongside of each other, each following its own linear course of historical progress. I contend that diasporic cultural identities are collaboratively produced and, refiguring the spatial imagery of diaspora, that diasporic histories are not parallel but regularly *intersect*. Even as distinct cultural identities are claimed through current articulations of diaspora, this cultural process of diasporic articulation must itself be recognized as an ontologically particular though currently popular style of identity formation.

As such, the problematic of cultural specificity may be effectively addressed through the further articulation of what may be called *critical difference in diaspora*. As the specificity of each diasporic history must be appreciated, so must the intercultural and collaborative production of diasporic identity be recognized. It is only through this interplay of "identity" and "difference" that the concept of cultural difference takes on any critical significance. For if claims of cultural specificity are regularly informed by the multiculturalist notion of absolute difference, then any politically challenging formation of diasporic identity must articulate this other sense of critical difference. Only thus may the proliferation of diasporic identities in current cultural politics be recognized not simply as an exhibitionist display of the diversity of cultures in the mosaic sense, but more saliently as a radical disruption of linear temporal historicity altogether.

INDO CARIBBEAN IDENTITY AND THE DOUBLY DIASPORIC

One such current diasporic formation is that of Indo-Caribbean identity. The term *Indo-Caribbean* itself is rather new, its earliest appearance in print and systematic use as far as I know dating from the mid-eighties in community newspapers and books published in Toronto. Certainly, there are many "East Indians" (another loaded discursive formation of diasporic identity, of course, popularly used both within the Caribbean and throughout its diaspora) from the Caribbean who do not identify as "Indo-Caribbean." However, many such as myself have come to claim this newly formed Indo-Caribbean identity, and the term seems to be gaining popularity, particularly outside of the Caribbean in the diasporic communities of the metropolitan cities of Europe and North America.

This Indo-Caribbean identity then, is *doubly diasporic*. For the Indo-Caribbean diaspora is founded upon two mo(ve)ments—the first marking the colonial institution of Indian indentureship in the Caribbean during the nineteenth and early twentieth centuries, and the second the neocolonial regulation of Caribbean migration to Europe and North America after World War II until the present. In the diasporic commemoration of these historical ruptures, indentureship and migration have become inextricably linked, the first mo(ve)ment rhetorically figured as the crossing of *K la P ni*, or the Dark Waters, upon the retrospective occasion of the second mo(ve)ment, which as yet remains nameless and perhaps is still unnamable. Those living in the Indo-Caribbean diaspora, then, claim the two diasporic homes of India *and* the Caribbean. As such, those who identify as Indo-Caribbean claim not only national citizenship in the multicultural state but also both Indian and Caribbean cultural identities. The historical emergence of Indo-Caribbean identity is thus intimately related to the formation of Afro-Caribbean and South Asian diasporic identities and further informed by the encounters between these and other diasporas in the metropolitan cities of Europe and North America.

This doubled sense of historical rupture is inscribed within the term *Indo-Caribbean* itself, the first mo(ve)ment of indentureship recalled through the prefix *Indo-* and the second mo(ve)ment of migration through the suffix *-Caribbean*. The recollection of India in this *Indo-* is not that of the politically independent secular state of the same name, but rather that of the cultural space of India that the indentured laborers left behind as home. This home of the first mo(ve)ment in Indo-Caribbean identity, then, is significantly different than the home of the South Asian diaspora. While the South Asian diaspora is founded upon a notion of home that redresses the political separation between the states of India, Pakistan, Sri Lanka, and Bangladesh, the thoroughly diasporic notion of a culturally integrated India still informs the articulation of Indo-Caribbean identity. What Seecharan (1993: 34) has notably called a "Gandhian India" thrives perhaps most strongly in the active memory of the Indian diaspora in the Caribbean.

Meanwhile, the Indo-Caribbean recollection in this *-Caribbean* is of a pan-Caribbean cultural space. While loyalty to the state and affinity to the local remain important to many Indo-Caribbean people, as expressed in their simultaneous claiming of various national and even town or village identities, these are qualified by this broader sense of the Caribbean. Samuel Selvon recalls the diasporic production of pan-Caribbean identity in Britain:

> When I left Trinidad in 1950 and went to England, one of my first experiences was living in a hostel with people from Africa and India and all over the Caribbean. It is strange to think I had to cross the Atlantic and be thousands of miles away, in a different culture and environment, for it to come about that, for the first time in my life, I was living among Barbadians and Jamaicans and others from my part of the world. If I had remained in Trinidad I might never have had the opportunity to be at such close quarters to observe and try to understand the differences and prejudices that exist from islander to islander. (1987: 16)

Selvon further comments that "among the immigrants abroad, when they talk of returning home the concept has widened into the greater area rather than to any particular island" (22). However, this articulation of pan-Caribbean identity is not unique to the Indo-Caribbean diaspora but is rather similar in other diasporic Caribbean communities. Stuart Hall likewise describes the historical emergence of Black identity during the seventies in Britain:

> Then Black erupted and people said, "Well, you're from the Caribbean, in the midst of this, identifying with what's going on, the Black population in England. You're Black."... People [began] to ask, "Are you from Jamaica, are you from Trinidad, are you from Barbados?" You can just see the process of divide and rule. "No. Just address me as I am. I know you can't tell the difference so just call me Black." (1991:55)

While Hall specifically addresses the development of British black politics in this passage, his use of examples of various Caribbean national or island identities is significant in its indication of the cultural formation of a pan-Caribbean identity within Britain. As such, this diasporic home of the second mo(ve)ment in Indo-Caribbean identity is collaboratively produced by Indo-, Afro-, and other diasporic Caribbean communities.

More precisely, however, this articulation of a doubled sense of diasporic identity indicates the creative collaboration of Indo- and Afro-Caribbean communities in particular on the ontological level. For Afro-Caribbean identity is similarly founded upon two diasporic mo(ve)ments—colonial slavery, commemorated as the Middle Passage, and neocolonial migration, again nameless and unnamable. Those living in the Afro-Caribbean diaspora also claim two diasporic homes—the integrated cultural space of Africa, undivided by colonial and now postcolonial borders, and the Caribbean, in its pan-regional sense. This articulation of doubled diaspora through the formation of Indo- and Afro-Caribbean identities is distinctly different from that of other hyphenated forms of cultural identity, thus radically altering the dialectics of diaspora and home. African-American diasporic identity, for example, though as a term of identity structurally similar to the term Afro-Caribbean, is constituted through only one diasporic mo(ve)ment, that of slavery. While the prefix *African-* recalls the historical rupture of the Middle Passage, the suffix *-American* refers not to any diasporic sense of dislocation but to national identity. Now, it is not that African Americans have not participated in any significant flow of migration since slavery. The large-scale migration of African Americans between the onsets of World War I and the Depression from the rural regions of the southern United States to the urban cities of the north is historically commemorated as the Great Migration, yet this historical episode does not discursively rupture African-American identity. It seems that American national identity is strong enough to have contained this potentially traumatic historical episode.

Both Indo- and Afro-Caribbean identities as doubly diasporic, then, further complicate the dialectics of diaspora and home on the ontological level. For these formations of cultural identity are doubly diasporic not so much in an arithmetic as in an exponential sense, or perhaps in the figurative sense through which the character of diaspora has doubled over on itself. In this stylish style of diasporic articulation, the place of home becomes even more ambiguous, its location even more slippery. Through the current international circulation of these doubly diasporic identities, what I have called an old and even traditional style of cultural identity has been radically modified, the Caribbean as a site of diaspora now transformed into a site of home, those barely traceable connections to India and Africa yet further rarefied.

INDENTURESHIP AND CRITICAL DIFFERENCE IN DIASPORA

However, this collaborative articulation of doubly diasporic Indo- and Afro-Caribbean identities certainly does not translate into any sort of cultural *equivalency* between them. Indo- and Afro-Caribbean diasporic communities enter into uneasy alliances at best when this strategy of equivalency is employed. Returning to the articulation of critical difference in diaspora, I revisit here the diasporic mo(ve)ments of indentureship and slavery, those foundational historical points through which Indo- and Afro-Caribbean cultural identities are respectively constituted. The deep ambivalence toward both diaspora and home within the formation of Indo-Caribbean identity itself is traced through a critical reading of some inaugural texts in the emerging field of Indo-Caribbean studies. This revision of Indo-Caribbean history contributes to my theoretical proposition for the articulation of critical difference in the intercultural politics of diaspora and furthermore, I suggest, may well be extended to current studies on slavery in the African diaspora and other diasporic studies.

In recently published works of Indo-Caribbean history, there is a recurrent concern with the resemblance of indentureship to slavery. While concessions are usually allowed for cultural specificity, indentureship is regularly paralleled with slavery. Thus, the Indo- and Afro-Caribbean experiences are constituted as discrete and, in a sense, replicable histories. This argument on indentureship has only recently gained acceptance within the Indo-Caribbean community, let alone the Afro-Caribbean one, yet it has quickly become a foundation in the new academic discourse of Indo-Caribbean studies. However, this parallel historical treatment of indentureship and slavery was developed well before the emergence of Indo-Caribbean studies and even before the discursive formation of Indo-Caribbean diasporic identity itself.

This line of argument on indentureship as a form of slavery was postulated and popularized by the historian Hugh Tinker in his book aptly titled *A New System of Slavery* (1974). As he states, this historical work "represents the first attempt to provide a comprehensive study of the whole process of emigration from rural India, across the seas to more than a dozen countries" (xiii), dealing with the indenture and other forms of labor recruitment of Indians in the Caribbean, Africa, and Southeast Asia. The book opens with a quote from the imperial official Lord Russell in 1840: "I should be unwilling to adopt any measure to favour the transfer of labourers from British India ... which may lead to ... a new system of slavery" (v). Tinker states the premise of his own work:

> The legacy of Negro slavery in the Caribbean and the Mascarenes was a new system of slavery, incorporating many of the repressive features of the old system, which induced in the Indians many of the responses of their African brothers [sic] in bondage. For ninety years after emancipation, sugar planters and sugar workers...worked out the inheritance of slavery. (19)

He justifies this conclusion as well as the title of his book in describing his course of study:

> When Lord John Russell's announcement was discovered...this seemed to promise the possibility of an arresting title: but it did not appear to represent a plain statement of the realities with which he was confronted. Only gradually did the accumulation of evidence produce the conclusion that indenture and other forms of servitude did, indeed, replicate the actual conditions of slavery. (xiv)

Tinker's work certainly constitutes a valuable historical project and is indispensable for anyone conducting research in the area of Indian labor overseas, including indentureship. Moreover, his bold argument on indentureship has been readily adopted and widely circulated within Indo-Caribbean studies. Although Tinker is not Indo-Caribbean himself, his book has become a fundamental cultural text in an incipient Indo-Caribbean canon. *A New System of Slavery* is treated as an authoritative source in Indo-Caribbean historical scholarship and regularly featured on the book tables at community events. Indeed, much current Indo-Caribbean scholarship is informed by this argument on indentureship as slavery, if not modeled outright upon the work of Tinker.

Brinsley Samaroo's "Two Abolitions: African Slavery and East Indian Indentureship" (1987) opens with the same quote by Lord Russell as does *A New System of Slavery*. The stated purpose of his essay is "to add to this debate by drawing further parallels between the systems of slavery and indentureship than those elaborated by Professor Tinker...[and] further, to indicate similar motivation and action among those who agitated against both systems" (25). Samaroo concludes that "[t]he movement for the abolition of indentureship bore many resemblances to that for the abolition of slavery" and summarizes that the historical forces "in both abolitions came together to end an era of slavery and of a new system of slavery" (38).

Basdeo Mangru's *Indenture and Abolition* (1993), while not directly referring to Tinker's work, resembles it in certain ways. Mangru's book also opens with a quote, but from the Indian nationalist Gopal Krishna Gokhale in 1910, stating of indentureship that "such a system by whatever name it may be called, must really border on the servile" (iv). Mangru describes indentureship as "a system the essential characteristics of which were reminiscent of slavery" (ix) and further notes that "[t]he anti-indenture campaign in India paralleled that of the antislavery movement in England" (xi). He goes on to call Indian indentured laborers in British Guiana "semi-slaves," arguing that they, "like the slave [s], [were] regarded merely as an instrument of production, one without any personality" (xii). He also cites Chief Justice Beaumont's statement on the entire Guianese political system as "a mercantile oligarchy founded on the foundations of slavery" (xii).

Frank Birbalsingh in his successive introductory articles to *Jahaji Bhai, Indenture and* Exile, and *Indo-Caribbean Resistance* increasingly emphasizes the parallel between indentureship and slavery, strengthening this argument from one introduction to the next. In the relatively cautious approach of his first article, he states that "[t]he first indentured immigrants occupied lodgings vacated by the former slaves, and were employed by the former slave owners. Hence the themes spawned by slavery/indenture are identical" (1988: 8). In his second article, Birbalsingh more forcefully posits a number of parallels between "the satanic device of slavery" and "the devilish stratagem of slavery's bedfellow—indenture" (1989: 9). He argues:

> For a long time, slave and indentured labour, under grossly exploitative conditions of colonial domination, bore similar dehumanizing burdens and executed the same back-breaking plantation tasks. There is much ... to support the view that this shared colonial victimization induced common attitudes of resistance and engendered unity of political purpose in Africans and Indians. (8)

He also refers to a common "exploitation [of] those who had crossed both the 'middle passage' from Africa, and the 'kala pani' (black water) from India" (10). In his third article, Birbalsingh this time explicitly argues:

> The appalling conditions under which indentured Indian immigrants existed suggests that they were slaves in everything but name; for they lived in the very quarters vacated by the freed Africans, and performed their exact tasks. ... Just as the brutality of slavery had provoked many slave rebellions, so did the hardships of indenture provoke resistance and retaliation. (1993: viii)

As such, the argument that indentureship parallels slavery has occupied a place of strategic importance in the articulation of Indo-Caribbean identity. Birbalsingh himself explains the complicated international political situation in which this strategy was adopted:

> [T]he better documented Afro-Caribbean suffering through slavery confer[s] a regional legitimacy that is acknowledged in the Euro-American metropolis which still controls the Third World as firmly as ever. (1988: 13)

> This condign sense of [the] historical legacy [of African slavery]...justifie[s] the dominance of an Afrocentric ethos in the Caribbean which, in turn, tend[s] to downplay, if not obscure the parallel Indo-Caribbean experience of indenture. (1993 xvi).

Of course, Birbalsingh is politically shrewd enough to qualify his criticism of Afrocentrism with appropriate deference to "the horror of the Atlantic slave trade, and the plight of its main victims—Afro-Americans and Afro-West Indians" and to the experience of "blacks in America and the Caribbean, who had endured the most heinous of all crimes, the trade in human beings as merchandise, across the Atlantic, for nearly four centuries" (1993: xvi).

Lastly, David Dabydeen and Samaroo in their introductory article to *Across the Dark Waters* (1996) place a heavy emphasis on the parallel between indentureship and slavery. The only subheading in this introduction is titled "A comparison with slavery," appearing rather anomalously in large, bold, and italicized print. Directly crediting Tinker, they argue that "East Indian indentureship turned out to be, as Hugh Tinker wrote, 'a new system of slavery'" (3). Dabydeen and Samaroo state that "[i]ndentureship, like slavery, furthered the creation of a new civilization in the Americas out of the blending of disparate traditions and the interaction of many peoples." Furthermore, employing a quotation by the wife of a ship captain on the preparation of indentured laborers for prospective purchasers, they simply state that "indentureship was hardly any different [from slavery]" (4).

Certainly, the project of a critical comparison between indentureship and slavery, as well as the publication of historical research on indentureship that is entailed in this project, is very valuable, and not only so as an "ethnic" concern in the academic field of Indo-Caribbean studies. However, the strategy of paralleling indentureship and slavery, *and thus Indo- and Afro-Caribbean diasporic identities,* is worth reconsidering for reasons besides the obvious legal distinctions between these labor systems and their historical variations. For this strategy affects the doubly diasporic meaning of Indo-Caribbean identity itself.

Firstly, the argument for indentureship as a form of slavery affects the meaning of Indianness, or the *Indo-* in Indo-Caribbean identity. The treatment of indentureship as slavery dismisses those choices made by Indian laborers themselves to migrate in search of employment opportunities and social mobility. The campaign of the Indian nationalists for the final abolition of indenture, achieved by 1920, and the further total prohibition of Indian labor migration, achieved in 1922, did not as such represent the interests of Indian migrant laborers. Yet in my research, only Walton Look Lai (1993: 136–37, 156, 177), however sketchily, and P.C. Emmer (1986), however problematically, challenge the assumption that indentured laborers favored the abolition of indenture. In another work theorizing the representation of Indian indentured laborers in the Caribbean, I systematically critique the politics of class, race, gender, and what I call *territoriality* in the abolition campaign of the Indian nationalists, and I further argue that Indians in the Caribbean advocated the reformation of labor migration rather than its abolition altogether.

This historical reading of indentureship challenges those ideological tenets of nationalism as developed by the colonial Indian elite, which continue to inform current articulations of both Indian national identity and South Asian and Indo-Caribbean cultural identities. In thus problematizing nationalist representations of Indian culture, the diasporic commemoration of indentureship may undermine monolithic notions of Indian identity. In this sense, the *Indo-* in Indo-Caribbean identity signifies that the Indo-Caribbean diaspora cannot be treated as a mere subcategory of the South Asian diaspora and that the meanings of Indianness are significantly different between as well as within Indo-Caribbean and South Asian identities.

Secondly, the argument for indentureship as a form of slavery also affects the meaning of Caribbeanness, or the *-Caribbean* in Indo-Caribbean identity. For this argument also relies upon the contention that Indian laborers entered the Caribbean in the same historical circumstances as did African laborers and that their responses to these circumstances of entry into the Caribbean were basically similar. This reluctance to theorize the critical differences between, let alone within, Afro-Caribbean and Indo-Caribbean diasporic experiences only marks a failure in the understanding of the relationship between Africans and Indians in the Caribbean. Indeed, writing as long ago as the publication of Tinker's work, John Gaffar La Guerre (1974) noted this failure in the Black Power movement in Trinidad, commenting that "the East Indians were asked to join with Negroes on the basis of 'blackness' and a common experience in the West Indies. Slavery and indentureship, they assumed, was enough to provide a common response to all oppression"

(102). Just as indentureship and slavery do not constitute a "common experience," let me suggest similarly that indentureship and slavery are not parallel *and Indo- and Afro-Caribbean identifies are not discrete*. That is, indentureship is not a replica of slavery. Rather, these diasporic histories intersect, crisscrossing and interweaving with each other in the entangled trajectories of labor migration and cultural identity.

It is not coincidental that what I have suggested is the central problematic of diaspora—the issue of cultural difference—is raised by La Guerre in his treatment of the Black Power movement and again in my own treatment of the emergence of Indo-Caribbean studies. For both of these occasions mark the historical formation of new diasporic identities, Afro- and Indo-Caribbean respectively. The argument for indentureship as a form of slavery exemplifies the problem of cultural relativization in the articulation of diasporic identities, in the diasporic spatialization of history, cultural identities are often posited as parallel, reflecting each other but never meeting. As such, the cultural politics of diaspora are often only too readily compatible with multiculturalist notions of cultural diversity, based as they are on the concept of *absolute difference*. However, the diasporic spatialization of history may be theoretically reconfigured to account for the regular intersection of cultural identities. Thus, the idea of cultural difference takes on critical significance as the current proliferation of the concept of diaspora itself becomes an important point of intersection among those engaged in this historical process. What I am arguing for, then, is the concept of *critical difference*. That is, while diaspora is a currently popular style of identity formation, a critical sense of cultural difference may yet be articulated both between and within diasporic identities. As the diasporic production of identity through the commemoration of a foundational historical mo(ve)ment is presently becoming an increasingly common strategy for cultural mobilization, the success of this strategy in resisting those newly dominant notions of multiculturalism depends upon the negotiation of social, political, and aesthetic differences among those communities constituted through diaspora.

The theorization of this issue of critical difference in diaspora is all the more urgent as it ultimately bears upon the historical appropriation of the concept of diaspora itself from Jewish cultural politics. For the very use of the term *diaspora* by Afro- and Indo-Caribbean and other diasporic communities necessitates this articulation of critical difference. If neither the powerful concept of diaspora is to be reserved exclusively for the Jewish community, nor various histories of displacement and disenfranchisement are to be measured against each other or some ahistorical ideal, then the task of theorizing the current proliferation of diasporic identities requires not the simple collapsing of, but rather a profound reckoning with, the politically significant differences between diasporic identities. Through this articulation of critical difference in diaspora, those absurd competitions between diasporic communities over the claim to the most oppressive form of cultural persecution might be replaced by some mutual realization of the political relationships between the many historical structures of dominance as well as the many historical projects of resistance.

The concept of critical difference in diaspora thus affects not only the treatment of indentureship and slavery within the academic field of Indo-Caribbean studies, but moreover the study of Indo- and Afro-Caribbean cultures themselves in all academic fields, including religious studies. For this concept challenges conventional notions of culture altogether. Accepting the concept of diaspora as style, we have to admit that culture is not a racial or even ancestral inheritance, but that it is continually fashioned and refashioned through the ongoing articulation of identity. Through this particular style of identity formation, home is constructed only in a dialectical relationship with diaspora. As such, India becomes a meaningful place for locating identity only when it has been left behind, the very desire for the return home thus inaugurated. And the same holds true of Africa. The notion of culture either lost or retained is thus radically problematized by this approach to diaspora, along with the conventional assumption that Africans in the Caribbean have lost their culture while Indians have retained theirs. Rather, both Afro- and Indo-Caribbean cultural identities have been creatively forged through the style of diaspora.

However, we must also account for the cultural differences between Afro- and Indo-Caribbean identities. And it is not a simple matter of time—that is, that Africans have lost more of their culture than have Indians because they have been in the Caribbean for a longer period. Time is not so simple, and after all, some African cultural forms are more popular now than they ever have been within the Caribbean. Yet certainly within the cultural field of religion, it may well seem that Indian institutions have indeed better survived the progression of time than have African traditions. But again, it is not so much a matter of cultural loss or retention as the specific social conditions of slavery and indentureship through which Africans and Indians were respectively introduced into the Caribbean. The system of indenture and subsequent settlement plans for Indians in the Caribbean facilitated exchange, travel, and communication between India and the Caribbean, as was not possible under slavery or post-emancipation plans for Africans in the Caribbean. Through the periodic visitations of governmental delegations and religious missionaries from India as well as the regular travels of individuals, Indians in the Caribbean were able not to retain any primordial Indian culture as such, but rather to participate in the same international upheavals that were radically transforming Indian society itself. The Hindu traditions of Sanatan Dharma and Arya Samaj and the Muslim traditions of Sunni and Shi'a exist today among Indians in the Caribbean, then, not simply because indentured laborers arrived on the sugar plantations already belonging to one of these religious traditions. It was what may be called the invention of religion within the modern world system—the division between "orthodox" and "reform" religious systems as well as the codification of Hinduism as a religion in itself—that resulted in the development of these traditions within both India and its diaspora. The concept of critical difference thus dissolves the absolutist notion of cultural difference, according to which, on the one hand, Africans in the Caribbean take no part in tradition, while on the other, Indians take no part in the modern.

In conclusion, then, working through the theoretical possibility of critical difference in diaspora, I suggest that the better strategy for claiming Indo-Caribbean identity may be pursued through articulating the difference rather than the parallel between indentureship and slavery, and hence between Indo-and Afro-Caribbean identities. Of course, this strategy is already the more successful one, if not within Indo-Caribbean studies, then within the popular Indo-Caribbean memory. While Africans in the Caribbean generally celebrate the abolition of slavery upon emancipation, Indians have long celebrated not the abolition of indentureship but rather their *arrival* in the Caribbean. On 5 May 1938 in British Guiana, the centenary of the arrival of Indians in the colony was celebrated. The British Guiana East Indian Association had requested that the day be declared an official holiday by the government, but their attempt was unsuccessful. Nonetheless, a public ceremony, an organizational session, a number of dinners, an evening fair, a dance drama, and the opening of a library were held in celebration of the centenary (Ruhomon 1988: 248, 290–92). Similarly, on 30 May 1945 in Trinidad, the centenary of the arrival of Indians in that colony was celebrated among "[t]he greatest concourse of Indians ever to have assembled in Trinidad" (Kirpalani et al. 1995: 119). Zoning regulations were lifted, while stores in the cities and major commercial centers were closed for the day and governmental departments closed for half of the day. A procession, public ceremony, a fair, and a dance were held, with over thirty thousand people in attendance during the evening (119). Presently, the celebration of Indian Arrival Day has been regularly observed as an annual event since 1978, when the first such celebration was organized by some Indo-Trinidadians from San Juan and Curepe (Singh 1987: 4).

This commemoration of diasporic history among Indians in the Caribbean certainly contradicts the argument that indentureship and slavery are parallel, as postulated in much current Indo-Caribbean scholarship. However, this contradiction does not necessarily imply any theoretical opposition between Indo-Caribbean popular culture and academic production. Indeed, their creative interaction has characterized the historical emergence of Indo-Caribbean identity in the late eighties and through the nineties. For this contradiction exists both within the popular Indo-Caribbean memory and within the academic field of Indo-Caribbean studies. In this popular Indo-Caribbean memory, a complex type of diasporic Indian nationalism has emerged. In the international development of Indian nationalism, diasporic Indians have not simply adopted the ideology of the Indian nationalist elite. Rather, not only have diasporic Indians been instrumental in the ideological formation of nationalism within India, but furthermore Indian nationalism has been articulated in radically different ways throughout India and its diaspora. In particular, diasporic Indians have articulated a quite peculiar sort of nationalism. The territorialist insistence on compulsory residence within India has not been entrenched in the popular memory of Indians in the Caribbean—that is, to be an Indian, you do not have to live inside India. The celebration of Indian arrival in the Caribbean attests to this ambivalence toward home in the formation of diasporic identity. Now, the academic field of Indo-Caribbean studies also displays this ambivalence toward indentureship. After all, those texts by Samaroo, Mangru, Birbalsingh, and Dabydeen in which the argument for indentureship as a form of slavery has been adopted from Tinker were themselves published on the occasions of the one hundred fiftieth anniversaries of Indian arrival in Guyana (1988) and Trinidad (1995). Indeed, the diasporic theme of Indian arrival in the Caribbean permeates both Indo-Caribbean popular culture and academic production, both in diaspora and at home.

The one hundred fiftieth anniversary of the arrival of Indians in British Guiana, also marking the earliest arrival of Indians in the Caribbean colonies, was celebrated in 1988 and that of the arrival of Indians in Trinidad and Jamaica in 1995. Between these celebrations, significant changes within the Caribbean had taken place as Indians were elected heads of state in Guyana and in Trinidad and Tobago, as leaders not of "ethnic" parties but of democratic parties with leftist sympathies to varying degrees. Indian Arrival Day was officially instituted as a national annual holiday in Trinidad and Tobago, as Emancipation Day had been some years before. Thus, in both popular and official arenas of Caribbean culture, the critical difference between Indian and African diasporic identities has already in some ways been recognized. Meanwhile, in the Indo-Caribbean diaspora of Toronto and other diasporic sites, Indian Arrival Day is also celebrated annually with an increasing popularity. Perhaps Indians finally *have* arrived in the Caribbean—yet only after a second migration from the Caribbean to the metropolitan cities of Europe and North America has profoundly transformed the diasporic identity occasioned by the first migration from India to the colonies of Africa, Southeast Asia, and the Caribbean.

Note
1. See my thesis, 'Dialectics of Diaspora and Home: Indentureship, Migration and Indo-Caribbean Identity' (Lokaisingh-Meighoo 1997).

Works Cited

Birbalsingh, Frank. 1988. Introduction. In *Jahaji Bhai: An Anthology of Indo-Caribbean Literature*, ed. Frank Birbalsingh. Toronto: TSAR.

Birbalsingh, Frank. 1989. Introduction. In *Indenture and Exile: The Indo-Caribbean Experience*, ed. Frank Birbalsingh. Toronto: TSAR.

Birbalsingh, Frank. 1993. Introduction. In *Indo-Caribbean Resistance*, ed. Frank Birbalsingh. Toronto: TSAR.

Dabydeen, David, and Brinsley Samaroo, eds. 1996. *Across the Dark Waters: Ethnicity and Indian Identity in the Caribbean*. London: Macmillan Caribbean.

Emmer, P C. 1986. The Meek Hindu; the Recruitment of Indian Indentured Labourers for Service Overseas, 1870–1916. In *Colonialism and Migration: Indentured Labour before and after Slavery*, ed. P.C. Emmer. Boston: Martinus Nijhoff Publishers.

Gilroy, Paul. 1993. The *Black Atlantic: Modernity and Double Consciousness*. Cambridge, Mass.: Harvard University Press.

Hall, Stuart. 1991. Old and New Identities, Old and New Ethnicities. In *Culture, Globalization and the World System*, ed. Anthony D. King. Binghamton: State University of New York.

Hebdige, Dick. 1993. *Subculture: The Meaning of Style*. 1979. New York: Routledge.

James, C.L.R. 1963. Appendix: From Toussaint L'Ouverture to Fidel Castro. *The Black Jacobins: Toussaint L'Ouverture and the San Domingo Revolution*. 2nd rev. ed. New York: Vintage Books.

Kirpalani, Murli J., et al., eds. 1945/1995. Indian Centenary Review: One Hundred Years of Progress, Trinidad 1845–1945. Reprinted in *In Celebration of 150 Yrs of the Indian Contribution to Trinidad and Tobago*, ed. Brinsley Samaroo et al. Port-of-Spain: Historical Publications.

La Guerre, John Gaffar. 1974. The East Indian Middle Class Today. *Calcutta to Caroni: The East Indians of Trinidad*. Trinidad: Longman Caribbean.

Lokaisingh-Meighoo, Sean. 1997. Dialectics of Diaspora and Home: Indentureship, Migration and Indo-Caribbean Identity. Masters thesis, York University.

Look Lai, Walton. 1993. *Indentured Labor, Caribbean Sugar: Chinese and Indian Migrants to the British West Indies, 1838–1918*. Baltimore: Johns Hopkins University Press.

Mangru, Basdeo. 1993. *Indenture and Abolition: Sacrifice and Survival on the Guyanese Sugar Plantations*. Toronto: TSAR.

Ruhomon, Peter. 1947/1988. *Centenary History of the East Indians in British Guiana, 1838–1938*. Georgetown: 150th Anniversary Committee of the Arrival of Indians in Guyana.

Samaroo, Brinsley. 1987. Two Abolitions: African Slavery and East Indians Indentureship. In *India in the Caribbean*, ed. David Dabydeen and Brinsley Samaroo. London Hansib/University of Warwick, Centre for Caribbean Studies.

Seecharan, Clem. 1993. *India and the Shaping of the Indo-Guyanese Imagination 1890–1920s*. Leeds: Peepal Tree.

Selvon, Samuel. 1979/1987. Three into One Can't Go – East Indian, Trinidadian, Westindian. In *India in the Caribbean*, ed. David Dabydeen and Brinsley Samaroo. London: Hansib/University of Warwick, Centre for Caribbean Studies.

Singh, I.J. Bahadur, ed. 1987. *Indians in the Caribbean*. New Delhi: Sterling Publishers.

Tinker, Hugh. 1974. *A New System of Slavery: The Export of Indian Labour Overseas 1830–1920*. New York: Oxford University Press.

West, Cornel. 1993. *Keeping Faith: Philosophy and Race in America*. New York: Routledge.

Re-Engineering Blackspace

Erna Brodber

There is one creative endeavour that I feel moved to talk about in this gathering and that is the completion of the task of emancipation. It is opportune I think that we spend some time thinking about this and entering it into our meditations, this task being one on which he whom this conference honours, Rex Nettleford, has applied much of his psychic and physical energy; has given the work of his head in formulating it into hypotheses and theories; his hands in writing not just for academics but for popular readership; has given his body (and imagination) to dancing and choreography forcing these issues onto the open stage; has given his voice on radio and TV, conducting the issues into the ears not only of the literate but of the illiterate of which our communities are well supplied. In this Rex Nettleford not only tells us that the work is there to be done but offers an approach to the task of completing emancipation. His life and work design a methodology: they recommend that we reach into our store of talents, identify them and this completed, apply all ten to the task at hand.

Who besides participants in this conference are the 'we' to which I refer? Rex Nettleford was the first academic that I heard on this University campus (Mona) refer to himself in an intellectual discourse as 'one of those Jamaicans of the colour of the black in the flag'. This young man had just come down from post-graduate work in Oxford; "bright can't done", had, in a public forum in 1964(?) in out-of-many-one colour Jamaica identified himself in terms of a specific colour and besides had put himself and that colour into the analytical scheme: two revolutions with one shot — self in scientific analysis and colour of self in scientific analysis. We here like him have skin colour. We could borrow his self-inclusive approach to our studies and while we make our deliberations of service to the task of emancipation, look at the man in the mirror, note his phenotype, reflect on his consequent experiences, develop our personal perspectives and openly bring this to bear on the issues at hand.

Kamau Brathwaite in 1974 presented the rationalisation for this self-inclusive colour-coded approach to discussions among Caribbean thinkers. In his *Contradictory Omens* (p33) he says

> "It is my conviction that we cannot begin to understand statements about 'West Indian culture', since it is so diverse and has so many subtly different orientations and interpretations, unless we know something about the speaker/writer's own socio-cultural background and orientation".

In this work he analyses Caribbean society and in particular Jamaican society to conclude that the plural society model with its clean lines does not represent the pure truth and modifies it into the 'orientation model' (p25) which sees Caribbean and Jamaican culture-areas in terms of two great traditions - African and European, creolizing into a socio-cultural continuum within which there are a number of inter-related orientations which sometimes overlap. The 'we' of the Caribbean, to paraphrase, are of different shadings on a black-white continuum and different orientations on the European-African cultural continuum. Our sensibilities are fashioned by our location on these twin continua. It is not enough to know you are black, you must know what your shade of black is, the nature of the experience it allows you and you must be able to identify the parallel point on the European-African cultural continuum to which that experience exposes you. For Brathwaite, it is a must that the Caribbean person entering into the intellectual arena knows, can and is willing to articulate his personal perspective as an important part of his conceptual framework. Brathwaite puts his money where his mouth is: he tells us where to find his self-analysis[1]

Brathwaite's fractionalising of the society is very valuable here. For him there are "four inter-related but significantly differing orientations

1. a Euro-centred elite which includes metropolitan experts and owners of significant property who have their being outside of the society,

2. a Euro-centred creole upper class of property owners who reside within the society and celebrate the values of the Euro-centred elite but are not accepted by them as brothers,

3. a creole intellectual elite who in reaction to the two other groups' ability to claim a space in Europe, have settled for the Caribbean as theirs trying now to make it as European as they can, and

4. the Afro-Caribbean (black) population, of illiterate labourers who with no access to the establishment and its values, have in the process of survival been creating what he calls a 'little tradition', rooted in the Caribbean space. The first of these orientations appear to belong to white faces, the second and third to a mixture of both and the last to black. In the hands of these last lies the development of a "real Alternative Tradition" a process which Brathwaite sees as stymied by the fact that "emancipation saw no change in the structure of the area; no change in the mercantilist system; no real change on the plantations".

Rex Nettleford recently drew our attention to the incomplete nature of the historical process which began in the British Caribbean in 1834. In *Emancipation - the Lesson and the Legacy: challenge to the Church, the Emancipation Commemoration Lecture 1994* (p4)[2], he says,

> "The legal emancipation of the enslaved Blacks was to make it possible for the development of a society of 'self-directed souls'..."

He rues the fact that these 'souls' and the society they were to create is still waiting and wanting. Brathwaite meets Nettleford - the emancipation process is not complete. Both agree that the completion of the emancipation process means change and that change is good for these societies. Brathwaite makes it clear that the change and the good would have had to (and I assume will have to) come from the acceptance by groups 1 to 3 of the tradition evolving out of the Afro-Caribbean population. Insistence is the other side of 'acceptance' - the more 'proactive' side as they say today. Had the 'Afro-Caribbean (black) population' insisted....but Brathwaite points out too that this group, this orientation, this potential catalyst is

> "losing ground fast as more and more of their number 'get' education, political power, material rewards within the world-powerful Euro-American mercantilist system" (p30).

The Blacks, the light of our world according to this analysis are losing their candle with time and their orientation can now neither be accepted nor can they insist that it be accepted by the whole. Nettleford's comment quoted above, intimates that we, his readers and audience, are part of the historical process began in 1834. Each of us then, called by name, has a place in time, in one of the generations since 1834. Each of us then has failed to bring emancipation to its fruition. Each of us has failed to be and has failed to get others to be 'self-directed souls'.

If Brathwaite and Nettleford are right in their analysis and are pointing their fingers at our generation as among those who are losing the candle and those who are failing to complete the task of emancipation, and if their prescription for change and the example they have set us are worthwhile, then the Caribbean scholar accepting the challenge to work at this task has to begin by finding his orientation, and positioning himself in relationship to the Afro-Caribbean one, that which had held the Alternative Tradition, and has to put this found self into the analysis. To thus position our personal selves as both Nettleford and Brathwaite have done, is to locate our personal 'I's' on that great big Caribbean cricket field as players, as batsmen, fielders, bowlers and so on working along with each other. Lloyd Best admonished intellectuals in a 1967 "cropover" article in *New World Quarterly* called, "Independent Thought and Caribbean Freedom" (p29) "we are the people too", so we in this room are really right out there with everybody else on the grounds mixing with them and their shades and orientations. Action is required from this collectivity of people. What is the game plan? At another time Lloyd Best dubbed academics 'intellectual workers' making the point that there is work for all people to do together, that there are different aspects of the work, the intellectual being just one of these. What is the game plan? What is the work? To align ourselves with the traditional Afro-Caribbean population and help it to carry on the job of providing an alternative for these societies, it is to this task, the re-defining of the role of the intellectual worker that I address my comments in this paper which I call *Re-engineering blackspace*.

The 311,070 persons of African ancestry emancipated in Jamaica in 1834 and fully so in 1838, owned no land and were outside of the political system – they had no vote. Few had family power – mates, children; few owned livestock. They owned no space. They had no army, no ships, no compass, no respected organised grouping. All they had was their individual minds and souls with which to create a viable space for themselves and their progeny in Jamaica and eventually to weld themselves in a nation or a respected part of a nation. As it was in Jamaica so it was in Africa of the diaspora except for the few reconstruction years in the US South. Real emancipation clearly has to eventuate in some accepted claim on space (physical and otherwise) in these countries to which our forefathers were brought and into which we were legally emancipated. This space, like any other shelter had to be engineered out of what exists. In 1834 we were asked to leave the old house:

> Slave before, mi ben slave before
> Mi no slave no more
> Bury mi foot chain
> Bury mi foot chain
> Down eena market square.[3]

But if not slave with a foot chain, who and with what? A new conceptual framework, frame of reference, portrait of self had to be constructed. The end product of this activity should be new blackspace. To work towards emancipation is to work towards a new definition of self and its possibilities, a new definition of the possibilities of our collective selves, is to re-engineer blackspace. This is the task.

According to Lloyd Best (p28) "… social change in the Caribbean has to and can only begin in the minds of Caribbean men" by which I think he means Caribbean people. He continues: "Thought is action for us" by which I know he means the intellectual class. In this matter of re-engineering blackspace, of completing the emancipation process, the part of the task awaiting the 'intellectual worker' is the development of philosophy, of creeds, of myths, of ideologies, of pegs on which to hang social and spiritual life, the construction of frames of reference. Are all intellectual workers of our varying ethnic shades and cultural orientations expected to work on this task of completing the emancipation process? Kamau Brathwaite in his summary to a discussion of his finding that a certain Caribbean custom was explained by Orlando Patterson by way of the "Euro-scientific tradition" when there was another (and more feasible explanation) in the Afro-tradition, helps us towards a reasonable answer. He says (p41)

> What I am suggesting here is not that there is a 'right' African explanation, or a 'wrong' Euro-scientific one, but that a proper understanding of ourselves can only be arrived at by a recognition of both traditions, both areas of explanation; and that for the Afro-Caribbean it will be increasingly more just to seek, in the first instance, African explanations and sources of overstating.

To extrapolate crudely there are issues more germane to one tradition than to the other, though the outcome will have relevance for both since they are, as postulated before, part of an on-going creolising complex. Completing the emancipation process lies in the domain of the Afro-orientation, of the children of the slaves legally freed in 1834. If the 'action' of those of them who are intellectuals is taught, then it is those who look in the mirror and see a black face who must manufacture the thoughts and other intellectual products that will eventuate in the change in the status of the black population, change of the status of the traditions of this majority force in territories such as Jamaica. If those who enter the intellectual factory must be able to identify their "socio-cultural background and orientation" (p33), then clearly these are the people who must now begin the self-examination for since this is an 'afro' issue, there are likely to be retrievable and needed data within the African tradition that might be of use and which they carry somewhere beneath their skin. In this paper I would like to draw the attention of those who identify themselves as black intellectuals ready for the liberating task of completing the process of emancipation and producing a society of 'self-directed souls', of which theirs must obviously be numbered, to the efforts of other philosophers in the Afro-tradition, in the hope that their efforts might be joined to expedite the job.

Nina Simone by way of introducing her popular song on the Black Gold Long Playing Record, *To be Young Gifted and Black* says: "This is not addressed primarily to white people; it doesn't put you down in anyway; it simply ignores you for my people need all the inspiration and love they can get". This paper seeks primarily to engage black people but it is very aware that their personal reconstruction and the extent to which they carry out the task of the first freedmen and freemen is the extent to which all racial and ethnic groups dealing with us are freed, for a skewed saucer at the bottom of the pile will cause all the others to fall and break. In any case, who is 'black'. If we are to follow the methodological strand we have been pursuing - "self-directed souls", "we are the people too", "the speaker/writer's own socio-cultural background and orientation...as a kind of navigational aid", we see that our definition of our phenotypical and social colour lies in our determination. It is not the social scientist's definition: it is what *you* see in the mirror.

So we here in this room have each identified our 'I'. If you find yourself to be black, you will have great difficulty in holding back the tears as you feel the lash on Cudjoe's back and watch with him as he sees his love raped by someone against whom to retaliate means certain death and the hope of ever protecting her; you are likely to feel the intense emptiness of Ottobah Cugoano kidnapped, tricked by those who look like you and sold to men of strange complexion and landed in Grenada's plantation far away from your Africa and your noble station. See his *Thoughts on the*

Evil and Wicked Traffic of the Slavery and Commerce on the Human Species submitted and published in Great Britain in 1738. If you see yourself as black, you can't help but feel. But how can the history of this West Indian futility be written? What tone shall the historian adopt? Shall he be as academic as Sir Allan Burns, protesting from time to time at some brutality, and setting West Indian brutality in the context of European brutality? Shall he, like Salvador de Madariaga weigh one set of brutality against another, and conclude that one has not been described in all its foulness and that this is unfair to Spain? Shall he like the West Indian historians, who can only now begin to face their history, be icily detached and tell the story of the slave trade as if it were just another aspect of mercantilism?

Thus asks Naipaul in that well quoted passage from his *Middle Passage*. No. You feel. To follow any of the minds above is to desert the Afro-tradition and the journey to blackspace. You feel, so "detached" is not your position: your story is not "just another aspect of mercantilism". You feel: can you still be the 'objective' scientist of the twentieth century? To feel and to feel attached is not to commit the academic sin of distorting. It is to claim your psychological space. Is to look through your 'uppentary'. From this perspective while empathising with Gugoano, you can as logically praise or blame him for accepting the story of his African captors. I have no quarrel with a text which asked its young readers to note certain things when they walked down Downing Street. My quarrel is with those who select this text for an ethnically Indian third form in a Trinidadian high school. The writers speak to English students who would want to and should want to and could walk down Downing Street. They seek to engage the students' emotions, bring their "I" into their classwork and allow them to identify with the people of their past. This approach I applaud and recommend for to assume your 'I' brings emotion, brings perspective, brings identification with our forefathers and allows us, should we follow suit, to do something George Beckford begged us to do, stop seeing slaves and to see instead 'enslaved persons'. To borrow another sentence from Lloyd Best in his article already mentioned (p30):

> To do this is to opt for the view of the people not as an abstraction - the masses, but as a community of persons.

To find the 'I' allows us then not only to be human but to see the people whom we as black Caribbean intellectuals want to serve, as humans with a potential for a range of action.

Lloyd Best's sentences before the one just quoted, create a point of departure for me.

> But there is much that is private experience, much that the people know; much that is real to the people. But the society is not moved only by what is real to individuals and groups. In an important sense, what is collectively real is what is politically significant. To arrive at that and then to make it common public property is our task.

I intend to show that Ethiopianism is a 'politically' significant product of the minds and souls of Caribbean people of the Afro-tradition, intent on laying down a philosophy towards the completion of the emancipation process; that it has re-engineered and can continue to re-engineer blackspace. As such it deserves the attention, even the assistance of today's Caribbean intellectuals.

Ethiopianism is "collectively real". It has been so at least since the late eighteenth century and still is alive today.

As Nettleford and others have taught us, in the religious ideology that Africans brought to the New World, physical death was not the end of life. Quite the contrary: it opened one to a new life as an ancestor, a living dead, having potential power over mortals. This understanding, transmitted orally, synchronised with a major tenet of Euro-American Christian philosophy, that there was to man, the possibility of everlasting life and communion with the 'passed' saints. This philosophy is literature based and, with learning to read and write denied to the enslaved, as well as, in some places religious instruction, Euro-American Christian philosophy came to them in whispers. As the whispering game we played as children demonstrates, we take from whispers what fits into our frame of reference. A particular aspect of Christianity was joined (or rejoined) with African religious ideology even before we began to handle the Bible, the centre piece of this Christianity. The notion of everlasting life and of a connection between the living and the dead strengthened the African notion of the existence of the 'I' and the 'I' in each human being and the eventual liberation of the corporeal 'I' into the more potent non-corporeal 'I'.

Though Africans came to the New World from several parts of Africa and several different political groups and were more likely to think of themselves as Ga and Ibo than African, a Euro-American consciousness dictated that they be labelled according to this consciousness. Thus in the New World all were 'African' and 'slave'. It was also a Euro-American consciousness which called them children of Ethiopia and drew their attention to Psalm 68 verse 31.

> Princes shall come out of Egypt Ethiopia shall soon stretch out her hands unto God.

Eighteenth century Euro-American missionaries justifying their christianising of the enslaved on the grounds that 'Ethiopia shall soon stretch forth her hands' were of their own volition singling out the enslaved population in the New World as elected by their God for a more mystic task than that of the hewing of wood and the drawing of water for their use. The enslaved African would naturally favour this reading and favour the Bible, this Euro-American authority on right and wrong, on ethical and spiritual issues. There is evidence that the use of the term was not particular to clerics. Brathwaite on page 30 of his *Contradictory Omens* calls us in inverted commas 'Ethiop's Authorized', a phrase he culls according to his footnote, from a poem published in London in 1764. Evidently the term, if not always the connotation was in public usage.

The enslaved person's reading of the Bible when literacy came to him, showed him mortals who had "stretch"(ed) their "hands unto God" and had their corporeal 'I's' liberated on earth. *Thy kingdom come on earth as it is in Heaven.* What couldn't happen if they the New World Ethiopians followed the Biblical injunction and "stretch(ed) (their) hands unto (this New World) God"? Cock's mouth had indeed caught Cock for in their definition of their slaves as African and Ethiopian, Euro-America had given their slaves as African and Ethiopian, Euro-American had given their slaves the basis of a liberating philosophy which they would develop into further philosophy, and action based on that philosophy. The enslaved African's reading of the Bible showed him several other references in it to Ethiopia. White-American religious groups of the eighteenth century had thought of America as the new Israel and of themselves as the chosen of God. "Cock mouth really did catch cock" for it was the word 'Ethiopia', and neither the word 'America' nor the word 'Britain' that appeared in the Bible. The conclusion: we, not they, are the people selected by this Christian God, is inescapable. By various intellectual strategies, the man Moses selected by God to be the world's greatest magician and with this gift to lead his people out of bondage, became a black man and the Israelites, black for 'Israel' now read 'Ethiopia'. We are without doubt God's people enslaved to be taught a lesson and prepared for greater work on earth, the light of the world.

This view of the New World black as (a) divinely selected and (b) selected for moral world leadership, is a crucial part of what is called 'Ethiopianism' and is the base of many intellectual workers who have located themselves within the Afro-tradition and have sought emancipation or to complete the emancipation process. The evidence of this in the early history of the enslaved African is clearest in North America in revolts of such as that which the brothers Gabriel and Martin Prosser attempted in Virginia in 1800 and Nat Turner in 1831 in Virginia[4]. The historians say that the Prossers likened themselves and their fellow bondsmen to biblical Israelites – one I suppose was Moses and the other Aaron – and argued that "God would stretch forth His (?) arm to save and would strengthen a hundred to overcome a thousand". Understandably. If the Ethiopian stretches forth his hand to God there has to be an accompanying stretching forth by God if action is to take place. So the Prossers marched on Henrico County, Virginia sure of their special relationship with God. Nat Turner felt too that he and his people were special to God. God had spoken to him as he had to the prophets of old and given him a special charge concerning a special people.[5]

There is evidence that persons enslaved here in Jamaica if they didn't see themselves as special to the God of the Christian church certainly saw themselves as especially close friends of some of his prophets. Edward (Kamau) Brathwaite[6] recalls an incident in which two black Baptists were sent to trial in 1816, in Black River "accused of fomenting rebellion". The leader of the rebellion had been charged with singing a certain song, obviously thought by the Establishment to be seditious.

He had countered that:

> "He had sung no songs but such as his brown priest had assured him were approved by John the Baptist ... [who] was a friend to the negroes ..." (page 211)

Sam Sharp and Deacon Bogle, were too, men steeped in their Bible. No doubt they saw themselves as special appointees to a special people.

The Prossers, Turner, Sharp, Bogle had done their research from the one book available to them and had applied it to their social situation and had designed an action-oriented strategy accordingly. They were intellectual workers. If we here have difficulty in seeing such 'unschooled minds' wearing the gown and the mortar board, then let us look at Edward Blyden praised in Europe and Asia as an academic. Blyden, the son of Danish West Indians transported from Africa and enslaved here, in 1878 and again in 1882 propounded a methodology for christianising the continent of Africa. Blyden began his argument with the fact that Greek intellectuals had presented Ethiopia as 'the place the Gods loved to dwell', not the malarial land it was currently being made out to be and that for them Ethiopians were a most highly venerated people not the despicable maneaters of current mythology. Ethiopia and Ethiopians were historically special. This condition dictated that those organising missionary work in Africa should pay attention to the lessons implied in God's dealings with Ethiopia. He has sent Philip to the Ethiopian Eunuch, made him baptise him and leave him to minister to his people. If Africa is to become a part of the larger Christian world and Blyden agreed that it should for Ethiopia would 'soon stretch forth her hand to God', then it must be missioned by people of African descent in much the same way as the Ethiopian Eunuch was baptised and left to convert his people. Blyden's programme added another element to Ethiopianism: what happens in and to Africa ought to be the business of Africans and Africans of the diaspora. These strands – the specialness of Africa and Africans and the responsibility of Africans of the diaspora towards Africa appear as well in the work and life of Alexander Crummel (1819–1898) the African-American Cambridge graduate and Bishop Turner of the African Methodist Episcopalian church who was one of the first of his stature to declare that "God is a negro".

All of the above-mentioned were clerics if also writers. Crummel's life and works are the subject of one of Wilson Jeremiah Moses monographs. Ethiopianism also entered the thought and frames of reference of the more unmistakable academic and of the literary artist. It appears in Dubois' *Children of the Moon*, in Lawrence Dunbar and obviously so in his *Ode to Ethiopia*. The political and literary efforts of our own Marcus Garvey were clearly influenced by this Ethiopianism. One of his popular lines, 'Africa for the Africans at home and abroad' smacks of Blyden, and his African National Anthem leaves no doubt concerning the presence of Ethiopianism in his conceptual framework. The lines "Ethiopia, the land of our fathers, Thou land where the gods loved to be" harks back to Blyden's exposition in his essay *Philip and the Eunuch*.

The internationalisation of the notion of Ethiopianism and behaviour in accordance with this, is very clear in the British West Indies of the 1930's. Our own Jamaican Una Marson sidetracked the more local concern of social work with children to apply herself to this cause in London. Sent there as secretary of the Save the Children Fund, to lobby on behalf of that group, Una Marson chose to work for Haile Selassie, exiled emperor of Ethiopia and the League of Coloured People. Ethiopianism according to the researches of the British government of the day was popular in Jamaica in the late 1930's. It blamed this complex of beliefs and feelings for the riots of the time. A secret document, "an extract from conclusions of a meeting of the cabinet held on Wednesday 25/5/1938" says concerning the riots in Jamaica:

> We had done a great deal for this island but nevertheless there were causes for discontent. In addition there was a good deal of racial feeling between coloureds and white people which had been much stimulated by events in Abyssinia and had now become serious. (Commonwealth Office, CO 137/839 file no 69056)

As the above indicates, Ethiopianism has its secular side. It also stimulated a secular programme. In 1938 C.L.R. James, an Afro-Trinidadian renaissance man, extremely well thought of in Trotskyite circles, left England for the US carried by his conviction that blacks were destined to be the vanguard of the international labour movement. He left the USA nearly twenty years later, even more convinced of the pivotal role that US blacks would have to play in the international socialist movement. If we interpose the phrase 'that God said' into the last sentence we see that this position fits very well into that of the clerics who had earlier maintained that blacks and particularly the New World variety, had been divinely selected for work of global significance. Padmore, (like James, a Trinidadian) of one of the generations of those freed in 1834, in 1935 parted company with the Communist International on the grounds that it was sacrificing the interest of black labour to that of the balance of power between white countries. He thereafter vowed to and did concern himself exclusively with making blacks into socialists. Crummel (according to Moses, his biographer) had stressed the "responsibility of the individual to the group" (p290). In other words, Blacks have to see to their own redemption before they take on the divine challenge of being the light of the world or the salt of the earth. Padmore's position is reminiscent of this. With scholars such as James and Padmore, Ethiopianism found in Pan-Africanism a secular arm, more to the taste of the 'schooled'. C.L.R. James wrote of Marcus Garvey:

> Up to 1918 blacks, as a whole, played no particular role in world politics. The world was not conscious of them except as objects. Blacks were not conscious of themselves. A spirit of frustration, humiliation, rebellion is not political consciousness. The man who both made blacks conscious of themselves and the world conscious of blacks as a force to be reckoned with in world politics was a Jamaican, Marcus Garvey. By 1925/26 Garveyism as a force was finished, but the political problem represented by black people had been placed before the world once and for all. Henceforth it had to be taken into consideration in all calculations on a national as well as on an international scale.

Is Ethiopianism 'politically significant'? Garvey had translated the Ethiopianist ideas of those before him into a populist instrument with which to carve out a black political space. Pan Africanism was to continue this work. It has been neglected by the more recent clerics, academics and political practitioners in Africa of the diaspora, in favour of insular nationalism, but it continues to be part of the 'unschooled' intellectuals of the Afro-tradition who feel that emancipation is incomplete. Chief among these in the post-Garvey days were the Rastafarians who in their different organisations have been honing, in particular, the religious aspects of the concept and designing a praxis.

The 'singers and players', whom says the Bible, 'will be there', have as rastafarians or others, been disseminating the ideas of Ethiopianism in its several forms.

> Emancipate yourself from mental slavery
> None but ourselves can free our minds

says the Rastafarian Bob Marley in a song that needs no referencing and he sings about himself in *Natty Dread* [ILPS 9281]

> Dread, Natty Dreadlocks
> Dreadlocks, Congo, Bongo I

Holding hands with Brathwaite and Nettleford, he continues:

> Children get your culture
> And don't stay here and jester
> Or the battle will be hotter
> And you won't get no supper

From the Trinidadian calypsonian - Superior comes[7]:

> No matter where you born, you still African, yes man.
> I don't care where you born, you still African

Black Stalin, Trinidadian calypso king for 1979, draws our attention to Ethiopianism as a political tool for uniting the Caribbean area. In this winning poem *Caribbean Unity* the two wings of Ethiopianism meet. Black Stalin points to the political gains in defining our collective selves as-

> ....one race
> From the same place
> That makes the same trip
> On the same ship

But he also recommends the religious aspect of Ethiopianism - Rastafarianism as the way forward:

> If the Rastafarian movement spreading
> But the Carifta dying slow
> Then is something Rasta done
> That the politician don't know...

Black Stalin locating his personal 'I' openly in Ethiopianism, takes a swing at the intellectuals who have barricaded themselves against this understanding, long part of the Afro-tradition:

> Mr West Indian politician
> You went to a big institution
> How come you can't unite
> Seven million
> When West Indian unity
> I know it is very easy
> If you only rap to your people
> And tell them like me

> That is one race
> From the same place
> That make the same trip
> On the same ship

Of Ethiopianism Wilson Jeremiah Moses, an authority on the history of black nationalism, has truly written in his *Golden Age of Black Nationalism*[8]

> Among black writers it made repeated appearances during the nineteenth century and by World War 1, Ethiopianism had become not only a trans-Atlantic political movement but a literary movement well-known among all black people from the Congo basin to the mountains of Jamaica to the sidewalks of New York. (p24)

It remains with us. It is there among the dreaded obeahmen who look to Solomon and Moses and their formulae, supposedly collated from ancient manuscripts and preserved and most certainly dispensed by the DeLaurence Company of Chicago. It remains among the Black Jews some of whom are still gathered in Caribbean. Not to mention the Rastafarian groups who have undertaken to keep Ethiopianism publicly alive so that we can "free ourselves from mental slavery" and begin to write the relevant songs, the "songs of freedom".

Ethiopianism is politically significant. It has historically created a continent of consciousness. African Methodist Episcopalians in South Africa sang the same songs and had the same hopes as African Methodist Episcopalians in British Guiana and the USA. Padmore felt that Ghana was as much his business as Trinidad was and Dubois found his way to Africa to be gathered up to his ancestors. It created for the enslaved persons emancipated in 1834 and 1863 a physical space which transcended geographical boundaries. As we have seen, it constructed a space for the enslaved African in Western religious thought, thoughts on which other generations worked to produce an instrument which created political and pyscho-physical space. "We" here "are the people too". Is it 'collectively real' for us, 'politically significant' for us?

Now that you who see black in the mirror feel this reality, you find yourself, like Jesus with Moses and Elijah at his transfiguration, only the souls you are talking with are Paul Cuffee an African-American who, caring about Africa, in 1815 began taking New World blacks back to Africa to help to build it; with the Prosser brothers, Nat Turner and Sam Sharpe who believed they were God's people and slavery was not the right way for them to live; with clerics Blyden, Crummel and Turner who felt that Africa was family and it was the divine duty of all 'Ethiopians' to make it the best that it could be; with the learned philosopher – Dubois, with James and Padmore; with Marcus Garvey; with Una Marson, with the large body of pop singers and calypsonians; with the Rastafarians, the black Jews and the obeahmen. What are they saying? Their words are in print and therefore more accessible to you than to anyone else. Can you help to write 'those songs of freedom'; help those young people who sit up late into the night to hear what Mutabaruka – a Jamaican dub poet can tell them to help them make sense of themselves? Can you do as Lloyd Best expects of intellectuals, make the information "common public property"? Can you join with the little tradition not to study it, not to report on it but to reason with it in a shared-learning mode, and help to build the myths, the ideologies, the religious and political philosophy that will make us what this tradition thinks it can be – the light of the world, the salt of the earth, that can help us to be what Rex Nettleford want to see – self-directed souls. The little tradition has laid a foundation. Finally, I ask of you as an old West Indian migrant to Britain once asked of me: please give the youth more than a past of slavery with which to carve out a blackspace in this white world. It is for the intellectuals in our society to tell those who are Ethiopianist that the Ethiopianism that attracts them has a distinguished and respected past.

Notes
1. Kamau Brathwaite, 'Timehri,' *Savacou* no. 2:33, UWI, Mona.
2. Rex Nettleford, *Emancipation – The Lesson and the Legacy: Challenge to the Church, the Emancipation Commemoration Lecture 1994*, Webster Memorial Church, July 1994, 4.
3. Collected from an informant in St James. See 'Conveniently Deafman,' 15, tape reference 63 St James in Erna Brodber, *Life in Jamaica in the Early Twentieth Century* a presentation of ninety oral accounts. ISER Doc Centre 1980.
4. Vincent Harding, 'Religion and Resistance among Antebellum Negroes, 1800–1860,' in *The Making of Black America*, ed. August Meir and Elliott Rudwick (New York Athenaeum, 1969).
5. Gayraud S. Wilmore, *Black Religion and Black Radicalism* (Maryknoll, NY: Orbis Books, 1984)
6. Kamau Brathwaite, *Creole Society in Jamaica* (London: Oxford University Press, 1971).
7. Davies Carole Boyce, 'The Africa Theme in Trinidad Calypso,' CQ 31, no 2:77
8. Wilson Jeremiah Moses, *Golden Age of Black Nationalism* (London: Oxford University Press, 1978).

Out on Main Street

Shani Mootoo

1.

Janet and me? We does go Main Street to see pretty pretty sari and bangle, and to eat we belly full a burfi and gulub jamoon, but we doh go too often because, yuh see, is dem sweets self what does give people like we a presupposition for untameable hip and thigh.

Another reason we shy to frequent dere is dat we is watered-down Indians – we ain't good grade A Indians. We skin brown, is true, but we doh even think 'bout India unless something happen over dere and it come on de news. Mih family remain Hindu ever since mih ancestors leave India behind, but nowadays dey doh believe in praying unless things real bad, because, as mih father always singing, like if is a mantra: "Do good and good will be bestowed unto you." So he is a veritable saint cause he always doing good by his women friends and dey chilren. I sure some a dem must be mih half sister and brother, oui!

Mostly, back home, we is kitchen Indians: some kind a Indian food every day, at least once a day, but we doh get cardamom and other fancy spice down dere so de food not spicy like Indian food I eat in restaurants up here. But it have one thing we doh make joke 'bout down dere: we like we meethai and sweetrice too much, and it remain overly authentic, like de day Naana and Naani step off de boat in Port of Spain harbour over a hundred and sixty years ago. Check out dese hips here nah, dey is pure sugar and condensed milk, pure sweetness!

But Janet family different. In de ole days when Canadian missionaries land in Trinidad dey used to make a bee-line straight for Indians from down South. And Janet great grandparents is one a de first South families dat exchange over from Indian to Presbyterian. Dat was a long time ago.

When Janet born, she father, one Mr. John Mahase, insist on asking de Reverend MacDougal from Trace Settlement Church, a leftover from de Canadian Mission, to name de baby girl. De good Reverend choose de name Constance cause dat was his mother name. But de mother a de child, Mrs. Savitri Mahase, wanted to name de child sheself. Ever since Savitri was a lil girl she like de yellow hair, fair skin and pretty pretty clothes Janet and John used to wear in de primary school reader – since she lil she want to change she name from Savitri to Janet but she own father get vex and say how Savitri was his mother name and how she will insult his mother if she gone and change it. So Savitri get she own way once by marrying this fella name John, and she do a encore, by calling she daughter Janet, even doh husband John upset for days at she for insulting de good Reverend by throwing out de name a de Reverend mother.

So dat is how my girlfriend, a darkskin Indian girl with thick black hair (pretty fuh so!) get a name like Janet.

She come from a long line a Presbyterian school teacher, headmaster and headmistress. Savitri still teaching from de same Janet and John reader in a primary school in San Fernando, and John, getting more and more obtuse in his ole age, is headmaster more dan twenty years now in Princes Town Boys' Presbyterian High School. Everybody back home know dat family good good. Dat is why Janet leave in two twos. Soon as A Level finish she pack up and take off like a jet plane so she could live without people only shoo-shooing behind she back..."But A A! Yuh ain't hear de goods 'bout John Mahase daughter, gyul? How yuh mean yuh ain't hear? Is a big thing! Everybody talking 'bout she. Hear dis, nah! Yuh ever see she wear a dress? Yes! Doh look at mih so. Yuh reading mih right!"

Is only recentish I realize Mahase is a Hindu last name. In de ole days every Mahase in de country turn Presbyterian and now de name doh have no association with Hindu or Indian whatsoever. I used to think of it as a Presbyterian Church name until some days ago when we meet a Hindu fella fresh from India name Yogdesh Mahase who never even hear of Presbyterian.

De other day I ask Janet what she know 'bout Divali. She say, "It's the Hindu festival of lights, isn't it?" like a line straight out a dictionary. Yuh think she know anything 'bout how lord Rama get himself exile in a forest for fourteen years, and how when it come time for him to go back home his followers light up a pathway to help him make his way out, and dat is what Divali lights is all about? All Janet know is 'bout going for drive in de country to see light, and she could remember looking forward, around Divali time, to the lil brown paper-bag packages full a burfi and parasad that she father Hindu students used to bring for him.

One time in a Indian restaurant she ask for parasad for dessert. Well! Since den I never go back in dat restaurant, I embarrass fuh so!

I used to think I was a Hindu *par excellence* until I come up here and see real flesh and blood Indian from India. Up here, I learning 'bout all kind a custom and food and music and clothes dat we never see or hear 'bout in good ole Trinidad. Is de next best thing to going to India, in truth, oui! But Indian store clerk on Main Street doh have no patience with us, specially when we talking English to dem. Yuh ask dem a question in English and dey insist on giving de answer in Hindi or Punjabi or Urdu or Gujarati. How I suppose to know de difference even! And den dey look at yuh disdainful disdainful – like yuh disloyal, like yuh is a traitor.

But yuh know, it have one other reason I real reluctant to go Main Street. Yuh see, Janet pretty fuh so! And I doh like de way men does look at she, as if because she wearing jeans and T-shirt and high-heel shoe and make-up and have long hair loose and flying about like she is a walking-talking shampoo ad, dat she easy. And de women always looking at she beady eye, like she loose and going to thief dey man. Dat kind a thing always make me want to put mih arm round she waist like, she is my woman, take yuh eyes off she! and shock de false teeth right out dey mouth. And den is a whole other story when dey see me with mih crew cut and mih blue jeans tuck inside mih jim-boots. Walking next to Janet, who so femme dat she redundant, tend to make me look like a gender dey forget to classify. Before going Main Street I does parade in front de mirror practicing a jiggly-wiggly kind a walk. But if I ain't walking like a strong-man monkey I doh exactly feel right and I always revert back to mih true colours. De men dem does look at me like if dey is exactly what I need a taste of to cure me good and proper. I could see dey eyes watching Janet and me, dey face growing dark as dey imagining all kind a situation and position. And de women dem embarrass fuh so to watch me in mih eye, like dey fraid I will jump up and try to kiss dem, or make pass at dem. Yuh know, sometimes I wonder if I ain't mad enough to do it just for a little bacchanal, nah!

Going for a outing with mih Janet on Main Street ain't easy! If only it wasn't for burfi and gulub jamoon! If only I had a learned how to cook dem kind a thing before I leave home and come up here to live!

2.

In large deep-orange Sanskrit-style letters, de sign on de saffron-colour awning above de door read "Kush Valley Sweets." Underneath in smaller red letters it had "Desserts Fit For The Gods." It was a corner building. The front and side was one big glass wall. Inside was big. Big like a gymnasium. Yuh could see in through de brown tint windows: dark brown plastic chair, and brown table, each one de length of a door, line up stiff and straight in row after row like if is a school room.

Before entering de restaurant I ask Janet to wait one minute outside with me while I rumfle up mih memory, pulling out all de sweet names I know from home, besides burfi and gulub jamoon: meethai, jilebi, sweetrice (but dey call dat kheer up here), and ladhoo. By now, of course, mih mouth watering fuh so! When I feel confident enough dat I wouldn't make a fool a mih Brown self by asking what dis one name? and what dat one name? we went in de restaurant. In two twos all de spice in de place take a flying leap in our direction and give us one big welcome hug up, tight fuh so! Since den dey take up permanent residence in de jacket I wear dat day!

Mostly it had women customers sitting at de tables, chatting and laughing, eating sweets and sipping masala tea. De only men in de place was de waiters, and all six waiters was men. I figure dat dey was brothers, not too hard to conclude, because all a dem had de same full round chin, round as if de chin stretch tight over a ping-pong ball, and dey had de same big roving eyes. I know better dan to think dey was mere waiters in de employ of a owner who chook up in a office in de back. I sure dat dat was dey own family business, dey stomach proudly preceeding dem and dey shoulders throw back in de confidence of dey ownership.

It ain't dat I paranoid, yuh understand, but from de moment we enter de fellas dem get over-animated, even armorously agitated. Janet again! All six pair a eyes land up on she, following she every move and body part. Dat in itself is something dat does madden me, oui! but also a kind a irrational envy have a tendency to manifest in me. It was like I didn't exist. Sometimes it could be a real problem going out with a good-looker, yes! While I ain't remotely interested in having a squeak of a flirtation with a man, it doh hurt a ego to have a man notice yuh once in a very long while. But with Janet at mih side, I doh have de chance of a penny shave-ice in de hot sun. I tuck mih elbows in as close to mih sides as I could so I wouldn't look like a strong man next to she, and over to de l-o-n-g glass case jam up with sweets I jiggle and wiggle in mih best imitation a some a dem gay fellas dat I see downtown Vancouver, de ones who more femme dan even Janet. I tell she not to pay de brothers no attention, because if any a dem flirt with she I could start a fight right dere and den. And I didn't feel to mess up mih crew cut in a fight.

De case had sweets in every nuance of colour in a rainbow. Sweets I never before see and doh know de names of. But dat was alright because I wasn't going to order dose ones anyway.

Since before we leave home Janet have she mind set on a nice thick syrupy curl a jilebi and a piece a plain burfi so I order dose for she and den I ask de waiter-fella, resplendent with thick thick bright-yellow gold chain and ID bracelet, for a stick a meethai for mihself. I stand up waiting by de glass case for it but de waiter/owner lean up on de back wall behind de counter watching me like he ain't hear me. So I say loud enough for him, and every body else in de room to hear, "I would like to have one piece a meethai please," and den he smile and lift up his hands, palms open-out motioning across de vast expanse a glass case, and he say, "Your choice! Whichever you want, Miss." But he still lean up against de back wall grinning. So I stick mih head out and up like a turtle and say louder, and slowly, "One piece a meethai – dis one!" and I point sharp to de stick a flour mix with ghee, deep fry and den roll up in sugar. He say, "That is koorma, Miss. One piece only?"

Mih voice drop low all by itself. "Oh ho! Yes, one piece. Where I come from we does call dat meethai." And den I add, but only loud enough for Janet to hear, "And mih name ain't 'Miss.'"

He open his palms out and indicate de entire panorama a sweets and he say, "These are all meethai, Miss. Meethai is Sweets. Where are you from?"

I ignore his question and to show him I undaunted, I point to a round pink ball and say, "I'll have one a dese sugarcakes too please." He start grinning broad broad like if he half-pitying, half-laughing at dis Indian-in-skin-colour-only, and den he tell me, "That is called chum-chum, Miss." I snap back at him, "Yeh, well back home we does call dat sugarcake, Mr. Chum-chum."

At de table Janet say, "You know, Pud [Pud, short for Pudding; is dat she does call me when she feeling close to me, or sorry for me], it's true that we call that 'meethai' back home. Just like how we call 'siu mai' 'tim sam.' As if 'dim sum' is just one little piece a food. What did he call that sweet again?"

"Cultural bastards, Janet, cultural bastards. Dat is what we is. Yuh know, one time a fella from India who living up here call me a bastardized Indian because I didn't know Hindi. And now look at dis, nah! De thing is: all a we in Trinidad is cultural bastards, Janet, all a we. *Toutes bagailles!* Chinese people, Black people, White people. Syrian. Lebanese. I looking forward to de day I find out dat place inside me where I am nothing else but Trinidadian, whatever dat could turn out to be."

I take a bite a de chum-chum, de texture was like grind-up coconut but it had no coconut, not even a hint a coconut taste in it. De thing was juicy with sweet rose water oozing out a it. De rose water perfume enter mih nose and get trap in mih cranium. Ah drink two cup a masala tea and a lassi and still de rose water perfume was on mih tongue like if I had a overdosed on Butchart Gardens.

Suddenly de door a de restaurant spring open wide with a strong force and two big burly fellas stumble in, almost rolling over on to de ground. Dey get up, eyes red and slow and dey skin burning pink with booze. Dey straighten up so much to over-compensate for falling forward, dat dey find deyself leaning backward. Everybody stop talking and was watching dem. De guy in front put his hand up to his forehead and take a deep Walter Raleigh bow, bringing de hand down to his waist in a rolling circular movement. Out loud he greet everybody with "Alarm o salay koom." A part a me wanted to bust out laughing. Another part make mih jaw drop open in disbelief. De calm in de place get rumfle up. De two fellas dem, feeling chupid now because nobody reply to dey greeting, gone up to de counter to Chum-chum trying to make a little conversation with him. De same booze-pink alarm-o-salay-koom-fella say to Chum-chum, "Hey, howaryah?"

Chum-Chum give a lil nod and de fella carry right on, "Are you Sikh?"

Chum-chum brothers converge near de counter, busying dey-selves in de vicinity. Chum-chum look at his brothers kind a quizzical, and he touch his cheek and feel his forehead with de back a his palm. He say, "No, I think I am fine, thank you. But I am sorry if I look sick, Sir."

De burly fella confuse now, so he try again.

"Where are you from?"

Chum-chum say, "Fiji, Sir."

"Oh! Fiji, eh! Lotsa palm trees and beautiful women, eh! Is it true that you guys can have more than one wife?"

De exchange make mih blood rise up in a boiling froth. De restaurant suddenly get a gruff quietness 'bout it except for a woman I hear whispering angrily to another woman at de table behind us, "I hate this! I just hate it! I can't stand to see our men humiliated by them, right in front of us. He should refuse to serve them, he should throw them out. Who on earth do they think they are? The awful fools!" And de friend whisper back, "If he throws them out all of us will suffer in the long run."

I could discern de hair on de back a de neck a Chum-chum brothers standing up, annoyed, and at de same time de brothers look like dey was shrinking in stature. Chum-chum get serious, and he politely say, "What can I get for you?"

Pinko get de message and he point to a few items in de case and say, "One of each, to go please."

Holding de white take-out box in one hand he extend de other to Chum-chum and say, "How do you say 'Excuse me, I'm sorry' in Fiji?"

Chum-chum shake his head and say, "It's okay. Have a good day."

Pinko insist, "No, tell me please. I think I just behaved badly, and I want to apologize. How do you say 'I'm sorry' in Fiji?"

Chum-chum say, "Your apology is accepted. Everything is okay." And he discreetly turn away to serve a person who had just entered de restaurant. De fellas take de hint dat was broad like daylight, and back out de restaurant like two little mouse.

Everybody was feeling sorry for Chum-chum and Brothers. One a dem come up to de table across from us to take a order from a woman with a giraffe-long neck who say, "Brother, we mustn't accept how these people think they can treat us. You men really put up with too many insults and abuse over here. I really felt for you."

Another woman gone up to de counter to converse with Chum-chum in she language. She reach out and touch his hand, sympathy-like. Chum-chum hold the one hand in his two and make a verbose speech to her as she nod she head in agreement generously. To italicize her support, she buy a take-out box a two burfi, or rather, dat's what I think dey was.

De door a de restaurant open again, and a bevy of Indian-looking women saunter in, dress up to weaken a person's decorum. De Miss Universe pageant traipse across de room to a table. Chum-chum and Brothers start smoothing dey hair back, and pushing de front a dey shirts neatly into dey pants. One brother take out a pack a Dentyne from his shirt pocket and pop one in his mouth. One take out a comb from his back pocket and smooth down his hair. All a dem den converge on dat single table to take orders. Dey begin to behave like young pups in mating season. Only, de women dem wasn't impress by all this tra-la-la at all and ignore dem except to make dey order, straight to de point. Well, it look like Brothers' egos were having a rough day and dey start roving 'bout de room, dey egos and de crotch a dey pants leading far in front dem. One brother gone over to Giraffebai to see if she want anything more. He call she "dear" and put his hand on she back. Giraffebai straighten she back in surprise and reply in a not-too-friendly way. When he gone to write up de bill she see me looking at she and she say to me, "Whoever does he think he is! Calling me dear and touching me like that! Why do these men always think that they have permission to touch whatever and wherever they want! And you can't make a fuss about it in public, because it is exactly what those people out there want to hear about so that they can say how sexist and uncivilized our culture is."

I shake mih head in understanding and say, "Yeah. I know. Yuh right!"

De atmosphere in de room take a hairpin turn, and it was man aggressing on woman, woman warding off a herd a man who just had dey pride publicly cut up a couple a times in just a few minutes.

One brother walk over to Janet and me and he stand up facing me with his hands clasp in front a his crotch, like if he protecting it. Stiff stiff, looking at me, he say, "Will that be all?"

Mih crew cut start to tingle, so I put on mih femmest smile and say, "Yes, that's it, thank you. Just the bill please." De smartass turn to face Janet and he remove his hands from in front a his crotch and slip his thumbs inside his pants like a cowboy 'bout to do a square dance. He smile, looking down at her attentive fuh so, and he say, "Can I do anything for you?"

I didn't give Janet time fuh his intent to even register before I bulldoze in mih most un-femmest manner, "She have everything she need, man, thank you. The bill please." Yuh think he hear me? It was like I was talking to thin air. He remain smiling at Janet, but she, looking at me, not at him, say, "You heard her. The bill please."

Before he could even leave de table proper, I start mih tirade. "But A A! Yuh see dat? Yuh could believe dat! De effing so-and-so! One minute yuh feel sorry fuh dem and next minute dey harassing de heck out a you. Janet, he crazy to mess with my woman, yes!" Janet get vex with me and say I overreacting, and is not fuh me to be vex, but fuh she to be vex. Is she he insult, and she could take good enough care a sheself.

I tell she I don't know why she don't cut off all dat long hair, and stop wearing lipstick and eyeliner. Well, who tell me to say dat! She get real vex and say dat nobody will tell she how to dress and how not to dress, not me and not any man. Well I could see de potential dat dis fight had coming, and when Janet get fighting vex, watch out! It hard to get a word in edgewise, yes! And she does bring up incidents from years back dat have no bearing on de current situation. So I draw back quick quick but she don't waste time; she was already off to a good start. It was best to leave right dere and den.

Just when I stand up to leave, de doors dem open up and in walk Sandy and Lise, coming for dey weekly hit a Indian sweets. Well, with Sandy and Lise is a dead giveaway dat dey not dressing fuh any man, it have no place in dey life fuh man-vibes, and dat in fact dey have a blatant penchant fuh women. Soon as dey enter de room yuh could see de brothers and de couple men customers dat had come in minutes before stare dem down from head to Birkenstocks, dey eyes bulging with disgust. And de women in de room start shoo-shooing, and putting dey hand in front dey mouth to stop dey surprise, and false teeth, too, from falling out. Sandy and Lise spot us instantly and dey call out to us, shameless, loud and affectionate. Dey leap over to us, eager to hug up and kiss like if dey hadn't seen us for years, but it was really only since two nights aback when we went out to dey favourite Indian restaurant for dinner. I figure dat de display was a genuine happiness to be seen wit us in dat place. While we stand up dere chatting, Sandy insist on rubbing she hand up and down Janet back – wit friendly intent, mind you, and same time Lise have she arm round Sandy waist. Well, all cover get blown. If it was even remotely possible dat I wasn't noticeable before, now Janet and I were over-exposed. We could a easily suffer from hypothermia, specially since it suddenly get cold cold in dere. We say goodbye, not soon enough, and as we were leaving I turn to acknowledge Giraffebai, but instead a any recognition of our buddiness against de fresh brothers, I get a face dat look like it was in de presence of a very foul smell.

De good thing, doh, is dat Janet had become so incensed 'bout how we get scorned, dat she forgot I tell she to cut she hair and to ease up on de make-up, and so I get save from hearing 'bout how I too jealous, and how much I inhibit she, and how she would prefer if I would grow *my* hair, and wear lipstick and put on a dress sometimes. I so glad, oui! dat I didn't have to go through hearing how I too demanding a she, like de time, she say, I prevent she from seeing a ole boyfriend when he was in town for a couple hours *en route* to live in Australia with his new bride (because, she say, I was jealous dat ten years ago dey sleep together.) Well, look at mih crosses, nah! Like if I really so possessive and jealous!

So tell me, what yuh think 'bout dis nah, girl?

Colonisation in Reverse

Louise Bennett

Wat a joyful news, Miss Mattie,
I feel like me heart gwine burs'
Jamaica people colonisin
Englan in reverse.

By de hundred, by de t'ousan
From country and from town,
By de ship-load, by de plane-load
Jamaica is Englan boun.

Dem a-pour out o' Jamaica,
Everybody future plan
Is fe get a big-time job
An settle in de mother lan.

What a islan! What a people!
Man an woman, old an young
Jusa pack dem bag an baggage
An tun history upside dung!

Some people don't like travel,
But fe show dem loyalty
Dem all a-open up cheap-fare-
To-Englan agency.

An week by week dem shippin off
Dem countryman like fire,
Fe immigrate an populate
De seat o' de Empire.

Oonoo see how life is funny,
Oonoo see de tunabout,
Jamaica live fe box bread
Outa English people mout'.

For wen dem catch a Englan,
An start play dem different role,
Some will settle down to work
An some will settle fe de dole.

Jane say de dole is not too bad
Because dey payin' she
Two pounds a week fe seek a job
Dat suit her dignity.

Me say Jane will never find work
At the rate how she dah-look,
For all day she stay pon Aunt Fan couch
An read love-story book.

Wat a devilment a Englan!
Dem face war an brave de worse,
But I'm wonderin' how dem gwine stan'
Colonisin' in reverse.

Inglan is a Bitch

Linton Kwesi Johnson

w'en mi jus' come to Landan toun
mi use to work pan di andahgroun
but workin' pan di andahgroun
y'u don't get fi know your way aroun'

Inglan is a bitch
dere's no escapin' it
Inglan is a bitch
dere's no runnin' whey fram it

mi get a lickle jab in a big 'otell
an' awftah a while, mi woz doin' quite well
dem staat mi aaf as a dish—washah
but w'en mi tek a stack, mi noh tun clack—
watchah!

Inglan is a bitch
dere's no escapin' it
Inglan is a bitch
noh baddah try fi hide fram it

w'en dem gi' you di lickle wage packit
fus dem rab it wid dem big tax rackit
y'u haffi struggle fi mek en's meet
an' w'en y'u goh a y'u bed y'u jus' cant sleep

Inglan is a bitch
dere's no escapin' it
Inglan is a bitch fi true
a noh lie mi a tell, a true

mi use to work dig ditch w'en it cowl noh bitch
mi did strang like a mule, but, bwoy, mi did fool
den awftah a while mi jus' stap dhu ovahtime
den awftah a while mi jus' phu dung mi tool

Inglan is a bitch
dere's no escapin' it
Inglan is a bitch
y'u haffi know how fi suvvive in it

well mi dhu day wok an' mi dhu nite wok
mi dhu clean wok an' mi dhu dutty wok
dem seh dat black man is very lazy
but if y'u si how mi wok y'u woulda sey mi crazy

Inglan is a bitch
dere's no escapin' it
Inglan is a bitch
y'u bettah face up to it

dem have a lickle facktri up inna Brackly
inna disya facktri all dem dhu is pack crackry
fi di laas fifteen years dem get mi laybah
now awftah fifteen years mi fall out a fayvah

Inglan is a bitch
dere's no escapin' it
Inglan is a bitch
dere's no runnin' whey fram it

mi know dem have work, work in abundant
yet still, dem mek mi redundant
now, at fifty—five mi gettin' quite ol'
yet still, dem sen' mi fi goh draw dole

Inglan is a bitch
dere's no escapin' it
Inglan is a bitch fi true
is whey wi a goh dhu 'bout it?

The Star-Apple Kingdom

Derek Walcott

There were still shards of an ancient pastoral
in those shires of the island where the cattle drank
their pools of shadow from an older sky,
surviving from when the landscape copied such subjects as
"Herefords at Sunset in the Valley of the Wye."
The mountain water that fell white from the mill wheel
sprinkling like petals from the star-apple trees,
and all of the windmills and sugar mills moved by mules
on the treadmill of Monday to Monday, would repeat
in tongues of water and wind and fire, in tongues
of Mission School pickaninnies, like rivers remembering
their source, Parish Trelawny, Parish St. David, Parish
St. Andrew, the names afflicting the pastures,
the lime groves and fences of marl stone and the cattle
with a docile longing, an epochal content.
And there were, like old wedding lace in an attic,
among the boas and parasols and the tea-coloured
daguerreotypes, hints of an epochal happiness
as ordered and infinite to the child
as the great house road to the Great House
down a perspective of casuarinas plunging green manes
in time to the horses, an orderly life
reduced by lorgnettes day and night, one disc the sun,
the other the moon, reduced into a pier glass:
nannies diminished to dolls, mahogany stairways
no larger than those of an album in which
the flash of cutlery yellows, as gamboge as
the piled cakes of teatime on that latticed
bougainvillea verandah that looked down toward
a prospect of Cuyp-like Herefords under a sky
lurid as a porcelain souvenir with these words:
"Herefords at Sunset in the Valley of the Wye."

Strange, that the rancour of hatred hid in that dream
of slow rivers and lily-like parasols, in snaps

of fine old colonial families, curled at the edge
not from age or from fire or the chemicals, no, not at all,
but because, off at its edges, innocently excluded
stood the groom, the cattle boy, the housemaid, the gardeners,
the tenants, the good Negroes down in the village,
their mouths in the locked jaw of a silent scream.
A scream which would open the doors to swing wildly
all night, that was bringing in heavier clouds,
more black smoke than cloud, frightening the cattle
in whose bulging eyes the Great House diminished;
a scorching wind of a scream
that began to extinguish the fireflies,
that dried the water mill creaking to a stop
as it was about to pronounce Parish Trelawny
all over, in the ancient pastoral voice,
a wind that blew all without bending anything,
neither the leaves of the album nor the lime groves;
blew Nanny floating back in white from a feather
to a chimerical, chemical pin speck that shrank
the drinking Herefords to brown porcelain cows
on a mantelpiece, Trelawny trembling with dusk,
the scorched pastures of the old benign Custos; blew
far the decent servants and the lifelong cook,
and shriveled to a shard that ancient pastoral
of dusk in a gilt-edged frame now catching the evening sun
in Jamaica, making both epochs one.

He looked out from the Great House windows on
clouds that still held the fragrance of fire,
he saw the Botanical Gardens officially drown
in a formal dusk, where governors had strolled
and black gardeners had smiled over glinting shears
at the lilies of parasols on the floating lawns,
the flame trees obeyed his will and lowered their wicks,
the flowers tightened their fists in the name of thrift,
the porcelain lamps of ripe cocoa, the magnolia's jet
dimmed on the one circuit with the ginger lilies
and left a lonely bulb on the verandah,
and, had his mandate extended to that ceiling
of star-apple candelabra, he would have ordered
the sky to sleep, saying, I'm tired,
save the starlight for victories, we can't afford it,
leave the moon on for one more hour, and that's it.
But though his power, the given mandate, extended
from tangerine daybreaks to star-apple dusks,

his hand could not dam that ceaseless torrent of dust
that carried the shacks of the poor, to their root-rock music,
down the gullies of Yallahs and August Town,
to lodge them on thorns of maca, with their rags
crucified by cactus, tins, old tires, cartons;
from the black Warieka Hills the sky glowed fierce as
the dials of a million radios,
a throbbing sunset that glowed like a grid
where the dread beat rose from the jukebox of Kingston.
He saw the fountains dried of quadrilles, the water-music
of the country dancers, the fiddlers like fifes
put aside. He had to heal
this malarial island in its bath of bay leaves,
its forests tossing with fever, the dry cattle
groaning like winches, the grass that kept shaking
its head to remember its name. No vowels left
in the mill wheel, the river. Rock stone. Rock stone.

The mountains rolled like whales through phosphorous stars,
as he swayed like a stone down fathoms into sleep,
drawn by that magnet which pulls down half the world
between a star and a star, by that black power
that has the assassin dreaming of snow,
that poleaxes the tyrant to a sleeping child.
The house is rocking at anchor, but as he falls
his mind is a mill wheel in moonlight,
and he hears, in the sleep of his moonlight, the drowned
bell of Port Royal's cathedral, sees the copper pennies
of bubbles rising from the empty eye-pockets
of green buccaneers, the parrot fish floating
from the frayed shoulders of pirates, sea-horses
drawing gowned ladies in their liquid promenade
across the moss-green meadows of the sea;
he heard the drowned choirs under Palisadoes,
a hymn ascending to earth from a heaven inverted
by water, a crab climbing the steeple,
and he climbed from that submarine kingdom
as the evening lights came on in the institute,
the scholars lamplit in their own aquarium,
he saw them mouthing like parrot fish, as he passed
upward from that baptism, their history lessons,
the bubbles like ideas which he could not break:
Jamaica was captured by Penn and Venables,
Port Royal perished in a cataclysmic earthquake.

Before the coruscating façades of cathedrals
from Santiago to Caracas, where the penitential archbishops
washed the feet of paupers (a parenthetical moment
that made the Caribbean a baptismal font,
turned butterflies to stone, and whitened like doves
the buzzards circling municipal garbage),
the Caribbean was borne like an elliptical basin
in the hands of acolytes, and a people were absolved
of a history which they did not commit;
the slave pardoned his whip, and the dispossessed
said the rosary of islands for three hundred years,
a hymn that resounded like the hum of the sea
inside a sea-cave, as their knees turned to stone,
while the bodies of patriots were melting down walls
still crusted with mute outcries of *La Revolución!*
"San Salvador, pray for us, St. Thomas, San Domingo,
ora pro nobis, intercede for us, Sancta Lucia
of no eyes," and when the circular chaplet
reached the last black bead of Sancta Trinidad
they began again, their knees drilled into stone,
where Colón had begun, with San Salvador's bead,
beads of black colonies round the necks of Indians.
And while they prayed for an economic miracle,
ulcers formed on the municipal portraits,
the hotels went up, and the casinos and brothels,
and the empires of tobacco, sugar, and bananas,
until a black woman, shawled like a buzzard,
climbed up the stairs and knocked at the door
of his dream, whispering in the ear of the keyhole:
"Let me in, I'm finished with praying, I'm the Revolution.
I am the darker, the older America."

She was as beautiful as a stone in the sunrise,
her voice had the gutturals of machine guns
across khaki deserts where the cactus flower
detonates like grenades, her sex was the slit throat
of an Indian, her hair had the blue-black sheen of the crow.
She was a black umbrella blown inside out
by the wind of revolution, La Madre Dolorosa,
a black rose of sorrow, a black mine of silence,
raped wife, empty mother, Aztec virgin
transfixed by arrows from a thousand guitars,
a stone full of silence, which, if it gave tongue
to the tortures done in the name of the Father,
would curdle the blood of the marauding wolf,

the fountain of generals, poets, and cripples
who danced without moving over their graves
with each revolution; her Caesarean was stitched
by the teeth of machine guns, and every sunset
she carried the Caribbean's elliptical basin
as she had once carried the penitential napkins
to be the footbath of dictators, Trujillo, Machado,
and those whose faces had yellowed like posters
on municipal walls. Now she stroked his hair
until it turned white, but she would not understand
that he wanted no other power but peace,
that he wanted a revolution without any bloodshed,
he wanted a history without any memory,
streets without statues,
and a geography without myth. He wanted no armies
but those regiments of bananas, thick lances of cane,
and he sobbed, "I am powerless, except for love."
She faded from him, because he could not kill;
she shrank to a bat that hung day and night
in the back of his brain. He rose in his dream.

The soul, which was his body made as thin
as its reflection and invulnerable
without its clock, was losing track of time;
it walked the mountain tracks of the Maroons,
it swung with Gordon from the creaking gibbet,
it bought a pack of peppermints and cashews
from one of the bandanna'd mammies outside the ward,
it heard his breath pitched to the decibels
of the peanut vendors' carts, it entered a municipal wall
stirring the slogans that shrieked his name: SAVIOUR!
and others: LACKEY! he melted like a spoon
through the alphabet soup of CIA, PNP, OPEC,
that resettled once he passed through with this thought:
I should have foreseen those seraphs with barbed-wire hair,
beards like burst mattresses, and wild eyes of garnet,
who nestled the Coptic Bible to their ribs, would
call me Joshua, expecting him to bring down Babylon
by Wednesday, after the fall of Jericho; yes, yes,
I should have seen the cunning bitterness of the rich
who left me no money but these mandates:

His aerial mandate, which
contained the crows whose circuit
was this wedding band that married him to his island.

His marine mandate, which
was the fishing limits
which the shark scissored like silk with its teeth
between Key West and Havana;
his terrestrial:
the bled hills rusted with bauxite;
paradisal:
the chimneys like angels sheathed in aluminium.

In shape like a cloud
he saw the face of his father,
the hair like white cirrus blown back
in a photographic wind,
the mouth of mahogany winced shut,
the eyes lidded, resigned
to the first compromise,
the last ultimatum,
the first and last referendum.

One morning the Caribbean was cut up
by seven prime ministers who bought the sea in bolts—
one thousand miles of aquamarine with lace trimmings,
one million yards of lime-coloured silk,
one mile of violet, leagues of cerulean satin—
who sold it at a markup to the conglomerates,
the same conglomerates who had rented the water spouts
for ninety-nine years in exchange for fifty ships,
who retailed it in turn to the ministers
with only one bank account, who then resold it
in ads for the Caribbean Economic Community,
till everyone owned a little piece of the sea,
from which some made saris, some made bandannas;
the rest was offered on trays to white cruise ships
taller than the post office; then the dogfights
began in the cabinets as to who had first sold
the archipelago for this chain store of islands.

Now a tree of grenades was his star-apple kingdom,
over fallow pastures his crows patrolled,
he felt his fist involuntarily tighten
into a talon that was strangling five doves,
the mountains loomed leaden under martial law,
the suburban gardens flowered with white paranoia
next to the bougainvilleas of astonishing April;
the rumours were a rain that would not fall:

that enemy intelligence had alerted the roaches'
quivering antennae, that bats flew like couriers,
transmitting secrets between the embassies;
over dials in the war rooms, the agents waited
for a rifle crack from Havana; down shuttered avenues
roared a phalanx of Yamahas. They left
a hole in the sky that closed on silence.

He didn't hear the roar of the motorcycles
diminish in circles like those of the water mill
in a far childhood; he was drowned in sleep;
he slept, without dreaming, the sleep after love
in the mineral oblivion of night
whose flesh smells of cocoa, whose teeth are white
as coconut meat, whose breath smells of ginger,
whose braids are scented like sweet-potato vines
in furrows still pungent with the sun.
He slept the sleep that wipes out history,
he slept like the islands on the breast of the sea,
like a child again in her star-apple kingdom.
Tomorrow the sea would gleam like nails
under a zinc sky where the barren frangipani
was hammered, a horizon without liners;
tomorrow the heavy caravels of clouds would wreck
and dissolve in their own foam on the reefs
of the mountains, tomorrow a donkey's yawn
would saw the sky in half, and at dawn
would come the noise of a government groaning uphill.
But now she held him, as she holds us all,
her history-orphaned islands, she to whom
we came late as our muse, our mother,
who suckled the islands, who, when she grows old
with her breasts wrinkled like eggplants,
is the head-tie mother, the bleached-sheets-on-the-river-rocks
    mother,
the gospel mother, the t'ank-you-parson mother
who turns into mahogany, the lignum-vitae mother,
her sons like thorns,
her daughters dry gullies that give birth to stones,
who was, in our childhood, the housemaid and the cook,
the young grand' who polished the plaster figure
of Clio, Muse of history, in her seashell grotto
in the Great House parlour, Anadyomene washed
in the deep Atlantic heave of her housemaid's hymn.

In the indigo dawn the palms unclenched their fists,
his eyes opened the flowers, and he lay as still
as the waterless mill wheel. The sun's fuse caught,
it hissed on the edge of the skyline, and day exploded
its remorseless avalanche of dray carts and curses,
the roaring oven of Kingston, its sky as fierce
as the tin box of a patties cart. Down the docks
between the Levantine smells of the warehouses
nosed the sea-wind with its odour of a dog's damp fur.
He lathered in anger and refreshed his love.
He was lathered like a horse, but the instant
the shower crowned him and he closed his eyes,
he was a bride under lace, remarrying his country,
a child drawn by the roars of the mill wheel's electorate,
those vows reaffirmed; he dressed, went down to breakfast,
and sitting again at the mahogany surface
of the breakfast table, its dark hide as polished
as the sheen of mares, saw his father's face
and his own face blent there, and looked out
to the drying garden and its seeping pond.

What was the Caribbean? A green pond mantling
behind the Great House columns of Whitehall,
behind the Greek façades of Washington,
with bloated frogs squatting on lily pads
like islands, islands that coupled as sadly as turtles
engendering islets, as the turtle of Cuba
mounting Jamaica engendered the Caymans, as, behind
the hammerhead turtle of Haiti-San Domingo
trailed the little turtles from Tortuga to Tobago;
he followed the bobbing trek of the turtles
leaving America for the open Atlantic,
felt his own flesh loaded like the pregnant beaches
with their moon-guarded eggs—they yearned for Africa,
they were lemmings drawn by magnetic memory
to an older death, to broader beaches
where the coughing of lions was dumbed by breakers.
Yes, he could understand their natural direction
but they would drown, sea-eagles circling them,
and the languor of frigates that do not beat wings,
and he closed his eyes, and felt his jaw drop
again with the weight of that silent scream.

He cried out at the turtles as one screams at children
with the anger of love, it was the same scream

which, in his childhood, had reversed an epoch
that had bent back the leaves of his star-apple kingdom,
made streams race uphill, pulled the water wheel backwards
like the wheels in a film, and at that outcry,
from the raw ropes and tendons of his throat,
the sea-buzzards receded and receded into specks,
and the osprey vanished.
        On the knee-hollowed steps
of the crusted cathedral, there was a woman in black,
the black of moonless nights, within whose eyes
shone seas in starlight like the glint of knives
(the one who had whispered to the keyhole of his ear),
washing the steps, and she heard it first.
She was one of a flowing black river of women
who bore elliptical basins to the feet of paupers
on the Day of Thorns, who bore milk pails to cows
in a pastoral sunrise, who bore baskets on their heads
down the haemophilic red hills of Haiti,
now with the squeezed rag dripping from her hard hands
the way that vinegar once dropped from a sponge,
but she heard as a dog hears, as all the underdogs
of the world hear, the pitched shriek of silence.
Star-apples rained to the ground in that silence,
the silence was the green of cities undersea,
and the silence lasted for half an hour
in that single second, a seashell silence, resounding
with silence, and the men with barbed-wire beards saw
in that creak of light that was made between
the noises of the world that was equally divided
between rich and poor, between North and South,
between white and black, between two Americas,
the fields of silent Zion in Parish Trelawny,
in Parish St. David, in Parish St. Andrew,
leaves dancing like children without any sound,
in the valley of Tryall, and the white, silent roar
of the old water wheel in the star-apple kingdom;
and the woman's face, had a smile been decipherable
in that map of parchment so rivered with wrinkles,
would have worn the same smile with which he now
cracked the day open and began his egg.

Horizons of Caribbean Studies: An Afterword-Overture

Aisha Khan

The convention of an 'Afterword' is something of an oxymoron. Its charge is to provide a bird's eye view of that which has preceded it, to be a reflective capstone of conversation. Rather than think of an After-Word as the last word, I see it as an overture, a discussion of some key themes that serves as a point of departure to something more expansive and prolonged. The intention of this volume is to offer a union of the best missions of cultural studies, the best missions of ethnography, and the most faithful of vernacular representations. It is a statement of the art, a summary presentation that encapsulates the essence of its subjects. In the words of its editors, Yanique Hume and Aaron Kamugisha, this collection calls for recognizing that the study of the Caribbean necessarily involves an interrogation of culture (treated appropriately broadly here as lifeworlds and the consequences of human social interaction) in terms of political struggle and intellectual introspection. Caribbean study, moreover, involves self-reflexivity, as Hume and Kamugisha argue; that is to say, referencing itself as a source which establishes the questions and assesses the answers, not simply the source from which illustrative examples are derived.

Periodizing the story of the Caribbean, as we can see, is an exercise in classification, revealing as much about the categories devised (historiographical interpretation) as about what is being categorized (historical occurrence). If sufficiently dramatic, stories may seem to tell themselves. No story does. Every particle of human experience is filtered through a telling, or, really, multiple (potentially infinite) tellings. Parsing the Caribbean has left us with different sorts of watershed moments, which appear as given. Instead, they are highlights chosen according to defining criteria. Thus, 'moments' have different durations as well as chronologies. Juxtaposed together, durations and chronologies produce different stories.

This region is typically understood in certain, familiar terms. Notable among these is the half-millennium slice – the iconic five centuries that contain such big pictures as the stories of modernity, slavery, and capitalism. There are also single century markers, each of which individually delineates iconic narratives that explain the Caribbean as a particular kind of place in the world. For example, a series of events in twentieth-century Caribbean created reverberations that either indicated or suggested the possibilities for great transformations. We have the political independence of several formerly British Caribbean colonies; the labour unrest, ethnic conflict, and reformist moves toward socialist forms of governance in Cuba, Guyana, Jamaica, and Grenada; the Black Power Revolution; the Caribbean Basin Initiative's attempt to quell Leftist movements in the Caribbean and Central America through trade agreements that liberalized access to US markets; massive out-migrations, 'industrialization by invitation,' and increasing dependence on mineral resources in the era of import substitution, and, in some cases, their increasing extraction for world markets; the active, if often covert role of US foreign policy – for example, security assistance programs, economic aid, and the promotion of particular ideologies.

Specified further still, designated periods that bracket smaller, more specific portions of time communicate their own powerful symbols for scholars and observers of and in the region. For example, the Haitian Revolution (which can mean 1791–1804, or some decades prior and subsequent to those monumental 13 years), or the Columbian 'Age of Discovery' (1492–1542, the inaugural, and most pervasive period of Amerindian genocide in the Caribbean), or the mid-nineteenth century (the abolition of slavery, or the systemization and implementation of indentured labour). Words like *epoch*, *age*, and *era* carry implications about the significance of what they contain – events, actors, locations; even such minimal moments as a *day* can defy its literal definition of 'twenty-four hours' to symbolize epic impact (positive or negative), such as May 30 (1845), Indian Arrival Day in the Republic of Trinidad and Tobago; or September 23 (1868), the *Grito de Lares*, Puerto Rico's first major revolt against Spanish rule; or January 12 (2010), the catastrophic earthquake in Haiti.

These vicissitudes hold various sorts of meaning and sway for the Caribbean region, depending on vantage point. For those who see such forces as migration, economic booms, economic recessions, and new governing structures as the promise of a better future, these are times of hope and inspiration. For those who see such forces as threats to a preferred and safe status quo, they are times of danger and loss. Hope and inspiration, danger and loss are perceptions that can emanate from within the region itself or from the region's 'front yard' or former 'front yards' (i.e., North America, Western Europe). Perceptions about Caribbean historical and social watersheds also can come from territories neither strictly 'within' it nor 'external' to the region, for example, what some late twentiethcentury observers saw as the creeping 'Central Americanization' of the Caribbean – i.e., the Global North-supported political repression, burgeoning neoliberalism, and free market flexible accumulation immersing the Caribbean as it had engulfed Central America. Academics, policy wonks, and activists throughout the Americas developed and engaged in discourses about the quantity and quality of change, about the quality of life, and about appropriate ways of going about tracking and directing these perturbations. In other words, then, not only is periodization arbitrarily construed, each construction highlights (or trumpets) its own message and that message's importance.

Hume and Kamugisha urge readers to use this collection to hone our critical gaze on the power/knowledge that is generated from epistemological traditions imposed from metropolitan and/or colonial vantage points. In the same spirit of querying and critique, the intention of my afterword is not to summarize the more than a century of brilliant Caribbean scholarship presented in this anthology, but rather to encourage readers to take Hume and Kamugisha's mission to heart: to investigate and interrogate all discourses and ways of knowing, whether abiding or cutting edge. It is only by keeping our conversations open, informed, and alive that will we reach the kind of goals to which *Caribbean Cultural Thought* is so committed.

Ironically, in their own projects of self-presentation, anthologies such as *Caribbean Cultural Thought* grapple with agendas that can seem at cross-purposes. In their introduction, Hume and Kamugisha rightly point to the genre-defying scholarship of such regional luminaries as C.L.R. James and Frantz Fanon. Hume and Kamugisha desire to see a reinvigoration of this kind of scholarship in Caribbean studies. Such men (and women) of Caribbean arts and letters were indeed 'renaissance thinkers' whose work transcends disciplinary boundaries as well as the lines between scholarship and activism that thinkers (renaissance and otherwise) connected to institutions typically contend with. Hence the editors present a vision of a future that returns to understanding power, and what power produces, as a matter of engaged political struggle; theorization is always a matter of subject position-driven dialogues with the domination and resistance that created the Caribbean we know today. What we also know today, perhaps more acutely than when 'the ivory tower' was spoken of as if somehow removed from 'real life,' is that the market forces of competition (exacerbated by neoliberalism) and the hyper-specialization of expertise for niche markets has helped discourage genre-defying scholarship.

Acknowledgement of such discouragement is audible among those committed to such scholarship. For example, an explicit mission of research and analysis that gave voice to multiple discourses, different intellectual histories, numerous unstable formations, and different 'conjunctures and moments in the past' (Hall 1996, 263) emerged from the Birmingham Centre for Contemporary Cultural Studies in the mid-1960s in the form of 'cultural studies.' Although it 'does have some stake in the choices it makes,' cultural studies 'refuses to be a master discourse or meta-discourse of any kind' (Hall 1996, 263). A number of discussions about the genesis of cultural studies as a twin project of activism and scholarship, and the advance of Cultural Studies as a creature of academic institutionalization, lament the disciplining that puts cultural studies 'in danger of losing its edge' (Sardar and Van Loon 1999, 171; Barker 2002). Indeed, Stuart Hall shrugs in apparent disapproval that he is 'completely dumbfounded' by American cultural studies, which has seen an 'enormous explosion' of 'rapid professionalization and institutionalization' (Hall 1996, 273–74). In Britain, he says, 'we are always aware of institutionalization as a moment of profound danger...Why? Well, would it be excessively vulgar to talk about such things as how many jobs there are, how much money there is around, and how much pressure that puts on people to do what they think of as critical political work and intellectual work of a critical kind while also looking over their shoulders at the promotions stakes and the publication stakes, and so on' (Hall 1996, 274). Yet the production and authorization of such counter-knowledges that these scholars are calling for might not only benefit from but require professionalization and institutionalization. As Renato Rosaldo observes, in the North American academy 'interdisciplinary cultural studies lacks the annual rites of intensification that reflect and produce the status of true disciplines...' (Rosaldo 1994, 525). In his view, faculty appointments, material support, and the regular renewal afforded by corporate bodies like professional associations (Rosaldo, 525) represent conditions of possibility rather than moments of jeopardy. Pace Hall and his colleague, Rosaldo see institutional, disciplining power as necessary (perhaps a necessary evil) to the establishment and maintenance of opportunities to learn against the grain. My point is not simply that perspective is everything (although it is a lot), but that cultural analysis must include, and perhaps even begin with considering the ways and occasions it can speak its mind.

In calling for a 'miscellany of approaches' (Sardar and Van Loon 1999, 3) and an activist engagement that enhances its outsider status, the project of cultural studies seeks to keep its agenda intact. This effort will always involve the struggle to reconcile the cross-purposes of celebrating certain against-the-grain ways of learning and knowing, and having to do so, in large part, by conventional, with-the-grain means. While there are some interesting parallels between the idea of 'cultural studies' and the idea of 'the Caribbean' (to which Hume and Kamugisha gesture), one complication lies in the application of the cultural studies agenda to this region. As Andrew Edgar and Peter Sedgwick (1999, 101) explain, the cultural studies approach to culture 'is explicitly opposed to the celebration of high or elite culture'. As blanket proposition and theoretical goal, this disputation works. Yet it does not address the problem of avoiding the replication of established hierarchies while highlighting vernacular expressions. In other words, not all forms of cultural production are valued as equally worthy or impressive. In the world of arts and letters the principal standard of measurement is a Western-derived calculus of 'high' and 'low' culture. Dismissing this standard as elitist is itself a privileged gesture, since allegedly 'low' culture producers also have political investment in seeing themselves as producing (or capable of producing) 'high' culture, as possessing lofty ancestries, and as being extraordinary as defined by hegemonic criteria. The trick is to distinguish between looking at the totality of producers (not just the elites or claimers of 'high' culture) while maintaining a creative skepticism about the hierarchies of cultural and symbolic capital that all producers hold. As Stuart Hall argues, useful scholarship must deal with the 'dirtiness' of the 'semiotic game' and step out of the 'clean air of meaning and textuality and theory to the something nasty down below' (Hall 1996, 263). But interest in the 'lived culture' of different classes (Edgar and Sedgwick 1999, 43) and in 'wrestling with the angels' (Hall 1996, 265) requires being able to ethnographically seek and acknowledge that people value certain forms of capital over others while, simultaneously, questioning the bases upon which those valuations rest.

Another sort of cross-purpose conundrum involves methodology: extrapolating from people's experience to formulate models explaining (or predicting) that experience. On the one hand, there is in Caribbean studies today the assertion that the approaches best suited to understanding the region are to think in terms of fluidity rather than stasis, surprise rather than predictability, and becoming rather than being. On the other hand, that perspective, and assertions about its best-suited methods are predicated on an inevitable objectification of 'the Caribbean'. This creation-of-the-object-of-study foregrounds selected features as representative, which reproduces another iconic Caribbean (albeit according to different, ostensibly improved, criteria). The problem of capture, so to speak, is always present in theory-building. There have been many ways to address this question, from looking for particular 'retentions' (e.g., Herskovits (1958), to pondering an 'absence of ruins' (e.g., Patterson 1982; Price 1985; Walcott 1974), to seeking formative watersheds and historical moments; to theorizing cultural 'creolization' (e.g., Ortiz 1995; Glissant 1995); to looking to 'flows' of people and things, and more. Perhaps analogous to this in everyday life practice (rather than in theory) is the tension described by Edward Kamau Brathwaite (1974) as 'psychic marronage,' or the maintenance of certain 'communicative canons' among subordinated peoples in the face of impositions of 'large scale pressures of dominance' by those in power. In lived experience, too, the prevailing ideological canopy is always tested by outliers and non-compliers, and imaginations are always shadowed by prior events and currents. Thus, everything hangs in the balance between abiding and fading, recognizable and indecipherable, but emblems always emerge.

Let us take the idea of 'diaspora', a fixture in contemporary theorizing about the Caribbean, as an example. It is generally assumed by scholars of the region to reveal a new and improved understanding of culture there, where culture is unbound, on the move, indistinctly shared among communities (whether 'local,' 'national' or 'transnational'), and not necessarily conforming to Western academic notions of ethnos, or peopleness, which have assumed (until relatively recently) a natural, necessary connection between identity and place. With its inherently dissident energy (Hall 1990), 'diaspora' becomes a kind of curative antithesis of bounded and isolated, routed as opposed to rooted, persons and identities. What we might call *staccato histories* – disjointed, disconnected, clipped – have come to be a measure of particularly *Caribbean* lives; staccato histories seem to trouble the linear, progressivist narratives of nation-states and global modernization. Thus 'diaspora,' becomes a key technology of Caribbean self-making, capturing the presumed restive essence of the place (and I use that word deliberately because the idea of 'essence' remains), where identities have long been punctuated by the question mark, 'who are we?' more frequently than the affirmative, 'who we are.' 'Diaspora consciousness,' 'diaspora identity,' 'diasporic discourse,' and 'diaspora aesthetic' characterize local lives and persons. Those who are 'obliged to uproot themselves from home, place and family' form culturally variegated new settlements whose way of life and forms of consciousness are 'diasporic,' and thus whose 'diasporic dilemma' is itself an identity (Hall 2008, 346–47). As Stuart Hall asks, how is the sense of self understood when one's lived reality is movement among places, histories, cultures, and religions (Hall 2008)?

Disentangling the sources of a diaspora identity is also complicated by language: to what extent does the *name* create the *thing*? Can conceptualizing identity be an objective exercise in description, or is this exercise necessarily a retrospective, and arbitrary determination? All theories and models try, by way of explanation, to capture the action from which generalizations are derived. But this sort of, as it were, stop-motion animation process must sacrifice what falls between the boundaries of the theory or model, what cannot be contained because it does not fit (the question or the answer). The fascinating challenge is to be a simultaneous translator, recognizing, for example, both the fluidity of *lives* in the midst and the freeze-frame of *Life* from a distance. The gamble of prioritizing real life, of course, is the discovery that the 'ideal' and the 'real' contradict each other, or at least are not a good match. While this tension is a central raison d'etre of anthropology, it keeps theory-building on its toes. Diaspora identities can also be deployed to better ground oneself *in* place, *within* the nation-state, rather than uniformly in resistance to integration/absorption – as, for example, among many Indo-Caribbean peoples (e.g., Khan 2006).

Blurred boundaries/borders have always been a particularly Caribbean problematic: those around unstable and contested categories and classifications, and those around scholarly discourse shaped significantly by dialogue and exchange among interlocutors. All categories are artificial in that some generalization and selection are needed to establish boundaries. The idea of 'borderlessness,' however, becomes a different sort of challenge, yet nonetheless imperative, in the crafting of theories. Theory-building is itself border-creating, not border-denying. More likely what we strive for is multi-bordered scholarship rather than scholarship without borders. From this perspective, 'diaspora' is best approached as an existential, and introspective, question, not a terminal last stop in theory-building. In this light, movement, border ambiguity, uprootedness, and similar Caribbean-defining metaphors about fluidity and open-endedness can work with the vernacular, without abrasion, highlighting rather than overshadowing. 'Diaspora' is neither a thing nor a condition, per se; it is a process, or sets of processes, of movement and agency, that simultaneously involve practices and thoughts about those practices. As a moving target and not a final resting place, diaspora neither prefigures in broad strokes nor encircles in narrow ones.

Another challenge in dealing with emblematic identity (nicely illustrated in *Caribbean Cultural Thought*) is how to understand 'place' and its relationship to 'belonging.' In the justifiable enthusiasm to dislodge the association of (putative) natural and homogeneous cultural authenticity from bounded and 'original' locations, proponents at times lose sight of the fact that places are emotionally constituted and involve continuous face-to-face interaction (e.g., Giddens 1984). Thus the attachment of cultures to places can create sites from which hegemonic criteria for belonging are challenged in substantive rather than abstract ways. As bell hooks, for example, argues, identity and political struggle are necessarily linked. Rather than look to reject identity, she argues, we must understand it as a stage in subjectivity formation that can generate ways of being that are adversarial to the pressures of assimilation and imitation (Hooks 1990).

In the Caribbean we see a pull between two kinds of epistemological (and political) projects: the region as symbolizing the defiance of lodging culture in place due to its essential qualities of fluidity and hybridity, and the region as symbolizing the affirmation of lodging culture in place due to its history of being denied 'ruins'– i.e., cultural heritage and traditions. Caribbean cultural thought reflects both of these projects of self-making, the struggle to locate culture and interpret authenticity in the face of so-called 'mimicked' cultural reproduction and 'artificial' rather than 'organic' cultural genesis. The Caribbean exemplifies the wisdom of theoretically dislodging culture from place, and authenticity from natural origins while at the same time interrogating the meaning of 'natural,' the significance of 'culture,' and the ability to claim and redefine them. The Caribbean reminds us that decoupling 'culture' from 'place' and presenting these as consisting of performative flows without clear limits (as much contemporary cultural theory does), requires a sense of ownership of one's history and possession of culture. Perhaps the key is that we have to feel stable to be able to valorize instability. As has been pointed out in recent scholarship on the Caribbean (and on diaspora and globalization, generally), but merits mention again here, such things as flux and flow can be in real experience distressing pressures contrary to what people who live those fluxes and flows may prefer. Caribbean cultural thought contains a warning against its own romanticization.

The problem with the idea of absolute identities is that it suggests that people operate automatically, according to inherent cultural, psychological, etc., impulses that are always-already there. The idea of identities as contingent, indeterminate, and conflicted points us toward looking at the way people operate in terms of their own agency and forms of consciousness – as actors with the capacity to define themselves, to make their own worlds, who perceive things in certain ways and move accordingly. What is not to be missed in the Caribbean, as elsewhere, are instances of culture-place symmetry, not, certainly, in any sense predictable according to prefigured essentials, but recognizable as significant among those who cast and cherish such symmetries, even if their ideas about culture-place – belonging – are not always as subversive as our current ideals might anticipate.

Among the most exciting aspects of *Caribbean Cultural Thought* is its invitation to further consider the whole notion of a 'Pan' Caribbean. 'Pan' may connote the underlying commonalities that bind together through time and space and power the cultural confetti of local lives; it may connote a 'meta-discourse' that does much the same thing, albeit condensing rather than individuating those lives; or, equally productively, it may connote the challenges of how to locate and valorize difference within the commonality. Yet 'pan' discourages resting on final instances – the conceit of theory. Knowing no finality, no closure, no fixity, no uniformity, no complete compliance: these are the features and the aspirations shared by a region archetypally understood to be iconic of them, and by a scholarly endeavour typically understood to be defined by them. Is the Caribbean a perfect subject for revitalized, genre-defying cultural studies enhanced by ethnography and vernacular representations? Or is the Caribbean subject to the classificatory practices that such scholarship promotes? The beauty of the Caribbean, and of the expanse of works collected in this anthology, is illustrating how the Caribbean and its study are both a subject for and subject to its myriad interlocutors.

References

Barker, Chris. 2002. *Making Sense of Cultural Studies*. London: Sage Publications.
Brathwaite, Edward Kamau. 1974. *Contradictory Omens*. Mona, Jamaica: Savacou.
Edgar, Andrew and Peter Sedgwick, eds. 1999. *Key Concepts in Cultural Theory*. London: Routledge.
Giddens, Anthony. 1984. *The Constitution of Society*. Cambridge: Polity Press.
Glissant, Edouard. 1995. Creolization in the Making of the Americas. In *Race, Discourse, and the Origin of the America*, ed. Vera L. Hyatt and Rex Nettleford, 268–75. Washington, DC: Smithsonian Institution Press.

Hall, Stuart. 1990. Cultural Identity and Diaspora. In *Identity, Community, Culture, Difference*. Edited by Jonathan Rutherford. London: Lawrence and Wishart.

———. 1996. Cultural Studies and Its Theoretical Legacies. In *Stuart Hall: Critical Dialogues in Cultural Studies*, ed. David Morley and Kuan-Hsing Chen, 262–75. London: Routledge.

———. 2008. Colonialism, Globalization and Diaspora: Stuart Hall in Conversation with Pnina Werbner. In *Anthropology and the New Cosmopolitanism*, ed. Pnina Werbner, 345–60. Oxford: Berg.

Herskovits, Melville. 1958. *The Myth of the Negro Past*. Boston: Beacon Press.

Hooks, Bell. 1990. *Yearning*. Boston, MA: South End Press.

Khan, Aisha. 2006. Caribbean 'Community'? Deciphering a Regional Cipher. In *The Seductions of Community: Emancipations, Oppressions, Quandaries*, ed. Gerald Creed, 143–74. Santa Fe: School of American Research.

Ortiz, Fernando. 1995/2012. *Cuban Counterpoint: Tobacco and Sugar*. Durham: Duke University Press.

Patterson, Orlando. 1982. Recent Studies on Caribbean Slavery and the Atlantic Slave Trade. *Latin American Research Review* 17 (3): 251–75.

Price, Richard. 1985. An Absence of Ruins? Seeking Caribbean Historical Consciousness. *Caribbean Review* XIV (3): 24–29, 45.

Rosaldo, Renato. 1994. Whose Cultural Studies? *American Anthropologist* 96 (3): 524–29.

Sardar, Ziauddin and Borin Van Loon. 1999. *Introducing Cultural Studies*. Cambridge: Icon Books.

Walcott, Derek. 1974. The Muse of History. In *Is Massa Day Dead? Black Moods in the Caribbean*, ed. Orde Coombs. New York: Anchor Books.